OPERATIONS MANAGEMENT
Strategy and Analysis

Fourth Edition

OPERATIONS MANAGEMENT

Strategy and Analysis

Fourth Edition

Lee J. Krajewski
University of Notre Dame

Larry P. Ritzman
Boston College

Addison-Wesley Publishing Company

Reading, Massachusetts · Menlo Park, California · New York
Don Mills, Ontario · Wokingham, England · Amsterdam · Bonn
Sydney · Singapore · Tokyo · Madrid · San Juan · Milan · Paris

WORLD STUDENT SERIES

Executive Editor: Michael Payne
Senior Sponsoring Editor: Julia Berrisford
Editorial Assistant: Kate Morgan
Senior Development Editor: Stephanie Botvin
Managing Editor: Kazia Navas
Senior Production Supervisor: Kathy Diamond
Associate Production Supervisor: Patricia Oduor
Copyeditor: Jerrold Moore
Editorial/Production Service: Lifland et al., Bookmakers
Text Designer: Rebecca Lemna
Technical Art Consultant: Susan London-Payne
Art Buyer: Joseph Vetere
Technical Illustrator: Scientific Illustrators
Reflective Illustrator: James Bryant
Photo Researcher: Susan Holtz
Permissions Editor: Mary Dyer
Cover Designer: Eileen R. Hoff
Prepress Buying Manager: Sarah McCracken
Typesetter: American Composition & Graphics, Inc.
Film Output: Pre-Press Co., Inc.
Supervisor of Manufacturing: Hugh Crawford
Printer: R. R. Donnelley & Sons

About the Cover

We chose our cover images to reflect the diversity of operations management today. With applications ranging from traditional "smokestack" industries to high-tech manufacturing and the service sector, as well as from domestic companies to international corporations, operations management more than ever is an integral part of business.

ISBN 0-201-40016-2

2 3 4 5 6 7 8 9 10 DOW 99989796

Dedicated with love
to our families

Judie Krajewski
Gary, Jeff, Dan, and Jon
Virginia and Jerry
Virginia and Larry

Barbara Ritzman
Karen and Matt; Lisa and Todd
Kristin, Cody, and Alayna
Kathryn and Paul; Mildred and Ray

About the Authors

LEE J. KRAJEWSKI

LARRY P. RITZMAN

Lee J. Krajewski is the William R. and F. Cassie Daley Professor of Manufacturing Strategy at the University of Notre Dame. Prior to joining Notre Dame, Lee was a faculty member at The Ohio State University, where he received the University Alumni Distinguished Teaching Award and the College of Business Outstanding Faculty Research Award. He initiated the Center for Excellence in Manufacturing Management and served as its director for three years. In addition, he received the National President's Award and the National Award of Merit of the American Production and Inventory Control Society and was elected a Fellow of the Decision Sciences Institute.

Lee's career spans more than twenty-six years of research and education in the field of operations management. He has designed and taught courses at both graduate and undergraduate levels on topics such as manufacturing strategy, introduction to operations management, operations design, and manufacturing planning and control systems.

Currently the editor of *Decision Sciences*, Lee was the founding editor of the *Journal of Operations Management* (1980–1983) and has served on several editorial boards. Widely published himself, Lee has contributed numerous articles to such journals as *Decision Sciences, Informational Systems and Operations Research, Management Science, Harvard Business Review,* and *Interfaces,* to name just a few. Lee's areas of specialization include manufacturing strategy, manufacturing planning and control systems, and master production scheduling.

Larry P. Ritzman is the Thomas J. Galligan, Jr. Professor in Operations and Strategic Management at Boston College. He previously served at The Ohio State University for twenty-three years, where he acted as department chairperson and received several awards for both teaching and research. He received his doctorate at Michigan State University, having had prior industrial experience at the Babcock and Wilcox Company. Over the years, he has been privileged to teach and learn more about operations management with numerous students at all levels—undergraduate, MBA, executive MBA, and doctorate.

Particularly active in the Decision Sciences Institute, Larry has served as Council Coordinator, Publications Committee Chair, Track Chair, Vice President, Board Member, Executive Committee Member, Doctoral Consortium Coordinator, and President. He was elected a Fellow of the Institute in 1987 and has received three best-paper awards. He is a frequent reviewer, discussant, and session chair for several other professional organizations.

Larry's areas of particular expertise are operations strategy, production and inventory systems, forecasting, multistage manufacturing, disaggregation, scheduling, and layout. An active researcher, Larry's publications have appeared in such journals as *Decision Sciences, Journal of Operations Management, Production and Operations Management, Harvard Business Review,* and *Management Science.* He has served in various editorial capacities for several journals.

PREFACE

We firmly believe that, to gain a competitive edge, organizations need sound operations strategies. This is particularly true today, given the pressures of global competition and the need to satisfy ever more demanding customers. The Fourth Edition of *Operations Management: Strategy and Analysis* reaffirms our view in light of the issues currently facing operations managers. We approach the operations function as a powerful tool for achieving organizational objectives and strategies.

Our aim is to help students become effective managers in today's competitive environment. With this purpose in mind, we set ourselves several goals for the Fourth Edition. First, because many students taking this course will go on to become managers in service and manufacturing organizations in a wide variety of functional areas, we wanted to focus on the challenge of both managing and understanding the interrelatedness of the operations function. Second, to help students discover the excitement of the dynamic field of operations management, we wanted to make the subject matter as lively as possible, by showing operations in action at numerous service and manufacturing firms, presenting discussion questions designed to prompt lively class discussions, and including cases of real-world firms that would encourage open debate of important issues. Third, to put the subject in an appropriate context, we wanted students to gain an understanding of what operations managers do, to realize that operations management involves many cross-functional links, and to learn more about the tools that operations managers use to make better operating decisions.

The Textbook

The Fourth Edition of *Operations Management: Strategy and Analysis* contains comprehensive coverage of the basic concepts and issues taught in an introductory operations management (OM) course. It also provides thorough coverage of the material tested on the American Production and Inventory Control Society certification exams for the Certified Production and Inventory Management and Certified Integrated Resource Management programs.

Philosophy. This revision reflects our philosophy that OM texts should address both the strategic importance and the analytic tools of operations management. Strategic and managerial issues have been woven into the fabric of each chapter to emphasize that the decisions made by operations managers in each topical area should be consistent with a corporate strategy shared by managers in all functional areas. We present the operations tools and techniques for solving problems in the context of achieving a firm's overall goals and strategies.

Organization. We have chosen to organize the text so that it moves from strategic choices to design decisions to operating decisions. Chapters 1, 2, and 3 are introductory chapters, which explore how organizations use the operations function to gain a competitive edge. Discussion centers on strategic issues related to developing customer-driven operations strategies; process choice, improvement, and reengineering; and critical cross-functional linkages. These concepts are solidified with detailed tours of two real organizations—a hospital and a steel company.

Chapters 4 and 5 deal with the important issues associated with quality. In the Fourth Edition, the chapter on quality management has been renamed Total Quality Management, and much new material has been incorporated to reflect current thought on quality management, including ideas on teamwork, employee involvement, continuous improvement, benchmarking, and quality function deployment. Also new are sections on tools for quality improvement and ISO 9000. The focus of Chapter 5, Statistical Process Control, has been redirected more toward statistical principles than mathematical mechanics, and coverage has been expanded to include the topic of process capability.

Chapters 6–9 address the decisions that managers make in designing an operating system to meet their firm's needs. Issues include work-force management and job design, capacity, location, and layout.

Having determined the appropriate design for their operations, managers must make successful operating decisions. Chapters 10–17 examine the issues that managers face as they coordinate day-to-day activities consistent with an overall operations strategy. Topics covered include forecasting, materials management, independent-demand inventory systems, aggregate planning, material requirements planning and master production scheduling, just-in-time systems, operations and work-force scheduling, and project scheduling and control.

If students are to gain a better understanding of the importance of operations management, they must learn how it is practiced in the real world. Our general approach is to paint concepts in broad strokes and then to follow up with current real-world applications whenever possible.

Flexibility.   One of our objectives was to write a textbook that offers considerable flexibility in order and depth of coverage (qualitative or quantitative) and in level (undergraduate or graduate). Thus instructors will find that the organization of the text allows smooth adaptation to various course syllabi. Once Chapters 1 and 2 have been covered, instructors can easily rearrange chapters to suit their individual teaching needs.

A major change from the Third to the Fourth Edition is in the treatment of quantitative methods used in operations. The nine supplements (labeled A through I) have been totally reorganized, rewritten for greater accessibility, and interspersed where appropriate within the main text (rather than collected at the end of the book, as they were in the Third Edition). Each topical supplement is complete within itself and includes a full problem set. This new arrangement is intended to make it easier and more pedagogically effective for instructors to incorporate this material into their courses if they desire.

Coverage.   The measure of success in the textbook business is acceptance in the marketplace. We are pleased that the first three editions of our book were so well received. The challenge in preparing a new edition was deciding what to retain and what to change. In doing so, we relied greatly on feedback from both professors and students. Following are highlights of the revisions made to enhance coverage of the ever-changing field of operations management.

• *Cross-Functional Connections.*   Chapter 1 emphasizes the role of operations management and how it can interface with all functional areas to improve organizational effectiveness. This theme is reinforced throughout the text, as in Chapter 11, where a discussion of cross-functional coordination of materials management has been added.

• *Customer-Driven Operations Strategy.* Chapter 2 explains how corporate strategy recognizes customer needs and demand and communicates them to operations in the form of competitive priorities. This theme is then carried throughout the text. The rationale for a firm's positioning strategy and its impact on various functional areas have been clarified in this edition.

• *Process Choice.* New material on the basic types of processes and how they are related to competitive priorities has been added to a completely revised chapter on process management. Process choice is a critical issue in the development of effective operations strategies, and we refer to it throughout the text.

• *Total Quality Management.* Chapter 4 now provides extensive coverage of continuous improvement, employee involvement, teamwork, benchmarking, quality functional deployment, and six tools of TQM: checklists, histograms, Pareto charts, scatter diagrams, cause-and-effect diagrams, and graphs. Chapter 5 contains expanded discussion of statistical process control methods, including how to assess process capability.

• *International Operations.* New material has been added on global competition and international quality standards such as ISO 9000. Information on international operations has been incorporated throughout the text.

• *Current Developments in Operations.* Discussions of the impact on operations management of important new developments in such areas as outsourcing, virtual corporations, reengineering, horizontal organizations, employee and team incentive plans, ethics, and environmental concerns have been added throughout the text.

• *Inventory Management.* A completely new supplement on inventory models contains an explanation of the economic lot size model and expanded coverage of the one-period and quantity-discount models. Chapter 12 now covers continuous review systems under conditions of constant demand with constant lead time and variable demand with variable lead time. An overview of an emerging form of just-in-time systems, JIT II, has been incorporated into Chapter 15.

• *Service Operations.* In this edition we have achieved a better balance between service and manufacturing examples and problems. In addition, we have expanded the discussion of staffing plans in the service sector in Chapter 13 and the use of just-in-time systems for service operations in Chapter 15.

• *Decision Making.* A new supplement on decision making covers decision theory, multiple criteria, and decision trees.

• *Quantitative Tools.* Supplements on techniques have been expanded and the mathematics made less formal and more intuitive. The linear programming supplement has been completely revised to include graphic sensitivity analysis and to be more computer oriented. Examples of the use of the computer have been incorporated throughout this edition.

• *Cases.* Eleven new cases complement the cases in the Third Edition, so virtually every chapter has at least one short case.

• *Problems and Study Questions.* With the addition of 150 new problems and 120 new study questions, this edition has 20 percent more problems and questions than the Third Edition.

Approach and Pedagogy.   In the Fourth Edition, our message to the student is clear: This text presents *practical* approaches to solving operations problems, and the solutions to those problems can and do make a difference in a firm's competitiveness.

We continue to provide a balanced treatment of manufacturing and services throughout the text. This approach not only reflects the realities of the global economy, but also helps the student view the field of operations management as a cohesive whole. Although there are separate sections addressing services where appropriate, a key goal was to provide a variety of service and manufacturing examples *throughout* the text.

In addition to presenting concepts as clearly and accessibly as possible, we have used pedagogical features to reinforce important ideas. The Fourth Edition includes the following pedagogical features, designed to motivate students and make this textbook a better teaching and learning tool.

- *Full-Color Art.*   Full-color drawings and photographs throughout the Fourth Edition help bring the subject alive and help the student visualize operations in action. We planned the use of color carefully to enhance the pedagogy of the text—complex diagrams are easier to understand because key elements are color-coded in a consistent manner.

- *Chapter Outlines.*   A chapter outline provides a quick overview of the topics covered in each chapter and supplement.

- *Chapter-Opening Vignettes.*   Each chapter opens with an example of how a company actually dealt with the specific operations issues addressed in the chapter.

- *Questions from Managers.*   In the margins are questions linked to the material being discussed. These voices from the real world highlight key concepts and permit a quick review of these concepts.

- *"The Big Picture."*   Five full-color, two-page spreads present the layouts of the Lower Florida Keys Hospital, Chaparral Steel, King Soopers Bakery, the Addison-Wesley warehouse, and the Coors Field baseball stadium to reinforce various topics. The Addison-Wesley and Coors Field layouts are new to the Fourth Edition.

- *Managerial Practices.*   Boxed inserts show operations management in action at various firms. Balanced between service and manufacturing organizations, these inserts present current examples of how companies—successfully or unsuccessfully—meet the operations challenges facing them.

- *Examples.*   Formerly labeled applications, the examples are a popular feature designed to help students more easily understand the quantitative material. Whenever a new technique is presented, an example is immediately provided to walk the student through the solution.

- *Chapter Highlights.*   A bulleted list of the key points appears at the end of each chapter.

- *Key Terms.*   Key terms are boldfaced and defined the first time they appear in the text. These terms also are listed at the end of each chapter, with a page reference to permit easy review.

- *Solved Problems.*   At the end of each chapter, detailed solutions demonstrate how to solve problems with the techniques presented in the chapter. These solved problems reinforce basic concepts and serve as models for students to refer to when doing the problems that follow.

• *Formula Review and Formula Review Card.* A summary of the chapter's important formulas is provided at the end of each chapter. New to the Fourth Edition is a detachable formula review card, included for easy review and reference.

• *End-of-Chapter Problem Material.* Most chapters have three types of problem material: study questions, discussion questions, and problems. A great deal of effort was expended to update, enliven, and increase the number of questions and problems in the Fourth Edition. We are grateful to Nile Leach for his excellent contribution to the problem materials for this edition. Although we were involved in all aspects of production of the problem materials, Nile provided 150 new problems, revised many of the existing problems, and ensured the overall accuracy and appropriate grading (in terms of increasing level of difficulty) of the problem sets.

• *Cases.* Most chapters now end with at least one case. These cases can either serve as a basis for classroom discussion or provide an important capstone problem to the chapter, challenging students to grapple with the issues of the chapter in a less structured and more comprehensive way. Many of the cases can be used as in-class exercises without prior student preparation. These real-world cases are powerful tools for student involvement, and we are indebted to Dr. Brooke Saladin (Wake Forest University) for preparing them for eleven of our chapters. Brooke also provided detailed casenotes for each case, including excellent suggestions for teaching them. We are also indebted to Professor Robert Bregman (University of Houston) and Professor Sue Perrott Siferd (Arizona State University) for providing one case each. Casenotes for all seventeen cases are provided in the *Instructor's Manual*.

Ancillary Materials

From an instructor's perspective, having a good textbook to work with is only half the battle. We are committed to creating a total package that will maximize the student's learning potential and ease the instructor's burden. To this end, the following ancillary support is available.

Instructor's Manual. The *Instructor's Manual* includes suggested course outlines, teaching notes and detailed lecture notes for each chapter, lecture notes that can be distributed to students for class sessions, casenotes for all the cases found in the main text, and a formula review section.

Solutions Manual. Written by Nile Leach and thoroughly checked for accuracy, this manual—intended for instructors, who may in turn choose to share it with students—provides complete solutions to all problems in the text. The appendix provides detailed printouts of solutions to selected computer problems presented in the text.

Test Item File and Computerized Testbank. The nearly 2000 items in the testing material have been coded according to level of difficulty. Every effort has been made to include a balance of conceptual and technique-oriented questions.

New to this version are four or five short-answer questions and one or two essay questions per chapter to further test the student's conceptual understanding of the material and critical thinking skills. The computerized testbank allows instructors to custom design their examinations. It is available in both IBM PC (and compatibles) and Macintosh versions.

Transparency Masters. The *Transparency Masters* feature key figures, diagrams, and problems from the book. Many of these masters are new visuals which do not appear in the text; they consist of lists or partial solutions designed to complement the annotated course outline and lecture notes in the *Instructor's Manual.*

Full-Color Acetates. Over 100 full-color acetates depicting key figures and diagrams in the text are available to adopters.

Study Guide. Contained in the *Study Guide* are detailed chapter notes, self-testing questions, additional review problems, and solutions for all chapters and supplements. Written by Nile Leach, the *Study Guide* is available for purchase by students.

Computer Models for Operations Management (CMOM). CMOM is an easy-to-learn and easy-to-use stand-alone package developed and newly updated by Owen P. Hall of Pepperdine University. The CMOM package was used to solve the computer problems presented at the ends of various chapters and supplements. This software provides a survey of the analytical tools for solving many of the quantitative problems encountered in an operations course. Basic requirements include an IBM PC with 256K memory and DOS 2.1 or later version.

Videos. Several video options are available for the Fourth Edition. We continue to offer *OM in Action.* These videos, made specifically to accompany this text, provide a series of plant tours that teach operations management. These tours include process choice at a large commercial bakery, total quality management as applied at an exclusive hotel chain, capacity and queuing at a bank, and independent demand inventory at the Addison-Wesley warehouse. A series of MacNeil/Lehrer Business Reports is also available, as is a video from Chaparral Steel, one of the plant tours included in the book.

ACKNOWLEDGMENTS

Revising a textbook is a major project, and we could not have accomplished the task without the help of a great many people. The entire Addison-Wesley publishing team has been a joy to work with. Those most closely involved with the project and for whom we hold the greatest admiration include Julie Berrisford, our senior sponsoring editor, whose ability to instill harmony where chaos could reign was instrumental in helping us create a quality product; Stephanie Botvin, senior development editor, who helped us decide what material had to be cut (as painful as it was) and guided our efforts at making the text much more understandable; Kate Morgan, editorial assistant, who further enhanced her skills to tactfully pour coals on our fire in the right places; Jerrold Moore, copyeditor, who has the enviable ability to turn our prose into polished text; Sally Lifland, editorial/production coordinator, who feigned good humor when we upended her dummy proofs; and Susan London-Payne, technical art consultant, whose patience with author changes to the artwork was greatly appreciated.

We wish to thank our colleagues who provided extremely useful guidance for the Fourth Edition. They include the following:

Jerry Allison
University of Central Oklahoma

Joe Biggs
California Polytechnic State University, San Luis Obispo

Raymond Boykin
California State University, Chico

Injazz Chen
Cleveland State University

Ken Cutright
Ohio University

Warren Fisher
Stephen F. Austin State University

Jeff Heyl
Lincoln University, NZ

Thomas Johnson
University of South Florida

Manuel Laguna
University of Colorado, Boulder

N. Paul Loomba
CUNY, Bernard M. Baruch College

W. Rocky Newman
Miami University of Ohio

William A. Ruch
Arizona State University

Gerald Shapiro
Virginia Polytechnic Institute and State University

Ramesh Soni
Indiana University of Pennsylvania

David West
Bryant College

Don Williams
Abilene Christian University

Jack Yurkiewicz
Pace University

We also are indebted to Cheng Li, California State University–Los Angeles, and Richard E. Peschke, Moorhead State University, for checking the accuracy of all examples and solved problems in the text.

Special thanks go to several colleagues who provided major inputs to the Fourth Edition. Nile Leach did an outstanding job with the Solved Problems, Study Questions, Discussion Questions, and Problems in the text, as well as authoring the *Solutions Manual*, parts of the *Instructor's Manual*, and *Study Guide*. His skills at making the material interesting to students will add much to the success of this edition. Brooke Saladin wrote eleven excellent cases of real-world situations to fit the material in the text. His contributions make it easy for instructors to add excitement to their classes. Owen P. Hall provided the computer solutions to selected problems in the text and updated his CMOM package, thereby greatly improving the linkage of our material to the computer. David McKenna, Boston College, helped us make significant improvements to the linear programming supplement with his ideas and writings that clearly demonstrated through graphic and algebraic analysis the meaning of shadow prices, coefficient sensitivity, and ranging. We also thank John Lehigh, Executive Director of the Denver Metropolitan Major League Baseball Stadium District, for the background material for the Coors Field Big Picture, and Dave Krajewski of Grace Cocoa for the details of the production process for making chocolate drops, described in the opener to Chapter 5.

Our appreciation for helpful suggestions and moral support is extended to our colleagues in the Department of Management Sciences, The Ohio State University, especially W. C. Benton, Bill Berry, Dave Collier, Keong Leong, and Peter Ward. We gratefully acknowledge the many comments and suggestions from our past and present Ph.D. students who have relayed their experiences in the classroom to us. We also thank Paul Sainsbury, Boston College, for his help in proofing, doing library research, and developing materials for the test item file.

Finally, we thank our families for putting up with the long conference calls, countless express deliveries just as we were walking out the door for an outing, and long periods of solitude followed by crankiness. As always, Judie and Barb were 100 percent supportive of our efforts, even though we still owe them an elegant dinner for this revision.

L. J. K.
South Bend, Indiana

L. P. R.
Medfield, Massachusetts

BRIEF CONTENTS

CONTENTS

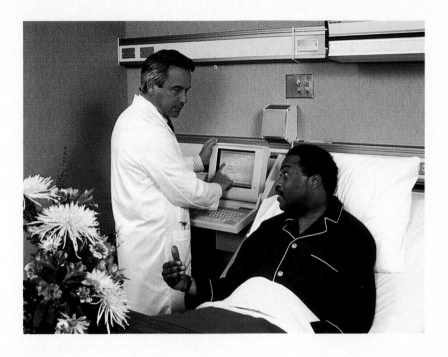

Supplement F   Simulation Analysis   323

Chapter 8   Location   336

Chapter 15 Just-in-Time Systems 721

Chapter One

OPERATIONS AS A COMPETITIVE WEAPON

The K2 Corporation (named for the world's second-highest mountain) is a world-class manufacturer of ski equipment and uses operations management as a competitive weapon. The way the operations function handles new product introductions, manufacturing processes, job designs, capacities, inventory levels, and schedules allows it to implement effectively the company's overall strategy.

To support the company's competitive efforts, operations devotes some facilities to high-volume stock items and others to low-volume customized products. Consistent quality, an important part of K2's competitive plan, is the responsibility of each operator at each workstation; operators are trained to monitor critical quality measures. To handle product variety, K2 installed general-purpose machinery to allow easy changeovers from one product to another. It also invested in a technology that gives designers greater control over ski performance. Production and machine maintenance are managed carefully because the plant runs at full capacity. The company prepares for heavy seasonal sales with a production plan that calls for building finished goods inventories from January to May.

The ski industry includes a competitive service sector, with numerous mountain resorts for both beginners and skilled athletes. Operations management also plays an important role in this segment of the ski market. Ski the Summit, in Colorado, offers three full-service resorts and four ski areas with 9 skiable mountains. It also provides such services as ski lessons, helicopter skiing, snowmobiling, and sleigh rides, as well as a variety of restaurants and social events.

Ski the Summit's operations are carefully designed for each service. For example, lifts are de-

Ski the Summit consists of four Colorado resorts—Copper Mountain, Keystone, Arapahoe Basin, and Breckenridge. Where gold, copper, and silver once reigned as the precious minerals, snow now attracts over three million skiers annually.

signed within safety guidelines for high-volume, low-cost operations. The more elegant restaurants are designed for low-volume, high-quality meals. Scheduled events must begin on time, and careful capacity planning keeps costs down and quality of service high. Extensive off-season promotions help stabilize demand.

These two companies—one in manufacturing and the other in services—are making operations management a key weapon in gaining competitive advantage. So it is with many of the real company examples presented in this text.

Operations management deals with the production of goods and services that people buy and use every day. It is the function that enables organizations to achieve their goals through efficient acquisition and utilization of resources. Manufacturers of skis, steel, and computers need operations management. So do ski resorts, health care providers, banks, and retailers. Every organization, whether public or private, manufacturing or service, has an operations function. The management of that function is the focus of this book. We explore with you the role of operations within the total organization. We explain what operations managers do, as well as some of the latest tools and concepts they use to support key decisions. By selecting appropriate techniques and strategies, successful operations managers can give their companies a competitive edge, making operations management one of the most exciting and challenging careers the modern business world offers.

◆ WHAT IS OPERATIONS MANAGEMENT?

Like other industrial societies, the United States is a society of organizations, ranging from sports teams, schools, and churches to hospitals, legal institutions, military bases, and large and small businesses. These formal groups enable people to produce a vast range of products and services that would be beyond the capabilities of the individual. Operations management is crucial to each type of organization because only through successful management of people, capital, and materials can an organization meet its goals.

At one time, the term "operations management" referred primarily to manufacturing production. The growing economic importance of a wide range of nonmanufacturing business activities, however, broadened the scope of the operations management function. Today, the term **operations management** refers to the direction and control of the processes that transform inputs into finished goods and services. This function is essential to systems producing goods and services in both profit and nonprofit organizations.

As Fig. 1.1 illustrates, operations management is part of a production system. Inputs include human resources (workers and managers), capital (equipment and facilities), purchased materials and services, land, and energy. The numbered circles represent the operations through which products, services, or customers may pass during the transformation process. The type of transforma-

FIGURE 1.1

The Operations Management System

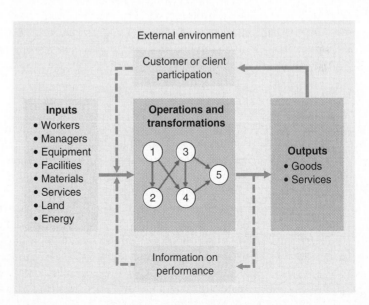

tion may vary. For example, at a factory the transformation would be a physical or chemical change of raw materials into products. At an airline it would be the movement of passengers and their luggage from one location to another. At a school it would be the education of students. And at a hospital it would be the healing of sick or wounded patients. The facilities vary accordingly: a machine center, two or more airport terminals, a classroom, and a hospital room.

The dashed lines in Fig. 1.1 represent two special types of input: participation by customers or clients and information on performance from internal and external sources. Participation by customers or clients occurs when they not only receive the outputs but also take an active part in the transformation process itself, such as students participating in a class discussion. Information on performance includes internal reports on customer service or inventory management and external information from market research, government reports, or telephone calls from suppliers. The operations manager needs all types of information to manage the production system.

Inputs and outputs vary among different industries. For example, inputs to the operations of a jewelry store include merchandise, the store building, registers, the jeweler, and customers; the output of the store is customer sales. Inputs to a factory manufacturing blue jeans include denim, machines, the plant, workers, managers, and services provided by outside consultants; the output of the factory is clothing. However, the underlying transformation process holds true for all production systems.

◆ DIFFERENCES AND SIMILARITIES BETWEEN MANUFACTURING AND SERVICES

In the early history of operations management and until the middle of the twentieth century, the focus was on manufacturing organizations, and the field was thus called *industrial management* or *production management*. Service organizations, because they performed almost at handicraft levels, were largely ignored. Times have changed. Today's managers apply concepts of quality, process analysis, job design, facility location, capacity, layout, inventory, and scheduling to both manufacturing and the provision of services. The benefits are improved quality, reduced costs, and increased value to the customers, all of which give the firm a competitive edge.

Differences

How do service operations differ from manufacturing operations?

The differences between manufacturing and service organizations fall into the eight categories shown in Fig. 1.2. However, these distinctions actually represent the ends of a continuum. The first distinction arises from the physical nature of the product. Manufactured goods are *physical, durable* products. Services are *intangible, perishable* products—often being ideas, concepts, or information.

The second distinction also relates to the physical nature of the product. Manufactured goods are outputs that can be produced, stored, and transported in anticipation of future demand. Creating *inventories* allows managers to cope with peaks and valleys in demand by smoothing output levels. By contrast, services cannot be preproduced. Without inventories as a cushion against erratic customer demand, service organizations are more constrained by time.

FIGURE 1.2

Continuum of Characteristics of Manufacturing and Service Organizations

More like a manufacturing organization

More like a service organization

- Physical, durable product
- Output can be inventoried
- Low customer contact
- Long response time
- Regional, national, or international markets
- Large facilities
- Capital intensive
- Quality easily measured

- Intangible, perishable product
- Output cannot be inventoried
- High customer contact
- Short response time
- Local markets
- Small facilities
- Labor intensive
- Quality not easily measured

A third distinction is *customer contact*. Most customers for manufactured products have little or no contact with the production system. Primary customer contact is left to distributors and retailers. However, in many service organizations the customers themselves are inputs and active participants in the process. For example, at a college the student studies, attends lectures, takes exams, and finally receives a diploma. Hospitals, jails, and entertainment centers are other places where the customer is present during the provision of most of the services. Some service operations have low customer contact at one level of the organization and high customer contact at other levels. For example, the branch offices of parcel delivery, banking, and insurance organizations deal with customers daily,

H&R Block tax preparers assist customers in filing their tax returns. Temporary store-front operations offer taxpayers convenience and allow the firm to maximize customer contact during the busy tax season of January through April.

but their central offices have little direct customer contact. Similarly, the backroom operations of a jewelry store require little customer contact, whereas sales counter operations involve a high degree of contact.

A related distinction is *response time* to customer demand. Manufacturers generally have days or weeks to meet customer demand, but many services must be offered within minutes of customer arrival. The purchaser of a forklift truck may be willing to wait 16 weeks for delivery. By contrast, a grocery store customer may grow impatient after waiting five minutes in a checkout line. Because customers for services usually arrive at times of their choosing, service operations may have difficulty matching capacity with demand. Furthermore, arrival patterns may fluctuate daily or even hourly, creating even more short-term demand uncertainty.

Two other distinctions concern the *location* and *size* of an operation. Manufacturing facilities often serve regional, national, or even international markets and therefore generally require larger facilities, more automation, and greater capital investment than for service facilities. In general, services cannot be shipped to distant locations. For example, a hairstylist in Manhattan cannot give a haircut to someone in Topeka. Thus service organizations requiring direct customer contact must locate relatively near their customers.

A final distinction is the measurement of *quality*. As manufacturing systems tend to have tangible products and less customer contact, quality is relatively easy to measure. The quality of service systems, which generally produce intangibles, is harder to measure. Moreover, individual preferences affect assessments of service quality, making objective measurement difficult. For example, one customer might value a friendly chat with the salesclerk during a purchase, whereas another might assess quality by the speed and efficiency of a transaction.

Similarities

Despite these distinctions, the similarities between manufacturing and service organizations are compelling. Every organization has processes that must be designed and managed effectively. Some type of technology, be it manual or computerized, must be used in each process. Every organization is concerned about quality, productivity, and the timely response to customers. A service organization, like a manufacturer, must make choices about the capacity, location, and layout of its facilities. Every organization deals with suppliers of outside services and materials, as well as scheduling problems. Matching staffing levels and capacities with forecasted demands is a universal problem. Finally, the distinctions between manufacturing and service organizations can get cloudy. Consider how the first three distinctions in Fig. 1.2 can get blurred.

• Manufacturers do not just offer products, and service organizations do not just offer services. Both types of organizations normally provide a package of goods and services. Customers expect both good service and good food at a restaurant and both good service and quality goods from a retailer. Manufacturing firms offer many customer services, and a decreasing proportion of the value added by them directly involves the transformation of materials.

• Despite the fact that service organizations cannot inventory their outputs, they must inventory the *inputs* for their products. These inputs must undergo further transformations during provision of the service. Hospitals, for example, must maintain an adequate supply of medications. As a result, wholesale and retail firms hold 44 percent of the U.S. economy's inventory. In addition, manufacturing firms that make customized products or limited-shelf-life products cannot inventory their outputs.

• As for customer contact, many operations in a service organization have little customer contact, such as the back-room operations of a bank or the baggage handling area at an airport. Moreover, as they seek ways to improve quality, both manufacturing and service organizations are beginning to realize that everyone in an organization has customers—outside customers or inside customers in the next office, shop, or department who rely on their inputs. A customer focus is needed in managing operations, whether in services or in manufacturing.

Clearly, operations management is relevant to both manufacturing and service operations. You need to know about operations management, regardless of the type of organization you work in or the function that most interests you.

◆ TRENDS IN OPERATIONS MANAGEMENT

Several business trends are currently having a great impact on operations management: the growth of the service sector; productivity changes; global competitiveness; quality, time, and technological change; continuous improvement; and other, wider issues. In this section we look at these trends and their implications for operations managers.

Service Sector Growth

The service sector of the economy is significant. As Fig. 1.3 shows, services may be divided into three main groups:

What are the implications of recent employment and productivity trends in the service sector?

1. government (local, state, and federal);
2. wholesale and retail sales; and
3. other services (transportation, public utilities, communication, health, financial services, real estate, insurance, repair services, business services, and personal service).

FIGURE 1.3

Percentage of Jobs in the U.S. Service Sector

Source: *Economic Report of the President,* February 1994, pp. 318–319.

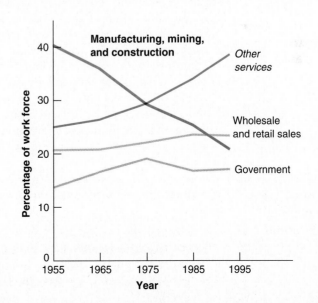

Between 1955 and 1993 the number of U.S. jobs in service-producing industries rose from 60 to 79 percent of total nonfarm jobs. Manufacturing and other goods-producing industries currently account for the remaining 21 percent of jobs in the United States. Although the absolute number of manufacturing jobs has increased (from 20.5 to 23 million), the percentage of manufacturing jobs in the total economy has declined. Similar increases in the percentage of the work force in service jobs are taking place in the other industrial countries. For example, the share of the work force in service jobs is well above 60 percent in Britain, Canada, France, and Japan.

Nonetheless, manufacturing remains a significant part of the U.S. economy. The value of manufacturing output (in real dollars) rose 22 percent in just the last decade. Moreover, the service and manufacturing sectors of the economy are complementary. For example, the output of many firms is purchased by other firms as inputs. More than 25 percent of these intermediate outputs, such as express mail and consulting services, are classified as services but go to companies in the nonservice sector.

Productivity Changes

Productivity is the value of outputs (goods and services) produced divided by the values of input resources (wages, cost of equipment, and the like) used:

$$\text{Productivity} = \frac{\text{Output}}{\text{Input}}$$

Many measures of productivity are possible, and all are rough approximations. Managers usually pick several reasonable measures and monitor their trends to spot areas needing improvement. For example, a manager at an insurance firm might measure office productivity as the number of insurance policies processed per employee each week. A manager at a carpet company might measure the productivity of installers as the number of square yards of carpet installed per hour. Both of these measures reflect *labor productivity,* which is an index of the output per person or hour worked. Similar measures may be used for *machine productivity,* where the denominator is the number of machines. Accounting for several inputs simultaneously is also possible. *Multifactor productivity* is an index of the output provided by more than one of the resources used in production. For example, it may be the value of the output divided by the sum of labor, materials, and overhead costs. When developing such a measure, you must convert the quantities to a common unit of measure, typically dollars.

EXAMPLE 1.1

Productivity Calculations

Calculate the productivity for the following operations:

a. Three employees processed 600 insurance policies last week. They worked 8 hours per day, 5 days per week.

b. A team of workers made 400 units of a product, which has a standard cost of $10 each. The accounting department reported that for this job the actual costs were $400 for labor, $1000 for materials, and $300 for overhead.

Solution

a. Labor productivity $= \dfrac{\text{Policies processed}}{\text{Employee hours}}$

   $= \dfrac{600 \text{ policies}}{(3 \text{ employees})(40 \text{ hours/employee})} = 5 \text{ policies/hour}$

b. Multifactor productivity $= \dfrac{\text{Quantity at selling price}}{\text{Labor cost} + \text{Materials cost} + \text{Overhead cost}}$

   $= \dfrac{(400 \text{ units})(\$10/\text{unit})}{\$400 + \$1000 + \$300} = \dfrac{\$4000}{\$1700} = 2.35$

Comparing these numbers with past performance might reveal opportunities for improvement.

Operations managers play a key role in determining productivity. Their challenge is to increase the value of output relative to the cost of input. If they can generate more output or output of better quality using the same amount of input, productivity increases. If they can maintain the same level of output while reducing the use of resources, productivity also increases.

At the national level, productivity typically is measured as the *dollar value of output per unit of labor.* This measure depends on the quality of the products and services generated in a nation and on the efficiency with which they are produced. Productivity is the prime determinant of a nation's standard of living. If the value of output per work hour goes up, the nation benefits from higher overall income levels, because the productivity of human resources determines employee wages. Conversely, lagging or declining productivity lowers the standard of living. Wage or price increases not accompanied by productivity increases lead to inflationary pressures rather than real increases in the standard of living.

U.S. Productivity. Figure 1.4(a) shows that the growth rate in productivity for manufacturing and services in the U.S. economy slowed down in the last three decades. (The graph reflects manufacturing and services combined but excludes farms, which represent less than 5 percent of U.S. output and employment.) Productivity is measured as the dollar value of output per hour worked, and percentage changes are shown. During the 1950s the annual productivity increase averaged 2.6 percent, but by the 1980s the annual increase averaged only 1.0 percent. The upturn so far in the 1990s is encouraging, but low productivity growth is still cause for concern.

Extremely low productivity increases in services (less than 0.1 percent per year) have slowed overall growth. Figure 1.4(b) shows that major trading partners such as Japan and Germany are experiencing the same problem. In the United States productivity increases in manufacturing during the 1980s averaged 2.9 percent per year, well ahead of the 1.0 percent for the economy as a whole. The whole economy's increase during the 1990s has been a respectable 1.7 percent. In contrast, productivity in the service sector was basically flat, despite the billions of dollars spent on computers and office technology. Many economists expect this trend to continue for the rest of the 1990s, although there are signs of improvement. Government deregulation of the telecommunications and airline industries and a surge of investment abroad in services are stimulating productivity increases. These events expose service firms to greater competition and increase

FIGURE 1.4

U.S. and Worldwide Productivity Growth

Sources: "America the Super-Fit," *The Economist,* February 13, 1993, p. 67; *Economic Report of the President,* February 1994, p. 323; "International Comparisons Data," *Monthly Labor Review,* June 1993. Figures for Germany refer to West Germany.

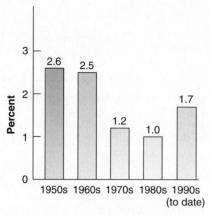

(a) Average annual growth in productivity (output per hour) for U.S. business sector over five decades.

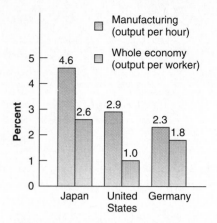

(b) Average annual productivity growth by sector and country in the 1980s.

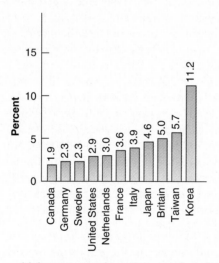

(c) Average annual growth in manufacturing productivity (output per hour) worldwide during the 1980s.

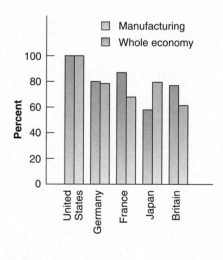

(d) Current value added per hour worked by sector and country.

the motivation to increase productivity. Perhaps in the next decade investment in information technology will begin to pay off for service organizations.

Some Possible Explanations.   One explanation for lower productivity in services than in manufacturing is the unreliability of the statistical data on the service sector. Quantifying the real value (rather than the cost) of outputs from some parts of the service sector, such as the government, health services, or education, is more difficult than measuring that of manufacturing outputs. Furthermore, productivity advances vary greatly by industry within the service sector. In software development and telecommunications, for example, U.S. industry is preeminent. Distribution systems, sophisticated health care, and advanced education are other bright spots. The vitality of the service sector is crucial to the U.S. economy; if productivity stagnates in services, the overall standard of living will decline. Thus productivity growth in services remains a concern.

What are the causes of recent productivity trends and shifts in shares of world markets?

Analysts have offered many other explanations for the mixed results on U.S. productivity. These explanations include the increased costs imposed by federal and state regulations governing occupational safety, health, and environmental protection; low investment in new equipment and facilities during the late 1970s and 1980s; the changing composition of the work force and changing attitudes toward work; and high wages and stringent union contracts. However, such explanations are incomplete. For example, Japanese firms operate successfully in the United States—using U.S. workers and paying U.S. costs, while achieving higher productivity and quality than their U.S. counterparts. Managerial Practice 1.1 on the next page describes two such Japanese-owned facilities. The lesson from these Japanese firms is that managers and employees can increase productivity and maintain high wages, salaries, and living standards through careful attention to operations management.

Global Competition

Today businesses accept that, to prosper, they must view customers, suppliers, facility locations, and competitors in global terms. Most products today are global composites of materials and services from throughout the world. Parts for your U.S. Zenith TV are assembled in Mexico, and your Gap polo shirt is sewn in Honduras from cloth cut in the United States. Sitting in the theater you munch a Nestlé's Crunch bar (Swiss) while watching a Columbia Pictures movie (Japanese) at a Cineplex theater (Canadian).

Two decades ago, imports of products and services were equivalent to just over 5 percent of total U.S. output; now they are over 13 percent. In Japan, imports climbed from 10 percent in 1970 to 14 percent today. In manufacturing, U.S. firms are competing with Asian and European firms. Figure 1.4(c) shows that East Asian countries such as South Korea and Taiwan achieved remarkable productivity gains during the 1980s. Developing countries such as Brazil, China, India, Malaysia, and Mexico are expected to become important in global terms in the future. And regional trading blocks such as ECC and NAFTA further change the competitive landscape.

Because of stiffening competition, U.S. firms have experienced declining shares of the domestic and international markets in steel, appliances and household durable goods, machinery, and chemicals. Industries hardest hit include the semiconductor, computer, steel, machine tools, consumer electronics, shipbuilding, telecommunications, and automobile industries. For example, Japan's share of the U.S. automobile market was 0.2 percent in 1965, 20 percent in 1980, and 23 percent in 1994.

Firms in banking, law, data processing, airlines, and consulting are beginning to face many of the same international pressures as U.S. manufacturers. For example, more than 260 foreign banks now operate in the United States; they have increased their share of domestic banking from 14 percent in 1982 to over 21 percent today. The world trade in services now stands at more than $600 billion.

Figure 1.4(d) suggests that, although the productivity gap is narrowing, U.S. workers are still more productive than their counterparts in other large economies. The average value added per hour worked is well above the productivity achieved elsewhere (in the whole economy and particularly in manufacturing). Even in manufacturing, Japanese productivity is 20 percent less than that in the United States. In globally competitive manufacturing industries, the United States attracts 37 percent of sales, Japan 32 percent, and Europe 31 percent. In

Managerial Practice 1.1

▶ *Successful Japanese-Owned Facilities in the United States*

Toyota Motor Corporation

In setting up New United Motor Manufacturing, Inc. (NUMMI), Toyota Motor Corporation joined forces with General Motors to revamp a mothballed GM plant in Fremont, California. Even though NUMMI is operating with GM's work force, in GM's building, and with much of GM's technology, productivity has skyrocketed because of the way its managers organized and operate the plant: The NUMMI managers set up a typical Toyota production system with just-in-time delivery and a flexible production line run by teams of workers in charge of their own jobs. As a result, NUMMI now operates with 3100 employees, compared to 5000 at some GM plants, and production costs are comparable to Toyota's costs in Japan. Now, GM executives are visiting the Toyota-managed factory to learn how it achieves high quality and productivity.

Honda of America

Honda of America Manufacturing Company now makes Accords in Marysville, Ohio, at approximately the same cost and almost the same quality as its parent in Japan. Dealers had originally pleaded with Honda not to build cars in the United States, believing that American workers could not build them as well as the Japanese. Time has shown that the key factor instead is Honda's management style. Managers use a hands-on approach attuned to correcting problems, simplifying

product designs, limiting inventories, simplifying layouts, and passing on to workers and supervisors the responsibility for improving production techniques. Flexible teams, just-in-time delivery, attention to quality, and employee loyalty are hallmarks of this approach.

Management at Honda of America's Marysville, Ohio, plant presents teams with awards for improving production techniques. This team, known as the "Return of the Engine Clippers," won Honda's Very Best award in the Eighteenth General Presentations.

Source: "Crisis Is Galvanizing Detroit's Big Three," *Wall Street Journal,* May 2, 1991.

fact, the United States garners 48 percent of corporate profits in these industries, particularly in energy equipment, aerospace, data processing and software, electronic components, beverages and tobacco, and health and personal care products. These achievements come from knowledge, skills, and technology that U.S. firms built over the years. However, global competitors are making inroads that could lead to living standard erosion unless U.S. industries improve productivity further.

Competition Based on Quality, Time, and Technology

What can be done to compete better in terms of quality, time, and technology?

Another trend in operations management has been an increasing emphasis on competing on the basis of quality, time, and technological advantage. Part of the success of foreign competitors has been their ability to provide products and services of high quality at reasonable prices. During the 1970s and 1980s, customers grew more attuned to the *quality* of the good or service being purchased.

Without quality products or services, a firm loses its ability to compete in the marketplace, and its cost structure can also become uncompetitive. Operations managers, in conjunction with the managers of other functional departments, are giving more attention to quality than ever. Total quality management, which is introduced in Chapter 4, is a way of involving everyone in the organization in continuously improving quality. Statistical process control, covered in Chapter 5, is a set of useful statistical tools for monitoring quality performance.

Another important trend is that more firms are competing on the basis of *time:* filling orders earlier than the competition, introducing new products or services quickly, and reaching the market first. Honda used this ability to thwart Yamaha's attempt to replace Honda as the world's largest motorcycle manufacturer. Honda's strategy was to introduce a wide variety of products so quickly that Yamaha would be unable to keep up. Within 18 months, Honda introduced or replaced 113 models of motorcycles. Yamaha was unable to keep up, and its sales all but dried up.

Another increasingly important factor in operations management is accelerating *technological change.* It affects the design of new products and services and the production processes themselves. Many new opportunities are coming from advances in computer technology. Robots and various forms of information technology are but two examples, with U.S. firms alone spending $200 billion each year on information technology. The *Internet*—part of the telecommunications "information highway"—has emerged as a vital tool linking firms internally and linking firms externally with customers and strategic partners. This computer network has global e-mail and data exchange capabilities, with more than 100 countries already linked to it. Introducing any new technology involves risk, and employee attitudes toward it depend on how the change is managed. The right choices and effective management of technology can give a firm a competitive advantage.

Continuous Improvement

How can operations be continuously improved?

Many firms are aggressively seeking better ways to operate because of the stiff competition (both domestic and global) in productivity, quality, and time. The philosophy of **continuous improvement** seeks ways to improve operations. It means selecting valid performance measures, getting internal and external feedback on current performance, setting goals for future improvement, and enlisting everyone in the change process. Just-in-time systems (sometimes referred to as *lean manufacturing*) are driven by the goal of continuous improvement and focus on the customer's needs, particularly for lower costs, improved quality, and speedier delivery.

The spirit of continuous improvement resides in looking for new ideas to innovate and stay ahead of the competition. To foster a creative, competitive environment, some firms are *restructuring* by pushing responsibilities down the organization, removing people and management layers, and empowering employees to get more fully involved in making key decisions. Other firms are going even further, relying on teams to achieve cross-functional coordination and overcome the barriers that often separate functions in the business. Some firms have moved toward the *horizontal* (or *molecular*) *organization,* where an employee team representing the different functional areas is organized around each market and the corresponding process. The pyramid organization structure is gone, along with its top-down decision-making process. The goal, sometimes called **mass customization** (or *batch of one*), is to achieve closer contact with customers, giving them more individual attention while still providing quick delivery and the efficiencies of mass production. Other firms are **reengineering** their processes, a philosophy that calls for the radical redesign of essential business processes. Its aim is change—ignoring the way things have "always been done" in the industry or firm and redesigning the processes or product from scratch. Using ample doses of strong management leadership and new technologies, reengineering focuses on business processes rather than functional departments.

We examine these approaches, and others, in subsequent chapters. Some of them, such as mass customization, at first appear to be ideal for every organization. But they must be evaluated carefully for the unique environment in which each firm operates. Further, what may be best for one operation in a firm may not be best for another. What *is* always true, however, is that the individuals in an organization should never become complacent. Instead they need to seek ways, both incremental and radical, to improve operations. To remain competitive, the firm as a whole must be nimble enough to embrace change. The firm that does so, sometimes called a *learning organization*, will gain competitive advantage.

Environmental, Ethical, and Work-Force Diversity Issues

How do ethics and the environment affect operations?

Business challenges are always changing, and so must management education. Two recent studies, the Porter–McKibbin Report and the Graduate Management Admission Council Report, offer criticisms applicable to both U.S. and European business schools. These reports encourage business schools to turn out managers versed in basic environmental, ethical, and workplace diversity concerns. They decry the fact that too many business students, both undergraduates and graduates, are unprepared to face the difficult "soft" issues of the fast-changing global marketplace.

One expert suggests a more ethical approach to business in which firms

- have responsibilities that go beyond producing goods and services at a profit,
- help solve important social problems,
- respond to a broader constituency than shareholders alone,
- have impacts beyond simple marketplace transactions, and
- serve a range of human values that go beyond economic values.

Business ethicists argue that managers' decisions about the design and operation of production systems should take into account such social issues as unsafe workplaces, discrimination against minorities and women, toxic wastes, poisoned drinking water, poverty, air quality, and global warming. In the past many people viewed environmental problems as quality of life issues; in the 1990s many people see them as survival issues. Interest in a clean, healthy environment is increasing. Industrial nations have a particular burden because their combined populations, representing only 25 percent of the total global population, consume 70 percent of all resources. Just seven nations, including the United States and Japan, produce almost half of all greenhouse gases. The United States and some European nations now spend 2 percent of their gross domestic product on environmental protection, a figure environmentalists believe should increase.

In keeping with the ethic that private industry should do social good, Cummins Engine Company donated money to the American Red Cross for relief for Chicago tornado victims in August 1990. Many Cummins employees and their families live in this area.

◆ OPERATIONS MANAGEMENT AND THE ORGANIZATION

We have described how operations management affects competitive advantage in both manufacturing and service sectors. In this section we explore the role of operations management within the organization, the way it interacts with other functional areas, and how it can be used as a competitive weapon.

Operations Management As a Functional Area

Figure 1.5 shows that operations is but one of several functions within an organization. Large companies generally assign each function to a separate department, which assumes responsibility for certain activities. However, many of these functions are interrelated. Thus coordination and effective communication are essential to achieving organizational goals.

FIGURE 1.5 *Operations Management as a Function*

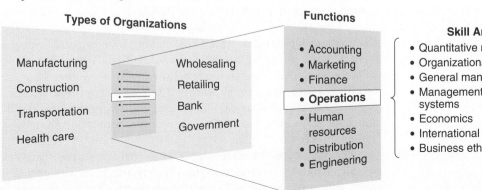

15

In large organizations, the *operations* (or *production*) *department* is usually responsible for the actual transformation of inputs into finished products or services. *Accounting* collects, summarizes, and interprets financial information. *Marketing* generates demand for the company's output. *Finance* secures and invests the company's capital assets. *Human resources* (or *personnel*) hires and trains employees. *Distribution* transports inputs and outputs. *Engineering* develops product and service designs and production methods. However, some organizations never need to perform certain functions. Other organizations may save money by contracting for a function, such as engineering, when they need it, rather than maintain an in-house department. In small businesses, the owners might manage one or more functions, such as marketing or operations, themselves.

Operations managers draw on many skill areas: quantitative analysis to solve problems; knowledge of information systems to manage vast quantities of data; concepts of organizational behavior to aid in designing jobs and managing the work force; and an understanding of international business methods to gain useful ideas about facility location, technology, and inventory management.

Operations serves as an excellent career path to upper management positions in many organizations. A recent survey of manufacturing firms showed that over 45 percent of the chief executives appointed in 1987 had an operations background. In manufacturing firms, the head of operations usually holds the title vice-president of manufacturing (or production or operations); the corresponding title in a service organization might be vice-president (or director) of operations. Reporting to the vice-president are the managers of other production departments, such as materials, industrial engineering, quality assurance, and plant supervision.

Operations Management As an Interfunctional Concern

Figure 1.6 shows that the operations function intersects with each of the other functional areas. The overlaps imply that decisions made in one area affect and are affected by the decisions made in the other areas. Too often organizations allow artificial barriers to be erected between functional areas and departments. In these situations, jobs or tasks move sequentially from marketing to engineering to operations. The result is often slow or poor decision making because each department bases its decisions solely on its own limited perspective, not the organization's overall perspective. A new approach being tried by many organizations is to replace linear decision making with more cross-functional coordination and flatter organizational structures. For example, Hallmark Cards formed cross-functional teams and cut its product development time by 50 percent.

Decisions in Operations.   Decision making is an essential aspect of all management activity, including the operations function. Although the specifics of each situation vary, decision making generally involves the same basic steps: (1) recognize and clearly define the problem, (2) collect the information needed to analyze possible alternatives, and (3) choose and implement the most feasible alternative. Supplement A at the end of Chapter 2 covers some tools that assist the decision-making process.

The *types* of decisions that operations managers participate in with others or actually make themselves may be divided into three categories: strategic decisions, design decisions, and operating decisions. In the following paragraphs, as

FIGURE 1.6

*Interfunctional
Connections*

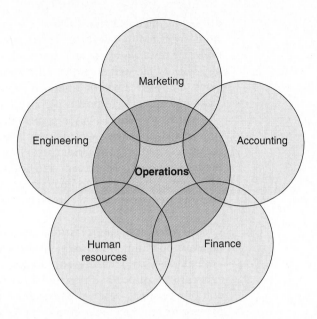

we identify some of the key decisions that affect operations, we cite the chapter (in parentheses) in which these issues are discussed.

We begin with the *strategic decisions* that affect the future direction of the company. For example, operations managers must help decide what the company's competitive priorities will be (2), whether to organize resources around products or processes (3), and what the quality objectives (4) and control methods (5) will be.

Next are the *design decisions* concerning the production system. Here the operations manager's recommendations and decisions often require long-term commitments. For example, the manager must help determine how specialized or enlarged the jobs should be (6), what the system's capacity should be (7), where to locate facilities (8), and how to organize departments and plan the facility's physical layout (9).

Operating decisions (sometimes called the *operations infrastructure*) deal with operating the facility after it has been built. At this stage the operations manager decides on the best forecasting approach (10), which suppliers to deal with (11), how to manage inventory (12), how to control output levels over shorter periods of time (13), when to release purchase or production orders and in what quantities (14), whether to implement just-in-time techniques (15), what customers or jobs to give top priority (16), and how to schedule resources (17).

Linking Decision Areas. The operations manager's decisions should reflect corporate strategy. Also, plans, policies, and actions within operations should be linked and mutually supportive. For example, process, quality, capacity, and inventory decisions must not be made independently. Even though individual choices may make sense on their own, collectively they might not add up to the best result.

Strategy and Analysis. A manager must deal with strategic issues (the "big picture"), as well as analytical or tactical issues. This book's subtitle, Strategy *and* Analysis, emphasizes the point. A course in operations management is not just about "concepts" or just about "numbers"—it has both dimensions. In the list of operations management (OM) decisions, note that long-range (or strategic) decisions are listed first and that tactical decisions are covered in later chapters. The importance of these tactical decisions should not be underestimated. For example, scheduling, which requires detailed analysis and numerous interrelated decisions, can have a major financial impact on a firm with millions of dollars at stake in completing a power plant or a hotel on time.

    Much of tactical planning depends on careful analysis. Fortunately, operations managers have a wide variety of analytic techniques at their disposal. These techniques range from simple pencil-and-paper techniques to sophisticated computer techniques. We present and illustrate both types of techniques throughout this book, often in a supplement at the end of the chapter. Both strategy and analysis are necessary and should complement each other.

Cross-Functional Coordination.   Cross-functional coordination is essential to effective operations management. However, many of the decision areas listed are not unique to an operations department. For instance, marketing or finance managers also must deal with quality, process, layout, and staffing issues. Thus, if operations develops new ways to achieve quality, lower costs, or speed deliveries, the rest of the organization may want to exploit these methods. Managing such interdependencies requires coordination and understanding across functional boundaries. As tomorrow's manager, you must understand the fundamentals of operations, regardless of your skill area.

    Consider how other functional areas interact with operations. Perhaps the strongest connection is with the marketing function, which determines the need for new products and services and the size of demand for existing ones. Operations managers must bring together human and capital resources to handle these demands effectively. The operations manager must consider facility locations and relocations to serve new markets, and the design of layouts for service organizations must match the image that marketing seeks to convey to the customer. Marketing and sales make delivery promises to customers, which must be related to current operations capabilities. Marketing's demand forecasts guide the operations manager in planning output rates and capacities.

    The operations manager also needs feedback from the accounting function to understand current performance. Financial measures help the operations manager assess labor costs, the long-term benefits of new technologies, and quality improvements. Accounting can help the operations manager monitor the production system's vital signs by developing multiple tracking methods. The operations manager can then spot problems and prescribe remedies. Accounting also has an impact on OM because of the order-fulfillment cycle, which begins when the customer places an order and is completed when operations hands it off to accounting for billing.

    In securing and investing the company's capital assets, the finance function influences operations' decisions relative to investments in new technology, layout redesign, capacity expansion, and even inventory levels. Similarly, the human resources function interacts with operations to hire and train workers and aids in changeovers related to new process and job designs. Human resources can help make promotions and transfers into and out of operations easier, thereby encouraging cross-functional understanding. The engineering function also can have a big impact on operations. In designing new products, engineering needs to consider technical trade-offs. It must ensure that product designs do not create costly specifications or exceed operations capabilities.

Achieving Cross-Functional Coordination.   Several approaches may be used to achieve cross-functional coordination. Each organization should select some blend of them to get everyone pulling in the same direction.

How can coordination be achieved with other functional areas?

- A unified strategy should be developed by management as a starting point, giving each department a vision of what it must do to help fulfill the overall organizational strategy.

- The organizational structure and management hierarchy can be redesigned to promote cross-functional coordination. Drawing departmental lines around areas of specialization may work against integration by creating insular views and "turf battles." Cross-functional coordination increases when management pushes decision-making responsibility lower in the organization. One technique for doing so is to group traditional functional areas around each major product or service and create interfunctional coordinating units that tie two or more functions together.

- The goal-setting process and reward systems can encourage cross-functional coordination. So can bringing people together from different functional areas—through task forces or committees—to make decisions and solve problems. Task forces are temporary, whereas committees are more permanent.

- Improvements to information systems also can boost coordination. Information must in part be tailored to the needs of each functional manager. However, sharing information helps harmonize the efforts of managers from different parts of the organization and enables them to make decisions consistent with organizational goals. The information system provides the inputs to decisions made throughout the organization. With telecommunications advances such as e-mail, voice mail, and video conferencing, people from around the world can interact with increasing ease.

- Informal social systems are another device that can be used to encourage better understanding across functional lines. Joint cafeteria facilities, exercise rooms, and social events can help build a sense of family and working together, as can corporate training and development programs.

- Employee selection and promotion also can help foster more cross-functional coordination by encouraging broad perspectives and common goals. Of course, employees must first be competent in their own skill areas.

The best mix of approaches depends on the organization. Some organizations need more coordination than others. The need is greatest when functions are dispersed (owing to organizational structure or geographical distance), organizations are large, and many products or services are customized. The need is also crucial in service organizations that have high customer contact and provide services directly to the customer.

Operations Management As a Competitive Weapon

Business and government leaders increasingly are recognizing the importance of involving the whole organization in making strategic decisions in order to compete globally. Because the organization usually commits the bulk of its human and financial assets to operations, operations is an important function in meeting global competition. More than 25 years ago, Wickham Skinner suggested that the production system could be either a competitive weapon or a millstone (see Skinner, 1969). He concluded that, all too often, operations policies covering in-

Managerial Practice 1.2

▶ *Meeting the Competitive Challenge*

IKEA

The Swedish furniture operation IKEA has transformed itself into the world's largest retailer of home furnishings. In an industry where few companies move beyond their home-country base, IKEA created a global network of more than 100 stores (*location*). Its innovative operational strategies keep costs down while maintaining quality (*competitive priorities*). It offers a new brand of division of labor by asking its customers to assemble the final products and take them home (*process management*). Products are grouped to offer not just chairs and tables but designs for entire rooms (*layout*). The supplier network is central to IKEA's success (*materials management*): For example, the back and seat of one chair model come from Poland, whereas the legs are made in France. IKEA has 1800 suppliers, located in more than 50 countries around the world. It distributes its products through 14 large warehouses in different parts of the world (*location* and *distribution*), with the largest one being 1.2 million square feet in size (*capacity*). Most ordering is done electronically (*process management*). Cash registers at each store relay information to the nearest warehouse and to corporate headquarters (*inventory*).

Cincinnati Milacron

Cincinnati Milacron faces a real challenge as it seeks to reestablish itself as a world-class manufacturer of facto-

ry machinery. It has not earned an acceptable profit since 1981. Milacron got ahead of the market: It could not find customers willing to spend $10 million to $20 million for its new robots and flexible manufacturing systems. Meanwhile, aggressive Japanese producers seized half the U.S. market for machine tools. Milacron executives aim to rebuild the company's capability to manufacture quality products more cheaply than competitors. They are concentrating on three basic product lines: machine tools, plastics machinery, and consumable industrial products such as grinding wheels (*corporate strategy*). Milacron is creating so-called focused factories (*capacity* and *layout*), each of which specializes in one type of product, such as lathes or machining centers. The goal is to bring people who design, manufacture, and service machines into closer contact with the buyer. Each factory is a profit center, which helps avoid unnecessary spending on product development. The last phase of the strategy is to redesign many machines to make them more efficient to manufacture and more reliable (*product planning*). The minimum goal is a 30 percent cost reduction on each machine. One division has already slashed manufacturing costs by 40 percent, partly by halving the number of parts required (*master production scheduling*). It is now going after an additional 15 percent of cost by automating parts making and streamlining assembly (*process management*).

ventory levels, schedules, and capacity reflect incorrect assumptions about corporate strategy and may work against a firm's strategic goals. This lack of understanding can waste a firm's resources for years.

Largely because of foreign competition and the explosion of new technologies, recognition is growing that a firm competes not only by offering new products and services, creative marketing, and skillful finance, but also with unique competencies in operations. The organization that can offer superior products and services at lower prices is a formidable competitor.

What are companies doing to make operations a competitive weapon?

To conclude this chapter, Managerial Practice 1.2 demonstrates what four companies are doing to improve quality and productivity and how management can use operations as a competitive weapon. These examples offer insight into the role that operations managers play in an organization.

The steps taken by these companies cover almost every decision area (shown in parentheses) in operations management. Note that each decision area in oper-

Dillard Stores

Dillard Department Stores sells the latest fashions in gleaming, marble-inlaid stores (*layout*), succeeding in a deeply troubled industry. It continues to show double-digit returns even as its competitors falter. Dillard disproves the conventional wisdom that department stores handling moderately priced merchandise are dead. It does so by offering a combination of upscale merchandise, wide selection, and decent prices (*competitive priorities*). Aiming at baby-boomer shoppers of the 1990s, who tend to head to the closest mall, Dillard operates only four downtown stores (*location*). Its low overhead means that its operating costs are 2 percentage points lower than competitors'. One reason Dillard can hold costs down is its sophisticated data collection system (*process management*). Management keeps tabs on sales at every cash register in every store. Sales data show, for example, whether Hickey-Freeman suits are selling as fast as expected in Kansas City or how Estée Lauder's latest line is doing nationwide. Such information helps in managing inventory levels (*inventory*) and also makes possible tracking the productivity of every salesclerk.

Clerks have a quota to meet; those who exceed it get raises (*work-force management*). When Dillard recently acquired the J.C. Ivey chain of 22 department stores, it installed over one weekend new point-of-sale registers that tie into Dillard's Arkansas headquarters. By Monday morning, Dillard's managers were tracking what was and wasn't selling. Dillard also has a quick response program that allows it to get merchandise into stores at breakneck speed (*materials management*). Goods from 187 of its suppliers are restocked in 12 days or less.

Shenandoah Life Insurance

Shenandoah Life Insurance installed a new computer system (*technology*) to help issue new life insurance policies to customers who were replacing old ones. The Roanoke, Virginia, company also revamped its procedures so that clerks are less specialized (*process management*) and work in teams (*job design*). Over a three-year period, the number of transactions processed rose by 28 percent while the number of workers handling them fell 15 percent.

Sources: "From Value Chain to Value Constellation: Designing Interactive Strategy," *Harvard Business Review* (July–August, 1993); "Milacron Wolfpack Goes in for the Kill," *Wall Street Journal*, August 14, 1990; "Two Disparate Firms Find Keys to Success in Troubled Industries," *Wall Street Journal*, May 29, 1991. Updated November, 1994.

ations management plays a vital role in the attempt to gain competitive advantage. These descriptions indicate that there are many roads to success within operations, not one single cure or magic formula.

CHAPTER REVIEW

Solved Problem 1

Student tuition at Boehring University is $100 per semester credit hour. The state supplements school revenue by matching student tuition, dollar for dollar. Average class size for a typical three-credit course is 50 students. Labor costs are $4000 per class, materials costs are $20 per student per class, and overhead costs are $25,000 per class.

a. What is the *multifactor* productivity ratio?
b. If instructors work an average of 14 hours per week for 16 weeks for each three-credit class of 50 students, what is the *labor* productivity ratio?

Solution   a. Multifactor productivity is the ratio of the value of output to the value of input resources.

$$\text{Value of output} = \left(\frac{50 \text{ students}}{\text{class}}\right)\left(\frac{3 \text{ credit hours}}{\text{student}}\right)\left(\frac{\$100 \text{ tuition} + \$100 \text{ state support}}{\text{credit hour}}\right)$$

$$= \$30{,}000/\text{class}$$

Value of input = Labor + Materials + Overhead

$$= \frac{\$4000 + \left(\dfrac{\$20}{\text{student}} \times 50 \text{ students}\right) + \$25{,}000}{\text{class}}$$

$$= \$30{,}000/\text{class}$$

$$\text{Multifactor productivity} = \frac{\text{Output}}{\text{Input}} = \frac{\$30{,}000/\text{class}}{\$30{,}000/\text{class}} = 1.00$$

b. Labor productivity is the ratio of the value of output to labor hours. The value of output is the same as in part (a), or $30,000/class, so

$$\text{Labor hours of input} = \left(\frac{14 \text{ hours}}{\text{week}}\right)\left(\frac{16 \text{ weeks}}{\text{class}}\right) = 224 \text{ hours/class}$$

$$\text{Labor productivity} = \frac{\text{Output}}{\text{Input}} = \frac{\$30{,}000/\text{class}}{224 \text{ hours/class}}$$

$$= \$133.93/\text{hour}$$

Solved Problem 2

Natalie Attired makes fashionable garments. During a particular week employees worked 360 hours to produce a batch of 132 garments, of which 52 were "seconds" (meaning that they were flawed). Seconds are sold for $90 each at Attired's Factory Outlet Store. The remaining 80 garments are sold to retail distribution, at $200 each. What is the *labor* productivity ratio?

Solution
$$\text{Value of output} = \left(52 \underset{\text{garments}}{\text{defective}} \times \frac{\$90}{\underset{\text{garment}}{\text{defective}}}\right) + \left(80 \text{ garments} \times \frac{\$200}{\text{garment}}\right)$$

$$= \$20{,}680$$

Labor hours of input = 360 hours

$$\text{Labor productivity} = \frac{\text{Output}}{\text{Input}} = \frac{\$20{,}680}{360 \text{ hours}}$$

$$= \$57.44/\text{hour}$$

Formula Review

1. Productivity is the ratio of output to input, or

$$\text{Productivity} = \frac{\text{Output}}{\text{Input}}$$

Chapter Highlights

- Every organization must have an operations function to transform inputs into outputs. Inputs include human resources (workers and managers), capital resources (equipment and facilities), purchased materials and services, land, and energy. Outputs are goods and services.

- Service organizations, (in contrast to manufacturing organizations) tend to have intangible products that cannot be inventoried, more direct contact with the customer, shorter response times, local markets, smaller facilities, labor-intensive operations, and less measurable quality. Although there are differences between manufacturing and service organizations, the concepts of productivity, quality, process management, job design, capacity, facility location, layout, inventory, scheduling, and the use of technology apply to both.

- Several trends are at work in operations management: Service sector employment is growing; productivity is lagging, particularly in the service sector; and global competition is intensifying. The pursuit of better quality, competition based on time, rapid technological change, global competition, and continuous improvement are also important trends. Awareness in business education of environmental, ethical, and work-force diversity concerns is increasing.

- Operations managers draw on a variety of skill areas. They play a key role in determining productivity, which in turn is the prime determinant of a nation's standard of living.

- Decision areas in which operations managers are involved include product and service plans, competitive priorities, positioning strategy, process management, quality management and control, new technologies, job design, capacity, location, layout, materials management, production and staffing plans, master production scheduling, inventory, and scheduling.

- Decision areas within operations must be linked. For example, quality, process, capacity, and inventory decisions affect one another and should not be made independently. Strategy (long-range plans) and tactical analysis (for short-range decision making) should complement each other.

- The pyramid organization structure, with its top-down decision-making process, is being replaced with flatter organizations that require cross-functional coordination and understanding. For operations to be a competitive weapon, it must be viewed as an interfunctional concern. Tomorrow's manager of every function must understand operations.

Key Terms

continuous improvement *13*	operations management *3*	reengineering *14*
mass customization *14*	productivity *8*	

Study Questions

1. Identify the inputs and outputs of four of the following types of firms:
   a. Hotel
   b. Public warehouse
   c. Paper mill
   d. Newspaper company
   e. Supermarket
   f. Home office of bank

2. Identify the largest employer in your hometown or county. What are its inputs, outputs, and transformation processes?

3. What are the usual distinctions between manufacturing and service organizations? Identify at least two types of firms that do not fit the pattern and explain the reasons for your choices.

4. Do employment shifts to the service sector mean that the demand for goods is declining? Do you expect these employment trends to continue at the same pace? Explain.

5. What does the productivity trend in Fig. 1.4(a) mean? Do you expect it to continue? Explain.

6. Why is productivity of particular interest to operations managers?

7. Which skill areas contribute significantly to the field of operations management? What does this imply about the skills needed by operations managers?

8. Do businesses really have responsibilities that go beyond producing goods and services at a profit? Make a list of additional responsibilities that you would support and a list of those that you would question.

9. Explain how cross-functional coordination improves an organization's ability to compete on the basis of time.

10. Marketing at the Model T automobile company has conducted a customer survey showing that customers prefer a choice of paint color. Presently, all Model T's are painted black. If Model T management decides to offer green paint, predict how this decision might af-

fect the following functional areas: product design, purchasing, industrial engineering, operations, quality, manufacturing engineering, finance, human resources, accounting, distribution, and sales and service.

11. A manufacturer of printed circuit boards develops a new method of attaching electronic components to circuit boards. Instead of inserting wires from the electronic components through holes and soldering to make the electrical connection, assembly is accomplished by pressing components into slots in the surface of the board. A more reliable solderless electrical connection is made by having the component fit tightly into its slot. What is the effect of this new technology on product design, purchasing, the environment, quality, operations, marketing, and service?

12. The registration procedure at Western State University will change from essentially a manual process to one that involves the use of an interactive computer network. Students will use personal computers to access the network, determine the availability of classes, and register. Predict which functions of WSU will be affected by this change and in what ways.

13. List at least three types of decisions that deal with the design of a production system, and write a sample question that each one would answer. Do the same for three types of decisions that deal with the operation of the production system.

14. Explain how linking decisions can help make operations a competitive weapon.

Discussion Questions

1. Make a list of possible endings to this sentence: "The responsibility of a business is to _____" (for example, ". . . *make money*" or ". . . *provide health care for its employees*"). Make a list of the responsibilities of business that you would support and a list of those that you would not support. Form a small group, and compare your lists with those of the others in the group. Discuss the issues and try to arrive at a consensus. An alternative discussion question: "The responsibility of a student is to _____."

2. Multinational corporations are formed to meet global competition. Although they operate in several countries, their workers do not have international unions. Some union leaders complain that multinationals are in a position to play off their own plants against each other to gain concessions from labor. What responsibilities do multinational corporations have to their host countries? To their employees? To their customers? To their shareholders? Would you support provisions of international trade treaties to address this problem? Form a small group, and compare your views with those of the others in the group. Discuss the issues and try to obtain a consensus.

Problems

1. Under Coach Bjourn Toulouse, several football seasons for the Big Red Herrings have been disappointing. Only better recruiting will return the Big Red Herrings to winning form. Because of the current state of the program, Boehring University fans are unlikely to support increases in the $192 season ticket price. Improved recruitment will increase overhead costs to $31,000 per class section from the current $25,000 per class section (refer to Solved Problem 1). The university's budget plan is to cover recruitment costs by increasing the average class size to 60 students. Labor costs remain constant at $4000 per three-credit course. Material costs are about $20 per student for each three-credit course. Tuition is $100 per semester credit, which is matched by state support of $100 per semester credit.
   a. What is the productivity ratio? Compared to the result obtained in Solved Problem 1, did productivity increase or decrease?
   b. If instructors work an average of 16 hours per week for 16 weeks for each three-credit class of 60 students, what is the *labor* productivity ratio?

2. Natalie Attired makes fashionable garments. After attending "Quality at the Source" training, employees worked 360 hours to produce a batch of 128 garments. Of these, 8 were "seconds," or defective garments, which are sold for $90 each at Attired's Factory Outlet Store. The remaining 120 garments are sold to retail distribution for $200 per unit.
   a. What is the *labor* productivity ratio?
   b. Last week's output of 132 garments was valued at $20,680 (refer to Solved Problem 2). The cost of materials was $70 per garment. If Attired shares 50 percent of productivity gains with its employees, what is the total amount of the bonus the employees receive for reducing defects?

3. Suds and Duds Laundry washed and pressed the following numbers of dress shirts per week.

Week	Work Crew	Hours	Shirts
1	Sud and Dud	24	68
2	Sud and Jud	46	130
3	Sud, Dud, and Jud	62	152
4	Sud, Dud, and Jud	51	125
5	Dud and Jud	45	131

Calculate the *labor* productivity ratio for each week. Explain the labor productivity pattern exhibited by the data.

4. Compact disc players are produced on an automated assembly line. The standard cost of compact disc players is $105 per unit (labor, $15; materials, $60; and overhead, $30). The sales price is $200 per unit.

   a. To achieve a 5 percent multifactor productivity improvement by reducing materials costs only, by what percentage must those costs be reduced?

   b. To achieve a 5 percent multifactor productivity improvement by reducing labor costs only, by what percentage must those costs be reduced?

   c. To achieve a 5 percent multifactor productivity improvement by reducing overhead costs only, by what percentage must those costs be reduced?

Advanced Problem

5. The Big Black Bird Company (BBBC) has a large order for special plastic-lined military uniforms to be used in an urgent Mideast operation. Working the normal two shifts of 40 hours, BBBC usually produces 2500 uniforms per week at a standard cost of $120 each. Seventy employees work the first shift, and 30 employees work the second shift. The contract price is $200 per uniform. Because of the urgent need, BBBC is authorized to use around-the-clock production, six days per week. When each of the two shifts works 72 hours per week, production increases to 4000 uniforms per week but at cost of $144 each.

   a. Did the productivity ratio increase, decrease, or remain the same? If it changed, by what percentage did it change?

   b. Did the labor productivity ratio increase, decrease, or remain the same? If it changed, by what percentage did it change?

   c. Did weekly profits increase, decrease, or remain the same?

CASE

Chad's Creative Concepts

Chad's Creative Concepts designs and manufactures wood furniture. Founded by Chad Thomas on the banks of Lake Erie in Sandusky, Ohio, the company began by producing custom-made wooden furniture for vacation cabins located along the coast of Lake Erie and on nearby Kelly's Island and Bass Island. Being an "outdoors" type of person himself, Chad Thomas originally wanted to bring "a bit of the outdoors" inside. Chad's Creative Concepts developed a solid reputation for its creative designs and high-quality workmanship. Sales eventually encompassed the entire Great Lakes region. Along with this growth came additional opportunities.

Traditionally, the company had focused entirely on custom-made pieces of furniture, with the customer specifying the kind of wood from which the piece would be made. As the company's reputation grew and sales increased, the sales force began selling some of the more popular types of furniture pieces to retail furniture outlets. This move into retail outlets led Chad's Creative Concepts into the production of a more standard line of furniture. Buyers of this line were much more price sensitive and imposed more stringent delivery requirements than did clients for the custom line. The custom-designed furniture continued to dominate the company's sales, accounting for

60 percent of the volume and 75 percent of the dollar sales. Currently, the company operates a single manufacturing facility in Sandusky, where both custom and standard furniture pieces are manufactured. The equipment is mainly general purpose in nature in order to provide the flexibility needed for producing custom pieces of furniture. The layout groups saws together in one section of the facility, lathes in another, and so on. The quality of the finished product reflects the quality of the wood chosen and the craftsmanship of the individual workers. Both the custom and the standard furniture pieces compete for processing time on the same equipment by the same craftspeople.

During the past few months, sales of the standard line steadily increased, leading to more regular scheduling of this line. However, when scheduling trade-offs had to be made, the custom furniture was always given priority because of its higher sales and profit margins. Thus, scheduled lots of standard furniture pieces were left sitting around the plant in various stages of completion.

As he reviews the progress of Creative Concepts, Thomas is pleased to note that the company has grown. Sales of custom furniture remain strong, and sales of standard pieces are steadily increasing. However, finance and accounting have indicated that profits are not what they should be. Costs associated with the standard furniture line are rising. Dollars are being tied up in inventory, both of raw materials and of work in process. Expensive public warehouse space has to be rented to accommodate the inventory volume. Thomas also is concerned with increased lead times for both custom and standard orders, which are causing longer promised delivery times. Capacity is being pushed, and no space is left in the plant for expansion. Thomas decides that the time has come to take a careful look at the overall impact this new standard furniture line is having on his operations.

Questions

1. What types of decisions must Chad Thomas make daily for his company's operations to run effectively? Over the long run?

2. How did sales and marketing affect operations when they began to sell standard pieces to retail outlets?

3. How has the move to producing standard furniture pieces affected the company's financial structure?

4. What might Thomas have done differently to avoid some of the problems he now faces?

Source: This case was prepared by Dr. Brooke Saladin, Wake Forest University, as a basis for classroom discussion.

Selected References

Bowen, David E., Richard B. Chase, Thomas G. Cummings, and Associates. *Service Management Effectiveness*. San Francisco: Jossey-Bass, 1990.

Buchholz, Rogene A. "Corporate Responsibility and the Good Society: From Economics to Ecology," *Business Horizons*, July–August 1991, pp. 19–31.

Cohen, Stephen S., and John Zysman. *Manufacturing Matters: The Myth of the Post-Industrial Economy*. New York: Basic Books, 1987.

Collier, David A. *Service Management: Operating Decisions*. Englewood Cliffs, N.J.: Prentice-Hall, 1987.

Commission on Admission to Graduate Management Education. *Leadership for a Changing World: The Future Role of Graduate Management Education*. Los Angeles: Graduate Management Admission Council (GMAC), 1990, pp. 1–43.

"Economic Trends," *Business Week*, December 21, 1992.

Hammer, Michael, and James Champy. *Reengineering the Corporation: A Manifesto for Business Revolution*. New York: HarperCollins, 1994.

Hayes, Robert H., and William J. Abernathy. "Managing Our Way to Economic Decline." *Harvard Business Review* (July–August 1980), pp. 67–77.

Hayes, Robert H., and Gary P. Pisano. "Beyond World-Class: The New Manufacturing Strategy." *Harvard Business Review* (January–February 1994), pp. 77–86.

Heskett, James L., W. Earl Sasser, Jr., and Christopher Hart. *Service Breakthroughs: Changing the Rules of the Game*. New York: Free Press, 1990.

Heyl, Jeff E., Jon L. Bushnell, and Linda A. Stone. *Cases in Operations Management*. Reading, MA: Addison-Wesley, 1994.

"The Horizontal Corporation," *Business Week*, December 20, 1993, pp. 76–81.

Mabert, Vincent A., and Michael J. Showalter. *Cases in Operations Management*. Plano, Texas: Business Publications, 1984.

"Management Education," *The Economist*, March 2, 1991, pp. 2–26.

McKenna, Regis. "Marketing Is Everything." *Harvard Business Review* (January–February 1991), pp. 65–79.

Parker, Glenn. *Cross-Functional Teams*. San Francisco: Jossey Bass, 1994.

Pine, B. Joseph. *Mass Customization: The New Frontier in Business Competition*. Boston: Harvard Business School Press, 1993.

Pine, B. Joseph, B. Victor, and A. C. Boynton. "Making Mass Customization Work." *Harvard Business Review* (September–October 1993), pp. 108–119.

Porter, Lyman W., and Lawrence E. McKibbin. *Management Education and Development: Drift or Thrust into 21st Century?* New York: McGraw-Hill, 1988.

Porter, Michael E. "The Competitive Advantage of Nations." *Harvard Business Review* (March–April 1990), pp. 73–93.

Post, James E. "Managing As If the Earth Mattered," *Business Horizons*, July–August 1991, pp. 32–38.

Roach, Stephen S. "Services Under Siege—The Restructuring Imperative." *Harvard Business Review* (September–October 1991), pp. 82–91.

"Reengineering: The Hot New Managing Tool," *Fortune*, August 23, 1994, pp. 41–48.

Schmenner, Roger W. *Service Operations Management*. Englewood Cliffs, N.J.: Prentice-Hall, 1995.

Senge, Peter M. "The Leader's New Work: Building Learning Organizations." *Sloan Management Review* (Fall 1990), pp. 7–23.

Shapiro, Benson P. "Functional Integration: Getting All the Troops To Work Together." Harvard Business School Paper 9-587-122, 1987, pp. 1–18.

Skinner, Wickham. "Manufacturing—Missing Link in Corporate Strategy." *Harvard Business Review* (May–June 1969), pp. 136–145.

"Under Pressure, Business Schools Devise Changes," *Wall Street Journal*, April 23, 1991, p. 15.

Wheelwright, Steven C. "Manufacturing Strategy: Defining the Missing Link." *Strategic Management Journal*, vol. 5 (1984), pp. 71–91.

Womack, James P., Daniel T. Jones, and Daniel Roos. *The Machine That Changed the World*. New York: HarperPerennial, 1991.

Chapter Two

OPERATIONS STRATEGY

The Foxboro Company has been a worldwide supplier of industrial automation control equipment since 1906. The company had been highly successful, but by 1986 the outlook was bleak. Many of Foxboro's customers were laying off large numbers of employees, which would affect Foxboro's sales. After studying the company's customers and competitors, Foxboro's management boldly decided to introduce a "next generation" industrial automation system offering—the Intelligent Automation Series. Management determined that customers would demand high quality, speedy delivery, and competitive price. In addition, product orders would involve small volumes but considerable variety. Foxboro's previous experience had been with large volumes and little variety of products. Finally, management determined that Foxboro would need to switch from electromechanical technology to electronic technology.

An engineer makes final checks on the Foxboro Company's Intelligent Automation system.

Management recognized the important role of operations in making the change to the new product line. Operations managers assembled the equipment, trained the employees, and developed the information and planning systems necessary to achieve high product quality, speedy delivery, and competitive cost. The results were impressive. By 1992, the plant required only 2.5 days to ship an order. Inventory levels had been reduced by 79 percent from original levels. Clerical positions in manufacturing had been replaced by an electronic network information system. The need for space in a purchased-parts warehouse had been reduced by 90 percent and the need for plant floor space by 36 percent. Plant profits rose 33 percent in both 1991 and 1992, and the plant achieved its promised shipping dates 99 percent of the time. All told, the changes implemented by Foxboro demonstrated that operations could be a competitive weapon for Foxboro.

The experience at the Foxboro Corporation is an example of a successful customer-driven operations strategy. At the corporate level, management recognized that there was a threat to the corporation and that new markets should be explored. After analyzing the company's customers and competitors, marketing management suggested the new product line and how to sell it successfully. Operations management designed the processes and systems needed to support the marketing plan.

Developing a customer-driven operations strategy begins with a process called **market analysis,** which categorizes the firm's customers, identifies their needs, and assesses competitors' strengths. This analysis occurs in conjunction with an analysis of the external environment. Next, the organization formulates its **corporate strategy,** which provides a framework of goals for the entire organi-

How does operations strategy relate to corporate strategy?

zation. Once the firm has determined the customers it wants to serve, it must develop its **competitive priorities,** or the capabilities and strengths that the firm's operating system must possess to meet customer demand. The competitive priorities and the future directions the firm will take, such as global strategies and new products or services, provide input for **functional strategies,** or the goals and long-term plans of each functional area. Through its strategic planning process, each functional area is responsible for identifying ways to develop the capabilities it will need to implement functional strategies and achieve corporate goals. This input, along with the current status and capability of each area, is fed back into the corporate strategic planning process to indicate whether corporate strategy should be modified. Figure 2.1 shows how corporate strategy, market analysis, competitive priorities, and functional strategies are linked.

FIGURE 2.1

Competitive Priorities: Link Between Corporate Strategy and Functional Area Strategies

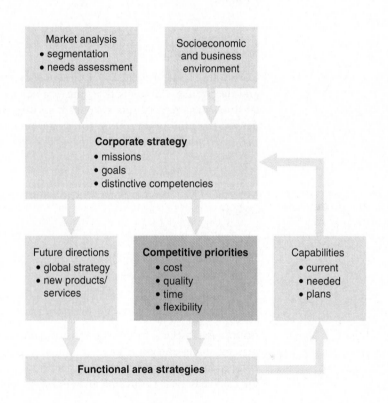

In this chapter we focus on **operations strategy,** which specifies how operations can help implement the firm's corporate strategy. Basically, operations strategy involves linking design decisions (discussed in Part Two) and operating decisions (discussed in Part Three). Continuous cross-functional interaction must occur in implementing operations strategy—or any other functional strategy. For example, operations needs feedback from marketing to determine how much capacity to allocate to particular product lines, and operations must work with finance regarding the timing and funding of capacity additions. Thus, in identifying the operational capabilities needed for the future, the operations manager must work closely with the managers of other functional areas to respond to competitive threats. In this chapter we explain how corporate strategy and operations strategy should be linked and the types of feedback needed during the development of these strategies.

◆   CORPORATE STRATEGY

Whatever the type of organization, top management's responsibility is to plan the organization's long-term future. Corporate strategy is an organization's plan that defines the business(es) the company will pursue, new opportunities and threats in the environment, and growth objectives the company should achieve. It also addresses business strategy, or how a firm can differentiate itself from the competition. Choices could include producing standardized products versus customized products or competing on the basis of cost advantage versus responsive delivery. Corporate strategy provides an overall direction that serves as the framework for carrying out all the organization's functions. In this section we discuss the basic choices involved in corporate strategy and how global markets affect strategic planning.

Strategic Choices

Corporate strategy defines the direction of the organization over the long term and determines the goals that must be achieved for the organization to be successful. Management sets corporate strategy by making three strategic choices: determining the organization's mission, monitoring and adjusting to changes in the environment, and identifying and developing the organization's distinctive competencies.

Mission.   An organization's *mission statement* answers fundamental questions such as

- What business are we in? Where should we be ten years from now?
- Who are our customers (or clients)?
- What are our basic beliefs?
- What are the key performance objectives, such as profits, growth, or market share, by which we measure success?

An understanding of the firm's mission helps managers conceptualize and design new products and services. If its mission is too broadly defined, the firm could enter areas in which it has no expertise. If the mission is too narrowly defined, the firm may miss promising growth opportunities.

Environment.   The external business environment in which a firm competes changes continually, so an organization needs to adapt to that environment continually. Adaptation begins with **environmental scanning,** the process by which managers monitor the trends within the socioeconomic environment, including the industry, the marketplace, and society, for potential opportunities or threats. Foxboro's environmental scanning showed that layoffs occurring at its primary customers reflected falling demand for the customers' products and hence for Foxboro's own products. This realization precipitated a bold move into a new market requiring a new technology.

A crucial reason for environmental scanning is to stay ahead of the competition. Competitors may be gaining an edge by broadening product lines, improving quality, or lowering costs. New entrants into the market or competitors who offer substitutes for the firm's product or service may threaten continued prof-

How can management identify and deal with environmental change when formulating corporate strategy?

itability. Other important environmental concerns include economic trends, technological changes, political conditions, social changes (such as attitudes toward work), the availability of vital resources, and the collective power of customers or suppliers. Witness the social and political movement to discourage cigarette smoking and ban it from public places: to survive, major cigarette manufacturers have had to diversify into other products or increase their efforts in overseas markets where smoking is still socially acceptable.

Environmental changes may cause a company to reconsider its current strategies. In the late 1980s and early 1990s, businesses have faced a particularly turbulent environment, requiring introspective looks at their strategies. Some markets grew slowly, technology became increasingly complicated and expensive, product and service life cycles became shorter, and foreign competition increased in intensity. Some companies managed to cope with such changes, but others could not. Precision Tune, the largest U.S. franchiser of automobile tune-ups, faced an external threat when automakers began designing cars with fuel-injection systems that rarely required adjusting. Precision Tune extended its services to include all parts related to engine performance. It also offers a 12 month/12,000 mile warranty on most services and repairs, as well as several customer price incentives. The new strategy caused sales to surge 78 percent in the last five years. Other companies facing similar threats haven't fared as well. Rusty Jones, once a major player in rust proofing, lost business because U.S. automakers extended corrosion protection guarantees to 100,000 miles. Fewer people wanted to pay for further protection; as a result Rusty Jones filed for protection from creditors under Chapter 11 of the federal bankruptcy code.

Distinctive Competencies. Good managerial skill alone cannot overcome environmental changes. Rather, corporate strategy must be changed to meet them. Firms succeed by taking advantage of what they do particularly well—that is, the organization's unique strengths. **Distinctive competencies** are the unique resources and strengths that management considers when formulating strategy. They include the following.

1. *Work force.* A well-trained and flexible work force is an advantage that allows organizations to respond to market needs in a timely fashion. This is particularly important in service organizations where the customer comes in direct contact with the employees.

2. *Facilities.* Having well-located facilities—offices, stores, and plants—is a major advantage because of the long lead time needed to build new ones. Expansion into new products or services may be accomplished quickly. In addition, facilities that are flexible and can handle a variety of products or services at different levels of volume provide a competitive advantage.

3. *Market and financial know-how.* An organization that can easily attract capital from stock sales, market and distribute its products, or differentiate its products from similar products on the market has a competitive edge.

4. *Systems and technology.* Organizations with expertise in information systems will have an edge in industries that are data—and information—intensive, such as the banking industry. Having the patents on a new technology is also a big advantage. When Oscar-Meyer held the patent on a new vacuum-pack technology for processed lunch meats, it had a decided market advantage. Competitors had to pay a premium to Oscar-Meyer for its use.

A study by Porter (1990) showed that companies achieving international leadership employed strategies that took advantage of their distinctive competencies. They achieved competitive advantage by designing new products, installing new production technologies, adapting training programs, using quality control techniques, and improving supplier relationships. Some innovations resulted from revolutionary changes in strategy, but others were a series of small, incremental changes. Successful companies anticipated environmental changes both domestically and in foreign operations. For example, Sweden's Volvo anticipated the growing international concern for product safety and gained competitive advantage by emphasizing the safety features of its cars in its advertising campaigns. This strategy required a major change in the way the autos were manufactured. Emphasizing existing features can give a firm a competitive advantage for a while, but relentless improvement also is required to sustain this advantage. Many other automobile manufacturers now compete on safety features. Competitors will eventually overtake a company that stops innovating and upgrading. For example, through incremental changes Korean companies have already matched the ability of Japanese companies to mass produce standard color TV sets and VCRs, and Brazilian companies have assembled technologies comparable to those of Italian rivals in casual leather footwear.

Global Strategies

What role does operations play in entering international markets?

Identifying opportunities and threats today requires a global perspective. A global strategy may include buying foreign parts or services, combatting threats from foreign competitors, or planning ways to enter markets outside traditional national boundaries. Although warding off threats from global competitors is necessary, firms should also actively seek to penetrate foreign markets. One way for a firm to open foreign markets is to create a **strategic alliance.** A strategic alliance is an agreement with another firm that may take the form of a

1. collaborative effort,
2. joint venture, or
3. licensing of technology.

A **collaborative effort** often arises when one organization has distinctive competencies that another needs but is unwilling (or unable) to duplicate. The two organizations agree to work together to the mutual benefit of both. Such arrangements are common in buyer–supplier relationships, such as a U.S. firm supplying parts to a foreign manufacturer, but also may be used in nontraditional ways. For example, Kodak entered into agreements with IBM, Businessland, and DEC to handle all its information systems, thereby relieving Kodak of the need for an information systems department. In such an arrangement procedures for maintaining data confidentiality must be carefully specified.

In a **joint venture** two firms agree to jointly produce a product or service. This approach often is used by firms to gain access to foreign markets. For example, a firm wanting to do business in Singapore might set up a joint venture with a firm in Singapore. The outside firm normally supplies the technology and much of the expertise associated with producing the product or service, and the local firm supplies the resources for the operation, including local workers and knowledge of labor practices. Often this sort of technology transfer is necessary for

Managerial Practice 2.1

▶ *Strategic Alliances Are Risky*

In 1992 McDonnell Douglas, looking for Asian partners in building new jetliners, planned to form an Asian consortium—involving Taiwan, Singapore, and South Korea—to buy up to 49 percent of the firm's commercial business. The key link was the Taiwanese deal. McDonnell Douglas offered to sell to the fledgling Taiwan Aerospace Corporation up to 40 percent of its airliner business for $2 billion. The arrangement seemed perfect: The Taiwanese company had plenty of cash and wanted to enter the civilian aerospace industry, and McDonnell Douglas needed cash and access to Asian markets.

What seemed perfect to the two companies, however, appeared flawed to the Taiwanese legislature, which had to approve the deal. Many legislators believed that the investment was too large for the value that Taiwan was to receive. Critics of the proposed investment thought that Taiwan already had much of the technological know-how needed to get into the civilian market and that McDonnell Douglas should increase the amount of its technology to be transferred in the deal. Critics also pointed out that an additional $2 billion would be needed for production facilities and development. These costs would have to be absorbed by the Taiwanese company. The legislature ordered an outside review of the arrangement and would not vote on the issue until that review was complete.

McDonnell Douglas also had plans for a joint venture in China to produce planes in Shanghai. Although the firm expected to get contracts for 150 planes for China's domestic routes, the Civil Aviation Administration of China, the country's major carrier, preferred to buy from Boeing. As a result, orders to McDonnell Douglas shrunk to only 40 planes. Together, these experiences with strategic alliances have jeopardized the company's plans for a strong Asian presence.

Source: "McDonnell Douglas' Far East Hopes Are Dimming," *Business Week,* March 9, 1992.

doing business in the Far East, and the outcome is sometimes risky, as Managerial Practice 2.1 shows.

Licensing technology is a form of strategic alliance in which one company licenses its production or service methods to another firm. Licenses may be used to gain access to foreign markets. For example, 84 percent of all laser printers sold today use print-engine technology licensed by Canon of Japan.

Another way to enter global markets is to locate operations in a foreign country. However, managers must recognize that what works well in their home country might not work well in another country. The economic and political environment or the customers' needs may be very different. For instance, McDonald's discovered that attracting customers to its Moscow restaurants was not going to be easy after rising food costs forced prices up 300 percent. Two years after the first store opened, the number of customers had dropped from 60,000 a year to only 30,000. McDonald's was criticized for catering to the wealthy as the price of a lunch approached the minimum monthly salary of Muscovites. Consequently, McDonald's executives announced that, to help reduce prices, the restaurants would not charge customers the government-imposed 28 percent value-added tax. As McDonald's still had to pay the taxes normally passed along to the customer, the impact on profits was enormous. The experience of McDonald's demonstrates that, to be successful, corporate strategies must recognize the customs and economic situation in other countries.

At McDonald's restaurants in Germany, beer is on the menu because Germans expect to be able to drink beer with their meals. However, for the most part, the menu uses English names for the foods.

◆ MARKET ANALYSIS

One key to success in formulating a customer-driven operations strategy for both manufacturing and service firms is understanding what the customer wants and how to provide it better than the competition does. Market analysis first divides the firm's customers into market segments. Then it identifies the needs of each market segment so that the appropriate operations system can be designed. In this section we define the concepts of market segmentation and needs assessment.

Market Segmentation

Market segmentation is the process of identifying groups of customers with enough characteristics in common to make possible the design and presentation of products or services that the group needs. For instance, The Gap, Inc. has targeted teenagers and young adults needing casual clothes and, for its GapKids stores, the parents or guardians of infants through 12-year-olds. Chaparral Steel has three market segments—standard steel customers, special bar quality steel customers, and mixed steel customers—each with different product needs. In general, to identify market segments the analyst must determine the characteristics that clearly differentiate each segment. A sound marketing program can then be devised and an effective operating system developed to support the marketing plan.

Once a market segment has been identified, the needs of the customers can be incorporated into the design of the product or service and the operations system for its production. The following characteristics are among those that can be used to determine market segments.

1. *Demographic factors.* Age, income, educational level, occupation, and location are examples of factors that can differentiate markets.

2. *Psychological factors.* Factors such as pleasure, fear, innovativeness, and boredom can serve to segment markets. For example, people with a fear of

crime constitute a market segment that has prompted a host of new products and services for protection.

3. *Industry factors.* Customers may utilize specific technologies (such as electronics, robotics, or microwave telecommunications), use certain materials (such as rubber, oil, or wood), or participate in a particular industry (such as banking, health care, or automotive). These factors are used for market segmentation when the firm's customers use the firm's product or service to produce another product or service for sale.

At one time managers thought of all customers as members of a homogeneous mass market. Today, however, managers realize that two customers may use the same product for very different reasons. Identifying the key factors in each market segment is the starting point for a customer-driven operations strategy.

Needs Assessment

The second step in the market analysis is to make a **needs assessment,** which identifies the needs of each segment and assesses how well competitors are addressing those needs. Once this has been done, the firm can differentiate itself from its competitors. The needs assessment should include both the tangible and the intangible attributes or features a customer desires. These attributes and features, known as the **customer benefit package** (Collier, 1994), consist of a core product or service and a set of peripheral products or services. The customer benefit package is viewed by the customer as a whole, not as separate products and services. For example, when you purchase an automobile, the core product is the car itself—its features and qualities. However, the peripheral services playing a key role in whether you will buy the car include the manner in which you are treated by the salesperson, the availability of financing, and the quality of post-sale service at the dealership. Thus the customer benefit package is the automobile plus the peripheral services at the dealership. Customers will not be completely satisfied without the entire customer benefit package.

Understanding the customer benefit package for a market segment enables management to identify ways to gain competitive advantages in the market. Each market segment has market needs that can be related to product or service, process, or demand attributes. Market needs may be grouped into the following categories.

- *Product/service needs*—attributes of the product or service, such as price, quality, and degree of customization desired.

- *Delivery system needs*—attributes of the process and the supporting systems and resources needed to deliver the product or service, such as availability, convenience, courtesy, safety, delivery speed, and delivery dependability.

- *Volume needs*—attributes of the demand for the product or service, such as high or low volume, degree of variability in volume, and degree of predictability in volume.

- *Other needs*—other attributes not directly relating to operations, such as reputation and number of years in business, technical after-sale support, accurate and reliable billing and accounting systems, ability to invest in international financial markets, competent legal services, and product/service design capability.

Any customer benefit package may meet several market needs. The distinction between them often blurs in the mind of the customer. For the customer, the customer benefit package as a whole is what matters.

◆ COMPETITIVE PRIORITIES

Should an organization emphasize price, quality, time or flexibility?

A customer-driven operations strategy reflects a clear understanding of the long-term goals of the organization and a cross-functional effort between marketing and operations to follow the needs of the marketplace and translate those needs into desirable capabilities, which we call competitive priorities. Managerial Practice 2.2 shows how corporate strategy led to competitive priorities for one of the business units at Varian Associates, Inc.

Market analysis identifies the market needs that can be exploited to gain competitive advantage in each market segment. Translating these needs into desirable capabilities for each of the functional areas of the firm is followed by implementation of the selected capabilities. Other terms used in the literature to refer to these competitive priorities are core content and content variables, dimensions of competition, external performance measures, manufacturing tasks, order winners and qualifiers, organizational priorities and generic capabilities, production competence, and service winners and qualifiers. These terms have somewhat different meanings and each has its own advantages, but they essentially address the same issue: translating market needs into operations terms. In this section we focus on the capabilities that relate to the product or service itself, delivery system, and volume factors. A firm gains an advantage by outperforming competitors in terms of one or more of these capabilities. There are eight competitive priorities, which fall into four groups.

Cost	1. Low-cost operations
Quality	2. High-performance design
	3. Consistent quality
Time	4. Fast delivery time
	5. On-time delivery
	6. Development speed
Flexibility	7. Customization
	8. Volume flexibility

Cost

Lowering prices can increase demand for products or services, but it also reduces profit margins if the product or service cannot be produced at lower cost. To compete based on cost, operations managers must address labor, materials, scrap, overhead, and other costs, to design a system that lowers the cost per unit of the product or service. Often, lowering costs requires additional investment in automated facilities and equipment.

Quality

Two competitive priorities deal with quality. The first, **high-performance design,** may include superior features, close tolerances, and greater durability; helpfulness, courteousness, and availability of service employees; convenience of access to service locations; and safety of products or services. High-performance design

Managerial Practice 2.2

▶ *Linking Corporate Strategy to Operations Through Competitive Priorities*

Varian Associates, Inc., a $1.37 billion company in Palo Alto, California, has developed products such as microwave tubes used for radar devices, nuclear magnetic resonance, electronic vacuum pumps, and semiconductors. The company's distinctive competencies include capabilities to manipulate and deposit materials on semiconductor wafers. These competencies led to domination of the market for implanters and sputtering systems for coating semiconductors. However, even its superior technological advantages weren't enough to keep Varian immune to competitive pressures. Varian had become overdiversified and had lost the focus it once had on its core competencies.

In 1990 Tracey O'Rourke was hired as CEO and given the task of getting Varian back on track. O'Rourke set a target of 10 percent return on sales, a big jump from the 1 to 4 percent returns of the past. Then he developed a three-phased strategic plan.

Phase I

Varian divested itself of 11 businesses and product lines, reduced its employees from 12,400 to 8400, and focused on four core businesses: analytical instruments, oncology systems, semiconductor production equipment, and electron devices.

Phase 2

Management determined that quality, customer satisfaction, shorter time to market for new products, and operations flexibility were key market needs. These factors translated into competitive priorities for each business

unit. For the oncology unit, which produces products such as medical radiotherapy accelerators useful for cancer therapy, radiotherapy simulators, and high-energy linear accelerators for nondestructive testing, the market needs determined by market analysis translated into competitive priorities of quality and fast delivery time. To improve the quality of the purchased parts, operations managers formed partnerships with key suppliers. Suppliers with certified quality levels enjoy a three- to five-year exclusive contract, access to training, tooling and technical assistance, streamlined administrative procedures, and forward visibility of schedules in return for on-time, high-quality components. This also makes the operating system more flexible and cost effective. In addition, the oncology unit managers made fast delivery time a priority. By analyzing the process for setting up and certifying new equipment, managers found several hundred problems that caused delays. In all, some 95 hours were cut from the setup and installation time.

Phase 3

To maintain the growth and profitability of the company, managers must continually look for ways to improve their operations.

Even though Varian is only part way through its program, the oncology unit has done very well. Earnings have increased by $58 million, inventories have shrunk by 30 percent since 1985, and costs have dropped 22 percent since 1987.

Source: "Varian," *Industry Week*, October 19, 1992.

determines the level of operations performance required in making a product or performing a service. The operations system for Club Med, the all-inclusive resorts with entertaining, dining, recreation, and hotel facilities, has much more demanding requirements for customer service than does a no-frills motel.

The second quality priority, **consistent quality,** measures the frequency with which the product or service meets design specifications. Customers want products or services that consistently conform to the specifications they contracted for, have come to expect, or saw advertised. For example, customers of a foundry expect castings to meet specific tolerances for length, diameter, and surface finish. Similarly, bank customers expect that the bank will not make errors when recording customer account numbers. To compete on the basis of consistent quality, managers need to design and monitor operations to reduce errors.

Club Med–Playa Blanca, located in the Mexican state of Jalisco, is an all-inclusive resort offering a wide diversity of activities, including kayaking, horseback riding, wall climbing, and a circus workshop in addition to more typical beach activities such as snorkeling, scuba, sailing, and volleyball.

Time

Three competitive priorities deal with time. The first, **fast delivery time,** is the elapsed time between receiving a customer's order and filling it. Industrial buyers often call this **lead time.** An acceptable delivery time can be a year for a major customized machine, several weeks for scheduling elective surgery, and minutes for an ambulance. Firms can shorten delivery times by storing inventory (manufacturing) or having excess capacity (manufacturing or service).

The second time priority, **on-time delivery,** measures the frequency with which delivery-time promises are met. Manufacturers measure on-time delivery as the percentage of customer orders shipped when promised, with 95 percent often considered the goal. A service firm such as a supermarket might measure on-time delivery as the percentage of customers who wait in the checkout line for less than three minutes.

The third time priority, **development speed,** measures how quickly a new product or service is introduced, covering the elapsed time from idea generation through final design and production. Getting the new product or service to market first gives the firm an edge on the competition, which is difficult to overcome in a rapidly changing business environment. Development speed is especially important in the fashion apparel industry. The Limited, for example, can design a new garment, transmit the design to Hong Kong, produce the garment, ship it back to the United States, and put it on store shelves in less than 25 weeks.

Many companies seek to maintain or increase their customer base by focusing on the competitive priorities of development speed and fast delivery time.

Managerial Practice 2.3

▶ *Time-Based Competition*

Many companies have used time as a means of differentiating themselves in the marketplace. Here are the stories of four companies that have taken advantage of time-based competition.

Reducing Response Times

As a customer have you ever been frustrated waiting for a retailer to get authorization for a credit card purchase? CompuServe, Inc. and VISA International are offering a service that will cut credit card transaction time to less than eight seconds. The advantage to customers is the shorter wait times in checkout lines. The advantages to retailers include reducing the time required to process a transaction and reducing the number of phone lines needed because both voice and data travel over a single circuit. A retail clerk's terminal is connected with equipment that sends signals directly via the local telephone company's central office through CompuServe's network to VISA.

Another example of reducing response times is provided by Atlas Door, which gained the number one competitive position in an industry previously dominated by large, established firms by focusing on fast delivery times. Atlas makes industrial doors, a product with limitless options in width, height, and material. It reorganized its factories to allow for a uniform flow of products, thereby reducing the manufacturing time of each product. It also streamlined and automated order-entry, engineering, pricing, and scheduling processes. Today, Atlas can schedule and price 95 percent of telephoned orders while the caller is still on the line. Finally, Atlas developed a system to ensure that all the parts for a shipment to a construction site would be available at the same time. As a result, Atlas can respond to an order in a few weeks; the industry average is four months. This quicker response time allows Atlas to charge premium prices. Because its time-efficient processes yield lower manufacturing costs, it also enjoys big profits.

Atlas's competitors did not recognize the thrust of the time-based strategy and still think it will gravitate toward the industry averages as volume increases. However, the enormous lead that Atlas presently enjoys will be very difficult—perhaps impossible—to overcome.

More Products in Less Time

Firms also can use time-based competition by focusing on development speed rather than fast delivery times—but with equally devastating results. Motorola Incorporated introduced its MicroTac pocket-sized cellular phone in 1989. By the time its competitors entered the market almost two years later, Motorola had sold over $1 billion worth of the 10.7 ounce phones. The new product even won two of the highest Japanese awards for top quality. Motorola was able to rush the new design into production by using new 3-D computer-aided design software (developed by Toronto-based Alias Research), which is much faster than traditional design methods. Using the software compresses the design process and electronically links every step from sketching to creating molds.

Another example of time-based competition is Hewlett-Packard's response to a shrinking market share. In one year HP introduced three new workstations, two ground-breaking printers, a palmtop PC, a new microprocessor chip, and 60 new test and measurement systems. It shortened the life cycle of products by introducing new products to replace them. In 1991 approximately 60 percent of HP's orders were for products less than two years old, compared to only 45 percent in 1989. The company accomplished much of this turnaround by eliminating dozens of committees that had been used to evaluate all decisions. Previously months had been needed to give the OK to a new project; in the meantime market opportunities were lost. Clearly, Motorola and Hewlett-Packard have used development speed to their competitive advantage.

Sources: "Pushing Design to Dizzying Speed," *Business Week,* October 21, 1991; "Service Will Check Credit Cards in 8 Seconds," *Columbus Dispatch,* January 2, 1994; "Suddenly Hewlett-Packard Is Doing Everything Right," *Business Week,* March 23, 1992.

With **time-based competition** managers carefully define the steps and time needed to deliver a product or service and then critically analyze each step to determine whether time can be saved without compromising quality. Managerial Practice 2.3 shows how companies can use time-based competition to advantage.

Flexibility

Some firms give top priority to two types of flexibility. **Customization** is the ability to accommodate the unique needs of each customer and changing product or service designs. Products or services are tailored to individual preferences and may not have long lives. A hairdresser works with the customer to design a hair style that may be unique to the individual. The life of that service may not be longer than a week. Alternatively, a customized plastic bottle for a shampoo manufacturer may last for years. Customization typically implies that the operating system must be flexible to handle specific customer needs and changes in designs.

Volume flexibility is the ability to accelerate or decelerate the rate of production quickly to handle large fluctuations in demand. The time between peaks may be years, as with the cycles in the home-building industry or political campaigns. It may be months, as with a ski resort or the manufacture of lawn fertilizers. It may even be hours, as with the systematic swings in demand from hour to hour at a major postal facility where mail is sorted and dispatched.

To illustrate how competitive priorities relate to market segments, consider American Airlines and two market segments: first-class passengers and coach-class passengers. The core services in the customer benefit packages for both market segments are identical: transportation to the customer's destination. However, the peripheral services are quite different. A needs assessment would reveal that, relative to coach-class passengers, first-class passengers require more comfortable seats, better meals and beverages, more frequent service from cabin attendants, and priority in boarding. In addition, personalized service (cabin attendants refer to customers by name), courtesy, and low volumes characterize this segment. Both first-class and coach-class passengers require dependability, but coach-class passengers are satisfied with standardized services (no surprises), courteous cabin attendants, and low prices. In addition, this market segment has high volumes. Consequently, we can say that the competitive priorities for the first-class market segment are *high-performance design, customization,* and *on-time delivery,* whereas the competitive priorities for the coach-class market segment are *low-cost operations, consistent quality,* and *on-time delivery.* Managerial Practice 2.4 further illustrates some competitive priorities by referring to the practices of actual firms.

In American Airlines' first-class cabin, customers receive amenities such as wider seats, hot towels after meals, and personalized attention.

Managerial Practice 2.4

▶ *Competitive Priorities of Various Firms*

Low-Cost Operations

In the early 1990s John Deere & Co., manufacturer of farming equipment, faced a period of weakening demand for farm equipment and intensified competition from rivals such as Caterpillar, Inc. Deere Chief Executive Hans W. Becherer understood that to be competitive Deere had to become a low-cost producer and improve quality. He believed that the easiest way to attack the problem was to involve the work force. For example, groups of workers meet weekly to discuss ways to improve product design to reduce manufacturing costs. In some plants, the company allowed teams of workers to do their own scheduling of overtime and vacations in addition to changing production procedures. A team in East Moline found a way to bring 12 assembly steps together to one site, cutting costs by more than 10 percent.

High-Performance Design

President Toshifumi Suzuki of 7-Eleven Japan believes in listening to the voice of the customer. A new $200 million computer system monitors inventories at the convenience stores and tracks consumer preferences by approximate age and sex. Any product that does not sell is immediately discontinued, leaving shelf space for items that customers really want. Seventy percent of the 3000 items a store carries are replaced annually. In addition, the stores have become one-stop errand centers where customers can send faxes, develop film, make photocopies, and even pay utility and insurance bills.

Consistent Quality

McDonald's restaurants are known for uniform design specifications. Eating at McDonald's is definitely a different experience from dining at a five-star restaurant. However, you can count on the same menu and standards of quality from one order to the next and from one restaurant to the next.

On-Time Delivery

Federal Express not only offers fast delivery time (overnight delivery) but also promises that parcels will be "absolutely, positively" delivered on time. Meeting delivery promises comes at a cost. Second-day delivery, priced at $2.90 by the U.S. Postal Service, can cost as much as $10 at Federal Express.

Customization

When hit by an industrywide slump, National Semiconductor Corporation decided to enter the growing market for custom-designed computer chips. Rather than mass produce the product and sell it through a catalog, the company designs each chip to suit the customer's specific requirements. A custom-made chip can cost as much as $1 million. Japan dominates the market for commodity memory chips, but U.S. producers such as National Semiconductor lead in the vital market of specialized, design-intensive chips.

Sources: "The New Soul of John Deere," *Business Week,* January 31, 1994; "Listening to Shoppers' Voices," *Business Week/Reinventing America,* 1992; "Masters of the Game," *Business Week,* October 12, 1992; "Don't Renew the Semiconductor Cartel," *Wall Street Journal,* May 20, 1991.

Trade-Offs

You might wonder why firms have to choose among competitive priorities. Why not compete in all areas at once and dramatically improve the firm's competitive position? Depending on the situation, firms *can* improve on all competitive priorities simultaneously. For example, in a manufacturing firm, scrap from mistakes in operations and reworking defective parts and products sometimes account for 20 to 30 percent of a product's cost. By reducing defects and improving quality, the firm can sharply reduce costs, improve productivity, and reduce delivery time at the same time.

Unfortunately, at some point further improvements in one area require a trade-off with one or more of the others. A survey of manufacturing companies indicated that raising the degree of customization or producing high-performance design products may lead to both higher costs and higher prices (Wood, 1991). For example, Rolls Royce produces cars with top-of-the-line specifications, making premium prices necessary. However, delivery lead times of six months are slower than those of other car manufacturers because of the painstaking hand-assembly process.

Sometimes trade-offs are not possible because a competitive priority has become a requirement, called an **order qualifier**, to do business in a particular market segment (Hill, 1994). In such situations, customers will not place orders for products or services from the firm unless a certain level of performance in a competitive priority can be demonstrated. Fulfilling the order qualifier will not ensure competitive success in a market; it will only get the firm into a position to compete in the market. For example, in the TV set market, one measure of quality is product reliability. Customers expect to purchase a set that will not require repairs for many years. Products that do not live up to that level of quality do not last long in the market. The electronics industry in general is moving to the point where product reliability is an order qualifier. Alternatively, in the automobile repair industry, quality has not yet become an order qualifier in all segments, so trade-offs between low-cost operations and quality can be used to gain an advantage in the market.

◆ SHIFTS IN COMPETITIVE PRIORITIES

Competitive priorities for a product or service shift over time. In this section we address two explanations for shifts in competitive priorities: product or service life cycles and entrance–exit market strategies.

Product or Service Life Cycles

What impact do product life cycles have on competitive priorities?

A firm that fails to introduce new products or services periodically will eventually decline. Sales and profits from any product decrease over time, so the pressure is on management to introduce new products before existing ones hit their peak. A **life cycle** consists of the five stages through which a product or service passes: product or service planning, introduction, growth, maturity, and decline. Figure 2.2 depicts sales and profits associated with each stage. Let's first consider these stages and then briefly look at the management of product or service life cycles.

Product or Service Planning.   During the product or service planning stage, ideas for new goods or services are generated, screened, and translated into final designs. Sales have not yet begun, so profits attributed to a product or service are negative because development costs are being incurred. Operations must be involved to ensure that production capabilities are adequate for the new product or service. In a process called **concurrent engineering** (or sometimes *simultaneous engineering* or *interactive design*), design engineers, manufacturing specialists,

FIGURE 2.2

Life Cycle of a Product or Service

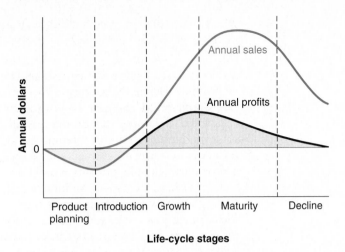

marketers, buyers, and quality specialists work jointly to design the product or service and select the production process. Ford Motor Company, for example, gives full responsibility for each new product to a program manager, who forms a product team representing every major part of the organization. In such a system, each department can raise concerns or anticipate problems while there is still time to alter the product. Changes are much simpler and less costly at this step than after the product or service has been introduced to the market. Working together also is a tradition at Honda, where animated discussions among representatives of all departments have earned the nickname *waigaya,* which loosely translates as "hubbub."

Introduction.   At the introduction stage, sales begin and profits go from negative to positive. Operations is still refining production efforts, which can best be characterized as fluid and evolving. Marketing efforts may be modest (as with introducing new prescription drugs) or nearing their peak (as with publishing new textbooks). At this stage, sales volumes have not peaked and annual profits are small, even though unit profit margins may be large. Operations typically must be able to handle design changes and volume and mix changes quickly and efficiently as the market for the product or service establishes itself.

Growth.   The product or service next enters a stage of rapid growth. Early in this stage, sales jump dramatically and profits rise. The mandate for operations is to keep up with demand and increase output; efficiency is less of a concern. The growth stage can be particularly difficult for a new business. Take the case of Hollywood makeup artist Bob Sidell, whose makeup work helped bring science-fiction creations (such as E.T.) alive. Sidell started his own mail-order company, California Cosmetics Incorporated, with a $4000 investment. In just three years the company grew into a $10-million-a-year business. However, the company suffered from a common ailment of new businesses: rapid but unsustainable growth. Operations couldn't handle the volume of business. Orders were being botched. Complaints were mounting. Total returns and nondeliveries of products climbed to 17 percent. Sidell and his partner decided that the only way to survive was to slow the company's short-term growth, which allowed California Cosmetics to set up its operating procedures.

Maturity.   During the maturity stage, sales level off, volumes are high, and profits begin to decline. New competitors create pressures to reduce prices and, as a result, unit profit margins. Now operations must stress low-cost operations or work with marketing to ease the pressure by differentiating the product or service. Product or service differentiation at the maturity stage can pose problems for operations because changes may be required in the way the product or service is produced while the pressure is still on to keep costs low.

For example, personal computers have entered the maturity stage and are becoming commodities that customers buy as cheaply as possible. This condition forces operations to deliver products at low cost. Companies that upgrade the architecture of their computers can differentiate their products and charge higher prices so that profit margins remain acceptable. However, such a move requires close cooperation between marketing and operations.

Decline.   Finally, the product or service enters a decline stage and ultimately becomes obsolete. Volumes decrease, and operations must return to low-volume production of the product or service. There may be tremendous pressure for low-cost operations if the firm tries to maintain sales levels by cutting prices in a dying market. Alternatively, the firm may choose to raise prices as the product becomes less common, as in the case of replacement parts for old equipment. These extremes pose different environments for operations. Often, a better, less expensive product or service takes the place of the old one. As sales and profits decrease, the firm finally discontinues the old one.

Life cycles vary greatly from one product or service to another. Coleco Industries, a Connecticut toy maker, sought ways to avoid bankruptcy and court protection just three years after riding high on the huge success of its Cabbage Patch Kids line. However, Morton has marketed salt for many years without changing its product much.

Managing Life Cycles.   A **life-cycle audit** determines the stage a product or service is in, based on how changes in sales and profits compare to those of prior years. For example, when both sales and profits are dropping, the product is in either the late maturity stage or the decline stage, as shown in Fig. 2.2. Life-cycle audits spot needs to revitalize or eliminate existing products and to introduce new ones.

When a life-cycle audit indicates that a product or service has reached maturity or entered decline, management has several options. The firm can stay with it for a few more years, find ways to squeeze costs still more, or revise and rejuvenate it. Revision might mean improving performance, as with a mix for a faster rising cake. Or it could be an update of an old standby, as with Mattel's revamp of the Barbie doll. Barbie, Mattel's 33-year-old best-seller, had been showing her age. In response to competition from Hasbro's new rock-star doll, Jem, Mattel gave Barbie an after-hours wardrobe of miniskirts, a modern hairdo, and a rock band. Barbie is now flourishing more than at any time since her introduction, with expected worldwide sales of $1 billion by 1995. Mattel is counting on overseas markets for much of its growth over the next several years.

EXAMPLE 2.1

Conducting a Life-Cycle Analysis

Management collected the following data in preparation for a life-cycle audit of one of its products, a packaging material sold to industrial buyers.

Performance Measure	This Year's Performance	Change from Last Year	Average Annual Change, Past Four Years
Annual sales	$30.8 million	+1.0%	+15.8%
Unit price	$1.12/lb	+2.2%	+8.5%
Unit profit margin	$0.16/lb	−0.3%	+3.2%
Total profits	$4.4 million	+1.5%	+22.5%

Solution Sales are stabilizing, having grown only 1 percent during the past year. Average annual growth was much higher during prior years, at 15.8 percent. Unit price growth has slowed, and unit profit margins are beginning to shrink. Total profit also is leveling off. All of these signs suggest the *early maturity* stage.

Entrance–Exit Strategies

The life cycle of a product within a company may be quite different from its cycle within an industry. For example, a firm may decide to pull out of a particular market, although the industry will continue to produce these products or services for years to come. An **entrance–exit strategy** is a firm's choice of when to enter a market and when to leave it. Choice of one of the three basic strategies discussed next has important implications for the operations function.

Enter Early and Exit Late. The most natural strategy is for a firm to enter the market when a product or service is first introduced by the industry and stay with it until the end of its life cycle. Polaroid and Xerox are examples of companies that developed a new product and grew with it throughout its life cycle. By entering the market early, the firm gets a head start. This added experience may allow the early entrant to produce a better product at a lower cost than can late entrants, at least initially.

This strategy requires operations to switch from a low-volume, flexible production system to a high-volume, low-cost system. Such a shift is always a challenge because it means changing to a whole new way of doing things. Several companies in the personal computer industry, including Apple and Commodore International, experienced similar growing pains when they moved from small, freewheeling ventures to large corporations.

Enter Early and Exit Early. A second possible strategy, favored by small, product-innovative firms, is to enter a market to gain competitive advantage, but to drop the product when it reaches the maturity stage and profit margins begin to shrink. In this strategy operations management maintains a small, flexible production system that can be adapted readily to changing products or services. Quarterdeck Office Systems, Inc., a small computer software company in Redmond, Washington, provides a good example. The company competes against Microsoft's market domination by offering software that gives a computer more memory capacity and the ability to run more than one program at once. Quarterdeck's narrow focus and fast reflexes help it combat an aggressive and far larger rival. Although its products are doing well, Quarterdeck is already developing new products, such as a program that allows personal computers to communicate with larger computers that don't use DOS.

Enter Late and Exit Late. Under this strategy a firm waits in the wings until other, innovative firms introduce a new product. If the product clearly shows significant market appeal and the prospect of high sales volumes, the firm enters the market with an automated, efficient production facility. For operations, the task is to provide low unit costs and maintain high output levels. Marketing may set prices considerably lower than those of their competitors to ensure the high-volume sales necessary for low unit costs. Entering the market late helps operations avoid a transition from low to high volumes. The firm can exploit its mass-marketing capabilities, establish distribution channels, and gain access to capital markets to finance the massive investment needed for top efficiency. An example in the service sector is United Parcel Service, the package delivery giant with 237,000 employees and $12.4 billion in revenues. UPS muscled into the overnight express business to compete head to head with Federal Express, the innovator in overnight express delivery. UPS has invested $1.5 billion in improvements to its system of tracking and scheduling deliveries. It now guarantees 10:30 A.M. next-day delivery in more locations than Federal Express and offers discounts to large-volume customers.

◆ POSITIONING STRATEGY

Figure 2.3 shows how corporate strategy is translated into strategic choices, design, and operating decisions. In this section we focus on the core of operations strategy: positioning strategy.

FIGURE 2.3

Positioning Strategy: The Connection Between Corporate Strategy and Key Operations Management Decisions

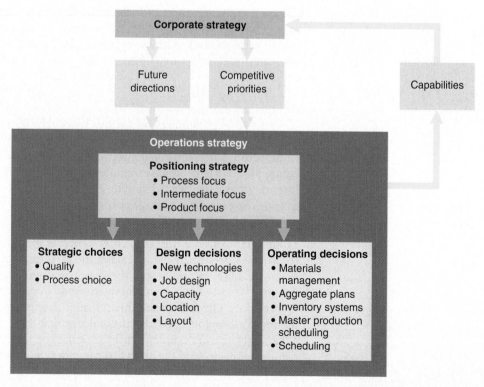

What is the best positioning strategy for the operations system?

Based on the firm's competitive priorities for its products or services, the operations manager must select a **positioning strategy**, which determines how the operations system is organized. A system organized around the processes used to produce the product or service is called a **process-focused strategy**. A system organized around the product or service itself is called a **product-focused strategy.** Process-focused and product-focused strategies are the extremes; many other strategies fall between the two.

This fundamental decision sets the stage for all operations decisions that follow. Positioning strategy does not define the specific processes to use or the specific resources to organize; rather, it identifies the nature of the operations that are required to accomplish the goals of the organization. It also serves as a check on whether the firm is organized in a manner consistent with the markets it is trying to serve.

Firms using a process-focused strategy tend to produce a wide range of customized (made-to-order) low-volume products or services. Different types of machines or employees are grouped to handle all products or services requiring a specific function to be performed, and various products or services move from one process to another. For example, in a manufacturing firm, drilling and welding machines would be located together. In a bank, separate departments would handle accounts payable and credit checks. In other words, the equipment and employees are organized around the process. However, each product or customer may not need every process. This situation creates an unpredictable *jumbled flow pattern* of products or customers through the facility, as shown in Fig. 2.4(a). Products or customers may have to compete for resources: Note that products 1 and 3 must compete for the same resources at operation A. Note also that product 1 follows an A–B–D routing pattern, product 2 follows a D–E–C routing pat-

FIGURE 2.4

Two Different Positioning Strategies

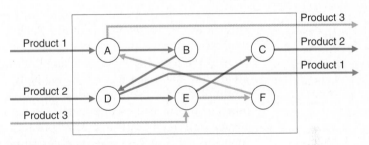

(a) Process focused

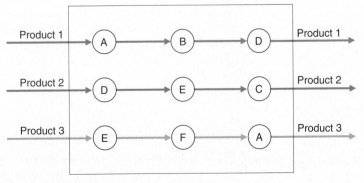

(b) Product focused

tern, and product 3 follows an E–F–A routing pattern. When a company is producing customized, low-volume products or services, organizing resources around similar processes is most efficient because dedicating resources to individual products or services would lead to duplication of many operations and leave resources idle.

A **job shop** is a production system with a process focus that takes on many types of small jobs and competes on the basis of resource flexibility. The flows of the product through the system are jumbled because each product can require a different sequence of resources. The more than 100,000 small job shops in the United States supply an estimated 75 percent of all machined metal parts used in products made by larger companies. Job shops employ the bulk of blue-collar workers. Other firms typically using a process-focused strategy include building contractors, law firms, architectural firms, and general medical practices.

At the other extreme is the product-focused strategy, in which the equipment and work force are organized around the product or service. A product-focused strategy fits high-volume production of a few standard products. Packaging and assembly operations often make products appear more diverse than they really are. For example, the same soft drink might be packaged in a bottle or a can, offering a degree of variety to the customer. The plant may have a line for bottles and another for cans. This type of production system is often called a **flow shop** because all products follow in a linear pattern. This system duplicates operations, but products and services don't have to compete for limited resources. For example, in Fig. 2.4(b), there are two operations A in the facility, one dedicated to product 1 and one to product 3. The routing pattern for each of the three products is straightforward, with several operations devoted to the same product or service. Firms typically using a product-focused strategy include fast-food restaurants, automobile assembly plants, and car washes, as well as electronic product manufacturers.

The line flows and high volumes of product-focused operations lend themselves to highly automated facilities. Such facilities can operate around the clock to offset the huge capital investment required. Borden's pasta-making plant in St. Louis is the nation's largest, making 250 million pounds annually. The 300,000 square foot plant is a marvel of simplicity. Grain is milled into flour at an adjacent mill and sped to the plant a few hundred yards away via giant pneumatic tubes. The flour is then distributed to one of eight pasta-making machines, each costing $5 million and capable of producing 6000 pounds of pasta per hour. A sophisticated touch screen computer system is used to schedule the machines. After pressing and drying, the mixture is forced through large dies, some weighing more than 200 pounds, to produce one of 65 different shapes of pasta. The product goes on to storage bins, each capable of holding 10,000 pounds of pasta until it is ready for packaging. Only 230 workers are needed to operate the plant. Production processes are automated so that the workers never touch the product. Packaging is computerized: 1200 different shapes and brands are sorted, put in the right boxes, and automatically stored. The plant operates 24 hours per day, 363 days a year.

A Continuum of Strategies

A firm's positioning strategy can vary from one facility to another, or even between areas of a single facility, depending on the product or service produced at each one. Further, numerous strategies exist between the two extremes of process focus and product focus. This continuum of choices is represented in Fig. 2.5 by the diagonal from the process focus to the product focus. The most frequently occupied positions are on this diagonal. Few firms position themselves very far outside the diagonal, and virtually none occupy positions in the white area.

The **intermediate strategy** lies halfway between the process focus and the product focus strategies. Product or service volumes are relatively high, and the system must be capable of handling several customer orders at a time. In manufacturing, if demand is sufficiently predictable, operations can produce some standardized products or components in advance of receiving actual customer orders. The general flow pattern is still jumbled, but dominant paths emerge. For example, in some parts of the facility, the manager may dedicate resources to one product or group of similar parts. Types of businesses that utilize this strategy include heavy equipment manufacturers, garment manufacturers, caterers, automobile repair shops, and small branch offices of service facilities such as brokerage firms and advertising agencies.

Although service operations managers can identify the appropriate place to position their operations relative to service volumes, the degree of customer contact is another factor they should consider. When services must be tailored to each customer's needs, a process-focused strategy allows the firm to achieve customized, low-volume production involving high degrees of face-to-face contact. Such would be the case for a hair stylist, dentist, or doctor. An intermediate strategy fits better when face-to-face contact and back-room processing are balanced.

FIGURE 2.5

A Continuum of Positioning Strategies

Source: After Robert H. Hayes and Steven C. Wheelwright, "Link Manufacturing Process and Product Life Cycles," *Harvard Business Review,* January–February 1979, pp. 133–140.

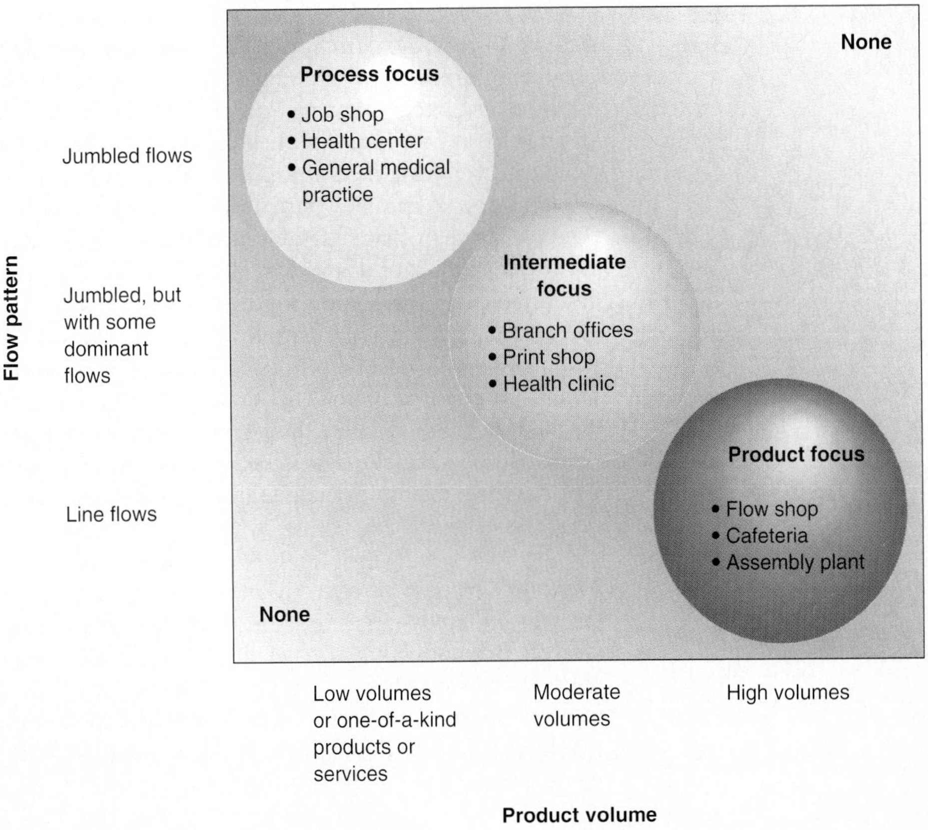

For example, in the front office of a bank customers and employees interact frequently with one another, while in the back office there is little customer contact and high use of automation and high-volume production methods to process volumes of checks and check credit references. A product-focused strategy is best in service facilities involving standardized services, high volumes, and no face-to-face contact. Such facilities include home offices, distribution centers, and power plants.

Manufacturing Strategies Based on Positioning Strategy

Three fundamental manufacturing strategies are based on positioning strategy: make-to-stock, assemble-to-order, and make-to-order.

Make-to-Stock Strategy.   Product-focused manufacturing firms tend to use a **make-to-stock strategy,** in which the firms hold items in stock for immediate delivery, thereby minimizing customer delivery times. This strategy is feasible because most product-focused firms produce high volumes of relatively few standardized products, for which they can make reasonably accurate forecasts. Examples of products produced with a make-to-stock strategy include garden tools, electronic components, soft drinks, and chemicals.

The term **mass production** is often used to define firms using a make-to-stock strategy. Because their environment is stable and predictable, mass-production firms typically have a bureaucratic organization, and workers repeat narrowly defined tasks. The competitive priorities for these companies are typically consistent quality and low costs.

Assemble-to-Order Strategy.   The **assemble-to-order strategy** is an approach to producing products with many options from relatively few major assemblies and components, after customer orders are received. The intermediate positioning strategy is appropriate for this situation because high-volume components and major assemblies can be produced with a product-focused strategy, whereas components and assemblies with lower volumes can be produced with a process-focused strategy. The assemble-to-order strategy addresses two competitive priorities: customization and fast delivery time. Operations holds assemblies and components in stock until a customer order arrives. Then, the specific product the customer wants is assembled from the appropriate assemblies and components. Stocking finished products would be economically prohibitive because the numerous possible options make forecasting relatively inaccurate. For example, a manufacturer of upscale upholstered furniture can produce hundreds of a particular style of sofa, no two alike, to meet the customer's selection of fabric and wood. Other examples include upscale farm tractors, automatic teller machines, and industrial scales.

Make-to-Order Strategy.   Many process-focused firms use a **make-to-order strategy,** whereby operations produces products to customer specifications. This strategy provides a high degree of customization. Because most products, components, and assemblies are custom-made, the production process has to be flexible to accommodate the variety. Job shops use a make-to-order strategy. Examples of products suited to the make-to-order strategy include specialized medical equipment, castings, and expensive homes.

The ultimate use of the make-to-order strategy is **mass customization,** or dynamically creating the processes necessary to produce custom products. In the ideal mass-customization firm, the people, processes, and technologies are reconfigured continually to give customers exactly what they want in an ever-changing environment. Managers must create an environment where these resources can be integrated rapidly in the best combination or sequence for the custom products. The goal of mass-customized firms is low-cost, high-quality, customized products.

However appealing the concept, mass customization is relatively untested. Achieving low costs is a big hurdle, and the required organizational changes are severe. Nonetheless, as some firms are attempting to implement it, this strategy is something to watch.

Positioning Strategy and Competitive Priorities

Operations managers use positioning strategy to translate product or service plans and competitive priorities into decisions throughout the operations function. Table 2.1 shows how positioning strategies relate to competitive priorities. In process-focused operations, the emphasis is on high-performance design quality, customization, and volume flexibility. Low-cost operations and quick delivery times are less important as competitive priorities, although these features could be used to gain a market niche. Thus a process focus meshes well with product or service plans favoring customization, short life cycles, or early exit from the life cycle. A product focus is appropriate when product plans call for standard products or services and long life cycles. Low-cost operations, quick delivery times, and consistent quality are the top competitive priorities. In Chapter 3 we discuss how operations puts the positioning strategy into practice by choosing the proper processes. In the remainder of this chapter we show how two firms, one in manufacturing and the other in services, chose different positioning strategies and linked their strategic choices and their design and operating decisions to those strategies.

TABLE 2.1   *Linking Positioning Strategy with Competitive Priorities*

Positioning Strategy	
Process Focus	**Product Focus**
More customized products and services, with low volumes	More standardized products and services, with high volumes
Shorter life cycles	Longer life cycles
Products and services in earlier stages of life cycle	Products and services in later stages of life cycle
An entrance–exit strategy favoring early exit	An entrance–exit strategy favoring late exit
High-performance design quality	Consistent quality
More emphasis on customization and volume flexibility	More emphasis on low cost
Long delivery times	Short delivery times

◆ TOURING A PROCESS-FOCUSED FACILITY:
   LOWER FLORIDA KEYS HEALTH SYSTEM*

The Lower Florida Keys Health System (LFKHS), a full-service acute care community hospital, serves the residents from Marathon to Key West, Florida. Some services, such as chemical dependency and eating disorders, draw from a larger market area. Although the patient population seems fairly stable, with no significant growth, the population may be shifting north because of the cost of living in Key West. If political relations with Cuba continue to thaw, however, the patient population could change, with LFKHS providing some care to that market. The Keys have a normal population of about 75,000, of which about 30,000 are in the LFKHS service area.

   The hospital is typical of relatively small facilities, with 550 employees, 420 of them full-time. This total does not include the 55 doctors who practice at the hospital but who are not strictly hospital employees. The emergency room (ER) typically sees 50 to 60 people per day. Inpatients stay in the hospital an average of 5.4 days. LFKHS's annual gross revenue is about $34 million, which generates a surplus of $0.7 million.

Service Plans, Competitive Priorities, and Quality

This general-purpose hospital offers a broad range of services to its patients, from treating cuts in the emergency room to obstetrics to major surgery. Its service capabilities stop just short of full trauma care. Given its small size and low volumes, it cannot offer standardized services at cut-rate prices. The services and procedures given to a patient tend to be "customized," with little opportunity for batching. Because of considerable shifts in volume, administrators give high priority to changing staffing levels easily to match daily workload requirements. Insufficient staffing jeopardizes service quality, whereas excessive staffing hurts the hospital's financial performance.

   Management also emphasizes quality as a competitive priority. Quality is everyone's responsibility, but a quality assurance (QA) coordinator designs, develops, and implements policies and procedures that enhance quality performance. Accreditation and third-party payers (insurance) are requiring increasingly sophisticated quality assurance programs. To date the hospital has emphasized after-the-fact inspection and corrective action. A *utilization review* is done for every patient when service is completed. All charts and records are reviewed to be sure that hospital personnel did what they were supposed to do. Little has been done yet in the way of continuous quality improvement or forming quality teams to find ways to improve quality performance continuously.

Process Management, Technology, and Job Design

Hospitals can be quite capital intensive, owing to the advanced technology that is now available and expected by patients. For example, a CAT scan machine can cost $2 million, and intensive-care monitoring equipment can have a $250,000 price tag. LFKHS's investment in equipment and facilities is $12 million, or $28,571 per full-time employee. This total may seem high, but it is less than the total investment of some larger hospitals that enjoy higher patient volumes.

*We are indebted to Jeff E. Heyl and Linda Stone for background information on this tour.

Owing to its small size, LFKHS acquires certain services from other organizations, rather than perform them in-house. For example, pharmacy operations are subcontracted. Contractors handle all orders and procure themselves whatever materials they need to provide their services. In contrast, larger hospitals have sufficiently high volumes to justify performing these services in-house.

Some areas in the hospital, such as the emergency room, insist that employees have broad education and experience so that they have the greatest possible flexibility in meeting patient needs. Accreditation standards require at least one registered nurse (RN) on duty at all times on each floor. Employee cross-training is a hospitalwide approach, even for areas where services are more standardized. Salaries and wages are comparable to those in the Miami area, where nurses are paid $15 to $16 per hour. Within classes of employment wages generally don't vary much, although experience and merit do affect wages within job classifications.

The procedures performed throughout the hospital are rigidly specified by traditional health care approaches, with little employee involvement in methods improvement. A patient's "routing" through the hospital is highly individualized; few patients have exactly the same routing. Scheduled admissions follow a predetermined basic routing upon arrival, depending on the reason for their hospitalization. Different surgical procedures involve slightly different routings. Patients admitted from the emergency room have less well-defined routings because there has been no advance planning. As actual services are performed on the patient, cost data are collected. The materials area affixes individual stickers for items to charts for later posting. Employee hours are recorded in less detail, but time and task linkage is noted.

Capacity and Location

LFKHS is a relatively small facility with a total capacity of 149 beds. On average, about 75 percent of the beds are occupied. During the peak season (December through April) occupancy (called the *hospital census*) is 90 percent; for the rest of the year it falls to slightly below 70 percent. Occasionally the emergency room runs out of beds, and surgery can be scheduled in only three operating rooms at a time. Regular admissions are scheduled around bed availability. Facility and equipment capacities tend to be the key limiting factor because there is no shortage of talented nurses and doctors in the area.

The hospital's location is quite rural, with only one road serving the island. The nearest major hospital is in Miami, 130 miles away. The Key West location brings with it some other specific problems: There are a significant number of AIDS cases, unusual for a rural setting; the emergency room gets victims of a large number of moped bike and head-on car accidents; and the homeless population is fairly large.

THE BIG PICTURE: Layout and Flow at LFKHS

The Big Picture illustration on pages 54–55 shows the layout of LFKHS's main hospital facility. Activities are grouped according to function. Volumes are too low and unpredictable to set aside many human and capital resources exclusively for a particular type of patient—except for maternity patients. The first floor thus houses such overall functions as the emergency room, labs, administrative offices, radiology, materials receiving, and the operating rooms. The second floor

Larry is a typical emergency room admission, who has twisted his ankle while jogging on the beach. He hobbles into the emergency room (ER) entrance (1) and sits down to fill out a patient history while he waits (2). Soon a nurse escorts him to an ER triage room (3), where she checks the severity of his injury. He returns to a seat in the waiting room (4), until an ER bed (5) opens up for him.

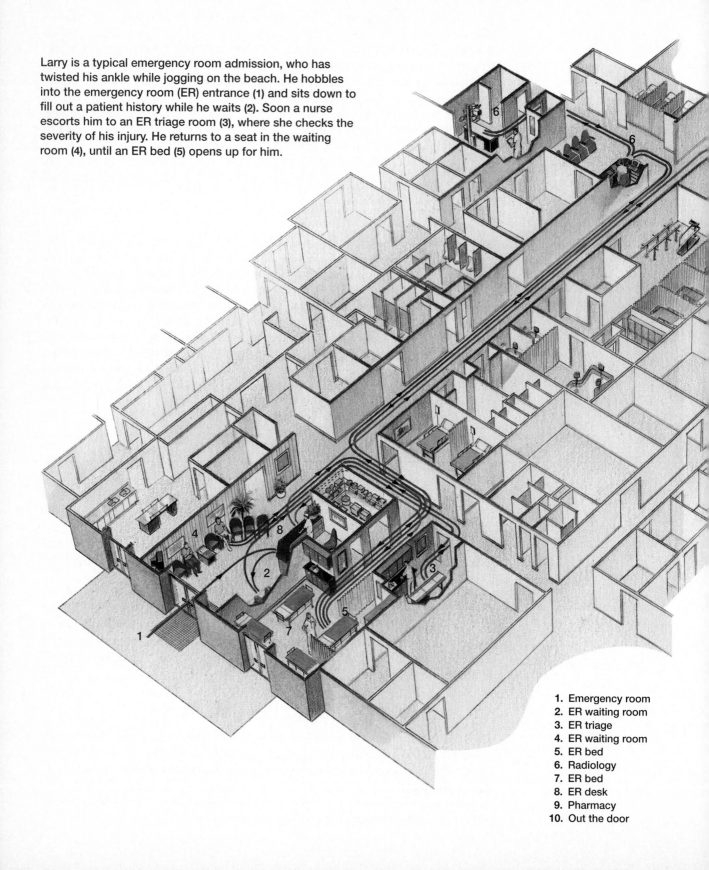

1. Emergency room
2. ER waiting room
3. ER triage
4. ER waiting room
5. ER bed
6. Radiology
7. ER bed
8. ER desk
9. Pharmacy
10. Out the door

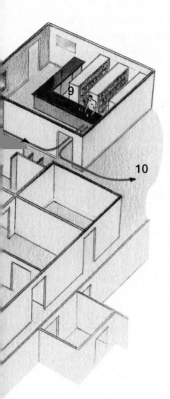

9

10

There a nurse and doctor palpate the ankle and question Larry about the level and type of pain he's experiencing. The doctor determines that an X ray will be necessary, and Larry is wheeled to the Radiology Department (6), where the radiologist takes the X rays. Larry then returns to his bed in the ER (7). Shortly, the doctor returns to tell him that he has a simple strain; suggests ice, compression, and elevation; and prescribes a muscle relaxant. Larry checks out at the ER desk (8) and picks up his prescription at the hospital pharmacy (9) on his way out the door (10). *(Note: As of this writing, necessary pharmaceuticals are issued directly from the ER.)*

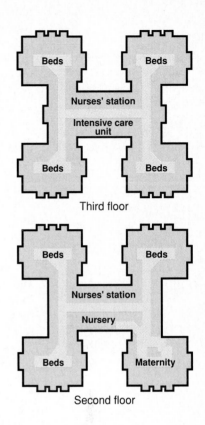

Beds   Beds

Nurses' station

Intensive care
unit

Beds   Beds

Third floor

Beds   Beds

Nurses' station

Nursery

Beds   Maternity

Second floor

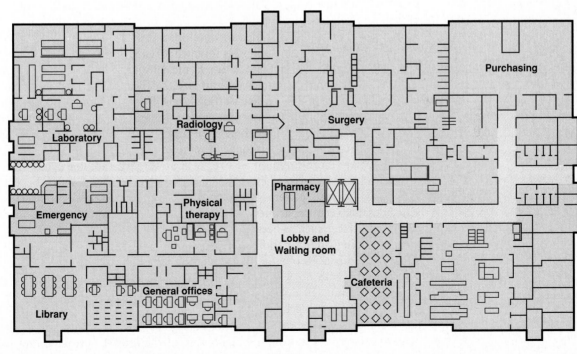

Purchasing

Laboratory

Radiology

Surgery

Pharmacy

Emergency

Physical
therapy

Lobby and
Waiting room

Cafeteria

Library

General offices

First floor

has three wards devoted to patient care, including maternity. The third floor has four more wards, as well as the intensive care unit. Nurses' stations are centrally located on each patient-care floor.

The customized services provided to each patient cause jumbled patient flows, with lots of individual handling. For simplicity, only one patient's path is shown in the illustration. The number of stops patients make during their stay varies greatly. Some patients make only 3 or 4 stops, but others may require 20 or more.

Materials Management, Staffing Plans, Inventory, and Scheduling

Some 6300 items, valued at $900,000, are held in inventory. They include all medical and surgical supplies except drugs (which are provided by a contractor). There are two separate types of inventory: (1) surgical inventory maintained by and used in surgical services to support only their activities and (2) supplies to support the patient wards. The former contains about 3500 items, valued at $600,000.

Typical items in the latter category are dressings, IV supplies, hypodermics, and maintenance materials. Each day much of the inventory is put in standard "kits" on carts and distributed to the wards. The carts are different, depending on the ward. Returned carts are exchanged, typically daily, for new ones. Owing to the hospital's small size and rural location, it has limited clout with its suppliers to achieve price or delivery concessions. The suppliers generally are large centralized distributors, and delivery time can be as long as two weeks for some items. A large Miami hospital may get delivery on the same order in two days. LFKHS has about 45 regular suppliers and 300 specialty suppliers. The purchasing policy is to monitor the inventory for the various items and place replenishment orders when the inventory gets low enough. There is some sense of how big lot sizes should be, although the determination is informal. Some specialty items, such as replacement hips, are never stocked but ordered as needed for specific patients.

Staffing plans and schedules are developed at the departmental level and typically cover one month. Planning is somewhat reactive, particularly in the ER. If the hospital census and patient *acuity* (a measure of the severity of patients' illnesses) increase, so does the day's staff size. At the same time, financial success depends on not having excessive staffing levels. Regular admissions are known at least a day in advance and sometimes much sooner. For example, surgical procedures that require special equipment or supplies require much longer planning lead times. Schedules are developed in more detail and further ahead for departments that are more capital intensive, such as surgery, radiology, and other specialties. However, even these schedules are dynamic and must be changed frequently because patient loads can change unexpectedly. Coordination of schedules between departments is informal, although some effort is made for critical interfaces such as between ER and radiology.

Scheduling rules for staff, rooms, shifts, and patients vary from one department to another. Rooms and beds often are assigned on a first-come, first-served basis, with some sensitivity to the nature of treatment and individual preferences. Staff schedules vary by department. Many departments use informal self-scheduling approaches once basic requirements have been established. Staff members make their requests, and the department director adjusts them to achieve the desired staffing levels. Because of the intense customer contact of a hospital system—and the need for around-the-clock availability for many services—many employees work nontraditional work hours. Per diem is the alternative of choice to handle short-term surges in work requirements. If per diem personnel are scheduled and turn out not to be needed, the extra staff is sent home early.

◆ TOURING A PRODUCT-FOCUSED FACILITY: CHAPARRAL STEEL*

Chaparral Steel started in 1973 as a joint venture between Texas Industries, Inc. (TXI), of Dallas, Texas, and Co-Steel, Inc., of Toronto, Canada. Groundbreaking in Midlothian, just outside of Dallas, took place in the fall of 1973. The first heat (batch of steel) was melted in May 1975. The rolling mill started running three months later. Chaparral went public in 1988, with TXI owning approximately 80 percent of the stock and the rest traded on the New York Stock Exchange. Co-Steel, however, is now the largest shareholder of TXI, and its president is on the TXI board of directors.

Gordon Forward, president of Chaparral Steel, seeks to keep the company innovative and on the leading edge of technology. Chaparral is clearly an international producer and marketer, having received Japanese Industrial Standard certification in 1989, which allows the company to sell steel in Japan. In 1991, some 7 percent of Chaparral's shipments were to Europe and Asia. Canada and Mexico are included in the company's home (domestic) market. Within the United States, most sales are to the Sunbelt.

Chaparral's facilities and operating philosophy reflect the latest advances in worldwide steel making. A customer orientation runs throughout the organization, a team concept blurs the lines between marketing and the other functional areas; and decision making is pushed down to the lowest levels of the organization, with an emphasis on action rather than on bureaucratic procedures. For instance, production workers often are included in the selection, purchase, and installation of major pieces of production equipment.

Chaparral's customers are large steel buyers, who are evaluated by the sales department before the company takes on new business. For example, a customer should have the potential to buy at least 600 tons per year to qualify as a purchaser from the mill. This ensures continuity and stable demand for Chaparral's high-volume operation. Company sales totaled $420 million in 1991.

Product Plans, Competitive Priorities, and Quality

Chaparral prides itself on providing good prices, fast delivery, and consistent quality. As for "customer orientation," Chaparral intends to be the easiest company from which to buy steel. Initially, the plant was able to produce 250,000 tons of steel per year; now it can produce 2 million. With the exception of certain specialty steels, it is a high-volume producer of standardized products.

The three rolling mills at Chaparral—the Bar Mill, the Medium Section Mill, and the Large Section Mill—determine the range of hot-rolled products the mill can produce. Customers can order standard products in different lengths and sizes; standard products are made to stock and can be cut to length as needed.

*We are indebted to Jeff E. Heyl and Linda Stone for background information on this tour.

In addition to three standard mixes of steel, Chaparral produces a variety of special carbon and alloy steel bars for the forging and cold finishing industries. Sales of a customized product, special bar quality (SBQ) steel, account for about 15 percent of all sales dollars.

In response to customer requests, Chaparral is increasing the steel quality. The large steel companies have refused to upgrade their standards because they sell by the ton, not by grade. The 50 grade is a higher grade than the normal A36, and many large mills have a difficult time achieving this grade. By making 50 grade the standard and totally eliminating A36, Chaparral can make one class of billet to satisfy the majority of its customers' needs. Chaparral's low-cost position allows it to make 50 grade for less than most mills can make A36.

Quality assurance is maintained throughout the manufacturing process. Chaparral has a policy of building quality into its products at the source, rather than depending on inspections at the end of the process. The quality control department trains all employees to recognize and remove questionable products as soon as they are discovered. The quality control lab will do any necessary chemical testing to determine quality problems and how to fix them. During the process, a front and a back sample are drawn from each heat (batch). For construction materials, the lab tests only for tensile strength. For SBQ sales, the lab may perform a variety of tests, depending on the customer's specifications. Among these are the Rockwell hardness test, the bend test, the turndown test, magnafluxing, and the Sharpie impact test—all of which have specific standards and procedures. In addition, SBQ material is hot bed–inspected (on the cooling bed after rolling) for seams and cracks.

Quality control personnel travel frequently to assist customers in the use of Chaparral products and to gather information for development of new products. Several people from quality control have even been integrated into the sales department to sell SBQ steel to customers.

Process Management

Historically, the steel industry has been labor and energy intensive. However, Chaparral Steel is much more capital intensive and innovative in its choice of technologies. The manufacturing process is capital intensive, with total property, plant, and equipment worth about $292.3 million at the end of 1991, or just over $314,000 per employee. The average labor content was 1.6 worker hours per ton produced.

The main production stages at Chaparral are melting, continuous casting, and rolling. First, *melting* is done in computer-assisted, high-powered electric arc furnaces. The melt charge, or raw material, consists exclusively of scrap metal, rather than the iron ore used in most steel-making operations. Chaparral's automobile shredder alone supplies more than 200,000 tons of prepared scrap per year. The shredder has both ferrous and nonferrous separators, as well as a wet scrubber, to assure that the charge is of acceptable quality. A furnace can melt a batch of metal in two hours, called the charge-to-tap time.

The next stage is *continuous casting,* which converts the molten metal into long steel bars called billets. Continuous casting eliminates several steps in the traditional steel-making process of pouring ingots. Chaparral has casters for each of its rolling mills. The four-strand curved mold caster supplies billets up to 49 feet in length to the Bar Mill, the smallest of the rolling mills. The five-strand caster supplies somewhat wider and shorter billets to the Medium Section Mill.

The average yield of both these casters is more than 90 percent, which is the percentage of the melt poured from the ladle that is converted to finished product. The newest mill, the Large Section Mill, has been built to utilize an internally developed "near net shape" caster. Instead of casting a rectangular billet, it casts one that is closer to the desired end shape of the beam. The casters have been carefully analyzed to improve quality. For example, electromagnetic stirring goes on within the molds, giving the billets superior surface and interior quality characteristics.

The billets go next to one of the *rolling* mills, where they must be heated to 2200° Fahrenheit in gas-fired reheat furnaces. At this temperature the billet becomes pliable and can be easily deformed. The heated billets are fed into a vertical reducing unit by a set of pinch rolls. The hot steel then moves untouched through 16 in-line stands, which progressively roll it into the desired product shape. In the Large Section Mill, the product has to be rolled fewer times to get the desired end shape. An old-style mill might call for 50 passes through rollers to accomplish what the Large Section Mill can do in 8 to 12. The result is considerable savings in processing costs across the board. Energy costs were cut by about 55 percent, and labor costs also are down, with only 0.25 labor hour per ton required in this mill.

The rolling mills are continuous in design, with a sophisticated computerized control system assisting production personnel in maintaining precise roll speed at each stand. The computer automatically prints out metal bundle tags, which include the heat number, theoretical weight, and piece count.

The formed bars next travel to an automatic cooling bed. The cooled bars are then transferred to the cold shear, where they are cut to standard lengths of from 20 to 60 feet. The sheared bars are automatically collected, strapped in bundles of 2 to 5 tons each, and tagged. Finally, they are moved to the warehouse for storage or to the shipping yard to await distribution. Angle and channel products are processed slightly differently. They are bulk-bundled, stored in the yard, and then restraightened off-line at the Bar Mill Straightener.

A special shop machines the mill rolls, which are installed on the in-line stands to create the desired product shapes. The rolls are massive, weighing between 5 and 7 tons each and costing from $8000 to $19,000. Three in-shop lathes, each costing about $500,000, machine the rolls from raw materials. The 1300 different rolls needed to make different products are stored in the ⅛-mile-long shop, from which they can be rolled into place to set up the line for the next product to be rolled.

Technology and Job Design

Chaparral has found especially innovative ways to use state-of-the-art technologies—in particular, the computer—directly in steel production. New technology is introduced frequently, even if it means replacing equipment that has not yet been fully depreciated.

Everyone on the nonunionized work force is encouraged to be innovative and to seek better ways to do his or her job. The culture at Chaparral encourages all employees to acquire new knowledge and then provides them with the freedom to apply what they have learned.

Lloyd Schmelzle, vice-president of operations, expects first-line supervisors not only to run their operations but also to keep their processes ahead of the competition. The new bar gauge system in the Bar Mill, spearheaded by two first-line supervisors and installed by the plant's maintenance department, is a good example. The system shows on a computer screen, both graphically and numerically, the shape of the steel bar being formed. This capability gives the floor operator instant feedback as he or she modifies the bar's shape—while safely enclosed in an observation pulpit. This particular innovation allowed the process to keep up with the mill's expanding capacity, which has increased to 200,000 tons per year. It also cut labor to 0.8 labor hour per ton, in contrast to the 6 labor hours per ton for most producers.

The educational process never ends for the Chaparral worker. A 3½ year program, covering mechanical, electrical, and statistical fundamentals as well as the safe operation of plant equipment, is mandatory for all employees. Beyond this program, a variety of classes are available on site to help employees develop a broad range of skills to further their careers. The company's educational program applies primarily to job-related skills, but Chaparral is supportive of employees taking classes in various subjects at local colleges. The company believes in the development of well-rounded employees. Teams of managers and workers, drawn from a mix of departments and functional areas, have been sent on numerous occasions to observe and learn from electrical furnace operations at other plants.

The manager of the Bar Mill encourages workers to find ways to automate themselves out of their own jobs, so that productivity can be increased and employees can move on to improving other jobs. Chaparral people are prepared for change and do not resist it. All employees are expected to prepare someone else to do their jobs and to grow on the job themselves. There is considerable cross-training throughout the organization. This type of job enlargement is coupled with financial incentives: Chaparral treats employees as partners, providing them with profit sharing and stock ownership plans.

Capacity and Location

Chaparral has just one plant. Its operations are located on 300 acres of land, and the plant covers about 75 acres. The plant operates 24 hours a day, 7 days a week. In 1974 the plant contained one furnace and had a capacity of 250,000 tons per year. Capacity was then expanded to 500,000 tons through the use of computers, larger ladles and transformers, and more efficient operating procedures. In 1983 a $200 million expansion featured a second furnace that immediately boosted capacity by another 300,000 tons per year. With the opening of the Large Section Mill, the plant's capacity rose to 2 million tons per year.

Capacity is well understood and a top management concern. The shredder is a good example. Its total capacity, when operated over three shifts, is 500,000 tons per year. However this output rate can be exceeded for short periods of time. For example, the record daily production was 2664 tons. Maintenance on the shredder is extensive, averaging 30 to 40 percent of the total hours worked.

THE BIG PICTURE: Layout and Flow at Chaparral Steel

The Big Picture illustration on pages 62–63 shows that the process flow through the Bar Mill is linear, following a one-directional route from the reheat furnace to storage of the finished product. An overhead crane is used to change the mill rolls on the line. At the end of the process, electromagnetic cranes and forklifts move material off the mill to storage. With these exceptions, materials handling tends to be automated and to follow fixed paths. For example, the steel flows down through the rolling mills automatically. Compare this linear, high-volume flow with the jumbled, customized flows at Lower Florida Keys Health System.

Materials Management, Production Plans, Scheduling, and Inventory

Chaparral recognizes the value of long-term relationships with its suppliers. In the past, departments did their own buying because management believed that the departments knew best what they needed. Currently, Chaparral is pursuing a new strategy of centralized purchasing. It recruited the former general manager of steel production to assist in the acquisition of raw materials. Whereas the company had been operating on a just-in-time delivery basis, it is now investigating nearby warehousing of some of the raw materials necessary for production, as well as barter with Russia for some materials. Chaparral does not buy in large quantities just to gain quantity discounts. Much of the material it buys can be had in spot markets, and the purchasing people watch these very closely, to buy quantities when the spot prices are low. They do not use blanket orders or long-term contracts because of the volatile nature of their raw material prices.

Most steel companies use a broker to get their scrap for them, who in turn receives a percentage of the job. Chaparral's vice-president of raw materials negotiates with each supplier individually every month. This approach gives Chaparral a competitive price advantage. Sources of scrap metal include crushed cars, which are then put through the shredder; turnings from machine shop operations; home scrap (leftover material from Chaparral processes); and plant and structural materials. Chaparral tends to deal with the same scrap suppliers, thus forming long-term but somewhat informal relationships.

Chaparral develops production plans three months into the future. Such planning is essential to maximize facility utilization and to establish accurate due dates for customer orders. Because of its high volumes and fairly standardized products, Chaparral can respond to unexpected demand shifts by swapping production between product groups to meet customer demands.

The Bar Mill sets up to make a product for 5 to 7 days at a time, making different sizes of the product during that week. For example, it might set up for reinforcing bars ("rebar") and make three different sizes. The Bar Mill tends to run one size for several days, then switch to the next. Setup times range from 1 to 3 hours. Changes tend to go from smaller to larger sizes.

The Medium Section Mill sets up to make beams for 5 to 7 days, making several different sizes during that week. By and large, the setups are independent of size. Most changeovers take about 5 or 6 hours.

The three-month production schedule is prepared by the production scheduler. It is reviewed at a weekly production meeting, where small revisions are made. The basic schedule comes from firm orders and requests from marketing. If the actual demand is less than capacity, additional production is scheduled (for which there is no stated demand), to ensure that the mills run at full capacity. Demand is considered seasonal, because much of the demand for construction materials is in the summer.

Finished goods inventory is maintained at the mill for a variety of bundle sizes, grades, and lengths. It is stored in either the 80-foot-wide or the 100-foot-

The Chaparral Steel plant covers some 75 acres. In the aerial view below, one sees the sites of the Bar Mill (**A**), the Medium Section Mill (**B**), the Large Section Mill (**C**), and the melt shop and continuous caster (**D**). The entire process is continuous in design, with a sophisticated computerized control system assisting personnel. At lower right is a floor plan of the Bar Mill, with an expanded cutaway on the opposite page highlighting the linear flow of the steel as it passes through operations.

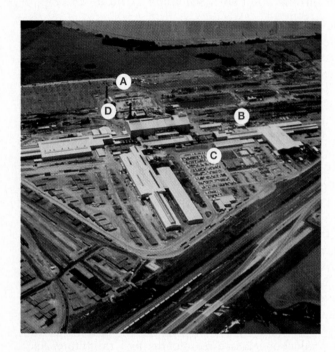

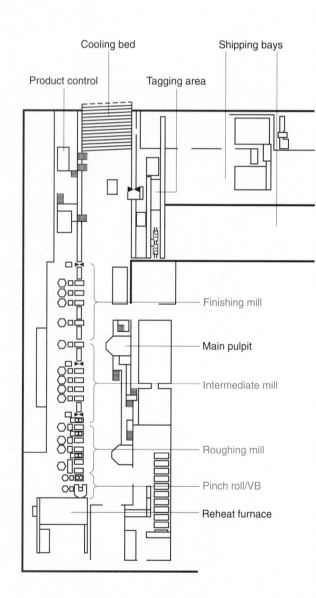

Computer consoles in the control pulpit.

A truncated (for space reasons) version of the Bar Mill, used for the plant's small, hot-rolled products. A four-strand mold caster (D in the aerial photo at left) supplies billets to the Bar Mill, where they are heated in the reheat furnace (1). The heat-softened billets then pass through the pinch rolls and VB (2) and move in a linear path (bottom to top) through the 16 in-line stands (3), which roll them into the desired shape. The mill is equipped with a computerized control system.

From the main control pulpit (4), an operator can read out status and maintain precise roll speed at each stand. The off-line machine shop (5) machines and stores the massive mill rolls, which workers can move into place with the help of overhead cranes (6), to set up the line for each new product. The formed bars travel to the cooling bed (7). From there they come back to the cold shear, where they are cut, bundled, and tagged for storage or shipment (8).

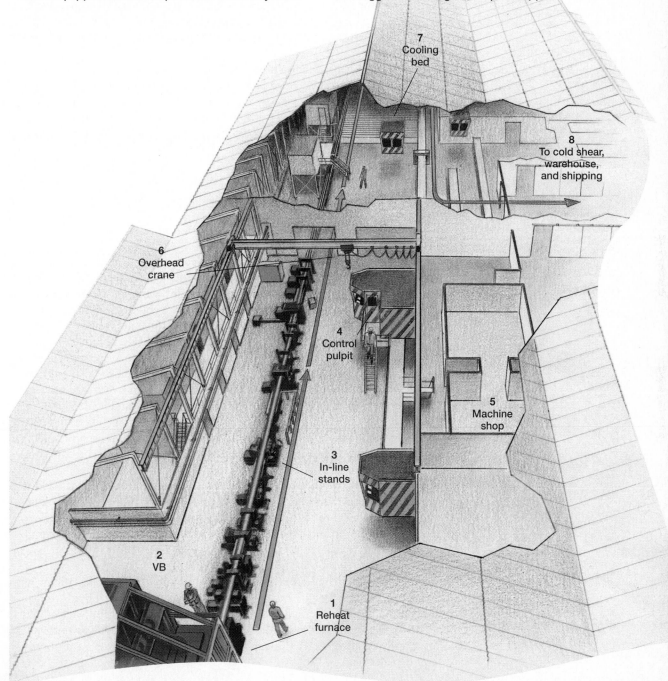

7
Cooling bed

8
To cold shear, warehouse, and shipping

6
Overhead crane

4
Control pulpit

5
Machine shop

3
In-line stands

2
VB

1
Reheat furnace

wide warehouse or in the shipping yard to await distribution. Chaparral recently opened a remote inventory warehouse in Pittsburgh, for even timelier delivery to the Northeast. The normal amount of crushed car inventory kept to feed the shredder is 25,000 tons, or approximately 6.5 weeks' supply. Finished goods inventory amounted to $45,230,000 in 1991. Of that amount, work in process accounted for $6,282,000. Raw materials, including scrap and crushed cars, totaled $10,193,000.

The new computerized order system allows customers direct access to check inventory levels, open orders, and pricing, and eventually to place orders. The quick response time allows customers to get by with lower inventory levels, giving Chaparral a competitive edge. Chaparral ships by common carrier, customer truck, and rail car, at a rate of about 30 rail car loads, or 120 truck loads, per day.

In terms of performance measures, Chaparral monitors production per hour, yield, alloys used per ton, electricity per ton, and tons per hour per employee. But tons shipped (produced) is the bottom line—the number that matters the most. A sign at the plant entrance shows yesterday's tonnage. As at any similar type of facility, running at nearly full capacity is the best way for Chaparral to make money.

◆ DIFFERENCES BETWEEN LFKHS AND CHAPARRAL STEEL

What impact does positioning strategy have on other operating decisions?

The sharp contrast between LFKHS and Chaparral Steel, summarized in Table 2.2, gives a sense of how decisions in operations must mesh. Clearly, the two firms utilize different positioning strategies. Product or service plans and competitive priorities on which these strategies are based also differ. LFKHS has a process focus. The hospital's service plans call for low-volume, customized services. Chaparral Steel has a product focus. The product volumes at Chaparral are huge: 2 million tons of steel per year, most of which is for standardized products. Its dominant competitive priorities are low cost, fast delivery, and consistent quality. The opposite is true at LFKHS, where competitive priorities cover a broad range of services customized to individual patients. LFKHS also has considerable volume flexibility, as it can adjust its capacity with overtime and part-time help to match staffing requirements with patient census and acuity.

Although LFKHS has advanced and expensive technologies in certain areas, its operation is labor intensive. Its financial health depends heavily on its being able to manage its labor costs. Chaparral Steel is quite different. To be cost competitive, it must use automation and technology to the fullest.

Capacity policies at the two organizations also are quite different. Facility utilization is much lower at LFKHS, which is equipped to handle peak season demand from December through April. Operating at a 75 percent capacity utilization level allows the hospital to handle unexpected surges in patient demand. Such a big capacity cushion would be too expensive for capital-intensive Chaparral.

Materials management at LFKHS is only informally related to suppliers; its volumes are too small to give it much clout. By contrast, Chaparral tends to deal long term, though still informally, with its suppliers of scrap metal. It also has more control over customer demand. By maintaining finished goods inventory at the mill, Chaparral protects itself much more than LFKHS can from variations in customer demand.

TABLE 2.2 *Linkages at LFKHS and Chaparral*

Decision Area	Process Focus at LFKHS	Product Focus at Chaparral
Product or service plan	Low-volume, customized service	High-volume, standardized products
Competitive priorities	Customized services, consistent quality, and volume flexibility	Low cost, fast delivery, and consistent quality
Process design	Labor intensive	Capital intensive
Capacity	Lower utilization	Higher utilization
Materials management	Informal supplier relationships	Formal supplier relationships
Scheduling	Fluid	Planned far ahead

Finally, scheduling procedures are quite different. The process focus and amount of customer contact at LFKHS require fluid scheduling procedures. Detailed plans are not made very far ahead because of the uncertainties involved. In contrast, at Chaparral the concern is for top efficiency, and the simplicity of line flows demands elaborate scheduling and day-to-day monitoring of performance.

CHAPTER REVIEW

Chapter Highlights

- Corporate strategy is the process of determining the organization's mission, monitoring and adjusting to changes in the external environment, and exploiting distinctive competencies. Firms taking a global view may form strategic alliances through collaborative efforts, joint ventures, or licensing of technology.
- Market analysis is key to formulating a customer-driven operations strategy. Market segmentation and needs assessment are methods of pinpointing elements of a product or service that satisfy customers.
- Customer-driven operations strategy requires translating market needs into desirable capabilities for the operations function, called competitive priorities. There are eight priorities: low-cost operations, high-performance design, consistent quality, fast delivery time, on-time delivery, development speed, customization, and volume flexibility. Trade-offs among them are often necessary. Management must decide on which dimensions the firm's production system should excel.
- With time-based competition, managers seek to save time on the various steps taken to deliver a product or service.
- A life cycle consists of five stages: product and service planning, introduction, growth, maturity, and decline. Concurrent engineering during product and service planning involves operations and other functions early in the development and testing of a new product or service.
- Life-cycle audits identify the need to eliminate existing product lines and introduce new ones. Three strategies for entering and exiting the life cycle of a product or service are enter early and exit late, enter early and exit early, and enter late and exit late. Each places a different demand on the production system. For example, entering early and exiting late forces operations to shift their priorities from low volume and product customization to high volume and low cost.
- Product and service planning is an ongoing activity that is the starting point for designing and operating a production system.
- Positioning strategy determines the fundamental nature of operations. Strategies range from a process focus to a product focus. Intermediate strategies form a continuum between these extremes.
- A process focus organizes equipment and human resources around processes. This focus fits with the low volumes, high flexibility, general-purpose equipment, jumbled flow patterns, labor-intensive technologies, low capacity utilization, informal relationships with suppliers and customers, large work-in-process inventories, and fluid schedules characteristic of job shops. The more customer contact at a service facility, the greater is the tendency toward a process focus.
- A product focus organizes resources around specific products, resulting in straightforward flow patterns characteristic of assembly lines and flow shops. It fits high volumes and standardized products.

Key Terms

assemble-to-order strategy *50*	flow shop *48*	market segmentation *34*
collaborative effort *32*	functional strategies *29*	mass customization *51*
competitive priorities *29*	high-performance design *36*	mass production *50*
concurrent engineering *42*	intermediate strategy *49*	needs assessment *35*
consistent quality *37*	job shop *48*	on-time delivery *38*
corporate strategy *28*	joint venture *32*	operations strategy *29*
customer benefit package *35*	licensing technology *33*	order qualifier *42*
customization *40*	lead time *38*	process-focused strategy *47*
development speed *38*	life cycle *42*	product-focused strategy *47*
distinctive competencies *31*	life-cycle audit *44*	positioning strategy *47*
entrance–exit strategy *45*	make-to-order strategy *50*	strategic alliance *32*
environmental scanning *30*	make-to-stock strategy *50*	time-based competition *39*
fast delivery time *38*	market analysis *28*	volume flexibility *40*

Study Questions

1. What questions does an organizational mission statement answer?
2. What indicates that an organization has too narrow a mission?
3. How are environmental scanning, adjusting to environmental change, and distinctive competencies related?
4. What are the differences among a collaborative effort, a joint venture, and a licensing agreement?
5. Contrast mass production with mass customization.
6. Give an example of each component of the customer benefit package for each of the following products.
   a. An insurance policy
   b. An airline trip
   c. Dental work
7. An air package delivery company, a passenger airline, and an airplane manufacturer all say that time is a competitive priority. Explain how these three companies might use time to measure performance but still have significantly different competitive priorities.
8. Explain how time-based competition can be used to gain a market niche.
9. What methods are used by your campus bookstore to deal with the crush of textbook sales at the beginning of each semester (or when the first midterm exams are scheduled)? With which two of the eight competitive priorities is your bookstore most concerned? For example, is it helpful, courteous (high-performance) service combined with low cost?
10. What dimensions of competitive priorities seem to be the most important for each of the following companies?
    a. McDonald's
    b. McDonnell Douglas
    c. Old MacDonald's (farm)
11. What positioning strategy seems best for each of the following types of companies? Briefly defend your choice.
    a. Résumé preparation service
    b. Local photocopy shop
    c. Paper mill
    d. Regional personal-check printer
    e. Recycling center
12. What positioning strategy seems best for each of the following types of companies? Briefly defend your choice.
    a. Builder of space launch vehicles
    b. Machine shop subcontractor to aerospace and defense contractors
    c. Aluminum refinery
    d. Microwave oven manufacturer
    e. Communications tower builder
    f. Radar detector manufacturer
13. What positioning strategy seems best for each of the following types of companies? Briefly defend your choice.
    a. Fossil-fired electric generation station
    b. Builder of fossil-fired electric generation stations
    c. Designer of fossil-fired electric generation stations
    d. Campus bookstore
    e. College campus
    f. Savings and loan branch office
14. Why do firms offering more customized, low-volume products tend to
    a. compete less on short customer delivery times and low costs?
    b. be less capital intensive?
15. Why do firms with a product focus tend to
    a. plan production and inventory levels further into the future?
    b. have more formalized supplier relationships?
    c. have less inventory accumulate at the work-in-process stage?
16. How does the concept of life cycles illustrate the ongoing need for product and service planning?
17. The Sealtight Company is a well-diversified manufac-

turer in the packaging business. It makes a variety of packaging materials and sells them to industrial buyers. Management is currently conducting a life-cycle audit to identify the current stage of each product in its life cycle. The profiles for two products are shown in Table 2.3.

a. In which stage is product A? Product B? Explain your answers.

b. For which product would low cost be a higher competitive priority? Why?

18. Singh DeCajon buys the rights to popular television shows and sells them to independent television stations and to international television markets. Management is currently conducting a life-cycle audit to identify the current stage of two shows. The profiles for the two products are shown in Table 2.4.

a. In which stage is product A? Product B? Explain your answers.

b. For which product would low cost be a higher competitive priority? Why?

19. How does the decision on when to enter and exit the life cycle of a product or service affect the operations function? With which entrance–exit strategy would a product focus make most sense?

20. What information is required to have a *customer-driven* operations strategy?

21. Is volume flexibility needed more by LFKHS or by Chaparral Steel? How is it achieved, and what is the impact on the predictability of an employee's upcoming work schedule? What is the impact on facility utilization?

22. Where is extensive customer contact needed more—at LFKHS or at Chaparral Steel? How does this requirement influence the location of customers for each facility? How does it affect the amount of inventory held by each?

TABLE 2.3 *Product Profiles*

Product	Performance Measure	This Year's Performance	Change from Last Year	Average Annual Change over Past Four Years
A	Annual sales	$42.1 million	−3.1%	+1.2%
	Unit price	$1.53/lb	0.0%	+0.5%
	Unit profit margin	$0.22/lb	−2.1%	−0.5%
	Total profit contribution	$6.0 million	−7.4%	+0.2%
B	Annual sales	$5.4 million	+72.1%	+35.0%
	Unit price	$1.30/lb	+7.0%	+6.8%
	Unit profit margin	$0.70/lb	+12.1%	+15.1%
	Total profit contribution	$2.9 million	+80.1%	+37.2%

TABLE 2.4 *Product Profiles*

Product	Performance Measure	This Year's Performance	Change from Last Year	Average Annual Change over Past Two Years
A "The June and Ozzie Stone Show"	Annual sales	$20.3 million	−31.6%	+7.2%
	Unit price	$210,000/episode	0.0%	+14.5%
	Unit profit margin	$40,000/episode	−12.1%	+17.5%
	Total profit contribution	$3.2 million	−17.4%	+8.2%
B "Dysfunctional Family Matters"	Annual sales	$5.4 million	+78.2%	NA
	Unit price	$310,000/episode	+7.0%	NA
	Unit profit margin	$190,000/episode	+12.1%	NA
	Total profit contribution	$4.9 million	+84.4%	NA

Discussion Questions

1. A sign on the way to an abandoned mine reads: "Choose your ruts carefully; you will be in them for the next 15 miles." How does this caution apply to positioning strategy and competitive priorities?

2. Look through the business section of a newspaper or weekly news magazine. Find an example of a company that is changing its mission (not simply adding capacity for its current business). Is the mission changing because of trends, threats, or opportunities identified by an environmental scan? Was the previous mission too broad or too narrow? What corrective actions are reported? What are the expected impacts on the organization associated with narrowing a mission that was too broad (or vice versa)?

3. Westinghouse recently sold the financial services part of its business. Find a similar example of a company that is narrowing its mission. Review the list of distinctive competencies presented in this chapter. Does the lack of a distinctive competency explain why the company is narrowing its mission?

4. Which global market is growing the fastest? (It is not the United States.) Find an example of a local operation whose primary market is not in the United States.

5. Suppose you were conducting a market analysis for a new textbook about technology management. What would you need to know to identify a market segment? How would you make a needs assessment? What would be the customer benefit package?

6. Escher's Fish and Fowl Restaurant has decided to excel in all eight competitive priorities. Is this a good idea? Explain.

7. A local fast-food restaurant processes several customer orders at once. Service clerks cross paths, sometimes nearly colliding, while they trace different paths to fill customer orders. If customers order a special combination of toppings on their hamburger, they must wait for quite some time while the special order is cooked. How would you modify the restaurant's operations to achieve competitive advantage? Because demand surges at lunchtime, volume flexibility is a competitive priority in the fast-food business. How would you achieve volume flexibility?

8. Kathryn Shoemaker established Grandmother's Chicken Restaurant in Middlesburg five years ago. It features a unique recipe for chicken, "just like grandmother used to make." The facility is homey, with relaxed and friendly service. Business has been good during the past two years, for both lunch and dinner. Customers normally wait about 15 minutes to be served, although complaints about service delays have increased. Shoemaker is currently considering whether to expand the current facility or open a similar restaurant in neighboring Uniontown, which has been growing rapidly.

   a. What types of strategic plans must Shoemaker make?

   b. What environmental forces could be at work in Middlesburg and Uniontown that Shoemaker should consider?

   c. What are the possible distinctive competencies of Grandmother's?

9. For 20 years Russell's Pharmacy has been located on the town square of River City, the only town for 20 miles in any direction. River City's economy is dominated by agriculture and generally rises and falls with the price of corn. But Russell's Pharmacy enjoys a steady business. Jim Russell is on a first-name basis with the entire town, except for his divorce lawyer. He provides friendly, accurate service, listens patiently to health complaints, and knows the family health history of everyone. He keeps an inventory of the medicines required by regular customers but sometimes has a one-day delay to fill new prescriptions. However, he can't obtain drugs at the same low price as the large pharmacy chains can. There's trouble right here in River City. Several buildings around the town square are now abandoned or used as storerooms for old cars. The town is showing signs of dying off right along with the family farm. Twenty miles upstream, situated on a large island in the river, is the growing town of Large Island. Russell is considering a move to the Conestoga Mall in Large Island.

   a. What types of strategic plans must Russell make?

   b. What environmental forces could be at work that Russell should consider?

   c. What are the possible distinctive competencies of Russell's Pharmacy?

10. Wild West, Inc. is a regional telephone company that inherited nearly 100,000 employees and 50,000 retirees from AT&T. Wild West has a new mission: to diversify. It calls for a 10 year effort to enter the financial services, real estate, cable TV, home shopping, entertainment, and cellular communication services markets—and to compete with other telephone companies. Wild West plans to provide cellular and fiber optic communication services in markets with established competitors, such as in the United Kingdom, and in markets with essentially no competition, such as Russia and former Eastern Bloc countries.

    a. What types of strategic plans must Wild West make? Is the "do nothing" option viable? If Wild West's mission appears too broad, which businesses would you trim first?

    b. What environmental forces could be at work that Wild West should consider?

    c. What are the possible distinctive competencies of Wild West? What weaknesses should it avoid or mitigate?

11. Give an example of how an order qualifier affected one of your recent selection decisions, such as your selection of a college or a bicycle.
12. You are planning to design a new air-powered hand tool. Which functions would you have represented in your concurrent engineering effort? Why? In the past, your design engineers did their work in isolation. What hurdles might you anticipate in implementing concurrent engineering?

C A S E

BSB, Inc.: The Pizza Wars Come to Campus

Renee Kershaw, manager of food services at a medium-sized private university in the southeast, has just had the wind taken out of her sails. She had decided that, owing to the success of her year-old pizza food service, the time had come expand pizza-making operations on campus. However, yesterday the university president announced plans to begin the construction of a student center on campus that would house, among other facilities, a new food court. In a departure from past university policy, this new facility would permit and accommodate food-service operations from three private organizations: Dunkin' Donuts, Taco Bell, and Pizza Hut. Until now, all food service on campus had been contracted out to BSB, Inc.

Campus Food Service

BSB, Inc. is a large, nationally operated food services company serving client organizations. The level of service provided varies, depending on the type of market being served and the particular contract specifications. The company is organized into three market-oriented divisions: corporate, airline, and university/college. Kershaw, of course, is employed in the university/college division.

At this particular university, BSB, Inc. is under contract to provide food services for the entire campus of 6000 students and 3000 faculty, staff, and support personnel. Located in a city of approximately 200,000 people, the campus was built on land donated by a wealthy industrialist. Because the campus is somewhat isolated from the rest of the town, students wanting to shop or dine off campus have to drive into town.

The campus itself is a "walking" campus, with dormitories, classrooms, and supporting amenities such as a bookstore, sundry shop, barber shop, branch bank, and food-service facilities all within close proximity. Access to the campus by car is limited, with peripheral parking lots provided. The university also provides space, at a nominal rent, for three food-service facilities. The primary facility, a large cafeteria housed on the ground floor of the main administration building, is located in the center of campus. This cafeteria is open for breakfast, lunch, and dinner daily. A second location, called the Dogwood Room, serves an upscale luncheon buffet on weekdays only on the second floor of the administration building. The third facility is a small grill located in the corner of a recreational building near the dormitories. The grill is open from 11 A.M. to 10 P.M. daily and until midnight on Friday and Saturday nights. Kershaw is responsible for all three operations.

The Pizza Decision

BSB, Inc. has been operating the campus food services for the past 10 years—ever since the university decided that its mission and distinctive competences should focus on education, not on food service. Kershaw has been at this university for 18 months. Previously, she had been assistant manager of food services at a small university in the northeast. After three to four months of getting oriented to the new position, she had begun to conduct surveys to determine customer needs and market trends.

An analysis of the survey data indicated that students were not as satisfied with the food operations as Kershaw had hoped. A significant percentage of the food being consumed by students was not being purchased at the BSB facilities:

Percentage of food prepared in dorm rooms	20
Percentage of food delivered from off campus	36
Percentage of food consumed off campus	44

The reasons most commonly given by students were (1) lack of variety in food offerings and (2) tight, erratic schedules that didn't always fit with cafeteria serving hours. Three other findings from the survey were of concern to Kershaw: (1) the large percentage of students with cars, (2) the large percentage of students with refrigerators and microwave ovens in their rooms, and (3) the number of times students ordered food delivered from off campus.

Percentage of students with cars on campus	84
Percentage of students having refrigerators/ microwaves in their rooms	62
Percentage of food that students consume outside BSB, Inc. facilities	43

In response to the market survey, Kershaw decided to expand the menu at the grill to include pizza. Along with expanding the menu, she also started a delivery service that covered the entire campus. Now students would have not only greater variety but also the convenience of having food delivered quickly to their rooms. To accommodate these changes, a pizza oven was installed in the grill and space was allocated to store pizza ingredients, to make cut-and-box pizzas, and to stage premade pizzas that were ready to cook. Existing personnel were trained to make pizzas, and additional personnel were hired to deliver them by bicycle. In an attempt to keep costs down and provide fast delivery, the combinations of toppings available were limited. That way a limited number of "standard pizzas" could be preassembled, ready to cook as soon as an order was received.

The Success

Kershaw believed that her decision to offer pizza service in the grill was the right one. Sales over the past 10 months had steadily increased, along with profits. Follow-up customer surveys indicated a high level of satisfaction with the reasonably priced and speedily delivered pizzas. However, Kershaw realized that success brought with it other challenges.

The demand for pizzas had put a strain on the grill's facilities. Initially, space was taken from other grill activities to accommodate the pizza oven, preparation, and staging areas. As the demand for pizzas grew, so did the need for space and equipment. The capacities of existing equipment and space allocated for making and cooking pizzas now were insufficient to meet demand, and deliveries were being delayed. To add to the problem, groups were beginning to order pizzas in volume for various on-campus functions.

Finally, a closer look at the sales data showed that pizza sales were beginning to level off. Kershaw wondered whether the capacity problem and resulting increase in delivery times were the reasons. However, something else had been bothering her. In a recent conversation, Mack Kenzie, the grill's supervisor, had told Kershaw that over the past couple of months requests for pizza toppings and

combinations not on the menu had steadily increased. She wondered whether her on-campus market was being affected by the "pizza wars" off campus and the proliferation of specialty pizzas.

The New Challenge

As she sat in her office, Kershaw thought about yesterday's announcement concerning the new food court. It would increase competition from other types of snack foods (Dunkin' Donuts) and fast foods (Taco Bell). Of more concern, Pizza Hut was going to put in a facility offering a limited menu and providing a limited selection of pizzas on a "walk up and order" basis. Phone orders would not be accepted nor would delivery service be available.

Kershaw pondered several crucial questions: Why had demand for pizzas leveled off? What impact would the new food court have on her operations? Should she expand her pizza operations? If so, how?

Questions

1. How would you describe the mission of BSB, Inc. on this campus? Does BSB, Inc. enjoy any competitive advantages or distinctive competencies?
2. Initially, how did Renee Kershaw choose to use her pizza operations to compete with off-campus eateries? What were her competitive priorities?
3. What impact will the new food court have on Kershaw's pizza operations? What competitive priorities might she choose to focus on now?
4. If she were to change the competitive priorities for the pizza operation, how might that affect her operating processes and capacity decisions?
5. What would be a good positioning strategy for Kershaw's operations on campus to meet the food court competition?

Source: This case was prepared by Dr. Brooke Saladin, Wake Forest University, as a basis for classroom discussion.

Selected References

Adam, E. E., Jr., and P. M. Swamidass. "Assessing Operations Management from a Strategic Perspective." *Journal of Management,* vol. 15, no. 2 (1989), pp. 181–203.

Berry, W. L., C. Bozarth, T. Hill, and J. E. Klompmaker. "Factory Focus: Segmenting Markets from an Operations Perspective." *Journal of Operations Management,* vol. 10, no. 3 (1991), pp. 363–387.

Blackburn, Joseph. *Time-Based Competition: The Next Battleground in American Manufacturing.* Homewood, Ill.: Business One–Irwin, 1991.

Cleveland, G., R. G. Schroeder, and J. C. Anderson. "Production Competence: A Proposed Theory." *Decision Sciences,* vol. 20, no. 4 (1989), pp. 655–688.

Collier, David A. *The Service Quality Solution.* Milwaukee, Wis.: ASQC Quality Press; and Burr Ridge, Illinois: Irwin Professional Publishing, 1994.

Dean, James W., Jr., and Gerald I. Susman. "Organizing for Manufacturable Design." *Harvard Business Review* (January–February 1989), pp. 28–36.

Ferdows, Kasra, and Arnoud De Meyer. "Lasting Improvements in Manufacturing Performance: In Search of a New Theory." *Journal of Operations Management,* vol. 9, no. 2 (April 1990), pp. 168–184.

Fitzsimmons, James A., and Mona Fitzsimmons. *Service Management for Competitive Advantage.* New York: McGraw-Hill, 1994.

Giffi, Craig A., Aleda V. Roth, and Gregory M. Seal. *Competing in World-Class Manufacturing: America's 21st Century Challenge.* Homewood, Ill.: Business One–Irwin, 1991.

Heskett, James L. *Managing the Service Economy.* Boston: Harvard Business School Press, 1986.

Heskett, James L., and Leonard A. Schlesenger. "The Service-Driven Service Company." *Harvard Business Review* (September–October 1991), pp. 71–81.

Hill, Terry. *Manufacturing Strategy: Text and Cases.* Homewood, Ill.: Irwin, 1994.

Kekre, Sunder, and Kannan Srinivasan. "Broader Product Line: A Necessity to Achieve Success?" *Management Science,* vol. 36, no. 10 (October 1990), pp. 1216–1231.

Kim, Jay S. "Beyond the Factory Walls: Executive Summary of 1994 U.S. Manufacturing Futures Survey." Boston University, 1994.

Leong, G. K., D. L. Snyder, and P. T. Ward. "Research in the Process and Content of Manufacturing Strategy." *OMEGA,* vol. 18, no. 2 (1990), pp. 109–122.

Merrills, Roy. "How Northern Telecom Competes on Time." *Harvard Business Review* (July–August 1989), pp. 108–114.

Pine, B. Joseph, II, Bart Victor, and Andrew C. Boynton. "Making Mass Customization Work." *Harvard Business Review* (September–October 1993), pp. 108–119.

Porter, Michael E. "The Competitive Advantage of Nations." *Harvard Business Review* (March–April 1990), pp. 73–93.

"Pushing Design to Dizzying Speed," *Business Week,* October 21, 1991, p. 64.

Roth, Aleda V., and Marjolijn van der Velde. "Operations as Marketing: A Competitive Service Strategy." *Journal of Operations Management,* vol. 10, no. 3 (December, 1993), pp. 303–328.

Schmenner, Roger W. *Plant Tours and Service Tours in Operations Management,* 3rd ed. New York: Macmillan, 1991.

Sharma, Deven. "Manufacturing Strategy: An Empirical Analysis." Unpublished dissertation, Ohio State University, 1987.

Skinner, Wickham. *Manufacturing in the Corporate Strategy.* New York: John Wiley & Sons, 1978.

Stalk, George Jr. "Time—The Next Source of Competitive Advantage." *Harvard Business Review* (July–August 1988), pp. 41–51.

Vickery, S. K., C. Droge, and R. R. Markland. "Production Competence and Business Strategy: Do They Affect Business Performance?" *Decision Sciences,* vol. 24, no. 2, 1993, pp. 435–456.

Wheelwright, Steven C., and Robert H. Hayes. "Competing Through Manufacturing." *Harvard Business Review* (January–February 1985), pp. 99–109.

Wheelwright, Steven C., and W. Earl Sasser, Jr. "The New Product Development Map." *Harvard Business Review* (May–June 1989), pp. 112–125.

Wood, Craig H. "Operations Strategy: Decision Patterns and Measurement." Unpublished dissertation, Ohio State University, 1991.

Decision Making

Operations managers make many choices as they deal with the various decision areas listed in Chapter 1. Although the specifics of each situation vary, decision making generally involves the same basic steps: (1) recognize and clearly define the problem, (2) collect the information needed to analyze possible alternatives, and (3) choose and implement the most feasible alternative.

Sometimes hard thinking in a quiet room is sufficient. At other times reliance on more formal procedures is needed. Here we present four such formal procedures: break-even analysis, the preference matrix, decision theory, and the decision tree.

- Break-even analysis helps the manager identify how much change in volume or demand is necessary before a second alternative becomes better than the first one.

- The preference matrix helps a manager deal with multiple criteria that cannot be evaluated with a single measure of merit, such as total profit or cost.

- Decision theory helps the manager choose the best alternative when outcomes are uncertain.

- A decision tree helps the manager when decisions are made sequentially—when today's best decision depends on tomorrow's decisions and events.

◆ BREAK-EVEN ANALYSIS

To evaluate an idea for a new product or service or to assess the performance of an existing one, determining the volume of sales at which the product or service breaks even is useful. The **break-even point** is the volume at which total revenues equal total costs. Use of this technique is known as **break-even analysis.** Break-even analysis can also be used to compare production methods by finding the volume at which two different processes have equal total costs.

Evaluating Products or Services

We begin with the first purpose: to evaluate the profit potential of a new or existing product or service. This technique helps the manager answer questions such as the following:

- Is the predicted sales volume of the product or service sufficient to break even (neither earning a profit nor sustaining a loss)?

- How low must the variable cost per unit be to break even, given prices and forecasts of sales?

- How low must the fixed cost be to break even?
- How do price levels affect the break-even volume?

Break-even analysis is based on the assumption that all costs related to the production of a specific product or service can be divided into two categories: variable costs and fixed costs.

The **variable cost,** *c,* is the portion of the total cost that varies directly with volume of output: costs per unit for materials, labor, and usually some fraction of overhead. If we let Q equal the number of units produced and sold per year, total variable cost $= cQ$. The **fixed cost,** *F,* is the portion of the total cost that remains constant regardless of changes in levels of output: the annual cost of renting or buying new equipment and facilities (including depreciation, interest, taxes, and insurance), salaries, utilities, and portions of the sales or advertising budget. Thus the total cost of producing a good or service equals fixed costs plus variable costs times volume, or

$$\text{Total cost} = F + cQ$$

The variable cost per unit is assumed to be the same no matter how many units Q are sold, and thus total cost is linear. If we assume that all units produced are sold, total annual revenues equal revenue per unit sold, p, times the quantity sold, or

$$\text{Total revenue} = pQ$$

If we set total revenue equal to total cost, we get the break-even point as

$$pQ = F + cQ$$
$$(p - c)Q = F$$
$$Q = \frac{F}{p - c}$$

We can also find this break-even quantity graphically. Because both costs and revenues are linear relationships, the break-even point is where the total revenue line crosses the total cost line.

EXAMPLE A.1

Finding the Break-Even Quantity

A hospital is considering a new procedure to be offered at \$200 per patient. Fixed cost per year would be \$100,000, with total variable costs of \$100 per patient. What is the break-even quantity for this service? Use both algebraic and graphic approaches to get the answer.

Solution   The formula for the break-even quantity yields

$$Q = \frac{F}{p - c} = \frac{100,000}{200 - 100} = 1000 \text{ patients}$$

To solve graphically we plot two lines—one for costs and one for revenues. Two points determine a line, so we begin by calculating costs and revenues for two different output levels. The following table shows the results for $Q = 0$ and $Q = 2000$. We selected zero as the first point because of the ease of plotting total revenue (0) and total cost (F). However, we could have used any two reasonably spaced output levels.

Quantity (patients) (Q)	Total Annual Cost ($) (100,000 + 100Q)	Total Annual Revenue ($) (200Q)
0	100,000	0
2000	300,000	400,000

We can now draw the cost line through points (0, 100,000) and (2000, 300,000). The revenue line goes between (0, 0) and (2000, 400,000). As Fig. A.1 indicates, these two lines intersect at 1000 patients, the break-even quantity.

FIGURE A.1   *Graphic Approach to Break-Even Analysis*

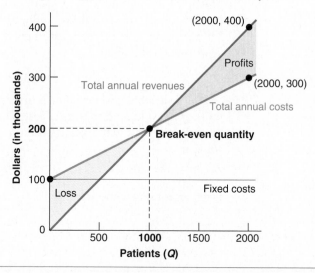

Break-even analysis cannot tell a manager whether to pursue a new product or service idea or drop an existing line. The technique can only show what is likely to happen for various forecasts of costs and sales volumes. To evaluate a variety of "what if" questions, we use an approach called **sensitivity analysis,** a technique for systematically changing parameters in a model to determine the effects of such changes. The concept can be applied later to other techniques, such as linear programming (see Supplement I). Here we assess the sensitivity of total profit to different pricing strategies, sales volumes forecasts, or cost estimates.

EXAMPLE A.2

Sensitivity Analysis of Sales Forecasts

If the most pessimistic sales forecast for the proposed service in Fig. A.1 were 1500 patients, what would be the procedure's total contribution to profit and overhead per year?

Solution   The graph shows that even the pessimistic forecast lies above the break-even volume, which is encouraging. The product's total contribution, found by subtracting total costs from total revenues, is

$$pQ - (F + cQ) = 200(1500) - [100,000 + 100(1500)]$$

$$= \$50,000$$

Evaluating Processes

Often choices must be made between two processes or between an internal process and buying the service or material on the outside. In such cases we assume that the decision does not affect revenues. The operations manager must study all the costs and advantages of each approach. Rather than find the quantity where total costs equal total revenues, the analyst finds the quantity for which the total costs for two alternatives are equal. For the make-or-buy decision, it is the quantity for which the total "buy" cost equals the total "make" cost. Let F_b equal the fixed cost (per year) of the buy option, F_m equal the fixed cost of the make option, c_b equal the variable cost (per unit) of the buy option, and c_m the variable cost of the make option. Thus the total cost to buy is $F_b + c_b Q$, and the total cost to make is $F_m + c_m Q$. To find the break-even quantity, we set the two cost functions equal and solve for Q:

$$F_b + c_b Q = F_m + c_m Q$$

$$Q = \frac{F_m - F_b}{c_b - c_m}$$

The make option should be considered, ignoring qualitative factors, only if its variable costs are lower than those of the buy option. The reason is that the fixed costs for making the product or service are typically higher than the fixed costs for buying. Under these circumstances, the buy option is best if production volumes are less than the break-even quantity. Beyond that quantity, the make option becomes best.

EXAMPLE A.3

Break-Even Analysis for Make-or-Buy Decisions

The manager of a fast-food restaurant featuring hamburgers is adding salads to the menu. There are two options, and the price to the customer will be the same for each. The make option is to install a salad bar stocked with vegetables, fruits, and toppings and let the customer assemble the salad. The salad bar would have to be leased and a part-time employee hired. The manager estimates the fixed costs at $12,000 and variable costs totaling $1.50 per salad. The buy option is to have preassembled salads available for sale. They would be purchased from a local supplier at $2.00 per salad. Offering preassembled salads would require installation and operation of additional refrigeration, with an annual fixed cost of $2400. The manager expects to sell 25,000 salads per year.

What is the break-even quantity?

Solution The formula for the break-even quantity yields

$$Q = \frac{F_m - F_b}{c_b - c_m}$$

$$= \frac{12,000 - 2400}{2.0 - 1.5}$$

$$= 19,200 \text{ salads}$$

The break-even quantity is 19,200 salads. As the 25,000-salad sales forecast exceeds this amount, the make option is preferred. Only if the restaurant expected to sell fewer than 19,200 salads would the buy option be better.

◆   PREFERENCE MATRIX

Decisions often must be made in situations where multiple criteria cannot be naturally merged into a single measure (such as dollars). For example, a manager deciding in which of two cities to locate a new plant would have to consider such unquantifiable factors as quality of life, worker attitudes toward work, and community reception in the two cities. These important factors cannot be ignored. A **preference matrix** is a table that allows the manager to rate an alternative according to several performance criteria. The criteria can be scored on any scale, such as from 1 (worst possible) to 10 (best possible) or from 0 to 1, as long as the same scale is applied to all the alternatives being compared. Each score is weighted according to its perceived importance, with the total of these weights typically equaling 100. The total score is the sum of the weighted scores (weight times score) for all the criteria. The manager can compare the scores for alternatives against one another or against a predetermined threshold.

EXAMPLE A.4

Evaluating an Alternative with a Preference Matrix

The following table shows the performance criteria, weights, and scores (1 = worst, 10 = best) for a new product: a thermal storage air conditioner. If management wants to introduce just one new product and the highest total score of any of the other product ideas is 800, should the firm pursue making the air conditioner?

Performance Criterion	Weight (*A*)	Score (*B*)	Weighted Score (*A* × *B*)
Market potential	30	8	240
Unit profit margin	20	10	200
Operations compatibility	20	6	120
Competitive advantage	15	10	150
Investment requirement	10	2	20
Project risk	5	4	20
		Weighted score =	750

Solution   Because the sum of the weighted scores is 750, it falls short of the 800 threshold, so management would not pursue the thermal storage air conditioner idea at this time.

Not all managers are comfortable with the preference matrix technique. It requires the manager to state criterion weights before examining the alternatives, although the proper weights may not be readily apparent. Perhaps only after seeing the scores for several alternatives can the manager decide what is important and what is not. Because a low score on one criterion can be compensated for or overridden by high scores on others, the preference matrix method also may cause managers to ignore important signals. In Example A.4, the investment required for the thermal storage air conditioner might exceed the firm's financial capability. In that case the manager should not even be considering the alternative, no matter how high its score.

◆ DECISION THEORY

Decision theory is a general approach to decision making when the outcomes associated with alternatives are often in doubt. It helps operations managers with decisions on process, capacity, location, and inventory, because such decisions are about an uncertain future. Decision theory can also be used by managers in other functional areas. With decision theory, a manager makes choices using the following process.

1. List the feasible *alternatives*. One alternative that should always be considered as a basis for reference is to do nothing. A basic assumption is that the number of alternatives is finite. For example, in deciding where to locate a new retail store in a certain part of the city, a manager could theoretically consider every grid coordinate on the city's map. Realistically, however, the manager must narrow the number of choices to a reasonable number.

2. List the *events* (sometimes called *chance events* or *states of nature*) that have an impact on the outcome of the choice but are not under the manager's control. For example, the demand experienced by the new facility could be low or high, depending not only on whether the location is convenient to many customers, but also on what the competition does and general retail trends. Then group events into reasonable categories. For example, suppose that the average number of sales per day could be anywhere from 1 to 500. Rather than have 500 events, the manager could represent demand with just 3 events: 100 sales/day, 300 sales/day, or 500 sales/day. The events must be mutually exclusive and exhaustive, meaning that they do not overlap and that they cover all eventualities.

3. Calculate the *payoff* for each alternative in each event. Typically the payoff is total profit or total cost. These payoffs can be entered into a **payoff table,** which shows the amount for each alternative if each event occurs. For 3 alternatives and 4 events, the table would have 12 payoffs (3×4). If significant distortions will occur if the time value of money is not recognized, the payoffs should be expressed as present values or internal rates of return (see Appendix 1). For multiple criteria with important qualitative factors, use the weighted scores of a preference matrix approach as the payoffs.

4. Estimate the likelihood of each event, using past data, executive opinion, or other forecasting methods. Express it as a *probability,* making sure that the probabilities sum to 1.0. Develop probability estimates from past data if the past is considered a good indicator of the future.

5. Select a *decision rule* to evaluate the alternatives, such as choosing the alternative with the lowest expected cost. The rule chosen depends on the amount of information the manager has on the event probabilities and the manager's attitudes toward risk.

Using this process, we examine decisions under three different situations: certainty, uncertainty, and risk.

Decision Making Under Certainty

The simplest situation is when the manager knows which event will occur. Here the decision rule is to pick the alternative with the best payoff for the known event. The best alternative is the highest payoff if the payoffs are expressed as profits. If the payoffs are expressed as costs, the best alternative is the lowest payoff.

A manager is deciding whether to build a small or a large facility. Much depends on the future demand that the facility must serve, and demand may be small or large. The manager knows with certainty the payoffs that will result under each alternative, shown in the following payoff table. The payoffs (in $000) are the present values (see Appendix 1) of future revenues minus costs for each alternative in each event.

Alternative	Possible Future Demand	
	Low	High
Small facility	200	270
Large facility	160	800
Do nothing	0	0

What is the best choice if future demand will be low?

Solution   In this example, the best choice is the one with the highest payoff. If the manager knows that future demand will be low, the company should build a small facility and enjoy a payoff of $200,000. The larger facility has a payoff of only $160,000. The "do nothing" alternative is dominated by the other alternatives; that is, the outcome of one alternative is no better than the outcome of another alternative for each event. Because the "do nothing" alternative is dominated, the manager doesn't consider it further.

Decision Making Under Uncertainty

Here we assume that the manager can list the possible events but cannot estimate their probabilities. Perhaps a lack of prior experience makes it difficult for the firm to estimate probabilities. In such a situation, the manager can use one of four decision rules.

1. *Maximin*—Choose the alternative that is the "best of the worst." This rule is for the *pessimist,* who anticipates the "worst case" for each alternative.
2. *Maximax*—Choose the alternative that is the "best of the best." This rule is for the *optimist,* who has high expectations and prefers to "go for broke."
3. *Laplace*—Choose the alternative with the best *weighted payoff*. To find the weighted payoff, give equal importance (or, alternatively, equal probability) to each event. If there are n events, the importance (or probability) of each is $1/n$, so they add up to 1.0. This rule is for the *realist.*
4. *Minimax Regret*—Choose the alternative with the best "worst regret." Calculate a table of regrets (or opportunity losses), where the rows represent the alternatives and the columns represent the events. A regret is the difference between a given payoff and the best payoff in the same column. For an event it shows how much is lost by picking a given alternative instead of the one that is best for this event. The regret can be lost profit or increased cost, depending on the situation.

Decisions Under
Uncertainty

Reconsider the payoff matrix in Example A.5. What is the best alternative for each decision rule?

Solution

a. *Maximin:* An alternative's worst payoff is the *lowest* number in its row of the payoff matrix, because the payoffs are profits. The worst payoffs ($000) are

Alternative	Worst Payoff
Small facility	200
Large facility	160

The best of these worst numbers is $200,000, so the pessimist would build a small facility.

b. *Maximax:* An alternative's best payoff ($000) is the *highest* number in its row of the payoff matrix, or

Alternative	Best Payoff
Small facility	270
Large facility	800

The best of these best numbers is $800,000, so the optimist would build a large facility.

c. *Laplace:* With two events, we assign each a probability of 0.5. Thus the weighted payoffs ($000) are

Alternative	Weighted Payoff
Small facility	$0.5(200) + 0.5(270) = \mathbf{235}$
Large facility	$0.5(160) + 0.5(800) = \mathbf{480}$

The best of these weighted payoffs is $480,000, so the realist would build a large facility.

d. *Minimax Regret:* If demand turns out to be low, the best alternative is a small facility and its regret is 0 (or $200 - 200$). If a large facility is built when demand turns out to be low, the regret is 40 (or $200 - 160$).

	Regret		
Alternative	Low Demand	High Demand	Maximum Regret
Small facility	$200 - 200 = \mathbf{0}$	$800 - 270 = \mathbf{530}$	530
Large facility	$200 - 160 = \mathbf{40}$	$800 - 800 = \mathbf{0}$	40

The column on the right shows the worst regret for each alternative. To minimize the maximum regret, pick a large facility. The biggest regret is associated with having only a small facility and high demand.

Decision Making Under Risk

Here we assume that the manager can list the events and estimate their probabilities. The manager has less information than with decision making under certainty but more information than with decision making under uncertainty. For this intermediate situation, the *expected value* decision rule is widely used. The expected value for an alternative is found by weighting each payoff with its associated probability and then adding the weighted payoff scores. The alternative with the best expected value (highest for profits and lowest for costs) is chosen.

This rule is much like the Laplace decision rule, except that the events are no longer assumed to be equally likely (or equally important). The expected value is what the *average* payoff would be if the decision could be repeated time after time. Of course, the expected value decision rule can result in a bad outcome if the wrong event occurs. However, it gives the best results if applied consistently over a long period of time. The rule should not be used if the manager is inclined to avoid risk.

EXAMPLE A.7

Decisions Under Risk

Reconsider the payoff matrix in Example A.5. For the expected value decision rule, which is the best alternative if the probability of small demand is estimated to be 0.4 and the probability of large demand is estimated to be 0.6?

Solution   The expected value for each alternative is

Alternative	Expected Value
Small facility	$0.4(200) + 0.6(270) = \textbf{242}$
Large facility	$0.4(160) + 0.6(800) = \textbf{544}$

Choose a large facility, because its expected value is the highest at $544,000.

Value of Perfect Information

Suppose that a manager has a way of improving the forecasts—say, through more expensive market research or studying past trends. Assume that the manager, although unable to affect the probabilities of the events, can predict the future without error. The **value of perfect information** is the amount by which the expected payoff will improve if the manager knows which event will occur. It can be found with the following procedure.

1. Identify the best payoff for each event.
2. Calculate the expected value of these best payoffs by multiplying the best payoff for each event by the probability that it will occur.
3. Subtract the expected value of the payoff without perfect information from the expected value of the payoff with perfect information. This difference is the value of perfect information.

What is the value of perfect information to the manager in Example A.7?

Solution   The best payoff for each event is the highest number in its column of the payoff matrix, or

Event	Best Payoff
Low demand	200
High demand	800

The expected values, with and without perfect information, are

$$EV_{perfect} = 200(0.4) + 800(0.6) = 560$$

$$EV_{imperfect} = 160(0.4) + 800(0.6) = 544$$

Therefore the value of perfect information is $560,000 - $544,000 = $16,000.

DECISION TREES

A decision tree is a general approach to a wide range of OM decisions, such as product planning, process management, capacity, and location. It is particularly valuable for evaluating different capacity expansion alternatives when demand is uncertain and sequential decisions are involved. For example, a company may expand a facility in 1996 only to discover in 1998 that demand is much higher than forecasted. In that case, a second decision may be necessary to determine whether to expand once again or build a second facility.

A **decision tree** is a schematic model of alternatives available to the decision maker, along with their possible consequences. The name derives from the tree-like appearance of the model. It consists of a number of square *nodes*, representing decision points, that are left by *branches* (which should be read from left to right), representing the alternatives. Branches leaving circular, or chance, nodes represent the events. The probability of each chance event, *P(E)*, is shown above each branch. The probabilities for all branches leaving a chance node must sum to 1.0. The conditional payoff, which is the payoff for each possible alternative–event combination, is shown at the end of each combination. Payoffs are given only at the outset, before the analysis begins, for the end points of each alternative–event combination. In Fig. A.2 on the next page, for example, payoff 1 is the financial outcome the manager expects if alternative 1 is chosen and then chance event 1 occurs. No payoff can be associated yet with any branches farther to the left, such as alternative 1 as a whole, because it is followed by a chance event and is not an end point. Payoffs often are expressed as the present value (see Appendix 1) of net profits. If revenues are not affected by the decision, the payoff is expressed as net costs.

After drawing a decision tree, we solve it by working from right to left, calculating the *expected payoff* for each node as follows.

FIGURE A.2

A Decision Tree Model

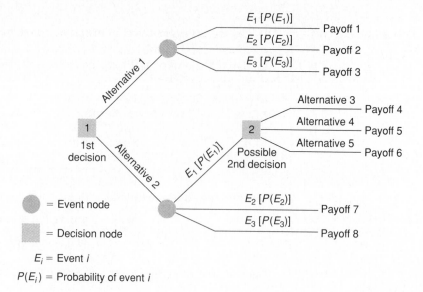

1. For an event node, multiply the payoff of each event branch by the event's probability. Add these products to get the event node's expected payoff.

2. For a decision node, pick the alternative that has the best expected payoff. If an alternative leads to an event node, its payoff is equal to that node's expected payoff (already calculated). "Saw off," or "prune," the other branches not chosen by marking two short lines through them. The decision node's expected payoff is the one associated with the single remaining unpruned branch.

We continue this process until the leftmost decision node is reached. The unpruned branch extending from it is the best alternative to pursue. If multistage decisions are involved, the manager must await subsequent events before deciding what to do next. If new probability or payoff estimates are obtained, the manager should repeat the process.

EXAMPLE A.9

Analyzing a Decision Tree

A retailer must decide whether to build a small or a large facility at a new location. Demand at the location can be either small or large, with probabilities estimated to be 0.4 and 0.6, respectively. If a small facility is built and demand proves to be high, the manager may choose not to expand (payoff = $223,000) or to expand (payoff = $270,000). If a small facility is built and demand is low, there is no reason to expand and the payoff is $200,000. If a large facility is built and demand proves to be low, the choice is to do nothing ($40,000) or to stimulate demand through local advertising. The response to advertising may be either modest or sizable, with their probabilities estimated to be 0.3 and 0.7, respectively. If it is modest, the payoff is estimated to be only $20,000; the payoff grows to $220,000 if the response is sizable. Finally, if a large facility is built and demand turns out to be high, the payoff is $800,000.

Draw a decision tree. Then analyze it to determine the expected payoff for each decision and event node. Which alternative—building a small facility or building a large facility—has the higher expected payoff?

Solution   The decision tree in Fig. A.3 shows the event probability and the payoff for each of the seven alternative–event combinations. The first decision is whether to build a small or a large facility. Its node is shown first, to the left, because it is the decision the retailer must make now. The second decision node—whether to expand at a later date—is reached only if a small facility is built and demand turns out to be high. Finally the third decision point—whether to advertise—is reached only if the retailer builds a large facility and demand turns out to be low.

F I G U R E   A.3   *Decision Tree for Retailer*

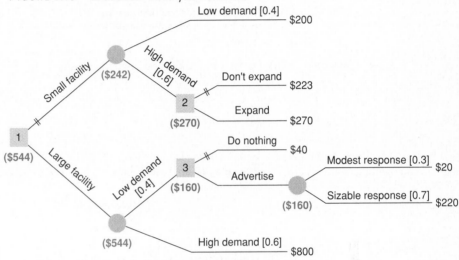

Now we can begin the analysis of the decision tree, calculating the expected payoffs from right to left, shown on Fig. A.3 beneath the appropriate event and decision nodes.

1. For the event node dealing with advertising, the expected payoff is 160, or the sum of each event's payoff weighted by its probability [0.3(20) + 0.7(220)].
2. The expected payoff for decision node 3 is 160 because *Advertise* (160) is better than *Do nothing* (40). Prune the *Do nothing* alternative.
3. The payoff for decision node 2 is 270 because *Expand* (270) is better than *Don't expand* (223). Prune *Don't expand*.
4. The expected payoff for the event node dealing with demand, assuming that a small facility is built, is 242 [or 0.4(200) + 0.6(270)].
5. The expected payoff for the event node dealing with demand, assuming that a large facility is built, is 544 [or 0.4(160) + 0.6(800)].
6. The expected payoff for decision node 1 is 544 because the large facility's expected payoff is largest. Prune *Small facility*.

The best alternative is to build the large facility. This initial decision is the only one the retailer makes now. Subsequent decisions are made after learning whether demand actually is low or high.

SUPPLEMENT REVIEW

Solved Problem 1

The owner of a small manufacturing business has patented a new device for washing dishes and cleaning dirty kitchen sinks. Before trying to commercialize the device and add it to her existing product line, she wants reasonable assurance of success. Variable costs are estimated at $7 per unit produced and sold. Fixed costs are about $56,000 per year.

a. If the selling price is set at $25, how many units must be produced and sold to break even? Use both algebraic and graphic approaches.
b. Forecasted sales for the first year are 10,000 units if the price is reduced to $15. With this pricing strategy, what would be the product's total contribution to profits in the first year?

Solution   a. Beginning with the algebraic approach, we get

$$Q = \frac{F}{p - c} = \frac{56,000}{25 - 7}$$

$$= 3111 \text{ units}$$

Using the graphic approach, shown in Fig. A.4, we first draw two lines:

$$\text{Total revenue} = 25Q$$

$$\text{Total cost} = 56,000 + 7Q$$

The two lines intersect at $Q = 3111$ units, the break-even quantity.

FIGURE A.4

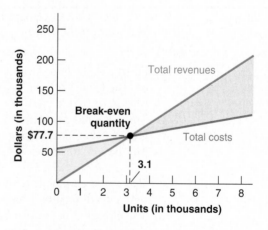

b. Total profit contribution = Total revenue − Total cost

$$= pQ - (F + cQ)$$

$$= 15(10,000) - [56,000 + 7(10,000)]$$

$$= \$124,000$$

Solved Problem 2

Binford Tool Company is screening three new product ideas, A, B, and C. Resource constraints allow only one of them to be commercialized. The performance criteria and ratings, on a scale of 1 (worst) to 10 (best), are shown in the following table. The Binford managers give equal weights to the performance criteria. Which is the best alternative, as indicated by the preference matrix method?

	Rating		
Performance Criterion	**Product A**	**Product B**	**Product C**
1. Demand uncertainty and project risk	3	9	2
2. Similarity to present products	7	8	6
3. Expected return on investment (ROI)	10	4	8
4. Compatibility with current manufacturing process	4	7	6
5. Competitive advantage	4	6	5

Solution Each of the five criteria receives a weight of ⅕ or 0.20.

Product	Calculation	Total Score
A	$(0.20 \times 3) + (0.20 \times 7) + (0.20 \times 10) + (0.20 \times 4) + (0.20 \times 4)$	= 5.6
B	$(0.20 \times 9) + (0.20 \times 8) + (0.20 \times 4) + (0.20 \times 7) + (0.20 \times 6)$	= 6.8
C	$(0.20 \times 2) + (0.20 \times 6) + (0.20 \times 8) + (0.20 \times 6) + (0.20 \times 5)$	= 5.4

The best choice is product B. Products A and C are well behind in terms of total weighted score.

Solved Problem 3

Adele Weiss manages the campus flower shop. Flowers must be ordered three days in advance from her supplier in Mexico. Although Valentine's Day is fast approaching, sales are almost entirely last-minute, impulse purchases. Advance sales are so small that Weiss has no way to estimate the probability of low (25 dozen), medium (60 dozen), or high (130 dozen) demand for red roses on the big day. She buys roses for $15 per dozen and sells them for $40 per dozen. Construct a payoff table. Which decision is indicated by each of the following decision criteria?

a. Maximin
b. Maximax
c. Laplace
d. Minimax regret

Solution The payoff table for this problem is

	Demand for Red Roses		
Alternative	**Low (25 dozen)**	**Medium (60 dozen)**	**High (130 dozen)**
Order 25 dozen	$625	$625	$625
Order 60 dozen	$100	$1500	$1500
Order 130 dozen	($950)	$450	$3250
Do nothing	$0	$0	$0

a. Under the maximin criteria, Weiss should order 25 dozen, because if demand is low, Weiss's profits are $625.

b. Under the maximax criteria, Weiss should order 130 dozen. The greatest possible payoff, $3250, is associated with the largest order.

c. Under the Laplace criteria, Weiss should order 60 dozen. Equally weighted payoffs for ordering 25, 60, and 130 dozen are about $625, $1033, and $917, respectively.

d. Under the minimax regret criteria, Weiss should order 130 dozen. The maximum regret of ordering 25 dozen occurs if demand is high: $3250 − $625 = $2625. The maximum regret of ordering 60 dozen occurs if demand is high: $3250 − $1500 = $1750. The maximum regret of ordering 130 dozen occurs if demand is low: 625 − (−$950) = **$1575**.

Solved Problem 4

White Valley Ski Resort is planning the ski lift operation for its new ski resort. Management is trying to determine whether one or two lifts will be necessary; each lift can accommodate 250 people per day. Skiing normally occurs in the 14-week period from December to April, during which the lift will operate seven days per week. The first lift will operate at 90 percent capacity if economic conditions are bad, the probability of which is believed to be about a 0.3. During normal times the first lift will be utilized at 100 percent capacity, and the excess crowd will provide 50 percent utilization of the second lift. The probability of normal times is 0.5. Finally, if times are really good, the probability of which is 0.2, the utilization of the second lift will increase to 90 percent. The equivalent annual cost of installing a new lift, recognizing the time value of money and the lift's economic life, is $50,000. The annual cost of installing two lifts is only $90,000 if both are purchased at the same time. If used at all, each lift costs $200,000 to operate, no matter how low or high its utilization rate. Lift tickets cost $20 per customer per day.

a. Should the resort purchase one lift or two?

b. What is the value of perfect information?

Solution   a. The decision tree is shown in Fig. A.5. The payoff ($000) for each alternative–event branch is shown in the following table. The total revenues from one lift operating at 100 percent capacity are $490,000 (or 250 customers × 98 days × $20/customer-day).

Alternative	Economic Condition	Payoff Calculation (Revenue − Cost)
One lift	Bad times	0.9(490) − (50 + 200) = 191
	Normal times	1.0(490) − (50 + 200) = 240
	Good times	1.0(490) − (50 + 200) = 240
Two lifts	Bad times	0.9(490) − (90 + 200) = 151
	Normal times	1.5(490) − (90 + 400) = 245
	Good times	1.9(490) − (90 + 400) = 441

b. The value of perfect information is

Economic Condition	Best Payoff	Probability	Weighted Payoff
Bad times	$191,000	0.3	$ 57,300
Normal times	$245,000	0.5	$122,500
Good times	$441,000	0.2	$ 88,200
Expected value with perfect information			$268,000
Without perfect information, part (a)			$256,000
The value of perfect information is			$ 12,000

FIGURE A.5

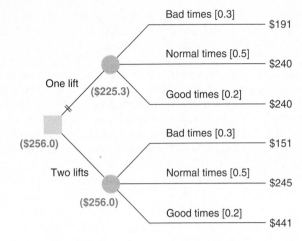

Formula Review

1. Break-even volume: $Q = \dfrac{F}{p - c}$

2. Evaluating processes, make-or-buy indifference quantity: $Q = \dfrac{F_m - F_b}{c_b - c_m}$

Supplement Highlights

- Break-even analysis can be used to evaluate the profit potential of products and services. It can also be used to compare alternative production methods. Sensitivity analysis can be used to predict the effect of changing forecasts, costs, or prices.
- At times, decision alternatives cannot be evaluated in light of a single performance measure such as profit or cost. The preference matrix is a method of rating alternatives according to several objectives. The technique calls for important objectives to receive more weight in the decision, but determining in advance which objectives are important may be difficult.
- Applications of decision theory in operations management include decisions on process, capacity, location, and inventory. Decision theory is a general approach to decision making under conditions of certainty, uncertainty, or risk.

Key Terms

break-even analysis 72
break-even point 72
decision theory 77
decision tree 81

fixed cost 73
payoff table 77
preference matrix 76
sensitivity analysis 74

value of perfect information 80
variable cost 73

Study Questions

1. Explain how break-even analysis can be used to
   a. screen product ideas.
   b. compare alternative processes or alternative facility locations.
2. A newlywed couple used the preference matrix to decide among several apartments. They scored available apartments against weighted performance criteria. The criteria included rent, proximity to work and recreational opportunities, security, and other neighborhood characteristics associated with the couple's values and life-style. Upon completing the analysis, they found that the best apartment indicated by the technique happened to be next door to the bride's parents!

   Evaluate the application of the preference matrix in this decision situation.

3. Explain why the accuracy of demand forecasts and cost estimates becomes important in break-even analysis when the margin between price and cost is small.

4. When we cannot estimate the probability of alternative future events, decisions are made under uncertainty. In such cases do you tend to the maximin, maximax, Laplace, or minimax regret method of making decisions? Does your decision-making style match your pessimistic, optimistic, or realist character? Does your approach to decisions vary in some situations? What situations encourage you to take risks (maximax)? Which cause you to favor minimax regret?

5. The expected value criterion gives good results if applied consistently over the long run. Congratulations! You've been promoted to Director of the Metropolitan Major League Baseball Stadium District. Your city is building a new stadium and you must decide among alternative designs calling for 30,000, 42,000, and 50,000 seats. What might cause difficulty if you use a decision tree and the expected value criterion to evaluate these alternatives?

6. You have calculated the value of perfect information. An expert in forecasting offers to provide you with consulting services for 90 percent of the value of perfect information. Should you accept the offer?

Problems

Problems 1–11 show a variety of applications for break-even analysis. Problems 1–4 apply break-even analysis to product or service planning decisions (Chapter 2). Problems 12 and 13 demonstrate use of the preference matrix for product or service planning, and problem 14 applies the preference matrix to location decisions. Decision theory problems 15, 16, and 19–22 apply to capacity decisions (discussed in Chapter 7). Problems 17 and 18 use decision trees to evaluate fairly complex product or service planning decisions.

Break-Even Analysis

1. Mary Williams, owner of Williams Products, is evaluating whether to introduce a new product line. After thinking through the production process and the costs of raw materials and new equipment, Williams estimates the variable costs of each unit produced and sold at $5 and the fixed costs per year at $46,500.
   a. If the selling price is set at $17 each, how many units must be produced and sold to break even? Use both graphic and algebraic approaches to get your answer.
   b. Williams forecasts sales of 8000 units for the first year if the selling price is set at $12.50 each. What would be the total contribution to profits from this new product during the first year?
   c. If the selling price is set at $11.50, Williams forecasts that first-year sales would increase to 10,000 units. Which pricing strategy ($12.50 or $11.50) would result in the greater total contribution to profits?
   d. What other considerations would be crucial to the final decision about making and marketing the new product?

2. A product at the Jennings Company has enjoyed reasonable sales volumes, but its contributions to profits have been disappointing. Last year, 17,500 units were produced and sold. The selling price is $22 per unit, c is $18, and F is $80,000.

   a. What is the break-even quantity for this product? Use both graphic and algebraic approaches to get your answer.
   b. Jennings is considering ways to either stimulate sales volumes or decrease variable costs. Management believes that sales can be increased by 30 percent or that c can be reduced to 85 percent of its current level. Which alternative leads to higher contributions to profits, assuming that each is equally costly to implement? (*Hint*: Calculate profits for both alternatives and identify the one having the greatest profits.)
   c. What is the percentage change in the per unit profit contribution generated by each alternative in part b?

3. An interactive television service that costs $7 per month to provide can be sold on the information highway for $12 per client per month. If a service area includes a potential of 10,000 customers, what is the most a company could spend on annual fixed costs to acquire and maintain the equipment?

4. A restaurant is considering adding fresh brook trout to its menu. Customers would have the choice of catching their own trout from a simulated mountain stream or simply asking the waiter to net the trout for them. Operating the stream would require $10,600 in fixed costs per year. Variable costs are estimated to be $6.70 per trout. The firm wants to break even if 800 trout dinners are sold per year. What should be the price of the new item?

5. Goliath Manufacturing must implement a manufacturing process that reduces the amount of toxic byproducts. Two processes have been identified that provide the same level of toxic by-product reduction. The first process would incur $205,000 of fixed costs and $650 per unit of variable costs. The second process has fixed costs of $145,000 and variable costs of $800 per unit.

a. What is the break-even quantity beyond which the first process is more attractive?

b. What is the difference in total cost if the quantity produced is 500 units?

6. A news clipping service is considering modernization. Rather than manually clipping and photocopying articles of interest and mailing them to its clients, employees electronically input stories from most widely circulated publications into a database. Each new issue is searched for key words, such as a client's company name, competitors' names, type of business, and the company's products, services, and officers. When matches occur, affected clients are instantly notified via an on-line network. If the story is of interest, it is electronically transmitted, so the client often has the story and can prepare comments for follow-up interviews before the publication hits the street. The manual process has fixed costs of $400,000 per year and variable costs of $6.20 per clipping mailed. The price charged the client is $8.00 per clipping. The computerized process has fixed costs of $1,300,000 per year and variable costs of $2.25 per story electronically transmitted to the client.

a. If the same price is charged for either process, what is the annual volume beyond which the automated process is more attractive?

b. The present volume of business is 225,000 clippings per year. Many of the clippings sent with the current process are not of interest to the client or are multiple copies of the same story appearing in several publications. The news clipping service believes that by improving service and by lowering the price to $4.00 per story, modernization will increase volume to 900,000 stories transmitted per year. Should the clipping service modernize?

c. If the forecasted increase in business is too optimistic, at what volume will the new process break even?

7. Hahn Manufacturing has been purchasing a key component of one of its products from a local supplier. The current purchase price is $1500 per unit. Efforts to standardize parts have succeeded to the point that this same component can now be used in five different products. Annual component usage should increase from 150 to 750 units. Management wonders whether it is time to make the component in-house, rather than to continue buying it from the supplier. Fixed costs would increase by about $40,000 per year for the new equipment and tooling needed. The cost of raw materials and variable overhead would be about $1100 per unit, and labor costs would go up by another $300 per unit produced.

a. Should Hahn make rather than buy?

b. What is the break-even quantity?

c. What other considerations might be important?

8. A construction company is trying to decide whether to continue renting or to buy a concrete pump for its foundation and slab construction. The fixed annual cost for buying a new pump with hose and all other accessories is $8800, and annual maintenance costs would be another $2000 per year. One of the company's current employees would operate the pump, at a wage rate of $35 per hour. If the company doesn't buy the pump, it will continue to rent one for $125 per hour, including operator labor cost. The pump is normally needed for eight hours per pour.

a. What is the break-even quantity in number of pours?

b. If the company expects to have 40 pours per year, should it buy or continue to rent? What is the difference in annual costs at this volume?

9. The Tri-County Generation and Transmission Association is a nonprofit cooperative organization that provides electrical service to rural customers. Based on a faulty long-range demand forecast, Tri-County overbuilt its generation and distribution system. Tri-County now has much more capacity than it needs to serve its customers. Fixed costs, mostly debt service on investment in plant and equipment, are $82.5 million per year. Variable costs, mostly fossil fuel costs, are $25 per megawatt-hour (MWh, or million watts of power used for one hour). The new person in charge of demand forecasting prepared a short-range forecast for use in next year's budgeting process. That forecast calls for Tri-County customers to consume 1 million MWh of energy next year.

a. How much will Tri-County need to charge its customers per MWh to break even next year?

b. The Tri-County customers balk at that price and conserve electrical energy. Only 95 percent of forecasted demand materializes. What is the resulting surplus or loss for this nonprofit organization?

10. Earthquake, drought, fire, economic famine, flood, and a pestilence of TV court reporters have caused an exodus from the City of Angels to Boulder, Colorado. The sudden increase in demand is straining the capacity of Boulder's electrical system. Boulder's alternatives have been reduced to buying 150,000 MWh of electric power from Tri-County G&T at a price of $75 per MWh, or refurbishing and recommissioning the abandoned Pearl Street Power Station in downtown Boulder. Fixed costs of that project are $10 million per year, and variable costs would be $35 per MWh. Should Boulder build or buy?

11. Tri-County G&T sells 150,000 MWh per year of electrical power to Boulder at $75 per MWh, has fixed costs of $82.5 million per year, and has variable costs of $25 per MWh. If Tri-County has 1,000,000 MWh of demand from its customers (other than Boulder) what will Tri-County have to charge to break even?

Preference Matrix

12. The Forsite Company is screening three ideas for new services. Resource constraints allow only one idea to be commercialized at the present time. The following estimates have been made for the five performance criteria that management believes to be most important.

	Rating		
Performance Criterion	Service A	Service B	Service C
Capital equipment investment required	0.6	0.8	0.3
Expected return on investment (ROI)	0.7	0.3	0.9
Compatibility with current work-force skills	0.4	0.7	0.5
Competitive advantage	1.0	0.4	0.6
Compatibility with EPA requirements	0.2	1.0	0.5

a. Calculate a total weighted score for each alternative. Use a preference matrix and assume equal weights for each performance criterion. Which alternative is best? Worst?

b. Suppose that the expected ROI is given twice the weight assigned to each of the remaining criteria. (Sum of weights should remain the same as in part a.) Does this modification affect the ranking of the three potential services?

13. You are in charge of analyzing five new product ideas and have been given the information shown in Table A.1 (1 = worst, 10 = best). Management has decided that criteria 2 and 3 are equally important, criterion 1 is five times as important as criterion 2, and criterion 4 is three times as important as criterion 2. Only two new products can be introduced, and a product can be introduced only if its score exceeds 70 percent of the maximum possible total points. Which product ideas do you recommend?

14. Schlemiel, Schlimazel, Hasenpfeffer, Inc. collected the following information on where to locate a brewery (1 = poor, 10 = excellent).

		Location Score	
Location Factor	Factor Weight	Milwaukee	Boulder
Construction costs	10	8	5
Utilities available	10	7	7
Business services	20	4	7
Real estate cost	30	7	4
Quality of life	10	4	8
Transportation	20	7	6

a. Which location, A or B, should be chosen on the basis of the total weighted score?

b. If the factors were weighted equally, would the choice change?

Decision Theory

15. B&K Construction has received favorable publicity from guest appearances on a public TV home improvement program. Public TV programming decisions seem to be unpredictable, so B&K can't estimate the probability of continued benefits from its relationship with the show. Demand for home improvements next year may be either low or high. But B&K must decide now whether to hire more employees, do nothing, or develop subcontracts with other home improvement contractors. B&K has developed the following payoff table (top of next page). Which alternative is best, according to each of the following decision criteria?

a. Maximin

b. Maximax

c. Laplace

d. Minimax regret

Table A.1   *Analysis of New Product Ideas*

	Rating				
Performance Criterion	Product A	Product B	Product C	Product D	Product E
Compatibility with current manufacturing	8	7	3	6	8
Expected return on investment (ROI)	3	8	4	7	7
Compatibility with current work-force skills	7	5	7	6	2
Unit profit margin	7	6	9	1	6

	Demand for Home Improvements	
Alternative	Low	High
Hire	($250,000)	$625,000
Subcontract	$100,000	$415,000
Do nothing	$250,000	$300,000

16. Once upon a time in the old West, Fletcher, Cooper, and Wainwright (the Firm) was deciding whether to make arrows, barrels, or Conestoga wagons. The Firm understood that demand for products would vary, depending on U.S. government policies concerning the development of travel routes to California. If land routes were chosen and treaties with Native Americans could not be negotiated, the demand for arrows would be great. Success in those negotiations would favor demand for Conestoga wagons. If the water route was chosen, the success of negotiations would be irrelevant. Instead, many barrels would be needed to contain goods during the long sea voyage around Cape Horn. Although the Firm was expert at forecasting the effect of policy on its business, it couldn't estimate the probability of the U.S. government favoring one policy over another. Based on the Firm's forecasted demand, which alternative is best, according to each of the following decision criteria?
    a. Maximin
    b. Maximax
    c. Laplace

	Forecasted Demand		
Policy	Arrows	Barrels	Conestoga Wagons
Land, no treaty	9,000,000	300,000	5,000
Land with treaty	5,000,000	200,000	50,000
Sea	2,500,000	500,000	3,000

	Product		
Price and Costs	Arrows	Barrels	Conestoga Wagons
Fixed costs	$60,000	$80,000	$100,000
Variable costs per unit	$0.05	$1.50	$50
Price per unit	$0.15	$3.00	$75

17. Returning to Problem 16, assume that Fletcher, Cooper, and Wainwright has contributed to the reelection campaign and legal defense fund for the Chair of the House Ways and Means Committee. In return the Firm learns that the probability of choosing the sea route is 0.2, the probability of developing the land route and successful treaty negotiations is 0.3, and the probability of developing the land route and unsuccessful negotiations is 0.5.
    a. Draw a decision tree to analyze the problem. Calculate the expected value of each product alternative.
    b. The Chair informs Fletcher, Cooper and Wainwright that a more accurate forecast of events is available "for a price." What is the value of perfect information?

Decision Tree

18. Analyze the decision tree in Fig. A.6. What is the expected payoff for the best alternative?

FIGURE A.6

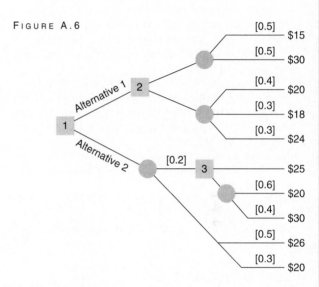

19. A manager is trying to decide whether to buy one machine or two. If only one is purchased and demand proves to be excessive, the second machine can be purchased later. Some sales will be lost, however, because the lead time for producing this type of machine is six months. In addition, the cost per machine will be lower if both are purchased at the same time. The probability of low demand is estimated to be 0.25, and of high demand, 0.75. The after-tax net present value of the benefits from purchasing the two machines together is $94,000 if demand is low and $165,000 if demand is high.

    If one machine is purchased and demand is low, the net present value is $115,000. If demand is high, the manager has three options. Doing nothing has a net present value of $115,000; subcontracting, $140,000; and buying the second machine, $126,000.
    a. Draw a decision tree for this problem.
    b. How many machines should the company buy initially? What is the expected payoff for this alternative?

20. A manager is trying to decide whether to build a small, medium, or large facility. Demand can be low, average, or high, with the estimated probabilities being 0.25, 0.40, and 0.35, respectively.

    A small facility is expected to earn an after-tax net present value of just $18,000 if demand is low. If demand is average, the small facility is expected to earn $75,000; it can be increased to average size to earn a net present value of $60,000. If demand is high, the small facility is expected to earn $75,000 and can be expanded to average size to earn $60,000 or to large size to earn $125,000.

    A medium-sized facility is expected to lose an estimated $25,000 if demand is low and earn $140,000 if demand is average. If demand is high, the medium-sized facility is expected to earn a net present value of $150,000; it can be expanded to a large size for a net payoff of $145,000.

    If a large facility is built and demand is high, earnings are expected to be $220,000. If demand is average for the large facility, the present value is expected to be $125,000; if demand is low, the facility is expected to lose $60,000.
    a. Draw a decision tree for this problem.
    b. What should management do to achieve the highest expected payoff?

21. A manufacturing plant has reached full capacity. The company must build a second plant—either small or large—at a nearby location. The probabilities are 0.40 for low demand and 0.60 for high demand.

    If demand is low, the large plant has a present value of $5 million and the small plant, $8 million. If demand is high, the large plant pays off with a present value of $17 million and the small plant with a present value of only $10 million. However, the small plant can be expanded later if demand proves to be high, for a present value of $15 million.
    a. Draw a decision tree for this problem.
    b. What should management do to achieve the highest expected payoff?

22. A firm is adding a new product line and must build a new plant. Demand will be either favorable or unfavorable, with probabilities of 0.60 and 0.40, respectively. If a large plant is built and demand is favorable, the after-tax net present value of benefits is estimated at $1,520,000. If demand is unfavorable, the loss with the large plant will be $20,000.

    If a small plant is built and demand is unfavorable, the net present value is $760,000, after deducting the costs to build and equip the plant. If demand proves to be favorable, the firm can maintain the small facility or expand it. Maintaining the small facility has a present value of $950,000; expanding, it has a present value of $570,000.
    a. Draw a decision tree for this problem.
    b. What should management do to achieve the highest expected payoff?

Selected References

Bierman, Harold, Jr., Charles P. Bonini, and Warren H. Hausman. *Quantitative Analysis for Business Decisions.* Homewood, Ill.: Irwin, 1986.

Clemen, Robert T. *Making Hard Decisions: An Introduction to Decision Analysis.* Boston: PWS-Kent, 1991.

Taylor, Bernard W. III. *Introduction to Management Science.* Needham Heights, Mass.: Allyn & Bacon, 1990.

Chapter Three

PROCESS MANAGEMENT

Senior executives at Banca di America e di Italia (BAI) reengineered their processes to become a "paperless bank" and become competitive once again with other European banks. They created two cross-functional teams to diagnose and redesign the bank's processes without considering the constraints of the current organization. The executives assigned their best people to the design teams and made significant investments in information technology and skill training. The teams divided the transactions that customers make into 10 categories, such as deposits, credit cards, money orders, and the like. They carefully documented the flow of activities needed to complete each process. Once a detailed picture emerged, they redesigned each process from scratch. For example, the check–deposit transaction previously had 64 operations and required 9 forms. It now involves only 25 operations and 2 forms. The redesigned processes were then given to the technology team, which focused on storing data and creating the necessary software. As a result of the redesigned processes, BAI was able to add 50 new banks without any new personnel. The number of employees per branch dropped from 8 to 4. The 2 hours formerly needed to close the cashier positions have been reduced to 10 minutes. Revenues have

Reengineering can improve a bank's back-room operations as well as its front-office operations. A bank can reduce both time and errors by replacing a manual check-cashing process with an automated one.

doubled, and BAI executives attribute 24 percent of the increase to the reengineered processes.

One essential issue in the design of a production system is deciding what process to use in making the products or providing the services. Deciding on a process involves many different choices in selecting human resources, equipment, and materials. Processes are involved in how marketing prepares a market analysis, how accounting bills customers, how a retail store provides services on the sales floor, and how a manufacturing plant performs its assembly operations. Process decisions are strategic and can affect an organization's ability to compete over the long run.

Process decisions affect what the firm achieves with the competitive priorities of quality, flexibility, time, and cost. For example, firms can improve their ability to compete on the basis of time by examining each step of their processes and finding ways to respond more quickly to the customer. Productivity (and therefore cost) is affected by choices made when the process is designed. However, process management is an ongoing activity, with the same principles applying to both first-time and redesign choices.

We begin by defining five basic decisions about process: process choice, vertical integration, resource flexibility, customer involvement, and capital intensity. Increasing a process's capital intensity often results in the introduction of new technologies, so we turn next to managing technological change. We conclude with some basic approaches to analyzing and modifying processes: reengineering and the use of flow diagrams and process charts to improve processes. As you will learn in Chapters 4 and 5, evaluating process decisions is a first step in improving quality. Process design also affects job design, as you will see in Chapter 6.

◆ WHAT IS PROCESS MANAGEMENT?

Process management is the selection of inputs, operations, work flows, and methods for producing goods and services. Input selection includes choosing the mix of human skills, raw materials, outside services, and equipment consistent with an organization's positioning strategy and its ability to obtain these resources. Operations managers must determine which operations will be performed by workers and which by machines.

Process decisions must be made when

- a new or substantially modified product or service is being offered,
- quality must be improved,
- competitive priorities have changed,
- demand for a product or service is changing,
- current performance is inadequate,
- competitors are gaining by using a new process or technology, or
- the cost or availability of inputs has changed.

Not all these situations lead to changes in the current process. Process decisions must recognize costs, and sometimes the costs of change clearly outweigh the benefits. Process decisions must take into account other choices concerning quality, capacity, layout, and inventory. Process decisions also depend on where products and services are in their life cycles, on competitive priorities, and on positioning strategy. Ethics and the environment are other considerations, as Managerial Practice 3.1 on the next page shows.

◆ MAJOR PROCESS DECISIONS

Whether dealing with processes for offices, service organizations, or manufacturing firms, operations managers must consider five common process decisions. **Process choice** determines whether resources are organized around the product or process in order to implement the positioning strategy. The process choice decision depends on the volumes and degree of customization. **Vertical integration** is the degree to which a firm's own production system handles the entire chain of processes from raw materials to sales and service. The more a firm's production system handles the raw materials, other inputs, and outputs, the greater is the degree of vertical integration. **Resource flexibility** is the ease with which employees and equipment can handle a wide variety of products, output levels, duties,

Managerial Practice 3.1

▶ *Process Management: Ethics and the Environment*

Ethics

Wall Street has been in love with Nucor Corporation, which has transformed itself from a backwater fabricator into the seventh largest U.S. steel company. Its minimills, which spin gleaming sheet steel out of scrapped cars and refrigerators, are efficient and profitable. Most of its 15 minimills are situated in small towns, where they employ and train people who never thought that they would make so much money. "Every manager wondering what it takes to compete in the twenty-first century needs to know the Nucor story," said Ann McLaughlin, the former U.S. secretary of labor. But there is another side of the Nucor story. Since 1980, its worker death rate has been the highest in the steel industry. Eleven employees have died as a result of accidents. Six more have died in accidents during construction of new plants. A review of court and safety documents and interviews with employees suggest that Nucor's work processes may have a human cost.

And the Environment

The chemical industry's record on the environment has been bad, and its production processes still account for almost half of all toxic pollution produced in the United States. Things are changing, however. Chemical companies are beginning to view waste produced by their processes as a measure of efficiency. The more unusable by-products a process creates, the less efficient it is. Some companies plan to sharply cut air emissions and waste by using recycling and less toxic materials with an ultimate goal of "closed loop" manufacturing that emits no discharges. For example, Hammermill Papers has pumped $95 million into its Lock Haven, Pennsylvania, plant to make 100 percent recycled copier paper in a color that it calls "earth white." And Dow Chemical Company's new ethylene plant in Fort Saskatchewan, Alberta, will release just 10 gallons of cleaned-up wastewater per minute into the North Saskatchewan River, down from the current plant's 360 gallons per minute. The process also will use 40 percent less energy. It will cost 8 percent more than usual, but Dow expects to recoup that in lower maintenance costs.

Sources: "Nucor Steel's Sheen Is Marred by Deaths of Workers at Plants," *Wall Street Journal*, May 10, 1991; "The Next Trick for Business: Taking a Cue from Nature," *Business Week*, May 11, 1992; "How Much Green in 'Green' Paper?", *Business Week*, November 1, 1993.

and functions. **Customer involvement** reflects the ways in which the customer becomes a part of the production process and the extent of this involvement. **Capital intensity** is the mix of equipment and human skills in a production process; the greater the relative cost of equipment, the greater is the capital intensity.

Process Choice

How can a positioning strategy best be implemented?

Process choice is the starting point for designing well-functioning processes. Figure 3.1 shows four basic choices for implementing positioning strategy: project, batch, line, and continuous. The best choice depends on the volume and degree of customization of the product and services produced.

Project Process.   A project process lies at the high-customization, low-volume end of the continuum. The sequence of operations—and the process at each one—is unique to each project, creating one-of-a-kind or low-volume products or services made to customer order. Typically project processes are of long duration and large scale. Products cannot be produced ahead of time because the spe-

FIGURE 3.1

Process Choice, Volume, and Customization

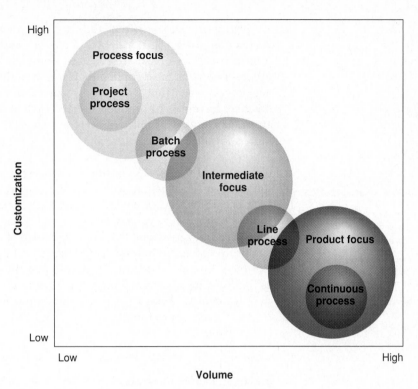

cific needs of the next customer are unknown. Each new order is handled as a single unit, often by project teams. Firms choosing a project process (or *unit process*) sell themselves on the basis of their capabilities, rather than on specific products or services. Examples are firms that specialize in event planning, running a political campaign, putting together training programs, constructing a new hospital, introducing a new product, creating a new software package, providing health care, handling special-delivery mail, making customized cabinets, or shipbuilding.

Batch Process. A batch process has average volumes, but too much variety in products or services for the firm to be able to dedicate resources to each one. Instead the products and services share resources, with the firm producing a batch of one product and then switching production to the next one. Eventually the first product or service is produced again. There is no standard sequence of operations through the facility. Some of the components going into the final product or service may be produced in advance, even though the final outputs are made to order. Project and batch processes are more process focused, with resources organized around the process. Examples of batch processes are scheduling air travel for a group, making components that feed an assembly line, and manufacturing capital equipment.

Line Process. A line process is more product focused, with resources organized around the product or service. Volumes are high, and products and services are standardized. Materials and customers move linearly from one operation to the next according to a fixed sequence. Production is in small lots, often with a lot size of 1. Each operation performs the same process over and over again, with little variability. Some product variety is possible but is carefully controlled by adding standard options to the main product or service. Manufactured products are held in inventory so that they are ready when a customer places an order. Production orders are not directly linked to customer orders, as is the case with project processes or batch processes. Sometimes called *mass production,* a line process is what is most commonly featured in the popular press as a manufacturing process, even though it is only one of several process choices prevalent in practice. Examples of products created by line processes are automobiles, appliances, and toys. Examples of services using line processes are fast-food restaurants and cafeterias.

Continuous Process.   A continuous process is the extreme end of high-volume, standardized production with rigid line flows. Usually one primary material, such as a liquid, gas, or powder, moves without stopping through the facility. The process often is very capital intensive and often is operated around the clock to maximize utilization and to avoid expensive shutdowns and startups. Continuous processes are found almost exclusively in manufacturing. Examples are petroleum refineries, chemical plants, and plants making beer, steel, and food (such as Borden's huge pasta-making plant). Firms with such facilities are also referred to as the *process industry.* An electric generation plant represents one of the few continuous processes found in the service sector.

THE BIG PICTURE: Process Choice at King Soopers Bakery

In the Big Picture illustration on pages 100–101, we literally lifted the roof of the multiproduct bakery King Soopers, a division of Kroger Company, in Denver, Colorado, to show you process choice at work. King Soopers makes three types of baked goods—custom decorated cakes, pastries, and bread—with widely varying volumes and customization. It uses three different production processes to meet the demands.

The custom cake process is a low-volume process, as shown by the bar graph of relative volumes to the right. It starts with basic cakes of the appropriate sizes, which are made from a batch process (not shown). From that point on, the product is highly customized and cakes are produced to order. A process-focused strategy is used, and the process choice is best described as a *project process.* Customers can choose some standard selections from a catalog, but often request one-of-a-kind designs. Frosting colors and cake designs are limited only by the worker's imagination.

The pastry process has higher volumes, but not enough for each product to have dedicated resources. It uses an intermediate positioning strategy, with the process choice best described as a *batch process.* Dough is mixed in relatively small batches and sent to the proofing room (not shown), where general-purpose equipment feeds the batch of dough through rollers. Special fixtures, each unique to the product being made, cut the dough into the desired shapes. A great deal of product variety is handled, with each batch making about 1000 units before a change is made to the next pastry.

The bread line is a high-volume process, making 7000 loaves per hour. The bread is a standardized product made to stock, and production is not keyed to specific customer orders. King Soopers uses a product-focused strategy for bread, and the process choice is a *line process.* Once the line starts, it must run until empty so that no dough is left in the mixers overnight and no bread is left in the hot oven. The line usually does not operate around the clock, and in this sense is not a continuous process.

Managerial Practice 3.2

▶ *Choosing the Right Amount of Vertical Integration*

More Integration

Dozens of U.S. corporations, frustrated with rising corporate health care costs, are *increasing* their vertical integration. They are spurning the health insurance industry and dealing with health care providers. In doing so, they are betting that they can do it better and cheaper by applying the same management attention to health care that they do to their core businesses. For example, Baxter International, a big medical supply company in Deerfield, Illinois, contracted with 200 doctors to provide health care for Baxter's employees. Corporations such as Baxter negotiated discounts and set quality guidelines with health care providers. Their staff regularly visited the providers to review data on trends in costs and procedures, to be sure that the savings resulting from discounts aren't eroded by increased use of services. They subsidized employee health care costs directly rather than rely on an insurance company to provide this service. Such vertical integration requires purchasing power and a knowledgeable staff.

Less Integration

Other companies, such as Japanese companies operating assembly plants in the United States, use *less* vertical integration. In contrast with GM, Ford, and Chrysler, they buy more of the parts going into their automobiles from independent subcontractors. One big reason is that the suppliers pay lower wage rates. Although the Japanese firms and the Big Three pay virtually identical wages for assembly workers in their own plants, independent subcontractors pay their workers considerably less. The Japanese firms can take advantage of this differential by buying parts from outside firms at a lower cost than if they manufactured the parts themselves. The Big Three U.S. automakers are prevented from outsourcing by UAW union resistance and so must do more part fabrication in-house.

Sources: "Firms Perform Own Bypass Operations, Purchasing Health Care from the Source," *Wall Street Journal,* August 19, 1991; "UAW and Big Three Face Mutual Mistrust as Auto Talks Heat Up," *Wall Street Journal,* August 29, 1990.

Vertical Integration

Which services and products should be created in-house?

All businesses buy at least some inputs to their processes, such as professional services, raw materials, or manufactured parts, from other producers. King Soopers is no exception and buys such materials as flour, sugar, butter, and water. Management decides the level of vertical integration by looking at all the activities performed between acquisition of raw materials or outside services and delivery of finished products or services. The more processes in the chain the organization performs itself, the more vertically integrated it is. As Managerial Practice 3.2 illustrates, firms may have different strategies for procuring necessary resources.

Extensive vertical integration is generally attractive when input volumes are high because high volumes allow task specialization and greater efficiency. It is also attractive if the firm has the relevant skills and views the industry into which it is integrating as particularly important to its future success. It is unattractive when a supplier can provide the good or service with greater efficiency and at a lower cost. For example, most small restaurants and food-service operators buy precooked eggs for salad bars and sandwiches from suppliers, rather than process their own. Matching the efficiency of a supplier such as Atlantic Foods, where a team of six employees can peel 10,000 eggs in one shift, is difficult.

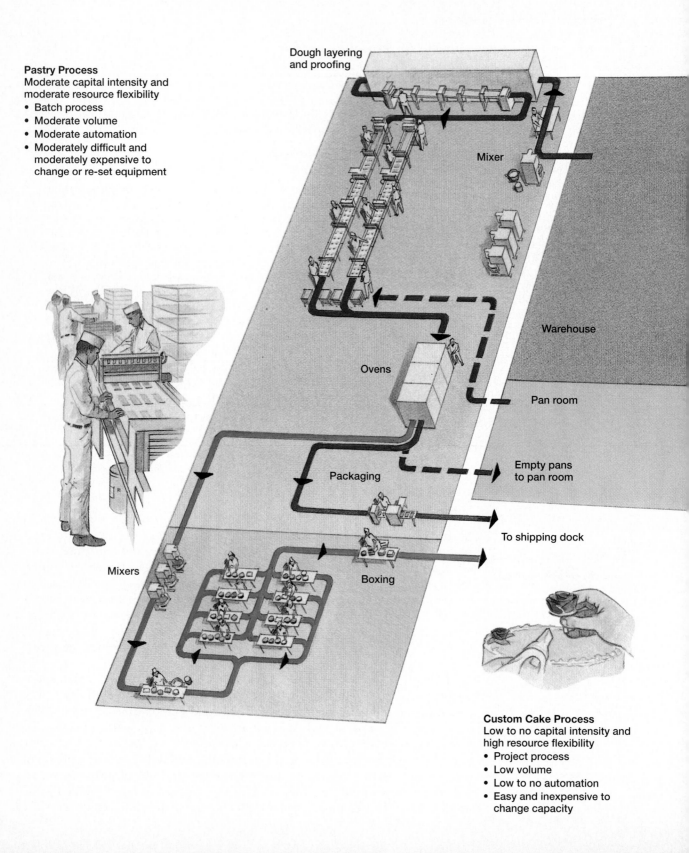

Pastry Process
Moderate capital intensity and
moderate resource flexibility
- Batch process
- Moderate volume
- Moderate automation
- Moderately difficult and
  moderately expensive to
  change or re-set equipment

Dough layering
and proofing

Mixer

Warehouse

Ovens

Pan room

Packaging

Empty pans
to pan room

To shipping dock

Mixers

Boxing

Custom Cake Process
Low to no capital intensity and
high resource flexibility
- Project process
- Low volume
- Low to no automation
- Easy and inexpensive to
  change capacity

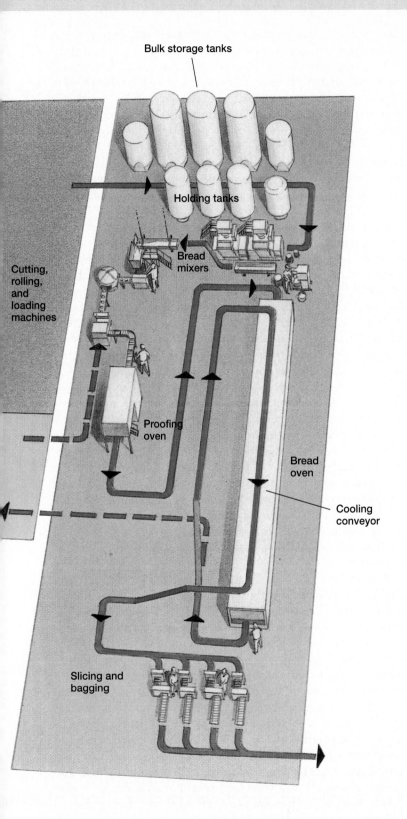

Bulk storage tanks

Holding tanks

Bread mixers

Cutting, rolling, and loading machines

Proofing oven

Bread oven

Cooling conveyor

Slicing and bagging

Bread Process
High capital intensity and low resource flexibility
- Line process
- High volume
- Difficult and expensive to change capacity

7000 loaves/hr

1000 pastries/hr

50 cakes/hr

Bread line

Pastry line

Cake line

Vertical integration can be in two directions. **Backward integration** represents movement toward the sources of raw materials and parts. (Managerial Practice 3.2 describes firms that choose more or less backward integration.) **Forward integration** means that the firm acquires more channels of distribution, such as its own distribution centers (warehouses) and retail stores. Village Meats, a fresh-meat supplier and the dominant source of hamburger for Wendy's International, is an example of a company that chose to decrease its forward integration. When Wendy's decided to have just one company deliver all its fresh, frozen, and dry products, Village Meats, which had been delivering its meat to Wendy's, chose to end its door-to-door deliveries. Becoming the sole distributor to Wendy's restaurants would have required the company to secure more warehouse space, handle frozen products, and purchase new trucks. The necessary investment was too much. Village Meats still supplies meat to Wendy's, but leaves the distribution to another firm.

Another example of decreasing forward integration is IBM's decision to allow versions of its minicomputer and mainframes to be marketed in Japan under the label of Mitsubishi Electric Corporation. IBM is becoming an *original-equipment manufacturer* (OEM) for this part of its market and leaving the sales and distribution to Japanese firms. This move allows IBM to enter otherwise closed markets, such as Japanese government agencies, because Japanese culture stresses dealing with Japanese rather than foreigners. This cultural value gives Mitsubishi Electric a distinctive competence over IBM for selling computers in Japan.

Increasing vertical integration can reduce resource flexibility if it requires a large investment in facilities and equipment. The Kroger grocery chain, for example, had heavily invested in equipment and facilities to produce house brands. When customer preferences shifted away from house brands and generic (no-brand) products and turned toward national brands, Kroger found itself with excess manufacturing capacity, which it had to find a way to utilize. It did so by making ice cream and frozen pizza dough for its competitors, which in turn sold the products under their own labels. About 20 percent of the sales from its plants are now to companies outside Kroger. Kroger also has sold some of its plants. Extensive vertical integration limited Kroger's resource flexibility and range of acceptable business opportunities.

A converse strategy to that of Kroger is followed by **hollow corporations**, small firms that contract with other firms for most of their production—and for many of their other functions. Hollow corporations have little backward integration; they sometimes are called *network companies* because employees spend most of their time on the telephone or at the computer, coordinating suppliers. If demand for the hollow corporation's products or services changes, its employees simply pass this message along to the suppliers, who change their output levels. Hollow corporations can move in and out of markets, riding the waves of fashion and technology. They are vulnerable to new competition, however, because the investment barriers to enter their businesses are low and because they lose business if their suppliers integrate forward or their customers integrate backward. A hollow corporation's risk of losing its business to suppliers or customers increases as product volumes increase and product life cycles lengthen. For example, Conner Peripherals has been very successful since entering the hard disk drive industry in 1986. Because product life cycles are so short, often measured in months, it designs products and lets outside suppliers manufacture them. This strategy avoids the need for Conner to invest in factories that may become obsolete as technology changes. If life cycles were longer, one of its big customers, such as Compaq Computer Corporation, might decide to make the computer drives itself and bypass Conner entirely.

Make or Buy. The decision about whether to implement backward integration is often referred to as the *make-or-buy decision*. In making that decision the operations manager must study all the benefits and costs of making the needed inputs and buying them from suppliers. Break-even analysis (see Supplement A) and financial analysis (see Appendix 1) are good starting points in making this decision. However, equally important are qualitative factors.

The "buy" decision of farming out an operation to a supplier, **outsourcing,** has both advantages and disadvantages. On the negative side, a firm may farm out a process that is crucial to its mission and lose control over that area of its business. It may even lose its ability to bring the work in-house at a later date. Customers may also be less satisfied with the final output. For example, if customers at a restaurant want to make a salad to their own tastes, they will be dissatisfied with preassembled salads provided by an outside supplier. Another disadvantage is that some "make" decisions require sizable capital investments. However, doing the work in-house may mean better quality and more timely delivery—and taking better advantage of the firm's human resources, equipment, and space.

Firms are doing more outsourcing than ever before. For example, the NCNB bank in Charlotte, North Carolina, outsourced the processing of card transactions and saved $5 million per year. Merrill Lynch, Sears Roebuck, and Texaco outsource their mailroom and photocopying operations to Pitney Bowes Management Services. Many firms do the same with payroll, security, cleaning, and other types of services, rather than employ personnel to provide these services. One recent survey showed that 35 percent of more than 1000 large corporations have increased the amount of outsourcing they do.

Two factors are contributing to this trend: global competition and information technology. Globalization creates more supplier options, and advances in information technology make coordination with suppliers easier. IKEA, the largest retailer of home furnishings, has 30 buying offices around the world to seek out suppliers. Its Vienna-based Business Service Department runs a computer database that helps suppliers find raw materials and new business partners. Cash registers at its stores around the world relay sales data to the nearest warehouse and its operational headquarters in Älmhult, Sweden, where information systems oversee shipping patterns worldwide.

Information technology allows suppliers to come together as a virtual corporation. In a **virtual corporation,** competitors actually enter into short-term partnerships to respond to market opportunities. Teams in different organizations and at different locations collaborate on production, design, and marketing, with information going electronically from place to place. They disband when the project is completed. Virtual corporations allow firms to change their positions flexibly in response to quickly changing market demands.

Own or Lease. When a firm decides to increase vertical integration, it must also decide whether to own or to lease the necessary facilities and equipment. The lease option is often favored for items affected by fairly rapid changes in technology, items that require frequent servicing, or items for which industry practices have made leasing the norm, as in the photocopier industry. Leasing is also common when a firm has a short-term need for equipment. For example, in the construction industry, where projects usually take months or years to complete, heavy equipment is often leased only as needed.

Resource Flexibility

Is general-purpose or special-purpose equipment needed, and how flexible should the work force be?

The choices that management makes concerning competitive priorities determine the degree of flexibility required of a company's resources—its employees, facilities, and equipment. For example, when new products and services call for short life cycles or high customization, employees need to perform a broad range of duties and equipment must be general purpose. Otherwise resource utilization will be too low for economical operation.

Work Force.   Operations managers must decide whether to have a **flexible work force.** Members of a flexible work force are capable of doing many tasks, either at their own workstations or as they move from one workstation to another. However, such flexibility often comes at a cost, requiring greater skills and thus more training and education. Nevertheless, benefits can be large: Worker flexibility can be one of the best ways to achieve reliable customer service and alleviate capacity bottlenecks. Resource flexibility is particularly crucial to process-focused positioning strategy, helping to absorb the feast-or-famine workloads in individual operations that are caused by low-volume production, jumbled routings, and fluid scheduling.

Some manufacturers, such as Corning, practice resource flexibility. At its recently opened plant in Blacksburg, Virginia, Corning trains its employees to have interchangeable skills. Workers must learn three skill modules—or families of skills—within two years to keep their jobs. A multiskilled work force is one reason the Blacksburg Corning plant turned a $2 million profit in its first eight months of production, instead of losing $2.3 million as projected for the start-up period. Training has been extensive, however: In the first year of production, 25 percent of all hours worked were devoted to training, at a cost of about $750,000.

Resource flexibility is also an issue in the service sector. Administrators of large urban hospitals must make decisions about staffing and degrees of specialization. Many hospitals choose to use all registered nurses (RNs), instead of a

At the Nissan truck and car manufacturing facility in Smyrna, Tennessee, teams receive training in the operations of each manufacturing station. Such training helps Nissan achieve a flexible work force.

mix of RNs, licensed vocational nurses (LVNs), and aides. Registered nurses have a higher educational level and earn more than LVNs and aides, but they are more flexible and can perform all nursing tasks.

The type of work force required also depends on the need for volume flexibility. When conditions allow for a smooth, steady rate of output, the likely choice is a permanent work force that expects regular full-time employment. If the process is subject to hourly, daily, or seasonal peaks and valleys in demand, the use of part-time or temporary employees to supplement a smaller core of full-time employees may be the best solution. However, this approach may not be practical if knowledge and skill requirements are too high for a temporary worker to grasp quickly.

Equipment. When a firm's product or service has a short life cycle and a high degree of customization, low production volumes mean that a firm should select flexible, general-purpose equipment. Figure 3.2 illustrates this relationship for two processes. Process 1 calls for inexpensive general-purpose equipment. It gets the job done but not at peak efficiency. Although fixed costs (F_1) are low, the variable unit cost (the slope of the total cost line) is high. Process 2 has high fixed costs (F_2), but it is a more efficient process and therefore has a lower variable unit cost. Such efficiency often is possible only because the equipment is designed for a narrow range of products or tasks.

FIGURE 3.2

Relationship Between Process Costs and Product Volume

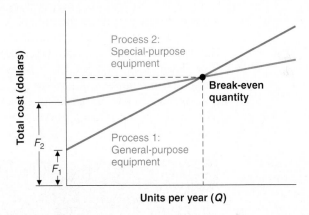

The break-even quantity in Fig. 3.2 is the quantity at which the total costs for the two alternatives are equal. At quantities beyond this point, the cost of process 1 exceeds that of process 2. Unless the firm expects to sell more than the break-even amount (which is unlikely with high customization), the capital investment of process 2 isn't warranted. An example of a firm that made the mistake of investing too heavily in specialized equipment is General Electric, which built a $52 million highly automated plant to make T700s jet engines—or similar-sized engines—and nothing else. Unfortunately, the Pentagon failed to order engines in the numbers anticipated, so the plant ran at only 60 percent of capacity—too low for efficient operation.

Customer Involvement

The fourth major process decision is the extent to which customers interact with the process. The amount of customer involvement may range from self-service to customization of product to deciding the time and place of service.

How much should customers be involved in processes?

Self-Service.   In many service industries, customer contact is crucial. At Wendy's restaurants, for instance, customers assemble their own salads. Self-service is the process decision of many retailers, particularly when price is a competitive priority. To save money, some customers prefer to do part of the process formerly performed by the manufacturer or dealer. Product-focused manufacturers of goods such as toys, bicycles, and furniture may also prefer to let the customer perform the final assembly because production, shipping, and inventory costs frequently are lower, as are losses from damage. The firms pass the savings on to customers as lower prices.

Product Selection.   A business that competes on customization frequently allows customers to come up with their own product specifications or even become involved in designing the product. A good example of customer involvement is in custom-designed and -built homes: The customer is heavily involved in the design process and inspects the work in process at various times. Customer involvement is not likely to end even when the owner occupies the house, because most builders guarantee their work for some extended time period.

Time and Location.   When services cannot be provided without the customer's presence, customers may determine the time and location of the service. If the service is delivered to the customer, client, or patient by appointment, decisions involving the location of such meetings become part of process design. Will customers be served only on the supplier's premises, will the supplier's employees go to the customers' premises, or will the service be provided at a third location? Operators of emergency ambulance services cannot provide service without a patient. They can't predict exactly when the next call for service will come in or where the ambulance will have to go, so they must design their response processes accordingly. Conversely, although certified public accountants frequently work on their clients' premises, both the time and the place are likely to be known well in advance.

At Wendy's Garden Spot salad bar, Wendy's customers customize the salad to their individual tastes. Self-service is one dimension of customer involvement.

Capital Intensity

How much should one depend on machinery and automated processes?

For either the design of a new process or the redesign of an existing one, an operations manager must determine the amount of capital intensity required. Capital intensity is the mix of equipment and human skills in the process; the greater the relative cost of equipment, the greater is the capital intensity. As the capabilities of technology increase and its costs decrease, managers face an ever-widening range of choices, from operations utilizing very little automation to those requiring task-specific equipment and very little human intervention. **Automation** is a system, process, or piece of equipment that is self-acting and self-regulating. Although automation is often thought to be necessary to gain competitive advantage, it has both advantages and disadvantages. Thus the automation decision requires careful examination.

One advantage of computer technology is that it can significantly increase productivity and improve quality. For example, Bailey Company, an independent Arby's roast beef restaurant franchisee based in Lakewood, Colorado, has installed a computerized order-taking system. Customers punch in their own orders, increasing employee efficiency at a time when fast-food restaurants face a labor shortage. The system allows one clerk to handle two terminals for two lines of customers and has improved both service time (by about 20 seconds per order) and order accuracy. The system also encourages sales by suggesting items such as soft drinks.

One big disadvantage of capital intensity can be the prohibitive investment cost for low-volume operations. Look at Fig. 3.2 again. Process 1, which uses general-purpose equipment, isn't capital intensive and therefore has small fixed costs, F_1. Although its variable cost per unit produced is high, as indicated by the slope of the total cost line, process 1 is well below the break-even quantity if volumes are low. Generally capital-intensive operations must have high utilization to be justifiable. Also, automation doesn't always align with a company's competitive priorities. If a firm offers a unique product or high-quality service, competitive priorities may indicate the need for skilled servers, hand labor, and individual attention rather than new technology. Arby's ordering system wouldn't be appropriate for an exclusive restaurant.

Some types of equipment may be acquired a piece at a time or leased, allowing the user to try the equipment out without making a large and risky initial capital investment. Examples of such equipment are photocopy machines, personal computers, and laser printers. However, many other technological choices involve large and costly systems—and a great deal more capital and risk.

Fixed Automation. Manufacturing uses two types of automation: fixed and flexible (or programmable). Particularly appropriate for line and continuous process choices, **fixed automation** produces one type of part or product in a fixed sequence of simple operations. Until the mid 1980s most U.S. automobile plants were dominated by fixed automation—and some still are. Chemical processing plants and oil refineries also utilize this type of automation.

Operations managers favor fixed automation when demand volumes are high, product designs are stable, and product life cycles are long. These conditions compensate for the process's two primary drawbacks: large initial investment cost and relative inflexibility. The investment cost is particularly high when a single, complex machine (called a *transfer machine*) must be capable of handling many operations. Because fixed automation is designed around a particular product, changing equipment to accommodate new products is difficult and costly. However, fixed automation maximizes efficiency and yields the lowest variable cost per unit.

Flexible Automation.   **Flexible** (or programmable) **automation** can be changed easily to handle various products. The ability to reprogram machines is useful in both process-focused and product-focused operations. A machine that makes a variety of products in small batches, in the case of a process focus, can be programmed to alternate between the products. When a machine has been dedicated to a particular product, as in the case of a product focus, and the product is at the end of its life cycle, the machine can simply be reprogrammed with a new sequence of operations for a new product. Cummins Engine Company, a manufacturer of diesel engines based in Columbus, Indiana, utilizes product-focused flexibility to handle frequent design modifications. For example, in the first 18 months after the introduction of new compression brakes for its engines, engineers made 14 design changes to the brakes. If the brakes had been made on less flexible machines, these improvements probably would have taken several years and millions of dollars to implement—and in fact might not have been made. Programmable automation gave Cummins a competitive advantage: It cut time to the market by two years, reduced annual warranty expenses by an estimated $300,000, and reduced costs to the customer by more than 30 percent.

Relationships Between Decisions

How should process decisions be coordinated?

Each of the five process decisions has an underlying relationship with volume. High volume occurs when demand for a product or service is heavy, when each unit made or served requires significant work content, and when parts or tasks are standard and therefore used often. Figure 3.3 shows how process choice and the other major process decisions are tied to volume. The solid vertical lines reflect the link between volume and the process choice, and the dashed horizontal lines represent the subsequent link between process choice and the other process decisions. High volumes typically mean

1. *a line or continuous process.*   For example, King Soopers uses a line process for its high-volume bread line.
2. *more vertical integration.*   High volumes create more opportunities for vertical integration.
3. *less resource flexibility.*   When volumes are high, there is no need for flexibility to utilize resources effectively, and specialization can lead to more efficient processes. King Soopers's bread line can make just one product—bread.
4. *less customer involvement.*   At high volumes, firms cannot meet the unpredictable demands required by full-service, customized orders. Exceptions include telephone exchanges, vending machines, and automatic bank tellers, mainly because these processes require minimal personalized attention.
5. *more capital intensity.*   High volumes justify the large fixed costs of an efficient operation. The King Soopers bread line is capital intensive. It is automated from dough mixing to placing the product on shipping racks. Expanding this process would be very expensive.

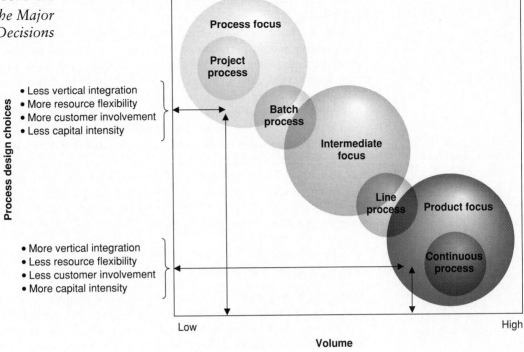

FIGURE 3.3
Volume and the Major Process Decisions

Process design choices

• Less vertical integration
• More resource flexibility
• More customer involvement
• Less capital intensity

• More vertical integration
• Less resource flexibility
• Less customer involvement
• More capital intensity

Process focus

Project process

Batch process

Intermediate focus

Line process

Product focus

Continuous process

Low   High

Volume

Low volumes typically mean

1. *a project or batch process.* For example, King Soopers uses a batch process for its pastry production.
2. *less vertical integration.* Low volumes eliminate most opportunities for vertical integration. King Soopers outsources frosting coloring and prune filling, because the volumes of customized cakes and pastries in which they are used are low.
3. *more resource flexibility.* When volumes are low, as in the custom cake process, workers are trained to handle all types of customer requests.
4. *more customer involvement.* King Soopers has more customer involvement with its custom cake process, because customers often order one-of-a-kind decorations not found in the catalog.
5. *less capital intensity.* The custom cake line is very labor intensive and requires little investment to equip the workers.

Of course, these are general tendencies rather than rigid prescriptions. Exceptions can be found, but these relationships provide a way of understanding how process decisions can be linked coherently.

Economies of Scope

Should more economies of scope be sought?

Note that capital intensity and resource flexibility vary inversely in Fig. 3.3. If capital intensity is high, resource flexibility is low. King Soopers produces a high-volume product (loaves of bread) efficiently on an automated (high-capital-intensity) bread line, with few people monitoring its operation, but the process has low resource flexibility. In contrast, the custom cake line produces a low volume of product because it requires high customization. To complete the unique customer orders, resources must be flexible, and because the process requires hand work, capital intensity is low.

In certain types of manufacturing operations, such as machining and assembly, programmable automation breaks this traditional inverse relationship between resource flexibility and capital intensity. It makes possible both high capital intensity and high resource flexibility, creating economies of scope. **Economies of scope** reflect the ability to produce multiple products more cheaply in combination than separately. In such situations, two conflicting competitive priorities—customization and low price—become more compatible. However, taking advantage of economies of scope requires that a family of parts or products have enough collective volume to utilize equipment fully, perhaps even making necessary the operation of machinery in multiple shifts. Adding a product to the family results in one-time programming (and sometimes fixture) costs. *Fixtures* are reusable devices that maintain exact tolerances by holding the product firmly in position while it is processed.

MANAGING TECHNOLOGICAL CHANGE

Changing a process's capital intensity means changing its technology. For our purposes, we define **technology** as any manual, automated, or mental process used to transform inputs into products or services. Each operation has a technology, even if it is manual. Invariably, managers have several technologies from which to choose. For example, the simple process of sawing lumber can be performed in at least four ways: a worker using a simple hand saw; a worker operating and controlling a portable power saw; a worker using a rigidly mounted power saw, which the worker must set up, load, and unload, but which automatically guides the lumber into the blade; or a high-speed, continuously running power saw, which automatically feeds and unloads lumber with infrequent worker intervention.

Because technology is changing so rapidly and because of the many technologies available, it is more important than ever for operations managers to make intelligent, informed decisions about automation. The stakes are high because such choices affect the human as well as the technical aspects of operations. Job satisfaction and positive employee attitudes can be maintained only if technological change is managed well.

We can't possibly cover all the technologies used in the manufacturing and service sectors in this chapter and, in particular, the numerous opportunities coming from advances in computer technology. However, Managerial Practice 3.3 illustrates such developments at the New York Stock Exchange, and Supplement B describes a new family of technologies called *computer-integrated manufacturing*. These two features will give you a sense of the widening array of possibilities. When you join an organization, you will need to learn more about the specific technologies it uses and new technologies that emerge.

This section presents some principles on the management of technological change that are valid for service and manufacturing organizations alike. We cover how technological choices link with operations strategy and how technology can create a competitive advantage. We conclude with some useful guidelines on managing innovation.

Managerial Practice 3.3

▶ *Technology at the New York Stock Exchange*

*A*utomated trading at the New York Stock Exchange (NYSE) involves the use of various computer and telecommunications technologies to receive buy or sell orders, make stock exchanges, report transactions and quotes, inform the entering party of the results, and report to the clearinghouse. Technological change is particularly difficult to implement at NYSE because multiple independent parties must be satisfied, transactions must be made more or less instantaneously, and prices must be set fairly and quickly. Volume variation is large: Capacity requirements may exceed 600 million shares on one day but be only 140 million the next. Essentially, the NYSE is electronically automated, with orders arriving at electronic speeds on stock specialists' computer terminals. Multiple additional participants can be called in to help handle transactions during particularly hectic periods through adjunct terminals.

One important part of the automation is the designated order turnaround (DOT) system, which helps report a transaction. A specialist on the trading floor reports the trade by summoning the information from the computer bank on a card that is fed into an optical reader for computer entry. The DOT "bunching" feature allows individual orders to be aggregated during volume surges according to parameters set by floor officials on-line, reducing the number of transactions to be handled.

Automation of the stock market is an ongoing process. For example, cathode ray tubes in terminal screens are being replaced with flat screen technology, taking less space and displaying more information. Such automation allowed NYSE to keep up with the deluge of orders during the stock market crash in mid October 1987. The volume that day was greater than anything that had occurred in the "back-office crises" of the 1960s.

Technology allows traders on the New York Stock Exchange floor to receive up-to-the-minute information on the movements of thousands of stock prices.

Linking Technology with Strategy

The right technological choices must link with operations strategy. As Fig. 3.3 demonstrates, volume is an important variable to consider in determining the amount of automation and capital intensity. Volume in turn is derived from corporate strategy and competitive priorities. If a firm succeeds in its priority to become the low-cost producer, it is likely to enjoy higher volumes and opt for more capital intensity. If sales do not materialize as expected after a considerable investment in automation, the firm's production system becomes a millstone, particularly if the equipment is not adaptable to other products or services.

Finding a Competitive Advantage

Managers in the global economy must be alert to all opportunities for improvement, and the rapid changes in technology make it a particularly important area to evaluate. The potential benefits from a new technology are far-ranging. The most obvious one is reducing the *direct costs* of labor and raw materials. For example, Fiat reduced its work force from 138,000 to 72,000 in nine years with its investment in robots. *Sales* can increase, as MCI Communications found when it spent $300 million to update its computer systems. It now can offer innovative residential calling services. *Quality* can improve, as illustrated by the new magnetic resonance imaging (MRI) machines that can diagnose heart and liver diseases without using X rays and radioactive materials. With MRIs, scanning times are reduced from about 45 to 20 minutes, which increases the number of patients who can be served, reduces costs per patient, and increases patient comfort. In manufacturing, Giddings & Lewis makes groups of machine tools by using automated materials-handling equipment and computer control. These systems reduce human error and thus improve product quality. In addition they yield *quicker delivery times* by reducing processing times. These reductions in turn allow for *smaller inventories*, with less inventory held on the shop floor. The *environment* might even improve: CSX Corporation replaced the mufflers on some of its unloading machinery with a noise cancellation system that eliminates the engine noise completely. The system, consisting of tiny speakers, a microphone, and a small signal processor, analyzes the noise and instantly generates identical waves that are 180° out of phase with the sound waves. The new technology eliminated the need for ear protection in a workplace that used to produce a noise level equivalent to the sound of a commercial jet during takeoff.

Investment costs of new technology can be forbidding, particularly for complex and expensive automation projects that require extensive facility overhaul. The investment also can be risky because of uncertainties in demand and in per unit benefits. Technology may have hidden costs, requiring more highly trained employees to maintain and operate the new equipment. This may generate employee resistance, create employee layoffs, and lower morale.

The operations manager must sort out the benefits and costs of different technological choices. Managing technology means more than choosing the right one: It also means supporting the technology throughout its implementation.

Some Guidelines

Operations managers must make informed decisions with courage and vision. Although they offer no guarantees of success, four useful guidelines have emerged from recent experience; they relate to simplification and initial planning, justification, the human side, and leadership.

What are some keys to successful technological change?

Simplification and Initial Planning. Before considering automation, a manager should simplify and streamline current operations to eliminate duplication and waste. The *base case* used to justify new automation should be what the current operation *can* achieve, not what it *is* achieving. Several plants have not lived up to expectations because automation preceded streamlining.

Management should plan automation to ensure that operations strategy and competitive priorities match technological choices. Operations managers should state precisely what they expect from automation. They should quantify costs and performance goals. When possible, they should consider approaching automation incrementally, as managers did successfully at plants such as Allen-Bradley, Caterpillar, and Hewlett-Packard.

Justification. When is investment in emerging technologies justified? Traditional techniques of financial analysis often are used to answer that question. However, the net present value method (see Appendix 1) would have rejected some very successful innovations. The problem with applying this technique is that labor savings are still used to justify most automation projects, but labor is a shrinking component—only 10 to 15 percent—of total costs. Focusing only on cost savings, rather than recognizing other more qualitative factors such as improved achievement in competitive priorities, understates the new technology's true value.

Allen-Bradley built a $15 million, 50 machine, flexible assembly facility to produce motor starters in 125 different configurations at a rate of 600 an hour. The company wanted to develop a manufacturing plant that would achieve the corporate strategy of competing on price. The company justified the operations strategy of investing in a fully automated facility on the basis of quality, cost, market share, competition, and profitability. "If there is a time to ignore conventional return-on-investment calculation, it's when your long-term goals are at stake," said Allen-Bradley's CEO.

Operations managers must look beyond the direct costs of automation to the impact of automation on customer service, delivery times, inventories, and resource flexibility. Quantifying such intangible goals as the ability to move quickly into a new market may be difficult. However, the smart operations manager must realize that a firm that fails to automate while its competitors do so can lose its competitive advantage. The result may be declining revenues and layoffs.

Thus justification still must begin with financial analysis techniques, but it must recognize *all* quantifiable factors that can be translated into dollar values. The resulting financial measure must be merged with the qualitative factors and intangibles, perhaps using the preference matrix approach (see Supplement A).

The Human Side. The jobs that people actually perform are largely determined by technology—that is, when technology changes, so do the jobs. Automation affects jobs at all levels: eliminating some, upgrading some, and downgrading others. Even when the changes resulting from automation are small, people-related issues may become large. The operations manager must anticipate such changes and prepare for them. Transition is easiest when automation is part of capacity expansion or a new facility and thus doesn't threaten existing jobs. In other situations early education and retraining are essential. Before Chrysler opened its automated plant in Sterling Heights, Michigan, it put its employees collectively through 900,000 labor hours of training.

Another key to successful implementation is involving employees in the design of new systems. When Ford revamped its plant to make the Aerostar mini-van, management reviewed proposed methods with workers directly responsible for specific operations. Employees made 434 suggestions, about 60 percent of which were adopted. Both the number and the percentage were considered quite good.

Leadership.   The operations manager should identify a team representing all affected departments to lead and coordinate new automation projects. A "project champion" who promotes the project at every opportunity and who has contagious enthusiasm should be in charge. This leader should be respected by all team members and preferably should have had experience dealing with equipment suppliers. Top management's ongoing support of the team must be evident throughout the project. Everyone should know that the operations manager is knowledgeable about the project, stands behind it, and will give it the resources it needs to succeed.

◆ DESIGNING PROCESSES

The five major process decisions represent broad, strategic issues. The next issue in process management is determining exactly how each process will be performed. Two different but complementary approaches exist for designing processes: process reengineering and process improvement. We begin with process reengineering, which is getting considerable attention today in management circles.

Process Reengineering

Reengineering is the fundamental rethinking and radical redesign of business processes to dramatically improve performance in areas such as cost, quality, service, and speed. Process reengineering is about reinvention, rather than incremental improvement. It is strong medicine and not always needed or successful. Pain, in the form of layoffs and large cash outflows for investments in information technology, almost always accompanies massive change. However, reengineering processes can have big payoffs. For example, Bell Atlantic reengineered its telephone business. After five years of effort, it cut the time to hook up new customers from 16 days to just hours. The changes caused Bell Atlantic to lay off 20,000 employees, but the company is decidedly more competitive.

A process selected for reengineering should be a core process, such as a firm's order fulfillment activities. Reengineering then requires focusing on that process, often using cross-functional teams, information technology, leadership, and process analysis.

Critical Processes.   The emphasis of reengineering should be on core business processes, rather than functional departments such as purchasing or marketing. By focusing on processes, managers may spot opportunities to eliminate unnecessary work and supervisory activities, rather than worry about defending turf. Reengineering should be reserved for essential processes, such as new-product development or customer service, because of the time and energy involved. Normal process improvement activities can be continued with the other processes. The processes selected should be broadly defined in terms of cost and customer value so that overall performance improves.

Do some of the organization's key processes need reengineering?

Strong Leadership.   Senior executives must provide strong leadership for reengineering to be successful. Otherwise, cynicism, resistance ("we tried that before"), and boundaries between functional areas can block radical changes. Managers can help overcome resistance to the new and different. They provide the clout to push the project through to completion. They also ensure that the project proceeds within a strategic context, with direct ties to corporate strategy and competitive priorities. Executives should set and monitor key performance objectives for the process, such as cost, quality, or speed of service. When Union Carbide decided to emphasize commodity chemicals rather than specialty products, its reengineering goal was low manufacturing cost and quick delivery. Top management also creates a sense of urgency, making a case for change that is compelling and constantly refreshed.

Cross-Functional Teams.   A team, consisting of members from each functional area affected by the process change, is charged with carrying out a reengineering project. For instance, in reengineering the process of handling an insurance claim, three departments should be represented: customer service, adjusting, and accounting. Team-building concepts, including team rewards based on the outcomes achieved, should be applied. Reengineering works best at high-involvement workplaces, where self-managing teams and employee empowerment (see Chapter 4) are the rule rather than the exception. Top-down and bottom-up initiatives can be combined—the top-down for performance targets and the bottom-up for deciding how to achieve the targets.

Information Technology.   Information technology is a major enabler of process engineering. Most reengineering projects design processes around information flows such as customer order fulfillment. The "process owners" who will actually be responding to marketplace happenings need information networks and computer technology to do their jobs better. The reengineering team must think through who needs the information, when they need it, and where. Restructuring an organization around information flows can eliminate many levels of management and work activity. For example, Wal-Mart reengineered its process so as to use information technology to eliminate wholesalers and drastically cut costs. Now, when a customer buys something, the information goes back instantly to the supplier's plant and is reflected in the manufacturing and shipping schedule.

Clean Slate Philosophy.   Reengineering requires a "clean slate" philosophy—that is, starting with the way the customer wants to deal with the company. To ensure a customer orientation, teams begin with internal and external customer objectives for the process. Often this means first establishing a price target for the product or service and deducting profits desired and then finding a process that provides what the customer wants at the price the customer will pay. Reengineers start from the future and work backward, unconstrained by current approaches.

Process Analysis.   Despite the clean slate philosophy, a reengineering team must understand things about the current process: what it does, how well it performs, and what factors affect it. Such understanding can reveal areas where new thinking will provide the biggest payoff. However, the emphasis is on understanding rather than analyzing the process in agonizing detail. Otherwise, the team will be blind to radically different approaches. At the same time, the team must look at every procedure involved in the process throughout the organization, mapping out each step and then questioning why it is done and eliminating steps that are not really necessary. Information on standing relative to the competition, process by process, is also valuable.

Process Improvement

Can flow diagrams and process charts be used to study and improve operations?

Process improvement is the systematic study of the activities and flows of each process to improve it. The relentless pressure to provide better quality at a lower price means that companies must continually review all aspects of their businesses. As the chief executive of Dana Corporation, a $4.9 billion producer of automotive parts, put it, "You have to get productivity improvements forever." Process improvement goes on, whether or not a process is reengineered. Further, reengineering uses process improvement tools and is followed after completion by process improvement efforts. For example, Wal-Mart keeps improving its reengineered process.

In this section we present two basic mapping techniques for analyzing processes: flow diagrams and process charts. We introduce more techniques for analyzing processes in Chapter 4, where their special focus is on quality improvement. These techniques systematically map the details of a process to allow better understanding of it. The analyst then can highlight tasks that can be simplified or indicate where productivity can otherwise be improved. Improvements can be made in quality, throughput time, cost, errors, safety, or on-time delivery. These techniques can be employed to design new processes and redesign existing ones and should be used periodically to study all operations. However, the greatest payoff is likely to come from applying them to operations having one or more of the following characteristics.

- The process is slow in responding to the customer.
- The process introduces too many quality problems or errors.
- The process is costly.
- The process is a bottleneck, with work piling up waiting to go through it.
- The process involves disagreeable work, pollution, or little value added.

Both analytic techniques involve breaking a process into detailed components. To do this, the manager should ask six questions:

1. *What* is being done?   4. *Where* is it being done?
2. *When* is it being done?   5. *How* long does it take?
3. *Who* is doing it?   6. *How* is it being done?

Answers to these questions are challenged by asking still another series of questions. *Why?* Why is the process even being done? Why is it being done where it is being done? Why is it being done when it is being done? Such questioning often can lead to creative answers that cause a breakthrough in process design. The analyst should brainstorm different aspects of the process, listing as many solutions as possible. Work elements can be streamlined, entire processes eliminated entirely, purchased materials usage cut, or jobs made safer. Most facilities can trim labor costs by eliminating unnecessary functions, such as parts inspection, warehousing, materials handling, and redundant supervision, among others—and reorganizing the process. For example, Eaton Corporation rearranged its plant in Marshall, Michigan, to use a conveyor to transport a rough forging automatically from machine to machine until it emerges as a polished gear for a truck differential. Computerized measuring machines, instead of human inspectors, ensure that automated turning centers cut gears to a precise size. Such changes come from a critical analysis of each process.

Flow Diagrams.   A **flow diagram** traces the flow of information, customers, employees, equipment, or materials through a process. There is no precise format, and the diagram can be drawn simply with boxes, lines, and arrows. Figure 3.4 is a diagram of an automobile repair process, beginning with the customer's call for an appointment and ending with the customer's pickup of the car and departure. In this figure, the dotted *line of visibility* divides activities that are directly visible to the customers from those that are invisible. Such information is particularly valuable for service operations involving considerable customer contact. Operations that are essential to success and where failure occurs most often are identified. Other formats are just as acceptable, and it is often helpful to show beside each box such process measurements as

1. total elapsed time,
2. quality losses,
3. error frequency,
4. capacity, or
5. cost.

Sometimes flow diagrams are overlaid on a facility's layout. To make this special kind of flow diagram, the analyst first does a rough sketch of the area in which the process is performed. On a grid the analyst plots the path followed by

FIGURE 3.4

Flow Diagram for Automobile Repair

Source: J. L. Heskett and R. Anthony, "Note on Service Mapping," Harvard Business School Publishing, No. 693-065, Winter 1993/1994, p. 5.

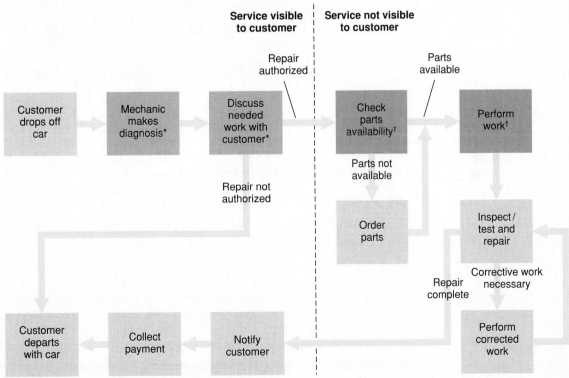

* = Points critical to the success of the service
† = Points at which failure is most often experienced

the person, material, or equipment, using arrows to indicate the direction of movement or flow. Figure 3.5 shows such a flow diagram for a car-wash facility, illustrating the flows of cars and customers. The facility used to have only one waiting line, but during peak periods the line of cars would extend back into the street, blocking traffic. The owner used a flow diagram to determine that a second waiting line could be added without changing the flow of the other operations. Now cars enter one of two lines from the street and alternate in forming a single line that rounds a sharp corner into the washing bay. Just before a car enters the bay, the customer leaves the car, walking through a separate door and hallway to the office to pay for the service. The car proceeds through the washing bay, and the customer exits through the hallway and a second door to rejoin the car after it is rolled to an open area and wiped down. The customer then gets back into the car and drives away. (Queuing and simulation analysis, described in Supplements E and F, are more extensive methods of studying waiting lines.)

FIGURE 3.5

Flow Diagram for a Car Wash Facility

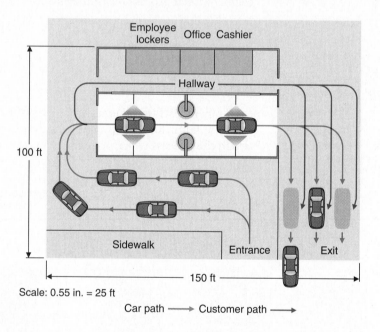

Scale: 0.55 in. = 25 ft

Car path ——→   Customer path ——→

Process Charts.   A **process chart** is an organized way of recording all the activities performed by a person, by a machine, at a workstation, with a customer, or on materials. For our purposes we group these activities into five categories:

- *Operation*—changes, creates, or adds something. Drilling a hole and serving a customer are examples of operations.

- *Transportation*—moves the study's subject from one place to another (sometimes called *materials handling*). The subject can be a person, a material, a tool, or a piece of equipment. A customer walking from one end of a counter to the other, a crane hoisting a steel beam to a location, and a conveyor carrying a partially completed product from one workstation to the next are examples of transportation.

- *Inspection*—checks or verifies something but does not change it. Checking for blemishes on a surface, weighing a product, and taking a temperature reading are examples of inspections.

- *Delay*—occurs when the subject is held up awaiting further action. Time spent waiting for materials or equipment, cleanup time, and time that workers, machines, or workstations are idle because there is nothing for them to do are examples of delays.
- *Storage*—occurs when something is put away until a later time. Supplies unloaded and placed in a storeroom as inventory, equipment put away after use, and papers put in a file cabinet are examples of storage.

Depending on the situation, other categories can be used. For example, subcontracting for outside services might be a category, or temporary storage and permanent storage might be two separate categories.

To complete a process chart for a new process, the analyst must identify each step performed. If the process is an existing one, the analyst can actually observe the steps, categorizing each step according to the subject being studied. The analyst then records the distance traveled and the time taken to perform each step. After recording all the activities and steps, the analyst summarizes the number of steps, times, and distances data. Figure 3.6 shows a process chart for a patient

FIGURE 3.6

Process Chart for Emergency Room Admission

			Summary			
Process: *Emergency room admission*			Activity	Number of steps	Time (min)	Distance (ft)
Subject Charted: *Ankle injury patient*						
Beginning: *Enter emergency room*						
Ending: *Leave hospital*			Operation ●	5	23	—
			Transport →	9	11	815
			Inspect ■	2	8	—
			Delay ▸	3	8	—
			Store ▼	—	—	—

Step no.	Time (min)	Distance (ft)	●	→	■	▸	▼	Step description
1	0.50	15		X				Enter emergency room, approach patient window
2	10.0	—	X					Sit down and fill out patient history
3	0.75	40		X				Nurse escorts patient to ER triage room
4	3.00	—			X			Nurse inspects injury
5	0.75	40		X				Return to waiting room
6	1.00	—				X		Wait for available bed
7	1.00	60		X				Go to ER bed
8	4.00	—				X		Wait for doctor
9	5.00	—			X			Doctor inspects injury and questions patient
10	2.00	200		X				Nurse takes patient to radiology
11	3.00	—	X					Technician x-rays patient
12	2.00	200		X				Return to bed in ER
13	3.00	—				X		Wait for doctor to return
14	2.00	—	X					Doctor provides diagnosis and advice
15	1.00	60		X				Return to emergency entrance area
16	4.00	—	X					Check out
17	2.00	180		X				Walk to pharmacy
18	4.00	—	X					Pick up prescription
19	1.00	20		X				Leave the building

with a twisted ankle being treated at Lower Florida Keys Hospital (see the Big Picture in Chapter 2). The process begins at the entrance and ends with the patient exiting after picking up the prescription. Such process charts are means to an end—continually improving the process. After a chart is prepared, for either a new or an existing process, it becomes the basis for brainstorming the process for improvement ideas. Examples 3.1–3.3 demonstrate the entire sequence, using an activity that can be easily understood—shaving.

EXAMPLE 3.1

Completing a Process Chart

The task is to analyze a process that most men perform each morning—shaving. The process begins when the shaver removes the shaving bowl and soap from the cabinet, where his tools are stored, and walks to the sink. He then lathers his face, shaves, and inspects the results. After rinsing the razor, he dries his face and cleans up the area.

Solution   Figure 3.7 shows the completed chart for the 18-step process. A summary of the times and distances traveled is shown in the upper right-hand corner of the process chart. The times sum to 16.2 minutes, and the shaver travels a total of 20 feet.

After the process is charted, the analyst estimates the annual cost of the entire process. It becomes a benchmark against which other methods for performing the process can be evaluated. Annual labor cost can be estimated by finding the product of (1) time in hours to perform the process each time, (2) variable cost per hour, and (3) number of times the process is performed each year, or

$$\begin{pmatrix} \text{Annual} \\ \text{labor cost} \end{pmatrix} = \begin{pmatrix} \text{Time to perform} \\ \text{the process} \end{pmatrix}\begin{pmatrix} \text{Variable costs} \\ \text{per hour} \end{pmatrix}\begin{pmatrix} \text{Number of times process} \\ \text{performed per year} \end{pmatrix}$$

EXAMPLE 3.2

Computing the Annual Labor Cost

The shaver values his time at $30 per hour (including fringe benefits) and shaves each day of the week. What is the annual labor cost of this process?

Solution

$$\text{Annual labor cost} = \left(\frac{16.2 \text{ min/day}}{60 \text{ min/hr}}\right)(\$30/\text{hr})(365 \text{ days/yr}) = \$2948$$

The calculations convert minutes to hours and then multiply this figure by the hourly rate and the number of hours per year spent on the process. Adding in the cost of materials, such as razor blades, would yield a sizable variable cost.

Next comes the creative part of process analysis. The analyst now asks the what, when, who, where, how long, and how questions, challenging each of the steps of the process charted. The summary of the process chart indicates which activities take the most time. To make a process more efficient, the analyst should question each delay and then analyze the operation, transportation, inspection, and storage activities to determine whether they can be combined, rearranged, or eliminated. There is always a better way, but someone must think of it. Improvements in productivity, quality, time, and flexibility can be significant.

FIGURE 3.7 *Process Chart for Shaving*

Process: *Shaving*								Summary			
Subject Charted: *Man*							Activity	Number of steps	Time (min)	Distance (ft)	
Beginning: *Remove tools*											
Ending: *Clear area*							Operation ●	4	6.2	—	
							Transport ➡	4	0.5	20	
							Inspect ■	1	0.5	—	
							Delay ❭	9	9.0	—	
							Store ▼	0	—	—	

Step no.	Time (min)	Distance (ft)	●	➡	■	❭	▼	Step description
1	0.1	5			X			Remove shaving bowl and soap from cabinet
2	0.1	5			X			Remove brush from cabinet
3	0.1					X		Turn warm water faucet on
4	3.0					X		Hold hand under faucet until water is warm
5	1.0					X		Create shaving lather with brush and warm water
6	1.0		X					Apply shaving lather to face
7	0.1					X		Plug sink
8	3.0					X		Turn faucet off when sink is half full
9	0.1	5			X			Remove razor from cabinet
10	0.5					X		Insert new razor blade
11	0.1		X					Draw blade across face
12	0.1					X		Rinse blade in sink
13	5.0		X					Repeat steps 11 and 12 until face is clear of stubble
14	0.5				X			Inspect face
15	0.2					X		Thoroughly rinse razor
16	0.1		X					Dry face with towel
17	0.2	5			X			Return shaving brush, bowl, and soap to cabinet
18	1.0					X		Unplug sink, drain completely, and clear area

EXAMPLE 3.3

Improving the Process

What improvement can be made in the process shown in Fig. 3.7?

Solution Brainstorming the process should generate at least 10 to 20 ideas. Don't try to evaluate each idea until as complete a list as possible has been compiled. Otherwise, the judgmental part of the mind blocks out the creative part. Begin your list with the following ideas.

1. *Don't shave.* It would save time—and might even be becoming—to eliminate the whole process and grow a beard.
2. *Don't use warm water.* A lot of time is lost just waiting for warm water.

CHAPTER REVIEW

Solved Problem 1

An automobile service is having difficulty providing oil changes in the 29 minutes or less mentioned in its advertising. You are to analyze the process of changing automobile engine oil. The subject of the study is the service mechanic. The process begins when the mechanic directs the customer's arrival and ends when the customer pays for the services.

Solution   Figure 3.8 shows the completed process chart. The process is broken into 21 steps. A summary of the times and distances traveled is shown in the upper right-hand corner of the process chart. The times add up to 28 minutes, which does not allow much room for error if the 29 minute guarantee is to be met, and the mechanic travels a total of 420 feet.

FIGURE 3.8

Process: *Changing engine oil*	**Summary**			
Subject Charted: *Mechanic*	Activity	Number of steps	Time (min)	Distance (ft)
Beginning: *Direct customer arrival*				
Ending: *Total charges, receive payment*				
	Operation ●	7	16.5	—
	Transport ➡	8	5.5	420
	Inspect ■	4	5.0	—
	Delay ◗	1	0.7	—
	Store ▼	1	0.3	—

Step no.	Time (min)	Distance (ft)	●	➡	■	◗	▼	Step description
1	0.8	50		X				Direct customer into service bay
2	1.8		X					Record name and desired service
3	2.3				X			Open hood, verify engine type, inspect hoses, check fluid levels
4	0.8	30		X				Walk to customer in waiting area
5	0.6		X					Recommend additional services
6	0.7					X		Wait for customer decision
7	0.9	70		X				Walk to storeroom
8	1.9		X					Look up filter number(s), find filter(s)
9	0.4				X			Check filter number(s)
10	0.6	50		X				Carry filter(s) to service pit
11	4.2		X					Perform under-car services
12	0.7	40	X					Climb from pit, walk to automobile
13	2.7		X					Fill engine with oil, start engine
14	1.3				X			Inspect for leaks
15	0.5	40		X				Walk to pit
16	1.0				X			Inspect for leaks
17	3.0		X					Clean and organize work area
18	0.7	80		X				Return to auto, drive from bay
19	0.3						X	Park the car
20	0.5	60		X				Walk to customer waiting area
21	2.3		X					Total charges, receive payment

Solved Problem 2

What improvement can you make in the process shown in Fig. 3.8?

Solution Your analysis should verify the following three ideas for improvement. You may also be able to come up with others.

1. *Move step 17 to step 21.*   Customers shouldn't have to wait while the mechanic cleans the work area.
2. *Store small inventories of frequently used filters in the pit.*   Steps 7 and 10 involve travel to the storeroom. If the filters are moved to the pit, a copy of the reference material must also be placed in the pit. The pit will have to be organized and well lighted.
3. *Use two mechanics.*   Steps 10, 12, 15, and 17 involve running up and down the steps to the pit. Much of this travel could be eliminated. The service time could be shortened by having one mechanic in the pit working simultaneously with another working under the hood.

Chapter Highlights

- Process management deals with *how* to make a product or service. Many choices must be made concerning the best mix of human resources, equipment, and materials.
- Process management is of strategic importance and is closely linked to the productivity levels a firm can achieve. It involves the selection of inputs, operations, work flows, and methods used to produce goods and services.
- Process decisions are made in the following circumstances: a new product is to be offered or an existing product modified, quality improvements are necessary, competitive priorities are changed, demand levels change, current performance is inadequate, new technology is available, or cost or availability of inputs changes.
- The five major process decisions are process choice, degree of capital intensity, resource flexibility, vertical integration, and customer involvement. Basic *process choices* may be categorized as project, batch, line, and continuous. *Capital intensity* concerns the mix of capital equipment and human skills in a process. *Resource flexibility* reflects the degree to which equipment is general purpose and individuals can handle a wide variety of work. *Vertical integration* concerns decisions about whether to make or buy parts and services. *Customer involvement* is the extent to which customers are allowed to interact with the production process. Self-service, product selection, and the timing and location of the interaction must all be considered.
- The variable underlying these relationships is volume. For example, high volume is associated with a line or continuous process, vertical integration, little resource flexibility, little customer involvement, and capital intensity.

- To achieve a competitive advantage, operations managers must pay continuing attention to technological advances. Potential benefits are associated with direct costs, quality, delivery times, inventories, and even the workplace environment.
- Fixed automation maximizes efficiency for high-volume products with long life cycles, but flexible (programmable) automation provides economies of scope. Flexibility is gained and setups are minimized because the machines can be reprogrammed to follow new instructions. Numerically controlled (NC) machines and robots are examples of programmable automation.
- Operations managers must make informed choices about investing in new automation. Success is more likely if the manager first simplifies current operations, sets goals, recognizes all costs and benefits, deals with people-related issues, and provides the necessary leadership and support. Operations strategy and the need to achieve a competitive advantage guide the selection of technologies. Successful technology management tactics include early planning, justification based on quantitative and qualitative analysis, considering the impact of technological change on the work force, and team-oriented leadership.
- Process reengineering uses cross-functional teams to rethink the design of critical processes. Process improvement is a systematic analysis of activities and flows that occurs continuously.
- Two basic mapping techniques for analyzing process activities and flows are flow diagrams and process charts. Both are ways to organize the detailed study of process components.

Key Terms

automation 107	flexible work force 104	process improvement 116
backward integration 102	flow diagram 117	process management 95
capital intensity 96	forward integration 102	reengineering 114
customer involvement 96	hollow corporations 102	resource flexibility 95
economies of scope 110	outsourcing 103	technology 110
fixed automation 107	process chart 118	vertical integration 95
flexible automation 108	process choice 95	virtual corporation 103

Study Questions

1. "Process management choices cannot be isolated from decisions in other areas of operations management." Comment on this statement from the standpoint of a bookstore manager. (*Hint:* Look over this book's table of contents to get some ideas.)

2. How much capital intensity do you recommend for a business having extremely unpredictable product demand? How much vertical integration? Explain.

3. The number of mail-order businesses has increased dramatically in the United States in the last 10 years. Compare the processes of a business selling ski equipment and clothing by direct mail to the processes of a retail store handling the same items. How do they differ in terms of capital intensity, resource flexibility, vertical integration, and customer involvement? How are they the same?

4. Suppose that you and a friend decide to start a business selling sandwiches and snacks in college dormitories late at night. What decisions must you make regarding vertical integration? How will your customers be involved in this process?

5. Explain the difference between fixed and flexible automation. Give examples of each.

6. Why are traditional financial analysis techniques criticized when used to justify automation projects? Must such projects just be accepted as a leap of faith and an act of hope?

7. Think of the process for registering for a course at your university or college. Identify elements of the process for which reengineering or process improvements are needed.

8. Consider some processes with which you are familiar, such as visiting the student health center, reselling textbooks, fueling an automobile, buying a beer, visiting a recycling center, or buying concert/sporting event tickets. Use the techniques presented in this chapter to suggest process improvements.

9. Compare the process of preparing and serving your own lunch at home with that of preparing and serving lunch to others at a local pizza parlor. What inputs in terms of materials, human effort, and equipment are involved in each process? How are these inputs similar? How are they different?

10. Suppose that a grocery store has decided to add an in-store bakery. The next decision to be made is whether to install a drive-in window for the bakery so that customers do not have to enter the store in order to purchase baked goods. The store manager expects that this window would do a high volume of business early in the morning, as people purchase donuts on their way to work. How is this window likely to affect other processes in the store? What tasks would bakery employees have to perform that they would not otherwise? How would customer involvement differ from that in the rest of the grocery operations?

11. King Soopers Bakery anticipates a peak demand for holiday cakes in December. What implications does this have for its work force? Should part-time employees be hired? Should there be more cross-training?

12. King Soopers management is considering offering customers a "menu" of 10 different custom cake options from which to choose. How might this change affect the custom cake line?

Discussion Questions

1. To give utilities an incentive to spend money on new pollution control technology, the EPA proposes that flue gas emission limits be changed to require slightly cleaner stacks than the older technology is capable of producing. To comply, some utilities will install the new technology. Some will not. Utilities that reduce emissions below the new requirements will receive "credits," which they can sell to utilities that choose not to install the pollution control technology. These utilities can then continue business as usual, so long as they have purchased enough credits to account for the extra pollution they create. The price of the credits will be determined by the free market.

   Form sides and discuss the ethical, environmental, and political issues and trade-offs associated with this proposition.

2. The Hydro-Electric Company (HEC) has three sources of power. A small amount of hydroelectric power is generated by damming wild and scenic rivers; a second source of power comes from burning coal, with emissions that create acid rain and contribute to global warming; and the third source of power comes from nuclear fission. HEC's coal-fired plants use obsolete pollution control technology, and an investment of several hundred million dollars would be required to update it. Environmentalists urge HEC to promote conservation and purchase power from suppliers that use the cleanest fuels and technology.

   However, HEC is already suffering from declining sales, which have resulted in billions of dollars invested in idle equipment. Its large customers are taking advantage of laws that permit them to buy power from low-cost suppliers. HEC must cover the fixed costs of idle capacity by raising rates charged to its remaining customers or face defaulting on bonds (bankruptcy). The increased rates motivate even more customers to seek low-cost suppliers, the start of a death spiral for HEC. To prevent additional rate increases, HEC implements a cost-cutting program and puts its plans to update pollution controls on hold.

   Form sides, and discuss the ethical, environmental, and political issues and trade-offs associated with HEC's strategy.

3. Chip "Hacker" Snerdly works for the sales department of Farr and Wyde, an office equipment supplier in a cutthroat competitive market. Farr and Wyde's competitors use voice-mailboxes to receive messages while they are calling on other customers. Snerdly discovers that a surprising number of voice-mailbox occupants don't bother to use passwords and others rarely change their passwords. So he listens to, copies, and deletes messages left for his competitors by their customers. Snerdly calls on those customers himself, knowing that they are in the market for office equipment. What are the ethical issues here? What policies are necessary to foil Snerdly?

4. The Dewpoint Chemical Company is deciding where to locate a fertilizer plant near the Rio Grande. What are the ethical, environmental, and political issues and trade-offs associated with locating a fertilizer plant on the north bank versus the south bank of the Rio Grande?

Problems

Problems 9 and 10 apply break-even analysis (discussed in Supplement A) to process decisions.

1. Your class has volunteered to work for Referendum #13 on the November ballot, which calls for free tuition and books for all college courses except operations management. Support for the referendum includes assembling 10,000 yard signs (preprinted water-resistant paper signs to be glued and stapled to a wooden stake) on a fall Saturday. Construct a flow diagram and a process chart for yard sign assembly. What inputs in terms of materials, human effort, and equipment are involved? Estimate the amount of volunteers, staples, glue, equipment, lawn and garage space, and pizza required.

2. Prepare a flow diagram for the three processes at King Soopers.

3. Suppose that you are in charge of a large mailing to the alumni of your college inviting them to contribute to a scholarship fund. The letters and envelopes have been individually addressed (mailing labels were not used). The letters are to be folded and stuffed into the correct envelopes, the envelopes are to be sealed, and a large commemorative stamp is to be placed in the upper right-hand corner of each envelope. Make a process chart for this activity, assuming that it is a one-person operation. Estimate how long it will take to stuff, seal, and stamp 2000 envelopes. Assume that the person doing this work is paid $8.00 per hour. How much will it cost to process 2000 letters, based on your time estimate? Consider how each of the following changes individually would affect the process.

   - Each letter has the greeting "Dear Alumnus or Alumna," instead of the person's name.
   - Mailing labels are used and have to be put on the envelopes.
   - Prestamped envelopes are used.
   - Envelopes are stamped by a postage meter.
   - Window envelopes are used.
   - A preaddressed envelope is included with each letter for contributions.
   a. Which of these changes would reduce the time and cost of the process?
   b. Would any of these changes be likely to reduce the effectiveness of the mailing? If so, which ones? Why?
   c. Would the changes that increase time and cost be likely to increase the effectiveness of the mailing? Why or why not?
   d. What other factors need to be considered for this project?

4. Diagrams of two self-service gasoline stations, both located on corners, are shown in Fig. 3.9(a) and (b). Both have two rows of four pumps and a booth at which an attendant receives payment for the gasoline. At neither station is it necessary for the customer to pay in advance. The exits and entrances are marked on the diagrams. Analyze the flows of cars and people through each station.

FIGURE 3.9

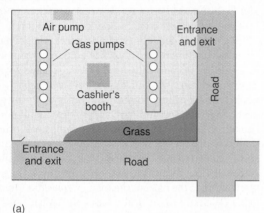

(a)

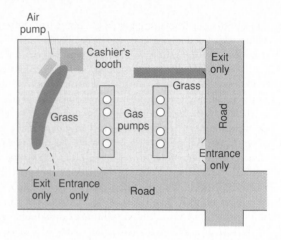

(b)

a. Which station has the more efficient flows from the standpoint of the customer?
b. Which station is likely to lose more potential customers who cannot gain access to the pumps because another car is headed in the other direction?
c. At which station can a customer pay without getting out of the car?

5. You have been asked by the management of the Just Like Home restaurant to analyze some of its processes. One of these processes is making a single-scoop ice cream cone. Cones can be ordered by a server (for table service) or by a customer (for takeout). Figure 3.10 illustrates the process chart for this operation.

FIGURE 3.10

Process: *Making one single-scoop ice cream cone*	Summary			
Subject Charted: *Server at counter*	Activity	Number of steps	Time (min)	Distance (ft)
Beginning: *Walk to cone storage area*				
Ending: *Give server or customer the cone*	Operation ●			—
	Transport ➜			
	Inspect ■			—
	Delay ❭			—
	Store ▼			—

Step no.	Time (min)	Distance (ft)	●	➜	■	❭	▼	Step description
1	0.20	5		X				*Walk to cone storage area*
2	0.05		X					*Remove empty cone*
3	0.10	5		X				*Walk to counter*
4	0.05		X					*Place cone in holder*
5	0.20	8		X				*Walk to sink area*
6	0.50					X		*Ask dishwasher to wash scoop*
7	0.15	8		X				*Walk to counter with clean scoop*
8	0.05		X					*Pick up empty cone*
9	0.10	2.5		X				*Walk to flavor ordered*
10	0.75		X					*Scoop ice cream from container*
11	0.75		X					*Place ice cream in cone*
12	0.25				X			*Check for stability*
13	0.05	2.5		X				*Walk to order placement area*
14	0.05		X					*Give server or customer the cone*

- The ice cream counter server earns $10 per hour (including variable fringe benefits).
- The process is performed 10 times per hour (on average).
- The restaurant is open 363 days a year, 10 hours a day.

a. Complete the summary (top right) portion of the chart.

b. What is the total labor cost associated with the process?

c. How can this operation be made more efficient? Draw a process chart of the improved process. What are the annual labor savings if this new process is implemented?

6. As a graduate assistant, your duties include grading and keeping records for operations management course homework assignments. Five sections for 40 students each are offered each semester. A few graduate students attend sections 3 and 4. Graduate students must complete some extra work to higher standards for each assignment. Every student delivers (or is supposed to deliver) directly to (under) the door of your office one homework assignment every Tuesday. Your job is to correct the homework, record grades, sort the papers by class section, sort by student last name in alphabetical order, and return the homework papers to the appropriate instructors (not necessarily in that order). There are some complications. A fair majority of the students sign their names legibly, others identify their work with the correct I.D. number, and a few do neither. Rarely do students identify their section number or graduate status. Prepare a list of process chart steps and place them in an efficient sequence.

7. At the Department of Motor Vehicles, the process of getting license plates for your car begins when you enter the facility and take a number. You walk 50 feet to the waiting area. During your wait, you count about 30 customers waiting for service. You notice that many customers become discouraged and leave. When a number is called, if a customer stands, the ticket is checked by a uniformed person, and the customer is directed to the available clerk. If no one stands up, several minutes are lost while the same number is called repeatedly. Eventually, the next number is called, and more often than not, that customer has left too. The DMV clerk has now been idle for several minutes, but doesn't seem to mind.

An unkempt man walks over to the ticket dispenser, picks up several tickets from the floor, and returns to his seat. A new arrival, carrying a stack of paper and looking like a car dealer, walks directly to the unkempt man. Some sort of transaction takes place. A few more numbers are called and it's the car dealer's number! After 4 hours, your number is called

and checked by the uniformed person. You walk 60 feet to the clerk, and the process of paying city sales taxes is completed in four minutes. The clerk then directs you to the waiting area for paying state personal property tax, 80 feet away. With a sinking heart, you take a different number and sit down with some different customers who are just renewing licenses. You notice the same unkempt man. A 1-hour, 40-minute wait this time, and after a walk of 25 feet you pay property taxes in a process that takes two minutes. Now that you have paid taxes you're eligible to pay registration and license fees. That department is 50 feet away, beyond the employees' cafeteria. As you walk by the cafeteria, you notice the unkempt man having coffee with a uniformed person.

The registration and license customers are called in the same order in which personal property taxes were paid. There is only a 10-minute wait and a 3-minute process. You receive your license plates, take a minute to abuse the license clerk, and leave exactly 6 hours after arriving.

Make a process chart to depict this process, and suggest improvements.

8. Refer to the process chart for the automobile oil change in Solved Problem 1. Calculate the annual labor cost if

- the mechanic earns $17 per hour (including variable fringe benefits),
- the process is performed twice per hour (on average), and
- the shop is open 350 days a year, 10 hours a day.

a. What is the total labor cost associated with the process?

b. If steps 7, 10, 12, and 15 were eliminated, estimate the annual labor savings associated with implementing this new process.

9. Dr. Gulakowicz is an orthodontist. She estimates that adding two new chairs will increase fixed costs by $105,000, including the annual equivalent cost of the capital investment and the salary of one more technician. Each new patient is expected to bring in $1925 per year in additional revenue, with variable costs estimated at $250 per patient. The two new chairs will allow her to expand her practice by as many as 200 patients annually. How many patients would have to be added for the new process to break even?

10. Two different manufacturing processes are being considered for making a new product. The first process is less capital intensive, with fixed costs of only $50,000 per year and variable costs of $400 per unit. The second process has fixed costs of $200,000 but variable costs of only $150 per unit. What is the break-even quantity, beyond which the second process becomes more attractive than the first?

CASE

Custom Molds, Inc.

Custom Molds, Inc. manufactures custom-designed molds for plastic parts and produces custom-made plastic connectors for the electronics industry. Located in Tucson, Arizona, Custom Molds, Inc. was founded by the father and son team of Tom and Mason Miller in 1975. Tom Miller, a mechanical engineer, had more than 20 years of experience in the connector industry with AMP, Inc., a large multinational producer of electronic connectors. Mason Miller had graduated from the University of Arizona in 1974 with joint degrees in chemistry and chemical engineering.

The company was originally formed to provide manufacturers of electronic connectors with a source of high-quality, custom-designed molds for producing plastic parts. The typical market was the product design and development divisions of those manufacturers. Custom Molds, Inc. worked closely with each customer to design and develop molds to be used in the customer's product development processes. Thus, virtually every mold made had to meet exacting standards and was somewhat unique. Orders for multiple molds would arrive when customers moved from the design and pilot-run stage of development to large-scale production of the newly designed parts.

As the years went by, Custom Molds, Inc.'s reputation grew as a designer and fabricator of precision molds. Building on this reputation, the Millers decided to expand into the limited manufacture of plastic parts. Ingredient mixing facilities and injection molding equipment were added, and by the mid 1980s Custom Molds, Inc. was expanding its reputation to include that of being a supplier of high-quality plastic parts. Because of limited capacity, the company concentrated its sales efforts on supplying parts that were used in limited quantities for research and development efforts and in preproduction pilot runs.

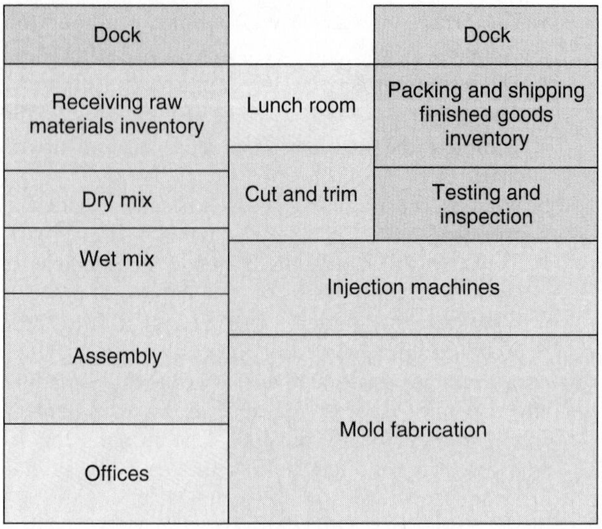

Production Processes

By 1985 the operations at Custom Molds, Inc. involved two distinct processes: one for fabricating molds and one for producing plastic parts. Although different, in many instances these two processes were linked, as when a customer would have Custom Molds, Inc. both fabricate a mold and produce the necessary parts to support the customer's R&D efforts. All fabrication and production operations were housed in a single facility. The layout was characteristic of a typical job shop, with like processes and similar equipment grouped together in various places in the plant. Figure 3.11 shows a schematic of the plant floor. Multiple pieces of various types of high-precision machin-

Dock		Dock
Receiving raw materials inventory	Lunch room	Packing and shipping finished goods inventory
Dry mix	Cut and trim	Testing and inspection
Wet mix		Injection machines
Assembly		
Offices		Mold fabrication

FIGURE 3.11   *Plant Layout*

ery, including milling, turning, cutting, and drilling equipment, were located in the mold fabrication area.

Fabricating molds is a skill-oriented, craftsman-driven process. When an order is received, a design team, comprising a design engineer and one of the 13 master machinists, reviews the design specifications. Working closely with the customer, the team establishes the final specifications for the mold and gives them to the master machinist for fabrication. It is always the same machinist who was assigned to the design team. At the same time the purchasing department is given a copy of the design specifications, from which it orders the appropriate raw materials and special tooling. The time needed to receive the ordered materials is usually three to four weeks. When the materials are received for a particular mold, the plant master scheduler reviews the workload of the assigned master machinist and schedules the mold for fabrication.

Fabricating a mold takes from two to four weeks, depending on the amount of work the machinist already has scheduled. The fabrication process itself takes only three to five days. Upon completion, the mold is sent to the testing and inspection area, where it is used to produce a small number of parts on one of the injection molding machines. If the parts meet the design specifications established by the design team, the mold is passed on to be cleaned and polished. It is then packed and shipped to the customer. One day is spent inspecting and testing the mold and a second day cleaning, polishing, packing, and shipping the mold to the customer. If the parts made by the mold do not meet the design specifications, the mold is returned to the master machinist for retooling and the process starts over. Currently, Custom Mold, Inc. has a published lead time of nine weeks for delivery of custom-fabricated molds.

The manufacturing process for plastic parts is somewhat different from that for mold fabrication. An order for parts may be received in conjunction with an order for a mold to be fabricated, or an order may be just for parts in instances where Custom Mold, Inc. has previously fabricated the mold and maintains it in inventory. If the mold is already available, the order is reviewed by a design engineer, who verifies the part and raw material specifications. If the design engineer has any questions concerning the specifications, the customer is contacted and any revisions to specifications are mutually worked out and agreed upon.

Upon acceptance of the part and raw material specifications, raw material orders are placed and production is scheduled for the order. Chemicals and compounds that support plastic parts manufacturing are typically ordered and received within one week. Upon receipt the compounds are first dry mixed and blended to achieve the correct composition, and then the mixture is wet mixed to the desired consistency (called slurry) for injection into the molding machines. When ready, the slurry is transferred to the injection molding area by an overhead pipeline and deposited in holding tanks adjacent to the injection machines. The entire mixing process takes only one day.

When the slurry is staged and ready, the proper molds are secured—from inventory or from the clean and polish operation if new molds were fabricated for the order—and the parts are manufactured. Although different parts require different temperature and pressure settings, the time to produce a part is relatively constant. Custom Mold, Inc. has the capacity to produce 5000 parts per day in the injection molding department; however, historically the lead time for handling orders in this department has averaged one week. Upon completion of molding, the parts are taken to the cut and trim operation, where they are disconnected and leftover flashing is removed. After being inspected, the parts may be taken to assembly or transferred to the packing and shipping area for shipment to the customer. If assembly of the final parts is not required, the parts can be on their way to the customer within two days of being molded.

Sometimes the final product requires some assembly. Typically, this entails attaching metal leads to the plastic connectors. If assembly is necessary, an additional three days is needed before the order can be shipped to the customer. Custom Mold, Inc. is currently quoting a three-week lead time for parts not requiring a mold to be fabricated.

The Changing Environment

In early 1991, Tom and Mason Miller began to realize that the electronics industry they supplied, along with their own business, was changing. Electronics manufacturers had traditionally used vertical integration into component parts manufacturing to reduce costs and ensure a timely supply of parts. By the late 1980s, this trend had changed. Manufacturers were developing strategic partnerships with parts suppliers to ensure the timely delivery of high-quality, cost-effective parts. This approach allowed funds to be diverted to other uses that could provide a larger return on investment.

The impact on Custom Mold, Inc. could be seen in the sales figures over the past three years. The sales mix was changing. Although the number of orders per year for mold fabrication remained virtually constant, orders for multiple molds were declining, as shown below.

	Number of Orders		
Order Size	Molds 1988	Molds 1989	Molds 1990
1	80	74	72
2	60	70	75
3	40	51	55
4	5	6	5
5	3	5	4
6	4	8	5
7	2	0	1
8	10	6	4
9	11	8	5
10	15	10	5
Total orders	230	238	231

The reverse was true for plastic parts, for which the number of orders per year had declined but for which the order sizes were becoming larger, as illustrated in the following table.

	Number of Orders		
Order Size	Parts 1988	Parts 1989	Parts 1990
50	100	93	70
100	70	72	65
150	40	30	35
200	36	34	38
250	25	27	25
500	10	12	14
750	1	3	5
1000	2	2	8
3000	1	4	9
5000	1	3	8
Total orders	286	280	277

During this same period Custom Mold, Inc. began having delivery problems. Customers were complaining that their orders for parts were taking four to five weeks instead of the stated three weeks and that the delays were disrupting production schedules. When asked about the situation, the master scheduler said that determining when a particular order could be promised for delivery was very difficult. The reason was that bottlenecks were occurring during the production process but where or when they would occur couldn't be predicted. They always seemed to be moving from one operation to another.

Tom Miller thought that he had excess labor capacity in the mold fabrication area. So, to help push through those orders that were behind schedule, he assigned one of the master machinists the job of identifying and expediting those late orders. However, that didn't seem to help much. Complaints about late deliveries were still being received. To add to the problems, two orders had been returned recently because of the number of defective parts. The Millers knew that something had to be done. The question was "What?"

Questions

1. What are the major issues facing Tom and Mason Miller?
2. Identify the individual processes on a flow diagram. What are the competitive priorities for these processes and the changing nature of the industry?
3. What alternatives might the Millers pursue? What key factors should they consider as they evaluate these alternatives?

Source: This case was prepared by Dr. Brooke Saladin, Wake Forest University, as a basis for classroom discussion.

Selected References

Abernathy, William J. "Production Process Structure and Technological Change." *Decision Sciences,* vol. 7, no. 4 (October 1976), pp. 607–619.

Alster, Norm. "What Flexible Workers Can Do," *Fortune,* February 13, 1989, pp. 62–66.

Brown, Donna. "Outsourcing: How Corporations Take Their Business Elsewhere." *Management Review* (February 1992), pp. 16–19.

Byrne, John A. "The Virtual Corporation," *Business Week,* February 8, 1993, pp. 98–102.

Collier, David A. *Service Management: The Automation of Services.* Reston, Va.: Reston, 1985.

Dixon, J. Robb, Peter Arnold, Janelle Heineke, Jay S. Kim, and Paul Mulligan. "Business Process Reengineering: Improving in New Strategic Directions." *California Management Review* (Summer 1994), pp. 1–17.

Goldhat, J. D., and Mariann Jelinek. "Plan for Economies of Scope." *Harvard Business Review* (November–December 1983), pp. 141–148.

Hall, Gene, Jim Rosenthal, and Judy Wade. "How to Make Reengineering Really Work." *Harvard Business Review* (November-December 1993), pp. 119–131.

Hammer, Michael, and James Champy. *Reengineering the Corporation: A Manifesto for Business Revolution.* New York: HarperBusiness, 1993.

Harrigan, K. R. *Strategies for Vertical Integration.* Lexington, Mass.: D. C. Heath, 1983.

Hill, Terry. *Manufacturing Strategy: Text and Cases.* Homewood, Ill.: Irwin, 1989.

Malhotra, Manoj K., and Larry P. Ritzman. "Resource Flexibility Issues in Multistage Manufacturing." *Decision Sciences,* vol. 21, no. 4 (Fall 1990), pp. 673–690.

Normann, Richard, and Rafael Ramírez. "From Value Chain to Value Constellation: Designing Interactive Strategy." *Harvard Business Review* (July–August 1993), pp. 65–77.

Port, Otis. "The Responsive Factory," *Business Week,* Enterprise 1993, pp. 48–51.

Porter, Michael E. "The Competitive Advantage of Nations." *Harvard Business Review* (March–April 1990), pp. 73–93.

"Reengineering: The Hot New Managing Tool," *Fortune,* August 23, 1994, pp. 41–48.

Ritzman, Larry P., Barry E. King, and Lee J. Krajewski. "Manufacturing Performance—Pulling the Right Levers." *Harvard Business Review* (March–April 1984), pp. 143–152.

Roth, Aleda V., and Marjolijn van der Velde. *The Future of Retail Banking Delivery Systems.* Rolling Meadows, Ill.: Bank Administration Institute, 1988.

Skinner, Wickham. "Operations Technology: Blind Spot in Strategic Management." *Interfaces,* vol. 14 (January–February 1984), pp. 116–125.

Swamidass, Paul M. "Manufacturing Flexibility." *OMA* Monograph 2, January 1988.

Wheelwright, Steven C., and Robert H. Hayes. "Competing Through Manufacturing." *Harvard Business Review* (January–February 1985), pp. 99–109.

Computer-Integrated Manufacturing

The popular press often writes about the factory of the future: a fully automated factory that manufactures a wide variety of products without human intervention. Although some "peopleless" factories do exist and others will be built, the major advances being made today occur in manufacturing operations where computers are being integrated into the process to help workers create high-quality products.

Computer-integrated manufacturing (CIM) is an umbrella term for the total integration of product design and engineering, process planning, and manufacturing by means of complex computer systems. Less comprehensive computerized systems for production planning, inventory control, or scheduling are often considered part of CIM. By using these powerful computer systems to integrate all phases of manufacturing, from initial customer order to final shipment, firms hope to increase productivity, improve quality, meet customer needs faster, and offer more flexibility. For example, McDonnell Douglas spent $10 million to introduce CIM in its Florida factory. The computer systems automatically schedule manufacturing tasks, keep track of labor, and send instructions to computer screens at workstations along the assembly line. Eliminating paperwork led to an increase of 30 percent in worker productivity. Less than 1 percent of U.S. manufacturing companies have approached full-scale use of CIM, but more than 40 percent are using one or more elements of CIM technology.

Computer-integrated manufacturing helps many manufacturing firms, even those with high wage rates, remain competitive in the global marketplace. The following sections describe several technologies that comprise CIM: computer-aided manufacturing, computer-aided design, numerically controlled machines, robots, automated materials handling, and flexible manufacturing systems.

◆ COMPUTER-AIDED MANUFACTURING

The component of CIM that deals directly with manufacturing operations is called **computer-aided manufacturing (CAM)**. CAM systems are used to design production processes and to control machine tools and materials flow through programmable automation.

◆ COMPUTER-AIDED DESIGN

Computer-aided design (CAD) is an electronic system for designing new parts or products or altering existing ones, replacing drafting traditionally done by hand. The heart of CAD is a powerful desktop computer and graphics software that allow a designer to manipulate geometric shapes. The designer can create drawings and view them from any angle on a display monitor. The computer can also simulate the reaction of a part to strength and stress tests. Using the design data stored in the computer's memory, manufacturing engineers and other users can quickly obtain printouts of plans and specifications for a part or product.

Analysts can use CAD to store, retrieve, and classify data about various parts. This information is useful in creating families of parts to be manufactured by the same group of machines. Computer-aided design saves time by enabling designers to access and modify old designs quickly, rather than start from scratch.

A *CAD/CAM system* integrates the design and manufacturing function by translating final design specifications into detailed machine instructions for manufacturing the part. CAD/CAM is quicker and less error prone than humans, and it eliminates duplication between engineering and manufacturing. The K2 Corporation, the largest U.S. manufacturer of Alpine skis, must continually redesign its products to meet changing customer needs. It produces about 20 different models in 12 different lengths. Its CAD/CAM workstations allow designers to convert the numerical descriptions for a new ski shape into drawings and tooling designs and to create machining instructions that can be used directly by the milling machines. Prototype skis are designed and produced for rapid testing, allowing K2 to respond rapidly to changing requirements in a competitive international market. An additional benefit is that K2 uses the system to make its own production machines, including a belt conveyor and an automated robotic ski topping system.

◆ NUMERICALLY CONTROLLED MACHINES

Numerically controlled (NC) machines are large machine tools programmed to produce small- to medium-sized batches of intricate parts. Following a preprogrammed sequence of instructions, NC machines drill, turn, bore, or mill many different parts in various sizes and shapes. The technology was developed in the early 1950s at the Massachusetts Institute of Technology to find more efficient methods of manufacturing jet aircraft for the U.S. Air Force.

Currently, NC machines are the most commonly used form of flexible (programmable) automation. Early models received their instructions from a punched tape or card. **Computerized numerically controlled (CNC) machines** are usually stand-alone pieces of equipment, each controlled by its own microcomputer. Since the early 1980s, Japanese industry has spent twice as much as North American or European industry on factory equipment, more than half of which was spent on CNC machines. Currently, more than 40 percent of the world's NC machines are at work in Japan.

◆ INDUSTRIAL ROBOTS

Robots are more glamorous than NC workhorses. The first industrial robot joined the GM production line in 1961. **Industrial robots** are versatile, computer-controlled machines programmed to perform various tasks. These "steel-collar" workers operate independently of human control. Most are stationary and mounted on the floor, with an arm that can reach into difficult locations. Figure B.1 shows the six standard movements of a robot's arm. Not all robots have every movement.

The robot's "hand," sometimes called an *end effector* or *tool*, actually does the work. The hand (not shown) can be changed to perform different tasks, in-

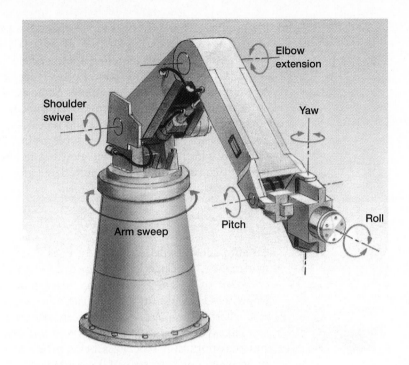

cluding materials handling, spot welding, spray painting, assembly, and inspection and testing. Second-generation robots equipped with sensors that simulate touch and sight have spawned new applications. For example, robots can wash windows, pick fruit from trees, mix chemicals in laboratories, and handle radioactive materials.

The initial cost of a robot depends on its size and function. Other potential costs include modifying both product and process to accommodate the robot, preparing the worksite, installing and debugging the robot, and retraining and relocating workers. Benefits from robot installation include less waste materials, more consistent quality, and labor savings. Robots are the drudges of the work force, performing highly repetitive tasks without tiring, taking a lunch break, or complaining.

By the late 1980s there were more than 20,000 robots in North America, 28,000 in Europe, and 80,000 in Japan. The conversion of U.S. industry to robots has fallen short of expectations: Less than 30 percent of manufacturers have even moderate experience with robots. One possible reason is that U.S. employers haven't faced a labor shortage, whereas in Japan a limited supply of workers led the government to subsidize robots. Cincinnati Milacron, the last big U.S. robot maker, recently left the robot business and returned to making basic machine tools. Robotics is but one of many possible technologies that can be used to gain a competitive advantage.

◆ AUTOMATED MATERIALS HANDLING

In both manufacturing and service industries, the choice of how, when, and by whom materials are handled is an important technological decision. **Materials handling** covers the processes of moving, packaging, and storing a product. Moving, handling, and storing materials costs time and money but adds no value to the product. Therefore operations managers are always looking for ways to reduce costs by automating the flow of materials to and from an operation.

Whether materials handling automation is justifiable depends on positioning strategy. When operations have a process focus, job paths vary and there is little repeatability in materials handling. Such variability means that workers must move materials and equipment in open-top containers, carts, or lift trucks. When operations have a product focus and repeatability is high, however, handling can be automated. In addition, other types of flexible automation are now available for firms with positioning strategies that fall between these two extremes. Let's look at two such technologies: automated guided vehicles and automated storage and retrieval systems.

AGVs

An **automated guided vehicle** (**AGV**) is a small, driverless, battery-driven truck that moves materials between operations, following instructions from either an on-board or a central computer. Most older models follow a cable installed below the floor, but the newest generation follows optical paths that can go anywhere with aisle space and a relatively smooth floor.

The AGV's ability to route around problems such as production bottlenecks and transportation blockages helps production avoid expensive, unpredictable shutdowns. Furthermore, AGVs enable operations managers to deliver parts as they are needed, thus reducing stockpiles of expensive inventories throughout the plant. The automotive industry now uses AGVs in some plants as mobile assembly stands, primarily for heavy loads. Workers prefer them to inflexible conveyors because the AGVs don't leave until the workers have done the job correctly at their own pace. NCR Corporation installed a $100,000 AGV system in one of its electronics fabrication facilities. Machines run along a 3000-foot guidepath at 1.5 miles per hour, ferrying parts between the stockroom, assembly stations, and the automated storage and retrieval system.

AS/RS

An **automated storage and retrieval system** (**AS/RS**) is a computer-controlled method of storing and retrieving materials and tools using racks, bins, and stackers. With support from AGVs, an AS/RS can receive and deliver materials without the aid of human hands. For example, IBM's new distribution center in Mechanicsburg, Pennsylvania, ships 105,000 spare computer parts and related publications each day—a staggering volume—using an AS/RS and 13 AGVs. Computer control assigns newly arrived materials to one of 37,240 storage locations. If optical sensors confirm that the materials will fit, the automated system moves them along to the proper location. Production at this highly automated facility has increased 20 percent, and accuracy of filled orders has reached 99.8 percent.

◆ FLEXIBLE MANUFACTURING SYSTEMS

A **flexible manufacturing system** (**FMS**) is a configuration of computer-controlled, semi-independent workstations where materials are automatically handled and machine loaded. An FMS is a type of flexible automation system.

Such systems require a large initial investment ($5 million to $20 million) but little direct labor to operate. An FMS system has three key components:

1. several computer-controlled workstations, such as CNC machines or robots, that perform a series of operations;
2. a computer-controlled transport system for moving materials and parts from one machine to another and in and out of the system; and
3. loading and unloading stations.

Workers bring raw materials for a part family to the loading points, where the FMS takes over. Computer-controlled transporters deliver the materials to various workstations, where they pass through a specific sequence of operations unique to each part. The route is determined by the central computer. The goal of using FMS systems is to synchronize activities and maximize the system's utilization. Because automation makes it possible to switch tools quickly, setup times for machines are short. This flexibility often allows one machine to perform an operation when another is down for maintenance and avoids bottlenecks by routing parts to another machine when one is busy.

Figure B.2 shows the layout of an FMS at the Mazak Corporation plant in Kentucky.* The plant produces turning and machining centers. Specific characteristics of this FMS include the following.

FIGURE B.2

A Flexible Manufacturing System at Mazak Corporation

Source: Courtesy of Vincent Mabert and Mazak Corporation. Reprinted by permission.

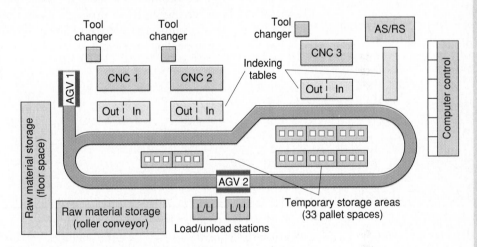

- The computer control room (right) houses the main computer, which controls the transporter and sequence of operations.
- Three CNC machines, each with its own microprocessor, control the details of the machining process.
- Two AGVs, which travel around a 200-foot-long oval track, move materials on pallets to and from the CNCs. When the AGVs' batteries run low, the central computer directs them to certain spots on the track for recharging.

*We are indebted to Vincent Mabert for much of the information about this FMS, including Fig. B.2.

- Indexing tables lie between each CNC and the track. Inbound pallets from an AGV are automatically transferred to the right side of the table, and outbound pallets holding finished parts are transferred to the left side for pickup.

- A tool changer located behind each CNC loads and unloads tool magazines. Each magazine holds an assortment of tools. A machine automatically selects tools for the next specific operation. Changing from one tool to another takes only 2 minutes.

- Two load/unload stations are manually loaded by workers; loading takes 10 to 20 minutes.

- An automatic AS/RS (upper right) stores finished parts. The AGV transfers parts on its pallet to an indexing table, which then transfers them to the AS/RS. The process is reversed when parts are needed for assembly into finished products elsewhere in the plant.

This particular system typifies the future that many envision for FMSs. It fits an intermediate positioning strategy involving medium-level variety (5 to 100 parts) and volume (annual production rates of 40 to 2000 units per part). The system can simultaneously handle small batches of many products. In addition, an FMS can be used a second way: At any given time, an FMS can produce low-variety, high-volume products in much the same way that fixed manufacturing systems do. However, when these products reach the end of their life cycles, the FMS can be reprogrammed to accommodate a different product. This flexibility makes FMS very appealing, especially to product-focused firms where life cycles are short.

SUPPLEMENT REVIEW

Supplement Highlights

- The concept of automation goes beyond the labor savings of displacing humans with machines. By totally integrating product design, engineering, process planning, and manufacturing through complex computer systems, computer-integrated manufacturing (CIM) allows companies to compete on the basis of time and flexibility while creating higher paying jobs. Computer-aided manufacturing (CAM) is the part of CIM that deals directly with manufacturing.

- A CAD/CAM system links computerized product design and production. It's the first step toward a paperless factory.

- Numerically controlled (NC) machines follow preprogrammed instructions to perform a variety of machining operations on parts having different sizes and shapes. Computerized numerically controlled (CNC) are distin-

guished by the use of a dedicated microcomputer for control. Industrial robots also are capable of a variety of tasks. However, their costs increase with size, the number of axes of rotation, and travel and sensory (sight, proximity) capability. These machines are used for flexibility, but not for high volume. Fixed automation is used for high-volume, standardized production.

- Two new methods used to automate materials handling systems are the automated guided vehicle (AGV) and the automated storage and retrieval system (AS/RS).

- Programmable automation includes flexible manufacturing systems (FMSs), which consist of several computer-controlled workstations, an interconnecting transport system, and areas for loading and unloading. An FMS is very expensive to acquire but is flexible enough to accommodate new product families.

Key Terms

automated guided vehicle
 (AGV) *134*
automated storage and retrieval
 system (AS/RS) *134*
computer-aided design
 (CAD) *131*

computer-aided manufacturing
 (CAM) *131*
computer-integrated manufacturing
 (CIM) *131*
computerized numerically controlled
 (CNC) machines *132*

flexible manufacturing system
 (FMS) *134*
industrial robots *132*
materials handling *133*
numerically controlled (NC)
 machines *132*

Study Questions

1. What is computer-integrated manufacturing (CIM)? Is it a good choice for all manufacturers? Why or why not?
2. What are some of the advantages of computer-aided design (CAD)?
3. What do numerically controlled (NC) machines and robots have in common?
4. The Japanese government began to subsidize the development and use of robots at a time when a labor shortage was forecast. What is the effect of a labor shortage on productivity ratios? On the standard of living? What factors could have contributed to a labor shortage in Japan?
5. What is materials handling? Why is it said that "the best materials handling is no handling at all"? Compare materials handling in two industries, one with a product focus and one with a process focus.
6. In what ways do an AGV and an AS/RS qualify as programmable automation?
7. What are the elements of a flexible manufacturing system (FMS)? Why is this kind of system flexible?
8. On the Ford assembly line, a robot reaches through the passenger side of a Taurus to perform spot welds near the fire wall while the car continues to move down the line. What types of motion are required of the robot?
9. A bicycle manufacturer uses a robot to weld frames. What types of motion are required of the robot? What would create a need to change the program for the robot?
10. What characteristics make a task a good candidate for automation?

Discussion Questions

1. Fiat's widespread use of robots was an economic success, helping improve its global competitiveness. Much of the savings resulted from reducing its work force from 138,000 to 72,000. There was a human cost of displaced workers, however. Finding another job in the Turin region is particularly difficult because Fiat is the dominant employer. Was Fiat's automation decision defensible on ethical grounds? What steps can a firm take to be a responsible and ethical employer when cutbacks are necessary?
2. "The central problem of America's economic future is that the nation is not moving quickly enough out of high-volume, standardized production. The extraordinary success of the half-century of the management era has left the United States a legacy of economic inflexibility. Thus our institutional heritage now imperils our future." [Robert B. Reich, "The Next American Frontier," *The Atlantic Monthly,* March 1983, pp. 43–58.]

   This quote from Dr. Reich, an economist later appointed Secretary of Labor by President Clinton, suggests that American managers weren't moving rapidly enough away from high-volume mass production. If so, into what type of production or other type of business should they have been moving? Keep in mind that the U.S. economy was already dominated by services and that we couldn't all sell one another insurance. What is the relationship between high-volume standardized production and economic inflexibility? What characterized the corporate investment decisions of the 1980s? Were those investments generally guided by a desire to increase economic flexibility?

Selected References

Ayers, Robert U., and Duane C. Butcher. "The Flexible Factory Revisited." *American Scientist,* vol. 81 (September–October 1993), pp. 448–459.

Doyle, Lawrence E., Carl A. Keyser, James L. Leach, George F. Schrader, and Morse B. Singer. *Manufacturing Processes and Materials for Engineers,* 3rd ed. Englewood Cliffs, N.J.: Prentice-Hall, 1985.

Gerwin, Donald. "Do's and Don'ts of Computerized Manufacturing." *Harvard Business Review* (March–April 1982), pp. 107–116.

Giffi, Craig A., Aleda V. Roth, and Gregory M. Seal. *Competing in World-Class Manufacturing: America's 21st Century Challenge.* Homewood, Ill.: Business One–Irwin, 1991.

Gold, Bela. "CAM Sets New Rules for Production." *Harvard Business Review* (November–December 1982), pp. 88–94.

Groover, Mikell P., and E. W. Zimmers, Jr. *CAD/CAM: Computer-Aided Design and Manufacturing.* Englewood Cliffs, N.J.: Prentice-Hall, 1984.

Jaikumar, Jay. "The Boundaries of Business: The Impact of Technology." *Harvard Business Review* (September–October 1991), pp. 100–101.

Kaplan, Robert S. "Must CIM Be Justified by Faith Alone?" *Harvard Business Review* (March–April 1986), pp. 87–95.

Norri, Hamid. *Managing the Dynamics of New Technology: Issues in Manufacturing Management.* Englewood Cliffs, N.J.: Prentice-Hall, 1990.

Rosenthal, Stephen. "Progress Toward the Factory of the Future." *Journal of Operations Management,* vol. 4, no. 3 (May 1984), pp. 203–229.

Skinner, Wickham. "Operations Technology: Blind Spot in Strategic Management." *Interfaces,* vol. 14, no. 1 (January–February 1984), pp. 116–125.

Starr, Martin K., and Alan J. Biloski. "The Decision to Adopt New Technology—Effects on Organizational Size." *Omega,* vol. 12, no. 4 (1984), pp. 353–361.

Stecke, Kathryn E., and James J. Solberg. "Loading and Control Policies for a Flexible Manufacturing System." *International Journal of Production Research,* vol. 19, no. 5 (1981), pp. 481–490.

Chapter Four

TOTAL QUALITY MANAGEMENT

The Federal Express Corporation (FedEx) started in 1973 with a fleet of eight small aircraft. Today, it employs 103,900 employees worldwide at more than 1600 sites and processes 2 million shipments daily using 469 airplanes. Since 1987, overall customer satisfaction with FedEx's service has averaged better than 94 percent. There are several key reasons for FedEx's success. First, a well-developed and thoroughly employed management evaluation system called SFA (survey/feedback/action) involves employees in the development of action plans for improvement. Second, employees receive extensive training to improve the quality of service. They are encouraged to be innovative and to make their own decisions. FedEx provides the information and the technology employees need to continually improve their performance. Finally, the company replaced its old measure of quality performance—percentage of on-time deliveries—with a 12-component index that comprehensively describes how performance is viewed by customers. Measures such as the numbers of invoice adjustments, damaged packages, lost packages, and missed pickups are

Federal Express pioneered the next-day package delivery service and continues to be a leader in the industry.

included. Quality action teams use the index to detect weekly, monthly, and annual trends when searching for the root causes of problems in service quality.

The challenge for business today is to produce quality products or services efficiently. Federal Express is just one example of a company that has met the challenge and is using quality as a competitive weapon. This chapter is the first of two that address the topic of quality. Here we explore the competitive implications of quality, focusing on the philosophy of total quality management which many firms have embraced. **Total quality management (TQM)** stresses three principles: customer satisfaction, employee involvement, and continuous improvements in quality. As Fig. 4.1 indicates, TQM also involves benchmarking, product and service design, process design, purchasing, and problem-solving tools. In Chapter 5 we address statistical process control, which consists of techniques useful for appraising and monitoring quality in operating systems.

◆ QUALITY: A MANAGEMENT PHILOSOPHY

Anyone born in 1970 or later probably takes for granted consumer demand for high-quality products and services and the need for firms to improve their operations to make quality a competitive priority. However, quality was not always a top priority. In international markets, the quality of products coming out of Japan in the 1950s and 1960s was very poor, owing to the destruction of Japa-

FIGURE 4.1

TQM Wheel

nese industry by Allied bombing during World War II. Following the war, Japan had to rebuild its industrial base completely. Starting in the 1970s, Japanese manufacturers, with the help of American consultants such as W. Edwards Deming, began making quality a competitive priority. At the time, U.S. automobile manufacturers scoffed at the ability of the small, fuel-efficient Japanese cars to compete against their large luxury sedans. However, the energy crisis in the mid 1970s created a demand for fuel efficiency and, coupled with the consumers' belief that Japanese cars were of better quality than U.S.-built cars, opened the door for Japanese manufacturers to gain an advantage in the marketplace. The quality practices used in the automobile industry spilled over into other Japanese industries. By the 1980s U.S. car manufacturers realized that they needed to listen to the customer or lose market share. In a short 30 years Japanese manufacturers turned quality levels once considered a joke into global standards of excellence. Today, the gap in quality between Japanese automobiles and those produced by others is narrowing dramatically. Nonetheless, the lesson learned by firms worldwide is clear: The global economy of the 1990s dictates that companies provide the customer with an ever-widening array of products and services having high levels of quality.

In Chapter 2 we identified two competitive priorities that deal with quality: high-performance design and consistent quality. These priorities characterize an organization's competitive thrust. Strategic plans that recognize quality as an essential competitive priority must be based on some operational definition of quality. In this section we discuss various definitions of quality and emphasize the importance of bridging the gap between consumer expectations of quality and operating capabilities.

Customer-Driven Definitions of Quality

How do customers perceive the quality of services?

Customers define **quality** in various ways. In a general sense, quality may be defined as meeting or exceeding the expectations of the customer. For practical purposes, it is necessary to be more specific. Quality has multiple dimensions in the mind of the customer, and one or more of the following definitions may apply at any one time.

Conformance to Specifications.   Customers expect the products or services they buy to meet or exceed certain advertised levels of performance. In manufacturing, specifications might be a tolerance for the critical dimensions of a part, the length of time between repairs, or a certain performance level. For example, Seagate, a disk drive manufacturer, emphasizes the high-performance design of its disk drives by advertising that the drives have a "mean time between failures" of 30,000 hours. All the components of the disk drive must conform to their individual specifications to achieve the desired performance of the complete product. To the person on the shop floor, quality is defined as the specifications on the part to be processed. To the customer, quality is measured by the performance of the complete product and the time between failures.

In service systems also, conformance to specifications is important, even though tangible outputs are not produced. Specifications for a service operation may relate to on-time delivery or response time. Bell Canada measures the performance of its operators in Ontario by the length of time to process a call (called "handle time"). If the group average time exceeds the standard of 23 seconds, managers work with the operators to reduce it.

Value.   Another way customers define quality is through value, or how well the product or service serves its intended purpose at a price customers are willing to pay. How much value a product or service has in the mind of the customer depends on the expectations the customer had before purchasing the product or service. For example, if you spent $2.00 for a plastic ballpoint pen and it served you well for three months, you might feel that the purchase was worth the price. Your expectations for the product were met or exceeded. However, if the pen lasted only two days, you might be disappointed and feel that the value was not there.

Fitness for Use.   In assessing fitness for use, or how well the product or service performs its intended purpose, the customer may consider the mechanical features of a product or the convenience of a service. Other aspects of fitness for use include appearance, style, durability, reliability, craftsmanship, and serviceability. For example, you may judge your dentist's quality of service on the basis of the age of her equipment. Or you may define the quality of the entertainment center you purchased on the basis of how easy it was to assemble and how well it housed your equipment.

Support.   Often the product or service support provided by the company is as important to customers as the quality of the product or service itself. Customers get upset with a company if financial statements are incorrect, responses to warranty claims are delayed, or advertising is misleading. Good product support can make up for quality failures in other areas. For example, if you just had a brake job done, you would be upset if the brakes began squealing again a week later. If the manager of the brake shop offers to redo the work at no additional charge, the company's intent to satisfy the customer is clear.

Psychological Impressions.   People often evaluate the quality of a product or service on the basis of psychological impressions: atmosphere, image, or aesthetics. In the provision of services, where the customer is in close contact with the provider, the appearance and actions of the provider are very important. Nicely dressed, courteous, friendly, and sympathetic employees can affect the customer's perception of service quality. For example, rumpled, discourteous, or grumpy waiters can undermine a restaurant's best efforts to provide high-quality service. In manufacturing, product quality often is judged on the basis of the knowledge and personality of salespeople, as well as the product image presented in advertisements.

Quality as a Competitive Weapon

Attaining quality in all areas of a business is a difficult task. To make things even more difficult, consumers change their perceptions of quality. For instance, changes in consumer life-styles and in economic conditions have drastically altered customer perceptions of automobile quality. When the oil crisis hit in the mid 1970s, consumer preferences shifted from power and styling to fuel economy. To the 1980s preference for quality of design and performance has been added a demand for greater safety in the 1990s. By failing to identify these trends and respond to them quickly in the 1970s and 1980s, U.S. automakers lost opportunities to maintain or increase their market shares relative to foreign competition. Today, U.S. automakers are staging a comeback by being more aware that the customer has a choice and by anticipating customer preferences.

In general, a business's success depends on the accuracy of its perceptions of customer expectations and its ability to bridge the gap between consumer expectations and operating capabilities. Consumers are much more quality-minded now than in the past and in many cases prefer to spend more for a product that lasts longer or a service that is delivered promptly and thoroughly. A survey of 2000 business units conducted by the Strategic Planning Institute of Cambridge, Massachusetts, indicated that a high-quality product has a better chance of gaining market share than does a low-quality product. Moreover, perception plays as important a role as performance: A product or service that is *perceived* by customers to be of higher quality stands a much better chance of gaining market share than does one *perceived* to be of low quality, even if the actual levels of quality are the same.

Good quality can also pay off in higher profits. High-quality products and services can be priced higher than comparable lower quality ones and yield a greater return for the same sales dollar. Poor quality erodes the firm's ability to compete in the marketplace and increases the costs of producing its product or service. For example, by improving conformance to specifications, a firm can increase its market share *and* reduce the cost of its products or services, which in turn increases profits. Management is more able to compete on price as well as on quality. Managerial Practice 4.1 shows how Alaska Airlines' turnaround was based on high-performance design.

◆ EMPLOYEE INVOLVEMENT

One of the important "spokes" of the TQM wheel is employee involvement. A complete program in employee involvement includes changing organizational culture, fostering individual development through training, establishing awards and incentives, and encouraging teamwork.

Managerial Practice 4.1

▶ *High Quality Pays Off for Alaska Airlines*

In the 1960s Alaska Airlines had a poor reputation for on-time departures and arrivals. Many passengers called the company "Elastic Airlines" in reference to the unreliability of its schedules. In the 1970s, under new management, the airline improved its schedule reliability and began an unbroken string of profitable years. In 1979 it changed its strategy of low-frills treatment and primarily in-state service. It opened service in Washington, Oregon, California, and Mexico and used high-performance design to attract customers from its larger competitors. The focus was on business travelers who were willing to pay full fares.

The service was outstanding. Fresh salmon was served in coach on the regular runs and venison on the Alaskan runs. Leg room was increased by taking out seats. The airline spent $12 million on guidance equipment so that schedules could be safely maintained even in foggy weather, a condition that often plagues the northwest United States. Beginning in 1979 the company's revenues grew 24 percent annually to $1.05 billion in 1990. In the eyes of management, it still had not reached its full potential. In February 1991, *Air Transport World* named Alaska Airlines its airline of the year, and in July 1991 *Consumer Reports* ranked the airline first on all dimensions measured.

What is the secret? Alaska Airlines relies heavily on its employees, who go through frequent training sessions focused on customer service. In addition, top management emphasizes that customers should be treated as if they were guests in the employees' homes. Management also conducted focus group sessions with customers to pick up suggestions for improved service. All told, Alaska Airlines used quality as a competitive weapon in a very competitive industry.

Source: "Northern Hospitality," *Business Week,* October 25, 1991.

Cultural Change

How can employees be included in the quality improvement process?

The challenge of quality management is to instill an awareness of the importance of quality in all employees and to motivate employees to improve product quality. This often requires changing the business culture of an organization. Change must come from the top levels of management. For example, in the late 1970s Scandinavian Airline System (SAS) was rapidly losing market share and suffering financial losses because of increased competition and rising fuel prices. Jan Carlzon, president of SAS, decided that SAS could distinguish itself from the competition by being a customer-driven company based on service quality. He set out to influence the norms and values of the people who deliver the service. His most important step was to introduce the concept of the "moment of truth," when a customer directly encounters an SAS representative. These encounters often define the quality of service in the minds of passengers. SAS carries more than 12 million passengers a year, and each passenger meets an average of five SAS front-line employees. Therefore customers encounter SAS services more than 60 million times in a typical year, and in each encounter the customer forms an opinion of SAS. This concept drove home the importance of the employee in the delivery of quality services. After one year the company had started to earn profits again, and in six years it had increased the profit margin to 10 percent.

Quality is a responsibility to be shared by the entire organization, especially the workers who actually make the product or service. With TQM, everyone is expected to contribute to the overall improvement of quality—from the administrator who finds cost-saving measures to the salesperson who learns a new customer need to the engineer who designs a product with fewer parts to the manager who communicates clearly with other department heads. In other words, TQM involves all the functions that relate to a product or service.

One of the main challenges in developing the proper culture for TQM is to define *customer* for each employee. In general, customers are internal and external. **External customers** are the people or firms who buy the product or service. In this sense the entire firm is a single unit that must do its best to satisfy the external customer. Some employees, especially those having little contact with external customers, may have difficulty seeing how their jobs contribute to the whole effort. However, each employee also has one or more **internal customers**—employees in the firm who rely on the output of other employees. For example, a machinist who drills holes in a component and passes it on to a welder has the welder as her customer. Even though the welder is not an external customer, he will have many of the same definitions of quality as an external customer, except that they will relate to the component instead of a complete product. All employees must do a good job of serving their internal customers if external customers ultimately are to be satisfied. The notion of internal customers applies to all parts of a firm. For example, accounting must prepare accurate and timely reports for management, and purchasing must provide high-quality materials on time for operations.

In TQM, everyone in the organization must share the view that quality control is an end in itself. Errors or defects should be caught and corrected at the source, not passed along to an internal customer. This philosophy is called *quality at the source*. In addition, firms should avoid trying to "inspect quality into the product" by using inspectors to weed out defective products or unsatisfactory services after all operations have been performed. In some manufacturing firms workers have the authority to stop a production line if they spot quality problems. At Kawasaki's U.S. plant, lights of different colors strung along the assembly lines indicate the severity of the quality problem detected. Workers activate a yellow light to indicate that a problem has been detected and a red light when the problem is serious enough to stop the line. If the line is stopped, the problem must be resolved quickly, because each lost minute results in less output and costs money. However, in TQM, quality consistency has a higher priority than the level of output.

Individual Development

On-the-job training programs can help improve quality. Teaching new work methods to experienced workers or training new employees in current practices can increase productivity and reduce the number of product defects. Some companies train workers to perform related jobs so as to help them understand how quality problems in their own work can cause problems for other workers. Honda of America, Inc. gives more than 100,000 hours of classroom instruction each year (taught by Honda associates to other Honda associates) in the Anna and Marysville, Ohio, plants.

Managers too need to develop new skills—not only those directly relating to their own duties, but also those needed to teach their subordinates. Many companies are putting their managers through "train-the-trainer" programs that give managers the skills to train others in quality improvement practices.

Managers informally discuss a case during a Xerox management training seminar.

Awards and Incentives

The prospect of merit pay and bonuses can give employees some incentive for improving quality. Companies may tie monetary incentives directly to quality improvements. For example, at Honda of America, Inc. an employee incentive program puts money into the pockets of associates whose suggestions for improvements in equipment or procedures have paid off. Associates are responsible for assembling all the necessary information and implementing the suggestion if it is approved. In 1990, Honda associates received approximately $190,000 in cash awards and five Honda Civic automobiles as part of this program.

Nonmonetary awards, such as recognition in front of co-workers, also can motivate quality improvements. Each month some companies select an employee who has demonstrated quality workmanship and give that person special recognition, such as a privileged parking spot, a dinner at a fine restaurant, or a plaque. Typically the event is reported in the company newsletter.

Teamwork

How can quality improvement teams be developed in a company?

Employee involvement, also called *worker participation* or *labor–management jointness,* is a key tactic for improving quality. One way to achieve employee involvement is by the use of **teams,** which are small groups of people who have a common purpose, set their own performance goals and approaches, and hold themselves accountable for success. Teams differ from the more typical "working group" because

- the members have a common commitment to an overarching purpose that all believe in and that transcends individual priorities;
- the leadership roles are shared rather than held by a single, strong leader;
- performance is judged not only by individual contributions, but also by collective "work products" that reflect the joint efforts of all the members;
- open-ended discussion, rather than a managerially defined agenda, is prized at meetings; and
- the members of the team do real work together, rather than delegating to subordinates.

Management plays an important role in determining whether teams are successful. Survey results suggest that the following approaches lead to more successful teams (Katzenbach and Smith, 1993).

1. The team's project should be meaningful, with well-defined performance standards and direction.
2. Particular attention should be paid to creating a positive environment at the first few meetings.
3. Team members should create clear rules on issues such as attendance, openness, constructive confrontation, and commitment to the team.
4. To foster a sense of accomplishment, the team should set a few immediate performance-oriented tasks and goals that will allow them to achieve some early successes.
5. People outside the team should be consulted for fresh facts and information.
6. If possible, team members should spend lots of time together to foster creative insights and personal bonding.
7. Managers should look for ways beyond direct compensation to give the *team* positive reinforcement.

A team at Tokyo Nissan studies ways to improve productivity and quality.

The three approaches to teamwork most often used are problem-solving teams, special-purpose teams, and self-managing teams. All three use some amount of **employee empowerment,** which moves responsibility for decisions further down the organizational chart—to the level of the employee actually doing the job.

Problem-Solving Teams.   First introduced in the 1920s, problem-solving teams, also called **quality circles,** became more popular in the late 1970s after the Japanese had used them successfully. Problem-solving teams are small groups of supervisors and employees who meet to identify, analyze, and solve production and quality problems. The philosophy behind this approach is that the people who are directly responsible for making the product or providing the service will be best able to consider ways to solve a problem. Also, employees take more pride and interest in their work if they are allowed to help shape it. The teams typically consist of 5 to 12 volunteers, drawn from different areas of a department or from a group of employees assigned to a particular task, such as automobile assembly or credit application processing. The teams meet several hours a week to work out quality and productivity problems and make suggestions to management. Such teams are used extensively by Japanese-managed firms in the United States. The Japanese philosophy is to encourage employee inputs while maintaining close control over their job activities. Although problem-solving teams can successfully reduce costs and improve quality, they die if management fails to implement a good proportion of the suggestions generated.

The Wilson Sporting Goods Company plant in Humboldt, Tennessee, has used problem-solving teams to rebound from a dismal market share of 2 percent in the golf ball business in 1985 to 17 percent in 1992. Problem-solving teams focused on achieving better customer service and reducing costs of production. For example, employees in the injection molding area, where Du Pont Surlyn covers are applied in the production of two-piece balls, found ways to reduce the defect rate from 15 percent in 1985 to only 1.4 percent in 1992. Plantwide, the employees working in problem-solving teams helped reduce defective workmanship by 67 percent and generated savings of $9.5 million.

Special-Purpose Teams.   An outgrowth of the problem-solving teams, **special-purpose teams** address issues of paramount concern to management, labor, or both. For example, management may form a special-purpose team to design and introduce new work policies or new technologies or to address customer service problems. Essentially, this approach gives workers a voice in high-level decisions. Special-purpose teams, which first appeared in the United States in the early 1980s, are beginning to become more popular.

Special-purpose teams usually consist of representatives from several different departments or functions. Such was the case at Victory Memorial Hospital in Waukegan, Illinois, where a cross-functional team was assembled to address complaints of lengthy delays in treating patients (Davis, 1993). The predominance of complaints came from level-two patients—patients who were not in immediate danger but were in pain. A team of representatives from Diagnostic Services, Admitting, Emergency, Patient Accounts, Medical Laboratory, Quality Assurance, and Telemetry found that the three most likely causes for the lengthy delays were (1) waiting for a sample from patients suspected of urinary tract infections, (2) waiting for lab test results, and (3) waiting for a physical exam. The team recommended various solutions, including having the admitting nurse start the patient specimen process as soon as the ailment has been assessed, drawing an extra tube of blood at the time the initial sample is taken to reduce delays when the doctor asks for additional tests, and adding another emergency treatment room with an examining table. The TQM process at Victory Memorial reduced the average length of stay from 9.1 to 6.7 days, reduced receivables from 73.6 to 59.3 days, reduced inventory investment from $270,000 to $200,000, improved patient satisfaction by 30 percent, and improved employee satisfaction generally.

Self-Managing Teams. The **self-managing teams** approach takes worker participation to its highest level: A small group of employees work together to produce a major portion, or sometimes all, of a product or service. Members learn all the tasks involved in the operation, rotate from job to job, and take over managerial duties such as work and vacation scheduling, ordering supplies, and hiring. In some cases team members design the process and have a high degree of latitude as to how it takes shape. Self-managing teams essentially change the way work is organized because employees have control over their jobs. Only recently have self-managing teams begun to catch on in the United States, but some have increased productivity by 30 percent or more in their firms. Managerial Practice 4.2 shows how a self-managed team at Huffy Bicycles made a significant change in the process of making bicycles.

All three approaches to teamwork may lead to **organizational restructuring,** which in this case means creating a flatter organization by eliminating some supervisors and middle managers. Restructuring is a natural result of employee empowerment: Because employees actually take over some supervisory duties, there is less need for traditional supervisors and their middle-management bosses.

An operator in the Wilson Sporting Goods Humboldt plant inspects golf ball cores for injection defects. She is a member of a self-managed team responsible for placing the ball core in the press, injecting the core, trimming the flash, and inspecting for defects. She follows one batch at a time through this process.

Managerial Practice 4.2

▶ *Huffy Bicycles Increases Production Flexibility with the Help of a Self-Managed Work Team*

The traditional method of production at Huffy Bicycles has been the assembly line. High volumes of standard bicycles can be produced and assembled efficiently on these lines. However, as a global competitor, Huffy faced the challenge of meeting the special requirements of foreign markets. Manufacturing an international bike that had unique dimensions for fenders, a special light, and a utility rack posed difficulties for Huffy's manufacturing process. The volumes for that bike were low because of its newness and special features. Inserting low-volume orders into the schedule of the high-volume assembly lines caused much disruption, and shipping schedules and quality standards could not be consistently met.

Huffy created a self-managed team, called the Alternative Work Structure Team, to improve the flexibility of the assembly process and allow Huffy to take advantage of the opportunities of the foreign markets. No managers were directly involved, and the team was given decision-making powers to make changes. The team consisted of volunteers from four assembly groups, a utility worker, and a team technician. Initially the team addressed the problem by taking fully assembled, packaged models from the warehouse and adding the parts required by the foreign markets. However, this process quickly became inefficient, as volumes for the bike increased from 3000 units to 18,000 units per year. The team assessed the economics of tooling costs and labor hours for assembling the bikes from the frame up and decided to abandon its first approach and do the complete assembly.

The team realized that its members had to become highly trained, multiskilled assemblers to build high-specification bikes in a flexible manner. Using a special area of the plant, they designed an entirely new assembly layout. Then they determined the skills that each team member would have to master and devised a training schedule for learning them. When quality problems such as nonconformance to specifications or missing or wrong parts arose, the team brainstormed ways to correct them. The solution resulted in further training in part identification, shop documentation, and blueprint reading.

Achievements of the Alternative Work Structure Team included

- more efficient assembly of specialized models,
- elimination of downtime associated with running specialized models on the assembly lines,
- reduction of $4.00 per unit in the assembly of foreign bikes,
- better control of quality while the job is being done,
- more flexible operators educated in all aspects of assembly,
- better communication within the team compared to assembly-line communication, and
- ability to produce all models with minimal process change.

Source: Presentation of the Alternative Work Structure Team, Huffy Bicycles, at the Case Studies in Team Excellence Competition, The Ohio Manufacturers' Association, Columbus, Ohio, October 6, 1993.

Some Concerns. Worker participation may seem to be an ideal way to maintain or improve a firm's competitiveness, but not everyone thinks it's a good idea. Some United Auto Workers leaders, for example, view worker participation as just another ploy to motivate employees to work harder for the same pay. They fear that it is merely an attempt to undermine the authority of the union. Interestingly, some companies that move to self-managing teams initially experience high turnover rates because some employees don't want to accept the additional responsibilities and to switch from job to job. At its Salisbury plant, GE experienced a 14 percent turnover rate for two years after it went to team-based production. In addition, organizational restructuring involving reductions in managerial positions is often resisted by first-line supervisors who would lose their jobs and by other managers who do not like giving workers decision-making authority. Some employees have expressed concern that with fewer managerial positions to be filled, their prospects for advancement are limited. Nonetheless, most managers and employees favor worker participation in some form. Studies show that about 25 percent of the workers volunteer for problem-solving teams in plants where such action is voluntary. Another 70 percent are passive supporters, and only 5 percent are opposed ("The Payoff from Teamwork," 1989).

Not all firms utilizing work teams use self-managing teams. In fact, most of these companies utilize the problem-solving, or quality circle, approach. The teams are used only to help solve problems, not to provide more employee autonomy, and workers still perform subdivided, repetitive tasks.

◆ CONTINUOUS IMPROVEMENT

Continuous improvement, based on a Japanese concept called *kaizen,* is the philosophy of continually seeking ways to improve operations. It involves identifying benchmarks of excellent practice and instilling a sense of employee ownership of the process. The focus can be on reducing the length of time required to process requests for loans in a bank, the amount of scrap generated at a milling machine, or the number of employee injuries. Continuous improvement also can focus on problems with customers or suppliers, such as customers who request frequent changes in shipping quantities and suppliers that fail to maintain high quality. The bases of the continuous improvement philosophy are the beliefs that virtually any aspect of an operation can be improved and that the people most closely associated with an operation are in the best position to identify the changes that should be made. Consequently, employee involvement plays a big role in continuous improvement programs. The idea is not to wait until a massive problem occurs before acting. For example, CIGNA Property and Casualty Companies determined that its processing time for adjusting a claim wasn't out of line with respect to the industry but that it could be improved. CIGNA made time (delivery speed) a competitive priority by streamlining its small-claims adjustment process and increasing its staff in other areas.

Getting Started with Continuous Improvement

Instilling a philosophy of continuous improvement in an organization may be a lengthy process, and several steps are essential to its eventual success.

1. Train employees in the methods of statistical process control (SPC) and other tools for improving quality.
2. Make SPC methods a normal aspect of daily operations.
3. Build work teams and employee involvement.
4. Utilize problem-solving techniques within the work teams.
5. Develop a sense of operator ownership of the process.

We discuss the methods of statistical process control in Chapter 5 and the various data-based tools for improving quality later in this chapter. Note that employee involvement is central to the philosophy of continuous improvement. However, the last two steps are crucial if the philosophy is to become part of everyday operations. Problem solving addresses the aspects of operations that need improvement and evaluates alternatives for achieving improvements. A sense of operator ownership emerges when employees feel as if they own the processes and methods they use and take pride in the quality of the product or service they produce. It comes from participation on work teams and in problem-solving activities, which instill in employees a feeling that they have some control over their workplace.

Problem-Solving Process

Most firms actively engaged in continuous improvement train their work teams to use the **plan–do–check–act cycle** for problem solving. Another name for this approach is the Deming Wheel. Figure 4.2 shows this cycle, which lies at the heart of the continuous improvement philosophy. The cycle comprises the following steps.

1. *Plan.*   The team selects a process (activity, method, machine, or policy, for example) that needs improvement. The team then documents the selected process, usually by analyzing data (using the tools we discuss later in the chapter); sets qualitative goals for improvement; and discusses various ways to achieve the goals. After assessing the benefits and costs of the alternatives, the team develops a plan with quantifiable measures for improvement.

2. *Do.*   The team implements the plan and monitors progress. Data are collected continuously to measure the improvements in the process. Any changes in the process are documented, and further revisions are made as needed.

3. *Check.*   The team analyzes the data collected during the *do* step to find out how closely they correspond to the goals set forth in the *plan* step. If major shortcomings exist, the team may have to reevaluate the plan or stop the project.

4. *Act.*   If the results are successful, the team documents the revised process so that it becomes the standard procedure for all who may use it. The team may then instruct other employees in use of the revised process.

FIGURE 4.2

Plan–Do–Check–Act Cycle

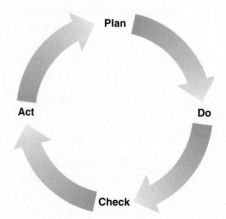

Problem-solving projects often focus on those aspects of operations that do not add value to the product or service. Value is added during operations such as machining a part or serving a customer. No value is added in activities such as inspecting parts for quality defects or routing requests for loan approvals to several different departments. The idea of continuous improvement is that activities that do not add value are wasteful and should be reduced or eliminated. Figure 4.3 illustrates schematically how reducing time on non–value added activities such as

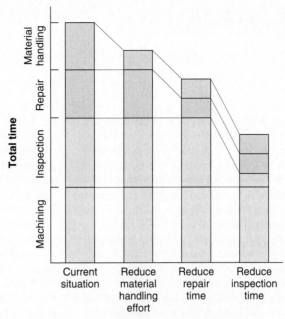

FIGURE 4.3

Continuous Improvement Projects to Reduce the Total Time to Produce a Product and Get It to the Customer

materials handling, repairs, and inspection reduces the time needed to deliver a product to a customer after an order has been received. Managerial Practice 4.3 shows how a team at the Timken Company identified several areas for improvement and made changes to increase effectiveness.

◆ THE COSTS OF POOR QUALITY

What are the costs of poor quality?

Most experts on the costs of poor quality estimate losses in the range of 20 to 30 percent of gross sales for defective or unsatisfactory products. For example, "dirty" electric power supplied by utility companies to manufacturers can be very costly. Tiny power surges, sags, and outages, often less than a millisecond long, rarely faze old manufacturing equipment but wreak havoc on new equipment that relies heavily on delicate computer chips. In one instance, General Motors' computer-run robots on its minivan assembly line in Baltimore kept shutting down. Finally the problem was traced to the local utility's faulty underground wiring: Current surges and outages were shutting down the robot's computers. Such blackouts can cost a manufacturer as much as $500,000 per hour.

Four major categories of costs are associated with quality management: prevention, appraisal, internal failure, and external failure.

Prevention

Prevention costs are associated with preventing defects before they happen. They include the costs of redesigning the process to remove the causes of poor quality, redesigning the product to make it simpler to produce, training employees in the methods of continuous improvement, and working with suppliers to increase the quality of purchased items or contracted services. In order to improve quality, firms have to increase their expenditure of time, effort, and money. We explore these costs further later in this chapter.

Managerial Practice 4.3

▶ *Continuous Improvement at the Timken Company*

ontinuous improvement projects may seem small and inconsequential by themselves, yet taken collectively add up to something worthwhile. Regardless of their size, the best projects are those that emanate from the employees themselves. Such was the case at the Timken Company, the world's leading manufacturer of precision engineered and manufactured bearings and alloy steels. The Small Industrial Bearings division produces more than 1000 different parts and assembles several thousand combinations, which are shipped to customers around the world. Department 80, which is responsible for assembly lines 8, 9, and 10, was experiencing problems with scheduling, high scrap rates, and low output rates. The employees, all members of the United Steel Workers of America, decided that they could make improvements and formed a team consisting of assembly operators, job-setters, maintenance personnel, a manufacturing tool engineer, and a shop floor supervisor.

The activity in Department 80 consisted of four basic operations in each assembly line, with each line requiring at least four operators. Flexibility had been introduced to the lines by adding pieces of equipment, but each line had grown to an unwieldy length of 18 pieces of equipment. The operators could operate only one machine at a time, leaving most of the machines idle at any particular time. In reality, there was no flexibility. In addition, work-in-process inventory investment was high because many partially completed products had to wait to be processed. This large work-in-process inventory also led to high inspection costs, because when an error was detected, many units had to be checked for the defect.

The team concluded that the key to the majority of the problems was the high work-in-process inventories, and members brainstormed ideas for improvement. The team decided to attack the problem by changing the arrangement of the equipment. The long lines were converted to short C-shaped lines, and the equipment was positioned closer together. The closer positioning enabled operators to run more than one piece of equipment at a time and reduced the need for high levels of inventory between each operation. In just 10 weeks the team's work

- increased output by 35 percent,
- reduced floor space for the assembly operations by 13,000 square feet,
- increased flexibility in product production,
- doubled equipment utilization, and
- increased labor utilization by 45 percent.

Source: The Timken Company team presentation at the Leadership Forum '93, The Ohio Manufacturers' Association, Cleveland, Ohio, November 11, 1993.

Appraisal

Appraisal costs are incurred in assessing the level of quality attained by the operating system. Appraisal helps management identify quality problems. As preventive measures improve quality, appraisal costs decrease, because fewer resources are needed for quality inspections and the subsequent search for causes of any problems that are detected. We discuss appraisal costs for quality audits and statistical quality control programs in more detail in Chapter 5.

Internal Failure

Internal failure costs result from defects that are discovered during the production of a product or service. They fall into two major cost categories: *yield losses,* which are incurred if a defective item must be scrapped, and *rework costs,* which are incurred if the item is rerouted to some previous operation(s) to correct the defect or if the service must be redone. For example, if the final inspector at an automobile paint shop discovers that the paint on a car has a poor finish, the car may have to be completely resanded and repainted. The additional time spent correcting such a mistake results in lower productivity for the sanding and painting departments. In addition, the car may not be finished by the date on which the customer is expecting it. Such activities are great candidates for continuous improvement projects.

External Failure

External failure costs arise when a defect is discovered after the customer has received the product or service. For instance, suppose that you have the oil changed in your car and the oil filter is improperly installed, causing the oil to drain onto your garage floor. You might insist that the company pay for the car to be towed and restore the oil and filter immediately. External failure costs to the company include the towing and additional oil and filter costs, as well as the loss of future revenue because you decide never to take your car back there for service. Dissatisfied customers talk about bad service or products to their friends, who in turn tell others. If the problem is bad enough, consumer protection groups alert the media. The potential impact on future profits is difficult to assess, but without doubt external failure costs erode market share and profits.

External failure costs also include warranty service and litigation costs. A **warranty** is a written guarantee of the producer's responsibility to replace or repair defective parts or to perform the service to the customer's satisfaction. Usually, a warranty is given for some specified period. For example, television repairs are usually guaranteed for 90 days and new automobiles for three years or 36,000 miles, whichever comes first. Warranty costs must be considered in the design of new products or services, particularly as they relate to reliability (discussed later in this chapter).

Encountering defects and correcting them after the product is in the customer's hands is costly. As Fig. 4.4 shows, the closer a product is to its finished state, the costlier it is to find and correct defects. When the product has been shipped to the customer, the cost to fix a defect skyrockets. For example, sending a customer engineer from IBM to a remote computer installation to find out what is wrong and fix it is far more expensive than finding and correcting the defect in the factory. An extreme example is provided by the Hubble space telescope. Placed in orbit from a space shuttle in 1990, the telescope proved to have

FIGURE 4.4

The Costs of Detecting a Defect

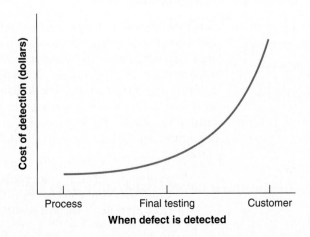

blurred vision resulting from an improperly ground lens. A test costing a few hundred thousand dollars could have detected the problem while the telescope was still on earth. Instead, NASA had to send a team of astronauts on a shuttle mission to correct the defect at a cost of more than $600 million.

Defective products can injure and even kill consumers who purchase them. Such a defect could arise from poor product design and/or nonconformance to specifications. An increasing number of states are adopting strict product liability laws that force companies to pay damages—often large amounts—to injured plaintiffs or heirs, even when they have not proved that the manufacturer was negligent in designing the product. All that needs to be shown is that a product was defective and that it caused the injury or death. For example, the Ford Motor Company, whose 23 million automatic transmissions manufactured from 1968 to 1980 were alleged to slip from park into reverse if the engine was left running, at one time faced more than 1000 lawsuits exceeding $500 million in claims for injuries and deaths supposedly caused by the transmissions. In Tacoma, Washington, a two-year-old child died from food poisoning after eating a meal at a Jack-in-the-Box restaurant. As many as 300 people were infected with the same *E. coli* bacteria that killed the boy. Sales at Jack-in-the-Box restaurants dropped 20 percent after the poisonings, and many managers and employees had to be laid off.

Litigation costs include not only legal fees but also the time and effort of employees appearing for the company in court. In addition, there is the cost of bad publicity. For instance, Procter & Gamble's Rely tampon, allegedly a cause of toxic shock syndrome, and Merrell-Dow Pharmaceuticals' Bendectin, allegedly a cause of birth defects, eventually were taken off the market by their manufacturers because of media reports. Regardless of whether the company is ultimately judged to be at fault in a court of law, the cost of litigation is enormous and the negative publicity can be damaging for a long time.

◆ IMPROVING QUALITY THROUGH TQM

Programs of employee involvement and continuous improvement are aimed at improving quality in a general sense. However, TQM often focuses on benchmarking, product and service design, process design, and purchasing.

Benchmarking

How good is the company's quality relative to that of competitors?

Benchmarking is a continuous, systematic process that measures products, services, and practices against those of industry leaders. Companies use benchmarking to understand better how outstanding companies do things so that they can improve their own operations. Typical measures used in benchmarking include cost per unit, service upsets (breakdowns) per customer, processing time per unit, customer retention rates, revenue per unit, return on investment, and customer satisfaction levels. Those involved in continuous improvement efforts rely on benchmarking to formulate goals and targets for performance. Benchmarking consists of four basic steps:

1. *Planning.* Identify the process to be benchmarked, identify the firm(s) to be used for comparison, determine the measures of process performance for analysis, and collect the data.

2. *Analysis.* Determine the gap between your firm's current performance and that of the benchmark firm(s), and identify the causes of significant gaps.
3. *Integration.* Establish goals, and obtain the support of managers who must provide the resources for accomplishing the goals.
4. *Action.* Develop cross-functional teams of those most affected by the changes, develop action plans and team assignments, implement the plans, monitor progress, and recalibrate benchmarks as improvements are made.

The benchmarking process is similar to the plan–do–check–act cycle in continuous improvement, but benchmarking focuses on setting quantitative goals for continuous improvement. *Competitive* benchmarking is based on comparisons with a direct industry competitor. *Functional* benchmarking compares areas such as administration, customer service, and sales operations with those of outstanding firms in any industry. For instance, Xerox benchmarked its distribution function against L. L. Bean's because Bean is renowned as the leading retailer in distribution efficiency and customer service. Functional comparisons can also be made in aggregate. McKinsey & Co. recently completed a functional benchmarking study of procurement which compared the performance of an average company to that of a world-class company.

Internal benchmarking involves using an organizational unit with superior performance as the benchmark for other units (Zeune, 1992). This form of benchmarking can be advantageous for firms that have several different business units or divisions. All forms of benchmarking are best applied in situations where a long-term program of continuous improvement is needed.

Product and Service Design

What factors in the operations system are causing major quality problems?

Because design changes often require changes in methods, materials, or specifications, they can increase defect rates. Change invariably increases the risk of making mistakes, so stable product and service designs can help reduce internal quality problems. If a firm needs to make design changes to remain competitive, it should carefully test new designs and redesign the product or service and/or the process with a focus on simplicity.

Effecting the two strategies involves a trade-off: Higher quality and increased competitiveness are exchanged for added time and cost. Ashton-Tate, producer of dBase software, suffered the penalties of inadequate planning and testing when it introduced its dBase IV in 1985. The program had bugs that caused it to crash even when doing simple routines, and it was issued to customers long after it had been promised. As a result, the product's U.S. market share plunged from 68 percent in 1985 to 48 percent in 1988. The loss in sales resulting from coding errors and delays could have been avoided by more thorough planning and checking during the design and testing stages. Between 1988 and 1991, dBase product developers performed extensive testing of 45,000 functions to weed out glitches. Nonetheless, profits plummeted, and in 1991 Borland International acquired Ashton-Tate.

Another dimension of quality related to product design is **reliability,** which refers to the probability that the product will be functional when used. Products often consist of a number of components that all must be operative for the product to be effective. Sometimes products can be designed with extra components (or subsystems) so that if one component fails another can be activated. For example, even though it would increase costs, Motorola is considering building redundancy such as spare transistor capacity or alternative signal paths into its microprocessor chips.

Suppose that a product has n major subsystems, each with its own reliability measure (the probability that it will operate when called upon). The reliability of each subsystem contributes to the quality of the total system; that is, the reliability of the complete product equals the product of all the reliabilities of the subsystems, or

$$r_s = (r_1)(r_2) \cdots (r_n)$$

where $\qquad r_s$ = reliability of the complete product

n = number of subsystems

r_n = reliability of the subsystem or component n

Suppose that a small portable radio designed for joggers has three major components: a motherboard with a reliability of 0.99, a housing assembly with a reliability of 0.90, and a headphone set with a reliability of 0.85. The reliability of the portable radio is

$$r_s = (0.99)(0.90)(0.85) = 0.76$$

The poor headsets and housings hurt the reliability of this product. Suppose that new designs resulted in a reliability of 0.95 for the housing and 0.90 for the headsets. Product reliability would improve to

$$r_s = (0.99)(0.95)(0.90) = 0.85$$

Manufacturers must be concerned about the quality of every component, because the product fails when any one of them fails.

Process Design

The design of the process used to produce the product or service greatly affects its quality. Managers at the First National Bank of Chicago noticed in 1985 that customers' requests for a letter-of-credit took four days to go through dozens of steps involving nine employees before a letter of credit would be issued. To improve the process and shorten the waiting time for customers, the bank trained letter-of-credit issuers to do all the tasks so that the customer could deal with just one person. In addition, customers were given the same employee each time they requested a letter. Today, First Chicago issues letters of credit in less than a day.

The purchase of new machinery can help prevent or overcome quality problems. Suppose that the design specification for the distance between two holes in a metal plate is 3.000 in. ± 0.0005 in. Suppose also that too many plates are defective; that is, the space between holes falls outside the design specification. One way to reduce the percentage of defective parts produced by the process would be to purchase new machinery with the capability of producing metal plates with holes 3.000 in. ± 0.0003 in. apart. The cost of the new machinery is the trade-off for reducing the percentage of defective parts and their cost.

One of the keys to obtaining high quality is concurrent engineering (Chapter 2), in which operations managers and designers work closely together in the initial phases of product or service design to ensure that production requirements and process capabilities are synchronized. The result is much better quality and shorter development time. NCR, an Atlanta company that makes terminals for checkout counters, used concurrent engineering to develop a new model in 22 months, or half the usual time. The terminal had 85 percent fewer parts and could be assembled in only two minutes. Quality rejects and engineering changes dropped significantly. The National Institute of Standards and Technology estimates that manufacturing firms using concurrent engineering need 30 to 70 percent less development time, require 20 to 90 percent less time to market, and produce 200 to 600 percent better quality.

Quality Function Deployment

A key to improving quality through TQM is linking the design of products or services to the processes that produce them. **Quality function deployment (QFD)** is a means of translating customer requirements into the appropriate technical requirements for each stage of product or service development and production. Bridgestone Tire and Mitsubishi Heavy Industries originated QFD in the late 1960s and early 1970s when they used quality charts that take customer requirements into account in the product design process. In 1978 Yoji Akao and Shigeru Mizuno published the first work on this subject, showing how design considerations could be "deployed" to every element of competition. Since then more than 200 U.S. companies have used the approach, including Digital Equipment, Texas Instruments, Hewlett-Packard, AT&T, ITT, Ford, Chrysler, General Motors, Procter & Gamble, Polaroid, and Deere & Company.

The core of the approach is a chart called the house of quality, which is a conceptual map for interfunctional planning and communications. Figure 4.5 on the next page shows a house of quality chart for improving the quality of a car door. The chart was constructed by answering the following six questions (Sanchez, Ramberg, Fiero, and Pignatiello, 1994).

1. *Voice of the customer.* What do our customers need and want? Customers were asked to list the attributes of car-door quality they felt were important. Customer attributes were grouped into two categories—"easy to open and close the door" and "isolation"—as shown in Fig. 4.5. The relative importance to the customer is listed as a percentage to the right of each attribute.

2. *Competitive analysis.* In terms of our customers, how well are we doing relative to our competitors? Customer perceptions of our car doors and those of our competitors for each attribute are listed on the right-hand side of the chart. For example, our car has an advantage over the other cars with respect to "no road noise," but none of the cars has an advantage regarding "stays open on a hill." The evaluations provide a place to start looking for ways to gain an advantage over the competition.

3. *Voice of the engineer.* What technical measures relate to our customers' needs? The engineering characteristics that are likely to affect one or more of the customer attributes are listed along the top of the chart. The plus signs mean that the engineers would like to increase the level of that characteristic, and the minus signs mean that the engineers would like to decrease the level. For example, our engineers would like to increase "road noise reduction" and decrease "energy to open the door."

4. *Correlations.* What are the relationships between the voice of the customer and the voice of the engineer? The nature of the relationship between customers' needs and engineering attributes needs to be specified. For example, reducing the amount of energy required to close the door will make closing the door easier, but increasing the door seal resistance will make closing the door more difficult.

FIGURE 4.5

Improving Car Door Quality

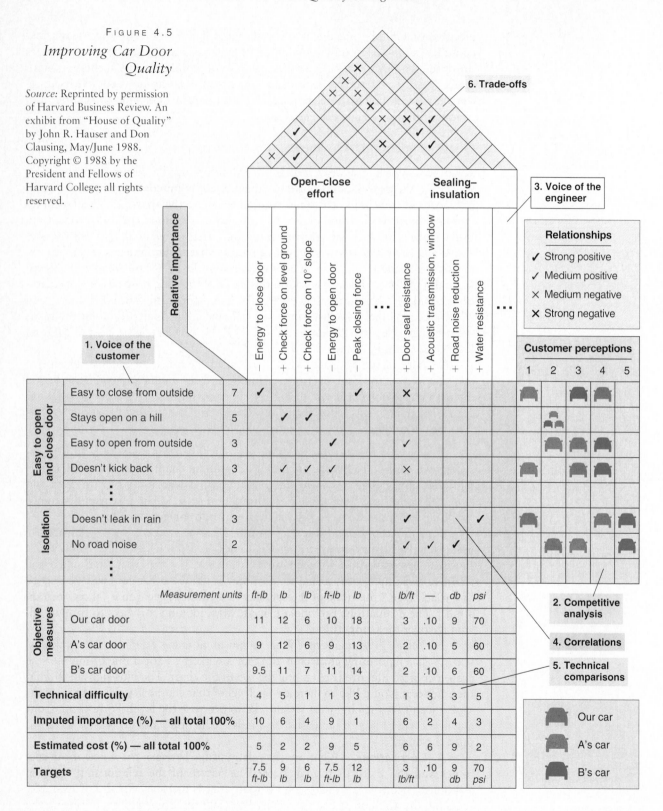

5. *Technical comparison.* How does our product or service performance compare to that of our competition? Comparing our door with those of the competition for each of the engineering characteristics allows the technical difficulty of working on each one to be assessed. For example, our door requires the greatest energy to close (11 ft-lb) and the greatest peak closing force (18 lb). A scale of 1 to 5 (where a rating of 5 means most difficult) conveys the relative technical difficulty of improving each dimension. In addition, the importance of each characteristic in responding to customer concerns can be assessed. For example, "easy to close the door from the outside" has high relative importance to customers and has a strong positive relationship with "reducing the energy to close the door." Consequently, "reducing the energy to close the door" receives the highest imputed importance (10 percentage points) of all the engineering characteristics. Estimated costs, again expressed as percentages, indicate relative importance.

Finally, in this step targets are assigned for the various engineering characteristics. Note that reducing the "energy to close the door" from 11 ft-lb to 7.5 ft-lb makes our car very competitive with the other cars. Other targets for the "open–close effort" category also were changed to improve the door.

6. *Trade-offs.* What are the potential technical trade-offs? Note that no changes were targeted in the current measures of engineering characteristics relating to the category "sealing-insulation." The reason is that those engineering characteristics and the ones included in the "open–close effort" category have some strongly negative relationships. These relationships are depicted at the top of the chart. For example, though "increasing road noise reduction" would have a strong positive impact on "no road noise," it would have a strong negative impact on "reducing the peak closing force" and "reducing energy to close the door." Because customers gave a low priority to "no road noise," no adjustments were made to "increasing road noise reduction."

The house of quality method provides a way to set targets and debate their effects on product quality. Engineering uses the data to focus on significant product design features. Marketing uses this input for determining marketing strategies. Operations uses the chart to identify the processes that are crucial to improving product quality in the eyes of the customer. As a result, the house of quality encourages interfunctional communication for the purpose of improving the quality of products and services.

Purchasing Considerations

Most businesses depend on outside suppliers for some of the materials, services, or equipment used in producing their products and services. Large companies have hundreds and even thousands of suppliers, some of which supply the same types of parts. The quality of these inputs can affect the quality of the firm's work, and purchased parts of poor quality can have a devastating effect. For example, the Ford Motor Company was forced to halt Tempo and Topaz production at its Kansas City, Missouri, and Oakville, Ontario, plants when a faulty engine part purchased from an outside supplier caused some gears in the engine to lose a few teeth during a test run. Approximately 5500 hourly workers were temporarily laid off. In addition, Ford lost about 2000 cars each day that production was stopped.

Both the buyer's approach and specification management are keys to controlling supplier quality. The firm's buyer must emphasize not only the cost and speed of delivery of the supplier, but also the quality of the product. A competent buyer will identify suppliers that offer high-quality products or services at a reasonable cost. After identifying these suppliers, the buyer should work with them to obtain essentially defect-free parts. To do so may require examining and evaluating trade-offs between receiving off-specification materials and seeking corrective action.

The specifications for purchased parts and materials must be clear and *realistic*. If specifications are drawn too tightly, the product may be uneconomical to produce or service later or too costly to produce. As a check on specifications, buyers in some companies initiate *process capability studies* for important products. These studies amount to trial runs of small product samples to ensure that all components, including the raw materials and purchased parts, work together to form a product that has the desired quality level at a reasonable cost. Analysis of study results may identify unrealistic specifications and the need for changes.

Management needs to allow sufficient time for the purchasing department to identify several low-cost, qualified suppliers and to analyze the information they submit. An unrealistic deadline can lead to poor selection based on incomplete information about supplier qualifications. In addition, improved communication between purchasing and other departments, such as engineering and quality control, is needed when those departments must provide information to assess supplier qualifications and the supplier's manufacturing process.

Tools for Improving Quality

How can areas for quality improvement be identified?

The first step in improving the quality of an operation is data collection. Data can help uncover operations requiring improvement and the extent of remedial action needed. There are seven tools for organizing and presenting data to identify areas for quality improvement: checklists, histograms and bar charts, Pareto charts, scatter diagrams, cause-and-effect diagrams, graphs, and control charts. We cover control charts as part of our discussion of statistical process control in Chapter 5. In this section we demonstrate the use of the other six to emphasize the breadth of applications possible. We conclude this section with an example showing how several of the approaches can be used together to focus on causes and remedies for a specific quality problem.

Checklists.   Data collection through the use of a checklist is often the first step in the analysis of quality problems. A **checklist** is a form used to record the frequency of occurrence of certain product or service characteristics related to quality. The characteristics may be measurable on a continuous scale (such as weight, diameter, time, or length) or on a yes-or-no basis (such as paint discoloration, odors, rude servers, or too much grease).

Histograms and Bar Charts.   The data from a checklist often can be presented succinctly and clearly with histograms or bar charts. A **histogram** summarizes data measured on a continuous scale, showing the frequency distribution of some quality characteristic (in statistical terms, the central tendency and dispersion of the data). Often the mean of the data is indicated on the histogram. A **bar chart** is a series of bars representing the frequency of occurrence of data characteristics measured on a yes-or-no basis. The bar height indicates the number of times a particular quality characteristic was observed.

Pareto Charts. When managers discover several quality problems that should be addressed, which should be attacked first? Vilfredo Pareto, a nineteenth-century Italian scientist whose statistical work focused on inequalities in data, proposed that most of the "activity" is caused by relatively few of the factors. In a restaurant quality problem, the activity could be customer complaints and the factor could be "discourteous waiter." For a manufacturer, the activity could be product defects and a factor could be "missing part." Pareto's concept, called the 80–20 rule, is that 80 percent of the activity is caused by 20 percent of the factors. By concentrating on the 20 percent of the factors (the "vital few"), managers can attack 80 percent of the quality problems.

The few vital factors can be identified with a **Pareto chart,** a bar chart organized so that the factors are plotted in decreasing order of frequency. The factors are listed along the horizontal axis. The chart has two vertical axes, the one on the left showing frequency as in a histogram and the one on the right showing the cumulative percentage of frequency. The cumulative frequency curve identifies the few vital factors that warrant managerial attention.

Scatter Diagrams. Sometimes managers suspect that a certain factor is causing a particular quality problem. A **scatter diagram** is a plot of two variables showing whether they are related. Each point on the scatter diagram represents one data observation. For example, the manager of a castings shop may suspect that casting defects are a function of the diameter of the casting. A scatter diagram could be constructed by plotting the number of defective castings found for each diameter of casting produced. After the diagram was completed, any relationship between diameter and number of defects could be observed.

Cause-and-Effect Diagrams. An important aspect of TQM is linking each aspect of quality prized by the customer to the inputs, methods, and process steps that build a particular attribute into the product. One way to identify a design problem that needs to be corrected is to develop a **cause-and-effect diagram** that relates a key quality problem to its potential causes. First developed by Kaoru Ishikawa, the diagram helps management trace customer complaints directly to the operations involved. Operations that have no bearing on a particular defect aren't shown on the diagram for that defect.

The cause-and-effect diagram sometimes is called a *fishbone diagram*. The main quality problem is labeled as the fish's "head," the major categories of potential causes as structural "bones," and the likely specific causes as "ribs." When constructing and using a cause-and-effect diagram, an analyst identifies all the major categories of potential causes for the quality problem. For example, these might be personnel, machines, materials, and process. For each major category, the analyst lists all the likely causes of the quality problem. For example, under personnel might be listed "lack of training," "poor communication," and "absenteeism." Brainstorming helps the analyst identify and properly classify all suspected causes. The analyst then systematically investigates the causes listed on the diagram for each major category, updating the chart as new causes become apparent. The process of constructing a cause-and-effect diagram calls management and worker attention to the primary factors affecting product or service quality. Example 4.1 demonstrates the use of a cause-and-effect diagram by an airline.

EXAMPLE 4.1
Analysis of Flight Departure Delays

The operations manager for Checker Board Airlines at Port Columbus International Airport noticed an increase in the number of delayed flight departures. To analyze all the possible causes of that problem, he constructed a cause-and-effect diagram, shown in Fig. 4.6. The main problem, delayed flight departures, is the "head" of the diagram. He brainstormed all possible causes with his staff and together they identified several major categories: equipment, personnel, materials, procedures, and "other factors," which are beyond managerial control. Several suspected causes were identified for each major category.

The operations manager suspected that most of the flight delays were caused by problems with materials. Consequently, he had food service, fueling, and baggage handling operations examined. He learned that there weren't enough tow trucks for the baggage transfer operations and that planes were delayed waiting for baggage from connecting flights.

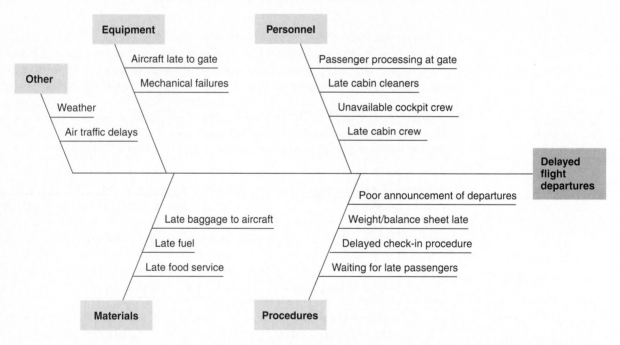

FIGURE 4.6

Cause-and-Effect Diagram for Flight Departure Delays

Source: Adapted from D. Daryl Wyckoff, "New Tools for Achieving Service Quality," *The Cornell Hotel and Restaurant Administration Quarterly,* November 1984, p. 89. © 1984 Cornell H.R.A. Quarterly. Used by permission. All rights reserved.

Graphs.   **Graphs** represent data in a variety of pictorial formats, such as line graphs and pie charts. *Line graphs* represent data sequentially with data points connected by line segments to highlight trends in the data. Line graphs are used in control charts (Chapter 5) and forecasting (Chapter 11). Pie charts represent quality factors as slices of a pie; the size of each slice is in proportion to the number of occurrences of the factor. Pie charts are useful for showing data from a group of factors that can be represented as percentages totaling 100 percent.

Data Snooping.   Each of the tools for improving quality may be used independently, but the power of these tools is greatest when they are used in conjunction with each other. In solving a quality problem, managers often must act as detectives, sifting data to clarify the issues involved and deducing the causes. We call this process *data snooping.* Example 4.2 demonstrates how the tools can be used for data snooping.

EXAMPLE 4.2

*Identifying Causes
of Poor Headliner
Quality*

The Wellington Fiber Board Company produces headliners, the fiberglass components that form the inner roof of passenger cars. Figure 4.7 shows the sequential application of several tools for improving quality.

Step 1. A checklist of different types of defects was constructed from last month's production records.

Step 2. A Pareto chart prepared from the checklist data indicated that broken fiber board accounted for 72 percent of the quality defects. The manager decided to dig further into the problem of broken fiber board.

Step 3. A cause-and-effect chart for broken fiber board identified several potential causes for the problem. The one strongly suspected by the manager was employee training.

FIGURE 4.7

*Application of the
Tools for Improving
Quality*

Step 4. The manager reorganized the production reports according to shift because the personnel on the three shifts had varied amounts of experience. A bar chart indicated that the second shift, with the least experienced work force, had most of the defects. Further investigation revealed that workers were not using proper procedures for stacking the fiber boards after the press operation, causing cracking and chipping.

Though the second shift was not responsible for all the defects, finding the source of many defects enabled the manager to improve the quality of her operations.

Step 1 Checklist

Headliner defects

Defect type	Tally	Total
A. Tears in fabric	////	4
B. Discolored fabric	///	3
C. Broken fiber board	JHT JHT JHT JHT JHT JHT JHT /	36
D. Ragged edges	JHT //	7
	Total	50

Step 2 Pareto Chart

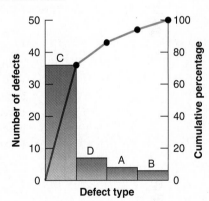

Step 3 Cause-and-Effect Diagram

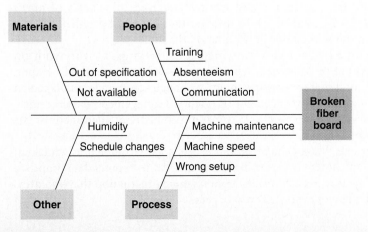

Step 4 Bar Chart

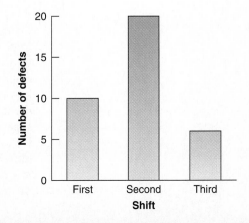

◆ PRESCRIPTIONS FOR EXCELLENCE IN QUALITY

How can a company meet the quality levels dictated by its competitive strategies?

Several individuals have strongly influenced companies in both manufacturing and service sectors to emphasize quality. Initially, their ideas found greater acceptance in Japan than in the United States. However, after having been thrashed in the marketplace by their international competitors, U.S. firms sought the help of these same consultants in the area of quality management.

W. Edwards Deming: Quality Is Management's Responsibility

W. Edwards Deming, considered to be the father of quality control in Japan, summarized the far-reaching, long-lasting effects of improving quality with his five-step chain reaction:

- first, costs decline because of less rework, fewer mistakes, fewer delays, and better use of time and materials, which
- results in improved productivity, which
- increases market share because of better quality and prices, which
- increases profitability, allowing the company to stay in business, which
- results in more jobs.

Deming created a list of 14 points that summarize his philosophy for achieving greater quality (Deming, 1982). His fundamental idea is that management is responsible for sending the message that quality is valued.

1. Create constancy of purpose toward improving the product or service. Decide to whom top management is responsible.
2. Adopt a new philosophy: The organization can no longer live with defective materials, poor workmanship, and unacceptable delays and mistakes. Management should embrace the philosophy that mistakes, defects, and unsuitable materials are no longer acceptable and should be eliminated.
3. Cease dependence on mass inspections. Require statistical evidence that the causes of defects have been eliminated, not just detected.
4. End the practice of buying products and services on the basis of price alone. Instead, use measures of quality along with price to make decisions. Eliminate suppliers that cannot provide statistical evidence of good quality.
5. Find problems and continually strive to improve all aspects of operations. Use statistical methods to uncover the sources of problems.
6. Institute modern methods of training on the job.
7. Improve supervision. Allow more time for supervisors to work with employees and to provide them with the tools to do their jobs. The responsibility of first-line supervisors must be changed from mere management by the numbers to management of quality. Management should remove the barriers to improved quality and productivity identified by the supervisors.
8. Drive out fear. Management should create an environment in which employees will not fear reporting problems or recommending improvements. This fear usually results from imagined retaliation that will affect the reporting worker or fellow workers.

9. Break down barriers between departments. Use the concepts of employee involvement by organizing teams of representatives from different departments to address particular problems of quality and productivity.
10. Eliminate numerical goals and slogans if the work force has not been provided with the means to achieve them.
11. Eliminate work standards (see Chapter 6) that merely prescribe numerical quotas and do not include measures of quality.
12. Remove barriers that stand between employees and their pride of workmanship.
13. Institute a vigorous program of education and retraining employees in new skills.
14. Structure management to accomplish the transformation represented by the preceding 13 points.

Deming developed his list in the years following World War II, when he went to Japan to develop a census of the war-torn nation. The Japanese were so impressed with his philosophy that in 1951 the Union of Japanese Scientists and Engineers instituted the **Deming Prize,** which is an annual award to firms demonstrating excellence in quality. Two objectives of the prize are to (1) disseminate statistical process control techniques throughout Japanese industry and (2) increase the public's awareness of quality management goals and techniques. Among Deming's U.S. clients, the most notable success story is that of the Ford Motor Company, which in the 1980s drastically improved the quality of its products to rival its Japanese competitors.

Management must develop the proper tools to manage quality—not only machines or hand tools, but also statistical methods to control processes or incoming materials and to help identify the sources of quality problems. Deming believed that statistical methods are the backbone of management's arsenal of tools for managing quality. We explore some of these methods in Chapter 5.

Joseph M. Juran: A Quality Trilogy

Juran, like Deming, pioneered the education of the Japanese in quality management and significantly affected the staggering quality improvement demonstrated by Japanese manufacturers during the past 40 years. Like Deming, he was not discovered by U.S. business until the early 1980s. Juran believes that over 80 percent of quality defects are caused by factors controllable by management. Consequently, management continually needs to seek improvements through sound quality management, which Juran defines as a trilogy of quality planning, control, and improvement.

Quality planning involves selecting the proper quality level and reliability and linking product and service design to process design to achieve the quality desired. Quality control compares products or services to standards and acts to correct discrepancies. This part of the trilogy, treated in detail in Chapter 5, provides the information necessary to identify needed improvements. Juran's final prescription is to get into the habit of making continuous improvements in quality. His recommendation for areas with chronic quality problems is to convince others that a breakthrough solution is needed and then analyze alternatives to the problem, select an alternative, implement it, and put controls in place to monitor the results. Juran believes that continuous improvement, hands-on management, and training are fundamental to achieving excellence in quality.

Phillip B. Crosby: Quality Is Free

Phillip B. Crosby, a corporate vice-president and director of quality at ITT for 14 years, gained a lot of attention when he published his book *Quality Is Free* in 1979. The conventional wisdom at the time was that each level of quality had some price. For example, reducing the level of defects from 8 percent to 3 percent would cost a lot. The basis for this belief was the notion that improvements in quality require the purchase of improved machines, better materials, or more skilled labor. In addition to the loss of materials to scrap, Crosby points out that poor quality has hidden costs: increased labor and machine hours, increased machine failures and downtime, customer delivery delays and lost future sales, and even increased warranty costs. Crosby believes that these costs typically dwarf the costs of the machines, materials, and training needed to foster high quality. The savings created by the reduction of hidden costs can offset the costs incurred to create the proper environment.

Crosby, now a consultant, advocates a goal of zero defects. In his view, to have any other goal is essentially a commitment to producing a certain amount of defective material. Continuous improvement should be the means that management uses to achieve zero defects.

◆ MALCOLM BALDRIGE NATIONAL QUALITY AWARD

All organizations will have to produce high-quality products and services if they are to be competitive in the years ahead. To emphasize that point, in August 1987, Congress signed into law the Malcolm Baldrige National Quality Improvement Act, creating the **Malcolm Baldrige National Quality Award.** Named for the late secretary of commerce, who was a strong proponent of enhancing quality as a means of reducing the trade deficit, the award promotes, recognizes, and publicizes quality strategies and achievements.

A maximum of two awards can be made each year in each of three categories: large manufacturers, large service companies, and small businesses in either manufacturing or services. As of 1992, 17 companies had received this prestigious award: 10 manufacturing firms, 3 service firms, and 4 small businesses. The more familiar firms include Motorola, IBM, Xerox, AT&T, Federal Express, and the Ritz-Carlton Hotel.

The application and four-stage review process for the Baldrige award is rigorous, but often the process helps companies define what quality means for them. The seven major criteria for the award are

1. leadership in creating and sustaining a visible quality culture,
2. effectiveness in collecting and analyzing information for quality improvement and planning,
3. effectiveness in integrating quality requirements into the strategic planning process,
4. success in utilizing the full potential of the work force for quality improvement,
5. effectiveness of the company's systems for assuring quality control,
6. results of quality achievement and improvement, as demonstrated by quantitative measures, and

President Ronald Reagan presented the first Malcolm Baldrige National Quality Awards at the White House in 1988. Pictured (from left) are Robert Glavin, CEO of Motorola; John Marous, CEO of Westinghouse; Arden Simms, CEO of Globe Metallurgical; Reagan; and Secretary of Commerce C. William Verity.

7. effectiveness of customer satisfaction systems to determine customer requirements.

Customer satisfaction underpins these seven criteria.

The Baldrige award has focused attention on the importance of quality and the operations factors that must be improved to achieve excellence. Millions of copies of the criteria have been mailed to organizations that have no intention of applying for the award; the guidelines have changed the thinking of many managers, who then have improved their operations. Organizations that applied for the award found that they received benefits even if they did not win. The main benefit is that they learned about their organization's strengths and weaknesses—and came up with ways to improve operations. Further testimony to the impact of this award is that 11 states and several foreign countries have used its guidelines as a model for their own awards. The Malcolm Baldrige National Quality Award is an important step in promoting the cause of quality in the United States and raising the awareness of good quality practice in the eyes of the public.

◆ INTERNATIONAL QUALITY STANDARDS

From a quality perspective, how can an organization prepare to do business in foreign markets?

If each country had its own set of standards, companies selling in international markets would have difficulty complying with quality documentation standards in the countries where they did business. To overcome this problem, the International Organization for Standardization devised a set of standards called ISO 9000 for companies doing business in the European Community.

What Is ISO 9000?

ISO 9000 is a set of standards governing the requirements for documentation of a quality program. Companies become certified by proving to a qualified external examiner that they have complied with all the requirements. Once certified, companies are listed in a directory so that potential customers can see which companies have been certified and to what level. Compliance with ISO 9000 standards says nothing about the actual quality of a product. Rather, it indicates to customers that companies can provide documentation to support whatever claims they make about quality.

ISO 9000 actually consists of five documents: ISO 9000–9004. ISO 9000 is an overview document, which provides guidelines for selection and use of the other standards. ISO 9001 is a standard that focuses on 20 aspects of a quality program for companies that design, produce, install, and service products. These aspects include management responsibility, quality system documentation, purchasing, product design, inspection, training, and corrective action. It is the most comprehensive and difficult standard to attain. ISO 9002 covers the same areas as ISO 9001 for companies that produce to the customer's designs or have their design and service activities at another location. ISO 9003 is the most limited in scope and addresses only the production process. ISO 9004 contains guidelines for interpreting the other standards.

Benefits of ISO 9000 Certification

Going through the certification process can take as long as 18 months and involve many hours of management and employee time. For example, ABB Process Automation, Inc., a manufacturer of control systems for pulp, paper, and chemical producers, spent 25,000 labor hours over nine months and $1.2 million, including a $200,000 audit fee, to achieve ISO 9001 certification. What are the benefits? The external benefits come from the potential sales advantage that companies in compliance have. Companies looking for a supplier will be more likely to select a company that has demonstrated compliance with ISO 9000 standards, all other factors being equal. Consequently, more and more U.S. firms are seeking certification to gain a competitive advantage over their rivals. As of 1992, only about 400 companies in the United States and 48 in Japan had achieved certification, whereas more than 20,000 European companies had been certified. As of 1994, certification in ISO 9000 was not a requirement for doing business in most industries and countries in Europe. However many managers of companies wanting to do business in Europe believe that certification is necessary because their competitors are seeking it.

Internal benefits relate directly to the company's TQM program. The Foxboro Company, which in 1991 became one of the first U.S. companies to be certified, develops, manufactures, engineers, and integrates control systems, analytical instruments, and sensing and control devices for the process industries. Certification in ISO 9001 forced the company to analyze and document its procedures, which is necessary for implementing continuous improvement, employee involvement, and similar programs. The benefits gained from the TQM and ISO certification processes were in four areas:

- *Delivery schedules.*   Delivery in 1992 was 98 percent on time, whereas in 1991 it was only 85 percent.

- *Inventory reduction.*   Inventories went down by about $40 million.

- *Materials reductions.*   Through team approaches, materials costs were reduced by 5 percent across the company, or by about $4 million.

- *Employee involvement.*   Employees noted improved communication and participation in decisions.

As demonstrated by the Foxboro example, the guidelines and requirements contained in the ISO standards provide companies with guidance in starting the TQM journey.

CHAPTER REVIEW

Solved Problem 1

Kathryn Chou is experiencing high repair costs for her snack vending machines. She suspects that the machines are being vandalized by customers who are irate because of low vending machine reliability. For the machines to work properly, all of the following must occur.

Subsystem	Reliability
Vending machine plugged in to power supply	0.97
Coins and bills read accurately	0.92
Customer pushes button matching selection	0.98
Vending machine is properly filled	0.98
Machine actually releases the product	0.85

What is the reliability of the vending operation?

Solution   The reliability of the system is the simultaneous occurrence of independent events expressed by the formula

$$r_s = (r_1)(r_2) \cdots (r_n)$$

Substituting $r_1 = 0.97$, $r_2 = 0.92$, ..., yields

$$r_s = (0.97)(0.92)(0.98)(0.98)(0.85)$$

$$= 0.7285, \text{ or about } 73\% \text{ reliability}$$

Solved Problem 2

Vera Johnson and Merris Williams manufacture vanishing cream. The following are the operations and reliabilities of their packaging operation.

Operation	Reliability
Mix	0.99
Fill	0.98
Cap	0.99
Label	0.97

Johnson and Williams ask their spouses to keep track of and analyze reported defects. They find the following.

Defect	Frequency
Lumps of unmixed product	7
Over- or underfilled jars	18
Jar lids didn't seal	6
Labels rumpled or missing	29
Total	60

a. What is the reliability of the packaging operation?
b. Draw a Pareto chart to identify the vital defects.

Solution   a. The formula is

$$r_s = (r_1)(r_2) \cdots (r_n)$$

Substituting $r_1 = 0.99$, $r_2 = 0.98$, . . . , gives

$$r_s = (0.99)(0.98)(0.99)(0.97)$$

$$= 0.9317, \text{ or about 93\% reliability}$$

Defective labels account for 48.33% of the total number of defects:

$$\frac{29}{60} \times 100\% = 48.33\%$$

Improperly filled jars account for 30% of the total number of defects:

$$\frac{18}{60} \times 100\% = 30.00\%$$

The cumulative percentage for the two most frequent defects is

$$48.33\% + 30.00\% = 78.33\%$$

Lumps represent $\dfrac{7}{60} \times 100\% = 11.67\%$ of defects; the cumulative percentage is

$$78.33\% + 11.67\% = 90.00\%$$

Defective seals represent $\dfrac{6}{60} \times 100\% = 10\%$ of defects; the cumulative percentage is

$$10\% + 90\% = 100.00\%$$

b. The Pareto chart is shown in Fig. 4.8.

FIGURE 4.8

Pareto Chart

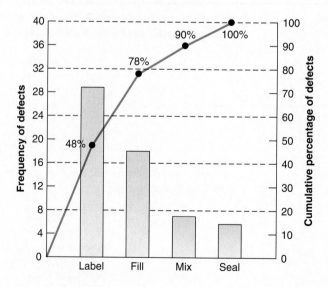

Formula Review

1. The reliability of a product: $r_s = (r_1)(r_2) \cdots (r_n)$

Chapter Highlights

- Total quality management stresses three principles: a customer-driven focus, employee involvement, and continuous improvements in quality.
- The consumer's view of quality may be defined in a variety of ways. The customer may make a quantitative judgment about whether a product or service meets specified design characteristics. In other situations, qualitative judgments about value, fitness for the customer's intended use, product or service support, and aesthetics may take on greater importance. One TQM responsibility of marketing is to listen to customers and report changing perceptions of quality.
- Quality can be used as a competitive weapon. High-performance design and consistent quality are competitive priorities associated with quality. World-class competition requires businesses to produce quality products or services efficiently.
- Responsibility for quality is shared by all employees in the organization. Employee involvement programs include leadership in changing organizational culture, individual development, awards and incentives, and teamwork. Three types of work teams are problem-solving teams, special-purpose teams, and self-managing teams.
- Managers need to develop skills for teaching their subordinates. The best improvement projects are those that emanate from the employees themselves. Employee-related strategies for improving quality include employee training, adequate monetary incentives, and quality circles.
- Employee empowerment results in flatter organizational hierarchies. This approach may be resisted by supervisors who would be displaced, by authoritarian managers, and by line employees reluctant to take on higher or more varied responsibilities.
- Continuous improvement involves identifying benchmarks of excellent practice and instilling a sense of ownership so that employees will continually identify changes and process improvements that should be made.
- Quality management is important because of its impact on market share, price, and profits and because of the costs of poor quality. The four major categories of costs associated with quality management are prevention, appraisal, internal failure, and external failure. If quality is to be improved, prevention costs must increase. Appraisal, internal failure, and external failure costs all decrease as quality is improved through preventive measures.
- Benchmarking is a comparative measure. It is used to establish goals for continuous improvement. Forms of benchmarking include competitive, functional, and internal.
- Concurrent engineering results in a better match between product design and production process capabilities. The higher quality and shorter product development times associated with concurrent engineering are competitive advantages.
- Quality improvement requires close cooperation among functions (design, operations, marketing, purchasing, and others). Quality function deployment (QFD) uses a chart called the "house of quality" to encourage interfunctional planning and communication.
- Keys to controlling supplier quality are the buyer's approach and specification management. The buyer must consider quality, delivery, and cost. Specifications must be clear and realistic. Improved communication between purchasing and other departments is needed.
- Approaches to organizing and presenting quality improvement data include checklists, histograms and bar charts, Pareto charts, scatter diagrams, cause-and-effect diagrams, graphs, and control charts.
- ISO 9000 is a set of quality standards for companies doing business in the European Community.

Key Terms

Study Questions

1. Your company makes Christmas tree lights. Give an example for each of the five ways your customers might define quality.

2. You own a small company that prepares income tax returns. How would you define quality in this situation?

3. A professor is considering several textbooks for a college course in operations management. Which of the definitions of quality are likely to be important in her decision? Can you judge a book by its cover? Why or why not?

4. Which responsibilities of the marketing function are essential to total quality management? In other words, how can marketing affect customers' definitions of quality? How can marketing contribute to continuous quality improvement?

5. Explain why poor quality can be expensive. How can quality be free?

6. As a manager, what can you do to help employees improve quality?

7. In which ways can product design affect quality? Process design? What can be done to link product design to process design?

8. A manufacturer noted for reliable automobiles included this slogan in advertisements: "Honda. We make it simple." How does simplicity relate to reliability?

9. Suppose that you are the purchasing manager of a company that buys raw materials from hundreds of suppliers, some of which supply the same raw materials. You are convinced that the quality of these materials, as measured by conformance to specifications, can be improved. What can you do in your relationships with suppliers to improve the quality of the raw materials your company needs? Describe how the engineering group's product designs and policies and performance measures set by top management affect your relationships with suppliers.

10. What are the benefits and costs of ISO 9000 certification?

11. What cultural changes would be required to implement Deming's 14 points to achieve greater quality in a college education?

12. What is the essence of the total quality management (TQM) concept? What do you think are the major impediments to TQM in the United States?

13. Use a cause-and-effect diagram to display and organize the potential causes of a problem such as "students arrive late to class." To get started, use the four categories of problem sources called the four M's: materials, machines, methods (or process), and person (originally man).

Problems

1. Contented Airlines (CA) is reluctant to begin service at the new Delayed Indefinitely Airport (DIA) until the automated baggage handling system can transport luggage to the correct location with at least 95 percent reliability. Lower reliability will result in damage to CA's reputation for quality service. The baggage system will not deliver to the right location if any of the following subsystems fail.

Subsystem	Reliability
Power supply	70.0% surge free
Scanner reading	99.8% accurate
Computer software	98.2% glitch free
Mechanical systems	97.5% jam free
Operators	96.0% error free

a. What is the reliability of the luggage system?

b. When the passenger shuttle system operates, power surges trip the motors on the baggage system. Each of the luggage system motors must then be manually reset. Installing surge protectors increases power supply reliability to 99.9 percent. What is the reliability of the luggage system?

c. What could be done to improve the reliability of the luggage system?

2. A semiconductor has three components. Component 1 has a reliability of 0.98; component 2, 0.95; and component 3, 0.85. What is the reliability of the semiconductor?

3. A space launch vehicle has 100 subsystems that must all check out "A-okay" before the rocket can be launched. If each of the subsystems has a reliability of 99%, what is the probability that the rocket will launch on schedule?

4. Each semester at Confucius University begins in chaos. Long lines of confused students form outside departmental offices. Students are not getting into the right class at the right place at the right time.

Problem	Probability
Students register for wrong course	0.05
Classroom assignment conflict	0.06
Class roster error occurs	0.01
Students misread class schedule	0.04
Error in published class schedule	0.01
Class canceled	0.03

On average, each student registers for five courses. What is the reliability of the registration process? In other words, what are the chances that a student will show up at the right place at the right time for the right class for all five courses?

5. The manager of Checkers Pizza collects data concerning customer complaints about delivery. Pizza is arriving late, or the wrong pizza is being delivered.

Problem	Frequency
Topping stuck to box lid	17
Pizza is late	35
Wrong topping/combination	9
Wrong style of crust	6
Wrong size	4
Pizza is partially eaten	3
Pizza never showed up	6

a. Use a Pareto chart to identify the "few vital" delivery problems.
b. Use a cause-and-effect diagram to identify potential causes of late pizza delivery.

6. Skosh, Smidgeon, and Tadd (SST) is a short-haul household furniture moving company. SST's labor force, selected from the local community college football team, is temporary and part-time. SST is concerned with recent complaints, as tabulated on the following tally sheet.

Complaint	Tally
Broken glass	///// ///// ///
Delivered to wrong address	///
Furniture rubbed together while on truck	///// ///// ///// //
Late delivery	///// //
Late arrival for pickup	///// ///// ///// /
Missing items	///// /////
Nicks and scratches from rough handling	///// ///// ///// ///// ///// ///
Soiled upholstery	///// /

a. Draw a bar chart and a Pareto chart to identify the most serious moving problems.
b. Use a cause-and-effect diagram to identify potential causes of complaints.

7. Titus Canby, manager of the Golden Valley Bank credit authorization department, recently noticed that a major competitor was advertising that applications for equity loans could be approved within two working days. As fast credit approval was a competitive priority, Canby wanted to see how well his department was doing relative to the competitor's. Golden Valley stamps each application with the date and time it is received and again when a decision is made. A total of 104 applications were received in March. The time required for each decision, rounded to the nearest hour, is shown in the table. Golden Valley's employees work 8 hours per day.

Decision Process Time	Frequency
7–9 hours	5
10–12 hours	12
13–15 hours	38
16–18 hours	19
19–21 hours	22
22–24 hours	0
25–27 hours	8
Total	104

a. Draw a histogram for these data.
b. Analyze the data. How is Golden Valley Bank doing with regard to this competitive priority?

8. Last year, the manager of the service department at North Woods Lincoln–Mercury instituted a customer opinion program to find out how to improve service. One week after service on a vehicle was performed, his assistant would call the customer to find out whether the work had been done satisfactorily and how service could be improved. After a year of gathering data, the assistant discovered that the complaints could be grouped into the following five categories.

Complaint	Frequency
Unfriendly atmosphere	7
Long wait for service	10
Price too high	19
Incorrect bill	5
Need to return to correct problem	49
Total	90

a. Draw a bar chart and a Pareto chart to identify the significant service problems.
b. Use a cause-and-effect diagram to identify potential causes of complaints.

9. Wellington Fiber Board makes roof liners for the automotive industry. The manufacturing manager is concerned about product quality. She suspects that one particular defect, tears in the fabric, is related to production run size. An assistant gathers the following data from production records.

Run	Size	Defects (%)	Run	Size	Defects (%)
1	1000	3.5	11	6500	1.5
2	4100	3.8	12	1000	5.5
3	2000	5.5	13	7000	1.0
4	6000	1.9	14	3000	4.5
5	6800	2.0	15	2200	4.2
6	3000	3.2	16	1800	6.0
7	2000	3.8	17	5400	2.0
8	1200	4.2	18	5800	2.0
9	5000	3.8	19	1000	6.2
10	3800	3.0	20	1500	7.0

a. Draw a scatter diagram for these data.

b. Does there appear to be a relationship between run size and percent defects? What implications does this have for Wellington's business?

10. University City enjoys two business seasons. During the school year, the economy is dominated by providing housing and other services for students. In the summer, the students leave and tourists overrun the town. For a long time the Lucky Star restaurant has hired university students to be waiters and waitresses. However, finding students to work during the summer always has been difficult. This year the owner hired servers from a local part-time employment agency to cover the summer months, and customer complaints seemed to be a problem.

Month	Last Year's Complaints	This Year's Complaints
January	3	4
February	5	3
March	4	6
April	5	3
May	5	4
June	4	8
July	6	14
August	5	13
September	6	8
October	4	2
November	2	4
December	3	3

a. Draw a line graph of the customer complaints by month for the past year and the year before.

b. Does there appear to be a relationship between complaints and student employment? Explain.

11. The operations manager for Checker Board Airlines at Port Columbus International Airport noticed an increase in the number of delayed flight departures. She brainstormed possible causes with her staff:

- Aircraft late to gate
- Acceptance of late passengers
- Passengers arrive late at gate
- Passenger processing delays at gate
- Late baggage to aircraft
- Other late personnel or unavailable items
- Mechanical failures

Draw a cause-and-effect diagram to organize the possible causes of delayed flight departures into the following major categories: equipment, personnel, material, procedures, and "other factors" beyond managerial control. Provide a detailed set of causes for each major cause identified by the operations manager, and incorporate them in your cause-and-effect diagram.

CASE

Cranston Nissan

Steve Jackson, General Manager of Cranston Nissan, slowly sifted through his usual Monday morning stack of mail. The following letter was one he would not soon forget.

Dear Mr. Jackson:

I am writing this letter so that you will be aware of a nightmare I experienced recently regarding the repair of my 300ZX in your body shop and subsequently in your service department. I will detail the events in chronological order.

August 28

I dropped the car off for repair of rust damage in the following areas:

> Roof—along the top of the windshield area
> Left rocker panel—under driver's door
> Left quarter panel—near end of bumper
> Rear body panel—under license plate

I was told it would take three or four days.

September 1

I called to inquire about the status of the car, since this was the fifth day the car was in the shop. I was told that I could pick up the car anytime after 2 P.M. My wife and I arrived at 5 P.M. The car was still not ready. In the meantime, I paid the bill of $443.17 and waited. At 6 P.M. the car was driven up dripping wet (presumably from a wash to make it look good). I got into the car and noticed the courtesy light in the driver's door would not turn off when the door was closed. I asked for help, and Jim Boyd, body shop manager, could not figure out what was wrong. His solution was to remove the bulb and have me return after the Labor Day holiday to have the mechanic look at it. I agreed and began to drive off. However, the voice warning, "Left door is open," repeatedly sounded. Without leaving the premises I returned to Mr. Boyd, advising him to retain the car until it was fixed—there was no way I could drive the car with that repeated recording. Mr. Boyd then suggested I call back the next day (Saturday) to see if the mechanic could find the problem. I must emphasize, I brought the car to the body shop on August 28 in perfect mechanical working condition—the repair work was for body rust. This point will become important as the story unfolds.

September 2
I called Jim Boyd at 10:30 A.M. and was told that the car had not been looked at yet. He promised to call back before the shop closed for the holiday, but he never did. I later learned that he did not call because "there was nothing to report." The car sat in the shop Saturday, Sunday, and Monday.

September 5
I called Jim Boyd to check on the status of the car. It was 4 P.M., and Mr. Boyd told me nothing had been done, but that it should be ready by the next day. At this point it was becoming obvious that my car did not have priority in the service department.

September 6
I called Jim Boyd again (about 4 P.M.) and was told that work had halted on the car because the service department needed authorization and they didn't know how much it would run. At the hint that I would have to pay for this mess I became very upset and demanded that the car be brought immediately to the mechanical condition it was in when it was dropped off on August 28. At this point Ted Simon, service department manager, was summoned, and he assured me that if the problem was caused by some action of the body shop, I would not be financially responsible. I had not driven the car since I dropped it off, and I could not fathom the evidence anyone could produce to prove otherwise.

September 7
Again late in the day, I called Mr. Simon, who said that Larry (in the service department) knew about the problem and switched me over to him. Larry said that they had narrowed it down to a wire that passed several spots where body work was performed. He said the work was very time consuming and that the car should be ready sometime tomorrow.

September 8
I called Mr. Simon to check on the status of the car once more. He told me that the wiring problem was fixed, but now the speedometer didn't work. The short in the wires was caused by the body work. Larry got on the phone and said I could pick up the car, but they would send the car out to a subcontractor on Monday to repair the speedometer. He said that when the mechanic test-drove the car he noticed the speedometer pinned itself at the top end, and Larry thought that someone must have done something while searching for the other problem. I asked him if there would be charges for this and he said there would not. My wife and I arrived to pick up the car at 5 P.M. I clarified the next steps with Larry and was again assured that the speedometer would be repaired at no charge to me.

The car was brought to me, and as I walked up to it I noticed that the rubber molding beneath the driver's door was hanging down. I asked for some help, and Mr. Simon came out to look at it. He said it must have been left that

way after the search process for the bad wire. He took the car back into the shop to screw it on. When it finally came out again, he said that he would replace the molding because it was actually damaged.

When I arrived home, I discovered that the anti-theft light on the dash would not stop blinking when the doors were closed. Attempting to activate the security system did not help. The only way I could get the light to stop flashing was to remove the fuse. In other words, now my security system was damaged. Needless to say, I was very upset.

September 11
On Sunday evening I dropped off the car and left a note with my keys in the "early bird" slot. The note listed the two items that needed to be done from the agreement of last Friday—the molding and the speedometer. In addition, I mentioned the security system problem and suggested that "somebody must have forgotten to hook something back up while looking for the wire problem." On Monday I received a call from someone in the service department (I think his name was John), who said that the problem in the security system was in two places—the hatchback lock and "some wires in the driver's door." The lock would cost me $76, and the cost for the rest was unknown. The verbal estimate was for a total of $110. I asked him why he did not consider this problem a derivative of the other problems. He said that both the body shop and the mechanic who worked on the wire problem said they could see no way that they could have caused this to happen.

I told the fellow on the phone to forget fixing the security system because I was not going to pay for it. At this point I just wanted the car back home, thinking I could address the problem later with someone such as yourself. I told him to have the speedometer fixed and again asked about charges for it. I was assured there would be none.

September 13
The service department called to say I could pick up the car anytime before 8 P.M. He also said that the molding had to be ordered because it was not in stock. The need for the part was known on September 8, and NOW the part must be ordered. This will cause me another trip to the shop.

When I went to the service department to pick up the car, I was presented a bill for $126. I asked what the bill was for, and I was shown an itemized list that included speedometer repair and searching for the security problem. I said my understanding was that there would be no charges. Somebody at the service desk was apprised of the problem and released the car to me with the understanding that the service manager would review the situation the next day.

My car was brought around to me by the same person who brought it to me September 8. As I got into the driver's seat, I noticed there was no rear view mirror—it was lying in the passenger's seat, broken off from its mounting. I was too shocked to even get mad. I got out of the car and

asked how something like this could happen without anyone noticing. Jim Boyd said someone probably did not
want to own up to it. He requisitioned a part and repaired
the mirror mounting.

Mr. Jackson, I realize this is a long letter, but I have
been so frustrated and upset over the past three weeks that
I had to be sure that you understood the basis for that
frustration. I am hoping you can look into this matter and
let me know what you think.

Sincerely,

Sam Monahan
555 South Main, Turnerville

Questions

Answer the following questions from the perspective of
TQM.

1. Categorize the quality problems in this case.
2. What are the probable causes of so many mishaps?
3. Prepare a cause-and-effect chart for "failure to remedy
   repair problem to customer satisfaction."
4. What specific actions should Jackson take
   immediately? What should some of his longer-term
   goals be?

Selected References

Aubrey, C. A., and L. A. Eldridge. "Banking on High Quality."
   Quality Progress, vol. 14, no. 12 (December 1981), pp. 14–19.

Collier, David A., *The Service Quality Solution*. New York: Irwin
   Professional Publishing; Milwaukee: ASQC Quality Press,
   1994.

"The Competitive Superiority Report," Gary Zuene, editor,
   Columbus, Ohio, 1992.

Crosby, Phillip B. *Quality Is Free*. New York: McGraw-Hill,
   1979.

Davis, Deborah. "Victory Memorial Solves Operations Problems
   with TQM." *Target*, vol. 9, no. 6 (November–December 1993),
   pp. 14–19.

Deming, W. Edwards. "Improvement of Quality and Productivity
   Through Action by Management." *National Productivity Review*, vol. 1, no. 1 (Winter 1981–1982), pp. 12–22.

Deming, W. Edwards. *Out of the Crisis*. Cambridge, Mass.: Massachusetts Institute of Technology Center for Advanced Engineering Study, 1986.

Feigenbaum, A. V. *Total Quality Control: Engineering and Management*, 3rd ed. New York: McGraw-Hill, 1983.

Garvin, David A. "How the Baldrige Award Really Works." Harvard Business Review (November–December 1991), pp. 80–93.

Garvin, David A. "Quality on the Line." *Harvard Business Review* (September–October 1983), pp. 65–75.

Hauser, John R., and Don Clausing. "The House of Quality."
   Harvard Business Review (May–June 1988), pp. 63–73.

Heskett, James L., W. Earl Sasser, Jr., and Christopher W. L. Hart.
   Service Breakthroughs: Changing the Rules of the Game. New
   York: The Free Press, 1990.

Hostage, G. M. "Quality Control in a Service Business." *Harvard
   Business Review* (July–August 1975), pp. 89–106.

Ishikawa, Kaoru. *Guide to Quality Control*. Tokyo: Asian Productivity Organization, 1972.

Juran, J. M., and Frank Gryna, Jr. *Quality Planning and Analysis,*
   2nd ed. New York: McGraw-Hill, 1980.

Kalinosky, Ian S., "The Total Quality System—Going Beyond ISO
   9000." *Quality Progress* (June 1990), pp. 50–53.

Katzenbach, Jon R., and Douglas K. Smith. "The Discipline of
   Teams." *Harvard Business Review* (March–April 1993), pp.
   111–120.

"The Payoff from Teamwork," *Business Week*, July 10, 1989,
   p. 58.

"Quality," *Business Week*, November 30, 1992, pp. 66–72.

Rabbitt, John T., and Peter A. Bergh. *The ISO 9000 Book*. White
   Plains, N.Y.: Quality Resources, 1993.

Reddy, Jack, and Abe Berger. "Three Essentials of Product Quality." *Harvard Business Review* (July–August 1983), pp.
   153–159.

Sanchez, S. M., J. S. Ramberg, J. Fiero, and J. J. Pignatiello, Jr.
   "Quality by Design." In *Concurrent Engineering*, A. Kusiak,
   editor. New York: John Wiley & Sons, Chapter 10, 1994.

Schonberger, Richard J. *Japanese Manufacturing Techniques*.
   New York: The Free Press, 1982.

Sullivan, Lawrence P. "The Power of Taguchi Methods." *Quality
   Progress*, vol. 20, no. 6 (June 1987), pp. 76–79.

"Want EC Business? You Have Two Choices," *Business Week*,
   October 19, 1992, pp. 58–59.

Chapter Five

STATISTICAL PROCESS CONTROL

race Cocoa's Chocolate Americas division produces chocolate drops and other chocolate products for customers such as Keebler, Nabisco, and Food Club. The production process for chocolate drops is highly automated and has a product focus. Some 150, 000 pounds of cocoa beans are unloaded, cleaned, and roasted each day. The roasted beans are ground into a liquid, called *liquor,* which is then blended with other ingredients according to a particular recipe for a given product to form a paste. The paste is heated to a specified temperature and then is pumped to a depositing machine that forms the paste into drops and controls their cooling. The drops then are packaged for delivery.

Grace utilizes total quality management (TQM) techniques with statistical process control (SPC) as the backbone. The degree of variability in agricultural commodities used for raw materials in the production of chocolate is high. For example, the fat content of cocoa beans varies according to the conditions under which the beans were grown. Fat content is crucial to determining the proper amount of each additive for blending into a specific product. Grace samples each batch of liquor just before the blending operation to measure fat content. If the sample is unacceptable, the liquor is reprocessed until it has the proper fat content. Because the fat content is standardized, the blending operation also can be standardized from batch to batch.

Grace's customers depend on having consistent quantities of chocolate drops. Customers have specifications such as 4000 ± 200 drops per pound and

At Grace Cocoa, operators must know both process control and machine operations.

gear their production processes accordingly. An essential step in production of the drops is operation of the depositing machine. Every hour, a random sample of 100 drops is taken from the production line, the total weight is recorded, and the average number of drops per pound is estimated. If the result is unacceptable, the operator of the machine explores the possible reasons for the problem (e.g., the temperature of the liquor entering the machine or the setting of the aperture that forms the drops). Adjustments require 15 minutes to take effect because of the time needed to clear the defective products. Operators must be well trained in both statistical process control techniques and machine operations because a mistake in the adjustment means that at least 30 minutes of production will be lost.

In Chapter 4 we explored the philosophy of total quality management (TQM) and defined five customer-driven characteristics of quality: conformance to specifications, value, fitness for use, support, and psychological impressions. Many organizations have begun to design quality into their processes through the continuous improvement methods discussed in Chapter 4. Quality improvement relies on continual monitoring of the inputs and outputs of the processes producing the products or services. When inputs and outputs can be measured or compared, statistical tools of TQM such as control charts can be useful for evaluating the degree of conformance to specifications.

Statistical process control (SPC) is the application of statistical techniques to determine whether the output of a process conforms to the product or service design. In SPC, tools called control charts are used primarily to prevent or detect production of defective products or services. Thus SPC can be used to alert management and workers when something is wrong and needs to be corrected. Some examples of problems that can be detected by SPC are

- a sudden increase in the proportion of defective gear boxes,
- an increase in the average number of complaints per day at a hotel,
- a consistently low measurement in the diameter of a crankshaft, and
- an increase in the number of claimants receiving late payment from an insurance company.

Let's consider the last situation. Suppose that the manager of the accounts payable department of an insurance company notices that the proportion of claimants receiving late payment has risen from an average of 0.05 to 0.08. The first question is whether the rise is a cause for alarm or just a random occurrence. Statistical process control can help the manager decide whether further action should be taken. If the rise in the proportion is large, the manager shouldn't conclude that it was just a random occurrence and should seek other explanations of the poor performance. Perhaps the number of claims significantly increased, causing an overload on the employees in the department. The decision might be to hire more personnel. Or perhaps the procedures being used are ineffective or the training of employees is inadequate.

Another approach to quality management, **acceptance sampling,** is the application of statistical techniques to determine whether a quantity of material should be accepted or rejected, based on the inspection or test of a sample. We discuss acceptance sampling in Supplement C. In addition, the statistical charts, graphs, and diagrams presented in Chapter 4 can be used to judge the quality of products or services. In this chapter we explore the techniques of statistical process control to understand better the role they play in decision making.

◆ SOURCES OF VARIATION

No two products or services are exactly alike because the processes that produce them contain many sources of variation, even if the process is working as it was intended. For example, the diameter of two crankshafts may vary because of differences in tool wear, material hardness, operator skill, or temperature during the period in which they were produced. Similarly, the time required to process a credit card application varies because of the load on the credit department, the financial background of the applicant, and the skills and attitudes of the employees. Nothing can be done to eliminate variation in process output completely, but management can investigate the *causes* of variation to minimize it.

Common Causes

There are two basic categories of variation in output: common causes and assignable causes. **Common causes of variation** are the purely random, unidentifiable sources of variation that are unavoidable with the current process. For example, a machine that fills cereal boxes will not put exactly the same amount of cereal in each box. If you weighed a large number of boxes filled by the machine and plotted the results in a scatter diagram, the data would tend to form a pattern that can be described as a *distribution*. Such a distribution may be characterized by its mean, spread, and shape.

1. The *mean* is the sum of the observations divided by the total number of observations:

$$\bar{x} = \frac{\sum_{i=1}^{n} x_i}{n}$$

where x_i = observation of a quality characteristic (such as weight)

         n = total number of observations

         $\bar{x}$ = mean

2. The *spread* is a measure of the dispersion of observations about the mean. Two measures commonly used in practice are the range and the standard deviation. The *range* is the difference between the largest observation in a sample and the smallest. The *standard deviation* may be calculated as

$$\sigma = \sqrt{\frac{\sum (x_i - \bar{x})^2}{n-1}} \quad \text{or} \quad \sigma = \sqrt{\frac{\sum x_i^2 - \frac{\left(\sum x_i\right)^2}{n}}{n-1}}$$

where σ = standard deviation

           n = total number of observations

           $\bar{x}$ = mean

           x_i = observation of a quality characteristic

Relatively small values for the range or the standard deviation imply that the observations are clustered near the mean.

3. Two common *shapes* of process distributions are symmetric and skewed. A *symmetric* distribution has the same number of observations above and below the mean. A *skewed* distribution has a preponderance of observations either above or below the mean.

If process variability comes solely from common causes of variation, the distribution is typically symmetric, with most observations near the center. Figure 5.1 shows the distribution for the box-filling machine when only common causes of variation are present. The mean weight is 425 grams, and the distribution is symmetric relative to the mean.

FIGURE 5.1

Process Distribution for the Box-Filling Machine When Only Common Causes of Variation Are Present

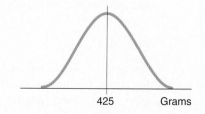

425   Grams

Assignable Causes

The second category of variation, **assignable causes of variation,** includes any variation-causing factors that can be identified and eliminated. Assignable causes of variation include an employee needing training or a machine needing repair. Let's return to the example of the box-filling machine. Figure 5.2 shows how assignable causes can change the distribution of output for the box-filling machine. The green curve is the process distribution when only common causes of variation are present. The purple lines depict a change in the distribution because of assignable causes. In Fig. 5.2(a), the purple line indicates that the machine put more cereal than planned in all the boxes, thereby increasing the average weight of each box. In Fig. 5.2(b), an increase in the variability of the weight of cereal in each box affected the spread of the distribution. Finally, in Fig. 5.2(c), the purple line indicates that the machine produced more lighter than heavier boxes. Such a distribution is skewed—that is, no longer symmetric to the average value.

FIGURE 5.2

Effects of Assignable Causes on the Process Distribution for the Box-Filling Machine

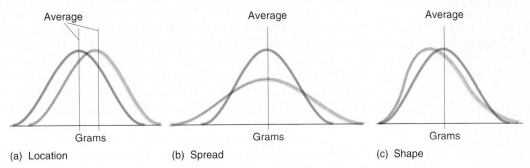

(a) Location   (b) Spread   (c) Shape

A process is said to be in statistical control when the dimensions of its distribution don't change over time. After the process is in statistical control, managers use SPC procedures to detect the onset of assignable causes so that they can be eliminated. Figure 5.3 shows the differences between a process that is in statistical control and one that isn't. In Fig. 5.3(a), the machine is generating different distributions of cereal box weight over time, indicating assignable causes that need to be eliminated. In Fig. 5.3(b), the distributions of weight are stable over time. Consequently, the process is in statistical control. Later, we discuss how SPC techniques can be used in continuous improvement projects to reduce process variability.

FIGURE 5.3

Effects of Assignable Causes on Process Control

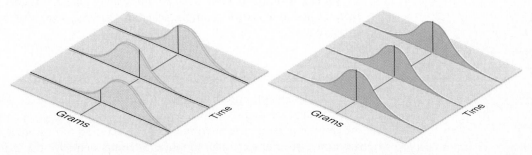

(a) Out of control (assignable causes present)   (b) In control (no assignable causes)

◆   THE INSPECTION PROCESS

Many companies use quality inspection improperly, merely to weed out the defectives before they reach the customer. This approach is doomed to failure because of the internal and external failure costs discussed in Chapter 4. In contrast, world-class companies combine early inspection with SPC to monitor quality and detect and correct abnormalities. Important decisions in implementing such a program include how to measure quality characteristics, what size sample to collect, and at which stage in the process to conduct inspections.

Quality Measurements

What trade-offs are involved in using attribute measurements instead of variable measurements of quality?

To detect abnormal variations in output, inspectors must be able to measure quality characteristics. Quality can be evaluated in two ways. One way is to measure **variables**—that is, characteristics of a product or service, such as weight, length, volume, or time, that can be *measured* on a continuous scale. For example, inspectors at Harley-Davidson measure the diameter of a piston to determine whether the product adheres to the specifications (within the allowable tolerance) and identify differences in diameter over time. Similarly, United Parcel Service managers monitor the length of time drivers spend delivering packages. The advantage of measuring a quality characteristic on a continuous scale is that if a product or service misses its quality specifications, the inspector knows by how much. The disadvantage is that such measurements typically involve special equipment, employee skills, exacting procedures, and time and effort.

Another way to evaluate quality is to measure a product's or service's **attributes**—that is, the characteristics that can be quickly *counted* for acceptable quality. The method allows inspectors to make a simple yes–no decision about whether a product or service meets the specifications. Attributes often are used when quality specifications are complex and measuring by variables is difficult or costly. Some examples of attributes that can be counted are the number of insurance forms containing errors that cause underpayments or overpayments, the proportion of radios inoperative at the final test, the proportion of airline flights arriving within 15 minutes of scheduled times, and the number of stove-top assemblies with spotted paint. The advantage of attributes counts is that less effort and fewer resources are needed than for making variables measurements. The disadvantage is that even though attributes counts can reveal that quality of performance has changed, they may not be of much use in indicating by how much. For example, a count may determine that the proportion of airline flights arriving within 15 minutes of their scheduled times has declined, but the result may not show how much beyond the 15-minute allowance the flights are arriving. For that, the actual deviation from the scheduled arrival, a variable, would have to be measured.

Sampling

The most thorough approach to inspection is to inspect each product or service at each stage for quality. This method, called *complete inspection,* is used when the costs of passing defects to the next workstation or customer outweigh the inspection costs. For example, suppliers of components for the space shuttles check each component many times before shipping it to a contractor. In such a situation, the cost of failure—injury, death, and the destruction of highly expensive

At its Safety Research and Development Lab, General Motors uses computer-monitored crash test dummies to check the safety of its car designs.

equipment—greatly exceeds the cost of inspection. Complete inspection virtually guarantees that defective units do not pass to the next operation or to the customer, a policy consistent with TQM. Nonetheless, when human inspectors are involved, even complete inspection may not uncover all defects. Inspector fatigue or imperfect testing methods may allow some defects to pass unnoticed. Firms can overcome these failings by using automated inspection equipment that can record, summarize, and display data. Many companies have found that automated inspection equipment can pay for itself in a reasonably short time.

A well-conceived **sampling plan** can approach the same degree of protection as complete inspection. A sampling plan specifies a **sample size,** which is a quantity of randomly selected observations of process outputs; the time between successive samples; and decision rules that determine when action should be taken. Sampling is appropriate when inspection costs are high because of the special knowledge, skills, procedures, and expensive equipment required to perform the inspections. Moreover, sampling is necessary *regardless of inspection costs* when the tests destroy the item being tested. For example, at its Milford, Michigan, Proving Ground facility, GM's Safety Research and Development Laboratory crash tests as many as 400 full-scale vehicles each year to learn the effect of impact on vehicles and occupants. GM obviously could not perform this test on every car.

Sampling Distributions. The purpose of sampling is to calculate a variable or attribute measure for some quality characteristic of the sample. That measure is then used to assess the performance of the process itself. For example, in the cereal box-filling example, an important quality dimension is the weight of the product in each box. Suppose that management wants the machine to produce boxes so that the average weight is 425 grams. That is, it wants the process distribution to have a mean of 425 grams. An inspector periodically taking a sample of 5 boxes filled by the machine and calculating the sample mean (a variable measure) could use it to determine how well the machine is doing.

Plotting a large number of these means would show that they have their own distribution, with a mean centered on 425 grams, as did the process distribution, but with much less variability. The reason is that means offset the highs and lows of the individual box weights. Figure 5.4 shows the relationship between the sampling distribution and the process distribution for the box weights.

FIGURE 5.4

Relationship Between the Distribution of Sample Means and the Process Distribution

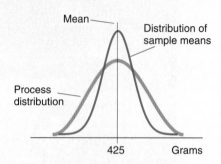

Some sampling distributions (e.g., for means and proportions) can be approximated by the *normal* distribution, allowing the use of the normal tables (see Appendix 2). Figure 5.5 shows the percentages of values within certain ranges of the normal distribution. For example, 68.26 percent of the sample will have values within ±1 standard deviation of the distribution mean. We can determine the probability that any particular sample result will fall outside certain limits. For example, there is a 4.56 percent chance (100 − 95.44) that a sample mean will fall more than two standard deviations from the mean. The ability to assign probabilities to sample results is important for the construction and use of control charts.

FIGURE 5.5

The Normal Distribution

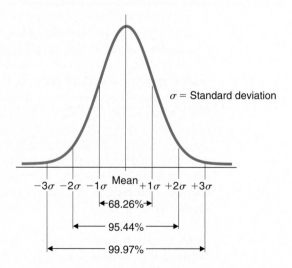

Control Charts. To determine whether observed variations are abnormal, the quality characteristic taken from the sample can be measured and plotted on a time-ordered diagram called a **control chart.** A control chart has a nominal value, or central line, which typically is a target that managers would like the process to achieve, and two control limits based on the sampling distribution of the quality measure. The control limits are used to judge whether action is required. The larger value represents the *upper control limit* (UCL), and the smaller value represents the *lower control limit* (LCL). Figure 5.6 shows how the control limits relate to the sampling distribution. A sample statistic that falls between the UCL and the LCL indicates that the process is exhibiting common causes of variation; a statistic that falls outside the control limits indicates that the process is exhibiting assignable causes of variation. Observations falling outside the control limits do not always mean poor quality. For example, the assignable cause may be a new billing procedure that was introduced to reduce the number of incorrect bills sent to customers. If the proportion of incorrect bills, the quality statistic from a sample of bills, falls below the LCL of the control chart, the new procedure has likely changed the billing process for the better and a new control chart should be constructed.

FIGURE 5.6

Relationship of Control Limits to Sampling Distribution and Observations from Three Samples

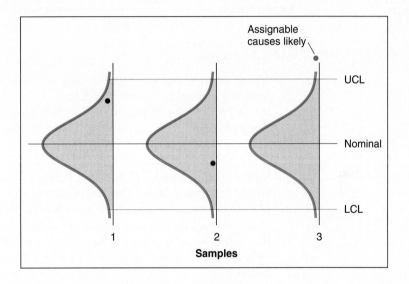

Managers use control charts in the following way.

1. Take a random sample from the process, measure the quality characteristic, and calculate a variable or attribute measure.
2. If the statistic falls outside the chart's control limits, look for an assignable cause.
3. Eliminate the cause if it degrades quality; incorporate the cause if it improves quality. Reconstruct the control chart with new data.
4. Repeat the procedure periodically.

Often a manager can tell that something is wrong even though the control limits have not been exceeded. Figure 5.7 contains five examples of control charts. Chart (a) shows a process that is in statistical control. No action is needed. However, chart (b) shows a pattern called a *run,* or a sequence of observations with a certain characteristic. In this case the run is a trend that could be the result of gradual tool wear, indicating the need to replace the tool or reset the machine to some value between the nominal value and the UCL to extend tool wear. For an airline company concerned with on-time performance, the cause may be a slow buildup of air traffic at the airport at the scheduled arrival times of its flights. Schedule changes may be in order. A typical rule is to take remedial

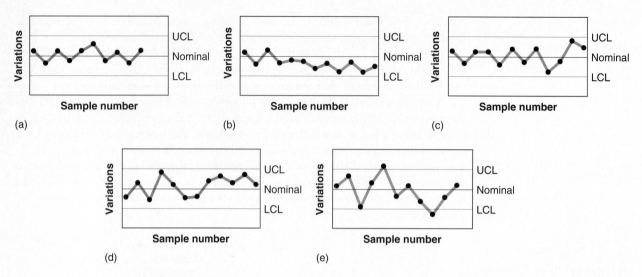

FᴵɢᴜʀᴇE 5.7   *Control Chart Examples*

action when there is a trend of five or more observations, even if the points haven't yet exceeded the control limits.

In chart (c) the process has taken a sudden change from its normal pattern. A manager should be concerned with such sudden changes even though the control limits haven't been exceeded. Chart (d) demonstrates another situation where action is needed even though the limits haven't been exceeded. Whenever a run of five or more observations above or below the nominal value occurs, the manager should look for a cause. The probability is very low that such a result could take place by chance. Finally, chart (e) indicates that the process went out of control twice because two sample results fell outside the control limits. The probability that the process distribution has changed is high. We discuss more implications of being out of statistical control when we discuss process capability later in this chapter.

Control charts are not perfect tools for detecting shifts in the process distribution because they are based on sampling distributions. Two types of error are possible with the use of control charts. A **type I error** occurs when the analyst concludes that the process is out of control based on a sample result that falls outside the control limits, when in fact it was due to pure randomness. A **type II error** occurs when the analyst concludes that the process is in control and only randomness is present, when actually the process is out of statistical control.

Figure 5.8 shows the consequences of these errors when the process average is the quality measure. In chart (a) the control limits for the sampling distribution were set for three standard deviations from the mean. We refer to these control limits as "three-sigma limits." In the leftmost curve the shaded portion shows the probability of making a type I error. For three-sigma limits, that probability is quite small. In the rightmost curve, the process average has shifted. The shaded portion of the curve now shows the probability of making a type II error, which is quite large. In chart (b) the control chart has only two-sigma control limits, a narrower spread than the three-sigma control chart. Now the probability of a type I error has increased, whereas the probability of a type II error has decreased, thus increasing the spread decreases type I errors while increasing type II errors.

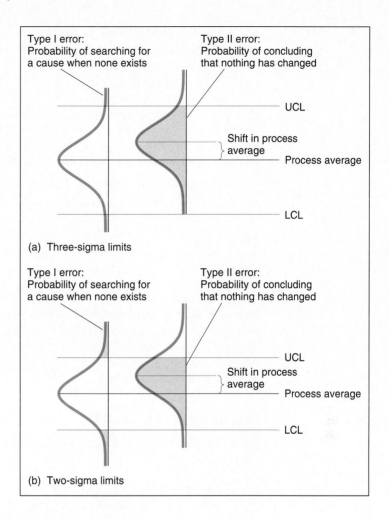

F I G U R E 5.8

Relationship of Control Limit Spread to Type I and Type II Errors

(a) Three-sigma limits

(b) Two-sigma limits

Inspection Station Location

Where should inspection stations be put?

To decide at which stage of the process to make inspections, management must identify the aspects of quality important to the consumer and the key steps in the process that affect those characteristics. A cause-and-effect diagram (see Chapter 4) is a good way of identifying these steps. Inspection stations usually occur in three different stages of the total process:

• *Raw material inputs.* The inspection of purchased materials ensures the proper quality of the inputs to the production process. At this stage, various acceptance-sampling plans, discussed in Supplement C, could be used.

• *Work in process.* At the work-in-process stage, an inspection station could be located after each step in the process. However, this approach could be very costly if testing requires highly skilled inspectors and/or expensive technology. A TQM program greatly reduces the need for inspection stations. However, even with a TQM program, some inspection stations would be needed, especially before costly operations or bottleneck operations. The cost of inspecting materials at any location should be balanced against the cost of passing defective materials to the next step.

• *Final product or service.*   In manufacturing systems, final product inspections are made just prior to stocking finished goods or shipping them to the customer. Product failures discovered at final inspection are costly because they may result in (1) scrapping the defective items or batch, (2) routing the defective items or batch to a previous step for rework, or (3) routing the defective items or batch to a special area for diagnosis and correction of the defects. In service operations, the customer often plays a major role in the final inspection process. For instance, a hair stylist works with the customer until the customer is satisfied, or a mechanic may take the customer for a test drive after repairing a car.

In deciding on the number and location of inspection stations, the operations manager must remember that quality cannot be inspected into the product; inspection can only detect that the process is not operating according to specifications and identify the need for corrective action.

◆   STATISTICAL PROCESS CONTROL METHODS

Statistical process control (SPC) methods are useful for both measuring the current quality of products or services and detecting whether the process itself has changed in a way that will affect quality. In this section we first discuss mean and range charts for variable measures of quality and then consider control charts for product or service attributes.

Control Charts for Variables

Control charts for variables monitor the mean and the variability of the process distribution.

R-Charts.   A range chart, or **R-chart,** is used to monitor process variability. To calculate the range of a set of sample data, the analyst subtracts the smallest from the largest measurement in each sample. If any of the data fall outside the control limits, the process variability is not in control.

The control limits for the R-chart are

$$\text{UCL}_R = D_4 \overline{R} \quad \text{and} \quad \text{LCL}_R = D_3 \overline{R}$$

where $\overline{R}$ = average of several past R values and the central line of the control chart

D_3, D_4 = constants that provide three standard deviation (three-sigma) limits for a given sample size

Values for D_3 and D_4 are contained in Table 5.1 and change as a function of the sample size. Note that the spread between the control limits narrows as the sample size increases. This change is a consequence of having more information on which to base an estimate for the process range.

$\overline{x}$-Charts.   An $\overline{x}$-chart (read "x-bar chart") is used to measure the mean. When the assignable causes of process variability have been identified and the process variability is in statistical control, the analyst can construct an $\overline{x}$-chart to control the process average. The control limits for the $\overline{x}$-chart are

$$\text{UCL}_{\overline{x}} = \overline{\overline{x}} + A_2 \overline{R} \quad \text{and} \quad \text{LCL}_{\overline{x}} = \overline{\overline{x}} - A_2 \overline{R}$$

where $\bar{\bar{x}}$ = central line of the chart and either the average of past sample means or a target value set for the process

A_2 = constant to provide three-sigma limits for the process mean

The values for A_2 are contained in Table 5.1. Note that the control limits use the value of $\bar{R}$; therefore the $\bar{x}$-chart must be constructed *after* the process variability is in control.

TABLE 5.1 *Factors for Calculating Three-Sigma Limits for $\bar{x}$-Chart and R-Chart*

Size of Sample (n)	Factor for UCL and LCL for $\bar{x}$-Charts (A_2)	Factor for LCL for R-Charts (D_3)	Factor for UCL for R-Charts (D_4)
2	1.880	0	3.267
3	1.023	0	2.575
4	0.729	0	2.282
5	0.577	0	2.115
6	0.483	0	2.004
7	0.419	0.076	1.924
8	0.373	0.136	1.864
9	0.337	0.184	1.816
10	0.308	0.223	1.777

Source: 1950 ASTM Manual on Quality Control of Materials, copyright © American Society for Testing Materials. Reprinted with permission.

EXAMPLE 5.1

Using $\bar{x}$- and R-Charts to Monitor a Process

The management of West Allis Industries is concerned about the production of a special metal screw used by several of the company's largest customers. The diameter of the screw is critical. It is designed to be 0.5025 in., and the average range has been 0.0020 in. Data from the last five samples are shown in the accompanying table. The sample size is 4. Is the process in control?

Data for the $\bar{x}$- and R-Charts:
Observations of Screw Diameter (in.)

Sample Number	Sample			
	1	2	3	4
1	0.5014	0.5022	0.5009	0.5027
2	0.5021	0.5041	0.5032	0.5020
3	0.5018	0.5026	0.5035	0.5023
4	0.5008	0.5034	0.5024	0.5015
5	0.5041	0.5056	0.5034	0.5039

Solution

Step 1.   To construct the R-chart, select the appropriate constants from Table 5.1 for a sample size of 4. The control limits are

$$\text{UCL}_R = D_4\overline{R} = 2.282(0.0020) = 0.00456 \text{ in.}$$

$$\text{LCL}_R = D_3\overline{R} = 0(0.0020) = 0 \text{ in.}$$

Step 2.   Compute the range for each sample by subtracting the lowest value from the highest value. For example, in sample 1 the range is $0.5027 - 0.5009 = 0.0018$ in. Similarly, the ranges for samples 2, 3, 4, and 5 are 0.0021, 0.0017, 0.0026, and 0.0022 in., respectively.

Step 3.   Plot the ranges on the R-chart, as shown in Fig. 5.9. None of the sample ranges fall outside the control limits. Consequently, the process variability is in statistical control. If any of the sample ranges had fallen outside of the limits, we would have had to search for the causes of the excessive variability.

FIGURE 5.9   *Range Chart for the Metal Screw, Showing That the Process Variability Is in Control*

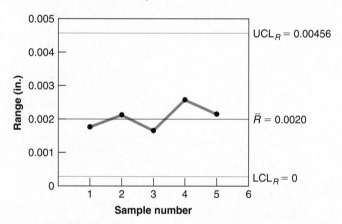

Step 4.   Now proceed to construct the $\overline{x}$-chart for the process average. The target for the screw diameter is 0.5025 in. and the average range has been 0.0020 in., so use $\overline{\overline{x}} = 0.5025$, $\overline{R} = 0.0020$, and A_2 from Table 5.1 for a sample size of 4 to construct the control limits:

$$\text{UCL}_{\overline{x}} = \overline{\overline{x}} + A_2\overline{R} = 0.5025 + 0.729(0.0020) = 0.5040 \text{ in.}$$

$$\text{LCL}_{\overline{x}} = \overline{\overline{x}} - A_2\overline{R} = 0.5025 - 0.729(0.0020) = 0.5010 \text{ in.}$$

Step 5.   Compute the mean for each sample. For example, the mean for sample 1 is

$$\frac{0.5014 + 0.5022 + 0.5009 + 0.5027}{4} = 0.5018 \text{ in.}$$

Similarly, the means of samples 2, 3, 4, and 5 are 0.5029, 0.5026, 0.5020, and 0.5043 in., respectively.

Step 6.   Plot the sample means on the control chart, as shown in Fig. 5.10.

FIGURE 5.10 *The $\bar{x}$-Chart for the Metal Screw, Showing That Sample 5 Is Out of Control*

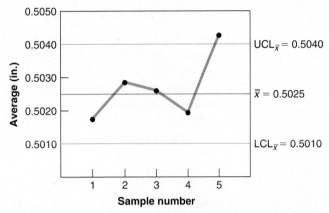

The mean of sample 5 falls above the upper control limit, indicating that the process average is out of control and that assignable causes must be explored, perhaps using a cause-and-effect diagram.

If the standard deviation of the process distribution is known, another form of the $\bar{x}$-chart may be used:

$$\text{UCL}_{\bar{x}} = \bar{\bar{x}} + z\sigma_{\bar{x}} \quad \text{and} \quad \text{LCL}_{\bar{x}} = \bar{\bar{x}} - z\sigma_{\bar{x}}$$

where $\sigma_{\bar{x}} = \sigma/\sqrt{n}$ = standard deviation of sample means

     σ = standard deviation of the process distribution

     n = sample size

     $\bar{\bar{x}}$ = average of sample means or a target value set for the process

     z = normal deviate

The advantage of using this form of the $\bar{x}$-chart is that the analyst can adjust the spread of the control limits by changing the value of z. This approach can be useful for balancing the effects of type I and type II errors.

EXAMPLE 5.2

Designing an $\bar{x}$-Chart Using the Process Standard Deviation

The Sunny Dale Bank monitors the time required to serve customers at the drive-by window because it is an important quality factor in competing with other banks in the city. After analyzing the data gathered in an extensive study of the window operation, bank management determined that the mean time to process a customer at the peak demand period has been 5 minutes with a standard deviation of 1.5 minutes. Management wants to monitor the mean time to process a customer by using a sample size of 6 customers. Design an $\bar{x}$-chart that has a type I error of 5 percent.

Solution

$$\bar{\bar{x}} = 5.0 \text{ minutes}$$
$$\sigma = 1.5 \text{ minutes}$$
$$n = 6 \text{ customers}$$
$$z = 1.96$$

The control limits are

$$\text{UCL}_{\bar{x}} = \bar{\bar{x}} + z\sigma/\sqrt{n} = 5.0 + 1.96(1.5)/\sqrt{6} = 6.20 \text{ minutes}$$

$$\text{LCL}_{\bar{x}} = \bar{\bar{x}} - z\sigma/\sqrt{n} = 5.0 - 1.96(1.5)/\sqrt{6} = 3.80 \text{ minutes}$$

The value for z can be obtained from Appendix 2 in the following way. The table gives the proportion of the total area under the normal curve from $-\infty$ to z. We want a type I error of 5 percent, or 2.5 percent of the curve above the upper control limit and 2.5 percent below the lower control limit. Consequently, we need to find the z value in the table that leaves only 2.5 percent in the upper portion of the normal curve (or 0.9750 in the table). That value is 1.96.

Control Charts for Attributes

Of the alternative attribute process charts available, which one can best be used in a given situation?

Two charts commonly used for quality measures based on product or service attributes are the p-chart and the c-chart. The p-chart is used for controlling the proportion of defective products or services generated by the process. The c-chart is used for controlling the number of defects when more than one defect can be present in a product or service.

p-Charts.   The **p-chart** is a commonly used control chart for attributes, whereby the quality characteristic is counted rather than measured and the entire item or service can be declared good or defective. For example, in the banking industry, the attributes counted might be the number of nonendorsed deposits or the number of incorrect financial statements sent. The method involves selecting a random sample, inspecting each item in it, and calculating the sample proportion defective, p, which is the number of defective units divided by the sample size.

Sampling with attributes involves a yes–no decision: The item or service either is or isn't defective. The underlying statistical distribution is based on the binomial distribution. However, for large sample sizes, the normal distribution provides a good approximation to it. The standard deviation of the distribution of proportion defective, σ_p, is

$$\sigma_p = \sqrt{\bar{p}(1 - \bar{p})/n}$$

where n = sample size

$\bar{p}$ = historical average population proportion defective or target value and central line on the chart

The central line on the p-chart may be the average of past sample proportion defective or a target that management has set for the process. We can use σ_p to arrive at the upper and lower control limits for a p-chart:

$$\text{UCL}_p = \bar{p} + z\sigma_p \quad \text{and} \quad \text{LCL}_p = \bar{p} - z\sigma_p$$

where z = normal deviate (number of standard deviations from the average)

The chart is used in the following way. A random sample of size n is taken, and the number of defective products or services is counted. The number of defectives is divided by the sample size to get a sample proportion defective, p, which is plotted on the chart. When a sample proportion defective falls outside the control limits, the analyst assumes that the proportion defective generated by the process has changed and searches for the assignable cause. The analyst may find no assignable cause because there is always a small chance that an "out of control" proportion will have occurred randomly. However, if the analyst discovers assignable causes, those sample data should not be used to calculate the control limits for the chart.

EXAMPLE 5.3

Using a p-Chart to Monitor a Process

The operations manager of the booking services department of Hometown Bank is concerned about the number of wrong customer account numbers recorded by Hometown personnel. Each week a random sample of 2500 deposits is taken, and the number of incorrect account numbers is recorded. The results for the past 12 weeks are shown in the following table. Is the process out of control? Use three-sigma control limits.

Sample Number	Wrong Account Numbers
1	15
2	12
3	19
4	2
5	19
6	4
7	24
8	7
9	10
10	17
11	15
12	3
Total	147

Solution

Step 1. Construct the *p*-chart, using past data to calculate $\bar{p}$.

$$\bar{p} = \frac{\text{Total defectives}}{\text{Total number of observations}} = \frac{147}{12(2500)} = 0.0049$$

$$\sigma_p = \sqrt{\bar{p}(1 - \bar{p})/n} = \sqrt{0.0049(1 - 0.0049)/2500} = 0.0014$$

$$\text{UCL}_p = \bar{p} + z\sigma_p = 0.0049 + 3(0.0014) = 0.0091$$

$$\text{LCL}_p = \bar{p} - z\sigma_p = 0.0049 - 3(0.0014) = 0.0007.$$

Step 2. Calculate the sample proportion defective. For sample 1 the proportion of defectives is $15/2500 = 0.0060$.

Step 3. Plot each sample proportion defective on the chart, as shown in Fig. 5.11 on the following page.

Sample 7 exceeds the upper control limit; thus the process is out of control and the reasons for the poor performance that week should be determined. The account numbers may have been incorrectly entered into the computer by a trainee, or an encoding machine may have been defective. After the problem is corrected, the analyst recalculates the control limits (discarding sample 7). The new $\bar{p}$ is 0.0045, the UCL_p is 0.0085, and the LCL_p is 0.0005. Now all data

FIGURE 5.11 *The p-Chart for Wrong Account Numbers, Showing That Sample 7 Is Out of Control*

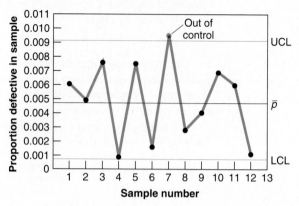

points fall within the control limits, so the process is in statistical control. Thus the *p*-chart provides a tool not only to measure product quality but also to indicate when the process needs adjustment.

c-Charts. Sometimes products have more than one defect per unit. For example, a roll of carpeting may have several defects, such as tufted or discolored fibers or stains from the production process. Other situations in which more than one defect may occur include defects in a television picture tube face panel, accidents at a particular intersection, and complaints at a hotel. When management is interested in reducing the number of defects per unit, another type of control chart, the **c-chart,** is useful.

The underlying sampling distribution for a *c*-chart is the Poisson distribution. It is based on the assumption that defects occur over a continuous region and that the probability of two or more defects at any one location is negligible. The mean of the distribution is $\overline{c}$ and the standard deviation is $\sqrt{\overline{c}}$. A useful tactic is to use the normal approximation to the Poisson so that the central line of the chart is $\overline{c}$ and the control limits are

$$\text{UCL}_c = \overline{c} + z\sqrt{\overline{c}} \quad \text{and} \quad \text{LCL}_c = \overline{c} - z\sqrt{\overline{c}}$$

EXAMPLE 5.4

Using a c-Chart to Monitor Defects per Unit

The Woodland Paper Company produces paper for the newspaper industry. As a final step in the process, the paper passes through a machine that measures various quality characteristics. When the process is in control, it averages 20 defects per roll.

    a. Set up a control chart for the number of defects per roll. Use two-sigma control limits.

    b. If the latest roll sampled contained 27 defects, is the process in control?

    c. If the latest roll contained only 5 defects, is the process in control?

Solution

    a. The average number of defects per roll is 20. Therefore

$$\text{UCL}_c = \overline{c} + z\sqrt{\overline{c}} = 20 + 2(\sqrt{20}) = 28.94$$

$$\text{LCL}_c = \overline{c} - z\sqrt{\overline{c}} = 20 - 2(\sqrt{20}) = 11.06$$

F ɪ ɢ ᴜ ʀ ᴇ   5.12   *The c-Chart for Defects per Roll of Paper*

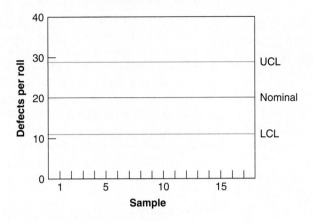

The control chart is shown in Fig. 5.12.
b. Because the latest roll had only 27 defects, or less than the upper control limit, the process is still in control.
c. Five defects is less than the lower control limit, and therefore the process is technically "out of control." However, the control chart indicates that something good has happened. Management should find the assignable cause and exploit it in order to reduce the average number of defects.

◆   SAMPLE SIZE CONSIDERATIONS

The most thorough method of process control would be to test each item (raw material, component, product, or service) to make sure that it satisfies design specifications. As we have stated, this isn't always possible. Consequently, the choice of sample size is crucial, and it has both economic and control implications.

Economic Implications

Because they are based on attributes, *p*-charts are useful when the acceptance decision is a simple yes or no. Although measuring quality attributes is easier than measuring variables, an attribute control chart may require 4 to 100 times the sample size required for a variable control chart. The reason is that the sample size for a *p*-chart must be large enough to detect at least one defective item on average. For example, the proportion defective for the past 12 weeks in the Hometown Bank example was 0.0045. To have a reasonable chance of observing at least one defect in each sample, we would need a sample size of 222. (We actually used a sample size of 2500 to have a better chance of observing defects in each sample.) The reason that smaller sample sizes can be used for $\bar{x}$-charts is that much more information can be derived from the variable measures. The analyst can determine that an item is defective and by how much. Consequently, unless measuring variables takes far more effort than measuring attributes, variable control charts usually are less expensive than attribute control charts.

Degree of Control

What are the implications of narrowing the control limits in a process control chart?

Another consideration is the effect of sample size on degree of control, or the ability to detect a shift in the process average. Recall that the standard deviation for the *p*-chart has *n* in the denominator. Also note that in Table 5.1 the value of A_2 decreases as the sample size increases. The relationship implies that, as the sample size increases, the control *limits* on the control charts move closer to the central line, or target process average. Thus the analyst is more likely to detect a shift in the process average when using a larger sample size. For example, for an $\bar{x}$-chart, sample sizes of 4 or 5 usually are sufficient to detect a relatively large shift in the process average (say, two standard deviations). However, a sample size three to five times larger would be needed to detect shifts of only one standard deviation. Here again, management must balance the cost of inspection against the cost of not detecting a shift in the process average.

Homogeneity

The sample should represent subgroups of output that are as homogeneous as possible. When significant deviations occur and assignable causes can be identified, the causes should show up as differences between subgroups and not as differences between members of a subgroup. Consider, for example, a two-shift operation, with each shift capable of producing 500 units. Choosing a sample size of 2000 could mask one of the assignable causes of quality problems: differences in output quality by shift. It might be better in this case to take samples that are homogeneous by shift, so that management can determine whether the problems occur during a particular shift.

◆ PROCESS CAPABILITY

What determines whether a process is capable of producing the products or services that customers demand?

Statistical process control techniques help managers achieve and maintain a process distribution that doesn't change in terms of its mean and variance. The control limits on the control charts signal when the mean or variability of the process changes. However, a process that is in statistical control may not be producing products or services according to their design specifications because the control limits are based on the mean and variability of the *sampling distribution*, not the design specifications. **Process capability** refers to the ability of the process to meet the design specifications for a product or service. Design specifications often are expressed as a **nominal value,** or target, and a **tolerance,** or allowance above or below the nominal value. For example, design specifications for the useful life of a light bulb might have a nominal value of 100 hours and a tolerance of ±20 hours. This tolerance gives an *upper specification* of 120 hours and a *lower specification* of 80 hours. The process producing the bulbs must be capable of producing within these design specifications; otherwise it will produce a certain proportion of defective bulbs.

Defining Process Capability

Figure 5.13 shows the relationship between a process distribution and the upper and lower specifications for the process producing light bulbs under two conditions. In Fig. 5.13(a) the process is capable because the extremes of the process distribution fall within the upper and lower specifications. In Fig. 5.13(b) the process is not capable because it produces too many bulbs with short lives.

FIGURE 5.13

Relationship Between Process Distribution and Specifications

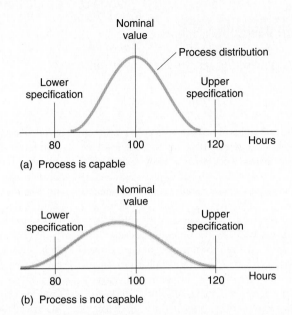

(a) Process is capable

(b) Process is not capable

Figure 5.13 shows clearly why managers are so concerned with reducing process variability. The less variability—represented by lower standard deviations—the less frequently bad output is produced. Figure 5.14 shows what reducing variability means for a process distribution that is a normal probability distribution. The firm with two-sigma quality (the tolerance limits equal the process distribution mean plus or minus two standard deviations) produces 4.56 percent defective parts, or 45,600 defective parts per million. The firm with four-sigma quality produces only 0.0063 percent defectives, or 63 defective parts per million. Finally, the firm with six-sigma quality produces only 0.0000002 percent defectives, or 0.002 defective parts per million. Managerial Practice 5.1 highlights Motorola's plan to achieve six-sigma quality.

FIGURE 5.14

Effects of Reducing Variability on Process Capability

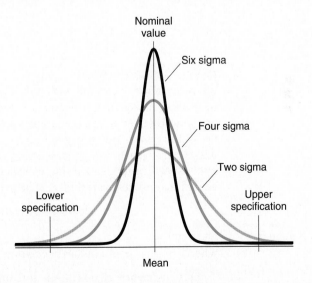

How can you determine quantitatively whether a process is capable? Two measures commonly are used in practice to assess the capability of a process: process capability ratio and process capability index.

Managerial Practice 5.1

▶ *Motorola's Six-Sigma Quality Program*

After discussing quality issues with customers, Motorola's management recognized the need to improve its products and customer services. These discussions resulted in Motorola's six-sigma quality program. For Motorola, *six-sigma capability* means that all processes should produce parts, assemblies, and products that meet design specifications 99.9999998 percent of the time. With the six-sigma goal, even if the average value for a quality characteristic of a part unexpectedly shifted by 1.5 standard deviations from the nominal value, the probability of producing the part within the design specifications would be 0.9999966. This probability implies that no more than 3.4 defects would be produced in 1 million operations.

The importance of this stringent goal becomes obvious when we look at the manufacture of a complete product. The MicroTac cellular phone has 400 parts that are assembled by robots and workers in only two hours. Suppose that the process average shifts by 1.5 standard deviations and the processes producing the parts are achieving only four-sigma capability. That is, 99.379 percent of the time each process produces a part within its specifications even after the shift in the process average. The probability that 400 parts will be nondefective is 0.08276. That is, there is only an 8.276 percent chance that a complete MicroTac will not require repair after final assembly. With six-sigma capability, the chances that any part will be defective are so remote that the probability of assembling a nondefective MicroTac increases to 0.99864.

Within three years after the program began, Motorola had reduced defective production to less than 200 parts per million. This performance helped Motorola win the coveted Malcolm Baldrige National Quality Award. The achievements of a team involved with the electrical component insertion line for a portable radio demonstrate the benefits of the program:

370 percent reduction in defects per million parts,
500 percent increase in quality, to 5.1 sigma capability,
40 percent reduction in manufacturing cycle time, and
60 percent increase in production with no additional personnel.

Sources: Sam Tomas, "Six Sigma: Motorola's Quest for Zero Defects," *APICS—The Performance Advantage*, July 1991, pp. 36–41; "The Rival Japan Respects," *Business Week*, November 13, 1989, pp. 108–118.

Process Capability Ratio. A process is *capable* if it has a process distribution whose extreme values fall within the upper and lower specifications for a product or service. As a general rule, most values of a process distribution fall within plus or minus three standard deviations of the mean. In other words, the range of values of the quality measure generated by the process is approximately six standard deviations. Hence, if a process is capable, the difference between the upper and lower specification, called the tolerance width, must be greater than six standard deviations (process variability). The **process capability ratio,** C_p, is defined as

$$C_p = \frac{\text{Upper specification} - \text{Lower specification}}{6\sigma}$$

where σ = standard deviation of the process distribution

If C_p is greater than 1.0, the tolerance range is greater than the range of actual process outputs. If C_p is less than 1.0, the process will produce products or services outside their allowable tolerance. Often firms will choose an arbitrary

A Motorola employee conducts a computer analysis on a cellular phone prior to its distribution.

critical value for the process capability ratio, such as 1.33, to establish a target for reducing process variability. The value is greater than 1.0 to allow for some change in the process distribution before bad output is generated.

Process Capability Index. The process is capable only when the capability ratio is greater than the critical value (e.g., 1.33) and the process distribution is centered on the nominal value of the design specifications. For example, the bulb-producing process may have a process capability ratio greater than 1.33. However, if the mean of the distribution of process output, $\overline{\overline{x}}$, is closer to either the upper or the lower specification, defective bulbs may still be generated. Thus, we need to compute a capability index that measures the potential for the process to generate bad outputs relative to either upper or lower specifications.

The **process capability index, C_{pk},** is defined as

$$C_{pk} = \text{Minimum of } \left[\frac{\overline{\overline{x}} - \text{Lower specification}}{3\sigma}, \frac{\text{Upper specification} - \overline{\overline{x}}}{3\sigma} \right]$$

We take the minimum of the two ratios because it gives the *worst case* situation. If C_{pk} is greater than a critical value greater than 1.0 (say, 1.33) and the process capability ratio is greater than its critical value, we can finally say the process is capable. If C_{pk} is less than 1.0, the process average is close to one of the tolerance limits and is generating defective output.

The capability index will always be less than or equal to the capability ratio. When C_{pk} equals the process capability ratio, the process is centered between the upper and lower specifications and hence the mean of the process distribution is centered on the nominal value of the design specifications.

EXAMPLE 5.5

Assessing the Process Capability of the Light-Bulb Production Process

The light-bulb production process yields bulbs with an average life of 90 hours and a standard deviation of 4.8 hours. The nominal value of the tolerance range is 100 hours, with an upper specification of 120 hours and a lower specification of 80 hours. The operations manager wants to determine whether the process is capable of producing the bulbs to specification.

Solution   To assess process capability, we calculate the process capability ratio and the process capability index:

$$C_p = \frac{120 - 80}{6(4.8)} = 1.39$$

Lower specification calculation: $\frac{90 - 80}{3(4.8)} = 0.69$

Upper specification calculation: $\frac{120 - 90}{3(4.8)} = 2.08$

$$C_{pk} = \text{Minimum of } [0.69, 2.08\ ] = 0.69$$

The process capability ratio of 1.39 tells us that the machine's variability is acceptable relative to the range of the tolerance limits. However, the process capability index tells us that the distribution of output is too close to the lower specification and that short-lived bulbs will be produced. The manager should look for ways to bring the average of the process closer to the nominal value of the design specifications.

Determining the Capability of a Process Using Continuous Improvement

To determine the capability of a process to produce within the tolerances, use the following steps.

Step 1.   Collect data on the process output, and calculate the mean and the standard deviation of the process output distribution.

Step 2.   Use the data from the process distribution to compute process control charts, such as an $\bar{x}$-chart or an R-chart.

Step 3.   Take a series of random samples from the process, and plot the results on the control charts. If at least 20 consecutive samples are within the control limits of the charts, the process is in statistical control. If the process is not in statistical control, look for assignable causes and eliminate them. Recalculate the mean and standard deviation of the process distribution and the control limits for the charts. Continue until the process is in statistical control.

Step 4.   Calculate the process capability ratio and the process capability index. If the results are acceptable, document any changes made to the process and continue to monitor the output by using the control charts. If the results are unacceptable, further explore assignable causes for reducing the variance in the output. As changes are made, recalculate the mean and standard deviation of the process distribution and the control limits for the charts and repeat step 3.

Managerial Practice 5.2 shows how a manufacturer of infant formula achieved process capability on a filling line by using continuous improvement.

Managerial Practice 5.2

▶ *Process Capability Study at Ross Products*

Ross Products, a division of Abbott Laboratories, produces a variety of pediatric and adult nutritional products under the brand names Similac and Ensure. Management wanted to assess the process capability of the 32-ounce-can filling line, which comprised several machines and conveyors. A critical quality measure is the weight of the cans after filling. The standard calls for specifications of 974 grams ± 14 grams.

Initial Capability Study

Initial capability of the multistation filling line was determined by measuring the output of the line and calculating the mean weight (or process average, $\bar{\bar{x}}$) and standard deviation, σ, of the process distribution. Using these data, an $\bar{x}$-chart and an R-chart were developed for the process. The sample size was six cans. After 35 consecutive samples (a total of 210 cans) were in statistical control (that is, the means and ranges of the samples fell within the control limits and no runs were present), the mean and standard deviation of the process distribution (all 210 cans) were recalculated. In addition, the process capability ratio and the process capability index were calculated:

$$\bar{\bar{x}} = 975.7 \text{ grams}$$
$$\sigma = 4.7581 \text{ grams}$$
$$C_p = 0.9808$$
$$C_{pk} = 0.8617$$

The overall variability of the filling line was unacceptable because the process was centered too close to the upper specification.

Attacking Assignable Causes

The capability study team brainstormed possible assignable causes for variation in the filling line process:

1. changeover procedures from product to product,
2. product splash when moving from filler to conveyor,
3. worn parts,
4. valve stems too long, too short, or not in appropriate location,
5. bowl level not constant during fill cycle,
6. foaming in filler bowl,
7. cylinder walls out of round, and
8. variation in dimensions of cans.

The team systematically addressed the likely assignable causes and collected data to determine the amount of improvement. First they changed all wearable parts on the filling machines. Then they addressed the operator-controlled sources of variation, such as valve stems in the wrong location. They also worked with the maintenance department to install new piston cylinders and to reduce splash at the point where the can moves from the filler to the conveyor. During this period the team continuously monitored output and evaluated it weekly.

Final Capability Analysis

After all known assignable causes were eliminated, the team again used output data to compute control limits for $\bar{x}$- and R-charts. Forty-six consecutive in-control samples yielded:

$$\bar{\bar{x}} = 976.1 \text{ grams}$$
$$\sigma = 2.891 \text{ grams}$$
$$C_p = 1.61$$
$$C_{pk} = 1.37$$

The team concluded that the changes it had made ensured long-term process capability for the design specifications currently in use.

Quality Engineering

How can quality engineering help us improve the quality of products and services?

Originated by Genichi Taguchi, **quality engineering** is an approach that involves combining engineering and statistical methods to reduce costs and improve quality by optimizing product design and manufacturing processes. Before Taguchi, managers often assumed that the goal in achieving quality was to produce products or services that fell anywhere within the design tolerances. Managers thought that the cost of achieving a quality level close to the tolerance limits equaled the cost of achieving a quality level right on the target value. Our discussion of process capability was based on that assumption. To use a football analogy, coaches know that, as long as the football goes anywhere between the goal posts, it counts as a field goal, or 3 points. Managers used to believe that they "scored" whenever parts, products, or services were produced anywhere within their tolerances.

Taguchi believes that unwelcome costs are associated with *any* deviation from a quality characteristic's target value. Taguchi's view is that there is a **quality loss function** of zero when the quality characteristic of the product or service is exactly on the target value and that the value rises exponentially as the quality characteristic gets closer to the tolerance limits. The rationale is that a product or service that barely conforms to the specifications is more like a defective product or service than a perfect one. In other words, just getting the football through the quality goal posts isn't good enough. Figure 5.15 shows Taguchi's quality loss function schematically. Taguchi concluded that managers should continually search for ways to reduce *all* variability from the target value in the production process and not be content with merely adhering to specification limits.

Using quality engineering techniques, engineers, managers, and production workers hypothesize critical factors affecting the quality of a selected product or service in team interaction sessions. They design and conduct an experiment to gather data and use statistical techniques to determine which factor(s) contribute most to quality problems. They then determine what would optimize performance and proceed to make the needed changes. A follow-up experiment is conducted to verify the results. Users believe that quality engineering aids communication among functional groups because it requires them to solve a problem cooperatively. It also permits efficient fine tuning of processes, requiring fewer adjustments with more predictable effects from each adjustment. That can be helpful in achieving and maintaining process capability.

FIGURE 5.15

Taguchi's Quality Loss Function

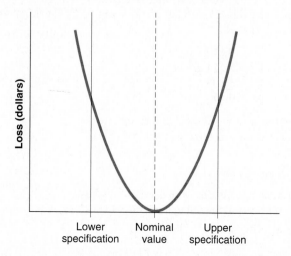

Loss (dollars)

Lower specification   Nominal value   Upper specification

CHAPTER REVIEW

Solved Problem 1

The Watson Electric Company produces incandescent light bulbs. The following data on the number of lumens for 40-watt light bulbs were collected when the process was in control.

	Observation			
Sample	1	2	3	4
1	604	612	588	600
2	597	601	607	603
3	581	570	585	592
4	620	605	595	588
5	590	614	608	604

a. Calculate control limits for an R-chart and an $\bar{x}$-chart.
b. Since these data were collected, some new employees were hired. A new sample obtained the following readings: 570, 603, 623, and 583. Is the process still in control?

Solution   a. To calculate $\bar{x}$, compute the mean for each sample. To calculate R, subtract the lowest value in the sample from the highest value in the same sample. For example, for sample 1,

$$\bar{x} = \frac{604 + 612 + 588 + 600}{4} = 601$$

$$R = 612 - 588 = 24$$

Sample	$\bar{x}$	R
1	601	24
2	602	10
3	582	22
4	602	32
5	604	24
Total	2991	112
Average	$\bar{\bar{x}} = 598.2$	$\bar{R} = 22.4$

The R-chart control limits are

$$\text{UCL}_R = D_4\bar{R} = 2.282(22.4) = 51.12$$

$$\text{LCL}_R = D_3\bar{R} = 0(22.4) = 0$$

The $\bar{x}$-chart control limits are

$$\text{UCL}_{\bar{x}} = \bar{\bar{x}} + A_2\bar{R} = 598.2 + 0.729(22.4) = 614.53$$

$$\text{LCL}_{\bar{x}} = \bar{\bar{x}} - A_2\bar{R} = 598.2 - 0.729(22.4) = 581.87$$

b. First check to see whether the variability is still in control based on the new data. The range is 53 (or $623 - 570$), which is outside the upper control limit for the R-chart. Even though the sample mean, 594.75, is within the control limits for the process average, process variability is not in control. A search for assignable causes must be conducted.

Solved Problem 2

The data processing department of the Arizona Bank has five keypunch operators. Each day their supervisor verifies the accuracy of a random sample of 250 records. A record containing one or more errors is considered defective and must be redone. The results of the last 30 samples are shown in the table. All were checked to make sure that none were out of control.

Sample	Number of Defective Records	Sample	Number of Defective Records	Sample	Number of Defective Records
1	7	11	18	21	17
2	5	12	5	22	12
3	19	13	16	23	6
4	10	14	4	24	7
5	11	15	11	25	13
6	8	16	8	26	10
7	12	17	12	27	14
8	9	18	4	28	6
9	6	19	6	29	11
10	13	20	11	30	9
				Total	300

a. Based on these historical data, set up a *p*-chart using $z = 3$.
b. Samples for the next four days showed the following.

Sample	Number of Defective Records
31	17
32	15
33	22
34	21

What is the supervisor's assessment of the keypunch process likely to be?

Solution a. From the table, the supervisor knows that the total number of defective records is 300 out of a total sample of 7500 [or 30(250)]. Therefore the central line of the chart is

$$\bar{p} = \frac{300}{7500} = 0.04$$

The control limits are

$$\text{UCL}_p = \bar{p} + z\sqrt{\frac{\bar{p}(1 - \bar{p})}{n}} = 0.04 + 3\sqrt{\frac{0.04(0.96)}{250}} = 0.077$$

$$\text{LCL}_p = \bar{p} - z\sqrt{\frac{\bar{p}(1 - \bar{p})}{n}} = 0.04 - 3\sqrt{\frac{0.04(0.96)}{250}} = 0.003$$

b. Samples for the next four days showed the following.

Sample	Number of Defective Records	Proportion
31	17	0.068
32	15	0.060
33	22	0.088
34	21	0.084

Samples 33 and 34 are out of control. The supervisor should look for the problem and, upon identifying it, take corrective action.

Solved Problem 3

The Minnow County Highway Safety Department monitors accidents at the intersection of Routes 123 and 14. Accidents at the intersection have averaged three per month.

a. Which type of control chart should be used? Construct a control chart with three-sigma control limits.
b. Last month seven accidents occurred at the intersection. Is this sufficient evidence to justify a claim that something has changed at the intersection?

Solution   a. The safety department can't determine the number of accidents that did *not* occur, so it has no way to compute a proportion defective at the intersection. Therefore the administrators must use a *c*-chart for which

$$UCL_c = \bar{c} + z\sqrt{\bar{c}} = 3 + 3\sqrt{3} = 8.20$$

$$LCL_c = \bar{c} - z\sqrt{\bar{c}} = 3 - 3\sqrt{3} = -2.196$$

There can't be a negative number of accidents, so the lower control limit in this case is adjusted to zero.

b. The number of accidents last month falls within the upper and lower control limits of the chart. We conclude that no assignable causes are present and that the increase in accidents was due to chance.

Solved Problem 4

Pioneer Chicken advertises "lite" chicken with 30 percent less calories. (The pieces are 33 percent smaller.) The process average distribution for "lite" chicken breasts is 420 calories, with a standard deviation of the population of 25 calories. Pioneer randomly takes samples of six chicken breasts to measure calorie content.

a. Design an $\bar{x}$-chart, using the process standard deviation.
b. The product design calls for the average chicken breast to contain 400 calories ± 100 calories. Calculate the process capability ratio (target = 1.33) and the process capability index. Interpret the results.

Solution   a. For the process standard deviation of 25 calories, the standard deviation of the sample mean is

$$\sigma_{\bar{x}} = \frac{\sigma}{\sqrt{n}} = \frac{25}{\sqrt{6}} = 10.2 \text{ calories}$$

$$\text{UCL}_{\bar{x}} = \bar{\bar{x}} + z\sigma_{\bar{x}} = 420 + 3(10.2) = 450.6 \text{ calories}$$

$$\text{LCL}_{\bar{x}} = \bar{\bar{x}} - z\sigma_{\bar{x}} = 420 - 3(10.2) = 389.4 \text{ calories}$$

b. The process capability ratio is

$$C_p = \frac{\text{Upper specification} - \text{Lower specification}}{6\sigma} = \frac{500 \text{ calories} - 300 \text{ calories}}{6(25)} = 1.333$$

The process capability index is

$$C_{pk} = \text{Minimum of} \left[\frac{\bar{\bar{x}} - \text{Lower specification}}{3\sigma}, \frac{\text{Upper specification} - \bar{\bar{x}}}{3\sigma} \right]$$

$$= \text{Minimum of} \left[\frac{420 - 300}{3(25)} = 1.60, \frac{500 - 420}{3(25)} = 1.07 \right] = 1.07$$

Because the process capability ratio is greater than 1.33, the process should be able to produce the product reliably within specifications. The process capability index is 1.07, so the current process is capable.

Formula Review

1. Mean: $\bar{x} = \dfrac{\displaystyle\sum_{i=1}^{n} x_i}{n}$

2. Standard deviation of a sample: $\sigma = \sqrt{\dfrac{\sum(x_i - \bar{x})^2}{n - 1}}$ or $\sigma = \sqrt{\dfrac{\sum x^2 - \dfrac{(\sum x_i)^2}{n}}{n - 1}}$

3. Control limits for variable process control charts

   a. *R*-chart, range of sample:

   $$\text{Upper control limit} = \text{UCL}_R = D_4 \bar{R}$$

   $$\text{Lower control limit} = \text{LCL}_R = D_3 \bar{R}$$

   b. $\bar{x}$-chart, sample mean:

   $$\text{Upper control limit} = \text{UCL}_{\bar{x}} = \bar{\bar{x}} + A_2 \bar{R}$$

   $$\text{Lower control limit} = \text{LCL}_{\bar{x}} = \bar{\bar{x}} - A_2 \bar{R}$$

   c. When the standard deviation of the process distribution, σ, is known:

   $$\text{Upper control limit} = \text{UCL}_{\bar{x}} = \bar{\bar{x}} + z\sigma_{\bar{x}}$$

   $$\text{Lower control limit} = \text{LCL}_{\bar{x}} = \bar{\bar{x}} - z\sigma_{\bar{x}}$$

   where $\sigma_{\bar{x}} = \dfrac{\sigma}{\sqrt{n}}$

4. Control limits for attribute process control charts

   a. *p*-chart, proportion defective:

   $$\text{Upper control limit} = \text{UCL}_p = \bar{p} + z\sigma_p$$

   $$\text{Lower control limit} = \text{LCL}_p = \bar{p} - z\sigma_p$$

   where $\sigma_p = \sqrt{\bar{p}(1 - \bar{p})/n}$

b. *c*-chart, number of defects:

$$\text{Upper control limit} = \text{UCL}_c = \bar{c} + z\sqrt{\bar{c}}$$

$$\text{Lower control limit} = \text{LCL}_c = \bar{c} - z\sqrt{\bar{c}}$$

5. Process capability ratio: $C_p = \dfrac{\text{Upper specification} - \text{Lower specification}}{6\sigma}$

6. Process capability index:

$$C_{pk} = \text{Minimum of} \left[\frac{\bar{\bar{x}} - \text{Lower specification}}{3\sigma}, \frac{\text{Upper specification} - \bar{\bar{x}}}{3\sigma} \right]$$

Chapter Highlights

- A key to meeting design specifications in a product or service is to reduce output variability. When a process is in a state of statistical control, outputs subject to common causes of variation follow a stable probability distribution. When assignable causes of variation are present, the process is out of statistical control. Statistical process control (SPC) methods are used to detect the presence of assignable causes of variation.
- Inspection stations may be located at three points in the process: where incoming materials are received, at selected points in the process, and at the end of the process. Inspection identifies whether processes need corrective action.
- Statistical process control charts are useful for measuring the current quality generated by the process and for detecting whether the process has changed to the detriment of quality. Thus *R*-charts are used to monitor process variability, $\bar{x}$-charts and *p*-charts identify abnormal variations in the process average, and *c*-charts are used for controlling the number of defects when a product or service process could result in several defects. The presence of abnormal variation triggers a search for assignable causes.
- Process variability should be in control before process average control charts are constructed. The reason is

that the average range is used in the calculation of control limits for process average control charts. Crucial decisions in the design of control charts are sample size and control limits.
- The use of *p*-charts requires a larger sample size than does the use of $\bar{x}$-charts, but the measurement of attributes may be easier than the measurement of variables. Larger samples provide greater protection in detecting a shift in the process average than do smaller samples. Also, the sample should be homogeneous with respect to potential causes of quality problems.
- The central line of a control chart can be the average of past averages of the quality measurement or a management target related to product specifications. The spread in control limits affects the chances of detecting a shift in the process average or range, as well as the chances of searching for assignable causes when none exist.
- A process can be in statistical control but still not be capable of producing all of its output within design specifications. The process capability ratio and the process capability index are quantitative measures used to assess the capability of a process.

Key Terms

acceptance sampling *181*
assignable causes of variation *183*
attributes *184*
c-chart *196*
common causes of variation *181*
control chart *186*
nominal value *198*
p-chart *194*

process capability *198*
process capability index (C_{pk}) *201*
process capability ratio (C_p) *200*
quality engineering *204*
quality loss function *204*
R-chart *190*
sample size *185*
sampling plan *185*

statistical process control (SPC) *181*
tolerance *198*
type I error *188*
type II error *188*
variables *184*
$\bar{x}$-chart *190*

Study Questions

1. Why is determining whether the cause of a variation is a "common" cause or an "assignable" cause important?
2. What competitive advantages result from using inspection to determine whether a process is in control instead of using inspection to weed out defects before they reach the customer?
3. What factors should be considered when choosing between sampling and complete inspections? What trade-offs are involved in inspecting for an attribute instead of a variable characteristic?
4. What factors should be considered regarding inspection station location?
5. What is the rationale for having upper and lower control limits in process control charts? Compare or contrast this approach to Taguchi's quality loss function.
6. What are the critical design parameters that must be specified for control charts? Explain how the design parameters are interrelated.
7. Quality characteristics for flexible disk production include hours of useful life, proportion of disks that cannot be formatted, and number of bad sectors on a disk. What type of control chart would be used to control each quality characteristic?
8. When designing control charts for a variable characteristic, why do we need two types of charts (R-chart and $\bar{x}$-chart)?
9. What are the implications of narrowing the control limits in a process control chart?
10. Explain how a process can be in statistical control but still produce bad products.
11. Why are managers concerned with reducing process variability?
12. What is the difference between a process capability ratio of 1.5 and a process capability index of 1.5? What do those quantitative measures mean?
13. When SPC indicates that an assignable cause of variation exists, what tools (described in Chapter 4) could be used to identify potential causes, relate causes to effects, and then organize the search for the root cause of the problem?

Problems

1. At Quayle Potatoe Chips, the filling process is set so that the average weight is 385 grams per bag. The average range for a sample of 7 bags is 13 grams. Use Table 5.1 to establish control limits for sample means and ranges for the filling process.
2. At Clinton Pharmaceuticals the filling process for its asthma inhaler is set to dispense 150 milliliters (mL) of steroid solution per container. The average range for a sample of 4 containers is 7 mL. Use Table 5.1 to establish control limits for sample means and ranges for the filling process.
3. Ross's Garage desires to create some colorful charts and graphs to illustrate how reliably its mechanics "get under the hood and fix the problem." Ross's goal for the proportion of customers that return for the same repair within the 30-day warranty period is 0.10. Each month, Ross tracks 100 customers to see whether they return for warranty repairs. The results are plotted as a proportion to report progress toward the goal. If the control limits are to be set at two standard deviations on either side of the goal, determine the control limits for this chart. In November, 15 of the 100 customers in the sample group returned for warranty repairs. Is the repair process in control?
4. The Canine Gourmet Company produces delicious dog treats for canines with discriminating tastes. Management wants the box-filling line to be set so that the process average weight per packet is 43.5 grams. To make sure that the process is in control, an inspector at the end of the filling line periodically selects a random box of eight packets and weighs each packet. When the process is in control, the range in the weight of each sample has averaged 10 grams.
   a. Design an R-chart and an $\bar{x}$-chart for this process.
   b. The results from the last five samples of eight packets are

Sample	$\bar{x}$	R
1	44	14
2	40	10
3	46	12
4	45	8
5	48	15

   Is the process in control? Explain.
5. The Marlin Company produces plastic bottles to customer order. The quality inspector randomly selects four bottles from the bottle machine and measures the outside diameter of the bottle neck, a critical quality dimension that determines whether the bottle cap will fit properly. The dimensions (in.) from the last six samples are

		Bottle		
Sample	1	2	3	4
1	0.604	0.612	0.588	0.600
2	0.597	0.601	0.607	0.603
3	0.581	0.570	0.585	0.592
4	0.620	0.605	0.595	0.588
5	0.590	0.614	0.608	0.604
6	0.585	0.583	0.617	0.579

a. Assuming that using only six samples is sufficient, use the data in the table to determine control limits for an R-chart and an $\bar{x}$-chart.

b. Suppose that the specifications for the bottle neck diameter are 0.600 ± 0.050 inch. If the population standard deviation is 0.012 inch, is the process capable of producing the bottle?

6. In an attempt to judge and monitor the quality of instruction, the administration of Mega-Byte Academy devised an examination to test students on the basic concepts that all should have learned. Each year, a random sample of 10 graduating students is selected for the test. The average score is used to track the quality of the educational process. Test results for the past 10 years are shown in Table 5.2.

Use these data to estimate the center and standard deviation for this distribution. Then calculate the two-sigma control limits for the process average. What comments would you make to the administration of the Mega-Byte Academy?

7. The Emerald Dormer is a luxury hotel in Key West, Florida. The hotel manager is interested in the overall quality of service provided to customers. Each customer is given a survey card. The survey card contains specific questions about various services, to be scored on a scale from 0 to 10, with 10 considered excellent. Customers receive a 5 percent discount on the bill for returning the card, so the program is very successful and only a few customers do not participate.

Each week, 100 cards are randomly selected, and points are totaled for each. A point total of 75 or less is considered a failure to provide adequate service to that customer. During a time when the manager felt that service was good, an average of 15 surveys per week still received scores of 75 or less.

a. Specify the control limits of a p-chart for the manager of the hotel. As service is considered so important, $z = 2$ is desired. The cost of searching for service quality problems is far outweighed by the cost of a shift in overall customer satisfaction with the service received.

b. The following are the results of the past five weeks of sampling.

Week	Number of Cards Having Score ≤ 75
March 1	12
March 8	18
March 15	26
March 22	6
March 29	21

Suppose that you are in charge of recording the results of the samples. What recommendations would you make to the manager about the overall service quality of the hotel?

TABLE 5.2   *Test Scores on Exit Exam*

					Student						
Year	1	2	3	4	5	6	7	8	9	10	Average
1	63	57	92	87	70	61	75	58	63	71	69.7
2	90	77	59	88	48	83	63	94	72	70	74.4
3	67	81	93	55	71	71	86	98	60	90	77.2
4	62	67	78	61	89	93	71	59	93	84	75.7
5	85	88	77	69	58	90	97	72	64	60	76.0
6	60	57	79	83	64	94	86	64	92	74	75.3
7	94	85	56	77	89	72	71	61	92	97	79.4
8	97	86	83	88	65	87	76	84	81	71	81.8
9	94	90	76	88	65	93	86	87	94	63	83.6
10	88	91	71	89	97	79	93	87	69	85	84.9

8. The Stosh Motor Company manufactures bolts for its model X-350 high-performance racing engine. If defective, the bolts typically have damaged threads or improper diameters. If a defective bolt is passed to the assembly line, there is a chance that the thread in the engine block hole will be damaged or that the bolt may work itself loose during operation of the engine. The historical proportion defective has averaged 0.015.

   a. Set up a *p*-chart for this process. Assume that management wants 99.74 percent of the normal variation to fall within the control limits ($z = 3$). The sample size is 250.

   b. The following numbers of defects were found in the last five samples. Is there a need for concern?

Sample	Number of Bad Bolts
1	2
2	8
3	6
4	10
5	1

9. The IRS is concerned with improving the accuracy of tax information given by its representatives over the telephone. Previous studies involved asking a series of questions of 20 IRS telephone representatives to determine the proportion of correct responses. Historically, the average proportion of correct responses has been 70 percent. Recently, IRS representatives have been receiving more training. On April 1, the tax questions were again asked of 20 randomly selected IRS telephone representatives. The proportions of correct answers were 0.88, 0.75, 0.63, 1.00, 0.75, 0.75, 0.88, 0.37, 1.00, 0.50, 0.50, 0.88, 1.00, 0.63, 0.75, 0.88, 0.88, 1.00, 0.38, and 0.75. Interpret the results of that study.

10. A travel agency is concerned with the accuracy and appearance of itineraries prepared for its clients. Defects can include errors in times, airlines, flight numbers, prices, car rental information, lodging, charge card numbers, and reservation numbers, as well as typographical errors. As the possible number of errors is nearly infinite, the agency measures the number of errors that do occur. The current process results in an average of 7 errors per itinerary.

    a. What are the two-sigma control limits for these defects?

    b. A client scheduled a trip to Chicago. Her itinerary contained 13 errors. Interpret this information.

11. Sam's Taylor Shop makes custom fancy shirts for cowboys. The shirts could be flawed in various ways, including flaws in the weave or color of the fabric, loose buttons or decorations, wrong dimensions, and uneven stitches. Sam randomly examined 10 shirts, with the following results.

Shirt	Defects
1	9
2	3
3	6
4	11
5	3
6	12
7	0
8	4
9	7
10	5

    a. Assuming that 10 observations are adequate for these purposes, determine the three-sigma control limits for defects per shirt.

    b. Suppose that the next shirt has 12 flaws. What can you say about the process now?

12. The Big Black Bird Company produces fiberglass camper tops. The process for producing the tops must be controlled so as to keep the number of dimples low. When the process was in control, the following defects were found in randomly selected sheets over an extended period of time.

Top	Dimples
1	7
2	9
3	14
4	11
5	3
6	12
7	8
8	4
9	7
10	6

    a. Assuming that 10 observations are adequate for these purposes, determine the three-sigma control limits for dimples per camper top.

    b. Suppose that the next camper top has 15 dimples. What can you say about the process now?

13. The production manager at Happy Soda, Inc. is interested in tracking the quality of the company's 12-ounce bottle filling line. The bottles must be filled within the tolerances set for this product because the dietary information on the label shows 12 ounces as the serving size. The design standard for the product calls for a fill level of 12.00 ± 0.10 ounces. The manager collected the following sample data (in fluid ounces per bottle) on the production process.

	Observation			
Sample	1	2	3	4
1	12.00	11.97	12.10	12.08
2	11.91	11.94	12.10	11.96
3	11.89	12.02	11.97	11.99
4	12.10	12.09	12.05	11.95
5	12.08	11.92	12.12	12.05
6	11.94	11.98	12.06	12.08
7	12.09	12.00	12.00	12.03
8	12.01	12.04	11.99	11.95
9	12.00	11.96	11.97	12.03
10	11.82	11.86	12.09	12.18
11	11.91	11.99	12.05	12.10
12	12.01	12.00	12.06	11.97
13	11.98	11.99	12.06	12.03
14	12.02	12.00	12.05	11.95
15	12.00	12.05	12.01	11.97

a. Are the process average and range in statistical control?
b. Is the process capable of meeting the design standard? Explain.

14. The Pony Express Burger Corral is a fast-food restaurant. Although customers are attracted by the distinctive taste of the Pony Burger, they may never return if their order is not correctly filled. Pony Express was concerned with errors in filling orders at its drive-up window. It hired several "quality scouts" to randomly place 100 orders while the process seemed to be in control. The completed orders were then checked for accuracy. The table shows the results of the survey.

Use these data to estimate the average number of defects per order and determine the two-sigma control limits for a *c*-chart. A quality scout just used the drive-up window and now checks her order. Her Pony Burger has mustard on it although she ordered it without ketchup or mustard. Three handfuls of ketchup and mustard packets are in the sack, but no napkins. And hot coffee has spilled because the lid wasn't properly sealed. Is the drive-up process in statistical control?

Defect	Frequency
Incomplete, shorted order	15
Unordered items dispensed	4
Wrong product dispensed	14
Wrong toppings	27
Wrong size drink	12
Drink lid not sealed	17
No drinking straw with soft drink order	8
No napkins	18
Far too many condiment packets	62
No salt with sandwich or fries order	10
Wrong change	7
Other	17

15. Tom Mauro manages the circulation department for *Today*, a large daily newspaper. The distribution center receives complaints about late or missed deliveries every day. The following is a history of customer complaints.

Week	Sun.	Mon.	Tue.	Wed.	Thur.	Fri.	Sat.
1	127	163	201	175	111	150	158
2	199	189	136	154	119	107	153
3	120	145	106	165	183	151	124
4	182	105	139	159	163	141	161
5	139	186	188	164	116	175	159

a. Assuming that these data are sufficient, use them to determine three-sigma control limits for the appropriate type of chart(s).
b. Suppose that the next week's complaints are

Week	Sun.	Mon.	Tue.	Wed.	Thur.	Fri.	Sat.
6	101	138	229	194	211	155	183

Is the process in statistical control?

16. Webster Chemical Company produces mastics and caulking for the construction industry. The product is blended in large mixers and then pumped into tubes and capped. Management is concerned about whether the filling process for tubes of caulking is in statistical control. The process should be centered on 8 ounces per tube. Several samples of eight tubes were taken, each tube was weighed, and the weights in Table 5.3 (next page) were obtained.

| TABLE 5.3 | | *Ounces of Caulking per Tube* | | | | | |

				Tube Number				
Sample	1	2	3	4	5	6	7	8
1	7.98	8.34	8.02	7.94	8.44	7.68	7.81	8.11
2	8.33	8.22	8.08	8.51	8.41	8.28	8.09	8.16
3	7.89	7.77	7.91	8.04	8.00	7.89	7.93	8.09
4	8.24	8.18	7.83	8.05	7.90	8.16	7.97	8.07
5	7.87	8.13	7.92	7.99	8.10	7.81	8.14	7.88
6	8.13	8.14	8.11	8.13	8.14	8.12	8.13	8.14

a. Assuming that only 6 samples are sufficient, determine whether the process is in statistical control.

b. A supervisor notes that the weighing scale was gummed up with caulking. Apparently, a tube was not properly capped. The sticky scale did not correctly read the variation in weights for the sixth sample. Delete that data item and recalculate the control charts. Is the process in statistical control?

17. The sticky scale in Problem 16 calls management's attention to whether caulking tubes are being properly capped. If a significant proportion of the tubes aren't being sealed, Webster is placing its customers in a messy situation. Tubes are packaged in large boxes of 144. Several boxes are inspected, and the following numbers of leaking tubes are found.

Sample	Tubes	Sample	Tubes	Sample	Tubes
1	3	8	6	15	5
2	5	9	4	16	0
3	3	10	9	17	2
4	4	11	2	18	6
5	2	12	6	19	2
6	4	13	5	20	1
7	2	14	1	Total	72

Calculate *p*-chart three-sigma control limits to assess whether the capping process is in statistical control.

18. At Webster Chemical Company, lumps in the caulking compound could cause difficulties in dispensing a smooth bead from the tube. Even when the process is in control, an average of 4 lumps per tube of caulk will remain. Testing for the presence of lumps destroys the product, so an analyst takes random samples. The following results are obtained.

Tube No.	Lumps	Tube No.	Lumps	Tube No.	Lumps
1	6	5	6	9	5
2	5	6	4	10	0
3	0	7	1	11	9
4	4	8	6	12	2

Determine the *c*-chart two-sigma upper and lower control limits for this process.

19. Webster Chemical's nominal weight for filling tubes of caulk is 8.00 ± 0.60 ounces. The target process capability ratio is 1.33. The current distribution of the filling process is centered on 8.054 ounces with a standard deviation of 0.192 ounce. Compute the process capability ratio and process capability index to assess whether the filling process is capable and set properly.

20. Specify the three-sigma upper and lower control limits for a variable process mean of 8.00, with a population standard deviation of 0.192 for a sample size of 8.

Advanced Problems

21. Canine Gourmet Super Breath dog treats are sold in boxes labeled with a net weight of 12 ounces (340 grams) per box. Each box contains eight individual 1½ ounce packets. To reduce the chances of shorting the customer, product design specifications call for the packet filling process average to be set at 43.5 grams so that the average net weight per box will be 348 grams. Tolerances are set for the box to weigh 348 ± 12 grams. The standard deviation for the *packet filling* process is 3.52 grams. The target process capability ratio is 1.33. One day, the packet filling process average weight drifts down to 43.0 grams. Is the packaging process capable? Is an adjustment needed?

22. The Mansfield Machinery Company makes hand-held tools on an assembly line that produces one product every minute. On one of the products, the critical quality dimension is the diameter (measured in thousandths of an inch) of a hole bored in one of the assemblies. Management wants to detect any shift in the process average diameter from 0.015 inch. Management considers the variance in the process to be in control. Historically, the average range has been 0.002 inch, regardless of the process average. Design an $\bar{x}$-chart to control this process, with a center line at 0.015 inch and the control limits set at three sigmas from the center line.

Management has provided the results of 80 minutes of output from the production line, as shown in Table 5.4. During this 80 minutes the process average changed once. All measurements are in thousandths of an inch.

a. Set up an $\bar{x}$-chart with $n = 4$. The frequency should be sample four, then skip four. Thus your first sample would be for minutes 1–4, the second would be for minutes 9–12, and so on. When would you stop the process to check for a change in the process average?

b. Set up an $\bar{x}$-chart with $n = 8$. The frequency should be sample eight, then skip four. When would you stop the process now? What can you say about the desirability of large samples on a frequent sampling interval?

23. Using the data from Problem 22, continue your analysis of sample size and frequency by trying the following plans.

a. Using the $\bar{x}$-chart for $n = 4$, try the frequency sample four, then skip eight. When would you stop the process in this case?

b. Using the $\bar{x}$-chart for $n = 8$, try the frequency sample eight, then skip eight. When would you consider the process to be out of control?

c. Using your results from a and b, determine what trade-offs you would consider in choosing between them.

24. The plant manager at Northern Pines Brewery decided to gather data on the number of defective bottles generated on the line. Every day a random sample of 250 bottles was inspected for fill level, cracked bottles, bad labels, and poor seals. Any bottle failing to meet the standard for any of these criteria was counted as a reject. The study lasted 30 days and yielded the data in Table 5.5. Based on the data, what can you tell the manager about the quality of the bottling line? Do you see any nonrandom behavior in the bottling process? If so, what might cause this behavior?

25. Red Baron Airlines serves hundreds of cities each day, but competition is increasing from smaller companies

---

TABLE 5.4   *Sample Data for Mansfield Machinery Company*

Minutes	Diameter										
1–12	15	16	18	14	16	17	15	14	14	13	16	17
13–24	15	16	17	16	14	14	13	14	15	16	15	17
25–36	14	13	15	17	18	15	16	15	14	15	16	17
37–48	18	16	15	16	16	14	17	18	19	15	16	15
49–60	12	17	16	14	15	17	14	16	15	17	18	14
61–72	15	16	17	18	13	15	14	14	16	15	17	18
73–80	16	16	17	18	16	15	14	17

TABLE 5.5   *Sample Data for Northern Pines Brewery*

Samples	Number of Rejected Bottles in Sample of 250									
1–10	4	9	6	12	8	2	13	10	1	9
11–20	4	6	8	10	12	4	3	10	14	5
21–30	13	11	7	3	2	8	11	6	9	5

affiliated with major carriers. One of the key competitive priorities is on-time arrivals and departures. Red Baron defines *on time* as any arrival or departure that takes place within 15 minutes of the scheduled time. To stay on top of the market, management has set the high standard of 98 percent on-time performance. The operations department was put in charge of monitoring the performance of the airline. Each week, a random sample of 300 flight arrivals and departures was checked for schedule performance. Table 5.6 contains the numbers of arrivals and departures over the last 30 weeks that did not meet Red Baron's definition of on-time service. What can you tell management about the quality of service? Do you see any nonrandom behavior in the process? If so, what might cause the behavior?

TABLE 5.6   *Sample Data for Red Baron Airlines*

Samples	Number of Late Planes in Sample of 300 Arrivals and Departures									
1–10	3	8	5	11	7	2	12	9	1	8
11–20	3	5	7	9	12	5	4	9	13	4
21–30	12	10	6	2	1	8	4	5	8	2

Selected References

Barnard, William, and Thomas F. Wallace, *The Innovation Edge.* Essex Junction, Vt.: Oliver Wight Publications, Inc., 1994.

Charbonneau, Harvey C., and Gordon L. Webster. *Industrial Quality Control.* Englewood Cliffs, N.J.: Prentice-Hall, 1978.

Crosby, Philip B. *Quality Is Free: The Art of Making Quality Certain.* New York: McGraw-Hill, 1979.

Deming, W. Edwards. *Out of the Crisis.* Cambridge, Mass.: MIT Center for Advanced Engineering Study, 1986.

Denton, D. Keith. "Lessons on Competitiveness: Motorola's Approach." *Production and Inventory Management Journal* (Third Quarter 1991), pp. 22–25.

Duncan, Acheson J. *Quality Control and Industrial Statistics*, 5th ed. Homewood, Ill.: Richard D. Irwin, 1986.

Gitlow, Howard S., Shelly Gitlow, Alan Oppenheim, and Rosa Oppenheim. *Tools for the Improvement of Quality.* Homewood, Ill.: Richard D. Irwin, 1989.

Juran, J. M., and F. M. Gryna, Jr. *Quality Planning and Analysis*, 2nd ed. New York: McGraw-Hill, 1980.

Tiffany, Susan. "Grace Cocoa Unveils Engineering Marvel." *Candy Industry* (April 1993), pp. 22–29.

Acceptance Sampling

Acceptance sampling is an inspection procedure used to determine whether to accept or reject a specific quantity of material. As more firms initiate total quality management (TQM) programs and work closely with suppliers to ensure high levels of quality, the need for acceptance sampling will decrease. The TQM concept is that no defects should be passed from a producer to a customer, whether the customer is an external or internal customer. However, in reality, many firms must still rely on checking their materials inputs. The basic procedure is straightforward.

1. A random sample is taken from a large quantity of items and tested or measured relative to the quality characteristic of interest.
2. If the sample passes the test, the entire quantity of items is accepted.
3. If the sample fails the test, either (a) the entire quantity of items is subjected to 100 percent inspection and all defective items repaired or replaced or (b) the entire quantity is returned to the supplier.

We first discuss the decisions involved in setting up acceptance sampling plans. We then address several attribute sampling plans. We conclude with a discussion of the use of the computer in acceptance sampling.

◆ ACCEPTANCE PLAN DECISIONS

Acceptance sampling involves the producer (or supplier) of a material and the consumer (or buyer). Consumers need acceptance sampling to limit the risk of rejecting good quality materials or accepting bad quality materials. Consequently, the consumer, sometimes in conjunction with the producer through contractual agreements, specifies the parameters of the plan. Any company can be both a producer of goods purchased by another company and a consumer of goods or raw materials supplied by another company.

Quality and Risk Decisions

Two levels of quality are considered in the design of an acceptance sampling plan. The first is the **acceptable quality level (AQL),** or the quality level desired by the *consumer*. The producer of the item strives to achieve the AQL, which typically is written into a contract or purchase order. For example, a contract might call for a quality level not to exceed 1 defective unit in 10,000, or an AQL of 0.0001. The **producer's risk** (α) is the risk that the sampling plan will fail to verify an acceptable lot's quality and thus reject it—a type I error. Most often the producer's risk is set at 0.05, or 5 percent.

Although producers are interested in low risk, they often have no control over the consumer's acceptance sampling plan. Fortunately, the consumer also is interested in a low producer's risk because sending good materials back to the producer (1) disrupts the consumer's production process and increases the likelihood of shortages in materials, (2) adds unnecessarily to the lead time for finished products or services, and (3) creates poor relations with the producer.

The second level of quality is the **lot tolerance proportion defective (LTPD)**, or the worst level of quality that the consumer can tolerate. The LTPD is a definition of bad quality that the consumer would like to reject. Recognizing the high cost of defects, operations managers have become more cautious about accepting materials of poor quality from suppliers. Thus sampling plans have lower LTPD values than in the past. The probability of accepting a lot with LTPD quality is the **consumer's risk** (β), or the type II error of the plan. A common value for the consumer's risk is 0.10, or 10 percent.

Sampling Plans

All sampling plans are devised to provide a specified producer's and consumer's risk. However, it is in the consumer's best interest to keep the average number of items inspected (ANI) to a minimum because that keeps the cost of inspection low. Sampling plans differ with respect to ANI. Three often-used attribute sampling plans are the single-sampling plan, the double-sampling plan, and the sequential-sampling plan. Analogous plans also have been devised for variable measures of quality.

Single-Sampling Plan.   The **single-sampling plan** is a decision rule to accept or reject a lot based on the results of one random sample from the lot. The procedure is to take a random sample of size (n) and inspect each item. If the number of defects does not exceed a specified acceptance number (c), the consumer accepts the entire lot. Any defects found in the sample are either repaired or returned to the producer. If the number of defects in the sample is greater than c, the consumer subjects the entire lot to 100 percent inspection or rejects the entire lot and returns it to the producer. The single-sampling plan is easy to use but usually results in a larger ANI than the other plans. After briefly describing the other sampling plans, we focus our discussion on this plan.

Double-Sampling Plan.   In a **double-sampling plan** management specifies two sample sizes (n_1 and n_2) and two acceptance numbers (c_1 and c_2). If the quality of the lot is very good or very bad, the consumer can make a decision to accept or reject the lot on the basis of the first sample, which is smaller than in the single-sample plan. To use the plan, the consumer takes a random sample of size n_1. If the number of defects is less than or equal to c_1, the consumer accepts the lot. If the number of defects is greater than c_2, the consumer rejects the lot. If the number of defects is between c_1 and c_2, the consumer takes a second sample of size n_2. If the combined number of defects in the two samples is less than or equal to c_2, the consumer accepts the lot. Otherwise, it is rejected. A double-sampling plan can significantly reduce the costs of inspection relative to a single-sampling plan for lots with a very low or very high proportion defective because a decision can be made after taking the first sample. However, if the decision requires two samples, the sampling costs can be greater than those for the single-sampling plan.

Sequential-Sampling Plan.   A further refinement of the double-sampling plan is the **sequential-sampling plan,** in which the consumer randomly selects items from the lot and inspects them one by one. Each time an item is inspected, a decision is made to (1) reject the lot, (2) accept the lot, or (3) continue sampling, based on the cumulative results so far. The analyst plots the total number of defectives against the cumulative sample size, and if the number of defectives is less than a certain acceptance number (c_1), the consumer accepts the lot. If the number is greater than another acceptance number (c_2), the consumer rejects the lot. If the number is somewhere between the two, another item is inspected. Figure C.1 illustrates a decision to reject a lot after examining the fortieth unit. Such charts can be easily designed with the help of statistical tables.

FIGURE C.1

Sequential-Sampling Chart

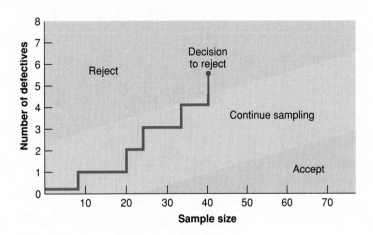

The ANI is generally lower for the sequential-sampling plan than for any other form of acceptance sampling, resulting in lower inspection costs. For very low or very high values of the proportion defective, sequential sampling provides a lower ANI than any comparable sampling plan. However, if the proportion of defective units falls between the AQL and the LTPD, a sequential-sampling plan could have a larger ANI than a comparable single- or double-sampling plan (although that is unlikely). In general, the sequential-sampling plan may reduce the ANI to 50 percent of that required by a comparable single-sampling plan and consequently save substantial inspection costs.

◆ OPERATING CHARACTERISTIC CURVES

Analysts create a graphic display of the performance of a sampling plan by plotting the probability of accepting the lot for a range of proportions of defective units. This graph, called an **operating characteristic (OC) curve,** describes how well a sampling plan discriminates between good and bad lots. Undoubtedly, every manager wants a plan that accepts lots with a quality level better than the AQL 100 percent of the time and accepts lots with a quality level worse than the AQL 0 percent of the time. This ideal OC curve for a single-sampling plan is shown in Fig. C.2 on the next page. However, such performance can be achieved only with 100 percent inspection. A typical OC curve for a single-sampling plan, plotted in red, shows the probability α of rejecting a good lot (producer's risk) and the probability β of accepting a bad lot (consumer's risk). Consequently, managers are left with choosing a sample size n and an acceptance number c to achieve the level of performance specified by the AQL, α, LTPD, and β.

FIGURE C.2

Operating Characteristic Curves

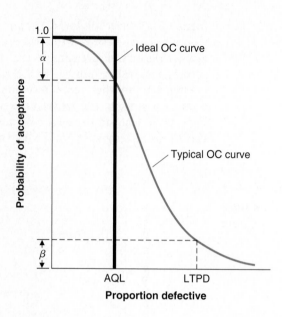

Drawing the OC Curve

The sampling distribution for the single-sampling plan is the binomial distribution because each item inspected is either defective (a failure) or not (a success). The probability of accepting the lot equals the probability of taking a sample of size n from a lot with a proportion defective of p and finding c or fewer defective items. However, if n is greater than 20 and p is less than 0.05, the Poisson distribution can be used as an approximation to the binomial to take advantage of tables prepared for the purpose of drawing OC curves (see Appendix 3). To draw the OC curve, look up the probability of accepting the lot for a range of values of p. For each value of p,

1. multiply p by the sample size n,
2. find the value of np in the left column of the table,
3. move to the right until you find the column for c, and
4. record the value for the probability of acceptance, P_a.

When p = AQL, the producer's risk, α, is 1 minus the probability of acceptance. When p = LTPD, the consumer's risk, β, equals the probability of acceptance.

EXAMPLE C.1

Constructing an OC Curve

The Noise King Muffler Shop, a high-volume installer of replacement exhaust muffler systems, just received a shipment of 1000 mufflers. The sampling plan for inspecting these mufflers calls for a sample size $n = 60$ and an acceptance number $c = 1$. The contract with the muffler manufacturer calls for an AQL of 1 defective muffler per 100 and an LTPD of 6 defective mufflers per 100. Calculate the OC curve for this plan, and determine the producer's risk and the consumer's risk for the plan.

Solution   Let $p = 0.01$. Then multiply n by p, to get $60(0.01) = 0.60$. Locate 0.60 in the table in Appendix 3. Move to the right until you reach the column for $c = 1$. Read the probability of acceptance: 0.878. Repeat this process for a range of p values. The following table contains the remaining values for the OC curve.

Note that the plan provides a producer's risk of 12.2 percent and a consumer's risk of 12.6 percent. Both values are higher than the values usually acceptable for plans of this type (5 percent and 10 percent, respectively). Figure C.3 shows the OC curve and the producer's and consumer's risks.

Values for the Operating Characteristic Curve with $n = 60$ and $c = 1$

Proportion Defective (p)	np	Probability of c or Less Defects (P_a)	Comments
0.01 (AQL)	0.6	0.878	$\alpha = 1.000 - 0.878 = 0.122$
0.02	1.2	0.663	
0.03	1.8	0.463	
0.04	2.4	0.308	
0.05	3.0	0.199	
0.06 (LTPD)	3.6	0.126	$\beta = 0.126$
0.07	4.2	0.078	
0.08	4.8	0.048	
0.09	5.4	0.029	
0.10	6.0	0.017	

FIGURE C.3   *The OC Curve for Single-Sampling Plan with $n = 60$ and $c = 1$*

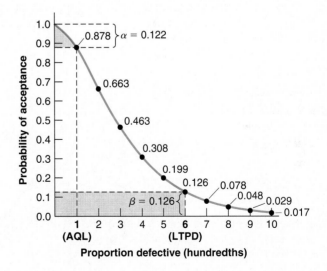

Explaining Changes in the OC Curve

Example C.1 raises the question of how management can change the sampling plan to reduce the probability of rejecting good lots and accepting bad lots. To answer this question, let's see how n and c affect the shape of the OC curve. In the Noise King example, a better single-sampling plan would have a lower producer's risk and a lower consumer's risk.

Sample Size Effect.   What would happen if we increased the sample size to 80 and left the acceptance level, c, unchanged at 1? We can use the tables in Appendix 3. If the proportion defective of the lot is p = AQL = 0.01, then np = 0.8 and the probability of acceptance of the lot is only 0.809. Thus the producer's risk is 0.191. Similarly, if p = LTPD = 0.06, the probability of acceptance is 0.048. Other values of the producer's and consumer's risks are shown in the following table.

n	Producer's Risk (p = AQL)	Consumer's Risk (p = LTPD)
60	0.122	0.126
80	0.191	0.048
100	0.264	0.017
120	0.332	0.006

These results, shown in Fig. C.4, yield the following principle: *Increasing n while holding c constant increases the producer's risk and reduces the consumer's risk.* For the producer of the mufflers, keeping $c=1$ and increasing the sample size makes getting a lot accepted by the customer tougher—only 2 bad mufflers will get the lot rejected. And the likelihood of finding those two defects is greater in a sample of 120 than in a sample of 60. Consequently, the producer's risk increases. For the management of Noise King, the consumer's risk goes down because a random sample of 120 mufflers from a lot with 6 percent defectives is less likely to have only 1 or less defective mufflers.

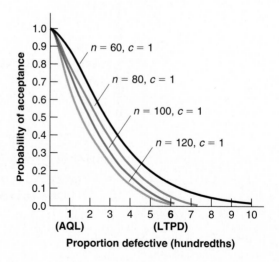

FIGURE C.4

Effects of Increasing Sample Size While Holding Acceptance Number Constant

Acceptance Level Effect.   Suppose that we keep the sample size constant at 60 but change the acceptance level. Again, we use the tables in Appendix 3.

c	Producer's Risk (p = AQL)	Consumer's Risk (p = LTPD)
1	0.122	0.126
2	0.023	0.303
3	0.003	0.515
4	0.000	0.706

The results are plotted in Fig. C.5. They demonstrate the following principle: *Increasing c while holding n constant decreases the producer's risk and increases the consumer's risk.* The producer of the mufflers would welcome an increase in the acceptance number because it makes getting the lot accepted by the consumer easier. If the lot has only 1 percent defectives (the AQL) with a sample size of 60, we would expect only 0.01(60) = 0.6 defect in the sample. An increase in the acceptance number from 1 to 2 lowers the probability of finding more than 2 defects and consequently lowers the producer's risk. However, raising the acceptance number for a given sample size increases the risk of accepting a bad lot. Suppose that the lot has 6 percent defectives (the LTPD). We would expect to have 0.6(60) = 3.6 defectives in the sample. An increase in the acceptance number from 1 to 2 increases the probability of getting a sample with 2 or less defects and therefore increases the consumer's risk.

FIGURE C.5

Effects of Increasing Acceptance Number While Holding Sample Size Constant

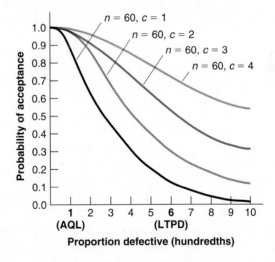

Thus, to improve Noise King's single-sampling acceptance plan, management should increase the sample size, which reduces the consumer's risk, *and* increase the acceptance number, which reduces the producer's risk. An improved combination can be found by trial and error using tables like those in Appendix 3. Alternatively, a computer can be used to find the best combination. For any acceptance number, the computer determines the sample size needed to achieve the desired producer's risk and compares it to the sample size needed to meet the consumer's risk. It selects the smallest sample size that will meet both the producer's risk and the consumer's risk. The following computer printout shows that a sample size of 111 and an acceptance number of 3 are best. This combination actually yields a producer's risk of 0.026 and a consumer's risk of 0.10 (not shown). The risks are not exact because c and n must be integers.

```
                    CMOM - Quality Control
                    Acceptance Sampling Plan

                          Data Entered

        Acceptable Quality Level (AQL)          : 0.0100
        Producer's Risk (Alpha)                 : 0.0500
        Lot Tolerance Percent Defective (LTPD)  : 0.0600
        Consumer's Risk (Beta)                  : 0.1000

                    CMOM - Quality Control
                    Acceptance Sampling Plan

                          Solution
```

	AQL BASED		LTPD BASED	
Acceptance Number	Expected Defectives	Sample Size	Expected Defectives	Sample Size
0	0.0513	5	2.3025	38
1	0.3553	36	3.8896	65
2	0.8176	82	5.3223	89
3 *	1.3663	137	6.6807	111
4	1.9702	197	7.9937	133
5	2.6130	261	9.2747	155
6	3.2854	329	10.5322	176
7	3.9810	398	11.7710	196
8	4.6953	470	12.9946	217
9	5.4253	543	14.2061	237
10	6.1689	617	15.4067	257

```
        Sample Size (n) = 111      Acceptance Level = 3
```

◆   AVERAGE OUTGOING QUALITY

We have shown how to choose the sample size and acceptance number for a single-sample plan, given AQL, α, LTPD, and β parameters. To check whether the performance of the plan is what we want, we can calculate the plan's **average outgoing quality** (AOQ), which is the expected proportion of defects that the plan will allow to pass. We assume that all defective items in the lot will be replaced with good items if the lot is rejected and that any defective items in the sample will be replaced if the lot is accepted. This approach is called **rectified inspection**. The equation for AOQ is

$$AOQ = \frac{p(P_a)(N - n)}{N}$$

where

p = true proportion defective of the lot

P_a = probability of accepting the lot

N = lot size

n = sample size

The analyst can calculate AOQ to estimate the performance of the plan over a range of possible proportion defectives in order to judge whether the plan will provide an acceptable degree of protection. The maximum value of the average outgoing quality over all possible values of the proportion defective is called the **average outgoing quality limit (AOQL)**. If the AOQL seems too high, the parameters of the plan must be modified until an acceptable AOQL is achieved.

EXAMPLE C.2

Calculating the AOQL

Suppose that Noise King is using rectified inspection for its single-sampling plan. Calculate the average outgoing quality limit for a plan with $n = 110$, $c = 3$, and $N = 1000$. Use Appendix 3 to estimate the probabilities of acceptance for values of the proportion defective from 0.01 to 0.08 in steps of 0.01.

Solution   Use the following steps to estimate the AOQL for this sampling plan:

Step 1.   Determine the probabilities of acceptance for the desired values of p. These are shown in the following table. However, the values for $p = 0.03$, 0.05, and 0.07 had to be interpolated because the table doesn't have them. For example, P_a for $p = 0.03$ was estimated by averaging the P_a values for $np = 3.2$ and $np = 3.4$, or $(0.603 + 0.558)/2 = 0.580$.

Proportion Defective (p)	np	Probability of Acceptance (P_a)
0.01	1.10	0.974
0.02	2.20	0.819
0.03	3.30	0.581 = (0.603 + 0.558)/2
0.04	4.40	0.359
0.05	5.50	0.202 = (0.213 + 0.191)/2
0.06	6.60	0.105
0.07	7.70	0.052 = (0.055 + 0.048)/2
0.08	8.80	0.024

Step 2.   Calculate the AOQ for each value of p.

For $p = 0.01$: $0.01(0.974)(1000 - 110)/1000 = 0.0087$
For $p = 0.02$: $0.02(0.819)(1000 - 110)/1000 = 0.0146$
For $p = 0.03$: $0.03(0.581)(1000 - 110)/1000 = 0.0155$
For $p = 0.04$: $0.04(0.359)(1000 - 110)/1000 = 0.0128$
For $p = 0.05$: $0.05(0.202)(1000 - 110)/1000 = 0.0090$
For $p = 0.06$: $0.06(0.105)(1000 - 110)/1000 = 0.0056$
For $p = 0.07$: $0.07(0.052)(1000 - 110)/1000 = 0.0032$
For $p = 0.08$: $0.08(0.024)(1000 - 110)/1000 = 0.0017$

The plot of the AOQ values is shown in Fig. C.6 on the next page.

Step 3.   Identify the largest AOQ value, which is the estimate of the AOQL. In this example, the AOQL is 0.0155 at $p = 0.03$.

FIGURE C.6   *Average Outgoing Quality Curve for the Noise King Muffler Service*

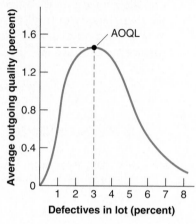

Managerial Practice C.1

▶ *Computerized SQC at Hay & Forage Industries*

Hay & Forage Industries (HFI) produces farm equipment such as windrowers, hay handling equipment, forage harvesters, tractors, balers, mowers, rotary cutters, backhoes, and tillers. In the mid 1970s the company experienced losses because of troubles in the farming industry. Over the next decade it suffered from intense national and global competition. In response to these pressures, management launched an aggressive quality enhancement program in an attempt to survive, grow, and increase market share. HFI adopted a computerized process control decision support system (PCDSS) capable of monitoring vast amounts of data crucial to maintaining product quality as well as recommending sampling plans and control charts. After some investigation, management determined that HFI had inadequate acceptance sampling plans. The company inventories about 2000 parts from 200 suppliers and produces many more of its own. A desirable sampling plan for one product and supplier may not be feasible for other products or suppliers. With PCDSS, management now develops a single-sampling plan for each internally manufactured part. Because the proportion

defective varies from day to day, management can use the most recent data to determine the average outgoing quality of each production lot. In addition, process control information can be shared by various departments at HFI. The actual proportion of defective products obtained from control charts is reported to the design engineering and marketing departments. As a result, design engineers can produce more meaningful product specifications and marketing managers have more reliable information on product quality.

Since 1987, the quality program at HFI has resulted in a 30 percent decrease in the proportion defective for most parts and a 60 percent decrease in some cases. The PCDSS creates more economical sampling plans that provide as good or better protection. Management spends 50 percent less time designing control charts and sampling plans, analyzing causes and effects, and training operators. Finally, HFI has increased sales dollars and increased the size of its work force from 500 to 725, despite an ongoing recession in the farming industry.

Source: Jinoos Hosseini and Nassar S. Fard, "A System for Analyzing Information to Manage the Quality-Control Process," *Interfaces,* vol. 21, no. 2 (March–April 1991), pp. 48–58.

♦ COMPUTERS AND STATISTICAL QUALITY CONTROL
PROCEDURES

At large companies such as United Parcel Service, American Airlines, Ford Motor Company, and Hewlett-Packard, computers are essential in implementing statistical quality control. Often thousands of parts, products, or services require monitoring, which involves determining quality measures; standards and inspection procedures; criteria for accepting, reworking, or rejecting materials; process control parameters; design specifications; costs; and historical quality performance of internal processes and suppliers. Computers enable managers to access the vast amounts of data collected in order to develop control charts, acceptance sampling plans, and frequency diagrams and correlations. Managerial Practice C.1 provides an example of the use of computers for acceptance sampling in a manufacturing firm.

SUPPLEMENT REVIEW

Solved Problem

An inspection station has been installed between two production processes. The feeder process, when operating correctly, has an acceptable quality level of 3 percent. The consuming process, which is expensive, has a specified lot tolerance proportion defective of 8 percent. The feeding process produces in batch sizes; if a batch is rejected by the inspector, the entire batch must be checked and the defective items reworked. Consequently, management wants no more than a 5 percent producer's risk and, because of the expensive process that follows, no more than a 10 percent chance of accepting a lot with 8 percent defectives or worse.

a. Determine the appropriate sample size, n, and the acceptable number of defective items in the sample, c.
b. Calculate values and draw the OC curve for this inspection station.
c. What is the probability that a lot with 5 percent defectives will be rejected?

Solution a. For AQL = 3%, LTPD = 8%, α = 5%, and β = 10%, use Appendix 3 and trial and error to arrive at a sampling plan. If n = 180 and c = 9,

$$np = 180(0.03) = 5.4$$

$$\alpha = 0.049$$

$$np = 180(0.08) = 14.4$$

$$\beta = 0.092$$

Sampling plans that would also work are n = 200, c = 10; n = 220, c = 11; and n = 240, c = 12.

b. The table on the next page contains the data for the OC curve. Appendix 3 was used to estimate the probability of acceptance. Figure C.7 shows the OC curve.

Proportion Defective (p)	np	Probability of c or Less Defects (Pₐ)	Comments
0.01	1.8	1.000	
0.02	3.6	0.996	
0.03 (AQL)	5.4	0.951	$\alpha = 1 - 0.951 = 0.049$
0.04	7.2	0.810	
0.05	9.0	0.587	
0.06	10.8	0.363	
0.07	12.6	0.194	
0.08 (LTPD)	14.4	0.092	$\beta = 0.092$
0.09	16.2	0.039	
0.10	18.0	0.015	

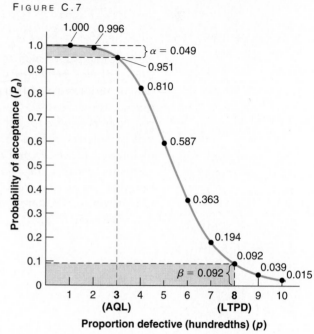

FIGURE C.7

c. According to the table, the probability of accepting a lot with 5 percent defectives is 0.587. Therefore the probability that a lot with 5 percent defects will be rejected is 0.413, or $1.00 - 0.587$.

Formula Review

1. Average outgoing quality: $\text{AOQ} = \dfrac{p(P_a)(N - n)}{N}$

Supplement Highlights

- Acceptance sampling is concerned with the decision to accept or reject a batch (or lot) of goods. The design of the acceptance sampling process includes decisions about sampling versus complete inspection, attribute versus variable measures, AQL, α, LTPD, β, sample size, and the acceptable number of defective items in the sample.
- Management can select the best plan (choosing sample size n and acceptance number c) by using an operating characteristic (OC) curve.
- Attribute sampling can be done with single-sampling, double-sampling, or sequential-sampling plans. When the lot proportion defective is either very low or very high, the last two have an advantage over single-sampling plans because the average number of items (ANI) needed to make a decision is smaller.
- When less than 100 percent of the lot is inspected, the sample may not be an accurate representation of the lot.

There are risks of accepting poor quality materials or rejecting good quality materials. The OC curves provide a graphic display of the performance of a sampling plan. They show how the probability of accepting a lot decreases with an increasing proportion defective in the lot.

- When rectified inspection is used to replace defective items with good items, the material leaving the inspection area (outgoing) will have a very high quality level. The average outgoing quality will depend on the original quality of the lot and the sampling plan used to identify and correct defects. Sampling plan parameters may be adjusted to provide an acceptable average outgoing quality limit.
- Computers are used to monitor vast amounts of quality performance data and to develop sampling plans that may cover thousands of parts, products, and services.

Key Terms

acceptable quality level (AQL) *217*
acceptance sampling *217*
average outgoing quality (AOQ) *224*
average outgoing quality limit (AOQL) *225*

consumer's risk (β) *218*
double-sampling plan *218*
lot tolerance proportion defective (LTPD) *218*
operating characteristic (OC) curve *219*

producer's risk (α) *217*
rectified inspection *224*
sequential-sampling plan *218*
single-sampling plan *218*

Problems

1. For $n = 180$, $c = 3$, AQL = 0.5%, and LTPD = 4%, find α and β.

2. You are responsible for purchasing bearings for the maintenance department of a large airline. The bearings are under contract from a local supplier, and you must devise an appropriate acceptance sampling plan for them. Management has stated in the contract that the acceptable quality level is 1 percent defective. In addition, the lot tolerance proportion defective is 4 percent, the producer's risk is 5 percent, and the consumer's risk is 10 percent.
   a. Specify an appropriate acceptance sampling plan that meets all these criteria.
   b. Draw the OC curve for your plan. What is the resultant producer's risk?
   c. Determine the AOQL for your plan. Assume a lot size of 3000.

3. The Lustre-Potion Shampoo Company purchases the label that is pasted on each bottle of shampoo it sells. The label contains the company logo, the name of the product, and directions for the product's use. Sometimes the printing on the label is blurred or the colors are not right. The company wants to design an acceptance sampling plan for the purchased item. The acceptable quality level is 10 defectives per 1000 labels, and the lot tolerance proportion defective is 5 percent. Management wants to limit the producer's risk to 5 percent or less and the consumer's risk to 10 percent or less.
   a. Specify a plan that satisfies those desires.
   b. What is the probability that a shipment with 3 percent defectives will be rejected by the plan?
   c. Determine the AOQL for your plan. Assume that the lot size is 2000 labels.

4. Your company supplies sterile syringes to a distributor of hospital supplies. The contract states that quality should be no worse than 0.2 percent defective, or 20 parts in 10,000. During negotiations, you learned that the distributor will use an acceptance sampling plan with $n = 400$ to test quality.
   a. If the producer's risk is to be no greater than 5 percent, what is the lowest acceptance number, c, that should be used?
   b. The syringe production process averages 25 defective parts in 10,000. With $n = 400$ and the acceptance level suggested in part a, what is the probability that a shipment will be returned to you?
   c. Suppose that you want a less than 5 percent chance that your shipment will be returned to you. For the data in part b, what acceptance number, c, should you have suggested in a? What is the producer's risk for that plan?

5. A buyer of electronic components has a lot tolerance proportion defective of 40 parts in 10,000, with a consumer's risk of 10 percent. If the buyer will sample 2000 components out of the shipment, what acceptance number, c, would the buyer want? What is the producer's risk if the AQL is 10 parts per 10,000?

6. Consider a certain raw material for which a single-sampling attribute plan is needed. The AQL is 1 percent, and the LTPD is 4 percent. Two plans have been proposed. Under plan 1, $n = 100$ and $c = 3$; under plan 2, $n = 200$ and $c = 6$. Are the two plans equivalent? Substantiate your response by determining the producer's risk and the consumer's risk for each plan.

7. You presently have an acceptance sampling plan in which $n = 40$ and $c = 1$, but you are unsatisfied with its performance. The AQL is 1 percent, and the LTPD is 5 percent.
   a. What are the producer's and consumer's risks for this plan?
   b. While maintaining the same 1:40 ratio of $c:n$ (called the acceptance proportion), increase c and n to find a sampling plan that will decrease the producer's risk to 5 percent or less *and* the consumer's risk to 10 percent or less. What producer's and consumer's risks are associated with this new plan?
   c. Compare the AOQLs for your plan and the old plan. Assume a lot size of 1000 units.

8. For AQL = 2%, LTPD = 8%, and $n = 200$, what value(s) of the acceptance number, c, would result in the producer's risk and the consumer's risk *both* being under 5 percent?

9. For AQL = 2% and $c = 5$, what is the largest value of n that will result in a producer's risk of under 5

percent? Using that sample size, determine the consumer's risk when LTPD = 8%.

10. For c = 11 and LTPD = 8%, what value of n results in a 10 percent consumer's risk?

11. Design a sampling plan for AQL = 0.1%, LTPD = 0.5%, producer's risk ≤ 5%, and consumer's risk ≤ 10%.

12. Design a sampling plan for AQL = 0.01% (100 parts per million), LTPD = 0.05% (500 ppm), producer's risk ≤ 5%, and consumer's risk ≤ 10%. This problem is similar to Problem 11. As AQL decreases by a factor of 10, what is the effect on the sample size, n?

Advanced Problems

A computer package is recommended for solving Problems 13–15.

13. Suppose that AQL = 0.5%, α = 5%, LTPD = 2%, β = 6%, and N = 1000.
    a. Find the AOQL for the single-sampling plan that best fits the given parameter values.
    b. For each of the following experiments, find the AOQL for the best single-sampling plan. Change only the parameter indicated, holding all others at their original values.
       i. Change N to 2000.
       ii. Change AQL to 0.8 percent.
       iii. Change LTPD to 6 percent.
    c. Discuss the effects of changes in the design parameters on plan performance, based on the three experiments in part b.

14. Mark Edwards is the quality assurance manager at an engine plant. The summer intern assigned to Edwards is a student in operations management at a local university. The intern's first task is to calculate the follow-

ing parameters, based on the SPC information at the engine plant:

$$AQL = 0.2\%, \quad \beta = 1\%, \quad \alpha = 2\%,$$
$$N = 1000, \quad LTPD = 2.5\%$$

a. Find the AOQL for the single-sampling plan that best fits the given parameter values.
b. For each of the following experiments, find the AOQL for the best single-sampling plan. Change only the parameter indicated, holding all others at their original values.
   i. Change N to 2000.
   ii. Change AQL to 0.3 percent.
   iii. Change LTPD to 4 percent.
c. Discuss the effects of changes in the design parameters on plan performance, based on the three experiments in part b.

15. The receiving manager at Breakthrough Technologies, Inc. wants to devise a sampling plan for an incoming lot of 1000 disk drive units. The plan will be based on the following parameters:

$$AQL = 0.02, \quad \alpha = 0.05, \quad LTPD = 0.08, \quad \beta = 0.10$$

a. Formulate a sampling plan that includes the sample size, n, and the acceptable number of defectives, c.
b. Develop an OC curve.
c. What is the probability that a lot with 4 percent defectives will be accepted? With 6 percent defectives?
d. Determine the AOQL for this plan. What is the impact on AOQL if the lot size is increased to 2000?

Selected References

Besterfield, D. H. *Quality Control*, 2nd ed. Englewood Cliffs, N.J.: Prentice-Hall, 1986.

U.S. Department of Defense. *Military Standard (MIL-STD-414), Sampling Procedures and Tables for Inspection by Variables for Percent Defective*. Washington, D.C.: Government Printing Office, 1957.

U.S. Department of Defense. *Military Standard (MIL-STD-105), Sampling Procedures and Tables for Attributes*. Washington, D.C.: Government Printing Office, 1963.

Chapter Six

WORK-FORCE MANAGEMENT

The Timken Company produces 2 million roller bearings a week for global customers who use them in products ranging from trailers to rail cars. A roller bearing reduces the friction of a wheel as it rotates on an axle. In the mid 1980s Timken management decided to close one of its two high-volume bearing plants. The Bucyrus, Ohio, plant was spared, but the employees were demoralized. As Jim Benson, general manager of the Bucyrus plant, recalls, "The workers told me, 'There's no future for us. It's only a matter of time.' "

The managers and employees of the Bucyrus plant decided to prove themselves wrong. Self-directed teams, initiated in 1990, cut across functional boundaries and allowed employees to make operating decisions formerly reserved for managers. For example, the teams address problems related to machine setup and maintenance, previously handled by two separate functions. An associate who has an idea can work with his or her immediate supervisor without going through several layers of management for approval. Members of the teams rotate through six positions responsible for equipment, quality, cost performance, safety and housekeeping, training, and human resources. An extensive training program was put in place; in one year 800 employees had more than 21,790 hours of instruction. Team accomplishments are recognized on a " Recognition Wall." Some of the accomplishments over a six-year period include the following.

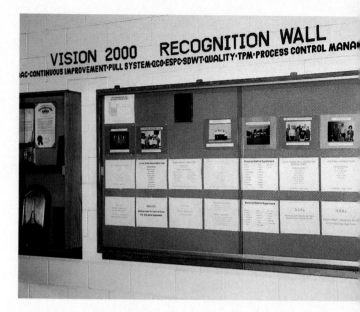

At Timken Company's Bucyrus, Ohio, plant, the Recognition Wall honors achievements made by teams through continuous improvement.

- Quality of the shipped product is at the seven-sigma level—only 0.31 defect per million bearings.
- Inventory levels have been reduced 25 percent, thereby reducing costs.
- Production schedules are met 98 percent of the time compared to only 74 percent earlier, dramatically improving on-time deliveries.

The more participative approach to the management of the plant has convinced the workers that they have a future.

The Timken plant in Bucyrus has undergone a significant change in the way it is being managed. The work force has been given much more latitude in the operations of the plant and as a result has made the plant much more competitive. Training and employee recognition played a big role, and the formation of self-directed teams cut across traditional functional boundaries. In this chapter we discuss both new and traditional approaches to work-force management.

◆ ORGANIZATIONAL RESTRUCTURING

We begin by defining an organizational structure that promotes cross-functional interaction, called the horizontal organization. We then discuss some of the incentive plans that companies use to recognize and reward employees and look at training programs that companies use to support work teams.

Horizontal Organizations

The most valuable resource any organization has is its employees. Putting up artificial boundaries in the organization that thwart the creativeness and problem-solving abilities of the employees wouldn't seem to make sense. Yet, that is what a traditional organization, called a vertical organization, tends to do. A **vertical organization** has departments such as marketing, operations, finance, human resources, and engineering. Employees look to their bosses for direction and authorization for actions; they are loyal to their own disciplines, and little communication occurs across functional boundaries. For example, in many traditional companies, marketing managers do not understand the problems of operations managers; operations managers do not talk to engineers; and there is little coordination between the functional areas and the human resources department.

Some companies, such as AT&T, DuPont, General Electric, and Motorola, are trying a new organizational model called the horizontal organization. In the **horizontal organization** the hierarchy and functional or departmental boundaries are eliminated and the organization is run by multidisciplinary teams. The idea is to manage *across* functional areas as opposed to managing *down* a hierarchical structure. The organization might have only three or four layers of management between the CEO and the members of a team. The focus in these organizations is the customer, not the interests of functional areas.

Is a horizontal organization appropriate for the firm?

Key Elements.   The horizontal organization has seven key elements.

1. *Organization is around the process.*   Often, three to five processes are crucial to the success of the organization. For example, a manufacturer's core processes may be product development (market analysis, market strategy, research and development, and design and engineering), customer support (advertising and customer service), and sales and fulfillment (pricing, sales, production, and shipping), with teams organized around each process.

2. *The organizational hierarchy is flat.*   Teams analyze processes to reduce the number of activities in each to a minimum, eliminating work that does not add value to the product or service.

3. *Teams manage the organization.*   Teams are the major building blocks in a horizontal corporation. At the top might be vice-presidents of strategy and planning and support services, the chief operating officer, and the chairperson of the board of directors, who is responsible for the performance of the entire organization. Below that level are teams comprising managers and employees from various disciplines, each organized around a core process. Each team has its own purpose and is held accountable for measurable performance goals.

4. *Customers drive performance.*   Customer satisfaction is the key performance measure in a horizontal corporation. This element also is part of total quality management programs (see Chapter 4).

5. *Management rewards team performance.* The appraisal and pay systems are designed to reward team efforts, rather than individual efforts. Employees acquiring multiple skills needed by their team are rewarded for their efforts.

6. *Teams maintain supplier and customer contact.* Team members are in contact with suppliers and customers. When appropriate, supplier or customer representatives take active roles on the teams.

7. *Training programs are provided for all employees.* Employees are offered training programs to improve their general skills in problem solving, leadership, and communication and their administrative skills. Information is provided in raw form so that the employees can analyze it and arrive at their own conclusions.

Links to Operations Strategy. For most companies, becoming a horizontal organization requires a major cultural transformation from the use of managers and employees who are specialists (as in a typical vertical organization) to the use of managers and employees who are generalists (as in a horizontal organization). The transformation may dramatically improve a company's competitiveness. Most attempts to create horizontal organizations to date have focused on the lower levels of the organization (middle management to hourly employees) rather than the executive level.

The process of changing an organizational structure can be painful, and many companies do not want to go through with it. The decision should be linked to operations strategy. A vertical organization may suit some mass-production industries better than a horizontal organization because of the repetitive nature of the operations and the competitive priority of low costs. Horizontal organizations are flexible. Firms whose competitive priorities include product development speed, high-performance design, customization, or high levels of product variety may find horizontal structures more suited to their needs. Companies should first decide what it takes to be successful in the marketplace and then decide whether a horizontal organization will support their organizational and operational strategies.

Incentive Plans

Incentive and recognition plans that reward workers individually or as team or group members encourage productivity improvements. A 1992 survey of 2000 companies by Hewitt Associates indicated that 61 percent of the companies surveyed had such plans, compared to only 47 percent in 1990. This interest in incentive plans reflects management's concern over properly rewarding excellence in the workplace, especially with the increase in the formation of work teams. Traditional incentive schemes do not always work because they reward individual behavior rather than team behavior. Seven incentive plans are commonly used; three are classified as individual based, two as team based, and two as group based.

> **S**hould individual-, team-, or group-based incentive plans be used to improve productivity?

Individual-Based Plans. Incentive plans for individuals may be based on piece rate, pay for skills, or bonus points.

Piece rate is a traditional compensation plan based on output: the number of units created or services performed during a day or week. For example, workers performing a telephone survey may be paid for the number of contacts they make. Output levels are based on what management, and sometimes the employees or the union, considers a fair day's work. Such plans do not promote team efforts nor do they encourage high-quality work.

In *pay-for-skills plans,* employees are rewarded for skills they acquire that make them more valuable members of their team. For example, at Mettler-Toledo, a manufacturer of weight indicators and circuit boards, employees receive $0.20 an hour more when they complete training and receive certification in a new skill. This incentive plan supports team efforts because it increases the diversity of skills of the team members and allows more flexibility in their assignments.

In a *bonus-point* plan, employees accumulate points for participating in employee involvement activities. Rewards are given after a certain number of points have been earned. For example, Honda of America awards employees points for participating in a quality circle working on a complex plant change. Honda's quality circles determine their own projects, and employees contribute as much time as they wish. Employees who earn 2500 bonus points receive a Honda Civic. Honda has awarded seven Civics to employees; the first car was awarded only 2½ years after the program was announced. Other rewards are available for fewer bonus points.

Team-Based Plans. Where incentives are tied to production/quality goals, teams may receive financial incentives. In other cases the reward is public recognition.

In organizations where members receive an increase in pay for achieving a given output quota (say, 1000 units per day) that is tied to a standard for quality (say, 99 percent defect-free), bonus payments may be made for exceeding those *production/quality goals.* Rewarding the team rather than individuals promotes teamwork and innovation.

Many companies believe that employees have an intrinsic desire for excellence and a need for public recognition of their accomplishments. Public recognition may take the form of displays of the team's efforts in the office or plant, articles in the company newsletter, or company banquets. Often, *public recognition plans* do not involve added compensation for employees. Teams can also receive recognition by competing against teams from other companies in sponsored events, such as the National Team Excellence Award contest sponsored by the Association for Quality and Participation.

Group-Based Plans. Two ways of rewarding groups are profit sharing and gain sharing.

Profit sharing rewards employees when the company as a whole meets certain profitability levels. Although profit sharing plans differ widely, a typical plan would require that, after a certain minimum return on investment (or profit level) has been achieved for the year, half of the profits in excess of the minimum be put into retained earnings for the company and the other half into a bonus pool for the employees. Individual bonuses are based on the number of hours worked or the employee's base pay. Bonuses can be large in good years and nothing in bad years.

Like profit sharing, *gain sharing* rewards the collective performance of a group, but it focuses on the costs of output, which are more under the control of employees than are profits. Employees share the benefits from quality and productivity improvements with the company. This incentive plan is often associated with participative forms of management because it promotes group efforts to improve productivity.

A study authorized by the U.S. Department of Labor in 1993 indicated that in 800 manufacturing companies in Michigan the presence of either profit sharing or gain sharing resulted in higher productivity and that these plans were more prevalent in firms that paid higher wages. In addition, the value added to products because of these plans exceeded the resultant increase in wages.

Training Programs

In a global marketplace, firms face changing market conditions brought on by new competitors and changing customer preferences. Firms must rely on their employees to anticipate possible problems, develop new products and services, and increase quality to remain competitive. As employees become more involved in team work, their need for social and communication skills, quality management skills, administrative skills, and technical skills increases. The emphasis on efficient processes and high quality requires that employees have a broader base of skills so that they can take on a greater variety of assignments and communicate with employees in other areas. Firms engage in a variety of training programs, including the following.

- *General training.* These programs address topics such as leadership, communication, project management, problem solving, mathematics, statistical process control methods, critical thinking, and even remedial English. Some firms encourage employees to take courses outside their functional areas, possibly at a local university or community college if their own training facility cannot satisfy the need.

- *Administrative training.* Courses in employment practices, performance appraisals, and management skills are offered to employees who have been designated team leaders.

Participants in an Outward Bound Professional Development Program in Joshua Tree National Monument, California, work on a map and compass exercise to find the evening's camp. The setting creates a situation outside of the office in which to assess leadership, teamwork, and communication skills.

- *Technical training.* These courses focus on the specific aspects of a person's job or a related job with the goal of increasing the employee's skills.

Organizational restructuring involves much more than we have been able to cover in this section. However, the work force clearly plays an important role in a firm's competitiveness. Even if a horizontal organization model is not appropriate for a firm, operations managers need to revisit traditional approaches to incentive programs and training.

◆ JOB DESIGN

Job design specifies a job's content, the employee skills and training needed to perform that job, and the degree of specialization appropriate for the job. Job design is an important part of a firm's operations strategy because it defines the amount of flexibility needed in the work force. Successful job design

- improves efficiency through analysis of the job's work elements,
- improves productivity through consideration of technical and human factors,
- increases the quality of the final product or service, and
- increases worker satisfaction.

Traditional job design was invented more than 100 years ago by Frederick Taylor. His approach, known as **scientific management,** is based on the philosophy that any operation can be improved by breaking it into components and studying the work content of each component to improve work methods. Taylor believed that managers should study jobs scientifically, using careful analysis, experimentation, and tools such as flow diagrams and process charts to find the most economic way to perform a task. Later in this chapter we discuss some of Taylor's techniques for studying work methods and arriving at standards.

Taylor stressed the need for managers to train workers in the new method in order to improve efficiency. He believed that management must accept the responsibility for coordinating work so that output is not restricted by poor planning and timing. Taylor also believed that scientific management would work only if the economic benefits of increased output were shared by both management and workers—that is, workers received greater pay for increased productivity.

Taylor's methods dealt primarily with the engineering aspects of job design: ways to best reach, grasp, and move objects; the number of repetitions to be performed before a rest was needed; and the best physical position for the worker. Undoubtedly, scientific management techniques practiced by industrial engineers contributed greatly to the rise in U.S. productivity between 1900 and 1950.

Many managers have applied Taylor's concepts to increase productivity in both manufacturing and service industries. These applications often led to job specialization and vertical organizations. New approaches to job design being used by some organizations today involve team building and developing cross-functional linkages. These approaches consider the behavioral aspects of a worker's job performance, such as the effects of safety, noise, ventilation, illumination, and monotony. In this section we address an aspect of job design that concerns managers—the degree of job specialization—because it relates directly to the discussion of organizational restructuring.

Should jobs be specialized or enlarged?

Job Specialization

A job with a high degree of **specialization** involves a narrow range of tasks, a high degree of repetition, and, presumably, great efficiency and high quality. For example, an appliance repairperson specializing in refrigerators can quickly diagnose problems and make the correct repairs based on previous experience; a heart specialist can diagnose and treat heart problems better than a general practitioner. Consider the tasks required in a fast-food restaurant where the employees take the order, prepare and package the meal, and accept payment. This job design becomes inefficient as the volume of orders increases because the employees start bumping into each other. Alternatively, the tasks could be divided into two jobs: one an order taker who also keeps the french-fryer going, draws drinks, packages the meal, and accepts the payment; the other a burger maker who does all the grill work. Specialization results in benefits such as

- less training time needed per employee because the methods and procedures are limited,
- faster work pace, leading to more output in less time, and
- lower wages paid because education and skill requirements are lower.

However, the arguments against job specialization suggest that narrowly defined jobs lead to

- poor employee morale, high turnover, and lower quality because of the monotony and boredom of repetitive work;
- the need for more management attention because the total activity is broken down into a large number of jobs for a large number of employees, all of whom have to be coordinated to produce the entire product or service; and
- less flexibility to handle changes or employee absences.

The degree of specialization should relate directly to the competitive priorities of the firm. A high degree of specialization tends to support the competitive priorities of a product-focused firm: low costs, consistent quality, and little product variety. A low degree of specialization tends to support the competitive priorities of a process-focused firm: customization, high performance design, and volume flexibility. However, some firms that compete on the basis of low costs and consistent quality (e.g., Motorola and AT&T) are exploring organizational models based on less specialization.

Alternatives to Specialization

People work for a variety of reasons: economic needs (to earn a living), social needs (to be recognized and to belong to a group), and individual needs (to feel important and to feel in control). These factors influence how people perform their jobs. In narrowly designed jobs, workers have fewer opportunities to control the pace of work, receive gratification from the work itself, advance to a better position, show initiative, and communicate with fellow workers. Alternative strategies to overcome the boredom of highly specialized jobs include job enlargement, job rotation, and job enrichment.

Job Enlargement. The *horizontal* expansion of a job—that is, increasing the range of tasks at the same level—is called **job enlargement.** The employee completes a larger proportion of the total work required for the product or service. Typically this approach requires that workers have various skills, and it is often accompanied by training programs and wage increases. Besides reducing boredom, job enlargement has the potential to increase employee satisfaction because the worker feels a greater sense of responsibility, pride, and accomplishment. For example, the AT&T Credit Corporation, which processes telephone equipment lease applications, is organized so that teams of workers perform all three major leasing functions for a customer: receiving applications and checking credit ratings, drawing up contracts, and collecting payments. Other financial institutions often devote three separate departments to these functions and design the jobs with a high degree of specialization. Employees at AT&T Credit Corporation feel responsibility for the quality of the service and understand how their activities contribute to the total service. With this job design the AT&T Credit Corporation processes up to 800 applications a day, more than double the number of a bank using the traditional job design processes.

Job Rotation. A system whereby workers exchange jobs periodically, thus getting more diversity in task assignment, is called **job rotation.** This approach is most effective when the jobs require an equal level of skill. For example, workers at a family restaurant may rotate duties from busing tables to cooking meals to taking orders from the patrons. Because workers learn many aspects of the job, job rotation increases the skills of the work force, giving management the flexibility to replace absent workers or to move workers to different workstations as necessary. In addition, rotating jobs can give each worker a better appreciation for the production problems of others and the value of passing only good quality to the next person.

Job Enrichment. The most comprehensive approach to job design is **job enrichment,** which entails a *vertical* expansion of job duties. That is, workers have greater control and responsibility for an entire process, not just a specific skill or operation. This approach supports the development of employee *empowerment* and *self-managed teams,* whereby employees make basic decisions about their jobs. For example, a chef at an elegant restaurant may be given the responsibility of purchasing ingredients at the market and arranging her own work schedule. Job enrichment generally increases job satisfaction because it gives workers a sense of achievement in mastering many tasks, recognition and direct feedback from users of the output, and responsibility for the quality of the output.

◆ WORK STANDARDS

Now that we have explored some aspects of job design let's turn to measuring output rates. The rate of output is influenced by positioning strategy, process choice, technology, and job design. Creating a commonly accepted basis for comparison requires development of a **work standard,** or the time required for a trained worker to perform a task following a prescribed method with normal effort and skill. Robots of the same type perform the same repetitive tasks with little variation in output rate, but human output is more difficult to evaluate because skill, effort, and stamina vary from one employee to another.

Work Standards As a Management Tool

Managers use work standards in the following ways.

How can work standards be used to achieve continuous improvements in operations?

1. *Establishing prices and costs.*   Managers can use labor and machine time standards to develop costs for current and new products, create budgets, determine prices, and arrive at make-or-buy decisions.
2. *Motivating workers.*   Standards can be used to define a day's work or to motivate workers to improve their performance. For example, under an incentive compensation plan, workers can earn a bonus for output that exceeds the standard.
3. *Comparing alternative process designs.*   Time standards can be used to compare different routings for an item and to evaluate new work methods and new equipment.
4. *Scheduling.*   Managers need time standards to assign tasks to workers and machines in ways that effectively utilize resources. We discuss scheduling in more detail in Chapter 16.
5. *Capacity planning.*   Managers can use time standards to determine current and projected capacity requirements for given demand requirements. We investigate capacity planning and long-term capital investment in Chapter 7. Work-force staffing decisions, discussed in Chapter 13, also may require time estimates.
6. *Performance appraisal.*   A worker's output can be compared to the standard output over a period of time to evaluate worker performance and productivity.

Areas of Controversy

Work standards often are a source of conflict between management and labor. When an organization uses output standards as the basis for pay, unions or workers may object if they believe that standards are set "too high" and management may object if they believe that standards are set "too low." Both groups benefit from setting *achievable* standards because setting output standards at either extreme makes planning for appropriate capacity levels difficult, increases costs, and reduces profits.

Managers themselves disagree over the use of engineered work standards to increase productivity. Some managers believe that employees need to be involved in determining work standards, that time studies dehumanize workers, and that the costs of large industrial engineering staffs and the hidden costs of labor–management conflicts outweigh the benefits of elaborate standards. Others believe that using engineered standards for piecework incentives actually defeats their purpose of increasing worker productivity because employees will have little incentive to improve their work methods. Workers also may lose sight of quality as they race to meet standards. However, as Managerial Practice 6.1 shows, when firms involve employees in defining their own work standards, Frederick Taylor's ideas can still increase productivity.

Managerial Practice 6.1

▶ *Allowing Workers to Define Their Own Work Standards*

When General Motors and Toyota announced their plan in 1983 to create the New United Motor Manufacturing, Inc. (NUMMI), the companies had two different goals. GM wanted to learn about Toyota's successful production system, and Toyota wanted to ease trade frictions that had arisen because of its competition with U.S. car companies. Toyota also wanted to see whether Japanese management methods could be used with U.S. workers. The site chosen for the new venture, GM's Fremont, California, plant, had had the worst productivity and employee absenteeism record in the corporation before being shut down in 1982. To avoid union backlashes at GM's other plants, NUMMI management had to re-employ over 1700 workers from the previous work force.

NUMMI's Toyota-trained management embraced Frederick Taylor's principles of measuring the activities of workers in minute detail and then standardizing and accelerating their tasks to increase productivity. At the "old" Fremont plant, GM had employed 80 industrial engineers to design jobs and set work standards; however workers often did not accept these because they were not consulted in establishing them. To overcome the problems of the past, NUMMI management organized the workers into 350 teams of six to eight people, including a team leader. The employees in each team were trained in work measurement and analysis methods and given the assignment to design all the team's jobs by first timing each other with stopwatches and then exploring ways to improve their own performance. Team members were trained in more than one job, and tasks were rotated among team members.

The approach has been successful for several reasons. First, the workers believe that they are a key to the factory's success. In addition, the no-layoff policy provides employees with the security of knowing that improvements to the process will not result in job loss. Finally, giving workers extensive training and consulting them

At the NUMMI plant in Fremont, California, a worker assembles a Geo Prism in accordance with worker-designed work standards.

frequently have fostered trust in management. Two years after the new venture started,

- productivity and quality were twice that of the "old" Fremont plant, greater than that of any other GM assembly plant, and almost as high as that of Toyota's long-established factories;
- drug and alcohol abuse on the job had disappeared;
- absenteeism had almost stopped; and
- Toyota had added another assembly line and expanded the work force.

Although NUMMI's approach includes employee involvement, it has not reduced white-collar jobs. These employees provide support to the shop-floor workers. Also, the teams are *not* encouraged to improvise new work methods. Improvements come from refinement of standards or the formulation of new ones.

Source: Paul Adler, "Time-and-Motion Regained," *Harvard Business Review* (January–February 1993), pp. 97–108.

◆ METHODS OF WORK MEASUREMENT

The key to creating a work standard is defining *normal* performance. Suppose, for example, that the manager of a fast-growing company that manufactures frozen pizza wants to create a standard for pizza assembly. To assemble the pizza, a worker spreads sauce over the pizza shell, adds pepperoni and cheese, places the pizza in a box, and puts the assembled product on a cart for fast freezing. The entire process takes 20 seconds. At this pace a worker could assemble 1440 pizzas in an eight-hour day.

Before settling on 20 seconds as the standard, however, the manager must consider whether all the employees have the skills of the observed worker. He may be exceptionally energetic, experienced, and efficient. Moreover, the estimate of 20 seconds per pizza did not account for fluctuations in pace or scheduled rest periods. Generally, the time per unit observed over a short period for one employee should not be used as a standard for an extended period of time for all employees.

Work measurement is the process of creating labor standards based on the judgment of skilled observers. Methods of work measurement available to the manager include

1. the time study method,
2. the elemental standard data approach,
3. the predetermined data approach, and
4. the work sampling method.

The method chosen often depends on the purpose of the data. For example, when an analyst needs a high degree of precision in comparing actual work method results to standards, a stopwatch study or predetermined times might be required. Alternatively, an analyst who wants to estimate the percentage of time that an employee is idle while waiting for materials requires a work sampling method. Moreover, an analyst may use more than one approach to obtain needed work measurement information.

How can time standards be obtained to compare alternative process designs or project future capacity requirements?

Time Study Method

The method used most often for setting time standards for a job is called a **time study**, which consists of four steps.

Step 1: Selecting Work Elements. Each work element should have definite starting and stopping points to facilitate taking stopwatch readings. Work elements that take less than three seconds to complete should be avoided because they are difficult to time. The work elements selected should correspond to a standard work method that has been running smoothly for a period of time in a standard work environment. Incidental operations not normally involved in the task should be identified and separated from the repetitive work.

Step 2: Timing the Elements. After the work elements have been identified, the analyst times a worker trained in the work method to get an initial set of observations. The analyst may use either the *continuous method*, recording the stopwatch reading for each work element upon its completion, or the *snap-back method*, resetting the stopwatch to zero upon completion of each work element. For the latter method, the analyst uses two watches, one for recording the previous work element and the other for timing the present work element.

If the sample data include a single, isolated time that differs greatly from other times recorded for the same element, the analyst should investigate the cause of the variation. An "irregular occurrence," such as a dropped tool or a machine failure, should not be included in calculating the average time for the work element. The average observed time based only on representative times is called the **select time** ($\bar{t}$). Irregular occurrences can be covered in the allowances that we discuss later.

Step 3: Determining Sample Size. Typically, those who use the time study method to set standards want an average time estimate that is very close to the true long-range average most of the time. A formula, based on the normal distribution, allows the analyst to determine the sample size, n, required:

$$n = \left[\left(\frac{z}{p} \right) \left(\frac{\sigma}{\bar{t}} \right) \right]^2$$

where n = required sample size

p = precision of the estimate as a proportion of the true value

$\bar{t}$ = select time for a work element

σ = standard deviation of representative observed times for a work element

z = number of normal standard deviations needed for the desired confidence

Typical values of z for this formula are

Desired Confidence (%)	z
90	1.65
95	1.96
96	2.05
97	2.17
98	2.33
99	2.58

For example, a z value of 1.96 represents ± 1.96 standard deviations from the mean, leaving a total of 5 percent in the tails of the standardized normal curve. The precision of the estimate, p, is expressed as a proportion of the true (but unknown) average time for the work element.

EXAMPLE 6.1

Estimating the Sample Size in a Time Study

A coffee cup packaging operation has four work elements. A preliminary study provided the following results.

Work Element	Standard Deviation, σ (minutes)	Select Time, $\bar{t}$ (minutes)	Sample Size
1. Get two cartons	0.0305	0.50	5
2. Put liner in carton	0.0171	0.11	10
3. Place cups in carton	0.0226	0.71	10
4. Seal carton and set aside	0.0241	1.10	10

Work element 1 was observed only 5 times because it occurs once every two work cycles. The study covered the packaging of 10 cartons. Determine the appropriate sample size if the estimate for the select time for any work element is to be within 4 percent of the true mean 95 percent of the time.

Solution   For this problem,

$$p = 0.04 \text{ and } z = 1.96$$

The sample size for each work element must be calculated, and the largest must be used for the final study so that all estimates will meet or exceed the desired precision.

Work element 1: $n = \left[\left(\dfrac{1.96}{0.04} \right) \left(\dfrac{0.0305}{0.500} \right) \right]^2 = 9$

Work element 2: $n = \left[\left(\dfrac{1.96}{0.04} \right) \left(\dfrac{0.0171}{0.11} \right) \right]^2 = 58$

Work element 3: $n = \left[\left(\dfrac{1.96}{0.04} \right) \left(\dfrac{0.0226}{0.71} \right) \right]^2 = 3$

Work element 4: $n = \left[\left(\dfrac{1.96}{0.04} \right) \left(\dfrac{0.0241}{1.10} \right) \right]^2 = 2$

All fractional calculations were rounded to the next largest integer. To be sure that all select times are within 4 percent of the true mean 95 percent of the time, we must have a total of 58 observations because of work element 2. Consequently, we have to observe the packaging of 48 (or $58 - 10$) more cartons.

Step 4:   Setting the Standard.   The final step is to set the standard. To do so, the analyst first determines the normal time for each work element by judging the pace of the observed worker. The analyst must assess not only whether the worker's pace is above or below average but also a **performance rating factor (RF)** that describes *how much* above or below average the worker's performance on each work element is. Setting the performance rating requires the greatest amount of judgment. Usually only a few workers are observed during a study. If the workers are fast, basing the standard on their average time wouldn't be fair, particularly if a wage incentive plan is involved. Conversely, if the workers are slow, basing the standard on their normal time would be unfair to the company. Further, workers may slow their pace when they are being observed in a time study. Thus the analyst has to make an adjustment in the average observed time to estimate the time required for a trained operator to do the task at a normal pace. Analysts go through training programs to ensure consistency of ratings over many analyses.

The analyst must also factor in the frequency of occurrence, *F*, of a particular work element in a work cycle. Some work elements may not be performed every cycle. The analyst finds the **normal time (NT)** for any work element by multiplying the select time $(\bar{t})$, the frequency (*F*) of the work element per cycle, and the rating factor (RF):

$$NT = \bar{t}(F)(RF)$$

To find the **normal time for the cycle (NTC)**, the analyst sums the normal time for each element:

$$NTC = \Sigma NT$$

EXAMPLE 6.2

Determining the Normal Time

Suppose that 48 additional observations of the coffee cup packaging operation were taken and the following data were recorded.

Work Element	$\bar{t}$	F	RF
1	0.53	0.50	1.05
2	0.10	1.00	0.95
3	0.75	1.00	1.10
4	1.08	1.00	0.90

Because element 1 occurs only every other cycle, its average time per cycle must be half its average observed time. That's why $F_1 = 0.50$ for that element. All others occur every cycle. What are the normal times for each work element and for the complete cycle?

Solution The normal times are calculated as follows.

Work element 1: $\quad NT_1 = 0.53(0.50)(1.05) = 0.28$ minute
Work element 2: $\quad NT_2 = 0.10(1.00)(0.95) = 0.10$ minute
Work element 3: $\quad NT_3 = 0.75(1.00)(1.10) = 0.83$ minute
Work element 4: $\quad NT_4 = 1.08(1.00)(0.90) = \underline{0.97}$ minute
$\qquad\qquad\qquad\qquad\qquad\qquad\qquad\qquad$ Total $= 2.18$ minutes

The normal time for the complete cycle is 2.18 minutes.

We cannot use the normal time of 2.18 minutes for the cycle as a standard because it doesn't allow for fatigue, rest periods, or unavoidable delays that occur during an average workday. Hence we must add some **allowance time** to the normal time to adjust for these factors. The **standard time (ST)** then becomes

$$ST = NTC(1 + A)$$

where $\quad A =$ proportion of the normal time added for allowances

Most allowances range from 10 to 20 percent of normal time and cover factors that may be difficult to measure. However, work sampling can be used to estimate some of those factors.

EXAMPLE 6.3

Determining the Standard Time

Management needs a standard time for the coffee cup packaging operation. Suppose that $A = 0.15$ of the normal time. What is the standard time for the coffee cup packaging operation, and how many cartons can be expected per eight-hour day?

Solution For $A = 0.15$ of the normal time,

$$ST = 2.18(1 + 0.15) = 2.51 \text{ minutes/carton}$$

For an eight-hour day, this translates into a production standard of

$$\frac{480 \text{ minutes/day}}{2.51 \text{ minutes/carton}} = 191 \text{ cartons/day}$$

Overall Assessment of Time Study.   Time study methods have some limitations. They should not be used to set standards for jobs in which the nature of the task is different each time, such as a student solving a problem, a professor preparing a lecture, or an automobile mechanic diagnosing the cause of a nonroutine problem. In addition, an inexperienced person should not conduct time studies because errors in recording information or in selecting the work elements to include can result in unreasonable standards. Finally, some workers may object to time study because of the subjectivity involved. Nonetheless, time studies conducted by an experienced observer usually provide a satisfactory, although imperfect, tool for setting equitable time standards.

Elemental Standard Data Approach

If a plant requires thousands of work standards, the time and cost required for the time study method may be prohibitive. When a high degree of similarity exists in the work elements of certain jobs, analysts often use **elemental standard data** to derive standards for various jobs. In this approach, analysts use a work measurement approach, such as time study, to compile standards for the common elements. The standards are stored in a database. If the time required for a work element depends on certain variable characteristics of the jobs, an equation that relates these characteristics to the time required can also be stored in a database. Once established, the database can provide the data needed to estimate the normal times for jobs requiring these work elements with varying characteristics. However, allowances still must be added to arrive at standard times for the jobs.

In addition to reducing the number of time studies needed, the elemental standard data approach can help managers develop standards for new work before production begins. This feature is helpful in product costing, pricing, and production planning.

Although the use of the elemental standard data approach reduces the need for time studies, they can't be eliminated. The analyst develops the normal times for the database using methods such as the time study method and should periodically use time study methods to check the standards developed by the elemental standard data approach. Specifying all the job variables that affect times for each work element may be difficult; consequently, this method may not produce good estimates for the normal time.

Predetermined Data Approach

The predetermined data approach eliminates the need for time studies altogether. The analyst divides each work element into a series of micromotions common to a variety of tasks. The analyst then consults a published database that contains the normal times for these micromotions, along with modifications for job variables. The normal time for any task can be developed by accessing the database.

One of the most commonly used predetermined data systems is **methods time measurement (MTM)**. Actually, there are several MTM databases, but we focus on the most accurate, MTM-1. In MTM-1 the basic micromotions are reach, move, disengage, apply pressure, grasp, position, release, and turn. The normal times for these micromotions, modified for job variables, were developed by trained observers, who applied performance ratings to observations of motion picture studies of workers in various industrial settings.

Each micromotion is measured in time measurement units (TMUs). One TMU equals 0.0006 minute. Setting standards from predetermined data involves several steps.

1. Break each work element down into its basic micromotions.
2. Find the proper tabular value for each micromotion. Tabular values account for mitigating factors such as weight, distance, size of object, and degree of difficulty.
3. Add the normal time for each motion from the tables to get the normal time for the total job.
4. Adjust the normal time for allowances to give the standard time.

For example, suppose that a worker must move an 18-pound object with both hands to an exact location 20 inches away. The hands are not in motion prior to the move. To find the TMU value for this action, we first go to Table 6.1 on the next page, which describes the *move* motion. The table allows for differences in weight, distance moved, and circumstances of the move. Note that case C describes the circumstances of this move. Under column C, the entry for 20 inches is 22.1 TMUs. Now make adjustments for the weight of the object. The worker is using two hands, so the weight *per hand* is 9 pounds, which is greater than 7.5 pounds and less than 12.5 pounds in the weight allowance columns. The dynamic factor is 1.11, and the static factor is 3.9 TMUs. To find the final TMU value for this move activity, we multiply the tabular TMU value for the distance moved by the dynamic factor and add the static factor: 22.1(1.11) + 3.9 = 28 TMUs. There are similar tables for other motions.

The predetermined data approach offers some advantages over the other approaches we have discussed. First, standards can be set for new jobs before production begins, which cannot be done with the time study method. Second, new work methods can be compared without conducting a time study. Third, a greater degree of consistency in the setting of time standards is provided because the sources of error in time studies, such as data recording errors, are reduced. Finally, this approach lessens the problem of biased judgment, since performance ratings are no longer needed in the derivation of a standard.

The predetermined data approach also has its drawbacks. Work must be broken down into micromotions, making this method impractical for firms with a process focus and low repeatability. Moreover, the sample of workers used to develop the predetermined data may not be representative of the workers in a particular facility. Further, performance time variations can result from a complex array of factors. For example, the time needed to move an object may depend on the shape of the object, but the MTM-1 charts do not recognize this factor. Also, the method assumes that the times associated with the micromotions simply can be summed to get the total time for a task. This assumption disregards the possibility that the actual time may depend on the specific *sequence* of motions. Finally, there is a danger that the approach will be misused. Although the approach appears easy to use, considerable training and experience are required to identify all the micromotions and accurately judge the mitigating factors of the motion.

TABLE 6.1   *MTM Predetermined Data for the Move Micromotion*

Distance Moved (in.)	Time TMU				Wt. Allowance			Case and Description
	A	B	C	Hand in Motion B	Wt. (lb) Up to	Dynamic Factor	Static Constant (TMU)	
¾ or less	2.0	2.0	2.0	1.7				
1	2.5	2.9	3.4	2.3	2.5	1.00	0	
2	3.6	4.6	5.2	2.9				
3	4.9	5.7	6.7	3.6	7.5	1.06	2.2	A Move object to other hand or against stop.
4	6.1	6.9	8.0	4.3				
5	7.3	8.0	9.2	5.0	12.5	1.11	3.9	
6	8.1	8.9	10.3	5.7				
7	8.9	9.7	11.1	6.5	17.5	1.17	5.6	
8	9.7	10.6	11.8	7.2				
9	10.5	11.5	12.7	7.9	22.5	1.22	7.4	
10	11.3	12.2	13.5	8.6				B Move object to approximate or indefinite location.
12	12.9	13.4	15.2	10.0	27.5	1.28	9.1	
14	14.4	14.6	16.9	11.4				
16	16.0	15.8	18.7	12.8	32.5	1.33	10.8	
18	17.6	17.0	20.4	14.2				
20	19.2	18.2	22.1	15.6	37.5	1.39	12.5	
22	20.8	19.4	23.8	17.0				
24	22.4	20.6	25.5	18.4	42.5	1.44	14.3	C Move object to exact location.
26	24.0	21.8	27.3	19.8				
28	25.5	23.1	29.0	21.2	47.5	1.50	16.0	
30	27.1	24.3	30.7	22.7				
Additional	0.8	0.6	0.85		TMU per inch over 30 inches			

Source: Copyright © by the MTM Association for Standards and Research. No reprint permission without written consent from the MTM Association, 16–01 Broadway, Fair Lawn, NJ 07410.

Work Sampling Method

How can the amount of time that employees spend on unproductive activities be estimated?

Work sampling involves estimating the proportions of time spent by people and machines on activities, based on a large number of observations. These activities might include producing a product or service, doing paperwork, waiting for instructions, waiting for maintenance, or being idle. The underlying assumption is that the proportion of time during which the activity is observed in the sample will be the proportion of time spent on the activity in general. Data from work sampling also can be used to estimate how effective machines or workers are, estimate the allowances needed to set standards for use with other work measurement methods, determine job content, and help assess the cost of jobs or activities.

Work Sampling Procedure. Conducting a work sampling study involves the following steps.

1. Define the activities.
2. Design the observation form.
3. Determine the length of the study.
4. Determine the initial sample size.
5. Select random observation times using a random number table.
6. Determine the observer schedule.
7. Observe the activities and record the data.
8. Decide whether additional sampling is required.

A work sampling study should be conducted over a period of time that is representative of normal work conditions, in which each activity occurs a representative number of times. For example, if an activity occurs only once a week, the study should probably span several months. However, if the activity occurs continuously throughout the week and from week to week throughout the year, the study might cover only several weeks.

Sample Size. The goal of work sampling is to obtain an estimate of the proportion of time spent on a particular activity that does not differ from the true proportion by more than a specified error. That is, the analyst wants to take a sample, calculate the sample proportion, $\hat{p}$, and be able to say that the following interval contains the true proportion with a specified degree of precision:

$$\hat{p} - e \leq \hat{p} \leq \hat{p} + e$$

where $\hat{p}$ = sample proportion (number of occurrences divided by the sample size)

e = maximum error in the estimate

The sample size affects the degree of precision that can be expected from work sampling for any desired level of statistical confidence. Work sampling involves estimating proportions, so the sampling distribution is the binomial distribution. However, large sample sizes are required for this approach, and the normal approximation to the binomial distribution can be used to determine the appropriate sample size. Figure 6.1 on the next page shows the confidence interval for a work sampling study. The maximum error can be computed as

$$e = z\sqrt{\frac{\hat{p}(1 - \hat{p})}{n}}$$

where n = sample size

z = number of standard deviations needed to achieve the desired confidence

FIGURE 6.1
*Confidence Interval for
a Work Sampling Study*

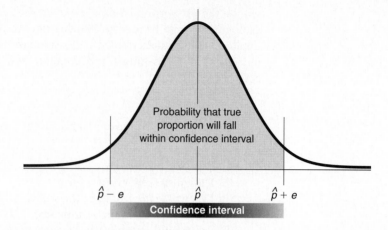

Because *n* is in the divisor of the equation, as *n* increases, the maximum error decreases. To determine the proper sample size for a given error, the analyst uses the formula for *e* to solve for *n*:

$$n = \left(\frac{z}{e}\right)^2 \hat{p}(1 - \hat{p})$$

Initially, the analyst may have to make a reasonable guess for the proportion of time an activity takes, use the formula to determine *n*, and then compute an estimate of the proportion based on the sample. The new estimate for the proportion can be used in the formula for *n* to determine whether additional sampling is required.

Sampling Schedule.   The times of day the analyst gathers the sample data should be selected at random over the length of the study. This approach reduces the amount of bias in the data. For example, if employees know that they will be observed each day at 2:30 P.M., some of them may alter their behavior at that time. If that happens, the data won't represent actual performance. After determining the observation times to be used, the analyst can develop a schedule for the observer.

EXAMPLE 6.4

*Using Work
Sampling Data for
Decision Making*

The hospital administrator at a private hospital is considering a proposal for installing an automated medical records storage and retrieval system. To determine the advisability of purchasing such a system, the administrator needs to know the proportion of time that registered nurses (RNs) and licensed vocational nurses (LVNs) spend accessing records. Presently these nurses must either retrieve the records manually or have them copied and sent to their wards. A typical ward, staffed by eight RNs and four LVNs, is selected for the study.

a. The hospital administrator estimates that accessing records takes about 20 percent of the RNs' time and about 5 percent of the LVNs' time. The administrator wants 95 percent confidence that the estimate for each category of nurses falls within ±0.03 of the true proportion. What should the sample size be?

b. The hospital administrator estimates that the annual amortization cost and expenses for maintaining the new automated medical records storage and retrieval system will be $150,000. The supplier of the new system estimates that the system will reduce the amount of time the nurses spend accessing records by 25 percent. The total annual salary expense for RNs in the hospital is $3,628,000, and for LVNs it is $2,375,000. The hospital administrator assumes that nurses could productively use any time saved by the new system. The pilot work sampling study resulted in the data shown in Fig. 6.2. Should the administrator purchase the new system?

Solution

a. Using estimates for the proportion of time spent accessing records of 0.20 for RNs and 0.05 for LVNs, an error of ± 0.03 for each, and a 95 percent confidence interval ($z = 1.96$), we recommend the following sample sizes.

$$\text{RN:} \quad n = \left(\frac{1.96}{0.03}\right)^2 (0.20)(0.80) = 683$$

$$\text{LVN:} \quad n = \left(\frac{1.96}{0.03}\right)^2 (0.05)(0.95) = 203$$

Eight RNs and four LVNs can be observed on each trip. Therefore 683/8 = 86 (rounded up) trips are needed for the observations of RNs, and only 203/4 = 51 (rounded up) trips are needed for the LVNs. Thus 86 trips through the ward will be sufficient for observing both nurse groups. This number of trips will generate 688 observations of RNs and 344 observations of LVNs. It will provide many more observations than are needed for the LVNs, but the added observations may as well be recorded as the observer will be going through the ward anyway.

b. Before using the estimates from the work sampling study, we must be sure that additional sampling is not required. Figure 6.2 shows that RNs accessed records 124 times and LVNs only 28 times. The CMOM output on the next page shows that the proportion of working time spent on accessing records is 0.1802 for the RNs and 0.0814 for the LVNs. Thus the original estimates were off the mark. The computer uses the new estimates for the proportions in the same formulas we used in part a to revise the sample sizes. However, the new sample sizes are *smaller* than those already used, so no additional sampling is required. If the sample sizes were too small for the proportions found, additional sampling would have to be performed. In addition, the confidence interval shows the range possible in the "true" proportions, based on the results of the pilot study. For example, the actual proportion of time spent by the RNs on accessing records could be as low as 0.15 and as high as 0.21.

FIGURE 6.2 *Results of the Initial Study*

	Activity				
	Accessing records	Attending to patients	Other support activities	Idle or break	Total observations
RN	124	258	223	83	688
LVN	28	251	46	19	344

Data Entered

Number of Work Elements :   2

Level of Confidence   :   0.9500

Test Statistic   :   1.9600

Absolute Error   :   0.0300

	Sample Size	Number of Working Tallies
WE1	688	124
WE2	344	28

CMOM - Work Measurement - Work Sampling

Solution

Work Element	Working Time	Delay Time	--Confidence Interval-- Lower	Upper	Required Sample Size
WE1	0.1802	0.8198	0.1515	0.2090	631
WE2	0.0814	0.9186	0.0525	0.1103	320

Because the nurses will not be using the system all the time, we use the supplier's estimate of 25 percent in determining the value of the time spent accessing records. Estimated annual net savings from the purchase of the automatic medical records storage and retrieval system are

Net savings = 0.25[($3,628,000)(0.18) + ($2,375,000)(0.08)] − $150,000
            = $60,760

However, the confidence intervals indicate that the true proportions could be as low as 0.15 for RNs and 0.05 for LVNs. If that "worst case" situation occurred, the net savings would be

Net savings = 0.25[($3,628,000)(0.15) + ($2,375,000)(0.05)] − $150,000
            = $15,737

Based on the results of the work sampling study, the new system appears to be a good investment, provided the nurses can spend the time saved productively on other duties.

Overall Assessment of Work Sampling.   The work sampling method is used frequently to estimate the proportion of time that people or machines spend on particular activities because it offers certain advantages over other approaches. No special training is required for the observers, no stopwatches are needed, and several studies can be conducted simultaneously. In addition, workers themselves often prefer this method of work measurement because it typically is directed at the activities of groups, rather than individuals.

The major disadvantage to work sampling is the large number of brief observations required to provide a reasonable degree of precision for the estimate. Unlike the other approaches discussed, this method usually is not used for setting standards for repetitive, well-defined jobs.

By calling up computerized medical records, doctors and nurses can consult and update patients' charts instantly. Bedside stations monitor vital signs, medication, and medical instructions.

Managerial Considerations in Work Measurement

In light of new management philosophies and technologies, managers should re-examine work measurement techniques that have been used since the days of Frederick Taylor. In particular, managers should consider the implications of TQM and increased automation.

TQM. Programs such as total quality management (TQM) and continuous improvement rely on employee inputs to improve operations. Traditional work measurement techniques seem repressive and not applicable to TQM or continuous improvement. However, traditional work measurement techniques *can* be used in the spirit of continuous improvement, as at GM-Toyota's NUMMI plant. Employees must be trained in the use of these techniques, which should be applied for the purpose of making improvements and keeping costs down.

Increased Automation. When a firm increases its level of automation, its methods of work measurement must also change. There is less need to use traditional work measurement techniques to develop work standards for automated operations because many computer-controlled machines can gather data on their operations. Hence standards for the machines can be set without having to sample unit processing times. Application of the techniques discussed in this chapter can then focus on less prevalent activities that are largely controlled by the pace of workers.

In Supplement D we discuss workers' learning curves because of their implications for work measurement.

CHAPTER REVIEW

Solved Problem 1

For a time study of a health insurance claims adjusting process, the analyst uses the continuous method of recording times. The job is divided into four work elements. Shown in Fig. 6.3 on the next page are the performance rating factors, RF, and the continuous method recorded times, *r*, for each work element.

FIGURE 6.3

Operation: Insurance claim processing		Date: 10/07		Observer: Jennifer Johnson					
Work Element		**Observations**					$\bar{t}$	RF	σ
		1	2	3	4	5			
1. Check form completion and signatures	t	0.50	0.55	0.45	0.60	0.50	0.52	1.1	0.0570
	r	0.50	3.30	5.70	8.20	10.85			
2. Enter claim amounts, check math	t	0.20	0.15	0.25	0.35	0.25	0.24	1.2	0.0742
	r	0.70	3.45	5.95	8.55	11.10			
3. Determine proportion of claim to be disallowed	t	0.75	0.60	0.55	0.70	0.65	0.65	1.2	0.0791
	r	1.45	4.05	6.50	9.25	11.75			
4. Generate form letter, enter data for check	t	1.30	1.20	1.10	1.10	1.30	1.20	0.9	0.1000
	r	2.75	5.25	7.60	10.35	13.05			

a. Calculate the normal time for this job.
b. Calculate the standard time for this job, assuming that the allowance is 20 percent of the normal time.
c. What is the appropriate sample size for estimating the time for element 2 within ± 10 percent of the true mean with 95 percent confidence?

Solution a. To get the normal time for this job, we must first determine the observed time, t, for each work element for each cycle. We calculate the time for each observation by finding the difference between successive recorded times, r. For example, the time for the fifth observation of the first work element is the difference between the recorded time when that element was completed (at 10.85 minutes) and the time when the fourth observation of the fourth work element was completed (at 10.35 minutes): 10.85 minutes − 10.35 minutes = 0.50 minute. Similarly, the time for the fifth observation of the second work element is 11.10 minutes − 10.85 minutes = 0.25 minute. With no extreme variation in the observed times for the work elements, they are representative of the process. All the data can be used for calculating the average observed time, called the select time, $\bar{t}$, and the standard deviation of the observed times, σ. The results of those calculations are given in Fig. 6.3. Every work element occurs during every cycle, so the frequency, F, equals 1. The normal times are calculated as

$$NT = \bar{t}\,(F)(RF)$$

Work element 1: $NT_1 = (0.52)(1)(1.1) = 0.572$ minute
Work element 2: $NT_2 = (0.24)(1)(1.2) = 0.288$ minute
Work element 3: $NT_3 = (0.65)(1)(1.2) = 0.780$ minute
Work element 4: $NT_4 = (1.20)(1)(0.9) = \underline{1.080}$ minutes
Total $= 2.720$ minutes

b. Standard time = (Normal time per cycle)(1.0 + Allowances), or

$$ST = NTC(1.0 + A) = 2.72(1.0 + 0.2)$$
$$= 3.264 \text{ minutes}$$

c. The appropriate sample size for 95 percent confidence that the select time for work element 2 is within ± 10 percent of the true mean is

$$n = \left[\left(\frac{z}{p}\right)\left(\frac{\sigma}{\bar{t}}\right)\right]^2 = \left[\left(\frac{1.96}{0.10}\right)\left(\frac{0.0742}{0.24}\right)\right]^2$$

$$= 36.72, \quad \text{or } 37 \text{ observations}$$

Solved Problem 2

A library administrator wants to determine the proportion of time the circulation clerk is idle. The following information was gathered randomly by using work sampling.

Day	Number of Times Clerk Busy	Number of Times Clerk Idle	Total Number of Observations
Monday	8	2	10
Tuesday	7	1	8
Wednesday	9	3	12
Thursday	7	3	10
Friday	8	2	10
Saturday	6	4	10

If the administrator wants a 95 percent confidence level and a degree of precision of ± 4 percent, how many more observations are needed?

Solution The total number of observations made was 60. The clerk was observed to be idle 15 times. The initial estimate of the proportion is $\hat{p} = 15/60 = 0.25$. The required sample size for a precision of ± 4 percent is

$$n = \frac{z^2 \hat{p}(1 - \hat{p})}{e^2} = \frac{(1.96)^2(0.25)(0.75)}{(0.04)^2}$$

$$= 450.19, \quad \text{or } 451 \text{ observations}$$

As 60 observations have already been made, an additional 391 are needed.

Formula Review

1. Required sample size in a time study: $n = \left[\left(\dfrac{z}{p} \right) \left(\dfrac{\sigma}{\bar{t}} \right) \right]^2$

2. Normal time for a work element: $\text{NT} = \bar{t}(F)(\text{RF})$

3. Normal time for the cycle: $\text{NTC} = \Sigma\text{NT}$

4. Standard time: $\text{ST} = \text{NTC}(1 + A)$

5. Required sample size in a work sampling study: $n = \left(\dfrac{z}{e} \right)^2 \hat{p}(1 - \hat{p})$

   where $e = z\sqrt{\dfrac{\hat{p}(1 - \hat{p})}{n}}$

Chapter Highlights

- Some organizations are changing from vertical to horizontal structures. The horizontal organization has only a few levels (a flat organizational chart) and is organized around customers and processes, rather than functional areas. Cross-functional teams manage projects. Rewards are based on customer-driven, team performance measures. Functional boundaries and policies that act as hurdles to creative problem solving are removed. Horizontal organizations have a competitive advantage when product development speed, high performance design, or customization is important.

- Scientific management is an engineering approach to job design. The method is concerned with the best physical position of the worker, most efficient ways to grasp and move objects, and the number of repetitions that results in fatigue. The scientific management approach often leads to job specialization and vertical organization. New approaches to job design consider both the technical and the social requirements of the job, with the focus on the work group instead of the individual worker.

- Whether jobs are to be narrowly or broadly defined is a

job design decision. Advantages of narrowly defined jobs are short learning time, fast work pace, and low labor costs. Disadvantages are creation of more idle time for some workers, increased materials handling and coordination, and adverse behavioral consequences. Broadly defined jobs may be achieved through job enlargement, job rotation, and job enrichment. These alternative strategies help overcome the boredom of highly specialized jobs.

- Work measurement results are useful for comparing alternative process designs, scheduling, capacity planning, pricing and costing, appraising performance, and developing incentive plans. Work measurement data are used most often for estimating and costing, followed by incentive plan development, scheduling, and performance appraisal.
- The most common method of setting time standards for a job is time study. After dividing the job into a series of smaller work elements, the analyst measures the time required for a trained worker using the prescribed work method to complete a certain number of cycles. The worker's pace is rated, and allowances are added to arrive at a standard.
- The elemental standard data approach relies on time standards that have been determined for common work elements. Time standards for other jobs containing the same elements are compiled by retrieving the standards from a database.
- The predetermined data approach further divides each work element into a series of micromotions. The analyst consults a database to estimate the time required for each and develops standards for a work element by adding its micromotion times.
- Work sampling is used most often to estimate the proportion of time spent on various broader activities associated with production processes. Although a large number of random observations are needed to make the estimates, little training on the part of the observer is required.
- Employees can be trained to perform work measurement studies on their own. Work measurement should be undertaken in the spirit of making continuous improvements rather than to justify reductions in the work force.

Key Terms

Study Questions

1. How does a horizontal organization affect opportunities for promotion and advancement?
2. What are the differences in skills needed by vertical and horizontal organizations? What effect will organizational restructuring have on distinctive competencies? On the roles of managers?
3. What are the key elements of a horizontal organization?
4. What important aspect of work does scientific management ignore?
5. What are the arguments for and against narrowly defined jobs?
6. What is the difference between job enlargement and job enrichment? How do they relate to the arguments for and against narrowly defined jobs?

7. What opportunities do workers lack in some work environments? Compare an assembly line worker in a highly automated plant to a secretary in a busy law office. Which opportunities is each likely to have? Which opportunities is each worker likely to lack?
8. An instructor for an introductory class in operations management positions all her students on the 50 yard line of the football field. She declares that anyone who does not reach the goal line in five seconds will fail the course. Discuss this intriguing way of grading a class in terms of defining a standard.
9. The Italian Maiden Pizza Company produces pizza for resale in the frozen food section of large supermarkets. Recently, product designs for a new deep-dish product were finalized. Which work measurement

technique should be used to develop time standards for making this product before production actually begins?

10. A colleague of yours comments that a time study with the use of a standard stopwatch is a precise method for determining work standards. What is your reply?

11. Your company builds concrete patio floors to customer specifications. The activities are (1) consulting with the customer to prepare the specifications, (2) drawing the plans, (3) digging the foundation, (4) building the forms, and (5) laying the concrete. What method would you use to develop a time standard for installing patio floors?

12. Two of your assistants are arguing over the precision required for a work sampling study. The proportion of time spent by a group of your employees manually filling out forms for customer orders turned out to be 0.28 in a recent pilot study. There is a proposal to bring in a network of microcomputers to speed this process. One assistant believes that the estimate should be within ± 0.01 of the true proportion, and the other believes that a precision of ± 0.05 is sufficient. The pilot study had a sample size of 100. What would you consider in choosing a sample size for this study?

Problems

1. A worker assembled 10 parts in 50 minutes during a time study. The analyst rated the worker at 95 percent. The allowance for fatigue, personal time, and other contingencies is 20 percent of the normal time.
   a. Calculate the normal time for this job.
   b. Calculate the standard time for this job.

2. The manager of Swifty Car Lube wants a labor standard for oil changes. Sandy Johnson completed 20 oil changes in a total of 178 minutes. Sandy is considered an above-average worker and was rated at 110 percent. The allowance is 10 percent of the normal time.
   a. Calculate the normal time for oil changes.
   b. Calculate the standard time for oil changes.

3. A time study involving the preparation of hamburgers at Bill's fast-food restaurant used the snap-back method to obtain the data (in minutes) shown in Table

6.2. Allowances typically constitute 15 percent of normal time. The schedule calls for 300 hamburgers to be prepared during the lunch rush. If each part-time employee works 190 minutes per day, how many employees will be needed?

4. A cook at Bill's restaurant (see Problem 3) has devised a new method of quickly flipping and pressing hamburgers that he believes will save time in cooking the second side of hamburgers (work element 3 in Table 6.2). The cook asked a peer to conduct a time study for this work element, with the results shown in Table 6.3. This cook is renowned for superior strength and speed in hamburger flipping and pressing. The rating factor for this study is 1.2. Allowances typically constitute 15 percent of the normal time.

TABLE 6.2   *Time Study Results of Hamburger Preparation*

Work Element	Observation 1	2	3	4	5	$\bar{t}$	F	RF	NT
1. Prepare patty	0.45	0.41	0.50	0.48	0.36		1	0.9	
2. Cook first side	0.85	0.81	0.77	0.89	0.83		1	1.2	
3. Flip, press, and cook other side	0.60	0.55	0.59	0.58	0.63		1	1.2	
4. Assemble	0.31	0.24	0.27	0.26	0.32		1	1.0	
								Normal time per cycle (NTC) =	

TABLE 6.3   *Work Element 3 Time Study*

Work Element	Observation 1	2	3	4	5	6	7	8	9	10
Revised work element 3	0.45	0.31	0.50	0.48	0.39	0.31	0.44	0.29	0.33	0.40

a. What is the average of select times for revised work element 3? For the revised normal time?

b. What is the revised normal time per cycle? The revised standard time?

c. The managers seem very interested in this revised method for work element 3. They say that if they could be sure the average of the select times for this study was within ±13 percent of the true average time for this new method, they could afford to buy health insurance for the part-time cooks. How many observations would be required to be 98 percent confident that the average of select times for this study was within ±13 percent of the true mean?

d. The cook is not only quick with a spatula but also quick with a calculator and a bit suspicious of management's motives. If the average of the select times found in part a were inflated by 13 percent, how many cooks would Bill's restaurant need?

5. The information (in minutes) shown in Table 6.4 pertains to a package filling operation at the Black Sheep Wool Company. When three bags are full, the third work element involves transporting the three bags down the lane. What is the normal cycle time for this operation?

6. A time analyst for the Thicket Bros. speedway pit crew observed the mechanic in charge of changing both front tires during a pit-stop practice session. Her job is divided into six work elements and a preparation time between drills. The element times (in seconds) for the first six cycles, recorded on a continuous basis, are shown in Table 6.5.

a. Calculate the normal time for changing tires.

b. What sample size is appropriate for estimating the average time for work element 3 within ±5 percent of the true mean with 95 percent confidence?

7. A time study has been conducted on a cellular telephone assembly operation. The data shown in Table 6.6 (in minutes) were obtained. How many additional observations are needed if the estimate of time for work element 1 is to be within ±3 percent of the true mean with 95 percent confidence?

8. Consider the recorded observations of 10 cycles of the cup packaging operation, shown in Figure 6.4.

a. Determine the select times for each work element, the normal time for the cycle, and the standard time per package.

b. Suppose that we want a sample size that gives an average time within ±5 percent of the true average

TABLE 6.4   *Time Study Results of the Package Filling Operation*

Work Element	Observation												F	RF
	1	2	3	4	5	6	7	8	9	10	11	12		
1. Fill bag	0.20	0.22	0.24	0.18	0.20	0.21	0.22	0.19	0.24	0.18	0.19	0.25	1.00	1.2
2. Sew closed	0.40	0.38	0.37	0.41	0.41	0.40	0.36	0.37	0.41	0.42	0.39	0.36	1.00	0.8
3. Transport			0.82			0.84			0.73			0.85	0.33	1.1

TABLE 6.5   *Pit Crew Time Study Data*

Work Element	Observation						F	RF
	1	2	3	4	5	6		
1. Wait for car lift	2.9	—	69.0	—	155.6	—	0.5	1.0
2. Remove lugs	6.2	24.3	72.6	91.0	159.6	176.8	1.0	0.9
3. Switch tires	12.6	31.4	79.4	98.3	165.8	183.2	1.0	1.2
4. Tighten lugs	16.7	35.2	82.9	103.2	169.3	187.4	1.0	0.8
5. Move to right side	20.5	—	87.2	—	172.5	—	0.5	1.2
6. Clear away for drop	—	37.3	—	105.9	—	189.4	0.5	0.9
Prepare for next drill	—	65.8	—	153.0	—	—	na	na

TABLE 6.6   *Cellular Telephone Time Study Data*

Work Element	Observation 1	2	3	4	5	6	7	8	F	RF
1. Assemble unit	0.78	0.70	0.75	0.80	0.79	0.82	0.81	0.80	1.0	1.2
2. Insert batteries	0.20	0.21	0.16	0.19	0.23	0.25	0.24	0.26	1.0	1.0
3. Test	0.61	0.60	0.55	0.57	0.63	0.61	0.62	0.60	1.0	0.9
4. Package	0.41	0.36	0.45	0.37	0.39	0.40	0.43	0.44	1.0	1.1

FIGURE 6.4

Operation: Coffee cup packaging		**Date:** 1/23			**Observer:** B. Larson								
Work Element		**Observations** 1	2	3	4	5	6	7	8	9	10	$\bar{t}$	F	RF
1. Get two cartons	t													
	r	0.48		4.85		9.14		13.53		17.83			0.5	1.05
2. Put liner in carton	t													
	r	0.59	2.56	4.94	6.82	9.25	11.23	13.61	15.50	17.93	19.83		1.0	0.95
3. Place cups in carton	t													
	r	1.33	3.24	5.65	7.51	9.98	11.93	14.29	16.24	18.64	20.55		1.0	1.10
4. Seal carton, set aside	t													
	r	2.43	4.39	6.72	8.60	11.10	13.04	15.38	17.32	19.74	21.68		1.0	0.90
Normal time for cycle:														
Allowances (% of total time): 15%							Standard time:				minutes per piece		

95 percent of the time. Did we make enough observations? If not, how many more should we make?

c. Suppose that all we wanted was a precision of ±10 percent. How many additional observations would we need?

9. A package delivery service is developing a standard for the number of urban residential deliveries per day. It needs to estimate the proportion of the day the drivers spend outside their vehicles while delivering packages to customers' doors. A summer intern is hired to make a preliminary work sampling study, with the following results. To be 95 percent confident that the work sampling study will be accurate within ±2 percent, how many observations should the company make?

Day	Percentage of Time Delivering Package	Total Observations
1	15	127
2	29	186
3	10	114
4	18	125
5	24	157
6	11	148
7	13	143

10. A professor is concerned that her lecture style causes her to spend more time looking at notes, the board, and visual aids than making eye contact with students. She estimates that she spends 40 percent of the time

making eye contact. A semester consists of 29 lectures of 75 minutes each plus several testing sessions that should not be included in the study. She asks her graduate assistant to design a work sampling study to estimate the proportion of time she spends making eye contact accurate to within ± 3 percent with 90 percent confidence.

a. How many observations will the graduate assistant need to make?

b. On average, how many minutes will elapse between random observations?

11. Mayor Jonathan (Johnny) Johnson of Graft City is running for reelection. At a big rally in the city park, volunteers will assemble signs "A vote for Johnny is a vote for Graft," to be placed on front lawns and city property. To ensure that the rally will go smoothly, the Mayor directs the public works department to conduct a preliminary time study to estimate the rate of work and number of city workers that will be needed to make signs during the rally. The results (in seconds) are shown in Figure 6.5.

a. Because of the chaos and uncontrolled environment at the city park rally, allowances will be 25 percent of the normal time. Determine the normal time for the cycle and the standard time.

b. The Mayor doesn't like to leave things to chance. Suppose that he wants 99 percent confidence that each work element's average time from the study is within ± 5 percent of the true average. Did the public works department make enough observations? If not, how many more should be made?

12. The information systems department of Evergreen Life Insurance Company wants to determine the proportion of time that the data entry operator is idle.

The following information was gathered randomly using work sampling.

Date	Number of Times Clerk Busy	Number of Times Clerk Idle	Total Number of Observations
8/22	11	2	13
8/23	12	3	15
8/24	11	3	14
8/25	12	4	16
8/26	13	1	14
8/27	13	3	16
8/28	6	6	12

If the department wants a 95 percent confidence level and a degree of precision of ± 0.05, how many more observations are needed?

13. The manager of the Twin-Fork post office is interested in the amount of time that window clerks spend on ancillary services such as selling special issue stamp sets or commemorative T-shirts and helping customers with passport applications. Three clerks, each earning $25,000 per year, staff the windows. When they are not needed at the window, they sort mail for the carriers. The results of a preliminary work sampling study are shown in Table 6.7, where entries reflect number of occurrences.

a. For a degree of precision of ± 0.05, is the sample size adequate for special stamp sets? For T-shirts? For passports? What proportion of time do the clerks spend on each activity?

b. If a machine to sell special stamps could be purchased outright for $3500, would you recommend buying it? Discuss.

FIGURE 6.5

Operation: Yard sign assembly		Date: 9/27				Observer: Jerimiah (Jerry) Johnson							
Work Element		**Observations**										$\bar{t}$	F	RF
		1	2	3	4	5	6	7	8	9	10			
1. Get stake and sign	t													
	r	8	39	70	107	293	332	358	405	433	463		1.0	1.05
2. Put glue on stake	t													
	r	14	46	75	112	302	336	365	410	436	467		1.0	0.8
3. Place sign, four staples	t													
	r	25	60	90	277*	319	347	387	421	449	489		1.0	0.9
4. Check assem., set aside	t													
	r	30	64	97	283	327	350	396	427	454	494		1.0	1.2

Normal time for cycle:

Allowances (% of total time): 25%   Standard time: _____ seconds per piece

*This observation isn't representative.

14. As manager of an encoding department in a bank, you are concerned about the amount of time your encoder clerks have to spend cleaning their machines because of malfunctions. You obtained a proposal to modify the design of the machines to reduce the number of malfunctions. The modification will reduce the amount of time spent cleaning the machines by 75 percent. You employ 25 encoder clerks at an average salary of $24,000 for working 2000 hours per year. To help you decide whether the proposal is worth considering, you had a pilot work sampling study made, which provided the following results.

Activity	Observations
Processing checks	52
Cleaning machine	15
Other duties	25
Breaks	8
Total	100

a. Estimate the value of the annual labor savings from modifying the encoding machine design.
b. Construct a 95 percent confidence interval for your estimate. Would you suggest a larger sample size? Why? *Hint:* Base your confidence interval on the normal approximation to the binomial distribution where the standard error is

$$\sigma_p = \sqrt{\hat{p}(1 - \hat{p})/n}$$

Advanced Problem

15. The packing manager for Lamps-"R"-Us, Inc. is interested in setting production standards for the company's lamp packing line. The production process comprises eight steps:

1. Obtain lamp components.
2. Assemble lamp.
3. Test lamp.
4. Get carton.
5. Place lamp in carton.
6. Insert two liners in carton.
7. Seal carton.
8. Place carton in storage.

The total operating time per day is 480 minutes (8 × 60), and the time allowance factor is 15 percent. The manager performed a time study of the production process, using a sample size of 10 observations. Table 6.8 shows the raw data (in minutes), frequency of work element per cycle, F, and estimated performance rating factor, RF, obtained. How many units per day can the manager expect from the packing line?

TABLE 6.7 *Twin-Fork Work Sampling Data*

Day	Selling Postage	Priority Mail	Special Stamp Sales	T-Shirt Sales	Passports	Other	Total
1	6	1	1			2	10
2	6	1		1	1	1	10
3	9			1			10
4	6	1	1		1	1	10
5	8			1		1	10
6	7	2	1				10
7	7	1		1	1		10
8	6	1	1			2	10
9	8	1				1	10
10	6	3		1			10

TABLE 6.8 *Lamps-R-Us Time Study Data*

	Observation											
Element	1	2	3	4	5	6	7	8	9	10	F	RF
1	1.27	1.27	1.24	1.25	1.20	1.26	1.24	1.27	1.26	1.24	1	1.05
2	2.10	2.09	2.18	2.17	2.09	2.08	2.15	2.18	2.14	2.12	1	0.95
3	0.60	0.59	0.64	0.67	0.65	0.68	0.61	0.62	0.64	0.60	1	1.05
4	0.39	0.42	0.32	0.40	0.34	0.36	0.37	0.38	0.40	0.32	1	0.90
5	0.51	0.53	0.45	0.44	0.47	0.49	0.45	0.50	0.46	0.50	1	0.95
6	0.26		0.29		0.30		0.27		0.28		0.5	1.00
7	0.86	0.91	0.89	0.86	0.84	0.85	0.91	0.88	0.86	0.84	1	1.10
8	1.19	1.18	1.20	1.16	1.21	1.15	1.16	1.20	1.18	1.17	1	1.00

The Facilities Maintenance Problem at Midwest University

Sean Allen is the manager in charge of facilities maintenance at Midwest University. Located on a 500-acre tract of land outside St. Louis, Missouri, Midwest University is home to 15,000 students. Allen is responsible for maintaining all the physical facilities on campus, which comprise 60 buildings. They include dormitories, academic buildings, administration and office buildings, two athletic stadiums, and a basketball coliseum. To carry out this function Allen manages a large, diverse work force that has traditionally been segmented by skilled craft into electricians, carpenters, plumbers, painters, heating and air conditioning specialists, masons, dry wallers, and so on. Allen also is responsible for the custodial and cleaning crews for each facility.

A recurring nightmare for Allen has been the inability of facilities maintenance to respond quickly to work-order requests. A review of the data indicated that a response time of 5 to 10 days wasn't unusual. This was unacceptable.

Allen applied what he had learned in a series of continuous improvement workshops that focused on problem identification, data collection and analysis, and problem resolution. He soon discovered that 85 percent of the work-order requests took less than an hour to handle. Furthermore, almost 40 percent of the requests were for routine maintenance items such as clogged drains, burned out light bulbs, and loose towel racks. His analysis led him to the conclusion that an ineffective organizational structure was a primary cause of the long response times.

Facility maintenance personnel were grouped by craft and centrally located at the physical plant offices. As work orders were received, Allen would try to prioritize the requests and allocate craft personnel to fix the problem. Scheduling work to be done was complicated. Both the importance of the job and the location had to be considered.

Maintenance personnel often spent a large portion of their time traveling back and forth across campus, going from one job to the next. Allen also discovered that jobs frequently could not be completed because more than one type of craft was required. For instance, repairing a set of wall-mounted bookshelves in a dormitory room required both a carpenter and a painter. Personnel in each craft were scheduled independently.

As Allen thought about what to do, he kept coming back to what he had learned in the continuous improvement workshops about "getting closer to the customer" and establishing cross-functional work teams that focus on processes, not outputs. A new structure with enhanced job responsibilities might just be the answer. The big questions were "What kind of organizational structure would make sense?" and "How could he minimize time spent traveling back and forth across campus and more effectively utilize his skilled craftspeople?"

Finally, there was the issue of implementation. After he had designed a new organizational structure and established new job responsibilities, how could he get the facilities maintenance personnel to support the changes? One phrase kept going through Allen's mind: "You get what you measure." In addition, any reorganization would mean a realignment of employee performance evaluation and recognition procedures.

Questions

1. How would you restructure the facilities maintenance organization at Midwest University?
2. What can Sean Allen do to alleviate the problem of excessive travel time for work crews?
3. As Allen redesigns job responsibilities, how should he evaluate his personnel's performance? What should he measure? How should he reward employees?

Source: This case was prepared by Dr. Brooke Saladin, Wake Forest University, as a basis for classroom discussion.

Selected References

Hammer, Michael. "Reengineering Work: Don't Automate, Obliterate." *Harvard Business Review* (July–August 1990), pp. 104–112.

Herzberg, F. "One More Time: How Do You Motivate Employees?" *Harvard Business Review* (September–October 1987), pp. 109–120.

"The Horizontal Corporation," *Business Week,* December 20, 1993, pp. 76–81.

Knights, David, Hugh Willmott, and David Collision, eds. *Job Redesign.* Hants, England: Gower, 1985.

"Motorola: Training for the Millennium," *Business Week,* March 28, 1994, pp. 158–162.

Niebel, Richard W. *Motion and Time Study,* 8th ed. Homewood, Ill.: Richard D. Irwin, 1988.

"The Payoff from Teamwork," *Business Week,* July 10, 1989, p. 58.

Schonberger, Richard J. *Building a Chain of Customers: Linking Business Functions to Create the World Class Company.* New York: Free Press, 1990.

Trist, Eric L. "The Sociotechnical Perspective." In A. H. Vande Ven and W. F. Joyce, eds., *Perspectives on Organization Design.* New York: John Wiley & Sons, 1981.

"What the Experts Forgot to Mention," *Inc.,* September 1993, pp. 66–77.

"When the Going Gets Tough, Boeing Gets Touchy-Feely," *Business Week,* January 17, 1994, pp. 65–67.

Learning Curves

In today's dynamic workplace, change occurs rapidly. Where there is change, there also is learning. With instruction and repetition, workers learn to perform jobs more efficiently and thereby reduce the number of direct labor hours per unit. Like workers, organizations learn. **Organizational learning** involves gaining experience with products and processes, achieving greater efficiency through automation and other capital investments, and making other improvements in administrative methods or personnel. Productivity improvements may be gained from better work methods, tools, product design, or supervision, as well as from individual worker learning. These improvements mean that existing standards must be continually evaluated and new ones set. Managerial Practice D.1 shows how organizational learning paid off for Samsung, the world's leading microwave oven producer.

◆ THE LEARNING EFFECT

The learning effect can be represented by a line called a **learning curve,** which displays the relationship between the total direct labor per unit and the cumulative quantity of a product or service produced. The learning curve relates to a repetitive job or task and represents the relationship between experience and productivity: The time required to produce a unit decreases as the operator or firm produces more units. The curve in Fig. D.1 is a learning curve for one process. It shows that the process time per unit continually decreases until the 140th unit is produced. At that point learning is negligible and a standard time for the operation can be developed. The terms *manufacturing progress function* and *experience curve* also have been used to describe this relationship, although the experience curve typically refers to total value-added costs per unit rather than labor hours. The principles underlying these curves are identical to those of the learning curve, however. Here we use the term *learning curve* to depict reductions in either total direct labor per unit or total value-added costs per unit.

FIGURE D.1

Learning Curve Showing the Learning Period and the Time When Standards Are Calculated

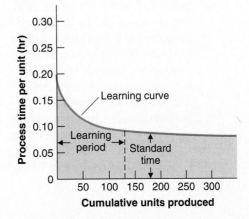

263

Managerial Practice D.1

▶ *The Learning Curve Effect at Samsung*

In 1976, Yun Soo Chu, a young engineer at Korean giant Samsung, received an unexpected assignment—design a microwave oven. While visiting the United States, J. U. Chung, a vice-president at Samsung, had become intrigued with a new kind of oven, one that was heated not by electricity or gas but by microwaves. His goal was to penetrate the market early and produce a low-cost product for export. He asked Chu to head up a team to design a microwave oven for Samsung. Chu began by buying leading microwave ovens and studying how they were made. He had to purchase equipment and materials he didn't have, such as presses and magnetron tubes, the heart of the oven. Chu spent one year of 80 hour workweeks to complete the first prototype, only to have it melt when he turned it on. Not until June 1978 did Chu and his team produce a prototype that worked.

The production team, on a makeshift assembly line, began making one oven a day, then two, and then five, as employees began to learn how to assemble the ovens. However, by mid 1979 Samsung had made only 1460 ovens. Convinced that Samsung could compete in the world microwave market and buoyed by a few initial orders, Samsung decided to improve the production efficiency of the microwave line. I. J. Jang, a production engineer, immersed himself in learning about the product and visiting leading Japanese manufacturers of microwave ovens. Despite his long hours redesigning the assembly line, some bugs remained. Samsung operated the line during the day, and Jang studied it at night to work out the problems. Production improved to 10 ovens a day, then 15. Soon the company was making 1500 per month.

By the end of 1981 Samsung had increased annual production a hundredfold, from little more than 1000 the year before to over 100,000, by improving methods and adding assembly lines. By 1982, annual production was 200,000. In 1983, it was 750,000, and in 1984, over 1 million. With each milestone, management celebrated the achievement—but only briefly. The next day all were back at work, looking for ways to increase production and quality while reducing costs.

Source: Ira C. Magaziner and Mark Patinkin, "Fast Heat: How Korea Won the Microwave War," *Harvard Business Review* (January–February 1989), pp. 83–92.

Background

The learning curve was first developed in the aircraft industry prior to World War II, when analysts discovered that the direct labor input per airplane declined with considerable regularity as the cumulative number of planes produced increased. A survey of major airplane manufacturers revealed that a series of learning curves could be developed to represent the average experience for various categories of airframes (fighters, bombers, and so on), despite the different amounts of time required to produce the first unit of each type of airframe. Once production started, the direct labor for the eighth unit was only 80 percent of that for the fourth unit, the direct labor for the twelfth was only 80 percent of that for the sixth, and so on. In each case, each doubling of the quantity reduced production time by 20 percent. Because of the consistency in the rate of improvement, the analysts concluded that the aircraft industry's rate of learning was 80 percent between doubled quantities of airframes. Of course, for any given product and company, the rate of learning may be different.

Learning Curves and Competitive Strategy

Learning curves enable managers to project the manufacturing cost per unit for any cumulative production quantity. Firms that choose to emphasize low price as a competitive strategy rely on high volumes to maintain profit margins. These firms strive to move down the learning curve (lower labor hours per unit or lower costs per unit) by increasing volume. This tactic makes entry into a market by competitors difficult. For example, in the electronics component industry, the cost of developing an integrated circuit is so large that the first units produced must be priced high. As cumulative production increases, costs (and prices) fall. The first companies in the market have a big advantage because newcomers must start selling at lower prices and suffer large initial losses.

However, market or product changes can disrupt the expected benefits of increased production. For example, Douglas Aircraft management assumed that it could reduce the costs of its new jet aircraft by following a learning curve formula and committing to fixed delivery dates and prices. Continued engineering modification of its planes disrupted the learning curve, and the cost reductions were not realized. The resulting financial problems were so severe that Douglas Aircraft was forced to merge with McDonnell Company.

◆ DEVELOPING LEARNING CURVES

In the following discussion and applications we focus on direct labor hours per unit, although we could as easily have used costs. When we develop a learning curve, we make the following assumptions.

- The direct labor required to produce the $n + 1$st unit will always be less than the direct labor required for the nth unit.
- Direct labor requirements will decrease at a declining rate as cumulative production increases.
- The reduction in time will follow an exponential curve.

In other words, the production time per unit is reduced by a fixed percentage each time production is doubled. We can use a logarithmic model to draw a learning curve. The direct labor required for the nth unit, k_n, is

$$k_n = k_1 n^b$$

where

k_1 = direct labor hours for the first unit

n = cumulative number of units produced

$b = \dfrac{\log r}{\log 2}$

r = learning rate

We can also calculate the cumulative average number of hours per unit for the first n units with the help of Table D.1 on the next page. It contains conversion factors that, when multiplied by the direct labor hours for the first unit, yield the average time per unit for selected cumulative production quantities.

TABLE D.1   *Conversion Factors for the Cumulative Average Number of Direct Labor Hours per Unit*

	80% Learning Rate (n = cumulative production)						90% Learning Rate (n = cumulative production)				
n		n		n		n		n		n	
1	1.00000	19	0.53178	37	0.43976	1	1.00000	19	0.73545	37	0.67091
2	0.90000	20	0.52425	38	0.43634	2	0.95000	20	0.73039	38	0.66839
3	0.83403	21	0.51715	39	0.43304	3	0.91540	21	0.72559	39	0.66595
4	0.78553	22	0.51045	40	0.42984	4	0.88905	22	0.72102	40	0.66357
5	0.74755	23	0.50410	64	0.37382	5	0.86784	23	0.71666	64	0.62043
6	0.71657	24	0.49808	128	0.30269	6	0.85013	24	0.71251	128	0.56069
7	0.69056	25	0.49234	256	0.24405	7	0.83496	25	0.70853	256	0.50586
8	0.66824	26	0.48688	512	0.19622	8	0.82172	26	0.70472	512	0.45594
9	0.64876	27	0.48167	600	0.18661	9	0.80998	27	0.70106	600	0.44519
10	0.63154	28	0.47668	700	0.17771	10	0.79945	28	0.69754	700	0.43496
11	0.61613	29	0.47191	800	0.17034	11	0.78991	29	0.69416	800	0.42629
12	0.60224	30	0.46733	900	0.16408	12	0.78120	30	0.69090	900	0.41878
13	0.58960	31	0.46293	1000	0.15867	13	0.77320	31	0.68775	1000	0.41217
14	0.57802	32	0.45871	1200	0.14972	14	0.76580	32	0.68471	1200	0.40097
15	0.56737	33	0.45464	1400	0.14254	15	0.75891	33	0.68177	1400	0.39173
16	0.55751	34	0.45072	1600	0.13660	16	0.75249	34	0.67893	1600	0.38390
17	0.54834	35	0.44694	1800	0.13155	17	0.74646	35	0.67617	1800	0.37711
18	0.53979	36	0.44329	2000	0.12720	18	0.74080	36	0.67350	2000	0.37114

EXAMPLE D.1

Using Learning Curves to Estimate Direct Labor Requirements

A manufacturer of diesel locomotives needs 50,000 hours to produce the first unit. Based on past experience with products of this sort, you know that the rate of learning is 80 percent.

a. Use the logarithmic model to estimate the direct labor required for the fortieth diesel locomotive and the cumulative average number of labor hours per unit for the first 40 units.

b. Draw a learning curve for this situation.

Solution

a. The estimated number of direct labor hours required to produce the fortieth unit is

$$k_{40} = 50{,}000(40)^{(\log 0.8)/(\log 2)} = 50{,}000(40)^{-0.322} = 50{,}000(0.30488)$$

$$= 15{,}244 \text{ hours}$$

We calculate the cumulative average number of direct labor hours per unit for the first 40 units with the help of Table D.1. For a cumulative production of 40 units and an 80 percent learning rate, the factor is 0.42984. The cumulative average direct labor hours per unit is $50{,}000(0.42984) = 21{,}492$ hours.

b. Plot the first point at (1, 50,000). The second unit's labor time is 80 percent of the first, so multiply $50{,}000(0.80) = 40{,}000$ hours. Plot the second point at (2, 40,000). The fourth is 80 percent of the second, so multiply $40{,}000(0.80) = 32{,}000$ hours. Plot the point (4, 32,000). The result is shown in Fig. D.2.

FIGURE D.2 *The 80 Percent Learning Curve*

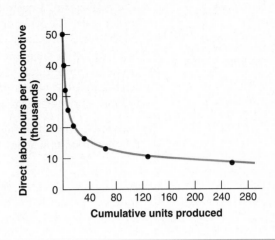

USING LEARNING CURVES

Learning curves can be used in a variety of ways. Let's look briefly at their use in bid preparation, financial planning, and labor requirement estimation.

Bid Preparation

Estimating labor costs is an important part of preparing bids for large jobs. Knowing the learning rate, the number of units to be produced, and wage rates, the estimator can arrive at the cost of labor by using a learning curve. After calculating expected labor and materials costs, the estimator adds the desired profit to obtain the total bid amount.

Financial Planning

Learning curves can be used in financial planning to help the financial planner determine the amount of cash needed to finance operations. Learning curves provide a basis for comparing prices and costs. They can be used to project periods of financial drain, when expenditures exceed receipts. They can also be used to determine a contract price by identifying the average direct labor costs per unit for the number of contracted units. In the early stages of production the direct labor costs will exceed that average, whereas in the later stages of production the reverse will be true. This information enables the financial planner to arrange financing for certain phases of operations.

Labor Requirement Estimation

For a given production schedule, the analyst can use learning curves to project direct labor requirements. This information can be used to estimate training requirements and develop hiring plans. We show how such information is used in production and staffing plans in Chapter 13.

EXAMPLE D.2

Using Learning Curves to Estimate Labor Requirements

The manager of a custom manufacturer has just received a production schedule for an order for 30 large turbines. Over the next five months, the company is to produce 2, 3, 5, 8, and 12 turbines, respectively. The first unit took 30,000 direct labor hours, and experience on past projects indicates that a 90 percent learning curve is appropriate; therefore the second unit will require only 27,000 hours. Each employee works an average of 150 hours per month. Estimate the total number of full-time employees needed each month for the next five months.

Solution   The following table shows the production schedule and cumulative number of units scheduled for production through each month.

Month	Units per Month	Cumulative Units
1	2	2
2	3	5
3	5	10
4	8	18
5	12	30

We first need to find the cumulative average time per unit using Table D.1 and the cumulative total hours through each month. We then can determine the number of labor hours needed each month. The calculations for months 1–5 are as follows.

Month	Cumulative Average Time per Unit	Cumulative Total Hours for All Units
1	30,000(0.95000) = 28,500	28,500(2) = 57,000
2	30,000(0.86784) = 26,035	26,035(5) = 130,175
3	30,000(0.79945) = 23,983	23,983(10) = 239,830
4	30,000(0.74080) = 22,224	22,224(18) = 400,032
5	30,000(0.69090) = 20,727	20,727(30) = 621,810

Calculate the number of hours needed for a particular month by subtracting its cumulative total hours from that of the previous month.

Month 1:   57,000 −   0 =   57,000 hours
Month 2:   130,175 −   57,000 =   73,175 hours
Month 3:   239,830 − 130,175 = 109,655 hours
Month 4:   400,032 − 239,830 = 160,202 hours
Month 5:   621,810 − 400,032 = 221,778 hours

The required number of employees equals the number of hours needed each month divided by 150, the number of hours each employee can work.

Month 1:   57,000/150 =   380 employees
Month 2:   73,175/150 =   488 employees
Month 3:   109,655/150 =   731 employees
Month 4:   160,202/150 = 1068 employees
Month 5:   221,778/150 = 1479 employees

◆ MANAGERIAL CONSIDERATIONS
IN THE USE OF LEARNING CURVES

Although learning curves can be useful tools for operations planning, managers should keep several issues in mind when using them. First, an estimate of the learning rate is necessary in order to use learning curves, and it may be difficult to get. Using industry averages can be risky because the type of work and competitive niches can differ from firm to firm. The learning rate depends on factors such as product complexity and the rate of capital additions. The simpler the product, the less pronounced is the learning rate. A complex product offers more opportunity to improve work methods, materials, and processes over the product's life. Replacing direct labor hours with automation alters the learning rate, giving less opportunity to make reductions in the required hours per unit. Typically, the effect of each capital addition on the learning curve is significant.

Another important estimate is that of the time required to produce the first unit because the entire learning curve is based on it. The estimate may have to be developed by using a work measurement method such as the predetermined data approach.

Learning curves provide their greatest advantage in the early stages of new product or service production. As the cumulative number of units produced becomes large, the learning effect is less noticeable.

Learning curves are dynamic because they are affected by various factors. For example, a short product or service life cycle means that firms may not enjoy the flat portion of the learning curve for very long before the product or service is changed or a new one is introduced. In addition, organizations utilizing team approaches will have different learning rates than they had before they introduced teams. Total quality management and continual improvement programs also will affect learning curves.

Finally, managers should always keep in mind that learning curves are only approximations to actual experience.

SUPPLEMENT REVIEW

Solved Problem

The Minnesota Coach Company has just been given the following production schedule for ski-lift gondola cars. This product is considerably different from any others the company has produced. Historically, the company's learning rate has been 80 percent on large projects. The first unit took 1000 hours to produce.

Month	Units	Cumulative Units
1	3	3
2	7	10
3	10	20
4	12	32
5	4	36
6	2	38

a. Estimate how many hours would be required to complete the thirty-eighth unit.

b. If the budget only provides for a maximum of 30 direct labor employees in any month and a total of 15,000 direct labor hours for the entire schedule, will the budget be adequate? Assume that each direct labor employee is productive for 150 work hours each month.

Solution   a. We use the learning curve formulas to calculate the time required for the thirty-eighth unit:

$$b = \frac{\log r}{\log 2} = \frac{\log 0.8}{\log 2} = \frac{-0.09691}{0.30103} = -0.32193$$

$$k_n = k_1 n^b = (1000 \text{ hours})(38)^{-0.32193}$$

$$= (1000 \text{ hours})(0.3100) = 310 \text{ hours}$$

b. Table D.1 gives the data needed to calculate the cumulative number of hours through each month of the schedule. Table D.2 shows these calculations.

TABLE D.2   *Cumulative Total Hours*

Month	Cumulative Units	Cumulative Average Time per Unit	Cumulative Total Hours for All Units
1	3	1000(0.83403) = 834.03 hr/u	(834.03 hr/u)(3 u) = 2,502.1 hr
2	10	1000(0.63154) = 631.54 hr/u	(631.54 hr/u)(10 u) = 6,315.4 hr
3	20	1000(0.52425) = 524.25 hr/u	(524.25 hr/u)(20 u) = 10,485.0 hr
4	32	1000(0.45871) = 458.71 hr/u	(458.71 hr/u)(32 u) = 14,678.7 hr
5	36	1000(0.44329) = 443.29 hr/u	(443.29 hr/u)(36 u) = 15,958.4 hr
6	38	1000(0.43634) = 436.34 hr/u	(436.34 hr/u)(38 u) = 16,580.9 hr

The cumulative amount of time needed to produce the entire schedule of 38 units is 16,580.9 hours, which exceeds the 15,000 hours budgeted. By finding how much the cumulative total hours increased each month, we can break the total hours into monthly requirements. Finally, the number of employees required is simply the monthly hours divided by 150 hours per employee per month. The calculations are shown in Table D.3.

TABLE D.3   *Direct Labor Employees*

Month	Cumulative Total Hours for Month	Direct Labor Workers by Month
1	2502.1 − 0 = 2502.1 hr	(2502.1 hr)/(150 hr) = 16.7, or 17
2	6315.4 − 2502.1 = 3813.3 hr	(3813.3 hr)/(150 hr) = 25.4, or 26
3	10,485.0 − 6315.4 = 4169.6 hr	(4169.6 hr)/(150 hr) = 27.8, or 28
4	14,678.7 − 10,485.0 = 4193.7 hr	(4193.7 hr)/(150 hr) = 28.0, or 28
5	15,958.4 − 14,678.7 = 1279.7 hr	(1279.7 hr)/(150 hr) = 8.5, or 9
6	16,580.9 − 15,958.4 = 622.5 hr	(622.5 hr)/(150 hr) = 4.2, or 5

The schedule is feasible in terms of the maximum direct labor required in any month because it never exceeds 28 employees. However, the total cumulative hours is 16,581, which exceeds the budgeted amount by 1581 hours. Therefore the budget will not be adequate.

Formula Review

1. Learning curve: $k_n = k_1 n^b$

Supplement Highlights

- When creating a product or service involves a substantial amount of human effort and thought, those involved will learn from the experience. If the situation recurs, the organization will benefit from previous experience and will be able to provide the product or service in less time. As the volume for the same product or service increases, the output per unit of time also increases.
- In situations where significant learning takes place as production increases, learning curves can be used to prepare bids, estimate financial requirements over the life of a contract, and estimate the amount of direct

labor needed to meet a production schedule. If the learning rate is 90 percent, for example, each doubling of production volume reduces the direct labor required per unit by 10 percent.
- Firms using a low-price strategy strive to move down the learning curve to reduce labor hours and costs per unit by increasing volume. This approach makes entry into a market by competitors very costly.
- Product design changes can disrupt the learning effect.

Key Terms

learning curve *263*
organizational learning *263*

Study Questions

1. In Chapter 2, Fig. 2.5 depicts the continuum of positioning strategies. Relate what Fig. 2.5 shows to the concepts of learning curves and competitive strategy.
2. Which results in fewer direct labor hours per unit: an 80 percent learning curve or a 90 percent learning curve? Explain.
3. Why don't simple tasks such as dusting furniture exhibit the learning effect as clearly as do complex projects such as manufacturing airplanes?
4. What is the relationship between automation and the learning effect?
5. As a product's design evolves during the introduction and growth stages of its life cycle, design changes sometimes are not implemented the moment they are ready. Instead, design changes may be accumulated

and implemented in a group. From your understanding of learning curves, why is this strategy useful?
6. When new products are introduced, the price and profit margins usually are high. For example, the earliest ballpoint pens were priced at about $500; the first digital watches, at about $1500; and the first compact disc players, at about $3000. This short-term strategy results in a rapid payback of development costs and a rapid entrance of competitors attracted by large profit margins. Another strategy is to introduce the product at a low price and low profit margin. How can the learning effect cause the latter to be an effective long-term strategy? Contrast the risks of the two strategies.

Problems

1. Mass Balance Company is manufacturing a new digital scale for use by a large chemical company. The order is for 40 units. The first scale took 60 hours of direct labor. The learning rate is estimated to be 80 percent.
   a. What is the estimated time for the third unit?
   b. What is the estimated time for the fortieth unit?
   c. What is the estimated total time for producing all 40 units?

   d. What is the average time per unit for producing the last 10 units (#31–#40)?
2. Cambridge Instruments is an aircraft instrumentation manufacturer. It has received a contract from the U.S. Department of Defense to produce 30 radar units for a military fighter plane. The first unit took 85 hours to produce. Based on past experience with manufacturing similar units, Cambridge estimates that the learning rate is 93 percent. How long will it take to

produce the fifth unit? The tenth? The fifteenth? The final unit?

3. A large grocery corporation has developed the following schedule for converting frozen food display cases to use CFC-free refrigerant.

Week	Units
1	20
2	65
3	100
4	140
5	120

Historically, the learning rate has been 90 percent on such projects. The budget allows for a maximum of 40 direct labor employees per week and a total of 7000 direct labor hours for the entire schedule. Assume 40 work hours per week. If the first unit took 30 hours to convert, is this schedule feasible? If not, how can it be altered? Are additional costs involved in altering it?

4. Freddie and Jason have just opened the Texas Toothpick, a chain-saw sharpening and repair service located on Elm Street. The Texas Toothpick promises same-week repair service. Freddie and Jason are concerned that a projected dramatic increase in demand as the end of October nears will cause service to deteriorate. Freddie and Jason have had difficulty attracting employees, so they are the only workers available to complete the work. Safety considerations require that they each work no more than 40 hours per week. The first chain-saw sharpening and repair required 7 hours of work, and an 80 percent learning curve is anticipated.

Week	Units	Cumulative Units
October 2–6	8	8
October 9–13	19	27
October 16–20	10	37
October 23–27	27	64

a. How many total hours are required to complete 64 chain saws?
b. How many hours of work are required for the week ending on Friday, the 13th?
c. Will Freddie and Jason be able to keep their same-week service promise during their busiest week just before Halloween?

5. The Bovine Products Company recently introduced a new automatic milking system for cows. The company just completed an order for 16 units. The last unit required 15 hours of labor, and the learning rate is estimated to be 90 percent on such systems. Another customer has just placed an order for the same system. This company, which owns many farms in the Midwest, wants 48 units. How many total labor hours will be needed to satisfy this order?

6. Suppose that you are bidding on a project and need to know how much to charge per unit. Assume that the product has an 80 percent learning rate. The contract calls for 100 units. You estimate that the first unit will cost $3500 for labor.
a. What is the total labor cost for the contract quantity?
b. At what point during production will the company begin to make a profit on each unit of the contract if you bid $1200 labor per unit (plus materials at cost)?

Advanced Problems

An electronic spreadsheet would be helpful in solving Problem 11.

7. The personnel manager at Powerwest Inc. wants to estimate the direct and cumulative average direct labor hours for producing 30 locomotive train units during the next year. He estimates from past experience that the learning rate is 90 percent. The production department estimates that manufacturing the first unit will take 30,000 hours. Each employee averages 200 hours per month. The production rate forecast is

Month	Production Rate (units)	Month	Production Rate (units)
January	2	July	2
February	3	August	4
March	2	September	3
April	4	October	3
May	3	November	1
June	2	December	1

a. How many direct hours are required to produce the thirtieth unit?
b. How many total hours are needed to produce all 30 units?
c. What is the maximum number of employees required next year?
d. If the learning rate were changed to 0.85, what would be the impact on the total hours and the number of employees needed to produce 30 units?

8. The Really Big Six Corporation will hire 1000 new accountants this year. Managers are considering whether to make or to buy office furniture for the new hires. Big can purchase office furniture for $1500 per accountant, or it can make the desks itself. Equipment to

assemble furniture can be scrounged from the company's carpenter shop. That old equipment has already been fully depreciated. Materials cost $400 per desk, and labor (and benefits) costs $25 per hour. Big hired a local shop to build a prototype desk. That desk required 100 hours of labor. If the learning curve is 90 percent, should Big make or buy the desks?

9. Although the learning curve never completely levels off to a horizontal line, if work standards are to be developed, there must be a point at which, for all practical purposes, learning is said to have stopped. If we have an 80 percent learning curve and say that the learning effect will be masked by other variables when the improvement in successive units is less than 0.5 percent, at about what unit number can the standard be set?

10. The Compton Company is manufacturing a solar grain dryer that requires methods and materials never before used by the company. The order is for 80 units. The first unit took 46 direct labor hours, whereas the tenth unit took only 24 direct labor hours.

   a. Estimate the rate of learning that occurred for this product.

   b. Use the learning rate in part a to estimate direct labor hours for the eightieth unit.

11. The Hand-To-Mouth Company (HTM) has $200,000 in cash, no inventory, and a 90 percent learning curve. To reduce the complexity of this problem, ignore the hiring and training costs associated with dramatically increased production. Employees are paid $20 per hour every Friday for that week's work. HTM has received an order to build 1000 oak desks over the next 15 weeks. Materials cost $400 per desk. Suppliers make deliveries each Monday and insist on cash upon delivery. The first desk takes 100 hours of direct labor to build. HTM will be paid $1500 per desk two weeks after the desks are delivered. Should HTM take this order?

Week	Units	Week	Units	Week	Units
1	2	6	24	11	88
2	4	7	64	12	100
3	8	8	128	13	100
4	12	9	128	14	100
5	14	10	128	15	100
				Total	1000

Selected References

Abernathy, William J., and Kenneth Wayne. "Limits of the Learning Curve." *Harvard Business Review* (September–October 1974), pp. 109–119.

Senge, Peter M. "The Leader's New Work: Building Learning Organizations." *The Sloan Management Review* (Fall 1990), pp. 7–23.

Yelle, Louis E. "The Learning Curve: Historical Review and Comprehensive Survey." *Decision Sciences*, vol. 10, no. 2 (April 1979), pp. 302–328.

Chapter Seven

CAPACITY

Recent experience by American Airlines demonstrates the strategic and dynamic nature of capacity planning. During the 1980s American became the nation's largest carrier, with annual revenues exceeding $10 billion. It pursued an aggressive growth strategy, doubling its fleet size and tripling its revenues. When domestic growth dipped below its double-digit pace, American looked overseas, snapping up $1 billion of routes in 1989 and 1990. However, its initial efforts to go global—with routes to South America, Europe, and the Pacific Rim—have been only partially successful to date. One reason is that American lacked enough long-haul aircraft: The orders that it had placed for $20 billion in new aircraft provided only limited relief because it did not plan for enough widebodies. Additionally, American lost its bid for some prized overseas routes, such as the Chicago–Tokyo route, awarded by the U.S. Department of Transportation. American cut back its capacity expansion, by delaying or not exercising its purchase options with aircraft manufacturers for future deliveries. Despite the cutback, American's existing fleet of 622 planes is second in capacity only to that of Aeroflot and is larger than those of British Airways, Air France, and

American Airlines uses the Dallas/Fort Worth International Airport as one of its hubs. Aggressive expansion in the 1980s gave the airline the youngest fleet in the industry. It then switched to a wait-and-see capacity strategy and curbed its equipment purchases, awaiting an improvement in business conditions.

Lufthansa combined. This capacity positions the airline to be a world leader in international air traffic, in a market for which demand is expected to nearly double by the year 2000.

After deciding what products or services should be offered and how they should be made, management must plan the system's capacity. American Airlines' experience demonstrates how important capacity plans are to an organization's future. **Capacity** is the maximum rate of output for a facility. The facility can be a workstation or an entire organization. The operations manager must provide the capacity to meet current and future demand, or else the organization will miss opportunities for growth and profits.

Capacity plans are made at two levels. Long-term capacity plans, which we describe in this chapter, deal with investments in new facilities and equipment. These plans look at least two years into the future, but construction lead times alone can force much longer time horizons. Currently, U.S. firms invest $617 billion annually in *new* plant and equipment. Service industries account for more than 68 percent of the total. Such sizable investments require top-management participation and approval because they are not easily reversed. Short-term capacity plans focus on work-force size, overtime budgets, inventories, and decisions that we explore in later chapters.

◆ CAPACITY PLANNING

Capacity planning is central to the long-term success of an organization. Too much capacity can be as agonizing as too little, as Managerial Practice 7.1 demonstrates. When choosing a capacity strategy, managers have to consider questions such as the following: Should we have one large facility or several small ones? Should we expand capacity before the demand is there or wait until demand is more certain? A systematic approach is needed to answer these and similar questions and to develop a capacity strategy appropriate for each situation.

Measures of Capacity

How should the maximum rate of output be measured?

No single capacity measure is applicable to all types of situations. Hospitals measure capacity as the number of patients that can be treated per day; a retailer measures capacity as annual sales dollars generated per square foot; an airline measures capacity as available seat-miles (ASMs) per month; a theater measures capacity as number of seats; and a job shop measures capacity as number of machine hours. In general, capacity can be expressed in one of two ways: output measures or input measures.

Output measures are the usual choice of product-focused firms. Nissan Motor Company states capacity at its Tennessee plant to be 450,000 vehicles per year. That plant produces only one type of vehicle, making capacity easy to measure. However, many organizations produce more than one product or service. For example, a restaurant may be able to handle 100 take-out customers *or* 50 sit-down customers per hour. It might also handle 50 take-out *and* 25 sit-down customers or many other combinations of the two types of customers. As the amount of customization and variety in the product mix becomes excessive, output-based capacity measures become less useful. Output measures are best utilized when the firm provides a relatively small number of standardized products and services.

Input measures are the usual choice of process-focused firms. For example, in a photocopy shop, capacity can be measured in machine hours or number of machines. Just as product mix can complicate output capacity measures, so too can demand complicate input measures. Demand, which invariably is expressed as an output rate, must be converted to an input measure. Only after making the conversion can a manager compare demand requirements and capacity on an equivalent basis. For example, the manager of a copy center must convert its annual demand for copies from different clients to the number of machines required.

Utilization. Capacity planning requires a knowledge of current capacity and its utilization. **Utilization,** or the degree to which equipment, space, or labor is currently being used, is expressed as a percentage:

$$\text{Utilization} = \frac{\text{Average output rate}}{\text{Maximum capacity}} \times 100\%$$

The average output rate and the capacity must be measured in the same terms—that is, time, customers, units, or dollars. The utilization rate indicates the need for adding extra capacity or eliminating unneeded capacity. The greatest difficulty in calculating utilization lies in defining *maximum capacity,* the denominator in the ratio. Two definitions of maximum capacity are useful: design capacity and effective capacity.

Managerial Practice 7.1

▶ *The Agony of Too Much—and Too Little—Capacity*

The commercial real estate market in most major U.S. cities has been suffering from excess capacity, with many properties vacant. The glut was caused in part by the recession in the early 1990s. At the same time many tenants, especially those in the financial industry, were undergoing restructurings expected to cut demand for office space for years to come. In 1991, the vacancy rate for office space was 26 percent in Miami, Oklahoma City, Phoenix, and Dallas alike; it was 20 percent nationwide. Values declined as much as 30 percent in some markets, and the capacity glut hurt everyone. For example, the CenTrust Tower in Miami, a 47-story building built by a failed savings and loan for $165 million, was sold for only $38 million. To make matters worse, the real estate industry suffered from "rollover risk," in which tenants from high-priced buildings were lured by cheaper rents to empty buildings. Said one banking consultant in Washington, D.C., "The entire market is being cannibalized."

The aircraft industry experienced the opposite problem in the late 1980s—not enough capacity. The world's airlines reequipped their fleets to carry more passengers on existing planes and vied to buy a record number of new commercial passenger jets. Orders received by Boeing, Airbus, and McDonnell Douglas surged to more than 2600 planes. McDonnell Douglas alone had a backlog of some $18 billion in firm orders for its MD-80 and new MD-11 widebody—enough to keep its plant fully utilized for more than three years. Despite the number of orders, Douglas's commercial aircraft division announced a startling loss, Airbus struggled to make money, and even mighty Boeing fought to improve subpar margins. Capacity shortage caused many problems for McDonnell Douglas: Its suppliers were unable to keep pace, its doubled work force was inexperienced and less productive, and considerable work had to be subcontracted to other plants. The result was that costs skyrocketed and profits plummeted. By the start of the 1990s the capacity pressure was relieved because American had cut back on the hypergrowth strategy that had set the pace for the entire airline industry in the 1980s.

Sources: "Office Buildings, Under Pressure Already, Face Threat to Their Leases," *Wall Street Journal*, September 27, 1991; "Planemakers Have It So Good, It's Bad," *Business Week*, May 8, 1989.

Design Capacity. Sometimes also called *peak capacity,* **design capacity** is the maximum output that a process or facility can achieve under ideal conditions. When capacity is measured relative to equipment alone, the appropriate measure is **rated capacity:** an engineering assessment of maximum annual output, assuming continuous operation except for an allowance for normal maintenance and repair downtime. Design capacity can be sustained for only a short time, such as a few hours in a day or a few days in a month. A firm reaches it by using extraordinary measures, such as excessive overtime, extra shifts, temporarily reduced maintenance activities, overstaffing, and subcontracting. Although they can help with temporary peaks, these options can't be sustained for long. Employees do not want to work excessive overtime for extended periods, and overtime and night-shift premiums drive up costs.

Effective Capacity. The maximum output that a process or firm can economically sustain under normal conditions is its **effective capacity.** In some organizations, effective capacity implies a one-shift operation; in others it implies a three-shift operation. For this reason, the Census Bureau in its surveys defines *capacity* as the greatest level of output the firm can *reasonably sustain* using realistic employee work schedules and the equipment currently in place.

A bus powered by a Cummins engine drives past Big Ben in London. In the past, Cummins Engine experienced quarterly losses despite record high sales. By increasing production capacity, and thereby not having to operate at peak capacity, Cummins posted a net earning of $70.2 million in the last quarter of 1994.

When operating close to design capacity, a firm can make minimal profits or even lose money despite high sales levels. Such was the case with the aircraft manufacturers mentioned in Managerial Practice 7.1. Similarly, Cummins Engine Company reacted a few years ago to an unexpected demand surge caused by the weakened dollar by working at peak capacity: The plant operated three shifts, often seven days a week. Overtime soared and exhausted workers dragged down productivity. Productivity also suffered when Cummins called back less skilled workers, laid off during an earlier slump. These factors together caused Cummins to report a quarterly loss of $6.2 million, even as sales jumped.

EXAMPLE 7.1

Calculating Utilization

If operated around the clock under ideal conditions, the fabrication department of an engine manufacturer can make 100 engines per day. Management believes that a maximum output rate of only 45 engines per day can be sustained economically over a long period of time. Currently the department is producing an average of 50 engines per day. What is the utilization of the department, relative to design capacity? Effective capacity?

Solution   The two utilization measures are

$$\text{Utilization}_{\text{design}} = \frac{\text{Average output rate}}{\text{Design capacity}} = \frac{50}{100} \times 100\% = 50\%$$

$$\text{Utilization}_{\text{effective}} = \frac{\text{Average output rate}}{\text{Effective capacity}} = \frac{50}{45} \times 100\% = 111\%$$

Even though fabrication department operations fall well short of the design capacity, they are beyond the output rate judged to be the most economical. They could be sustained at that level only through the use of considerable overtime.

Increasing Maximum Capacity. Most facilities have multiple operations, and often their effective capacities are not identical. A **bottleneck** is an operation that has the lowest effective capacity of any operation in the facility and thus limits the system's output. Figure 7.1(a) shows a facility where operation 2 is a bottleneck that limits the output of the facility to 50 units per hour. In effect, the facility can produce only as fast as the slowest operation. Figure 7.1(b) shows the facility when the capacities are perfectly balanced, making every operation a bottleneck. True expansion of a facility's capacity occurs only when bottleneck capacity is increased. In Fig. 7.1(a), initially adding capacity at operation 2 (and not operation 1 or 3) will increase system capacity. However, when operation 2's capacity reaches 200 units per hour, as in Fig. 7.1(b), all three operations must be expanded simultaneously to increase capacity further.

FIGURE 7.1   *Capacity Bottlenecks at a Three-Operation Facility*

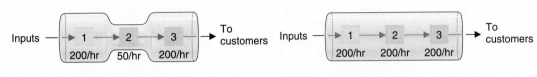

(a) Operation 2 a bottleneck   (b) All operations bottlenecks

If a facility is process-focused, such as a job shop, it doesn't enjoy the simple line flows shown in Fig. 7.1. Its operations may process many different items, and the demands on any one operation could vary considerably from one day to the next. Bottlenecks can still be identified by computing the average utilization of each operation. However, the variability in workload also creates *floating bottlenecks*. One week the mix of work may make operation 1 a bottleneck, and the next week it may make operation 3 the constraint. This type of variability increases the complexity of day-to-day scheduling. In this situation, management prefers lower utilization rates, which allow greater slack to absorb unexpected surges in demand.

Economies of Scale

What is the maximum reasonable size for a facility?

Historically, organizations have accepted a concept known as **economies of scale,** which states that the average unit cost of a good or service can be reduced by increasing its output rate. There are four principal reasons why costs go down when output increases: fixed costs are spread over more units, construction costs are reduced, costs of purchased materials are cut, and process advantages are found.

Spreading Fixed Costs. In the short term, certain costs do not vary with changes in the output rate. These fixed costs include heating costs, debt service, and management salaries. Depreciation of plant and equipment already owned is also a fixed cost in the accounting sense. When the output rate—and therefore the facility's utilization rate—increases, the average unit cost drops because fixed costs are spread over more units. Because increments of capacity often are rather large, a firm initially might have to buy more capacity than it needs. However, demand increases in subsequent years can then be absorbed without additional fixed costs.

Reducing Construction Costs.   Certain activities and expenses are required in building small and large facilities alike: building permits, architects' fees, rental of building equipment, and the like. Doubling the size of the facility usually does not double construction costs. The construction cost of equipment or a facility often increases relative to its surface area, whereas its capacity increases in proportion to its cubic volume. For example, the cost of steel to build an oil tanker increases more slowly than the tanker's capacity increases. Industries such as breweries and oil refineries benefit from strong economies of scale because of this phenomenon.

Cutting Costs of Purchased Materials.   Higher volumes can reduce the costs of purchased materials and services. They give the purchaser a better bargaining position and the opportunity to take advantage of quantity discounts. Retailers such as Wal-Mart Stores and Toys 'R' Us reap significant economies of scale because their national and international stores sell huge volumes of each item. Producers who rely on a vast network of suppliers (e.g., Toyota) and food processors (e.g., Kraft General Foods) also can buy inputs for less because of the quantity they order. In the personal computer business, large firms can negotiate volume discounts on the components that determine up to 80 percent of a PC's costs. Thus Compaq can sell its base model for just $100 more than it costs a smaller firm, making only 200 to 500 units a month, for materials alone. The small producers are being squeezed out of the PC business.

Finding Process Advantages.   High-volume production provides many opportunities for cost reduction. At a higher output rate, the process shifts toward a product-focused strategy, with resources dedicated to individual products. Firms may be able to justify the expense of more efficient technology or more specialized equipment. The benefits from dedicating resources to individual products or services may include speeding up the learning effect, lowering inventory, improving process and job designs, and reducing the number of changeovers. For exam-

Retailer Toys 'R' Us reaps the benefits of economies of scale because its network of national and international stores allows it to sell high volumes of each item.

Managerial Practice 7.2

▶ *Economies of Scale at Work*

Hospitals

Hospital bills in Kalamazoo, a metropolitan area of only 200,000, are the second highest in Michigan and among the highest in the nation. The reason is that the two archrival hospitals in Kalamazoo are not getting the full benefit from economies of scale. Borgess Medical Center and Bronson Methodist Hospital each have their own heart programs, maternity wards, state-of-the-art emergency rooms, and radiology services. They even each have their own helicopter ambulances—two of only 90 in the entire country. Operating both helicopter units costs a total of $5 million a year, and combining their operations would save at least $1 million, even if both choppers were kept running. In general, hospital costs in two-hospital towns like Kalamazoo are 30 percent higher than in one-hospital communities, where consolidat-ed volumes allow the hospital to enjoy greater economies of scale.

Coca-Cola Enterprises

Coca-Cola Enterprises, one of Coca-Cola Company's biggest bottlers, is putting economies of scale to work for it. It has been consolidating many of its smaller, disparate bottlers. The strategy is to cut production costs significantly below those of the rest of the industry. It bought 34 bottlers for about $3.6 billion and then molded them into a single operation. It cut its work force by 20 percent, to 20,000, and cut costs by merging distribution and raw materials buying. Its merger with Johnston Coca-Cola Bottling Group, executives say, will consolidate operations still more and reap the benefits of even bigger, better economies of scale.

Sources: "Rival Operations," *Wall Street Journal,* June 6, 1990; "Coke Still Searching for Bottling Formula," *Wall Street Journal,* September 6, 1991.

ple, higher volumes allow James River Corporation, a paper manufacturer, to achieve greater efficiency than manufacturers producing a wide variety of products in small volumes, because the mill can set up its machines for one long run of a certain grade of paper and not have to make as many adjustments for different grades.

Managerial Practice 7.2 gives examples of economies of scale in health care and bottling organizations. The economies of scale come from all four sources—spreading fixed costs, reducing construction costs, cutting purchasing costs, and finding process advantages.

Diseconomies of Scale

The concept of economies of scale is valid, but at some point a facility becomes so large that **diseconomies of scale** set in; that is, the average cost per unit increases as the facility's size increases. The reason is that excessive size can bring complexity, loss of focus, and inefficiencies that raise the average unit cost of a product or service. There are too many layers of employees and bureaucracy, and management loses touch with employees and customers. The organization is less agile and loses the flexibility to respond to changing demands. Many large companies become so involved in analysis and planning that they innovate less and avoid risks. The result is that small companies outperform corporate giants in numerous industries.

Figure 7.2 illustrates the transition from economies of scale to diseconomies of scale. The 500-bed hospital shows economies of scale because the average unit cost at its *best operating level*, represented by the blue dot, is less than that of the 250-bed hospital. However, further expansion to a 750-bed hospital leads to higher average unit costs and diseconomies of scale. One reason the 500-bed hospital enjoys greater economies of scale than the 250-bed hospital is that the cost of building and equipping it is less than twice the cost for the smaller hospital. The 750-bed facility would enjoy similar savings. Its higher average unit costs can be explained only by diseconomies of scale, which outweigh the savings realized in construction costs.

FIGURE 7.2

Economies and Diseconomies of Scale

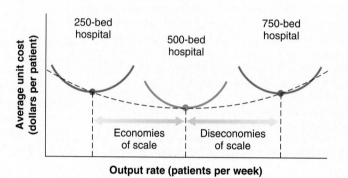

Economies of scale vary by industry, and so managers often set policies regarding the maximum size for any one facility. Employee ceilings of 300 are common for industries such as metal working. For example, Dana Corporation, a $5 billion supplier of steel to U.S., European, and Japanese automakers, has a cap of 200 employees at all but a few of its 120 plants. When a division gets too big, it simply gets split in half. For industries such as transportation equipment or electronics, where economies of scale are particularly strong, the limits are as large as 6000 employees. The real challenge in setting such limits is predicting how costs will change for different output rates and facility sizes.

Focused Factories

Is there enough focus in the facilities?

Before 1970, many firms were willing to endure the additional complexity that went with size. The nature of competition changed during the 1970s: Large scale no longer guaranteed an advantage. Quality and flexibility gained importance, rapid technological change shortened life cycles, and the demand for more customized products made maintaining high production volumes difficult. Many companies began to reevaluate the usefulness of large facilities and created **focused factories,** splitting large plants that produced all of the company's products at one location into several specialized smaller plants (Skinner, 1974). The theory is that narrowing the range of demands on a facility will lead to better performance because the operations manager can concentrate on fewer tasks and lead a work force toward a single goal. The General Electric Aircraft Engine Group once concentrated production in two large complexes but now has eight smaller satellite plants. Hewlett-Packard, S. C. Johnson and Sons, AT&T, Japan's Ricoh, Mitsubishi Electric, Nippon Telephone & Telegraph, and Britain's Imperial Chemical Industries PLC are some of the firms that have gone to smaller plants and focused operations. In some situations a plant that used to produce all the components and assemble the final product may split into one that produces the components and one that assembles the final product, so that each can focus on its own individual process technology.

Even within a large facility, focus can be gained by having *plants within plants* (PWPs), or separate operations with individualized competitive priorities, technology, and work force under the same roof. Boundaries for PWPs may be established by physically separating subunits or simply by revising organizational relationships. The advantages of PWPs are fewer layers of management, greater ability to rely on team problem solving, and shorter lines of communication between departments.

Service industries also have implemented focused factories. Specialty retailers, such as The Gap and The Limited, opened stores that have smaller, more accessible spaces. These focused facilities chipped away at the business of large department stores throughout the 1980s. Using the same philosophy, some department stores are focusing on specific customers or products. For example, Federated Department Stores wants to capitalize on its furniture departments, and J. C. Penney is pushing hard to boost its apparel image. Department stores have remodeled stores to create the effect of having many small "boutiques" under one roof. In the transportation industry, Roadway Services—a $3.7 billion giant—created a company within a company by starting Global Air to focus on the international package delivery business. Much of Southwest Airlines' success has been credited to its ability to maintain its image as a small, efficient company, even though it has grown to a $1.7 billion operation. Small size often means a more flexible, agile organization that competes particularly well on the basis of short lead times.

The Gap, a retailer of clothing for men, women, and children, uses a standard design for all its mall outlets. The stores are focused facilities, specializing in casual clothing at reasonable prices.

Capacity Strategies

Operations managers must examine three dimensions of capacity strategy before making capacity decisions: sizing capacity cushions, timing and sizing expansion, and linking capacity and other operating decisions.

Sizing Capacity Cushions.   Average utilization rates should not get too close to 100 percent. When they do, that usually is a signal to increase capacity or decrease order acceptance so as to avoid declining productivity. The **capacity cushion** is the amount of reserve capacity that a firm maintains to handle sudden increases in demand or temporary losses of production capacity; it measures the amount by which the average utilization (in terms of *effective* capacity) falls below 100 percent. Specifically,

$$\text{Capacity cushion} = 100\% - \text{Utilization rate (\%)}$$

How much capacity cushion is best for various processes?

From 1948 to 1993 U.S. manufacturers maintained an average cushion of 18 percent, with a low of 9 percent in 1966 and a high of 27 percent in 1982. The appropriate size of the cushion varies by industry. In the capital-intensive paper industry, where machines can cost hundreds of millions of dollars each, cushions well under 10 percent are preferred. Electric utilities also are capital intensive but consider cushions of 15 to 20 percent in electric generating capacity to be optimal to avoid brownouts and loss of service to customers.

Businesses find large cushions appropriate when demand varies. In certain service industries (e.g., groceries), demand on some days of the week is predictably higher than on other days, and there are even hour-to-hour patterns. Long customer waiting times are not acceptable because customers grow impatient if they have to wait in a supermarket checkout line for more than a few minutes. Prompt customer service requires supermarkets to maintain a capacity cushion large enough to handle peak demand.

Large cushions also are necessary when future demand is uncertain, particularly if resource flexibility is low. One large bank operated its computer for six months at an average 77 percent load on the central processing unit (CPU) during peak demand. Top management believed that the capacity cushion was more than ample and rejected a proposal to expand capacity. During the next six months, however, the average CPU utilization during peaks unexpectedly surged to 83 percent, causing a dramatic decline in customer service. The 17 percent capacity cushion proved to be too small to meet the bank's customer service objectives. Waiting line analysis and simulation (see Supplements E and F) can help managers anticipate better the relationship between capacity cushion and customer service.

Another type of demand uncertainty occurs with a changing product mix. Though total demand might remain stable, the load can shift unpredictably from one work center to another as the mix changes. In the case of American Airlines, uncertainty in the product mix—domestic flights versus international flights—caused the company to estimate incorrectly how much of its capacity to devote to widebody planes for international travel. Similarly, the auto industry, emerging from a punishing recession in 1994, faced the challenge of shifting its capacity from midsized cars to pickup trucks when consumer preferences shifted. High customization also leads to uncertainty. An example is a municipal court system, where the capacity in courtroom hours varies with the nature of the trials and whether a jury is needed. The mix varies from week to week and month to month.

Supply uncertainty also favors large capacity cushions. Capacity often comes in large increments, so expanding even by the minimum amount possible may create a large cushion. Consider the new Gamma Knife machine, which emits gamma radiation to treat brain tumors and lesions. It is used on only a few types of tumors, and a hospital purchasing the machine may find that it has purchased greater capacity than it needs. Most of the 16 units currently owned by U.S. hospitals are idle all but two days per week.

Firms also need to build in excess capacity to allow for employee absenteeism, vacations, holidays, and any other delays. Penalty costs for overtime and subcontracting can create the need for further increases in capacity cushions.

The argument in favor of small cushions is simple: Unused capacity costs money. For capital-intensive firms, minimizing the capacity cushion is vital. Since the mid 1970s, airlines have expanded capacity by cramming about 20 percent more seats into the same size aircraft. Studies indicate that businesses with high capital intensity achieve a low return on investment when the capacity cushion is high. This strong correlation doesn't exist for labor-intensive firms, however. Their return on investment is about the same because the lower investment in equipment makes high utilization less critical. Small cushions have other advantages; they reveal inefficiencies that may be masked by capacity excesses—problems with absenteeism, for example, or unreliable suppliers. Once managers and workers have identified such problems, they often can find ways to correct them.

Timing and Sizing Expansion.   The second issue of capacity strategy is when to expand and by how much. Figure 7.3 illustrates two extreme strategies: the *expansionist strategy,* which involves large, infrequent jumps in capacity, and the *wait-and-see strategy,* which involves smaller, more frequent jumps.

Should an expansionist or a wait-and-see strategy be followed?

During an industrywide slump in 1987 and 1988, The Limited, a firm with seven specialty apparel store divisions, opted for an expansionist strategy by aggressively opening new outlets and expanding existing ones. As a result of the store expansions and clustering of stores from its seven divisions, The Limited became one of the largest specialty store tenants in hundreds of malls. In a shopping center in Columbus, Ohio, The Limited divisions account for 125,000 square feet, or 25 percent of the total. That amount of space earns concessions such as prime locations, cheaper rents, and even money from developers to help with construction costs. By 1990, The Limited's holdings had grown by 27 percent, to 3419 stores, and its sales by 68 percent, to $5.2 billion. The best strategy for a firm can change over time. American Airlines followed an expansionist strategy in the 1980s, when it aggressively pursued overseas routes. After several setbacks, including lack of proper equipment and rising fuel costs because of the Persian Gulf War, American adopted a less risky wait-and-see strategy.

FIGURE 7.3   *Two Capacity Strategies*

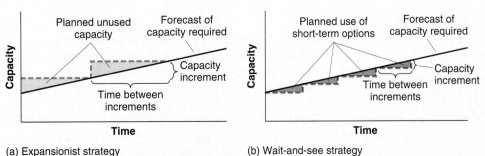

(a) Expansionist strategy   (b) Wait-and-see strategy

The timing and sizing of expansion are related; that is, if demand is increasing and the time between increments increases, the size of the increments must also increase. The expansionist strategy, which stays ahead of demand, minimizes the chance of sales lost to insufficient capacity. The wait-and-see strategy lags behind demand, relying on short-term options such as use of overtime, temporary workers, subcontractors, stockouts, and postponement of preventive maintenance to meet any shortfalls. However, these options have their drawbacks. For example, overtime requires payment of time-and-a-half wages for some employees and may result in lower productivity or quality during overtime hours; union agreements may even limit the amount of allowable overtime. Nonetheless, some mix of short-term options might make the wait-and-see strategy best in certain situations.

Several factors favor the expansionist strategy. Expansion may result in economies of scale and a faster rate of learning, thus helping a firm reduce its costs and compete on price. This strategy might increase the firm's market share or act as a form of preemptive marketing. By making a large capacity expansion or announcing that one is imminent, the firm uses capacity to preempt expansion by other firms. These other firms must sacrifice some of their market share or risk burdening the industry with overcapacity. To be successful, however, the pre-empting firm must have the credibility to convince the competition that it will carry out its plans—and must signal its plans before the competition can act.

The conservative wait-and-see strategy is to expand in smaller increments, such as by renovating existing facilities rather than building new ones. Because the wait-and-see strategy follows demand, it reduces the risks of overexpansion based on overly optimistic demand forecasts, obsolete technology, or inaccurate assumptions regarding the competition. However, this strategy has different risks, such as being preempted by a competitor or being unable to respond if demand is unexpectedly high. The wait-and-see strategy has been criticized as a short-term strategy typical of some U.S. management styles. Managers on the fast track to corporate advancement tend to take fewer risks. They earn promotions by avoiding the big mistake and maximizing short-term profits and return on investment. The wait-and-see strategy fits this short-term outlook but can erode market share over the long run.

Management may choose one of these two strategies or one of the many between these extremes. With strategies in the more moderate middle, firms may expand more frequently (on a smaller scale) than with the expansionist strategy, but do not always lag behind demand as with the wait-and-see strategy. An intermediate strategy could be to *follow-the-leader,* expanding when others do. If others are right, so are you, and nobody gains a competitive advantage. If they make a mistake and overexpand, so have you, but everyone shares in the agony of overcapacity.

Linking Capacity and Other Decisions.   Capacity decisions should be closely linked to strategies and operations throughout the organization. When managers make decisions about location, resource flexibility, and inventory, they must consider the impact on capacity cushions. Capacity cushions buffer the organization against uncertainty, as do resource flexibility, inventory, and longer customer lead times. If a system is well balanced and a change is made in some other decision area, then the capacity cushion may need change to compensate. Examples of such links with capacity include the following.

How should capacity and competitive priorities be linked? Capacity and other types of decisions?

- *Competitive priorities.* A change in competitive priorities that emphasizes faster deliveries requires a larger capacity cushion to allow for quick response and uneven demand, if holding finished goods inventory is infeasible or uneconomical.

- *Quality management.* A drive to obtain higher levels of quality allows for a smaller capacity cushion because there will be less uncertainty caused by yield losses.

- *Capital intensity.* An investment in expensive new technologies makes a process more capital-intensive and increases pressure to have a smaller capacity cushion to get an acceptable return on the investment.

- *Resource flexibility.* A change to less worker flexibility requires a larger capacity cushion to compensate for the operation overloads that are more likely to occur with a less flexible work force.

- *Inventory.* A change to less reliance on inventory in order to smooth the output rate requires a larger capacity cushion to meet increased demands during peak periods.

- *Scheduling.* A change to a more stable environment allows a smaller cushion because products or services can be scheduled with more assurance.

As an example of how capacity and a firm's competitive priorities are linked, consider the subsidiary of a large goods manufacturer that sold 85 percent of its output to other divisions in the company, with the remaining 15 percent going to outside customers. The capacity of one of its processes was tight, and the company was considering expanding capacity to attract more outside customers. However, to attract new customers in a different market segment, the subsidiary would have to shift its competitive priorities; this low-cost supplier to the company's other divisions would have to place higher priority on customization and the premium quality demanded by new customers. The subsidiary's management decided against the expansion because of poor coupling with its other goals and policies.

A survey of managers of manufacturing firms illustrates the link between capacity and other decisions. Managers were asked which of eight broad categories of processes (such as packaging, changing shapes of metals, and assembling) were performed in their plants. The results show that managers opt for a more focused factory (fewer processes in the same facility) when a standardized product is being produced.

One crucial linkage is between capacity and location decisions. A firm that is expanding eventually must add new facilities and find suitable locations for them, whereas a multisite firm that is downsizing often must identify which locations to eliminate. During the last decade, General Motors cut back its capacity by shutting down several factories to stop large losses in its North American automobile operation. It faced tough choices between closing older factories with cooperative and productive work forces and abandoning expensive, modern plants where labor relations were poor. The UAW contract made closing a facility quite costly, so some plants that otherwise should have been closed remained open.

Finally, because capacity decisions are linked with the other functional areas, careful integration of plans is required. Marketing is involved because of its knowledge of market segments and projections of demand. Capacity decisions today have much to do with market position 10 years hence. Finance is involved because expansion requires significant capital outlays that must be taken from retained earnings or obtained from outside sources. Human resources is involved because capacity changes have hiring and training implications—and can also mean painful layoffs and downsizing. Cross-functional understanding is a key to wise capacity strategy.

◆ A SYSTEMATIC APPROACH TO CAPACITY DECISIONS

How can capacity plans be systematically developed?

Although each situation is somewhat different, a four-step procedure generally can help managers make sound capacity decisions. In describing this procedure, we assume that management has already performed the preliminary step of determining existing capacity.

1. Estimate future capacity requirements.
2. Identify gaps by comparing requirements with available capacity.
3. Develop alternative plans for filling the gaps.
4. Evaluate each alternative, both qualitatively and quantitatively, and make a final choice.

Step 1: Estimate Capacity Requirements

The foundation for estimating long-term capacity needs is forecasts of demand, productivity, competition, and technological changes that extends well into the future. Unfortunately, the further ahead you look, the more chance you have of making an inaccurate forecast. (See Chapter 10 for a more detailed discussion of quantitative and qualitative forecasting methods.)

The demand forecast has to be converted to a number that can be compared directly with the capacity measure being used. Suppose that capacity is expressed as the number of available machines at an operation. When just one product (service) is being processed, the number of machines required, M, is

$$M = \frac{Dp}{N\,[1 - (C/100)]}$$

where D = number of units (customers) forecast per year
p = processing time (in hours per unit or customers)
N = total number of hours per year during which the process operates
C = desired capacity cushion

The denominator is the total number of hours, N, available for the year, multiplied by a proportion that accounts for the desired capacity cushion, C. The proportion is simply $1.0 - C$, where C is converted from a percentage to a proportion by dividing by 100.

If multiple products or services are involved, extra time is needed to change over from one product or service to the next. **Setup time** is the time required to change a machine from making one product or service to making another. The total setup time is found by dividing D by the number of units made in each lot, which gives the number of setups per year, and then multiplying by the time per setup. For example, if the annual demand is 1200 units and the average lot size is 100, there are $1200/100 = 12$ setups per year. Accounting for both processing and setup time when there are multiple products (services), we get

$$M = \frac{[Dp + (D/Q)s]_{\text{product 1}} + [Dp + (D/Q)s]_{\text{product 2}} + \cdots + [Dp + (D/Q)s]_{\text{product } n}}{N[1 - (C/100)]}$$

where
$$Q = \text{number of units in each lot}$$
$$s = \text{setup time (in hours) per lot}$$

Always round up the fractional part unless it is cost efficient to use short-term options such as overtime or stockouts to cover any shortfalls.

EXAMPLE 7.2

Estimating Requirements

A copy center in an office building prepares bound reports for two clients. The center makes multiple copies (the lot size) of each report. The processing time to run, collate, and bind each copy depends on, among other factors, the number of pages. The center operates 250 days per year, with one eight-hour shift. Management believes that a capacity cushion of 15 percent (beyond the allowance built into time standards) is best. Based on the following table of information, determine how many machines are needed at the copy center.

Item	Client X	Client Y
Annual demand forecast (copies)	2000	6000
Standard processing time (hour/copy)	0.5	0.7
Average lot size (copies per report)	20	30
Standard setup time (hours)	0.25	0.40

Solution

$$M = \frac{[Dp + (D/Q)s]_{\text{product 1}} + [Dp + (D/Q)s]_{\text{product 2}} + \cdots + [Dp + (D/Q)s]_{\text{product } n}}{N[1 - (C/100)]}$$

$$= \frac{[2000(0.5) + (2000/20)(0.25)]_{\text{client X}} + [6000(0.7) + (6000/30)(0.40)]_{\text{client Y}}}{(250 \text{ days/year})(1 \text{ shift/day})(8 \text{ hours/shift})](1.0 - 15/100)}$$

$$= \frac{5305}{1700} = 3.12$$

Rounding up to the next integer gives a requirement of four machines.

Step 2: Identify Gaps

A **capacity gap** is any difference (positive or negative) between projected demand and current capacity. Identifying gaps requires use of the correct capacity measure. Complications arise when multiple operations and several resource inputs are involved. For example, in the early 1970s, airline executives incorrectly concluded that airlines having the larger share of seats flown attract a larger share of total passengers. In other words, fly more seats to get more passengers. Many airlines responded by buying more jumbo jets, but competitors flying smaller planes were more successful. The correct measure of capacity was the number of departures rather than the number of seats. Thus several airlines had to adjust the capacity imbalance between small and large planes by buying smaller planes and discontinuing use of some jumbo jets. Expanding the capacity of some operations may increase overall capacity. However, if one operation is a bottleneck, capacity can be expanded only if the capacity of the bottleneck operation is expanded.

EXAMPLE 7.3

*Identifying Capacity
Gaps*

Grandmother's Chicken Restaurant is experiencing a boom in business. The owner expects to serve a total of 80,000 meals this year. Although the kitchen is operating at 100 percent capacity, the dining room can handle a total of 105,000 diners per year. Forecasted demand for the next five years is as follows.

Year 1:	90,000 meals
Year 2:	100,000 meals
Year 3:	110,000 meals
Year 4:	120,000 meals
Year 5:	130,000 meals

What are the capacity gaps in Grandmother's kitchen and dining room through year 5?

Solution   The kitchen is currently the bottleneck at a capacity of 80,000 meals per year. Based on the demand forecast, the capacity gap for the kitchen is

Year 1:	$90,000 - 80,000 = 10,000$
Year 2:	$100,000 - 80,000 = 20,000$
Year 3:	$110,000 - 80,000 = 30,000$
Year 4:	$120,000 - 80,000 = 40,000$
Year 5:	$130,000 - 80,000 = 50,000$

Before year 3, the capacity of the dining room (105,000) is greater than demand. In year 3 and subsequently, there are capacity gaps for the dining room:

Year 3:	$110,000 - 105,000 = 5000$
Year 4:	$120,000 - 105,000 = 15,000$
Year 5:	$130,000 - 105,000 = 25,000$

Step 3: Develop Alternatives

The next step is to develop alternative plans to cope with projected gaps. One alternative, called the **base case**, is to do nothing and simply lose orders from any demand that exceeds current capacity. Other alternatives are various timing and sizing options for adding new capacity, including the expansionist and wait-and-see strategies illustrated in Fig. 7.3. Additional possibilities include expanding at a different location and using short-term options such as overtime, temporary workers, and subcontracting.

Step 4: Evaluate the Alternatives

In this final step, the manager evaluates each alternative, both quantitatively and qualitatively.

Qualitative Concerns.   Qualitatively, the manager has to look at how each alternative fits the overall capacity strategy and other aspects of the business not covered by the financial analysis. Of particular concern might be uncertainties about demand, competitive reaction, technological change, and cost estimates. Some of these factors cannot be quantified and have to be assessed on the basis of judgment and experience. Others can be quantified, and the manager can analyze each alternative by using different assumptions about the future. One set of assumptions could represent a worst case, where demand is less, competition is greater, and construction costs are higher than expected. Another set of assumptions could represent the most optimistic view of the future. This type of "what if" analysis allows the manager to get an idea of each alternative's implications before making a final choice.

Quantitative Concerns. Quantitatively, the manager estimates the change in cash flows for each alternative over the forecast time horizon, compared to the base case. **Cash flow** is the difference between the flows of funds into and out of an organization over a period of time, including revenues, costs, and changes in assets and liabilities. The manager is concerned here only with calculating the cash flows attributable to the project.

EXAMPLE 7.4

Evaluating the Alternatives

One alternative for Grandmother's Chicken Restaurant is to expand both the kitchen and the dining room now, bringing their capacities up to 130,000 meals per year. The initial investment would be $200,000, made at the end of this year (year 0). The average meal is priced at $10, and the before-tax profit margin is 20 percent. The 20 percent figure was arrived at by determining that, for each $10 meal, $6 covers variable costs and $2 goes toward fixed costs (other than depreciation). The remaining $2 goes to pre-tax profit.

What are the pre-tax cash flows from this project for the next five years, compared to those of the base case of doing nothing?

Solution   Recall that the base case of doing nothing results in losing all potential sales beyond 80,000 meals. With the new capacity, the cash flow would equal the extra meals served by having a 130,000 meal capacity, multiplied by a profit of $2 per meal. In year 0, the only cash flow is $-$200,000 for the initial investment. In year 1, the 90,000 meal demand will be completely satisfied by the expanded capacity, so the incremental cash flow is $(90,000 - 80,000)(2) =$ $20,000. For subsequent years, the figures are as follows.

Year 2:   Demand = 100,000; Cash flow = $(100,000 - 80,000)2 = \$40,000$
Year 3:   Demand = 110,000; Cash flow = $(110,000 - 80,000)2 = \$60,000$
Year 4:   Demand = 120,000; Cash flow = $(120,000 - 80,000)2 = \$80,000$
Year 5:   Demand = 130,000; Cash flow = $(130,000 - 80,000)2 = \$100,000$

Because the owner is evaluating an alternative that provides enough capacity to meet all demand through year 5, the added meals served are identical to the capacity gaps in Example 7.3. That wouldn't be true if the new capacity were smaller than the expected demand in any year. To find the added meals in that case, we would subtract the base case capacity from the new capacity (rather than the demand). The result would be smaller than the capacity gap.

Before completing the evaluation of this capacity alternative, the owner must examine qualitative concerns. For example, the homey atmosphere that the restaurant has projected may be lost with expansion. Furthermore, other alternatives should be considered, such as the one in Solved Problem 2 at the end of the chapter.

◆   TOOLS FOR CAPACITY PLANNING

What tools can help in planning capacities?

Long-term capacity planning requires demand forecasts for an extended period of time. Unfortunately, forecast accuracy declines as the forecasting horizon lengthens. In addition, anticipating what competitors will do increases the uncertainty of demand forecasts. Finally, demand during any period of time isn't evenly distributed; peaks and valleys of demand may (and often do) occur within the time period. These realities necessitate the use of capacity cushions. In this section we introduce two decision tools that more formally deal with demand uncertainty and variability: waiting line models and decision trees. Waiting line models account for the random, independent behavior of many customers, in terms of both their time of arrival and their processing needs. Decision trees allow anticipation of events such as competitor actions.

Waiting Line Models

Waiting line models often are useful in capacity planning. Waiting lines tend to develop in front of a work center, such as an airport ticket counter, a machine center, or a central computer, because the arrival time between jobs or customers varies and the processing time may vary from one customer to the next. Waiting line models use probability distributions to provide estimates of average customer delay time, average length of waiting lines, and utilization of the work center. Managers can use this information to choose the most cost-effective capacity, balancing customer service and the cost of adding capacity.

Supplement E provides a fuller treatment of waiting line models. It introduces formulas for estimating important characteristics of a waiting line, such as average customer waiting time and average facility utilization, for different facility designs. For example, a facility might be designed to have one or multiple lines at each operation and to route customers through one or multiple operations. Given the estimating capability of these formulas and cost estimates for waiting and idle time, managers can select cost-effective designs and capacity levels that also provide the desired level of customer service. More complex waiting line problems must be analyzed with simulation (see Supplement F).

Decision Trees

A decision tree can be particularly valuable for evaluating different capacity expansion alternatives when demand is uncertain and sequential decisions are involved. For example, the owner of Grandmother's Chicken Restaurant (see Example 7.4) may expand the restaurant now, only to discover in year 4 that demand growth is much higher than forecasted. In that case, she needs to decide whether to expand further. In terms of construction costs and downtime, expanding twice is likely to be much more expensive than building a large facility from the outset. However, making a large expansion now when demand growth is low means poor facility utilization. Much depends on the demand.

Figure 7.4 shows a decision tree for this view of the problem, with new information provided. Demand growth can be either low or high, with probabilities of 0.4 and 0.6, respectively. The initial expansion in year 1 (square node 1) can either be small or large. The second decision node (square node 2), whether to expand at a later date, is reached only if the initial expansion is small and demand

FIGURE 7.4

A Decision Tree for Capacity Expansion (Payoffs in Thousands of Dollars)

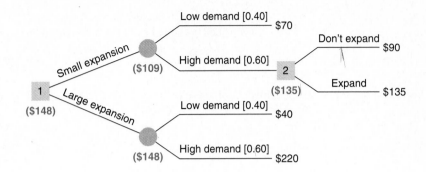

turns out to be high. If demand is high and if the initial expansion was small, a decision must be made about a second expansion in year 4. Payoffs for each branch of the tree are estimated. For example, if the initial expansion is large, the financial benefit is either $40,000 or $220,000, depending on whether demand is low or high. Weighting these payoffs by the probabilities yields an expected value of $148,000. This expected payoff is higher than the $109,000 payoff for the small initial expansion, so the best choice is to make a large expansion in year 1. Supplement A describes decision trees in more depth, including how to draw them and analyze them.

CHAPTER REVIEW

Solved Problem 1

You have been asked to put together a capacity plan for a critical bottleneck operation at the Surefoot Sandal Company. Your capacity measure is number of machines. Three products (men's, women's, and children's sandals) are manufactured. The time standards (processing and setup), lot sizes, and demand forecasts are given in the following table. The firm operates two 8-hour shifts, 5 days per week, 50 weeks per year. Experience shows that a capacity cushion of 5 percent is sufficient.

| | Time Standards | | | |
Product	Processing (hr/pair)	Setup (hr/lot)	Lot Size (pairs/lot)	Demand Forecast (pairs/yr)
Men's sandals	0.05	0.5	240	80,000
Women's sandals	0.10	2.2	180	60,000
Children's sandals	0.02	3.8	360	120,000

a. How many machines are needed?
b. If the operation currently has two machines, what is the capacity gap?

Solution a. The number of hours of operation per year, N, is

$$N = (2 \text{ shifts/day})(8 \text{ hours/shift})(250 \text{ days/machine-year})$$
$$= 4000 \text{ hours/machine-year}$$

The number of machines required, *M*, is the sum of machine hour requirements for all three products divided by the number of productive hours available for one machine:

$$M = \frac{[Dp + (D/Q)s]_{men} + [Dp + (D/Q)s]_{women} + [Dp + (D/Q)s]_{children}}{N[1 - (C/100)]}$$

$$= \frac{[80,000(0.05) + (80,000/240)0.5] + [60,000(0.10) + (60,000/180)2.2] + [120,000(0.02) + (120,000/360)3.8]}{4000[1 - (5/100)]}$$

$$= \frac{14,567 \text{ hours/year}}{3800 \text{ hours/machine-year}} = 3.8, \quad \text{or 4 machines}$$

b. The capacity gap is 1.8 machines (3.8 − 2). Two more machines should be purchased, unless management decides to use short-term options to fill the gap.

Solved Problem 2

The base case for Grandmother's Chicken Restaurant (see Example 7.3) is to do nothing. The capacity of the kitchen in the base case is 80,000 meals per year. A capacity alternative for Grandmother's Chicken Restaurant is a two-stage expansion. This alternative expands the kitchen at the end of year 0, raising its capacity from 80,000 meals per year to that of the dining area (105,000 meals per year). If sales in year 1 and year 2 live up to expectations, the capacities of both the kitchen and the dining room will be expanded at the *end* of year 3 to 130,000 meals per year. The initial investment would be $80,000 at the end of year 0 and an additional investment of $170,000 at the end of year 3. The pre-tax profit is $2 per meal. What are the before-tax cash flows for this alternative through year 5, compared with the base case?

Solution   Table 7.1 shows the cash inflows and outflows. The year 3 cash flow is unusual in two respects. First, the cash inflow from sales is $50,000 rather than $60,000. The increase in sales over the base is 25,000 meals (105,000 − 80,000) instead of 30,000 meals (110,000 − 80,000) because the restaurant's capacity falls somewhat short of demand. Second, a cash outflow of $170,000 occurs at the end of year 3, when the second-stage expansion occurs. The net cash flow for year 3 is $50,000 − $170,000 = −$120,000.

TABLE 7.1   *Cash Flows for Two-Stage Expansion at Grandmother's Chicken Restaurant*

Year	Projected Demand (meals/yr)	Projected Capacity (meals/yr)	Calculation of Incremental Cash Flow Compared to Base Case (80,000 meals/yr)	Cash Inflow (Outflow)
0	80,000	80,000	Increase kitchen capacity to 105,000 meals =	($80,000)
1	90,000	105,000	90,000 − 80,000 = (10,000 meals)($2/meal) =	$20,000
2	100,000	105,000	100,000 − 80,000 = (20,000 meals)($2/meal) =	$40,000
3	110,000	105,000	105,000 − 80,000 = (25,000 meals)($2/meal) =	$50,000
			Increase total capacity to 130,000 meals =	($170,000)
				($120,000)
4	120,000	130,000	120,000 − 80,000 = (40,000 meals)($2/meal) =	$80,000
5	130,000	130,000	130,000 − 80,000 = (50,000 meals)($2/meal) =	$100,000

Solved Problem 3

Penelope and Peter Legume own a small accounting service and one personal computer. If their customers keep organized records, either of the owners can use the computer to prepare one tax return per hour, on average. During the first two weeks of April, both Legumes work seven 12-hour shifts. This allows them to use their computer around the clock.

a. What is the design (or peak) capacity, measured in tax returns per week?
b. The Legumes normally operate from 9 A.M. to 7 P.M., five days per week. What is their effective capacity, measured in tax returns per week?
c. During the third week of January, the Legumes processed 40 tax returns. What is their utilization, as a percentage of effective capacity?

Solution   a.   Peak capacity = (12 hours/shift)(2 shifts/day)(7 days/week)(1 return/hour)
= 168 returns/week

b. Although both Legumes may be present in the shop, the capacity is limited by the number of hours their one computer is available:

Effective capacity = (10 hours/day)(5 days/week)(1 return/hour)
= 50 returns/week

c. Utilization is the ratio of output to effective capacity:

$$\text{Utilization} = \frac{40 \text{ returns/week}}{50 \text{ returns/week}} \times 100\%$$

$$= 80\%$$

Formula Review

1. Utilization, expressed as a percentage:

$$\text{Utilization} = \frac{\text{Average output rate}}{\text{Maximum capacity}} \times 100\%$$

2. Capacity cushion, C, expressed as a percentage:

$$C = 100\% - \text{Utilization}(\%)$$

3. a. Capacity requirement for one product:

$$M = \frac{Dp}{N[1 - (C/100)]}$$

b. Capacity requirement for multiple products:

$$M = \frac{[Dp + (D/Q)s]_{\text{product 1}} + [Dp + (D/Q)s]_{\text{product 2}} + \cdots + [Dp + (D/Q)s]_{\text{product } n}}{N[1 - (C/100)]}$$

Chapter Highlights

- Operations managers plan for timely acquisition, use, and disposition of capacity.
- Long-term capacity planning is crucial to an organization's success because it often involves large investments in facilities and equipment and because such decisions are not easily reversed.
- Capacity can be stated in terms of either input or output measures. Output measures giving the number of prod-

ucts or services completed in a time period are useful when a firm provides *standardized* products or services. However, a statement of the number of *customized* products or services completed in a time period is meaningless, because the work content per unit varies. Demand for customized products and services must be translated into input measures, such as labor hours, machine hours, and material requirements.

- Operating at design, or peak, capacity calls for extraordinary effort under ideal conditions that usually are not sustainable. Maximum output under normal conditions is called effective capacity. The operation having the lowest effective capacity is called a bottleneck and limits the capacity of the entire system. Variable work loads and changing product mix complicate measuring capacity and can cause different operations to become bottlenecks under varying circumstances. Such floating bottlenecks make determining a firm's effective capacity difficult.

- Economies of scale derive from spreading fixed costs, reducing construction costs, reducing purchased materials costs, and obtaining process advantages. Diseconomies of scale cause some firms to focus their operations and move to smaller, rather than larger, facilities.

- The desirable amount of capacity cushion varies, depending on competitive priorities, cost of unused capacity, resource flexibility, supply uncertainties, shelf life, variability and uncertainty of demand, and other factors.

- Three capacity strategies are expansionist, wait-and-see, and follow-the-leader. The expansionist strategy is attractive when there are economies of scale, learning effects, and a chance for preemptive marketing. The wait-and-see strategy minimizes risk by relying more on short-term options. The follow-the-leader strategy maintains the current balance between competitors.

- Capacity choices must be linked to other operations management decisions.

- The four steps in capacity planning are (1) estimate capacity requirements, (2) identify gaps, (3) develop alternatives, and (4) evaluate the alternatives.

- Waiting line models help the manager choose the capacity level that best balances customer service and the cost of adding more capacity. As waiting line problems involve more servers, mathematical models quickly become very complex. Simulation is used to analyze most multiple-server waiting line situations. Decision trees are schematic models that can be helpful in evaluating different capacity expansion alternatives when demand is uncertain and sequential decisions are involved.

Key Terms

base case *290*	cash flow *291*	focused factories *282*
bottleneck *279*	design capacity *277*	rated capacity *277*
capacity *275*	diseconomies of scale *281*	setup time *288*
capacity cushion *284*	economies of scale *279*	utilization *276*
capacity gap *289*	effective capacity *277*	

Study Questions

1. What factors make capacity planning a particular challenge?

2. What are the different ways of responding to capacity gaps?

3. What capacity measure would you recommend for a drive-in window at a bank? For an entire toy manufacturing plant? What complications might you run into when using these measures?

4. What types of estimates and forecasts are needed for capacity planning?

5. Three operations, A, H, and C, are arranged in series. For an eight-hour shift, the effective capacities are 24, 18, and 20 units per day, respectively. What is the effective capacity of the system? To increase production, 33 percent overtime was authorized at operation H and 20 percent at operation C. Soon after the overtime was authorized, the average output rate for the system rose to 21 units per day, which is less than the

24 units per day expected. Explain three likely reasons the average output rate fell below expectations.

6. A young boy has set up a lemonade stand on the corner of College Street and Air Park Boulevard. Temperatures in the area climb to 110° during the summer. The intersection is near a major university and a large construction site. Explain to this young entrepreneur how his business might benefit from economies of scale.

7. Explain to the young entrepreneur in Question 6 some conditions that might lead to diseconomies of scale.

8. What are the economies of scale in operations management class size? As class size increases, what symptoms of diseconomies of scale appear?

9. What economies of scale are associated with a shift from a process focus to a product focus? Why are commodities such as steel, oil, paper, and beer produced in large facilities?

10. PacTel recently spun off its cellular telephone business under the name Air Touch. Air Touch then allied with US West's cellular business. The combined operations will be positioned to provide personal communication services in most of the contiguous states west of the Mississippi. Which principles from this chapter are apparent in this strategy?

11. Most capital-intensive businesses tend to shy away from expansionist strategies. Why don't electric utilities use the wait-and-see strategy?

12. Explain how the wait-and-see strategy risks reduced market share. Explain the risk of technological advancement associated with the expansionist strategy.

13. Two electric utilities each must satisfy a 3000 megawatt demand. The first utility generates electricity using a large number of 50 to 100 megawatt power plants. The second utility owns a small number of 500 to 1000 megawatt power plants. Which utility needs the larger capacity cushion? Why?

14. Example 7.3 describes a one-stage expansion for Grandmother's Chicken Restaurant, whereas Solved Problem 2 describes a two-stage expansion. Which alternative resembles the expansionist strategy? The wait-and-see strategy? What qualitative factors favor the wait-and-see strategy?

15. John B. Galipault, president of the Aviation Safety Institute, said: "Airlines since the mid 1970s have stuffed 20 percent more seats into the same size aircraft." The standard first-class and coach configuration of an MD-11 holds about 300 passengers. With narrower, more upright seats and coach seating throughout, an MD-11 will seat about 410 passengers. Some 747s presently fly with 568 passengers. Double-deck airplanes are being designed to carry even more passengers. What are the trade-offs between safety and capacity utilization? What other facility changes are associated with increasing the number of passengers per plane?

Problems

1. Peter Moss operates Pete's Garage and Manhole Cover Recycling Center at the corner of Lookout Highway and Ruff Road. Pete's Garage has one bay dedicated to wheel alignments. Although the recycling center is open at night, the garage normally is open only on weekdays from 7 A.M. to 6 P.M. and on Saturdays from 7 A.M. to noon. An alignment takes an average of 40 minutes to complete, although Pete charges customers for two hours according to a nationally published mechanic's labor-standard manual. During March, the height of pothole season, Pete's Garage is open from 7 A.M. to 9 P.M. on weekdays and from 7 A.M. to 5 P.M. on Saturdays.

   a. What are the garage's peak and effective capacities, in alignments per week?

   b. During the second week in March, Pete's Garage completed 100 alignments. What is the utilization as a percentage of effective capacity? As a percentage of peak capacity?

2. Sterling Motors is a telephone/mail-order dealer in British auto parts. Sterling has six telephones for receiving orders. Order takers answer the telephones, check inventory availability, and prepare picking tickets for the warehouse stockpickers. One order may consist of several lines, with a different part or multiple of a part ordered on each line. Each order taker can prepare picking tickets at a rate of one line every three minutes. The telephones are normally answered weekdays from 6 A.M. to 4 P.M., Pacific Time. Stockpickers can fill and package parts at a rate of one line every five minutes. Sterling employs eight stock pickers, who normally work weekdays from 8 A.M. to 5 P.M. (except for lunch hours).

   a. What is the effective capacity of order taking, in lines per week? Stockpicking?

   b. For three weeks after the spring catalog is mailed in May, the eight warehouse employees work 10 hours per day between 7 A.M. and 6 P.M., six days per week. What is the peak capacity of the system, in lines per week?

   c. During the second week of May, Sterling filled 5000 order lines. What is the utilization as a percentage of effective capacity? As a percentage of peak capacity?

3. The Dahlia Medical Center has 20 labor rooms, 16 combination labor/delivery rooms, 2 delivery rooms, and 1 special delivery room reserved for complicated births. All of these facilities operate around the clock. Time spent in labor rooms varies from hours to days, with an average of about a day. The average uncomplicated delivery requires about one hour in a delivery room.

   During an exceptionally busy three-day period, 120 healthy babies were born at or received by Dahlia Medical Center. Sixty-five babies were born in separate labor and delivery rooms, 45 were born in combined labor/delivery rooms, 6 were born en route to the hospital, and only 4 babies required a labor room and the complicated-delivery room. Which of the facilities (labor rooms, labor/delivery rooms, delivery rooms) had the greatest utilization rate?

4. The Clip Joint operates three barber's chairs in the student center. During the week before semester break and the week before graduation, The Clip Joint experiences peak demands. Military style haircuts take 1 minute each, and other styles require 20 minutes each.

Operating from 9 A.M. to 6 P.M. on the six days before semester break, The Clip Joint completes 100 military style haircuts and 450 other haircuts. During a comparable six-day week before graduation, The Clip Joint completes 800 military haircuts and 400 other haircuts. In which week is utilization higher?

5. An automobile brake supplier operates on two eight-hour shifts, five days per week, 52 weeks per year. Table 7.2 shows the time standards, lot sizes, and demand forecasts for three components. Because of demand uncertainties, the operations manager obtained three demand forecasts (pessimistic, expected, and optimistic). The manager believes that a 20 percent capacity cushion is best.

    a. What is the minimum number of machines needed? The expected number? The maximum number?

    b. If the operation currently has three machines and the manager is willing to expand capacity by 20 percent through short-term options in the event that the optimistic demand occurs, what is the capacity gap?

6. Up, Up, and Away is a producer of kites and windsocks. Relevant data on a bottleneck operation in the shop for the upcoming fiscal year are given in the following table.

Item	Kites	Windsocks
Demand forecast	30,000 units/year	12,000 units/year
Lot size	20 units	70 units
Standard processing time	0.3 hour/unit	1.0 hour/unit
Standard setup time	3.0 hours/lot	4.0 hours/lot

The shop works two shifts per day, eight hours per shift, 200 days per year. There currently are four machines, and a 25 percent capacity cushion is desired. How many machines should be purchased to meet the upcoming year's demand without resorting to any short-term capacity solutions?

7. Trak, Inc. manufactures touring bikes and mountain bikes in a variety of frame sizes, colors, and compo-

nent combinations. Identical bicycles are produced in lots of 100. The projected demand, lot size, and time standards are shown in the following table.

Item	Touring	Mountain
Demand forecast	2000 units/year	15,000 units/year
Lot size	100 units	100 units
Standard processing time	½ hour/unit	⅔ hour/unit
Standard setup time	1.0 hour/lot	1.0 hour/lot

The shop currently works eight hours a day, five days a week, 50 weeks a year. Trak has five workstations, each producing one bicycle in the time shown in the table. The shop maintains a 20 percent capacity cushion. How many workstations will Trak require next year to meet the expected demand without using overtime and without decreasing its current capacity cushion?

8. The lock box department at Bank 21 handles the processing of monthly loan payments to the bank, monthly and quarterly premium payments to a local insurance company, and bill payments for 85 of the bank's largest commercial customers. The payments are processed by machine operators, with one operator per machine. An operator can process one payment in 0.25 minute; setup times are negligible. The operation requires a capacity cushion of 20 percent. The average monthly (not annual) volume of payments processed through the department currently is 400,000 but is expected to increase by 20 percent. The department operates eight hours per shift, two shifts per day, 260 days per year. How many machines (not operators) will be needed to satisfy the new total processing volume? (Round up to the next whole integer.)

9. Worcester Athletic Club is considering expanding its facility to include two adjacent suites. The owner will remodel the suites in consideration of a seven-year lease. Expenditures for rent, insurance, utilities, and exercise equipment leasing would increase by $45,000

TABLE 7.2   *Capacity Information for Automotive Brake Supplier*

	Time Standard			Demand Forecast		
Component	Processing (hr/unit)	Setup (hr/lot)	Lot Size (units/lot)	Pessimistic	Expected	Optimistic
A	0.05	1.0	60	15,000	18,000	25,000
B	0.20	4.5	80	10,000	13,000	17,000
C	0.05	8.2	120	17,000	25,000	40,000

per year. This expansion would increase Worcester's lunch time rush hour capacity from the present 150 members to 225 members. A maximum of 30 percent of the total membership attends the Athletic Club during any one lunch hour. Therefore Worcester's facility can presently serve a total membership of 500. Membership fees are $40 per month. Based on the following membership forecasts, determine what before-tax cash flows the expansion will produce for the next several years.

Year	1	2	3	4	5	6	7
Membership	450	480	510	515	530	550	600

10. Arabelle is considering expanding the floor area of her high-fashion import clothing store, The French Prints of Arabelle, by increasing her leased space in the upscale Cherry Creek Mall from 2000 square feet to 3000 square feet. The Cherry Creek Mall boasts one of the country's highest ratios of sales value per square foot. Rents (including utilities, security, and similar costs) are $110 per square foot per year. Salary increases related to French Prints' expansion are shown in the following table, along with projections of sales per square foot. The purchase cost of goods sold averages 70 percent of the sales price. Sales are seasonal, with an important peak during the year-end holiday season.

Year	Quarter	Sales (per sq ft)	Incremental Salaries
1	1	$ 90	$12,000
	2	60	8,000
	3	110	12,000
	4	240	24,000
2	1	99	12,000
	2	66	8,000
	3	121	12,000
	4	264	24,000

a. If Arabelle expands French Prints at the end of year 0, what will her quarterly before-tax cash flows be through year 2?

b. Project the quarterly before-tax cash flows assuming that the sales pattern (10 percent annually compounded increase) continues through year 3.

11. The Magic World amusement park has the opportunity to expand its size now (the end of year 0) by purchasing adjacent property for $150,000 and adding attractions at a cost of $350,000. This expansion is expected to increase attendance by 20 percent over projected attendance without expansion. The price of admission is $30, with a $2 increase planned for the beginning of year 3. Additional operating costs are ex-

pected to be $100,000 per year. Estimated attendance for the next five years, *without expansion*, follows.

Year	1	2	3	4	5
Attendance	30,000	34,000	36,250	38,500	41,000

a. What are the before-tax combined cash flows for years 0 through 5 that are attributable to the park's expansion?

b. Ignoring tax, depreciation, and the time value of money, determine how long it will take to recover (pay back) the investment.

12. Rex Saul owns a drugstore that is experiencing significant growth. He employs one pharmacist (besides himself) and is trying to decide whether to hire a third pharmacist to expand the drugstore's capacity. With two pharmacists, Saul's current effective capacity is 5000 prescriptions per quarter. Sales are seasonal. Forecasts of demand for prescriptions, expressed in prescriptions filled per quarter, for the next two years follow.

Year	Quarter	Prescriptions (per quarter)	Projected Average Price (per prescription)
1	1	5400	$22.00
	2	6600	$20.00
	3	3600	$24.00
	4	6300	$30.00
2	1	6300	$32.00
	2	7700	$30.00
	3	4200	$34.00
	4	7350	$40.00

The new pharmacist would be paid $4000 per month in year 1 and $4200 per month in year 2. The before-tax profit from additional sales (not counting the new pharmacist's salary) is 35 percent of the price. What are the projected quarterly incremental before-tax cash flows attributable to this expansion?

13. Roche Brothers is considering a capacity expansion of its supermarket. The landowner will build the addition to suit, in return for $200,000 upon completion and a five-year lease. The increase in rent for the addition is $10,000 per month. The annual sales projected through year 5 follow. The current effective capacity is equivalent to 500,000 customers per year. Assume a 2 percent pre-tax profit on sales.

Year	1	2	3	4	5
Customers	560,000	600,000	685,000	700,000	715,000
Average sales per customer	$50.00	$53.00	$56.00	$60.00	$64.00

a. If Roche expands its capacity to serve 700,000 customers per year now (end of year 0), what are the projected annual incremental pre-tax cash flows attributable to this expansion?

b. If Roche expands its capacity to serve 700,000 customers per year at the end of year 2, the landowner will build the same addition for $240,000 and a three-year lease at $12,000 per month. What are the projected annual incremental pre-tax cash flows attributable to this expansion alternative?

Advanced Problems

Problem 17 requires reading of Supplement A (Decision Making).

14. Mel Opp, Danny Strange, and Arnold Balmer build several models of robots. Balmer has great strength and can build the robots while working alone. Opp and Strange prefer to work as a team. Table 7.3 gives the processing and setup times. The robot manufacturing facility operates 2000 hours per year.

    a. If the work is equally divided so that Balmer produces the same number of robots as Opp and Strange produce as a team, what is the utilization as a percentage of effective capacity?

    b. If the work is divided so that Balmer makes 66 Mavericks, 128 Angels, and 170 Terminators while Opp and Strange produce the remainder of demand, what is the utilization as a percentage of effective capacity?

15. Truck-Tuff, a producer of bed liners for pickup trucks, is currently operating at its capacity of 2000 liners per day. Daily demand has risen to 2500 liners per day; thus Truck-Tuff is losing potential business owing to lack of capacity. The contribution to profit is $20 per liner. An expansion to produce another 1000 liners per day would cost $8 million.

    a. If the before-tax payback period is four years, should Truck-Tuff expand?

    b. What is the lowest demand per day that would satisfy the payback period requirement of four years?

16. Two new alternatives have come up for expanding Grandmother's Chicken Restaurant (see Solved Problem 2). They involve more automation in the kitchen and feature a special cooking process that retains the original-recipe taste of the chicken. Although the process is more capital intensive, it would drive down labor costs, so that the pre-tax profit for *all* sales (not just the sales from the capacity added) would go up, from 20 to 22 percent. This gain would increase the pre-tax profit by 2 percent of each sales dollar through $800,000 (80,000 meals $\times$ $10) and by 22 percent of each sales dollar between $800,000 and the new capacity limit. Otherwise, the new alternatives are much the same as those in Example 7.4 and Solved Problem 2.

Alternative 1: Expand both the kitchen and the dining area now (at the end of year 0), raising the capacity to 130,000 meals per year. The cost of construction, including the new automation, would be $336,000 (rather than the earlier $200,000).

Alternative 2: Expand only the kitchen now, raising its capacity to 105,000 meals per year. At the end of year 3, expand both the kitchen and the dining area to the 130,000 meals per year volume. Construction and equipment costs would be $424,000, with $220,000 at the end of year 0 and the remainder at the end of year 3. As with alternative 1, the contribution margin would go up to 22 percent.

With both new alternatives, the salvage value would be negligible. Compare the cash flows of all alternatives. Should Grandmother's Chicken Restaurant expand with the new or the old technology? Should it expand now or later?

17. Acme Steel Fabricators has experienced booming business for the past five years. The company fabricates a wide range of steel products, such as railings, ladders, and light structural steel framing. The current manual method of materials handling is causing excessive inventories and congestion. Acme is considering the purchase of an overhead rail-mounted hoist system or a forklift truck to increase capacity and improve manufacturing efficiency.

The annual pre-tax payoff from the system de-

TABLE 7.3   *Capacity Information for Robot Manufacturer*

| Robot Model | Balmer | | Opp and Strange | | Lot Size (units/lot) | Annual Demand Forecast |
	Processing (hr/unit)	Setup (hr/unit)	Processing (hr/unit)	Setup (hr/unit)		
Maverick	5	3.0	4	2.0	6	144
Angel	2	4.0	1.5	2.0	8	320
Terminator	4	5.0	3	3.0	10	400

pends on future demand. If demand stays at the current level, the probability of which is 0.50, annual savings from the overhead hoist will be $10,000. If demand rises, the hoist will save $25,000 annually because of operating efficiencies in addition to new sales. Finally, if demand falls, the hoist will result in an estimated annual loss of $65,000. The probability is estimated to be 0.30 for higher demand and 0.20 for lower demand.

If the forklift is purchased, annual payoffs will be $5,000 if demand is unchanged, $10,000 if demand rises, and −$25,000 if demand falls.

   a. Draw a decision tree for this problem, and compute the expected value of the payoff for each alternative.
   b. Which is the best alternative, based on the expected values?

18. The vice-president of operations at Dintell Corporation, a major supplier of passenger-side automotive air bags, is considering a $50 million expansion at the firm's Fort Worth production complex. The most recent economic projections indicate a 0.60 probability that the overall market will be $400 million per year over the next five years and a 0.40 probability that the market will be only $200 million per year during the same period. The marketing department estimates that Dintell has a 0.50 probability of capturing 40

percent of the market and an equal probability of obtaining only 30 percent of the market. The cost of goods sold is estimated to be 70 percent of sales. For planning purposes the company currently uses a 12 percent discount rate, a 40 percent tax rate, and the MARCS depreciation schedule. The criteria for investment decisions at Dintell are (1) the net expected present value must be greater than zero; (2) there must be at least a 70 percent chance that the net present value will be positive; and (3) there must be no more than a 10 percent chance that the firm will lose more than 20 percent of the initial value.

Use a computer package with decision trees and financial analysis, such as CMOM, to help answer the following questions. Supplement A and Appendix 1 also will be helpful.

   a. Based on the stated criteria, determine whether Dintell should fund the project.
   b. What effect will a probability of 0.70 of capturing 40 percent of the market have on the decision?
   c. What effect will an increase in the discount rate of 15 percent have on the decision? A decrease of 10 percent?
   d. What effect will the need for another $10 million in the third year have on the decision?

C A S E

Fitness Plus

Fitness Plus is a full-service health and sports club in Greensboro, North Carolina. The club provides a range of facilities and services to support three primary activities: fitness, recreation, and relaxation. Fitness activities generally take place in four areas of the club: the aerobics room, which can accommodate 35 people per class; a room equipped with free weights; a workout room with 24 pieces of Nautilus equipment; and a large cardiovascular workout room containing 29 pieces of cardiovascular equipment. This equipment includes nine stairsteppers, six treadmills, six life-cycle bikes, three airdyne bikes, two cross-aerobics machines, two rowing machines, and one climber. Recreational facilities comprise eight racquetball courts, six tennis courts, and a large outdoor pool. Fitness Plus also sponsors softball, volleyball, and swim teams in city recreation leagues. Relaxation is accomplished through yoga classes held twice a week in the aerobics room, whirlpool tubs located in each locker room, and a trained massage therapist.

Situated in a large suburban office park, Fitness Plus opened its doors in 1984. During the first two years, membership was small and use of the facilities was light. By 1988, membership had grown as fitness began to play a large role in more and more people's lives. Along with this growth came increased use of club facilities. Records indicate that, in 1988, an average of 15 members per hour checked into the club during a typical day. Of course, the actual number of members per hour varied by both day and time. On some days during a slow period, only six to eight members would check in per hour. At a peak time, such as Mondays from 4:00 P.M. to 7:00 P.M., the number would be as high as 40 per hour.

The club was open from 6:30 A.M. to 11:00 P.M. Monday through Thursday. On Friday and Saturday the club closed at 8:00 P.M., and on Sunday the hours were 12:00 noon to 8:00 P.M.

As the popularity of health and fitness continued to grow, so did Fitness Plus. By May 1993, the average number of members arriving per hour during a typical day had increased to 25. The lowest period had a rate of 10 members per hour; during peak periods 80 members per hour checked in to use the facilities. This growth brought complaints from members about overcrowding and unavailability of equipment. Most of these complaints centered on the Nautilus, cardiovascular, and aerobics fitness areas. The owners began to wonder whether the club was indeed too small for its membership. Past research had indicated that individuals work out an average of 60 minutes per visit. Data collected from member surveys showed the following facilities usage pattern: 30 percent of the members do aerobics, 40 percent use the cardiovascular equipment, 25 percent use the Nautilus machines, 20 percent use the free weights, 15 percent use the racquetball courts, and 10 percent use the tennis courts. The owners wondered whether they could use this information to estimate how well existing capacity was being utilized.

If capacity levels were being stretched, now was the time to decide what to do. It was already May, and any expansion of the existing facility would take at least four months. The owners knew that January was always a peak membership enrollment month and that any new capacity needed to be ready by then. However, other factors had to be considered. The area was growing both in terms of population and geographically. The downtown area had just received a major facelift, and many new offices and businesses were moving back to it, causing a resurgence in activity.

With this growth came increased competition. A new YMCA was offering a full range of services at a low cost.

Two new health and fitness facilities had opened within the past year in locations 10 to 15 minutes from Fitness Plus. The first, called the Oasis, catered to the young adult crowd and restricted the access of children under 16 years old. The other facility, Gold's Gym, provided excellent weight and cardiovascular training only.

As the owners thought about the situation, they had many questions: Were the capacities of the existing facilities constrained, and if so, where? If capacity expansion was necessary, should the existing facility be expanded? Because of the limited amount of land at the present site, expansion of some services might require reducing the capacity of others. Finally, owing to increased competition and growth downtown, was now the time to open a facility to serve that market? A new facility would take six months to renovate, and the financial resources were not available to do both.

Questions

1. What method would you use to measure the capacity of Fitness Plus? Has Fitness Plus reached its capacity?
2. Which capacity strategy would be appropriate for Fitness Plus? Justify your answer.
3. How would you link the capacity decision being made by Fitness Plus to other types of operating decisions?

Selected References

"Avoiding Plant Failures Grows More Difficult for Many Industries," *Wall Street Journal*, January 8, 1981.

Bott, Kevin, and Larry P. Ritzman. "Irregular Workloads with MRP Systems." *Journal of Operations Management*, vol. 3, no. 4 (1983), pp. 169–182.

Bowman, Edward H. "Scale of Operations—An Empirical Study." *Operations Research* (June 1958), pp. 320–328.

Buffa, Elwood S. *Meeting the Competitive Challenge: Manufacturing Strategy for U.S. Companies.* Homewood, Ill.: Dow Jones–Irwin, 1984.

Hayes, Robert H., and Steven C. Wheelwright. *Restoring Our Competitive Edge: Competing Through Manufacturing.* New York: John Wiley & Sons, 1984.

"How Goliaths Can Act Like Davids," *Business Week/Enterprise* (1993), pp. 192–200.

Sassar, W. Earl. "Match Supply and Demand in Service Industries." *Harvard Business Review* (November–December 1976), pp. 133–140.

Schmenner, Roger W. *Making Business Location Decisions.* Englewood Cliffs, N.J.: Prentice-Hall, 1982.

Skinner, Wickham. "The Focused Factory." *Harvard Business Review* (May–June 1974), pp. 113–121.

Waiting Line Models

Anyone who has had to wait at a stoplight, at McDonald's, or at the registrar's office has experienced the dynamics of waiting lines. Perhaps one of the best examples of effective management of waiting lines is that of Walt Disney World. One day there may be only 25,000 customers, but on another day there may be 90,000. Careful analysis of process flows, technology for people-mover (materials handling) equipment, capacity, and layout keeps the waiting times for attractions to acceptable levels.

The analysis of waiting lines is of concern to managers because it affects design, capacity planning, layout planning, inventory management, and scheduling. In this supplement we discuss why waiting lines form, the uses of waiting line models in operations management, and the structure of waiting line models. We also discuss the decisions managers address with the models.

WHY WAITING LINES FORM

A **waiting line** is one or more "customers" waiting for service. The customers can be people or inanimate objects such as machines requiring maintenance, sales orders waiting for shipping, or inventory items waiting to be used. A waiting line forms because of a temporary imbalance between the demand for service and the capacity of the system to provide the service. In most real-life waiting line problems, the demand rate varies; that is, customers arrive in unpredictable intervals. Most often the rate of producing the service also varies, depending on customer needs. Suppose that bank customers arrive at an average rate of 15 per hour throughout the day and that the bank can process an average of 20 customers per hour. Why would a waiting line ever develop? The answers are that the customer arrival rate varies throughout the day and the time to process a customer can vary. During the noon hour, 30 customers may arrive at the bank. Some of them may have complicated transactions, requiring above-average process times. The waiting line may grow to 15 customers for a period of time before it eventually disappears. Even though the bank manager provided for more than enough capacity on average, waiting lines can still develop.

Waiting lines can develop even if the time to process a customer is constant. For example, a subway train is computer-controlled to arrive at stations along its route. Each train is programmed to arrive at a station, say, every 15 minutes. Even with the constant service time, waiting lines develop while customers wait for the next train or can't get on a train because of the size of the crowd at a busy time of the day. Consequently, variability in the rate of demand determines the sizes of the waiting lines in this case. In general, if there is no variability in the demand or service rates and enough capacity has been provided, no waiting lines form.

◆ USES OF WAITING LINE THEORY

Waiting line theory applies to service as well as manufacturing firms, relating customer arrival and service system processing characteristics to service system output characteristics. In our discussion, we use the term *service* broadly—the act of processing a customer. The service system might be hair cutting at a hair salon or processing a production order of parts on a certain machine. Other examples of customers and services include lines of theater goers waiting to purchase tickets, trucks waiting to be unloaded at a warehouse, machines waiting to be repaired by a maintenance crew, and patients waiting to be examined by a physician. Regardless of the situation, waiting line problems have several common elements.

◆ STRUCTURE OF WAITING LINE PROBLEMS

Analyzing waiting line problems begins with a description of the situation's basic elements. Each specific situation will have different characteristics, but four elements are common to all situations:

1. an input, or **customer population,** that generates potential customers;
2. a waiting line of customers;
3. the **service facility,** consisting of a person (or crew), a machine (or group of machines), or both necessary to perform the service for the customer; and
4. a **priority rule,** which selects the next customer to be served by the service facility.

Figure E.1 shows these basic elements. The **service system** describes the number of lines and the arrangement of the facilities. After the service has been performed, the served customers leave the system.

FIGURE E.1
Basic Elements of
Waiting Line Models

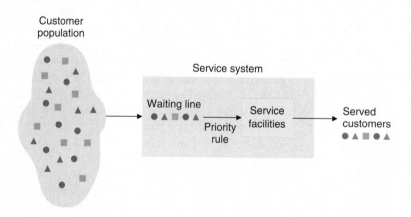

Customer Population

A customer population is the source of input to the service system. If the potential number of new customers for the service system is appreciably affected by the number of customers already in the system, the input source is said to be *finite*. For example, suppose that a maintenance crew is assigned responsibility for the repair of 10 machines. The customer population for the maintenance crew is 10 machines in working order. The population generates customers for the maintenance crew as a function of the failure rates for the machines. As more machines fail and enter the service system, either waiting for service or being repaired, the customer population becomes smaller and the rate at which it can generate another customer falls. Consequently, the customer population is said to be finite.

Alternatively, an *infinite* customer population is one in which the number of customers in the system doesn't affect the rate at which the population generates new customers. For example, consider a mail-order operation for which the customer population consists of shoppers who have received a catalog of products sold by the company. Because the customer population is so large and only a small fraction of the shoppers place orders at any one time, the number of new orders it generates isn't appreciably affected by the number of orders waiting for service or being processed by the service system. In this case the customer population is said to be infinite.

Customers in waiting lines may be *patient* or *impatient,* which has nothing to do with the colorful language a customer may use while waiting in line for a long time on a hot day. In the context of waiting line problems, a patient customer is one who enters the system and remains there until being served; an impatient customer is one who either decides not to enter the system (balks) or leaves the system before being served (reneges). For the methods used in this supplement, we make the simplifying assumption that all customers are patient.

The Service System

The service system may be described by the number of lines and the arrangement of facilities.

Number of Lines.   Waiting lines may be designed to be a *single line* or *multiple lines.* Figure E.2 shows an example of each arrangement. Generally, single lines are utilized at airline counters, inside banks, and at some fast-food restaurants, whereas multiple lines are utilized in grocery stores, at drive-in bank operations,

FIGURE E.2

Waiting Line Arrangements

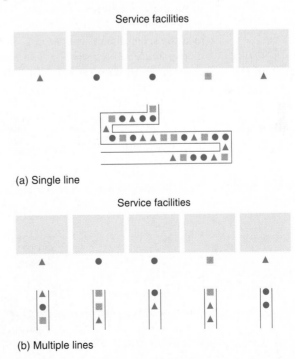

(a) Single line

(b) Multiple lines

and in discount stores. When multiple servers are available and each one can handle general transactions, the single-line arrangement keeps servers uniformly busy and gives customers a sense of fairness. Customers believe that they are being served on the basis of when they arrived, not how well they guessed their waiting time when selecting a particular line. The multiple-line design is best when some of the servers provide a limited set of services. In this arrangement, customers select the services they need and wait in the line where that service is provided, such as at a grocery store where there are special lines for customers paying with cash or having fewer than 10 items.

Sometimes, queues are not organized neatly into "lines." Machines that need repair on the production floor of a factory may be left in place, and the maintenance crew comes to them. Nonetheless, we can think of such machines as forming a single line or multiple lines, depending on the number of repair crews and their specialties. Likewise, passengers who telephone for a taxi also form a line even though they may wait at different locations.

Arrangement of Service Facilities.   Service facilities consist of the personnel and/or equipment necessary to perform the service for the customer. Figure E.3 shows examples of the five basic types of service facility arrangements. Managers should choose an arrangement based on customer volume and the nature of services performed. Some services require a single step, also called a **phase**, whereas others require a sequence of steps.

In the *single-channel, single-phase* system, all services demanded by a customer can be performed by a single-server facility. Customers form a single line and go through the service facility one at a time. Examples are a drive-through car wash and a machine that must process several batches of parts.

The *single-channel, multiple-phase* arrangement is used when the services are best performed in sequence by more than one facility, yet customer volume or other constraints limit the design to one channel. Customers form a single line and proceed sequentially from one service facility to the next. An example of this arrangement is a McDonald's drive-through where the first facility takes the order, the second takes the money, and the third provides the food.

The *multiple-channel, single-phase* arrangement is used when demand is large enough to warrant providing the same service at more than one facility or

FIGURE E.3

Examples of Service Facility Arrangements

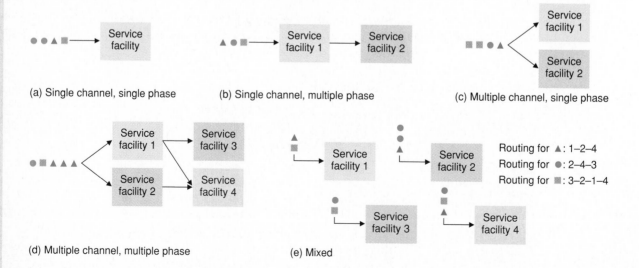

(a) Single channel, single phase

(b) Single channel, multiple phase

(c) Multiple channel, single phase

(d) Multiple channel, multiple phase

(e) Mixed

when the services offered by the facilities are different. Customers form one or more lines, depending on the design. In the single-line design, customers are served by the first available server, as in the lobby of a bank. If each channel has its own waiting line, customers wait until the server for their line can serve them, as at a bank's drive-through facilities.

The *multiple-channel, multiple-phase* arrangement occurs when customers can be served by one of the first-phase facilities but then require service from a second-phase facility, and so on. In some cases, customers cannot switch channels after service has begun; in others they can. An example of this arrangement is a Laundromat. Washing machines are the first-phase facilities, and dryers are the second-phase facilities. Some of the washing machines and dryers may be designed for extra-large loads, thereby providing the customer a choice of channels.

The most complex waiting line problem involves customers who have unique sequences of required services; consequently, service can't be described neatly in phases. A *mixed* arrangement is used in such a case. In the mixed arrangement, waiting lines can develop in front of each facility, as in a job shop where each customized job may require the use of various machines and different routings.

Priority Rule

The priority rule determines which customer to serve next. Most service systems that you encounter use the first-come, first-served (FCFS) rule. The customer at the head of the waiting line has the highest priority, and the customer who arrived last has the lowest priority. Other priority disciplines might take the customer with the earliest promised due date (EDD) or the customer with the shortest expected processing time (SPT). We focus on FCFS in this supplement and discuss EDD and SPT in Chapter 16.

A **preemptive discipline** is a rule that allows a customer of higher priority to interrupt the service of another customer. For example, in a hospital emergency room, patients with the most life-threatening injuries receive treatment first, regardless of their order of arrival. Modeling of systems having complex priority disciplines is usually done using computer simulation (see Supplement F).

◆ PROBABILITY DISTRIBUTIONS

The sources of variation in waiting line problems come from the random arrivals of customers and the variations in service times. Each of these sources can be described with a probability distribution.

Arrival Distribution

Customers arrive at service facilities randomly. The variability of customer arrivals often can be described by a Poisson distribution, which specifies the probability that n customers will arrive in T time periods:

$$P(n) = \frac{(\lambda T)^n}{n!}e^{-\lambda T} \quad \text{for } n = 0, 1, 2, \ldots$$

where $\quad P(n) =$ probability of n arrivals in T time periods

$\lambda =$ average number of customer arrivals per period

$e = 2.7183$

The mean of the Poisson distribution is λT, and the variance also is λT. The Poisson distribution is a discrete distribution; that is, the probabilities are for a specific number of arrivals per unit of time.

EXAMPLE E.1

Calculating the Probability of Customer Arrivals

Customers arrive at a complaint desk in a large department store at the rate of two customers per hour. What is the probability that four customers will arrive during the next hour?

Solution   In this case $\lambda = 2$ customers per hour, $T = 1$ hour, and $n = 4$ customers. The probability that four customers will arrive in the next hour is

$$P(4) = \frac{[2(1)]^4}{4!}e^{-2(1)} = \frac{16}{24}e^{-2} = 0.090$$

Another way to specify the arrival distribution is to do it in terms of customer **interarrival times**—that is, the time between customer arrivals. If the customer population generates customers according to a Poisson distribution, the *exponential distribution* describes the probability that the next customer will arrive in the next T time periods. As the exponential distribution also describes service times, we discuss the details of this distribution in the next section.

Service Time Distribution

The exponential distribution describes the probability that the service time of the customer at a particular facility will be no more than T time periods. The probability can be calculated by using the formula

$$P(t \leq T) = 1 - e^{-\mu T}$$

where μ = mean number of customers completing service per period

t = service time of the customer

T = target service time

The mean of the service time distribution is $1/\mu$, and the variance is $(1/\mu)^2$. As T increases, the probability that the customer's service time will be less than T approaches 1.0.

For simplicity, let's look at an example using a single-channel, single-phase arrangement.

EXAMPLE E.2

Calculating the Service Time Probability

The clerk at a customer complaint desk can serve an average of three customers per hour. What is the probability that a customer will require less than 10 minutes of service?

Solution   We must have all the data in the same time units. Because $\mu = 3$ customers per *hour*, we convert minutes of time to hours, or $T = 10$ minutes = 10/60 hour = 0.167 hour. Then

$$P(t \leq T) = 1 - e^{-\mu T}$$

$$P(t \leq 0.167 \text{ hr}) = 1 - e^{-3(0.167)} = 1 - 0.61 = 0.39$$

Some characteristics of the exponential distribution don't always conform to an actual situation. The exponential distribution model is based on the assumption that each service time is independent of those that preceded it. In real life, however, productivity may improve as human servers learn about the work. Another assumption underlying the model is that very small, as well as very large, service times are possible. However, real-life situations often require a fixed-length startup time, some cutoff on total service time, or nearly constant service time.

◆ USING WAITING LINE MODELS TO ANALYZE OPERATIONS

Operations managers can use waiting line models to balance the gains that might be made by increasing the efficiency of the service system against the costs of doing so. In addition, managers should consider the costs of *not* making improvements to the system: Long waiting lines or long waiting times may cause customers to balk or renege. Managers should therefore be concerned about the following operating characteristics of the system.

1. *Line length.* The number of customers in the waiting line reflects one of two conditions. Short queues could mean either good customer service or too much capacity. Similarly, long queues could indicate either low server efficiency or the need to increase capacity.

2. *Number of customers in system.* The number of customers in queue and being served also relates to service efficiency and capacity. A large number of customers in the system causes congestion and may result in customer dissatisfaction, unless more capacity is added.

3. *Waiting time in line.* Long lines do not always mean long waiting times. If the service rate is fast, a long line can be served efficiently. However, when waiting time seems long, customers perceive the quality of service to be poor. Managers may try to change the arrival rate of customers or design the system to make long wait times seem shorter than they really are. For example, at Walt Disney World customers in line for an attraction are entertained by videos and also are informed about expected waiting times, which seems to help them endure the wait.

4. *Total time in system.* The total elapsed time from entry into the system until exit from the system may indicate problems with customers, server efficiency, or capacity. If some customers are spending too much time in the service system, there may be a need to change the priority discipline, increase productivity, or adjust capacity in some way.

5. *Service facility utilization.* The collective utilization of service facilities reflects the percentage of time that they are busy. Management's goal is to maintain high utilization and profitability without adversely affecting the other operating characteristics.

The best method for analyzing a waiting line problem is to relate the five operating characteristics and their alternatives to dollars. However, placing a dollar figure on certain characteristics (such as the waiting time of a shopper in a grocery store) is difficult. In such cases, an analyst must weigh the cost of implementing the alternative under consideration against a subjective assessment of the cost of *not* making the change.

We now present three models and some examples showing how waiting line models can help operations managers make decisions. We analyze problems requiring the single-server, multiple-server, and finite-source models, all of which are single phase. References to more advanced models are cited at the end of this supplement.

Single-Server Model

The simplest waiting line model involves a single server and a single line of customers. To further specify the model, we make the following assumptions.

1. The customer population is infinite and all customers are patient.
2. The customers arrive according to a Poisson distribution, with a mean arrival rate of λ.
3. The service distribution is exponential, with a mean service rate of μ.
4. Customers are served on a first-come, first-served basis.
5. The length of the waiting line is unlimited.

With these assumptions we can apply various formulas to describe the operating characteristics of the system:

$$\rho = \text{average utilization of the system}$$

$$= \frac{\lambda}{\mu}$$

$$P_n = \text{probability that } n \text{ customers are in the system}$$

$$= (1 - \rho)\rho^n$$

$$L = \text{average number of customers in the service system}$$

$$= \frac{\lambda}{\mu - \lambda}$$

$$L_q = \text{average number of customers in the waiting line}$$

$$= \rho L$$

$$W = \text{average time spent in the system, including service}$$

$$= \frac{1}{\mu - \lambda}$$

$$W_q = \text{average waiting time in line}$$

$$= \rho W$$

EXAMPLE E.3

Calculating the Operating Characteristics of a Single-Channel, Single-Phase System

The manager of a grocery store in the retirement community of Sunnyville is interested in providing good service to the senior citizens who shop in his store. Presently, the store has a separate check-out counter for senior citizens. On average, 30 senior citizens per hour arrive at the counter, according to a Poisson distribution, and are served at an average rate of 35 customers per hour, with exponential service times. Find the following averages.

a. Utilization of the checkout clerk
b. Number of customers in the system
c. Number of customers in line
d. Time spent in the system
e. Waiting time in line

Solution The check-out counter can be modeled as a single-channel, single-phase system. We use the equations for the operating characteristics of the *single-server model* to calculate the average characteristics.

a. The average utilization of the checkout clerk is

$$\rho = \frac{\lambda}{\mu} = \frac{30}{35} = 0.857, \text{ or } 85.7\%$$

b. The average number of customers in the system is

$$L = \frac{\lambda}{\mu - \lambda} = \frac{30}{35 - 30} = 6 \text{ customers}$$

c. The average number of customers in line is

$$L_q = \rho L = 0.857(6) = 5.14 \text{ customers}$$

d. The average time spent in the system is

$$W = \frac{1}{\mu - \lambda} = \frac{1}{35 - 30} = 0.20 \text{ hour, or } 12 \text{ minutes}$$

e. The average time spent waiting in line is

$$W_q = \rho W = 0.857(0.20) = 0.17 \text{ hour, or } 10.28 \text{ minutes}$$

EXAMPLE E.4

Analyzing Service Rates with the Single-Server Model

The manager of the Sunnyville grocery in Example E.3 wants answers to the following questions.

a. What service rate would be required to have customers average only eight minutes in the system?
b. For that service rate, what is the probability of having more than four customers in the system?
c. What service rate would be required to have only a 10 percent chance of exceeding four customers in the system?

Solution

a. We use the equation for the average time in the system and solve for μ.

$$W = \frac{1}{\mu - \lambda}$$

$$8 \text{ minutes} = 0.133 \text{ hour} = \frac{1}{\mu - 30}$$

$$0.133\mu - 0.133(30) = 1$$

$$\mu = 37.52 \text{ customers/hour}$$

b. The probability that there will be more than four customers in the system equals 1 minus the probability that there are four or fewer customers in the system.

$$P = 1 - \sum_{n=0}^{4} P_n$$

$$= 1 - \sum_{n=0}^{4} (1 - \rho)\rho^n$$

and

$$\rho = \frac{30}{37.52} = 0.80$$

Then

$$P = 1 - 0.2(1 + 0.8 + 0.8^2 + 0.8^3 + 0.8^4)$$

$$= 1 - 0.672 = 0.328$$

Therefore there is a nearly 33 percent chance that more than four customers will be in the system.

c. We use the same logic as in part b, except that μ is now a decision variable. The easiest way to proceed is to find the correct average utilization first, by trial and error, and then solve for the service rate.

$$P = 1 - (1 - \rho)(1 + \rho + \rho^2 + \rho^3 + \rho^4)$$

Try $\rho = 0.7$:

$$0.10 \overset{?}{=} 1 - (0.3)(1 + 0.7 + 0.49 + 0.343 + 0.240) = 0.168$$

$$0.10 \neq 0.168$$

Try $\rho = 0.6$:

$$0.10 \overset{?}{=} 1 - (0.4)(1 + 0.6 + 0.36 + 0.216 + 0.1296) = 0.078$$

$$0.10 \neq 0.078$$

Try $\rho = 0.63$:

$$0.10 \overset{?}{=} 1 - (0.37)(1 + 0.63 + 0.3969 + 0.2500 + 0.1575) = 0.099$$

$$0.10 \cong 0.099$$

Therefore, for a utilization rate of 63 percent, the probability of more than four customers in the system is 10 percent. For $\lambda = 30$, the service rate must be

$$\frac{30}{\mu} = 0.63$$

$$\mu = 47.62 \text{ customers/hour}$$

The manager must now find a way to increase the service rate from 35 per hour to approximately 48 per hour. She can increase the service rate in several different ways, ranging from employing a high school student to help bag the groceries to installing electronic point-of-sale equipment that reads the prices from bar-coded information on each item.

Multiple-Server Model

With the multiple-server model, customers form a single line and choose one of s servers when one is available. The service system has only one phase. We make the following assumption in addition to those for the single-server model: There are s identical servers, and the service distribution for each server is exponential, with a mean service time of $1/\mu$.

With these assumptions, we can apply several formulas to describe the operating characteristics of the service system:

ρ = average utilization of the system

$$= \frac{\lambda}{s\mu}$$

P_0 = probability that zero customers are in the system

$$= \left[\sum_{n=0}^{s-1} \frac{(\lambda/\mu)^n}{n!} + \frac{(\lambda/\mu)^s}{s!} \left(\frac{1}{1-\rho} \right) \right]^{-1}$$

P_n = probability that n customers are in the system

$$= \begin{cases} \dfrac{(\lambda/\mu)^n}{n!} P_0, & 0 < n < s \\ \dfrac{(\lambda/\mu)^n}{s!s^{n-s}} P_0, & n \geq s \end{cases}$$

L_q = average number of customers in line

$$= \frac{P_0(\lambda/\mu)^s \rho}{s!(1-\rho)^2}$$

W_q = average waiting time of customers in line

$$= \frac{L_q}{\lambda}$$

W = average time spent in the system, including service

$$= W_q + \frac{1}{\mu}$$

L = average number of customers in the service system

$$= \lambda W$$

EXAMPLE E.5

Estimating Idle Time and Hourly Operating Costs with the Multiple-Server Model

The management of the American Parcel Service terminal in Verona, Wisconsin, is concerned about the amount of time the company's trucks are idle, waiting to be unloaded. The terminal operates with four unloading bays. Each bay requires a crew of two employees, and each crew costs $30 per hour. The estimated cost of an idle truck is $50 per hour. Trucks arrive at an average rate of three per hour, according to a Poisson distribution. On average, a crew can unload a semi-trailer rig in one hour, with exponential service times. What is the total hourly cost of operating the system?

Solution   The *multiple-server model* is appropriate. To find the total cost of labor and idle trucks, we must calculate the average waiting time in the system and the average number of trucks in the system. However, we first need to calculate the average number of trucks in line and the average waiting time in line.

The average utilization of the four bays is

$$\rho = \frac{\lambda}{\mu s} = \frac{3}{1(4)} = 0.75, \text{ or } 75\%$$

For this level of utilization, we can now compute the probability that no trucks are in the system:

$$P_0 = \left[\sum_{n=0}^{4-1} \frac{(3/1)^n}{n!} + \frac{(3/1)^4}{4!} \left(\frac{1}{1 - 0.75} \right) \right]^{-1}$$

$$= \frac{1}{1 + 3 + \dfrac{9}{2} + \dfrac{27}{6} + \dfrac{81}{24} \left(\dfrac{1}{1 - 0.75} \right)} = 0.0377$$

The average number of trucks in line is

$$L_q = \frac{P_0(\lambda/\mu)^s \rho}{s!(1 - \rho)^2} = \frac{0.0377(3/1)^4(0.75)}{4!(1 - 0.75)^2} = 1.53 \text{ trucks}$$

The average waiting time in line is

$$W_q = \frac{L_q}{\lambda} = \frac{1.53}{3} = 0.51 \text{ hour}$$

The average time spent in the system is

$$W = W_q + \frac{1}{\mu} = 0.51 + \frac{1}{1} = 1.51 \text{ hours}$$

Finally, the average number of trucks in the system is

$$L = \lambda W = 3(1.51) = 4.53 \text{ trucks}$$

We can now calculate the hourly costs of labor and idle trucks:

Labor cost: $30(s) = $30(4)$ = $120.00
Idle truck cost: $50(L) = $50(4.53) =$ 226.50
                  Total hourly cost = $346.50

Finite-Source Model

We now consider a situation in which all but one of the assumptions of the single-server model are appropriate. In this case the customer population is finite, having only N potential customers. If N is greater than 30 customers, the single-server model with the assumption of an infinite customer population is adequate. Otherwise, the finite-source model is the one to use. The formulas used to calculate the operating characteristics of the service system are

P_0 = probability that zero customers are in the system

$$= \left[\sum_{n=0}^{N} \frac{N!}{(N-n)!}\left(\frac{\lambda}{\mu}\right)^n\right]^{-1}$$

ρ = average utilization of the server

$$= 1 - P_0$$

L_q = average number of customers in line

$$= N - \frac{\lambda + \mu}{\lambda}(1 - P_0)$$

L = average number of customers in the system

$$= N - \frac{\mu}{\lambda}(1 - P_0)$$

W_q = average waiting time in line

$$= L_q[(N-L)\lambda]^{-1}$$

W = average time in the system

$$= L[(N-L)\lambda]^{-1}$$

EXAMPLE E.6

Analyzing Maintenance Costs with the Finite-Source Model

The Worthington Gear Company installed a bank of 10 robots about three years ago. The robots greatly increased the firm's labor productivity, but recently attention has focused on maintenance. The firm does no preventive maintenance on the robots because of the variability in the breakdown distribution. Each machine has an exponential breakdown (or interarrival) distribution with an average time between failures of 200 hours. Each machine hour lost to downtime costs $30, which means that the firm has to react quickly to machine failure. The firm employs one maintenance person, who needs 10 hours on average to fix a robot. Actual maintenance times are exponentially distributed. The wage rate is $10 per hour for the maintenance person, who can be put to work productively elsewhere when not fixing robots. Determine the daily cost of labor and robot downtime.

Solution   The *finite-source model* is appropriate for this analysis because there are only 10 machines in the customer population and the other assumptions are satisfied. Here, $\lambda = 1/200$, or 0.005 breakdown per hour, and $\mu = 1/10 = 0.10$ robot per hour. To calculate the cost of labor and robot downtime, we need only to estimate L, the average number of robots in the maintenance system. However, to demonstrate the use of the finite-source model, we will compute all the operating statistics.

The probability that the maintenance system is empty is

$$P_0 = \left[\sum_{n=0}^{N} \frac{N!}{(N-n)!}\left(\frac{\lambda}{\mu}\right)^n\right]^{-1} = \frac{1}{\displaystyle\sum_{n=0}^{10} \frac{10!}{(10-n)!}\left(\frac{0.005}{0.10}\right)^n} = 0.538$$

The average utilization of the maintenance person is

$$\rho = 1 - P_0 = 1 - 0.538 = 0.462, \text{ or } 46\%$$

The average number of robots waiting to be repaired is

$$L_q = N - \frac{\lambda + \mu}{\lambda}(1 - P_0) = 10 - \frac{0.005 + 0.10}{0.005}(1 - 0.538) = 0.30 \text{ robot}$$

The average number of robots in line and being repaired is

$$L = N - \frac{\mu}{\lambda}(1 - P_0) = 10 - \frac{0.10}{0.005}(1 - 0.538) = 0.76 \text{ robot}$$

The average waiting time of robots for the maintenance person is

$$W_q = L_q[(N - L)\lambda]^{-1} = \frac{0.30}{(10 - 0.76)(0.005)} = 6.49 \text{ hours}$$

Finally, the average time that a failed robot spends waiting for service and being repaired is

$$W = L[(N - L)\lambda]^{-1} = \frac{0.76}{(10 - 0.76)(0.005)} = 16.45 \text{ hours}$$

The daily cost of labor and robot downtime is

Labor cost:	($10/hour)(8 hours/day)	= $ 80.00
Idle robot cost:	(0.76 robot)($30/robot hour)(8 hours/day)	= 182.40
		Total daily cost = $262.40

◆   DECISION AREAS FOR MANAGEMENT

After analyzing a waiting line problem, management can improve the service system by making changes in one or more of the following areas.

1. *Arrival rates.*   Management often can affect the rate of customer arrivals, λ, through advertising, special promotions, or differential pricing. For example, a telephone company uses differential pricing to shift residential long-distance calls from daytime hours to evening hours.

2. *Number of service facilities.*   By increasing the number of service facilities, such as tool cribs, toll booths, or bank tellers, or by dedicating some facilities in a phase to a unique set of services, management can increase system capacity.

3. *Number of phases.*   Managers can decide to allocate service tasks to sequential phases if they determine that two sequential service facilities may be more efficient than one. For instance, in the assembly-line problem discussed in Chapter 9, the decision concerned the number of phases needed along the assembly line. Determining the number of workers needed on the line also involves assigning a certain set of work elements to each one. Changing the facility arrangement can increase the service rate, μ, of each facility and the capacity of the system.

4. *Number of servers per facility.*   Managers can influence the service rate by assigning more than one person to a service facility.

5. *Server efficiency.* By adjusting the capital-to-labor ratio, devising improved work methods, or instituting incentive programs, management can increase the efficiency of servers assigned to a service facility. Such changes are reflected in μ.

6. *Priority rule.* Managers set the priority rule to be used, decide whether to have a different priority rule for each service facility, and decide whether to allow preemption (and, if so, under what conditions). Such decisions affect the waiting times of the customers and the utilization of the servers.

7. *Line arrangement.* Managers can influence customer waiting times and server utilization by deciding whether to have a single line or a line for each facility in a given phase of service.

Obviously, these factors are interrelated. An adjustment in the customer arrival rate, λ, might have to be accompanied by an increase in the service rate, μ, in some way. Decisions about the number of facilities, the number of phases, and waiting line arrangements also are related.

For each of the problems we analyzed with the waiting line models, the arrivals had a Poisson distribution (or exponential interarrival times), the service times had an exponential distribution, the service facilities had a simple arrangement, and the priority discipline was first come, first served. Waiting line theory has been used to develop other models in which these criteria are not met, but these models are very complex. Many times, the nature of the customer population, the constraints on the line, the priority rule, the service time distribution, and the arrangement of the facilities are such that waiting line theory is no longer useful. In these cases, simulation, which we discuss in Supplement F, often is used.

SUPPLEMENT REVIEW

Solved Problem 1

A photographer at the post office takes passport pictures at an average rate of 20 pictures per hour. The photographer must wait until the customer blinks or scowls, so the time to take a picture is exponentially distributed. Customers arrive at a Poisson distributed average rate of 19 customers per hour.

a. What is the utilization of the photographer?
b. How much time will the average customer spend at the photograph step of the passport issuing process?

Solution a. The assumptions in the problem statement are consistent with a single-server model. Utilization is

$$\rho = \frac{\lambda}{\mu} = \frac{19}{20} = 0.95$$

b. The average customer time spent at the photographer's station is

$$W = \frac{1}{\mu - \lambda} = \frac{1}{20 - 19} = 1 \text{ hour}$$

Solved Problem 2

The Mega Multiplex Movie Theater has three concession clerks serving customers on a first-come, first-served basis. The service time per customer is exponentially distributed with an average of 2 minutes per customer. Concession customers wait in a single line in a large lobby, and arrivals are Poisson distributed with an average of 81 customers per hour. Previews run for 10 minutes before the start of each show. If the average time in the concession area exceeds 10 minutes, customers become dissatisfied.

a. What is the average utilization of the concession clerks?
b. What is the average time spent in the concession area?

Solution a. The problem statement is consistent with the multiple-server model, and the average utilization rate is

$$\rho = \frac{\lambda}{s\mu} = \frac{81 \text{ customers/hour}}{(3 \text{ servers})\left(\dfrac{60 \text{ minutes/server hour}}{2 \text{ minutes/customer}}\right)} = 0.90$$

The concession clerks are busy 90 percent of the time.

b. The average time spent in the system, W, is

$$W = W_q + \frac{1}{\mu}$$

Here

$$W_q = \frac{L_q}{\lambda}, \quad L_q = \frac{P_0(\lambda/\mu)^s \rho}{s!(1-\rho)^2}, \quad \text{and} \quad P_0 = \left[\sum_{n=0}^{s-1} \frac{(\lambda/\mu)^n}{n!} + \frac{(\lambda/\mu)^s}{s!}\left(\frac{1}{1-\rho}\right)\right]^{-1}$$

We must solve for P_0, L_q, and W_q, in that order, before we can solve for W:

$$P_0 = \left[\sum_{n=0}^{s-1} \frac{(\lambda/\mu)^n}{n!} + \frac{(\lambda/\mu)^s}{s!}\left(\frac{1}{1-\rho}\right)\right]^{-1}$$

$$= \frac{1}{1 + \dfrac{(81/30)}{1} + \dfrac{(2.7)^2}{2} + \left[\dfrac{(2.7)^3}{6}\left(\dfrac{1}{1-0.9}\right)\right]}$$

$$= \frac{1}{1 + 2.7 + 3.645 + 32.805} = \frac{1}{40.15} = 0.0249$$

$$L_q = \frac{P_0(\lambda/\mu)^s \rho}{s!(1-\rho)^2} = \frac{0.0249(81/30)^3(0.9)}{3!(1-0.9)^2} = \frac{0.4411}{6(0.01)} = 7.352 \text{ customers}$$

$$W_q = \frac{L_q}{\lambda} = \frac{7.352 \text{ customers}}{81 \text{ customers/hour}} = 0.0908 \text{ hour}$$

$$W = W_q + \frac{1}{\mu} = 0.0908 \text{ hour} + \frac{1}{30} \text{ hour} = (0.1241 \text{ hour})\left(\frac{60 \text{ minutes}}{\text{hour}}\right) = 7.45 \text{ minutes}$$

With three concession clerks, customers will spend an average of 7.45 minutes in the concession area.

Solved Problem 3

The Severance Coal Mine serves six trains having exponentially distributed interarrival times averaging 30 hours. The time required to fill a train with coal varies with the number of cars, weather-related delays, and equipment breakdowns. The time to fill a train can be approximated by a negative exponential distribution with a mean of 6 hours 40 minutes. The railroad requires the coal mine to pay very large demurrage charges in the event that a train spends more than 24 hours at the mine. What is the average time a train will spend at the mine?

Solution The problem statement describes a finite-source model, with $N = 6$. The average time spent at the mine is $W = L[(N - L)\lambda]^{-1}$, with $1/\lambda =$ mean time between arrivals for a finite input source, or 30 hours/train, $\lambda = 0.8$ train/day, and $\mu = 3.6$ trains/day. In this case,

$$P_0 = \left[\sum_{n=0}^{N} \frac{N!}{(N-n)!}\left(\frac{\lambda}{\mu}\right)^n\right]^{-1} = \frac{1}{\displaystyle\sum_{n=0}^{6} \frac{6!}{(6-n)!}\left(\frac{0.8}{3.6}\right)^n}$$

$$= \frac{1}{\left[\frac{6!}{6!}\left(\frac{0.8}{3.6}\right)^0\right] + \left[\frac{6!}{5!}\left(\frac{0.8}{3.6}\right)^1\right] + \left[\frac{6!}{4!}\left(\frac{0.8}{3.6}\right)^2\right] + \left[\frac{6!}{3!}\left(\frac{0.8}{3.6}\right)^3\right] + \left[\frac{6!}{2!}\left(\frac{0.8}{3.6}\right)^4\right] + \left[\frac{6!}{1!}\left(\frac{0.8}{3.6}\right)^5\right] + \left[\frac{6!}{0!}\left(\frac{0.8}{3.6}\right)^6\right]}$$

$$= \frac{1}{1 + 1.33 + 1.48 + 1.32 + 0.88 + 0.39 + 0.09} = \frac{1}{6.49} = 0.1541$$

$$L = N - \frac{\mu}{\lambda}(1 - P_0) = 6 - \left[\frac{3.6}{0.8}(1 - 0.1541)\right] = 2.193 \text{ trains}$$

$$W = L[(N - L)\lambda]^{-1} = \frac{2.193}{(3.807)0.8} = 0.72 \text{ day}$$

Arriving trains will spend an average of 0.72 day at the coal mine.

Formula Review

1. Customer arrival Poisson distribution: $P_n = \dfrac{(\lambda T)^n}{n!} e^{-\lambda T}$

2. Service-time exponential distribution: $P(t \leq T) = 1 - e^{-\mu T}$

	Single-Server Model	Multiple-Server Model	Finite Source Model
Average utilization of the system	$\rho = \dfrac{\lambda}{\mu}$	$\rho = \dfrac{\lambda}{s\mu}$	$\rho = 1 - P_0$
Probability that n customers are in the system	$P_n = (1 - \rho)\rho^n$	$P_n = \begin{cases} \dfrac{(\lambda/\mu)^n}{n!} P_0, & 0 < n < s \\[2mm] \dfrac{(\lambda/\mu)^n}{s!\,s^{n-s}} P_0, & n \geq s \end{cases}$	
Probability that zero customers are in the system	$P_0 = 1 - \rho$	$P_0 = \left[\displaystyle\sum_{n=0}^{s-1} \dfrac{(\lambda/\mu)^n}{n!} + \dfrac{(\lambda/\mu)^s}{s!}\left(\dfrac{1}{1-\rho}\right) \right]^{-1}$	$P_0 = \left[\displaystyle\sum_{n=0}^{N} \dfrac{N!}{(N-n)!}\left(\dfrac{\lambda}{\mu}\right)^n \right]^{-1}$
Average number of customers in the service system	$L = \dfrac{\lambda}{\mu - \lambda}$	$L = \lambda W$	$L = N - \dfrac{\mu}{\lambda}(1 - P_0)$
Average number of customers in the waiting line	$L_q = \rho L$	$L_q = \dfrac{P_0(\lambda/\mu)^s \rho}{s!(1-\rho)^2}$	$L_q = N - \dfrac{\lambda + \mu}{\lambda}(1 - P_0)$
Average time spent in the system, including service	$W = \dfrac{1}{\mu - \lambda}$	$W = W_q + \dfrac{1}{\mu}$	$W = L[(N-L)\lambda]^{-1}$
Average waiting time in line	$W_q = \rho W$	$W_q = \dfrac{L_q}{\lambda}$	$W_q = L_q[(N-L)\lambda]^{-1}$

Supplement Highlights

- Waiting lines form when customers arrive at a faster rate than they are being served. Because customer arrival rates vary, surprisingly long waiting lines will occur even when the system's designed service rate is substantially higher than the average customer arrival rate.
- Four elements are common to all waiting line problems: a customer population, a waiting line, a service system, and a priority rule for determining which customer is to be served next.

- Waiting line models have been developed for use in analyzing service systems. If the assumptions made in creating a waiting line model are consistent with an actual situation, the model's formulas can be solved to predict the performance of the system with respect to server utilization, average customer waiting time, and the average number of customers in the system.

Key Terms

customer population *304*
interarrival times *308*
phase *306*
preemptive discipline *307*

priority rule *304*
service facility *304*
service system *304*
waiting line *303*

Study Questions

1. A 900-seat college lecture hall is being designed, and cost is an important consideration. Studies show that an average of 30 students can pass through a doorway in one minute. Therefore the average capacity of a doorway is 1800 students per hour. For each one-hour lecture, a maximum of 900 students file into the hall, and 900 leave. Therefore the lecture hall is designed to have only one doorway. Would waiting lines occur? Why or why not?

2. All other things being equal, in which situation in each pair would you expect better customer service?
   a. 1. The pool of customers is equal to 9, and the probability that each customer will need service during one hour equals 1/3.
      2. The pool of customers is infinite, and the average arrival rate is 3 customers per hour.
   b. 1. The service time is exponentially distributed, with an average of 15 minutes per customer.
      2. The service time is constant at 15 minutes per customer.
   c. 1. There are multiple service lines, with one customer waiting line for each service line.
      2. There are multiple service lines, with one common customer waiting line.
   d. 1. A single-server model has $\lambda = 3$ and $\mu = 4$.
      2. A multiple-server model has $\lambda = 6$, $\mu = 4$, and $s = 2$.

3. What is the difference between balking and reneging? What is the difference between multiple channels and multiple phases?

4. The most common priority rule encountered in the U.S. service economy is also the least common priority rule encountered in the U.S. manufacturing economy. Why?

5. What is the relationship between the Poisson distribution and the exponential distribution?

6. In the single-server model, as the arrival rate increases as a proportion of the service rate, the probability that no customers are in the system decreases. What can be said about the probability that one customer is in the system? Does it increase, decrease, remain constant, or do something else?

Problems

1. The Howard, Smith, and Parke law firm produces many legal documents that must be typed for clients and the firm. Requests average four pages of documents per hour, and they arrive according to a Poisson distribution. The secretary can type five pages per hour on average according to an exponential distribution.
   a. What is the average utilization rate of the secretary?
   b. What is the probability that more than four pages of documents are waiting or being typed?
   c. What is the average number of documents waiting to be typed?
   d. What is the average waiting time for documents in the waiting line?

2. The Mayberry telephone directory assistance operator receives calls at a rate of 120 per hour according to a Poisson distribution. The average time required to process a call is 20 seconds, exponentially distributed. Assuming that the single-server waiting line model applies, answer the following questions.
   a. What is the probability that three or more calls are in the system?
   b. What is the average time required for the operator to answer?
   c. What is the average number of calls waiting to be answered?

3. Moore, Aiken, and Payne is a dental clinic serving the needs of the general public on a first-come, first-served basis. The clinic has three dental chairs, each staffed by a dentist. Patients arrive at the rate of five per hour, according to a Poisson distribution, and don't balk or renege. The average time required for a dental checkup is 30 minutes, according to an exponential distribution.
   a. What is the probability that no patients are in the clinic?
   b. What is the probability that six or more patients are in the clinic?
   c. What is the average number of patients waiting?
   d. What is the average total time that a patient spends in the clinic?

4. Floyd's barbershop has three barber's chairs. Patrons are served on a first-come, first-served basis and arrive at the rate of nine customers per hour, according to a Poisson distribution. The time required for a haircut averages 15 minutes, according to an exponential distribution.
   a. What is the probability that no customers are in the shop?
   b. What is the probability that five or more customers are in the shop?
   c. What is the average number of customers in the waiting area?
   d. What is the average waiting time in the waiting line?

5. Consider further the barbershop described in Problem 4. Suppose that the owner wants to allow more idle time for sweeping the floor and discussing events of the day. He believes that the added expense of remodeling the shop to accommodate four barber's chairs can be offset by slightly increased prices, if the resulting average waiting time per customer is less than five minutes. Assuming that the price change will not affect the rate of customer arrivals, should Floyd remodel the barber shop?

6. Blue Niles hosts a psychology talk show on KRAN radio. Niles's advice averages 10 minutes per caller, but varies according to an exponential distribution. The average time between calls is 25 minutes, exponentially distributed. Generating calls in this local market is difficult, so Niles does not want to lose any calls to busy signals. The radio station has only three telephone lines. What is the probability that a caller receives a busy signal?

7. The supervisor at the Ace Job Shop wishes to determine the staffing policy that minimizes total operating costs. The average arrival rate at the tool crib, where tools are dispensed to the workers, is eight machinists per hour. Each machinist's pay is $18 per hour. The supervisor can staff the crib either with a junior attendant who is paid $5 per hour and can process 10 arrivals per hour or with a senior attendant who is paid $9 per hour and can process 12 arrivals per hour. Which attendant should be selected, and what would be the total estimated hourly cost?

8. The daughter of the owner of a local hamburger restaurant is preparing to open a new fast-food restaurant called Hasty Burgers. Based on the arrival rates at her father's outlets, she expects customers to arrive at the drive-in window according to a Poisson distribution, with a mean of 20 customers per hour. The service rate is flexible; however, the service times are expected to follow an exponential distribution. The drive-in window is a single-server operation.

   a. What service rate is needed to keep the average number of customers in the service system (waiting line and being served) to four?

   b. For the service rate in part a, what is the probability that more than four customers are in line and being served?

   c. For the service rate in part a, what is the average waiting time in line for each customer? Does this average seem satisfactory for a fast-food business?

Advanced Problems

9. Three employees in the maintenance department are responsible for repairing the video games at Pinball Wizard, a video arcade. A maintenance worker can fix one video game machine every eight hours on average, with an exponential distribution. An average of one video game machine fails every three hours, according to a Poisson distribution. Each down machine costs the Wizard $10 per hour in lost income. A new maintenance worker would cost $8 per hour.

   Should the manager hire any new personnel? If so, how many? What would you recommend to the manager, based on your analysis?

10. The College of Business and Public Administration at Benton University has a copy machine on each floor for faculty use. Heavy use of the five copy machines causes frequent failures. Maintenance records show that a machine fails every 2.5 days (or $\lambda = 0.40$ failure/day). The college has a maintenance contract with the authorized dealer of the copy machines. Because the copy machines fail so frequently, the dealer has assigned one person to the college to repair them. This person can repair an average of 2.5 machines per day. Using the finite-source model, answer the following questions.

    a. What is the average utilization of the maintenance person?

    b. On average, how many copy machines are being repaired or waiting to be repaired?

    c. What is the average time spent by a copy machine in the repair system (waiting and being repaired)?

11. Bryant Manufacturing has six essential machines in its plant that fail frequently. On average, a machine fails every four days. The repair person assigned full-time to maintain the machines can fix an average of two machines per day. Using the finite-source model, answer the following questions.

    a. What is the repair person's average utilization?

    b. How many machines are being repaired or waiting to be repaired, on average?

    c. What is the average time spent by a machine in the repair system (waiting and being repaired)?

Selected References

Cooper, Robert B. *Introduction to Queuing Theory,* 2nd ed. New York: Elsevier–North Holland, 1980.

Hillier, F. S., and G. S. Lieberman. *Introduction to Operations Research,* 2nd ed. San Francisco: Holden-Day, 1975.

Moore, P. M. *Queues, Inventories and Maintenance.* New York: John Wiley & Sons, 1958.

Saaty, T. L. *Elements of Queuing Theory with Applications.* New York: McGraw-Hill, 1961.

Simulation Analysis

Simulation is the act of reproducing the behavior of a system using a model that describes the operations of the system. Once the model has been developed, the analyst can manipulate certain variables to measure the effects of changes on the operating characteristics of interest. A simulation model cannot prescribe what should be done about a problem. Instead, it can be used to study alternative solutions to the problem. The alternatives are systematically used in the model, and the relevant operating characteristics are recorded. After all the alternatives have been tried, the best one is selected.

The waiting line models presented in Supplement E are not simulation models because they describe the operating characteristics with known equations. With simulation, the equations describing the operating characteristics are unknown. Using a simulation model, the analyst actually generates customer arrivals, puts customers into waiting lines, selects the next customer to be served by using some priority discipline, serves that customer, and so on. The model keeps track of the number in line, waiting time, and the like during the simulation and calculates the averages and variances at the end.

Simulation also may be used in other ways. For example, pilots are tested periodically on flight simulators. The cockpit of the simulator is identical to that of a real plane, but it is inside a large building. Through the use of computer graphics and other visual and mechanical effects, a pilot seems to be actually flying a plane. The pilot's reactions to various unexpected situations are measured and evaluated.

◆ REASONS FOR USING SIMULATION

Simulation is useful when waiting line models become too complex. There are other reasons for using simulation for analyzing operations management problems. First, when the relationship between the variables is nonlinear or when there are too many variables and/or constraints to handle with optimizing approaches, simulation models can be used to estimate operating characteristics or objective function values and analyze a problem.

Second, simulation models can be used to conduct experiments without disrupting real systems. Experimenting with a real system can be very costly. For example, a simulation model can be used to estimate the benefits of purchasing and installing a new flexible manufacturing system without first installing such a system. Also, the model could be used to evaluate different configurations or processing decision rules without disrupting production schedules.

Third, simulation models can be used to obtain operating characteristic estimates in much less time than is required to gather the same operating data from a real system. This feature of simulation is called **time compression**. For example, a simulation model of airport operations can generate statistics on airplane arrivals, landing delays, and terminal delays for a year in a matter of minutes on a computer. Alternative airport designs can be analyzed and decisions made quickly.

Finally, simulation is useful in sharpening managerial decision-making skills through gaming. A descriptive model that relates managerial decisions to important operating characteristics (such as profits, market share, and the like) can be developed. From a set of starting conditions, the participants make periodic decisions with the intention of improving one or more operating characteristics. In such an exercise a few hours' "play" can simulate a year's time. Gaming also enables managers to experiment with new ideas without disrupting normal operations.

Although simulation is used extensively in practice for the various reasons cited above, many analysts still think of it as the method of last resort. Mathematical analysis is preferred because it finds the optimal solution for the problem, whereas simulation requires the analyst to try various alternatives and possibly obtain a suboptimal solution. In addition, simulation modeling usually is very expensive because of the detail required in the computer model. Spending thousands of hours on programming and debugging complex models is not uncommon. Optimizing approaches, if they apply, usually are less expensive.

◆ THE SIMULATION PROCESS

The simulation process includes data collection, random-number assignment, model formulation, and analysis. This process is known as **Monte Carlo simulation,** after the European gambling capital, because of the random numbers used to generate the simulation events.

Data Collection

Simulation requires extensive data gathering on costs, productivities, capacities, and probability distributions. Typically, one of two approaches to data collection is used. Statistical sampling procedures are used when the data are not readily available from published sources or when the cost of searching for and collecting the data is high. Historical search is used when the data are available in company records, governmental and industry reports, professional and scientific journals, or newspapers.

EXAMPLE F.1
*Data Collection for
a Simulation*

The Specialty Steel Products Company produces items such as machine tools, gears, automobile parts, and other specialty items in small quantities to customer order. Because the products are so diverse, demand is measured in machine-hours. Orders for products are translated into required machine-hours, based on time standards for each operation. Management is concerned about capacity in the lathe department. Assemble the data necessary to analyze the addition of one more lathe machine and operator.

Solution   Historical records indicate that lathe department demand varies from week to week as follows.

Weekly Production Requirements (hr)	Relative Frequency
200	0.05
250	0.06
300	0.17
350	0.05
400	0.30
450	0.15
500	0.06
550	0.14
600	0.02
Total	1.00

To gather these data, all weeks with requirements of 175.00–224.99 hours were grouped in the 200-hour category, all weeks with 225.00–274.99 hours in the 250-hour category, and so on. The average weekly production requirements for the lathe department are

$$200(0.05) + 250(0.06) + 300(0.17) + \cdots + 600(0.02) = 400 \text{ hours}$$

Employees in the lathe department work 40 hours per week on 10 machines. However, the number of machines actually operating during any week may be less than 10. Machines may need repair, or a worker may not show up for work. Historical records indicate that actual machine hours were distributed as follows.

Regular Capacity (hr)	Relative Frequency
320 (8 machines)	0.30
360 (9 machines)	0.40
400 (10 machines)	0.30

The average number of operating machine hours in a week is

$$320(0.30) + 360(0.40) + 400(0.30) = 360 \text{ hours}$$

The company has a policy of completing each week's workload on schedule, using overtime and subcontracting if necessary. The maximum amount of overtime authorized in any week is 100 hours, and requirements in excess of 100 hours are subcontracted to a small machine shop in town. Lathe operators receive $10 per hour for regular time. However, management estimates that the cost for overtime work is $25 per hour per employee, which includes premium-wage, variable overhead, and supervision costs. Subcontracting costs $35 per hour, exclusive of materials costs.

To justify adding another machine and worker to the lathe department, weekly savings in overtime and subcontracting costs should be at least $650. These savings would cover the cost of the additional worker and provide for a reasonable return on machine investment. Management estimates from prior experience that with 11 machines the distribution of weekly capacity machine hours would be

Regular Capacity (hr)	Relative Frequency
360 (9 machines)	0.30
400 (10 machines)	0.40
440 (11 machines)	0.30

Random-Number Assignment

Before we can begin to analyze this problem with simulation, we must specify a way to generate demand and capacity each week. Suppose that we want to simulate 100 weeks of lathe operations with 10 machines. We would expect that 5 percent of the time (5 weeks of the 100) we would have a demand for 200 hours. Similarly, we would expect that 30 percent of the time (30 weeks of the 100) we would have 320 hours of capacity. However, we can't use these averages of demand in our simulation, because a real system doesn't operate that way. Demand may be 200 hours one week but 550 hours the next.

We can obtain the effect we want by using a random-number table to determine the amount of demand and capacity each week. A **random number** is a number that has the same probability of being selected as any other number. Appendix 4 contains five-digit random numbers.

The events in a simulation can be generated in an unbiased way if random numbers are assigned to the events in the same proportion as their probability of occurrence. We expect a demand of 200 hours 5 percent of the time. If we have 100 random numbers (00–99), we can assign 5 numbers (or 5 percent of them) to the event "200 hours demanded." Thus we can assign the numbers 00–04 to that event. If we randomly choose numbers in the range of 00–99 enough times, 5 percent of the time they will fall in the range of 00–04. Similarly, we can assign the numbers 05–10, or 6 percent of the numbers, to the event "250 hours demanded." In Table F.1, we show the allocation of the 100 random numbers to the demand events in the same proportion as their probability of occurrence. We similarly assigned random numbers to the *capacity* events for 10 machines. The capacity events for the 11-machine simulation would have the same random-number assignments, except that the events would be 360, 400, and 440 hours, respectively.

TABLE F.1   *Random-Number Assignments to Simulation Events*

Event: Weekly Demand (hr)	Probability	Random Numbers	Event: Existing Weekly Capacity (hr)	Probability	Random Numbers
200	0.05	00–04	320	0.30	00–29
250	0.06	05–10	360	0.40	30–69
300	0.17	11–27	400	0.30	70–99
350	0.05	28–32			
400	0.30	33–62			
450	0.15	63–77			
500	0.06	78–83			
550	0.14	84–97			
600	0.02	98–99			

Model Formulation

Formulating a simulation model entails specifying the relationships among the variables. Simulation models consist of decision variables, uncontrollable variables, and dependent variables. **Decision variables** are controlled by the decision maker and will change from one run to the next as different events are simulated.

For example, the number of lathe machines is the decision variable in the Specialty Steel Products problem in Example F.1. **Uncontrollable variables**, however, are random events that the decision maker can't control. At Specialty Steel Products, the weekly production requirements and the *actual* number of machine hours available are uncontrollable variables for the simulation analysis. Dependent variables reflect the values of the decision variables and the uncontrollable variables. At Specialty Steel Products, operating characteristics such as idle time, overtime, and subcontracting hours are dependent variables.

The relationships among the variables are expressed in mathematical terms so that the dependent variables can be computed for any values of the decision variables and uncontrollable variables. For example, in the simulation model for Specialty Steel Products, the methods of determining weekly production requirements and actual capacity availability must be specified first. Then the methods of computing idle-time hours, overtime hours, and subcontracting hours for the values of production requirements and capacity hours can be specified.

Analyzing simulation models requires a computer for virtually all real problems. Simulation programming can be done in a variety of computer languages, including general-purpose programming languages such as BASIC, FORTRAN, or Pascal. The advantage of general-purpose programming languages is that they are available on most computer systems. Special simulation languages, such as GPSS, SIMSCRIPT, and SLAM, also are available. These languages simplify programming because they have macroinstructions for the commonly used elements of simulation models. These macrostatements automatically contain the computer instructions needed to generate arrivals, keep track of waiting lines, and calculate the statistics on the operating characteristics of a system.

EXAMPLE F.2

Formulating a Simulation Model

Formulate a simulation model for Specialty Steel Products that will estimate idle-time hours, overtime hours, and subcontracting hours for a specified number of lathes. Design the simulation model to terminate after 20 weeks of simulated lathe department operations.

Solution   Let's use the first two rows of random numbers in Appendix 4 for the demand events and the third and fourth rows for the capacity events. Because they are five-digit numbers, we use only the first two digits of each number for our random numbers. The choice of the rows in the random-number table was arbitrary. The important point is that we must be consistent in drawing random numbers and should not repeat the use of numbers in any one simulation.

To simulate a particular capacity level, we proceed as follows.

1. Draw a random number from Appendix 4 from the first two rows. Start with the first number in the first row, then go to the second number in the first row, and so on.
2. Find the random-number interval for production requirements associated with the random number.
3. Record the production hours (PROD) required for the current week.
4. Draw another random number from Appendix 4 from row 3 or row 4. Start with the first number in row 3, then go to the second number in row 3, and so on.
5. Find the random-number interval for capacity (CAP) associated with the random number.

6. Record the capacity hours available for the current week.
7. If CAP ≥ PROD, then IDLE HR = CAP − PROD.
8. If CAP < PROD, then SHORT = PROD − CAP.
   If SHORT ≤ 100, then OVERTIME HR = SHORT
   and SUBCONTRACT HR = 0.
   If SHORT > 100, then OVERTIME HR = 100
   and SUBCONTRACT HR = SHORT − 100.
9. Repeat steps 1–8 until you have simulated 20 weeks.

Analysis

Table F.2 contains the simulations for the two capacity alternatives at Specialty Steel Products. We used a unique random-number sequence for weekly production requirements for each capacity alternative and another sequence for the existing weekly capacity to make a direct comparison between the capacity alternatives.

TABLE F.2   *20-Week Simulations of Alternatives*

				10 Machines				11 Machines			
Week	Demand Random Number	Weekly Production (hr)	Capacity Random Number	Existing Weekly Capacity (hr)	Idle Hours	Overtime Hours	Sub-contract Hours	Existing Weekly Capacity (hr)	Idle Hours	Overtime Hours	Sub-contract Hours
1	71	450	50	360		90		400		50	
2	68	450	54	360		90		400		50	
3	48	400	11	320		80		360		40	
4	99	600	36	360		100	140	400		100	100
5	64	450	82	400		50		440		10	
6	13	300	87	400	100			440	140		
7	36	400	41	360		40		400			
8	58	400	71	400				440	40		
9	13	300	00	320	20			360	60		
10	93	550	60	360		100	90	400		100	50
11	21	300	47	360	60			400	100		
12	30	350	76	400	50			440	90		
13	23	300	09	320	20			360	60		
14	89	550	54	360		100	90	400		100	50
15	58	400	87	400				440	40		
16	46	400	82	400				440	40		
17	00	200	17	320	120			360	160		
18	82	500	52	360		100	40	400		100	
19	02	200	17	320	120			360	160		
20	37	400	19	320		80		360		40	
			Total		490	830	360		890	590	200
			Weekly average		24.5	41.5	18.0		44.5	29.5	10.0

Based on the 20-week simulations, we would expect average weekly overtime hours (highlighted in red) to be reduced by 41.5 − 29.5 = 12 hours and subcontracting hours (highlighted in gray) to be reduced by 18 − 10 = 8 hours per week. The average weekly savings would be

Overtime:	(12 hours)($25/hour) =	$300
Subcontracting:	(8 hours)($35/hour) =	280
	Total savings per week =	$580

This amount falls short of the minimum required savings of $650 per week. Does that mean that we should not add the machine and worker? Before answering, let's look at Table F.3, which shows the results of a *1000-week* simulation for each alternative. The costs (highlighted in blue) are quite different from those of the 20-week simulations. Now the savings are estimated to be $1851.50 − $1159.50 = $692 and exceed the minimum required savings for the additional investment. This result emphasizes the importance of selecting the proper run length for a simulation analysis. We can use statistical tests to check for the proper run length.

TABLE F.3 *Comparison of 1000-Week Simulations*

	10 Machines	11 Machines
Idle hours	26.0	42.2
Overtime hours	48.3	34.2
Subcontract hours	18.4	8.7
Cost	$1851.50	$1159.50

Simulation analysis can be viewed as a form of hypothesis testing, whereby the results of a simulation run provide sample data that can be analyzed statistically. Data can be recorded and compared with the results from other simulation runs. Statistical tests also can be made to determine whether differences in the alternative operating characteristics are statistically significant. Commonly used statistical methods include *analysis of variance, t-tests,* and *regression analysis*. These techniques require replication of each simulation experiment. For example, if we wanted to test the null hypothesis that the difference between total weekly costs is zero, we would have to run the simulation model several times for each capacity alternative. Each time, we would use a different set of random numbers to generate weekly production requirements and weekly existing capacity. The number of replications is analogous to the sample size in statistical terminology. If we can show that the weekly cost for 11 machines is significantly different (in a statistical sense) from the weekly cost for 10 machines, we can be more confident of the estimate of the difference between the two.

Even though a difference between simulation experiments may be statistically significant, it may not be *managerially* significant. For example, suppose that we developed a simulation model of a car wash operation. We may find, by changing the speed of the car wash from 3 minutes per car to 2.75 minutes per car, that we can reduce the average waiting time per customer by 0.20 minute. Even though this may be a statistically significant difference in the average waiting time, the difference is so small that customers may not even notice it. What is managerially significant often is a judgment decision.

SUPPLEMENT REVIEW

Solved Problem

A manager is considering production of several products in an automated facility. The manager would purchase a combination of two robots. The two robots (named Mel and Danny) in series are capable of doing all the required operations. Every batch of work will contain ten units. A waiting line of several batches will be maintained in front of Mel. When Mel completes his portion of the work, the batch will then be transferred directly to Danny.

Each robot incurs a setup before it can begin processing a batch. Each unit in the batch has equal run time. The distributions of the setup times and run times for Mel and Danny are identical. But, as Mel and Danny will be performing different operations, simulation of each batch requires four random numbers from the table. The first random number determines Mel's setup time, the second determines Mel's run time per unit, and the third and fourth random numbers determine Danny's setup and run times, respectively.

Setup Time (min)	Probability	Run Time per Unit (sec)	Probability
1	0.10	5	0.10
2	0.20	6	0.20
3	0.40	7	0.30
4	0.20	8	0.25
5	0.10	9	0.15

Estimate how many units will be produced in an hour. Then use the first column of random numbers to simulate 60 minutes of operation for Mel and Danny.

Solution   Except for the time required for Mel to set up and run the first batch, we assume the two robots run simultaneously. The expected average setup time per batch is given by

$$[(0.1 \times 1 \text{ min}) + (0.2 \times 2 \text{ min}) + (0.4 \times 3 \text{ min}) + (0.2 \times 4 \text{ min}) + (0.1 \times 5 \text{ min})]$$

$$= 3 \text{ minutes, or } 180 \text{ seconds per batch}$$

The expected average run time per batch (of ten units) is

$$[(0.1 \times 5 \text{ sec}) + (0.2 \times 6 \text{ sec}) + (0.3 \times 7 \text{ sec}) + (0.25 \times 8 \text{ sec}) + (0.15 \times 9 \text{ sec})]$$

$$= 7.15 \text{ seconds/unit} \times 10 \text{ units/batch} = 71.5 \text{ seconds per batch}$$

Thus the total of average setup and run times per batch is 251.5 seconds. In an hour's time we might expect to complete about 14 batches (3600 seconds/251.5 seconds = 14.3). However, this estimate is probably too high.

Keep in mind that Mel and Danny operate in sequence and that Danny cannot begin to do work until it has been completed by Mel (see batch 2 of Table F.4). Nor can Mel start a new batch until Danny is ready to accept the previous one. Refer to batch 6, where Mel completes this batch at time 25:50 but cannot begin the seventh batch until Danny is ready to accept the sixth batch at time 28:00.

Mel and Danny completed only 12 batches in one hour. Even though the robots used the same probability distributions and therefore have perfectly balanced production ca-

TABLE F.4   *Simulation Results for Mel and Danny*

			Mel						Danny			
Batch No.	Start Time	Random No.	Setup	Random No.	Process	Completion Time	Start Time	Random No.	Setup	Random No.	Process	Completion Time
1	0:00	71	4 min	50	7 sec	5 min 10 sec	5:10	21	2 min	94	9 sec	8 min 40 sec
2	5:10	50	3 min	63	8 sec	9 min 30 sec	9:30	47	3 min	83	8 sec	13 min 50 sec
3	9:30	31	3 min	73	8 sec	13 min 50 sec	13:50	04	1 min	17	6 sec	15 min 50 sec
4	13:50	96	5 min	98	9 sec	20 min 20 sec	20:20	21	2 min	82	8 sec	23 min 40 sec
5	20:20	25	2 min	92	9 sec	23 min 50 sec	23:50	32	3 min	53	7 sec	28 min 0 sec
6	23:50	00	1 min	15	6 sec	25 min 50 sec	28:00	66	3 min	57	7 sec	32 min 10 sec
7	28:00	00	1 min	99	9 sec	30 min 30 sec	32:10	55	3 min	11	6 sec	36 min 10 sec
8	32:10	10	2 min	61	8 sec	35 min 30 sec	36:10	31	3 min	35	7 sec	40 min 20 sec
9	36:10	09	1 min	73	8 sec	38 min 30 sec	40:20	24	2 min	70	8 sec	43 min 40 sec
10	40:20	79	4 min	95	9 sec	45 min 50 sec	45:50	66	3 min	61	8 sec	50 min 10 sec
11	45:50	01	1 min	41	7 sec	48 min 00 sec	50:10	88	4 min	23	6 sec	55 min 10 sec
12	50:10	57	3 min	45	7 sec	54 min 20 sec	55:10	21	2 min	61	8 sec	58 min 30 sec
13	54:20	26	2 min	46	7 sec	57 min 30 sec	58:30	97	5 min	31	7 sec	64 min 40 sec

pacities, Mel and Danny did not produce the expected capacity of 14 batches because Danny was sometimes idle while waiting for Mel (see batch 6) and Mel was sometimes idle while waiting for Danny (see batch 8). This loss-of-throughput phenomenon occurs whenever variable processes are closely linked, whether those processes are mechanical, such as Mel's and Danny's, or functional, such as production and marketing. The simulation shows the need to place between the two robots sufficient space to store several batches to absorb the variations in process times. Subsequent simulations could be run to show how many batches are needed.

Supplement Highlights

- Simulation is used to model the important operating characteristics of complex waiting line situations. Information that isn't attainable through the use of waiting line formulas, such as the maximum number in line and the effect of disruptions to steady-state operations, also can be collected.
- Simulation models consist of decision variables (e.g., number of servers), uncontrollable variables (e.g., incidence of machine breakdowns), and dependent variables (e.g., utilization or the maximum number in line). Dependent variables reflect the behavior of the system defined by the decision variables as it is affected by uncontrollable variables. For example, simulation of three machines (decision variable) may show that when one machine breaks down for two hours (uncontrollable variable), the maximum number in line grows to seven customers (dependent variable).

Key Terms

Problems

1. Eagle Dry Cleaners specializes in same-day dry cleaning. Customers drop off their garments early in the morning and expect them to be ready for pickup on their way home from work. There is a risk, however, that the work needed on a given garment cannot be done that day, depending on the type of cleaning required. Historically, an average of 15 garments have had to be held over to the next day. The outlet's manager is contemplating expanding to reduce or eliminate that backlog. A simulation model was developed with the following distribution for garments per day.

Number	Probability	Random Numbers
50	0.10	00–09
60	0.25	10–34
70	0.30	35–64
80	0.25	65–89
90	0.10	90–99

With expansion, the maximum number of garments that could be dry cleaned per day is

Number	Probability	Random Numbers
60	0.30	00–29
70	0.40	30–69
80	0.30	70–99

In the simulation for a specific day, the number of garments needing cleaning (NGNC) is determined first. Next, the maximum number of garments that could be dry cleaned (MNGD) is determined. If MNGD ≥ NGNC, all garments are dry cleaned for that day. If MNGD < NGNC, then (NGNC − MNGD) garments must be added to the number of garments arriving the next day to obtain the NGNC for the next day. The simulation continues in this manner.

a. Assuming that the store is empty at the start, simulate 15 days of operation. Use the following random numbers, the first determining the number of arrivals and the second setting the capacity:

(49, 77), (27, 53), (65, 08), (83, 12), (04, 82), (58, 44), (53, 83), (57, 72), (32, 53), (60, 79), (79, 30), (41, 48), (97, 86), (30, 25), (80, 73)

Determine the average daily number of garments held overnight, based on your simulation.

b. If the cost associated with garments being held over is $25 per garment per day and the added cost of expansion is $100 per day, is the expansion a good idea?

2. The Precision Manufacturing Company is considering the purchase of an NC machine and has narrowed the possible choices to two models. The company produces several products, and batches of work arrive at the NC machine every 6 minutes. The number of units in the batch has the following discrete distribution.

Number of Units in Batch	Probability
3	0.1
6	0.2
8	0.3
14	0.2
18	0.2

The distributions of the setup times and processing times for the two NC models follow. Assume that the work in a batch shares a single setup and that each unit in the batch has equal processing time. Simulate two hours (or 12 batch arrivals) of operation for the two NC machines. Which one would you recommend if both machines cost the same to purchase, operate, and maintain?

NC Machine 1

Setup Time (min)	Probability	Run Time per Unit (sec)	Probability
1	0.10	5	0.10
2	0.20	6	0.20
3	0.40	7	0.30
4	0.20	8	0.25
5	0.10	9	0.15

NC Machine 2

Setup Time (min)	Probability	Run Time per Unit (sec)	Probability
1	0.05	3	0.20
2	0.15	4	0.25
3	0.25	5	0.30
4	0.45	6	0.15
5	0.10	7	0.10

3. In Problem 2, what factors would you consider if the initial cost of NC Machine 1 was $5000 less than that of NC Machine 2?

4. The 30 management professors at Omega University

(ΩU) find out that telephone calls made to their offices aren't being picked up. A call-forwarding system redirects calls to the management office after the fourth ring. A department office assistant answers the telephone and takes messages. An average of 90 telephone calls per hour are placed to the management faculty, and each telephone call consumes about one minute of the assistant's time. The calls arrive according to a Poisson distribution with an average of 1.5 calls per minute, as shown in Fig. F.1(a). Because the professors spend much of their time in class and in conferences, there is only a 40 percent chance that they will pick up a call themselves, as shown in Fig. F.1(b). If two or more telephone calls are forwarded to the office during the same minute, only the first call will be answered.

a. Without using simulation, make a preliminary guess of what proportion of the time the assistant will be on the telephone and what proportion of the telephone calls will not be answered.

b. Now use the random number table, starting with the top of the second column to simulate the situation for one hour starting at 10:00 a.m. Table F.5 will get you started.

c. What proportion of the time is the office assistant on the telephone? What proportion of the telephone calls are not answered? Are these proportions close to what you expected?

FIGURE F.1

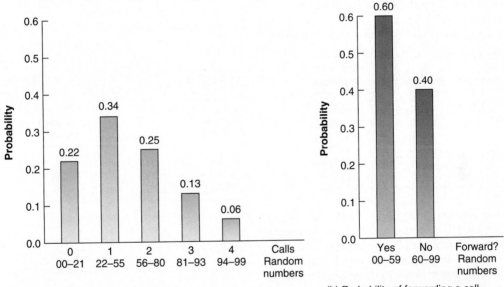

(a) Number of telephone calls placed

(b) Probability of forwarding a call

TABLE F.5   *Office Assistant Simulation*

Time	RN	Number of Calls Made	RN	1st Call Forwarded? (Yes/No)	RN	2nd Call Forwarded? (Yes/No)	RN	3rd Call Forwarded? (Yes/No)	RN	4th Call Forwarded? (Yes/No)	Number of Calls Not Answered	Assistant Idle (✔)
10:00	68	2	30	Yes	54	Yes					1	
10:01	76	2	36	Yes	32	Yes					1	
10:02	68	2	04	Yes	07	Yes					1	
10:03	98	4	08	Yes	21	Yes	28	Yes	79	No	2	
10:04	25	1	77	No							0	✔
10:05	51	1	23	Yes							0	
10:06	67	2	22	Yes	27	Yes					1	
10:07	80	2	87	No	06	Yes					0	✔
10:08	03	0									0	✔
10:09	03	0									0	✔
10:10	33	1	78	No							0	✔

5. The management chair at ΩU is considering installing a voice-mail system. Monthly operating costs are $20 per voice-mailbox, but the system will reduce the amount of time the office assistant spends answering the telephone by 50 percent. The department has 32 telephones. Use the results of your simulation in Problem 4 to estimate the proportion of the assistant's time presently spent answering the telephone. The office assistant's salary (and overhead) is $2000 per month. Should the management chair order the voice-mailbox system?

6. The Capital City Shuttle takes people from the downtown business district to the airport. The shuttle bus has a capacity of 12 people and takes one hour to make the round trip to and from the airport. If more than 12 people arrive during the hour, the excess must wait until the next trip and the service charge to them is discounted by 15 percent. The following table shows the arrival distribution at the downtown depot.

Number	Probability	Random Numbers
10	0.20	00–19
11	0.35	20–54
12	0.20	55–74
13	0.15	75–89
14	0.05	90–94
15	0.05	95–99

a. Suppose that the owner of the shuttle charges $10 per person. Disregarding any revenues that might be generated on the trip from the airport, estimate the average hourly revenue for the trip from downtown to the airport. Base your estimate on a simulation of eight hours, using the following random numbers.

87, 44, 29, 02, 97, 20, 71, 15

b. What is the average utilization of the shuttle bus from downtown to the airport?

7. Swift Airlines has a large service center to overhaul and maintain its fleet of passenger jets. A maximum of two jets per day can be serviced by the company's maintenance crew. Aircraft arrive at the service center according to the following distribution.

Number	Probability	Random Numbers
1	0.33	00–32
2	0.34	33–66
3	0.33	67–99

If a jet arrives at the service center but cannot receive any maintenance the same day, it must wait overnight in the hangar for service the next day. Use the following random numbers.

24, 05, 19, 53, 20, 80, 58, 32, 93, 77

a. Simulate the arrival and servicing of aircraft for ten days.

b. Determine the maximum number of aircraft held overnight in any one day.

8. A machine center handles four types of clients: A, B, C, and D. The manager wants to assess the number of machines required to produce goods for these clients. Setup times for changeover from one client to another are negligible. Annual demand and processing times are uncertain; demand may be low, normal, or high. The probabilities for these three events are shown in the following tables.

Client A

Demand (units/yr)	Probability	Processing Time (hr/ unit)	Probability
3000	0.10	10	0.35
3500	0.60	20	0.45
4200	0.30	30	0.20

Client B

Demand (units/yr)	Probability	Processing Time (hr/ unit)	Probability
500	0.30	60	0.25
800	0.50	90	0.50
900	0.20	100	0.25

Client C

Demand (units/yr)	Probability	Processing Time (hr/unit)	Probability
1500	0.10	12	0.25
3000	0.50	15	0.60
4500	0.40	20	0.15

Client D

Demand (units/yr)	Probability	Processing Time (hr/unit)	Probability
600	0.40	60	0.30
650	0.50	70	0.65
700	0.10	80	0.05

a. Explain how simulation could be used to generate a probability distribution for the total number of machine hours required per year to serve the clients.

b. Simulate one year, using the following random numbers. For example, use random number 78 for client A's demand and 10 for client A's processing time.

78, 10, 62, 72, 11, 28, 16, 99

Selected References

Christy, D. P., and H. J. Watson. "The Application of Simulation: A Survey of Industry Practice." *Interfaces*, vol. 13, no. 5 (October 1983), pp. 47–52.

Ernshoff, J. R., and R. L. Serson. *Design and Use of Computer Simulation Models.* New York: Macmillan, 1970.

Hillier, F. S., and G. S. Lieberman. *Introduction to Operations Research*, 2nd ed. San Francisco: Holden-Day, 1975.

Law, A. M., and W. D. Kelton. *Simulation Modeling and Analysis*, 2nd ed. New York: McGraw-Hill, 1991.

Meier, R. C., W. T. Newell, and H. L. Pazer. *Simulation in Business and Economics.* Englewood Cliffs, N.J.: Prentice-Hall, 1969.

Naylor, T. H., et al. *Computer Simulation Techniques.* New York: John Wiley & Sons, 1966.

Solomon, S. L. *Simulation of Waiting Lines.* Englewood Cliffs, N.J.: Prentice-Hall, 1983.

Watson, H. J. *Computer Simulation in Business.* New York: John Wiley & Sons, 1981.

Chapter Eight

LOCATION

Commuters hurrying to work from subway and rail line stations in Boston can't avoid walking past an Au Bon Pain Company cafe. This fast-growing chain is known for its gourmet sandwiches, freshly baked French bread, and croissants. It is the latest to embrace the unconventional strategy of locating retail outlets close together. Au Bon Pain has clustered 16 cafes in the downtown area alone, with many less than 100 yards apart. It is exporting this same location strategy to New York, Philadelphia, Washington, D.C., and other cities. Although putting too many outlets close together can hurt individual store sales in some cases, the advantages can outweigh the drawbacks. Clustering shops can reduce advertising expenses, make for easier supervision, and attract customers from the competition. This saturation approach won't work in suburban or residential areas because Au Bon Pain is not a "destination restaurant" that people drive to. It works best in high-density cities where the shops attract hordes of impulse buyers with little time to shop or eat lunch.

With numerous urban cafes located close to offices and stores, Au Bon Pain attracts commuters passing by.

In a typical year in the United States, manufacturing firms build more than 3000 new plants and expand 7500 others, while service industries build and remodel innumerable stores, office buildings, warehouses, and other facilities. Choosing where to locate new manufacturing facilities, service organizations, or branch offices is a strategic decision. The location of a business's facilities has a significant impact on the company's operating costs, the prices it charges for goods and services, and its ability to compete in the marketplace.

Analyzing location patterns to discover a firm's underlying strategy is fascinating. For example, why does White Castle often locate restaurants near manufacturing plants? Why do competing new-car sales showrooms cluster near one another? White Castle's strategy is to cater to blue-collar workers. As a result it tends to locate near the target population and away from competitors such as Wendy's and McDonald's. In contrast, managers of new-car showrooms deliberately locate near one another because customers prefer to do their comparative shopping in one area. In each case, management's location decision reflects a particular strategy.

Recognizing the strategic impact of location decisions, we first examine the most important trend in location patterns: the globalization of operations. We then consider qualitative factors that influence location choices. We end with some analytic techniques for making single- or multiple-facility location decisions.

◆ THE GLOBALIZATION AND GEOGRAPHIC DISPERSION OF OPERATIONS

Should facilities be opened overseas?

In the past, industries tended to concentrate in specific areas—for example, fabricated metals manufacturers in the industrial belt of the United States and international banking firms in London and New York City. Today this tendency to concentrate in certain geographic regions is lessening. Although electric machinery and electronics remain key industries in New England, and sport shoes in Korea, these industries and many others have become more geographically diversified. Geography and distance are becoming increasingly irrelevant in location decisions, owing to improved communication technologies such as e-mail, faxes, video conferencing, and overnight delivery. An important exception is manufacturing firms that utilize just-in-time systems (described in Chapter 15), which rely on supplier proximity. The trend of separating operations and putting thousands of miles between them has been applied by large corporations as well as small and medium-sized companies. For example, a high-fashion designer may choose to locate its headquarters in New York City because it is the center of fashion, its warehouses in Ohio because it is centrally located, customer-service toll-free numbers in Des Moines because Iowans speak with an all-American accent, and manufacturing facilities in Hong Kong because people in Asia are skilled in textile work and receive lower wages.

The term **globalization** describes businesses' deployment of facilities and operations around the world. Worldwide exports now account for more than 30 percent of worldwide gross national product, up from 12 percent in 1962. For years, U.S. firms have built production facilities overseas. That trend continues, and foreign businesses have begun building facilities in this country. Michigan now has nearly 300 Japanese companies, a sixfold increase in eight years. Mostly auto-related, they have located near Detroit to buy from or sell to the Big Three automakers (General Motors, Ford, and Chrysler) and to hire U.S. engineers for their own growing U.S. operations. In the service sector there have been high-profile Japanese acquisitions: Columbia Pictures, CBS Records, Universal Studios, and a majority interest in New York's Rockefeller Center. At the end of 1994, total foreign investment in U.S. service and manufacturing industries exceeded $404 billion. Europe accounts for 64 percent of the total, with the United Kingdom leading the way at 29 percent. Japanese firms account for another 21 percent.

Globalization also results in more exports to and imports from other countries, often called *offshore* sales and imports. Offshore sales and purchases by U.S. manufacturers have increased to 14 percent of total sales and 10 percent of total purchases. The volume of corporate voice, data, and teleconferencing traffic between countries is growing at an annual rate of 15 to 20 percent—about double the corporate domestic rate—indicating how businesses are increasingly bridging national boundaries.

Reasons for Globalization

Four developments have spurred the trend toward globalization: improved transportation and communication technologies, loosened regulations on financial institutions, increased demand for imported goods, and lowered international trade barriers.

Improved Transportation and Communication Technologies.   Improvements in communications technology and transportation are breaking down the barriers of time and space between countries. For example, air transportation can move goods quickly from, say, Kansas City to New York or even from Osaka, Japan, to Kansas City. Telecommunications (voice and data) technology—including electronic mail, facsimile machines, the Internet, and sophisticated toll-free telephone arrangements—allows facilities to serve larger market areas and allows firms to centralize some operations and provide support to branches located near their customers. It also permits managers around the world to communicate quickly, increasing the possibilities for cooperation.

Opened Financial Systems.   During the 1980s, U.S. banking regulators removed interest rate ceilings, which allowed banks to attract more foreign investors by offering higher rates. At the same time, foreign banks removed barriers to entry. As a result, the world's financial systems have become more open, making it easier for firms to locate where capital, supplies, and resources are cheapest.

Increased Demand for Imports.   Import penetration of the major economies is increasing, as political barriers to international trade have crumbled. Imported goods and services now are the equivalent of about 13 percent of total output in the United States and 14 percent in Japan, up considerably from earlier decades. Penetration has been increased by locating production facilities in foreign countries because a local presence reduces customer aversion to buying imports. For example, Elasticos Selectos, a Mexico City–based elastics concern, built a plant in the United States primarily to gain customers who demand a Made-in-the-U.S.A. label.

Reduced Import Quotas and Other Trade Barriers.   Producing goods or service in the country where the customers live also circumvents import quotas and other trade barriers, such as India's restrictions on certain imports. During the 1980s, Japanese automakers including Honda, Mazda, Mitsubishi, Nissan, and Toyota located production facilities in the United States to avoid import quotas and negative public opinion. The recent development of regional trading blocks, such as the European Union (better known by its former name—European Community, or EC) and the North American Free Trade Agreement (NAFTA), also make trade between countries easier. So does the General Agreement on Tariffs and Trade (GATT), a tariff-cutting world trade agreement.

Disadvantages to Globalization

Of course, there also can be disadvantages to operations in other countries. A firm may have to relinquish proprietary technology if it turns over some of its component manufacturing to offshore suppliers or if suppliers need the firm's technology to achieve the desired quality and cost goals.

There may be political risks. Each nation can exercise its sovereignty over the people and property within its borders. The extreme case is nationalization, in which a government may take over a firm's assets without paying compensation. Also, a firm may alienate customers back home if jobs are lost to offshore operations.

Employee skills may be lower in foreign countries, requiring additional training time. Korean firms moved much of their sports shoe production to low-wage Indonesia and China, but they still manufacture hiking shoes and in-line roller skates in Korea because of the greater skills required.

When a firm's operations are scattered, customer response times can be longer. Effective cross-functional connections also may be more difficult if face-to-face discussions are needed.

Hot Spots of Global Economic Activity

Where is global economic activity particularly visible?

Globalization fosters an increasingly interdependent world economy. Figure 8.1 shows a few areas where the trend toward globalization is particularly visible.

Mexico.   American, Japanese, South Korean, and European firms have opened nearly 2000 plants employing almost 500,000 workers in **maquiladoras,** or industrial parks, along the northern border of Mexico. The *maquilas*, or plants in the maquiladoras, assemble foreign parts and reexport the finished product to the United States. For example, Ford opened a new plant in Hermosillo to make the Escort and is expanding its multivalve four-cylinder engine plant in Chihuahua. These plants take advantage of cheaper Mexican labor, which lowers the sticker price on Ford's cars and trucks. The massive devaluation of the peso in 1982 put Mexico's wages in the ballpark with those of newly industrialized Asian countries. A firm facing a $10 per hour average payroll cost in the United States can save $15,000 annually per employee by moving to Mexico. The incentive of inexpensive labor must be balanced, however, against lower productivity, less work-force stability, an inefficient rail system, dusty roads, and considerable training requirements. For example, the cost to connect a new plant to Mexico's underdeveloped electric grid can be as high as $200,000.

European Community.   The EC has dropped most internal trade barriers, and significant economic expansion is expected in Western Europe over the next two decades. Multinational firms are positioning themselves to be treated as *EC corporations,* with the ability to trade freely within the EC and avoid import quotas or duties by locating local production facilities in Europe. For a company to qualify as an EC corporation, it must manufacture a product's core parts within the EC. For example, Whirlpool Corporation acquired Philips's European appliance business in order to qualify as an EC company and gain a share in the growing European market for appliances. Whirlpool expects European appliance sales to grow 4 percent per year. Only 14 percent of European households currently own clothes dryers and only 19 percent have dishwashers. Japanese multinationals—Toyota, Honda, Nissan, Sony, Matsushita, Fujitsu, and the Mitsubishi companies—also are pouring staggering amounts of money into manufacturing plants in Europe. Nissan, Toyota, and Honda have committed $2.6 billion to major manufacturing investments in Britain alone. They hope to capture a larger share of the $180 billion European automobile market, the largest in the world.

Eastern Europe and the Former Soviet Union.   With the political collapse of the former communist countries in Eastern Europe and the former Soviet Union, many firms began looking increasingly to those markets as a source of new customers, suppliers, and partners. Although the pace of growth may be less certain

FIGURE 8.1 *Global Hot Spots*

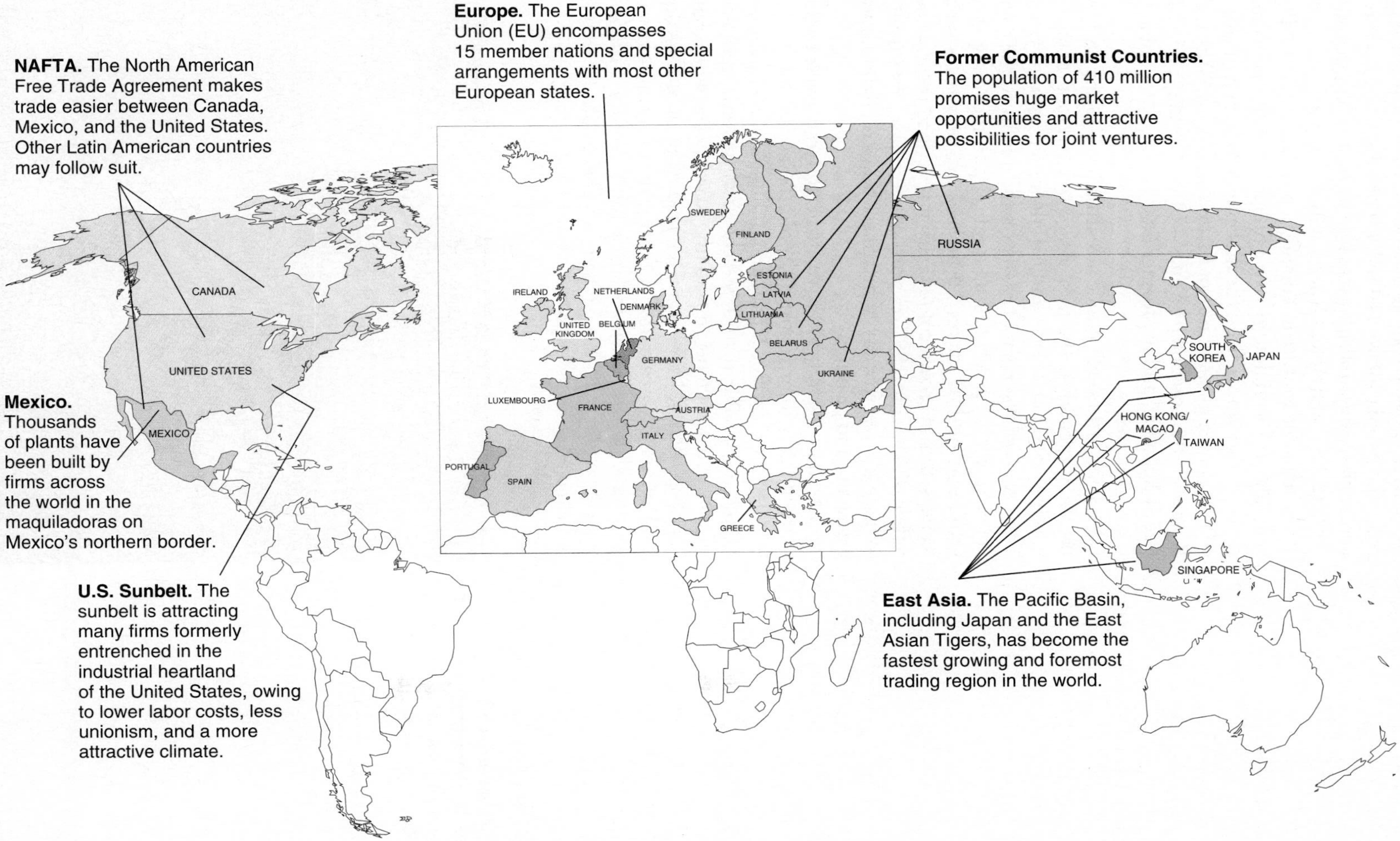

NAFTA. The North American Free Trade Agreement makes trade easier between Canada, Mexico, and the United States. Other Latin American countries may follow suit.

Mexico. Thousands of plants have been built by firms across the world in the maquiladoras on Mexico's northern border.

U.S. Sunbelt. The sunbelt is attracting many firms formerly entrenched in the industrial heartland of the United States, owing to lower labor costs, less unionism, and a more attractive climate.

Europe. The European Union (EU) encompasses 15 member nations and special arrangements with most other European states.

Former Communist Countries. The population of 410 million promises huge market opportunities and attractive possibilities for joint ventures.

East Asia. The Pacific Basin, including Japan and the East Asian Tigers, has become the fastest growing and foremost trading region in the world.

CANADA

UNITED STATES

MEXICO

IRELAND
UNITED KINGDOM
LUXEMBOURG
PORTUGAL
SPAIN
FRANCE
BELGIUM
NETHERLANDS
DENMARK
GERMANY
ITALY
AUSTRIA
GREECE
SWEDEN
FINLAND
ESTONIA
LATVIA
LITHUANIA
BELARUS
UKRAINE
RUSSIA

RUSSIA

SOUTH KOREA
JAPAN
HONG KONG/
MACAO
TAIWAN
SINGAPORE

there than in other regions because of the enormous political and economic turmoil, the population of 410 million promises huge market opportunities. Foreign companies are establishing joint ventures in local manufacturing at an accelerating pace. For example, General Motors may invest as much as $400 million by 1996 in a joint venture in Poland to produce a midsized Opel automobile in Warsaw and $150 million in two Hungarian ventures to make various automobile parts. It also won a five-year agreement to supply nearly $1 billion of pollution-control and engine-control parts to Volga Auto Works, the largest automaker in Russia. In the computer business, IBM is setting up joint ventures in Russia, the Czech Republic, and the former East Germany (now part of Germany).

East Asia.   Although public attention has focused on Japan because of its manufacturing capability, the *East Asian tigers* (Hong Kong, Taiwan, Singapore, and South Korea) are rapidly industrializing areas with growing economic strength. Their economies depend heavily on the export of their manufactured goods. Taiwan exports 70 percent of its total output, including garments, electronics, software, and steel; it makes 20 percent of the world's personal computers. Hong Kong, a British crown colony until it reverts to the jurisdiction of the People's Republic of China in 1997, exports 90 percent of its manufacturing output. Owing to its small size, this city-state concentrates on light industries such as electronics, garments, and printing.

The East Asian tigers have attracted large investments from foreign firms and share in many joint ventures. Apple, Texas Instruments, and General Electric, as well as Matsushita of Japan, are among the 170 foreign firms with plants in Singapore responsible for 60 percent of all manufacturing output. Four major domestic conglomerates in South Korea (Daewoo, Samsung, Hyundai, and Lucky-Goldstar), known as the *chaebol*, account for 40 percent of the country's total output. Korea attracts foreign investment, particularly from the United States and Japan. Daewoo has a joint venture with Suzuki to build Japanese minicars and trucks. Kia Motors, another South Korean firm, is partly owned by Ford and Mazda and builds the Ford Festiva for the U.S. market.

TIS, an independent marketing company, provides the necessary distribution operations to service a small but growing market for Apple Computer in Eastern Europe.

Globalization of Services. In 1990 the value of world trade in services reached $600 billion, or roughly 20 percent of total world trade. Banking, law, information services, airlines, education, consulting, and restaurant services are particularly active globally. For example, McDonald's opened a record 220 restaurants offshore in just one year. Small companies also are beginning to export their services. The Tokyo city government gave a New York architect a $50 million contract to design and build a $1 billion International Forum complex in downtown Tokyo, and India's Steel Authority hired a Silver Spring, Maryland, consulting firm to design and implement quality systems for its five major steel plants.

Managing Global Operations

How should global operations be managed, and what are their biggest challenges?

All the concepts and techniques described in this book apply to operations throughout the world. However, location decisions involve added complexities when a firm sets up facilities abroad, as Managerial Practice 8.1 on the next page illustrates. One recent study (see Klassen and Whybark, 1994) found that the most important barrier to effective global manufacturing operations is that many firms don't take a global view of their market opportunities and competitors. Global markets impose new standards on quality and time. Managers should not think about domestic markets first and then global markets later, if at all. Also, they must have a good understanding of their competitors, which requires greater appraisal capabilities when the competitors are global rather than domestic. Other important challenges of managing multinational operations include other languages and customs, different management styles, unfamiliar laws and regulations, and different costs.

Other Languages. The ability to communicate effectively is important to all organizations. Most U.S. managers are fluent only in English and thus are at a disadvantage when dealing with managers in Europe or Asia who are fluent in several languages. For example, despite the vast potential for trade with Russia, few American students are studying Russian.

Different Norms and Customs. Several U.S. franchisers, such as Century 21 Real Estate, Levi Strauss, and Quality Inns International, found that even when the same language is spoken, different countries have unique norms and customs that shape business values. The goals of the firm, attitudes toward work, customer expectations, desire for risk taking, and other business values can vary dramatically from one part of the world to another. For example, more than two-thirds of the managers surveyed in Japan believe that business should take an active role in environmental protection, whereas only 25 percent of Mexican managers agree (see Kanter, 1991).

Work-Force Management. Employees in different countries prefer different management styles. Managers moving to operations in another country often must reevaluate their on-the-job behavior (e.g., superior–subordinate relationships), assumptions about workers' attitudes, and hiring and promotion practices. Practices that work well in one country may be ineffective in another.

Unfamiliar Laws and Regulations. Managers in charge of overseas plants must deal with unfamiliar labor laws, tax laws, and regulatory requirements. The after-tax consequences of an automation project, for instance, can be quite

Managerial Practice 8.1

▶ *Managerial Challenges with Global Operations*

Mexico

The maquiladoras help firms do business in a country that has different traditions and culture. The maquiladoras provide what other industrial parks around the world provide: plants built to the clients' specifications and other physical facilities such as roads, sewers, and power lines. But, in addition, the maquiladora manager helps the foreign firm recruit, train, and pay all the Mexicans in the work force—including supervisors and engineers. The maquiladora manager also guides the maquila's relationships with the local government and local community. The foreigner runs the business part of the organization, and the maquiladora manager handles the social tasks.

European Community

In the EC, more managers are crossing borders from one European country to another, often at critical stages in their careers. Responsibilities of these "Euromanagers" are shifting from national to regional, or pan-European, units. Companies must stay in touch with local conditions. They need managers who can think big while understanding local nuances, who can deal skillfully with a variety of cultures and bring a diverse team together. The best kind of manager in an international setting is a flexible one. Getting along with colleagues is important in a foreign setting, where extra effort is needed to build understanding and trust.

Eastern Europe and the Former Soviet Union

The political uncertainty in Eastern Europe and the former Soviet Union complicates the problems of doing business there. The Denver-based phone company US West found itself in a jam in August 1991. The August coup attempt in Russia unfolded just two weeks before a scheduled ceremony to officially switch on St. Petersburg's (formerly Leningrad) new cellular telephone system. When the coup unraveled the ceremony went on as scheduled, but that experience taught foreign firms several lessons: the importance of getting into a country early, understanding how its power structure works, establishing relationships with several layers of officials, being willing to change plans on short notice, and learning how to sidestep potential conflicts in dealing with officials.

East Asia

Distance and language differences can handicap a firm's ability to work with its new overseas managers. Concord Camera opened a Chinese assembly plant 15 miles north of Hong Kong, where the going wage was $8 a week instead of the $8 an hour paid at its New Jersey home base. The new operation turned out to be a nightmare. Feedback to Concord's home office was minimal, almost all of it coming through one manager whom the company wound up suing for "wrongful actions."

Sources: "Mexico's Ugly Duckling—the Maquiladora," *Wall Street Journal,* October 4, 1990; "Firms in Europe Try to Find Executives Who Can Cross Borders in a Single Bound," *Wall Street Journal,* January 25, 1991; "Playing Politics," *Wall Street Journal,* October 4, 1991; "Small Firms Face Big Headaches in Far-Flung Ventures," *Wall Street Journal,* July 1, 1991; "Innocents Abroad," *Wall Street Journal,* April 15, 1991.

different from country to country because of different tax laws. Legal systems also differ. Some policies and practices that are illegal in one country might be acceptable or even mandated elsewhere in the world.

Unexpected Cost Mix. Firms may shift some of their operations to another country because of lower costs of inventory, labor, materials, and real estate. However, these same differences may mean that policies that worked well in one economic environment—such as automating a process—might be a mistake in the new environment.

Federal Express's attempt to expand in Europe illustrates several of these complexities. FedEx entered the European market well after competitors such as

ANY EXPRESS COMPANY CAN FIND TOPEKA. TRY THE SUBURBS OF ABU HADRIYAH.

TOPEKA? NO PROBLEM. BUT WHAT ABOUT A TOWN IN THE MIDDLE EAST? BIG PROBLEM. UNLESS YOU USE DHL. BECAUSE ONLY DHL USES ITS OWN LOCAL PEOPLE, WITH LOCAL KNOW-HOW, TO DELIVER PACKAGES TO PLACES AS DIFFERENT AS CAIRO OR ABU HADRIYAH. WHICH, OF COURSE, IS RIGHT UP THE DESERT FROM AL MUBARRAZ. 1-800-CALL-DHL.

DHL, an American overnight package delivery service, had much more success initially in establishing global operations.

DHL and TNT, and problems cropped up immediately. Setting up a U.S.-style hub-and-spoke system, which permits standardized sorting and tracking of parcels, proved to be difficult. Governments saw FedEx as foreign competition to domestic mail services and delayed granting landing rights for certain flights. To speed up the process, FedEx bought a total of 21 European transportation firms between 1983 and 1990, a costly strategy that left the company with decidedly "unexpresslike" operations. The company didn't adapt its services to European languages and customs. Until recently, it printed all shipping bills and sales brochures in English, and it cut off pickups after 5 P.M., even though workers in some countries (e.g., Spain and Italy) work as late as 8 P.M.

In dealing with global operations, managers must decide how much of the firm's operations to shift overseas and how much control the home office should retain. Four distinct approaches may be used in managing international operations. *Global* firms rely on their home offices for strategic direction and are highly centralized. *International* firms are less centralized but still depend heavily on the home office. *Multinational* firms are highly decentralized, with each company subsidiary operating relatively autonomously. *Transnational* firms have a worldwide vision but allow each company to operate independently. A transnational manager must be able to manage highly decentralized organizations that have a complex mix of product strategies, cultures, and consumer needs.

◆ FACTORS AFFECTING LOCATION DECISIONS

Which factors are dominant in picking a new location? Secondary?

Facility location is the process of determining a geographic site for a firm's operations. Managers of both service and manufacturing organizations must weigh many factors when assessing the desirability of a particular site, including proximity to customers and suppliers, labor costs, and transportation costs. As Managerial Practice 8.2 suggests, when GM decided on the location of its Saturn facility, it gave particular weight to union attitudes, outbound transportation costs, quality of life, and the availability of utilities. Managers generally can disregard factors that do not meet at least one of the following two conditions.

1. The factor must be sensitive to location. That is, managers should not consider a factor that is not affected by the location decision. For example, if community attitudes are uniformly good at all of the locations under consideration, community attitudes should not be considered as a factor.

2. The factor must have a high impact on the company's ability to meet its goals. For example, although different locations will be at different distances from suppliers, if shipments and communication can take place by overnight delivery and faxing, distance to suppliers should not be considered as a factor.

Managers can divide location factors into dominant and secondary factors. Dominant factors are those which are derived from competitive priorities (cost, quality, time, and flexibility) and have a particularly strong impact on sales or costs. For example, a labor-intensive plant might require low wage costs to remain competitive. Secondary factors also are important, but management may downplay or even ignore some of them if other factors are more important. Thus for GM's Saturn plant, which makes many parts on site, inbound transportation costs were considered a less important secondary factor.

Dominant Factors in Manufacturing

Six groups of factors dominate location decisions for new U.S. manufacturing plants. Listed in order of importance, they are

1. favorable labor climate,
2. proximity to markets,
3. quality of life,
4. proximity to suppliers and resources,
5. proximity to the parent company's facilities, and
6. utilities, taxes, and real estate costs.

Favorable Labor Climate.   A favorable labor climate may be the most important factor in location decisions for labor-intensive firms in industries such as textiles, furniture, and consumer electronics. Labor climate is a function of wage rates, training requirements, attitudes toward work, worker productivity, and union strength. Many executives perceive weak unions or a low probability of union organizing efforts as a distinct advantage. One indicator of this attitude is that, although 50 percent of U.S. industry is unionized, only 20 percent of new plants being opened have unions.

Proximity to Markets.   After determining where the demand for goods and services is greatest, management must select a location for the facility that will supply that demand. Locating near markets is particularly important when the final

Managerial Practice 8.2

▶ *GM's Saturn Plant in Tennessee*

General Motors Corporation needed a location for its new Saturn manufacturing complex for small cars. The facility was planned to be the most integrated car operation in the United States, with many parts made by one of several feeder plants located on site. After considering 60 different location factors and more than 1000 possible sites in two dozen states, GM selected Spring Hill, Tennessee, because it offered the "best balance." Saturn Corporation headquarters and the engineering staff remained in Michigan near Detroit.

Spring Hill is near Nashville, a metropolitan area offering a variety of educational and cultural activities.

Major rail and highway routes provide access to most customers within a 500-mile radius. The state offers a stable economic climate, with adequate water and electric power. Although a Michigan site would have been closer to existing suppliers, that factor was unimportant because the Spring Hill facility would make most major parts on site.

Although Tennessee is a right-to-work state, which guarantees an open shop, the Saturn facility is operated by a UAW work force. The contract is quite innovative, providing for an unprecedented degree of worker flexibility and more of a "consensus decision-making" structure.

Source: "GM Is Expected to Put Saturn Complex in Tennessee as UAW Board Votes Pact," *Wall Street Journal*, January 29, 1985.

goods are bulky or heavy and *outbound* transportation rates are high. For example, manufacturers of products such as plastic pipe and heavy metals all emphasize proximity to their markets.

Quality of Life. Good schools, recreational facilities, cultural events, and an attractive life-style contribute to **quality of life.** This factor is relatively unimportant on its own, but it can make the difference in location decisions. In the United States during the past two decades, more than 50 percent of new industrial jobs went to nonurban regions. A similar shift is taking place in Japan and Europe. Reasons for this movement include high costs of living, high crime rates, and general decline in the quality of life in many large cities.

Proximity to Suppliers and Resources. Industries dependent on inputs of bulky, perishable, or heavy raw materials emphasize proximity to suppliers and resources. In such cases *inbound* transportation costs become a dominant factor, encouraging these firms to locate facilities near suppliers. For example, locating paper mills near forests and food processing facilities near farms is practical. Another advantage of locating near suppliers is the ability to maintain lower inventories.

Proximity to the Parent Company's Facilities. In many companies, plants supply parts to other facilities or rely on other facilities for management and staff support. These ties require frequent coordination and communication, which can become more difficult as distance increases.

Utilities, Taxes, and Real Estate Costs. Other important factors that may emerge include utility costs (telephone, energy, and water), local and state taxes, financing incentives offered by local or state governments, relocation costs, and land costs. For example, companies building new facilities in California are concerned about the high cost of land (about $100,000 an acre) near San Francisco, Los Angeles, and San Diego. Many are finding refuge in the state's Central Valley communities, long considered less desirable and therefore less expensive than the more glamorous coastal cities. Florestone Products, a maker of bath and shower products, decided to build its new plant in the Central Valley, 150 miles from the company's headquarters and existing plant, and bought 15 acres for only $150,000 for its $4.2 million plant. The same acreage in the San Francisco area would have cost $1.5 million.

Other Factors.   Still other factors may need to be considered, including room for expansion, construction costs, accessibility to multiple modes of transportation, the cost of shuffling people and materials between plants, insurance costs, competition from other firms for the work force, local ordinances (such as pollution or noise control regulations), community attitudes, and many others. For global operations, firms are emphasizing local employee skills and education and the local infrastructure. Many firms are concluding that large, centralized manufacturing facilities in low-cost countries with poorly trained workers are not sustainable. Smaller, flexible facilities serving multiple markets allow the firm to deal with nontariff barriers such as sales volume limitations, regional trading blocks, political risks, and exchange rates.

Dominant Factors in Services

The factors mentioned for manufacturing firms also apply to service industries, with one important addition: the impact that the location might have on sales and customer satisfaction. Customers usually care about how close a service facility is, particularly if the process requires considerable customer contact.

How does the location decision for service facilities differ from that for manufacturing facilities?

Proximity to Customers.   Location is a key factor in determining how conveniently customers can carry on business with a firm. For example, few people will patronize a remotely located dry cleaner or supermarket if another is more convenient. Thus the influence of location on revenues tends to be the dominant factor.

Transportation Costs and Proximity to Markets.   For warehousing and distribution operations, transportation costs and proximity to markets are extremely important. With a warehouse nearby, many firms can hold inventory closer to the customer, thus reducing delivery time and promoting sales. For example, Invacare Corporation of Elyria, Ohio, gained a competitive edge in the distribution of home health care products by decentralizing inventory into 32 warehouses across the country. Invacare sells wheelchairs, hospital beds, and other patient aids, some of which it produces and some of which it buys from other firms, to small dealers who sell to consumers. Previously the dealers, often small mom-and-pop operations, had to wait three weeks for deliveries, which meant that a lot of their cash was tied up in excess inventory. With Invacare's new distribution network, the dealers get daily deliveries of products from one source. Invacare's location strategy shows how timely delivery can be a competitive advantage.

Location of Competitors.   One complication in estimating the sales potential at different locations is the impact of competitors. Management must not only con-

Should a firm be a leader or a follower in picking locations for new retail outlets?

sider the current location of competitors but also try to anticipate their reaction to the firm's new location. Avoiding areas where competitors are already well established often pays. However, in some industries, such as new-car sales showrooms and fast-food chains, locating near competitors is actually advantageous. The strategy is to create a **critical mass,** whereby several competing firms clustered in one location attract more customers than the total number who would shop at the same stores at scattered locations. Recognizing this effect, some firms use a follow-the-leader strategy when selecting new sites.

Site-Specific Factors.   Retailers also must consider the level of retail activity, residential density, traffic flow, and site visibility. Retail activity in the area is important, as shoppers often decide on impulse to go shopping or to eat in a restaurant. Traffic flows and visibility are important because businesses' customers arrive in cars. Management considers possible traffic tie-ups, traffic volume and direction by time of day, traffic signals, intersections, and the position of traffic medians. Visibility involves distance from the street and size of nearby buildings and signs. High residential density ensures nighttime and weekend business, as long as the population in the area fits the competitive priorities and target market segment.

◆ LOCATING A SINGLE FACILITY

Having examined trends and important factors in location, we now consider more specifically how a firm can make location decisions. In this section we consider the case of locating only one new facility. Where the facility is part of a firm's larger network of facilities, we assume that there is no interdependence; that is, a decision to open a restaurant in Tampa, Florida, is independent of whether the chain has a restaurant in Austin, Texas. Let's begin by considering how to decide whether a new location is needed, and then we will examine a systematic selection process aided by the load–distance method to deal with proximity.

Selecting On-Site Expansion, New Location, or Relocation

Should a firm expand on site, add a new facility, or relocate the existing facility?

Management must first decide whether to expand on site, build another facility, or relocate to another site. A survey of *Fortune* 500 firms showed that 45 percent of expansions were on site, 43 percent were in new plants at new locations, and only 12 percent were relocations of all facilities. On-site expansion has the advantage of keeping management together, reducing construction time and costs, and avoiding splitting up operations. As indicated in Chapter 7, however, a firm may overexpand a facility, at which point diseconomies of scale set in. Poor materials handling, increasingly complex production control, and simple lack of space all are reasons for building a new plant or relocating the existing one.

The advantages of building a new plant or moving to a new retail or office space are that the firm does not have to rely on production from a single plant, can hire new and possibly more productive labor, can modernize with new technology, and can reduce transportation costs. Most firms that choose to relocate are small (less than 10 employees). They tend to be single-location companies cramped for space and needing to redesign their production processes and layouts. More than 80 percent of all relocations are within 20 miles of the first location, which enables the firm to retain its current work force.

Comparing Several Sites

A systematic selection process begins after there is a perception or evidence that opening a retail outlet, warehouse, office, or plant in a new location will increase profits. A team may be responsible for the selection decision in a large corporation, or an individual may make the decision in a small company. The process of selecting a new facility location involves a series of steps.

1. Identify the important location factors, and categorize them as dominant or secondary.

2. Consider alternative regions; then narrow the choices to alternative communities and finally to specific sites.

3. Collect data on the alternatives from location consultants, state development agencies, city and county planning departments, chambers of commerce, land developers, electric power companies, banks, and on-site visits (see Managerial Practice 8.3).

4. Analyze the data collected, beginning with the *quantitative* factors—factors that can be measured in dollars, such as annual transportation costs or taxes. These dollar values may be broken down into separate cost categories (e.g., inbound and outbound transportation, labor, construction, and utilities) and separate revenue sources (e.g., sales, stock or bond issues, and interest income). These financial factors can then be converted to a single measure of financial merit and used to compare two or more sites.

5. Bring the qualitative factors pertaining to each site into the evaluation. A *qualitative* factor is one that can't be evaluated in dollar terms, such as community attitudes or quality of life. To merge quantitative and qualitative factors, some managers review the expected performance of each factor, while others assign each factor a weight of relative importance and calculate a weighted score for each site, using a preference matrix. What is important in one situation may be unimportant or less important in another. The site with the highest weighted score is best.

After thoroughly evaluating between 5 and 15 sites, those making the study prepare a final report containing site recommendations, along with a summary of the data and analyses on which they are based. An audiovisual presentation of the key findings usually is delivered to top management in large firms.

EXAMPLE 8.1

Calculating Weighted Scores in a Preference Matrix

A new medical facility, Health-Watch, is to be located in Erie, Pennsylvania. The following table shows the location factors, weights, and scores (1 = poor, 5 = excellent) for one potential site. The weights in this case add up to 100 percent. A weighted score will be calculated for each site. What is the weighted score for this site?

Location Factor	Weight	Score
Total patient miles per month	25	4
Facility utilization	20	3
Average time per emergency trip	20	3
Expressway accessibility	15	4
Land and construction costs	10	1
Employee preferences	10	5

Managerial Practice 8.3

▶ *Data Collection with the Tiger File*

The Census Bureau's new Tiger file is a minutely detailed computerized map of the entire United States. Tiger's formal name is the Topologically Integrated Geographic Encoding and Reference file. It lists in digital form every highway, street, bridge, and tunnel in the 50 states. When combined with a database such as the results of the 1990 census or a company's own customer files, Tiger gives desktop computer users the ability to ask various "what if" questions and print out the answers in map form. Retailers, bankers, franchisers, vehicle fleet operators, marketers, and even political consultants are excited about the information they have access to with the combined Tiger–census file. For example, by combining population, age, and income figures with geography, retailers can pinpoint on a computer screen map the most attractive locations for a new store. And package delivery companies can use Tiger technology to figure out the most efficient routes for their truck fleets. Software companies are scrambling to take advantage of this statistical mother lode.

Using information collected through the 1990 census, a worker plots Census Bureau data on a map.

Source: "Businesses Map Plans for Use of Tiger Geographical Files," *Wall Street Journal,* June 8, 1990.

Solution The weighted score (WS) for this particular site is calculated by multiplying each factor's weight by its score and adding the results:

$$WS = (25 \times 4) + (20 \times 3) + (20 \times 3) + (15 \times 4) + (10 \times 1) + (10 \times 5)$$
$$= 100 + 60 + 60 + 60 + 10 + 50$$
$$= 340$$

The total weighted score of 340 can be compared with the total weighted scores for other sites being evaluated.

Applying the Load–Distance Method

Should a firm locate near its suppliers, work force, or customers?

In the systematic selection process, the analyst must identify attractive candidate locations and compare them on the basis of quantitative factors. The load–distance method can facilitate this step. Several location factors relate directly to distance: proximity to markets, average distance to target customers, proximity to suppliers and resources, and proximity to other company facilities. The **load–distance method** is a mathematical model used to evaluate locations based on proximity factors. The objective is to select a location that minimizes the total weighted loads moving into and out of the facility. The distance between two points is expressed by assigning the points to grid coordinates on a map. (A similar approach is used for layout planning in Chapter 9.)

Distance Measures.   Suppose that a new warehouse is to be located to serve Pennsylvania. It will receive inbound shipments from several suppliers, including one in Erie. If the new warehouse were located at State College, what would be the distance between the two facilities? If shipments travel by truck, the distance depends on the highway system and the specific route taken. Computer software is available for calculating the actual mileage between any two locations in the same country. However, for a rough calculation, which is all that is needed for the load–distance method, either a Euclidean or rectilinear distance measure may be used.

Euclidean distance is the straight-line distance, or shortest possible path, between two points. To calculate this distance, we create a graph. We place point *A* on the grid to represent the supplier's location in Erie. Then we place point *B* on the grid to represent the possible warehouse location at State College. In Fig. 8.2 the distance between points *A* and *B* is the length of the hypotenuse of a right triangle, or

$$d_{AB} = \sqrt{(x_A - x_B)^2 + (y_A - y_B)^2}$$

where

$$d_{AB} = \text{distance between points } A \text{ and } B$$

$$x_A = x\text{-coordinate of point } A$$

$$y_A = y\text{-coordinate of point } A$$

$$x_B = x\text{-coordinate of point } B$$

$$y_B = y\text{-coordinate of point } B$$

FIGURE 8.2

Distance Between Erie (Point A) and State College (Point B)

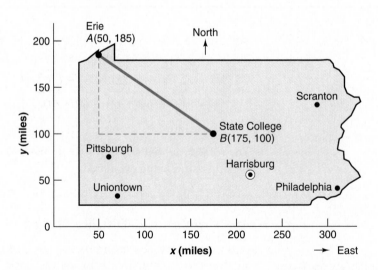

Rectilinear distance measures distance between two points with a series of 90° turns, as along city blocks. Essentially, this distance is the sum of the two dashed lines representing the base and side of the triangle in Fig. 8.2. The distance traveled in the *x*-direction is the absolute value of the difference in *x*-coordinates. Adding this result to the absolute value of the difference in the *y*-coordinates gives

$$d_{AB} = |x_A - x_B| + |y_A - y_B|$$

EXAMPLE 8.2

Calculating Distances

What is the Euclidean distance between points *A* and *B* in Fig. 8.2? The rectilinear distance?

Solution   Calculating the Euclidean distance, we get

$$d_{AB} = \sqrt{(50 - 175)^2 + (185 - 100)^2}$$

$$= 151.2 \text{ miles}$$

The rectilinear distance,

$$d_{AB} = |50 - 175| + |185 - 100|$$

$$= 210 \text{ miles}$$

is longer. The two measures give quite different numbers: 151.2 versus 210 miles. However, we are interested in the *relative* performance of different locations. Hence we simply use one of the distance measures consistently throughout the calculations.

Calculating a Load–Distance Score.   Suppose that a firm planning a new location wants to select a site that minimizes the distances that loads, particularly the larger ones, must travel to and from the site. Depending on the industry, a *load* may be shipments from suppliers, between plants, or to customers, or it may be customers or employees traveling to or from the facility. The firm seeks to minimize its load–distance, or *ld,* score, generally by choosing a location so that large loads go short distances.

To calculate a load–distance, *ld,* score for any potential location, we use either of the distance measures and simply multiply the loads flowing to and from the facility by the distances traveled. These loads may be expressed as tons or number of trips per week.

EXAMPLE 8.3

Calculating Load–Distance Scores

The new Health-Watch facility is targeted to serve seven census tracts in Erie, Pennsylvania. Figure 8.3 on the next page shows the coordinates for the center of each census tract, along with the projected populations, measured in thousands. Customers will travel from the seven census tract centers to the new facility when they need health care. Two locations being considered for the new facility are at (5.5, 4.5) and (7, 2), which are the centers of census tracts C and F. If we use the population as the loads and use rectilinear distance, which location is better in terms of its total *ld* score?

Solution   We want to calculate the *ld* score for each location. The distance between census tract A at (2.5, 4.5) and the first alternative location at (5.5, 4.5) is 3 miles in the east–west direction plus 0 miles in the north–south direction, or 3 miles. The *ld* score equals the distance multiplied by the population (measured in thousands), or 6. Using the coordinates from Fig. 8.3, we calculate the *ld* score for each tract:

Census Tract	(x, y)	Population (l)	Locate at (5.5, 4.5) Distance (d)	ld	Locate at (7, 2) Distance (d)	ld
A	(2.5, 4.5)	2	3 + 0 = 3	6	4.5 + 2.5 = 7	14
B	(2.5, 2.5)	5	3 + 2 = 5	25	4.5 + 0.5 = 5	25
C	(5.5, 4.5)	10	0 + 0 = 0	0	1.5 + 2.5 = 4	40
D	(5, 2)	7	0.5 + 2.5 = 3	21	2 + 0 = 2	14
E	(8, 5)	10	2.5 + 0.5 = 3	30	1 + 3 = 4	40
F	(7, 2)	20	1.5 + 2.5 = 4	80	0 + 0 = 0	0
G	(9, 2.5)	14	3.5 + 2 = 5.5	77	2 + 0.5 = 2.5	35
			Total	239	Total	168

Summing the scores for all tracts gives a total *ld* score of 239 when the facility is located at (5.5, 4.5) versus an *ld* score of 168 at location (7, 2). Therefore the location in census tract F is a better location.

FIGURE 8.3   *Calculating Load–Distance Scores for Two Possible Locations*

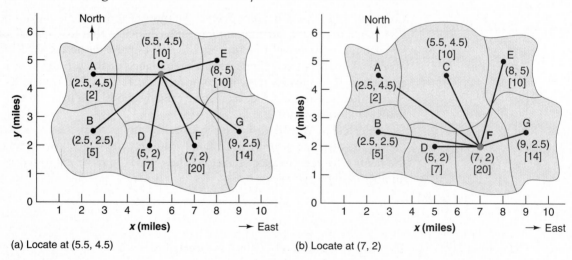

(a) Locate at (5.5, 4.5)   (b) Locate at (7, 2)

Note: The numbers in parentheses are census tract coordinates; the numbers in brackets are the populations of the census tracts in thousands.

We should evaluate still other candidate locations before making a decision. Figure 8.4 gives *ld* scores for several alternative locations (shown as dots). The best location appears to be at about (7, 2), at least on the basis of *ld* scores. Should an acceptable medical facility site not be available in the immediate area, the grid shows the implications of selecting a location elsewhere. For example, a two-mile deviation directly north to (7, 4) increases the score to only 197, which is less of a penalty than the same deviation to the east or west.

FIGURE 8.4

*Load–Distance
Scores for Several
Alternative
Locations*

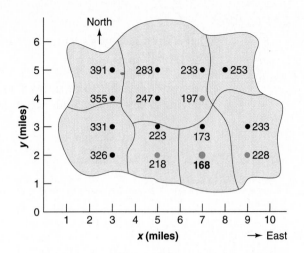

We could solve directly for the optimal location in Example 8.3.[†] However, practical considerations rarely allow managers to select this exact location. For example, land may not be available there at a reasonable price, or other location factors may make the site undesirable. Further, the rectilinear distance measure may be unrealistic. For such reasons, an analysis such as the one in Fig. 8.4 is particularly useful. Any distance measure can be used with these procedures.

Patterned Search. Testing different locations with the load–distance model is relatively simple if some systematic search process is followed. One such process is a patterned search, which is a quick method for finding the ideal location. The analyst begins by testing the location at the **center of gravity** of the target area. The center of gravity's x-coordinate, denoted x^*, is found by multiplying each point's x-coordinate (x_i) by its load (l_i), summing these products $(\sum l_i x_i)$, and then dividing by the sum of the loads $(\sum l_i)$. The y-coordinate, denoted y^*, is found the same way with the y-coordinates used in the numerator. The formulas are

$$x^* = \frac{\sum_i l_i x_i}{\sum_i l_i} \quad \text{and} \quad y^* = \frac{\sum_i l_i y_i}{\sum_i l_i}$$

This location usually isn't the optimal one for the Euclidean or rectilinear distance measures, but it still is an excellent starting point.

The analyst next evaluates locations in the vicinity of the center of gravity—say, one-half mile north, south, east, and west. If one or more of these locations has a load–distance score lower than the starting solution, the best one becomes the new starting solution. The analyst continues the process by searching in the near vicinity of this new starting solution. When further directional changes uncover no better solution, the current "starting solution" becomes the final solution. Patterned search has the advantage of speed but doesn't yield the added information that a full grid search does.

[†]As long as rectilinear distance is assumed, the optimal site can be found using the *cross-median* technique. See Fitzsimmons and Sullivan (1982) and Problem 23 at the end of this chapter.

What is the target area's center of gravity for the Health-Watch medical facility in Example 8.3?

Solution   To calculate the center of gravity, we begin with the information in the following table, where population is given in thousands.

Census Tract	(x, y)	Population (*l*)	*lx*	*ly*
A	(2.5, 4.5)	2	5	9
B	(2.5, 2.5)	5	12.5	12.5
C	(5.5, 4.5)	10	55	45
D	(5, 2)	7	35	14
E	(8, 5)	10	80	50
F	(7, 2)	20	140	40
G	(9, 2.5)	14	126	35
	Totals	68	453.5	205.5

Next we solve for x^* and y^*:

$$x^* = \frac{453.5}{68} = 6.67$$

$$y^* = \frac{205.5}{68} = 2.96$$

The center of gravity is (6.66, 2.96), which isn't necessarily optimal. It is in the general vicinity of location (7, 2), which was found to be best from the grid search in Fig. 8.4. Using the center of gravity as a starting point, we can now begin a patterned search in its vicinity.

Computer support simplifies the analysis still further. The following printout is CMOM output for the Health-Watch medical facility. The center of gravity is as before, and the output shows that its total *ld* score is 140. The computer also tested some 50,000 locations in the vicinity of the center of gravity to determine that (7, 2.25) is the optimal solution, with a total *ld* score of only 135.

```
        CMOM -- Location Analysis -- Load-Distance
                      Euclidean


                       Solution


                      X            Y
                  Coordinate   Coordinate   Load-Dist

Center of Gravity    6.67         2.96         140
Optimal              7            2.25         135
```

Using Break-Even Analysis

Break-even analysis (see Supplement A) can help a manager compare location alternatives on the basis of quantitative factors that can be expressed in terms of total cost. It is particularly useful when the manager wants to define the ranges over which each alternative is best. The basic steps for graphic and algebraic solutions are as follows.

1. Determine the variable costs and fixed costs for each site. Recall that *variable* costs are the portion of the total cost that varies directly with the volume of output. Recall that fixed costs are the portion of the total cost that remains constant regardless of output levels.
2. Plot the total cost lines—the sum of variable and fixed costs—for all the sites on a single graph.
3. Identify the approximate ranges for which each location has the lowest cost.
4. Solve algebraically for the break-even points over the relevant ranges.

EXAMPLE 8.5

Break-Even Analysis for Location

An operations manager has narrowed the search for a new facility location to four communities. The annual fixed costs (land, property taxes, insurance, equipment, and buildings) and the variable costs (labor, materials, transportation, and variable overhead) are

Community	Fixed Costs per Year	Variable Costs per Unit
A	$150,000	$62
B	$300,000	$38
C	$500,000	$24
D	$600,000	$30

a. Plot the total cost curves for all the communities on a single graph. Identify on the graph the approximate range over which each community provides the lowest cost.
b. Using break-even analysis, calculate the break-even quantities over the relevant ranges.
c. If the expected demand is 15,000 units per year, what is the best location?

Solution

a. To plot a community's total cost line, let's first compute the total cost for two output levels: $Q = 0$ and $Q = 20,000$ units per year. For the $Q = 0$ level, the total cost is simply the fixed costs. For the $Q = 20,000$ level, the total cost (fixed plus variable costs) is

Community	Fixed Costs	Variable Costs (Cost per unit)(No. of units)	Total Costs (Fixed + Variable)
A	$150,000	$62(20,000) = $1,240,000	$1,390,000
B	$300,000	$38(20,000) = $ 760,000	$1,060,000
C	$500,000	$24(20,000) = $ 480,000	$ 980,000
D	$600,000	$30(20,000) = $ 600,000	$1,200,000

Figure 8.5 shows the graph of the total cost lines. The line for Community A goes from (0, 150) to (20, 1390). The graph indicates that Community A is best for low volumes, B for intermediate volumes, and C for high volumes. We should no longer consider Community D, as both its fixed *and* its variable costs are higher than Community C's.

FIGURE 8.5   *Break-Even Analysis of Four Candidate Locations*

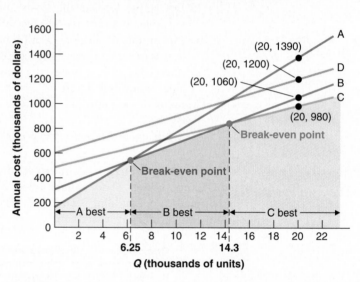

b. The break-even quantity between A and B lies at the end of the first range, where A is best, and the beginning of the second range, where B is best. We find it by setting their total cost equations equal to each other and solving:

$$\begin{array}{cc} \text{(A)} & \text{(B)} \\ \$150,000 + \$62Q & = \$300,000 + \$38Q \end{array}$$

$$Q = 6250 \text{ units}$$

The break-even quantity between B and C lies at the end of the range over which B is best and the beginning of the final range where C is best. It is

$$\begin{array}{cc} \text{(B)} & \text{(C)} \\ \$300,000 + \$38Q & = \$500,000 + \$24Q \end{array}$$

$$Q = 14,286 \text{ units}$$

No other break-even quantities are needed. The break-even point between A and C lies above the shaded area, which doesn't mark either the start or the end of one of the three relevant ranges.

c. The graph shows that 15,000 units lies in the high-volume range, so Community C is the best choice.

◆   LOCATING WITHIN A NETWORK OF FACILITIES

When a firm with a network of existing facilities plans a new facility, one of two conditions exists: Either the facilities operate independently (e.g., a chain of restaurants, health clinics, banks, or retail establishments) or the facilities interact (e.g., component manufacturing plants, assembly plants, and warehouses). Independently operating units can be located by treating each as a separate single facility, as described in the preceding section. Locating interacting facilities introduces new issues, such as how to allocate work between the facilities and how to determine the best capacity for each. Changing work allocations in turn affects the size (or capacity utilization) of the facilities. Thus the multiple-facility location problem has three dimensions—location, allocation, and capacity—that must be solved simultaneously. In many cases, the analyst can identify a workable solution merely by looking for patterns in the cost, demand, and capacity data and using trial-and-error calculations. In other cases, more formal approaches can help.

In manufacturing or distribution systems, management can choose the sources of demand (plants, warehouses, distributors, or retail outlets) that each new facility will serve. One approach is to divide the total market into regions, with a facility in each region. Dividing the market into regions determines each facility's capacity and work allocation: Each facility serves its region and must have enough capacity to do so. One goal of management may be to make all facilities similar in size to obtain economies of scale. The only remaining decision, then, concerns the specific location for each facility within its region. Single-facility location techniques, such as full grid search or patterned search, can be used for this purpose.

In service or retail systems, the customers often choose the facility that serves them. This condition requires a different approach to location, allocation, and capacity decisions. Using a simple trial-and-error approach, the analyst first selects some tentative facility locations. Making an assumption about how customers select specific locations and how sales might be affected by location proximity, the analyst obtains allocation and capacity estimates for each location. After evaluating the solutions obtained, the analyst can similarly test other reasonable locations.

The Transportation Method

What is the best way to partition work among various facilities?

The **transportation method** is a quantitative approach that can help solve multiple-facility location problems. We use it here to determine the allocation pattern that minimizes the cost of shipping products from two or more plants, or *sources of supply,* to two or more warehouses, or *destinations.*[*] The transportation method is described more fully in Supplement G.

The transportation method does not solve *all* facets of the multiple-facility location problem. It only finds the *best* shipping pattern between plants and warehouses for a particular set of plant locations, each with a given capacity. The analyst must try a variety of location–capacity combinations and use the transportation method to find the optimal distribution for each one. Distribution costs (variable shipping and possibly variable production costs) are but one important input in evaluating a particular location–allocation combination. Investment costs and other fixed costs also must be considered, along with various qualitative factors. This complete analysis must be made for each reasonable location–capacity combination. Because of the importance of making a good decision, this extra effort is well worth its cost.

---

[*]It can also be used to determine an optimal production plan (see Chapter 13) or an optimal allocation of service accounts to service centers.

Setting Up the Initial Tableau. Whether a transportation problem is to be solved manually or by computer, it first must be formatted in a standard matrix, sometimes called a *tableau*. The basic steps in setting up an initial tableau are as follows.

1. Create a row for each plant (existing or new) being considered and a column for each warehouse.
2. Add a column for plant capacities and a row for warehouse demands, and then insert their specific numerical values.
3. Insert the unit costs in the upper right-hand corner of each cell.

The Sunbelt Pool Company is considering building a new 500-unit plant, because business is booming. One possible location is Atlanta. Figure 8.6 shows a tableau with its plant capacity, warehouse requirements, and shipping costs. The tableau shows, for example, that shipping one unit from the existing Phoenix plant to warehouse 1 costs $5.00. Costs are assumed to increase linearly with the size of the shipment; that is, the cost is the same *per unit* regardless of the size of the total shipment.

In the transportation method, the sum of the shipments in a row must equal the corresponding plant's capacity. For example, in Fig. 8.6, the total shipments from the Atlanta plant to warehouses 1, 2, and 3 must add up to 500. Similarly, the sum of shipments to a column must equal the corresponding warehouse's demand requirements. For example, shipments to warehouse 1 from Phoenix and Atlanta must total 200 units. The transportation method also requires that the sum of the capacities equal the sum of the demands.*

FIGURE 8.6

Initial Tableau

Plant	Warehouse			Capacity
	1	2	3	
Phoenix	5.0	6.0	5.4	400
Atlanta	7.0	4.6	6.6	500
Requirements	200	400	300	900 / 900

Finding a Solution. After the initial tableau has been set up, the goal is to find the least-cost allocation pattern that satisfies all demands and exhausts all capacities. This pattern can be found by using the transportation method (see Supplement G). This method guarantees the optimal solution. The initial tableau is filled in with a feasible solution that satisfies all warehouse demands and exhausts all plant capacities. Then a new tableau is created, defining a new solution that has a lower total cost. This iterative process continues until no improve-

---

*In many real problems, the sums will be unequal. If so, we add either an extra row (a *dummy plant*) or an extra column (a *dummy warehouse*) to the tableau. This case of unbalanced capacities and demands is discussed more fully in Supplement G. Some software packages automatically add the dummy row or column.

ments can be made in the current solution, signaling that the optimal solution has been found. Solution with a computer package, which performs the calculations for you, is an efficient option. All that must be input is the information for the initial tableau. This option is best utilized when the problem is large, with many plants and warehouses.

Whatever the solution method, the number of nonzero shipments in the optimal solution will never exceed the sum of the numbers of plants and warehouses minus 1. The Sunbelt Pool Company has 2 plants and 3 warehouses, so there need not be more than 4 (or $3 + 2 - 1$) shipments in the optimal solution.

EXAMPLE 8.6	The following printout is CMOM output for the Sunbelt Pool Company. Verify
Interpreting the Optimal Solution	that each plant's capacity is exhausted and that each warehouse's demand is filled. Also confirm that the total transportation cost of the solution is $4580.

Data Entered

Number of Columns: 3

Number of Rows   :   2

Model

	W1	W2	W3	CAP
PHOEN	5	6	5.4	400
ATLAN	7	4.6	6.6	500
REQTS	200	400	300	900

Solution

	W1	W2	W3	CAP
PHOEN	200	0	200	400
ATLAN	0	400	100	500
REQTS	200	400	300	900

Total Payoff :   4580

Solution   Phoenix ships 200 units to warehouse 1 and 200 units to warehouse 3, exhausting its 400-unit capacity. Atlanta ships 400 units of its 500-unit capacity to warehouse 2 and the remaining 100 units to warehouse 3. All warehouse demand is satisfied: Warehouse 1 is fully supplied by Phoenix and warehouse 2 by Atlanta. Warehouse 3 receives 200 units from Phoenix and 100 units from Atlanta, satisfying its 300-unit demand. The total transportation cost is $200(\$5.00) + 200(\$5.40) + 400(\$4.60) + 100(\$6.60) = \$4580$.

The Larger Solution Process.   The optimal solution in Example 8.6 doesn't necessarily mean that the best choice is to open an Atlanta plant. It just means that the best allocation pattern for the current choices on the other two dimensions of this multiple-facility location problem (i.e., a capacity of 400 units at Phoenix and the new plant's location at Atlanta) results in total *transportation* costs of $4580. Other costs and various qualitative factors also must be considered as additional parts of a complete evaluation. For example, the annual profits earned from the expansion must be balanced against the land and construction costs of a new plant in Atlanta. Thus management might use the preference matrix approach (see Example 8.1) to account for the full set of location factors.

The analyst should also evaluate other capacity and location combinations. For example, one possibility is to expand at Phoenix and build a smaller plant at Atlanta. Alternatively, a new plant could be built at another location, or several new plants could be built. The analyst must repeat the analysis for each such likely location strategy.

Other Methods of Location Analysis

Many location analysis problems are even more complex than those discussed so far. Consider the complexity that a medium-sized manufacturer faces when distributing products through warehouses, or *distribution centers,* to various demand centers. The problem is to determine the number, size, allocation pattern, and location of the warehouses. There could be thousands of demand centers, hundreds of potential warehouse locations, several plants, and multiple product lines. Transportation rates depend on the direction of shipment, product, quantity, rate breaks, and geographic area.

Such complexity requires use of a computer for a comprehensive evaluation. Three basic types of computer models have been developed for this purpose: heuristic, simulation, and optimization.

Heuristics.   Solution guidelines, or rules of thumb, that find feasible—but not necessarily the best—solutions to problems are called **heuristics.** Their advantages include efficiency and an ability to handle general views of a problem. The patterned search procedure described earlier for single-facility location problems is a typical heuristic procedure. One of the first heuristics to be computerized for location problems was proposed more than three decades ago to handle several hundred potential warehouse sites and several thousand demand centers (Kuehn and Hamburger, 1963). Many other heuristic models are available today for analyzing a variety of situations.

Simulation.   A modeling technique that reproduces the behavior of a system is called **simulation.** Discussed in greater detail in Supplement F, simulation allows manipulation of certain variables and shows the effect on selected operating characteristics. Simulation models allow the analyst to evaluate different location alternatives by trial and error. It is up to the analyst to propose the most reasonable alternatives. Simulation handles more realistic views of a problem and involves the analyst in the solution process itself. For each run, the analyst inputs the facilities to be opened, and the simulator typically makes the allocation decisions based on some reasonable assumptions that have been written into the computer program. The Ralston Purina Company used simulation to assist in locating warehouses to serve 137 demand centers, 5 field warehouses, and 4 plants. Random demand at each demand center by product type was simulated over a period of time. Demand was met by the closest warehouse having available inventory. Data were produced by simulating inventory levels, transportation costs, warehouse operating costs, and backorders. Ralston-Purina implemented the result of the simulation, which showed that the least-cost alternative would be to consolidate the five field warehouses into only three.

Optimization. The transportation method was one of the first optimization procedures for solving one part (the allocation pattern) of multiple-facility location problems. In contrast to heuristics and simulation, **optimization** involves procedures to determine the "best" solution. Even though this approach might appear to be preferable, it has a limitation, because optimization procedures generally utilize simplified and less realistic views of a problem. However, the payoffs can be substantial. Hunt-Wesson Foods applied optimization techniques to the company's network. As a result of the analysis, five changes were made, reportedly saving millions of dollars.

CHAPTER REVIEW

Solved Problem 1

An electronics manufacturer must expand by building a second facility. The search has been narrowed to four locations, all acceptable to management in terms of dominant factors. Assessment of these sites in terms of seven location factors is shown in Table 8.1. For example, location A has a factor score of 5 (excellent) for labor climate; the weight for this factor (20) is the highest of any.

TABLE 8.1 *Factor Information for Electronics Manufacturer*

		Factor Score for Each Location			
Location Factor	Factor Weight	A	B	C	D
1. Labor climate	20	5	4	4	5
2. Quality of life	16	2	3	4	1
3. Transportation system	16	3	4	3	2
4. Proximity to markets	14	5	3	4	4
5. Proximity to materials	12	2	3	3	4
6. Taxes	12	2	5	5	4
7. Utilities	10	5	4	3	3

Calculate the weighted score for each location. Which location should be recommended?

Solution Based on the weighted scores in Table 8.2, location C is the preferred site, although location B is a close second.

TABLE 8.2   *Calculating Weighted Scores for Electronics Manufacturer*

		Weighted Score for Each Location			
Location Factor	Factor Weight	A	B	C	D
1. Labor climate	20	100	80	80	100
2. Quality of life	16	32	48	64	16
3. Transportation system	16	48	64	48	32
4. Proximity to markets	14	70	42	56	56
5. Proximity to materials	12	24	36	36	48
6. Taxes	12	24	60	60	48
7. Utilities	10	50	40	30	30
Totals	100	348	370	374	330

Solved Problem 2

The operations manager for Mile-High Beer has narrowed the search for a new facility location to seven communities. Annual fixed costs (land, property taxes, insurance, equipment, and buildings) and variable costs (labor, materials, transportation, and variable overhead) are shown in Table 8.3.

TABLE 8.3   *Fixed and Variable Costs for the Mile-High Beer*

Community	Fixed Costs per Year	Variable Costs per Barrel
Aurora	$1,600,000	$17.00
Boulder	$2,000,000	$12.00
Colorado Springs	$1,500,000	$16.00
Denver	$3,000,000	$10.00
Englewood	$1,800,000	$15.00
Fort Collins	$1,200,000	$15.00
Golden	$1,700,000	$14.00

a. Which of the communities can be eliminated from further consideration because they are dominated (both variable and fixed costs are higher) by another community?

b. Plot the total cost curves for all remaining communities on a single graph. Identify on the graph the approximate range over which each community provides the lowest cost.

c. Using break-even analysis (see Supplement A), calculate the break-even quantities to determine the range over which each community provides the lowest cost.

Solution   a. Aurora and Colorado Springs are dominated by Fort Collins, as both fixed and variable costs are higher for those communities than for Fort Collins. Englewood is dominated by Golden.

b. Figure 8.7 shows that Fort Collins is best for low volumes, Boulder for intermediate volumes, and Denver for high volumes. Although Golden isn't dominated by any community, it is the second or third choice over the entire range. Golden doesn't become the lowest cost choice at any volume.

FIGURE 8.7

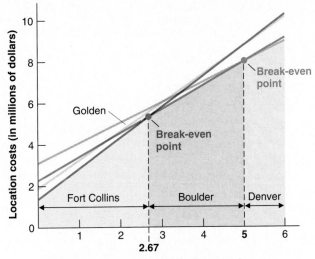

Barrels of beer per year (in hundred thousands)

c. The break-even point between Fort Collins and Boulder is

$$\$1,200,000 + \$15Q = \$2,000,000 + \$12Q$$

$$Q = 266,667 \text{ barrels per year}$$

The break-even point between Denver and Boulder is

$$\$3,000,000 + \$10Q = \$2,000,000 + \$12Q$$

$$Q = 500,000 \text{ barrels per year}$$

Solved Problem 3

A supplier to the electric utility industry has a heavy product, and transportation costs are high. One market area includes the lower part of the Great Lakes region and the upper portion of the Southeastern region. More than 600,000 tons are to be shipped to eight major customer locations, as shown in Table 8.4.

TABLE 8.4 *Markets for Electric Utilities Supplier*

Customer Location	Tons Shipped	*xy*-Coordinates
Three Rivers, Mich.	5,000	(7, 13)
Fort Wayne, Ind.	92,000	(8, 12)
Columbus, Ohio	70,000	(11, 10)
Ashland, Ky.	35,000	(11, 7)
Kingsport, Tenn.	9,000	(12, 4)
Akron, Ohio	227,000	(13, 11)
Wheeling, W.V.	16,000	(14, 10)
Roanoke, Va.	153,000	(15, 5)

a. Calculate the center of gravity, rounding distance to the nearest tenth.
b. Calculate the load–distance score for this location, using rectilinear distance.

Solution   a. The center of gravity is (12.4, 9.2).

$$\sum_i l_i = 5 + 92 + 70 + 35 + 9 + 227 + 16 + 153 = 607$$

$$\sum_i l_i x_i = 5(7) + 92(8) + 70(11) + 35(11) + 9(12) + 227(13) + 16(14) + 153(15)$$

$$= 7504$$

$$x^* = \frac{\sum_i l_i x_i}{\sum_i l_i} = \frac{7504}{607} = 12.4$$

$$\sum_i l_i y_i = 5(13) + 92(12) + 70(10) + 35(7) + 9(4) + 227(11) + 16(10) + 153(5) = 5572$$

$$y^* = \frac{\sum_i l_i y_i}{\sum_i l_i} = \frac{5572}{607} = 9.2$$

b. The load–distance score is

$$ld = \sum_i l_i d_i = 5(5.4 + 3.8) + 92(4.4 + 2.8) + 70(1.4 + 0.8) + 35(1.4 + 2.2)$$
$$+ 9(0.4 + 5.2) + 227(0.6 + 1.8) + 16(1.6 + 0.8) + 153(2.6 + 4.2)$$
$$= 2662.4$$

where $d_i = |x_i - x^*| + |y_i - y^*|$

Solved Problem 4

The Arid Company makes canoe paddles to serve distribution centers in Worchester, Rochester, and Dorchester from existing plants in Battle Creek and Cherry Creek. Annual demand is expected to increase as projected in the bottom row of the tableau shown in Fig. 8.8. Arid is considering locating a plant near the headwaters of Dee Creek. Annual capacity for each plant is shown in the right column of the tableau. Transportation costs per paddle are shown in the tableau in the small boxes. For example, the cost to ship one paddle from Battle Creek to Worchester is $4.37. The optimal allocations are also shown. For example, Battle Creek ships 12,000 units to Rochester. What are the estimated transportation costs associated with this allocation pattern?

FIGURE 8.8

Source	Destination			Capacity
	Worchester	Rochester	Dorchester	
Battle Creek	$4.37	$4.25 / 12,000	$4.89	12,000
Cherry Creek	$4.00 / 6,000	$5.00 / 4,000	$5.27	10,000
Dee Creek	$4.13	$4.50 / 6,000	$3.75 / 12,000	18,000
Demand	6,000	22,000	12,000	40,000

Solution   The total cost is $167,000.

Ship 12,000 units from Battle Creek to Rochester @ $4.25.	Cost = $51,000
Ship 6,000 units from Cherry Creek to Worchester @ $4.00.	Cost = $24,000
Ship 4,000 units from Cherry Creek to Rochester @ $5.00.	Cost = $20,000
Ship 6,000 units from Dee Creek to Rochester @ $4.50.	Cost = $27,000
Ship 12,000 units from Dee Creek to Dorchester @ $3.75.	Cost = $45,000
	Total $167,000

Formula Review

1. Euclidean distance: $d_{AB} = \sqrt{(x_A - x_B)^2 + (y_A - y_B)^2}$

2. Rectilinear distance: $d_{AB} = |x_A - x_B| + |y_A - y_B|$

3. Load–distance score: $ld = \sum_i l_i d_i$

4. Center of gravity: $x^* = \dfrac{\sum_i l_i x_i}{\sum_i l_i}$ and $y^* = \dfrac{\sum_i l_i y_i}{\sum_i l_i}$

Chapter Highlights

- The globalization of operations affects both manufacturing and service industries. More facilities are being located in other countries, and offshore sales (and imports) are increasing. Four factors that spur globalization are improved transportation and communications technologies, opened financial systems, increased demand for imports, and fewer import quotas and other trade barriers. Offsetting the advantages of global operations are differences in language, regulations, and culture that create new management problems.

- Location decisions depend on many factors. For any situation some factors may be disregarded entirely; the remainder may be divided into dominant and secondary factors.

- Favorable labor climate, proximity to markets, quality of life, proximity to suppliers and resources, and proximity to other company facilities are important factors in most manufacturing plant location decisions. Proximity to markets, clients, or customers usually is the most important factor in service industry location decisions. Competition is a complicating factor in estimating the sales potential of a location. Having competitors' facilities nearby may be an asset or a liability, depending on the type of business.

- One way of evaluating qualitative factors is to calculate a weighted score for each alternative location by using the preference matrix approach. The load–distance method brings together concerns of proximity (to markets, suppliers, resources, and other company facilities) during the early stages of location analysis. By making a full grid or patterned search of an area, an analyst identifies locations resulting in lower *ld* scores. The center of gravity of an area is a good starting point for making a patterned search. Break-even analysis can help compare location alternatives when location factors can be expressed in terms of variable and fixed costs.

- Multiple-facility problems have three dimensions: location, allocation, and capacity. In manufacturing or distribution systems, trial-and-error methods begin with a proposed allocation and capacity plan. Preferred locations can then be determined by using single-facility techniques. In services, customers often choose the facility that serves them. In that case, trial-and-error methods begin with a proposed set of multiple-facility locations, followed by allocation and capacity estimates for each location.

- The transportation method is a basic tool for finding the best allocation pattern for a particular combination of location–capacity choices. Transportation costs are recalculated for each location–capacity combination under consideration. The transportation method's single criterion for determining the best shipping pattern is minimum transportation costs. To complete the location study, the analysis must be expanded to account for the full set of location factors.

- Location analysis can become complex for multiple facilities. A variety of computerized heuristic, simulation, and optimization models have been developed over the last two decades to help analysts deal with this complexity.

Key Terms

center of gravity *355*

critical mass *349*

Euclidean distance *352*

facility location *346*

globalization *338*

heuristics *362*

load–distance method *351*

maquiladoras *340*

optimization *363*

quality of life *347*

rectilinear distance *352*

simulation *362*

transportation method *359*

Study Questions

1. What factors have expanded the range of possible locations?

2. Where is international activity particularly evident in the world today?

3. Why does an overseas location confront a manager with a different set of problems?

4. Some observers say that maquiladoras allow U.S. companies to have their unskilled jobs done across the border while preserving the jobs of their skilled and knowledgeable workers in the United States. What ethical issues, if any, are involved with this use of maquiladoras?

5. Describe briefly the dominant factors in plant location, and identify a business for which each would be crucial.

6. Which location factor is particularly important to service industries? How is it related to competitors' locations?

7. What are the advantages of building another plant versus expanding on site?

8. Under what conditions does a firm usually choose to relocate rather than expand on site?

9. An automobile manufacturer is considering closing its current large facility in a rustbelt city, which has strong unions, high wages, high taxes, severe winters, a decaying urban infrastructure, and stringent environmental regulations, and relocating to a rural area in the sunbelt, which has advantages in all the factors mentioned. What obligations, if any, does the manufacturer have to the city in which its facility is presently located?

10. A major league baseball owner is considering moving his team from its current city in the rustbelt to a city in the sunbelt. The sunbelt city offers a larger television market and a new stadium and holds the potential for greater fan support. What ethical obligations, if any, does the owner have to the city in which the team is presently located?

11. Describe the conditions under which the use of each of the following tools for facility location decisions would be appropriate: preference matrix, break-even analysis, transportation method, heuristics, and simulation.

12. "Euclidean and rectilinear distances differ. Furthermore, neither is correct in terms of actual distance. Therefore neither should be used for location analysis." Comment on this statement.

13. A full grid search is less efficient than a patterned search but may be preferable. Why?

14. At what point does a multiple-facility location problem break down into several single-facility location problems?

15. Why does the trial-and-error solution method for a multiple-facility problem depend on whether it is the customer or the producer who decides how the work is to be allocated?

16. What are the advantages and disadvantages of heuristic, simulation, and optimization computer models for multiple-facility location analysis?

17. "The transportation method is an optimization technique, but becomes part of a heuristic when applied to the multiple-facility location problem." Explain this statement.

Problems

1. Calculate the weighted score for each location (A, B, C, and D) shown in Table 8.5. Which location would you recommend?

2. John and Marcia Darling are newlyweds trying to decide among several available rentals. Alternatives were scored on a scale of 1 to 5 (5 = best) against weighted performance criteria, as shown in Table 8.6. The criteria included rent, proximity to work and recreational opportunities, security, and other neighborhood characteristics associated with the couple's values and lifestyle. Alternative A is an apartment, B is a bungalow, C is a condo, and D is a downstairs apartment in Marcia's parents' home.

   Which location is indicated by the preference matrix? What qualitative factors might cause this preference to change?

TABLE 8.5 *Factors for Locations A–D*

Location Factor	Factor Weight	Factor Score for Each Location			
		A	B	C	D
1. Labor climate	5	5	4	3	5
2. Quality of life	30	2	3	5	1
3. Transportation system	5	3	4	3	5
4. Proximity to markets	25	5	3	4	4
5. Proximity to materials	5	3	2	3	5
6. Taxes	15	2	5	5	4
7. Utilities	15	5	4	2	1
Total	100				

TABLE 8.6 *Factors for Newlyweds*

Location Factor	Factor Weight	Factor Score for Each Location			
		A	B	C	D
1. Rent	25	3	1	2	5
2. Quality of life	20	2	5	5	4
3. Schools	5	3	5	3	1
4. Proximity to work	10	5	3	4	3
5. Proximity to recreation	15	4	4	5	2
6. Neighborhood security	15	2	4	4	4
7. Utilities	10	4	2	3	5
Total	100				

3. Two alternative locations are under consideration for a new plant: Knoxville, Tennessee, and Dayton, Ohio. The Knoxville location is superior in terms of costs. However, management believes that sales volume would decline if this location were chosen, because it is farther from the market and the firm's customers prefer local suppliers. The selling price of the product is $200 per unit in either case. Use the following information to answer the questions below.

Location	Annual Fixed Cost	Variable Cost per Unit	Forecast Demand per Year
Knoxville	$1,800,000	$60	25,000 units
Dayton	$2,400,000	$85	30,000 units

Determine which location yields the higher total profit contribution per year.

4. Fall-Line, Inc. is a Great Falls, Montana, manufacturer of a variety of downhill skis. Fall-Line is considering four locations for a new plant: Aspen, Colorado; Medicine Lodge, Kansas; Broken Bow, Nebraska; and Wounded Knee, South Dakota. Annual fixed costs and variable costs per pair of skis are shown in the following table.

Location	Annual Fixed Costs	Variable Costs per Pair
Aspen	$8,000,000	$250
Medicine Lodge	$2,400,000	$130
Broken Bow	$3,400,000	$ 90
Wounded Knee	$4,500,000	$ 65

a. Plot the total cost curves for all the communities on a single graph (see Solved Problem 2). Identify on the graph the range in volume over which each location would be best.

b. What break-even quantity defines each range?

Although Aspen's fixed and variable costs are dominated by those of the other communities, Fall-Line believes that both the demand and the price would be higher for skis made in Aspen than for skis made in the other locations. The following table shows those projections.

Location	Price per Pair	Forecast Demand per Year
Aspen	$500	60,000 pairs
Medicine Lodge	$350	45,000 pairs
Broken Bow	$350	43,000 pairs
Wounded Knee	$350	40,000 pairs

c. Determine which location yields the highest total profit contribution per year.

d. Is this location decision sensitive to forecast accuracy? At what minimum sales volume does Aspen become the location of choice?

5. Wiebe Trucking, Inc. is planning a new warehouse to serve the West. Denver, Santa Fe, and Salt Lake City are under consideration. For each location, annual fixed costs (rent, equipment, and insurance) and average variable costs per shipment (labor, transportation, and utilities) are listed in the following table. Sales projections range from 450,000 to 600,000 shipments per year.

Location	Annual Fixed Costs	Variable Costs per Shipment
Denver	$4,000,000	$6.25
Santa Fe	$4,300,000	$5.50
Salt Lake City	$3,800,000	$7.25

a. Plot the total cost curves for all the locations on a single graph.

b. Which city provides the lowest overall costs?

6. The operations manager for Hot House Roses has narrowed the search for a new facility location to seven communities. Annual fixed costs (land, property taxes, insurance, equipment, and buildings) and variable costs (labor, materials, transportation, and variable overhead) are shown in the following table.

Community	Fixed Costs per Year	Variable Costs per Dozen
Aurora, Colo.	$210,000	$7.20
Flora, Ill.	$200,000	$7.00
Garden City, Kan.	$150,000	$9.00
Greensboro, N.C.	$280,000	$6.20
Roseland, La.	$260,000	$6.00
Sunnyvale, Calif.	$420,000	$5.00
Watertown, Mass.	$370,000	$8.00

a. Which of the communities can be eliminated from further consideration because they are dominated (both variable and fixed costs are higher) by another community?

b. Plot the total cost curves for the remaining communities on a single graph. Identify on the graph the approximate range over which each community provides the lowest cost.

c. Using break-even analysis (see Supplement A), calculate the break-even quantities to determine the range over which each community provides the lowest cost.

7. Ethel and Earl Griese narrowed their choice for a new oil refinery to three locations. Fixed and variable costs are as follows.

Location	Fixed Costs per Year	Variable Costs per Unit
Albany	$ 350,000	$980
Baltimore	$1,500,500	$240
Chattanooga	$1,100,000	$500

a. Plot the total cost curves for all the communities on a single graph. Identify on the graph the range in volume over which each location would be best.

b. What break-even quantities define each range?

8. Excel Foods is planning a new warehouse to serve the Midwest. St. Louis, Chicago, and Cincinnati are under consideration. For each location, the annual fixed costs (rent, equipment, and insurance) and the variable costs (labor, transportation, and utilities) are

listed. Sales projections indicate that the market will be between 250,000 and 450,000 units per year.

Location	Fixed Costs	Variable Costs per Unit
Chicago	$3,500,000	$8.35
Cincinnati	$3,350,000	$8.25
St. Louis	$3,425,000	$8.60

a. Plot the total cost curves for all the locations on a single graph.

b. Which city provides the lowest overall costs?

9. The following three points are the locations of important facilities in a transportation network: (10, 20), (20, 40), and (50, 0). The coordinates are in miles.

a. Calculate the Euclidean distances (in miles) between each of the three pairs of facilities.

b. Calculate these distances using rectilinear distances.

10. The following three points are the locations of important facilities in a transportation network: (20, 20), (50, 10), and (50, 60). The coordinates are in miles.

a. Calculate the Euclidean distances (in miles) between each of the three pairs of facilities.

b. Calculate these distances using rectilinear distances.

11. Centura High School is to be located at the population center of gravity of three communities: Boelus, population 228; Cairo, population 737; and Dannebrog, population 356. The coordinates (on a grid of square miles) for the communities are provided in Fig. 8.9. Where should Centura High School be located? (Round to 0.1 mile.) What factors may result in locating at the site indicated by this technique?

FIGURE 8.9

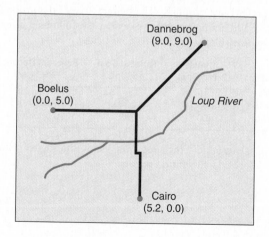

12. Val's Pizza is looking for a single central location to make pizza for delivery only. This college town is arranged on a grid with arterial streets as shown in Fig. 8.10. The main campus, located at point A in the grid at 14th and R streets, is the source of 4000 pizza orders per week. Three smaller campuses are located at 52nd and V, at 67th and Z, and at 70th and South. Orders from the smaller campuses average 1000 pizzas a week. In addition, the State Patrol headquarters at 10th and A orders 500 pizzas per week.

FIGURE 8.10

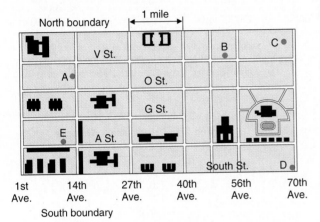

a. At about what intersection should Val start looking for a suitable site? (Estimate coordinates for the major demands accurate to the nearest ¼ mile, and then find the center of gravity.)

b. What is the rectilinear weekly load–distance score for this location?

c. If the delivery person can travel 1 mile in two minutes on arterial streets and ¼ mile per minute on residential streets, going from the center of gravity location to the farthest demand location will take how long?

13. The best location found manually so far for Fig. 8.4 was (7, 2), with a load–distance score of 168. Search in the neighborhood of this point for a better solution. Using rectilinear distances, try (6.5, 2), (7, 2.5), and (7, 1.5).

14. Reconsider Solved Problem 3, evaluating the four points that are one unit of distance north, east, south, and west of the center of gravity. Use rectilinear distances. Does this limited pattern search yield a better solution?

15. A larger and more modern main post office is to be constructed at a new location in Davis, California. Growing suburbs have shifted the population density from where it was 40 years ago, when the current facility was built. Annette Werk, the postmaster, asked her assistants to draw a grid map of the seven points where mail is picked up and delivered in bulk. The coordinates and trips per day to and from the seven mail source points and the current main post office, M, are shown in the following table. M will continue to act as a mail source point after relocation.

Mail Source Point	Round Trips per Day (*l*)	*xy*-Coordinates (miles)
1	6	(2, 8)
2	3	(6, 1)
3	3	(8, 5)
4	3	(13, 3)
5	2	(15, 10)
6	7	(6, 14)
7	5	(18, 1)
M	3	(10, 3)

a. Calculate the center of gravity as a possible location for the new facility (round to the nearest whole number).

b. Compare the load–distance scores for the location in part a and the current location, using rectilinear distance.

16. Paramount Manufacturing is investigating which location would best position its new plant relative to two suppliers (located in cities A and B) and one market area (represented by city C). Management has limited the search for this plant to those three locations. The following information has been collected.

Location	*xy*-Coordinates (miles)	Tons per Year	Freight Rate ($/ton-mile)
A	(100, 200)	4,000	3
B	(400, 100)	3,000	1
C	(100, 100)	4,000	3

a. Which of the three locations gives the lowest total cost, based on Euclidean distances? *Hint:* The annual cost of inbound shipments from supplier A to the new plant is $12,000 per mile (4000 tons per year × $3 per ton-mile).

b. Which location is best, based on rectilinear distances?

c. What are the coordinates of the center of gravity?

17. A personal computer manufacturer plans to locate its assembly plant in Taiwan and to ship its computers back to the United States through either Los Angeles or San Francisco. It has distribution centers in

TABLE 8.7   *Distances and Costs for PC Manufacturer*

		Distribution Center (units/year)		
		Chicago (10,000)	*Atlanta* (7500)	*New York* (12,500)
Port of Entry	Los Angeles			
	Distance (miles)	1800	2600	3200
	Shipping cost ($/unit)	0.0017/mile	0.0017/mile	0.0017/mile
	San Francisco			
	Distance (miles)	1700	2800	3000
	Shipping cost ($/unit)	0.0020/mile	0.0020/mile	0.0020/mile

Atlanta, New York, and Chicago and will ship to them from whichever city is chosen as the port of entry on the West Coast. Overall transportation cost is the only criterion for choosing the port. Use the load–distance model and the information in Table 8.7 to select the more cost-effective city.

Advanced Problems

Use a computer package, such as CMOM, to help solve Problems 24–28.

18. Suppose that two medical facilities, rather than one, are to serve the census tracts shown in Fig. 8.3. One option is to build them at locations C and G.
    a. Assuming that the patients in each tract will go to the nearest facility, determine how much capacity each facility needs (in terms of total population served). Are the capacities well balanced?
    b. What is the total load–distance score for this solution, based on rectilinear distance?
19. Reconsidering Problem 18, use trial and error to find a better solution than opening medical facilities at locations C and G. Limit your search to locations B, C, D, and G, and continue to use rectilinear distance.
    a. What is the total load–distance score of your improved solution?
    b. How much capacity is needed at each medical facility in your solution?
20. A different option is being considered for building two medical facilities, rather than one, to serve the census tracts shown in Fig. 8.3. Facility 1 would serve the western area (census tracts A, B, C, and D) and facility 2 the eastern area (census tracts E, F, and G).
    a. Use the center of gravity to find locations for the two facilities (round to the nearest tenth).
    b. How much capacity does each facility need (in terms of total population served)? Are the capacities well balanced?
    c. What is the total load–distance score for this solution, based on rectilinear distance?

21. Management wants to locate two facilities to serve two groups of demand points. The following data were collected.

Demand Point	xy-Coordinates (miles)	Trips per Day (*l*)
A	(0, 10)	10
B	(15, 30)	15
C	(20, 15)	20
D	(30, 30)	30
E	(40, 45)	15

   a. Draw a grid map showing the locations of the demand points.
   b. Divide the points into two groups, north and south. The north facility will serve B, D, and E, whereas the south facility will serve A and C. Let the facility locations be the centers of gravity of the two areas, rounded to the nearest whole numbers. What is the total load–distance score for the entire system, based on Euclidean distance?
   c. Repeat part b for an east–west division. The west facility will serve A, B, and C, and the east facility will serve D and E. Is this solution better or worse than the one in part b?
22. PG Oil Company plans to open two new filling stations in a region encompassing population centers A through H. The objective is to maximize proximity to population centers. It is assumed that customers will go to the nearest available facility. A map of the area is shown in Fig. 8.11. The numbers are the actual distances between centers. Locations B and F are highway intersections, rather than population centers. Population densities and distances between each pair of points are given in Table 8.8. For example, the shortest distance from A to E (and vice versa) is 62.

FIGURE 8.11

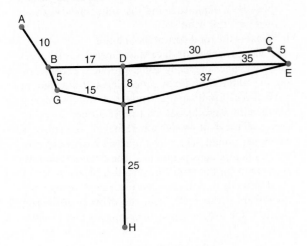

the median value calculated in part a. Identify the facility that corresponds to the last load that entered the sum. Its x-coordinate is optimal for the new facility.

c. Repeat part b, except order the facilities by *y*-coordinate, from smallest to largest. The *y*-coordinate of the facility corresponding to the last load entering the sum is optimal for the new facility.

d. How does the optimal solution compare with the best location shown in Fig. 8.4 in terms of the load–distance score?

24. The operations manager of Immediate Access Health Care, Inc. wants to locate a new emergency response facility in Fresno, California. She divided the city into 12 zones and estimated the number of emergency responses per day per zone. The zone coordinates (x, y) and load factors are as follows.

Zone	(x, y)	Load	Zone	(x, y)	Load
11	(0.5, 0.5)	20	23	(1.5, 2.5)	11
12	(0.5, 1.5)	15	24	(1.5, 3.5)	7
13	(0.5, 2.5)	22	31	(2.5, 0.5)	18
14	(0.5, 3.5)	12	32	(2.5, 1.5)	25
21	(1.5, 0.5)	9	33	(2.5, 2.5)	20
22	(1.5, 1.5)	4	34	(2.5, 3.5)	17

a. What is the center of gravity?

b. Which coordinates minimize the *ld* score, based on Euclidean distances?

c. Which coordinates minimize the *ld* score, based on rectilinear distances?

d. Which location would you recommend to the manager?

e. What is the impact on the optimal location (based on coordinates) if the load for zone 11 is doubled?

25. The Pelican Company has four distribution centers (A, B, C, and D) that require 50,000, 40,000, 60,000, and 40,000 gallons of diesel fuel, respectively, per month for their long-haul trucks. Three fuel wholesalers (1, 2, and 3) have indicated their willingness to supply up to 60,000, 80,000, and 50,000 gallons of fuel, respectively. The total cost (shipping plus price) of delivering 1000 gallons of fuel from each wholesaler to each distribution center is shown in the following table.

| Wholesaler | Distribution Center | | | |
	A	B	C	D
1	1.70	1.60	1.60	1.60
2	1.50	1.80	1.60	1.70
3	1.80	1.50	1.80	1.60

TABLE 8.8 *Data for PG Oil Company*

| From | To | | | | | | | | Population Density |
	A	B	C	D	E	F	G	H	
A	—	10	57	27	62	30	15	55	5
B	10	—	47	17	52	20	5	45	0
C	57	47	—	30	5	38	52	63	10
D	27	17	30	—	35	8	22	33	20
E	62	52	5	35	—	37	52	62	20
F	30	20	38	8	37	—	15	25	0
G	15	5	52	22	52	15	—	40	4
H	55	45	63	33	62	25	40	—	20

a. Management wants to limit consideration to these eight points and is giving particular attention to a plan for locating facilities at C and H. Calculate the total load–distance score for this plan.

b. Try at least one other plan that you think might improve on this score.

23. Continuing to assume rectilinear distance, use the cross-median technique (see the footnote on page 355) to find the optimal location for the problem in Example 8.3.

a. First calculate the median value, which is one-half the sum of the loads to all facilities.

b. Order the facilities by *x*-coordinate, starting with the facility having the smallest and ending with the one having the largest. Maintaining this order, add the facility loads until the total reaches or exceeds

a. Set up the initial tableau for this transportation problem.

b. Determine the optimal solution. Show that all capacities have been exhausted and that all demands can be met with this solution.

c. What is the total cost of the solution?

26. The Acme Company has four factories that ship products to five warehouses. The shipping costs, requirements, and capacities are shown in Fig. 8.12.

FIGURE 8.12

Factory	Shipping Cost per Case to Warehouse					Capacity
	W1	W2	W3	W4	W5	
F1	$1	$3	$4	$5	$6	80,000
F2	$2	$2	$1	$4	$5	60,000
F3	$1	$5	$1	$3	$1	60,000
F4	$5	$2	$4	$5	$4	50,000
Demand	60,000	70,000	50,000	30,000	40,000	250,000

a. Find the optimal solution. Show that all capacities have been exhausted and that all demands can be met with this solution.

b. What is the total cost of the solution?

27. The Summit Company has three warehouses that ship products to five retail outlets. The shipping costs, requirements, and capacities are shown in Fig. 8.13.

FIGURE 8.13

Warehouse	Shipping Cost per Case to Retail					Capacity
	R1	R2	R3	R4	R5	
W1	$4	$3	$1	$5	$6	60,000
W2	$2	$2	$3	$4	$5	30,000
W3	$1	$5	$1	$3	$2	50,000
Demand	20,000	30,000	40,000	10,000	40,000	140,000

a. Find the optimal solution. Show that all capacities have been exhausted and that all demands can be met with this solution.

b. What is the total cost of the solution?

28. The vice-president of JavaMart International, a regional supplier of trendy coffee products, is considering the addition of a new processing and distribution facility. The company currently has two processing plants with a production cost of $2.50 per pound of coffee. The cost of production at the proposed plant is $2.00 per pound. The new plant will have a capacity of 5 million pounds per month. The estimated monthly demand (in thousands of pounds), plant capacities (in thousands of pounds), and per unit shipping costs (in dollars per pound) from the existing processing plants to the five wholesale operators are given below.

	Wholesale Outlet					
	1	2	3	4	5	Capacity
Plant 1	0.50	0.75	0.90	1.10	1.25	2000
Plant 2	0.80	0.45	1.15	0.80	1.00	4000
Demand	1500	750	2000	500	750	

a. What are the optimal total operating cost and transportation schedule for the existing system?

b. If the transportation costs from the new plant to the five wholesale outlets are $1.10, $0.75, $0.90, $0.55, and $0.65, respectively, how much can operating costs be reduced?

c. Which one of the existing plants should be closed if the new plant is built?

d. What would be the impact on the optimal solution if the demand by wholesale outlets 2 and 4 each increased by 1 million pounds per month?

C A S E

Imaginative Toys

When Gerald Kramb arrived at the company offices early on Monday, July 1, 1991 to review the end-of-the-year sales and operating figures, several pressing matters commanded his attention. Sales had been much stronger than projected in 1990–1991, and existing production capacity had been fully utilized, with excessive overtime, to meet demand. Sales forecasts for the coming year indicated further rapid growth in demand, and Kramb knew that added capacity was needed. Several alternatives were available to the company, and he wanted to be sure that all the key factors were considered in making the decision.

Imaginative Toys was founded in Seattle, Washington, in 1975. When he founded the company, Gerald Kramb envisioned that Imaginative Toys would develop and produce toys that "reach children's imagination and bring out their creativity." He liked to call these toys "learning toys." Two product lines quickly emerged as the mainstays of the company: construction toys that were similar to Lincoln Logs and Legos and maze and mind toys that focused on solving puzzles and developing hand–eye coordination. The toys were quickly accepted in the marketplace and became a popular choice for day care centers, preschool facilities, and elementary schools, as well as for parents.

Keys to success in this market were continual development of innovative products and a high level of product quality. Toys needed to be both creative and durable. Two other important factors were timing and availability. New products had to be ready to be introduced at the spring toy shows. Then, sufficient capacity was needed to fill retail orders by late summer in order to be ready for the Christmas buying season. Hence, Kramb knew that any capacity expansion decisions had to be made soon to meet next spring's production needs.

Because of the long-term nature of the decision, Kramb had asked Pat Namura, the marketing director, to prepare a four-year sales forecast. This forecast projected strong growth in sales during the four-year period for several reasons. First, the 1960s baby-boomers' children were reaching preschool and elementary school age, and child care facilities were rapidly expanding to accommodate these children, whose parents typically both worked. A second factor was the growth of international markets. Domestic sales remained strong, but international sales were growing at the rate of 25 percent per year. An important factor to consider was that, in a trendy business such as toys, the European market was one to two years behind the U.S. market. Namura attributed this lag to less developed television programming targeted toward children.

Finally, Imaginative Toys had just launched a new line of toys, and initial sales figures were very promising. The new line of toys was called Transformers. Much like a puzzle, each of the transformers could be rearranged and snapped together to form from two to four different toys. Designs were patterned after the robotic characters in children's Saturday morning cartoon shows. Namura was sure that this new line was just beginning to take off.

As Kramb reviewed the alternatives, he wished that expanding existing facilities were a viable option. Were the necessary space available, adding to the Seattle facilities would put much less pressure on the company's already thin management structure. As it was, suitable space was nowhere to be found in the Seattle area. However, the processes used to manufacture the three product lines could be replicated easily at any location. All three line processes were labor intensive, with plastic parts molding being the only skilled position. The construction toys consisted of molded plastic parts that were assembled into kits and packaged for shipment. The maze and mind toys required some parts fabrication from wood and metal materials. Then these parts were assembled into toys that were packed for shipment. The transformers were made from molded plastic parts that were then assembled with various fasteners and packed for shipment. The operating costs breakdown across all three toy lines was estimated to be 30 percent materials, 30 percent labor, 20 percent overhead, and 20 percent transportation and distribution. Obtaining the raw materials used to manufacture the toys would not be a problem for any location.

Kramb and his staff had researched two alternative locations for expansion. One was in a maquiladora in Nogales, Mexico, across the border from Tucson, Arizona. The improving trade relations and projected relaxation of tariffs and duties made this an attractive alternative. Labor costs also could be substantially reduced. If skilled labor was not available to mold and fabricate the parts, these operations could be done in the United States and the parts could be shipped across the border to Nogales for assembly and packaging.

The second alternative was to locate in Europe. A plastic injection molding company outside Brussels had decided to close and was looking for a buyer. Labor costs would be comparable to those in Seattle, but transportation cost would be 10 to 15 percent higher on toys shipped back to the U.S. market. However, the Brussels location was attractive because of the European community's projected single-market program. It was designed to bring free movement of people, goods, capital, and services to the EC by January 1, 1993. The 1988 Cecchini report developed for the European Commission forecasted an increase of 5 percent in the gross EC product from this program. By producing in Brussels, Imaginative Toys also could avoid the 6 percent tariff on goods entering the EC.

As Kramb prepared to meet with his staff, he wondered how the company would be affected by expanding to a multisite operation. Conceivably, the decision would be to expand into both Mexico and Europe. If the sales projections held, the demand would support a three-plant network.

Questions

1. In making the location decision, what factors would you consider to be dominant? Secondary?
2. What role, if any, do the competitive priorities of Imaginative Toys play in the location decision?

Source: This case was prepared by Dr. Brooke Saladin, Wake Forest University, as a basis for classroom discussion.

Selected References

Bartlett, Christopher, and Sumantra Ghoshal. *Managing Across Borders.* Boston: Harvard Business School Press, 1989.

"The Best Cities for Business," *Fortune,* November 4, 1991, pp. 52–84.

"The Boom Belt," *Business Week,* September 27, 1993, pp. 98–104.

Fitzsimmons, James A. "A Methodology for Emergency Ambulance Development." *Management Science,* vol. 19, no. 6 (February 1973), pp. 627–636.

Fitzsimmons, James A., and Robert S. Sullivan. *Service Operations Management.* New York: McGraw-Hill, 1982.

Fulton, Maurice. "New Factors in Plant Location." *Harvard Business Review* (May–June 1971), pp. 4–17, 166–168.

Geoffrion, Arthur M. "Better Distribution Planning with Computer Models." *Harvard Business Review* (July–August 1976), pp. 92–99.

"A Global Fight in the Tire Industry," *New York Times,* March 10, 1988.

Hamel, Gary, and C. K. Prahalad. "Do You Really Have a Global Strategy?" *Harvard Business Review* (July–August 1985), pp. 139–148.

Harms, Craig S. "A Comparison of Facility Location Techniques." Unpublished doctoral dissertation, Ohio State University, 1984.

Harris, Philip R., and Robert T. Moran. *Managing Cultural Differences.* Houston: Gulf, 1987.

Hayes, Robert H., and Steven C. Wheelwright. *Restoring Our Competitive Edge: Competing Through Manufacturing.* New York: John Wiley & Sons, 1984.

Kanter, Rosabeth Moss. "Transcending Business Boundaries: 12,000 World Managers View Change." *Harvard Business Review* (May–June 1991), pp. 151–164.

Khumawala, Basheer M., and D. Clay Whybark. "A Comparison of Some Recent Warehouse Location Techniques." *The Logistics Review,* vol. 7, no. 3 (Spring 1971).

Kim, Jay S., and Jeffrey G. Miller. "Building the Value Factory: A Progress Report for U.S. Manufacturing." Manufacturing Roundtable, Boston University, 1992.

Klassen, Robert D., and D. Clay Whybark. "Barriers to the Management of International Operations." *Journal of Operations Management,* vol. 11, no. 4 (March 1994), pp. 385–396.

Kolesar, P., and W. E. Walker. "An Algorithm for the Dynamic Relocation of Fire Companies." *Operations Research,* vol. 22, no. 2 (March–April 1974), pp. 249–274.

Kuehn, Alfred A., and Michael J. Hamburger. "A Heuristic Program for Locating Warehouses." *Management Science,* vol. 9, no. 4 (July 1963), pp. 643–666.

Love, Robert F., James G. Morris, and George O. Weslowsky. *Facilities Location: Models and Methods.* New York: North-Holland, 1988.

Magaziner, Ira C., and Mark Patinkin. *The Silent War.* New York: Random House, 1989.

Markland, Robert E. "Analyzing Geographical Discrete Warehousing Networks by Computer Simulation." *Decision Sciences,* vol. 4, no. 2 (April 1973), pp. 216–236.

MacCormack, Alan D., Lawrence James Newman III, and David B. Rosenfield. "The New Dynamics of Global Manufacturing Site Location." *Sloan Management Review* (Summer 1994), pp. 69–77.

Porter, Michael E. "The Competitive Advantage of Nations." *Harvard Business Review* (March–April 1990), pp. 73–93.

Schmenner, Roger W. *Making Business Location Decisions.* Englewood Cliffs, N.J.: Prentice-Hall, 1982.

Schmenner, Roger W. "Multiple Manufacturing Strategies Among the *Fortune* 500." *Journal of Operations Management,* vol. 2, no. 2 (February 1982), pp. 77–86.

Skinner, Wickham. *Manufacturing in the Corporate Strategy.* New York: John Wiley & Sons, 1978.

"Spanning the Globe," *Wall Street Journal,* October 4, 1991.

Sugiura, Hideo. "How Honda Localizes Its Global Strategy." *Sloan Management Review* (Fall 1990), pp. 77–82.

Transportation Method

In Chapter 8 we introduced the transportation method to help solve multiple-facility location problems. We demonstrated how quantitative solutions can be obtained with the help of a computer software package. Here we present what goes into such a package so that you can understand more fully the underlying logic. This material also will help you understand what the computer does, and doesn't do, in finding the optimal solution. The transportation method actually is a special type of linear programming, which we consider in Supplement I.

Outline

SOLVING
TRANSPORTATION
PROBLEMS

DEGENERACY

◆ SOLVING TRANSPORTATION PROBLEMS

The transportation method is an iterative procedure for solving problems when we want to minimize the cost of shipping products from m plants or sources of supply to n destinations. (The same approach may be used to solve profit maximization problems and to obtain optimal production plans, as discussed in Chapter 13.) Here we apply the transportation method to plant location, where the sources are plants and the destinations are warehouses. The transportation method involves four basic steps.

1. Translate the problem description into an initial tableau, which represents the plants as rows and the warehouses as columns. Each cell in the tableau represents a shipping route from a plant to a warehouse. Add cost, demand, and capacity data.
2. Generate an initial feasible solution.
3. Incrementally improve the initial solution until no further improvements are possible, which means that the solution is optimal. At each iteration an entering route and an exiting route must be identified before moving from one solution to the next.
4. Identify and evaluate the final solution.

The last three steps are usually solved on the computer because of the massive amount of data processing required for realistically large problems. However, you must still perform the first step, which can require considerable creativity. Here we examine all four steps so that you can solve such a problem from beginning to end.

The Initial Tableau

We begin by putting the problem in the format of a standard matrix called a *tableau*. The rows in the tableau (except the last one) represent plants, either existing or proposed. The columns (except the last one) represent warehouses. The last row shows each warehouse's demand, and the last column each plant's capacity. Each cell in the tableau indicates how much the plant in the cell's row should ship to the warehouse in its column. The cost to ship one unit from a plant to a warehouse is shown in the upper right-hand corner of the corresponding cell. For profit maximization problems, the profit per unit shipped is shown. In the transportation method, the sum of the allocations to a row must equal the capacity of that row; similarly, the sum of the allocations to a column must equal the requirements for that column. These two sets of constraints are called **rim conditions**. The sum of the capacities must always equal the sum of the requirements.

EXAMPLE G.1
Formulating the Initial Tableau

The Giant Farmer Company processes food for sale in discount food stores. It has two plants: one in Chicago and one in Houston. The company also operates warehouses in Miami, Denver, Lincoln, and Jackson. Forecasts indicate that demand soon will exceed supply and that a new plant with a capacity of 8000 cases per week is needed. The question is where to locate the new plant. Two potential sites are Buffalo and Atlanta, and management wants to determine which location will minimize shipping costs. The following data on capacities, forecasted demand, and shipping costs have been gathered.

Plant	Capacity (cases per week)	Warehouse	Demand (cases per week)
Chicago	10,000	Miami	7,000
Houston	7,500	Denver	9,000
New plant	8,000	Lincoln	4,500
Total	25,500	Jackson	5,000
		Total	25,500

Plant	Shipping Cost to Warehouse (per case)			
	Miami	Denver	Lincoln	Jackson
Chicago	$7	$ 2	$4	$5
Houston	$3	$ 1	$5	$2
Buffalo (alternative 1)	$6	$ 9	$7	$4
Atlanta (alternative 2)	$2	$10	$8	$3

Set up the initial tableau, with the Buffalo option as the new plant's location.

FIGURE G.1   *Initial Tableau for the Giant Farmer Company Problem*

Plant	Warehouse				Capacity
	Miami	Denver	Lincoln	Jackson	
Chicago	7	2	4	5	100
Houston	3	1	5	2	75
Buffalo	6	9	7	4	80
Requirements	70	90	45	50	255 / 255

Solution The initial tableau is shown in Fig. G.1. There is a row for each plant and a column for each warehouse. To simplify calculations, capacity and demand quantities are shown in hundreds of units and shipping costs in dollars per case. After solving this revised problem, convert the solution to the original problem by multiplying the shipments and total cost by 100. Note that the total capacity of 25,500 units per week equals total requirements.

In many real problems, capacity may exceed requirements, or vice versa. If so, we have to adjust the model to satisfy the rim conditions. If capacity exceeds requirements by *r* units, we create an additional *column* in the tableau representing a *dummy warehouse* with a demand for *r* units and make the shipping costs in the newly created cells $0. Shipments to dummy warehouses are not really made, but represent unused plant capacity. Similarly, if requirements exceed capacity by *r* units, we create a new *row* representing a *dummy plant* with a capacity of *r* units. We assign shipping costs equal to the stockout costs in the new cells. If stockout costs are unknown or the same for all warehouses, we simply assign shipping costs of $0 per unit to each cell in the dummy row. The optimal solution will not be affected, because the shortage of *r* units is required in all cases.

Figure G.2 shows the initial tableau for the Giant Farmer Company when the Buffalo plant's capacity is expanded to 100 units. In this case a dummy warehouse with a 20-unit demand requirement is added to maintain the rim conditions. In the final solution at least one plant will be shown to be shipping to the dummy warehouse. These shipments will not really be made, which is why the unit costs are shown to be $0. The sum of the shipments to the dummy warehouse is equal to the unused capacity of the system.

FIGURE G.2

Initial Tableau with Dummy Warehouse for the Giant Farmer Company Problem

Plant	Warehouse					Capacity
	Miami	Denver	Lincoln	Jackson	Dummy	
Chicago	7	2	4	5	0	100
Houston	3	1	5	2	0	75
Buffalo	6	9	7	4	0	100
Requirements	70	90	45	50	20	275 / 275

Generating an Initial Solution

The transportation method requires an initial solution, which allocates quantities to cells to meet the rim conditions. Two procedures for specifying an initial solution are the northwest-corner method and Vogel's approximation method (VAM).

The Northwest-Corner Method.   The quickest way to arrive at an initial solution to a transportation problem is to use the **northwest-corner method.** As the name indicates, the procedure starts in the northwest (upper left-hand) corner of the tableau and allocates as many units as possible to that cell *without exceeding* the row capacity or the column requirement. This allocation will completely satisfy either the row or the column constraint. In our example (we restore Buffalo's capacity to 80 units for the rest of the supplement), we can allocate 70 units to the Chicago–Miami route, which eliminates Miami from further allocations, as shown in Fig. G.3.

FIGURE G.3

Initial Solution Using the Northwest-Corner Approach

Plant	Warehouse				Capacity
	Miami	Denver	Lincoln	Jackson	
Chicago	7 70	2 30	4	5	100
Houston	3	1 60	5 15	2	75
Buffalo	6	9	7 30	4 50	80
Requirements	70	90	45	50	255 / 255

Total cost = 70($7) + 30($2) + 60($1) + 15($5) + 30($7) + 50($4) = $1095

We continue to make allocations to satisfy each row or column quantity but do not exceed any of the rim conditions. Thus the sequence of allocations would be to Chicago–Denver (eliminating the first row), Houston–Denver (eliminating the second column), Houston–Lincoln (eliminating the second row), and so on.

The total cost for this initial solution is $109,500, as calculated at the bottom of Fig. G.3. In general, the northwest-corner method does not yield a low-cost initial solution. This result is to be expected, as costs were not considered in the allocation process. Usually we must trade off arriving at an initial solution quickly with doing more work later to find the optimal solution.

Vogel's Approximation Method (VAM).   Although **Vogel's approximation method (VAM)** requires more work than the northwest-corner method, it normally provides an initial solution that is much closer to the optimal solution. The more useful initial solution results from inclusion of the objective function in making the allocations. Application of VAM to our problem is shown in Fig. G.4.

We begin by calculating a penalty cost for each row and column. The penalty cost for each row is the difference between the lowest cost element in a row and the *next largest* cost element in that row. We obtain the penalty cost for each column in the same manner. For example, in our problem the penalty cost for the first row is $2 (or $4 − $2), and the penalty cost for the first column is $3 (or $6 − $3).

In making our first allocation, we choose the row or column having the largest penalty cost because it is like an opportunity cost. That is, if we don't allocate as many units as possible now to the cell with lowest cost in that row or column, we may have to allocate units later to the cell with the next largest cost in that row or column. The largest cost penalty is $3, for column 1, so we allocate as many units as we can to the lowest cost cell in the first column. This is the Houston–Miami route, the allocation is for 70 units, and this allocation satisfies the Miami requirements. If we have a tie in penalty costs, we arbitrarily choose between the tied rows or columns.

In the second iteration (and thereafter), we have to recalculate the penalty costs to determine whether any have changed because of the last allocation. In this case, only the third-row penalty cost changes because we eliminated column 1. The $3 penalty cost for the third row is now the largest, so we allocate 50 units to the lowest cost cell. Even though 80 units of capacity are available in row 3 (Buffalo), the requirement in column 4 (Jackson) is only 50 units.

The rest of the iterations are straightforward. In iteration 3, row 2 has the highest penalty cost. However, we can allocate only 5 units to the lowest cost cell because we had previously allocated 70 units to that row and the capacity is 75

FIGURE G.4

Initial Solution Using VAM

(a) Iteration 1

(b) Iteration 2

FIGURE G.4 (CONT)

Plant	Warehouse				Capacity	VAM costs
	Miami	Denver	Lincoln	Jackson		
Chicago	7	2	4	5	100	$2
Houston	3 70	1 5	5	2	75	$4
Buffalo	6	9	7	4 50	80	$2
Requirements	70	90	45	50	255 / 255	
VAM costs	—	$1	$1	—		

(c) Iteration 3

Plant	Warehouse				Capacity	VAM costs
	Miami	Denver	Lincoln	Jackson		
Chicago	7	2 85	4	5	100	$2
Houston	3 70	1 5	5	2	75	—
Buffalo	6	9	7	4 50	80	$2
Requirements	70	90	45	50	255 / 255	
VAM costs	—	$7	$3	—		

(d) Iteration 4

Plant	Warehouse				Capacity
	Miami	Denver	Lincoln	Jackson	
Chicago	7	2 85	4 15	5	100
Houston	3 70	1 5	5	2	75
Buffalo	6	9	7 30	4 50	80
Requirements	70	90	45	50	255 / 255

Total cost = 70($3) + 85($2) + 5($1) + 15($4) + 30($7) + 50($4) = $855

(e) Final allocation

units. We can eliminate column 2 in the fourth iteration by allocating 85 units to the Chicago–Denver route. The final allocation is obvious at this point. Two cells need allocations, and their values are prescribed by the rim conditions. The total cost of this initial solution is $85,500, which is $24,000 less than the cost generated by the northwest-corner method.[†]

Improving the Solution, Iteration by Iteration

Now that we have a feasible solution, we must find a way to improve it. This improvement process requires a series of iterations. With each iteration, a new solution is obtained that is at least as good as the solution obtained in the preceding iteration. This process ensures that we will eventually reach a solution that cannot be improved upon and therefore is optimal. Three steps are involved at each iteration.

1. Select an **entering route**, which is a nonallocated cell (or route) in the preceding iteration that will be introduced in the new solution.
2. Select an **exiting route**, which is an allocated cell (or route) in the preceding iteration that will be removed in the new solution to make way for the entering route.
3. Transform the tableau to reflect the impact of this change on all cells, including the cells representing the entering and exiting routes.

Select the Entering Route.   Of the approaches to selecting the entering route in a transportation problem, the so-called **stepping-stone method** is the most intuitive.[‡] It is named for the procedure utilized. In general terms, we begin by selecting a nonallocated cell for evaluation. Hypothetically, we allocate one unit to the cell, then adjust the currently allocated cells to balance the affected row capacities and column requirements alternately, without violating the rim conditions. In this respect, the tableau is like a shallow pond of water, with the allocated cells serving as stepping stones. Starting with the nonallocated cell, we move from allocated cell to allocated cell, each time moving at a right angle to the last move, alternately subtracting one unit from and adding one unit to the allocated cells, until we end up at the nonallocated cell again. In so doing, we create a *loop* and satisfy all rim conditions. Fortunately, there is only one loop for each nonallocated cell. We can calculate the net cost advantage from this loop.

Consider Fig. G.5 on the next page, which represents the initial solution derived from VAM in Fig. G.4. An asterisk (*) indicates an allocated cell, and the solid square (■) indicates the nonallocated cell that we will evaluate first. The dashed line shows the loop for this cell. The cost of shipping one unit from Chicago to Jackson is $5, but, as Jackson requires only 50 units, we must reduce the Buffalo–Jackson shipment by one unit, *saving* $4. This change leaves Buffalo

---

[†]Regardless of the method used for determining an initial solution, the number of allocated cells must equal $m + n - 1$, where m = number of rows and n = number of columns. If we have more than that number, we didn't allocate as much as we could to each cell at each step. Having fewer creates degeneracy, a condition covered in the last section.

[‡]Another approach, called the *modified-distribution* (MODI) *method*, actually requires less work but is based on concepts beyond the scope of this supplement. This approach is discussed in Krajewski and Thompson (1981).

FIGURE G.5

Loop for the Chicago–Jackson Route

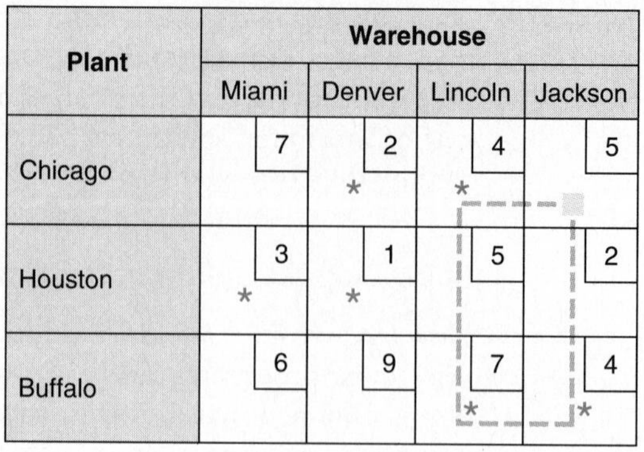

Plant	Warehouse			
	Miami	Denver	Lincoln	Jackson
Chicago	7	2 *	4 *	5
Houston	3 *	1 *	5	2
Buffalo	6	9	7 *	4 *

Net contribution to total cost/unit = $5 − $4 + $7 − $4 = $4

one unit short of its capacity of 80 units, but we know that all of its capacity will be needed because the total requirement from all warehouses equals the total capacity of the plants. Consequently, we add one unit to the Buffalo–Lincoln route, *increasing* costs by $7. In so doing, we have allocated to Lincoln one more unit than it requires, so we reduce the Chicago–Lincoln shipment by one unit, *saving* $4. This completes the loop, and the net contribution to total costs is $4 (or $5 − $4 + $7 − $4). Because the net contribution is positive, opening a route from Chicago to Jackson isn't profitable at this time. It would add $4 to the total cost for each unit shipped.

Figure G.6 shows the loops for the remaining nonallocated cells, and Table G.1 shows the calculation of the net contributions for each one. Note that some loops are more complicated than others. The Houston–Jackson loop crosses itself, which is permissible as long as the intersection is at a right angle. The Buffalo–Denver loop passes over the Houston–Denver cell because, if we had stopped there, the only right-angle move would have been Houston–Miami. From that position, there is no right-angle move to an allocated cell. Finally, we should mention that loops can be traversed in two directions.

We can now identify the entering route for our problem. Table G.1 indicates that the only route that would reduce costs is Buffalo–Miami. In general, we would pick the route with the largest negative net contribution for cost maximization problems and the route with the largest positive net contribution for profit maximization problems.

FIGURE G.6   *Loops for the Remaining Nonallocated Cells*

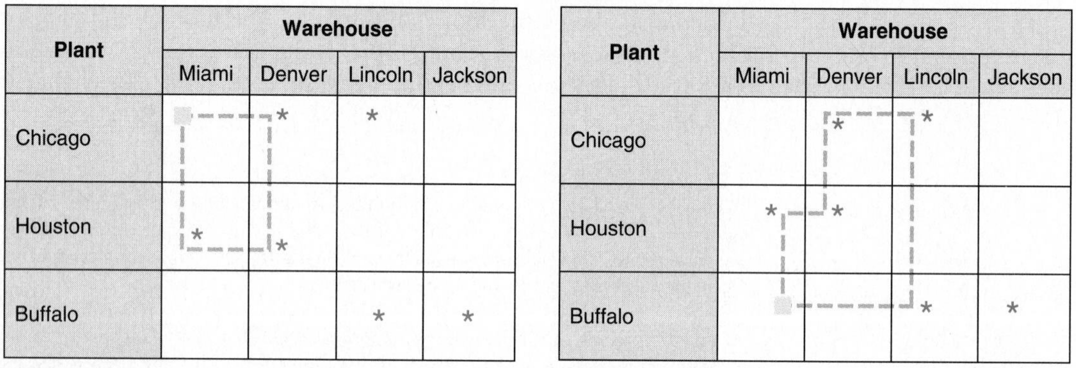

Plant	Warehouse			
	Miami	Denver	Lincoln	Jackson
Chicago		*	*	
Houston	*	*		
Buffalo			*	*

(a) Chicago–Miami

Plant	Warehouse			
	Miami	Denver	Lincoln	Jackson
Chicago		*	*	
Houston	*	*		
Buffalo			*	*

(b) Buffalo–Miami

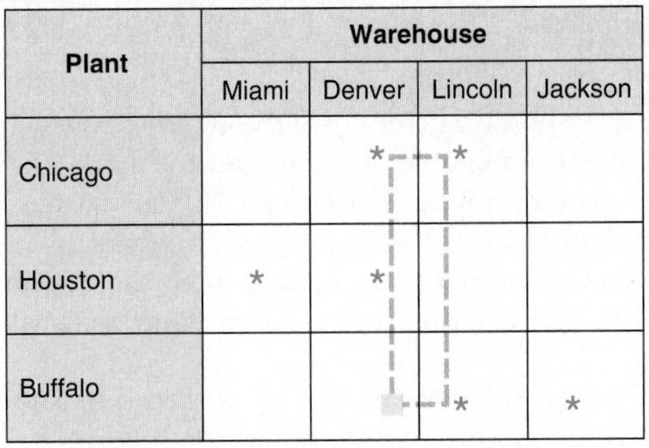

(c) Buffalo–Denver

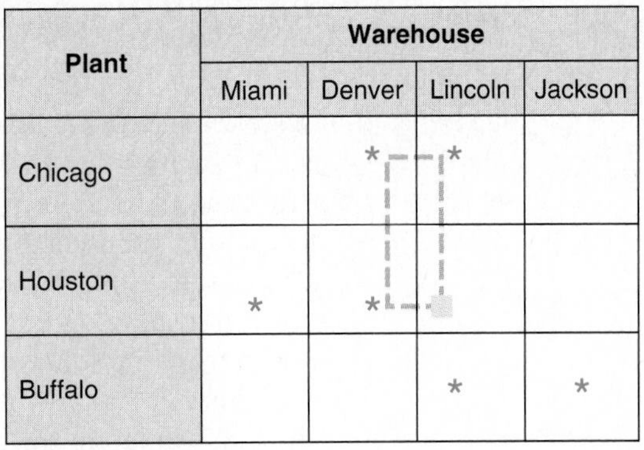

(d) Houston–Lincoln

FIGURE G.6 (CONT)

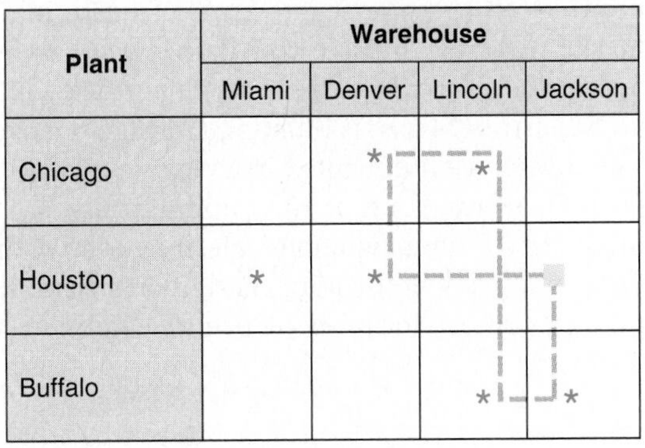

(e) Houston–Jackson

TABLE G.1 *Net Contributions for Nonallocated Cells*

Shipment Change		Cost Change	Shipment Change		Cost Change
Chicago–Miami			*Houston–Lincoln*		
Add 1 unit	Chicago–Miami	+ $7	Add 1 unit	Houston–Lincoln	+ $5
Subtract 1 unit	Houston–Miami	− $3	Subtract 1 unit	Chicago–Lincoln	− $4
Add 1 unit	Houston–Denver	+ $1	Add 1 unit	Chicago–Denver	+ $2
Subtract 1 unit	Chicago–Denver	− $2	Subtract 1 unit	Houston–Denver	− $1
Net contribution		+ $3	Net contribution		+ $2
Buffalo–Miami			*Houston–Jackson*		
Add 1 unit	Buffalo–Miami	+ $6	Add 1 unit	Houston–Jackson	+ $2
Subtract 1 unit	Houston–Miami	− $3	Subtract 1 unit	Buffalo–Jackson	− $4
Add 1 unit	Houston–Denver	+ $1	Add 1 unit	Buffalo–Lincoln	+ $7
Subtract 1 unit	Chicago–Denver	− $2	Subtract 1 unit	Chicago–Lincoln	− $4
Add 1 unit	Chicago–Lincoln	+ $4	Add 1 unit	Chicago–Denver	+ $2
Subtract 1 unit	Buffalo–Lincoln	− $7	Subtract 1 unit	Houston–Denver	− $1
Net contribution		− $1	Net contribution		+ $2
Buffalo–Denver					
Add 1 unit	Buffalo–Denver	+ $9			
Subtract 1 unit	Chicago–Denver	− $2			
Add 1 unit	Chicago–Lincoln	+ $4			
Subtract 1 unit	Buffalo–Lincoln	− $7			
Net contribution		+ $4			

Select the Exiting Route.   After we have determined the entering route, we allocate as many units to that route as possible. To maintain the same number of shipments (allocated cells) as before, one of the current shipments must be reduced to 0. (Reducing more than one cell to 0 requires special care, as we show in the last section.) By analyzing the loop for the entering route, we determine the maximum shipping quantity for the entering route and the route that will be removed from the solution.

Figure G.7 shows the tableau for the initial solution that we developed using VAM and the loop for the Buffalo–Miami route. The $(+)$ or $(-)$ in the circle of each cell in the loop indicates that we must add or subtract a unit from that cell to satisfy the rim conditions. Note that each row and column affected has one positive cell and one negative cell. To determine the maximum quantity that can be shipped from Buffalo to Miami, we examine the negative cells because these are the cells for which shipping quantities will be reduced. In this example, they are Houston–Miami (70 units), Chicago–Denver (85 units), and Buffalo–Lincoln (30 units). Consequently, the maximum quantity that we can ship on the Buffalo–Miami route is the minimum of (70, 85, 30), or 30 units. To ship any more than 30 units would result in a negative quantity in the Buffalo–Lincoln cell and would violate the nonnegativity restriction. As the Buffalo–Lincoln route has the minimum allocation of negative cells in the loop, we remove it from the solution.

FIGURE G.7

*Loop for the
Buffalo–Miami Route*

Plant	Warehouse				Capacity
	Miami	Denver	Lincoln	Jackson	
Chicago	7	2 — 85	4 + 15	5	100
Houston	70 3 —	1 + 5	5	2	75
Buffalo	6 +	9	7 — 30	4 50	80
Requirements	70	90	45	50	255 / 255

Transform the Tableau.   Figure G.8 shows the new solution to the problem after 30 units have been added to each positive cell and subtracted from each negative cell. The values in the circles are the net contributions for each nonallocated cell and are calculated in the same manner as previously.

Identifying and Evaluating the Final Solution

The criteria for optimality in transportation problems are the following.

Minimization problems: If the net contributions of all nonallocated cells are 0 or *positive,* the current solution is optimal.

FIGURE G.8

Transformed Array
Showing Optimal
Solution

Plant	Warehouse				Capacity
	Miami	Denver	Lincoln	Jackson	
Chicago	7 +$3	2 55	4 45	5 +$3	100
Houston	3 40	1 35	5 +$2	2 +$1	75
Buffalo	6 30	9 +$5	7 +$1	4 50	80
Requirements	70	90	45	50	255 / 255

Total cost = 40($3) + 30($6) + 55($2) + 35($1) + 45($4) + 50($4) = $825

> *Maximization problems:* If the net contributions of all nonallocated cells are 0 or *negative,* the current solution is optimal.

Because the net contributions of all six nonallocated cells in Fig. G.8 are positive and because this is a minimization problem, the solution shown is optimal—provided that we locate a new plant in Buffalo with an 80-unit capacity. If one or more of the net contributions were still negative, we would have to do another iteration of the tableau. The process took only one iteration beyond the initial one. The best distribution plan, with the total transportation cost of $82,500, is for Chicago to serve Denver and Lincoln with 55 and 45 units, respectively. Houston supplies Miami with 40 units and Denver with 35 units. Finally, Buffalo ships 30 units to Miami and fully satisfies Jackson's demand for 50 units.

For alternative 2, locating the new plant in Atlanta, the solution yields a total transportation cost of $57,500. We leave the solution process to you. If transportation cost is the overriding consideration, the new plant should be located in Atlanta. However, management usually considers many other factors before making a final plant location decision. (See Chapter 8.)

◆ DEGENERACY

An optimal solution need never be more than $m + n - 1$ allocated cells, so the transportation method restricts its search to such solutions. For example, the final solution in Fig. G.8 has 6 (or $3 + 4 - 1$) plant–warehouse shipments. It is possible, however, to have fewer than $m + n - 1$ allocated cells, a situation called degeneracy. **Degeneracy** can occur in the derivation of an initial solution when we satisfy a row constraint and a column constraint simultaneously with one allocation, or when we introduce a new route into the solution and more than one negative cell in the loop has the same minimum allocation. Degeneracy is troublesome because without $m + n - 1$ allocated cells, we cannot create a loop for each nonallocated cell.

The procedure for dealing with degeneracy involves the allocation of an infinitesimal quantity, ϵ (the lowercase Greek letter epsilon), to as many nonallocated cells as necessary to bring the total number of allocated cells to $m + n - 1$. We choose only those nonallocated cells having loops that cannot be formed without the ϵ allocation. Because the value of ϵ is so small, it doesn't enter into the total cost of the solution or the shipping quantity for any route; its only use is in identifying the loops for nonallocated cells. We treat the cell with ϵ as a typical allocated cell in our calculations and continue with the stepping-stone method until we reach optimality.

Figure G.9(a) revises the Miami and Denver demand requirements so that degeneracy occurs when we apply the northwest-corner approach to find an initial solution (compare with Fig. G.3). Figure G.9(b) shows one way of dealing with it—positioning ϵ in the Chicago–Denver route. This placement allows all six remaining nonallocated cells to be evaluated. Some experimentation may be needed to find an acceptable spot for ϵ because not every placement will allow evaluation of all six nonallocated cells. For example, we could put ϵ in the Chicago–Lincoln cell but not in the Houston–Jackson cell. For the latter case the Buffalo–Miami route cannot be evaluated.

FIGURE G.9

Identifying and Dealing with Degeneracy

Plant	Warehouse				Capacity
	Miami	Denver	Lincoln	Jackson	
Chicago	7 / 100	2	4	5	100
Houston	3	1 / 60	5 / 15	2	75
Buffalo	6	9	7 / 30	4 / 50	80
Requirements	100	60	45	50	255 / 255

(a) Tableau with degeneracy using northwest-corner approach

Plant	Warehouse				Capacity
	Miami	Denver	Lincoln	Jackson	
Chicago	7 / 100	2 / ϵ	4	5	100
Houston	3	1 / 60	5 / 15	2	75
Buffalo	6	9	7 / 30	4 / 50	80
Requirements	100	60	45	50	255 / 255

(b) Tableau with added allocation

SUPPLEMENT REVIEW

Solved Problem 1

Fire Brand makes picante sauce in El Paso and New York City. Distribution centers are located in Atlanta, Omaha, and Seattle. For the capacities, locations, and shipment costs per case shown in Fig. G.10, start with the northwest-corner initial solution and use the stepping-stone method to determine the shipping pattern that will minimize transportation costs. What are the estimated transportation costs associated with this optimal allocation pattern?

FIGURE G.10

Source	Destination			Capacity
	Atlanta	Omaha	Seattle	
El Paso	$4	$5	$6	12,000
New York City	$3	$7	$9	10,000
Demand	8,000	10,000	4,000	22,000

Solution The northwest-corner initial solution is shown in Fig. G.11.

FIGURE G.11

Source	Destination			Capacity
	Atlanta	Omaha	Seattle	
El Paso	$4 8,000	$5 4,000	$6	12,000
New York City	$3	$7 6,000	$9 4,000	10,000
Demand	8,000	10,000	4,000	22,000

First Iteration
First use Fig. G.12 to select the entering route.

FIGURE G.12

Source	Destination			Capacity
	Atlanta	Omaha	Seattle	
El Paso	$4	$5	$6	12,000
New York City	$3	$7	$9	10,000
Demand	8,000	10,000	4,000	22,000

The net contribution to total cost/unit for the El Paso–Seattle loop is $+$ \$6 $-$ \$5 $+$ \$7 $-$ \$9 $=$ $-$\$1. The net contribution to total cost/unit for the New York–Atlanta loop is $+$ \$3 $-$ \$7 $+$ \$5 $-$ \$4 $=$ $-$\$3. The New York–Atlanta route offers the greater opportunity to reduce costs.

Then use Fig. G.13 to select the exiting route.

FIGURE G.13

Source	Destination			Capacity
	Atlanta	Omaha	Seattle	
El Paso	\$4 − 8,000	\$5 + 4,000	\$6	12,000
New York City	\$3 +	\$7 − 6,000	\$9 4,000	10,000
Demand	8,000	10,000	4,000	22,000

The smallest negative shipping quantity is New York–Omaha, which is the exiting route.

Finally, transform the tableau, as shown in Fig. G.14, by subtracting 6000 units from each negative cell and adding 6000 to each positive cell. No units are sent from New York to Omaha in this iteration.

FIGURE G.14

Source	Destination			Capacity
	Atlanta	Omaha	Seattle	
El Paso	\$4 2,000	\$5 10,000	\$6	12,000
New York City	\$3 6,000	\$7	\$9 4,000	10,000
Demand	8,000	10,000	4,000	22,000

Second Iteration

First use Fig. G.15 to select the entering route.

FIGURE G.15

Source	Destination			Capacity
	Atlanta	Omaha	Seattle	
El Paso	\$4 *	\$5 *	\$6	12,000
New York City	\$3 *	\$7	\$9 *	10,000
Demand	8,000	10,000	4,000	22,000

The net contribution to total cost/unit for the El Paso–Seattle loop is $+$ \$6 $-$ \$4 $+$ \$3 $-$ \$9 $=$ $-$\$4. The net contribution to total cost/unit for the New York–Omaha loop is

$+\$7 - \$5 + \$4 - \$3 = +\$3$. The El Paso–Seattle route offers the only opportunity to reduce costs in this iteration.

Then use Fig. G.16 to select the exiting route.

FIGURE G.16

Source	Destination			Capacity
	Atlanta	Omaha	Seattle	
El Paso	$4 − 2,000	$5 10,000	$6 +	12,000
New York City	$3 + 6,000	$7	$9 − 4,000	10,000
Demand	8,000	10,000	4,000	22,000

The smallest negative shipping quantity is El Paso–Atlanta, which is the exiting route.

Finally, transform the tableau, as shown in Fig. G.17, by subtracting 2000 units from each negative cell and adding 2000 to each positive cell. No units are sent from El Paso to Atlanta in this iteration.

FIGURE G.17

Source	Destination			Capacity
	Atlanta	Omaha	Seattle	
El Paso	$4	$5 10,000	$6 2,000	12,000
New York City	$3 8,000	$7	$9 2,000	10,000
Demand	8,000	10,000	4,000	22,000

Determine whether the optimal answer has been found. The El Paso–Atlanta route is positive: $+\$4 - \$3 + \$9 - \$6 = +\$4$. The New York–Omaha route is negative: $+\$7 - \$9 + \$6 - \$5 = -\$1$. Therefore, a better solution exists.

Third Iteration
The entering route is New York–Omaha, as shown in Fig. G.18.

FIGURE G.18

Source	Destination			Capacity
	Atlanta	Omaha	Seattle	
El Paso	$4	$5 *	$6 *	12,000
New York City	$3 *	$7	$9 *	10,000
Demand	8,000	10,000	4,000	22,000

The exiting route is New York–Seattle, as shown in Fig. G.19.

Source	Destination			Capacity
	Atlanta	Omaha	Seattle	
El Paso	$4	$5 — 10,000 +	$6 + 2,000	12,000
New York City	$3 8,000	$7 +	$9 — 2,000	10,000
Demand	8,000	10,000	4,000	22,000

Transform the tableau, as shown in Fig. G.20, by subtracting 2000 units from each negative cell and adding 2000 to each positive cell. No units are sent from El Paso to Atlanta in this iteration.

Source	Destination			Capacity
	Atlanta	Omaha	Seattle	
El Paso	$4	$5 8,000	$6 4,000	12,000
New York City	$3 8,000	$7 2,000	$9	10,000
Demand	8,000	10,000	4,000	22,000

This is the optimal shipping arrangement because the El Paso–Atlanta route is positive (+$4 − $5 + $7 − $3 = +$3), and the New York–Seattle route is positive (+$9 − $6 + $5 − $7 = +$1).

Optimal Solution

Ship 8000 cases from El Paso to Omaha @ $5:	$ 40,000
Ship 4000 cases from El Paso to Seattle @ $6:	$ 24,000
Ship 8000 cases from New York City to Atlanta @ $3:	$ 24,000
Ship 2000 cases from New York City to Omaha @ $7:	$ 14,000
Minimum transportation costs	$102,000

Much time and effort could have been saved if we had used VAM to find the initial solution. For this problem, the VAM initial solution is the optimal solution.

Supplement Highlights

- The transportation method is an iterative procedure for solving problems when we want to minimize the cost of shipping products from *m* plants or sources of supply to *n* destinations. It can be applied to plant location or production planning problems and also to maximization problems.

- The four basic steps in solving such problems are to create an initial tableau, find an initial feasible solution, improve the solution incrementally until optimality is reached, and evaluate the final solution.
- Each tableau requires that the rim conditions be satisfied. When the initial tableau is created, rim conditions

may require that a dummy plant or dummy warehouse be added.

- The northwest-corner method and Vogel's approximation method (VAM) are two ways to generate the initial solution.
- The stepping-stone method transforms the initial solution into an optimal solution. An entering route and exiting route are selected to create an improved solution at the next iteration. Optimality is detected in a tableau when the net contributions for all nonallocated cells are 0 or positive for minimization problems or 0 or negative for maximization problems.
- Degeneracy occurs in a solution when fewer than $m + n - 1$ cell allocations are greater than 0; it can be handled by the ϵ allocation method.

Key Terms

degeneracy *387*
entering route *383*
exiting route *383*
northwest-corner method *380*

rim conditions *378*
stepping-stone method *383*
Vogel's approximation method (VAM) *380*

Study Questions

1. What is the trade-off between methods for generating initial solutions and the effort required to find the optimal solution?
2. How is the setup of the initial tableau arranged for a situation where existing sources have greater total capacity than existing demands?
3. When the stepping-stone method is applied to minimize transportation costs, what is indicated when we calculate the loop for a nonallocated cell and arrive at a negative number?
4. A manufacturer uses the transportation method to create monthly production plans covering 12 months of forecasted demand. Production resources exceed total demand. They include regular time, overtime, and subcontracted production. How many rows and columns are needed to set up this transportation model? How many cells? See Problem 7.

Problems

1. Pucchi, Inc. makes designer dog collars in Chihuahua, Mexico; Saint Bernard, Ohio; and Yorkshire, New York. Distribution centers are located in Baustin, Vegas, Nawlns, and New Yawk. The shipping costs, requirements, and capacities are shown in Fig. G.21. Use the transportation method to find the shipping schedule that minimizes shipping cost.

FIGURE G.21

Factory	Shipping Cost per Collar to Distribution Centers					Capacity
	Baustin	Vegas	Nawlns	New Yawk	Dummy	
Chihuahua	$8	$5	$4	$9	$0	12,000
Saint Bernard	$4	$6	$3	$3	$0	7,000
Yorkshire	$2	$8	$6	$1	$0	4,000
Demand	4,000	6,000	3,000	8,000	2,000	23,000

2. The Ajax International Company has four factories that ship products to five warehouses. The shipping costs, requirements, and capacities are shown in Fig. G.22. Use the transportation method to find the shipping schedule that minimizes shipping cost.

FIGURE G.22

Factory	Shipping Cost per Case to Warehouse						Capacity
	W1	W2	W3	W4	W5	Dummy	
F1	$1	$3	$3	$5	$6	$0	50,000
F2	$2	$2	$1	$4	$5	$0	80,000
F3	$1	$5	$1	$3	$1	$0	80,000
F4	$5	$2	$4	$5	$4	$0	40,000
Demand	45,000	30,000	30,000	35,000	50,000	60,000	250,000

20,000 paint cans, respectively, per month. Three paint-can suppliers (1, 2, and 3) have indicated their willingness to supply as many as 40,000, 30,000, and 20,000 cans per month, respectively. The shipping costs per 100 cans are shown in Fig. G.23, along with capacity and demand quantities in hundreds of cans.

FIGURE G.23

Supplier	Shipping Cost per 100 Cans to Plant					Capacity
	A	B	C	D	Dummy	
S1	$54	$48	$50	$46		400
S2	$52	$50	$54	$48		300
S3	$46	$48	$50	$52		200
Demand	300	200	100	200	100	900

3. Consider further the Ajax International Company situation described in Problem 2. Ajax has decided to close F3 because of high operating costs. In addition, the company has decided to add 50,000 units of capacity to F4. The logistics manager is worried about the effect of this move on transportation costs. Presently, F3 is shipping 30,000 units to W4 and 50,000 units to W5 at a cost of $140,000 [or 30,000(3) + 50,000(1)]. If these warehouses were to be served by F4, the cost would increase to $350,000 [or 30,000(5) + 50,000(4)]. As a result, the Ajax logistics manager has requested a budget increase of $210,000 (or $350,000 − $140,000).
   a. Should the logistics manager get the budget increase?
   b. If not, how much would you budget for the increase in shipping costs?
4. Consider the facility location problem at the Giant Farmer Company described in Example G.1.
   a. Find the minimum cost shipping plan for a new plant in Atlanta.
   b. Find the minimum cost plan for an alternative plant in Memphis. The shipping costs per case from Memphis are $3 to Miami, $11 to Denver, $6 to Lincoln, and $5 to Jackson.
5. The Bright Paint Company has four factories (A, B, C, and D) that require 30,000, 20,000, 10,000, and

Currently supplier 1 is shipping 20,000 cans to plant B and 20,000 cans to D. Supplier 2 is shipping 30,000 cans to A, and supplier 3 is shipping 10,000 gallons to C. Does the present delivery arrangement minimize the total cost to the Bright Paint Company? If not, find a plan that does so.

6. The Chambers Corporation produces and markets an automotive theft deterrent product, which it stocks in various warehouses throughout the country. Recently, its market research group compiled a forecast indicating that a significant increase in demand will occur in the near future, after which demand will level off for the foreseeable future. The company has decided to satisfy this demand by constructing new plant capacity. Chambers already has plants in Baltimore and Milwaukee and has no desire to relocate those facilities. Each plant is capable of producing 600,000 units per year.

After a thorough search, the company developed three site and capacity alternatives. *Alternative 1* is to build a 600,000-unit plant in Portland. *Alternative 2* is to build a 600,000-unit plant in San Antonio. *Alternative 3* is to build a 300,000-unit plant in Portland and a 300,000-unit plant in San Antonio. The company has four warehouses that distribute the product to retailers. The market research study provided the following data.

Warehouse	Expected Annual Demand
Atlanta (AT)	500,000
Columbus (CO)	300,000
Los Angeles (LA)	600,000
Seattle (SE)	400,000

The logistics department compiled the following cost table that specified the cost per unit to ship the product from each plant to each warehouse in the most economical manner, subject to the reliability of the various carriers involved.

	Warehouse			
Plant	AT	CO	LA	SE
Baltimore	$0.35	$0.20	$0.85	$0.75
Milwaukee	$0.55	$0.15	$0.70	$0.65
Portland	$0.85	$0.60	$0.30	$0.10
San Antonio	$0.55	$0.40	$0.40	$0.55

As one part of the location–capacity decision, management wants an estimate of the total distribution cost for each alternative. Use the transportation method to calculate these estimates.

7. Use the transportation method to plan production to meet the projected quarterly demand for a microbrewery, as shown in Fig. G.24. The costs of production are $10 for regular time and $12 for overtime. Backorders are not permitted. In other words, beer cannot be produced in April (second quarter) to satisfy demand that occurred in February (first quarter). To prevent solutions that would involve backorders, an arbitrarily high cost (such as $99) is placed in cells that would represent a backorder. The cost minimization process will avoid planning production in those cells. Producing and storing beer early in the year for later consumption is possible, but costly and not desirable. The cost of storing one barrel for one quarter of the year is $1.50. If the production plan doesn't fully utilize the available regular time, the workers are still paid. The cost for unused regular-time capacity is $6 per barrel under capacity. Demand and capacity quantities are in barrels. *Hint:* The manual tableau method described in Chapter 13 does not necessarily find the optimal solution if (1) backorders are allowed or (2) the cost of unused capacity is greater than $0. Here the second condition applies, and so the transportation method must be used instead of the tableau method.

FIGURE G.24

Source of Product	Demand				Unused Capacity	Capacity
	First Quarter	Second Quarter	Third Quarter	Fourth Quarter		
Initial inventory	$0.00	$1.50	$3.00	$4.50	$4.50	100
First quarter regular time	$10.00	$11.50	$13.00	$14.50	$6.00	900
First quarter overtime	$12.00	$13.50	$15.00	$16.50	$0.00	300
Second quarter regular time	$99	$10.00	$11.50	$13.00	$6.00	900
Second quarter overtime	$99	$12.00	$13.50	$15.00	$0.00	300
Third quarter regular time	$99	$99	$10.00	$11.50	$6.00	800
Third quarter overtime	$99	$99	$12.00	$13.50	$0.00	200
Fourth quarter regular time	$99	$99	$99	$10.00	$6.00	600
Fourth quarter overtime	$99	$99	$99	$12.00	$0.00	150
Demand	500	900	1200	1200	450	4250

8. In Problem 7, suppose that another local microbrewer has some excess capacity and is willing to make 500 barrels of beer per production quarter to the same recipe and specifications for $12.50 per barrel. Given this additional capacity, determine the lowest cost production plan, ignoring proprietary concerns about the recipe. *Hint:* The subcontractor becomes an additional source of supply for each quarter, with a capacity of 500 barrels and a cost of $12.50 per barrel.

Selected References

Anderson, David R., Dennis J. Sweeney, and Thomas A. Williams. *An Introduction to Management Science: Quantitative Approaches to Decision Making.* St. Paul, Minn.: West, 1988.

Bierman, Harold, Charles P. Bonini, and Warren H. Hausman. *Quantitative Analysis for Business Decisions.* Homewood, Ill.: Richard D. Irwin, 1986.

Cook, Thomas M., and Robert A. Russell. *Introduction to Management Sciences.* Englewood Cliffs, N.J.: Prentice-Hall, 1993.

Krajewski, L. J., and H. E. Thompson. *Management Science: Quantitative Methods in Context.* New York: John Wiley & Sons, 1981.

Markland, Robert E., and James R. Sweigart. *Quantitative Methods: Applications to Managerial Decision Making.* New York: John Wiley & Sons, 1987.

Taylor, Bernard W. III, *Introduction to Management Science.* Needham Heights, Mass.: Allyn & Bacon, 1990.

Wagner, Harvey M. *Principles of Operations Research,* 2nd ed. Englewood Cliffs, N.J.: Prentice-Hall, 1975.

Chapter Nine

LAYOUT

WHAT IS LAYOUT PLANNING?

STRATEGIC ISSUES

CREATING HYBRID LAYOUTS

DESIGNING PROCESS LAYOUTS

DESIGNING PRODUCT LAYOUTS

CASE: Hightec, Inc.

CASE: The Pizza Connection

Citicorp's headquarters branch in New York City has a new layout. Before the renovation, there were 19 teller windows at one end of the lobby, a service desk at the other end, and customers shuttling back and forth between them. If, for example, a customer went to the service desk to get account information, she would be directed to a teller. If she wanted to order more checks, the teller would send her to the service desk. Now customers entering the renovated facility face a service desk where a "concierge" handles routine questions and directs the customer to a banker when she needs more help. The sleek, futuristic lobby is filled with light and has triple the old number of automated teller machines to handle the simplest transactions. The bankers themselves sit at semicircular desks devoid of papers and even personal photos so that customers feel that it is their space. Their computer terminals swivel so that customers can see the screens. The number of teller windows has been cut from 19 to 8, but the bank's hours have been extended to 6 P.M. from 3 P.M. There also is a room in the

Citicorp chose an uncluttered open layout for the lobby of its banking headquarters on Manhattan's Park Avenue.

back where tellers can take turns reconciling their cash drawers without shutting down a window. The new layout is more customer oriented and has boosted the number of transactions and profits.

Facility layout decisions translate the broader decisions about a firm's competitive priorities, process, and capacity into actual physical arrangements of people, equipment, and space. In this chapter we examine layout in a variety of settings, along with techniques of layout analysis.

◆ WHAT IS LAYOUT PLANNING?

What are some key layout questions that need to be addressed?

Layout planning involves decisions about the physical arrangement of economic activity centers within a facility. An **economic activity center** can be anything that consumes space: a person or group of people, a teller window, a machine, a workbench or workstation, a department, a stairway or an aisle, a timecard rack, a cafeteria or storage room, and so on. The goal of layout planning is to allow workers and equipment to operate most effectively. Before a manager can make decisions regarding physical arrangement, four questions must be addressed.

1. *What centers should the layout include?* Centers should reflect process decisions and maximize productivity. For example, a central storage area for tools is most efficient for certain processes, but keeping tools at individual workstations makes more sense for other processes.

2. *How much space and capacity does each center need?* Inadequate space can reduce productivity, deprive employees of privacy, and even create

health and safety hazards. However, excessive space is wasteful, can reduce productivity, and can isolate employees unnecessarily.

3. *How should each center's space be configured?* The amount of space, its shape, and the elements in a center are interrelated. For example, placement of a desk and chair relative to the other furniture is determined by the size and shape of the office, as well as the activities performed there. Providing a pleasing atmosphere also should be considered as part of the layout configuration decisions, especially in retail outlets and offices.

4. *Where should each center be located?* Location can significantly affect productivity. For example, employees who must frequently interact with one another face to face should be placed in a central location rather than in separate, remote locations to reduce time lost traveling back and forth.

The location of a center has two dimensions: (1) *relative location,* or the placement of a center relative to other centers, and (2) *absolute location,* or the particular space that the center occupies within the facility. Both affect a center's performance. Look at the grocery store layout in Fig. 9.1(a). It shows the location of five departments, with the dry groceries department allocated twice the space of each of the others. The location of frozen foods relative to bread is the same as the location of meats relative to vegetables, so the distance between the first pair of departments is equal to the distance between the second pair of departments. Relative location is normally the crucial issue when travel time, materials handling cost, and communication effectiveness are important.

Now look at the plan in Fig. 9.1(b). Although the relative locations are the same, the absolute locations have changed. This modified layout might prove unworkable. For example, the cost of moving the meats to the northwest corner could be excessive. Or customers might react negatively to the placement of vegetables in the southwest corner, preferring them to be near the entrance.

<table>
<tr><td>FIGURE 9.1

Identical Relative Locations and Different Absolute Locations</td><td>

Frozen foods	Dry groceries	Meats
Bread		Vegetables

(a) Original layout

</td><td>

Meats	Dry groceries	Frozen foods
Vegetables		Bread

(b) Revised layout

</td></tr>
</table>

◆ STRATEGIC ISSUES

How should layout reflect competitive priorities?

Layout choices can help immensely in communicating an organization's product plans and competitive priorities. As Managerial Practice 9.1 on page 401 illustrates, if a retailer plans to upgrade the quality of its merchandise, the store layout should convey more exclusiveness and luxury.

Layout has many practical and strategic implications. Altering a layout can affect an organization and how well it meets its competitive priorities by

- facilitating the flow of materials and information,
- increasing the efficient utilization of labor and equipment,
- increasing customer convenience and sales at a retail store,

- reducing hazards to workers,
- improving employee morale, and
- improving communication.

The type of operation determines layout requirements. For example, in warehouses, materials flow and stockpicking costs are dominant considerations. In retail stores, customer convenience and sales may dominate, whereas communication effectiveness and team building may be crucial in an office.

Among the several fundamental layout choices available to managers are whether to plan for current or future (and less predictable) needs, whether to select a single-story or multistory design, whether to open the planning process to employee suggestions, what type of layout to choose, and what performance criteria to emphasize. Because of their strategic importance, we focus on the last two choices.

Layout Types

Should a layout be process, product, hybrid, or fixed position?

The choice of layout type depends largely on the firm's positioning strategy. There are four basic types of layout: process, product, hybrid, and fixed position.

Process Layout.   When positioning strategy calls for low-volume, high-variety production, the operations manager must organize resources (employees and equipment) around the process. A **process layout,** which groups workstations or departments according to function, accomplishes this purpose. For example, in the metal-working job shop shown in Fig. 9.2(a), all drills are located in one area of the machine shop and all milling machines are located in another. The process layout is most common when the same operation must intermittently produce many different products or serve many different customers. Demand levels are too low or unpredictable for management to set aside human and capital resources exclusively for a particular product line or type of customer. Advantages of a process layout over a product layout [illustrated by Fig. 9.2 (b), where centers are arranged in a linear path] include the following.

1. Resources are relatively general purpose and less capital intensive.
2. The process layout is less vulnerable to changes in product mix or new marketing strategies and is therefore more flexible.

FIGURE 9.2
Two Layout Types

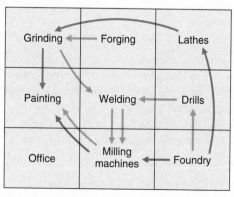

(a) Layout of a job shop

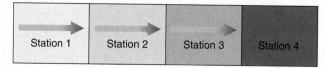

(b) Layout of a production line

▶ *Retailers Match Layouts to Strategies*

J. C. Penney

J. C. Penney is changing its strategy. It is moving from being a low-cost department store to offering better quality merchandise in more attractive stores. Although the stores still offer bottom-of-the-line prices, the overall price mix is up. At the Penney's in Dallas's NorthPark Center, the average price of women's career dresses is $105, up 50 percent from two years earlier. Penney also is emphasizing its specialties. Planners eliminated some departments (e.g., appliances, lawn and garden, paint, hardware, automotive, home electronics, and sporting goods) and expanded others (e.g., apparel, jewelry, and luggage). Penney has upgraded its stores with parquet and carpeting, new mannequins, softer lighting, brash chrome-and-glass fixtures, wood paneling, and more attractive displays of merchandise. Over the past five years, annual revenue has grown 16 percent and net income has more than doubled, to $802 million.

The Limited redesigned its facilities to project a hip, European image.

The Limited

The Limited Inc., the specialty clothing retailer, is reformulating its recipe for success by changing the look of its stores. Once a small outlet geared to teenagers, the store has quadrupled in size and changed its look to that of a European boutique in order to attract older customers. From the grainy wood floors to the black lacquered display cases, the store serves as a stage for trendy sportswear for women. A separate division, Structure, has been created to market men's sportswear. While rivals left their store layouts basically unchanged, The Limited tripled the size of its stores and spent millions on a fresh look. The look is intended to entice customers to spend more time in its stores and pay more for merchandise.

Wal-Mart

Wal-Mart, the discount giant that is the largest U.S. retailer, is experimenting with a prototype store in Rogers, Arkansas to appeal to customers who are as concerned about service as about low prices. With wide aisles, less cramped racks, sitting areas for customers, and attractive displays, the store looks more like an upscale department store than a discount store. As in department stores, the displays organize related products—such as shower curtains, towels, and ceramic bathroom accessories—into visual "vignettes" that encourage sales of "multiples," or related products. Unlike department stores, however, the store has the same bargain-basement prices offered in all its outlets. Many retailing executives consider Wal-Mart the leader in attention to the layout details that help shape shoppers' attitudes. The chain is particularly adept at striking the delicate balance needed to convince customers that its prices are low without making people feel that its stores are cheap.

Sources: "Penney Moves Upscale in Merchandise But Still Has to Convince Public," *Wall Street Journal*, June 7, 1990; "Limited Inc., on New Tack, Pulls Ahead of Retail Gang," *Wall Street Journal*, February 24, 1989; "Wal-Mart's Store of the Future Blends Discount Prices, Department-Store Feel," *Wall Street Journal*, May 17, 1991.

3. Equipment utilization is higher. When volumes are low, dedicating resources to each product or service (as is done with a product layout) would require more equipment than pooling the requirements for all products does.*

*However, management won't allow utilization to get too high. A larger capacity cushion with process layouts absorbs the more unpredictable demands of customized products and services.

4. Employee supervision can be more specialized, an important factor when job content requires a good deal of technical knowledge.

A process focus, with the accompanying process layout, has its disadvantages.

1. Processing rates tend to be slower.
2. Productive time is lost in changing from one product or service to another.
3. More space and capital are tied up in inventory, which helps workstations to work independently despite their variable output rates.
4. The time lags between job starts and end points are relatively long.
5. Materials handling tends to be costly.
6. Diversity in routings and jumbled flows necessitate the use of variable path devices, such as carts rather than conveyors.
7. Production planning and control is more difficult.

A major challenge in designing a process layout is to locate centers so that they bring some order to the apparent chaos of the process-focused operation.

Product Layout.   When a firm's positioning strategy calls for repetitive or continuous production, the operations manager dedicates resources to individual products or tasks. This strategy is achieved by a **product layout**, illustrated by Fig. 9.2(b), in which workstations or departments are arranged in a linear path. As in an automated car wash, the product or customer moves along in a smooth, continuous flow. Resources are arranged around the product's route, rather than shared across many products. (Later we demonstrate that some product layouts, called *mixed-model lines,* can handle several products as long as their processing requirements are similar.) Product layouts are common in high-volume types of operations. Although product layouts often follow a straight line, a straight line isn't always best, and layouts may take an L, O, S, or U shape. A product layout often is called a *production line* or an *assembly line.* The difference between the two is that an assembly line is limited to assembly processes, whereas a production line can be used to perform other processes such as machining.

Product layouts often rely heavily on specialized, capital-intensive resources. When volumes are high, the advantages of product layouts over process layouts include

1. faster processing rates,
2. lower inventories, and
3. less unproductive time lost to changeovers and materials handling.

There's less need to decouple one operation from the next, allowing management to cut inventories. The Japanese refer to a product focus as *overlapped operations,* whereby materials move directly from one operation to the next without waiting in queues. The disadvantages of product layouts include

1. greater risk of layout redesign for products or services with short or uncertain lives,
2. less flexibility, and
3. low resource utilization for low-volume products or services.

For product layouts, deciding where to locate centers is easy because operations must occur in a prescribed order. For example, in a car wash, the routing of the car must proceed from *washing* to *rinsing* to *drying;* rinsing and drying should be placed next to each other in the layout. This arrangement, which simply follows the product's routing, ensures that all interacting pairs of centers are as close together as possible or have a common boundary. The challenge of product layout is to group activities into workstations and achieve the desired output rate with the least resources. The composition and number of workstations are crucial decisions, which we explore later in the chapter.

Hybrid Layout.   More often than not, a positioning strategy combines elements of both a product and a process focus. This intermediate strategy calls for a **hybrid layout,** in which some portions of the facility are arranged in a process layout and others are arranged in a product layout. Hybrid layouts are used in facilities having both fabrication and assembly operations, as would be the case if both types of layout shown in Fig. 9.2 were in the same building. Fabrication operations—in which components are made from raw materials—have a process focus, whereas assembly operations—in which components are assembled into finished products—have a product focus. Operations managers often create a hybrid layout when introducing a flexible manufacturing system (FMS). A FMS (see Supplement B) is a group of computer-controlled workstations where materials are automatically handled and machine loaded. Group technology (GT) cells and one worker, multiple machines (OWMM) lines, which we cover later, are other types of hybrid layouts. These technologies help achieve repeatability, even when product volumes are too low to justify dedicating a single line to one product, by bringing together all resources needed to make a family of parts in one center. The rest of the facility represents a process layout.

A retail store is an example of a hybrid layout in a nonmanufacturing setting. The manager may group similar merchandise, enabling customers to find desired items easily (a process layout). At the same time the layout often leads customers along predetermined paths, such as up and down aisles (a product layout). The intent is to maximize exposure to the full array of goods, thereby stimulating sales.

Fixed-Position Layout.   The fourth basic type of layout is the **fixed-position layout.** In this arrangement, the product is fixed in place; workers, along with their tools and equipment, come to the product to work on it. This type of layout

This aerial view of National Steel and Shipbuilding Company in San Diego shows a Princess Line cruise ship as well as various United States Navy ships undergoing repairs in dry dock. The shipyard provides an example of a fixed-position layout, because the ship stays in place and the workers and their tools come to it to make the repairs.

makes sense when the product is particularly massive or difficult to move, as in shipbuilding, assembling locomotives, making huge pressure vessels, building dams, or repairing home furnaces. A fixed-position layout minimizes the number of times that the product must be moved and often is the only feasible solution.

Performance Criteria

What performance criteria should be emphasized?

Other fundamental choices facing the layout planner concern *performance criteria,* which may include one or more of the following factors.

- Level of capital investment
- Requirements for materials handling
- Ease of stockpicking
- Work environment and "atmosphere"

- Ease of equipment maintenance
- Employee attitudes
- Amount of flexibility needed
- Customer convenience and level of sales

Managers must decide early in the process which factors to emphasize in order to come up with a good layout solution. In most cases, multiple criteria are used. For example, a warehouse manager may emphasize ease in stockpicking, flexibility, and amount of space needed (capital investment), whereas a retail store manager may emphasize flexibility, atmosphere, customer convenience, and sales. Sales are particularly important to retailers, which place items with high profitability per cubic foot of shelf space in the most prominent display areas and impulse-buy items near the entrance or checkout counter.

Capital Investment.   Floor space, equipment needs, and inventory levels are assets which the firm buys or leases. These expenditures are an important criterion in all settings. If an office layout is to have partitions to increase privacy, the cost rises. Even increasing space for filing cabinets can add up. A four-drawer lateral file occupies about nine square feet, including the space needed to open it. At $25 per square foot, that translates into a floor space "rental" of $225 a year. Renovation costs also can be significant. Recent remodeling at J. C. Penney, Sears, and Kmart stores had a total price tag of almost $5 billion. For a manufacturer, renovation costs depend in part on whether management selects a process or a product layout. A process focus reduces equipment needs but may increase needs for space and inventory.

Materials Handling.   Relative locations of centers should restrict large flows to short distances. Centers between which frequent trips or interactions are required should be placed close to one another. In a manufacturing plant, this approach minimizes materials handling costs. In a warehouse, stockpicking costs are reduced by storing items typically needed for the same order next to one another. In a retail store, customer convenience improves if items are grouped predictably to minimize customer search and travel time. In an office, communication and cooperation often improve when people or departments that must interact frequently are located near one another, because telephone calls and memos can be poor substitutes for face-to-face communication. Spatial separation is one big reason why cross-functional coordination between departments can be challenging.

Managerial Practice 9.2

▶ *Layout Flexibility at Work*

Real estate developers have found ways to change the layout of vacant properties and "recycle" them for new uses. A Los Angeles developer converted a men's clothing store into a restaurant, a movie palace into a performing arts center, and several historic office buildings into new offices. Elsewhere a Dallas office building was converted into condominiums, a Denver shopping center became a church, and an Ohio tire factory got new life as an industrial mall. Recycling *new* office buildings, which are vacant in some cities because of a capacity glut, is proving to be a more intractable problem. These layouts are less flexible because their large floor areas leave too much space too far removed from windows to allow conversion to apartments, and the structures aren't designed to support the weight required for industrial or warehouse use.

Honda of America Manufacturing doesn't have flexibility problems with the second auto plant that it built in the United States at East Liberty, Ohio. Touted as a twenty-first-century manufacturing facility, the plant was big enough and laid out in such a way that it can accommodate more lines. As the plant manager said, "Maybe we can expand without expanding," by adding more production lines within the 1.4 million square foot building. The immediate purpose of the new plant is to build Civics, at a rate of 600 cars per day.

Sources: "Developers Recycle Vacant Properties," *Wall Street Journal*, September 23, 1991; "Honda Aims for Flexibility at New Auto Plant," *The Columbus Dispatch*, April 12, 1990.

Flexibility. A flexible layout allows a firm to adapt quickly to changing customer needs and preferences and is best for many situations (see Managerial Practice 9.2). **Layout flexibility** means either that the facility remains desirable after significant changes occur or that it can be easily and inexpensively adapted in response to them. The changes can be in the mix of customers served by a store, goods made at a plant, space requirements in a warehouse, or organizational structure in an office. Using modular furniture and partitions, rather than permanent load-bearing walls, is one way to minimize the cost of office layout changes. So can having wide bays (fewer columns), heavy-duty floors, and extra electrical connections in a plant.

Other Criteria. Other criteria that may be important include labor productivity, machine maintenance, work environment, and organizational structure. Labor productivity can be affected if certain workstations can be operated by common personnel in some layouts but not in others. Downtime spent waiting for materials can be caused by materials handling difficulties resulting from poor layout. Equipment maintenance can be made difficult by inadequate space or poor access. The work environment, including temperature, noise level, and safety, can be layout related; its counterpart in an office or store is the atmosphere created by the layout. Office layouts can reinforce the organizational structure by grouping all members of the same department in the same area, or they can encourage interfunctional cooperation by grouping people by project rather than by function. Some warehouse layouts facilitate stockpicking on a FIFO (first-in, first-out) basis, minimizing loss from spoilage or limited shelf life. Finally, employee attitudes may depend on whether the layout allows workers to socialize, reflects equitably the employees' levels of responsibility, or puts workers under the watchful eyes of a supervisor.

◆ CREATING HYBRID LAYOUTS

Can some miniature product
layouts be created in a
facility?

When volumes aren't high enough to justify dedicating a single line of multiple workers to a single product, managers still may be able to derive the benefits of product layout—line flows, simpler materials handling, low setups, and reduced labor costs—by creating product layouts in some portions of the facility. Two techniques for creating hybrid layouts are one worker, multiple machines (OWMM) stations and group technology (GT) cells. Flexible automation (see Chapter 3 and Supplement B) is a third way to achieve the benefits of high-volume production when volumes for individual items are low.

One Worker, Multiple Machines

If volumes aren't sufficient to keep several workers busy on one production line, the manager might set up a line small enough to keep one worker busy. This is the theory behind the **one worker, multiple machines (OWMM) line,** in which a worker operates several different machines simultaneously to achieve a line flow. Having one worker operate several identical machines isn't unusual. For example, in the semiconductor industry one worker operates several saws that cut silicon bars into slices for computer chips. However, with an OWMM line, several different machines are in the line.

Figure 9.3 illustrates a five-machine OWMM line which is being used to produce a flanged metal part, with the machines encircling one operator in the center. (A U shape also is common.) The operator moves around the circle, performing tasks (typically loading and unloading) that haven't been automated. Different products or parts can be produced on an OWMM line by changing the machine setups. If the setup on one machine is especially time-consuming for one

FIGURE 9.3

One Worker, Multiple Machines (OWMM) Line

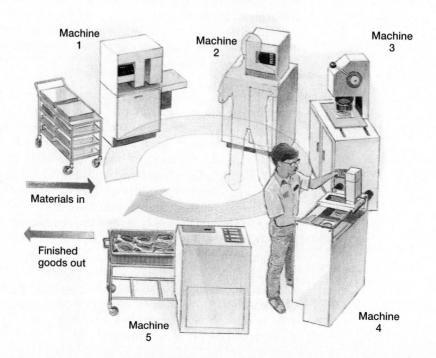

part, management can add a duplicate machine to the cell for use whenever that part is being produced.

An OWMM arrangement reduces both inventory and labor requirements. Inventory is cut because, rather than piling up in queues, materials move directly into the next operation. Labor is cut because more work is automated. The addition of several low-cost automated devices can maximize the number of machines included in an OWMM arrangement: automatic tool changers, loaders and unloaders, start and stop devices, and fail-safe devices that detect defective parts or products. Japanese manufacturers are applying the OWMM concept widely because of their desire to achieve low inventories. For example, the Mitsubishi Electric Company converted more than 25 percent of its machine operations to OWMM.

Group Technology

A second option for achieving product layouts with low-volume processes is **group technology (GT)**. This manufacturing technique groups parts or products with similar characteristics into *families* and sets aside groups of machines for their production. Families may be based on size, shape, manufacturing or routing requirements, or demand. The goal is to find a set of products with similar processing requirements and minimize machine changeover or setup. For example, all bolts might be assigned to the same family because they all require the same basic processing steps regardless of size or shape. Figure 9.4 shows 13 parts belonging to the same family.

FIGURE 9.4

Thirteen Parts Belonging to the Same Family

Source: Mikell P. Groover, *Automation, Production Systems, and Computer-Aided Manufacturing* (Englewood Cliffs, N.J.: Prentice-Hall, 1980), p. 540. Reprinted by permission.

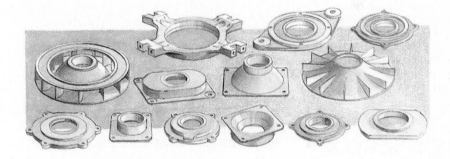

Once parts have been grouped into families, the next step is to organize the machine tools needed to perform the basic processes on these parts into separate areas called *cells*. The machines in each cell require only minor adjustments to accommodate product changeovers from one part to the next in the same family. By simplifying product routings, GT cells reduce the time a job is in the shop. Queues of materials waiting to be worked on are shortened or eliminated. Frequently, materials handling is automated so that, after loading raw materials into the cell, a worker doesn't handle machined parts until the job has been completed. To summarize, GT cells provide the following benefits over traditional process layouts:

- Less setup time
- Lower work-in-process inventory
- Less materials handling
- Reduced cycle time
- Increased opportunities for automation

Figure 9.5 compares process flows before and after creation of GT cells. Figure 9.5(a) shows a shop floor where machines are grouped according to function: lathing, milling, drilling, grinding, and assembly. After lathing, a part is moved to one of the milling machines, where it waits in line until it has a higher priority than any other job competing for the machine's capacity. When the milling operation on the part is finally done, the part is moved to a drilling machine, and so on. The queues can be long, creating significant time delays. Flows of materials are very jumbled because the parts being processed in any one area of the shop have so many different routings.

By contrast, the manager of the shop shown in Figure 9.5(b) has identified three product families that account for a majority of the firm's production. One family always requires two lathing operations followed by one operation at the milling machines. The second family always requires a milling operation followed by a grinding operation. The third family requires the use of a lathe, milling machine, and drill press. For simplicity, only the flows of parts assigned to these three families are shown. The remaining parts are produced at machines

FIGURE 9.5

Process Flows Before and After the Use of GT Cells

Source: Mikell P. Groover, *Automation, Production Systems, and Computer-Aided Manufacturing* (Englewood Cliffs, N.J.: Prentice-Hall, 1980), pp. 540–541. Reprinted by permission.

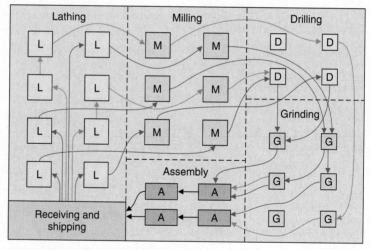

(a) Jumbled flows in a job shop without GT cells

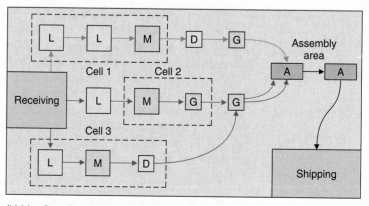

(b) Line flows in a job shop with three GT cells

Managerial Practice 9.3

▶ *Cummins Engine Uses Group Technology*

Cummins Engine Company, a manufacturer of diesel engines based in Columbus, Indiana, uses group technology to achieve high-volume production for some of the 100,000 parts in its catalog. Cummins made the transition from a process layout to cellular production by reorganizing into product departments, each responsible for a family of related products. One engine family has 86 different flywheels, 49 flywheel housings, 17 starter motors, and 12 possible mountings. Components were classified according to volume, predictability of demand, stability of design, and changeover times. Management grouped machines into cells: U-shaped clusters that move a part from lathe to grinder to milling machine with little interruption. Work-in-process inventory is handed off from machine to machine without "resting" and thus goes from one operation to the next smoothly.

The Columbus plant has 15 cells, each machining a comparatively small group of related parts: a water pump line, a flywheel line, a manifold line, and so on. These hybrid layouts, dedicated to a narrower range of parts, required the purchase of some new machines. However, Cummins invested only $60,000 for new machines, $105,000 for additional fixtures and tools, and about $40,000 to move equipment around. In the first year, floor space requirements were reduced by 25 percent, scrap by 30 percent, and work-in-process inventory by 90 percent. More than a million dollars was saved in labor cost. The hybrid layout allows high-volume and low-volume systems to coexist in the same facility.

Source: "Cummins Engine Flexes Its Factory," *Harvard Business Review* (March–April 1990), pp. 120–127.

outside the cells and still have jumbled routings. Some equipment might have to be duplicated, as when a machine is required for one or more cells and for operations outside the cells. However, by creating three GT cells, the manager has definitely created more line flows and simplified routings. Managerial Practice 9.3 describes how Cummins Engine Company successfully uses group technology.

◆ DESIGNING PROCESS LAYOUTS

How can a better process layout be found for a facility?

The approach to designing a layout depends on whether a process layout or a product layout has been chosen. A fixed-position format basically eliminates the layout problem, whereas the design of the hybrid layout partially uses process-layout principles and partially uses product-layout principles.

Process layout involves three basic steps, whether the design is for a new layout or for revising an existing one: (1) gather information, (2) develop a block plan, and (3) design a detailed layout.

Step 1: Gather Information

Longhorn Machine is a machine shop that produces a variety of small metal parts on general-purpose equipment. A full shift of 26 workers and a second shift of 6 workers operate its 32 machines. Three types of information are needed to begin designing a revised layout for Longhorn Machine: space requirements by center, available space, and closeness factors.

Space Requirements by Center. Longhorn has grouped its processes into six different departments: burr and grind, NC equipment, shipping and receiving, lathes and drills, tool crib, and inspection. The exact space requirements of each department, in square feet, are listed below.

Department	Area Needed (square feet)
1. Burr and grind	1000
2. NC equipment	950
3. Shipping and receiving	750
4. Lathes and drills	1200
5. Tool crib	800
6. Inspection	700
Total	5400

The layout designer must tie space requirements to capacity plans, calculate the specific equipment and space needs for each center, and allow circulation space such as aisles and the like.

Available Space. A **block plan** allocates space and indicates placement of each department. When describing a new facility layout, the plan need only provide the facility's dimensions and space allocations. When an existing facility layout is being modified, the current block plan also is needed. Longhorn's available space is 90 feet by 60 feet, or 5400 square feet. The designer could begin the design by dividing the total amount of space into six equal blocks (900 square feet each), even though inspection needs only 700 square feet and lathes and drills needs 1200 square feet. The equal space approximation shown in Fig. 9.6 is good enough until the detailed layout stage, when larger departments (such as lathes and drills) are assigned more block spaces than smaller departments.

Closeness Factors. The layout designer must also know which centers need to be located close to one another. Location is based on the number of trips between centers and qualitative factors.

Following is Longhorn's **trip matrix**, which gives the number of trips (or some other measure of materials movement) between each pair of departments per day.

FIGURE 9.6

Current Block Plan for Longhorn Machine

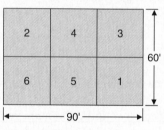

Trip Matrix

Department						
	1	**2**	**3**	**4**	**5**	**6**
1. Burr and grind	—	20		20		80
2. NC equipment		—	10		75	
3. Shipping and receiving			—	15		90
4. Lathes and drills				—	70	
5. Tool crib					—	
6. Inspection						—

The designer estimates the number of trips between centers by using routings and ordering frequencies for typical items made at the plant, by carrying out statistical sampling, or by polling supervisors and materials handlers. Only the right-hand portion of the matrix, which shows the number of trips in *both* directions, is used. For example, there are 75 trips per day between departments 2 (NC equipment) and 5 (tool crib). Showing the merged flow totals eliminates the need to add the flow in one direction to the flow in the other direction. The totals give clues as to which departments should be located close together. For example, the largest number of trips is between departments 3 and 6 (at 90 trips), with 1 and 6 close behind (at 80 trips). Thus the designer should locate department 6 near both 1 and 3, which is not the arrangement in the current layout.

A **REL chart** (REL is short for *relationships*), which reflects the qualitative judgments of managers and employees, can be used in place of a trip matrix. Following is a REL chart for Longhorn Machine. An A rating represents the judgment that locating two particular departments close to each other is absolutely necessary; E is for especially important, I for important, O for ordinary closeness, U for unimportant, and X for undesirable. The A rating is higher than the E, but as the assessment is qualitative, the designer doesn't know by how much. One advantage of a REL chart is that the manager can account for multiple performance criteria when selecting closeness ratings, whereas a trip matrix focuses solely on materials handling or stockpicking costs. For example, the desired closeness between departments 1 and 2 is rated E because of two considerations: ease of supervision and materials handling.

REL Chart

Department	Closeness Rating Between Departments					
	1	2	3	4	5	6
1. Burr and grind	—	E (3, 1)	U	I (2, 1)	U	A (1)
2. NC equipment		—	O (1)	U	E (1)	I (6)
3. Shipping and receiving			—	O (1)	U	A (1)
4. Lathes and drills				—	E (1)	X (5)
5. Tool crib					—	U
6. Inspection						—

Closeness Ratings

Rating	Definition
A	Absolutely necessary
E	Especially important
I	Important
O	Ordinary closeness
U	Unimportant
X	Undesirable

Explanation Codes

Code	Meaning
1	Materials handling
2	Shared personnel
3	Ease of supervision
4	Space utilization
5	Noise
6	Employee attitudes

Other Considerations. Finally, the information gathered for Longhorn includes performance criteria that depend on the *absolute* location of a department. Longhorn has two criteria based on absolute location:

1. Shipping and receiving (department 3) should remain where it is because it is next to the dock.
2. Lathes and drills (department 4) should remain where it is because relocation costs would be prohibitive.

Noise levels and management preference are other potential sources of performance criteria that depend on absolute location. A REL chart or trip matrix cannot reflect these criteria, because it reflects only *relative* location considerations. The layout designer must list them separately.

Step 2: Develop a Block Plan

The second step in layout design is to develop a block plan that best satisfies performance criteria and area requirements. The most elementary way to do so is by trial and error. Because success depends on the designer's ability to spot patterns in the data, this approach doesn't guarantee the selection of the best or even a nearly best solution. When supplemented by the use of a computer to evaluate solutions, however, such an approach often compares quite favorably with more sophisticated computerized techniques.

E X A M P L E   9.1

Developing a Block Plan

Develop an acceptable block plan for Longhorn, using trial and error. The goal is to minimize materials handling costs.

Solution A good place to start is with the largest closeness ratings in the trip matrix (say, 70 and above). Beginning with the largest number of trips and working down the list, you might plan to locate departments as follows:

Departments 3 and 6 close together   Departments 2 and 5 close together
Departments 1 and 6 close together   Departments 4 and 5 close together

Departments 3 and 4 should remain at their current locations because of the "other considerations."

If after several attempts you cannot meet all five requirements, drop one or more and try again. If you can meet all five easily, add more (such as for interactions below 70).

The block plan in Fig. 9.7 shows a trial-and-error solution that satisfies all five requirements. We started by keeping departments 3 and 4 in their original locations. As the first requirement is to locate departments 3 and 6 close to each other, we put 6 in the southeast corner of the layout. The second requirement is to have departments 1 and 6 close together, so we placed 1 in the space just to the left of 6, and so on.

F I G U R E   9.7   *Proposed Block Plan*

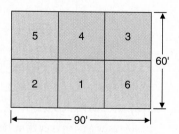

When *relative* locations are a primary concern, such as for effective materials handling, stockpicking, and communication, the load–distance method can be used to compare alternative block plans. Recall from Chapter 8 that we find the total load–distance, or *ld,* score by multiplying each load by the distance traveled and then summing over all of the loads. Here the loads are just the numbers in the trip matrix. Each load goes between two centers (each represented by a row and a column in the matrix). The distance (actual, Euclidean, or rectilinear) between them is calculated from the block plan being evaluated. Of course, the loads need not be trips; any numerical closeness measure related to distance will do.

EXAMPLE 9.2

Calculating the Total Desirability Score

How much better, in terms of the *ld* score, is the proposed block plan? Use the rectilinear distance measure.

Solution   The accompanying table lists each pair of departments that has a nonzero closeness factor in the trip matrix. For the third column, calculate the rectilinear distances between the departments in the current layout. For example, in Fig. 9.6, departments 1 and 2 are in the southeast and northwest blocks of the plant, respectively. The distance between the centers of these blocks is 3 units (two horizontally and one vertically). For the fourth column, we multiply the loads by the distances and then add the results for a total *ld* score of 785 for the current plan. Similar calculations for the proposed plan in Fig. 9.7 produce an *ld* score of only 400. For example, between departments 1 and 2 is just 1 unit of distance (one horizontally and none vertically).

Department Pair	Closeness Factor, *l*	Current Plan		Proposed Plan	
		Distance *d*	Load–Distance Score, *ld*	Distance, *d*	Load–Distance Score, *ld*
1, 2	20	3	60	1	20
1, 4	20	2	40	1	20
1, 6	80	2	160	1	80
2, 3	10	2	20	3	30
2, 5	75	2	150	1	75
3, 4	15	1	15	1	15
3, 6	90	3	270	1	90
4, 5	70	1	70	1	70
			ld = 785		*ld* = 400

To be exact, we could multiply the two *ld* total scores by 30 because each unit of distance represents 30 feet. However, the relative difference between the two totals remains unchanged.

Although the *ld* score in Example 9.2 for the proposed layout represents an almost 50 percent improvement, the designer may be able to do better. However, the designer must first determine whether the revised layout is worth the cost of relocating four of the six departments (all but 3 and 4). If relocation costs are too high, a less expensive proposal must be found.

The following computer output helps in finding a better solution. It shows the *ld* score for the original layout and offers some clues about a better layout.

Much of the 785 score comes from trips between departments 3 and 6 (270) and between departments 1 and 6 (160). One option is to switch the locations of departments 5 and 6, putting department 6 closer to both departments 1 and 3. Additional output (not shown) indicates that the *ld* score for this revised plan drops to 610 and that only two departments have to be relocated. Perhaps this compromise is better.

CMOM - Process Layout

Proposed Plan

2	4	3
6	5	1

Solution

Department Pair	Closeness Rating	Distance	Score
1,2	20	3	60
1,4	20	2	40
1,6	80	2	160
2,3	10	2	20
2,5	75	2	150
3,4	15	1	15
3,6	90	3	270
4,5	70	1	70
		Total	785

Step 3: Design a Detailed Layout

After finding a satisfactory block plan, the layout designer translates it into a detailed representation, showing the exact size and shape of each center, the arrangement of elements (e.g., desks, machines, and storage areas), and the location of aisles, stairways, and other service space. These visual representations can be two-dimensional drawings, three-dimensional models, or even computer-aided graphics. This step helps decision makers discuss the proposal and problems that might otherwise be overlooked. The depiction of Addison-Wesley's distribution center, on pages 420–421, is a good example of a detailed layout.

Aids for Process Layout Decisions

Finding an acceptable block plan is a complex process in real-life situations. A company with 20 departments has 2.43×10^{18} possible layouts if each of the 20 departments can be assigned to any of the 20 locations. Fortunately, several computationally feasible aids are now available for helping managers make process layout decisions.

The **automated layout design program (ALDEP)** is a computer software package that uses REL chart information to construct a good layout. Being a heuristic method, it generally provides good—but not necessarily the best—solutions. ALDEP constructs a layout from scratch, adding one department at a time. The program picks the first department randomly. The second department must have a strong REL rating with the first (say, A or E), the third must have a strong rating with the second, and so on. When no department has a strong rating with the department just added, the system again randomly selects the next department. The program computes a score (somewhat different from the *ld* score used earlier) for each solution generated and prints out the layouts having the best scores for the manager's consideration.

Another powerful computer software package, the **computerized relative allocation of facilities technique (CRAFT)**, is a heuristic method that uses a trip matrix, including materials flow rates, transportation costs, and an initial block layout. Working from an initial block plan (or starting solution), CRAFT evaluates all possible paired exchanges of departments. The exchange that causes the greatest reduction in the total *ld* score is incorporated into a new starting solution. This process continues until no other exchanges can be found to reduce the *ld* score. The starting solution at this point is also the final solution, which is printed out, along with the *ld* score.

Other models have been developed to handle multiple floors and relocation costs. Goal programming, a special form of linear programming, has been used to optimize a solution with several criteria simultaneously. One particularly intriguing development is a method that integrates the last two steps of layout planning (the block plan and detailed layout). A detailed configuration (called a *design unit*) is preassigned to each center and must be maintained throughout the solution process. This constraint prevents unusual shapes from occurring and helps the manager visualize the final layout better.

Warehouse Layouts

Warehouses are similar to manufacturing plants in that materials are moved between activity centers. Much of the preceding discussion on manufacturing layouts applies to warehouses. However, warehouses are a special case because a warehouse's central process is one of storage, rather than physical or chemical change. Figure 9.8 illustrates the simplest type of warehousing layout. The A-1 Distribution Systems warehouse receives items at the dock and moves them to a storage area. Later, stockpickers withdraw inventory to fill individual customer orders. For example, the following table shows that 280 trips per week are made between the dock and the storage area for toasters.

FIGURE 9.8

Layout for A-1 Distribution Systems Warehouse

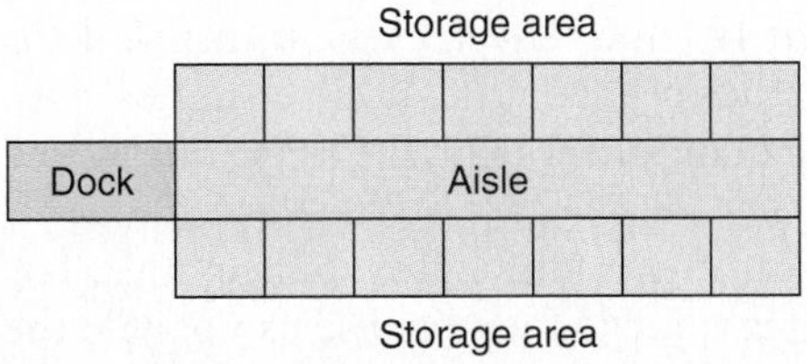

Department	Trips to and from Dock	Area Needed (blocks)
1. Toasters	280	1
2. Air conditioners	160	2
3. Microwaves	360	1
4. Stereos	375	3
5. TVs	800	4
6. Radios	150	1
7. Bulk storage	100	2

A Layout Solution.   We could find a layout solution by the method used in Examples 9.1 and 9.2. However, because all travel takes place between the dock and individual departments and there is no travel between departments, we can use an even simpler method, which is guaranteed to minimize the *ld* score. The decision rule is as follows.

1. *Equal areas.*   If all departments require the same space, simply place the one generating the most trips closest to the dock, the one generating the next largest number of trips next closest to the dock, and so on.
2. *Unequal areas.*   If some departments need more space than others, give the location closest to the dock to the department with the largest ratio of trip frequency to block space. The department with the second highest ratio gets the next closest location, and so on.

EXAMPLE 9.3
Determining a Warehouse Layout

Determine a new layout for the A-1 Distribution Systems warehouse that minimizes the *ld* score.

Solution   Because the departments have different area requirements, we must first obtain the ratio of trips to block spaces:

Department	Ratio	Rank
1. Toasters	280/1 = 280	2
2. Air conditioners	160/2 = 80	6
3. Microwaves	360/1 = 360	1
4. Stereos	375/3 = 125	5
5. TVs	800/4 = 200	3
6. Radios	150/1 = 150	4
7. Bulk storage	100/2 = 50	7

Department 3 (microwaves) has the highest ratio and therefore ranks first. Although 360 trips per week are involved, the department occupies only one block of space. Ranking the remaining departments by their ratios, we get 1, 5, 6, 4, 2, and 7. Figure 9.9 shows the layout derived from this ranking. Department 3 had first choice and could have been placed in either of the two locations nearest the dock. We chose the north one and assigned the south one to department 1.

FIGURE 9.9   *Best Block Plan for A-1 Distribution Systems Warehouse*

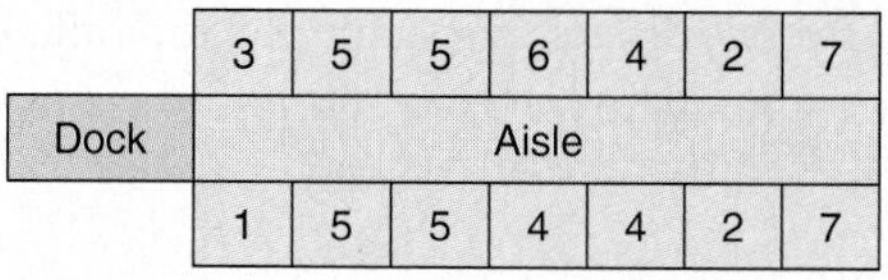

Additional Layout Options.   Although one advantage of the layout just proposed is its simplicity, other options might be more effective. First, demand for different items often is seasonal. Thus an efficient layout might place radios close to the dock for Christmas but move air conditioners near the dock during the summer.

Second, various ways of utilizing space offer additional layout options. For example, an 82,000 square foot, 32 foot high, racked warehouse can handle the

What type of layout pattern makes sense for a warehouse?

same volume as a 107,000 square foot, low-ceilinged warehouse, with the higher stockpicking productivity of the high-ceilinged warehouse offsetting the added rack and equipment costs. Another space-saving design assigns all incoming materials to the nearest available space, rather than to a predetermined area where all like items are clustered. A computer system tracks the location of each item. When it's time to retrieve an item, the system prints its location on the shipping bill and identifies the shortest route for the stockpicker. Canadiana Outdoor Products, in Brampton, Ontario, introduced a computer system with terminals mounted on lift trucks. This arrangement allows drivers to track the exact location and contents of each storage bin in the warehouse. With this new system, Canadiana can handle quadrupled sales with less storage space.

Third, different layout patterns offer still more layout options. The warehouse in Fig. 9.8 has an *out-and-back pattern,* where items are picked one at a time, but there are other options. In a *route collection system,* the stockpicker selects a variety of items to be shipped to a customer. In a *batch picking system,* the stockpicker gathers the quantity of an item required to satisfy a group of customer orders to be shipped in the same truck or rail car. Finally, in the *zone system,* the stockpicker gathers all needed items in her assigned zone and places them on a powered conveyor line. Figure 9.10 illustrates the zone system for a warehouse. The conveyor line consists of five feeder lines and one trunk line. When the merchandise arrives at the control station, an operator directs it to the correct tractor trailer for outbound shipment. The advantage of the zone system is that pickers do not need to travel throughout the warehouse to fill orders; they are responsible only for their assigned zones.

FIGURE 9.10

Zone System for a Warehouse

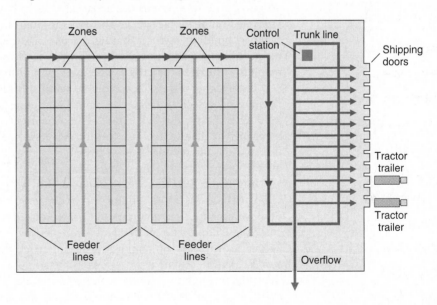

THE BIG PICTURE: Layout of Addison-Wesley Distribution Center*

Addison-Wesley's Distribution Center (DC) consists of four buildings comprising some 400,000 square feet. The first building opened in 1966, and the last one was completed in 1990. Essentially, all four buildings are under one roof, but each was designed and built for a specific purpose. The Big Picture diagram on

*We are indebted to Jeff E. Heyl for researching the information for this tour.

pages 420–421 shows the basic layout of the four buildings. The oldest buildings, 1 and 2, cover about 156,000 square feet. They are used for all the order-filling operations, returns, and order shipping. Building 1 also houses general office space (A). The 257,000 square feet of buildings 3 and 4 is dedicated to warehouse facilities. In addition to greater floor areas, these buildings also have considerably higher ceilings to provide even more storage space.

The DC currently holds about 16 million books in inventory and processes between 2000 and 5000 orders per day. It stores and processes books for primary and secondary schools, colleges and universities, and trade, or popular, bookstores. Demand is highly seasonal, with the peak period being the summer, as schools and colleges prepare for the start of classes. Shipments average less than 1 million units per month from February through April but exceed 2.5 million in July and August. During peak periods, employment swells to 175 workers, from the off-peak average of 125.

The DC has about 65,000 stocking locations in total, and buildings 3 and 4 have about 30,000 pallet locations. Often the facility runs at about 90 percent utilization of stocking locations. Any time a distribution facility is this full, bottlenecks inevitably arise, with the resulting problems.

Four separate processes are performed in the DC. The first is the receipt of new book shipments. The DC receives about 35 million pounds of books each year, delivered on about 1500 individual trucks, from printing plants around the country and the world. Shipments of full pallets of books are received in building 4 (B). The computer system assigns a stocking location, usually based on the type of title: School books generally go into building 4, and college and trade books go into building 3. Books are assigned randomly to locations within each building based on available space. The racks in building 4 are closer together than the racks in building 3, necessitating the use of different materials handling equipment. Building 4 requires narrow, wire-guided forklifts, whereas more traditional manually operated forklifts can be used in building 3.

The second process is the picking and shipping of customer orders. All orders are processed through the central computer system early each morning. By 5:00 A.M. the system has printed the pick lists, shipping orders, and replenishment orders. The warehouse forklift drivers come in at 5:30 A.M., get their pick lists and mobile scanners, and start picking the day's orders from the warehouse and delivering them to the required locations.

In advance of the peak summer season, a "golden zone" of the 80 fastest-selling titles is set up in building 1 (C). These 80 titles comprise about 50 percent of all shipments. The quantity and titles stocked are based on ABC analysis (discussed in Chapter 11) of demand forecasted by Addison-Wesley's sales and marketing staff. Cases of books are picked from the golden zone in response to specific orders. As the case is picked, the shipping label is placed on a conveyor that runs through the middle of the golden zone. Whenever a forklift driver picks and moves a pallet of books, mobile scanners linked to the computer system verify the title and quantity so that stock locations can be replenished.

Books not in the golden zone but for which there are full-case orders are withdrawn daily at adjoining locations in buildings 3 and 4 (D) in response to specific orders. Full cases are picked from the pallets and placed on conveyors (E) that merge with the one from the golden zone and transport the full cases to the shipping area in building 1.

For orders of less-than-case quantities, open cases of the required titles are placed in one of the 17,000 designated stocking locations in flow racks (F). The computer system tracks the status of each location and assigns titles to racks at random when space is available. Employees called loose-book pickers work through the pick list, filling a box with the titles ordered. If the order is large enough to fill a box, the pick list is placed inside the completed box, the shipping label is affixed to the outside, and the open box is placed on a floor-level conveyor to the packaging area (G).

In the packaging area, the box passes over a computerized weigh-in-motion scale, which compares the total weight of the package to the sum of the weights of individual titles. Boxes with incorrect weights are pushed aside automatically for checking. Boxes with correct weights are filled with an environmentally safe packing material, sealed, and sent on the conveyor system to the shipping area (H).

As a final check of their contents, all full boxes pass over another weigh-in-motion scale before being shipped. A laser scans the shipping label, and the system automatically routes the box to one of eight loading docks (I), depending on the type of shipping required and the destination. Workers in the shipping department organize the boxes and load them on trucks for shipment to customers.

Some of the loose-book orders are for quantities too small for a box. These orders are picked like any other loose-book order but follow another conveyor to the wrap line (J). Here the books are wrapped in protective coverings, shipping labels are applied to the packages, and the completed packages are placed in a hopper. The system automatically prepares shipping manifests, and the full hoppers are wheeled to the shipping dock to await pickup by the appropriate carrier. Almost every order, from individual-book orders to multiple-case orders, is shipped within 24 hours of the time it is received at the DC.

The third basic process is the receipt and restocking of returned books. The amount of returns is surprisingly large, about 60,000 shipments per year, comprising about 12.5 percent of the overall volume. Returns from schools and colleges occur when bookstores order more books than they actually sell to students. All returns are received in building 3, where they are staged for processing (K). Operators unpack the returned boxes and check each item for damage; damaged books are sent to a local recycler. The operator scans acceptable books for the identifying ISBN number on the bar code and places the items in one of four boxes according to instructions from the computer system. When these boxes are full, the system assigns the boxes to one of 5400 holding locations in the returns staging carousel (L). The carousel is a two-story set of movable storage shelves where returned books are held until enough have been received to fill a case. When full, cases are sealed and sent back to the warehouse for restocking.

The final basic process is media assembly. Some of the orders received by the DC call for a special mix of materials. For example, an order may call for a computer disk to be bundled with a textbook for sale in a college bookstore. In the media assembly area (M), workers assemble components into a shrink-wrapped package and rebox the product for shipment to the customer. Although the demand has been relatively small in the past and much of the work has been subcontracted, demand for this type of customization is increasing. The DC management is considering how this area might be expanded within the existing buildings.

Cases of the fastest-selling titles are stacked outside the flow racks in the golden zone (C).

A floor-level conveyor transports boxes of books to the packaging area (G).

Returned books are temporarily stored in the 5400 locations in the returns staging carousel (L).

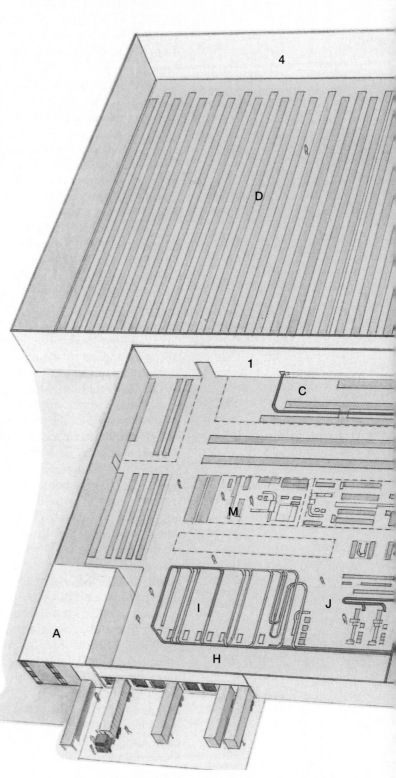

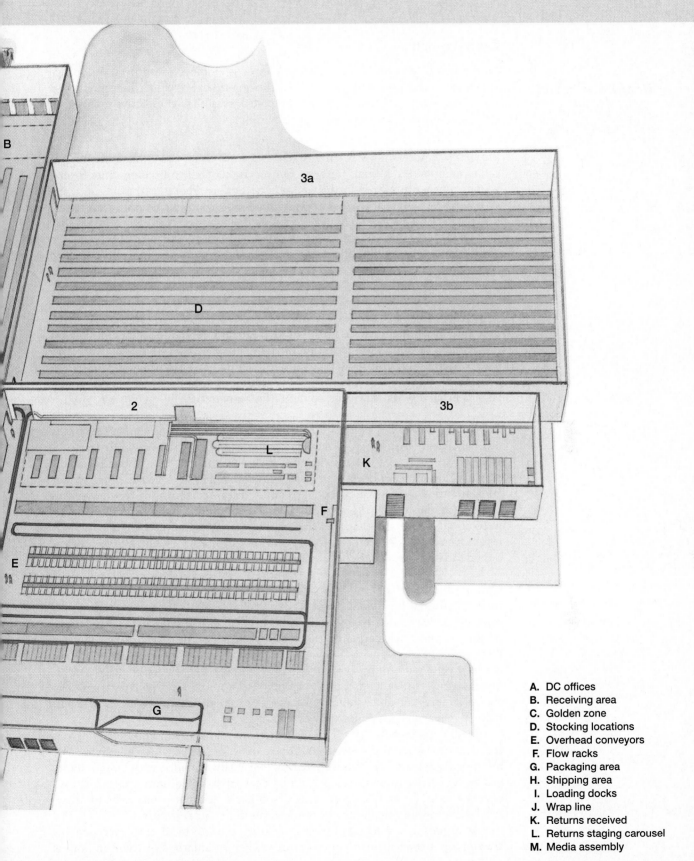

A. DC offices
B. Receiving area
C. Golden zone
D. Stocking locations
E. Overhead conveyors
F. Flow racks
G. Packaging area
H. Shipping area
I. Loading docks
J. Wrap line
K. Returns received
L. Returns staging carousel
M. Media assembly

Office Layouts

What is the best trade-off between proximity and privacy for an office layout?

More than 40 percent of the U.S. work force is employed in offices, and office layout can affect both productivity and the quality of work life. In a recent survey, three-fourths of 1400 employees polled said that productivity could be raised by improvements in their work environments.

Proximity.   Accessibility to co-workers and supervisors can enhance communication and develop mutual interest. Conversations tend to become more formal as individuals are placed farther apart. The famous Hawthorne study in 1939 showed that the physical work setting influences group formation. In the study, management used spatial language to tell workers in the experimental group that they were important. Management changed both absolute and relative locations of the workers by moving them to a separate room and away from the watchful eyes of a supervisor. The revised layout facilitated contact between workers and the setting of group norms. More recent studies confirm that proximity to others can help clarify what is expected of an employee on the job and in other ways.

Most formal procedures for designing office layouts try to maximize the proximity of workers whose jobs require frequent interaction. Data collected on the frequency and importance of interactions can be used in a REL chart or a trip matrix. Certain procedures can be used to identify natural clusters of workers to be treated as a center in a block plan. The goal of such approaches is to design layouts around work flows and communication patterns.

Privacy.   Another key factor in office design—and one that is somewhat culturally dependent—is privacy. Outside disruptions and crowding can hurt a worker's performance. At Sperry Rand's and McDonald's world headquarters, employee reactions to open offices were favorable. However, when a newspaper company tried to increase worker proximity by going from private work spaces to an open-plan office, the results were disappointing. Employees felt as if they were in a fishbowl and that they had little control over their environment. Studies at several state government departments revealed a strong link between privacy and satisfaction with the supervisor and the job.

Options in Office Layout.   Providing both proximity and privacy for employees poses a dilemma for management. Proximity is gained by opening up the work area. Privacy is gained by more liberal space standards, baffled ceilings, doors, partitions, and thick carpeting that absorbs noise—expensive features that reduce layout flexibility. Thus management must generally arrive at a compromise between proximity and privacy. Four different approaches are available: traditional layouts, office landscaping, activity settings, and electronic cottages. The choice requires an understanding of work requirements, the work force itself, and top management's philosophy of work.

Traditional layouts call for closed offices for management and those employees whose work requires privacy and open areas (or bullpens) for all others. The resulting layout may be characterized by long hallways lined with closed doors, producing considerable isolation, and by open areas filled uniformly with rows of desks. In traditional layouts each person has a designated place. Its location, size, and furnishing signify the person's status in the organization.

An approach developed in Germany during the late 1950s puts everyone (including top management) in an open area. The headquarters of Johnson Wax is

Managerial Practice 9.4

▶ *Telecommuting at Pacific Bell*

Pacific Bell, a subsidiary of Pacific Telesis Group, has a formal telecommuting policy. More than 1000 of its managers work fairly regularly from sites other than their primary offices. The company opened two full-blown satellite offices four years ago, each able to accommodate 18 managers who communicate with co-workers and the outside world via personal computers, modems, facsimile machines, copying equipment, and laser printers.

One of the managers in sales support, for example, works at a neighborhood satellite just 15 minutes from his home. He used to make a 26-mile commute to the downtown Los Angeles office, which took an hour when everything went well and up to 2½ hours when it rained. Free from the time-consuming commute and the distractions of Pacific Telesis's main office, he feels that he is functioning more efficiently. He prefers working at an office to working at home, where there are distractions such as doing dishes, mowing the lawn, or seeing what's in the refrigerator. Like other satellite workers, he visits the main office from time to time.

This advertising salesperson stops at a satellite office in Venice, California to make use of mail, computer, and storage facilities. With his laptop computer and portable telephone, he can access information and send faxes while visiting clients.

Source: "Close to You," *Wall Street Journal,* June 4, 1990.

designed with open offices. So is Hewlett-Packard's Waltham, Massachusetts, plant. Shoulder-high dividers partition the space. The idea is to achieve closer cooperation among employees at *all* levels. However, the corporate nurse still keeps earplugs on hand for employees bothered by noise. An extension of this concept is called *office landscaping:* Attractive plants, screens, and portable partitions increase privacy and cluster or separate groups. Movable workstations and accessories help maintain flexibility. Because the workstations (or cubicles) are only semiprivate, employees might have trouble concentrating or might feel uncomfortable trying to hold sensitive discussions. Construction costs are as much as 40 percent less than for traditional layouts, and rearrangement costs are less still.

Activity settings represent a relatively new concept for achieving both proximity and privacy. The full range of work needs is covered by multiple workplaces, including a library, teleconferencing facility, reception area, conference room, special graphics area, and shared terminals. Employees move from one activity setting to the next as their work requires during the day. Each person also gets a small, personal office as a home base.

Some futurists expect more and more employees to work at home or in neighborhood offices, connected to the main office by computer. Called *telecommuting* or *electronic cottages,* this approach represents a modern-day version of the cottage industries that existed prior to the Industrial Revolution. Besides saving on commuting time, it offers flexibility in work schedules. Many working men and women with children, for example, prefer such flexibility. More than nine million Americans already have a taste of this arrangement, working at least part of the week at home. However, telecommuting can have drawbacks, such as lack of equipment, too many family disruptions, and too few opportunities for socialization and politicking. Some managers at Hartford Insurance complained that they couldn't supervise—much less get to know—employees they couldn't see. Managerial Practice 9.4 discusses the telecommuting policy of another company, Pacific Bell.

◆ DESIGNING PRODUCT LAYOUTS

How can a better product layout for a facility be determined?

Product layouts raise management issues entirely different from those of process layouts. Often called a production or assembly line, a product layout arranges workstations in sequence. The product moves from one station to the next until its completion at the end of the line. Typically, one worker operates each station, performing repetitive tasks. Little inventory is built up between stations, so stations cannot operate independently. Thus the line is only as fast as its slowest workstation. In other words, if the slowest station takes 45 seconds per unit, the line's fastest possible output is one product every 45 seconds.

Line Balancing

Line balancing is the assignment of work to stations in a line so as to achieve the desired output rate with the smallest number of workstations. Normally, one worker is assigned to a station. Thus the line that produces at the desired pace with the fewest workers is the most efficient one. Line balancing must be performed when a line is set up initially, when a line is rebalanced to change its hourly output rate, or when product or process changes. The goal is to obtain workstations with well-balanced workloads (for example, every station takes roughly 45 seconds per unit produced).

The analyst begins by separating the work into **work elements,** the smallest units of work that can be performed independently. The analyst then obtains the labor standard (see Chapter 6) for each element and identifies the work elements, called **immediate predecessors,** that must be done before the next can begin.

Precedence Diagram.   Most lines must satisfy some technological precedence requirements—that is, certain work elements must be done before the next can begin. However, most lines also allow for some latitude and more than one sequence of operations. To help you visualize immediate predecessors better, let's run through the construction of a **precedence diagram.*** We denote the work elements by circles, with the time required to perform the work shown below each circle. Arrows lead from immediate predecessors to the next work element.

---

*Precedence relationships and precedence diagrams are important in the entirely different context of project scheduling, as discussed in Chapter 17.

EXAMPLE 9.4
Constructing a Precedence Diagram

Green Grass, Inc., a manufacturer of lawn and garden equipment, is designing an assembly line to produce a new fertilizer spreader, the Big Broadcaster. Using the following information on the production process, construct a precedence diagram for the Big Broadcaster.

Work Element	Description	Time (sec)	Immediate Predecessor(s)
A	Bolt leg frame to hopper	40	None
B	Insert impeller shaft	30	A
C	Attach axle	50	A
D	Attach agitator	40	B
E	Attach drive wheel	6	B
F	Attach free wheel	25	C
G	Mount lower post	15	C
H	Attach controls	20	D, E
I	Mount nameplate	18	F, G
	Total	244	

Solution   Figure 9.11 shows the complete diagram. We begin with work element A, which has no immediate predecessors. Next, we add elements B and C, for which element A is the only immediate predecessor. After entering labor standards and arrows showing precedence, we add elements D and E, and so on. The diagram simplifies interpretation. Work element F, for example, can be done anywhere on the line after element C is completed. However, element I must await completion of elements F and G.

FIGURE 9.11   *Precedence Diagram for Assembling the Big Broadcaster*

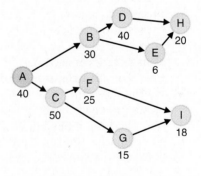

Desired Output Rate.   The goal of line balancing is to match the output rate to the production plan. For example, if the production plan calls for 4000 units per week and the line operates 80 hours per week, the desired output rate ideally would be 50 units (4000/80) per hour. Matching output to demand ensures on-time delivery and prevents buildup of unwanted inventory. However, managers should avoid rebalancing a line too frequently, because each time a line is rebalanced, many workers' jobs on the line must be redesigned, temporarily hurting productivity and sometimes even requiring a new detailed layout for some stations.

What should be a line's output rate?

Some automobile plants avoid frequent changes by eliminating a shift entirely when demand falls and inventory becomes excessive, rather than gradually scaling back the output rate.

Managers can also add shifts to increase equipment utilization, which is crucial for capital-intensive facilities. However, higher pay rates or low demand may make multiple shifts undesirable or unnecessary.

As the desired output rate from a line increases, fewer work elements can be assigned to a station and jobs become more specialized. For example, General Motors added a second shift to its Orion Township plant in Michigan. The line was designed to assemble 67 Cadillacs and Oldsmobiles an hour, an output rate that implies considerable job specialization and a fairly fast moving line.

Cycle Time.   After determining the desired output rate for a line, the analyst can calculate the line's cycle time. A line's **cycle time** is the maximum time allowed for work on a unit at each station.* If the time required for work elements at a station exceeds the line's cycle time, the station will be a bottleneck, preventing the line from reaching its desired output rate. The target cycle time is the reciprocal of the desired hourly output rate:

$$c = \frac{1}{r}$$

where c = cycle time in hours per unit

                      r = desired output rate in units per hour

For example, if the line's desired output rate is 60 units per hour, the cycle time is $c = 1/60$ hour per unit, or 1 minute.

Theoretical Minimum.   To achieve the desired output rate, managers use line balancing to assign every work element to a station, making sure to satisfy all precedence requirements and to minimize the number of stations, *n,* formed. If each station is operated by a different worker, minimizing *n* also maximizes worker productivity. Perfect balance is achieved when the sum of the work-element times at each station equals the cycle time, *c,* and no station has any idle time. For example, if the sum of each station's work-element times is 1 minute, which is also the cycle time, there is perfect balance. Although perfect balance usually is unachievable in practice, owing to the unevenness of work-element times and the inflexibility of precedence requirements, it sets a benchmark, or goal, for the smallest number of stations possible. The **theoretical minimum (TM)** for the number of stations is

$$TM = \frac{\Sigma t}{c}$$

where Σt = total time required to assemble each unit (the sum of all work-element standard times)

             c = cycle time

For example, if the sum of the work-element times is 15 minutes and the cycle time is 1 minute, TM = 15/1, or 15 stations. Any fractional values obtained for TM are rounded up because fractional stations are impossible.

*Except in the context of line balancing, *cycle time* is the elapsed time between starting and completing a job. Some researchers and practitioners prefer the term *lead time.*

Idle Time, Efficiency, and Balance Delay. Minimizing n automatically ensures (1) minimal idle time, (2) maximal efficiency, and (3) minimal balance delay. Idle time is the total unproductive time for all stations in the assembly of each unit:

$$\text{Idle time} = nc - \Sigma t$$

where
n = number of stations

c = cycle time

Σt = total standard time required to assemble each unit

Efficiency is the ratio of productive time to total time, expressed as a percentage:

$$\text{Efficiency (\%)} = \frac{\Sigma t}{nc}(100)$$

Balance delay is the amount by which efficiency falls short of 100 percent:

$$\text{Balance delay (\%)} = 100 - \text{Efficiency}$$

As long as c is fixed, we can optimize all three goals by minimizing n.

EXAMPLE 9.5

Calculating the Cycle Time, Theoretical Minimum, and Efficiency

Green Grass's plant manager has just received marketing's latest forecasts of Big Broadcaster sales for the next year. She wants its production line to be designed to make 2400 spreaders per week for at least the next 3 months. The plant will operate 40 hours per week.

a. What should be the line's cycle time?
b. What is the smallest number of workstations that she could hope for in designing the line for this cycle time?
c. Suppose that she finds a solution that requires only five stations. What would be the line's efficiency?

Solution

a. First convert the desired output rate (2400 units per week) to an hourly rate by dividing the weekly output rate by 40 hours per week to get $r = 60$ units per hour. Then the cycle time is

$$c = \frac{1}{r} = \frac{1}{60} \text{ hour/unit} = 1 \text{ minute/unit}$$

b. Now calculate the theoretical minimum for the number of stations by dividing the total time, Σt, by the cycle time, $c = 1$ minute = 60 seconds. Assuming perfect balance, we have

$$\text{TM} = \frac{\Sigma t}{c} = \frac{244 \text{ seconds}}{60 \text{ seconds}} = 4.067, \qquad \text{or 5 stations}$$

c. Now calculate the efficiency of a five-station solution, assuming for now that one can be found:

$$\text{Efficiency (\%)} = \frac{\Sigma t}{nc}(100) = \frac{244}{5(60)}(100) = 81.3\%$$

Thus if the manager finds a solution that achieves TM, the efficiency (sometimes called the *theoretical maximum efficiency*) will be only 81.3 percent.

Finding a Solution.   Often many assembly-line solutions are possible, even for such simple problems as Green Grass's. As for process layouts, computer assistance is available. For example, one software package considers every feasible combination of work elements that doesn't violate precedence or cycle-time requirements. The combination that minimizes the station's idle time is selected. If any work elements remain unassigned, a second station is formed, and so on.

The approach that we use here is even simpler. We select a work element from a list of candidates and assign it to a station. We repeat this process until all stations have been formed, using k as a counter for the station being formed.

Step 1.   Start with station $k = 1$. Make a list of candidate work elements to assign to station k. Each candidate must satisfy three conditions.

  a. It has not yet been assigned to this or any previous station.
  b. All its predecessors have been assigned to this or a previous station.
  c. Its time does not exceed the station's idle time, which accounts for all work elements already assigned. If no work elements have been assigned, the station's idle time equals the cycle time.

If no such candidates can be found, go to step 4.

Step 2.   Pick a candidate. Two decision rules are commonly used for selecting from the candidate list.

  a. Pick the candidate with the *longest work-element time.* This heuristic rule assigns as quickly as possible those work elements most difficult to fit into a station and saves work elements having shorter times for fine tuning the solution.
  b. Pick the candidate having the *largest number of followers.* Figure 9.11 shows, for example, that work element C has three followers and E has one follower. This rule helps keep options open for forming subsequent stations. Otherwise, precedence requirements may leave only a few possible sequences of work elements, all causing an unnecessary amount of station idle time as a result.

Assign the candidate chosen to station k. If two or more candidates are tied, arbitrarily choose one of them.

Step 3.   Calculate the cumulative time of all tasks assigned so far to station k. Subtract this total from the cycle time to find the station's idle time. Go to step 1, and generate a new list of candidates.

Step 4.   If some work elements are still unassigned, but none are candidates for station k, create a new station, station $k + 1$, and go to step 1. Otherwise, you have a complete solution.

EXAMPLE 9.6	Find a line-balancing solution for the Green Grass, Inc. problem. Use the manual

EXAMPLE 9.6
Finding a Solution

Find a line-balancing solution for the Green Grass, Inc. problem. Use the manual solution procedure, the largest work-element time rule to pick candidates, and a cycle time of 1 minute.

Solution   The following worksheet shows how to proceed, and the first few iterations reveal the pattern. Beginning with the first station, S1 ($k = 1$), the precedence diagram shows that only element A can be a candidate. It is the only one with all immediate predecessors (none, in this case) already assigned. With element A assigned, station S1 has an idle time of 20 seconds ($60 - 40$). Elements B and C cannot now become candidates for station S1, because their times exceed 20 seconds, and so S1 is complete. For the second station ($k = 2$), elements B and C are candidates, and we choose C because it has the larger work-element time. With station S2 now consisting of element C, its idle time equals 10 seconds ($60 - 50$). No candidates remain because adding the time of element B, F, or G brings the work content of S2 over the cycle time ($c = 60$). We continue through the procedure until we have assigned all work elements. The final solution calls for only five stations, as shown in Fig. 9.12. As $n = $ TM $= 5$, we can do no better than this with a 60-second cycle time.

FIGURE 9.12   *Big Broadcaster Precedence Diagram Solution Using Longest Work-Element Time Rule*

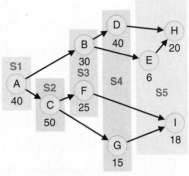

When implementing this solution, we must observe precedence requirements within each station. For example, the worker at station S5 can do element I at any time but cannot start element H until element E is finished.

Worksheet

Station (Step 1)	Candidate (Step 2)	Choice (Step 3)	Cumulative Time (sec) (Step 4)	Idle Time ($c = 60$ sec) (Step 4)
S1	A	A	40	20
S2	B, C	C	50	10
S3	B, F, G	B	30	30
	E, F, G	F	55	5
S4	D, E, G	D	40	20
	E, G	G	55	5
S5	E, I	I	18	42
	E	E	24	36
	H	H	44	16

The solution process can be eased by computer support. The following computer output for the Green Grass problem is based on the longest work-element time rule. It shows the results of much of our manual calculations in Examples 9.5 and 9.6.

```
                CMOM - Layout Design - Line Balancing

                   Solution (Longest Work-Element Time)
  Station                      Time      #Tasks     Task Assignments

     1      Total Time:         40         1        A
            Station Slack:      20

     2      Total Time:         50         1        C
            Station Slack:      10

     3      Total Time:         55         2        B F
            Station Slack:       5

     4      Total Time:         55         2        D G
            Station Slack:       5

     5      Total Time:         44         3        E H I
            Station Slack:      16


            Number of Work Elements                     : 9

            Cycle Time                                  : 60

            Theoretical Minimum Number of Stations : 5

            Number of Stations in Solution              : 5

            Sum of the Work Elements                    : 244

            Efficiency (%)                              : 81.33
```

Computer-based techniques tend to give acceptable, though not necessarily optimal, results. Human judgment and pattern recognition often can improve computer-generated solutions.

Other Considerations

In addition to balancing a line for a given cycle time, managers must also consider four other options: pacing, behavioral factors, number of models produced, and cycle times.

Pacing.   The movement of product from one station to the next after the cycle time has elapsed is called **pacing.** Automated materials handling has a big advantage, but it also has a disadvantage. Capacity losses, difficulties in aligning components that are being assembled, or missing components mean that either the entire line must be slowed down or unfinished work must be pulled off the line to be completed later. *Paced lines* have no buffer inventory, making them particularly susceptible to capacity losses and variability in work-element times. *Unpaced lines* require that inventory storage areas be placed between stations. These storage areas make unexpected downtime at one station less likely to delay work downstream, but they increase space and inventory costs.

Behavioral Factors.   The most controversial aspect of product layouts is behavioral response. Studies have shown that installing production lines increases levels of absenteeism, turnover, and grievances. Paced production and high

What can be done to humanize product layouts?

specialization (say, cycle times of less than two minutes) lower job satisfaction. Workers generally favor inventory buffers as a means of avoiding mechanical pacing. One study even showed that productivity increased on unpaced lines.

Many companies are exploring job enlargement and rotation to increase job variety and reduce excessive specialization. For example, New York Life has redesigned the jobs of workers who process and evaluate claims applications. Instead of using a production line approach with several workers doing specialized tasks, New York Life has made each worker solely responsible for an entire application. This approach increased worker responsibility and raised morale. In manufacturing, at its plant in Kohda, Japan, Sony Corporation dismantled the conveyor belts on which as many as 50 people assembled camcorders. It set up tables for workers to assemble an entire camera themselves, doing everything from soldering to testing. Output per worker is up 10 percent, because the approach frees efficient assemblers to make more product instead of limiting them to a conveyor belt's speed. And if something goes wrong, only a small section of the plant is affected. This approach also allows the line to match actual demand better and avoid frequent shutdowns because of inventory buildups.

Such efforts aren't always as successful because some workers react unfavorably to enlarged jobs. The new format, sometimes called a *craft line* because the workers are jacks-of-all-trades, usually is less efficient at making heavy, high-volume goods, such as automobiles. In fact, AB Volvo closed its much-publicized craft lines at two auto factories in Sweden.

Another option for increasing worker satisfaction is to involve worker groups in making decisions about who is assigned to each station, when jobs are rotated, which specific work elements are assigned to a station, and even how tasks are performed. Management identifies for each group the type of work to be done, specifies the desired daily output rate, and provides the necessary resources. Each group decides the rest. The quality circles pioneered in Japanese industry, which are now becoming more widespread in the United States, are another example of employee involvement.

Other ways to promote positive behavior include arranging station layouts to facilitate social interaction, creating stations where two or more people work together, and giving particular attention to personnel selection. Some workers don't enjoy line work; others actually prefer it. Even a factory's furnishings can make a difference. The Saab assembly plant in labor-starved Sweden is light and spacious, with walls and equipment in matching colors. On the top floor, a restaurant commands a view over the Oresund sound.

Number of Models Produced. A **mixed-model line** produces several items belonging to the same family, such as the Cadillac de Ville and Oldsmobile 98 models. In contrast, a single-model line produces one model with no variations. Mixed-model production enables a plant to achieve both high-volume production *and* product variety. However, it complicates scheduling and increases the need for good communication about the specific parts to be produced at each station. Care must be taken to alternate models so as not to overload some stations for too long. Despite these difficulties, the mixed-model line may be the only reasonable choice when product plans call for many customer options, as volumes may not be high enough to justify a separate line for each model.

Should a mixed-model line be considered?

Cycle Times. A line's cycle time depends on the desired output rate (or sometimes on the maximum number of workstations allowed). In turn, the maximum line efficiency varies considerably with the cycle time selected. Thus exploring a range of cycle times makes sense. A manager might go with a particularly efficient solution even if it doesn't match the output rate. The manager can compensate for the mismatch by varying the number of hours the line operates through overtime, extending shifts, or adding shifts. Multiple lines might even be the answer.

Another possibility is to let finished-goods inventory build up for some time and then rebalance the line at a lower output rate to deplete the excess. Use of this strategy should be weighed against the costs of rebalancing. Japanese automobile manufacturing strategy calls for rebalancing lines about 12 times a year. In the United States, the overall average is only about 3 times per year. The Japanese strategy minimizes inventories and balance delay. The primary disadvantage of the Japanese approach is that it disrupts production during the changeover from one line configuration to another. Greater worker flexibility, cross-training, and job rotation, which are additional elements of the Japanese approach, can minimize such disruptions.

CHAPTER REVIEW

Solved Problem 1

A defense contractor is evaluating its machine shop's current process layout. Figure 9.13 shows the current layout, and the table shows the trip matrix for the facility. Safety and health regulations require departments E and F to remain at their current locations.

FIGURE 9.13

Current Layout

E	B	F
A	C	D

Trips Between Departments

Department	A	B	C	D	E	F
A	—	8	3		9	5
B		—		3		
C			—		8	9
D				—		3
E					—	3
F						—

a. Use trial and error to find a better layout.
b. How much better is your layout than the current one, in terms of the *ld* score? Use rectilinear distance.

Solution   a. In addition to keeping departments E and F at their current locations, a good plan would locate the following department pairs close to each other: A and E, C and F, A and B, and C and E. Figure 9.14 was worked out by trial and error and satisfies all these requirements. Start by placing E and F at their current locations. Then, because C must be as close as possible to both E and F, put C between them. Place A directly south of E, and B next to A. All of the heavy traffic concerns have now been accommodated. Department D is located in the remaining space.

FIGURE 9.14

Proposed Layout

E	C	F
A	B	D

Department Pair	Number of Trips (1)	Current Plan Distance (2)	Current Plan Load x Distance (1) × (2)	Proposed Plan Distance (3)	Proposed Plan Load x Distance (1) × (3)
A, B	8	2	16	1	8
A, C	3	1	3	2	6
A, E	9	1	9	1	9
A, F	5	3	15	3	15
B, D	3	2	6	1	3
C, E	8	2	16	1	8
C, F	9	2	18	1	9
D, F	3	1	3	1	3
E, F	3	2	6	2	6
			ld = 92		*ld* = 67

b. The table reveals that the *ld* score drops from 92 for the current plan to 67 for the revised plan, a 27 percent reduction.

Solved Problem 2

Using rectilinear distances, develop a layout for the warehouse docking area shown in Fig. 9.15. Each of seven departments (A–G) requires one block space—except C, which needs two spaces. The daily trips to and from the dock are 390 for A, 180 for B, 220 for C, 250 for D, 160 for E, 120 for F, and 220 for G.

FIGURE 9.15

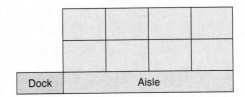

Solution Sequencing departments by the ratio of trips per block space, we get A, D, G, B, E, F, and C, as shown in the table. Giving preference to those higher in the sequence produces the layout shown in Fig. 9.16. There are other optimal solutions because some locations are equidistant from the dock.

FIGURE 9.16

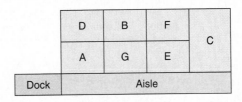

Department	Trips	Block Space	Trips per Block Space
A	390	1	390
D	250	1	250
G	220	1	220
B	180	1	180
E	160	1	160
F	120	1	120
C	220	2	110

Solved Problem 3

A company is setting up an assembly line to produce 192 units per eight-hour shift. The following table identifies the work elements, times, and immediate predecessors.

Work Element	Time (sec)	Immediate Predecessor(s)
A	40	None
B	80	A
C	30	D, E, F
D	25	B
E	20	B
F	15	B
G	120	A
H	145	G
I	130	H
J	115	C, I
Total	720	

a. What is the desired cycle time?
b. What is the theoretical minimum number of stations?
c. Use the largest work-element time rule to work out a solution, and show your solution on a precedence diagram.
d. What are the efficiency and balance delay of the solution found?

Solution   a. Substituting in the cycle-time formula, we get

$$c = \frac{1}{r} = \frac{8 \text{ hours}}{192 \text{ units}} (3600 \text{ seconds/hour}) = 150 \text{ seconds/unit}$$

b. The sum of the work-element times is 720 seconds, so

$$TM = \frac{\Sigma t}{c} = \frac{720 \text{ seconds/unit}}{150 \text{ seconds/unit-station}} = 4.8, \quad \text{or 5 stations}$$

which may not be achievable.

c. The precedence diagram is shown in Fig. 9.17. Each row in the following table represents one iteration of application of the largest work-element time rule in assigning work elements to workstations.

Station	Candidate(s)	Choice	Work-Element Time (sec)	Cumulative Time (sec)	Idle Time (c = 150 sec)
S1	A	A	40	40	110
	B	B	80	120	30
	D, E, F	D	25	145	5
S2	E, F, G	G	120	120	30
	E, F	E	20	140	10
S3	F, H	H	145	145	5
S4	F, I	I	130	130	20
	F	F	15	145	5
S5	C	C	30	30	120
	J	J	115	145	5

FIGURE 9.17

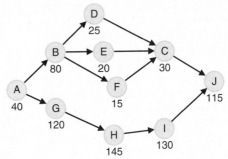

d. Calculating the efficiency, we get

$$\text{Efficiency} = \frac{\Sigma t}{nc}(100) = \frac{720 \text{ seconds/unit}}{5(150 \text{ seconds/unit})}(100)$$

$$= 96\%$$

Thus the balance delay is only 4 percent $(100 - 96)$.

Formula Review

1. Cycle time (in seconds): $\quad c = \frac{1}{r}(3600 \text{ seconds/hour})$
2. Theoretical minimum number of workstations: $\quad \text{TM} = \frac{\Sigma t}{c}$
3. Idle time (in seconds): $\quad nc - \Sigma t$
4. Efficiency (%): $\quad \frac{\Sigma t}{nc}(100)$
5. Balance delay (%): $\quad 100 - \text{Efficiency}$

Chapter Highlights

- Layout decisions go beyond placement of economic activity centers. Equally important are which centers to include, how much space they need, and how to configure their space.
- There are four layout types: process, product, hybrid, and fixed position. Management's choice should reflect its positioning strategy. A process focus calls for a process layout, whereas a product focus calls for a product layout. Hybrid layouts, such as OWMM, GT cells, and FMS, reflect an intermediate positioning strategy.
- Capital investment, materials handling cost, and flexibility are important criteria in judging most layouts. Entirely different criteria, such as encouraging sales or communication, might be emphasized for stores or offices.
- If product volumes are too low to justify dedicating a production line to a single product, obtaining overlapped operations may still be possible. In such cases the one worker, multiple machines (OWMM) concept or group technology (GT) cells, where machines are arranged to produce families of parts, may be feasible.

- Designing a process layout involves gathering the necessary information, developing an acceptable block plan, and translating the block plan into a detailed layout. Information needed for process layouts includes space requirements by center, available space, the block plan for existing layouts, closeness ratings, and performance criteria relating to absolute location concerns. Closeness ratings can be tabulated on either a trip matrix or a REL chart. A manual approach to finding a block plan begins with listing key requirements, which may be based on high closeness ratings or on other considerations. Trial and error is then used to find a block plan that satisfies most of the requirements. A load–distance score is helpful in evaluating the plan for relative location concerns. Several computer-based models, such as ALDEP and CRAFT, are now available to aid layout decision making.
- The simplest warehouse situation is the out-and-back pattern. Departmental proximity to the dock depends on the ratio of trip frequency to space needs. Other patterns are the route collection, batch picking, and the zone systems.

- The effect of a layout on people is particularly apparent in offices. Layout affects productivity and the quality of work life. Four approaches to proximity–privacy trade-offs are traditional layouts, office landscaping, activity settings, and electronic cottages.
- In product layouts, workstations are arranged in a somewhat naturally occurring, commonsense sequence as required for high-volume production of only one product or a family of products. Because the physical arrangement is determined by the product's design, management concerns become line balance, pacing, behavior, number of models, and cycle times.
- In line balancing, tasks are assigned to stations so as to satisfy all precedence and cycle-time constraints while minimizing the number of stations required. Balancing minimizes idle time, maximizes efficiency, and minimizes delay. The desired output rate from a line depends not only on demand forecasts but also on frequency of rebalancing, capacity utilization, and job specialization. One approach to line balancing is to create one station at a time. A work element selected from a list of candidates is added to a station at each iteration. Two commonly used decision rules for making this choice are the longest work-element time and largest number of followers rules.

Key Terms

automated layout design program (ALDEP) *415*
balance delay *427*
block plan *410*
computerized relative allocation of facilities technique (CRAFT) *415*
cycle time *426*
economic activity center *398*
fixed-position layout *403*

group technology (GT) *407*
hybrid layout *403*
immediate predecessors *424*
layout flexibility *405*
layout planning *398*
line balancing *424*
mixed-model line *431*
one worker, multiple machines (OWMM) line *406*

pacing *430*
precedence diagram *424*
process layout *400*
product layout *402*
REL chart *411*
theoretical minimum (TM) *426*
trip matrix *410*
work elements *424*

Study Questions

1. What are the strategic choices that must be made in designing a layout? With which other types of decisions is layout strongly connected? Explain.
2. How does a process layout differ from a product layout? Illustrate each with an example that you have encountered.
3. A proper layout can affect an organization in many ways. Review the ways listed on pages 399–400. What advantage does a U-shaped assembly line have over a straight assembly line?
4. Identify the types of layout performance criteria that might be most important in the following settings.
   a. Airport
   b. Bank
   c. Classroom
   d. Office of product designers
   e. Law firm
   f. Fabrication of sheet metal components
   g. Parking lot
   h. Human resources/ personnel
5. What is the one worker, multiple machines (OWMM) concept? What is a group technology (GT) cell? What do they have in common? How do they differ?
6. An office of 120 employees must be redesigned to accommodate 30 new employees. At the same time it should be made as effective as possible. You want to improve communication, find space for everyone, create a good work environment, and minimize adverse reactions to space reductions and relocation.

   a. What information would you gather? How?
   b. How would you analyze this information?
   c. How much employee involvement would you recommend? Why?

7. Consider the layout of a retail store you recently visited as a customer. What criteria seemed most important to those who designed it? Why?
8. Think of a small- to medium-sized class that you have taken where there was no assigned seating. Did you tend to sit in the same seat each time? Which criterion discussed for office layouts were you implicitly satisfying?
9. Layouts are often designed to fit current work activities and interaction patterns. These, in turn, are partially shaped by the existing layout. Comment on this apparent circularity.
10. What information is needed before you can solve a line-balancing problem?
11. Give an example of a *relative* location consideration and an *absolute* location consideration.
12. Assembly-line cycle time is the inverse of the desired output rate. For example, an output rate of 20 units per hour results in a cycle time of 1/20 hour per unit, which is equivalent to 180 seconds per unit. Why might other cycle times of about 180 seconds per unit be considered?

13. In Solved Problem 3, what positive and negative effects are associated with increasing the production rate from 192 units per 8 hours to 198 units per 8 hours? What would need to be done to increase production to 200 units per 8 hours?

14. Why might employee dissatisfaction be high on assembly lines? What steps might help to alleviate this problem? Will these steps always lead to higher satisfaction and productivity? Explain.

15. Workers trying to keep up with paced lines may have to choose between quality and keeping up with the pace imposed on them. Unpaced lines are less stressful because inventory positioned between workstations absorbs temporary capacity losses and work-element time variability. However, unpaced lines increase space and inventory costs. Can stress, inventory, and space requirements all be reduced at the same time? If so, explain how.

Problems

1. Baker Machine Company is a job shop specializing in precision parts for firms in the aerospace industry. Figure 9.18 shows the current block plan for the key manufacturing centers of the 75,000 square foot facility. Referring to the trip matrix, use rectilinear distance (the current distance from inspection to shipping and receiving is 3 units) to calculate the change in the load–distance, *ld,* score if Baker exchanges the locations of the tool crib and inspection.

Trip Matrix

Department	Trips Between Departments					
	1	2	3	4	5	6
1. Burr and grind	—	8	3		9	5
2. NC equipment		—		3		
3. Shipping and receiving			—		8	9
4. Lathes and drills				—		3
5. Tool crib					—	3
6. Inspection						—

FIGURE 9.18

2. Use trial and error to find a particularly good block plan for Baker Machine (see Problem 1). Because of excessive relocation costs, shipping and receiving (de-

partment 3) must remain at its current location. Compare *ld* scores to evaluate your new layout, again assuming rectilinear distance.

3. The head of the information systems group at Conway Consulting must assign six new analysts to offices. The following trip matrix shows the expected frequency of contact between analysts. The block plan in Fig. 9.19 shows the available office locations (1–6) for the six analysts (A–F). Assume equal-sized offices and rectilinear distance. Owing to their tasks, analyst A must be assigned to location 4 and analyst D to location 3. What are the best locations for the other four analysts? What is the *ld* score for your layout?

Trip Matrix

Analyst	Contacts Between Analysts					
	A	B	C	D	E	F
Analyst A	—		6			
Analyst B		—		12		
Analyst C			—	2	7	
Analyst D				—		4
Analyst E					—	
Analyst F						—

FIGURE 9.19

4. A department in an insurance company is now designing its layout for newly built office space. From statistical samplings over the past three months, the analyst developed the trip matrix shown below for daily trips between the department's offices.

Trip Matrix

	Trips Between Departments					
Department	**A**	**B**	**C**	**D**	**E**	**F**
A	—	10	75			140
B		—			95	
C			—		130	130
D				—	10	
E					—	95
F						—

a. If other factors are equal, which two offices should be located closest together?

b. Figure 9.20 shows an alternative layout for the department. What is the total load–distance score for this plan, based on rectilinear distance and assuming that offices A and B are 3 units of distance apart?

FIGURE 9.20

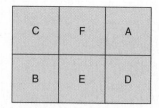

c. Switching which two departments will most improve the total load–distance score?

5. A firm with four departments has the following trip matrix and the current block plan shown in Fig. 9.21.

FIGURE 9.21 *Current Block Plan*

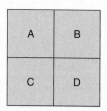

Trip Matrix

	Trips Between Departments			
Department	**A**	**B**	**C**	**D**
A	—	12	10	8
B		—	20	6
C			—	0
D				—

a. What is the load–distance score for the current layout? (Assume rectilinear distance.)

b. Develop a better layout. What is its total load–distance score?

6. The department of philosophy at a university in Ontario must assign six faculty members to their new offices. The trip matrix shown indicates the expected number of contacts per day between professors. The available office spaces (1–6) for the six faculty members are shown in Fig. 9.22. Assume equal-sized

Trip Matrix

	Contacts Between Professors					
Professor	**A**	**B**	**C**	**D**	**E**	**F**
A	—		4			
B		—	12			10
C			—	2	7	
D				—		4
E					—	
F						—

FIGURE 9.22 *Available Space*

offices. The distance between offices 1 and 2 (and between offices 1 and 3) is 1 unit.

a. Because of their academic positions, professor A must be assigned to office 1, professor C must be assigned to office 2, and professor D must be assigned to office 6. Which faculty members should be assigned to offices 3, 4, and 5, respectively, to minimize the total load–distance score? (Assume rectilinear distance.)

b. What is the load–distance score of your solution?

7. As director of the Office of Budget Management for Michigan's state government, Todd Paul manages a department of 120 employees assigned to eight different sections. Because of budget cuts, 30 employees from another department have been transferred and must be placed somewhere within the existing space. While changing the layout, Paul wants to improve communication and create a good work environment. One special consideration is that the state controlling board (section 2) should occupy the northeast location. The trip matrix shown in Table 9.1 was developed from questionnaires sent to each of the 120 current employees. It contains section names, area requirements, and closeness ratings.

a. Develop a square block plan (4 rows and 4 columns) for Paul.

b. What behavioral issues does Paul need to address when revising the layout?

8. Figure 9.23 shows the block layout configuration for a warehouse docking area. Using the information in the table, determine the best layout for an out-and-back pattern if each department must be assigned contiguous space on only one side of the aisle.

Trips and Space Requirements

Department	Trips to and from Dock	Area Needed (blocks)
A	250	2
B	180	1
C	390	3
D	320	4
E	100	1
F	190	2
G	220	1

FIGURE 9.23 *Dock and Storage Space*

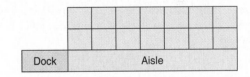

9. The layout configuration for a warehouse docking area is shown in Fig. 9.24. Using the information in the table on the next page on travel frequencies and area requirements for departments A–G, determine the best layout for an out-and-back selection pattern.

FIGURE 9.24 *Dock and Storage Space*

TABLE 9.1 *Trip Matrix*

Section	Trips Between Sections								Area Needed (blocks)
	1	2	3	4	5	6	7	8	
1. Administration	—	3	2	10		2	2		1
2. State controlling board		—		3		2	2		5
3. Program clearinghouse			—			2	2	6	1
4. Social services				—	5	3	2		2
5. Institutions					—	8			3
6. Accounting						—			2
7. Education							—		1
8. Internal audit								—	1

Trips and Space Requirements

Departments	Trips to and from Dock	Area Needed (blocks)
A	330	3
B	240	1
C	180	2
D	460	4
E	300	1
F	60	1
G	280	2

10. Big Reaper plans to produce several new and larger truck models at its Seattle manufacturing facility. Four major warehousing areas in the plant, divided into 12 equal sections, will be used to store the parts and components needed for the new models. Based on current inventory and output plans, the average number of trips per day between storage and the assembly line has been estimated for each of seven basic categories of parts. The number of storage sections needed for each category and the distance from each section to the assembly line have also been calculated. (See the tables.) Assign each category of parts to one or more storage sections so as to provide the right amount of space for each. Find the assignment that minimizes travel from storage to the assembly line. Owing to size restrictions, part category G cannot be assigned to sections 1 and 2.

Part Category	Trips per Day	Number of Sections Needed (blocks)
A	80	1
B	140	2
C	60	1
D	240	4
E	320	2
F	150	1
G	60	1

Section	Distance to Assembly Line	Section	Distance to Assembly Line
1	60	7	190
2	80	8	230
3	90	9	300
4	110	10	305
5	140	11	320
6	160	12	360

11. Use the longest work-element time rule to balance the assembly line described in the table and Figure 9.25 so that it will produce 40 units per hour. Break ties using the largest number of followers rule.
    a. What is the cycle time?
    b. What is the theoretical minimum number of work-stations?
    c. Which work elements are assigned to each work-station?
    d. What are the resulting efficiency and balance delay percentages?

Work Element	Time (sec)	Immediate Predecessor(s)
A	40	None
B	80	A
C	30	A
D	25	B
E	20	C
F	15	B
G	60	B
H	45	D
I	10	E, G
J	75	F
K	15	H, I, J
Total	415	

FIGURE 9.25

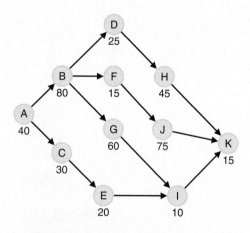

12. A company wants to set up a line to produce 60 units per hour. The work elements and their precedence relationships are shown on the following page.
    a. What is the theoretical minimum number of stations?
    b. How many stations are required if the longest work-element time method is used?
    c. How many stations are required if the largest number of followers method is used?
    d. Suppose that a solution requiring five stations is obtained. What is its efficiency?

Work Element	Time (sec)	Immediate Predecessor(s)
A	40	None
B	30	A
C	50	A
D	40	B
E	6	B
F	25	C
G	15	C
H	20	D, E
I	18	F, G
J	30	H, I
Total	274	

Work Element	Time (min)	Immediate Predecessor(s)
A	1.8	None
B	0.4	None
C	1.6	None
D	1.5	A
E	0.7	A
F	0.5	E
G	0.8	B
H	1.4	C
I	1.4	D
J	1.4	F, G
K	0.5	H
L	1.0	J
M	0.8	I, K, L

13. The Illinois Appliance Company is installing a line to produce a vacuum cleaner, and you, as the operations manager, are responsible for designing the line. The line has to produce 480 units per day, and the company operates two 8-hour shifts each day. The work elements, time requirements, and immediate predecessor(s) are as follows.

Work Element	Time (sec)	Immediate Predecessor(s)
A	55	None
B	45	A
C	25	B
D	20	B
E	40	B
F	50	D
G	70	D
H	45	F, G
I	20	E
J	80	C, H, I

a. What is the theoretical number of stations?

b. If you balance the line using the longest work-element time rule, which elements are assigned to station 2?

14. The *trim line* at PW is a small subassembly line that, along with other such lines, feeds into the final chassis line. The entire assembly line, which consists of more than 900 workstations, is to make PW's new E cars. The trim line itself involves only 13 work elements and must handle 20 cars per hour. In addition to the usual precedence constraints, there are two *zoning constraints*. First, work elements 11 and 12 should be assigned to the same station; both use a common component, and assigning them to the same station conserves storage space. Second, work elements 8 and 10 cannot be performed at the same station. Work-element data follow.

a. Draw a precedence diagram.

b. What cycle time (in minutes) results in the desired output rate?

c. What is the theoretical minimum number of stations?

d. Using trial and error, balance the line as best you can.

e. What is the efficiency of your solution?

15. An assembly line must produce 40 wall air conditioners per hour. The following data give the necessary information.

Work Element	Time (sec)	Immediate Predecessor(s)
A	20	None
B	55	A
C	25	B
D	40	B
E	5	B
F	35	A
G	14	D, E
H	40	C, F, G

a. Draw a precedence diagram.

b. What cycle time (in seconds) ensures the desired output rate?

c. What is the theoretical minimum number of stations? the theoretical maximum efficiency?

d. Use the longest work-element rule to design the line. What is its efficiency?

e. Can you find any way to improve the line's balance? If so, explain how.

Advanced Problems

A computer package is recommended for Problems 18, 21, 22b, 24b, and 26.

16. CCI Electronics makes various products for the communications industry. One of its manufacturing plants

makes a device for sensing when telephone calls are placed. A from–to matrix is shown in Table 9.2; the current layout appears in Fig. 9.26. Management is reasonably satisfied with the current layout, although it has heard some complaints about the placement of departments D, G, K, and L. Use information in the from–to matrix to create a trip matrix, and then find a revised block plan for moving only the four departments about which complaints have been made. Show that the load–distance score is improved. Assume rectilinear distance.

FIGURE 9.26   *Current Block Plan*

L	H	B	K
F	I	J	A
C	D	E	G

17. A paced assembly line has been devised to make electric can openers, as the following data show.

Station	Work Element Assigned	Work-Element Time (min)
S1	A	1.8
S2	D, E	0.5, 0.8
S3	C	2.0
S4	B, F, G	0.6, 0.6, 0.7
S5	H, I, J	0.5, 0.2, 0.9
S6	K	1.5

a. What is the maximum hourly output rate from this line? (*Hint:* The line can go only as fast as its slowest workstation.)
b. What cycle time corresponds to this maximum output rate?
c. If a worker is at each station and the line operates at this maximum output rate, how much idle time is lost during each 8-hour shift?
d. What is the line's efficiency?

18. The director of operations at the Good Samaritan Medical Center, an outpatient clinic, is interested in developing a block plan for a new facility. The director desires a layout consisting of four rows and five columns that will accommodate a total of 12 departments. The southwest block in the new complex is reserved for the utilities room (e.g., electrical). Table 9.3 shows the trip matrix and required areas.

TABLE 9.2   *From–To Matrix*

Department	A	B	C	D	E	F	G	H	I	J	K	L
Trips Between Departments												
A. Network lead forming	—											80
B. Wire forming and subassembly		—							50	70		
C. Final assembly			—			120						
D. Inventory storage				—	40							
E. Presoldering			80		—					90		
F. Final testing						—	120					
G. Inventory storage		30					—	40	50			
H. Coil winding								—	80			
I. Coil assembly		70		40					—	60		
J. Network preparation	90									—		
K. Soldering		80									—	
L. Network insertion			60									—

a. Develop an effective block plan and calculate its total rating score.
b. Identify the department pairs that contribute the most to the total rating score.
c. Develop a revised layout that reduces the total rating score based on the results in part b.
d. What would be the impact on your layout plan if management wanted to locate administrative offices in the northwest corner?

19. Sanders Manufacturing seeks a better layout for its plant. The table shows the departments to be located on the first floor of the plant.

Department	Area Needed (square feet)
1 Materials storage	1,300
2 Forming	500
3 Machining	1,000
4 Painting	600
5 Assembly	1,400
6 Stamping	1,200
7 Saw	800
8 Inspection	700
82 Elevator	100
83 Stairs	200
84 Office	800
99 Aisle	2,200
Total	10,800

Figure 9.27 divides the available space into 9 rows and 12 columns. Each block represents 100 square feet, which means that 13 blocks should be allocated to materials storage, 5 blocks to forming, and so on. Productive space is lost to the elevator, stairs, office, and aisle. Their positions, along with those for departments 1 and 6, must remain fixed. Table 9.4 is a

FIGURE 9.27 *Available Space*

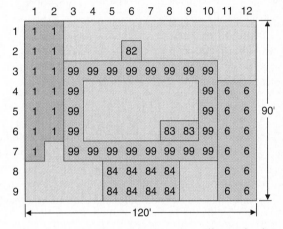

Note: Productive space lost to elevator, stairs, office, and aisle is shown in beige, as are required locations for departments 1 and 6.

TABLE 9.3 *Trip Matrix*

	Trips Between Departments												Area Needed (blocks)
Department	1	2	3	4	5	6	7	8	9	10	11	12	
1. Management	—	2	1	5	2	15	3	8	10	2	2	6	1
2. Surgery		—	20	1	6	4	10		1	3	1	3	4
3. Recovery			—			2	4	3				4	3
4. Admissions				—	2	3		8	4	3	5		2
5. Laboratory					—	4	10	2	5	2	9	2	2
6. Training						—					12	1	1
7. Supplies							—	2				3	1
8. Accounting								—	8	2		4	1
9. Information									—	2		3	1
10. Staff lounge										—		2	1
11. Receiving											—	5	1
12. Security												—	1

REL chart. The letters indicate the closeness score, whereas the numbers in parentheses explain the reason for the rating. For example, the forming department and the assembly department must be close to each other (rating = A) because personnel are shared and supervision is easier. There are two additional considerations:

Closeness Ratings		Explanation Codes	
Rating	**Definition**	**Code**	**Meaning**
A	Absolutely necessary	1	Materials handling
E	Especially important	2	Shared personnel
I	Important	3	Ease of supervision
O	Ordinary closeness	4	Space utilization
U	Unimportant	5	Noise
X	Undesirable	6	Employee attitudes

- Owing to noise factors and the need for special foundations, the stamping department should be put in the southeast corner.
- Materials storage should be on the northwest side, since this is where the shipping and receiving dock will be placed.

Develop an acceptable layout for Sanders, working the remaining departments around the prepositioned departments.

20. The ALDEP score is computed differently from the *ld* score used earlier. First, the letter ratings are converted into numerical equivalents, as, for example, in the following table.

Points	REL Letter	Description
6	A	Absolutely necessary
4	E	Especially important
3	I	Important
2	O	Ordinary closeness
0	U	Unimportant
5	X	Undesirable

(These numerical equivalents are arbitrary, and others could just as easily be used.) Second, these numerical equivalents are added to the total ALDEP score whenever they belong to departments that touch somewhere along their borders—except in the case of X, where points are added when borders do not touch.

21. The manager of the Tastegood Pizza Parlor wants to organize the tasks involved in the preparation and de-

TABLE 9.4 *REL Chart*

	Closeness Ratings Between Departments							
Department	**1**	**2**	**3**	**4**	**5**	**6**	**7**	**8**
1. Materials storage	—	O (1)	O (1)	U	E (1)	U	O (1)	E (1)
2. Forming		—	E (1)	U	A (2, 3)	U	I (1)	O (1)
3. Machining			—	I (1)	O (1)	U (1)	I (1)	U
4. Painting				—	E (2, 3)	O	U (1)	E (4)
5. Assembly					—	X (5, 6)	I (1)	I (1)
6. Stamping						—	I (1)	O (1)
7. Saw							—	I (1)
8. Inspection								—

livery of pizzas. The manager plans to produce 100 pizzas per 10-hour workday. The following table presents work-element times and precedence relationships.

Work Element	Time (min)	Immediate Predecessor(s)
A	2	None
B	3	A
C	1	B
D	5	B
E	5	C, D
F	4	E
G	1	D, E
H	2	F
I	6	G
J	4	H
K	2	I, J
L	6	K

a. Construct a precedence diagram for this process.
b. What cycle time corresponds to the desired output rate?
c. Try to identify the best possible line-balancing solution. What work elements are assigned to each station?
d. What is the impact on your solution if the time for work element 6 increases by 50 percent? decreases by 50 percent?

22. Green Grass, Inc. is expanding its product line to include a new fertilizer spreader called the Big Broadcaster. Operations plans to make the Big Broadcaster on a new assembly line, with most parts purchased from outside suppliers. Karen Annay, the plant manager, obtained the information shown in Table 9.5 concerning work elements, labor standards, and immediate predecessors for the Big Broadcaster.
a. Construct a precedence diagram for the Big Broadcaster.
b. Find a line-balancing solution using the longest work-element time rule so that the line will produce 2400 Big Broadcasters per week with one shift of 40 hours.
c. Calculate the efficiency and balance delay of your solution.

23. The table on the following page has been partially completed from the information in Problem 22 for the Big Broadcaster.
a. Complete the table by filling in the last column.
b. Find a line-balancing solution using the largest number of followers rule. Break ties using the largest work-element time rule. If a tie remains, pick the work element with the highest numerical label.
c. Calculate the efficiency and balance delay of your solution.

TABLE 9.5   *Big Broadcaster Assembly*

Work Element	Description	Time (sec)	Immediate Predecessor(s)	Work Element	Description	Time (sec)	Immediate Predecessor(s)
	Attach leg frame				*Attach free wheel*		
A	Bolt leg frame to hopper	51	None	L	Slip on free wheel	30	G
B	Insert impeller shaft into hopper	7	A	M	Place washer over axle	6	L
C	Attach agitator to shaft	24	B	N	Secure with cotter pin	15	M
D	Secure with cotter pin	10	C	O	Push on hub cap	9	N
	Attach axle				*Mount lower post*		
E	Insert bearings into housings	25	A	P	Bolt lower handle post to hopper	27	G
F	Slip axle through first bearing and shaft	40	E	Q	Seat post in square hole	13	P
G	Slip axle through second bearing	20	D, F	R	Secure leg to support strap	60	Q
	Attach drive wheel				*Attach controls*		
H	Slip on drive wheel	35	G	S	Insert control wire	28	K, O, R
I	Place washer over axle	6	H	T	Guide wire through slot	12	S
J	Secure with cotter pin	15	I	U	Slip T handle over lower post	21	T
K	Push on hub cap	9	J	V	Attach on-off control	26	U
				W	Attach level	58	V
				X	Mount nameplate	29	R
					Total	576	

Work Element	Number of Followers		Work Element	Number of Followers
A	23		M	
B	20		N	
C	19		O	
D	18		P	
E	19		Q	
F	18		R	
G	17		S	
H	8		T	
I	7		U	
J	6		V	
K	5		W	
L	8		X	

24. Green Grass's plant manager (see Problem 22) is willing to consider a line balance with an output rate of less than 60 units per hour if the gain in efficiency is sufficient. Operating the line longer (with either a second shift or overtime) and setting up two lines are ways to compensate for the lower rate.

   a. Calculate the theoretical maximum efficiency for output rates of 30, 35, 40, 45, 50, 55, and 60 units per hour. Is there any possible gain in efficiency when the output rate is reduced to as low as 30?

   b. Use the longest work-element time rule to explore solutions over the range of output rates for which efficiency gains might be achieved.

25. Mohan Assemblies, Inc. manufactures customized wire harnesses for kitchen appliances, snowmobiles, farm machinery, and motorcycles. Table 9.6 shows the trip matrix and areas needed, and Figure 9.28 shows the current layout of the plant.

   a. Develop a better layout, but keep departments 2, 16, and 99 (dead space) at their current positions.

   b. Use ALDEP to calculate scores for both plants (see Problem 20). How much better is your plan?

TABLE 9.6 *Trip Matrix*

Department	Trips Between Departments																	Area Needed (blocks)
	1	2	3	4	5	6	7	8	9	10	11	12	13	14	15	16	99	
1. Terminal storage	—	1		8	4		4											6
2. Shipping and receiving		—	1								2							6
3. Wire storage			—	8		5												6
4. Finished goods				—	11	16		1										6
5. Terminating					—	18	5			6			3	5	5			6
6. Cutting I						—	2											3
7. Cutting II							—	2		6			1	1	1			2
8. Painting								—		3								3
9. Processing									—									3
10. Work-in-process										—			3	2	3			10
11. Rest rooms											—							1
12. Supplies												—	2	2	1			4
13. Assembly I													—	2	2			4
14. Assembly II														—	1			4
15. Custom assembly															—			3
16. Offices																—		3
99. Dead space																	—	20

FIGURE 9.28

	1	2	3	4	5	6
1	4	4	2	2	99	99
2	4	4	2	2	3	3
3	4	4	2	2	3	3
4	5	1	1	1	3	3
5	5	1	1	1	10	10
6	5	6	6	6	10	10
7	5	7	7	11	10	10
8	5	9	9	9	10	10
9	5	8	8	8	10	10
10	12	12	12	99	99	99
11	13	14	12	99	99	99
12	13	14	15	99	99	99
13	13	14	15	99	99	99
14	13	14	15	99	99	99
15	16	16	16	99	99	99

TABLE 9.7   *Trip Matrix*

Department	Trips Between Departments							
	1	2	3	4	5	6	7	8
1. Reception	—	25	35	5	10	15		20
2. Business office		—	5	10	15			15
3. Examining room			—	20	30	20		10
4. X-ray				—	25	15		25
5. Laboratory					—	20		25
6. Surgery						—	40	
7. Postsurgery							—	15
8. Doctor's office								—

26. The associate administrator at Getwell Hospital wants to evaluate the layout of the outpatient clinic. Table 9.7 shows the interdepartmental flows (patients/day) between departments; Fig. 9.29 shows the current layout.

FIGURE 9.29   *Current Layout*

a. Determine the effectiveness of the current layout, as measured by the total *ld* score, using rectilinear distances.
b. Try to find the best possible layout based on the same effectiveness measure.
c. What is the impact on your new solution if it must be revised to keep department 1 at its present location?
d. How should the layout developed in part c be revised if the interdepartmental flow between the examining room and the X-ray department is increased by 50 percent? decreased by 50 percent?

CASE

Hightec, Inc.

"It's hard to believe," thought Glenn Moore as he walked into the employee lunch area, "that it has been only six years since I founded Hightec." He was not interested in lunch because it was only 9:30 A.M. His purpose was to inspect the new microcomputer, which had just been purchased to improve management of the company's inventory and accounting functions. The computer had to be housed at the rear of the employee lunch area,

right next to the coffee, hot soup, and hot chocolate vending machines. There was absolutely no room for the computer elsewhere.

Hightec is a manufacturer of transducers, which convert gas or liquid pressure into an electrical signal. Another form of the device converts weight or force into an electrical signal. A typical customer order is for only 3 to 10 units. The firm currently rents a 12,000 square foot, L-shaped building housing four basic sections: the office area, an engineering area, a machine shop, and an assembly area. The 80 employees comprise machinists, engineers, assemblers, secretaries, and salespeople.

Although Moore concentrated on finance and marketing during the first two years of Hightec's existence, his activities now are more concerned with production costs, inventory, and capacity. Sales have been increasing about 30 percent per year, and this growth is expected to continue. Specific symptoms of Hightec's problems include the following.

- Space limitations have delayed the purchase of a numerical control machine and a more efficient testing machine. Both promise greater capacity and higher productivity, and their cost is easily justified.

- The machine shop is so crowded that equipment not in constant use had to be moved into the inventory storage area.

- More machines are being operated on second and third shifts than would normally be justified. Productivity is falling, and quality is slipping.

- Approximately 10 percent of the work force's time is spent moving materials to and from the inventory storage area, where inventory at all stages of production is kept. The chaotic supply room makes finding wanted parts difficult, and considerable time is lost searching.

- Approximately 1000 square feet of storage space must be rented outside the plant.

- Lack of capacity has forced Moore to forgo bidding on several attractive jobs. One salesperson is particularly disgruntled because she lost a potentially large commission.

- Several office workers have complained about the cramped quarters and lack of privacy. The quality of employee space also leaves an unfavorable impression on prospective customers who visit the plant.

- Additional help was just hired for the office. To make room for their desks, Moore had to discard his favorite

TABLE 9.8   REL Chart

Department	\multicolumn{15}{c}{Closeness Rating Between Departments}	Area Needed (blocks*)
	1	2	3	4	5	6	7	8	9	10	11	12	13	14	15	
1. Administrative office	—	I	A	E	U	A	E	O	O	O	O	I	E	O	U	3
2. Conference room		—	U	U	U	U	U	U	U	U	U	U	U	U	U	1
3. Engineering & mtls. mgt.			—	I	U	U	O	A	E	E	I	E	E	U	O	2
4. Production manager				—	U	A	A	A	A	A	I	I	E	O	A	1
5. Lunch room					—	U	U	U	U	U	U	U	U	U	U	2
6. Computer						—	A	X	U	U	U	O	I	U	U	1
7. Inventory storage							—	A	O	O	O	O	U	U	U	2
8. Machine shop								—	A	X	I	O	U	U	I	6
9. Assembly area									—	A	A	I	U	I	A	7
10. Cleaning										—	O	O	U	U	U	1
11. Welding											—	O	U	U	U	1
12. Electronic												—	E	U	U	1
13. Sales & accounting													—	O	U	2
14. Shipping and receiving														—	U	1
15. Load test															—	1

*Each block represents approximately 595 square feet.

tropical plant, which started as a cutting when Hightec was formed and had sentimental value.

The Options

Glenn Moore has identified three options for increasing capacity at Hightec. The first is to renew the rental contract on the current facility for another five years and rent portable units to ease the cramped conditions. He discarded it as being inadequate for a growing problem. The second option is to purchase land and build a new 19,000 square foot facility. The most attractive site would cost $100,000 for land, and the construction cost is estimated at $40 per square foot. His cost of capital is about 15 percent.

The third option is to renew the rental contract on the current building for another five years and rent an adjacent 7000 square foot building only 30 feet from the current one. The rental cost of both buildings would be $2800 per month. Choice of this third option would necessitate building a $15,000 corridor connecting the buildings. However, Moore estimates the relocation costs (such as for moving and installing the machines and the loss of regular-time capacity) to be $20,000 less than with the second alternative.

The Layout

Regardless of which option Moore chooses, he must improve on the existing layout. It suffers in terms of materials handling costs and departmental coordination. When Moore initially designed it, he located the office first and then fit the other departments around it as best he could. The main consideration for the other departments was not to have the machine shop next to the cleaning room.

Moore put together the information needed for planning the new layout, as shown in Table 9.8 and Figure 9.30. The projected area requirements should be sufficient for the next five years. Both layouts provide for 19,000 square feet. The REL chart emphasizes materials handling and communication patterns.

FIGURE 9.30

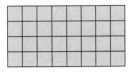

(a) Available space for new plan (Option 2)

(b) Available space for renting two buildings (Option 3)

Glenn Moore walked back to the office with a fresh cup of coffee in his hand. He hated hot chocolate, and it was too early for soup. He wondered what he should do next. Whatever the choice, he wanted a more attractive work environment for the engineering and materials-management staffs, currently located in a cramped, open-office setting. Attracting creative people in these areas had been difficult. He made a mental note that the adjacent building also is quite drab.

Questions

1. Which expansion option would you recommend to Glenn Moore? Justify your position.
2. Design an effective block plan and evaluate it. Cite any qualitative considerations that you believe make your design attractive.

C A S E

The Pizza Connection

Dave Collier owns and operates the Pizza Connection in Worthington, Ohio. The restaurant is a franchise of a large, national chain of pizza restaurants; its product and operations are typical of the industry. As Figure 9.31 shows, the facility is divided into two areas: customer contact and pizza production. Customers enter the facility and wait to be seated by a hostess. In the case of a carry-out order, the customer goes directly to the cashier at the front of the facility to place an order or to pick up a previously phoned-in order. Dine-in customers are served by waiters and waitresses; upon completion of their meal and receipt of the check from the server, they proceed to the cashier to pay their bill and leave. During peak hours at lunch and dinner the cashier's area becomes quite crowded with customers waiting for carry-out orders and dine-in customers trying to pay their bills.

The pizza production area is somewhat of a hybrid layout. Major operations that comprise the pizza production process, such as the preparation tasks, baking, and the cut and box tasks, are grouped together. These individual work centers are arranged in a process flow pattern around the production area.

Historically, Collier's operation has been very successful, benefiting from the rise in popularity of pizza that swept across the country during the past few years. To help take advantage of this trend, the franchiser's home office provided coordinated national and regional marketing and advertising support. It also provided strong product development support. This resulted in a new line of specialty pizzas designed to expand pizza's market appeal.

Recently, however, Collier has noticed a decline in sales. Over the past few months the number of customers has been declining steadily. After doing some research, he came to the following conclusions, which he felt explained the decline in sales.

To begin with, customer demand had changed. Providing high-quality pizza at a reasonable price no longer was enough. The customers now demanded speed, convenience, and alternative dining options. If they were dine-in patrons, they wanted to be able to get in, eat, and get out quickly. Phone-in, carry-out customers wanted their orders ready when they arrived. Also, restaurant "parties" were a growing trend. Little league baseball teams, youth soccer teams, and birthdays all had been part of a growing demand for "party space" in restaurants. The busy, fast-paced lifestyle of today's families was contributing to moving celebrations out of the home and into restaurants and activity centers such as Putt-Putt or the Discovery Zone.

Besides these changing market demands, Collier had seen competition for the consumer's dining dollar increase significantly in the geographical area his restaurant served. The number of dining establishments in the area had more than tripled during the last two years. They ranged from drive-through to dine-in options and covered the entire spectrum from Mexican to Chinese and chicken to burgers.

Collier wondered how he should respond to what he had learned about his market. He thought that a reconfiguration of the restaurant's layout would enable him to address some of these changing customer demands. He hoped a change in facilities would also help with labor turnover problems. Collier was having difficulty keeping trained servers, which he knew was driving up labor costs and causing a deterioration in service to his customers.

Questions

1. Reconfigure the layout in Figure 9.31 to respond to customers' demands for speed and convenience.
2. Explain how your new layout addresses the issues that Dave Collier identified.
3. How can the effectiveness of this new layout be measured?

Source: This case was prepared by Dr. Brooke Saladin, Wake Forest University, as a basis for classroom discussion.

FIGURE 9.31

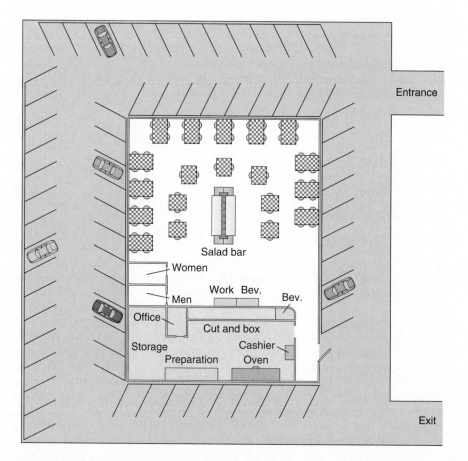

Selected References

Ackerman, K. B., and B. J. LaLonde. "Making Warehousing More Efficient." *Harvard Business Review* (March–April 1980), pp. 94–102.

"Bank Branches May Go the Way of Dime Stores and Dinosaurs," *Wall Street Journal,* December 16, 1993.

Farnum, Gregory T. "Integrating Stamping Operations." *Manufacturing Engineering* (September 1986), pp. 36–38.

Flynn, Barbara B., and F. Robert Jacobs. "An Experimental Comparison of Cellular (Group Technology) Layout with Process Layout." *Decision Sciences,* vol. 18, no. 4 (Fall 1987), pp. 562–581.

Francis, Richard L., Leon F. McGinnis, Jr., and John A. White. *Facility Layout and Location: An Analytical Approach,* 2nd ed. Englewood Cliffs, N.J.: Prentice-Hall, 1992.

Hoffman, T. R. "Assembly Line Balancing with a Precedence Matrix." *Management Science,* vol. 9, no. 4 (July 1963), pp. 551–562.

Homans, G. C. *The Human Group.* New York: Harcourt Brace, 1950.

Jacobs, F. Robert. "A Layout Planning System with Multiple Criteria and a Variable Domain Representation." *Management Science,* vol. 33, no. 8 (August 1987), pp. 1020–1034.

Kottas, J. F., and H. Lau. "Some Problems with Transient Phenomena When Simulating Unpaced Lines." Journal of Operations Management, vol. 1, no. 3 (February 1981), pp. 155–164.

Oldham, G. R., and D. J. Brass. "Employee Reactions to an Open-Plan Office: A Naturally Occurring Quasi-Experiment." *Administrative Science Quarterly,* vol. 24 (1979), pp. 267–294.

Pesch, Michael J., Larry Jarvis, and Loren Troyer. "Turning Around the Rust Belt Factory: The $1.98 Solution." *Production and Inventory Management Journal,* Second Quarter, 1993.

Pinto, Peter D., David Dannenbring, and Basheer Khumawala. "Assembly Line Balancing with Processing Alternatives." *Management Science,* vol. 29, no. 7 (July 1983), pp. 817–830.

Ritzman, Larry P., John W. Bradford, and F. Robert Jacobs. "A Multiple Objective Approach to Space Planning for Academic Facilities." *Management Science,* vol. 25, no. 9 (September 1979), pp. 895–906.

Schuler, Randall S., Larry P. Ritzman, and Vicki L. Davis. "Merging Prescriptive and Behavioral Approaches for Office Layout." *Journal of Operations Management,* vol. 1, no. 3 (February 1981), pp. 131–142.

Seehof, J. M., and W. O. Evans. "Automated Layout Design Program." *Journal of Industrial Engineering,* vol. 18, no. 12 (December 1967), pp. 690–695.

Steel, F. I. *Physical Settings and Organization Development.* Reading, Mass.: Addison-Wesley, 1973.

Stone, Philip J., and Robert Luchetti. "Your Office Is Where You Are." *Harvard Business Review* (March–April 1985), pp. 102–117.

Chapter Ten

FORECASTING

enredon produces low volumes of intricate, handcrafted, household furniture that is sold in 600 retail outlets. Because the demand for high-quality furniture is low, holding it in inventory is very expensive for retailers. Nonetheless, before the recession of the 1980s, Henredon's retailers carried large inventories to attract customers who demanded both high quality and timely service. The recession, however, changed the way retailers dealt with Henredon. They cut inventories to remain price competitive while pressuring Henredon to maintain quality levels and reduce delivery lead times to less than two months.

The average time required to manufacture and ship an order was 11 weeks before the recession. To meet the demand for faster delivery, Henredon needed to reduce the amount of time required to manufacture and ship orders. Accurate forecasts of demand were essential for meeting this competitive priority. The forecasting system in use before the recession based production and inventory schedules on the average of the last four months' demand for a product. This approach wasn't effective because more than 10 percent of Henredon's products were new each year and had no prior order history.

The new forecasting system treats new products differently from mature products. Forecasts for new products are based on a curve created from orders from semiannual furniture shows and Henredon's past experiences with similar products. The curve is

Craftspeople in the finishing area at Henredon Furniture put the final touches on an inlaid wooden table. Each piece of furniture is made to customer specifications for wood and finish.

used for the first 12 months of a product's life, after which traditional statistical forecasting techniques are used. Middle managers, as well as top management, provide inputs to the forecasts. More accurate forecasts provided by the system have helped cut the amount of time needed to manufacture and ship orders to about five weeks. This improvement increased customer service and reduced inventories. Henredon's orders during the recession increased 3 percent over the prerecessionary period even though, industry-wide, sales declined.

Why is forecasting important?

enredon's success demonstrates the value of forecasting. A **forecast** is a prediction of future events used for planning purposes. At Henredon, management needed accurate forecasts of retailer demands to reduce lead times and reduce inventory levels. Accurate forecasts allow schedulers to use machine capacity efficiently, reduce production times, and cut inventories. The manager of a fast-food restaurant needs to forecast the number of customers at various times of the day, along with the products they will want, in order to schedule the correct number of cooks and counter clerks. Managers may need forecasts to anticipate changes in prices or costs or to prepare for new laws or regulations, competitors, resource shortages, or technologies. Although forecasting methods provide useful estimates for planning purposes, they are rarely perfect.

Forecasting methods may be based on mathematical models using historical data available or qualitative methods drawing on managerial experience. In this chapter we explore several forecasting methods commonly used today and their advantages and limitations. We also identify the decisions that managers should make in designing a forecasting system.

◆ DEMAND CHARACTERISTICS

At the root of most business decisions is the challenge of forecasting customer demand. It is a difficult task because the demand for goods and services can vary greatly. For example, demand for lawn fertilizer predictably increases in the spring and summer months; however, the particular weekends when demands are heaviest may depend on uncontrollable factors such as the weather. Sometimes patterns are more predictable. Thus weekly demand for haircuts at a local barbershop may be quite stable from week to week, with daily demand being heaviest on Saturday mornings and lightest on Mondays and Tuesdays. Forecasting demand in such situations requires uncovering the underlying patterns from available information. In this section, we first discuss the basic components of demand and then address the factors that affect demand in a particular situation.

Components of Demand

The repeated observations of demand for a product or service in their order of occurrence form a pattern known as a **time series**. The five basic components of most demand time series are

1. *average,* or the sum of the demand observations for each period divided by the number of data periods;
2. *trend,* or systematic increase or decrease in the average of the series over time;
3. *seasonal influence,* or a predictable increase or decrease in demand depending on the time of day, week, month, or season;
4. *cyclical movements,* or less predictable increases or decreases in demand over longer periods of time (years or decades); and
5. *random* (unforecastable) *error.*

Cyclical movement arises from two influences. The first is the business cycle, which includes factors that cause the economy to go from recession to expansion over a number of years. The other influence is the product or service life cycle, which reflects the stages of demand from development through decline (see Chapter 2). Business cycle movement is difficult to predict because it is affected by national or international events, such as presidential elections or political turmoil in other countries. Predicting the rate of demand buildup or decline in the life cycle also is difficult. Sometimes firms estimate demand for a new product by starting with the demand history for the product it is replacing. For example, the demand rate for digital audiotapes might emulate the demand buildup for stereo cassette tapes in the early stages of their life cycle. The ability to make intelligent long-range forecasts depends on accurate estimates of cyclical movement.

Four of the components of demand—average, trend, seasonal influence, and cyclical movements—combine in varying degrees to define the underlying time pattern of demand for a product or service. The fifth component, random error, results from chance variation and thus cannot be predicted. Random error is the component of demand that makes every forecast wrong. Figure 10.1 shows the first four components of a demand time series, all of which contain random error. A time series may comprise any combination of these components.

FIGURE 10.1

Components of Demand

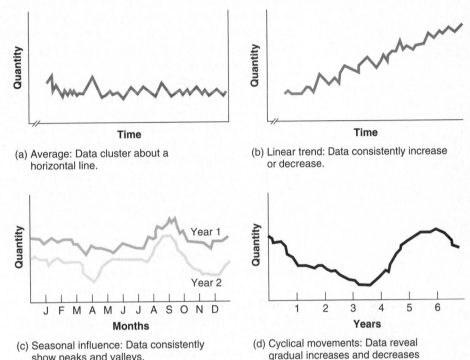

(a) Average: Data cluster about a horizontal line.

(b) Linear trend: Data consistently increase or decrease.

(c) Seasonal influence: Data consistently show peaks and valleys.

(d) Cyclical movements: Data reveal gradual increases and decreases over extended periods of time.

Factors Affecting Demand

What factors cause changes in the demand for a particular product or service over time? Generally, such factors can be divided into two major categories: external and internal.

External Factors.   External factors that affect demand for the firm's products or services are beyond management's control. A booming economy may positively influence demand, although the effect may not be the same for all products and services. Furthermore, certain economic activities such as changes in government regulations affect some products and services but not others. For example, a state law limiting the sulfur content of coal used in steam-powered electric generating plants reduces the demand for high-sulfur coal but doesn't affect the demand for electricity.

Certain government agencies and private firms compile statistics on general economic time series to help organizations predict the direction of change in demand for their products or services. Of prime importance is the *turning point*—that is, the period when the long-term rate of growth in demand for the firm's products or services will change. Although predicting the exact timing of turning points is impossible, some general economic time series have turning points that can be useful in estimating the timing of the turning points in a firm's demands.

Leading indicators, such as the rate of business failures, are external factors with turning points that typically precede the peaks and troughs of the general business cycle. For example, an upswing in residential building contracts might precede an increase in the demand for plywood by several weeks, for homeowners insurance by several months, and for furniture by one year. This indicator gives some advance warning to plywood manufacturers, insurance companies, and furniture manufacturers about possible demand increases. **Coincident indicators,** such as unemployment figures, are time series with turning points that generally match those of the general business cycle. **Lagging indicators,** such as retail sales, follow those turning points, typically by several weeks or months. Knowing that a series is a lagging indicator can be useful. For example, a firm needing a business loan for expansion should realize that interest rates will drop to a low point several weeks after the business cycle reaches its trough.

Let's look briefly at other external factors that affect demand. Consumer tastes can change quickly, as they often do in clothing fashions. The consumer's image of a product can be another big factor in changing demand. For example, in the last decade sales of tobacco products in the United States have dropped significantly because many people believe that those products can be hazardous to their health. In addition, competitors' actions regarding prices, advertising promotions, and new products also affect sales. For example, the United Parcel Service commercial showing the speedy delivery of a parcel reduces the demand for the services of competitors, such as FedEx or DHL. Finally, the success of one product or service affects the demand for complementary products or services. The Milwaukee plant of Harley-Davidson stimulates the sales of many motorcycle parts and components locally. Future demand for parts and components there depends on Harley-Davidson's success in that area.

Internal Factors.   Internal decisions about product or service design, price and advertising promotions, packaging design, salesperson quotas or incentives, and expansion or contraction of geographic market target areas all contribute to changes in demand volume. The term **demand management** describes the process of influencing the timing and volume of demand or adapting to the undesirable effects of unchangeable demand patterns. For example, automobile manufacturers use rebates to boost car sales.

How can demand be influenced?

Management must carefully consider the timing of demand, an extremely important factor in efficiently utilizing resources and production capacity. Trying to produce for peak customer demand during the peak demand period can be very costly. To avoid this situation, firms often use price incentives or advertising promotions to encourage customers to make purchases before or after traditional times of peak demand. For example, telephone companies encourage customers to make long distance calls after normal business hours by offering lower evening and weekend rates. This practice helps spread demand more evenly over the day. Another tactic is to produce two products that have different heavy seasonal demand periods. A producer of engines for tractor lawn mowers, for instance, might also make engines for snowmobiles to even out resource and production requirements over the year. In this way costly changes in work-force level and inventory can be minimized.

Finally, some companies schedule delivery dates for products or services according to the current workload and capacity. Doctors, dentists, and other professionals use this approach by asking patients to make appointments for their services. Manufacturers of custom-built products also work to backlogs of demand.

◆ DESIGNING THE FORECASTING SYSTEM

Before using forecasting techniques to analyze operations management problems, a manager must make three decisions: (1) what to forecast, (2) what type of forecasting technique to use, and (3) what type of computer hardware or software (or both) to use. We discuss each of these decisions before examining specific forecasting techniques.

Deciding What to Forecast

What makes a forecasting system best for any particular situation?

Although some sort of demand estimate is needed for the individual goods or services produced by a company, forecasting total demand for groups or clusters and then deriving individual product or service forecasts may be easiest. Also, selecting the correct unit of measurement (e.g., product or service units or machine hours) for forecasting may be as important as choosing the best method.

Level of Aggregation.   Few companies err by more than 5 percent when forecasting total demand for all their products. However, errors in forecasts for individual items may be much higher. By clustering several similar products or services in a process called **aggregation**, companies can obtain more accurate forecasts. Many companies utilize a two-tier forecasting system, first making forecasts for families of goods or services that have similar demand requirements and common processing, labor, and materials requirements and then deriving forecasts for individual items. For example, General Motors forecasts the demand for Saturn automobiles as a product family, then derives unit forecasts for the SL-1 and SL-2 models from the product family forecast. This approach maintains consistency between planning for the final stages of manufacturing (which requires the unit forecasts) and longer term planning for sales, profit, and capacity (which requires the product family forecasts). We return to this point when we discuss aggregate planning in Chapter 13.

Units of Measurement.   The most useful forecasts for planning and analyzing operations problems are those based on product or service units, such as Saturn SL-1's, express packages to deliver, or customers needing maintenance repairs for their cars, rather than dollars. Forecasts of sales revenue are not very helpful because prices often fluctuate. Thus, even though total sales in dollars might be the same from month to month, the actual number of units of demand could vary widely. Forecasting the number of units of demand—and then translating these estimates to sales revenue estimates by multiplying them by the price—often is the better method. If accurately forecasting the number of units of demand for a product or service isn't possible, forecasting the standard labor or machine *hours* required of each of the critical resources, based on historical patterns, often is better. For companies producing goods or services to customer order, estimates of labor or machine hours are important to scheduling and capacity planning.

Choosing the Type of Forecasting Technique

The forecaster's objective is to develop a useful forecast from the information at hand with the technique appropriate for the different characteristics of demand. This choice sometimes involves a trade-off between forecast accuracy and costs, such as software purchases, the time required to develop a forecast, and personnel training. Three general types of forecasting techniques are used for demand

When are time series methods best and when are causal or judgment methods best?

forecasting: judgment methods, causal methods, and time series analysis. **Judgment methods** translate the opinions of managers, expert opinions, consumer surveys, and sales force estimates into quantitative estimates. **Causal methods** use historical data on independent variables, such as promotional campaigns, economic conditions, and competitors' actions, to predict demand. **Time series analysis** is a statistical approach that relies heavily on historical demand data to project the future size of demand and recognizes trends and seasonal patterns. We describe each technique in more detail later in this chapter. First, however, let's consider the conditions under which these techniques are likely to be applied. Table 10.1 contains examples of demand forecasting applications and the typical planning horizon for each.

TABLE 10.1   *Demand Forecast Applications*

| | Time Horizon | | |
Application	Short Term (0–3 months)	Medium Term (3 months– 2 years)	Long Term (more than 2 years)
Forecast quantity	Individual products or services	Total sales Groups or families of products or services	Total sales
Decision area	Inventory management Final assembly scheduling Work-force scheduling Master production scheduling	Staff planning Production planning Master production scheduling Purchasing Distribution	Facility location Capacity planning Process management
Forecasting technique	Time series Causal Judgment	Causal Judgment	Causal Judgment

Short Term.   In the short term (here, 0–3 months in the future) managers typically are interested in forecasts of demand for individual products or services. There is little time to satisfy demand, so forecasts need to be as accurate as possible for planning purposes. Time series analysis is the method most often used for short-term forecasting. It is a relatively inexpensive and accurate way to generate the large number of forecasts required.

Although causal models can be used for short-term forecasts, they aren't used extensively for this purpose because they are much more costly than time series analysis and require more time to develop. In the short term, operations managers rarely can wait for development of causal models, even though they may be more accurate than time series models. Finally, managers use judgment methods for short-term forecasts when historical data are not available for a specific item, such as a new product. However, these forecast techniques also are more expensive than forecasts generated from time series analysis.

Medium Term.   The time horizon for the medium term is three months to two years into the future. The need for medium-term forecasts relates to capacity planning. The level of forecast detail required isn't as great as for the short term. Managers typically forecast total sales demand in dollars or in the number of units of a group (or family) of similar products or services. Causal models are commonly used for medium-term forecasts. These models typically do a good job of estimating the timing of turning points, as when slow sales growth will turn into rapid decline, which is useful to operations managers in both the medium and the long term.

Some judgment methods of forecasting also are helpful in identifying turning points. As we mentioned earlier, however, they are most often used when no historical data exist. Time series analysis typically doesn't yield accurate results in the medium or long term primarily because it assumes that existing patterns will continue in the future. Although this assumption may be valid for the short term, it is less accurate over longer time horizons.

Long Term.   For time horizons exceeding two years, forecasts usually are developed for total sales demand in dollars or some other common unit of measurement (e.g., barrels, pounds, or kilowatts). Accurate long-term forecasts of demand for individual products or services not only are very difficult to make but also are too detailed for long-range planning purposes. Three types of decisions—facility location, capacity planning, and process choice—require market demand estimates for an extended period into the future. Causal models and judgment methods are the primary techniques used for long-term forecasting. However, even mathematically derived causal model forecasts have to be tempered by managerial experience and judgment because of the time horizon involved and the potential consequences of decisions based on them.

Forecasting with Computers

In many short-term forecasting applications, computers are a necessity. Often companies must prepare forecasts for hundreds or thousands of products or services repetitively. For example, a large network of health care facilities must calculate demand forecasts for each of its services for every department. This undertaking involves voluminous data that must be manipulated frequently. Analysts must examine the time series for each product or service and arrive at a forecast.

The decision to invest in a computerized forecasting system is an important one, as Managerial Practice 10.1 demonstrates. Many forecasting software packages are available for all sizes of computers and offer a wide variety of forecasting capabilities and report formats. As you will learn when we discuss the forecasting techniques, the most arduous task associated with developing a good forecasting model is "fitting" it to the data. This task involves determining the values of certain model parameters so that the forecasts are as accurate as possible. Software packages provide varying degrees of assistance in this regard. The three categories of software packages (Yurkiewicz, 1993) are

1. *manual systems,* whereby the user chooses the forecasting technique and specifies the parameters needed for a specific forecasting model;
2. *semiautomatic systems,* whereby the user specifies the forecasting technique but the software determines the parameters for the model so that the most accurate forecasts are provided; and

Managerial Practice 10.1

▷ *Computerized Forecasting at John H. Harland Company*

The John H. Harland Company is a leading manufacturer of personalized bank checks. The firm manufactures more than 1000 checking products at 20 imprinting plants using complex manufacturing processes, including both make-to-stock and assemble-to-order strategies. The base materials—preprinted assemblies and components—are supplied by the central base stock facility and assorted suppliers. The plants then use the base materials to produce the products to their customers' orders. Competition is keen, and Harland competes on the basis of superior quality, customer service, and price. Consequently, the firm places a high premium on accurate forecasts to achieve high levels of customer service at low cost.

In 1987, the materials group was using simple, manual forecasting methods for each plant, taking a three-month average and modifying it based on their experience and judgment. This process was time-consuming and resulted in only marginal accuracy. Because of the poor forecasts, the plants often ran out of base materials. Dissatisfied with deteriorating inventory and scheduling performance, management purchased computer software that incorporates advanced statistical capabilities. The software simultaneously produces forecasts for thousands of items and features an "automatic forecasting expert system" that performs all the mathematical computations but allows for manual adjustments to the forecasts based on managerial judgment. With the new system the company's plants, located in 16 states, transmit inventory data via modem on the firm's IBM PS/2 computer network. The data then go to a mainframe computer for consolidation. Forecasts are generated for each time series so that the firm's production schedule for the next quarter can be developed.

John H. Harland Company uses an offset press to print personal checks. The sheets of preprinted stock are loaded in front and pass through the rollers for printing of personalized data.

Management credited the computerized forecasting system with the following benefits:

- A 15 percent reduction in inventory costs
- A reduction in schedule changes, from 20 percent to less than 10 percent
- A reduction in the time required to make a forecast, from two weeks to two days
- A 50 percent reduction in the staff assigned to forecasting

Source: "Forecasting Pays Dividends for Check Manufacturer," *P&IM Review with APICS News,* May 1990, pp. 38–39.

3. *automatic systems,* whereby the software examines the data and suggests not only the appropriate technique but also the best parameters for the model.

Software packages for forecasting typically can read data inputs from spreadsheet files, plot graphs of the data and the forecasts, and save forecast files for spreadsheet display of results. The prices of these programs range from $200 to $3000, depending on the data analysis functions they provide. The design of these programs for personal computers and their relatively low price place these packages within the reach of any business.

Marketing and operations usually select a forecasting software package jointly. Typically, an implementation team consisting of marketing and operations staff is charged with selecting a package from the wide variety available. Team members may ask their departments for a "wish list" and then categorize the wishes as "musts" and "wants." Final selection is based on (1) how well the package satisfies the musts and wants, (2) the cost of buying or leasing the package, (3) the level of clerical support required, and (4) the amount of programmer maintenance required.

◆ JUDGMENT METHODS

When adequate historical data are lacking, such as when a new product is introduced or technology is expected to change, firms rely on managerial judgment and experience to generate forecasts. In this section we discuss four of the more successful methods currently in use: sales force estimates, executive opinion, market research, and the Delphi method.

Sales Force Estimates

How can reasonable forecasts be obtained when no historical information is available?

Sometimes the best information about future demand comes from the people closest to the customer. **Sales force estimates** are forecasts compiled from estimates of future demands made periodically by members of a company's sales force. This approach has several advantages.

- The sales force is the group most likely to know which products or services customers will be buying in the near future, and in what quantities.
- Sales territories often are divided by district or region. Information broken down in this manner can be useful for inventory management, distribution, and sales force staffing purposes.
- The forecasts of individual sales force members can be combined easily to get regional or national sales.

But this approach also has several disadvantages.

- Individual biases of the salespeople may taint the forecast; moreover, some people are naturally optimistic, others more cautious.
- Salespeople may not always be able to detect the difference between what a customer "wants" (a wish list) and what a customer "needs" (a necessary purchase).
- If the firm uses individual sales as a performance measure, salespeople may underestimate their forecasts so that their performance will look good when they exceed their projections or may work only up until they reach their required minimum sales.

Executive Opinion

When a new product or service is contemplated, the sales force may not be able to make accurate demand estimates. **Executive opinion** is a forecasting method in which the opinions and experiences of one or more managers are summarized to arrive at a single forecast. Sometimes executive opinion is used to modify an existing sales forecast to account for unusual circumstances, such as a new sales promotion or unexpected international events.

This method of forecasting has several disadvantages. Executive opinion can be costly because it takes valuable executive time. Although that may be warranted under certain circumstances, it sometimes gets out of control. In addition, if executives are allowed to modify a forecast without collectively agreeing to the changes, the resulting forecast will not be useful. For example, suppose that the marketing manager sees the sales force estimates and, feeling a bit more optimistic than the sales force, increases the forecast to ensure the availability of enough product. After receiving the market forecasts, the manufacturing manager further increases the forecast to avoid being blamed for not meeting customer demand. When actual sales are much lower than the forecasts, everyone blames someone else for the extra inventory that was created. Hence the key to effective use of executive opinion is to ensure that the forecast reflects not a series of independent modifications but consensus among executives on a single forecast.

Market Research

Market research is a systematic approach to determine consumer interest in a product or service by creating and testing hypotheses through data-gathering surveys. Conducting a market research study includes

1. designing a questionnaire that requests economic and demographic information from each person interviewed and asks whether the interviewee would be interested in the product or service;
2. deciding how to administer the survey, whether by telephone polling, mailings, or personal interviews;
3. selecting a representative sample of households to survey, which should include a random selection within the market area of the proposed product or service; and
4. analyzing the information using judgment and statistical tools to interpret the responses, determine their adequacy, make allowance for economic or competitive factors not included in the questionnaire, and analyze whether the survey represents a random sample of the potential market.

Focus Suites of Philadelphia offers market research and focus group services. The private suites are equipped with one-way mirrors so that researchers can watch a focus group in session.

Market research may be used to forecast demand for the short, medium, and long term. Accuracy is excellent for the short term, good for the medium term, and only fair for the long term. Although market research yields important information, one shortcoming is the numerous qualifications and hedges typically included in the findings. For example, a finding might be "The new diet burger product received good customer acceptance in our survey; however, we were unable to assess its longer term acceptance once other competitor products make their appearance." Another is that the typical response rate for mailed questionnaires is poor (30 percent is often considered high). Yet another shortcoming is the possibility that the survey results do not reflect the opinions of the market. Finally, the survey might produce imitative, rather than innovative, ideas because the customer's reference point is often limited.

Delphi Method

The **Delphi method** is a process of gaining consensus from a group of experts while maintaining their anonymity. This form of forecasting is useful when there are no historical data from which to develop statistical models and when managers inside the firm have no experience on which to base informed projections. A coordinator sends questions to each member of the group of outside experts, who may not even know who else is participating. Anonymity is important when some members of the group tend to dominate discussion or command a high degree of respect in their fields. In an anonymous group, the members tend to respond to the questions and support their responses freely. The coordinator prepares a statistical summary of the responses along with a summary of arguments for particular responses. The report is sent to the same group for another round, and the participants may choose to modify their previous responses. These rounds continue until consensus is obtained.

The Delphi method can be used to develop long-range forecasts of product demand and new product sales projections. One of its more useful applications is that of **technological forecasting.** The quick pace of technological change makes keeping abreast of the latest advances difficult. The Delphi method can be used to obtain a consensus from a panel of experts who can devote their attention to following scientific advances, changes in society, governmental regulations, and the competitive environment. The results can provide direction for a firm's research and development staff.

The Delphi method has some shortcomings, including the following major ones.

- The process can take a long time (sometimes a year or more). During that time the people considered to be experts may change, confounding the results or at least further lengthening the process.

- Responses may be less meaningful than if experts were accountable for their responses.

- There is little evidence that Delphi forecasts achieve high degrees of accuracy. However, they are known to be fair to good in identifying turning points in new product demand.

- Poorly designed questionnaires will result in ambiguous or false conclusions.

These shortcomings should be carefully considered before the Delphi method is used.

Research has shown that judgment forecasts, generated by practitioners with general forecasting experience in their industries and specific product knowledge, are superior to forecasts generated solely from statistical methods for time series involving a lot of of data variability (Sanders and Ritzman, 1992). However, for more stable time series, statistical methods are better. In the remainder of this chapter we focus on the statistical approaches commonly used in practice.

◆ CAUSAL METHODS: LINEAR REGRESSION

Causal methods are used when historical data are available and the relationship between the factor to be forecasted and other external or internal factors (e.g. government actions or advertising promotions) can be identified. These relationships are expressed in mathematical terms and can be very complex. Causal methods provide the most sophisticated forecasting tools and are very good for predicting turning points in demand and preparing long-range forecasts. We focus here on linear regression, one of the best-known and most commonly used causal methods.

In **linear regression,** one variable, called a **dependent variable,** is related to one or more **independent variables** by a linear equation. The dependent variable, such as demand for doorknobs, is the one the manager wants to forecast. The independent variables, such as advertising expenditures and new housing starts, are assumed to affect the dependent variable and thereby "cause" the results observed in the past. Figure 10.2 shows how a linear regression line relates to the data. In technical terms, the regression line minimizes the squared deviations from the actual data.

FIGURE 10.2

Linear Regression Line Relative to Actual Data

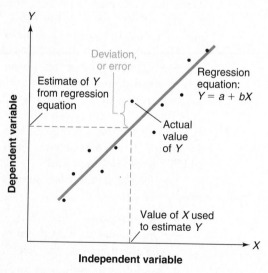

In the simplest linear regression models, the dependent variable is a function of only one independent variable, and therefore the theoretical relationship is a straight line:

$$Y = a + bX$$

where
Y = dependent variable
X = independent variable
a = Y-intercept of the line
b = slope of the line

The objective of linear regression analysis is to find values of a and b that minimize the sum of the squared deviations of the actual data points from the graphed line. The process of finding the values of a and b that minimize the sum of the squared deviations is complex, so we'll merely state the equations here:

$$a = \overline{Y} - b\overline{X} \qquad \text{and} \qquad b = \frac{\sum XY - n\overline{X}\overline{Y}}{\sum X^2 - n\overline{X}^2}$$

where
a = estimate of the Y-intercept
b = estimate of the slope of the line
$\overline{Y}$ = average of the Y-values
$\overline{X}$ = average of the X-values
n = number of data points in the sample

Regression analysis also provides measures of forecast accuracy. The three measures most often used are the correlation coefficient, the coefficient of determination, and the standard error of the estimate. All three can be used to judge whether the independent variable chosen for the model is a good choice.

The **correlation coefficient** measures the direction and strength of the linear relationship between the independent variable and the dependent variable. The correlation coefficient, r, is calculated as:

$$r = \frac{n\sum XY - \sum X \sum Y}{\sqrt{\left[n\sum X^2 - \left(\sum X\right)^2\right]\left[n\sum Y^2 - \left(\sum Y\right)^2\right]}}$$

Values of r can range from -1.00 to $+1.00$. A correlation coefficient of $+1.00$ implies that period-by-period changes in direction (increases or decreases) of the independent variable always are accompanied by changes in the same direction by the dependent variable. An r value of -1.00 means that decreases in the independent variable always are accompanied by increases in the dependent variable, and vice versa. A zero value of r means that there is no relationship between the variables. The closer the absolute value of r is to 1.00, the better the regression line fits the points.

The **coefficient of determination** measures the amount of variation in the dependent variable about its mean that is explained by the regression line. The coefficient of determination, r^2, is calculated as

$$r^2 = \frac{a\sum Y + b\sum XY - n\overline{Y}^2}{\sum Y^2 - n\overline{Y}^2}$$

The value of r^2 ranges from 0.00 to 1.00. Regression equations with a value of r^2 close to 1.00 are desirable because then the variations in the dependent variable and the forecast generated by the regression equation are closely synchronized.

Finally, the **standard error of the estimate** measures how closely the data on the dependent variable cluster around the regression line. The standard error of the estimate, σ_{YX}, is calculated as

$$\sigma_{YX} = \sqrt{\frac{\sum Y^2 - a\sum Y - b\sum XY}{n - 2}}$$

Although it is similar to the sample standard deviation, σ_{YX} measures the error from the dependent variable, Y, to the regression line, rather than the mean. When determining which independent variable to include in the regression equation, you should choose the one with the smallest value of σ_{YX}.

EXAMPLE 10.1

*Using Linear
Regression to
Forecast Product
Demand*

The person in charge of production scheduling for a company must prepare fore-casts of product demand in order to plan for appropriate production quantities. During a luncheon meeting, the marketing manager gives her information about the advertising budget for a brass door hinge. The following are sales and adver-tising data for the past five months.

Month	Sales (thousands of units)	Advertising (thousands of $)
1	264	2.5
2	116	1.3
3	165	1.4
4	101	1.0
5	209	2.0

The marketing manager says that next month the company will spend $1750 on advertising for the product. Use linear regression to develop an equation and a forecast for this product.

Solution   We assume that sales are the dependent variable and advertising ex-penditures are the independent variable. In other words, sales are linearly related to advertising expenditures. Using the data provided by the marketing manager, we calculate XY, X^2, and Y^2 for each period and then add the total in each col-umn to obtain $\sum XY$, $\sum X^2$, and $\sum Y^2$.

Month	Sales, Y	Advertising, X	XY	X^2	Y^2
1	264	2.5	660.0	6.25	69,696
2	116	1.3	150.8	1.69	13,456
3	165	1.4	231.0	1.96	27,225
4	101	1.0	101.0	1.00	10,201
5	209	2.0	418.0	4.00	43,681
Total	855	8.2	1560.8	14.90	164,259

Then,

$$\overline{X} = \frac{8.2}{5} = 1.64 \quad \text{and} \quad \overline{Y} = \frac{855}{5} = 171.00$$

Substituting into the equations for a and b gives

$$b = \frac{\sum XY - n\overline{X}\,\overline{Y}}{\sum X^2 - n\overline{X}^2} = \frac{1560.8 - 5(1.64)(171)}{14.9 - 5(1.64)^2} = \frac{158.60}{1.452} = 109.229$$

$$a = \overline{Y} - b\overline{X} = 171.00 - 109.229(1.64) = -8.136$$

The regression equation is

$$Y = -8.136 + 109.229X$$

and the regression line is shown in Fig. 10.3.

FIGURE 10.3   *Linear Regression Line for the Sales Data*

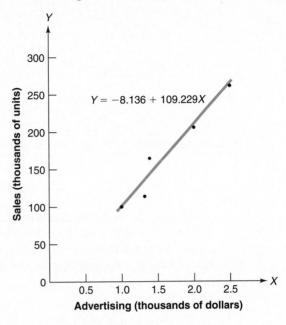

After arriving at this equation, we want to determine whether the choice of advertising is a good one for this forecasting equation. First we calculate the correlation coefficient:

$$r = \frac{n\Sigma XY - \Sigma X \Sigma Y}{\sqrt{\left[n\Sigma X^2 - (\Sigma X)^2\right]\left[n\Sigma Y^2 - (\Sigma Y)^2\right]}}$$

$$= \frac{5(1560.8) - (8.2)(855)}{\sqrt{\left[5(14.90) - (8.2)^2\right]\left[5(164,259) - (855)^2\right]}}$$

$$= \frac{7804 - 7011}{\sqrt{\left[74.5 - 67.24\right]\left[821,295 - 731,025\right]}} = 0.98$$

The value of r is very close to $+1.0$, which indicates a strong positive relationship between sales and advertising expenditures. Next we calculate the coefficient of determination:

$$r^2 = \frac{a\Sigma Y + b\Sigma XY - n\overline{Y}^2}{\Sigma Y^2 - n\overline{Y}^2} = \frac{-8.136(855) + 109.229(1560.8) - 5(171)^2}{164,259 - 5(171)^2}$$

$$= \frac{17,323.34}{18,054.00} = 0.96$$

The value of r^2 close to 1.0 indicates that advertising expenditures explain most of the variation in sales. The values for the coefficient of determination and the correlation coefficient indicate that the choice of advertising expenditures is a good one for predicting sales.

The standard error of the estimate for this regression equation is

$$\sigma_{YX} = \sqrt{\frac{\sum Y^2 - a\sum Y - b\sum XY}{n - 2}}$$

$$= \sqrt{\frac{164{,}259 - (-8.136)(855) - 109.229(1560.8)}{5 - 2}}$$

$$= \sqrt{\frac{730.66}{3}} = 15.61$$

As the advertising expenditure will be $1750, the forecast for month 6 is

$$Y = -8.136 + 109.229(1.75)$$

$$= 183.015, \quad \text{or } 183{,}015 \text{ units}$$

The production scheduler can use this forecast to determine the quantity of brass door hinges needed for month 6. Suppose that she has 62,500 units in stock. The requirement to be filled from production then is $183{,}015 - 62{,}500 = 120{,}015$ units, assuming that she doesn't want to lose any sales.

Regression analysis can provide useful guidance for important operations management decisions, such as inventory management, capacity planning, and process management. Often several independent variables may affect the dependent variable. For example, advertising expenditures, new corporation startups, and residential building contracts may be important for estimating the demand for door hinges. In such cases, *multiple regression analysis* is helpful in determining a forecasting equation for the dependent variable as a function of several independent variables. Multiple regression analysis is relatively costly because of the large amounts of data and subsequent analysis, although computers facilitate the process. Nonetheless, linear regression models are quite useful for predicting turning points and solving many planning problems.

◆ TIME SERIES METHODS

Rather than using independent variables for the forecast as regression models do, time series methods use historical information regarding only the dependent variable. These methods are based on the assumption that the dependent variable's past pattern will continue in the future. Time series analysis is used to identify the components of demand that influenced the historical pattern of the dependent variable and then develop a model to replicate it. In this section we focus on time series methods that address the average, trend, and seasonal influence components of demand. Before we discuss statistical methods, let's take a look at the simplest time series method for addressing all components of demand—the naive forecast.

Naive Forecast

A method often used in practice is the **naive forecast,** whereby the forecast for the next period equals the demand for the current period. So, if the actual demand for Wednesday is 35 customers, the forecasted demand for Thursday is 35 customers. If the actual demand on Thursday is 42 customers, the forecasted demand for Friday is 42 customers.

The naive forecast method may take into account a demand trend. The increase (or decrease) in demand observed between the last two periods is used to adjust the current demand to arrive at a forecast. Suppose that last week the demand was 120 units and the week before it was 108 units. Demand increased 12 units in one week, so the forecast for next week would be 120 + 12 = 132 units. If the actual demand next week turned out to be 127 units, the next forecast would be 127 + 7 = 134 units. The naive forecast method also may be used to account for seasonal influences. If the demand last July was 50,000 units, the forecast for this July is 50,000 units. Similarly, forecasts of demand for each month of the coming year may simply reflect actual demand in the same month last year.

The advantages of the naive forecast method are its simplicity and low cost. The method works best when the average, trend, or seasonal influences are stable and random errors are small. If random errors are large, using last period's demand to estimate next period's demand can result in highly variable forecasts that are not useful for planning purposes. Nonetheless, if its level of accuracy is acceptable, the naive forecast is an attractive approach for time series forecasting.

Estimating the Average

Every demand time series has two of the five components of demand: an average and random error. It *may* have trend, seasonal influence, or cyclical movements. We begin our discussion of statistical methods of times series forecasting with demand that has no trend, seasonal component, or cyclical movements. For all the methods of forecasting we discuss in this section, the forecast of demand for *any* period in the future is the average of the time series computed in the current period. For example, if the average of past demand calculated on Tuesday is 65 customers, the forecasts for Wednesday, Thursday, and Friday are 65 customers each day.

Consider Fig. 10.4, which shows patient arrivals at a medical clinic over the past 28 weeks. Assume that the demand pattern for patient arrivals has no trend, seasonal, or cyclical component. The time series has only an average and random error. As no one can predict random error, we focus on estimating the average. The statistical techniques useful for forecasting such a time series are (1) simple moving averages, (2) weighted moving averages, and (3) exponential smoothing.

F I G U R E 1 0 . 4

Weekly Patient Arrivals at a Medical Clinic

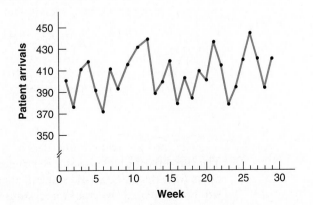

Simple Moving Averages.   The **simple moving average method** is used to estimate the average of a demand time series and thereby remove the effects of random fluctuation. It is most useful when demand has no pronounced trend or seasonal influences. Applying a moving average model simply involves calculating the average demand for the n most recent time periods and using it as the forecast for the next time period. Next period, after the demand is known, the oldest demand from the previous average is replaced by the most recent demand and the average is recalculated. In this way the n most recent demands are used, and the average "moves" from period to period.

Specifically, the moving average, A_t, can be calculated as

$$A_t = \frac{\text{Sum of last } n \text{ demands}}{n} = \frac{D_t + D_{t-1} + D_{t-2} + \cdots + D_{t-n+1}}{n}$$

where D_t = actual demand in period t

n = total number of periods in the average

A_t = average computed for period t

With the moving average method, the forecast of next period's demand equals the average calculated this period.

EXAMPLE 10.2

Using the Moving Average Method to Estimate Average Demand

a. Compute a *three-week* moving average forecast for the arrival of medical clinic patients in week 4. The numbers of arrivals for the last three weeks were

Week	Patient Arrivals
1	400
2	380
3	411

b. If the actual number of patient arrivals in week 4 is 415, what is the forecast for week 5?

Solution

a. The moving average at the end of week 3 is

$$A_3 = \frac{411 + 380 + 400}{3} = 397.0$$

Thus the forecast for week 4 is 397 patients.

b. The forecast for week 5 requires the actual arrivals from weeks 2–4, the three most recent weeks of data.

$$A_4 = \frac{415 + 411 + 380}{3} = 402.0$$

The forecast for week 5 is 402 patients. In addition, as we are now in week 4, the forecast for week 6 and beyond is also 402 patients.

The moving average may use as many periods of past demand as desired. The stability of the demand series generally determines how many periods to include (i.e., the value of n). Stable demand series are those for which the average (to be estimated by the forecasting method) only infrequently experiences

FIGURE 10.5

Comparison of Three-Week and Six-Week Moving Average Forecasts

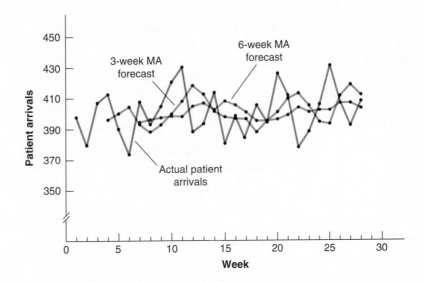

changes. Large values of *n* should be used for demand series that are stable and small values of *n* for those that are susceptible to changes in the underlying average. Consider Fig. 10.5, which compares actual patient arrivals to a three-week and a six-week moving average forecast for the medical clinic data. Note that the three-week moving average forecast varies more and reacts more quickly to large swings in demand. Conversely, the six-week moving average forecast is more stable because large swings in demand tend to cancel each other. We defer discussion of which of the two forecast methods is better for this problem until we discuss the criteria for choosing time series methods later in the chapter.

Including more historical data in the average by increasing the number of periods results in a forecast that is less susceptible to random variations. If the underlying average in the series is changing, however, the forecasts will tend to lag behind the changes for a longer time interval because of the additional time required to remove the old data from the forecast. We address other considerations in the choice of *n* when we discuss choosing a time series method.

Weighted Moving Averages.   In the simple moving average method, each demand has the same weight in the average—namely, $1/n$. In the **weighted moving average method,** each historical demand in the average can have its own weight. The sum of the weights equals 1.0. For example, in a *three-period* weighted moving average model, the most recent period might be assigned a weight of 0.50, the second most recent might be weighed 0.30, and the third most recent might be weighed 0.20. The average is obtained by multiplying the weight of each period by the value for that period and adding the products together:

$$A_t = 0.50D_t + 0.30D_{t-1} + 0.20D_{t-2}$$

The advantage of a weighted moving average method is that it allows you to emphasize recent demand over earlier demand. The forecast will be more responsive than the simple moving average forecast to changes in the underlying average of the demand series. Nonetheless, the weighted moving average forecast will still lag behind demand because it merely averages *past* demands. This lag is especially noticeable with a trend because the average of the time series is systematically increasing or decreasing.

The analyst for the medical clinic has assigned weights of 0.70 to the most recent demand, 0.20 to the demand one week ago, and 0.10 to the demand two weeks ago. Use the data for the first three weeks from Example 10.2 to calculate the weighted moving average forecast for week 4.

Solution   The average demand in week 3 is

$$A_3 = 0.70(411) + 0.20(380) + 0.10(400) = 403.7$$

Patients can't be divided into fractions, so we round the answer to the nearest whole number. The forecast for week 4 therefore is 404 patients.

Now suppose that the actual demand for week 4 is 415 patients. The new average and the forecast for week 5 would be

$$A_4 = 0.70(415) + 0.20(411) + 0.10(380) = 410.7$$

Rounding up, the forecast for week 5 is 411 patients.

The weighted moving average method has the same shortcomings as the simple moving average method: Data must be retained for n periods of demand to allow calculation of the average for each period. Keeping this amount of data isn't a great burden in simple situations, such as the preceding three-week and six-week examples. For a company that has to forecast many different demands, however, data storage and update costs may be high. Managers must balance the cost of keeping such detailed records against the usefulness of the forecasts.

Exponential Smoothing.   The **exponential smoothing method** is a sophisticated weighted moving average method that calculates the average of a time series by giving recent demands more weight than earlier demands. It is the most frequently used formal forecasting method because of its simplicity and the small amount of data needed to support it. Unlike the weighted moving average method, which requires n periods of past demand and n weights, exponential smoothing requires only three items of data: the estimated average of the series as of the last period; the demand for this period; and a smoothing parameter, alpha (α), which has a value between 0 and 1.0. To obtain an exponentially smoothed forecast we simply calculate a weighted average of the most recent demand and the average calculated last period. The equation for the forecast is

$$A_t = \alpha(\text{Demand this period}) + (1 - \alpha)(\text{Average calculated last period})$$

$$= \alpha D_t + (1 - \alpha)A_{t-1}$$

An equivalent equation is

$$A_t = A_{t-1} + \alpha(D_t - A_{t-1})$$

This form of the equation shows that the forecast for the next period equals the forecast for the current period plus a proportion of the forecast error for the current period.

As before, an average is calculated at the end of the current period and used as a forecast for the next period. The amount of emphasis given to the most recent demand levels can be adjusted by changing the smoothing parameter. Larger α values emphasize recent levels of demand and result in forecasts more responsive to changes in the underlying average. Smaller α values treat past demand more uniformly and result in more stable forecasts. This approach is analogous to adjusting the value of *n* in the moving average methods, except there smaller values of *n* emphasize recent demand and larger values give greater weight to past demand. In practice, various values of α are tried and the one producing the best forecasts is chosen. We discuss the choice of α further when we present the criteria for selecting time series methods.

Exponential smoothing requires an initial estimate of the average to get started. There are two ways to get this initial estimate: Either use last period's demand as the estimate or, if some historical data is available, calculate the average of several recent periods of demand. The effect of the initial estimate of the average on successive estimates of the average diminishes over time because, with exponential smoothing, the weights given to successive historical demands used to calculate the average decay exponentially. We can illustrate this effect with an example. If we let $\alpha = 0.20$, the estimate for the average in period *t* is

$$A_t = 0.20D_t + 0.80A_{t-1}$$

Using the equation for A_{t-1}, we expand the equation for A_t:

$$A_t = 0.20D_t + 0.80(0.20D_{t-1} + 0.80A_{t-2}) = 0.20D_t + 0.16D_{t-1} + 0.64A_{t-2}$$

Continuing to expand, we get

$$A_t = 0.20D_t + 0.16D_{t-1} + 0.128D_{t-2} + 0.1024D_{t-3} + \cdots$$

Eventually the weights approach zero. As with the weighted moving average method, the sum of the weights must equal 1.0, which is implicit in the exponential smoothing equation.

EXAMPLE 10.4

Using Exponential Smoothing to Estimate Average Demand

Again consider the patient arrival data in Example 10.2. It is now the end of week 3. Using $\alpha = 0.10$, calculate the exponential smoothing forecast for week 4.

Solution The exponential smoothing method requires estimating an initial value for the average. Suppose that we take the demand data for the past two weeks and average them, obtaining $(400 + 380)/2 = 390$ as an estimate of the past average. To obtain the forecast for week 4, using exponential smoothing with $\alpha = 0.10$, we calculate the average at the end of week 3 as

$$A_3 = 0.10(411) + 0.90(390) = 392.1$$

Thus the forecast for week 4 would be 392 patients. If the actual demand for week 4 proved to be 415, the new average for week 4 would be

$$A_4 = 0.10(415) + 0.90(392.1) = 394.4$$

and the forecast for week 5 would be 394 patients. Notice that we used A_3, and not the integer-value forecast for week 4, in the computation for A_4. In general, we round off only the final result to maintain as much accuracy as possible in the calculations.

Exponential smoothing has the advantages of simplicity and minimal data requirements. It is inexpensive to use and therefore very attractive to firms that make thousands of forecasts for each time period. However, its simplicity also is a disadvantage when the underlying average is changing, as in the case of a demand series with a trend. Like any method geared solely to the assumption of a stable average, exponential smoothing results will lag behind changes in the underlying average of demand. Higher α values may help reduce forecast errors when there is a change in the average of the time series; however, the lags will still be there if the average is changing systematically. Typically, if large α values (e.g. > 0.50) are required for an exponential smoothing application, chances are good that a more sophisticated model is needed because of a significant trend or seasonal influence in the demand series.

Including a Trend

Let's now consider a demand time series that has a trend. Although several forecasting methods that recognize a trend are available, we focus on exponential smoothing because it is so widely used in practice.

A trend in a time series is a systematic increase or decrease in the average of the series over time. Where a trend is present, exponential smoothing approaches must be modified; otherwise, the forecasts always will be below or above the actual demand. For example, assume that actual demand is steadily increasing at 10 units per period. Forecasts using exponential smoothing with $\alpha = 0.3$ will lag severely behind the actual demand even if the first forecast is perfect, as the following table shows.

	Actual Demand in Period t	Forecast for Period t
1	10	$A_0 = 10$
2	20	$A_1 = 0.30(10) + 0.70(10) = 10$
3	30	$A_2 = 0.30(20) + 0.70(10) = 13$
4	40	$A_3 = 0.30(30) + 0.70(13) = 18.1$

To improve the forecast we need to calculate an estimate of the trend. We start by calculating the *current* estimate of the trend, which is the difference between the average of the series computed in the current period and the average computed last period. To obtain an estimate of the long-term trend, you can average the current estimates. The method for estimating a trend is similar to that used for estimating the demand average with exponential smoothing.

The method for incorporating a trend in an exponentially smoothed forecast is called the **trend-adjusted exponential smoothing method.** With this approach the estimates for both the average and the trend are smoothed, requiring two smoothing constants. For each period we calculate the average and the trend:

$$A_t = \alpha(\text{Demand this period}) + (1 - \alpha)(\text{Average + Trend estimate last period})$$

$$= \alpha D_t + (1 - \alpha)(A_{t-1} + T_{t-1})$$

$$T_t = \beta(\text{Average this period} - \text{Average last period})$$
$$+ (1 - \beta)(\text{Trend estimate last period})$$

$$= \beta(A_t - A_{t-1}) + (1 - \beta)T_{t-1}$$

where A_t = exponentially smoothed average of the series in period t

         T_t = exponentially smoothed average of the trend in period t

         α = smoothing parameter for the average, with a value between 0 and 1

         β = smoothing parameter for the trend, with a value between 0 and 1

The forecast for next period is simply $A_t + T_t$. Estimates for last period's average and trend can be derived from past data or based on an educated guess if no historical data exist. To find values for α and β, often an analyst systematically adjusts α and β until the forecast errors are lowest. This process can be carried out in an experimental setting with the model used to forecast historical demands.

EXAMPLE 10.5

Using Trend-Adjusted Exponential Smoothing to Forecast a Demand Series with a Trend

Medanalysis, Inc. provides medical laboratory services to patients of Health Providers, a group of 10 family-practice doctors associated with a new health maintenance program. Managers are interested in forecasting the number of patients requesting blood analysis per week. Supplies must be purchased and a decision made regarding the number of blood samples to be sent to another laboratory because of capacity limitations at the main laboratory. Recent publicity about the damaging effects of cholesterol on the heart has caused a national increase in requests for standard blood tests. Medanalysis ran an average of 28 blood tests per week during the past four weeks. The trend over that period was 3 additional patients per week. This week's demand was for 27 blood tests. We use $\alpha = 0.20$ and $\beta = 0.20$ to calculate the forecast for next week.

Solution $\qquad A_0 = 28$ patients $\qquad$ and $\qquad T_0 = 3$ patients

The forecast for week 2 (next week) is

$$A_1 = 0.20(27) + 0.80(28 + 3) = 30.2$$

$$T_1 = 0.20(30.2 - 28) + 0.80(3) = 2.8$$

The forecast for week 2 is $30.2 + 2.8 = 33$ blood tests.

If the actual number of blood tests requested in week 2 proved to be 44, the updated forecast for week 3 would be

$$A_2 = 0.20(44) + 0.80(30.2 + 2.8) = 35.2$$

$$T_2 = 0.2(35.2 - 30.2) + 0.80(2.8) = 3.2$$

The forecast for week 3 is $35.2 + 3.2 = 38.4$, or 38 blood tests.

Figure 10.6 shows the CMOM trend-adjusted forecast (the blue line) for Medanalysis for a period of 15 weeks. At the end of each week CMOM calculated a forecast for the next week, using the number of blood tests for the current

FIGURE 10.6

Trend-Adjusted Forecast for Medanalysis

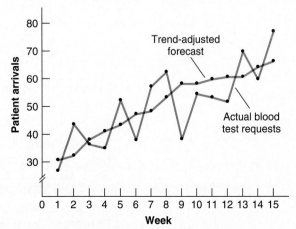

week. Note that the forecasts (shown in the printout below) vary less than actual demand because of the smoothing effect of the procedure for calculating the estimates for the average and the trend. By adjusting α and β, we may be able to come up with a better forecast.

CMOM - Forecasting - Smoothing with Trend Factoring

Data Entered

Number of Time Periods	:	15
Data Smoothing Coefficient	:	0.2000
Initial Data Value	:	28
Trend Smoothing Coefficient	:	0.2000
Estimate of Trend	:	3

	Dt		Dt		Dt		Dt
P1	27	P5	53	P9	39	P13	60
P2	44	P6	38	P10	55	P14	60
P3	37	P7	57	P11	54	P15	75
P4	35	P8	61	P12	52		

Solution

Period	Actual Demand	Smoothed Average	Trend Est.	Forecast	Forecast Error
P0	28	28	3	0	0
P1	27	30.20	2.84	31	-4
P2	44	35.23	3.27	33.04	10.96
P3	37	38.20	3.21	38.51	-1.51
P4	35	40.14	2.96	41.42	-6.42
P5	53	45.08	3.35	43.10	9.89
P6	38	46.35	2.93	48.43	-10.43
P7	57	50.83	3.24	49.29	7.71
P8	61	55.46	3.52	54.08	6.92
P9	39	54.99	2.72	58.98	-19.98
P10	55	57.17	2.61	57.71	-2.71
P11	54	58.63	2.38	59.78	-5.78
P12	52	59.21	2.02	61.01	-9.01
P13	60	60.99	1.97	61.23	-1.23
P14	60	62.37	1.85	62.96	-2.96
P15	75	66.38	2.28	64.22	10.77

CMOM - Forecasting - Smoothing with Trend Factoring

Summary

Average Demand	:	49.80
Mean Square Error	:	76.13
Mean Absolute Deviation	:	7.35
Forecast Value(16)	:	68.66
Forecast Value(17)	:	70.95
Forecast Value(18)	:	73.24

To make forecasts for periods beyond the next period, we multiply the trend estimate by the number of additional periods that we want in the forecast and add the result to the current average. For example, if we were at the end of week 2 and wanted to estimate the demand for blood tests in week 6 (that is, 4 weeks ahead), the forecast would be $35.2 + 4(3.2) = 48$ tests. The printout shows the forecasts for periods 16, 17, and 18. The trend-adjusted exponential smoothing method has the advantage of being able to adjust the forecast to *changes* in the trend. Nonetheless, when the trend is changing, the further ahead we project the trend estimate, the more tenuous the forecast becomes. Thus the use of time series methods should be restricted to short-term forecasting.

Seasonal Influences

Many organizations experience seasonal demand for their goods or services. Seasonal influences are regularly repeating upward or downward movements in demand measured in periods of less than one year (hours, days, weeks, months, or quarters). In this context, the time periods are called *seasons*. For example, customer arrivals at a fast-food shop on any day may peak between 11 A.M. and 1 P.M. and again from 5 P.M. to 7 P.M. Here the seasonal influence lasts a day, and each hour of the day is a season. Similarly, the demand for haircuts may peak on Saturday, week to week. In this case, the seasonal influence lasts a week, and the seasons are the days of the week. Seasonal influences may last a month, as in the weekly applications for driver's license renewals, or a year, as in the monthly volumes of mail processed and the monthly demand for automobile tires.

Various methods are available for forecasting time series with seasonal influences. We describe only the **multiplicative seasonal method**, whereby seasonal factors are multiplied by an estimate of average demand to arrive at a seasonal forecast. The four-step procedure presented here uses simple averages of past demand, although more sophisticated methods for calculating averages, such as a moving average or exponential smoothing approach, could be used. The description below is based on a seasonal influence lasting one year and seasons of one month, although the procedure can be used for any seasonal influence and season of any length.

1. For each year, calculate the average demand per season by dividing annual demand by the number of seasons per year. For example, if the total demand for a year is 6000 units and each month is a season, the average demand per season is $6000/12 = 500$ units.

2. For each year, divide the actual demand for a season by the average demand per season. The result is a *seasonal index* for each season in the year, which indicates the level of demand relative to the average demand. For example, suppose that the demand for March was 400 units. The seasonal index for March then is $400/500 = 0.80$, which indicates that March's demand is 20 percent below the average demand per month. Similarly, a seasonal index of 1.14 for April implies that April's demand is 14 percent greater than the average demand per month.

3. Calculate the average seasonal index for each season, using the results from step 2. Add the seasonal indices for a season and divide by the number of years of data. For example, suppose that you have calculated three seasonal indices for April: 1.14, 1.18, and 1.04. The average seasonal index for April is $(1.14 + 1.18 + 1.04)/3 = 1.12$. This is the index we will use for forecasting April's demand.

478

Members of the Steel-Rule Die Department at Hallmark Cards review a printed sheet of valentines. Hallmark's products are highly seasonal, and once their season is past, they are difficult to sell.

4. Calculate each season's forecast for next year. Begin by estimating the average demand per season for next year. Use the naive method, moving averages, exponential smoothing, or trend-adjusted exponential smoothing. Then obtain the seasonal forecast by multiplying the seasonal index by the average demand per season.

EXAMPLE 10.6

Using the Multiplicative Seasonal Method to Forecast the Number of Customers

The manager of the Stanley Steemer carpet cleaning company needs a quarterly forecast of the number of customers expected next year. The carpet cleaning business is seasonal, with a peak in the third quarter and a trough in the first quarter. Following are the quarterly demand data from the past four years.

Quarter	Year 1	Year 2	Year 3	Year 4
1	45	70	100	100
2	335	370	585	725
3	520	590	830	1160
4	100	170	285	215
Total	1000	1200	1800	2200

The manager wants to forecast customer demand for each quarter of year 5, based on her estimate of total year 5 demand of 2600 customers.

Solution

Step 1. The average number of customers per season is

Year 1: 1000/4 = 250   Year 2: 1200/4 = 300
Year 3: 1800/4 = 450   Year 4: 2200/4 = 550

Step 2. The seasonal indices are

Quarter	Year 1	Year 2	Year 3	Year 4
1	45/250 = 0.18	70/300 = 0.23	100/450 = 0.22	100/550 = 0.18
2	335/250 = 1.34	370/300 = 1.23	585/450 = 1.30	725/550 = 1.32
3	520/250 = 2.08	590/300 = 1.97	830/450 = 1.84	1160/550 = 2.11
4	100/250 = 0.40	170/300 = 0.57	285/450 = 0.63	215/550 = 0.39

Step 3. Note how the seasonal indices for each quarter fluctuate from year to year because of random effects. That's why the manager needs to compute the average seasonal index for each quarter.

Quarter	Average Seasonal Index
1	(0.18 + 0.23 + 0.22 + 0.18)/4 = 0.20
2	(1.34 + 1.23 + 1.30 + 1.32)/4 = 1.30
3	(2.08 + 1.97 + 1.84 + 2.11)/4 = 2.00
4	(0.40 + 0.57 + 0.63 + 0.39)/4 = 0.50

Step 4. Note that annual demand has been increasing each year. The manager extends that trend and projects an annual demand in year 5 of 2600 customers. Therefore the estimated average demand per quarter is 2600/4 = 650 customers. The manager then makes quarterly forecasts by multiplying the seasonal factors by the average demand per quarter.

Quarter	Forecast
1	650(0.20) = 130 customers
2	650(1.30) = 845 customers
3	650(2.00) = 1300 customers
4	650(0.50) = 325 customers

At the end of each year, the average seasonal factor for each quarter can be updated. We calculate the average of all historical seasonal factors for that quarter or, if we want some control over the relevance of past demand patterns, we calculate a moving average or single exponentially smoothed average.

The multiplicative seasonal method gets its name from the way seasonal factors are calculated and used. Multiplying the seasonal factor by an estimate of the average period demand implies that the seasonal influence depends on the level of demand. The peaks and valleys are more extreme when average demand is high, a situation faced most often by firms that produce goods and services having a seasonal demand. Figure 10.7(a) shows a time series with multiplicative seasonal influences. Note how the amplitude of the seasons increases, reflecting an upward trend in demand. The reverse occurs with a downward trend in demand. An alternative to the multiplicative seasonal method is the **additive seasonal method,** whereby seasonal effects are generated by adding a constant (say,

FIGURE 10.7

Comparison of Seasonal Influences

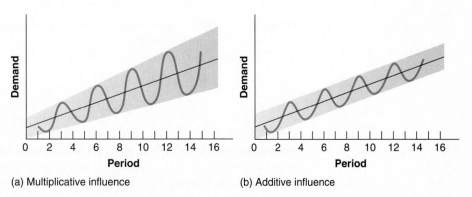

(a) Multiplicative influence

(b) Additive influence

50 units) to the estimate of average demand per season. This approach is based on the assumption that seasonal influence is constant, regardless of average demand. Figure 10.7(b) shows a time series with additive seasonal influences. Here, the amplitude of the seasons remains the same regardless of the level of demand.

◆ CHOOSING A TIME SERIES METHOD

We now turn to factors that managers must consider in selecting a method for time series forecasting. One important consideration is forecast performance, as determined by forecast errors. Managers need to know how to measure forecast errors and how to detect when something is going wrong with the forecasting system. After examining forecast errors and their detection, we discuss criteria that managers can use to choose an appropriate time series forecasting method.

Forecast Error

Forecasts almost always contain errors. Forecast errors can be classified as either *bias errors* or *random errors*. Bias errors are the result of consistent mistakes—the forecast is always too high or always too low. These errors often are the result of neglecting or not accurately estimating components of demand, such as a trend, seasonal influence, or cyclical movements. For example, if the demand for playing time on a country club's tennis courts is steadily increasing and the club manager is using the naive forecasting method with the demand last year as the forecast for this year, the forecast will always be low because he didn't take the trend into account.

The other type of forecast error, random error, results from unpredictable factors that cause the forecast to deviate from the actual demand. Forecasting analysts try to minimize the effects of bias and random errors by selecting appropriate forecasting models, but eliminating all forms of errors is impossible.

Measures of Forecast Error.   Before they can think about minimizing forecast error, managers must have some ways to measure it. **Forecast error** is simply the difference between the forecast and actual demand for a given period, or

$$E_t = D_t - F_t$$

where
$$E_t = \text{forecast error for period } t$$
$$D_t = \text{actual demand for period } t$$
$$F_t = \text{forecast for period } t$$

However, managers usually are more interested in measuring forecast error over a relatively long period of time.

The **cumulative sum of forecast errors (CFE)** measures the total forecast error:

$$\text{CFE} = \Sigma E_t$$

Large positive errors tend to be offset by large negative errors in the CFE measure. Nonetheless, CFE is useful in assessing bias in a forecast. For example, if a forecast is always lower than actual demand, the value of CFE will gradually get larger and larger. This increasingly large error indicates some systematic deficiency in the forecasting approach. Perhaps the analyst omitted a trend element or a cyclical influence, or perhaps seasonal influences changed from their historical pattern. We explain later how to use CFE to develop a tracking signal to indicate when you should be concerned about forecast performance.

The **mean squared error (MSE), standard deviation (σ),** and **mean absolute deviation (MAD)** measure the dispersion of forecast errors:

$$\text{MSE} = \frac{\Sigma E_t^2}{n}$$

$$\sigma = \sqrt{\text{MSE}}$$

$$\text{MAD} = \frac{\Sigma |E_t|}{n}$$

The mathematical symbol $|\ |$ is used to indicate the absolute value—that is, it tells us to disregard positive or negative signs. If MSE, σ, or MAD is small, the forecast is typically close to actual demand; a large value indicates the possibility of large forecast errors. The measures differ in the way they emphasize errors. Large errors get far more weight in MSE and σ because the errors are squared. MAD is a widely used measure of forecast error because managers can easily understand it; it is merely the mean of the forecast errors over a series of time periods, without regard to whether the error was an overestimate or an underestimate. MAD also is used in tracking signals and inventory control. In Chapter 12 we discuss how MAD or σ can be used to determine safety stocks for inventory items.

The **mean absolute percent error (MAPE)** relates the forecast error to the level of demand and is useful for putting forecast performance in the proper perspective:

$$\text{MAPE} = \frac{\Sigma \big[|E_t|(100) \big]/D_t}{n} \qquad \text{(expressed as a percentage)}$$

For example, an absolute forecast error of 100 results in a larger percentage error when the demand is 200 units than when the demand is 10,000 units.

EXAMPLE 10.7

Calculating Forecast Error Measures

The following table shows the actual sales of upholstered chairs for a furniture manufacturer and the forecasts made for each of the last eight months. We will calculate CFE, MSE, σ, MAD, and MAPE for this product.

Month, t	Demand, D_t	Forecast, F_t	Error, E_t	Error Squared, E_t^2	Absolute Error, $|E_t|$	Absolute Percent Error, $(|E_t|/D_t)(100)$
1	200	225	−25	625	25	12.5%
2	240	220	20	400	20	8.3
3	300	285	15	225	15	5.0
4	270	290	−20	400	20	7.4
5	230	250	−20	400	20	8.7
6	260	240	20	400	20	7.7
7	210	250	−40	1600	40	19.0
8	275	240	35	1225	35	12.7
		Total	−15	5275	195	81.3%

Solution   Using the formulas for the measures, we get

Cumulative forecast error: $\text{CFE} = -15$

Mean squared error: $\text{MSE} = \dfrac{\Sigma E_t^2}{n} = \dfrac{5275}{8} = 659.4$

Standard deviation: $\sigma = \sqrt{\text{MSE}} = \sqrt{659.4} = 25.7$

Mean absolute deviation: $\text{MAD} = \dfrac{\Sigma |E_t|}{n} = \dfrac{195}{8} = 24.4$

Mean absolute percent error: $\text{MAPE} = \dfrac{\Sigma \big[|E_t|(100) \big] / D_t}{n} = \dfrac{81.3\%}{8} = 10.2\%$

A CFE of -15 indicates that the forecast has a tendency to overestimate demand. The MSE, σ, and MAD statistics provide measures of forecast error variability. A MAD of 24.4 means that the average forecast error was 24.4 units. The value of σ, 25.7, indicates that the sample distribution of forecast errors has a standard deviation of 25.7 units. A MAPE of 10.2 percent implies that, on average, the forecast error was about 10 percent of actual demand. These measures become more reliable as the number of periods of data increases.

What types of controls are needed for the forecasting system?

Tracking Signals.   A **tracking signal** is a measure that indicates whether a method of forecasting is accurately predicting actual changes in demand. The tracking signal measures the number of MADs represented by the cumulative sum of forecast errors, the CFE. The CFE tends to be 0 when a correct forecasting system is being used. At any time, however, random errors can cause the CFE to be a nonzero number. The tracking signal formula is

$$\text{Tracking signal} = \frac{\text{CFE}}{\text{MAD}}$$

Each period, the CFE and MAD are updated to reflect current error and the tracking signal is compared to some predetermined limits. The MAD can be calculated in one of two ways: (1) as the simple average of all absolute errors (as demonstrated in Example 10.7) or (2) as a weighted average determined by the exponential smoothing method:

$$\text{MAD}_t = \alpha |E_t| + (1 - \alpha)\text{MAD}_{t-1}$$

The latter approach has certain advantages. Less historical data have to be retained for each estimate, and recent forecast performance can be emphasized more than past performance.

If forecast errors are normally distributed with a mean of 0, there is a simple relationship between σ and MAD:

$$\sigma = (\sqrt{\pi/2})(\text{MAD}) \cong 1.25(\text{MAD})$$

$$\text{MAD} = 0.7978\sigma \cong 0.8\sigma$$

where $\pi = 3.1416$

This relationship enables us to use the normal probability tables to specify limits for the tracking signal. If the tracking signal falls outside those limits, the forecasting model no longer is tracking demand adequately. A tracking system is useful when forecasting systems are computerized because it alerts analysts when forecasts are getting far from desirable limits. Table 10.2 shows the area of the normal probability distribution within the control limits of 1 to 4 MAD.

TABLE 10.2	*Percentage of the Area of the Normal Probability Distribution Within the Control Limits of the Tracking Signal*

Control Limit Spread (number of MAD)	Equivalent Number of σ*	Percentage of Area Within Control Limits[†]
±1.0	±0.80	57.62
±1.5	±1.20	76.98
±2.0	±1.60	89.04
±2.5	±2.00	95.44
±3.0	±2.40	98.36
±3.5	±2.80	99.48
±4.0	±3.20	99.86

*The equivalent number of standard deviations is found by using the approximation of MAD $\cong$ 0.8.

[†]The area of the normal curve included within the control limits is found in Appendix 2. For example, the cumulative area from $-\infty$ to 0.80 is 0.7881. The area between 0 and $+0.80\sigma$ is $0.7881 - 0.5000 = 0.2881$. Since the normal curve is symmetric, the area between -0.80σ and 0 is also 0.2881. Therefore the area between $±0.80\sigma$ is $0.2881 + 0.2881 = 0.5762$.

Figure 10.8 shows tracking signal results for 23 periods plotted in a *control chart*. The control chart is useful for determining whether any action needs to be taken to improve the forecasting model. In the example, the first 20 points cluster around 0, as we would expect if the forecasts are not biased. The CFE will tend toward 0. When the underlying characteristics of demand change but the forecasting model doesn't, the tracking signal eventually goes out of control. The steady increase after the 20th point in Fig. 10.8 indicates that the process is going out of control. The 21st and 22nd points are acceptable, but the 23rd point isn't.

FIGURE 10.8

Tracking Signal

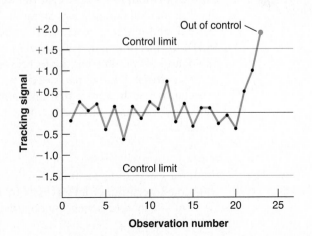

Choosing the limits for the tracking signal involves a trade-off between the cost of poor forecasts and the cost of checking for a problem when none exists. For example, suppose that CFE = 180 and MAD = 100; the tracking signal would be +1.8. If we set the control limits of the tracking signal at ±1.5, as in Fig. 10.8, a result of +1.8 would require a check of our forecasting method to see whether it needs to be revised because of changes in the demand pattern. Two modifications may be required: either a change in the model *form* (such as adding a trend estimate) or a change in the values of the smoothing parameters. However, even when the forecasting method is correct for the situation, the tracking signal can exceed the control limits of the chart by chance. In fact, with a limit of ±1.5 MAD on the control chart, the probability is 0.115 (one-half the area outside the control limits) that we will get a value of the tracking signal greater than +1.5 as a result of random variation. The value of 1.8 exceeds the upper limit on the chart, but that could have happened by chance. As in statistical process control charts, the choice of control limits must recognize the costs of searching for problems when none exist and the costs of not detecting poor performance.

Forecast Error Ranges.   Calculating MAD can also provide additional information. Forecasts that are stated as a single value, such as 1200 units or 26 customers, rarely are useful because they don't indicate the range of likely errors that the forecast typically generates. A far more useful approach is to provide the manager with a forecasted value and an error range. For example, suppose that the forecasted value for a product is 1000 units, with a MAD of 20 units. Table 10.2 shows that there is about a 95 percent chance that actual demand will fall within ±2.5 MAD of the forecast; that is, for a forecast of 1000 units, we can say with a 95 percent confidence level that actual demand will fall in the range of 950 to 1050 units. This information gives the manager a better feel for the uncertainty in the forecast and allows better planning for inventories, staffing levels, and the like.

Criteria for Selecting Time Series Methods

What is involved in choosing the best time series forecasting method?

Forecast error measures provide important information for choosing the best forecasting method for a product or service. They also guide managers in selecting the best values for the parameters needed for the method: n for the moving average method, the weights for the weighted moving average method, and α for the exponential smoothing method. The criteria to use in making forecast method and parameter choices include (1) minimizing bias, (2) minimizing MAD, (3) meeting managerial expectations of changes in the components of demand, and (4) minimizing the forecast error last period. The first two criteria relate to statistical measures based on historical performance, the third reflects expectations of the future that may not be rooted in the past, and the fourth is a way to use whatever method seems to be working best at the time a forecast must be made.

Using Statistical Criteria.   Statistical forecast measures can be used in the selection of a forecasting method. To illustrate the trade-offs that are considered in choosing a technique, let's return to the medical clinic example in Examples 10.2–10.4 and add single exponential smoothing with $\alpha = 0.2$. We focus on

MAD as a measure of forecast error dispersion, but we could also use the mean squared error or standard deviation. Table 10.3 shows the forecast error performance of the methods used for the medical clinic if all 28 periods of data are utilized.

TABLE 10.3   *Forecast Performance of Various Forecasting Methods for a Medical Clinic*

Method	Cumulative Sum of Forecast Errors (CFE—bias)	Mean Absolute Deviation (MAD)
Simple moving average		
Three-week ($n = 3$)	23.1	17.1
Six-week ($n = 6$)	69.8	15.5
Weighted moving average		
0.70, 0.20, 0.10	14.0	18.4
Exponential smoothing		
$\alpha = 0.1$	65.6	14.8
$\alpha = 0.2$	41.0	15.3

Let's begin by looking for the best value of n for moving average methods. Ideally, we would like to have forecasts with no bias and no MAD. As this is impossible, we face a trade-off between bias and MAD, as demonstrated in Table 10.3. A value of $n = 3$ weeks gives us a lower bias but a greater MAD than does a value of $n = 6$ weeks. Normally, preference is given to lower values of MAD. However, in this example, the two values of MAD are not that different, whereas the measures of bias are very different. A positive value for CFE indicates that, on balance, the forecasts have been too low. This result can be detrimental to clinic operations, particularly if purchasing procedures and staffing schedules are based on the raw forecasts. If the small difference in MAD isn't of concern to management, $n = 3$ seems like a good choice for the simple moving average method.

Similar considerations are involved in choosing α for exponential smoothing. Again, the differences in MAD are slight, but the differences in bias are considerable. Larger α values seem to result in less bias than do smaller values in this example. Consequently, if we were to use exponential smoothing, $\alpha = 0.2$ would be best.

Note that all three methods—the moving average method with $n = 3$, the weighted moving average method, and the exponential smoothing method with $\alpha = 0.2$—give significantly greater weight to the most recent levels of demand and less weight to earlier levels. This indicates that a trend or seasonal component of demand may be present in the time series. Here we are concerned only with simple methods based on the assumption that the only components of demand are its historical average and random error. If another component were present, we could continue to use simple methods and compensate by using low n values or high α values. Note that the weighted moving average method, with a weight of 0.70 for the most recent demand, provided the lowest bias and a MAD only slightly larger than the one produced by the moving average method with

$n = 3$. Of the three alternatives, the weighted moving average method would be a reasonable choice. However, to further reduce bias and/or MAD, methods that include a trend or seasonal influence should be explored. Regardless, a tracking signal should be used to monitor the performance of the forecasting method in the future.

Using Managerial Expectations.   Earlier in the chapter we identified several external and internal factors that can affect demand: a change in the average, the rate of a trend, or the timing and size of peaks in a seasonal demand series. Such changes can make forecasting methods that rely on historical customer demand data less relevant for projecting future demand. In some cases, time series forecasting models can be modified, with the parameters of the models used as policy variables that depict expectations of changes in the underlying components of demand. Managers can use two general guidelines in this regard.

1. For projections of more stable demand patterns, use lower α and β values or larger n values to emphasize historical experience.
2. For projections of more dynamic demand patterns, use higher α and β values or smaller n values. When the historical components of demand are changing, recent history should be emphasized.

Managers should monitor forecast error and modify the parameters as needed. In this way, managers can detect a poor choice and correct it.

Using the Forecast Error Last Period.   Does a more sophisticated forecasting model always produce a better forecast? Is there one best forecasting technique for all products or services? The answer to both questions is *no*. In 1984, Bernard Smith, an inventory manager at American Hardware Supply, recognized these realities of forecasting and developed what he called **focus forecasting,** which selects the best forecast from a group of forecasts generated by simple techniques.

> Is the most sophisticated forecasting system always the best one to use?

Smith was responsible for an inventory of 100,000 different items purchased by the company's 21 buyers. Originally, the company used a basic exponential smoothing system with a sophisticated method for projecting seasonal influences. The forecasts generated were supposed to be used to determine purchase quantities. However, the buyers altered 53 percent of the forecasted purchase quantities, mainly because they didn't understand exponential smoothing and consequently didn't trust the system. Their continual changes resulted in excessive purchases and inventory.

Smith decided to survey the buyers to find out how they arrived at their own forecasts. One buyer computed the percentage increase in demand experienced during the last period and used it to project the increase in demand for the next period. Another buyer simply used the demand from the last period as the forecast for the next period. Other buyers used similar simple methods for forecasting demand. Each buyer was responsible for a different group of items, and Smith had no reason to believe that any one of the methods would work for all items.

Using methods suggested by the buyers and adding some statistical methods, including exponential smoothing, Smith selected seven forecast methods as the basis for his focus forecasting technique. Every period the computer employs all seven methods to make forecasts for each item. Using historical data as the starting point for each method, the computer makes forecasts for the current period. The forecasts are compared to actual demand, and the method that produces the forecast with the least error is used to make the forecast for the next period. The method used for each item may change from period to period.

Each period the computer prints the forecast for each of the 100,000 items. Buyers can still override the computer forecast, although Smith claims that his system provides excellent short-term forecasts for American Hardware Supply. The system is used for expensive as well as inexpensive items and has much more credibility with the buyers than the previous system did.

CHAPTER REVIEW

Solved Problem 1

Chicken Palace periodically offers carryout five-piece chicken dinners at special prices. Let Y be the number of dinners sold and X be the price. Based on the historical observations and calculations in the following table, determine the regression equation, correlation coefficient, coefficient of determination, and standard error of the estimate. How many dinners can Chicken Palace expect to sell at $3.00 each?

Observation	Price, X	Dinners Sold, Y	XY	X^2	Y^2
1	$ 2.70	760	2052	7.2900	577,600
2	$ 3.50	510	1785	12.2500	260,100
3	$ 2.00	980	1960	4.0000	960,400
4	$ 4.20	250	1050	17.6400	62,500
5	$ 3.10	320	992	9.6100	102,400
6	$ 4.05	480	1944	16.4025	230,400
Total	$19.55	3300	9783	67.1925	2,193,400
Average	$ 3.258	550			

Solution We first determine the regression equation, where the number of dinners sold is a function of price:

$$b = \frac{\sum XY - n\overline{X}\,\overline{Y}}{\sum X^2 - n\overline{X}^2} = \frac{9783 - 6(3.258)(550)}{67.1925 - 6(3.258)^2} = \frac{-968.4}{3.5} = -276.28$$

$$a = \overline{Y} - b\overline{X} = 550 - (-276.28)(3.258) = 1450.12$$

Therefore the regression line is

$$Y = a + bX = 1450.12 - 276.28X$$

The correlation coefficient is

$$r = \frac{n\sum XY - \sum X\sum Y}{\sqrt{\left[n\sum X^2 - \left(\sum X\right)^2\right]\left[n\sum Y^2 - \left(\sum Y\right)^2\right]}}$$

$$= \frac{6(9783) - (19.55)(3300)}{\sqrt{\left[6(67.1925) - (19.55)^2\right]\left[6(2,193,400) - (3300)^2\right]}}$$

$$= \frac{58,698 - 64,515}{\sqrt{\left[20.9525\right]\left[2,270,400\right]}} = \frac{-5817}{6897.14} = -0.84$$

The coefficient of determination is the square of the correlation coefficient, or

$$r^2 = \frac{a\sum Y + b\sum XY - n\bar{Y}^2}{\sum Y^2 - n\bar{Y}^2} = \frac{1450.12(3300) + (-276.28)(9783) - 6(550)^2}{2,193,400 - 6(550)^2}$$

$$= \frac{4,785,396 - 2,702,847.2 - 1,815,000}{378,400} = \frac{267,548.8}{378,400} = 0.71$$

The standard error of the estimate indicates the amount of data dispersion:

$$\sigma_{YX} = \sqrt{\frac{\sum Y^2 - a\sum Y - b\sum XY}{n - 2}}$$

$$= \sqrt{\frac{2,193,400 - 1450.12(3300) - (-276.28)(9783)}{6 - 2}}$$

$$= \sqrt{\frac{110,851.2}{4}} = 166.47$$

The correlation coefficient ($r = -0.84$) shows reasonable correlation between the variables. The coefficient of determination ($r^2 = 0.71$) indicates that other variables (in addition to price) appreciably affect sales. The standard error of the estimate ($\sigma_{YX} = 166$) is large relative to average sales (550) and reflects the possibility of sizable forecast errors.

If the regression equation is satisfactory to the manager, estimated sales at a price of $3.00 per dinner may be calculated as follows:

$$Y = a + bX = 1450.12 - 276.28(3.00)$$

$$= 621.28, \quad \text{or 621 dinners}$$

Solved Problem 2

The Polish General's Pizza Parlor is a small restaurant catering to patrons with a taste for European pizza. One of its specialties is Polish Prize pizza. The manager must forecast weekly demand for these special pizzas so that he can order pizza shells weekly. Recently, demand has been as follows:

Week of	Pizzas	Week of	Pizzas
June 2	50	June 23	56
June 9	65	June 30	55
June 16	52	July 7	60

a. Forecast the demand for pizza for June 23–July 14 by using the simple moving average method with $n = 3$. Then repeat the forecast by using the weighted moving average method with $n = 3$ and weights of 0.50, 0.30, and 0.20, with 0.50 applying to the most recent demand.

b. Calculate the MAD for each method.

Solution   a. The simple moving average method and the weighted moving average method give the following results:

Current Week	Simple Moving Average Forecast for Next Week	Weighted Moving Average Forecast for Next Week
June 16	$\dfrac{52 + 65 + 50}{3}$ = 55.7, or 56	$[(0.5 \times 52) + (0.3 \times 65) + (0.2 \times 50)]$ = 55.5, or 56
June 23	$\dfrac{56 + 52 + 65}{3}$ = 57.7, or 58	$[(0.5 \times 56) + (0.3 \times 52) + (0.2 \times 65)]$ = 56.6, or 57
June 30	$\dfrac{55 + 56 + 52}{3}$ = 54.3, or 54	$[(0.5 \times 55) + (0.3 \times 56) + (0.2 \times 52)]$ = 54.7, or 55
July 7	$\dfrac{60 + 55 + 56}{3}$ = 57	$[(0.5 \times 60) + (0.3 \times 55) + (0.2 \times 56)]$ = 57.7, or 58

b. The mean absolute deviation is calculated as follows.

		Simple Moving Average		Weighted Moving Average	
Week	Actual Demand	Forecast	Absolute Errors, $\lvert E_t \rvert$	Forecast	Absolute Errors, $\lvert E_t \rvert$
June 23	56	56	$\lvert 56 - 56 \rvert$ = 0	56	$\lvert 56 - 56 \rvert$ = 0
June 30	55	58	$\lvert 55 - 58 \rvert$ = 3	57	$\lvert 55 - 57 \rvert$ = 2
July 7	60	54	$\lvert 60 - 54 \rvert$ = 6	55	$\lvert 60 - 55 \rvert$ = 5
		MAD =	$\dfrac{0 + 3 + 6}{3} = 3$	MAD =	$\dfrac{0 + 2 + 5}{3} = 2.3$

For this limited set of data, the weighted moving average method resulted in a slightly lower mean absolute deviation. However, final conclusions can be made only after analyzing much more data.

Solved Problem 3

The monthly demand for units manufactured by the Acme Rocket Company has been as follows.

Month	Units	Month	Units
May	100	September	105
June	80	October	110
July	110	November	125
August	115	December	120

a. Use the exponential smoothing method to forecast the number of units for June–January. The initial forecast for May was 105 units; $\alpha = 0.2$.
b. Calculate the absolute percentage error for each month from June through December and the MAD and MAPE of forecast error as of the end of December.
c. Calculate the tracking signal as of the end of December. What can you say about the performance of your forecasting method?

Solution   a.

Current Month, t	$A_t = \alpha D_t + (1 - \alpha)A_{t-1}$	Forecast Month, t + 1
May	0.2(100) + 0.8(105) = 104.0, or 104	June
June	0.2(80) + 0.8(104.0) = 99.2, or 99	July
July	0.2(110) + 0.8(99.2) = 101.4, or 101	August
August	0.2(115) + 0.8(101.4) = 104.1, or 104	September
September	0.2(105) + 0.8(104.1) = 104.3, or 104	October
October	0.2(110) + 0.8(104.3) = 105.4, or 105	November
November	0.2(125) + 0.8(105.4) = 109.3, or 109	December
December	0.2(120) + 0.8(109.3) = 111.4, or 111	January

b.

Month, t	Actual Demand, D_t	Forecast, A_t	Error, $E_t = D_t - A_t$	Absolute Error, $\lvert E_t \rvert$	Absolute Percentage Error, $(\lvert E_t \rvert / D_t)(100\%)$
June	80	104	−24	24	30.0%
July	110	99	11	11	10.0
August	115	101	14	14	12.2
September	105	104	1	1	0.9
October	110	104	6	6	5.4
November	125	105	20	20	16.0
December	120	109	11	11	9.2
Total	765		39	87	83.7%

$$\text{MAD} = \frac{\Sigma \lvert E_t \rvert}{n} = \frac{87}{7} = 12.4 \quad \text{and} \quad \text{MAPE} = \frac{\Sigma \lvert E_t \rvert / D_t(100)}{n} = \frac{83.7\%}{7} = 11.9\%$$

c. As of the end of December, the cumulative sum of forecast errors (CFE) is 39. Using the mean absolute deviation calculated in part b, we calculate the tracking signal:

$$\text{Tracking signal} = \frac{\text{CFE}}{\text{MAD}} = \frac{39}{12.4} = 3.14$$

The probability that a tracking signal value of 3.14 could be generated completely by chance is very small. Consequently, we should revise our approach. The long string of forecasts lower than actual demand suggests use of a trend method.

Solved Problem 4

The demand for Krispee Crunchies, a favorite breakfast cereal of people born in the 1940s, is experiencing a decline. The company wants to monitor demand for this product closely as it nears the end of its life cycle. The trend-adjusted exponential smoothing method is used with $\alpha = 0.1$ and $\beta = 0.2$. At the end of December, the January estimate for the average number of cases sold per month, A_t, was 900,000 and the trend, T_t, was −50,000 per month. The following table shows the actual sales history for January, February, and March. Generate forecasts for February, March, and April.

Month	Sales
January	890,000
February	800,000
March	825,000

Solution   We know the initial condition at the end of December and actual demand for January, February, and March. We must now update the forecast method and prepare a forecast for April. All data are expressed in thousands of cases. Our equations for use with trend-adjusted exponential smoothing are

$$A_t = \alpha D_t + (1 - \alpha)(A_{t-1} + T_{t-1})$$

$$T_t = \beta(A_t - A_{t-1}) + (1 - \beta)T_{t-1}$$

$$\text{Forecast} = A_t + T_t$$

For January we have

$$A_{\text{Jan}} = 0.1(890,000) + 0.9(900,000 - 50,000)$$
$$= 854,000 \text{ cases}$$

$$T_{\text{Jan}} = 0.2(854,000 - 900,000) + 0.8(-50,000)$$
$$= -49,200 \text{ cases}$$

Forecast for February $= A_{\text{Jan}} + T_{\text{Jan}} = 854,000 - 49,200 = 804,800$ cases

For February we have

$$A_{\text{Feb}} = 0.1(800,000) + 0.9(854,000 - 49,200)$$
$$= 804,320 \text{ cases}$$

$$T_{\text{Feb}} = 0.2(804,320 - 854,000) + 0.8(-49,200)$$
$$= -49,296 \text{ cases}$$

Forecast for March $= A_{\text{Feb}} + T_{\text{Feb}} = 804,320 - 49,296 = 755,024$ cases

For March we have

$$A_{\text{Mar}} = 0.1(825,000) + 0.9(804,320 - 49,296)$$
$$= 762,021.6, \quad \text{or } 762,022 \text{ cases}$$

$$T_{\text{Mar}} = 0.2(762,022 - 804,320) + 0.8(-49,296)$$
$$= -47,896.4, \quad \text{or } -47,897 \text{ cases}$$

Forecast for April $= A_{\text{Mar}} + T_{\text{Mar}} = 762,022 - 47,897 = 714,125$ cases

Solved Problem 5

The Northville Post Office experiences a seasonal pattern of daily mail volume every week. The following data for two representative weeks are expressed in thousands of pieces of mail.

Day	Week 1	Week 2
Sunday	5	8
Monday	20	15
Tuesday	30	32
Wednesday	35	30
Thursday	49	45
Friday	70	70
Saturday	15	10
Total	224	210

a. Calculate a seasonal factor for each day of the week.
b. If the postmaster estimates that there will be 230,000 pieces of mail to sort next week, forecast the volume for each day of the week.

Solution a. Calculate the average daily mail volume for each week. Then for each day of the week divide the mail volume by the week's average to get the seasonal factor. Finally, for each day, add the two seasonal factors and divide by 2 to obtain the average seasonal factor to use in the forecast (see part b).

Day	Week 1 Mail Volume	Week 1 Seasonal Factor (1)	Week 2 Mail Volume	Week 2 Seasonal Factor (2)	Average Seasonal Factor [(1) + (2)]/2
Sunday	5	5/32 = 0.15625	8	8/30 = 0.26667	0.21146
Monday	20	20/32 = 0.62500	15	15/30 = 0.50000	0.56250
Tuesday	30	30/32 = 0.93750	32	32/30 = 1.06667	1.00209
Wednesday	35	35/32 = 1.09375	30	30/30 = 1.00000	1.04688
Thursday	49	49/32 = 1.53125	45	45/30 = 1.50000	1.51563
Friday	70	70/32 = 2.18750	70	70/30 = 2.33333	2.26042
Saturday	15	15/32 = 0.46875	10	10/30 = 0.33333	0.40104
Total	224		210		
Average	224/7 = 32		210/7 = 30		

b. The average daily mail volume is expected to be 230,000/7 = 32,857 pieces of mail. Using the average seasonal factors calculated in part a, we obtain the following forecasts.

Day	Calculation	Forecast
Sunday	0.21146(32,857) =	6,948
Monday	0.56250(32,857) =	18,482
Tuesday	1.00209(32,857) =	32,926
Wednesday	1.04688(32,857) =	34,397
Thursday	1.51563(32,857) =	49,799
Friday	2.26042(32,857) =	74,271
Saturday	0.40104(32,857) =	13,177
	Total	230,000

Formula Review

1. Linear regression: $Y = a + bX$

   where the forecast, Y, is a dependent linear function of the independent variable, X, and where

   $$a = \overline{Y} - b\overline{X}$$

   $$\overline{Y} = \frac{\sum Y}{n}$$

   $$\overline{X} = \frac{\sum X}{n}$$

   $$b = \frac{\sum XY - n\overline{X}\,\overline{Y}}{\sum X^2 - n\overline{X}^2}$$

2. Correlation coefficient: $r = \dfrac{n\sum XY - \sum X \sum Y}{\sqrt{\left[n\sum X^2 - \left(\sum X\right)^2\right]\left[n\sum Y^2 \left(\sum Y\right)^2\right]}}$

3. Coefficient of determination: $r^2 = \dfrac{a\sum Y + b\sum XY - n\overline{Y}^2}{\sum Y^2 - n\overline{Y}^2}$

4. Standard deviation of the estimate: $\sigma_{YX} = \sqrt{\dfrac{\sum Y^2 - a\sum Y - b\sum XY}{n - 2}}$

5. Naive forecasting: Forecast $= D_t$

6. Estimating the average: Forecast $= A_t$

7. Simple moving average: $A_t = \dfrac{D_t + D_{t-1} + D_{t-2} + \cdots + D_{t-n+1}}{n}$

8. Weighted moving average:

$$A_t = \text{Weight}_1(D_t) + \text{Weight}_2(D_{t-1}) + \text{Weight}_3(D_{t-2}) + \cdots + \text{Weight}_n(D_{t-n+1})$$

9. Exponential smoothing: $A_t = \alpha D_t + (1 - \alpha)A_{t-1}$

10. Trend-adjusted exponential smoothing:

$$A_t = \alpha D_t + (1 - \alpha)(A_{t-1} + T_{t-1})$$

$$T_t = \beta(A_t - A_{t-1}) + (1 - \beta)T_{t-1}$$

$$\text{Forecast} = A_t + T_t$$

11. Forecast error:

$$E_t = D_t - F_t$$

$$\text{CFE} = \Sigma E_t$$

$$\text{MSE} = \frac{\Sigma E_t^2}{n}$$

$$\sigma = \sqrt{\text{MSE}}$$

$$\text{MAD} = \frac{\Sigma |E_t|}{n}$$

$$\text{MAPE} = \frac{\Sigma |E_t|/D_t(100)}{n}$$

12. Exponentially smoothed error: $\text{MAD}_t = \alpha |E_t| + (1 - \alpha)\text{MAD}_{t-1}$

13. Tracking signal: $\dfrac{\text{CFE}}{\text{MAD}}$,   or $\dfrac{\text{CFE}}{\text{MAD}_t}$

Chapter Highlights

- The five basic components of demand are the average, trend, seasonal influence, cyclical movements, and random error. Demand can be affected by external factors that are beyond management's control. Indicators of changes in external factors can help predict changes in demand for goods and services. Decisions about product design, price, and advertising are examples of internal decisions that may influence demand.

- Designing a forecasting system involves determining what to forecast, which forecasting technique to use, and how computerized forecasting systems can assist managerial decision making.

- Level of data aggregation and units of measure are important considerations in managerial decisions about what to forecast. Three general types of demand forecasting are used: judgment methods, causal methods, and time series methods.

- Judgment methods of forecasting are useful in situations where relevant historical data are lacking. Sales force estimates, executive opinion, market research, and the Delphi method are judgment methods. The Delphi method has been used to make forecasts of technological change. Judgment methods require the most human interaction and so are the most costly of these methods. Facility location and capacity planning are examples of long-term decisions that justify the expense of generating a judgment forecast.

- Causal forecasting methods hypothesize a functional relationship between the factor to be forecasted and other internal or external factors. Causal methods identify turning points in demand patterns but require more extensive analysis to determine the appropriate relationships between the item to be forecast and the external and internal factors. Causal methods tend to be used in medium-term production planning for product families. Linear regression is one of the more popular causal forecasting methods.

- Time series analysis is often used with computer systems to generate quickly the large number of short-term forecasts required for scheduling products or services. Simple moving averages, weighted moving averages, and exponential smoothing are used to estimate the average of a time series. The exponential smoothing technique has the advantage of requiring that only a minimal amount of data be kept for use in updating the forecast. Trend-adjusted exponential smoothing is a method for including a trend estimate in exponentially smoothed forecasts. Estimates for the series average and the trend are smoothed to provide the forecast.

- Although many techniques allow for seasonal influences, a simple approach is the multiplicative seasonal method, which is based on the assumption that the seasonal influence is proportional to the level of average demand.

- The cumulative sum of forecast errors (CFE), mean squared error (MSE), standard deviation of forecast errors (σ), mean absolute deviation (MAD), and mean absolute percent error (MAPE) are all measures of forecast error used in practice. The CFE and MAD are used to develop a tracking signal that determines when a forecasting method no longer is yielding acceptable forecasts. Forecast error measures also are used to select the best forecast methods from available alternatives.

Key Terms

additive seasonal method *479*
aggregation *457*
causal methods *458*
coefficient of determination *465*
coincident indicators *456*
correlation coefficient *465*
cumulative sum of forecast errors (CFE) *480*
Delphi method *463*
demand management *456*
dependent variable *464*
executive opinion *461*
exponential smoothing method *472*
focus forecasting *486*

forecast *453*
forecast error *480*
independent variables *464*
judgment methods *458*
lagging indicators *456*
leading indicators *456*
linear regression *464*
market research *462*
mean absolute deviation (MAD) *481*
mean absolute percent error (MAPE) *481*
mean squared error (MSE) *481*
multiplicative seasonal method *477*

naive forecast *468*
sales force estimates *461*
simple moving average method *470*
standard deviation (σ) *481*
standard error of the estimate *465*
technological forecasting *463*
time series *454*
time series analysis *458*
tracking signal *482*
trend-adjusted exponential smoothing method *474*
weighted moving average method *471*

Study Questions

1. The College of Business needs a forecast of demand for staff planning. List two external factors and one internal factor that could affect demand. Identify a leading indicator of demand. What options exist for managing demand? What should be forecast? In other words, what level of aggregation and what units of measurement are appropriate for forecasting demand?

2. It's spring break time. On S. Padre Island, Texas, Ivan Czajkow, the new manager of the Bates Motel, is concerned about the motel's water heater capacity. What causal factor(s) could help Ivan in predicting the demand for hot water? What demand management options might be effective?

3. An independent grocery has thousands of items in stock and must forecast demand for each one on a weekly basis. Which of the three approaches (time series analysis, causal, or judgment) would you recommend? Why?

4. A new movie theater in town gets an overflow crowd of teenagers for Friday and Saturday night showings of the horror movie *Bad Dreams on Mohican Way— Part 16* and very little attendance for other movies shown during the rest of the week. Discuss how demand management could be used to smooth the load on facilities over the week and during the day on Saturday.

5. If you had to choose among simple moving averages, weighted moving averages, and exponential smoothing to forecast demand for a product having no trend or seasonal components, which method would you choose? Why?

6. Create a simple example to show how an electronic spreadsheet could be set up to calculate simple moving averages or simple exponential smoothing.

7. A market survey company was experiencing difficulty in getting responses. Potential respondents would

hang up on telephone interviewers, throw away mailings, and avoid clipboard-toting interviewers at the shopping mall. A bubble gum manufacturer has hired the firm for a survey to taste-test sushi-flavored bubble gum. Tired of chasing respondents, the surveyor simply posted a sidewalk sign outside the office, located in the city's financial district: "$50 cash for 15 minutes of your time." The sign brought in plenty of eager survey subjects. The results of the survey predicted great success and the manufacturer invested heavily, but the product failed miserably. What went wrong?

8. The naive method uses the actual demand from the previous period as the forecast for the next period. Is exponential smoothing a naive forecasting method? Why or why not?

9. A production manager recommends that all exponentially smoothed forecasts have a low α value. A marketing manager recommends that all exponentially smoothed forecasts have a high α value. Describe demand patterns or situations for which each would be appropriate.

10. You have just spent eight months developing a method to forecast hourly volumes of checks to be processed by the encoding department of a large bank. Based on historical data, your method's forecasts resulted in a MAD of 500 checks. The first week you used the new method, the actual MAD was 1000 checks. Should you be concerned? Why or why not?

11. Describe how you could use simple linear regression in conjunction with the seasonal factors approach to seasonal forecasting.

12. As a consultant, you have been asked to look into the forecasting problems of a certain company. The company has been plotting the cumulative forecast error for each of its forecasts and using the results to judge the adequacy of its forecasting system. What are your reactions to this approach? What would you recommend?

13. As part of its product planning program, an automobile manufacturer is interested in determining when the gasoline engine will be replaced by some other source of power for the automobile. How would you go about making this prediction?

14. Ideally we would like forecasts with no bias and no MAD. Do random errors contribute more to bias or to MAD? How do forecasts with positive bias affect inventories?

15. You have received forecasts from two sources for the same product. The first forecast states that demand next month will be 500 units. The other says with 95 percent confidence that demand next month will be between 400 and 600 units. Which of the two forecasts would you prefer? Why?

Discussion Questions

1. Figure 10.9 shows summer air visibility measurements for Denver. The acceptable visibility standard is 100, with readings above 100 indicating clean air and good visibility and readings below 100 indicating temperature inversions, forest fires, volcanic eruptions, or collisions with comets.

FIGURE 10.9

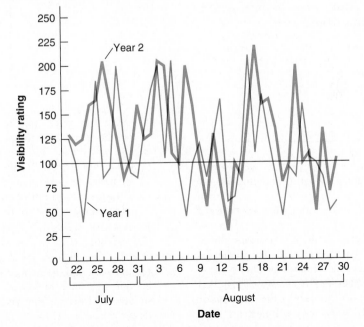

a. Is there a trend in the data? Which time series techniques might be appropriate for estimating the average of these data?

b. A medical center for asthma and respiratory diseases located in Denver has great demand for its services when air quality is poor. If you were in charge of developing a short-term (say, 3-day) forecast of visibility, which causal factor(s) would you analyze? In other words, which external factors hold the potential to significantly affect visibility in the *short term*?

c. Tourism, an important factor in Denver's economy, is affected by the city's image. Air quality, as measured by visibility, affects the city's image. If you were responsible for development of tourism, which causal factor(s) would you analyze to forecast visibility for the *medium term* (say, the next two summers)?

d. The federal government threatens to withhold several hundred million dollars in department of transportation funds unless Denver meets visibility standards within eight years. How would you proceed to generate a *long-term* judgment forecast of technologies that will be available to improve visibility in the next ten years?

2. Kay and Michael Passe publish *What's Happening?*— a biweekly newspaper to publicize local events.

What's Happening? has few subscribers; it typically is sold at checkout stands. Much of the revenue comes from advertisers of garage sales and supermarket specials. In an effort to reduce costs associated with printing too many papers or delivering them to the wrong location, Michael implemented a computerized system to collect sales data. Sales-counter scanners accurately record sales data for each location. Since the system was implemented, total sales volume has steadily declined. Selling advertising space and maintaining shelf space at supermarkets are getting more difficult.

Reduced revenue makes controlling costs all the more important. For each issue, Michael carefully makes a forecast based on sales data collected at each location. Then he orders papers to be printed and distributed in quantities matching the forecast. Michael's forecast reflects a downward trend, which *is* present in the sales data. Now only a few papers are left over at only a few locations. Although the sales forecast accurately predicts the actual sales at most locations, *What's Happening?* is spiraling toward oblivion. Kay suspects that Michael is doing something wrong in preparing the forecast but can find no mathematical errors. Tell her what's happening.

Problems

1. The owner of a computer store rents printers to some of her preferred customers. She is interested in arriving at a forecast of rentals so that she can order the correct quantities of supplies that go with the printers. Data for the last 10 weeks are shown below.

Week	Rentals	Week	Rentals
1	25	6	22
2	28	7	26
3	30	8	24
4	26	9	20
5	27	10	23

a. Prepare a forecast for weeks 6–10 by using a five-week moving average. What is the forecast for week 11?

b. Calculate the mean absolute deviation as of the end of week 10.

2. The Midwest Telephone Company provides phone installation services. The manager of the installers is interested in forecasting the demand for phone installation so that he can plan for the number of installers required. The numbers of weekly phone installation requests for the last 10 weeks were as follows:

Week	Installation Requests	Week	Installation Requests
1	15	6	19
2	18	7	20
3	12	8	26
4	27	9	29
5	23	10	32

a. Use a four-week moving average to forecast the number of requests for weeks 7, 8, 9, 10, and 11.

b. Use a six-week moving average to forecast the number of requests for weeks 7, 8, 9, 10, and 11.

c. Compare the performance of the two methods with a simple calculation of forecast error. Explain the relative performance of the two methods.

3. Karl's Copiers sells and repairs photocopy machines. The manager needs weekly forecasts of service calls so that he can schedule service personnel. The forecast for the week of July 3 was 23 calls. The manager uses exponential smoothing with $\alpha = 0.25$. Forecast the number of calls for the week of August 7, which is next week.

Week of	Actual Service Calls
July 3	27
July 10	36
July 17	31
July 24	24
July 31	23

4. The K&R Camera Shop sells all the latest cameras and accessories. To meet customer demand, the manager must forecast demand for the items she sells. Lately the XR-42S zoom lens has been very popular. Recent monthly demand for this item has been as shown:

Month	Number of Lenses Sold
1	12
2	17
3	15
4	20
5	18
6	23

   a. Forecast XR-42S demand for months 4–6, using a weighted moving average. The weights are 0.5, 0.3, and 0.2, where 0.5 refers to the most recent demand.
   b. Repeat part a, using exponential smoothing with $\alpha = 0.2$. Assume that the average at the end of month 2 was 15 lenses.
   c. What is the forecast for week 7, using each method? Based on these limited data, which method do you have more confidence in? Discuss.

5. A vending machine company recently started to carry a new brand of soda in its territory. Management is interested in estimating future sales volume to determine whether it should continue to carry the new brand or replace it with another brand. At the end of April the average monthly sales volume of the new soda was 700 cans and the trend was +50 cans per month. The actual sales volume figures for May, June, and July are 760, 800, and 820, respectively. Use trend-adjusted exponential smoothing with $\alpha = 0.2$ and $\beta = 0.1$ to forecast usage for June, July, and August.

6. Sunnyvale Bank in Yuma, Arizona, recently installed a new automatic teller machine to perform the standard banking services and handle loan applications and investment transactions. The new machine is a bit complicated to use, so management is interested in tracking its past use and projecting its future use. Additional machines may be needed if projected use is high enough.

   At the end of March the average monthly use was 600 customers and the trend was +60 customers per month. The actual use figures for April, May, and June are 680, 710, and 790, respectively. Use trend-adjusted exponential smoothing with $\alpha = 0.3$ and $\beta = 0.2$ to forecast usage for May, June, and July.

7. Consider the following data for the sales in units of a particular product over the past four weeks.

Week	Sales (units)
1	29
2	35
3	32
4	40

   a. Use exponential smoothing with $\alpha = 0.7$ to forecast sales for weeks 2–5. Assume that the average of the time series was 30 units just before week 1.
   b. Use trend-adjusted exponential smoothing with $\alpha = 0.1$ and $\beta = 0.1$ to forecast sales for weeks 2–5. Assume that the average of the series was 30 units and that the average trend was +3 units per week just before week 1.
   c. Compare the performance of these two methods, using appropriate measures of forecast error. Which method seems to fit the data better?

8. The following data are for calculator sales in units at an electronics store over the past five weeks.

Week	Sales
1	46
2	49
3	43
4	50
5	53

   Use trend-adjusted exponential smoothing with $\alpha = 0.2$ and $\beta = 0.2$ to forecast sales for weeks 3–6. Assume that the average of the time series was 45 units and that the average trend was +2 units per week just before week 1.

9. Forrest and Dan make boxes of chocolates for which the demand is uncertain. Forrest says, "That's life." But Dan believes that some demand patterns exist that could be useful for planning the purchase of sugar, chocolate, and shrimp. Forrest insists on placing a surprise chocolate-covered shrimp in some boxes so that "You never know what you'll get." Quarterly demand (in boxes of chocolates) for the last three years follows.

Quarter	Year 1	Year 2	Year 3
1	3,000	3,300	3,502
2	1,700	2,100	2,448
3	900	1,500	1,768
4	4,400	5,100	5,882
Total	10,000	12,000	13,600

ment quantities can be purchased. An example of the sales growth experienced during the last 50 months is the growth in demand for item EP-37, a laser printer cartridge, shown in Table 10.4.

a. Develop a trend-adjusted exponential smoothing solution for forecasting demand. Find the "best" parameters and justify your choices. Forecast demand for months 51–53.

b. A consultant to Midwest's management suggested that new office building leases would be a good leading indicator for company sales. He quoted a recent university study finding that new office building leases precede office equipment and supply sales by three months. According to the study findings, leases in month 1 would affect sales in month 4; leases in month 2 would affect sales in month 5; and so on. Use linear regression to develop a forecasting model for sales, with leases as the independent variable. Forecast sales for months 51–53.

c. Which of the two models provides better forecasts? Explain.

21. A certain food item at Wise Owl Supermarkets has the demand pattern shown in the following table. Find the "best" forecast you can for month 25 and justify your methodology. You may use some of the data to find the best parameter value(s) for your method and the rest to test the forecast model. Your justification should include both quantitative and qualitative considerations.

Month	Demand	Month	Demand
1	33	13	37
2	37	14	43
3	31	15	56
4	39	16	41
5	54	17	36
6	38	18	39
7	42	19	41
8	40	20	58
9	41	21	42
10	54	22	45
11	43	23	41
12	39	24	38

TABLE 10.4   *EP-37 Sales and Lease Data*

Month	EP-37 Sales	Leases	Month	EP-37 Sales	Leases
1	80	32	26	1296	281
2	132	29	27	1199	298
3	143	32	28	1267	314
4	180	54	29	1300	323
5	200	53	30	1370	309
6	168	89	31	1489	343
7	212	74	32	1499	357
8	254	93	33	1669	353
9	397	120	34	1716	360
10	385	113	35	1603	370
11	472	147	36	1812	386
12	397	126	37	1817	389
13	476	138	38	1798	399
14	699	145	39	1873	409
15	545	160	40	1923	410
16	837	196	41	2028	413
17	743	180	42	2049	439
18	722	197	43	2084	454
19	735	203	44	2083	441
20	838	223	45	2121	470
21	1057	247	46	2072	469
22	930	242	47	2262	490
23	1085	234	48	2371	496
24	1090	254	49	2309	509
25	1218	271	50	2422	522

22. The data for the visibility chart in Discussion Question 2 are shown in Table 10.5. The visibility standard is set at 100. Readings below 100 indicate that air pollution has reduced visibility, and readings above 100 indicate that the air is clearer.
    a. Use several methods to generate a visibility forecast for August 31 of the second year. Which of the methods seems to produce the best forecast?
    b. Use several methods to forecast the visibility index for the summer of the third year. Which of the methods seems to produce the best forecast? Support your choice.
23. Vinton A. (Bud) Vizier forecasts electrical demand for the Flatlands Public Power District (FPPD). The FPPD wants to take its Comstock power plant out of service for maintenance when demand is expected to be low. After shutdown, performing maintenance and getting the plant back on line takes two weeks. The utility has enough other generating capacity to satisfy 1550 megawatts (MW) of demand while Comstock is out of service. Table 10.6 shows weekly peak demands (in MW) for the past several autumns. When next fall should the Comstock plant be scheduled for maintenance?

24. The general manager at Comnet Communications, a regional telecommunications service, is interested in developing a forecast of yearly phone installations and quarterly sales. From the company's computer database she acquired the following numbers of monthly installations (in thousands) for the last three years.

Month	Year 1	Year 2	Year 3
January	23	28	49
February	21	32	52
March	24	34	45
April	26	38	43
May	22	31	44
June	27	32	40
July	25	40	46
August	27	38	48
September	24	42	54
October	23	44	50
November	29	45	48
December	31	47	56

TABLE 10.5 *Visibility Data*

Date	Year 1	Year 2	Date	Year 1	Year 2	Date	Year 1	Year 2
July 22	125	130	Aug. 5	105	200	Aug. 19	170	160
23	100	120	6	205	110	20	125	165
24	40	125	7	90	100	21	85	135
25	100	160	8	45	200	22	45	80
26	185	165	9	100	160	23	95	100
27	85	205	10	120	100	24	85	200
28	95	165	11	85	55	25	160	100
29	200	125	12	125	130	26	105	110
30	125	85	13	165	75	27	100	50
31	90	105	14	60	30	28	95	135
Aug. 1	85	160	15	65	100	29	50	70
2	135	125	16	110	85	30	60	105
3	175	130	17	210	150			
4	200	205	18	110	220			

TABLE 10.6 *Weekly Peak Power Demands*

	August		September				October					November	
Year	1	2	3	4	5	6	7	8	9	10	11	12	13
1	2050	1925	1825	1525	1050	1300	1200	1175	1350	1525	1725	1575	1925
2	2000	2075	2225	1800	1175	1050	1250	1025	1300	1425	1625	1950	1950
3	1950	1800	2150	1725	1575	1275	1325	1100	1500	1550	1375	1825	2000
4	2100	2400	1975	1675	1350	1525	1500	1150	1350	1225	1225	1475	1850
5	2275	2300	2150	1525	1350	1475	1475	1175	1375	1400	1425	1550	1900

The General Manager needs a forecast for the first three months of next year.

a. Calculate a forecast for January, February, and March of next year, based on minimizing MAD, using each of the following methods: three-period moving average, exponential smoothing, trend-adjusted exponential smoothing.

b. Develop linear regression forecasts for January, February, and March, with time as the independent variable.

c. Compare the forecasts in parts a and b. Which would you recommend? Why?

25. The marketing vice-president of Getsmart Computers, a regional computer distributor, wants to develop a quarterly sales forecast for the coming year (year 10). He obtained the following quarterly sales data (in thousands of dollars).

Year	Quarter			
	1st	2nd	3rd	4th
1	1115	1450	1845	1235
2	1320	1375	1678	940
3	1390	1615	2005	1145
4	1405	1595	2125	1225
5	1490	1690	2225	1280
6	1450	1630	2100	1220
7	1560	1810	2250	1335
8	1590	1970	2265	1390
9	1605	2010	2360	1410

Prepare a forecast for each quarter of year 10.

CASE

Yankee Fork and Hoe Company

The Yankee Fork and Hoe Company is a leading producer of garden tools ranging from wheelbarrows, mortar pans, and hand trucks to shovels, rakes, and trowels. The tools are sold in four different product lines ranging from the top-of-the-line Hercules products, which are rugged tools for the toughest jobs, to the Garden Helper products, which are economy tools for the occasional user. The market for garden tools is extremely competitive because of the simple design of the products and the large number of competing producers. In addition, more people are using power tools, such as lawn edgers, hedge trimmers, and thatchers, reducing demand for their manual counterparts. These factors compel Yankee to maintain low prices while retaining high quality and dependable delivery.

Garden tools represent a mature industry. Unless new manual products can be developed or there is a sudden resurgence in home gardening, the prospects for large increases in sales are not bright. Keeping ahead of the competition is a constant battle. No one knows this better than Alan Roberts, president of Yankee. He lived through the early years of rapid growth, which has now leveled off. The types of tools sold today are, by and large, the same ones sold 30 years ago. The only way to generate new sales and retain old customers is to provide superior customer service and produce a product with high customer value. This approach puts pressure on the manufacturing system, which has been having difficulties lately. Recently Roberts has been receiving calls from long-time customers, such as Sears and Tru-Value Hardware Stores, complaining about late shipments. These customers advertise promotions for garden tools and require on-time delivery.

Roberts knows that losing customers like Sears and Tru-Value would be disastrous. He decides to ask consultant Sharon Place to look into the matter and report to him in one week. Roberts suggests that she focus on the bow rake as a case in point because it is a high-volume product and has been a major source of customer complaints of late.

Planning Bow Rake Production

A bow rake consists of a head with 12 teeth spaced one inch apart, a hardwood handle, a bow that attaches the head to the handle, and a metal ferrule that reinforces the area where the bow inserts into the handle. The bow is a metal strip that is welded to the ends of the rake head and bent in the middle to form a flat tab for insertion into the handle. The rake is about 64 inches long.

Place decides to find out how Yankee plans bow rake production. She goes straight to Phil Stanton, who gives the following account:

Planning is informal around here. To begin, marketing determines the forecast for bow rakes by month for the next year. Then they pass it along to me. Quite frankly, the forecasts are usually inflated—must be their big egos over there. I have to be careful because we enter into long-term purchasing agreements for steel, and having it just sitting around is expensive. So, I usually reduce the forecast by 10 percent or so. I use the modified forecast to generate a monthly final assembly schedule, which determines what I need to have from the forging and woodworking areas. The system works well if the forecasts are good. But when marketing comes to me and says they are behind on customer orders, as they often do near the end of the year, it wreaks havoc with the schedules. Forging gets hit the hardest. For example, the presses that stamp the rake heads from blanks of steel can handle only 7000 heads per day, and the bow rolling machine can do only 5000 per day. Both operations are also required for many other products.

Because the marketing department provides crucial information to Stanton, Place decides to see the marketing manager, Ron Adams. Adams explains how he arrives at the bow rake forecasts.

Things don't change much from year to year. Sure, sometimes we put on a sales promotion of some kind, but we try to give Phil enough warning before the demand kicks in—usually a month or so. Basically, we use the time series of bow rake shipments as a starting point for the forecast. We use shipment data because they are hard numbers—what we actually shipped in

a given month. [See Table 10.7.] They reflect our physical capacity to produce. I meet with several managers from the various sales regions to modify the shipping data from last year for anticipated promotions, changes in the economy, and shortages we experienced last year. Even though we take a lot of time getting the forecast, it never seems to help us avoid customer problems.

The Problem

Place ponders the comments from Stanton and Adams. She understands Stanton's concerns about costs and keeping inventory low and Adams's concern about having enough rakes on hand to make timely shipments. Both are also somewhat concerned about capacity. Yet, she decides to check actual customer demand for the bow rake over the past four years (in Table 10.8) before making her final report to Roberts.

Questions

1. Comment on the forecasting system being used by Yankee. Suggest changes or improvements that you believe are justified.
2. Develop your own forecast for bow rakes for each month of the next year (year 5). Justify your forecast and the method you used.

TABLE 10.7 *Four-Year History of Bow Rake Shipments*

	Actual Shipments			
Month	Year 1	Year 2	Year 3	Year 4
1	38,459	42,604	36,067	39,403
2	45,778	38,960	34,589	38,308
3	36,375	35,560	41,720	43,698
4	38,987	37,980	39,500	40,309
5	17,480	23,638	29,269	27,247
6	16,304	7,921	19,680	11,571
7	17,260	22,475	10,754	22,502
8	10,649	13,397	21,909	19,712
9	22,890	20,400	20,491	14,802
10	35,717	56,980	53,040	38,298
11	105,793	85,678	80,304	110,256
12	75,209	74,244	78,432	77,655

TABLE 10.8 *Four-Year Demand History for the Bow Rake*

	Actual Demands*			
Month	Year 1	Year 2	Year 3	Year 4
1	53,630	51,078	53,977	50,040
2	56,289	59,298	60,998	63,781
3	17,345	20,223	22,568	23,266
4	26,199	25,970	26,504	28,140
5	23,099	24,705	26,932	27,566
6	15,700	13,400	16,421	15,898
7	16,560	17,788	13,045	18,209
8	18,200	16,465	18,991	17,690
9	15,510	17,433	21,604	22,887
10	55,088	57,400	59,297	54,777
11	84,188	85,455	81,521	83,709
12	71,088	73,886	74,699	75,432

*The number of units promised each month for delivery

Selected References

Adam, Everett E. "Individual Item Forecasting Model Evaluation." *Decision Sciences,* vol. 4, no. 4 (1973).

Box, George E. P., and Gwilym M. Jenkins. *Time Series Analysis: Forecasting and Control.* San Francisco: Holden-Day, 1970.

Chambers, John C., Satinder K. Mullick, and Donald D. Smith. "How to Choose the Right Forecasting Technique." *Harvard Business Review* (July–August 1971), pp. 45–74.

Gardner, Everette S. "The Strange Case of the Lagging Forecasts." *Interfaces,* vol. 14, no. 3 (May–June 1984), pp. 47–50.

Gardner, Everette S., and David G. Dannenbring. "Forecasting with Exponential Smoothing: Some Guidelines for Model Selection." *Decision Sciences,* vol. 11, no. 2 (April 1980), pp. 370–383.

Jenkins, Carolyn. "Accurate Forecasting Reduces Inventory and Increases Output at Henredon." *APICS—The Performance Advantage* (September 1992), pp. 37–39.

Kimes, Sheryl E., and James A. Fitzsimmons. "Selecting Profitable Hotel Sites at La Quinta Motor Inns." *Interfaces,* vol. 20, no. 2 (March–April 1990), pp. 12–20.

Mabert, Vincent A. "Forecast Modification Based on Residual Analysis: A Case Study of Check Volume Estimation." *Decision Sciences,* vol. 9, no. 2 (April 1978), pp. 285–296.

Makridakis, Spyros, Steven C. Wheelwright, and Victor E. McGee. *Forecasting: Methods and Applications,* 2nd ed. New York: John Wiley & Sons, 1983.

Sanders, Nada R., and Larry P. Ritzman. "The Need for Contextual and Technical Knowledge in Judgmental Forecasting." *Journal of Behavioral Decision Making,* vol. 5, no. 1 (January–March 1992), pp. 39–52.

Smith, Bernard. *Focus Forecasting: Computer Techniques for Inventory Control.* Boston: CBI Publishing, 1984.

Stratton, William B. "How to Design a Viable Forecasting System." *Production and Inventory Management,* vol. 20, no. 1 (First Quarter 1979), pp. 17–27.

Yurkiewicz, Jack. "Forecasting Software: Clearing Up a Cloudy Picture." *OR/MS Today* (February 1993), pp. 64–75.

Chapter Eleven

MATERIALS MANAGEMENT

un Microsystems, Incorporated, a computer
workstation maker in Mountain View, California, enjoyed seven years of sizzling growth in
the 1980s. But in 1989, its president announced a
$27 million loss for the fiscal fourth quarter. What
went wrong? Several serious problems in its forecasting, production planning, and inventory control systems affected Sun at the same time. An especially
troubling problem stemmed from Sun's new computerized record-keeping system for customer orders
and inventory control. Sun had spent years considering the transition from manual to computerized
record keeping and was understandably disappointed when it found that its new system didn't work.
For several weeks the company lost track of orders,
didn't track inventory well, and didn't get key reports. To close the books on its June quarter, Sun
had to finish some of the accounting work by hand.
Painful shortages of some key components, such as
color monitors, occurred. These shortages kept Sun
from filling many orders for a new Sun-designed microprocessor called Sparc. In addition, the company
failed to stop hiring when production, ordering, and
inventory problems caused sales to slow. Excess
labor costs caused profits to plummet. The record-

Sun Microsystems' computers are readied for shipment.

keeping systems didn't alert the company to the
problems soon enough. These miscues in managing
materials and production levels have been corrected.
Sun's sales exploded from $500 million in 1989 to
$4.7 billion in 1994, with net income growing to
$196 million. However, the miscues demonstrate
how important effective materials management is to
a firm's bottom line.

aterials management concerns short-range decisions about supplies, inventories, production levels, staffing patterns, schedules, and distribution. Decisions in these areas affect the entire organization, either
directly or indirectly. We begin by examining the important role materials and inventory play in the economy. We then describe materials management tasks, focusing on purchasing and distribution. We conclude by presenting several
important inventory concepts and management decisions.

◆ IMPORTANCE OF MATERIALS MANAGEMENT

Figure 11.1 shows the materials management cycle of acquisition, storage, conversion, storage, and distribution—illustrated in this case for baked goods. The
cycle begins with the purchase of materials or services from outside suppliers.
Raw materials are stored and then converted into goods or services by one or
more transformation processes. Manufacturers store semifinished and finished
goods and finally distribute the finished products to customers. For services, the
distribution step is unnecessary if customers come to the facility themselves for

FIGURE 11.1

The Materials Management Cycle, Illustrated for Baked Goods

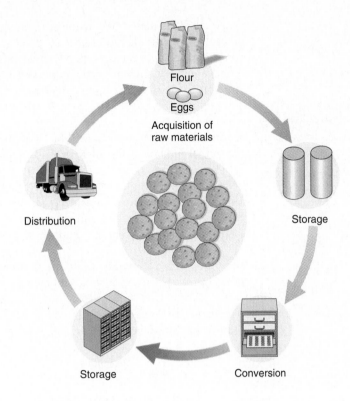

the services. This cycle repeats over and over, as the firm responds to changing customer demand. Materials management decisions have short time horizons and therefore are more tactical than strategic. However, they have a major cumulative effect and thus attract considerable managerial attention. Tactical decisions about materials are important for two reasons: (1) the central role of materials in production and (2) the impact of inventories on company profitability.

Central Role of Materials in the Economy

Managing materials is common to organizations in every segment of the economy: churches, governments, manufacturers, wholesalers, retailers, and universities. Manufacturers make products from materials they purchase from outside suppliers. Service industries use materials in the form of physical items purchased from suppliers. For example, churches buy bulletins for their services, envelopes, brochures, audiotapes, file folders, audio equipment, hymnals, and devotional readings. The typical U.S. manufacturer spent 40 percent of its total income from sales on purchased materials and services in 1945. The proportion rose to 50 percent in 1960 and now stands at more than 60 percent. This increase indicates that companies today are relying more on suppliers (less backward vertical integration) from around the world.

The percentage of income from sales spent on purchased materials varies from industry to industry. At one extreme, the petroleum refining industry spends more than 80 percent of its income from sales on materials; at the other extreme, the pharmaceutical industry spends only 25 percent. There is also some variation by country. Owing to the lack of natural resources in Japan, firms there spend an average of 7 percent more of their income from sales on materials than do North American and European firms. In general, most firms spend 45 to 65 percent on materials and 15 to 20 percent on labor; the remainder of their income goes for depreciation, taxes, dividends, and retained earnings. Because materials comprise such a large component of the sales dollar, companies can reap large profits with a small percentage reduction in the cost of materials.

EXAMPLE 11.1

Profit-Making Potential of Materials

A company's sales this year will be $100 million. Cost of materials represents 60 percent of income from sales, or $60 million; salaries, wages, and benefits take another 15 percent, or $15 million. A 10 percent gross profit (before taxes) is expected. To increase gross profits by $1 million next year, from $10 million to $11 million, management is considering three options: increase sales, reduce labor costs (through increased productivity), or reduce materials costs. Which option requires the least percentage change?

Solution   The following calculations show that the company could increase sales by *10 percent*, reduce labor costs by almost *7 percent*, or reduce materials costs by less than *2 percent* to achieve the same increase in profits. Because smaller percentage changes normally are easier (cost less) to achieve than large ones, changes in materials costs have a high profit-making potential.

Alternative	Percentage Change
1. Increase sales by $10 million	$\left(\dfrac{\$10\text{ million}}{\$100\text{ million}}\right)(100\%) = 10\%$
2. Reduce labor costs by $1 million	$\left(\dfrac{\$1\text{ million}}{\$15\text{ million}}\right)(100\%) \cong 7\%$
3. Reduce materials costs by $1 million	$\left(\dfrac{\$1\text{ million}}{\$60\text{ million}}\right)(100\%) \cong 2\%$

Impact of Inventory on Profitability

Materials also are important because of the investment tied up in them. In 1990, more than $1 trillion worth of goods were held in inventory in the U.S. economy—2.7 times the economy's monthly sales to consumers. In other words, the economy held 2.7 months' sales volume in inventory, down from 3.1 months' volume in the 1980s and 3.6 months' volume in the 1970s.

Inventory investment in the U.S. economy is almost double all business investment (by both manufacturing and service sectors) in new plants and equipment each year. Each dollar tied up in inventory is a dollar unavailable for investment in new products or services, technological improvements, or capacity increases.

Figure 11.2 shows that manufacturers hold most inventory (36 percent), followed by retailers with 25 percent and wholesalers at 23 percent. These percentages illustrate why all sectors of the economy are concerned with materials management.

FIGURE 11.2

Where Inventories Are Held

Source: *Economic Report of the President*, 1993.

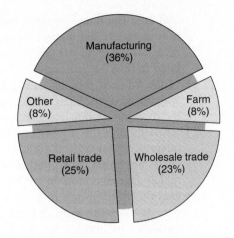

◆ FUNCTION OF MATERIALS MANAGEMENT

Some argue that, ideally, one person in a firm should make all materials management decisions because they are so interrelated. However, the sheer magnitude of this task in most firms—which may have thousands of employees and product items, hundreds of work centers, several plants, and hundreds of suppliers—makes that impossible. Trying to develop weekly plans even three months into the future for purchasing, inventory, output rates, work-force levels, and transportation schedules would be a mind-boggling job for one person.

Traditionally, organizations have divided the responsibility for materials management among three departments: purchasing, production control, and distribution. In this form of organization, called a **segmented structure,** the manager of each of these departments reports to a different person. The following table shows how manufacturing and service firms usually assign tasks in materials management. Tasks such as staff planning and work-force scheduling usually are decentralized. For example, branch managers at retail stores or banks develop schedules for the activities and employees in their own units.

What organizational structure is best, and what activities require the most coordination with other functions?

Materials Management Task	Manufacturing	Services
Supplier selection	Purchasing	Purchasing
Issuing purchase releases	Purchasing	Decentralized
Inbound transportation	Purchasing	Purchasing
Initiating purchase requests	Production control	Decentralized
Work-force schedules	Production control	Decentralized
Inventory control on site	Production control	Purchasing
Assigning priorities to work	Production control	Decentralized
Outbound transportation	Distribution	Decentralized
Inventory control at distribution centers	Distribution	Decentralized

Since the early 1960s, many firms have restructured to centralize most materials management tasks in one department and elevate its manager to a higher position in the company. This form of organization is called an **integrated structure,** and the unified new department typically is called *materials management,* although the name *logistics management* is used sometimes. This structure not only elevates the function but also recognizes that the various materials management tasks are all part of the same broad activity, bringing together all tasks related to flows of materials, from the purchase of raw materials to the distribution of the finished product or service. A majority of firms use hybrid structures, in which two of the three departments typically report to the same executive; often the distribution department continues reporting to marketing.

Although the organizational structure and management hierarchy can help integrate decisions and activities in the materials management cycle, considerable cross-functional coordination still is required. For example, marketing typically makes forecasts and processes incoming customer orders. Production control uses this information to put together work-force schedules and set work priorities. At the same time, marketing needs to know the current schedule and production capability when processing incoming orders so as to make realistic delivery promises. Once purchased materials are received or finished products shipped, accounting must follow through with payments or billing. Achieving better cross-functional coordination may mean pushing responsibilities lower in the organization, grouping traditional functions around each major product or service, or creating interfunctional coordinating units. Information systems and reward systems can also facilitate coordination across the functional boundaries.

Subsequent chapters of this book deal with most of the materials management tasks. Here, we provide a brief introduction to two functions not discussed later: purchasing and distribution.

Purchasing

Purchasing is the management of the acquisition process, which includes deciding which suppliers to use, negotiating contracts, and deciding whether to buy locally or centrally. Purchasing must satisfy the firm's long-term supply needs and support the firm's production capabilities. This task is crucial for any organization, whether retailer, service provider, or manufacturer. The inputs and outputs of downstream productive processes depend on how well the task is performed.

After introducing the basic steps in the acquisition process, we examine types of decisions that are particularly important, including supplier selection and relations, contracting, centralized buying, and local buying. As purchasing managers can have valuable input into value analysis (which, technically, isn't just a purchasing responsibility), we conclude this section with a brief discussion of that topic.

The Acquisition Process.   The usual steps in the acquisition process are the following:

1. *Recognize a need.*   The process begins when purchasing receives a request to buy outside materials or services. The request (called a *purchase requisition*) includes the item description, quantity and quality desired, and desired delivery date. At a manufacturing firm the purchasing department normally receives authority to buy from the production control department. Production control, in turn, is guided by the make-or-buy decisions that have been made in setting the process design (see Chapter 3). The purchasing department typically makes important inputs into these make-or-buy decisions because it is most

aware of supplier capabilities and performance. At a retailing firm, deciding what to buy is the same as deciding what merchandise to sell; marketing and purchasing decisions are intermingled.

2. *Select suppliers.* This step involves identifying suppliers capable of providing the items, grouping items that can be supplied by the same supplier, asking for bids on the needed items, evaluating the bids in terms of multiple criteria, and selecting a supplier. When a long-term contract has already been set up for an item, this step isn't necessary.

3. *Place the order.* The ordering procedure can be complex and time-consuming, as with expensive one-time purchases, or as simple as a phone call for a standard item routinely ordered from the same supplier. In some high-usage situations the supplier makes shipments daily or even shift by shift without being prompted by purchase orders. Some firms are linked by computer to suppliers, simplifying the ordering process even more.

4. *Track the order.* Tracking includes routine follow-up of orders so as to anticipate late deliveries or probable deviations from requested order quantities. Suppliers are contacted by letter, telex, fax, or telephone. Follow-up is particularly important for large purchases, when a delay is disruptive to production plans, or when a delay could mean loss of customer goodwill and future sales.

5. *Receive the order.* Incoming shipments usually must be checked for quantity and quality, with notices going to purchasing, the unit placing the purchase requisition, inventory control, and accounting. If the shipment isn't satisfactory, purchasing must decide whether to return it to the supplier. Records on punctuality, quality, quantity deviations, and price must be updated as part of supplier evaluation. Purchasing must coordinate closely with accounting so that suppliers are paid accurately and on time.

New technologies are making the acquisition process easier. **Electronic data interchange (EDI)** is the computer-to-computer exchange, over telephone lines or direct leased lines, between two or more companies of routine business documents having a standard format. The linkages soon may be by direct radio also. Special communications software translates documents into and out of a generic form, allowing organizations to exchange information even if they have different hardware and software components. Invoices, purchase orders, and payments are some of the routine documents that EDI can handle—it replaces the phone call or mailed document. For example, Chaparral Steel allows customers to have computer access to its sales database, to check inventory, and to place orders. EDI saves the cost of opening mail, directing it to the right department, checking the document for accuracy, and reentering the information into a computer system. It also improves accuracy, shortens response times, and can even cut inventory. Savings (ranging from $2 to $25 per document) are considerable in light of the hundreds to thousands of documents a firm typically handles daily.

Supplier Selection. Purchasing is the eyes and ears of the organization in the supplier marketplace, continuously seeking better buys and new materials from suppliers. To make the supplier selection decision and to review the performance of current suppliers, purchasing agents for some companies establish formal rating procedures. Competitive priorities (see Chapter 2) are a starting point in developing the list of performance criteria to be used. A recent study of food-service firms, for example, found on-time delivery and quality to be the top two criteria.

How should suppliers be selected, evaluated, and supported?

Three criteria almost always considered are price, quality, and delivery. Because a typical firm spends more than 60 percent of its total income from sales on purchased items, finding suppliers who charge low *prices* is one key to healthy profit margins. The *quality* of a supplier's materials also is important. The hidden costs of poor quality can be high, particularly if defects aren't detected until after considerable value has been added by subsequent manufacturing operations. For a retailer, poor quality can mean loss of customer goodwill and future sales.

Finally, shorter lead times and on-time *delivery* help the buying firm maintain acceptable customer service with less inventory. For example, Maimonides Medical Center, a 700-bed hospital in Brooklyn, buys many of its materials from one supplier. The supplier offers very short lead times from a nearby warehouse, which allowed Maimonides to pare its inventory from about $1200 to only $150 per bed. The benefits of fast, on-time deliveries also apply to the manufacturing sector. Many manufacturing firms seek just-in-time (JIT) delivery from their suppliers to minimize inventory levels. (JIT systems are intended to minimize inventory buildups by coordinating the flow of materials between production processes; see Chapter 15.) This constraint means that suppliers must have nearby plants or warehouses. Kasle Steel Corporation built a steel-processing plant adjacent to GM's Buick facility in Flint, Michigan, even though it already had two plants only 70 miles away. This new plant is part of a complex (called "Buick City") in which all parts are supplied to the GM facility by nearby plants. These clustered suppliers ship small quantities frequently to minimize the assembly plant's inventory. There is a 20-minute window during which a quantity of a particular part must be delivered; otherwise, the production line may have to be shut down.

Maimonides Medical Center is a 700-bed facility providing emergency, acute care, and outpatient services in Brooklyn, New York. The hospital serves a multi-ethnic community including Chinese, Latinos, Russians, and Orthodox Jews. By buying many materials from one supplier, the hospital realizes fast delivery times, low costs, and community goodwill.

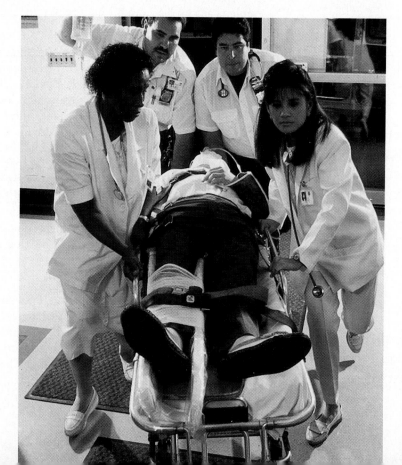

Supplier Relations. The type of relations maintained with suppliers can affect the quality, timeliness, and price of a firm's products and services. A firm can relate to a supplier either competitively or cooperatively, as described in Managerial Practice 11.1. The **competitive orientation,** which is particularly prevalent in North America, views negotiations between buyer and seller as a zero-sum game: Whatever one side loses, the other side gains. Short-term advantages are prized over long-term commitments. The buyer may try to beat the supplier's price down to the lowest survival level or to push demand to high levels during boom times and order almost nothing during recessions. In contrast, the supplier presses for higher prices for specific levels of quality, customer service, and volume flexibility. Which party wins depends largely on who has the most clout.

Which purchased materials and services give a firm its greatest purchasing clout? How can this clout be used effectively?

The *buyer* has more clout when	The *supplier* has more clout when
1. the buyer represents a significant share of the supplier's sales.	1. the buyer represents a small share of the supplier's sales.
2. the purchased item is standardized, with substitutes offered by other suppliers.	2. the purchased item is customized, and substitutes are not readily available.
3. the buyer could integrate backward into the supplier's business.	3. the buyer does not have enough volume to integrate backward.
4. the supplier could not integrate forward into the buyer's business.	4. the supplier has the volume and know-how to integrate forward.
5. switching to a new supplier is easy.	5. switching to a new supplier is costly.

Some large U.S. companies have used their clout to negotiate sizable travel discounts with the airlines. In 1990, they received special rates on 36 percent of their airline tickets, compared to 10 percent just the year before. The corporately negotiated discount fares are only about 25 percent of coach fare for the average trip. Leisure travelers and small businesses don't have the clout to negotiate such deals. Another example is managed care in the health industry. To reduce the high costs of employee health care, large companies set up networks of doctors and hospitals through an insurance carrier. Southwestern Bell held the increase in its health care costs to only 7 percent in 1989, which was less than half the national average increase, by using managed care.

The **cooperative orientation** to supplier relations is attracting more attention, particularly because of the success that certain Japanese firms have had with it. In this view, the buyer and seller are partners, each helping the other as much as possible. A cooperative orientation means long-term commitment, joint work on quality, and support by the buyer of the managerial, technological, and capacity development of the supplier. A cooperative orientation favors few suppliers of a particular item, with just one or two suppliers being the ideal number. With the increased order volumes, the supplier gains repeatability, which helps movement toward the product-focused strategy of high volume at a low cost. When contracts are large and a long-term relationship is assured, the supplier might even build a new facility and hire a new work force, perhaps relocating close to the buyer's plant. Reducing the number of suppliers also can help the buyer, as suppliers become almost an extension of the buyer.

A cooperative orientation means that the buyer shares more information with the supplier on its future buying intentions. This forward visibility allows suppliers to make better, more reliable forecasts of future demand. The buyer

Managerial Practice 11.1

▶ *Competitive Versus Cooperative Orientations*

Competitive Orientation

Phar-Mor was the largest and fastest growing deep-discount chain in the United States in 1991, when its sales surpassed $3 billion. You never know what you might find there. What Phar-Mor almost always has is low prices, from $0.99 movie rentals to greeting cards marked off 50 percent. Like the no-frills warehouse clubs that emerged in the 1980s, Phar-Mor appeals to penny-pinching consumers. The privately owned company, founded 12 years ago in Youngstown, Ohio, makes such bargains possible through bare-knuckle negotiating with its suppliers. "We're very aggressive in all our purchases," said David Shapira, the former chief executive officer. "We push people to where they squeak." Phar-Mor's lifeline is high volumes and clout, allowing it to drive down costs by buying in bulk and clearing out discontinued products.

The competitive orientation seemed to work well for Phar-Mor, but the company stumbled just one year later on an ethics issue related to inventory. Certain key executives had perpetrated a massive fraud, by overstating inventories to inflate the company's net worth (and therefore their compensation). After discovery of the fraud the company filed for Chapter 11 reorganization. A new CEO is helping make the firm profitable again.

Cooperative Orientation

Bumper Works, a 100-employee firm in Danville, Illinois, recently became the sole supplier of bumpers to U.S. facilities in which Toyota attaches rear bumpers and other accessories to trucks made in Japan. Toyota has helped its supplier make the bumpers better, cheaper, and faster. It flew a task force from Bumper Works to Japan for a round of meetings and tours to gain a better understanding of the Toyota manufacturing system. A Japanese manufacturing expert came to Danville and helped cut the time needed to change metal-stamping press dies from more than 90 minutes to 22 minutes. Later Toyota dispatched two more consultants from Japan who helped improve the plant's layout, train employees in new jobs, monitor production rates, label bins of parts for easier identification, improve quality, and cut inventory. Slowly, the approach is paying off. Productivity rose 60 percent and the number of defects fell by 80 percent from 1990 to 1991. Reducing wasted metal saved Bumper Works $0.55 per bumper. Toyota plans to start such cooperative efforts with its other suppliers.

Sources: "Brash Phar-Mor Chain Has Uneven Selection, But It's Always Cheap," *Wall Street Journal,* June 24, 1991; "These White Shoes Are Splattered with Mud," *Business Week,* September 7, 1992; "Japanese Auto Makers Help U.S. Suppliers Become More Efficient," *Wall Street Journal,* September 9, 1991.

visits suppliers' plants and cultivates cooperative attitudes. The buyer may even suggest ways to improve the suppliers' operations. This close cooperation with suppliers could even mean that the buyer doesn't need to inspect incoming materials. It also could mean more latitude with the specifications on purchase orders, involving the supplier more in designing parts, implementing cost-reduction ideas, and sharing in savings.

A 1994 survey of department stores showed that over half either had trimmed the number of their suppliers or planned to do so. Most apparel makers now vie for positions on a department store's most-favored-supplier list, making them the informal partners of their department store customers, as stores centralize and streamline their buying operations.

Reducing the number of suppliers may have the disadvantage of increased risk of an interruption in supply. Another disadvantage is that the supplier who is the sole source of a supply may have less motivation to continue improving its performance.

Thus neither orientation is always best. What works for one organization might not work for another. The Air Force recently used a competitive orientation by dividing a huge jet-engine contract between General Electric and the former exclusive contract holder, Pratt & Whitney, in order to cut costs. Other companies utilize a mixed strategy. A company can pursue a competitive strategy by seeking price reductions from its suppliers but also incorporate a cooperative element by paring the number of major suppliers and negotiating long-term contracts with them. This benefit can give suppliers enough volume to invest in cost-saving equipment and new capacity.

Contracting.   Purchasing must decide how to contract for each of the thousands of items that most firms buy. The procedure selected depends a great deal on volume and usage rates. When demand is low, as with customized items not held in inventory, a buyer has three options: competitive bidding, single-source contracting, and supplier catalogues.

Competitive bidding means that several suppliers are asked to submit formal quotations. The lowest *and* best (most capable) bidder receives the contract. In the private sector, competitive bidding isn't mandatory but is prudent for large expenditures, such as heavy equipment or a computer system. If the dollar value of the purchase is low or time is of the essence, single-source contracting or supplier catalogues may be best. With single-source contracting, a company negotiates a contract with a single supplier. This approach reduces purchasing lead time but doesn't guarantee the best buy, particularly if the buyer is unaware of comparative prices. Using supplier catalogues, the buyer simply looks through several and makes a selection. This method is best when the cost of any further search outweighs the benefits.

Contracting procedures can be quite different for standardized items for which demand is continuous. For such items, purchasing may preselect suppliers, rather than using competitive bidding. When requisitions are received from elsewhere in the organization, purchasing immediately sends to the preselected supplier a purchase order specifying the product, quantity, and delivery due date. This approach avoids delays caused by supplier selection procedures.

If demands are high enough, purchasing may preselect a supplier and negotiate contracts covering one or more years, with delivery dates, quantities, and even prices left open. Most long-term contracts are either *blanket* or *open-ended* contracts. A blanket contract covers a variety of items, whereas an open-ended contract allows items to be added or the contract period extended. Long-term contracts save paperwork and reserve supplier capacity. Suppliers prefer long-term contracts because they make future demand more certain, and suppliers are therefore able to grant buyers price concessions. Long-term contracts are consistent with the cooperative orientation to supplier relations.

Centralized Buying.   When an organization has several facilities (such as stores, hospitals, or plants), management must decide whether to buy locally or to buy centrally.

Centralized buying has the advantage of increasing purchasing clout. Savings can be significant, often on the order of 10 percent or more. Increased buying power can mean getting better service, ensuring long-term supply availability, or

Should long-term contracts be used? Should buying be centralized?

developing new supplier capability. The trend toward production and purchasing of parts from around the world favors centralization because of the specialized skills (e.g., understanding of foreign languages and cultures) needed to buy from foreign sources. Buyers also need to understand international commercial and contract law regarding the transfer of goods and services. Another trend that favors centralization is the growth of computer-based information systems, which give specialists at headquarters access to data previously available only at the local level.

Local Buying.   Probably the biggest disadvantage of centralized buying is loss of control at the local level. When plants or divisions are evaluated as profit or cost centers, centralized buying is undesirable for items unique to a particular facility. These items should be purchased locally whenever possible. The same holds for purchases that must be closely meshed with production schedules, as with just-in-time systems. Centralized purchasing often means longer lead times, involving another level in the firm's hierarchy. Perhaps the best solution is a compromise strategy, whereby both local autonomy and centralized buying are possible. For example, the corporate purchasing group at IBM negotiates contracts on a centralized basis only at the request of local plants. Then management at one of the facilities monitors the contract for all the participating plants.

Value Analysis.   A systematic effort to reduce the cost or improve the performance of items either purchased or produced is referred to as **value analysis.** It involves asking questions such as the following: What is the function of the item? Is the function necessary? Can a lower cost standard part that serves the purpose be identified? Can the item be simplified, or its specifications relaxed, to achieve a lower price? Value analysis should be performed periodically on large-dollar-volume items, for which potential savings are the greatest. It usually is done by a team, involving purchasing, production, and engineering. Each type of specialist brings a different perspective to the analysis.

Distribution

While purchasing deals with inbound materials, distribution deals with outbound flows. **Distribution** is the management of the flow of materials from manufacturers to customers and from warehouses to retailers, involving the storage and transportation of products. Distribution broadens the marketplace for a firm, adding time and place value to its products. Here we briefly consider three issues that distribution managers face: where to stock finished goods; what transportation mode to use; and scheduling, routing, and carrier selection.

Placement of Finished Goods Inventory.   A fundamental choice is where to stock inventory of finished goods. **Forward placement** means locating stock closer to customers at a warehouse (now usually called a *distribution center,* or DC) or with a wholesaler or retailer. Forward placement can have two advantages—fast delivery times and reduced transportation costs—which can stimulate sales.

Should distribution centers be added to position inventory closer to customers?

Finding the best way to position inventory is particularly important for international operations, as Managerial Practice 11.2 shows. Firms from around the world are trying to open DCs in strategic cities to support their sales activities in the European Community (EC) and the recently opened East European markets.

Managerial Practice 11.2

▶ *International Distribution Systems*

IKEA is a Scandinavian retailer that claims to be the world's largest-volume furniture chain, selling $3.8 billion per year of ready-to-assemble furniture and housewares in 100 stores worldwide. Its sales per square foot are about $350—three times the average for traditional furniture stores. But the company hasn't exactly taken America by storm. In the seven years after IKEA—pronounced "eye-key-ah"—opened its first mammoth U.S. store, near Philadelphia, it did so in just six other cities: Elizabeth, New Jersey; Burbank, California; Hicksville, New York; Washington; Baltimore; and Pittsburgh. But its U.S. sales increased by 68 percent in 1991, from $169 million to $284 million. The slow pace has nothing to do with its concept, merchandise, or innovative store layouts, which are praised even by rivals. "Our problem," says Anders Moberg, president of the Humlebaek (Denmark)–based retailer, "is with distribution—finding warehouses and setting up a network."

IKEA has tackled the issue by building huge distribution centers in Philadelphia and Montreal to serve eastern stores and, more recently, near Los Angeles to prepare for West Coast expansion. It opened two new stores in Los Angeles in 1992 and acquired three new store locations through merger. IKEA expects to add two or three stores a year. "Forty percent of our investment in the next three to five years will be in the U.S.," says Moberg.

Sources: "Why Competitors Shop for Ideas at IKEA," *Business Week,* October 9, 1989; "From Value Chain to Value Constellation: Designing Interactive Strategy," *Harvard Business Review* (July–August, 1993).

Forward placement might also reduce shipping costs. Shipments from a plant can be concentrated on a few routes (to the DCs), rather than fragmented for scattered customer locations. Outbound shipments from DCs to customer destinations may be large enough to justify discount rates. For example, General Foods mixes products received from various plants at its distribution centers and reships them to customers at reduced rates.

If competitive priorities call for customized products, storing an inventory of finished goods risks creating unwanted products. **Backward placement** means holding the inventory at the manufacturing plant or maintaining no inventory. Backward placement is advantageous when the demand in regions may be unpredictably high one month and low the next. In this case, backward placement pools demand so that the highs in some regions cancel the lows in others. Demand on a centralized inventory is less erratic and more predictable than demand on regional inventories. Inventories for the whole system can be lower, and costly reshipments from one DC to another can be minimized.

Ethan Allen provides a good example of the benefits of backward placement, often called the **pooling effect.** Originally, each of the 40 retailers of Ethan Allen products in the New York metropolitan area maintained its own inventory. The aggregate inventory value averaged $3 million, and customer service was poor. The probability that all items in a customer's order were on hand was only 0.25. Ethan Allen solved this dilemma by creating one large field warehouse to serve all 40 retailers. The retailers no longer need to carry separate inventories, except for display purposes. Inventory dropped to $700,000, and the probability of filling a customer's order from DC inventory increased to 0.80.

Selection of Transportation Mode.   The five basic modes of transportation are highway, rail, water, pipeline, and air. Each has its own advantages and limitations.

Highway transportation provides the flexibility of shipping to almost any location in the United States. No rehandling is needed, as is often the case with other modes that rely on trucks for pickup and delivery. Transit times are good, and rates are usually less than rail rates for small quantities and short hauls. Truckers haul 40 percent of U.S. freight, whereas railroads move 30 percent (down from 50 percent in 1947). Rail transportation can move large quantities very cheaply, but transit times are long and variable. This mode is usually best for shipping raw materials, rather than finished goods. Rail shipments often require pickup and delivery rehandling. Water transportation provides high capacity at low unit cost, but transit times are slow and large areas are inaccessible to waterborne carriers. Pipeline transportation is highly specialized, with limited geographical flexibility. It is limited to liquids, gases, or solids in slurry form. No packaging is needed, and operating costs per mile are low. Although most pipelines move petroleum, some companies use them to transport fish and coal. Air transportation is the fastest and most expensive mode. It represents only 1 percent of all freight moved, although that proportion is rising rapidly. Air transportation is limited by the availability of airport facilities and requires pickup and delivery rehandling.

In addition to these primary modes, special service modes and hybrids, such as parcel post, air express, bus service, freight forwarder, and piggyback, are available. Piggyback means that pickup and delivery are by truck but the truck's trailer is loaded on a rail car for the rest of the trip. Different forms of ownership and management are possible. A firm can integrate forward and become a *private carrier,* owning and operating its own fleet. It can instead leave the trans-

Roadnet software is used to control scheduling of delivery vehicles, to select the most efficient routes, and to choose the appropriate vehicle for the job.

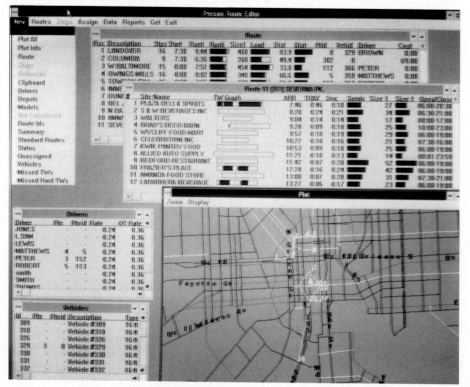

portation to a *contract carrier,* negotiating with the carrier for a specified amount, type, and frequency of shipment. A contract carrier doesn't provide service to the general public, instead serving specific customers. Or the firm can select a *common carrier,* which by law must serve all customers. This option gives the firm the least control over carrier availability but makes sense for low-volume producers with geographically dispersed markets.

Scheduling, Routing, and Carrier Selection.   Several activities are involved in the day-to-day control of freight movement. The shipping schedule must mesh with purchasing and production control schedules. It also reflects the trade-off between transportation costs and customer response times. Delaying a shipment for another two days so as to combine it with others may make possible a full carload rate for a rail shipment or a full truckload rate for a truck shipment. Routing choices also must be made. A manufacturer can gain a lower freight rate by selecting a routing that combines shipments to multiple customers. The firm may even negotiate lower overall rates if it develops routings by which large volumes can be shipped regularly. The choices are complex. Even before deregulation, the U.S. freight rate structure seemed chaotic to the uninitiated. Now rates and services vary markedly, depending on the specific mode and carrier chosen.

◆ INVENTORY CONCEPTS

An essential part of materials management is inventory control. **Inventory** is a stock of anything held to meet future demand. Inventory is created when the rate of receipts exceeds the rate of disbursements; it is depleted when disbursements exceed receipts. In this section we focus on basic terminology and fundamentals needed to understand inventory: accounting categories, the pressures for high and low inventories, and types of inventory.

Accounting Categories

Inventory for a manufacturing plant exists in three forms, or accounting categories: raw materials, work-in-process (WIP), and finished goods. Inventory can be held in various forms and locations, or stocking points. In the system shown in Fig. 11.3, raw materials are kept at two stocking points: the supplier's facility and the plant. Raw materials at the plant pass through one or more processes,

FIGURE 11.3

Inventory at Successive Stocking Points

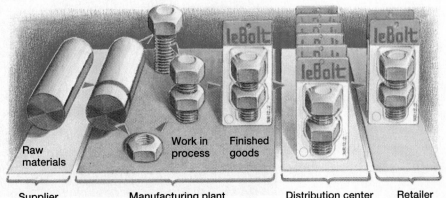

Raw materials

Work in process

Finished goods

Supplier   Manufacturing plant   Distribution center   Retailer

which transform them into various levels of WIP inventory. When this inventory is processed at the final operation, it becomes finished goods inventory. Finished goods can be held at the plant, a DC, and retail locations.

Materials flow systems can be more or less complex, depending on the size of the firm. A small retailer that must manage only in-store inventories can use a relatively simple system. A large retailer, such as Kroger, often integrates backward to include distribution centers and even manufacturing plants, creating a need for a more complex system. A process-focused manufacturer usually ships directly to the customer and thus can use a simple system with no intervening DCs or retail stocking points. A product-focused manufacturer may integrate backward to the point where it has its own feeder plants, which in turn supply its assembly plants. A multiplant operation is particularly challenging because inventories must be coordinated at more stocking points.

Pressures for Low Inventories

An inventory manager's job is to balance the conflicting costs and pressures that argue for both low and high inventories and determine appropriate inventory levels. The primary reason for keeping inventories low is that inventory represents a temporary monetary investment in goods on which a firm must pay (rather than receive) interest. **Inventory holding** (or carrying) **cost** is the cost of keeping items on hand, including interest, storage and handling, taxes, insurance, and shrinkage. When these cost components change with inventory levels, they are part of the holding cost. Companies usually state an item's holding cost per period of time as a percentage of its value. The annual cost to maintain one unit in inventory typically ranges from 20 to 40 percent of its value. Suppose that a firm's holding costs are 30 percent. If the average value of total inventory is 20 percent of sales, the cost to hold inventory is 6 percent [0.30(0.20)] of total sales. This cost is sizable in terms of gross profit margins, which often are less than 10 percent.

Let's examine the components of holding cost in order to understand the pressures for low inventories.

At the Union Camp paper mill in Virginia, finished goods are loaded onto rail cars for delivery to customers' plants, where the goods become their raw materials.

Interest or Opportunity Cost.   To finance inventory, a company may obtain a loan or forgo the opportunity of an investment promising an attractive return. Interest or opportunity cost, whichever is greater, usually is the largest component of holding cost, often as high as 15 percent.

Storage and Handling Costs.   Inventory takes up space and must be moved into and out of storage. Storage and handling costs may be incurred when a firm rents space on either a long-term or a short-term basis. There also is an opportunity cost for storage when a firm could use storage space productively in some other way.

Taxes, Insurance, and Shrinkage.   More taxes are paid if end-of-year inventories are high, and insurance on assets increases when there is more to insure. Shrinkage takes three forms. Pilferage, or theft of inventory by customers or employees, is a significant percentage of sales for some businesses. Obsolescence occurs when inventory cannot be used or sold at full value, owing to model changes, engineering modifications, or unexpectedly low demand. Deterioration through physical spoilage or damage results in lost value. Food and beverages, for example, lose value and might even have to be discarded when their shelf life is reached. When the rate of deterioration is high, building large inventories may be unwise.

Pressures for High Inventories

The fact that inventory held in the U.S. economy exceeds the $1.1 trillion mark suggests that there are pressures for large inventories, despite the expense. Let's look briefly at each type of pressure.

Customer Service.   Creating inventory can speed up delivery and improve on-time delivery. Inventory reduces the potential for stockouts and backorders, which are key concerns of wholesalers and retailers. A **stockout** occurs when a standard item is not on hand to satisfy demand for the item the moment it occurs, resulting in loss of the sale. A **backorder** is a customer order that cannot be filled when promised or demanded but is filled later. Customers may be willing to wait this time but later may take their business elsewhere. Inventory also increases the percentage of on-time deliveries, a key concern of manufacturers in ensuring customer satisfaction.

Ordering Cost.   Each time a firm places a new order, it incurs **ordering cost,** the cost of preparing a purchase order for a supplier or a production order for the shop. For the same item, the cost is the same, regardless of the order size: The purchasing agent must take the time to decide how much to order, select a supplier, and negotiate terms. Time also is spent on paperwork, follow-up, and receiving. In the case of a production order for a manufactured item, a blueprint and routing instructions often must accompany the shop order.

Setup Cost.   The cost involved in changing over a machine to produce a different component or item is the **setup cost.** It includes labor and time to make the changeover, cleaning, and new tools or fixtures. Scrap or rework costs can be substantially higher at the start of the run. Setup cost also is independent of order size, so there is pressure to order a large supply of the component and hold it in inventory.

Labor and Equipment Utilization.   By creating more inventory, management can increase work-force productivity and facility utilization in three ways. First, placing larger, less frequent production orders reduces unproductive setup time, which doesn't add value to a product or service. Second, holding inventory reduces the chance of costly rescheduling of production orders because the components needed to make the product aren't in inventory. Third, building inventories improves resource utilization by stabilizing the output rate for industries when demand is cyclical or seasonal. The firm uses inventory built during slack periods to handle extra demand in peak seasons and minimizes the need for extra shifts, hiring, layoffs, and overtime. Equipment capacities also may be less because capacity doesn't need to match peak demand.

Transportation Cost.   Sometimes, outbound transportation cost can be reduced by increasing inventory levels. Having inventory on hand allows more time to help ensure carload shipments and minimizes the need for expedited shipments by more expensive modes of transportation. As we have already noted, forward placement of inventory can reduce outbound transportation cost, even though the pooling effect is lessened and more inventory is necessary. Inbound transportation cost also may be reduced by creating more inventory. Sometimes, several items are ordered from the same supplier. Combining these orders and placing them at the same time may lead to rate discounts, thereby decreasing the costs of transportation and raw materials.

Quantity Discounts.   A firm often can reduce total payments to suppliers if it can tolerate higher inventory levels. Suppose that a firm learns that a key supplier is about to increase prices. It might be cheaper for the firm to order a larger quantity than usual—in effect delaying the price increase—even though inventory will increase temporarily. Similarly, a firm can take advantage of quantity discounts. A **quantity discount**, whereby the price per unit drops when the order is sufficiently large, is an incentive to order larger quantities.

Types of Inventory

Another perspective on inventory is to classify it by how it is created. In this context, there are four types of inventory for an item: cycle, safety, anticipation, and pipeline. These four types cannot be identified physically; that is, someone cannot divide up a pile of widgets and identify which ones are cycle inventory and which ones are pipeline inventory. However, conceptually, each of the four types comes into being in a different way. The way in which cycle inventory is created differs entirely from how safety stock is created. Once you understand these differences, you can prescribe different ways to reduce inventory, which we discuss in the next section.

Cycle Inventory.   Cycle inventory is increased by ordering in larger quantities so as to reduce the number of orders that must be placed each year and thus reduce costs. Determining how frequently to order, and in what quantity, is called **lot sizing.** Two principles apply.

1. The lot size, Q, varies directly with the elapsed time (or cycle) between orders. If a lot is ordered every five weeks, the average lot size must equal five weeks' demand. Large lot cycles go with infrequent orders.
2. The longer the time between orders, the greater the cycle inventory must be. **Cycle inventory** is the portion of total inventory that varies directly with lot size.

At the beginning of the interval, the cycle inventory is at its maximum, or Q. At the end of the interval, just before a new lot arrives, cycle inventory drops to its minimum, or 0. The average cycle inventory is the average of these two extremes:

$$\text{Average cycle inventory} = \frac{Q + 0}{2} = \frac{Q}{2}$$

This formula is exact only when the demand rate is constant and uniform. The formula provides a reasonably good estimate even when demand rates aren't constant. Factors other than the demand rate (e.g., scrap losses) also may cause estimating errors when this simple formula is used.

EXAMPLE 11.2

Calculating Cycle Inventory

The lot size of an item is 100 units, and the ordering cycle averages 2 months. What are the item's annual demand and cycle inventory?

Solution The first principle of cycle inventory tells us that 100 units is a 2-month supply, so a 12-month supply must be 6 times as large, or 600 units. The second principle and formula tell us that the average cycle inventory is 50, or 100/2.

Safety Stock Inventory. To avoid customer service problems and the hidden costs of unavailable components, companies hold safety stock. **Safety stock inventory** protects against uncertainties in demand, lead time, and supply. An unreliable supplier that deviates frequently from the requested lot size or promised delivery time makes maintaining safety stock desirable. Moreover, if a manufactured item is subject to significant amounts of scrap or rework, safety stock is needed. Having the item available when problems occur allows subsequent operations to continue.

To create safety stock, a firm places an order for delivery earlier than when the item is typically needed.[*] The replenishment order therefore arrives ahead of time, giving a cushion against uncertainty. For example, suppose that the average lead time from a supplier is 3 weeks but a firm orders 5 weeks in advance just to be safe. This policy creates a safety stock equal to 2 weeks of supply $(5 - 3)$. We discuss creating safety stock further in Chapter 12.

Anticipation Inventory. Inventory used to absorb uneven rates of demand or supply, which business often faces, is referred to as **anticipation inventory.** Manufacturers of air conditioners, for example, can experience 90 percent of their annual demand during just three months of a year. Such uneven demand may lead a

---

[*]When orders are placed at fixed intervals, there is a second way. For each new order placed, make its size greater than what is typically needed through the next delivery date.

manufacturer to stockpile anticipation inventory during periods of low demand so that output levels don't have to be increased much when demand peaks. Smoothing output rates with inventory can increase productivity because varying output rates and work-force size can be costly. Anticipation inventory also can help when supply, rather than demand, is uneven. A company may stock up on a certain purchased item if its suppliers are threatened with a strike or have severe capacity limitations.

Pipeline Inventory.   Inventory moving from point to point in the materials flow system is called **pipeline inventory**. Materials move from suppliers to a plant, from one operation to the next in the plant, from the plant to a DC or customer, and from the DC to a retailer. Pipeline inventory consists of orders that have been placed but not yet received.

Pipeline inventory between two points, for either transportation or production, can be measured as the average demand during lead time, $\overline{D}_L$, which is the average demand for the item per period (d) times the number of periods in the item's lead time (L) to move between the two points, or

$$\text{Pipeline inventory} = \overline{D}_L = dL$$

Note that the lot size doesn't directly affect the average level of the pipeline inventory. Increasing Q inflates the size of each order, so if an order has been placed but not received, there is more pipeline inventory for that lead time. But that increase is canceled by a proportionate decrease in the number of orders placed per year. The lot size can *indirectly* affect pipeline inventory, however, if increasing Q causes the lead time to increase. Here $\overline{D}_L$, and therefore pipeline inventory, will increase.

EXAMPLE 11.3

Estimating Inventory Levels

A plant makes monthly shipments to a wholesaler of a particular item in average lot sizes of 280 units. The wholesaler's average demand is 70 units per week, and the lead time from the plant is 3 weeks. On average, how much cycle inventory and pipeline inventory does the wholesaler carry?

Solution

$$\text{Cycle inventory} = \frac{Q}{2} = \frac{280}{2} = 140 \text{ units}$$

$$\text{Pipeline inventory} = \overline{D}_L = dL = (70 \text{ units/week})(3 \text{ weeks}) = 210 \text{ units}$$

The wholesaler's cycle inventory is 140 units, whereas the pipeline inventory (inventory in transit) is 210 units.

◆   INVENTORY MANAGEMENT

We conclude by mentioning the types of issues that managers must address to control inventories: inventory measures, inventory placement, inventory reduction, ABC analysis, and links to operations strategy. Such issues are relevant to the next five chapters, each of which deals with some phase of inventory management, either directly or indirectly.

Inventory Measures

How should inventory levels be measured and evaluated?

As we have shown, managers have valid reasons to hold inventory, but costs are associated with doing so. For this reason, managers closely monitor measures of inventory to keep them at acceptable levels. All methods of measuring inventory begin with a physical count of units, volume, or weight. However, inventories are measured in three basic ways: average aggregate inventory value, weeks of supply, and inventory turnover.

One unit of item A may be worth only pennies, whereas one unit of item B may be valued in the thousands of dollars. The **average aggregate inventory value** is the total value of all items held in inventory. It is an average because it usually represents the inventory investment over some period of time. This measure for an inventory consisting of only items A and B is

$$\begin{aligned}
\text{Average aggregate} \atop \text{inventory value} &= \left(\begin{array}{c}\text{Number of units of item A}\\\text{typically on hand}\end{array}\right)\left(\begin{array}{c}\text{Value of each}\\\text{unit of item A}\end{array}\right)\\
&+ \left(\begin{array}{c}\text{Number of units of item B}\\\text{typically on hand}\end{array}\right)\left(\begin{array}{c}\text{Value of each}\\\text{unit of item B}\end{array}\right)
\end{aligned}$$

Summed over all items in an inventory, this total value tells managers how much of a firm's assets are tied up in inventory. Manufacturing firms typically have about 25 percent of their total assets in inventory, whereas wholesalers and retailers average about 75 percent.

To some extent, managers can decide whether the aggregate inventory value is too low or too high by historical or industry comparison or by managerial judgment. However, they must also take demand into account by using the measures weeks of supply and inventory turnover. **Weeks of supply** is an inventory measure obtained by dividing the average aggregate inventory value by the sales per week at cost. (In some low-inventory operations, days or even hours are a better unit of time for measuring inventory.) The automobile industry, for example, carries about two months' supply of finished goods. The amount varies from company to company, with Ford having the lowest target level among the Big Three and General Motors the highest. The formula (expressed in weeks) is

$$\text{Weeks of supply} = \frac{\text{Average aggregate inventory value}}{\text{Weekly sales (at cost)}}$$

Although the numerator includes the value of all items (raw materials, WIP, and finished goods), the denominator represents only the finished goods sold—and at the cost to make them rather than the sale price after markups. This cost is referred to as the *cost of goods sold*. One reason for expressing value at cost is that inventory measures can be expressed for individual items and final sales dollars have meaning only for final products—not manufactured components or purchased items.

Inventory turnover (or *turns*) is an inventory measure obtained by dividing annual sales at cost by the average aggregate inventory value maintained during the year:

$$\text{Inventory turnover} = \frac{\text{Annual sales (at cost)}}{\text{Average aggregate inventory value}}$$

The "best" inventory level, even when expressed as turnover, cannot be determined easily. Although 6 or 7 turns per year is typical, the average high-tech firm settles for only about 3 turns. At the other extreme, some Japanese automobile firms report 40 turns per year.

EXAMPLE 11.4
Calculating Inventory Measures

A company averaged $2 million in inventory last year, and the cost of goods sold was $10 million. If the company has 52 business weeks per year, how many weeks of supply were held in inventory? What was the inventory turnover?

Solution   The average aggregate inventory value of $2 million translates into 10.4 weeks of supply and 5 turns per year, calculated as follows:

$$\text{Weeks of supply} = \frac{\$2 \text{ million}}{(\$10 \text{ million})/(52 \text{ weeks})} = 10.4 \text{ weeks}$$

$$\text{Inventory turnover} = \frac{\$10 \text{ million}}{\$2 \text{ million}} = 5 \text{ turns/year}$$

Inventory Placement

Should most inventory be held at the raw material, WIP, or finished goods level? Which items should be standards?

Just as distribution managers decide where to place finished goods inventory, manufacturing managers make similar decisions for raw materials and WIP within the plant. In general, managers make inventory placement decisions by designating an item as either a special or a standard. A **special** is an item made to order. If it is purchased, it is bought to order. Just enough are ordered to cover the latest customer request. A **standard** is an item that is made to stock and normally is available when needed. When a company makes more of its items as standards, particularly at the finished goods level, it places inventory closer to the customer.

Inventory held toward the finished goods level means short delivery times—but a higher dollar investment in inventory. Inventory placement at Shamrock Chemicals, a Newark, New Jersey, manufacturer of materials used in printing inks, illustrates this trade-off. Shamrock enjoys sales of more than $15 million because it can ship any of its products the same day a customer orders it. But because finished goods are treated as standards rather than specials, Shamrock is forced to maintain a large inventory. Holding inventory at the raw materials level would reduce the cost of carrying inventory—but at the expense of the quick customer response times that give Shamrock its competitive advantage. R. R. Donnelley, a large manufacturer of books, chooses an opposite strategy by positioning inventory back at the raw materials level (e.g., in rolled paper stock and ink).

Inventory Reduction

What are the options for reducing inventory wisely?

Managers always are eager to find cost-effective ways to reduce inventory. In Chapter 12 we examine various ways for finding optimal lot sizes. Here we discuss something more fundamental—the basic tactics (which we call *levers*) for reducing inventory. A primary lever is one that must be activated if inventory is to be reduced. A secondary lever reduces the penalty cost of applying the primary lever and the need for having inventory in the first place.

Cycle Inventory.   The primary lever is simply to reduce the lot size. Methods of just-in-time production (see Chapter 15) use extremely small lots, compared to traditional lot sizes equaling several weeks' (or even months') supply. However, making such reductions in Q without making any other changes can be devastating. For example, setup costs can skyrocket, which leads to use of the two secondary levers.

1. Streamline methods for placing orders and making setups, which reduces ordering and setup costs and allows Q to be reduced.
2. Increase repeatability to eliminate the need for changeovers. **Repeatability** is the degree to which the same work can be done over again. It can be increased through high product demand; use of specialization; devoting resources exclusively to a product; using the same part in many different products; flexible automation; the one worker, multiple machines concept; or group technology. (See Chapters 3 and 9.) Increased repeatability may justify new setup methods, reduce transportation costs, and allow quantity discounts from suppliers.

Safety Stock Inventory.   The primary lever for reducing safety stock inventory is to place orders closer to the time when they must be received. However, this approach can lead to unacceptable customer service—unless demand, supply, and delivery uncertainties can be minimized. Four secondary levers can be used.

1. Improve demand forecasts so that there are fewer surprises from customers. Perhaps customers can even be encouraged to order items before they need them.
2. Cut lead times of purchased or produced items to reduce demand uncertainty during lead time. For example, local suppliers with short lead times could be selected whenever possible.
3. Reduce supply uncertainties. Suppliers may be more reliable if production plans are shared with them, permitting them to make more realistic forecasts. Surprises from unexpected scrap or rework can be reduced by improving manufacturing processes. Preventive maintenance can minimize unexpected downtime caused by equipment failure.
4. Rely more on equipment and labor buffers, such as capacity cushions and cross-trained workers. These are the only buffers available to businesses in the service sector because they cannot inventory their services.

Anticipation Inventory.   The primary lever to reduce anticipation inventory is simply to match demand rate with production rate. Secondary levers are to level out customer demand in one of the following ways.

1. Add new products with different demand cycles so that a peak in the demand for one product compensates for the seasonal low for another.
2. Provide off-season promotional campaigns.
3. Offer seasonal pricing plans.

Pipeline Inventory.   An operations manager has direct control over lead time but not demand rate. Because pipeline inventory is a function of demand during lead time, the primary lever is to reduce the lead time. Two secondary levers can help managers cut the lead times.

1. Find more responsive suppliers and select new carriers for shipments between stocking locations, or improve materials handling within the

plant. Introducing a computer system could overcome information delays between a DC and retailer.
2. Decrease Q, at least in those cases where lead time depends on lot size.
Smaller jobs generally require less time to complete.

ABC Analysis

Thousands of items are held in inventory by a typical organization, but only a
small percentage of them deserve management's closest attention and tightest
control. **ABC analysis** is the process of dividing items into three classes according
to their dollar usage so that managers can focus on items that have the highest
dollar value. This method is the equivalent of creating a Pareto chart (see Chapter 4) except that it is applied to inventory rather than quality. As Fig. 11.4
shows, class A items typically represent only about 20 percent of the items but
account for 80 percent of the dollar usage. Class B items account for another 30
percent of the items but only 15 percent of the dollar usage. Finally, 50 percent of
the items fall in class C, representing a mere 5 percent of the dollar usage.

F I G U R E   11.4

*Typical Chart from
ABC Analysis*

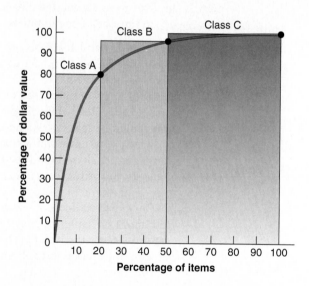

The goal of ABC analysis is to identify the inventory levels of class A items
and enable management to control them tightly by using the levers just discussed.
The analyst begins by multiplying the annual demand rate for one item by the
dollar value (cost) of one unit. After ranking the items on the basis of dollar
usage and creating the Pareto chart, the analyst looks for "natural" changes in
slope. The dividing lines in Fig. 11.4 between classes are inexact. Class A items
could be somewhat higher or lower than 20 percent of all items, but normally account for the bulk of the dollar usage.

A manager can direct that class A items be reviewed frequently to reduce the
average lot size and to keep their inventory records accurate. If the records show
an on-hand balance of 100 units but the actual balance is 200 units, costly inventory is being carried needlessly. If a class A item is bought outside the firm, purchasing may be able to reduce its cost through centralized buying, switching
suppliers, or more effective contract negotiation.

For class C items, much looser control is appropriate. A stockout of a class C item can be as crucial as for a class A item, but the inventory holding cost of class C items tends to be low. These features suggest that higher inventory levels can be tolerated and that more safety stock, larger lot sizes, and perhaps even a visual system, which we discuss in Chapter 12, may suffice for class C items.

Links to Operations Strategy

How can materials management be linked to other parts of operations strategy?

Managers must link their inventory and scheduling policies with operations strategy. Much depends on the positioning strategy chosen. Inventory choices for a process-focused firm, such as Lower Florida Keys Health System, should be quite different from those for a product-focused firm, such as Chaparral Steel. The general patterns are as follows.

Process Focus	Product Focus
1. More need for cushions	1. Less tolerance for cushions
2. More pressure for an integrated organizational structure	2. Less pressure for an integrated organizational structure
3. Shorter planning horizons	3. Longer planning horizons
4. Less formalized supplier and customer relationships	4. More formalized supplier and customer relationships
5. Information systems oriented to specific customer orders	5. Information systems oriented to forecasts and inventory records

Cushions.   One strategy for capacity planning (see Chapter 7) favors large capacity cushions that require extra equipment and result in lower utilization rates. Two other cushions are extra workers and high inventories. All firms use such cushions—but to varying degrees.

A firm with a product focus has less tolerance for cushions for three basic reasons. First, there is less need for a buffer because operations are less complex. For example, an operation with a product focus is characterized by high repeatability, standard products or services, low volume flexibility, and streamlined routings.

Second, there is less need to buffer against uncertainty. On the demand side, the higher volumes of a product focus make forecasting customer demand easier. Standard products or services mean fewer last-minute design changes from customers or engineers. On the supply side, higher volumes give a company more clout in finding reliable suppliers. The high volumes within the firm's own plant reduce the uncertainty in both lead times and production quantities caused by capacity bottlenecks, rework, and scrap. Short lead times mean small WIP inventories.

Third, a firm with a product focus is likely to emphasize low cost as a competitive priority. Minimal cushions are essential for high productivity and low costs. Large safety stock inventories and extra workers are a costly luxury.

Integrated Organizational Structure.   An integrated organizational structure—in which purchasing, production control, and distribution report to the same executive—requires a high degree of cross-functional coordination among these departments and with manufacturing and marketing.

Integration comes at a cost and should be pursued only when benefits exceed costs. Benefits are greatest in the uncertain environment of a process focus. Demand and supply uncertainties mean unexpected changes and updates, which in turn call for more coordination. Because a process-focused firm generally has a low finished goods inventory and few, if any, DCs to manage, making distribution part of an integrated structure doesn't add much complexity.

Firms with a product focus have a greater ability to create finished goods inventory, which can help decouple departments and create less need for close coordination. Distribution is more likely to be housed with marketing and separated from purchasing and production planning.

Planning Horizons.   Production plans and schedules project further into the future for a product focus for two reasons. First, forward scheduling is feasible. Increased demand and supply certainty means that schedules can be developed with greater assurance. A product-focused firm should experience few of the last-minute disruptions that are commonplace at process-focused firms. Second, a product focus creates a strong incentive to plan ahead. Maximizing facility and equipment utilization has top priority because the facility is so capital intensive. High utilization rates depend on forward scheduling.

Supplier and Customer Relationships.   Both supplier and customer relationships are more formal and extensive with a product focus. Firms negotiate annual supply contracts with key suppliers rather than use the full purchasing cycle for each new purchase. Contract terms tend to be more attractive than terms for individual purchases. With high volumes, a firm can exert more control over suppliers and expect better service. Distribution channels also are more formal because markets are more scattered, requiring a network of regional DCs. With a process focus and its customized products, positioning inventory at DCs close to the customer is impossible. Typically, shipments are made directly from the plant to the customer.

Information Systems.   Information requirements for a product focus are oriented to demand forecasts and current inventory levels. Items tend to be standards rather than the specials at process-focused firms, where information is oriented to the bidding process and specific customer orders and output plans are communicated by releasing jobs with detailed routing information.

CHAPTER REVIEW

Solved Problem 1

A distribution center (DC) experiences an average weekly demand of 50 units for one of its items. The product is valued at $650 per unit. Average inbound shipments from the factory warehouse average 350 units. Average lead time (including ordering delays and transit time) is 2 weeks. The DC operates 52 weeks per year; it carries a 1-week supply of inventory as safety stock and no anticipation inventory.

a. What is the average aggregate inventory value being held by the DC?
b. How many weeks of supply are held? What are annual sales? What is the inventory turnover?

c. What type of inventory (cycle, safety stock, or pipeline) is the best target for inventory reduction?

Solution a.

Type of Inventory	Calculation of Average Inventory Quantity	Calculation of Average Inventory Value
Cycle	$\dfrac{Q}{2} = \dfrac{350 \text{ units}}{2} = 175$ units	(175 units)($650/unit) = $113,750
Safety	1 week of supply = 50 units	(50 units)($650/unit) = $ 32,500
Anticipation	None	$ 0
Pipeline	dL = (50 units/week)(2 weeks) = 100 units	(100 units)($650/unit) = $ 65,000
	Average aggregate inventory = 325 units	Value = $211,250

b. Weeks of supply $= \dfrac{\text{Average aggregate inventory value}}{\text{Weekly sales (at cost)}} = \dfrac{\$211,250}{\$32,500/\text{week}} = 6.5$ weeks

Annual sales = (50 units/week)(52 weeks/year)($650/unit) = $1,690,000/year

Inventory turnover $= \dfrac{\text{Annual sales (at cost)}}{\text{Average aggregate inventory value}} = \dfrac{\$1,690,000}{\$211,250}$

$= 8$ turns/year

c. Cycle inventory, valued at $113,750, is the largest component of the average aggregate inventory value and thus is the best target for inventory reduction.

Solved Problem 2

Booker's Book Bindery divides inventory items into three classes according to their dollar usage. Calculate the usage values of the following inventory items and determine which is most likely to be classified as an A item.

Part Number	Description	Quantity Used per Year	Unit Value
1	Boxes	500	$3.00
2	Cardboard (square feet)	18,000	$0.02
3	Cover stock	10,000	$0.75
4	Glue (gallons)	75	$40.00
5	Inside covers	20,000	$0.05
6	Reinforcing tape (meters)	3,000	$0.15
7	Signatures	150,000	$0.45

Solution

Part Number	Description	Quantity Used per Year		Unit Value		Annual Dollar Usage
1	Boxes	500	×	$3.00	=	$ 1,500
2	Cardboard (square feet)	18,000	×	$0.02	=	$ 360
3	Cover stock	10,000	×	$0.75	=	$ 7,500
4	Glue (gallons)	75	×	$40.00	=	$ 3,000
5	Inside covers	20,000	×	$0.05	=	$ 1,000
6	Reinforcing tape (meters)	3,000	×	$0.15	=	$ 450
7	Signatures	150,000	×	$0.45	=	$67,500
					Total	$81,310

The annual dollar usage for each item is determined by multiplying the annual usage quantity by the value per unit. The items are sorted by annual dollar usage, in declining order. Finally, A–B and B–C class lines are drawn roughly according to the guidelines presented in the text. The A class in this problem includes only one item (signatures), which represents only 1/7, or 14 percent, of the items but accounts for 83 percent of annual dollar usage. The B class includes the next two items, which taken together represent 28 percent of the items and account for 13 percent of annual dollar usage. The final four items represent over half the number of items but only 4% of total annual dollar usage.

Part Number	Description	Annual Dollar Usage	Percentage of Total Dollar Usage	Cumulative Percent	Inventory Class
7	Signatures	$67,500	($67,500/$81,310)(100) = 83.0%	83.0%	A
3	Cover stock	$ 7,500	($7,500/$81,310)(100) = 9.2%	92.2%	B
4	Glue	$ 3,000	($3,000/$81,310)(100) = 3.7%	95.9%	B
1	Boxes	$ 1,500	($1,500/$81,310)(100) = 1.8%	97.7%	C
5	Inside covers	$ 1,000	($1,000/$81,310)(100) = 1.2%	98.9%	C
6	Reinforcing tape	$ 450	($450/$81,310)(100) = 0.6%	99.5%	C
2	Cardboard	$ 360	($360/$81,310)(100) = 0.4%	99.9%	C
	Total	$81,310			

Formula Review

1. Cycle inventory $= \dfrac{Q}{2}$

2. Pipeline inventory $= dL$

3. Weeks of supply $= \dfrac{\text{Average aggregate inventory value}}{\text{Weekly sales (at cost)}}$

4. Inventory turnover $= \dfrac{\text{Annual sales (at cost)}}{\text{Average aggregate inventory value}}$

Chapter Highlights

- Materials managers make decisions concerning the acquisition, storage, conversion, and distribution of goods and services. Purchased materials and services require more than 60 percent of the total income from sales for a typical manufacturer. Service organizations commonly need inventories of goods that are consumed in their operations. Inventory investment and materials management decisions play a central role in determining operating costs and profitability.
- Materials management decisions involve several departments that specialize in different aspects of the materials cycle. Many firms utilize integrated organizational structures, which bring purchasing, production control, and distribution under unified control.
- There are five steps in the acquisition cycle: receive a request to place an order, select a supplier, place the order, track the order, and receive the order. Electronic data interchange (EDI), the computer-to-computer communication of routine business documents, makes the acquisition process easier.

- Purchasing activities include selecting suppliers, developing supplier relations, negotiating contracts, and participating in value analysis teams.
- Distribution is responsible for finished goods inventory placement, transportation mode selection, and shipping schedule, route, and carrier selection. Forward placement of inventory at distribution centers (DCs) can cut delivery times and transportation costs, although the pooling effect is less and can result in higher inventory levels.
- Three accounting categories of inventory are raw materials, work-in-process, and finished goods.
- Inventory investment decisions involve trade-offs among the conflicting objectives of low inventory investment, good customer service, and high resource utilization. Benefits of good customer service and high resource utilization may be outweighed by costs of carrying large inventories, including interest or opportunity costs, storage and handling costs, taxes, insurance, shrinkage, and obsolescence. Order quantity decisions

are guided by a trade-off between the costs of holding inventories and the combined costs of ordering, setup, transportation, and purchased materials.

- Cycle, safety stock, anticipation, and pipeline inventories vary in size with order quantity, uncertainty, production rate flexibility, and lead time, respectively.
- Inventory placement at the plant level depends on whether an item is a standard or a special and on the trade-off between short customer response time and low inventory costs.
- ABC analysis helps managers focus on the few significant items that account for the bulk of investment in inventory. Class A items deserve the most attention, with less attention justified for class B and class C items.
- Materials management must fit operations strategy. When competitive priorities favor a product focus, the tendencies are for (1) low tolerance for cushions, (2) little pressure for an integrated organizational structure, (3) long planning horizons, (4) formalized supplier and customer relationships, and (5) information systems oriented to forecasts and inventory records.

Key Terms

ABC analysis *528*
anticipation inventory *523*
average aggregate inventory value *525*
backorder *521*
backward placement *517*
competitive orientation *513*
cooperative orientation *513*
cycle inventory *523*
distribution *516*
electronic data interchange (EDI) *511*

forward placement *516*
integrated structure *509*
inventory *519*
inventory holding cost *520*
inventory turnover *525*
lot sizing *522*
materials management *506*
ordering cost *521*
pipeline inventory *524*
pooling effect *517*
purchasing *510*
quantity discount *522*

repeatability *527*
safety stock inventory *523*
segmented structure *509*
setup cost *521*
special *526*
standard *526*
stockout *521*
value analysis *516*
weeks of supply *525*

Study Questions

1. An operations management consultant states: "The factors that make inventory attractive are the same ones that stand in the way of substantial improvements in efficiency." What are the reasons for carrying raw materials, work-in-process, and finished goods inventories? How can carrying inventory impede operating efficiency?

2. "Because organizations in the service sector do not manufacture products from raw materials, materials management concepts do not apply to them." Do you agree or disagree with this statement? Why?

3. It has been said that "if not controlled, work will flow to the competent people until they are submerged." What does this statement imply for centralizing materials management functions under one executive?

4. As a manufacturing firm grows to participate in international business, is the percentage of total income from sales spent on purchased materials and services likely to increase or decrease? Are materials management functions likely to be segmented or integrated? Are supplier relations likely to be more competitive or more cooperative? Is buying authority more likely to be central or local?

5. Suppose that you were a buyer charged with selecting one or more suppliers of an expensive, high-volume part going into a new product line. How would you proceed?

6. What steps would you take to make supplier relations more cooperative? Describe a situation that would favor competitive supplier relations.

7. In which situations would you favor
   a. long-term purchase contracts?
   b. centralized buying?

8. You have been asked to review the inventory policies of a large appliance manufacturer for which the dollar value of inventory now exceeds 40 percent of total sales. How would you go about identifying opportunities for inventory reduction? What are the advantages and disadvantages of forward placement of inventory?

9. The purpose of safety stock inventory is to protect against uncertainties in demand, lead time, and supply. What is the purpose of anticipation inventory?

10. What can be done to reduce the cost of buying and holding materials purchased from suppliers?

11. What are the benefits of making an ABC analysis of inventory item usage values?

12. Give three examples of how competitive priorities can affect choices made in materials management.

Discussion Questions

1. Under the Defense Industry Initiative on Business Ethics and Conduct, 46 contractors agreed to establish internal codes of ethics, to conduct training sessions, and to report suspected abuses.
   a. Is this an example of moving toward competitive or cooperative supplier relations?
   b. Suppose that you are a defense contracts manager. You have a friend in the military whom you have known for 20 years. As a gesture of friendship she offers useful inside information about a competing contractor's bid. What would you do if your company were part of the industry's ethics project? If your company were not in it?
   c. To build a win–win relationship with its suppliers, the armed forces made agreements calling for suppliers to be reimbursed for the costs of supplier training and employee morale-building programs. According to that agreement, your company decided to hold a private party for employees to "build morale." Because the expenses were to be reimbursed, the party planners were not very careful in making the arrangements and got carried away. They rented the city auditorium and hired a na-

   tionally known music group to provide entertainment. Furthermore, the planners didn't do a good job of contract negotiation and ended up paying five times the going rate for these services. The bill for the party now reaches your desk . . . $250,000! Under the terms of your agreement, your company is entitled to reimbursement of the entire amount. What should you do?

2. The USX Corporation fed caviar and filet mignon to executives of 300 of its biggest suppliers. The dinner was part of a two-day, $250,000 courtship to sell them on the virtues of relocating to Gary, Indiana. USX buys nearly $1 billion in products annually for its flagship plant in Gary and believes that greater supplier proximity would increase its inventory turnover.
   a. Explain how cycle, safety stock, and pipeline inventory could be reduced by having suppliers nearby.
   b. Is USX's approach to its suppliers ethically correct? How much does it differ from a salesperson's giving expensive presents to important customers?

Problems

1. A company enjoys $500 million in sales and a 15 percent gross profit margin (before taxes). Cost of materials is 60 percent of income from sales. The materials manager believes that $20 million can be saved through improved purchasing policies.
   a. What would be the percentage change in cost of materials?
   b. What percentage change in sales would be necessary to achieve the same result in gross profits?

2. Joan Pontius, the materials manager at Money Enterprises, is beginning to look for ways to reduce inventories. A recent accounting statement shows the following inventory investment by category: raw materials, $2,845,000; work-in-process, $5,670,000; and finished goods, $2,985,000. This year's cost of goods sold will be about $29.9 million. Assuming 52 business weeks per year, express total inventory as
   a. weeks of supply.   b. inventory turns.

3. One product line has eight turns per year and an annual sales volume (at cost) of $775,000. How much inventory is being held, on average?

4. Henderson Corporation supplies alloy ball bearings to auto manufacturers in Detroit. Because of its specialized manufacturing process, considerable work-in-process and raw materials are needed. The current inventory levels are $1,152,000 and $2,725,000, respectively. In addition, finished goods inventory is

$3,225,000, and sales (at cost) for the current year are expected to be about $24 million. Express total inventory as
   a. weeks of supply.   b. inventory turns.

5. The following data have been collected for a firm.

Cost of goods sold	$3,500,000
Gross profit	$ 700,000
Operating costs	$ 500,000
Operating profit	$ 200,000
Total inventory	$1,200,000
Fixed assets	$ 750,000
Long-term debt	$ 300,000

Assuming 52 business weeks per year, express total inventory as
   a. weeks of supply.   b. inventory turns.

6. A part is produced in lots of 500 units. It is assembled from two components worth $50 in total. The value added (for labor and variable overhead) in manufacturing one unit from its two components is $45, bringing the total cost per completed unit to $95. The typical lead time for the item is 5 weeks, and its annual demand is 1976 units. There are 52 business weeks per year.

a. How many units of the part are held, on average, in cycle inventory? What is the dollar value of this cycle inventory?

b. How many units of the part are held, on average, in pipeline inventory? What is the dollar value of this inventory? *Hint:* Assume that the typical job in pipeline inventory is 50 percent completed. Thus one-half the labor and variable overhead cost has been added, bringing the unit cost to $72.50 (or $50 + $45/2).

7. Sterling Incorporated, a manufacturer of consumer electric goods, has five DCs in different regions of the country. For one of its products, a high-performance VCR priced at $500 per unit, the average weekly demand at *each* DC is 75 units. Average shipment size to each DC is 400 units, and average lead time for delivery is 2 weeks. Each DC carries 2 weeks' supply as safety stock, but holds no anticipation inventory.

a. On average, how many dollars of pipeline inventory will be in transit to each DC?

b. How much total inventory (cycle, safety stock, and pipeline) does Sterling hold for all five DCs?

8. McKenzie Industries is considering using ABC analysis to focus attention on its most critical inventory items. A random sample of 20 items has been taken, and the dollar usages have been calculated as shown in the following table. Rank the items and assign them to an A, B, or C class.

Item	Dollar Usage	Item	Dollar Usage
1	9,200	11	300
2	400	12	10,400
3	33,400	13	70,800
4	8,100	14	6,800
5	1,100	15	57,900
6	600	16	3,900
7	44,000	17	700
8	900	18	4,800
9	100	19	19,000
10	700	20	15,500

9. Ben Dare Incorporated manufactures a motorcycle part in lots of 150 units. The raw materials cost for the part is $300, and the value added in manufacturing one unit from its components is $200, for a total cost per completed unit of $500. The lead time to make the part is 4 weeks, and the annual demand is 2000 units. The company operates 50 weeks per year.

a. How many units of the part are being held, on average, as cycle inventory?

b. How much pipeline inventory is being held, on average?

Advanced Problems

Problem 10 requires prior reading of Supplement A. Spreadsheet software would be helpful in calculating annual usage value and sorting the results in Problem 11.

10. The Dunnet Company purchases one of its essential raw materials from three suppliers. Dunnet's current policy is to distribute purchases equally among the three. The owner's son, Benjamin Darren Dunnet, has just graduated from business college. He proposes that these suppliers be rated (high numbers mean good performance) on six performance criteria weighted as shown in Table 11.1. A hurdle total score of 0.60 is proposed to screen suppliers. Purchasing policy would be revised to order raw materials from suppliers with performance scores greater than the hurdle total score, in proportion to their performance rating scores.

a. Use a preference matrix to calculate a total weighted score for each supplier.

b. Which supplier(s) survived the hurdle total score? Under the younger Dunnet's proposed policy, what proportion of orders would each supplier receive?

c. What advantages does the proposed policy have over the current policy?

TABLE 11.1 *Supplier Performance Scores*

		Rating		
Performance Criterion	Weight	Supplier A	Supplier B	Supplier C
1. Price	0.2	0.4	0.7	0.6
2. Quality	0.2	0.3	0.5	0.8
3. Delivery	0.2	0.4	0.5	0.7
4. Production facilities	0.1	0.6	0.9	0.6
5. Warranty and claims policy	0.2	0.7	0.6	0.7
6. Financial position	0.1	0.8	0.9	0.7

TABLE 11.2   *Inventory Items*

Item	Quantity per Year	Unit Value	Item	Quantity per Year	Unit Value
1. Axles	2,400	$ 2.850	14. Paint (gallons)	800	$42.00
2. Bolts	50,000	$ 0.038	15. Rivets	20,000	$ 0.003
3. Brake assemblies	4,800	$ 2.170	16. Seats	2,400	$ 5.260
4. Brake levers	4,800	$ 1.650	17. Shift levers	4,800	$ 1.500
5. Chains	2,400	$ 3.700	18. Spokes	200,000	$ 0.021
6. Control cable (meters)	8,000	$ 0.250	19. Sprockets	2,400	$ 8.180
7. Crank sets	2,400	$157.55	20. Tape (meters)	5,000	$ 0.121
8. Derailer assemblies	2,400	$ 82.45	21. Tires	4,800	$ 6.680
9. Fork assemblies	2,400	$ 39.36	22. Tubing, large (meters)	10,000	$ 9.250
10. Handlebar assemblies	2,400	$ 3.490	23. Tubing, small (meters)	8,000	$ 2.152
11. Head sets	2,400	$ 30.85	24. Welding rod (feet)	1,000	$ 1.251
12. Inner tubes	4,800	$ 2.490	25. Wheel rims	4,800	$ 5.250
13. Nuts	40,000	$ 0.019			

11. The Acme Bicycle Company (ABC) divides inventory items into three classes according to their dollar usage values, as shown in Table 11.2. Which items should be classified A, B, and C?

12. Suppose that a product has an annual demand of 390 units. The lot size is 130 units, and the lead time is 4 weeks. The firm operates 52 weeks per year.
    a. Over the course of a year, how many orders will be placed?
    b. During the 4-week lead time, 130 units will be in the pipeline; thus there will be 520 unit-weeks of pipeline inventory (4 weeks)(130 units). How many unit-weeks of pipeline inventory will there be during a year?
    c. Over a year's time, what will be the *average* number of units in pipeline inventory?
    d. Set up a mathematical expression for average pipeline inventory, using D for annual demand, Q for lot size, and L for lead time. How does your final expression, simplified, relate to the notion that average pipeline inventory is approximated by dL?

13. Finished-good item A is assembled from 1 unit of B and 4 units of purchased item E. Item B is manufactured from 1 unit of purchased item C and 1 unit of purchased item D. The weekly demand for item A averages 10 units. The demand for items B, C, D, and E can be derived from demand for A. The per unit purchase price is $30 for C, $40 for D, and $25 for E. The added cost to manufacture B from C and D is $70 per unit, bringing the value of one finished unit of B to $140 (or $30 + $40 + $70). The value of one unit of B is only $105 (or $30 + $40 + $70/2) if it is in the

pipeline as work-in-process inventory, assuming that it is half finished on the shop floor. Similar reasoning applies to item A, which costs $20 (value added only) to manufacture from B and E. Table 11.3 gives lead times and management's current policies on lot sizes, safety stock, and anticipation inventory. For example, the lot size of item D is (8 weeks)(10 units/week) = 80 units.

TABLE 11.3   *Lead Times and Policies*

		Inventory Policy (weeks of supply)		
Item	Lead Time (weeks)	Lot Size	Safety Stock	Anticipation Inventory
A	1	1	1	0
B	11	4	0	1
C	1	4	1	0
D	5	8	0	0
E	2	4	2	0

    a. What is the value of one unit of A upon completion?
    b. Calculate the average number of units held in inventory for each item, broken down as cycle, safety stock, anticipation, and pipeline inventory. Then convert your answer to dollar equivalents.
    c. How much inventory is being held in total? What is the inventory turnover?
    d. Which item and type of inventory is the best target for improvement?

CASE

Wolf Motors

John Wolf, president of Wolf Motors, had just returned to his office after visiting the company's newly acquired automotive dealership. It was the fourth Wolf Motors' dealership in a network that served a metropolitan area of 400,000 people. Beyond the metropolitan area, but within a 45-minute drive, were another 500,000 people. Each of the dealerships in the network marketed a different make of automobile and historically had operated autonomously.

Wolf was particularly excited about this new dealership because it was the first "auto supermarket" in the network. Auto supermarkets differed from traditional auto dealerships in that they sold multiple makes of automobiles at the same location. The new dealership sold a full line of Chevrolets, Nissans, and Volkswagens.

Starting 15 years ago with the purchase of a bankrupt Ford dealership, Wolf Motors had grown steadily in size and in reputation. Wolf attributed this success to three highly interdependent factors. The first was volume. By maintaining a high volume of sales and turning over inventory rapidly, economies of scale could be achieved, which reduced costs and provided customers with a large selection. The second factor was a marketing approach called the "hassle-free buying experience." Listed on each automobile was the "one price–lowest price." Customers came in, browsed, and compared prices without being approached by pushy salespersons. If they had questions or were ready to buy, a walk to a customer service desk produced a knowledgeable salesperson to assist them. Finally, and Wolf thought perhaps most important, was the after-sale service. Wolf Motors had established a solid reputation for servicing, diagnosing, and repairing vehicles correctly, in a timely manner, the first time.

High-quality service after the sale depended on three essential components. First was the presence of a highly qualified, well-trained staff of service technicians. Second was the use of the latest tools and technologies to support diagnosis and repair activities. And third was the availability of the full range of parts and materials necessary to complete the service and repairs without delay. Wolf invested in training and equipment to ensure that the trained personnel and technology were provided. What he worried about, as Wolf Motors grew, was the continued availability of the right parts and materials. This concern caused him to focus on the purchasing function and management of the service parts and materials flows.

Wolf thought back on the stories in the newspaper's business pages describing the failure of companies that hadn't planned appropriately for growth. These companies outgrew their existing policies, procedures, and control systems. Lacking a plan to update their systems, the companies experienced a myriad of problems that led to inefficiencies and an inability to compete effectively. He didn't want this to happen to Wolf Motors.

Each of the four dealerships purchased its own service parts and materials. Purchases were based on forecasts derived from historical demand data, which accounted for factors such as seasonality. Batteries and alternators had a higher failure rate in the winter, and air-conditioner parts were in higher demand during the summer. Similarly, freon was needed in the spring to service air conditioners for the summer months, whereas antifreeze was in demand in the fall to winterize automobiles. Forecasts also were adjusted for special vehicle sale and service promotions. Promotions for automobile sales meant an increased need for materials used to prep new cars. Dealers also would have special service promotions.

One thing that made the purchase of service parts and materials so difficult was the tremendous number of different parts that had to be kept on hand. Some of these parts would be used to service customer automobiles, and others would be sold over the counter. Some had to be purchased from the automobile manufacturers or their certified wholesalers to support the "guaranteed GM parts" promotion. Still other parts and materials such as oils, lubricants, and fan belts could be purchased from any number of suppliers. Purchasing had to remember that the success of the dealership depended on (1) lowering costs to support the hassle-free, one price–lowest price concept and (2) providing the right parts at the right time to support fast, reliable after-sale service.

As Wolf thought about the purchasing of service parts and materials, two things kept going through his mind: the amount of space available for parts storage and the level of financial resources available to invest in service parts and materials. The acquisition of the auto supermarket dealership put an increased strain on both factors with the need to support three different automobile lines at the same facility. Investment dollars were becoming scarce, and space was at a premium. Wolf wondered what could be done in the purchasing area to address some of these concerns and alleviate some of the pressures.

Questions

1. What recommendations would you make to John Wolf with respect to structuring the purchasing function for the Wolf Motors dealership network?
2. How might purchasing policies and procedures differ as the dealerships purchase different types of service parts and materials (e.g., lubricants versus genuine GM parts)?
3. How can inventory management concepts help John Wolf reduce investment and space requirements while maintaining adequate service levels?

Source: This case was prepared by Dr. Brooke Saladin, Wake Forest University, as a basis for classroom discussion.

Selected References

"Apparel Makers Are Refashioning Their Operations," *Wall Street Journal,* January 13, 1994.

Burt, D. *Proactive Purchasing.* Englewood Cliffs, N.J.: Prentice-Hall, 1984.

Corey, E. Raymond. "Should Companies Centralize Procurement?" *Harvard Business Review* (November–December 1978), pp. 102–110.

Dobler, Donald W., Lamar Lee, Jr., and David N. Burt. *Purchasing and Materials Management.* New York: McGraw-Hill, 1984.

"Doing the Unthinkable: Japan Inc.'s Suppliers Gasp as It Buys Abroad," *Business Week,* January 10, 1994.

Ellram, Lisa M., and Martha C. Cooper. "Supply Chain Management, Partnerships, and the Shipper–Third Party Relationship." *The International Journal of Logistics Management,* vol. 1, no. 2 (1990).

"Internal Operations Problems Leave Firm Reeling," *Wall Street Journal,* August 11, 1989.

Kelly, Scott W., and Michael J. Dorsch. "Ethical Climate, Organizational Commitment, and Indebtedness Among Purchasing Executives." *Journal of Personal Selling & Sales Management,* vol. 11, no. 4 (Fall 1991), pp. 55–66.

McLeavey, Dennis W., and S. L. Narasimhan. *Production Planning and Inventory Control.* Newton, Mass.: Allyn & Bacon, 1985.

Narasimhan, Ram. "An Analytical Approach to Supplier Selection." *Journal of Purchasing and Materials Management* (Winter 1983), pp. 27–32.

Reid, R. Dan, and Carl D. Riegel. "Purchasing Practices of Large Food Service Firms." Tempe, Arizona: Center for Advanced Purchasing Studies, 1989, pp. 20–21.

"Revolution in Japanese Retailing," *Fortune,* February 7, 1994.

Van Dierdonck, Roland, and Jeffrey G. Miller. "Designing Production Planning and Control Systems." *Journal of Operations Management,* vol. 1, no. 1 (August 1980), pp. 37–46.

Vollmann, Thomas E., William L. Berry, and D. Clay Whybark. *Manufacturing Planning and Control Systems.* Homewood, Ill.: Richard D. Irwin, 1988.

Chapter Twelve

INDEPENDENT DEMAND INVENTORY SYSTEMS

Retailers like to say that the rest of the year is a dress rehearsal for Christmas. During November and December many retailers ring up a third of their annual sales and half their profit. At J.C. Penney, Christmas planning is in full swing by early February, when its managers hammer out their holiday sales forecasts. They base their forecasts on the previous year's results and the economic outlook in order to determine how much space they will devote to each department. Buyers work backward from the sales plan and place orders four to eight months ahead of delivery. Not ordering enough inventory means lost sales and unhappy customers. Ordering too much inventory, which happens if sales slip below expectations, means that retailers must hold costly inventory or sell it at a loss. Thanks to computers, it's easier nowadays to track what is hot and what is not. And stores no longer have to unleash their clerks to mark down prices: They simply program discounts into electronic cash registers. The decision to slash prices is usually made at the highest

Retailers such as J.C. Penney expect to earn a high percentage of their annual sales during the Christmas shopping season.

management levels. Decisions on inventory levels, and the systems to control them, are vital to the retailer's success during the all-important Christmas season.

An important distinction between types of inventory is whether an item is subject to dependent or independent demand. J.C. Penney and other retailers must manage **independent demand items**—that is, items for which demand is influenced by market conditions and is not related to production decisions for any other item held in stock. Independent demand inventory includes four categories:

1. wholesale and retail merchandise;
2. service industry inventory, such as medical supplies for hospitals, stamps and mailing labels for post offices, and office supplies for law firms;
3. end-item and replacement part inventories at manufacturing firms; and
4. maintenance, repair, and operating (MRO) supplies at manufacturing firms—that is, items that do not become part of the final product, such as employee uniforms, fuel, paint, and machine repair parts.

Managing independent demand inventory can be tricky because demand is influenced by external factors. For example, the owner of a bookstore may not be sure how many copies of the latest best-seller customers will purchase during the coming month. As a result, she may decide to stock extra copies as a safeguard.

This chapter focuses on independent demand, which is the type of demand the bookstore owner and J.C. Penney face. Even though demand from any one customer is difficult to predict, low demand from some customers often is offset by high demand from others. Thus total demand for any independent demand item may follow a relatively smooth pattern, with some random fluctuations, as shown in Fig. 12.1. **Dependent demand items** are those required as components or inputs to a product or service. As we explain in Chapter 14, dependent demand items exhibit a very different pattern.

Independent Demand

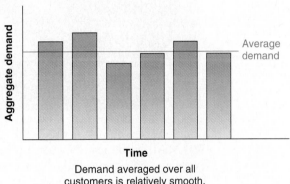

Demand averaged over all customers is relatively smooth.

We begin with practical issues of operating an actual inventory system: maintaining accurate records and deciding what types of computer support might be advisable. We then examine how to determine the appropriate lot size and frequency of placing new orders. We conclude by considering three common inventory control systems: continuous review, periodic review, and hybrid systems. Special cases of lot-sizing problems are presented in Supplement H.

◆ INVENTORY RECORDS

How much effort must be expended to maintain accurate inventory records?

Information on the amount of on-hand inventory and scheduled receipts is needed for both inventory management and accounting purposes. A **scheduled receipt,** often called an **open order,** is an order that has been placed but not yet received. Sometimes only periodic checks are made, as when a facility is shut down once a year for several days to count all inventory. At the other extreme are perpetual inventory records, in which a transaction report is made for each withdrawal and receipt. In manual systems, this information is posted to some type of written record. (Forms for manual record keeping include Kardex, visirecord, rotary wheel files, books, and logs.) In computerized systems, this information is maintained on disk or tape. Whether manual or computerized, records are updated the same way. For example, if an open order of 300 units is received, an inventory transaction must be made to increase on-hand inventory by that amount and to delete the 300-unit scheduled receipt from the record.

Computerized systems often are coupled with automated identification procedures, such as bar coding. A **bar code** is a pattern of wide and narrow black bands and alternating white spaces printed directly on the product or on an attached label. A computer, with the aid of an optical scanner or wand, reads the pattern and automatically records the price and updates inventory records.

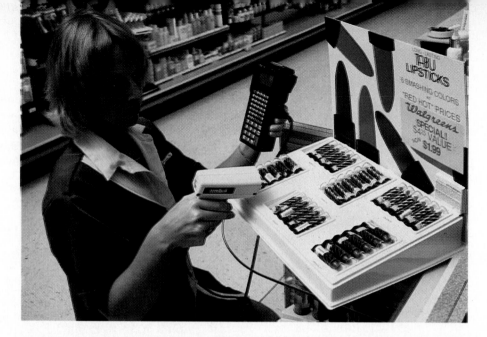

One important use of the computer is for inventory control. This Walgreen employee is monitoring stock with a laser gun that reads the product bar codes into a small computer connected to the manufacturer, allowing immediate placement of replenishment orders.

Computerized checkout procedures have helped retailers such as Walgreen and Wal-Mart dramatically increase productivity and manage inventory more accurately and efficiently. Today, grocery stores, manufacturers, supermarkets, warehouses, public libraries, VCR rental stores, retailers, hospitals, and even the U.S. Postal Service use bar codes.

Tracking Methods

One method of tracking inventory is to assign responsibility to specific employees for issuing and receiving materials and accurately reporting each transaction. A second method is to secure inventory behind locked doors or gates to prevent unauthorized or unreported withdrawals. This method also guards against storing new receipts in the wrong locations, where they can be lost for months. **Cycle counting** is a third method, whereby storeroom personnel physically count a small percentage of the total number of items each day, correcting errors they find. Class A items are counted most frequently. A final method, for computerized systems, is to make logic error checks on each transaction reported and fully investigate discrepancies. Examples of discrepancies are (1) actual receipts when there is no record of scheduled receipts, (2) disbursements that exceed the current on-hand balance, and (3) receipts with an inaccurate (nonexistent) part number.

These four methods can keep inventory record accuracy within acceptable bounds. Accuracy pays off mainly through better customer service, although some inventory reductions can be achieved by improving accuracy. A side benefit is that auditors may not require end-of-year counts if records prove to be sufficiently accurate.

Computer Support

Should a manual or a computerized system be used?

Because computers excel at manipulating massive amounts of data, many companies have computerized at least parts of their inventory systems. For example, Walgreen, one of the largest and most sophisticated U.S. retailers, implemented computer processing and automatic identification of its inventory at all five of its DCs. All Walgreen stores are then linked into the DC network, so store personnel can place replenishment orders directly from the actual shelf locations. The Benetton Group, an Italian manufacturer of jackets, skirts, and jeans, has become a truly global firm with active markets in 120 nations. Part of its success comes from its advanced inventory system, which develops production schedules directly from overnight inventory records transmitted to its Italian factories from stores all over the world. Recently Benetton fully integrated its suppliers into its inventory system.

Several inventory system software packages are generally available, in addition to the in-house systems developed by individual companies. Five of the most common uses of such packages are updating records, providing management reports, automating the reordering process, generating exception reports, and recomputing decision parameters. Managerial Practice 12.1 (on the next page) describes even more uses.

Updating Records.   At the time of each transaction, the computer updates on-hand inventory and scheduled receipts balances. Other information, such as recent demand rates, yield losses, price changes, lead times, and supplier performance, also can be updated and displayed on request.

Providing Management Reports.   Management can get reports on inventory investment that show measures such as dollar value of inventory, weeks of supply, and turns and compare them to measures from prior periods. The computer can also report on customer service measures (such as the number of stockouts) and the cost of operating the inventory system itself. Sometimes management compensation plans are geared to such performance measures. Eaton Corporation, a Cleveland-based manufacturer, bases incentive bonuses mainly on each unit's operating profit as a percentage of assets (including inventory) employed, instead of simply rewarding sales or profit gains.

Automating the Reordering Process.   An automatic reordering system can generate purchase orders and shop orders automatically. It also can generate **action notices**, which are signals to inventory analysts or buyers to place an order or to expedite an open order. Using action notices allows a decision maker to review the situation, possibly taking more things into account, before authorizing action to correct a deficiency. The computer saves considerable time because it brings only certain types of items and actions to the analyst's attention.

Generating Exception Reports.   Unusual situations needing management's attention may go unnoticed under manual systems. For example, actual lead times or demand rates might be deviating considerably from those forecast. Or a transaction report might show an impossibly large withdrawal, based on the current on-hand record. Computers can detect such exceptions to normal conditions and print out the data for the analyst to assess.

Recomputing Decision Parameters.   A computer program can recompute inventory decision parameters (e.g., when to reorder and in what quantity) when costs, lead times, or demands change. Computers also can be used to simulate changes to the system and make projections of changes to inventory and customer service levels.

Managerial Practice 12.1

▶ *Computerized Inventory Control for a Competitive Advantage*

A t Nissenbaum's auto junkyard in Somerville, Massachusetts, someone on the phone wants an engine for a 1979 Buick. Nissenbaum's, which seems to have everything, doesn't have one of those. So salesman David Butland turns to a nearby personal computer, types a brief message, and patches his request by satellite to 600 junkyards across the country. Within minutes, he is offered engines from Texas, California, and Maine. He buys the one from Maine for $550 and sells it to the customer for $700. "We probably boosted our looking-for-parts business by 75 percent since we got this," says Butland, patting the keyboard.

Philip Cavavetta buys merchandise for his Boston-area drugstore from two wholesalers. One of them, McKesson, is getting more of his business these days because "their computer system is so good," he explains. A clerk in his store walks down the aisles once a week with a McKesson-supplied computer in his palm. If the store is low on an item, the clerk waves his scanner over a label affixed to the shelf. The computer takes note and, when the clerk is finished, transmits the order to McKesson.

Wooster, Ohio's Rubbermaid Incorporated tracks its retail customers' inventories with a computer hookup to the retailers' point-of-sale data. This, says Rubbermaid President Wolf Schmidt, "avoids dead periods" between customer orders and shipments, thus helping retailers lower their inventory. Innovations such as this one are why Rubbermaid has been among the top 10 most admired companies since 1987 in *Fortune's* annual survey, and why it ranked No. 1 in 1994.

By using McKesson's Econolink electronic and inventory system, pharmacists can assure the availability of the medications their customers demand.

Sources: "Computer Finds a Role in Buying and Selling, Reshaping Businesses," *Wall Street Journal*, March 18, 1987; "America's Most Admired Company," *Fortune*, February 7, 1994.

◆ ECONOMIC ORDER QUANTITY

How large should cycle inventories be?

Recall from Chapter 11 that managers face conflicting pressures to keep inventories low enough to avoid excess inventory holding costs, but high enough to reduce the frequency of orders and setups. For example, a policy of replenishing inventory only every five months keeps ordering and setup costs low but raises the level of inventories and holding costs. A good starting point for balancing these conflicting pressures is finding the **economic order quantity (EOQ)**, which is the lot size that minimizes total annual inventory holding and ordering costs. The approach to determining the EOQ is based on the following assumptions.

1. The demand rate for the item is constant (e.g., always 10 units per day) and known with certainty.
2. The item is produced or purchased in lots, and a complete order for the item is received at once, rather than piecemeal. There are no constraints on the size of each lot, such as truck capacity or materials handling limitations.
3. The only two relevant costs are the inventory holding cost and the fixed cost per lot for ordering or setup.
4. Decisions for one item can be made independently of decisions for other items. For example, there is no advantage in combining several orders going to the same supplier.
5. There is no uncertainty in lead time or supply. Like the demand, the lead time is constant (e.g., always 14 days) and known with certainty. The amount received is exactly what was ordered.

The economic order quantity will be optimal when the five assumptions are satisfied. In reality, few situations are so simple and well-behaved. In fact, different lot-sizing approaches are needed to reflect quantity discounts, uneven demand rates, or interactions between items. We introduce some of these approaches in Supplement H, but the EOQ often is a reasonable first approximation of average lot sizes, even when several of the assumptions don't quite apply.

Calculating the EOQ

We begin by formulating the total costs for any lot size Q. Next we derive the EOQ, which is the Q that minimizes total costs. Finally, we describe how to convert the EOQ into a companion measure, which is the elapsed time between orders.

When the EOQ assumptions are satisfied, on-hand inventory behaves as shown in Fig. 12.2. A cycle begins with Q units held in inventory, which happens when a new order is received. Over the course of the cycle, on-hand inventory is used at a constant rate and falls to 0 precisely when the next lot is received. Because it varies uniformly between Q and 0, the average cycle inventory (see Chapter 11) equals one-half the lot size, Q.

FIGURE 12.2

Cycle-Inventory Levels

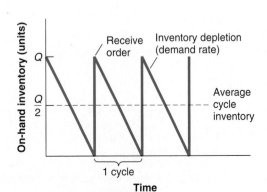

The annual holding cost for this amount of inventory, which increases linearly with Q, as Fig. 12.3(a) shows, is

Annual holding cost = (Average cycle inventory)(Unit holding cost)

The annual ordering cost is

Annual ordering cost = (Number of orders/year)(Ordering or setup cost)

The average number of orders per year is annual demand divided by Q. For example, if 1200 units must be ordered each year and the average lot size is 100 units, then 12 orders will be placed during the year. The annual ordering or setup cost decreases nonlinearly as Q increases, as shown in Fig. 12.3(b), because fewer orders are placed.

The total annual cost,[*] as graphed in Fig. 12.3(c), is the sum of the two cost components:

Total cost = Annual holding cost + Annual ordering or setup cost[†]

$$C = \frac{Q}{2}(H) + \frac{D}{Q}(S)$$

where C = total cost per year

   Q = lot size, in units

   H = cost of holding one unit in inventory for a year, often calculated as a percentage of the item's value (see Chapter 11)

   D = annual demand, in units per year

   S = cost of ordering or setting up one lot, in dollars per lot

FIGURE 12.3

Graphs of Annual Holding, Ordering, and Total Costs

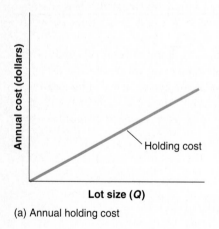

(a) Annual holding cost

(b) Annual ordering cost

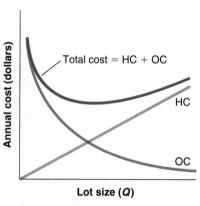

(c) Total annual cost

[*]Expressing the total cost on an annual basis usually is convenient (though not necessary). Any time horizon can be selected, as long as D and H cover the same period of time. If the total cost is calculated on a monthly basis, D must be monthly demand and H must be the cost of holding a unit for one month.

[†]The number of orders actually placed in any year is always a whole number, although the formula allows the use of fractional values. However, rounding isn't needed because what is being calculated is an average for multiple years. Such averages often are nonintegers.

EXAMPLE 12.1

*Costing Out a Lot-
Sizing Policy*

A museum of natural history opened a gift shop two years ago. Managing inventories has become a problem. Low inventory turnover is squeezing profit margins and causing cash-flow problems.

One of the top-selling items in the container group at the museum's gift shop is a birdfeeder. Sales are 18 units per week, and the supplier charges $60 per unit. The cost of placing an order with the supplier is $45. Annual holding costs are 25 percent of a feeder's value, and the museum operates 52 weeks per year. Management chose a 390-unit lot size so that new orders could be placed less frequently. What is the annual cost of the current policy of using a 390-unit lot size?

Solution   We begin by computing the annual demand and holding cost as

$$D = (18 \text{ units/week})(52 \text{ weeks/year}) = 936 \text{ units}$$

$$H = 0.25(\$60/\text{unit}) = \$15$$

Thus the annual cost is

$$C = \frac{Q}{2}(H) + \frac{D}{Q}(S)$$

$$= \frac{390}{2}(\$15) + \frac{936}{390}(\$45) = \$2925 + \$108 = \$3033$$

Figure 12.4 displays the impact of using several Q values for the birdfeeder in Example 12.1. Eight different lot sizes were evaluated in addition to the current one. Both holding and ordering costs were plotted, but their sum—the total cost curve—is the important feature. The graph shows that the best lot size, or EOQ, is the lowest point on the total cost curve, or between 50 and 100 units. Obviously, reducing the current lot-size policy ($Q = 390$) can result in significant savings.

FIGURE 12.4

*Total Inventory Cost
Function for Birdfeeder*

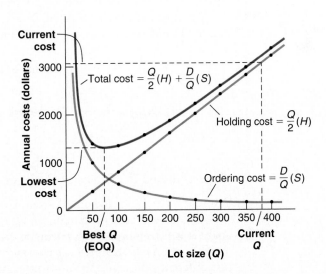

A more efficient approach is to use the EOQ formula:

$$EOQ = \sqrt{\frac{2DS}{H}}$$

This formula is obtained through calculus: We take the first derivative of the total cost function with respect to Q, set it equal to 0, and solve for Q. As Fig. 12.4 indicates, the EOQ is the order quantity for which annual holding cost equals annual ordering cost. When the annual holding cost for any Q exceeds the annual ordering cost, as with the 390-unit order in Fig. 12.4, we can immediately conclude that Q is too big. A smaller Q reduces holding cost and increases ordering cost, bringing them into balance. Similarly, if the annual ordering cost exceeds the annual holding cost, Q should be increased.

Sometimes inventory policies are based on the time between replenishment orders, rather than the number of units in the lot size. The **time between orders (TBO)** for a particular lot size is the average elapsed time between receiving (or placing) replenishment orders of Q units. Expressed as a fraction of a year, the TBO is simply Q divided by annual demand. When we use the EOQ and express time in terms of months, the TBO is

$$TBO_{EOQ} = \frac{EOQ}{D}(12 \text{ months/year})$$

EXAMPLE 12.2

Finding the EOQ, Total Cost, and TBO

For the birdfeeders in Example 12.1, calculate the EOQ and its total cost. How frequently will orders be placed if the EOQ is used?

Solution Using the formulas for EOQ and annual cost, we get

$$EOQ = \sqrt{\frac{2DS}{H}} = \sqrt{\frac{2(936)(45)}{15}} = 74.94, \quad \text{or 75 units}$$

$$C = \frac{75}{2}(\$15) + \frac{936}{75}(\$45) = \$562 + \$562 = \$1124$$

The EOQ is 75 units and the cost $1124. This cost is much less than the $3033 cost of the current policy of placing 390-unit orders.

The time between orders (TBO) when the EOQ is used is given below both in months and in weeks (assuming 52 business weeks per year):

$$TBO_{EOQ} = \frac{EOQ}{D}(12 \text{ months/year}) = \frac{75}{936}(12) = 0.96 \text{ month}$$

$$TBO_{EOQ} = \frac{EOQ}{D}(52 \text{ weeks/year}) = \frac{75}{936}(52) = 4.17 \text{ weeks}$$

Understanding the Effect of Changes

Subjecting the EOQ formula to sensitivity analysis can yield valuable insights into the management of inventories. Recall from Supplement A that sensitivity analysis is a technique for systematically changing crucial parameters to determine the effects of change. Let's consider the effects on the EOQ when we substitute different values into the numerator or denominator of the formula.

How often should demand estimates, cost estimates, and lot sizes be updated?

A Change in the Demand Rate. Because *D* is in the numerator, the EOQ (and therefore the best cycle inventory level) increases in proportion to the square root of the annual demand. Therefore when demand rises, lot size also should rise, but more slowly than actual demand. Interestingly, when the best cycle inventory is measured in terms of weeks of supply or inventory turnover—both of which account for the demand rate—it actually declines when demand increases. Conversely, when *D* declines, the best cycle inventory increases in terms of inventory turns or weeks of supply. This relationship explains why increasing repeatability, which in effect increases *D*, helps reduce costs (see Chapter 11 for the levers that can be used to reduce inventory).

A Change in the Setup Costs. Because *S* is in the numerator, increasing *S* increases the EOQ and, consequently, the average cycle inventory. Conversely, reducing *S* reduces the EOQ, allowing smaller lot sizes to be produced economically. This relationship explains why manufacturers are so concerned about cutting setup time and costs. When setup cost and setup time become trivial, a major impediment to small-lot production is removed.

A Change in the Holding Costs. Because *H* is in the denominator, the EOQ declines when *H* increases. Conversely, when *H* declines, the EOQ increases. Larger lot sizes are justified by lower holding costs.

Errors in Estimating D, H, and S. Total costs are fairly insensitive to errors, even when the estimates are wrong by a large margin. The reasons are that errors tend to cancel each other out and that the square root reduces the effect of the error. Suppose that we incorrectly estimate the holding cost to be double its true value—that is, we calculate EOQ using 2*H*, instead of *H*. For Example 12.1, this 100 percent error increases total cost by only 6 percent, from $1124 to $1192. Thus the EOQ lies in a fairly large zone of acceptable lot sizes.

◆ INVENTORY CONTROL SYSTEMS

The EOQ formula, or the models in Supplement H, can be used to help determine how much to order. Next, we look at methods to determine when to reorder. An inventory control system brings together both dimensions—sizing and timing—as it replenishes inventory. In this section we discuss and compare two inventory control systems: the continuous review system, called a *Q* system, and the periodic review system, called a *P* system. We close with a look at hybrid systems, which incorporate features of both *P* and *Q* systems.

Continuous Review (*Q*) System

A **continuous review (*Q*) system**, sometimes called a **reorder point (ROP) system** or fixed order quantity system, tracks the remaining inventory of an item each time a withdrawal is made, to determine whether it is time to reorder. In practice, these reviews are done frequently (e.g., daily) rather than continuously (after each withdrawal). The advent of computers and electronic cash registers linked to inventory records has made continuous reviews easier. At each review a decision is made about an item's inventory position. If it is judged too low, the system triggers a new order. The **inventory position (IP)** measures the item's ability to satisfy future demand. It includes scheduled receipts (SR) plus on-hand inventory (OH) minus backorders (BO), which are customer orders or commitments that are unfilled because an item is out of stock. More specifically,

Inventory position = On-hand inventory + Scheduled receipts − Backorders

$$IP = OH + SR - BO$$

When the inventory position reaches a predetermined minimum level, called the **reorder point (R)**, a fixed quantity Q of the item is ordered. In a continuous review system, although the order quantity Q is fixed, the time between orders can vary. Hence Q can be based on the EOQ, a price break quantity (the minimum lot size that qualifies for a quantity discount), a container size (such as a truckload), or some other quantity selected by management. Managerial Practice 12.2 shows how such a system works at two major retail chains.

Selecting the Reorder Point When Demand and Lead Time Are Certain.   So far, we have assumed that demand is constant and certain, making the reorder point easy to determine. In Example 12.1, suppose that the demand for feeders at the museum gift shop is always 18 per week, the lead time is always 2 weeks, and the supplier always ships on time the exact amount ordered. With both demand and lead time certain, the museum's buyer can wait until the inventory position drops to 36 units [or (18 units/week)(2 weeks)] to place a new order. Thus the reorder point, R, equals the *demand during lead time*, with no added allowance for safety stock.

Figure 12.5 shows how the system operates when demand and lead time are constant. The downward-sloping line represents the on-hand inventory, which is being depleted at a constant rate. When it reaches reorder point R (the horizontal line), a new order for Q units is placed. The on-hand inventory continues to drop throughout lead time L, until the order is received. At that time, which marks the end of the lead time, on-hand inventory jumps by Q units. A new order arrives just when inventory drops to 0. The time between orders (TBO) is the same for each cycle.

The inventory position IP shown in Fig. 12.5 corresponds to the on-hand inventory, except during the lead time. Just after a new order is placed, at the start of the lead time, IP increases by Q, as shown by the dashed line. The IP exceeds

FIGURE 12.5

Q System When Demand and Lead Time Are Constant and Certain

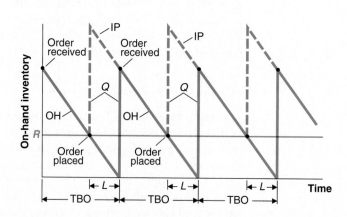

Managerial Practice 12.2

▶ *Inventory Control at Jordan Marsh and Wal-Mart*

Jordan Marsh is an apparel chain that carefully controls the inventory of its basic merchandise. Common items, such as jeans, underwear, and socks, are ordered automatically. A buyer sets the basic stock level, or reorder point, for each item. Once a stock level reaches this point, the system places a replenishment order. Champion, Haynes, and Levi Strauss & Company have become major suppliers in part because they deliver merchandise quickly and dependably. Wal-Mart has a similar approach. Its stores become "display opportunities" for the suppliers, which monitor and replenish from their offices. Wal-Mart also monitors supplier performance and switches suppliers if there are problems. Quick and dependable supplier deliveries pay off for the retailer, which can reduce the amount of safety stock that it must carry to provide the desired customer service levels.

Source: "As Stores Scrimp More and Order Less, Suppliers Take on Greater Risks, Costs," *Wall Street Journal,* December 10, 1991.

OH by this same margin throughout the lead time.* At the end of the lead time, when the scheduled receipts convert to on-hand inventory, IP = OH once again. The key point here is to compare IP, not OH, with R in deciding whether to reorder. A common error is to ignore scheduled receipts or backorders.

EXAMPLE 12.3
Determining Whether to Reorder

A withdrawal for an item has just been reported, leaving an on-hand inventory of only 10 units. Reorder point R is 100 and there are no backorders, but there is one open order for 200 units. Should a new order be placed?

Solution

$$IP = OH + SR - BO$$
$$= 10 + 200 - 0 = 210$$

As IP exceeds R (210 versus 100), don't reorder. Inventory is almost depleted, but there is no need to place a new order because the scheduled receipt is on the way.

How large should safety stocks be?

Selecting the Reorder Point When Demand and Lead Time Are Uncertain. In reality, demand and lead times aren't always predictable. For instance, the museum's buyer knows that *average* demand is 18 feeders per week and that the *average* lead time is 2 weeks. That is, a variable number of feeders may be purchased during the lead time, with an average demand during lead time of 36 feeders (assuming that each week's demand is identically distributed). Suppose that she sets R at 46 units, thereby placing orders before they typically are needed. This approach will create a safety stock, or stock held in excess of expected demand, of 10 units (46 − 36) to buffer against uncertain demand. In general,

Reorder point = Average demand during lead time + Safety stock

*A possible exception is the unlikely situation of long lead times, when more than one scheduled receipt is open at the same time.

Figure 12.6 shows how the Q system operates when demand and lead time are variable and uncertain. The wavy downward-sloping line indicates that demand varies from day to day. Its slope is steeper in the third cycle, which means that the demand rate is higher during this time period. The changing demand rate means that the time between orders changes, so $TBO_1 \neq TBO_2 \neq TBO_3$. The lead time also is a variable, so $L_1 \neq L_2 \neq L_3$. Because of uncertain demand and lead time, sales during lead time are unpredictable, and safety stock is added to hedge against lost sales. This addition is why R is at a higher level in Fig. 12.6 than in Fig. 12.5. It also explains why the on-hand inventory usually doesn't drop to 0 by the time a replenishment order arrives. The greater the safety stock, and thus the higher reorder point R, the less likely a stockout.

Because the average demand during lead time is determined largely by customers and suppliers, the real decision to be made when selecting R concerns the safety stock level. Deciding on a small or large safety stock is a trade-off between customer service and inventory holding costs. Cost minimization models can be used to find the best safety stock, but they require an estimate of stockout or backorder costs, which are usually difficult to estimate with any precision. The usual approach for determining R is for management—based on judgment—to set a reasonable service level policy and then determine the safety stock level that satisfies this policy.

FIGURE 12.6

Q System When Demand and Lead Time Are Uncertain

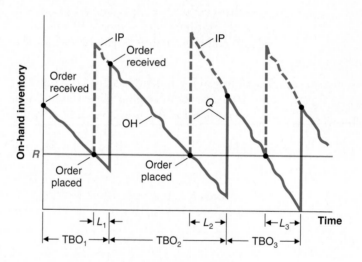

Choosing an Appropriate Service Level Policy. Managers must weigh the benefits of holding safety stock against the cost of holding it. One way to determine the safety stock is to set a **service level**, or **cycle-service level**—the desired probability of not running out of stock in any one inventory cycle. In a bookstore, the manager may select a 90 percent cycle-service level for a book. In other words, the probability is 90 percent that the demand will not exceed the supply during the lead time. The probability of running short *during the lead time*, creating a stockout or backorder, is only 10 percent (100 − 90). This stockout risk during the lead time is greater than the overall risk of stockout, because the risk is 0 for times outside of lead times.

To translate this policy into a specific safety stock level, we must know how the demand and lead times are distributed. If the demand and lead time vary little around their averages, safety stock (and thus reorder point R) can be small. Conversely, if the demand during lead time varies greatly from one cycle to the next, the safety stock must be large. Variability is measured with probability distributions.

We consider two types of probability distributions in the next two sections—the normal probability distribution and the discrete probability distribution. With the normal distribution, the inventory planner must know the mean (average) and standard deviation. These two parameters fully specify the probability distribution. With the discrete distribution, the planner specifies each possible demand during lead time, along with the probability that it will occur. With either distribution, forecasts of the needed parameters are based on past history or managerial judgment (see Chapter 10).

Finding the Safety Stock by Using a Normal Probability Distribution. When selecting the safety stock, the inventory planner often assumes that the demand during lead time L is normally distributed, as shown in Fig. 12.7. The average demand during the lead time is the center line of the graph, with 50 percent of the area under the curve to the left and 50 percent to the right. Thus if a cycle-service level of 50 percent was chosen, reorder point R would be the quantity represented by this center line. As R equals demand during the lead time plus the safety stock, the safety stock is 0 when R equals this average demand. Demand is less than average 50 percent of the time, and thus having no safety stock will be sufficient 50 percent of the time.

FIGURE 12.7

Finding Safety Stock with a Normal Probability Distribution for an 85 Percent Cycle-Service Level

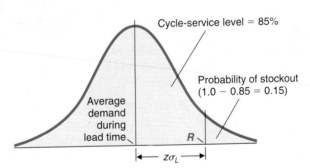

To provide a service level above 50 percent, the reorder point must be greater than average demand during the lead time. In Fig. 12.7, that requires moving the reorder point to the right of the center line so that more than 50 percent of the area under the curve is to the left of R. An 85 percent cycle-service level is achieved in Fig. 12.7, with 85 percent of the area under the curve to the left of R (in blue) and only 15 percent to the right (in pink). We compute the safety stock by multiplying the number of standard deviations from the mean needed to implement the cycle-service level (z) by the standard deviation of the demand during lead time probability distribution (σ_L):*

$$\text{Safety stock} = z\sigma_L$$

---

*For small manual systems, some inventory planners prefer to work with the mean absolute deviation (MAD), rather than the standard deviation, because it's easier to calculate. Recall from Chapter 10 that to convert MAD to the standard deviation, you simply multiply the MAD value by 1.25. Then proceed as usual to calculate the safety stock.

The higher the value of z, the higher the safety stock and the cycle-service level. If $z = 0$, there is no safety stock and stockouts will occur during 50 percent of the cycles.

EXAMPLE 12.4

Finding the Safety Stock and R by Using a Normal Probability Distribution

Returning to the birdfeeder example, suppose that demand during the lead time is normally distributed, with an average demand during the lead time of 36 units and $\sigma_L = 15$. What safety stock should be carried for a 90 percent cycle-service level? What is R?

Solution   The first step is to find z, the number of standard deviations to the right of average demand during the lead time that places 90 percent of the area under the curve to the left of that point. Look for 0.90 in the normal table in Appendix 2. The closest number is 0.8997, which corresponds to 1.2 in the row heading and 0.08 in the column heading. Adding these values gives a z of 1.28. With this information, you can calculate the safety stock and reorder point:

$$\text{Safety stock} = z\sigma_L = 1.28(15) = 19.2, \quad \text{or } 19$$

$$\text{Reorder point} = \text{Average demand during lead time} + \text{Safety stock}$$

$$= 36 + 19 = 55$$

Selecting the right amount of safety stock requires knowledge of σ_L, the standard deviation of demand during the lead time. Sometimes σ_L isn't directly available and must be calculated by combining information on the demand rate with information on the lead time. There are two reasons for this additional calculation.

1. Developing estimates first for demand, and then for the lead time, may be easier. Demand information comes from the customer, whereas lead times come from the supplier.
2. Records are not likely to be collected for a time interval that is exactly the same as the lead time. The same inventory control system is being used to manage thousands of different items, each with a different lead time. For example, if records report demand on a *weekly* basis, they can be used directly to compute the standard deviation of demand if the lead time is exactly one week. However, what is the standard deviation for demand during the lead time if the lead time is three weeks ?

Let's calculate σ_L for the case where demand is variable and uncertain, but the lead time is constant and certain. Suppose that we know the standard deviation of demand, σ_t, over some time interval t (say, days or weeks), where t isn't equal to the lead time. Let L be the constant lead time, expressed as a multiple (or fraction) of t. For example, if t represents a day and the lead time is 4 days, $L = 4$. We calculate σ_L as follows:

$$\sigma_L = \sigma_t\sqrt{L}$$

This formula comes from basic statistics. It is based on the assumption that the daily demand probability distributions are independent (i.e., demand one day doesn't affect demand the next day) and identical. The standard deviation of the sum of two or more identically distributed independent random variables is the square root of the sum of their variances. Here, the demand for each day in the lead time is an independent random variable. If the standard deviation of daily demand is 20 units and the lead time is 4 days,

$$\sigma_L = \sqrt{20^2 + 20^2 + 20^2 + 20^2}$$

which simplifies to $20\sqrt{4} = 40$.

More complex formulas or simulation must be used when both demand and the lead time are variable or when the supply is uncertain. In such cases, the safety stock must be larger than otherwise.

EXAMPLE 12.5

Finding the Safety Stock and R When σ_L Is Not Given

Records show that the average demand for an item is 50 units a week, with a standard deviation of 10 units. The lead time is constant at 5 weeks. Determine the safety stock and reorder point if management wants a 99 percent cycle-service level.

Solution   In this case, $t = 1$ week and $L = 5$, so

$$\sigma_L = \sigma_t\sqrt{L} = 10\sqrt{5} = 22.4$$

Consult the normal table for 0.99, which corresponds to a 99 percent cycle-service level. The closest number is 0.9901, which corresponds to a standard deviation of 2.33. With this information, we calculate the safety stock and reorder point as follows:

Safety stock $= z\sigma_L = 2.33(22.4) = 52.2$,   or 52

Reorder point = Average demand during lead time + Safety stock

$$= 5(50) + 52 = 302$$

Finding the Safety Stock by Using a Discrete Probability Distribution.   We can use the same general approach with other probability distributions. A manager is more likely to use a discrete probability distribution when data are unavailable and judgment is the main source of the estimates. A discrete probability distribution lists each possible demand during the lead time, along with its probability. This approach may be used when either demand or the lead time or both are uncertain because the probabilities are already stated in terms of demand during the lead time. If instead there are two distributions, one for demand and one for the lead time, simulation can be used to derive the joint probability distribution.

For simplicity, we assume that the demand levels listed are the only ones that can occur (nothing in between). We then select R from the list of demand levels in the distribution. The probabilities of demands at or less than the quantity chosen must equal or exceed the desired cycle-service level. We find the smallest value of R that meets this condition. For example, if the desired cycle-service level is 80 percent and R is set at 50 units, the probabilities of all demands ≤ 50 must equal or exceed 0.80, and R is the smallest such quantity.

Whereas with a normal distribution the safety stock is computed first and then added to average demand during the lead time, with a discrete distribution the sequence is reversed. We first find the desired R and then obtain the safety stock by subtracting expected demand during the lead time from R. To calculate the average value of the demand during lead time distribution, we multiply each demand by its probability and then sum the products. The result (see Supplement A) is average demand over many cycles.

Regardless of the distribution chosen, R must be known before a reorder point system can be implemented. And knowing the safety stock for each item is important to managers because they can then determine which safety stocks are most costly.

<table>
<tr><td></td><td colspan="6"></td></tr>
</table>

EXAMPLE 12.6

Finding the Safety Stock and R by Using a Discrete Probability Distribution

Based on past records and judgment, the director of materials management at the Lower Florida Keys Health System's hospital estimated the following probability distribution for demand during the lead time for one of the items that goes into the basic surgery carts.

Demand During Lead Time (units)	100	200	300	400	500	600
Probability	0.10	0.15	0.20	0.25	0.25	0.05

The manager selected a 95 percent cycle-service level (95 of 100 cycles). What reorder point should the manager use? What is the safety stock?

Solution   The reorder point, R, should be 500. The probability that this quantity is enough to avoid a stockout during the lead time is 0.95 (or $0.10 + 0.15 + 0.20 + 0.25 + 0.25$). A stockout will occur only when demand during the lead time is 600, which will happen only 5 percent of the time.

To find the safety stock, the manager first must know the average demand during the lead time, which is calculated as

$$\text{Demand during lead time} = 100(0.10) + 200(0.15) + \cdots + 600(0.05) = 355 \text{ units}$$

Substituting R (500) and expected demand during the lead time (355) into the basic equation for the reorder point and solving for the safety stock yields

$$\text{Reorder point} = \text{Average demand during lead time} + \text{Safety stock}$$

$$500 = 355 + \text{Safety stock}$$

$$\text{Safety stock} = 500 - 355 = 145 \text{ units}$$

Periodic Review (*P*) System

How can inventory be controlled if the time between replenishment orders should be fixed?

An alternative inventory control system is the **periodic review (*P*) system,** sometimes called a fixed interval reorder system or periodic reorder system, in which an item's inventory position is reviewed periodically rather than continuously. A new order is always placed at the end of each review, and the time between orders (TBO) is fixed at *P*. Demand is a random variable, so the total demand between reviews varies. In a *P* system, the lot size, *Q*, may change from one order to the next, and the time between orders is fixed. An example of a periodic review system is that of a soft-drink supplier making weekly rounds of grocery stores. Each week, the supplier reviews the store's inventory of soft drinks and restocks the store with enough items to meet demand until the next week.

We maintain four of the original assumptions: that the item is delivered in lots, that inventory holding cost is unaffected by lot sizing decisions, that decisions for one item are independent of decisions for other items, and that the amount received is exactly the amount ordered. However, we again allow for demand uncertainty. The periodic review system is shown in Fig. 12.8 for uncertain demand and constant lead time. The downward-sloping line again represents on-hand inventory. When the predetermined time, P, has elapsed since the last review, an order is placed to bring the inventory position, represented by the dashed line, up to the target inventory level, T. The lot size for the first review is Q_1, or the difference between inventory position IP_1 and T. As with the continuous review system, IP and OH differ only during the lead time. When the open order arrives, at the end of the lead time, OH and IP again are identical. Figure 12.8 shows that lot sizes vary from one cycle to the next; the inventory position is lower at the second review, meaning that a greater quantity is needed to achieve an inventory level of T.

FIGURE 12.8

P System When Demand Is Uncertain and Lead Time Is Certain

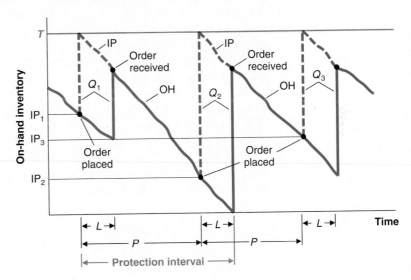

EXAMPLE 12.7

Determining How Much to Reorder

There is a backorder of 5 units of an item having no on-hand inventory. Now is the time to review. How much should be reordered if $T = 400$ and there are no scheduled receipts?

Solution

$$IP = OH + SR - BO$$

$$= 0 + 0 - 5 = -5 \text{ units}$$

$$T - IP = 400 - (-5) = 405 \text{ units}$$

That is, 405 units must be ordered to bring the inventory position up to T units.

Selecting the Time Between Reviews.   To run a *P* system, managers must make two decisions: the length of time between reviews and the target inventory level. Let's first consider the time between reviews, *P*. It can be any convenient interval, such as each Friday or every other Friday. Another option is to base *P* on the cost trade-offs of the EOQ. In other words, *P* can be set equal to the average time between orders for the economic order quantity, or TBO_{EOQ}. Because demand is variable, some orders will be larger than the EOQ and some will be smaller. However, the average lot size should equal the EOQ over time. If other models are used to determine the lot size (e.g., those described in Supplement H), we divide the lot size chosen by the annual demand, *D*, and use this ratio as *P*. It will be expressed as the fraction of a year between orders, which can be converted into months, weeks, or days as needed.

Selecting the Target Inventory Level.   Now let's consider how to calculate the target inventory level, *T*. Figure 12.8 reveals that an order must be large enough to make the inventory position, IP, last beyond the next review, which is period *P* away. The decision maker must wait one full period *P* to revise, correct, and reestablish the inventory position. Then a new order is placed, but it does not arrive until after the lead time, *L*. Therefore, as Fig. 12.8 shows, the decision maker needs a **protection interval** of *P* + *L*, the time interval for which inventory must be planned when each new order is placed. If the lead time varies, the protection interval is *P* plus the average lead time. A fundamental difference between the *Q* and *P* systems is the length of time needed for stockout protection. A *Q* system needs stockout protection only during the lead time because orders can be placed as soon as they are needed and will be received *L* periods later. A *P* system, however, needs stockout protection for the longer *P* + *L* protection interval because orders are placed only at fixed intervals.

Therefore in a *P* system, target inventory level *T* must equal the expected demand during protection interval *P* + *L*, plus enough safety stock to protect against demand and lead time uncertainty over this same protection interval. Thus

$$T = \begin{array}{c}\text{Average demand during} \\ \text{protection interval}\end{array} + \begin{array}{c}\text{Safety stock for} \\ \text{protection interval}\end{array}$$

Safety stock is computed for a *P* system much as it is for the *Q* system, except that it must cover demand uncertainty for a longer time. When using a normal probability distribution, we multiply the desired standard deviations to implement the cycle-service level (*z*) by the standard deviation of demand during the protection interval (σ_{P+L}). The value of *z* is the same as for a *Q* system. Thus

$$\text{Safety stock} = z\sigma_{P+L}$$

Based on our earlier logic for calculating σ_L when demand is variable and uncertain but the lead time is constant and known, we know that the protection interval is

$$\sigma_{P+L} = \sigma_t \sqrt{P + L}$$

Because a *P* system requires safety stock to cover demand uncertainty over a longer time period than a *Q* system, a *P* system requires more safety stock; that is, σ_{P+L} exceeds σ_L. Hence overall inventory levels are somewhat higher with a *P* system.

E XAMPLE 12.8

Calculating P and T

An item's demand is normally distributed with a mean of 40 units per week and a standard deviation in *weekly* demand of 15 units. The lead time is 3 weeks, and the business operates 52 weeks per year. A *P* system is used. What *P* approximates a 400-unit EOQ? What *T* is needed for an 80 percent cycle-service level? Round your final answers to the nearest integer.

Solution   We define first *D* and then *P*:

$$D = (40 \text{ units/week})(52 \text{ weeks/year}) = 2080 \text{ units}$$

$$P = \frac{\text{EOQ}}{D}(52) = \frac{400}{2080}(52) = 10 \text{ weeks}$$

We therefore would review the item every 10 weeks. We now find the standard deviation of demand over the protection interval $(P + L = 13)$. Here, *P* is the time between reviews expressed as a multiple (or fraction) of time interval t ($t = 1$ week because the data are expressed as demand *per week*):

$$\sigma_{P+L} = \sigma_t\sqrt{P + L} = 15\sqrt{13} = 54 \text{ units}$$

Before calculating *T*, we also need a *z* value. We find it for an 80 percent cycle-service level in Appendix 2 ($z = 0.84$). We now solve for *T*:

$$T = \text{Average demand during protection interval} + z\sigma_{P+L}$$

$$= (40 \text{ units/week})(13 \text{ weeks}) + 0.84(54 \text{ units}) = 565 \text{ units}$$

Every 10 weeks we would order the number of units needed to bring inventory position IP (counting the new order) up to the target inventory level of 565 units.

Comparative Advantages of the *Q* and *P* Systems

Neither the *Q* system nor the *P* system is best for all situations. Three *P*-system advantages must be balanced against three *Q*-system advantages. The advantages of one system are implicitly disadvantages of the other one.

The primary advantages of *P* systems are as follows.

What type of system—a *Q* system, a *P* system, or some hybrid—should be used to control inventories?

1. Administration of the system is convenient because replenishments are made at fixed intervals. Employees can set aside a day or part of a day regularly to concentrate on this particular task. Fixed replenishment intervals also are better for transportation systems that fix the time of pickups or deliveries on a daily, weekly, or even monthly basis, as they allow the route for pickups to be standardized.
2. Orders for multiple items from the same supplier may be combined into a single purchase order. This approach may result in a price break from the supplier and saves the buyer some paperwork, thereby reducing ordering costs. Suppliers also may prefer combined orders because all items in the order may be shipped at the same time, reducing transportation costs and increasing vehicle utilization.
3. The inventory position, IP, needs to be known only when a review is made (not continuously, as in a *Q* system) to determine when to reorder. However, this advantage is a moot point for firms using computerized

record-keeping systems, in which a transaction is reported upon each receipt or withdrawal. When inventory records are always current, the system is called a **perpetual inventory system.**

The primary advantages of Q systems are as follows.

1. The review frequency of each item may be individualized. Tailoring the review frequency to the item can reduce total ordering and holding costs.
2. Fixed lot sizes sometimes result in quantity discounts. Physical limitations related to truckload capacities, materials handling methods, and furnace capacities also may require a fixed lot size.
3. Lower safety stocks result in savings.

In conclusion, the choice between Q and P systems is not clearcut. Which one is better depends on the relative importance of its advantages in various situations. Management must weigh each alternative carefully in selecting the best system.

Hybrid Systems

What other types of systems are possible?

Various hybrid inventory control systems merge some but not all the features of the P and Q systems. We briefly examine three such systems: optional replenishment, base-stock, and visual.

Optional Replenishment System. Sometimes called the optional review, min–max, or s, S system, the **optional replenishment system** is much like the P system. It is used to review the inventory position at fixed time intervals and, if the position has dropped to (or below) a predetermined level, place a variable-sized order to cover expected needs. The new order is large enough to bring the inventory position up to a target inventory, similar to T for the P system. However, orders aren't placed after a review unless the inventory position has dropped to the minimum level set. The minimum level acts as reorder point R does in a Q system. Its effect is to ensure that a reasonable order quantity is placed. If the target is 100 and the minimum level is 60, the minimum order size is 40 (or 100 − 60). The optional review system avoids continuous reviews and so is particularly attractive when both review and ordering costs are significant.

Base-Stock System. In its simplest form, the **base-stock system** issues a replenishment order, Q, each time a withdrawal is made, for the same amount as the withdrawal. This one-for-one replacement policy maintains the inventory position at a base-stock level equal to the expected demand during the lead time plus safety stock. The base-stock level therefore is equivalent to the reorder point in a Q system. However, order quantities now vary to keep the inventory position at R at all times. Because this is the lowest IP possible to maintain a specified service level, the base-stock system may be used to minimize cycle inventory. More orders are placed, but each is smaller. This system is appropriate for very expensive items, such as replacement engines for jet airplanes. No more inventory is held than the maximum demand expected until a replacement order can be received.

The base-stock system often is modified in one of two ways. First, replenishment orders can be accumulated so that orders can be placed at fixed time intervals. For example, a distribution center may receive weekly shipments from a manufacturing plant, with the quantity shipped equaling the total withdrawals at the DC since the prior week's shipment. This system actually is a *P* system that uses small *P* values. Second, replenishment orders can be accumulated to achieve a fixed order quantity. This system actually is a *Q* system that uses very small *Q* values. It was introduced as part of the Kanban system by Toyota in Japan, as discussed in Chapter 15. Small-lot production in standard lot sizes is achieved, leading to minimal inventory levels.

Visual Systems. **Visual systems** allow employees to place orders when inventory visibly reaches a certain marker. For example, in the **single-bin system,** a maximum level is marked on the storage shelf or bin or on a measuring rod. The inventory level is brought up to the mark periodically—say, once a week. The single bin may be, for example, a gasoline storage tank at a service station or a storage bin for small parts at a manufacturing plant. This method is essentially a *P* system, with target inventory *T* and current IP established visually.

In the **two-bin system,** an item's inventory is stored at two different locations. Inventory is first withdrawn from the first bin. If it is empty, the second bin provides backup to cover demand until a replenishment order arrives. An empty first bin signals the need to place a new order. Premade order forms may be placed near the bins so that workers can send one to purchasing or even directly to the supplier. When the new order arrives, the second bin is restored to its normal level and the rest is put in the first bin. The two-bin system actually is a *Q* system, with the normal level in the second bin being reorder point *R*. The system also may be implemented with just one bin by marking the bin at the reorder point level. Sometimes the reorder point is even built into the product by the supplier. A calendar, with a notice inserted toward the end as a reminder to reorder for the new year, is a good example of a product with a built-in reorder point.

Both types of visual systems are easy to administer because records are not kept on the current inventory position. The historical usage rate can simply be reconstructed from past purchase orders. Visual systems are intended for use with low-value items that have a steady demand, such as nuts and bolts. Overstocking is common, but the extra inventory holding cost is minimal because the items have such little value.

CHAPTER REVIEW

Solved Problem 1

In Example 12.1 the economic order quantity, EOQ, is 75 units when annual demand, *D*, is 936 units/year, the setup cost, *S*, is $45, and the holding cost, *H*, is $15/unit/year. Suppose that we mistakenly estimate inventory holding cost to be $30/unit/year.

a. What is the new order quantity, *Q*, if *D* = 936 units/year, *S* = $45, and *H* = $30/unit/year?

b. What is the change in order quantity, expressed as a percentage of the economic order quantity (75 units)?

Solution   a. The new order quantity is

$$\text{EOQ} = \sqrt{\frac{2DS}{H}} = \sqrt{\frac{2(936)(\$45)}{\$30}} = \sqrt{2808} = 52.99, \qquad \text{or 53 units}$$

b. The percentage change is

$$\left(\frac{53 - 75}{75}\right)(100\%) = -29.33\%$$

The new order quantity (53) is about 29 percent smaller than the correct order quantity (75).

Solved Problem 2

In Example 12.2, the total cost, C, is \$1124/year.

a. What is the annual total cost when D = 936 units/year, S = \$45, H = \$15/unit/year, and Q is the result from Solved Problem 1a?
b. What is the change in total cost, expressed as a percentage of the total cost (\$1124)?

Solution   a. With 53 as the order quantity, the annual cost is

$$C = \frac{Q}{2}(H) + \frac{D}{Q}(S) = \frac{53}{2}(15) + \frac{936}{53}(45) = \$397.50 + \$794.72$$

$$= \$1192.22, \qquad \text{or about } \$1192$$

b. The percentage change is

$$\left(\frac{1192 - 1124}{1124}\right)(100\%) = 6.05\%, \qquad \text{or about } 6\%$$

A 100 percent error in estimating the holding cost caused the order quantity to be 29 percent too small, and that in turn increased annual costs by about 6 percent.

Solved Problem 3

A regional warehouse purchases hand tools from various suppliers and then distributes them on demand to retailers in the region. The warehouse operates 5 days per week, 52 weeks per year. Only when it is open can orders be received. The following data are estimated for ⅜-inch hand drills with double insulation and variable speeds.

> Average daily demand = 100 drills
> Standard deviation of daily demand (σ_t) = 30 drills
> Lead time (L) = 3 days
> Holding cost (H) = \$9.40/unit/year
> Ordering cost (S) = \$35/order
> Cycle-service level = 92%

The warehouse uses a continuous review (Q) system.

a. What order quantity, Q, and reorder point, R, should be used?
b. If on-hand inventory is 40 units, there is one open order for 440 drills, and there are no backorders, should a new order be placed?

Solution   a. The annual demand, D, is (5 days/week)(52 weeks/year)(100 drills/day) = 26,000 drills/year. The order quantity is

$$\text{EOQ} = \sqrt{\frac{2DS}{H}} = \sqrt{\frac{2(26,000)(\$35)}{\$9.40}} = \sqrt{193,617} = 440.02, \quad \text{or 440 drills}$$

$$\sigma_L = \sigma_t\sqrt{L} = (30 \text{ drills})\sqrt{3} = 51.96, \quad \text{or 52 drills}$$

Appendix 2 shows that a 92 percent cycle-service level corresponds to $z = 1.40$. Therefore

$$\text{Safety stock} = z\sigma_L = 1.40(52 \text{ drills}) = 72.8, \quad \text{or 73 drills}$$

$$\text{Average demand during the lead time} = 100(3) = 300 \text{ drills}$$

$$\text{Reorder point} = \text{Average demand during the lead time} + \text{Safety stock}$$

$$= 300 \text{ drills} + 73 \text{ drills} = 373 \text{ drills}$$

With a continuous review system, $Q = 440$ and $R = 373$.

b. Inventory position = On-hand inventory + Scheduled receipts − Backorders, or

$$\text{IP} = \text{OH} + \text{SR} - \text{BO} = 40 + 440 - 0 = 480 \text{ drills}$$

As IP (480) exceeds R (373), do not place a new order.

Solved Problem 4

Suppose that a periodic review (P) system is used at the warehouse, but otherwise the data are the same as in Solved Problem 3.

a. Calculate the P (in workdays) that gives approximately the same number of orders per year as the EOQ. Round your answer to the nearest day.

b. What is the value of the target inventory level, T?

c. It's time to review the item. On-hand inventory is 40 drills; there is a scheduled receipt of 440 drills, and there are no backorders. How much should be reordered?

Solution   a. The time between orders is

$$P = \frac{\text{EOQ}}{D}(260 \text{ days/year}) = \frac{440}{26,000}(260) = 4.4, \quad \text{or 4 days}$$

b. For a periodic review system,

$$\text{Safety stock} = z\sigma_{P+L} = z\sigma_t\sqrt{P + L} = 1.40(30)\sqrt{4 + 3} = 111.12, \quad \text{or 111 drills}$$

The target inventory level, T, is the average demand during the protection interval plus the safety stock, or

$$T = (100 \text{ drills/day})[(4 + 3) \text{ days}] + 111 \text{ drills} = 811 \text{ drills}$$

c. Inventory position is the amount on hand plus scheduled receipts minus backorders, or

$$\text{IP} = \text{OH} + \text{SR} - \text{BO} = 40 + 440 - 0 = 480 \text{ drills}$$

The order quantity is the target inventory level minus the inventory position, or

$$Q = T - \text{IP} = 811 \text{ drills} - 480 \text{ drills} = 331 \text{ drills}$$

In a periodic review system, the order quantity for this review period is 331 drills.

Solved Problem 5

The following discrete probability distribution has been estimated for demand (in units) during the lead time.

Demand	Probability
0	0.15
50	0.30
100	0.20
150	0.10
200	0.10
250	0.10
300	0.05
	1.00

a. With a continuous review system and a 75 percent cycle-service level, what is the reorder point?

b. What is the safety stock for this reorder point?

Solution   a. R should be 150 units because the probabilities of demand ≤ 150 sum to 0.75:

$$0.15 + 0.30 + 0.20 + 0.10 = 0.75$$

Demand	Probability	Cumulative Probability
0	0.15	0.15
50	0.30	0.45
100	0.20	0.65
150	0.10	0.75
200	0.10	0.85
250	0.10	0.95
300	0.05	1.00
	1.00	

b. The expected average demand during the lead time is

$$0(0.15) + 50(0.30) + 100(0.20) + 150(0.10) + 200(0.10) + 250(0.10) + 300(0.05)$$
$$= 110 \text{ units}$$

The reorder point, R, is the average demand during the lead time plus the safety stock. Therefore

$$\text{Safety stock} = 150 \text{ units} - 110 \text{ units} = 40 \text{ units}$$

Formula Review

1. Total annual cost = Annual holding cost + Annual ordering or setup cost

$$C = \frac{Q}{2}(H) + \frac{D}{Q}(S)$$

2. Economic order quantity: $\text{EOQ} = \sqrt{\dfrac{2DS}{H}}$

3. Inventory position = On-hand inventory + Scheduled receipts − Backorders

$$IP = OH + SR - BO$$

4. Continuous review system:

Reorder point (R) = Average demand during the protection interval + Safety stock

Protection interval = Lead time (L)

Safety stock = $z\sigma_L$

Standard deviation of demand during the lead time = $\sigma_L = \sigma_t\sqrt{L}$

Order quantity = EOQ

Replenishment rule: Order EOQ units when IP $\leq R$.

5. Periodic review system:

Target inventory level (T) = Average demand during the protection interval + Safety stock

Protection interval = Time between orders + Lead time = $P + L$

Reorder interval = Time between orders = P

Safety stock = $z\sigma_{P+L}$

Standard deviation of demand during the protection interval = $\sigma_{P+L} = \sigma_t\sqrt{P + L}$

Order quantity = Target inventory level − Inventory position = $T -$ IP

Replenishment rule: Every P time periods order $T -$ IP units.

Chapter Highlights

- Independent demand inventory management methods are appropriate for wholesale and retail merchandise, service industry supplies, finished goods and service parts replenishment, and maintenance, repair, and operating supplies.
- Inventory management decisions require accurate information on the amount of on-hand inventory, scheduled receipts, and backorders in order to determine the inventory position for every independent demand item. Accuracy is attained through cycle counting, automated identification methods such as bar coding, and error detection logic available in computer-based inventory management systems. Computerized systems are used to update records, provide management reports, reorder automatically, generate exception reports, and recompute decision parameters.
- A basic inventory management question is whether to order large quantities infrequently or to order small quantities frequently. The EOQ provides guidance for this choice by indicating the lot size that minimizes (subject to several assumptions) the sum of holding and ordering costs over some time period such as a year.

- In the continuous review (Q) system, the buyer places orders of a fixed lot size Q when the inventory position drops to the reorder point. In the periodic review (P) system, the quantity varies from order to order. Every P fixed time intervals, the buyer places an order to replenish the quantity consumed since the last order. The fixed replenishment interval in P systems tends to be an advantage when orders for several items from the same supplier can be combined to obtain quantity discounts or transportation savings. In P systems the protection interval is $P + L$, which is longer than protection interval L of Q systems, reflecting greater uncertainty. P systems require greater investment in safety stock to attain comparable service levels.
- Various hybrid inventory systems are used, including optional replenishment, base-stock, and visual systems. The base-stock system minimizes cycle inventory by maintaining the inventory position at the base-stock level. Visual systems, such as single-bin and two-bin systems, are adaptations of the P and Q systems that eliminate the need for records.

Key Terms

action notices 543
bar code 541
base-stock system 560
continuous review (Q) system 549
cycle counting 542
cycle-service level 552
dependent demand items 541
economic order quantity (EOQ)
    544

independent demand items 540
inventory position (IP) 550
open order 541
optional replenishment system 560
periodic review (P) system 556
perpetual inventory system 560
protection interval 558
reorder point (R) 550
reorder point (ROP) system 549

scheduled receipt 541
service level 552
single-bin system 561
time between orders (TBO) 548
two-bin system 561
visual systems 561

Study Questions

1. What is the relationship between an item's lot size and the frequency of ordering the item?
2. How are the best lot size, Q, and reorder point, R, affected by
   a. increases in demand?
   b. decreases in setup costs?
   c. increases in interest rates?
   d. forecast errors in D, H, or S?
3. Few, if any, products or services fit the EOQ assumptions (e.g., no variation in demand, lead time, or sup-

ply), so how can the EOQ model provide guidance in managing real-world inventories?
4. What costs should be considered in setting cycle-service policy?
5. What are the rewards and costs of having accurate inventory records? How can accuracy be increased?
6. Under what conditions would you prefer to use a Q system? a P system? a base-stock system? a visual system?

Discussion Question

What is the relationship between inventory and the eight competitive priorities? (See Chapter 2.) Suppose that two competing manufacturers, Company H and Company L, are similar except that Company H has much higher investments in raw materials, work-in-process, and finished goods inventory than Company L. In which of the eight competitive priorities will Company H have an advantage?

Problems

1. Full Court Press, Inc. buys slick paper in 1500 pound rolls for textbook printing. Annual demand is 1920 rolls. The cost per roll is $1000, and the annual holding cost is 30 percent of the cost. Each order costs $500.
   a. How many rolls should Full Court Press order at a time?
   b. What is the time between orders?
2. SOCKS, Inc. buys 200 blank cassette tapes per month for use in producing foreign language courseware. The ordering cost is $50. Holding cost is $0.24 per cassette per year.
   a. How many rolls should SOCKS order at a time?
   b. What is the time between orders?
3. Officer Krumpke buys doughnuts for the police department coffee-break room. The department consumes 4 dozen doughnuts per day, 7 days per week. She buys doughnuts from the nearby Dandy Dough-

nut shop for $3.00 per dozen. Dandy offers free delivery. Officer Krumpke's time involved in placing a telephone order for replenishment is valued at $1.75. Because of high risks of obsolescence and pilferage, the cost to carry 1 dozen doughnuts in inventory for 1 week is $0.20. How many dozen doughnuts should Officer Krumpke order at a time?
4. Louis Zephyr is a buyer for the Purgatory, Colorado, School District. Lou's duties include purchasing devil's food cake mix for the school system's cafeterias. The supplying firm, B. Elsie Bubba Company, specially makes each shipment of cake mix according to a tempting recipe specified by Purgatory schools. Production scheduling, several layers of bureaucracy, and remote locations result in high ordering costs and long lead times. Purgatory uses a continuous review inventory system.

   Demand is normally distributed, with an average

of 225 boxes of devil's food cake mix *per month* and a standard deviation of *monthly* demand of 35.36 boxes. Ordering costs are $123.21, and the lead time is 2 months. To hold a box of devil's food cake mix in inventory for a year costs $1.50. The desired cycle-service level is 90 percent.

   a. How many boxes of devil's food cake mix should Lou Zephyr buy at a time?

   b. What is the reorder point?

   c. Suppose that 100 boxes are in on-hand inventory and Lou has placed an order with B. Elsie Bubba for the quantity indicated in part a, which hasn't yet been delivered. However, cafeterias just have requested a total of 112 boxes. According to the continuous review system, what should Lou do?

5. An ophthalmologist's office operates 52 weeks per year, 6 days per week and uses a continuous review inventory system. It purchases disposable contact lenses for $11.70 per pair. The following information is available about these lenses.

Demand = 90 pairs/week

Order cost = $54/order

Annual holding cost = 27% of cost

Desired cycle-service level = 80%

Lead time = 3 weeks (18 working days)

Standard deviation of weekly demand = 15 pairs

Current on-hand inventory is 320 pairs, with no open orders or backorders.

   a. What is the EOQ? What would be the average time between orders (in weeks)?

   b. What should R be?

   c. An inventory withdrawal of 10 pairs was just made. Is it time to reorder?

   d. The store currently uses a lot size of 500 units (i.e., $Q = 500$). What is the annual holding cost of this policy? annual ordering cost? Without calculating the EOQ, how can you conclude from these two calculations that the current lot size is too large?

   e. What would be the annual cost saved by shifting from the 500-unit lot size to the EOQ?

6. Consider again the contact lens ordering policy for the ophthalmologist's office in Problem 5.

   a. Suppose that the weekly demand forecast of 90 pairs is incorrect and actual demand averages only 60 pairs per week. How much higher will total costs be, owing to the distorted EOQ caused by this forecast error?

   b. Suppose that actual demand is 60 pairs but that ordering costs are cut to only $6 by using electronic data interchange to automate order placing (see Chapter 11). However, the buyer doesn't tell any-

one, and the EOQ isn't adjusted to reflect this reduction in S. How much higher will total costs be, compared to what they could be if the EOQ were adjusted?

7. In a Q system, the demand rate for gizmos is normally distributed, with an average of 200 units *per week*. The lead time is 4 weeks. The standard deviation of *weekly* demand is 15 units.

   a. What is the standard deviation of demand during the 4-week lead time?

   b. What is the average demand during the 4-week lead time?

   c. What reorder point results in a cycle-service level of 99 percent?

8. In a continuous review system, the lead time for widgets is 3 weeks. Average demand during the lead time is normally distributed, with an average of 450 units. The standard deviation of *weekly* demand is 15 units. What cycle-service level is provided when the reorder point is set at 489 units?

9. In a perpetual inventory system, the lead time for dohickies is 5 weeks. The standard deviation of demand during the lead time is 85 units. The desired cycle-service level is 99 percent. The supplier of dohickies has streamlined operations and now quotes a 1-week lead time. How much can safety stock be reduced without reducing the 99 percent cycle-service level?

10. In a two-bin inventory system, the demand for whatchamacallits during the 2-week lead time is normally distributed, with an average of 53 units per week. The standard deviation of weekly demand is 5 units. What cycle-service level is provided when the normal level in the second bin is set at 120 units?

11. In a periodic review system, the lead time for doodads is 3 weeks and the review period is 2 weeks. The average demand rate is 216.4 units per week, with a standard deviation of weekly demand of 68 units.

   a. What is the standard deviation of demand during the protection interval?

   b. What is the average demand during the protection interval?

   c. What is the target inventory level if a 95 percent cycle-service level is desired?

12. In a P system, the lead time for gadgets is 2 weeks and the review period is 1 week. Demand during the protection interval averages 218 units, with a standard deviation of 40 units. What is the cycle-service level when the target inventory level is set at 300 units?

13. Potpourri retails a variety of kitchen cooking devices. It uses an optional replenishment system with a review period of 2 weeks, and its suppliers quote a 1-week lead time. Potpourri has $100,000 invested in safety stock and has asked you to estimate the effect on safety stock investment of changing its review period to 1 week.

14. Suppose that the ophthalmologist's office in Problem 5 uses a P system instead of a Q system. The average daily demand is 15 pairs (90/6), and the standard deviation of *daily* demand is 6.124 pairs ($15/\sqrt{6}$).
    a. What P (in working days) and T should be used to approximate the cost trade-offs of the EOQ?
    b. How much more safety stock is needed than with a Q system?
    c. It's time for the periodic review. How much should be ordered?

15. Your firm uses a continuous review system and operates 52 weeks per year. One of the items handled has the following characteristics.

    Demand (D) = 20,000 units/year

    Ordering cost (S) = $40/order

    Holding cost (H) = $2/unit/year

    Lead time (L) = 2 weeks

    Cycle-service level = 95%

    Demand is normally distributed, with a standard deviation of *weekly* demand of 100 units.

    Current on-hand inventory is 1040 units, with no scheduled receipts and no backorders.

    a. Calculate the item's EOQ. What is the average time, in weeks, between orders?
    b. Find the safety stock and reorder point that provide a 95 percent cycle-service level.
    c. For these policies, what are the annual costs of (i) holding the cycle inventory and (ii) placing orders?
    d. A withdrawal of 15 units just occurred. Is it time to reorder? If so, how much should be ordered?

16. Suppose that your firm uses a periodic review system, but otherwise the data are the same as in Problem 15.
    a. Calculate the P that gives approximately the same number of orders per year as the EOQ. Round your answer to the nearest week.
    b. Find the safety stock and the target inventory level that provide a 95 percent cycle-service level.
    c. How much larger is the safety stock than with a Q system?

17. A company begins a review of ordering policies for its continuous review system by checking the current policies for a sample of items. Following are the characteristics of one item.

    Demand (D) = 64 units/week   (Assume 52 weeks per year.)

    Ordering and setup cost (S) = $50/order

    Holding cost (H) = $13/unit/year

    Lead time (L) = 2 weeks

    Standard deviation of *weekly* demand = 12 units

    Cycle-service level = 88%

    a. What is the EOQ for this item?
    b. What is the desired safety stock?
    c. What is the reorder point?
    d. What are the cost implications if the current policy for this item is Q = 200 and R = 180?

18. Using the same information as in Problem 17, develop the best policies for a periodic review system.
    a. What value of P gives the same approximate number of orders per year as the EOQ? Round to the nearest week.
    b. What safety stock and target inventory level provide an 88 percent cycle-service level?

19. Wood County Hospital consumes 500 boxes of bandages per week. The price of bandages is $70 per box, and the hospital operates 52 weeks per year. The cost of processing an order is $60, and the cost of holding one box for a year is 15 percent of the value of the material.
    a. The hospital orders bandages in lot sizes of 900 boxes. What *extra cost* does the hospital incur, which it could save by using the EOQ method?
    b. Demand is normally distributed, with a standard deviation of weekly demand of 100 boxes. The lead time is ½ week. What safety stock is necessary if the hospital uses a continuous review system and a 97 percent cycle-service level is desired? What should be the reorder point?
    c. If the hospital uses a periodic review system, with P = 2 weeks, what should be the target inventory level, T?

20. A golf specialty wholesaler operates 50 weeks per year. Management is trying to determine an inventory policy for its 1-irons, which have the following characteristics.

    Demand (D) = 1000 units/year

    Demand is normally distributed.

    Standard deviation of *weekly* demand = 3 units

    Ordering cost = $20/order

    Annual holding cost (H) = $2/unit

    Desired cycle-service level = 85%

    Lead time (L) = 3 weeks

    a. If the company uses a periodic review system, what should P and T be? Round P to the nearest week.
    b. If the company uses a continuous review system, what should R be?

21. Clone Computer Mart estimates the distribution of demand during the lead time for boxes of flexible diskettes to be as follows.

Demand	Probability
20	0.20
40	0.40
60	0.20
80	0.10
100	0.10
	1.00

a. If a continuous review system is used, what reorder point provides an 80 percent cycle-service level?
b. What would be the safety stock?

22. Club Hardware estimates the following demand during lead time distribution for crescent wrenches.

Demand	Probability
0	0.20
25	0.20
50	0.20
75	0.20
100	0.10
125	0.10
	1.00

a. What reorder point R would result in a 90 percent cycle-service level?
b. How much safety stock would be provided with this policy?

Advanced Problems

Problems 23–26 require prior reading of Supplement F, and Problem 27 requires prior reading of Supplement I. A computer package is required for solving Problem 27.

23. The Georgia Lighting Center stocks more than 3000 lighting fixtures, including chandeliers, swags, wall lamps, and track lights. The store sells at retail, operates 6 days per week, and advertises itself as the "brightest spot in town." One expensive fixture is selling at an average rate of 5 units per day. The reorder policy is $Q = 40$ and $R = 15$. A new order is placed on the day the reorder point is reached. The lead time is 3 business days. For example, an order placed on Monday will be delivered on Thursday. Simulate the performance of this Q system for the next 3 weeks (18 workdays). Any stockouts result in lost sales (rather than backorders). The beginning inventory is 19 units, and there are no scheduled receipts. Table 12.1 simulates the first week of operation. Extend Table 12.1 to simulate operations for the next 2 weeks, given that demand for the next 12 business days is 7, 4, 2, 7, 3, 6, 10, 0, 5, 10, 4, and 7.
    a. What is the average daily ending inventory over the 18 days?
    b. How many stockouts occurred?

24. Simulate Problem 23 again, but this time use a P system with $P = 8$ and $T = 55$. Let the first review occur on the first Monday. As before, the beginning inventory is 19 units, and there are no scheduled receipts.
    a. What is the average daily ending inventory over the 18 days?
    b. How many stockouts occurred?

25. In Solved Problem 3, a Q system for hand drills was devised, with $Q = 440$ and $R = 373$. Simulate this system for a 21-day period by completing and extending Table 12.2 (next page). The daily demand is drawn from a normal distribution with a mean of 100 and standard deviation of 30. The demand for the next 16 business days is 60, 94, 87, 102, 42, 123, 140, 85, 67, 83, 123, 108, 88, 120, 138, and 74. The on-hand inventory at the start of day 1 is 40 units, and one scheduled receipt of 440 units is to arrive on this first day. The lead time for new orders is 4 business days. If a new order is placed on the first workday (Monday), it will be available on the fifth workday (Friday).

TABLE 12.1   *First Week of Operation*

Workday	Beginning Inventory	Orders Received	Daily Demand	Ending Inventory	Inventory Position	Order Quantity
1. Monday	19	—	5	14	14	40
2. Tuesday	14	—	3	11	51	—
3. Wednesday	11	—	4	7	47	—
4. Thursday	7	40	1	46	46	—
5. Friday	46	—	10	36	36	—
6. Saturday	36	—	9	27	27	—

TABLE 12.2   *First Week of Operation*

Workday	Beginning Inventory	Orders Received	Daily Demand	Ending Inventory	Inventory Position	Order Quantity
1. Monday	40	440	143	337	337	474
2. Tuesday	337	—	82	255	729	—
3. Wednesday	255	—	103	152	626	—
4. Thursday	152	—	127	25	526	—
5. Friday	25	474	85	414	414	397

a. What is the average daily ending inventory over the 21 days?

b. How many new orders were placed?

26. In Solved Problem 4, a *P* system for hand drills was devised, with $P = 4$ days and $T = 811$. Simulate this system for a 21-day period, using the same random demands.

   a. What is the average ending inventory over the 21 days?

   b. How many new orders were placed?

27. A problem often of concern to managers in the process industry is blending. Consider the task facing Lisa Rankin, procurement manager of a company that manufactures special additives. She must determine the proper amount of each raw material to purchase for the production of a certain product. Each gallon of the finished product must have a combustion point of at least 220°F. In addition, the gamma content (which causes hydrocarbon pollution) cannot exceed 6 percent by volume, and the zeta content (which cleans the internal moving parts of engines) must be at least 12 percent by volume. The three raw materials available vary with respect to these characteristics as shown in the following table.

| | Raw Material | | |
Characteristic	A	B	C
Combustion point (°F)	200	180	280
Gamma content (%)	4	3	10
Zeta content (%)	20	10	8

Raw material A costs \$0.60 per gallon, whereas raw materials B and C cost \$0.40 and \$0.50 per gallon, respectively. Lisa Rankin wants to minimize the cost of raw materials per gallon of product. She asks you to use linear programming to find the optimal proportion of each raw material per gallon of finished product. *Hint:* Express your decision variables as fractions of a gallon. The sum of the fractions must equal 1.00.

C A S E

Parts Emporium

It is June 6, Sue McCaskey's first day in the newly created position of materials manager for Parts Emporium. A recent graduate of a prominent business school, McCaskey is eagerly awaiting her first real-world problem. At approximately 8:30 A.M. it arrives in the form of status reports on inventory and orders shipped. At the top of an extensive computer printout is a handwritten note from Joe Donnell, the purchasing manager:

Attached you will find the inventory and customer service performance data. Rest assured that the individual inventory levels are accurate because we took a complete physical inventory count at the end of last week. Unfortunately, we do not keep compiled records in some of the areas as you requested. However, you're welcome to do so yourself. Welcome aboard!

A little upset that aggregate information isn't available, McCaskey decides to randomly select a small sample of approximately 100 items and compile inventory and customer service characteristics to get a feel for the "total picture." The results of this experiment reveal to her why Parts Emporium decided to create the position she now fills. It seems that the inventory is in all the wrong places. Although there is an *average* of approximately 60 days of inventory, customer service is inadequate. Parts Emporium tries to backorder the customer orders not immediately filled from stock, but some 10 percent of demand is being lost to competing distributorships. Because stockouts are costly relative to inventory holding costs, McCaskey believes that a cycle-service level of at least 95 percent should be achieved.

Parts Emporium, Inc. was formed in 1967 as a wholesale distributor of automobile parts by two disenchanted auto mechanics, Dan Block and Ed Spriggs. Originally located in Block's garage, the firm showed slow but steady growth until 1970, when it relocated to an old, abandoned meat-packing warehouse on Chicago's South Side. With increased space for inventory storage, the company was able to begin offering an expanded line of auto parts. This increased selection, combined with the trend toward longer car ownership, led to an explosive growth of the business in the mid to late 1970s. By 1991, Parts Emporium was the largest independent distributor of auto parts in the North Central region.

In 1993, Parts Emporium relocated in a sparkling new office and warehouse complex off Interstate 55 in suburban Chicago. The warehouse space alone occupied more than 100,000 square feet. Although only a handful of new products have been added since the warehouse was constructed, its utilization has increased from 65 percent to more than 90 percent of capacity. During this same period, however, sales growth has stagnated. These conditions motivated Block and Spriggs to hire the first manager from outside the company in the firm's history.

Sue McCaskey knows that although her influence to initiate changes will be limited, she must produce positive results immediately. Thus she decides to concentrate on two products from the extensive product line: the EG151 exhaust gasket and the DB032 drive belt. If she can demonstrate significant gains from proper inventory management for just two products, perhaps Block and Spriggs will give her the backing needed to change the total inventory management system.

The EG151 exhaust gasket is purchased from an overseas supplier, Haipei, Inc. Actual demand for the first 21 weeks of 1994 is shown in the table below.

Week	Actual Demand	Week	Actual Demand
1	104	12	97
2	103	13	99
3	107	14	102
4	105	15	99
5	102	16	103
6	102	17	101
7	101	18	101
8	104	19	104
9	100	20	108
10	100	21	97
11	103		

A quick review of past orders, shown in another document, indicates that a lot size of 150 units is being used and that the lead time from Haipei is fairly constant at 2 weeks. Currently, at the end of week 21, no inventory is on hand; 11 units are backordered, and there is a scheduled receipt of 150 units.

The DB032 drive belt is purchased from the Bendox Corporation of Grand Rapids, Michigan. Actual demand so far in 1994 is listed below.

Week	Actual Demand	Week	Actual Demand
11	18	17	50
12	33	18	53
13	53	19	54
14	54	20	49
15	51	21	52
16	53		

Because this product is new, data are available only since its introduction in week 11. Currently, 324 units are on hand; there are no backorders and no scheduled receipts. A lot size of 1000 units is being used, with the lead time fairly constant at 3 weeks.

The wholesale prices that Parts Emporium charges its customers are $12.99 for the EG151 exhaust gasket and $8.89 for the DB032 drive belt. Because no quantity discounts are offered on these two highly profitable items, gross margins based on current purchasing practices are 32 percent of the wholesale price for the exhaust gasket and 48 percent of the wholesale price for the drive belt.

Parts Emporium estimates its cost to hold inventory at 21 percent of its inventory investment. This percentage recognizes the opportunity cost of tying money up in inventory and the variable costs of taxes, insurance, and shrinkage. The annual report notes other warehousing expenditures for utilities and maintenance and debt service on the 100,000 square foot warehouse, which was built for $1.5 million. However, McCaskey reasons that these warehousing costs can be ignored because they won't change for the range of inventory policies that she is considering.

Out-of-pocket costs for Parts Emporium to place an order with suppliers are estimated to be $20 per order for exhaust gaskets and $10 per order for drive belts. On the outbound side, there can be delivery charges. Although most customers pick up their parts at Parts Emporium, some orders are delivered to customers. To provide this service, Parts Emporium contracts with a local company for a flat fee of $21.40 per order, which is added to the customer's bill. McCaskey is unsure whether to increase the ordering costs for Parts Emporium to include delivery charges.

Questions

1. Put yourself in Sue McCaskey's position and prepare a detailed report to Dan Block and Ed Spriggs on managing the inventory of the EG151 exhaust gasket and the DB032 drive belt. Be sure to present a proper inventory system and recognize all relevant costs.

2. By how much do your recommendations for these two items reduce annual cycle inventory, stockout, and ordering costs?

Source: This case was provided by Professor Robert Bregman, University of Houston.

Selected References

Bragg, Daniel Jay. "The Impact of Inventory Record Inaccuracy on Material Requirements Planning Systems." Unpublished dissertation, Ohio State University, 1984.

Buffa, Elwood S., and Jeffrey G. Miller. *Production-Inventory Systems: Planning and Control,* 3rd ed. Homewood, Ill.: Richard D. Irwin, 1979.

"Factors That Make or Break Season Sales," *Wall Street Journal,* December 9, 1991.

Fogerty, Donald W., and Thomas R. Hoffman. *Production and Inventory Management.* Cincinnati: South-Western, 1983.

Greene, James H. *Production and Inventory Control Handbook.* New York: McGraw-Hill, 1970.

Johnson, Lynwood A., and Douglas C. Montgomery. *Operations Research in Production Planning, Scheduling and Inventory Control.* New York: John Wiley & Sons, 1979.

Love, Stephen F. *Inventory Control.* New York: McGraw-Hill, 1979.

Ronen, David. "Inventory Service Measures—A Comparison of Measures." *International Journal of Operations and Production Management,* vol. 3, no. 2 (1983), pp. 37–45.

Silver, Edward A. "Operations Research in Inventory Management: A Review and Critique." *Operations Research,* vol. 9, no. 4 (July–August 1981).

Silver, Edward A., and Rein Peterson. *Decision Systems for Inventory Management and Production Planning.* New York: John Wiley & Sons, 1985.

Special Inventory Models

Many real-world problems require relaxation of certain assumptions on which the EOQ model is based. This supplement addresses three realistic situations that require going beyond the simple EOQ formulation.

1. *Noninstantaneous replenishment.* Particularly in situations where manufacturers use a continuous process to make a primary material such as a liquid, gas, or powder, production is not instantaneous, and thus inventory is replenished gradually rather than in lots.
2. *Quantity discounts.* There are three relevant annual costs: the inventory holding cost, the fixed cost for ordering and setup, and the cost of materials. Both for service and for manufacturing organizations, the unit cost of purchased materials sometimes depends on the order quantity.
3. *One-period decisions.* Retailers often face a situation in which demand is uncertain and occurs during just one period or season.

◆ NONINSTANTANEOUS REPLENISHMENT

If an item is being produced internally rather than purchased, finished units may be used or sold as soon as they are completed, without waiting until a full lot has been completed. For example, a restaurant that bakes its own dinner rolls begins to use some of the rolls from the first pan even before the baker finishes a five-pan batch. The inventory of rolls never reaches the full five-pan level, the way it would if the rolls all arrived at once on a truck sent by an external supplier or a cart driven by an internal materials handler.

Figure H.1 on the next page depicts the usual case where the production rate, *p*, exceeds the demand rate, *d*.* Cycle inventory accumulates faster than demand occurs; that is, there is a buildup of *p* − *d* units during the time when both production and demand occur. For example, if the production rate is 100 units per day and the demand is 5 units per day, the buildup is 95 (or 100 − 5) units each day. This buildup continues until the lot size, *Q*, has been produced, after which the inventory depletes at a rate of 5 units per day. Just as the inventory reaches 0, the next production interval begins. To be consistent, both *p* and *d* must be expressed in units for the same time interval, such as units per day or units per week. Here, we assume that they are expressed in units per day.

---

* If they were equal, production would be continuous with no buildup of cycle inventory. If the production rate is lower than the demand rate, sales opportunities are being missed on an ongoing basis. We will assume *p* > *d* in this supplement.

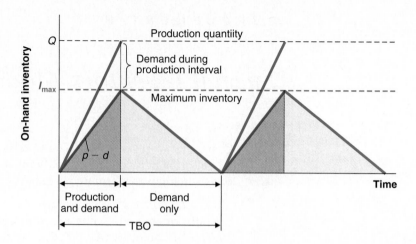

The $p - d$ buildup continues for Q/p days, because Q is the lot size and p units are produced each day. In our example, if the lot size is 300 units, the production interval is 3 days (300/100). Given the rate of buildup over the production interval, the maximum cycle inventory, I_{max}, is

$$I_{max} = \frac{Q}{p}(p - d) = Q\left(\frac{p - d}{p}\right)$$

Cycle inventory is no longer $Q/2$, as it was with the basic EOQ method (Chapter 12); instead it is $I_{max}/2$. Setting up the total cost equation for this production situation, where D is the annual demand, as before, and d is the daily demand, we get

Total cost = Annual holding cost + Annual ordering or setup cost

$$C = \frac{I_{max}}{2}(H) + \frac{D}{Q}(S) = \frac{Q}{2}\left(\frac{p - d}{p}\right)(H) + \frac{D}{Q}(S)$$

Based on this cost function, the optimal lot size, often called the **economic production lot size (ELS)**, is

$$ELS = \sqrt{\frac{2DS}{H}} \sqrt{\frac{p}{p - d}}$$

Because the second term is a ratio greater than 1, the ELS results in a larger lot size than the EOQ.

A plant manager of a chemical plant must decide the lot size for a particular chemical that has a steady demand of 30 barrels per day. The production rate is 190 barrels per day, annual demand is 10,500 barrels, setup cost is $200, annual holding cost is $0.21 per barrel, and the plant operates 350 days per year. Determine

    a. the economic production lot size (ELS).
    b. the total annual setup and inventory holding cost for this item.
    c. the TBO, or cycle length, for the ELS.
    d. the production time per lot.

Solution

a. Solving first for the ELS, we get

$$\text{ELS} = \sqrt{\frac{2DS}{H}} \sqrt{\frac{p}{p-d}} = \sqrt{\frac{2(10,500)(\$200)}{\$0.21}} \sqrt{\frac{190}{190-30}}$$

$$= 4873.4 \text{ barrels}$$

b. The annual total cost with the ELS is

$$C = \frac{Q}{2}\left(\frac{p-d}{p}\right)(H) + \frac{D}{Q}(S)$$

$$= \frac{4873.4}{2}\left(\frac{190-30}{190}\right)(\$0.21) + \frac{10,500}{4873.4}(\$200)$$

$$= \$430.91 + \$430.91 = \$861.82$$

c. Applying the TBO formula from Chapter 12 to the ELS, we get

$$\text{TBO}_{\text{ELS}} = \frac{\text{ELS}}{D}(350 \text{ days/year}) = \frac{4873.4}{10,500}(350)$$

$$= 162.4, \quad \text{or } 162 \text{ days}$$

d. The production time during each cycle is the lot size divided by the production rate:

$$\frac{\text{ELS}}{p} = \frac{4873.4}{190} = 25.6, \quad \text{or } 26 \text{ days}$$

◆ QUANTITY DISCOUNTS

In Chapter 11, we stated that quantity discounts, which are price incentives to purchase large quantities, create pressure to maintain a large inventory. For example, a supplier may offer a price of $4 per unit for orders between 1 and 99 units, a price of $3.50 per unit for orders between 100 and 199 units, and a price of $3.00 per unit for orders of more than 200 units. The item's price is no longer fixed, as assumed in the EOQ derivation; instead, if the order quantity is increased enough, the price is discounted. Hence a new approach is needed to find the best lot size—one that balances the advantages of lower prices for purchased materials and fewer orders (which are benefits of large order quantities) against the disadvantage of the increased cost of holding more inventory.

The total annual cost now includes not only the holding cost, $(Q/2)(H)$, and the ordering cost, $(D/Q)(S)$, but also the cost of purchased materials. For any per unit price level, P, the total cost is

$$\begin{array}{ccc} \text{Total} \\ \text{cost} \end{array} = \begin{array}{c} \text{Annual holding} \\ \text{cost} \end{array} + \begin{array}{c} \text{Annual ordering} \\ \text{cost} \end{array} + \begin{array}{c} \text{Annual cost} \\ \text{of materials} \end{array}$$

$$C = \frac{Q}{2}(H) + \frac{D}{Q}(S) + PD$$

The unit holding cost H usually is expressed as a percentage of the unit price because the more valuable the item held in inventory is, the higher the holding cost. Thus the lower the unit price, P, is, the lower H is. Conversely, the higher P is, the higher H is.

As when we calculated total cost in Chapter 12, the total cost equation yields U-shaped total cost curves. Adding the annual cost of materials to the total cost equation raises each total cost curve by a fixed amount, as shown in Fig. H.2(a). There are three cost curves—one for each price level. The top curve applies when no discounts are received; the lower curves reflect the discounted price levels. No single curve is relevant to all purchase quantities. The relevant, or *feasible*, total cost begins with the top curve, then drops down, curve by curve, at the price breaks. A *price break* is the minimum quantity needed to get a discount. In Fig. H.2, there are two price breaks: at $Q = 100$ and $Q = 200$. The result is a total cost curve, with steps at the price breaks.

Figure H.2(b) also shows three additional points—the minimum point on each curve, obtained with the EOQ formula at each price level. These EOQs do not necessarily produce the best lot size for two reasons.

1. The EOQ at a particular price level may not be feasible—the lot size may not lie in the range corresponding to its price. Figure H.2(b) illustrates two instances of an infeasible EOQ. First, the minimum point for the $3.00 curve appears to be about 175 units. However, the supplier's quantity discount schedule doesn't allow purchase of that small a quantity at the $3.00 unit price. Similarly, the EOQ for the $4.00 price level is greater than the first price break, so the price charged would be only $3.50.

2. The EOQ at a particular price level may be feasible but may not be the best lot size—the feasible EOQ may have a *higher* cost than is achieved by the EOQ or price break quantity on a *lower* price curve. In Fig. H.2(b), for example, the 200-unit price break quantity for the $3.00 price level has a lower total cost than the feasible EOQ for the $3.50 price level. A feasible EOQ always is better

FIGURE H.2

Total Cost Curves with Quantity Discounts

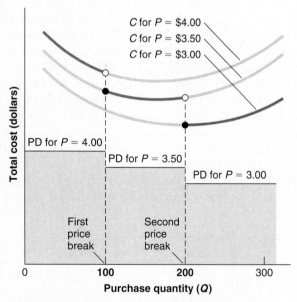

(a) Total cost curves with purchased materials added

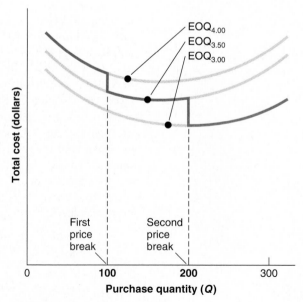

(b) EOQs and price break quantities

than any feasible point on cost curves with higher price levels, but not necessarily those with lower levels. Thus the only time we can immediately conclude, without comparing total costs, that a feasible EOQ is the best order quantity is when it is on the curve for the *lowest* price level. This conclusion isn't possible in Fig. H.2(b), because the only feasible EOQ is at the middle price level, $P = \$3.50$.

We must therefore pay attention only to feasible price–quantity combinations, shown as solid lines in Fig. H.2(b), as we search for the best lot size. The following two-step procedure may be used to find the best lot size.

Step 1. Beginning with the *lowest* price, calculate the EOQ for each price level until a feasible EOQ is found. It is feasible if it lies in the range corresponding to its price. Each subsequent EOQ is smaller than the previous one, because P, and thus H, gets larger and because the larger H is in the denominator of the EOQ formula.

Step 2. If the first feasible EOQ found is for the *lowest* price level, this quantity is the best lot size. Otherwise, calculate the total cost for the first feasible EOQ and for the larger price break quantity at each *lower* price level. The quantity with the lowest total cost is optimal.

EXAMPLE H.2

Finding Q with Quantity Discounts at LFKHS

A supplier for Lower Florida Keys Health System has introduced quantity discounts to encourage larger order quantities of a special catheter. The price schedule is

Order Quantity	Price per Unit
0–299	$60.00
300–499	$58.80
500 or more	$57.00

LFKHS estimates that its annual demand for this item is 936 units, its ordering cost is $45 per order, and its annual holding cost is 25 percent of the catheter's per unit price. What quantity of this catheter should the hospital order to minimize total costs?

Solution

Step 1. Find the first feasible EOQ, starting with the lowest price level:

$$\text{EOQ}_{57.00} = \sqrt{\frac{2DS}{H}} = \sqrt{\frac{2(936)(45)}{0.25(57.00)}}$$

$$= 77 \text{ units}$$

A 77-unit order actually costs $60 per unit, instead of the $57 per unit used in the EOQ calculation, so this EOQ is infeasible. Now try the $58.80 level:

$$\text{EOQ}_{58.80} = \sqrt{\frac{2DS}{H}} = \sqrt{\frac{2(936)(45)}{0.25(58.80)}}$$

$$= 76 \text{ units}$$

This quantity also is infeasible because a 76-unit order is too small to qualify for the $58.80 price. Try the highest price level:

$$EOQ_{60.00} = \sqrt{\frac{2DS}{H}} = \sqrt{\frac{2(936)(45)}{0.25(60.00)}} = 75 \text{ units}$$

This quantity is feasible, because it lies in the range corresponding to its price, $P = \$60.00$.

Step 2.   The first feasible EOQ of 75 doesn't correspond to the lowest price level. Hence we must compare its total cost with the price break quantities (300 units and 500 units) at the *lower* price levels ($58.80 and $57.00):

$$C = \frac{Q}{2}(H) + \frac{D}{Q}(S) + PD$$

$$C_{75} = \frac{75}{2}[(0.25)(\$60.00)] + \frac{936}{75}(\$45) + \$60.00(936) = \$57,284$$

$$C_{300} = \frac{300}{2}[(0.25)(\$58.80)] + \frac{936}{300}(\$45) + \$58.80(936) = \$57,382$$

$$C_{500} = \frac{500}{2}[(0.25)(\$57.00)] + \frac{936}{500}(\$45) + \$57.00(936) = \$56,999$$

The best purchase quantity is 500 units, which qualifies for the deepest discount. However, the solution doesn't always work out this way. When discounts are small, holding cost H is large, and demand D is small, small lot sizes are better even though price discounts are forgone.

Following is the computer output for this problem. It begins with a display of the input parameters, for the user to check for input accuracy. Then the output shows the optimal order quantity to be 500 units. The total costs for the first feasible EOQ and for larger price break quantities of the curves with lower price levels are shown. The best order quantity is the price break quantity for the curve with the lowest price (labeled the DC2 price level).

```
                 CMOM - Quantity Discount


                     Data Entered


     Demand                                      : 936

        Cost per Order                           : 45

     Holding Cost per Unit (% of unit price)   : 25

        Lead Time (% of period)                  : 0

     Base Unit Price                             : 60

        Number of Discount Categories            : 2

              Minimum Order      Discount (%)
     DC1          300                 2
     DC2          500                 5
```

```
                            Solution
          Optimal Order Quantity : 500

          Reorder Point           : 0

          Maximum Inventory       : 500

          Ordering Costs          : 84.2400

          Holding Costs           : 3562.4995

          Total Inventory Costs   : 3646.7383
```

Category	Item Cost	Order Quantity	Inventory Cost	Ordering Cost	Purchase Cost	Total Cost
DC0	60.00	74.94	562.05	562.05	56160.00	57284.10
DC1	58.80	300	2205.00	140.40	55036.80	57382.20
DC2	57.00	500	3562.50	84.24	53352.00	56998.74

◆ ONE-PERIOD DECISIONS

One of the dilemmas facing many retailers is how to handle seasonal goods such as winter coats. Often they can't be sold at full markup next year because of changes in styles. Furthermore, the lead time can be longer than the selling season, allowing no second chance to rush through another order to cover unexpectedly high demand.

This type of situation is often called the *newsboy problem.* If the newspaper seller doesn't buy enough papers to resell on the street corner, sales opportunities are lost. If the seller buys too many, the overage cannot be sold because nobody wants yesterday's newspaper.

The following process is a straightforward way to analyze such problems and decide on the best order quantity.

1. List the different levels of demand that are possible, along with the estimated probability of each. The discrete probability distribution that results is much like the one discussed in Chapter 12 for demand during lead time. The only difference is that demand now is the demand for the entire period or season.

2. Develop a *payoff table* (see Supplement A) that shows the profit for each purchase quantity, Q, at each assumed demand level, D. Each row in the table represents a different order quantity, and each column represents a different demand level. The payoff for a given quantity–demand combination depends on whether all units are sold at the regular profit margin during the regular season. There are two possible cases.

   a. If demand is high enough ($Q \leq D$) that all units are sold at the full profit margin, p, during the regular season,

   $$\text{Payoff} = (\text{Profit per unit})(\text{Purchase quantity})$$

   $$= pQ$$

   b. If the purchase quantity exceeds the eventual demand ($Q > D$), only
      D units are sold at the full profit margin, and the remaining units
      purchased must be disposed of at a loss, l, after the season. In this
      case,

$$\text{Payoff} = \left(\begin{array}{c} \text{Profit per unit sold} \\ \text{during season} \end{array} \right)(\text{Demand}) - \left(\begin{array}{c} \text{Loss per} \\ \text{unit} \end{array} \right)\left(\begin{array}{c} \text{Amount disposed of} \\ \text{after season} \end{array} \right)$$

$$= pD - l(Q - D)$$

3. Calculate the expected payoff for each Q (or row in the payoff table) by
   using the *expected value* decision rule described in Supplement A. For a
   specific Q, first multiply each payoff in the row by the demand probability associated with the payoff and then add these products.
4. Choose the order quantity Q with the highest expected payoff.

Using this decision process for all such items over many selling seasons will maximize profits. However, it is not foolproof, and it can result in an occasional bad
outcome.

EXAMPLE H.3

*Finding Q for One-
Time Inventory
Decisions*

One of many items sold at a museum of natural history is a Christmas ornament
carved from wood. The gift shop makes a $10 profit per unit sold during the sea-
son, but it takes a $5 loss per unit after the season is over. The following discrete
probability distribution for the season's demand has been identified.

Demand	10	20	30	40	50
Demand Probability	0.2	0.3	0.3	0.1	0.1

How many ornaments should the museum's buyer order?

Solution   Each demand level is a candidate for best order quantity, so the payoff
table should have five rows. For the first row, where $Q = 10$, demand is at least
as great as the purchase quantity. Thus all five payoffs in this row are

$$\text{Payoff} = pQ = (\$10)(10) = \$100$$

This formula can be used in other rows but only for those quantity–demand
combinations where all units are sold during the season. These combinations lie
in the upper right portion of the table, where $Q \leq D$. For example, the payoff
when $Q = 40$ and $D = 50$ is

$$\text{Payoff} = pQ = (\$10)(40) = \$400$$

The payoffs in the lower left portion of the table represent quantity–demand
combinations where some units must be disposed of after the season ($Q > D$).
For this case, the payoff must be calculated with the second formula. For example, when $Q = 40$ and $D = 30$,

$$\text{Payoff} = pD - l(Q - D) = (\$10)(30) - (\$5)(40 - 30) = \$250$$

Using this process, we obtain the following payoff table.

			D		
Q	**10**	**20**	**30**	**40**	**50**
10	$100	$100	$100	$100	$100
20	50	200	200	200	200
30	0	150	300	300	300
40	−50	100	250	400	400
50	−100	50	200	350	500

Now we calculate the expected payoff for each Q by multiplying the payoff for each demand quantity by the probability of that demand and then adding the results. For example, for $Q = 30$,

Payoff $= 0.2(\$0) + 0.3(\$150) + 0.3(\$300) + 0.1(\$300) + 0.1(\$300) = \$195$

Making these calculations for each row in the payoff table, we get

Order Quantity, *Q*	Expected Payoff
10	$100
20	170
30	195
40	175
50	140

Because $Q = 30$ has the highest payoff at $195, it is the best order quantity.

The need for one-time inventory decisions also can arise in manufacturing plants when (1) customized items (specials) are made (or purchased) to a single order *and* (2) scrap quantities are high.* A special item produced for a single order is never intentionally held in stock because the demand for it is too unpredictable. In fact, it may never be ordered again, so the manufacturer would like to make just the amount requested by the customer—no more, no less. The manufacturer also would like to satisfy an order in just one run to avoid an extra setup and a delay in delivering goods ordered. These two goals may conflict if the likelihood of some units being scrapped is high. Suppose that a customer places an order for 20 units. If the manager orders 20 units from the shop or from the supplier, one or two units may have to be scrapped. This shortage will force the manager to place a second (or even third) order to replace the defective units. Replacement can be costly if setup time is high and can also delay shipment to the customer. To avoid such problems, the manager could order more than 20 units the first time. If some units are left over, the customer might be willing to buy the extras or the manager might find an internal use for them. For example, some manufacturing companies set up a special account for obsolete materials. These materials can be "bought" by departments within the company at less than their normal cost, as an incentive to use them.

* The intent of TQM is to eliminate scrap. If successful, TQM makes this discussion moot.

SUPPLEMENT REVIEW

Solved Problem 1

Peachy Keen, Inc. makes mohair sweaters, blouses with Peter Pan collars, pedal pushers, poodle skirts, and other popular clothing styles of the 1950s. The average demand for mohair sweaters is 100 per week. Peachy's production facility has the capacity to sew 400 sweaters per week. Setup cost is $351. The value of finished goods inventory is $40 per sweater. The annual per unit inventory holding cost is 20 percent of the item's value.

a. What is the economic production lot size (ELS)?
b. What is the average time between orders (TBO)?
c. What is the total of the annual holding costs and setup costs?

Solution   a. The production lot size that minimizes total costs is

$$\text{ELS} = \sqrt{\frac{2DS}{H}} \sqrt{\frac{p}{p-d}} = \sqrt{\frac{2(100 \times 52)(\$351)}{0.20(\$40)}} \sqrt{\frac{400}{(400-100)}}$$

$$= \sqrt{456,300} \sqrt{\frac{4}{3}} = 780 \text{ sweaters}$$

b. The average time between orders is

$$\text{TBO} = \frac{\text{ELS}}{D} = \frac{780}{5200} = 0.15 \text{ year}$$

Converting to weeks, we get

$$\text{TBO} = (0.15 \text{ year})(52 \text{ weeks/year}) = 7.8 \text{ weeks}$$

c. The minimum total of ordering and holding costs is

$$C = \frac{Q}{2}\left(\frac{p-d}{p}\right)(H) + \frac{D}{Q}(S) = \frac{780}{2}\left(\frac{400-100}{400}\right)0.20 \times \$40 + \frac{5200}{780}(\$351)$$

$$= \$2340/\text{year} + \$2340/\text{year} = \$4680/\text{year}$$

Solved Problem 2

A hospital buys disposable surgical packages from Pfisher, Inc. Pfisher's price schedule is $50.25 per package on orders of 1 to 199 packages, and $49.00 per package on orders of 200 or more packages. Ordering cost is $64 per order, and annual holding cost is 20 percent of the per unit purchase price. Annual demand is 490 packages. What is the best purchase quantity?

Solution   We first calculate the EOQ at the *lowest* price:

$$\text{EOQ}_{\$49.00} = \sqrt{\frac{2DS}{H}} = \sqrt{\frac{2(490)(\$64)}{0.20(\$49.00)}} = \sqrt{6400} = 80 \text{ packages}$$

This solution is infeasible because, according to the price schedule, we can't purchase 80 packages at a price of $49 each. Therefore we calculate the EOQ at the next lowest price ($50.25):

$$\text{EOQ}_{\$50.25} = \sqrt{\frac{2DS}{H}} = \sqrt{\frac{2(490)(\$64)}{0.20(\$50.25)}} = \sqrt{6241} = 79 \text{ packages}$$

This EOQ is feasible, but $50.25 per package isn't the lowest price. Hence we have to determine whether total costs can be reduced by purchasing 200 units and thereby obtaining a quantity discount.

$$C = \frac{Q}{2}(H) + \frac{D}{Q}(S) + PD$$

$$C_{79} = \frac{79}{2}(0.20 \times \$50.25) + \frac{490}{79}(\$64) + \$50.25(490)$$

$$= \$396.98/\text{year} + \$396.96/\text{year} + \$24,622.50/\text{year} = \$25,416.44/\text{year}$$

$$C_{200} = \frac{200}{2}(0.20 \times \$49) + \frac{490}{200}(\$64) + \$49(490)$$

$$= \$980/\text{year} + \$156.80/\text{year} + \$24,010/\text{year} = \$25,146.80/\text{year}$$

Purchasing 200 units per order will save about \$270/year, compared to buying 79 units at a time.

Solved Problem 3

Swell Productions is sponsoring an outdoor conclave for owners of collectible and classic Fords. The concession stand in the T-Bird area will sell T-shirts, poodle skirts, and other souvenirs of the 1950s. Poodle skirts are purchased from Peachy Keen, Inc. for \$40 each and are sold during the event for \$75 each. If any skirts are left over, they can be returned to Peachy for a refund of \$30 each. Poodle skirt sales depend on the weather, attendance, and other variables. The following table shows the probability of various sales quantities. How many poodle skirts should Swell order from Peachy Keen for this one-time event?

Sales Quantity	Probability	Sales Quantity	Probability
100	0.05	400	0.34
200	0.11	500	0.11
300	0.34	600	0.05

Solution Table H.1 is the payoff table that describes this one-period inventory decision. The upper right portion of the table shows the payoffs when the demand, D, is greater than or equal to the order quantity, Q. The payoff is equal to the per unit profit (the difference between price and cost) multiplied by the order quantity. For example, when the order quantity is 100 and the demand is 200,

$$\text{Payoff} = (p - c)Q = (\$75 - \$40)100 = \$3500$$

TABLE H.1 *Payoffs*

			Demand, D				Expected Payoff
Q	100	200	300	400	500	600	
100	\$3,500	\$3,500	\$ 3,500	\$ 3,500	\$ 3,500	\$ 3,500	\$ 3,500
200	\$2,500	\$7,000	\$ 7,000	\$ 7,000	\$ 7,000	\$ 7,000	\$ 6,775
300	\$1,500	\$6,000	\$10,500	\$10,500	\$10,500	\$10,500	\$ 9,555
400	\$500	\$5,000	\$ 9,500	\$14,000	\$14,000	\$14,000	\$10,805
500	(\$500)	\$4,000	\$ 8,500	\$13,000	\$17,500	\$17,500	\$10,525
600	(\$1,500)	\$3,000	\$ 7,500	\$12,000	\$16,500	\$21,000	\$ 9,750
Probability	0.05	0.11	0.34	0.34	0.11	0.05	

The lower left portion of the table shows the payoffs when the order quantity exceeds the demand. Here, the payoff is the profit from sales, pD, minus the loss associated with returning overstock, $l(Q - D)$, where l is the difference between the cost and the amount refunded for each poodle skirt returned and $Q - D$ is the number of skirts returned. For example, when the order quantity is 500 and the demand is 200,

$$\text{Payoff} = pD - l(Q - D) = (\$75 - \$40)200 - (\$40 - \$30)(500 - 200) = \$4000$$

The highest expected payoff occurs when 400 poodle skirts are ordered:

$$\text{Expected payoff}_{400} = (\$500 \times 0.05) + (\$5,000 \times 0.11) + (\$9,500 \times 0.34)$$
$$+ (\$14,000 \times 0.34) + (\$14,000 \times 0.11) + (\$14,000 \times 0.05)$$
$$= \$10,805$$

Formula Review

Noninstantaneous Replenishment

1. Economic production lot size: $\text{ELS} = \sqrt{\dfrac{2DS}{H}} \sqrt{\dfrac{p}{p - d}}$

2. Maximum inventory: $(I_{\max}) = Q\left(\dfrac{p - d}{p}\right)$

3. Total cost = Annual holding cost + Annual setup cost

$$C = \frac{Q}{2}\left(\frac{p - d}{p}\right)(H) + \frac{D}{Q}(S)$$

4. Time between orders, in years: $\text{TBO}_{\text{ELS}} = \dfrac{\text{ELS}}{D}$

Quantity Discounts

5. Total cost = Annual holding cost + Annual setup cost + Annual cost of material

$$C = \frac{Q}{2}(H) + \frac{D}{Q}(S) + PD$$

One-Period Decisions

6. Payoff matrix: $\text{Payoff} = \begin{cases} pQ & \text{if } Q \leq D \\ pD - l(Q - D) & \text{if } Q > D \end{cases}$

Supplement Highlights

- When inventory items are made instead of bought, inventory is replenished gradually over some production period. This condition is called noninstantaneous replenishment. The amount of inventory accumulated during the production period is reduced by concurrent sales. Hence the maximum amount in inventory will be less than the production lot size. The economic lot size is a balance between annual holding and annual ordering costs. Sales during the production period have the effect of lowering the average inventory and annual holding costs, so balance is restored by increasing the size of each order. Larger orders reduce the number of orders placed during a year.

- When quantity discounts are available, the total relevant cost includes annual holding, ordering, and materials costs. Purchasing larger quantities to achieve price discounts reduces annual ordering and materials costs but usually increases annual holding costs. The order quantity is based on minimizing the total of relevant costs per year, instead of obtaining the minimum purchase price per unit.

- Retailers, as well as manufacturers of customized products, often face one-time inventory decisions. Demand uncertainty can lead to ordering too much or too little,

which can result in cost or customer-service penalties. A straightforward approach to one-time inventory decisions is to calculate the expected payoff over a range of reasonable alternatives and choose the one with the best expected payoff.

Key Term

economic production lot size (ELS)
  574

Study Questions

1. In noninstantaneous replenishment, what is the effect on order quantity as the demand rate increases to approach the production rate?
2. In noninstantaneous replenishment, the cycle inventory no longer is $Q/2$ but instead is $I_{max}/2$. What is the maximum amount of inventory in the instantaneous replenishment model?
3. What conditions can lead to the *simultaneous* reduction of all three elements of the total relevant costs (annual holding cost, annual ordering cost, and annual cost of materials)?
4. An important performance measure for the purchasing department in the Big Six Corporation is purchase price variance. As a reward for obtaining materials at

a lower price per unit, thereby generating favorable purchase price variance, buyers receive bonuses or increases in base pay. Predict the effect of this performance measure on inventory levels, total costs, quality, and the ability of Big Six to compete in the marketplace.

5. Which of the items in a campus bookstore are candidates for one-period inventory decisions? Find an example of an inventory item at a football game or basketball game that does *not* require a one-period inventory decision. What are the characteristics of that item in terms of its demand, price, risk of obsolescence, or storage cost that make it different from the others?

Problems

1. Big Purple, Inc. makes laser printer and photocopier toner cartridges. The demand rate is 625 EP cartridges per week. The production rate is 1736 EP cartridges per week, and the setup cost is $150. The value of inventory is $130 per unit, and the holding cost is 30 percent of the inventory value. What is the economic production lot size?
2. Hudson makes several models of computer monitors. Hudson's fastest 21-inch color monitor is named the Lizard. The demand rate is 3000 Lizards per month, and the production rate is 23,275 Lizards per month. The setup cost is $8000, the value of inventory is $1200 per unit, and the annual holding cost is 25 percent of the inventory value. What is the economic production lot size?
3. Suds's Bottling Company does bottling, labeling, and distribution work for several local microbreweries. The demand rate for Wortman's beer is 400 cases (24 bottles each) per week. Suds's bottling production rate is 2000 cases per week, and the setup cost is $1000.

The value of inventory is $10.40 per case, and the annual holding cost is 45 percent of the inventory value. What is the economic production lot size?

4. The Bucks Grande major league baseball team breaks an average of 4 bats per week. The team orders baseball bats from Corky's, a bat manufacturer noted for its access to the finest hardwood. The order cost is $70, and the annual holding cost per bat per year is 38 percent of the purchase price. Corky's price structure is

Order Quantity	Price per Unit
0–11	$54.00
12–143	$51.00
144 or more	$48.50

a. How many bats should the team buy per order?
b. What are the total annual costs associated with the best order quantity?

c. Corky discovers that, owing to special manufacturing processes required for the Bucks' bats, it has underestimated setup costs. Rather than raise prices, Corky adds another category to the price structure to provide an incentive for larger orders and reduce the number of setups required. If the Bucks buy 180 bats or more, the price will drop to $45 each. Should the Bucks revise the order quantity to 180 bats?

5. To boost sales, Pfisher (refer to Solved Problem 2) announces a new price structure for disposable surgical packages. Although the price break no longer is available at 200 units, Pfisher now offers an even greater discount if larger quantities are purchased. On orders of 1 to 499 packages, the price is $50.25 per package. For orders of 500 or more, the price per unit is $47.80. Ordering costs, annual holding costs, and annual demand remain at $64 per order, 20 percent of the per unit cost, and 490 packages per year, respectively. What is the new lot size?

6. A plumbing supply company received the following price schedule for a popular valve.

Order Quantity	Price per Valve
0–199	$1.60
200–399	$1.40
400 or more	$1.20

Annual demand is estimated at 6000 valves, and each order costs $10. If annual holding cost is 20 percent of the per unit purchase price, what is the best purchase quantity?

7. Mac-in-the-Box, Inc. sells computer equipment by mail and telephone order. Mac sells 1200 flat-bed scanners per year. Ordering cost is $400, and annual holding cost is 16 percent of the item's cost. The scanner manufacturer offers the following price structure to Mac-in-the-Box.

Order Quantity	Price per Unit
0–11	$610.00
12–143	$600.00
144 or more	$594.00

What order quantity minimizes total annual costs?

8. As inventory manager you must decide on the order quantity for an item that has an annual demand of 2000 units. Placing an order costs you $20 each time. Your annual holding cost, expressed as a percentage of average inventory value, is 20 percent. Your supplier has provided the following price schedule.

Minimum Order Quantity	Price per Unit
1	$2.50
200	$2.40
300	$2.25
1000	$2.00

What ordering policy do you recommend?

9. Matt Herron is the chief buyer at Investment Clothiers, a retail store known for excellence in apparel. It is time to order merchandise for the Christmas season. During a recent trip to Hong Kong, he spotted a particular men's overcoat that should sell quite well. Based on past experience, Herron expects demand to range from 100 to 400 coats. He estimates the probability distribution as follows.

Season's Demand	Probability
100	0.10
200	0.40
300	0.40
400	0.10
	1.00

The total cost to Investment Clothiers would be $50 per coat, and the retail price would be set at $90. Any coats left over after Christmas would be sold at $40 each. How many coats should Herron buy if he wants to maximize expected profits?

10. Kay's pastries are freshly baked and sold at several specialty shops throughout New York. When they are a day old, they must be sold at reduced prices. Daily demand is distributed as follows.

Demand	Probability
100	0.30
200	0.40
300	0.30

Each pastry sells for $1.00 and costs $0.60 to make. Each one not sold at the end of the day can be sold the next day for $0.30 as day-old merchandise. How many pastries should be baked each day?

11. The Aggies will host Tech in this year's homecoming football game. Based on advance ticket sales, the athletic department has forecast hot dog sales as shown in the following table. The school buys premium hot dogs for $1.25 and sells them during the game at

$3.00 each. Hot dogs left over after the game will be sold for $0.50 each to the Aggie student cafeteria to be used in making beanie weenie casserole.

Sales Quantity	Probability
2000	0.15
3000	0.30
4000	0.25
5000	0.20
6000	0.10

Use a payoff matrix to determine the number of hot dogs to prepare for the game.

12. The Akaga Corporation distributes robotics throughout Japan. The marketing manager estimates the demand for the next year at 60,000 units, with a standard deviation of 12,000 units. The base price for a robotic system is US$7500, and the cost of placing an order, including engineering, is US$2000. The estimated holding cost is 15 percent of the base price per unit per year. Management wants to maintain a cycle-service level of 95 percent (i.e., a stockout probability of 5 percent). The delivery lead time is 1 month. The supply vendor offers the following price discount schedule.

Minimum Order	Discount
5,000	1%
10,000	2%
30,000	3%

a. What optimal order quantity and reorder point minimize total costs?
b. What are the total inventory costs and safety stock level for the optimal policy?
c. Should the company take advantage of the price discount plan? If so, at what level?
d. What proportion of total costs are inventory costs with the optimal policy?
e. What is the impact on the optimal policy if the stockout probability is increased to 10 percent?

Selected References

Buffa, Elwood S., and Jeffrey G. Miller. *Production-Inventory Systems: Planning and Control,* 3rd ed. Homewood, Ill.: Richard D. Irwin, 1979.

"Factors That Make or Break Season Sales," *Wall Street Journal,* December 9, 1991.

Fogerty, Donald W., and Thomas R. Hoffman. *Production and Inventory Management.* Cincinnati: South-Western, 1983.

Johnson, Lynwood A., and Douglas C. Montgomery. *Operations Research in Production Planning, Scheduling and Inventory Control.* New York: John Wiley & Sons, 1979.

Love, Stephen F. *Inventory Control.* New York: McGraw-Hill, 1979.

Silver, Edward A., and Rein Peterson. *Decision Systems for Inventory Management and Production Planning.* New York: John Wiley & Sons, 1985.

Chapter Thirteen

AGGREGATE PLANNING

Whirlpool Corporation is a leading producer of room air conditioners. The demand for window units is highly seasonal and also depends on variations in the weather. Typically, Whirlpool begins production of room air conditioners in the fall and holds them as anticipation inventory until they are shipped in the spring. Building anticipation inventory in the slack season allows the company to level production rates over much of the year and yet satisfy demand in the peak periods (spring and summer) when retailers are placing most of their orders. However, when summers are hotter than usual, demand increases dramatically and stockouts can occur. If Whirlpool increases output and the summer is hot, it stands to increase its sales and market share. But if the summer is cool, the company is stuck with expensive inventories of unsold machines. Whirlpool prefers to make its production plans based on the average year, taking into account industry forecasts for total sales and traditional seasonalities.

Whirlpool Corporation's La Vergne, Tennessee manufacturing division produces air conditioners, which are subject to heavy seasonal demand.

Whirlpool, like many other companies, experiences seasonal shifts in demand for its products. Its strategy, called an **aggregate plan,** is a statement of its production rates, work-force levels, and inventory holdings based on estimates of customer requirements and capacity limitations. This statement is time-phased, meaning that the plan is projected for several time periods (such as months) into the future.

A manufacturing firm's aggregate plan, called a **production plan,** generally focuses on production rates and inventory holdings, whereas a service firm's aggregate plan, called a **staffing plan,** centers on staffing and other labor-related factors. For both types of company, the plan must balance conflicting objectives involving customer service, work-force stability, cost, and profit.

Based on the broad, long-term goals of a company, the aggregate plan specifies how the company will work for the next year or so toward those goals within existing equipment and facility capacity constraints. From these medium-range plans, managers prepare detailed operating plans. For manufacturing companies the aggregate plan links strategic goals and objectives with production plans for individual products and the specific components that go into them. In this chapter and Chapters 14 and 15, we demonstrate how this is done. For service firms the aggregate plan links strategic goals with detailed work-force schedules. We discuss this linkage in Chapter 16.

◆   THE PURPOSE OF AGGREGATE PLANS

In this section we explain why companies need aggregate plans and how they use them to take a macro, or big picture, view of their business. We also discuss how the aggregate plan relates to a company's long-term and short-term plans.

Aggregation

What items should be aggregated?

The aggregate plan is useful because it focuses on a general course of action, consistent with the company's strategic goals and objectives, without getting bogged down in details. For example, it allows Whirlpool's managers to determine whether they can satisfy budgetary goals without having to schedule each of the company's thousands of products and employees. Even if a planner could prepare such a detailed plan, the time and effort required to update it would make it uneconomical. For this reason, production and staffing plans are prepared by grouping together, or aggregating, similar products, services, units of labor, or units of time. For instance, a manufacturer of bicycles that produces 12 different models of bikes might divide them into two groups, mountain bikes and road bikes, for the purpose of preparing the aggregate plan. It might also consider its work-force needs in terms of units of labor needed per month. In general, companies aggregate products or services, labor, and time. Managerial Practice 13.1 shows some aggregate planning problems encountered in the auto industry and in package delivery services.

Product Families.   Recall that a group of products or services that have similar demand requirements and common processing, labor, and materials requirements is called a product family (see Chapter 10). Sometimes, product families relate to market groupings or, in the case of production plans, to specific manufacturing processes. A firm can aggregate its products or services into a set of relatively broad families, avoiding too much detail at this stage of the planning process. Common and relevant measurements, such as units, dollars, standard hours, gallons, or pounds, should be used. For example, consider the bicycle manufacturer that has aggregated all products into two families: mountain bikes and road bikes. This facilitates production planning for the assembly lines in the plant. A firm that specializes in quick oil changes might aggregate the services it offers into two categories: the basic service and special services.

Labor.   A company can aggregate labor in various ways, depending on work-force flexibility. For example, if workers at the bicycle manufacturer are trained to work on either mountain bikes or road bikes, for planning purposes management can consider its work force to be a single aggregate group, even though the skills of individual workers may differ.

Alternatively, management can aggregate labor along product family lines by splitting the work force into subgroups and assigning a different group to the production of each product family. Automobile manufacturers, such as Chrysler, use this approach, devoting production lines and even entire plants to separate product families. In service operations, such as a city government, workers are aggregated by the type of service they provide: fire fighters, police officers, sanitation workers, and administrators.

Managerial Practice 13.1

▷ *Typical Aggregate Planning Problems*

Automobile Industry

The peak demands for cars and trucks in 1994 created a problem for the Big Three automakers. With United Automobile Workers (UAW) wages ranging from $18 to $44 an hour, including benefits, achieving high productivity per labor hour was essential. The automakers thus were reluctant to hire more workers, fearing the pension and health care costs they would have to cover during the inevitable downturn. They also wanted to protect productivity gains made over the past decade, when they shrank their payrolls while sales increased. Part of their response was to hire temporary employees in the summer of 1994. However, they made up most of the shortfall by operating at record levels of overtime. Even this amount of overtime production fell short, costing the Big Three up to 200,000 vehicles of sales in 1994.

General Motors faced a particular dilemma in 1994, being pressed by investors to reduce its hourly work force and bring its productivity into line with Ford's. Its overtime rose at Buick City in Flint, Michigan, to the point where workers were averaging 17 hours of overtime a week. Although the UAW had mostly cooperated with automakers' efforts to shrink payrolls and improve productivity, it contended that its members were being worked too hard and couldn't sustain the overtime work pace. More than 11,000 workers went on strike. GM settled quickly because of the boom market and the effect the Flint shutdown would have on other GM plants; the company hired nearly 1000 new workers.

The industry's highest cost producer had to slow its drive to reduce costs because the strike had already cost GM the production of about 10,000 vehicles.

Delivery Services

United Parcel Service hires a large number of employees for its package-sorting hub. The work is hard and routine, and the hours are long. The high level of productivity demanded by UPS occasionally generates complaints from Teamsters Union members. When faced with the

Automated scanning equipment helps UPS sort 1.1 million air-delivery documents daily, relying primarily on full-time employees.

alternatives of hiring full-time or part-time employees, UPS managers prefer full-time employees so that they can train them and, by means of thoroughly researched process and job designs, instill a strong sense of teamwork and job satisfaction. Although the work is demanding, UPS typically has many more applications than openings when it recruits employees.

Federal Express also requires large numbers of employees for its package-sorting facilities. Its managers, however, prefer part-time employees. To enable next-day delivery, FedEx's facilities are designed and staffed to sort more than a million pieces of freight and express mail in only four hours during the middle of the night. A full complement of full-time employees couldn't be effectively utilized all day long, whereas part-time employees, with high energy levels, can be used to meet daily peak demands. College students are a good source of labor for these sorting facilities.

Sources: "Auto Workers Pushed to the Limit," *New York Times*, September 24, 1994; "GM, in a Switch, Agrees to Hire New Workers," *Wall Street Journal*, October 3, 1994; James Heskett, W. Earl Sasser, Jr., and Christopher Hart, *Service Breakthroughs: Changing the Rules of the Game* (New York: Free Press, 1990), pp. 197–198.

Companies that aggregate labor along product lines must plan for changes in economic conditions and consumer demand that may cause cutbacks in production of some product families and increases in production of others. When such shifts occur, labor may not be interchangeable. For example, in automobile assembly, production of different product families takes place in scattered locations. In such cases, planning for changes in work-force levels and the use of overtime by aggregating labor around product families is the most practical approach.

Time.   A **planning horizon** is the length of time covered by an aggregate plan. Typically, the planning horizon is one year, although it can differ in various situations. To avoid the expense and disruptive effect of frequent changes in output rates and the work force, adjustments usually are made monthly or quarterly. In other words, the company looks at time in the aggregate—months, quarters, or seasons, rather than days or hours. Some companies use monthly planning periods for the near portion of the planning horizon and quarterly periods for the later portion. In practice, planning periods reflect a balance between the needs for (1) a limited number of decision points to reduce planning complexity and (2) flexibility to adjust output rates and work-force levels when demand forecasts exhibit seasonal variations. The bicycle manufacturer, for example, may choose monthly planning periods so that timely adjustments to inventory levels can be made without excessively disruptive changes to the work force.

Relationship to Other Plans

How should an aggregate
plan fit with other plans?

A financial assessment of the organization's near future—that is, for one or two years ahead—is called either a business plan (in for-profit firms) or an annual plan (in nonprofit services). A **business plan** is a projected statement of income, costs, and profits. It usually is accompanied by budgets, a projected (pro forma) balance sheet, and a projected cash flow statement, showing sources and allocations of funds. The business plan unifies the plans and expectations of a firm's operations, finance, sales, and marketing managers. In particular, it reflects plans for market penetration, new product introduction, and capital investment. Manufacturing firms and for-profit service organizations, such as a retail store, firm of attorneys, or hospital, prepare such plans. A nonprofit service organization, such as the United Way or a municipal government, prepares a different type of plan, called an **annual plan** or **financial plan.**

Figure 13.1 illustrates the relationships among the business or annual plan, production or staffing plan (aggregate plan), and detailed production or work-force schedules. In the manufacturing sector, top management sets the company's strategic objectives for at least the next year in the business plan. It provides the overall framework of demand projections, functional area inputs, and capital budget from which the aggregate plan and the master production schedule (MPS) are developed. The production plan specifies corresponding product family production rates, inventory levels, and work-force levels. The **master production schedule,** in turn, specifies the timing and size of production quantities for each product in the product families. Thus the aggregate plan plays a key role in translating the strategies of the business plan into an operational plan for the manufacturing process.

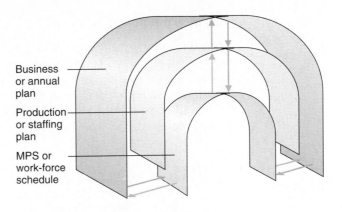

In the service sector, top management sets the organization's direction and objectives in the business plan (for-profit organization) or annual plan (nonprofit organization). In either case the plan provides the framework for the staffing plan and work-force schedule. The staffing plan presents the number and types of employees needed to meet the objectives of the business or annual plan. The **work-force schedule,** in turn, details the specific work schedule for each category of employee. For example, a staffing plan might allocate ten police officers for the day shift in a particular district; the work-force schedule might assign five of them to work Monday through Friday and the other five to work Wednesday through Sunday to meet the varying daily needs for police protection in that district. Thus the work-force schedule implements the staffing plan in much the same way that the master production schedule implements the production plan. (We present a more complete discussion of work-force scheduling in Chapter 16.)

As the arrows in Fig. 13.1 indicate, information flows in two directions: from the top down (broad to detailed) and from the bottom up (detailed to broad). If an aggregate plan can't be developed to satisfy the objectives of the business or annual plan, the business or annual plan might have to be adjusted. Similarly, if a feasible master production schedule or work-force schedule can't be developed, the aggregate plan might have to be adjusted. The planning process is dynamic, with plans periodically revised or adjusted based on two-way information flows.

An analogy for the three levels of plans in Fig. 13.1 is a student's calendar. Choosing a school based on career goals—a plan covering four or five years—corresponds to the highest planning level. Choosing classes based on that school's requirements—a plan for the next school year—corresponds to the middle planning level (or aggregate plan). Finally, scheduling group meetings and study times around work requirements in current classes—a plan for the next few weeks—corresponds to the most detailed planning level.

◆ MANAGERIAL IMPORTANCE OF AGGREGATE PLANS

In this section we concentrate on the managerial inputs, objectives, alternatives, and strategies associated with aggregate plans.

Managerial Inputs

What kind of cross-functional coordination is needed?

Figure 13.2 shows the types of information that managers from various functional areas supply to aggregate plans. One way of ensuring the necessary cross-functional coordination and supply of information is to create a committee of functional-area representatives. Chaired by a general manager, the committee has the overall responsibility to make sure that company policies are followed, conflicts are resolved, and a final plan is approved.

FIGURE 13.2

Managerial Inputs from Functional Areas to Aggregate Plans

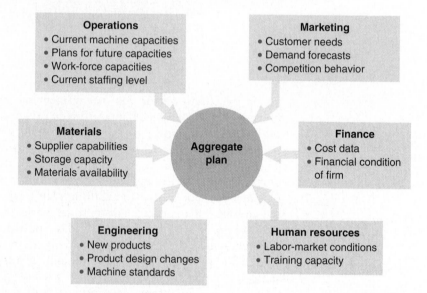

Typical Objectives

The many functional areas in an organization that give input to the aggregate plan typically have conflicting objectives for the use of the organization's resources. Six objectives usually are considered during development of a production or staffing plan:

1. *Minimize costs/maximize profits.* If customer demand isn't affected by the plan, minimizing costs will also maximize profits.
2. *Maximize customer service.* Improving delivery time and on-time delivery may require additional work-force, machine capacity, or inventory resources.
3. *Minimize inventory investment.* Inventory accumulations are expensive because the money could be used for more productive investments.
4. *Minimize changes in production rates.* Frequent changes in production rates can cause difficulties in coordinating the supplying of materials and require production line rebalancing.
5. *Minimize changes in work-force levels.* Fluctuating work-force levels may cause lower productivity because new employees typically need time to become fully productive.
6. *Maximize utilization of plant and equipment.* Firms with a product focus require uniformly high utilization of plant and equipment.

The weight given to each one in the plan involves cost trade-offs and consideration of nonquantifiable factors. For example, maximizing customer service with fast, on-time delivery can be improved by increasing—not minimizing—the stock of finished goods in a production plan. Or, for example, a staffing plan that minimizes costs may not minimize changes in work-force levels or maximize customer service.

Balancing these various objectives to arrive at an acceptable aggregate plan involves consideration of various alternatives. The two basic types of alternatives are reactive and aggressive. Aggressive alternatives are actions that adjust demand patterns, whereas reactive alternatives are actions that respond to given demand patterns.

Reactive Alternatives

What options should be considered in responding to uneven demand?

Reactive alternatives are actions that can be taken to cope with demand requirements. Typically, an operations manager controls reactive alternatives. That is, the operations manager accepts forecasted demand as a given and modifies work-force levels, overtime, vacation schedules, inventory levels, subcontracting, and planned backlogs to meet that demand.

Work-Force Adjustment. Management can adjust work-force levels by hiring or laying off employees. The use of this alternative can be attractive if the work force is largely unskilled or semiskilled and the labor pool is large. However, for a particular company, the size of the qualified labor pool may limit the number

During the busy tax season preceding and following April 15, the IRS increases the number of clerks employed to process tax returns.

of new employees that can be hired at any one time. Also, new employees must be trained, and the capacity of the training facilities themselves might limit the number of new hires at any one time. In some industries, laying off employees is difficult or unusual for contractual reasons (unions); in other industries, such as tourism and agriculture, seasonal layoffs and hirings are the norm.

Overtime and Undertime.   An alternative to work-force adjustment is the use of overtime and undertime. Overtime can be used to satisfy output requirements that cannot be completed on regular time. However, overtime is expensive (typically 150 percent of the regular-time pay rate). Moreover, in many cases, workers do not want to work a lot of overtime for an extended period of time, and excessive overtime may result in declining quality and productivity.

Undertime is used when labor capacity exceeds demand requirements. Workers are kept on the payroll rather than being laid off. This option is used by companies that have highly skilled, hard-to-replace employees (particularly firms with a process focus) or that confront contractual obstacles to laying off workers. In the latter case, undertime can cause inefficiency and higher unit costs.

Vacation Schedules.   A firm can shut down during an annual lull in sales, leaving a skeleton crew to cover operations and perform maintenance. Employees might be required to take all or part of their allowed vacation time during this period. Automakers, such as General Motors, sometimes use this alternative during the Christmas holiday period, not only to do maintenance work or install equipment, but also to reduce inventory. Use of this alternative depends on whether the employer can mandate the vacation schedules of its employees. In any case, employees may be strongly discouraged from taking vacations during peak periods or encouraged to take vacations during periods when replacement part-time labor is most abundant.

Anticipation Inventory.   A plant facing seasonal demand can stock anticipation inventory during light demand periods and use it during heavy demand periods. Although this approach stabilizes output rates and work-force levels, it can be costly because the value of the product is greatest in its finished state. Stocking components and subassemblies that can be assembled quickly when customer orders come in might be preferable to stocking finished goods.

Service providers generally cannot use anticipation inventory because services cannot be stocked. In some instances, however, services can be performed prior to actual need. For example, telephone company workers usually lay cables for service to a new subdivision before housing construction begins. They can do this work during a period when the workload for scheduled services is low.

Subcontractors.   Subcontractors can be used to overcome short-term capacity shortages, such as during peaks of the season or business cycle. Subcontractors can supply services, make components and subassemblies, or even assemble an entire product. If the subcontractor can supply components or subassemblies of equal or better quality less expensively than the company can produce them itself, these arrangements may become permanent. The major automakers, for example, typically subcontract for underbody frames, steering linkage components, and other items. In the service industry, book publishers are turning increasingly to freelance artists and copy editors as part of a downsizing trend.

Backlogs, Backorders, and Stockouts.   Another way in which firms with a process focus often cope with a high demand forecast is to plan for order backlogs. A **backlog** is an accumulation of customer orders that have been promised for delivery at some future date. Having a sizable backlog may be a good strategy, if on-time delivery and quality aren't sacrificed. Delivery lead times typically increase during seasonal peaks in demand. Firms with a process focus often use this method. The customer places an order for a customized product or service, and the firm promises it for later delivery. Job shops, TV repair shops, and automobile repair shops work to varying degrees to backlogs. Examples of backlogs in services are tickets for a concert and appointments to see a dentist.

Backorders and stockouts are used by firms with a product focus. A **backorder** is a customer order that isn't ready for the customer when promised or demanded, thereby delaying demand requirements to later periods. A **stockout** is an inability to satisfy the demand for a stock item when it occurs. In this case, the customer may go to a competitor, resulting in a lost sale. Generally, backorders and stockouts are to be avoided. Planned stockouts may be used, but only when the expected loss in sales and customer goodwill is less than the cost of using other reactive alternatives or aggressive alternatives, or adding the capacity needed to satisfy demand.

In conclusion, decisions about the use of each alternative for each period of the planning horizon specify the output rate for each period. In other words, the output rate is a function of the choices among these alternatives.

Aggressive Alternatives

How can demand be leveled to reduce operating costs?

Coping with seasonal or volatile demand by using reactive alternatives can be costly. Another approach is to attempt to change demand patterns to achieve efficiency and reduce costs. **Aggressive alternatives** are actions that attempt to modify demand and, consequently, resource requirements. Typically, marketing managers are responsible for specifying these actions in the marketing plan.

Complementary Products.   One way to even out the load on resources is to produce **complementary products** or services having similar resource requirements but different demand cycles. For example, a company producing garden tractors can also produce snowmobiles, making requirements for major components, such as engines, reasonably uniform year round. In the service sector, city parks and recreation departments can counterbalance seasonal staffing requirements for summer activities by offering ice skating, tobogganing, or indoor activities during the winter. The key is to find products and services that can be produced with existing resources and can level off the need for resources over the year.

Creative Pricing.   Promotional campaigns often increase sales with creative pricing. Examples include automobile rebate programs, price reductions for winter clothing in the late summer months, reduced prices on airline tickets for travel during off-peak periods, and "two for the price of one" automobile tire sales.

Planning Strategies

Managers often combine reactive and aggressive alternatives in various ways to arrive at an acceptable aggregate plan. For the remainder of this chapter, let's assume that the expected results of the aggressive alternatives have already been incorporated into the demand forecasts of product families or services. This assumption allows us to focus on the reactive alternatives that define output rates and work-force levels. There are two pure strategies for selecting the particular alternatives to be used: a chase strategy and a level strategy.

A **chase strategy** adjusts output rates or work-force levels to match demand over the planning horizon without using anticipation inventory or undertime. This strategy can be accomplished in many ways. For example, workers can be hired or laid off, or overtime and subcontracting can be used during peak periods. A chase strategy has the advantage of low inventory investment and backlogs. However, it has some drawbacks: the expense of continually adjusting output rates or work-force levels, the potential alienation of the work force, and the loss of productivity and of quality because of constant changes in the work force.

A **level strategy** maintains a constant output rate or work-force level over the planning horizon by using anticipation inventory and/or undertime. In manufacturing firms a constant production rate often is accomplished by maintaining a stable work force and building anticipation inventory to satisfy peak seasonal demands. Hiring, overtime, or subcontracting can be used if the work force is subject to attrition. In service firms a level strategy usually involves maintaining a stable work force and using undertime, overtime, and backlogs. The advantages are level output rates and a stable work force at the expense of increased inventory investment, undertime, overtime, or backlogs. Managerial Practice 13.2 shows how Hallmark uses a level strategy for competitive advantage.

A range of strategies lies between the chase strategy at one extreme and the level strategy at the other. The best strategy for a company may be a **mixed strategy** of some anticipation inventory buildup during slack periods, only a few work-force level changes, and overtime. Whether a company chooses a pure strategy or some mix, the strategy must reflect the organization's environment and planning objectives. For example, for the municipal street repair department, which faces seasonal demand shifts and needs an ample supply of unskilled labor, possible strategies include varying the work-force level, low use of overtime, and no subcontracting.

The aggregate plan not only is a product of managerial inputs from the various functional areas, but also has an impact on their activities. Thus aggregate plans significantly affect the direction of the firm over the near and intermediate future. In general, firms that have a process focus can adapt to volume flexibility rather easily and tend to meet variable demand with overtime, subcontracting, or work-force level changes, unless highly skilled, hard-to-find labor is involved. However, firms that have a product focus find volume flexibility difficult to handle and tend to meet fluctuating demand with anticipation inventory, scheduled vacations, or plant shutdowns.

◆ THE PLANNING PROCESS

Figure 13.3 shows the process for preparing aggregate plans. It is dynamic and continuing, as aspects of the plan are updated periodically when new information becomes available and new opportunities emerge.

Managerial Practice 13.2

▶ *Hallmark's Level Strategy*

Hallmark, a $2-billion-a-year producer of greeting cards, spends considerable sums to improve efficiency and has made significant gains—all without imposing layoffs. Hallmark has never used layoffs to adjust production rates of greeting cards, even though the business is highly competitive, exhibits little growth, and is very seasonal. Employee flexibility is the key to this strategy. The company's four plants produce millions of cards each day, along with gift wrapping paper and other party goods. Even though technology in the industry has made production processes increasingly more labor efficient, Hallmark's philosophy has been to retrain its employees continually to make them more flexible. For example, a cutting machine operator might also be a custom card imprinter, a painter, or a modular office assembler as needed. To keep workers busy, Hallmark shifts production from its Kansas City plant to branch plants in Topeka, Leavenworth, and Lawrence,

Kansas, to keep those plants fully utilized. It uses the Kansas City plant as its "swing facility"—when demand is down, these employees may take jobs in clerical positions, all at factory pay rates. They might also be in classrooms learning new skills.

According to CEO Irvine O. Hockaday, Hallmark must protect its employees from cyclical markets and other unexpected happenings beyond their control. The added job security, however, carries the expectation that employees' performance will be commensurate with their compensation package. The philosophy has paid dividends. For example, reducing setup times to support short production runs is crucial to keeping inventories and costs low. Employees have suggested ways to cut setup times significantly. A stable work-force policy has been a major factor in allowing Hallmark to capture some 42 percent of the $5.6 billion domestic card market.

Source: "Cutting Costs Without Cutting People," *Fortune,* May 25, 1987, pp. 26–31; "Loyal to a Fault," *Forbes,* March 14, 1994, pp. 58–60.

FIGURE 13.3

The Process for Preparing Aggregate Plans

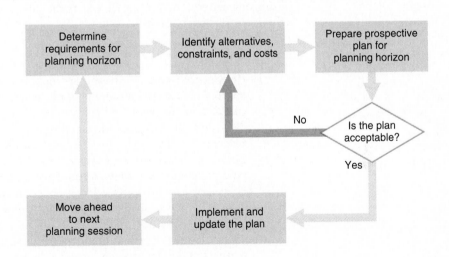

Determining Demand Requirements

The first step in the planning process is to determine the demand requirements for each period of the planning horizon using one of the many methods that we've already discussed. For staffing plans, the planner bases forecasts of staff requirements for each work-force group on historical levels of demand, managerial judgment, and existing backlogs for services. For example, a director of nursing in a hospital can develop a direct-care index for a nursing staff and translate a projection of the month-to-month patient census into an equivalent total amount of nursing care time—and thus number of nurses—required for each month of the year. A police department can develop a formula for patrol staffing that accounts for such factors as the number of calls for service by type, the number of street miles patrolled, and the number of businesses in the community, to determine weekly or monthly workloads and thus the number of police officers or vehicles required.

For production plans, however, the requirements represent the demand for finished goods and the external demand for replacement parts. The planner can derive future requirements for finished goods from backlogs (for a process focus) or from forecasts for product families made to stock (for a product focus). Sometimes, distributors or dealers indicate their requirements for finished goods in advance of actual orders, providing a reliable forecast of requirements from those sources.

Identifying Alternatives, Constraints, and Costs

The second step is to identify the alternatives, constraints, and costs for the plan. We presented the reactive alternatives used in aggregate plans earlier, so we now focus on constraints and costs.

Constraints represent physical limitations or managerial policies associated with the aggregate plan. Examples of physical constraints might include training facilities capable of handling only so many new hires at a time, machine capacities that limit maximum output, or inadequate inventory storage space. Policy constraints might include limitations on the amount of backordering or the use of subcontracting or overtime, as well as the minimum inventory levels needed to achieve desired safety stocks.

Typically, many plans can satisfy a specific set of constraints. The planner usually considers several types of costs when preparing aggregate plans:

1. *Regular-time costs.*   These costs include regular-time wages paid to employees plus contributions to such benefits as health insurance, dental care, Social Security, and retirement funds and pay for vacations, holidays, and certain other types of absence.

2. *Overtime costs.*   Overtime wages typically are 150 percent of regular-time wages, exclusive of fringe benefits. Some companies offer a 200 percent rate for working overtime on Sundays and holidays.

3. *Hiring and layoff costs.*   Hiring costs include the costs of advertising jobs, interviews, training programs for new employees, scrap from new employees, loss of productivity, and initial paperwork. Layoff costs include the costs of exit interviews, severance pay, retraining remaining workers and managers, and lost productivity.

4. *Inventory holding costs.*   Inventory holding costs include costs that vary with the *level* of inventory investment: the costs of capital tied up in inventory, variable storage and warehousing costs, pilferage and obsolescence costs, insurance costs, and taxes.

5. *Backorder and stockout costs.*   As discussed earlier, the use of backorders and stockouts involves costs of expediting past-due orders, costs of lost sales, and the potential cost of losing the customer's sales to competitors in the future (sometimes called loss of goodwill).

Preparing an Acceptable Plan

The third step is to prepare the aggregate plan. As shown in Fig. 13.3, developing an acceptable plan is an iterative process; that is, plans may need to go through several revisions and adjustments. A prospective, or tentative, plan is developed to start. A production plan with monthly periods, for example, must specify monthly production rates, inventory and backlog accumulations, subcontracted production, and monthly work-force levels (including hires, layoffs, and overtime). The plan must then be checked against constraints and evaluated in terms of strategic objectives. If the prospective plan isn't acceptable for either of those reasons, a new prospective plan must be developed. It may include new alternatives or proposed changes in physical or policy constraints. When the plan is acceptable to the representatives from all functional areas, implementation can begin.

Implementing and Updating the Plan

The final step is implementing and updating the aggregate plan. Implementation requires the commitment of managers in all functional areas. The planning committee may recommend changes in the plan during implementation or updating to balance conflicting objectives better. Acceptance of the plan does not necessarily mean that everyone is in total agreement, but it does imply that everyone will work to achieve it.

◆ AGGREGATE PLANNING FOR SERVICES

Should a level work-force strategy or some variable work-force strategy be used in providing services?

Here we use a *trial-and-error* approach of stating a strategy, then developing a plan, comparing the developed plan to other plans, and finally modifying the plan or strategy as necessary, until we are satisfied with the results. We demonstrate this approach by developing two staffing plans, the first based on a level strategy and the second on a chase strategy. We then evaluate them in terms of costs and seek ways to improve on them.

Level Strategy for Services

With the level strategy the constant number of employees that will satisfy demand over the planning horizon is determined by using the maximum amount of overtime in the peak period. The work-force level doesn't change, except possibly for hires or layoffs at the beginning of the first period if the current and desired constant work-force levels don't match. The level strategy can lead to considerable undertime, which is the amount of time by which capacity exceeds demand requirements, summed over all periods on the time horizon. If undertime is paid for, regular-time costs per period are found by multiplying the actual staff size by the full wage cost for the period. If undertime is not paid for, which is usually the case with part-time workers, an *equivalent staff size* must be calculated for each period—the number of part-time workers, working the maximum allowable time, that would be needed to cover the demand requirements without any undertime. This equivalent staff size, rather than the actual staff level, becomes the basis for calculating regular-time costs.

REI employs a high percentage of part-time workers, many of whom are college students, in its retail stores. They tend to be young people who participate in outdoor sports and are very familiar with the equipment that REI sells.

EXAMPLE 13.1
A Staffing Plan with the Level Strategy

The manager of a large distribution center must determine how many part-time stockpickers to maintain on the payroll. She wants to develop a staffing plan with a level strategy. Her objective is to keep the part-time work-force level with a minimum of undertime and stable without using backorders or subcontractors.

The manager divides the next year into 13 accounting periods, each one four weeks long. Each part-time employee can work a maximum of 20 hours per week on regular time, but the actual number can be less. The distribution center shortens each worker's day during slack periods, rather than pay undertime. Once on the payroll, each worker is used each day, but may work only a few hours. Overtime can be used during peak periods to avoid excessive undertime.

Work-force requirements are shown as the number of part-time employees required for each accounting period at the maximum regular time of 20 hours per week. For example, in accounting period 6, an estimated 20 part-time employees working 20 hours per week on regular time will be needed.

	Accounting Period													
	1	2	3	4	5	6	7	8	9	10	11	12	13	Total
Requirement*	5	6	8	15	17	20	15	15	10	16	14	14	12	167

* Number of part-time employees

Currently, 10 part-time clerks are employed. They haven't been subtracted from the requirements shown. The constraints on employment are as follows.

1. The size of training facilities limits the number of new hires in any period to no more than 10.

2. No backorders are permitted; demand must be met each period.
3. Overtime cannot exceed 25 percent of the regular-time capacity (that is, 5 hours) in any period. Therefore the most that any part-time employee can work is 1.25(20) = 25 hours per week.

Solution   For the level strategy, the manager begins by finding the number of part-time employees, at 25 hours per week (20 × 1.25), needed to meet the peak requirement. The most overtime that she can use is 25 percent of the regular-time capacity, w, so

$$1.25w = 20 \text{ employees required in peak period (period 6)}$$

$$w = \frac{20}{1.25} = 16 \text{ employees}$$

A 16-employee staff size minimizes the amount of undertime for the level strategy. As there already are 10 part-time employees, the manager should immediately hire 6 more. The complete plan is shown in the following table. The key entries are the staff levels of 16 for each period, the 6 people to be hired in period 1, and no hires or layoffs thereafter. A better solution would be to delay hiring until period 4 because the current work force is sufficient until then. However, this modification creates a hybrid strategy rather than the pure level strategy with a constant work force for the entire horizon, which is the strategy illustrated here.

	Accounting Period													
	1	**2**	**3**	**4**	**5**	**6**	**7**	**8**	**9**	**10**	**11**	**12**	**13**	**Total**
Requirement	5	6	8	15	17	20	15	15	10	16	14	14	12	167
Staff level	16	16	16	16	16	16	16	16	16	16	16	16	16	208
Equivalent staff	5	6	8	15	16	16	15	15	10	16	14	14	12	162
Hires	6	—	—	—	—	—	—	—	—	—	—	—	—	6
Layoffs	—	—	—	—	—	—	—	—	—	—	—	—	—	0
Overtime	—	—	—	—	1	4	—	—	—	—	—	—	—	5

Note: Equivalent staff is the equivalent number of employees working the maximum 20 hours per week.

In periods of undertime, the equivalent staff is identical to the requirements. Otherwise, when requirements exceed the staff level, it is equal to the staff level. (Excess requirements in periods 5 and 6 are met by using overtime.) In periods 1–4 and 7–13, the employees would be working less than the maximum 20 hours per week because the requirements do not exceed 16 employees. For example, in period 1, 16 employees are on the payroll, but only 100 hours [or 5(20)] per week are needed. Consequently, each employee might work only 6.25 hours per week. Alternatively, management could assign 7 employees to 4 hours per week and 9 employees to 8 hours per week.

The overtime row is calculated last; it is the amount by which the requirement exceeds the staff level. For example, in period 6 the overtime worked is the equivalent of 4 employees (or 20 − 16) working 20-hour weeks. Like undertime in slack periods, this overtime would be apportioned equitably to the 16 employees.

Chase Strategy for Services

The chase strategy adjusts work-force levels as needed to achieve requirements without using overtime, undertime, or subcontractors. The chase strategy can result in a large number of hires and layoffs. However, many employees, such as college students, prefer part-time work. With the chase strategy the equivalent staff row is identical to the requirements row, with no overtime in any period.

EXAMPLE 13.2

A Staffing Plan with the Chase Strategy

The manager now wants to find the staffing plan for the distribution center, using the chase strategy so as to avoid all overtime and undertime.

Solution   This strategy simply involves adjusting the work force as needed to meet demand, as shown in the following table.

| | **Accounting Period** | | | | | | | | | | | | | |
	1	2	3	4	5	6	7	8	9	10	11	12	13	Total
Requirement	5	6	8	15	17	20	15	15	10	16	14	14	12	167
Staff level	5	6	8	15	17	20	15	15	10	16	14	14	12	167
Equivalent staff	5	6	8	15	17	20	15	15	10	16	14	14	12	167
Hires	—	1	2	7	2	3	—	—	—	6	—	—	—	21
Layoffs	5	—	—	—	—	—	5	—	5	—	2	—	2	19
Overtime	—	—	—	—	—	—	—	—	—	—	—	—	—	0

Note: Equivalent staff is the equivalent number of employees working the maximum 20 hours per week.

The manager should plan to lay off 5 part-time employees immediately, because the current staff is 10 and the staff level required in period 1 is only 5. The work force then should steadily build to 20 by period 6. After that, the manager can reduce the work force except for the secondary peak in period 10, when she should hire 6 more employees.

Cost Calculations and Mixed Strategies

Along with qualitative considerations, the calculated cost of each plan determines whether the plan is satisfactory or whether a revised plan should be considered. The basic approach is to look at higher cost elements in each plan, which might provide clues for selecting a mixed strategy that could be better than the pure strategy considered. Spreadsheet programs make analyzing many alternatives easy. Innovations such as Excel's add-in solver present a whole new world of possibilities in developing sound aggregate plans. Special-purpose programs also are available. The CMOM output for the chase strategy is shown next. The plan's cost of $98,000 confirms the manual calculations in Example 13.3 for the chase strategy.

CMOM - Chase Strategy

Solution

	P1	P2	P3	P4	P5	P6	P7	P8	P9	P10	P11	P12	P13
Demand	5	6	8	15	17	20	15	15	10	16	14	14	12
Reg Out	5	6	8	15	17	20	15	15	10	16	14	14	12
Over Out	0	0	0	0	0	0	0	0	0	0	0	0	0
Total	5	6	8	15	17	20	15	15	10	16	14	14	12

Summary

Total Costs   : 98000

Total Demand   : 167

Total Capacity   : 167

Unused Capacity   : 0

Average Inventory : 0

EXAMPLE 13.3

Evaluating the Level and Chase Strategies

Compute the total cost for the two plans, and identify some mixed strategies that might give a better solution. The following costs can be assigned.

Regular-time wage rate	$500 per accounting period at 20 hours per week
Overtime wages	150 percent of the regular-time rate
Hires	$600 per person
Layoffs	$100 per person

Solution   The cost comparisons are shown in the following table.

Cost	Level Strategy	Chase Strategy
Regular time	162 worker periods @ $500 = $81,000	167 worker periods @ $500 = $83,500
Overtime	5 worker periods @ $750 = 3,750	0 worker periods @ $750 = 0
Hire	6 workers @ $600 = 3,600	21 workers @ $600 = 12,600
Layoff	0 workers @ $100 = 0	19 workers @ $100 = 1,900
	Totals $88,350	$98,000

Note: Regular-time wages are based on the equivalent staff available because workers in this case aren't paid undertime.

Not surprisingly, the level strategy is less expensive because undertime isn't a payroll cost. The chase strategy calls for a lot of hiring and laying off. If staffing couldn't be done with part-time employees with flexible work hours, the level strategy would be more expensive. Use of the level strategy in this situation makes sense—and the economics of the case verify it.

As for further improvements, the chase strategy might be improved by revising the plan to lay off five employees in period 9, hire six in period 10, and then lay off two in period 11. The level strategy could be improved by delaying the six hires until period 5. The amount of undertime can be reduced, which is always a goal even if undertime isn't paid.

MATHEMATICAL METHODS FOR AGGREGATE PLANNING

The major advantage of the trial-and-error approach is its simplicity; however, the planner still must make many choices for each period of the planning horizon. In manufacturing firms, these decisions relate to the amount of anticipation inventory to produce, the amount of overtime to use, the number of units to subcontract, and other factors.

Tableau Method of Production Planning

In this section we present and demonstrate the **tableau method** of production planning. It is based on the assumption that a demand forecast is available for each period, along with a capacity plan specifying the maximum capacities of regular time, overtime, and subcontractor production for each period. Another assumption is that all costs are linearly related to the amount of goods produced—that is, that a change in the amount of goods produced creates a proportionate change in costs.

With these assumptions, the tableau method yields the optimal mixed-strategy production plan over the planning horizon. To demonstrate this method, here we apply a manual approach to a simple case in which backorders are not a viable alternative.

Production Planning Without Backorders. We start with a table—called a tableau—of the capacity plan and demand forecast quantities, beginning inventory level, and costs for each period of the planning horizon. Figure 13.4 shows such a tableau for a four-period production plan, where

$$h = \text{holding cost per unit per period}$$

$$r = \text{cost per unit to produce on regular time}$$

$$c = \text{cost per unit to produce on overtime}$$

$$s = \text{cost per unit to subcontract}$$

$$I_0 = \text{beginning inventory level}$$

$$I_4 = \text{desired inventory level at the end of period 4}$$

$$R_t = \text{regular-time capacity in period } t$$

$$O_t = \text{overtime capacity in period } t$$

$$S_t = \text{subcontracting capacity in period } t$$

$$D_t = \text{forecasted demand for period } t$$

Note that each row in the tableau represents an alternative for supplying output. For example, the first row shows the beginning inventory (the amount

Should subcontracting be used to achieve short-term capacity increases or should some combination of inventory accumulation and overtime be used?

FIGURE 13.4

Production Planning Tableau

Alternatives		Time Period				Unused Capacity	Total Capacity
		1	2	3	4		
Period	Beginning inventory	0	h	2h	3h		I_0
1	Regular time	r	r + h	r + 2h	r + 3h		R_1
1	Overtime	c	c + h	c + 2h	c + 3h		O_1
1	Subcontract	s	s + h	s + 2h	s + 3h		S_1
2	Regular time	✕	r	r + h	r + 2h		R_2
2	Overtime	✕	c	c + h	c + 2h		O_2
2	Subcontract	✕	s	s + h	s + 2h		S_2
3	Regular time	✕	✕	r	r + h		R_3
3	Overtime	✕	✕	c	c + h		O_3
3	Subcontract	✕	✕	s	s + h		S_3
4	Regular time	✕	✕	✕	r		R_4
4	Overtime	✕	✕	✕	c		O_4
4	Subcontract	✕	✕	✕	s		S_4
Requirements		D_1	D_2	D_3	$D_4 + I_4$		

currently on hand) for the present time (period 0), which can be used to satisfy demands in any of the four periods. The second row is for regular-time production in period 1, which can also be used to satisfy demands in any of the four periods the plan will cover. The third and fourth rows are for production via two other alternatives (overtime and subcontracting) in period 1, for meeting demand in any of the four periods.

The columns represent the periods the plan must cover, plus the unused and total capacities available. The box in the upper right-hand corner of each cell shows the cost of producing a unit in one period and, in some cases, carrying the unit in inventory for sale in a future period. For example, in period 1 the regular-time cost to produce one unit is r (column 1). To produce the unit in period 1 for sale in period 2, the cost is $r + h$ (column 2) because we must hold the unit in inventory for one period. Satisfying a unit of demand in period 3 by producing in period 1 on regular time and carrying the unit for two periods costs $r + 2h$ (column 3), and so on. The large Xs indicate that backorders (or producing in a period to satisfy demand in a past period) aren't allowed.

The least expensive alternatives are those in which the output is produced and sold in the same period. However, we may not always be able to use those alternatives exclusively because of capacity restrictions. Finally, the per unit holding cost for the beginning inventory in period 1 is 0 because it is a function of previous production planning decisions. Similarly, the target inventory at the end of the planning horizon is added to the forecasted demand for the last period. No holding cost is charged because we have already decided to have a specified ending inventory; in this regard it is a sunk cost.*

Because no backorders are allowed, the following manual method for finding the optimal solution is adequate.

Step 1.   Put all capacities from the total capacity column into the unused capacity column.

Step 2.   In column 1 (period 1), allocate as much production as you can to the cell with the lowest cost but do not exceed the unused capacity in that row or the demand in that column.

Step 3.   Subtract your allocation from the unused capacity for that row. This quantity must never be negative. If negative unused capacities cannot be avoided, the solution is infeasible for that capacity plan. More capacity is needed.

Step 4.   If there is still some demand left, repeat step 2, allocating as much production as possible to the cell with the next-to-lowest cost. Repeat until the demand is satisfied.

Step 5.   Repeat steps 2 through 4 for periods 2 and beyond. Take each column separately before proceeding to the next. Be sure to check all cells with unused capacity (but without Xs) for the cell with the lowest cost in a column.

At the end of the procedure, the sum of all entries in a row must equal the total capacity for that row, and the sum of all entries in a column must equal the requirements for that column. Following this principle ensures that capacities are not exceeded and that all demands are met.

EXAMPLE 13.4

Preparing a Production Plan Using the Tableau Method

The Tru-Rainbow Company produces a variety of paint products for both commercial and private use. The demand for paint is highly seasonal, peaking in the third quarter. Current inventory is 250,000 gallons, and ending inventory should be 300,000 gallons.

Tru-Rainbow's manufacturing manager wants to determine the best production plan using the following demand requirements and capacity plan (expressed in thousands of gallons). The manager knows that the regular-time cost is $1.00 per unit, overtime cost is $1.50 per unit, subcontracting cost is $1.90 per unit, and inventory holding cost is $0.30 per gallon per quarter.

*If we were analyzing the implications of different ending inventory levels, the holding cost of the ending inventory would have to be added to the costs because ending inventory level would be a decision variable.

	Quarter				
	1	2	3	4	Total
Demand	300	850	1500	350	3000
Capacities					
Regular time	450	450	750	450	2100
Overtime	90	90	150	90	420
Subcontracting	200	200	200	200	800

The following constraints apply.

1. Maximum allowable overtime in any quarter is 20 percent of the regular-time capacity in that quarter.
2. The subcontractor can supply a maximum of 200,000 gallons in any quarter. Production can be subcontracted in one period and the excess held in inventory for a future period to avoid a stockout.
3. No backorders or stockouts are permitted.

Solution Figure 13.5 on the next page contains the tableau solution to the problem. The first step is for the analyst to transfer all capacities from the total capacity column to the unused capacity column. The total requirements sum to 3,300,000 gallons (or 300,000 + 850,000 + 1,500,000 + 650,000), which is less than the total capacity of 3,570,000 gallons. Therefore the analyst knows that at the end of the solution process he will have 270,000 gallons of unused capacity. Next he proceeds through steps 2–5 for each quarter, starting with quarter 1.

Quarter 1. The least expensive alternative in quarter 1 is to use the inventory on hand, so he allocates as much as he can: 250,000 gallons. That leaves a demand of 50,000 gallons to satisfy, so he allocates 50,000 gallons of quarter 1 regular-time capacity (the next least costly alternative) to satisfy demand in quarter 1 and reduces the unused capacity by 50,000. Quarter 1 demand has now been satisfied.

Quarter 2. The least expensive option is to allocate all regular-time production in quarter 2 to satisfy demand in that quarter. As the analyst is still short 400,000 gallons, the next least costly option is to allocate 400,000 gallons of quarter 1 regular-time production. These allocations satisfy quarter 2 demand, but now there is no more regular-time capacity left in quarters 1 and 2.

Quarter 3. The only capacities available in addition to the quarter 3 capacities are overtime and subcontracting in quarters 1 and 2. This condition implies that the company must produce anticipation inventories in quarters 1 and 2 to meet the peak demand in quarter 3. The analyst begins by allocating the maximum amount of quarter 3 regular-time capacity, the least costly alternative. Then, in order, he allocates as much as he can of quarter 3 overtime, quarter 2 overtime, quarter 3 subcontracting, quarter 1 overtime, and quarter 2 subcontracting. Finally, the analyst allocates 20,000 gallons of quarter 1 subcontracting capacity to meet quarter 3 demand.

Quarter 4. The least expensive option is to allocate all regular-time production to quarter 4. Then, in order, the analyst allocates all of the quarter 4 overtime and 110,000 gallons of quarter 4 subcontracting.

A quick check indicates that this plan is feasible: No unused capacities are negative, the sum of the allocations in each row (including the unused capacity)

FIGURE 13.5

The Tableau Solution for the Tru-Rainbow Problem

	Alternatives	Quarter 1	Quarter 2	Quarter 3	Quarter 4	Unused Capacity	Total Capacity
Quarter 1	Beginning inventory	0.00 / 250	0.30	0.60	0.90	2̶5̶0̶ 0	250
	Regular time	1.00 / 50	1.30 / 400	1.60	1.90	4̶5̶0̶ 4̶0̶0̶ 0	450
	Overtime	1.50	1.80	2.10 / 90	2.40	9̶0̶ 0	90
	Subcontract	1.90	2.20	2.50 / 20	2.80	2̶0̶0̶ 180	200
Quarter 2	Regular time	✕	1.00 / 450	1.30	1.60	4̶5̶0̶ 0	450
	Overtime	✕	1.50	1.80 / 90	2.10	9̶0̶ 0	90
	Subcontract	✕	1.90	2.20 / 200	2.50	2̶0̶0̶ 0	200
Quarter 3	Regular time	✕	✕	1.00 / 750	1.30	7̶5̶0̶ 0	750
	Overtime	✕	✕	1.50 / 150	1.80	1̶5̶0̶ 0	150
	Subcontract	✕	✕	1.90 / 200	2.20	2̶0̶0̶ 0	200
Quarter 4	Regular time	✕	✕	✕	1.00 / 450	4̶5̶0̶ 0	450
	Overtime	✕	✕	✕	1.50 / 90	9̶0̶ 0	90
	Subcontract	✕	✕	✕	1.90 / 110	2̶0̶0̶ 90	200
Requirements		300	850	1500	350 + 300 = 650	270	3570

equals the total capacity for that row, and the sum of the allocations for each quarter equals the demand for that quarter.

The total cost of this prospective production plan is equal to the sum of the products calculated by multiplying the allocation in each cell by the cost per unit in that cell. Computing this cost column by column yields a total cost of $4,010,000:

Quarter 1:	250($0) + 50($1.00)	= $ 50
Quarter 2:	400($1.30) + 450($1.00)	= 970
Quarter 3:	90($2.10) + 20($2.50) + 90($1.80) + 200($2.20) + 750($1.00) + 150($1.50) + 200($1.90)	= 2196
Quarter 4:	450($1.00) + 90($1.50) + 110($1.90)	= 794
		Total = 4010

To interpret the solution, we can convert Fig. 13.5 into the following table. For example, the total regular-time production in quarter 1 is 450,000 gallons (50,000 gallons to meet demand in quarter 1 and 400,000 gallons to help satisfy demand in quarter 2).

Quarter	Regular-Time Production	Overtime Production	Subcon-tracting	Total Production	Anticipation Inventory
1	450	90	20	560	250 + 560 − 300 = 510
2	450	90	200	740	510 + 740 − 850 = 400
3	750	150	200	1100	400 + 1100 − 1500 = 0
4	450	90	110	650	0 + 650 − 350 = 300
Totals	2100	420	530	3050	

Note: Anticipation inventory is the amount at the end of each quarter, where
Beginning inventory + Total production − Demand = Ending inventory

The anticipation inventory held at the end of each quarter is obtained in the last column. For any quarter, it is the quarter's beginning inventory plus total production (regular-time and overtime production, plus subcontracting) minus demand. For example, for quarter 1 the beginning inventory (250,000) plus the total from production and subcontracting (560,000) minus quarter 1 demand (300,000) results in an ending inventory of 510,000, which also is the beginning inventory for quarter 2.

Figure 13.6 shows graphically the inventory accumulation and consumption over the planning horizon. Inventory accumulates whenever production plus subcontracting exceeds quarterly demand. Conversely, anticipation inventories are consumed when production plus subcontracting is less than quarterly demand. Quarter 2 illustrates this scenario when total production plus subcontracting is only 740,000 gallons, but requirements are for 850,000 gallons, calling for consumption of 110,000 gallons from inventory.

FIGURE 13.6	*Prospective Tru-Rainbow Production Plan*

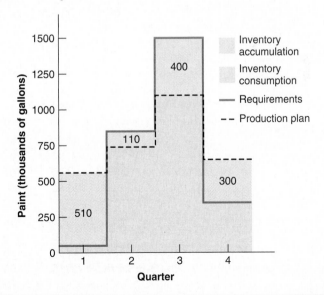

Additional Capacity Plans. The plan offered in Example 13.4 required the use of a lot of overtime and subcontracting. A better capacity plan—with increases in the work force to boost regular-time production capacity—might result in lower production costs, perhaps even low enough to offset the added capacity costs. A series of capacity plans can be tried and compared to find the best plan. Even though this process in itself involves trial and error, the tableau method yields the best mix of regular time, overtime, and subcontracting for each capacity plan.

Incorporating Backorders. Backorders also can be considered. For example, in Example 13.4, regular-time production in quarter 3 could be used to satisfy demand from quarter 2 by replacing the X in the quarter 2 cell for regular-time production in quarter 3 with some appropriate penalty cost. In effect, the X's in the Tru-Rainbow tableau represent costs large enough that we wouldn't consider backorders.

Computer Solution. In practice, we recommend using computers for complex problems, trial-and-error analysis of the capacity plan or demand forecasts, and problems involving backorders. For example, computer output from the CMOM package, which uses the transportation method, is shown below for the Tru-Rainbow Company. The first part summarizes the production, shipments, and ending inventories for each period; it confirms the plan found manually in Example 13.4. For example, the total regular-time production is 450,000 gallons in quarters 1, 2, and 4 in both solutions. Overtime, subcontracting, and inventory levels also are identical for every quarter. The second part of the computer output displays production costs first and then adds the inventory holding costs. The total cost of $4,010,000 is the same in both plans, when we exclude the cost of holding the 300,000 gallons at the end of the fourth quarter.

```
        CMOM - Tru-Rainbow Production Plan

          Production and Inventory Summary

                    P1     P2     P3     P4    Total
       Demand       300    850   1500    350   3000
       Init Invn    250    510    400      0   1160
       Production
         Regular    450    450    750    450   2100
         Overtime    90     90    150     90    420
         Subcontract 20    200    200    110    530
         Total      560    740   1100    650   3050
       Shipments
         On-time    300    850   1500    350   3000
         Backorders   0      0      0      0      0
         Total      300    850   1500    350   3000
       Ending Invn  510    400      0    300   1210
```

Cost Summary

	P1	P2	P3	P4	Total
Regular	450	450	750	450	2100
Overtime	135	135	225	135	630
Subcontract	38	380	380	209	1007
Total Prod	623	965	1355	794	3737
Backorders	0	0	0	0	0
Holding	153	120	0	90	363
Total Invn	153	120	0	90	363
Total Cost	776	1085	1355	794	4010
Total Cost*	776	1085	1355	884	4100

Total Costs   : 4010

Total Costs*   : 4100

Total Demand**   : 3300

Total Capacity   : 3570

Unused Capacity   : 270

Average Inventory*** : 296.2500

*   Includes holding cost of desired ending inventory in last period.
**   Includes desired ending inventory in last period.
*** Averaging beginning and ending inventories over all periods.

Linear Programming for Production Planning

The tableau method just discussed actually is a specialized form of linear programming (see Supplement I). Linear programming models for production planning seek the optimal production plan for a linear objective function and a set of linear constraints; that is, there can be no cross products or powers of decision variables or other types of nonlinear terms in the problem formulation. Linear programming models are capable of handling a large number of variables and constraints and, unlike the tableau method, are not limited to using a specific capacity plan. Linear programming models can determine optimal inventory levels, backorders, subcontractor quantities, production quantities, overtime production, hires, and layoffs. The major drawbacks are that all relationships between variables must be linear and that the optimal values of the decision variables may be fractional. The assumption of linearity is violated when certain costs (e.g., setup costs) are incurred only when specific product families are produced in a time period and do not get larger as the production quantity increases. Also, fractional values of the decision variables may cause difficulties when the variables represent discrete items, such as workers, tables, or trucks.

    Suppose that you must plan the production of a certain product family and do not want to use backorders. Each worker can produce 5000 units per month.

Subcontracting and overtime production are possible options to supplement regular-time production, although overtime is limited to 15 percent of the regular-time production in any month. Let

D_t = demand in month t (presumed known; not a variable)

W_t = workers on hand at the start of month t

H_t = hires at the start of month t

L_t = layoffs at the start of month t

I_t = inventory at the end of month t

S_t = subcontracted production in month t

O_t = overtime production in month t

Then for each month the following constraints are required:

$W_t = W_{t-1} + H_t - L_t$ (relationship for the number of workers)

$I_t = I_{t-1} + 5000W_t + O_t + S_t - D_t$ (relationship for the inventory level)

$O_t \leq 0.15(5000W_t)$ (relationship for the overtime limit)

There are six variables (D_t is not a decision variable) and three constraints for each month. If the production plan is to cover 12 months, you need 72 decision variables and 36 constraints. In addition you need to specify an objective function for minimizing costs or maximizing profits. For example, let

c_w = regular-time wages per worker per month

c_h = cost to hire one worker

c_L = cost to lay off one worker

c_I = cost to hold one unit of product for one month

c_s = cost to subcontract one unit of product

c_o = cost to produce one unit of product on overtime

An objective function for minimizing costs would be

$$TC = \sum_{t=1}^{12}(c_w W_t + c_h H_t + c_L L_t + c_I I_t + c_s S_t + c_o O_t)$$

Obviously, even for simple problems, this approach requires a considerable number of variables and constraints. Hence a computer is mandatory for production planning applications of linear programming. Nonetheless, the method is versatile in its ability to handle a wide variety and large number of variables and constraints.

Managerial Considerations

Other mathematical techniques, such as linear decision rules (Holt, Modigliani, and Simon, 1955), the search decision rule (Taubert, 1968), goal programming (Lee and Moore, 1974), and simulation (Lee and Khumawala, 1974), are available in addition to those covered here. All can be useful in developing sound aggregate plans, but they are only aids to the planning process. As you have seen in this chapter, the planning process is dynamic and often complicated by conflicting objectives. Analytic techniques can help managers evaluate plans and resolve conflicting objectives, but managers—not techniques—make the decisions.

After arriving at an acceptable production plan, management must implement it. However, the aggregate plan is stated in aggregate terms. The first step in implementation therefore is to disaggregate the plan—that is, break it down into specific products, work centers, and dates by using master production scheduling and materials requirements planning, the topic of Chapter 14, and work-force schedules, discussed in Chapter 16.

CHAPTER REVIEW

Solved Problem 1

The Cranston Telephone Company employs workers who lay telephone cables and perform various other construction tasks. The company prides itself on good service and strives to complete all service orders within the planning period in which they are received.

Each worker puts in 600 hours of regular time per planning period and can work as much as an additional 100 hours overtime. The operations department has estimated the following work-force requirements for such services over the next five planning periods.

Planning Period	1	2	3	4	5
Demand (hours)	21,000	18,000	30,000	12,000	24,000

Cranston pays regular-time wages of $6000 per employee per period for any time worked up to 600 hours (including undertime). The overtime pay rate is $15 per hour over 600 hours. Hiring, training, and outfitting a new employee costs $8000. Layoff costs are $2000 per employee. Currently, 40 employees work for Cranston in this capacity.

a. Develop a level work-force plan that allows for no delay in service and minimizes undertime. How many hours of undertime does this plan call for?
b. Prepare a chase strategy without use of overtime. What are the total numbers of employees hired and laid off?
c. Propose an effective mixed-strategy plan.
d. Calculate and compare the total costs of the three plans.

Solution a. The peak demand is 30,000 hours in period 3. As each employee can work 700 hours per period (600 on regular time and 100 on overtime), the level work force that minimizes undertime is 30,000/700 = 42.86, or 43, employees. The level strategy calls for three employees to be hired in the first quarter and for none to be laid off. The 43 employees work (43)(600) = 25,800 hours of regular time in each period. Demand for 30,000 hours in the third period requires 4200 hours (30,000 − 25,800) of overtime. Total undertime for the five periods is 28,200 hours.

| | **Planning Period** | | | | | |
	1	2	3	4	5	Total
Demand (hours)	21,000	18,000	30,000	12,000	24,000	105,000
Regular-time employee requirement	35	30	50	20	40	
Level-strategy work force	43	43	43	43	43	215
Hires	3	—	—	—	—	3
Layoffs	—	—	—	—	—	0
Overtime (hours)	—	—	4,200	—	—	4,200
Undertime (hours)	4,800	7,800	—	13,800	1,800	28,200

b. The chase-strategy work force is calculated by dividing the demand for each period by 600 hours, or the amount of regular-time work for one employee during one period. This strategy calls for a total of 40 workers to be hired and 40 to be laid off during the five-period plan.

| | **Planning Period** | | | | | |
	1	2	3	4	5	Total
Demand (hours)	21,000	18,000	30,000	12,000	24,000	
Regular-time employee requirement	35	30	50	20	40	
Chase-strategy work force	35	30	50	20	40	175
Hires	—	—	20	—	20	40
Layoffs	5	5	—	30	—	40

c. The following mixed-strategy plan uses a combination of hires, layoffs, and overtime to reduce total costs. The work force is reduced by 5 at the beginning of the first period, increased by 8 in the third period, and reduced by 8 in the fourth period.

| | **Planning Period** | | | | | |
	1	2	3	4	5	Total
Demand (hours)	21,000	18,000	30,000	12,000	24,000	
Regular-time employee requirement	35	30	50	20	40	
Mixed-strategy work force	35	35	43	35	35	183
Hires	—	—	8	—	—	8
Layoffs	5	—	—	8	—	13
Overtime (hours)	—	—	4,200	—	3,000	7,200
Undertime (hours)	—	3,000	—	9,000	—	12,000

d. The total cost of the level strategy is $1,377,000. The chase strategy results in a total cost of $1,450,000. The mixed-strategy plan was developed by trial and error and results in a total cost of $1,296,000. Further improvements to the mixed strategy are possible.

Cost	Level Strategy		Chase Strategy		Mixed Strategy	
Regular- time wages	215 worker-periods @ $6000	= $1,290,000	175 worker-periods @ $6000	= $1,050,000	183 worker-periods @ $6000	= $1,098,000
Overtime	4200 hrs @ $15/hr =	63,000			7200 hrs @ $15/hr =	108,000
Hire costs	3 workers @ $8000 =	24,000	40 workers @ $8000 =	320,000	8 workers @ $8000 =	64,000
Layoff costs			40 workers @ $2000 =	80,000	13 workers @ $2000 =	26,000
	Total costs	$1,377,000		$1,450,000		$1,296,000

Solved Problem 2

The Arctic Air Company produces residential air conditioners. The manufacturing manager wants to develop a production plan for the next year based on the following demand and capacity data (in hundreds of units).

	Period					
	Jan–Feb (1)	Mar–Apr (2)	May–Jun (3)	Jul–Aug (4)	Sep–Oct (5)	Nov–Dec (6)
Demand	50	60	90	120	70	40
Capacities						
Regular time	65	65	65	80	80	65
Overtime	13	13	13	16	16	13
Subcontractor	10	10	10	10	10	10

No cost is associated with unused regular time, overtime, or subcontractor capacity. Producing one air conditioning unit on regular time costs $1000, including $300 for labor. Producing a unit on overtime costs $1150. A subcontractor can produce a unit to Arctic Air specifications for $1250. Holding an air conditioner in stock costs $60 for each two-month period, and 200 air conditioners are currently in stock. The plan calls for 400 units to be in stock at the end of period 6. No backorders are allowed. Use the tableau method to develop the aggregate plan that minimizes costs.

Solution The tableau method used to obtain the optimal production plan is shown in Fig. 13.7 on the next page. Again, all production quantities are in hundreds of units. Note that demand in period 6 is 4400. That amount is the period 6 demand of 4000 plus the desired ending inventory of 400. The following table summarizes the production plan depicted in the figure. The anticipation inventory is measured as the amount at the end of each period.

Production Plan

Period	Regular-Time Production	Overtime Production	Subcontracting	Total
1	6,500	—	—	6,500
2	6,500	400	—	6,900
3	6,500	1,300	—	7,800
4	8,000	1,600	1,000	10,600
5	7,000	—	—	7,000
6	4,400	—	—	4,400

Anticipation Inventory

Period	Beginning Inventory Plus Total Production Minus Demand	Anticipation (Ending) Inventory
1	200 + 6500 − 5000	1700
2	1700 + 6900 − 6000	2600
3	2600 + 7800 − 9000	1400
4	1400 + 10,600 − 12,000	0
5	0 + 7000 − 7000	0
6	0 + 4400 − 4000	400

FIGURE 13.7

Period	Alternatives	Time Period 1	2	3	4	5	6	Unused Capacity	Total Capacity
Period	I_0	0 2	60	120	180	240	300	~~2~~ 0	2
1	R_1	1000 48	1060	1120 17	1180	1240	1300	~~65~~ ~~17~~ 0	65
1	O_1	1150	1210	1270	1330	1390	1450	13	13
1	S_1	1250	1310	1370	1430	1490	1550	10	10
2	R_2	X	1000 60	1060 5	1120	1180	1240	~~65~~ ~~5~~ 0	65
2	O_2	X	1150	1210	1270 4	1330	1390	~~13~~ 9	13
2	S_2	X	1250	1310	1370	1430	1490	10	10
3	R_3	X	X	1000 65	1060	1120	1180	~~65~~ 0	65
3	O_3	X	X	1150 3	1210 10	1270	1330	~~13~~ ~~10~~ 0	13
3	S_3	X	X	1250	1310	1370	1430	10	10
4	R_4	X	X	X	1000 80	1060	1120	~~80~~ 0	80
4	O_4	X	X	X	1150 16	1210	1270	~~16~~ 0	16
4	S_4	X	X	X	1250 10	1310	1370	~~10~~ 0	10
5	R_5	X	X	X	X	1000 70	1060	~~80~~ 10	80
5	O_5	X	X	X	X	1150	1210	16	16
5	S_5	X	X	X	X	1250	1310	10	10
6	R_6	X	X	X	X	X	1000 44	~~65~~ 21	65
6	O_6	X	X	X	X	X	1150	13	13
6	S_6	X	X	X	X	X	1250	10	10
	D	50	60	90	120	70	44	132	566

We compute the total cost column by column. This calculation is based on the assumption that workers aren't paid for undertime or are productively put to work elsewhere in the organization whenever they are not needed for this work. The total cost of this plan is $44,287,000.

Period	Calculation	Amount
1	2($0) + 4800($1000)	= $ 4,800,000
2	6000($1000)	= $ 6,000,000
3	1700($1120) + 500($1060) + 6500($1000) + 300($1150)	= $ 9,279,000
4	400($1270) + 1000($1210) + 8000($1000) + 1600($1150) + 1000($1250)	= $12,808,000
5	7000($1000)	= $ 7,000,000
6	4400($1000)	= $ 4,400,000
	Total	= $44,287,000

Chapter Highlights

- Aggregate plans (production plans or staffing plans) are statements of strategy that specify time-phased production or service rates, work-force levels, and (in manufacturing) inventory investment. These plans show how the organization will work toward longer term objectives while considering the demand and capacity that are likely to exist over a planning horizon of only a year or two. In manufacturing organizations, the plan linking strategic goals to the master production schedule is called the production plan. In service organizations, the staffing plan links strategic goals to the work-force schedule.

- To reduce the level of detail required in the planning process, products or services are aggregated into families, and labor is aggregated along product family lines or according to the general skills or services provided. Time is aggregated into periods of months or quarters.

- Managerial inputs are required from the various functional areas in the organization. This approach typically raises conflicting objectives, such as high customer service, a stable work force, and low inventory investment. Creativity and cross-functional compromise are required to reconcile these conflicts.

- The two basic types of alternatives are reactive and aggressive. Reactive alternatives take customer demand as a given. Aggressive alternatives attempt to change the timing or quantity of customer demand to stabilize production or service rates and reduce inventory requirements.

- Two pure, but generally high-cost planning strategies are the level strategy, which maintains a constant work-force size and production rate, and the chase strategy, which varies work-force level and production rate to match fluctuations in demand.

- Developing aggregate plans is an iterative process of determining demand requirements; identifying relevant constraints, alternatives, and costs; preparing and approving a plan; and implementing and updating the plan.

- Although trial-and-error techniques and linear programming techniques can help analyze complicated alternatives, aggregate planning is primarily an exercise in conflict resolution and compromise. Ultimately, decisions are made by managers, not by quantitative methods.

Key Terms

aggregate plan 589
aggressive alternatives 597
annual plan 592
backlog 597
backorder 597
business plan 592
chase strategy 598

complementary products 597
financial plan 592
level strategy 598
master production schedule 592
mixed strategy 598
planning horizon 592
production plan 589

reactive alternatives 595
staffing plan 589
stockout 597
tableau method 606
work-force schedule 593

Study Questions

1. What is an aggregate plan? Why are production plans aggregated into product families?
2. How does the aggregate plan relate to other plans?
3. Consider the statement "Production planning is the responsibility of manufacturing because it determines the use of manufacturing resources." Comment on that statement in light of the strategic importance of production planning.
4. Give reasons why executives representing the following areas should be interested in production planning.
   a. Marketing   d. Finance
   b. Manufacturing   e. Human resources
   c. Materials   f. Engineering
5. List the typical objectives of aggregate planning. Describe a situation that demonstrates the conflicting nature of those objectives.
6. What is the difference between *reactive* and *aggressive* alternatives in aggregate planning? List two examples of each.
7. The *chase* strategy and the *level* strategy represent two extremes in aggregate planning. Define each one and describe the type of environment in which each would work best.
8. Briefly describe the aggregate planning process and explain how inputs from functional areas in the organization are solicited and incorporated into production and staffing plans.
9. Compare and contrast the staffing plan in a service organization with a production plan in a manufacturing organization. In what ways are the objectives, alternatives, and planning processes different?
10. The Hometown Bank currently employs eight tellers to staff lobby stations for customer transactions. Customer demand for banking services is variable, with peaks coinciding with the end of the week, the end of the month, and holiday seasons. Because of this variability the tellers are idle much of the time. During rush periods, however, customers experience lengthy delays. Suppose that you are the operations manager of this bank.
    a. What staffing plan alternatives would you consider?
    b. What data would you need?
    c. What objectives would you consider?

Discussion Questions

1. Quantitative methods can help managers evaluate alternative production plans on the basis of cost. These methods require cost estimates for each of the controllable variables, such as overtime, subcontracting, hiring, firing, and inventory investment. Say that the existing work force is made up of 10,000 direct-labor employees having skills valued at $40,000 per year. The production plan calls for "creating alternative career opportunities"—in other words, laying off 500 employees. List the types of costs incurred when employees are laid off, and make a rough estimate of the length of time required for payroll savings to recover restructuring costs. If business is expected to improve in one year, are layoffs financially justified? What costs are incurred in a layoff that are difficult to estimate in monetary terms?
2. In your community some employers maintain stable work forces at all costs, and others furlough and recall workers seemingly at the drop of a hat. What are the differences in markets, management, products, financial position, skills, costs, and/or competition that could explain these two extremes in personnel policy?
3. As the fortunes of the Big Three domestic automakers improved in the mid 1990s, workers at one GM plant went on strike. The striking workers produced transmissions used in other GM plants. Almost immediately, many other GM plants shut down for lack of transmissions. Facing lost production during a hot market, GM management quickly acceded to labor's demands to recall more furloughed workers and schedule less overtime. What production planning decisions regarding the controllable variables (listed in Discussion Question 1) are apparent in this situation?

Problems

1. The Barberton Municipal Division of Road Maintenance is charged with road repair in the city of Barberton and surrounding area. Cindy Kramer, road maintenance director, must submit a staffing plan for the next year based on a set schedule for repairs and on the city budget. Kramer estimates that the labor hours required for the next four quarters are 6000, 12,000, 19,000, and 9000, respectively. Each of the 11 workers on the work force can contribute 520 hours per quarter. Payroll costs are $6240 in wages

per worker for regular time worked up to 520 hours, with an overtime pay rate of $18 for each overtime hour. Overtime is limited to 20 percent of the regular-time capacity in any quarter. Although unused over-time capacity has no cost, unused regular time is paid at $12 per hour. The cost of hiring a worker is $3000, and the cost of laying off a worker is $2000. Subcontracting is not permitted.

a. Find a level work-force plan that allows no delay in road repair and minimizes undertime. Overtime can be used to its limits in any quarter. What is the total cost of the plan and how many undertime hours does it call for?

b. Use a chase strategy without overtime. What is the total cost of this plan?

c. Propose a plan of your own. Compare your plan with those in parts a and b and discuss its comparative merits.

2. Jill B. Nimble's day care center estimates the following work-force requirements for its services over the next two years.

Quarter	1	2	3	4
Demand (hours)	4200	6400	3000	4800

Quarter	5	6	7	8
Demand (hours)	4400	6240	3600	4800

Each certified instructor puts in 480 hours per quarter regular time and can work an additional 120 hours overtime. Regular-time wages and benefits cost Nimble $7200 per employee per quarter for regular time worked up to 480 hours, with an overtime cost of $20 per hour. Unused regular time for certified instructors is paid at $15 per hour. There is no cost for unused overtime capacity. The cost of hiring, training, and certifying a new employee is $10,000. Layoff costs are $4000 per employee. Currently, eight employees work in this capacity.

a. Find a level work-force plan that allows for no delay in service and minimizes undertime. What is the total cost of this plan?

b. Use a chase strategy without overtime. What is the total cost of this plan?

c. Propose a low-cost, mixed-strategy plan and calculate its total cost.

3. Continuing Problem 2, now assume that Nimble is permitted to employ some uncertified, part-time instructors, provided they represent no more than 15 percent of the total work-force hours in any quarter. Each part-time instructor can work up to 240 hours

per quarter, with no overtime or undertime cost. Labor costs for part-time instructors are $12 per hour. Hiring and training costs are $2000 per uncertified instructor, and there are no layoff costs.

a. Propose a low-cost, mixed-strategy plan and calculate its total cost.

b. What are the primary advantages and disadvantages of having a work force consisting of both regular and temporary employees?

4. The Crop Chemical Company produces chemical fertilizers. The projected manufacturing requirements (in thousands of gallons) for the next four quarters are 80, 50, 80, and 130, respectively. Stockouts and backorders are to be avoided. A level production strategy is desired.

a. Determine the level quarterly production rate required to meet total demand for the year. Beginning inventory is zero.

b. Specify the anticipation inventories that will be produced.

c. Suppose that the requirements for the next four quarters are revised to 80, 130, 50, and 80, respectively. If total demand is the same, what level production rate is needed now?

5. Management at the Ross Corporation has determined the following demand schedule (in units).

Month	1	2	3	4
Demand	500	800	1000	1400

Month	5	6	7	8
Demand	2000	1600	1400	1200

Month	9	10	11	12
Demand	1000	2400	3000	1000

An employee can produce an average of 10 units per month. Each worker on the payroll costs $2000 in regular-time wages per month. Undertime is paid at the same rate as regular time. In accordance with the labor contract in force, Ross Corporation doesn't work overtime or use subcontracting. Ross can hire and train a new employee for $2000 and lay one off for $500. Inventory costs $32 per unit on hand at the end of each month. At present, 140 employees are on the payroll.

a. Prepare a production plan with a level strategy. The plan may call for a one-time adjustment of the work force before month 1.

b. Prepare a production plan with a chase strategy.
c. Compare and contrast the two pure-strategy plans on the basis of annual costs and other factors that you believe to be important.
d. Propose a mixed-strategy plan that is better than the two pure-strategy plans. Explain why you believe that your plan is better.

6. The Flying Frisbee Company has forecasted the following staffing requirements for full-time employees. Demand is seasonal, and management wants three alternative staffing plans to be developed.

Month	1	2	3	4
Requirement	2	2	4	6

Month	5	6	7	8
Requirement	18	20	12	18

Month	9	10	11	12
Requirement	7	3	2	1

The company currently has 10 employees. No more than 10 new hires can be accommodated in any month because of limited training facilities. No backorders are allowed, and overtime cannot exceed 25 percent of regular-time capacity in any month. There is no cost for unused overtime capacity. Regular-time wages are $1500 per month, and overtime wages are 150 percent of regular-time wages. Undertime is paid at the same rate as regular time. The hiring cost is $2500 per person, and the layoff cost is $2000 per person.

a. Prepare a staffing plan utilizing a level strategy.
b. Using a chase strategy, prepare a plan that is consistent with the constraint on hiring and minimizes use of overtime.
c. Prepare a low-cost, mixed-strategy plan.
d. Which strategy is most cost effective? What are the advantages and disadvantages of each plan?

7. The Little Shoe Company makes sandals for children. Management has just prepared a forecast of sales (in pairs of sandals) for next year and now must prepare a production plan. The company has traditionally maintained a level work-force strategy. Currently, there are eight workers, who have been with the company for a number of years. Each employee can produce 2000 pairs of sandals during a two-month planning period. Every year management authorizes

overtime in periods 1, 5, and 6, up to a maximum of 20 percent of regular-time capacity. Management wants to avoid stockouts and backorders and won't accept any plan that calls for such shortages. At present there are 12,000 pairs of sandals in finished goods inventory. The demand forecast is as follows.

Period	1	2	3
Sales	25,000	6,500	15,000

Period	4	5	6
Sales	19,000	32,000	29,000

a. Is the level work-force strategy feasible with the current work force, assuming that overtime is used in periods 1, 5, and 6? Explain.
b. Find two alternative plans that would satisfy management's concern over stockouts and backorders, disregarding costs. What trade-offs between these two plans must be considered?

Advanced Problems

Linear programming approaches, including the tableau method, are recommended for solving Advanced Problems 8–10. Additional applications of these techniques to production planning may be found in Supplement G, Review Problems 7 and 8, and in Supplement I, Review Problems 14, 18, and 19.

8. The Bull Grin Company makes a supplement for the animal feed produced by a number of companies. Sales are seasonal, but Bull Grin's customers refuse to stockpile the supplement during slack sales periods. In other words, the customers want to minimize their inventory investments, insist on shipments according to their schedules, and won't accept backorders.

   Bull Grin employs manual, unskilled laborers, who require little or no training. Producing 1000 pounds of supplement costs $830 on regular time and $910 on overtime. There is no cost for unused regular-time, overtime, or subcontractor capacity. These figures include materials, which account for 80 percent of the cost. Overtime is limited to production of a total of 20,000 pounds per quarter. In addition, subcontractors can be hired at $1000 per thousand pounds, but only 30,000 pounds per quarter can be produced this way.

   The current level of inventory is 40,000 pounds, and management wants to end the year at that level. Holding 1000 pounds of feed supplement in inventory per quarter costs $100. The latest annual forecast is shown in Table 13.1.

TABLE 13.1 *Forecasts and Capacities*

	Period				
	Quarter 1	Quarter 2	Quarter 3	Quarter 4	Total
Demand (pounds)	130,000	400,000	800,000	470,000	1,800,000
Capacities (pounds)					
Regular time	390,000	400,000	460,000	380,000	1,630,000
Overtime	20,000	20,000	20,000	20,000	80,000
Subcontract	30,000	30,000	30,000	30,000	120,000

Use the tableau method to find the optimal production plan and calculate its cost, or use trial-and-error to find a good production plan and calculate its cost.

9. Waverly Scale Company produces industrial scales for a variety of applications. The cost to Waverly for hiring a semiskilled worker for its assembly plant is $3000 and for laying one off is $2000. The plant averages an output of 36,000 scales per quarter with its current work force of 720 employees. Regular-time capacity is directly proportional to the number of employees. Overtime is limited to a maximum of 3000 scales per quarter, and subcontracting is limited to 1000 scales per quarter. The costs to produce one scale are $2430 on regular time (including materials), $2700 on overtime, and $3300 via subcontracting. Unused regular-time capacity costs $270 per scale. There is no cost for unused overtime or subcontractor capacity. The current level of inventory is 4000 scales, and management wants to end the year at that level. Customers do not tolerate backorders, and holding a scale in inventory per quarter costs $300. The demand for scales this coming year is

Quarter	1	2	3	4
Demand	10,000	41,000	77,000	44,000

Two work-force plans have been proposed, and management is uncertain as to which one to use. The table shows the number of employees per quarter under each plan.

Quarter	1	2	3	4
Plan 1	720	780	920	720
Plan 2	860	860	860	860

a. Which plan would you recommend to management? Explain, supporting your recommendation

with an analysis using either the tableau method or computer solution.

b. If management used creative pricing to get customers to buy scales in nontraditional time periods, the following demand schedule would result.

Quarter	1	2	3	4
Demand	20,000	54,000	54,000	44,000

Which work-force plan would you recommend now?

10. Gretchen's Kitchen is a fast-food restaurant located in an ideal spot near the local high school. Gretchen Lowe must prepare an annual staffing plan. The only menu items are hamburgers, chili, soft drinks, shakes, and french fries. A sample of 1000 customers taken at random revealed that they purchased 2100 hamburgers, 200 pints of chili, 1000 soft drinks and shakes, and 1000 bags of french fries. Thus for purposes of estimating staffing requirements, Lowe assumes that each customer purchases 2.1 hamburgers, 0.2 pint of chili, 1 soft drink or shake, and 1 bag of french fries. Each hamburger requires 4 minutes of labor, a pint of chili requires 3 minutes, and a soft drink/shake and a bag of fries each take 2 minutes of labor.

The restaurant currently has 10 part-time employees who work 80 hours a month on staggered shifts. Wages are $400 per month for regular time and $7.50 per hour for overtime. Hiring and training costs are $250 per new employee, and layoff costs are $50 per employee.

Lowe realizes that building up seasonal inventories of hamburgers (or any of the products) would not be wise because of shelf-life considerations. Also, any demand not satisfied is a lost sale and must be avoided. Three strategies come to mind.

- Utilize a level work-force strategy and use up to 20 percent of regular-time capacity on overtime.

- Maintain a base of 10 employees, hiring and laying off as needed to avoid any overtime.

- Utilize a chase strategy, hiring and firing employees as demand changes to avoid overtime.

When performing her calculations Lowe always rounds to the next highest integer for the number of employees. She also follows a policy of not using an employee more than 80 hours per month, except when overtime is needed. The projected demand by month (number of customers) for next year is as follows.

Jan.	3200	July	4800
Feb.	2600	Aug.	4200
Mar.	3300	Sept.	3800
Apr.	3900	Oct.	3600
May	3600	Nov.	3500
June	4200	Dec.	3000

a. Develop the schedule of service requirements for the next year.
b. Which of the strategies is most effective?
c. Suppose that an arrangement with the high school enables the manager to identify good prospective employees without having to advertise in the local newspaper. This source reduces the hiring cost to $50, which is mainly the cost of charred hamburgers during training. If cost is her only concern, will this method of hiring change Gretchen Lowe's strategy? Considering other objectives that may be appropriate, do you think she should change strategies?

CASE

Memorial Hospital

Memorial Hospital is a 265-bed regional health care facility located in the mountains of western North Carolina. The mission of the hospital is to provide quality health care to the people of Ashe County and the six surrounding counties. To accomplish this mission Memorial Hospital's CEO has outlined three objectives: (1) maxi-

mize customer service to increase customer satisfaction, (2) minimize costs to remain competitive, and (3) minimize fluctuations in work-force levels to help stabilize area employment.

The hospital's operations are segmented into eight major wards for the purposes of planning and scheduling the nursing staff. These wards are listed in Table 13.2 along with the number of beds, targeted patient-to-nurse ratios, and average patient census for each ward. The overall demand for hospital services has remained relative-

TABLE 13.2   *Ward Capacity Data*

Ward	Number of Beds	Patients per Nurse	Patient Census*
Intensive care	20	2	10
Cardiac	25	4	15
Maternity	30	4	10
Pediatric	40	4	22
Surgery	5	†	†
Post op	15	5	8 (T–F daily equivalent)‡
Emergency	10	3	5 (daily equivalent)‡
General	120	8	98

*Yearly average per day.

†The hospital employs 20 surgical nurses. Routine surgery is scheduled on Tuesdays and Fridays; five surgeries can be scheduled per day per operating room (bed) on these days. Emergency surgery is scheduled as needed.

‡Daily equivalents are used to schedule nurses because patients flow through these wards in relatively short periods of time. A daily equivalent of 5 indicates that, throughout a typical day, an average of five patients are treated in the ward.

ly constant over the past few years even though the population of the seven counties served has increased. This stable demand can be attributed to increased competition from other hospitals in the area and the rise in alternative health care delivery systems such as health maintenance organizations (HMOs). However, demand for Memorial Hospital's services does vary considerably by type of ward and time of year. Table 13.3 provides a historical monthly breakdown of the average daily patient census per ward.

The director of nursing for Memorial Hospital is Darlene Fry. Each fall she confronts one of the most challenging aspects of her job: planning the nurse staffing levels for the next calendar year. Although the average demand for nurses has remained relatively stable over the past couple of years, the staffing plan usually changes because of changing work policies, changing pay structures, and temporary nurse availability and cost. With fall quickly approaching, Fry has begun to collect information to plan next year's staffing levels.

The nurses at Memorial Hospital work a regular schedule of four 10-hour days per week. The average regular-time pay across all nursing grades is $12.00 per hour. Overtime may be scheduled when necessary. However, because of the intensity of the demands placed on nurses, only a limited amount of overtime is permitted per week. Nurses may be scheduled for up to 12 hours per day for a maximum of five days per week. Overtime is compensated at a rate of $18.00 per hour. In periods of extremely high demand, temporary part-time nurses may be hired for a limited period of time. Temporary nurses are paid $15.00 per hour. Memorial Hospital has a policy that limits the proportion of temporary nurses to 15 percent of the total nursing staff.

Finding, hiring, and retaining qualified nurses is a problem that hospitals have been facing for years. One reason is that various forms of private practice are luring many nurses away from hospitals with higher pay and greater flexibility. This situation has caused Memorial to guarantee its full-time staff nurses pay for a minimum of 30 hours per week, regardless of the demand placed on nursing services. In addition, each nurse receives a four-week paid vacation each year. However, vacation scheduling may be somewhat restricted by the projected demand for nurses during particular times of the year.

At present, the hospital employs 100 nurses, including 20 surgical nurses. The other 80 nurses are assigned to the remaining seven major areas of the hospital. The Personnel Department has told Fry that the average cost to the hospital for hiring a new full-time nurse is $400 and for laying off or firing a nurse is $150. Although layoffs are an option, Fry is aware of the hospital's objective of maintaining a level work force.

After looking over the information that she has collected, Darlene Fry decides that it is time to roll up her sleeves and get started.

Questions

1. Explain the alternatives available to Darlene Fry as she develops a nurse staffing plan for Memorial Hospital. How does each meet the objectives stated by the CEO?
2. Based on the data presented, develop a nurse staffing plan for Memorial Hospital. Explain your rationale for this plan.

Source: This case was prepared by Dr. Brooke Saladin, Wake Forest University, as a basis for classroom discussion.

TABLE 13.3   *Average Daily Patient Census per Month*

Ward						Month						
	J	F	M	A	M	J	J	A	S	O	N	D
Intensive care	13	10	8	7	7	6	11	13	9	10	12	14
Cardiac	18	16	15	13	14	12	13	12	13	15	18	20
Maternity	8	8	12	13	10	8	13	13	14	10	8	7
Pediatric	22	23	24	24	25	21	22	20	18	20	21	19
Surgery*	20	18	18	17	16	16	22	21	17	18	20	22
Post op†	10	8	7	7	6	6	10	10	7	8	9	10
Emergency†	6	4	4	7	8	5	5	4	4	3	4	6
General	110	108	100	98	95	90	88	92	98	102	107	94

*Average surgeries per day.
†Daily equivalents.

Selected References

Bowman, E. H. "Production Planning by the Transportation Method of Linear Programming." *Journal of the Operations Research Society,* vol. 4 (February 1956), pp. 100–103.

Hanssman, F., and S. W. Hess. "A Linear Programming Approach to Production and Employment Scheduling." *Management Technology,* vol. 1 (January 1960), pp. 46–51.

Holt, C., C. F. Modigliani, and H. Simon. "A Linear Decision Rule for Production and Employment Scheduling." *Management Science,* vol. 2, no. 2 (October 1955), pp. 1–30.

"An Industry's Race with Summer," *New York Times,* February 23, 1989.

Jones, C. H. "Parametric Production Planning." *Management Science,* vol. 15, no. 11 (July 1967), pp. 843–866.

Krajewski, L., and H. Thompson. "Efficient Employment Planning in Public Utilities." *Bell Journal of Economics and Management Science,* vol. 6, no. 1 (Spring 1975), pp. 314–326.

Lee, S. M., and L. J. Moore. "A Practical Approach to Production Scheduling." *Production and Inventory Management* (First quarter 1974), pp. 79–92.

Lee, W. B., and B. M. Khumawala. "Simulation Testing of Aggregate Production Planning Models in an Implementation Methodology." *Management Science,* vol. 20, no. 6 (February 1974), pp. 903–911.

Silver, E. A. "A Tutorial on Production Smoothing and Workforce Balancing." *Operations Research* (November–December 1967), pp. 985–1010.

Taubert, W. H. "A Search Decision Rule for the Aggregate Scheduling Problem." *Management Science,* vol. 14, no. 6 (February 1968), pp. 343–359.

Linear Programming

In many business situations, resources are limited and demand for them is great. For example, a limited number of vehicles may have to be scheduled to make multiple trips to customers, or a staffing plan may have to be developed to cover expected variable demand with the fewest employees. This supplement describes a technique called **linear programming**, which is useful for allocating scarce resources among competing demands. The resources may be time, money, or materials, and the limitations are known as constraints. Linear programming can help managers find the best allocation solution and provide information about the value of additional resources.

◆ BASIC CONCEPTS

Outline

Before we can demonstrate how to solve problems in operations management with linear programming, we must first explain several characteristics and mathematical assumptions of all linear programming models:

1. Objective function
2. Decision variables
3. Constraints
4. Feasible region
5. Parameters
6. Linearity
7. Nonnegativity

Linear programming is an *optimization* process. A single **objective function** states mathematically what is being maximized (e.g., profit or present value) or minimized (e.g., cost or scrap). The objective function provides the scorecard on which the attractiveness of different solutions is judged.

Decision variables represent choices that the decision maker can control. Solving the problem yields their optimal values. For example, a decision variable could be the number of units of a product to make next month or the number of units of inventory to hold next month. Linear programming is based on the assumption that decision variables are *continuous*—they can be fractional quantities and need not be whole numbers. Often this assumption is realistic, as when the decision variable is expressed in dollars, hours, or some other continuous measure. Even when the decision variables represent nondivisible units such as workers, tables, or trucks, we sometimes can simply round the linear programming solution up or down to get a reasonable solution that does not violate any constraints, or we can use a more advanced technique, called *integer programming*.

Constraints are limitations that restrict the permissible choices for the decision variables. Each limitation can be expressed mathematically in one of three ways: a less-than-or-equal-to ($\leq$), equal-to ($=$), or greater-than-or-equal-to ($\geq$) constraint. A $\leq$ constraint puts an upper limit on some function of decision variables and most often is used with maximization problems. For example, a $\leq$ constraint may specify the maximum number of customers who can be served or the capacity limit of a machine. An $=$ constraint means that the function must equal some value. For example, 100 (not 99 or 101) units of one product must be made. An $=$ constraint often is used for certain mandatory relationships, such as the fact that ending inventory always equals beginning inventory plus production minus sales. A $\geq$ constraint puts a lower limit on some function of decision variables. For example, a $\geq$ constraint may specify that production of a product must exceed or equal demand.

Every linear programming problem must have one or more constraints. Taken together, the constraints define a **feasible region,** which represents all permissible combinations of the decision variables. In some unusual situations, the problem is so tightly constrained that there is only one possible solution—or perhaps none. However, in the usual case the feasibility region contains infinitely many possible solutions, assuming that the feasible combinations of the decision variables can be fractional values. The goal of the decision maker is to find the best possible solution.

The objective function and constraints are functions of decision variables and parameters. A **parameter,** also known as a *coefficient* or *given constant,* is a value that the decision maker cannot control and that doesn't change when the solution is implemented. Each parameter is assumed to be known with **certainty.** For example, a computer programmer may know that running a software program will take three hours—no more, no less.

The objective function and constraint equations are assumed to be linear. **Linearity** implies proportionality and additivity—there can be no products (e.g., $10x_1x_2$) or powers (e.g., x_1^3) of decision variables. Suppose that the profit gained by producing two types of products (represented by decision variables x_1 and x_2) is $2x_1 + 3x_2$. Proportionality implies that one unit of x_1 contributes \$2 to profits and two units contribute \$4, regardless of how much of x_2 is produced. Similarly, each unit of x_2 contributes \$3, whether it is the first or the tenth unit produced. Additivity means that the total objective function value equals the profits from x_1 plus the profits from x_2.

Finally, we make an assumption of **nonnegativity,** which means that the decision variables must be positive or zero. A firm making spaghetti sauce, for example, cannot produce a negative number of jars. To be formally correct, a linear programming formulation should show a ≥ 0 constraint for each decision variable. Most computer software programs for linear programming, such as CMOM, contain these constraints already, so the analyst doesn't have to enter them as input data.

Although the assumptions of linearity, certainty, and continuous variables are restrictive, linear programming can help managers analyze many complex resource allocation problems. The process of building the model forces managers to identify the important decision variables and constraints, a useful step in its own right. Identifying the nature and scope of the problem represents a major step toward solving it. In a later section we show how sensitivity analysis can help the manager deal with uncertainties in the parameters and answer "what if" questions.

Formulating a Problem

Linear programming applications begin with the formulation of a *model* of the problem with the general characteristics just described. We illustrate the modeling process here with the **product-mix problem**—a one-period type of aggregate planning problem, the solution of which yields optimal output quantities (or product mix) of a group of products or services, subject to resource capacity and market demand constraints. Formulating a model to represent each unique problem, using the following three-step sequence, is the most creative and perhaps the most difficult part of linear programming.

> **Step 1.** *Define the decision variables.* What must be decided? Define each decision variable specifically, remembering that the definitions used in the objective function must be equally useful in the constraints. The definitions should be as specific as possible. Consider the following two alternative definitions:

$$x_1 = \text{product 1}$$

$$x_1 = \text{number of units of product 1 to be produced}$$
$$\text{and sold next month}$$

The second definition is much more specific than the first, making the remaining steps easier.

> **Step 2.** *Write out the objective function.* What is to be maximized or minimized? If it is next month's profits, write out an objective function that makes next month's profits a linear function of the decision variables. Identify parameters to go with each decision variable. For example, if each unit of x_1 sold yields a profit of \$7, the total profit from product x_1 equals $7x_1$. If a variable has no impact on the objective function, its objective function coefficient is 0. The objective function often is set equal to Z, and the goal is to maximize or minimize Z.

> **Step 3.** *Write out the constraints.* What limits the values of the decision variables? Identify the constraints and the parameters for each decision variable in them. As with the objective function, the parameter for a variable that has no impact in a constraint is 0. To be formally correct, also write out the nonnegativity constraints.

As a consistency check, make sure that the same unit of measure is being used on both sides of each constraint and in the objective function. For example, suppose that the right-hand side of a constraint is hours of capacity per month. Then if a decision variable on the left-hand side of the constraint measures the number of units produced per month, the dimensions of the parameter that is multiplied by the decision variable must be hours per unit because

$$\left(\frac{\text{hours}}{\text{unit}}\right)\left(\frac{\text{units}}{\text{month}}\right) = \left(\frac{\text{hours}}{\text{month}}\right)$$

Of course, you can also skip around from one step to another, depending on the part of the problem that has your attention. If you can't get past step 1, try a new set of definitions for the decision variables. There may be more than one way to model a problem correctly.

EXAMPLE I.1

*Formulating a
Linear
Programming Model*

The Stratton Company produces two basic types of plastic pipe. Three resources are crucial to the output of pipe: extrusion hours, packaging hours, and a special additive to the plastic raw material. The following data represent next week's situation. All data are expressed in units of 100 feet of pipe.

| | Product | | |
Resource	Type 1	Type 2	Resource Availability
Extrusion	4 hr	6 hr	48 hr
Packaging	2 hr	2 hr	18 hr
Additive mix	2 lb	1 lb	16 lb

The contribution to profits and overhead per 100 feet of pipe is $34 for type 1 and $40 for type 2. Formulate a linear programming model to determine how much of each type of pipe should be produced to maximize contribution to profits and to overhead.

Solution

Step 1. To define the decision variables that determine product mix, we let

x_1 = amount of type 1 pipe to be produced and sold next week, measured in 100-foot increments (for example, $x_1 = 2$ means 200 feet of type 1 pipe)

x_2 = amount of type 2 pipe to be produced and sold next week, measured in 100-foot increments

Step 2. Next, we define the objective function. The goal is to maximize the total contribution that the two products make to profits and overhead. Each unit of x_1 yields $34, and each unit of x_2 yields $40. For specific values of x_1 and x_2, we find the total profit by multiplying the number of units of each product produced by the profit per unit and adding them. Thus our objective function becomes

$$\text{Maximize:} \quad \$34x_1 + \$40x_2 = Z$$

Step 3. The final step is to formulate the constraints. Each unit of x_1 and x_2 produced consumes some of the critical resources. In the extrusion department, a unit of x_1 requires 4 hours and a unit of x_2 requires 6 hours. The total must not exceed the 48 hours of capacity available, so we use the $\leq$ sign. Thus the first constraint is

$$4x_1 + 6x_2 \leq 48 \quad \text{(extrusion)}$$

Similarly, we can formulate constraints for packaging and raw materials:

$$2x_1 + 2x_2 \leq 18 \quad \text{(packaging)}$$

$$2x_1 + x_2 \leq 16 \quad \text{(additive mix)}$$

These three constraints restrict our choice of values for the decision variables because the values we choose for x_1 and x_2 must satisfy all of them. Negative values for x_1 and x_2 don't make sense, so we add nonnegativity restrictions to the model:

$$x_1 \geq 0 \quad \text{and} \quad x_2 \geq 0 \quad \text{(nonnegativity restrictions)}$$

We can now state the entire model, made complete with the definitions of variables.

$$\text{Maximize:} \quad \$34x_1 + \$40x_2 = Z$$
$$\text{Subject to:} \quad 4x_1 + 6x_2 \leq 48$$
$$2x_1 + 2x_2 \leq 18$$
$$2x_1 + x_2 \leq 16$$
$$x_1 \geq 0 \quad \text{and} \quad x_2 \geq 0$$

where x_1 = amount of type 1 pipe to be produced and sold next week, measured in 100-foot increments

x_2 = amount of type 2 pipe to be produced and sold next week, measured in 100-foot increments

◆ GRAPHIC ANALYSIS

With the model formulated, we now seek the optimal solution. In practice, most linear programming problems are solved with the computer. However, insight into the meaning of the computer output—and linear programming concepts in general—can be gained by analyzing a simple two-variable problem with the **graphic method of linear programming.** Hence we begin with the graphic method, even though it isn't a practical technique for solving problems having three or more decision variables. The five basic steps are

1. plot the constraints,
2. identify the feasible region,
3. plot an objective function line,
4. find the visual solution, and
5. find the algebraic solution.

Plot the Constraints

We begin by plotting the constraint equations, disregarding the inequality portion of the constraints ($<$ or $>$). Making each constraint an equality ($=$) transforms it into the equation for a straight line. The line can be drawn as soon as we identify two points on it. Any two points reasonably spread out may be chosen; the easiest ones to find are the *axis intercepts,* where the line intersects each axis. To find the x_1 axis intercept, set x_2 equal to 0 and solve the equation for x_1. For the Stratton Company in Example I.1, the equation of the line for the extrusion process is

$$4x_1 + 6x_2 = 48$$

For the x_1 axis intercept, $x_2 = 0$ and so

$$4x_1 + 6(0) = 48$$
$$x_1 = 12$$

To find the x_2 axis intercept, set $x_1 = 0$ and solve for x_2:

$$4(0) + 6x_2 = 48$$
$$x_2 = 8$$

We connect points (0, 8) and (12, 0) with a straight line, as shown in Fig. I.1.

FIGURE I.1

Graph of the Extrusion Constraint

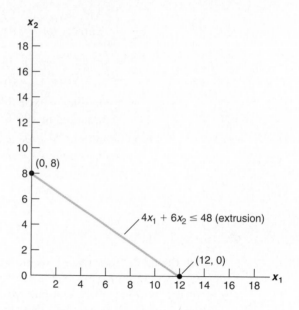

EXAMPLE I.2

Plotting the Constraints

For the Stratton Company problem, plot the other constraints: one for packaging and one for the additive mix.

Solution   The equation for the packaging process's line is $2x_1 + 2x_2 = 18$. To find the x_1 intercept, set $x_2 = 0$:

$$2x_1 + 2(0) = 18$$

$$x_1 = 9$$

To find the x_2 axis intercept, set $x_1 = 0$:

$$2(0) + 2x_2 = 18$$

$$x_2 = 9$$

The equation for the additive mix's line is $2x_1 + x_2 = 16$. To find the x_1 intercept, set $x_2 = 0$:

$$2x_1 + 0 = 16$$

$$x_1 = 8$$

To find the x_2 axis intercept, set $x_1 = 0$:

$$2(0) + x_2 = 16$$

$$x_2 = 16$$

With a straight line, we connect points $(0, 9)$ and $(9, 0)$ for the packaging constraint and points $(0, 16)$ and $(8, 0)$ for the additive mix constraint. Figure I.2 shows the graph with all three constraints plotted.

FIGURE I.2 *Graph of the Three Constraints*

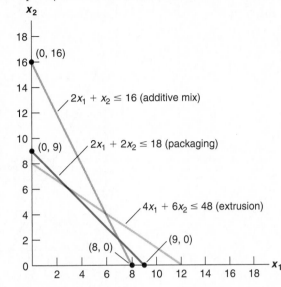

Identify the Feasible Region

The feasible region is the area on the graph that contains the solutions that satisfy all the constraints simultaneously, including the nonnegativity restrictions. To find the feasible region, locate first the feasible points for each constraint and then the area that satisfies all constraints. *Generally* the following three rules identify the feasible points for a given constraint.

1. For the = constraint, only the points on the line are feasible solutions.
2. For the ≤ constraint, the points on the line and the points below and/or to the left are feasible solutions.
3. For the ≥ constraint, the points on the line and the points above and/or to the right are feasible solutions.

Exceptions to these rules occur when one or more of the parameters on the left-hand side of a constraint are negative. In such cases, we draw the constraint line and test a point on one side of it. If the point doesn't satisfy the constraint, it is in the infeasible part of the graph. Suppose that a linear programming model has the constraints

$$2x_1 + x_2 \geq 10$$
$$2x_1 + 3x_2 \geq 18$$
$$x_1 \leq 7$$
$$x_2 \leq 5$$
$$-6x_1 + 5x_2 \leq 5$$
$$x_1, x_2 \geq 0$$

The feasible region is the shaded portion of Fig. I.3. The arrows shown on each constraint identify which side of each line is feasible. The rules work for all but the fifth constraint, which has a negative parameter, -6, for x_1. We arbitrarily

FIGURE I.3

Identifying the Feasible Region

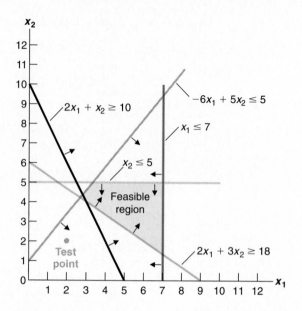

select $(2, 2)$ as the test point, which Fig. I.3 shows is below the line and to the right. At this point, we find $-6(2) + 5(2) = -2$. Because -2 doesn't exceed 5, the portion of the figure containing $(2, 2)$ is feasible, at least for this fifth constraint.

EXAMPLE I.3

Identifying the Feasible Region

Identify the feasible region for the Stratton Company problem.

Solution   Because there are only $\leq$ constraints and the parameters on the left-hand side of each constraint are not negative, the feasible portions are to the left of and below each constraint. The feasible region, shaded in Fig. I.4, satisfies all three constraints simultaneously.

FIGURE I.4   *The Feasible Region*

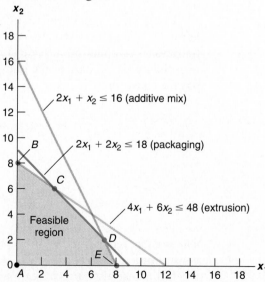

Plot an Objective Function Line

Now we want to find the solution that optimizes the objective function. Even though all the points in the feasible region represent possible solutions, we can limit our search to the corner points. A **corner point** lies at the intersection of two (or possibly more) constraint lines on the boundary of the feasible region. No interior points in the feasible region need be considered because at least one corner point is better than any interior point. Similarly, other points on the boundary of the feasible region can be ignored because there is a corner point that is at least as good as any of them.

In Fig. I.4 the five corner points are marked *A*, *B*, *C*, *D*, and *E*. Point *A* is the origin $(0, 0)$ and can be ignored because any other feasible point is a better solution. We could try each of the other corner points in the objective function and select the one that maximizes *Z*. For example, corner point *B* lies at $(0, 8)$. If we substitute these values into the objective function, the resulting *Z* value is 320:

$$34x_1 + 40x_2 = Z$$

$$34(0) + 40(8) = 320$$

However, we may not be able to read accurately the values of x_1 and x_2 for some of the points (e.g., *C* or *D*) on the graph. Algebraically solving two linear equations for each corner point also is inefficient when there are many constraints and thus many corner points.

The best approach is to plot the objective function on the graph of the feasible region for some arbitrary *Z* values. From these objective function lines we can spot the best solution visually. If the objective function is profits, each line is called an *iso-profit line* and every point on that line will yield the same profit. If *Z* measures cost, the line is called an *iso-cost line* and every point on it represents the same cost. We can simplify the search by plotting the first line in the feasible region—somewhere near the optimal solution, we hope. For the Stratton Company example, let's pass a line through point *E* $(8, 0)$. This point is a corner point. It might even be the optimal solution because it is far from the origin. To draw the line, we first identify its *Z* value as $34(8) + 40(0) = 272$. Therefore the equation for the objective function line passing through *E* is

$$34x_1 + 40x_2 = 272$$

To find a second point on this line, let's use the x_2 intercept, where $x_1 = 0$:

$$34(0) + 40x_2 = 272$$

$$x_2 = 6.8$$

Figure I.5 on the next page shows the iso-profit line that connects points $(8, 0)$ and $(0, 6.8)$.

Find the Visual Solution

We now eliminate corner points *A* and *E* from consideration as the optimal solution because better points lie above and to the right of the $Z = 272$ iso-profit line. Our goal is to maximize profits, so the best solution is a point on the iso-profit line *farthest* from the origin but still touching the feasible region. (For minimization problems, it is a point in the feasible region on the iso-cost line *closest* to the origin.) To identify which of the remaining corner points is optimal (*B*, *C*,

FIGURE I.5   *Passing an Iso-Profit Line Through (8, 0)*

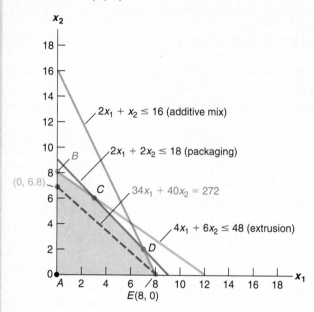

FIGURE I.6   *Drawing the Second Iso-Profit Line*

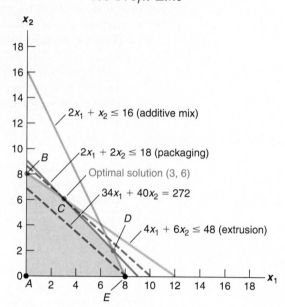

or D), we draw, parallel to the first line, one or more iso-profit lines that give better Z values (higher for maximization and lower for minimization). The line that just touches the feasible region identifies the optimal solution. For the Stratton Company problem, Fig. I.6 shows the second iso-profit line. The optimal solution is the last point touching the feasible region: point C. It appears to be in the vicinity of $(3, 6)$, but the visual solution isn't exact.

A linear programming problem can have more than one optimal solution. This situation occurs when the objective function is parallel to one of the faces of the feasible region. Such would be the case if our objective function in the Stratton Company problem were $\$38x_1 + \$38x_2$. Points $(3, 6)$ and $(7, 2)$ would be optimal, as would any other point on the line connecting these two corner points. In such a case, management probably would base a final decision on nonquantifiable factors. It is important to understand, however, that we need to consider only the corner points of the feasible region when optimizing an objective function.

Find the Algebraic Solution

To find an exact solution, we must use algebra. We begin by identifying the pair of constraints that define the corner point at their intersection. We then list the constraints as equations and solve them simultaneously to find the coordinates (x_1, x_2) of the corner point. Simultaneous equations can be solved several ways. For small problems the easiest way is as follows.

> **Step 1.**   Develop an equation with just one unknown. Start by multiplying both sides of one equation by a constant so that the coefficient for one of the two decision variables is *identical* in both equations. Then subtract one equation from the other and solve the resulting equation for its single unknown variable.

> **Step 2.**   Insert this decision variable's value into either one of the original constraints and solve for the other decision variable.

E X A M P L E   I.4

Finding the Optimal
Solution
Algebraically

Find the optimal solution algebraically for the Stratton Company problem. What is the value of Z when the decision variables have optimal values?

Solution

Step 1. Figure I.6 shows that the optimal corner point lies at the intersection of the extrusion and packaging constraints. Listing the constraints as equalities, we have

$$4x_1 + 6x_2 = 48 \quad \text{(extrusion)}$$

$$2x_1 + 2x_2 = 18 \quad \text{(packaging)}$$

We multiply each term in the packaging constraint by 2. The packaging constraint now is $4x_1 + 4x_2 = 36$. Next, we subtract the packaging constraint from the extrusion constraint. The result will be an equation from which x_1 has dropped out. (Alternatively, we could multiply the second equation by 3 so that x_2 drops out after the subtraction.) Thus

$$4x_1 + 6x_2 = 48$$
$$-(4x_1 + 4x_2 = 36)$$
$$\overline{}$$
$$2x_2 = 12$$
$$x_2 = 6$$

Step 2. Substituting the value of x_2 into the extrusion equation, we get

$$4x_1 + 6(6) = 48$$
$$4x_1 = 12$$
$$x_1 = 3$$

Thus the optimal point is $(3, 6)$. The Stratton Company should produce 300 feet of type 1 pipe and 600 feet of type 2 pipe next week. This solution gives a total profit of $34(3) + 40(6) = \$342$.

Slack and Surplus Variables

Figure I.6 shows that the optimal product mix will exhaust all the extrusion and packaging resources because, at the optimal corner point $(3, 6)$, the two constraints are equalities. Substituting the values of x_1 and x_2 into these constraints shows that the left-hand sides equal the right-hand sides:

$$4(3) + 6(6) = 48 \quad \text{(extrusion)}$$

$$2(3) + 2(6) = 18 \quad \text{(packaging)}$$

A constraint (such as the one for extrusion) that helps form the optimal corner point is called a **binding constraint** because it limits the ability to improve the objective function. If a binding constraint is *relaxed*, or made less restrictive, a better solution is possible. Relaxing a constraint means increasing the right-hand-side parameter for a $\leq$ constraint or decreasing it for a $\geq$ constraint. No improvement is possible from relaxing a constraint that is not binding, such as the additive mix constraint in Fig. I.6. If the right-hand side were increased from 16 to 17 and the problem solved again, the optimal solution wouldn't change. In other words, there is already more additive mix than needed.

For nonbinding inequality constraints, knowing how much the left and right sides differ is helpful. Such information tells us how close the constraint is to becoming binding. For a $\leq$ constraint, the amount by which the left-hand side falls short of the right-hand side is called **slack.** For a $\geq$ constraint, the amount by which the left-hand side exceeds the right-hand side is called **surplus.** To find the slack for a $\leq$ constraint algebraically, we *add* a slack variable to the constraint and convert it to an equality. Then we substitute in the values of the decision variables and solve for the slack. For example, the additive mix constraint in Fig. I.6, $2x_1 + x_2 \leq 16$, can be rewritten by adding slack variable s_1:

$$2x_1 + x_2 + s_1 = 16$$

We then find the slack at the optimal solution (3, 6):

$$2(3) + 6 + s_1 = 16$$

$$s_1 = 4$$

The procedure is much the same to find the surplus for a $\geq$ constraint, except that we *subtract* a surplus variable from the left-hand side. Suppose that $x_1 + x_2 \geq 6$ was another constraint in the Stratton Company problem, representing a lower bound on the number of units produced. We would then rewrite the constraint by subtracting a surplus variable s_2:

$$x_1 + x_2 - s_2 = 6$$

The slack at the optimal solution (3, 6) would be

$$3 + 6 - s_2 = 6$$

$$s_2 = 3$$

◆ SENSITIVITY ANALYSIS

Rarely are the parameters in the objective function and constraints known with certainty. Often they are just estimates of actual values. For example, the available packaging and extrusion hours for the Stratton Company are estimates that do not reflect the uncertainties associated with absenteeism or personnel transfers, and the required hours per unit to package and extrude may be work standards that essentially are averages. Likewise, profit contributions used for the objective function coefficients do not reflect uncertainties in selling prices and such variable costs as wages, raw materials, and shipping.

Despite such uncertainties, initial estimates are needed to solve the problem. Accounting, marketing, and work-standard information systems often provide these initial estimates. After solving the problem using these estimated values, the analyst can determine how much the optimal values of the decision variables and the objective function value Z would be affected if certain parameters had different values. This type of postsolution analysis for answering "what if" questions is called *sensitivity analysis.*

One way of conducting sensitivity analysis for linear programming problems is the brute-force approach of changing one or more parameter values and re-solving the entire problem. This approach may be acceptable for small problems but is inefficient if there are many parameters. For example, brute-force sensitivity analysis using 3 separate values for each of 20 objective function coefficients requires 3^{20}, or 3,486,784,401, separate solutions! Fortunately, efficient methods are available for getting sensitivity information without re-solving the entire problem, and they are routinely used in most linear programming computer software packages. Here we do sensitivity analysis on the objective function coefficients and the right-hand-side parameters of the constraints for a one-parameter-at-a-time change.

Objective Function Coefficients

We begin sensitivity analysis on the objective function of a two-variable problem by calculating the slope of the iso-profit (or iso-cost) lines. The equation of any straight line can be written as $y = mx + b$, where m is the slope of the line. In our graphic solution in Fig. I.6, we used x_2 rather than y, and x_1 rather than x. Thus the equation that reveals a line's slope will be $x_2 = mx_1 + b$. To put the objective function in this form, we solve the objective function for x_2 in terms of x_1 and Z:

$$34x_1 + 40x_2 = Z$$

$$40x_2 = -34x_1 + Z$$

$$x_2 = -\frac{34x_1}{40} + \frac{Z}{40}$$

Thus the slope m of the iso-profit lines for Stratton Company is $-34/40$, or -0.85. In general, it is the negative of the ratio found by dividing the objective function coefficient of x_1 by the objective function coefficient of x_2.

Now let's see what happens when an objective function coefficient changes. We define c_1 to be the profit contribution per 100 feet of x_1 and c_2 to be the profit contribution per 100 feet of x_2. The equation of the iso-profit line becomes

$$x_2 = -\frac{c_1 x_1}{c_2} + \frac{Z}{c_2}$$

If c_1 *increases* while c_2 stays constant, the slope becomes more negative (steeper), and the line rotates clockwise. For example, if c_1 increases to \$40, the slope becomes -1.00, or $-40/40$. But if c_1 *decreases*, the slope becomes less negative and the line rotates counterclockwise. If the reduction is substantial enough, the slope of the objective function will equal the slope of the extrusion constraint. When this happens, point B becomes an optimal corner point. If c_1 instead increases so that the slope of the objective function becomes more negative than the slope of the packaging constraint, corner point D becomes optimal. Similar conclusions also can be drawn about changes in c_2.

Range of Optimality. If the objective function coefficient makes the slope of the objective function greater than the slope of the packaging constraint but less than the slope of the extrusion constraint, point C remains the optimal solution. In Fig. I.7 on the next page, the area between the two binding constraints, extrusion and packaging, is shaded. Note that point C remains optimal if the objective function slope is greater than -1.00, the slope of the packaging constraint, and less than $-2/3$, the slope of the extrusion constraint. Thus the following relationship holds:

$$-1 \le -\frac{c_1}{c_2} \le -\frac{2}{3}$$

FIGURE I.7

*Finding the Range of
Optimality*

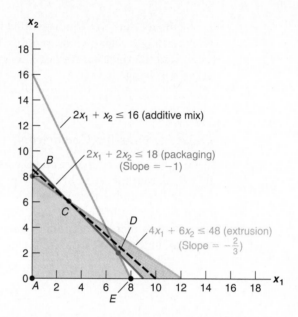

We use this relationship to find the range over which c_1 can vary without changing the optimality of point C, holding c_2 constant at \$40:

$$-1 \leq -\frac{c_1}{40} \leq -\frac{2}{3}$$

Because we seek the range for c_1, rather than $-c_1/40$, we multiply by -40. Multiplying by a negative number reverses the direction of the inequalities, so we get

$$40 \geq c_1 \geq 26.67$$

Rearranging terms for ease of reading yields

$$26.67 \leq c_1 \leq 40$$

Thus the objective function coefficient for x_1 ranges from a *lower limit* of \$26.67 through an *upper limit* of \$40. This **range of optimality** defines a lower and upper limit over which the optimal values of the decision variables remain unchanged. Of course, the value of Z would change as c_1 changed. For example, if c_1 increased from \$34 to \$40, the value of Z at point C would become 360:

$$40x_1 + 40x_2 = Z$$

$$40(3) + 40(6) = 360$$

EXAMPLE I.5

*Finding the Range
of Optimality for c_2*

What is the range of optimality for c_2 in the Stratton Company problem?

Solution   If we hold c_1 constant at \$34, the relationship for the slope of the iso-profit lines is

$$-1 \leq -\frac{34}{c_2} \leq -\frac{2}{3}$$

Because c_2 is in the denominator, defining one limit at a time is easiest. For the limit on the left, we get

$$-1 \leq -\frac{34}{c_2}$$

Multiplying by $-c_2$, we find the lower limit:

$$c_2 \geq 34$$

Now, taking the second relationship on the right, we have

$$-\frac{34}{c_2} \leq -\frac{2}{3}$$

Multiplying by $-c_2$, we obtain the upper limit:

$$34 \geq \frac{2c_2}{3}$$

$$51 \geq c_2$$

Putting both limits into one final expression, we find that c_2 can be as low as \$34 or as high as \$51 without changing the optimality of point C, or

$$34 \leq c_2 \leq 51$$

Coefficient Sensitivity. In the Stratton Company problem, the optimal point makes both decision variables greater than 0 (3 and 6). If c_1 were low enough (below 26.67), point B would be optimal, and the optimal value of x_1 would be 0. Sensitivity analysis can give us additional information about variables that have optimal values of 0. **Coefficient sensitivity** measures how much the objective function coefficient of such a decision variable must improve (increase for maximization or decrease for minimization) before the optimal solution changes and the decision variable becomes some positive number. The coefficient sensitivity for c_1 can be found in the following manner.

Step 1. Identify the direction of rotation (clockwise or counterclockwise) of the iso-profit (or iso-cost) line that improves c_1. Rotate the iso-profit (or iso-cost) line in this direction until it reaches a new optimal corner point that makes x_1 greater than 0.

Step 2. Determine which binding constraint has the same slope as the rotated iso-profit (or iso-cost) line at this new point. Solve for the value of c_1 that makes the objective function slope equal to the slope of this binding constraint.

Step 3. Set the coefficient sensitivity equal to the difference between this value and the current value of c_1.

E X A M P L E I . 6

Finding the Coefficient Sensitivity for a Revised Problem

Suppose that the Stratton Company problem is changed so that c_1 is \$20 rather than \$34. Figure I.8 shows that the highest iso-profit line now passes through point B, making it the optimal solution rather than point C. At point B, the optimal value of x_1 is zero. What is the coefficient sensitivity for c_1?

Solution We apply the three solution steps to the revised Stratton problem.

Step 1. This is a maximization problem, so c_1 improves as it *increases*. Increasing c_1 rotates the iso-profit line clockwise. Rotation continues until point C is reached—a corner point that makes x_1 a positive number (3).

FIGURE I.8   *Coefficient Sensitivity for the Revised Problem*

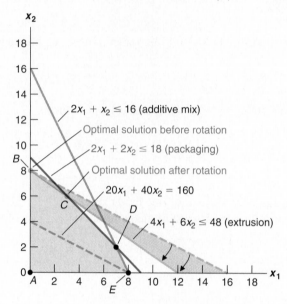

Step 2.   The binding constraint that has the same slope is extrusion. Solving for the c_1 that makes the two slopes equal, we get

$$-\frac{c_1}{40} = -\frac{2}{3}$$

$$c_1 = 26.67$$

Step 3.   The coefficient sensitivity is $6.67, or $26.67 − $20.

Therefore c_1 must increase by $6.67 before it is optimal to make x_1 greater than 0.

Right-Hand-Side Parameters

Now consider how a change in the right-hand-side parameter for a constraint may affect the feasible region and perhaps cause a change in the optimal solution. Let's return to the original Stratton Company problem, changing c_1 back from $20 to $34. However, we now consider adding one more hour to the packaging resource, increasing it from 18 to 19 hours.

Shadow Prices.   As Fig I.9 demonstrates, this change expands the feasible region, and the optimal solution changes from point C to point C'. Point C' is better in terms of Z because the added unit of a binding constraint will be used to make more product. To find the amount of improvement, we first find the new values of x_1 and x_2 by simultaneously solving the two binding constraints at point C', where

$$4x_1 + 6x_2 = 48 \qquad \text{(extrusion)}$$

$$2x_1 + 2x_2 = 19 \qquad \text{(packaging)}$$

FIGURE I.9

Enlarging the Feasible
Region by Relaxing the
Packaging Constraint
by One Hour

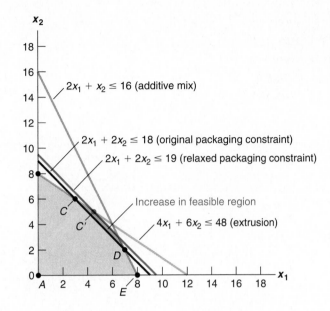

The optimal values are $x_1 = 4.5$ and $x_2 = 5$, and the new Z value is $34(4.5) + \$40(5) = \$353$. Because the value of Z was $342 with 18 hours of packaging, the value of one more hour of packaging is $11 (or $353 − $342).

The change in Z per unit of change in the value of the right-hand-side parameter of a constraint is called the shadow price. The **shadow price** is the marginal improvement in Z caused by relaxing the constraint by one unit. Relaxation means making the constraint less restrictive, which involves increasing the right-hand side for a $\leq$ constraint or decreasing it for a $\geq$ constraint. The shadow price also is the marginal loss in Z caused by making the constraint more restrictive by one unit. In our example, the shadow price for the packaging resource is $11 per hour. Thus, if scheduling additional packaging hours is possible, Stratton's management should be willing to pay a premium of up to $11 per hour over and above the normal cost for a packaging hour. However, if capacity is cut by one hour, profits will fall by $11.

Range of Feasibility. A lower limit and an upper limit define the **range of feasibility,** which is the interval over which the right-hand-side parameter can vary while its shadow price remains valid. If the right-hand side is increased beyond the upper limit or reduced beyond the lower limit, at least one other constraint becomes binding, which in turn alters the rate of change in Z. These two limits are established when, as the constraint line is relaxed or tightened, a new corner point on the feasible region is reached that makes a different constraint binding.

With 18 packaging hours, the optimal solution for the Stratton Company is $x_1 = 3$, $x_2 = 6$, 4 pounds of slack in the additive mix, and 0 slack for the other two constraints. We found that each additional packaging hour would increase profit by $11 (minus any premium cost of adding this additional capacity). Similarly, one fewer packaging hour would reduce profits by $11. However, $11 is the shadow price over a limited range of packaging hours. Let's begin by finding

FIGURE I.10

*Defining the Upper and
Lower Limits to
Packaging's Range of
Feasibility*

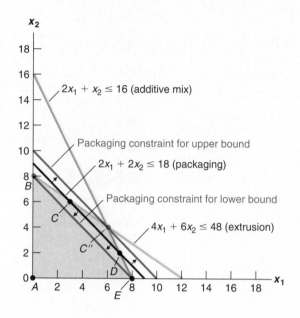

the *upper* limit over which this shadow price is valid. Figure I.10 shows the packaging constraint being relaxed and shifted to the right, away from the origin. When it reaches point C'', where it intersects the extrusion and additive mix constraints, the additive mix constraint and the extrusion constraint become binding. Until the packaging constraint reaches C'', relaxing it will expand the feasible region, as shown by the pink shading in the feasible region. With this expansion comes the improvement in Z, which is $11 per packaging hour added. However, any increase in packaging hours beyond what is used at point C'' will be worth $0 because the constraint will no longer be binding.

To find how many hours are used at point C'', we solve the additive mix and extrusion constraints simultaneously because C'' lies at their intersection. Doing so, we get $x_1 = 6$ and $x_2 = 4$. Substituting these values into the packaging constraint, we find that the upper limit on the shadow price of $11 is 20 packaging hours, or $2(6) + 2(4) = 20$.

EXAMPLE I.7

*Finding the Lower
Limit on the $11
Shadow Price*

What is the lower limit on the $11 shadow price for packaging hours?

Solution   Figure I.10 shows that reducing the packaging hours shifts the constraint to the left, toward the origin, reducing the feasible region and thus the value of Z. Eventually the constraint reaches corner point B, defined by the extrusion constraint and the x_1 nonnegativity constraint. Because a new constraint is binding (the x_1 nonnegativity constraint), B defines the lower limit on packaging's shadow price. We found earlier that, at point B, $x_1 = 0$ and $x_2 = 8$. Substituting these values into the packaging constraint, we determine the *lower* limit on the shadow price of $11 to be 16 packaging hours, or $2(0) + 2(8) = 16$.

In some cases, there may be no lower or upper limit to the range of feasibility. The additive mix constraint provides one example. Figure I.6 shows that this constraint isn't binding. Shifting the constraint upward still more doesn't expand the feasible region or improve Z. Thus the shadow price of the additive mix is $0. The right-hand side can be increased without limit—to infinity—and the shadow price remains at $0.

The additive mix constraint illustrates a final principle that always holds: When a constraint's slack or surplus variable is greater than 0, its shadow price is 0. In every optimal solution, either a constraint's slack (or surplus) variable is 0 or its shadow price is 0. For the additive mix, with its shadow price of $0, there are 4 pounds of slack at the optimal point C. Because $x_1 = 3$ and $x_2 = 6$ at C, only $2(3) + 1(6) = 12$ pounds of the additive mix are needed. The slack is 4 pounds $(16 - 12)$, because 16 pounds of the mix are available.

◆ COMPUTER SOLUTION

Most real-world linear programming problems are solved on a computer, so we concentrate here on understanding the use of linear programming and the logic on which it is based. The solution procedure in computer codes is some form of the **simplex method,** an iterative algebraic procedure for solving linear programming problems.

Simplex Method

The graphic analysis gives insight into the logic of the simplex method, beginning with the focus on corner points. One corner point will always be the optimum, even when there are multiple optimal solutions. Thus the simplex method starts with an initial corner point and then systematically evaluates other corner points in such a way that the objective function improves (or, at worst, stays the same) at each iteration. In the Stratton Company problem, an improvement would be an increase in profits. When no more improvements are possible, the optimal solution has been found.* The simplex method also helps generate the sensitivity analysis information that we developed graphically.

Each corner point has no more than m variables that are greater than 0, where m is the number of constraints (not counting the nonnegativity constraints). The m variables include slack and surplus variables, not just the original decision variables. Because of this property, we can find a corner point by simultaneously solving m constraints, where all but m variables are set equal to 0. For example, point B in Fig. I.6 has three nonzero variables: x_2, the slack variable for packaging, and the slack variable for the additive mix. Their values can be found by solving simultaneously the three constraints, with x_1 and the slack variable for extrusion equal to 0. After finding this corner point, the simplex method applies information similar to the coefficient sensitivity to decide which new corner point to find next that gives an even better Z value. It continues in this way until no better corner point is possible. The final corner point evaluated is the optimal one.

---

*For more information on how to perform the simplex method manually, see Cook and Russell (1993) or any other current textbook on management science.

Computer Output

Computer programs dramatically reduce the amount of time required to solve linear programming problems. Special-purpose programs can be developed for applications that must be repeated frequently. Such programs simplify data input and generate the objective function and constraints for the problem. In addition, they can prepare customized managerial reports. We illustrate computer usage below with CMOM (linear programming module).

Printout 1

Data Entered

Number of Variables	: 2
Number of $\leq$ Constraints	: 3
Number of = Constraints	: 0
Number of $\geq$ Constraints	: 0

Model

	X1	X2		RHS
Max-Z	34	40		
Ext	4	6	$\leq$	48
Pac	2	2	$\leq$	18
Add	2	1	$\leq$	16

Printout 2

Solution

Variable Label	Variable Value	Original Coefficient	Coefficient Sensitivity
X1	3	34	0
X2	6	40	0

Constraint Label	Original RHV	Slack or Surplus	Shadow Price
Ext	48	0	3
Pac	18	0	11
Add	16	4	0

Objective Function Value : 342

Printout 3

Sensitivity Analysis and Ranges

Objective Function Coefficients

Variable Label	Lower Limit	Original Coefficient	Upper Limit
X1	26.6667	34	40
X2	34	40	51

Right-Hand-Side Values

Constraint Label	Lower Limit	Original Value	Upper Limit
Ext	40	48	54
Pac	16	18	20
Add	12	16	no limit

Printout 1 shows the input data for the Stratton Company problem. The display, on screen, paper, or disk, allows you to double-check the data entries. CMOM prohibits any negative right-hand-side values. If a value is negative in the original problem formulation, multiply both sides of the constraint by -1 to reverse the signs of all parameters, and reverse the direction of the inequality. For example, $x_1 - 3x_2 \geq -10$ becomes $-x_1 + 3x_2 \leq 10$.

CMOM automatically adds slack and surplus variables as needed. The last half of Printout 1 gives the values and the type of constraint ($\leq$, $=$, or $\geq$). The user may choose to enter labels for the objective function, constraints, and right-hand-side values. Here, the extrusion constraint is labeled "Ext," and the right-hand-side values are labeled "RHS." Input data can be stored in a file for use during subsequent sessions.

Printout 2 shows the optimal solution for the Stratton Company problem, including the optimal values of the decision variables ($x_1 = 3$ and $x_2 = 6$), their objective function coefficients, and their coefficient sensitivities. In this example, the coefficient sensitivities provide no new insight because they are always 0 when decision variables have positive values in the optimal solution. For the constraints, Printout 2 shows the original right-hand-side values, the slack or surplus variables, and the shadow prices. For example, there are 4 pounds of additive mix slack. Packaging is a binding constraint because it has no slack. The shadow price of one more packaging hour is $11. All confirm our earlier calculations and the graphic analysis.

Printout 3 reports the range of optimality over which the objective function coefficients can vary without changing the optimal values of the objective function. Note that c_1, which currently has a value of $34, has a range of optimality from $26.67 to $40. The last part of Printout 3 gives the range of feasibility, over which the right-hand-side parameters can range without changing the shadow prices. For example, the $11 shadow price for packaging is valid over the range from 16 to 20 hours. Again, these findings are identical to the sensitivity analysis done graphically.

EXAMPLE I.8

*Using Shadow
Prices for Decision
Making*

The Stratton Company needs answers to three important questions: Would increasing capacities in the extrusion or packaging area pay if it cost an extra $8 per hour over and above the normal costs already reflected in the objective function coefficients? Would increasing packaging capacity pay if it cost an additional $6 per hour? Would buying more raw materials pay?

Solution   Expanding extrusion capacity would cost a premium of $8 per hour, so the company shouldn't expand; the shadow price for that capacity is only $3 per hour. However, expanding packaging hours would cost only $6 per hour more than the price reflected in the objective function, and the shadow price is $11 per hour. Hence the company should increase its packaging capacity. Finally, buying more raw materials would not pay because there is already a surplus of 4 pounds; the shadow price is 0 for that resource.

◆   OTHER APPLICATIONS

Many problems in operations management, and in other functional areas, have been modeled as linear programming problems. Knowing how to formulate a problem generally, the decision maker can then adapt it to the situation at hand.

The following list identifies some problems that can be solved with linear programming. Review problems at the end of this supplement and of other chapters illustrate many of these types of problems.

- **Aggregate planning**

  Production: Find the minimum-cost production schedule, taking into account hiring and layoff, inventory-carrying, overtime, and subcontracting costs, subject to various capacity and policy constraints.
  Staffing: Find the optimal staffing levels for various categories of workers, subject to various demand and policy constraints.
  Blends: Find the optimal proportions of various ingredients used to make products such as gasoline, paints, and food, subject to certain minimal requirements.

- **Distribution**

  Shipping: Find the optimal shipping assignments from factories to distribution centers or from warehouses to retailers.

- **Inventory**

  Stock control: Determine the optimal mix of products to hold in inventory in a warehouse.
  Supplier selection: Find the optimal combination of suppliers to minimize the amount of unwanted inventory.

- **Location**

  Plants or warehouses: Determine the optimal location of a plant or warehouse with respect to total transportation costs between various alternative locations and existing supply and demand sources.

- **Process management**

  Stock cutting: Given the dimensions of a roll or sheet of raw material, find the cutting pattern that minimizes the amount of scrap material.

- **Scheduling**

  Shifts: Determine the minimum-cost assignment of workers to shifts, subject to varying demand.
  Vehicles: Assign vehicles to products or customers and determine the number of trips to make, subject to vehicle size, vehicle availability, and demand constraints.
  Routing: Find the optimal routing of a product or service through several sequential processes, each having its own capacity and other characteristics.

SUPPLEMENT REVIEW

Solved Problem 1

O'Connel Airlines is considering air service from its hub of operations in Cicely, Alaska, to Rome, Wisconsin, and Seattle, Washington. O'Connel has one gate at the Cicely Airport, which operates 12 hours per day. Each flight requires 1 hour of gate time. Each flight to Rome consumes 15 hours of pilot crew time and is expected to produce a profit of $2500. Serving Seattle uses 10 hours of pilot crew time per flight and will result in a profit of $2000 per flight. Pilot crew labor is limited to 150 hours per day. The market for service to Rome is limited to nine flights per day.

a. Use the graphic method of linear programming to maximize profits for O'Connel Airlines.
b. Identify slack and surplus constraints, if any.
c. Find the range of optimality for c_1, the profit per flight to Rome.
d. Chris Hoover says that radio advertising would increase the demand for travel to Rome. What is the value of increasing demand (relaxing the market constraint) by one flight to Rome?
e. By how much would O'Connel's objective function increase if the Cicely Airport operated an extra hour per day? Would increased hours of operation result in increased service to Rome, Seattle, or both?
f. Maurice Foster strongly voices his opinion that O'Connel would benefit from hiring additional experienced pilots. What is the value of one additional hour of flight crew resources? What is the upper limit on the range of feasibility for flight crew time?

Solution   a. The objective function is to maximize profits, Z:

$$\text{Maximize:} \quad \$2500x_1 + \$2000x_2 = Z$$

where x_1 = number of flights per day to Rome, Wisconsin

               x_2 = number of flights per day to Seattle, Washington

The constraints are

$$x_1 + x_2 \leq 12 \qquad \text{(gate capacity)}$$

$$15x_1 + 10x_2 \leq 150 \qquad \text{(labor)}$$

$$x_1 \leq 9 \qquad \text{(market)}$$

$$x_1 \geq 0 \quad \text{and} \quad x_2 \geq 0$$

A careful drawing of iso-profit lines parallel to the one shown in Fig. I.11 will indicate that point D is the optimal solution. It is at the intersection of the labor and gate capacity constraints. Solving algebraically, we get

$$15x_1 + 10x_2 = 150 \qquad \text{(labor)}$$

$$\underline{-10x_1 - 10x_2 = -120} \qquad \text{(gate} \times -10\text{)}$$

$$5x_1 + 0x_2 = 30$$

$$x_1 = 6$$

$$6 + x_2 = 12 \qquad \text{(gate)}$$

$$x_2 = 6$$

FIGURE I.11

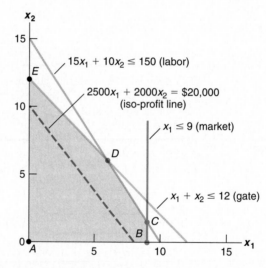

The maximum profit results from making six flights to Rome and six flights to Seattle:

$$\$2500(6) + \$2000(6) = \$27,000$$

b. The market constraint has three units of slack, so the demand for flights to Rome isn't fully met:

$$x_1 \leq 9$$

$$x_1 + s_3 = 9$$

$$6 + s_3 = 9$$

$$s_3 = 3$$

c. Point D remains optimal as long as the objective function slope $(-c_1/c_2)$ is between $-3/2$, the slope of the labor constraint, and -1.00, the slope of the gate capacity constraint, or

$$-\frac{3}{2} \le -\frac{c_1}{c_2} \le -1$$

Holding c_2 constant at 2000 yields

$$-\frac{3}{2} \le -\frac{c_1}{2000} \le -1$$

and multiplying by -2000 gives

$$3000 \ge c_1 \ge 2000 \qquad \text{or} \qquad 2000 \le c_1 \le 3000$$

d. As the market constraint already has slack, the optimal solution wouldn't improve with an increase in demand for service to Rome.
e. Figure I.12 shows what would happens if the gate were open for 13 hours instead of 12 hours. One increased hour of operation would increase service to Seattle from six to nine flights, but *decrease* service to Rome from six to four flights. The intersecting constraints are

$$
\begin{aligned}
x_1 + \quad x_2 &\le \; 13 \qquad \text{(gate capacity)}\\
15x_1 + 10x_2 &\le 150 \qquad \text{(labor)}
\end{aligned}
$$

Solving algebraically, we have

$$
\begin{aligned}
15x_1 + 10x_2 &= \quad 150 \qquad \text{(labor)}\\
-10x_1 - 10x_2 &= -130 \qquad \text{(gate} \times -10\text{)}\\
\hline
5x_1 + \quad 0x_2 &= \quad 20\\
x_1 &= 4\\
4 + x_2 &= 13 \qquad \text{(gate)}\\
x_2 &= 9
\end{aligned}
$$

FIGURE I.12

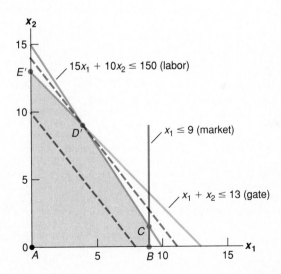

The objective function would be $\$2500(4) + \$2000(9) = \$28,000$, an increase of $\$1000$ over the previous solution. The shadow price for gate capacity is $\$1000$ per hour.

f. The intersecting constraints are

$$x_1 + x_2 \le 12 \quad \text{(gate capacity)}$$

$$15x_1 + 10x_2 \le 151 \quad \text{(labor)}$$

Solving algebraically, we get

$$15x_1 + 10x_2 = 151 \quad \text{(labor)}$$

$$\underline{-10x_1 - 10x_2 = -120} \quad \text{(gate} \times -10)$$

$$5x_1 + 0x_2 = 31$$

$$x_1 = 6.2$$

$$6.2 + x_2 = 12 \quad \text{(gate)}$$

$$x_2 = 5.8$$

The objective function would be $2500(6.2) + $2000(5.8) = $27,100$, an increase of $100 over the previous solution. The shadow price for flight crew time is $100 per hour. Increasing flight crew time would increase service to Rome and decrease service to Seattle. However, a one-hour change in flight crew time doesn't result in an integer change in the number of flights.

As more hours of flight crew time become available, the optimal solution shifts toward point *F*. Eventually, as Fig. I.13 shows, the market limit on flights to Rome (≤ 9) will bind the solution. Point *F* is at the intersection of the market and gate constraints, located at (9, 3). You may prove this result by algebraically solving for the intersection of those two constraints. Now we find the labor constraint that will also go through that point. When $x_1 = 9$ and $x_2 = 3$,

$$15x_1 + 10x_2 = 15(9) + 10(3) = 165$$

FIGURE I.13

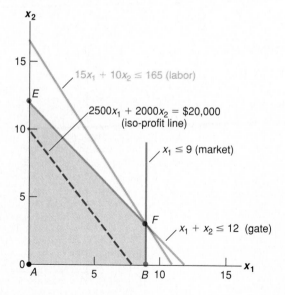

The labor constraint that passes through point (9, 3) is

$$15x_1 + 10x_2 \le 165$$

The right-hand side of the labor constraint has increased by $(165 - 150) = 15$ hours.

Therefore 15 more flight crew hours would improve the solution by (15)($100 shadow price) = $1500. Beyond this point, additional flight crew time would merely become a slack resource and not further improve the solution.

Solved Problem 2

Holling desires to minimize the cost of preparing at least 750 hors d'oeuvres for a celebration. Holling is considering two recipes: Dave's crab cakes (x_1) and Shelly's seafood surprise (x_2). The cost per unit is $0.30 for the crab cakes and $0.20 for the seafood surprise. Holling has a good supply of Alaskan king crab but must order at least 20 pounds at a time to obtain it at a reasonable price. The crab cake recipe requires 0.02 pound of crab meat per unit. Seafood surprise requires 0.04 pound per unit. Because of crab meat's short shelf life, Holling wants to use an entire order of crab meat in preparing the hors d'oeuvres. Again, at least 20 pounds of crab meat must be consumed.

a. Use the graphic method of linear programming to minimize Holling's costs.
b. Use coefficient sensitivity to determine the value of c_1, the cost of crab cakes, that would bring x_1 into the solution (make x_1 greater than 0).

Solution
a. The graphic solution (Fig. I.14) shows that the optimal solution occurs at point A. Thus 750 units of Shelly's seafood surprise and no crab cakes would be produced.

FIGURE I.14

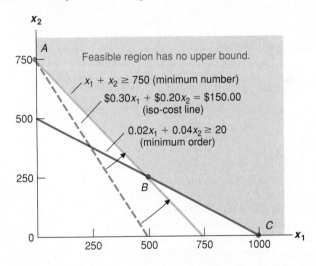

b. The per unit cost of crab cakes would have to be reduced to $0.20 to bring x_1 into the optimal solution. Improving c_1 results in a counterclockwise rotation of the iso-cost line. The objective function becomes parallel to the quantity constraint (at least 750 hors d'oeuvres produced). The slope of that constraint is -1.00. Solving for the value of c_1 that makes the objective function slope, $-c_1/c_2$, equal to -1.00 yields

$$-\frac{c_1}{c_2} = -1.00$$

$$-\frac{c_1}{\$0.20} = -1.00$$

$$c_1 = \$0.20$$

The coefficient sensitivity equals the difference between this value and the current value of c_1: $0.30 − $0.20 = $0.10. In other words, forcing the production of one crab cake into the solution incurs a penalty of $0.10.

Supplement Highlights

- Linear programming is an effective tool for solving complex resource allocation problems when the objective and constraints can be approximated by linear equations. Skill and creativity often are required to model a situation with a set of linear equations. After the model has been formulated, one of several available computer programs may be used to identify the optimal solution.
- Although only simple linear programming problems can be solved by using graphic analysis, the technique provides valuable insight into the way optimal solutions to complex problems are generated.

- In addition to identifying the optimal combination of decision variables, analysis of the solution will determine shadow price, coefficient sensitivity, and ranging information. Shadow prices are the values of additional resources. Coefficient sensitivity indicates the penalties associated with nonoptimal solutions. Ranging describes either how much coefficients can change without invalidating the solution or how much of a resource can be acquired without changing the value of its shadow price.

Key Terms

binding constraint 637
certainty 628
coefficient sensitivity 641
constraints 627
corner point 635
decision variables 627
feasible region 628

graphic method of linear
    programming 631
linear programming 627
linearity 628
nonnegativity 628
objective function 627
parameter 628

product-mix problem 629
range of feasibility 643
range of optimality 640
shadow price 643
simplex method 645
slack 638
surplus 638

Study Questions

1. In linear programming what is the distinction between a parameter and a decision variable?
2. Why is it difficult to use graphic analysis to solve practical linear programming problems?
3. A particular linear programming maximization problem has three less-than-or-equal-to constraints: (1) raw materials, (2) labor hours, and (3) storage space. The optimal solution occurs at the intersection of the raw materials and labor hours constraints, so those constraints are binding. Management is considering whether to authorize overtime. What useful information could the linear programming solution provide to management in making this decision? Suppose a warehouse becomes available for rent at bargain rates. What would management need to know in order to decide whether to rent the warehouse? How could the linear programming model be helpful?
4. What is a *slack* variable? Give an example of how slack variables can be useful in linear programming analysis.
5. What is meant by an iso-profit line? How is it similar to the iso-bars and iso-therms used on weather maps?

Discussion Question

1. A company wants to use linear programming for production planning but finds that the cost of firing workers isn't linear. Rather, it is approximated by the equation

$$\text{Firing cost} = \$4000F^{1.25}$$

where F is the number of workers fired during a month. How could this relation be modified to permit linear program formulation and modeling of this situation?

Problems

The use of linear programming software is suggested for Problems 7–19.

1. The Really Big Shoe is a manufacturer of basketball and football shoes. Ed Sullivan, the manager of marketing, must decide the best way to spend advertising resources. Each football team sponsored requires 120 pairs of shoes. Each basketball team requires 32 pairs of shoes. Football coaches receive $300,000 for shoe sponsorship, and basketball coaches receive $1,000,000. Sullivan's promotional budget is $30,000,000. The Really Big Shoe has a limited supply (4 liters or 4000 cubic centimeters) of flubber, a rare and costly compound used in promotional athletic shoes. Each pair of basketball shoes requires 3 cc of flubber, and each pair of football shoes requires 1 cc. Sullivan wants to sponsor as many basketball and football teams as resources allow.

   a. Create a set of linear equations to describe the objective function and the constraints.
   b. Use graphic analysis to find the visual solution.
   c. What is the maximum number of each type of team The Really Big Shoe can sponsor?

2. A business student at Nowledge College must complete a total of 65 courses to graduate. The number of business courses must be greater than or equal to 23. The number of nonbusiness courses must be greater than or equal to 20. The average business course requires a textbook costing $60 and 120 hours of study. Nonbusiness courses require a textbook costing $24 and 200 hours of study. The student has $3000 to spend on books.

   a. Create a set of linear equations to describe the objective function and the constraints.
   b. Use graphic analysis to find the visual solution.
   c. What combination of business and nonbusiness courses minimizes total hours of study?
   d. Identify the slack or surplus variables.

3. In Problem 2, suppose that the objective is to minimize the cost of books and that the student's total study time is limited to 12,600 hours.

   a. Use graphic analysis to determine the combination of courses that minimizes the total cost of books.
   b. Identify the slack or surplus variables.

4. Mile-High Microbrewery makes a light beer and a dark beer. Mile-High has a limited supply of barley, limited bottling capacity, and a limited market for light beer. Profits are $0.20 per bottle of light beer and $0.50 per bottle of dark beer.

   a. The following table shows resource availability of products at the Mile-High Microbrewery. Use the graphic method of linear programming to maximize profits. How many bottles of each product should be produced per month?

	Product		
	Light	Dark	Resource Availability
Resource	Beer (x_1)	Beer (x_2)	(per month)
Barley	0.1 g	0.6 gram	2000 g/month
Bottling	1 bottle	1 bottle	6000 bottles/month
Market	1 bottle		4000 bottles/month

   b. Identify any constraints with slack or surplus.
   c. Find the range of optimality for c_2, the profit per bottle of dark beer.
   d. Beth Richards says that sponsoring sporting events would increase the demand for Mile-High's light beer. What is the value of increasing demand for light beer?
   e. Jorge Gallegos suggests that the bottling constraint could be alleviated by subcontracting for additional bottling capacity. By how much would Mile-High's objective function increase if bottling capacity increased by one bottle per month? Would increased hours of operation result in increased production of light beer, dark beer, or both?
   f. What is the upper limit on the range of feasibility for bottling capacity?

5. The plant manager of a plastic pipe manufacturer has the opportunity to use two different routings for a particular type of plastic pipe. Routing 1 uses extruder A, and routing 2 uses extruder B. Both routings require the same melting process. The following table shows the time requirements and capacities of these processes.

Process	Time Requirements (hr/100 ft)		Capacity (hr)
	Routing 1	Routing 2	
Melting	1	1	45
Extruder A	3	0	90
Extruder B	0	4	160

Each 100 feet of pipe processed on routing 1 uses 5 pounds of raw material, whereas each 100 feet of pipe processed on routing 2 uses only 4 pounds. This difference results from differing scrap rates of the extruding machines. Consequently, the profit per 100 feet of pipe processed on routing 1 is $60 and on routing 2 is $80. A total of 200 pounds of raw material is available.

   a. Create a set of linear equations to describe the objective function and the constraints.
   b. Use graphic analysis to find the visual solution.
   c. What is the maximum profit?

d. Use coefficient sensitivity to determine the value of c_1, the profit per unit processed on routing 1, that would bring x_1 into the solution (make x_1 greater than 0).

6. A manufacturer of textile dyes can use two different processing routings for a particular type of dye. Routing 1 uses drying press A, and routing 2 uses drying press B. Both routings require the same mixing vat to blend chemicals for the dye before drying. The following table shows the time requirements and capacities of these processes.

Time Requirements (hr/kg)

Process	Routing 1	Routing 2	Capacity (hr)
Mixing	2	2	54
Dryer A	6	0	120
Dryer B	0	8	224

Each kilogram of dye processed on routing 1 uses 20 liters of chemicals, whereas each kilogram of dye processed on routing 2 uses only 15 liters. The difference results from differing yield rates of the drying presses. Consequently, the profit per kilogram processed on routing 1 is $50 and on routing 2 is $65. A total of 450 liters of input chemicals is available.

a. Write the constraints and objective function to maximize profits.
b. Use the graphic method of linear programming to find the optimal solution.
c. Identify any constraints with slack or surplus.
d. What is the value of an additional hour of mixing time? What is the upper limit of the range for which this shadow price is valid?

7. The Trim-Look Company makes several lines of skirts, dresses, and sport coats. Recently, a consultant suggested that the company reevaluate its South Islander line and allocate its resources to products that would maximize contribution to profits and to overhead. Each product requires the same polyester fabric and must pass through the cutting and sewing departments. The following data were collected for the study.

Processing Time (hr)

Product	Cutting	Sewing	Material (yd)
Skirt	1	1	1
Dress	3	4	1
Sport coat	4	6	4

The cutting department has 100 hours of capacity, sewing has 180 hours of capacity, and 60 yards of material are available. Each skirt contributes $5 to profits and overhead; each dress, $17; and each sport coat, $30.

a. Specify the objective function and constraints for this problem.
b. Use a computer package to solve the problem.

8. Consider Problem 7 further.

a. How much would you be willing to pay for an extra hour of cutting time? For an extra hour of sewing time? For an extra yard of material? Explain your response to each question.
b. Determine the range of right-hand-side values over which the shadow price would be valid for the cutting constraint and for the material constraint.

9. Polly Astaire makes fine clothing for big and tall men. A few years ago Astaire entered the sportswear market with the Sunset line of shorts, pants, and shirts. Management wants to make the amount of each product that will maximize profits. Each type of clothing is routed through two departments, A and B. Following are the relevant data for each product.

Processing Time (hr)

Product	Department A	Department B	Material (yd)
Shirt	2	1	2
Shorts	2	3	1
Pants	3	4	4

Department A has 120 hours of capacity, department B has 160 hours of capacity, and 90 yards of material are available. Each shirt contributes $10 to profits and overhead; each pair of shorts, $10; and each pair of pants, $23.

a. Specify the objective function and constraints for this problem.
b. Use a computer package to solve the problem.
c. How much should Astaire be willing to pay for an extra hour of department A capacity? Department B capacity? For what range of right-hand values are these shadow prices valid?

10. The Butterfield Company makes a variety of hunting knives. Each knife is processed on four machines. Following are the processing times required; machine capacities (in hours) are 1500 for machine 1, 1400 for machine 2, 1600 for machine 3, and 1500 for machine 4.

Processing Time (hr)

Knife	Machine 1	Machine 2	Machine 3	Machine 4
A	0.05	0.10	0.15	0.05
B	0.15	0.10	0.05	0.05
C	0.20	0.05	0.10	0.20
D	0.15	0.10	0.10	0.10
E	0.05	0.10	0.10	0.05

Each product contains a different amount of two basic raw materials. Raw material 1 costs $0.50 per ounce, and raw material 2 costs $1.50 per ounce. There are 75,000 ounces of raw material 1 and 100,000 ounces of raw material 2 available.

	Requirements (oz/unit)		Selling Price
Knife	Raw Material 1	Raw Material 2	($/unit)
A	4	2	15.00
B	6	8	25.50
C	1	3	14.00
D	2	5	19.50
E	6	10	27.00

a. If the objective is to maximize profit, specify the objective function and constraints for the problem. Assume that labor costs are negligible.

b. Solve the problem with a computer package using the simplex method.

11. The Nutmeg Corporation produces five different nut and mixed nut products: almond pack, walnut pack, gourmet pack, fancy pack, and thrifty pack. Each product (individual or mix) comes in a one-pound can. The firm can purchase almonds at $0.80 per pound, walnuts at $0.60 per pound, and peanuts at $0.35 per pound. Peanuts are used to complete each mix, and the company has an unlimited supply of them. The supply of almonds and walnuts is limited. The company can buy up to 3000 pounds of almonds and 2000 pounds of walnuts. The resource requirements and forecasted demand for the products follow. Use a computer package to solve this problem.

	Minimum Requirements (%)		Demand
Product	Almonds	Walnuts	(cans)
Almonds	100	—	1250
Walnuts	—	100	750
Gourmet	45	45	1000
Fancy	30	30	500
Thrifty	20	20	1500

a. What mix minimizes the cost of meeting the demand for all five products?

b. What is the impact on the product mix if only 2000 pounds of peanuts are available?

c. What is the impact on the product mix if the gourmet pack requires 50 percent almonds and 50 percent walnuts?

d. What is the impact on the product mix if demand for the fancy pack doubles?

12. A problem often of concern to managers in processing industries is blending. Consider the task facing Lisa Rankin, procurement manager of a company that manufactures special additives. She must determine the proper amount of each raw material to purchase for the production of a certain product. Each gallon of the finished product must have a combustion point of at least 220°F. In addition, the product's gamma content (which causes hydrocarbon pollution) cannot exceed 6 percent of volume, and the product's zeta content (which cleans the internal moving parts of engines) must be at least 12 percent by volume. Three raw materials are available. Each raw material has a different rating on these characteristics:

	Raw Material		
Characteristic	A	B	C
Combustion point (°F)	200	180	280
Gamma content (%)	4	3	10
Zeta content (%)	20	10	8

Raw material A costs $0.60 per gallon; raw materials B and C cost $0.40 and $0.50 per gallon, respectively. The procurement manager wants to minimize the cost of raw materials per gallon of product. Use linear programming to find the optimal proportion of each raw material for a gallon of finished product. *Hint:* Express the decision variables in terms of fractions of a gallon; the sum of the fractions must equal 1.00.

13. A small fabrication firm makes three basic types of components for use by other companies. Each component is processed on three machines. Following are the processing times; total capacities (in hours) are 1600 for machine 1, 1400 for machine 2, and 1500 for machine 3.

	Processing Time (hr)		
Component	Machine 1	Machine 2	Machine 3
A	0.25	0.10	0.05
B	0.20	0.15	0.10
C	0.10	0.05	0.15

Each component contains a different amount of two basic raw materials. Raw material 1 costs $0.20 per ounce, and raw material 2 costs $0.35 per ounce. There are 200,000 ounces of raw material 1 and 85,000 ounces of raw material 2 available.

Component	Requirement (oz/unit)		Selling Price ($/unit)
	Raw Material 1	Raw Material 2	
A	32	12	40
B	26	16	28
C	19	9	24

a. Assume that the company must make at least 1200 units of component B, that labor costs are negligible, and that the objective is to maximize profits. Specify the objective function and constraints for the problem.
b. Use a computer package to solve the problem.

14. The following is a linear programming model for analyzing the product mix of Maxine's Hat Company, which produces three hat styles:

Maximize: $\$7x_1 + \$5x_2 + \$2x_3 = Z$
Subject to: $3x_1 + 5x_2 + x_3 \le 150$ (machine A time)
$5x_1 + 3x_2 + 2x_3 \le 100$ (machine B time)
$x_1 + 2x_2 + x_3 \le 160$ (machine C time)
$x_1 \ge 0,\quad x_2 \ge 0,\quad$ and $\quad x_3 \ge 0$

The printout below shows the optimal solution to the problem. Consider each of the following statements independently, and state whether it is true or false. Explain each answer.
a. If the price of hat 3 were increased to $2.50, it would be part of the optimal product mix.
b. The capacity of machine C can be reduced to 65 hours without affecting profits.
c. If machine A had a capacity of 170 hours, the production output would remain unchanged.

Linear Programming
Maximization

Solution

Variable Label	Variable Value	Original Coefficient	Coefficient Sensitivity
X1	3.1250	7	0
X2	28.1250	5	0
X3	0	2	0.7500

Constraint Label	Original RHV	Slack or Surplus	Shadow Price
C1	150	0	0.2500
C2	100	0	1.2500
C3	160	100.6250	0

Objective Function Value: 162.5000

Sensitivity Analysis
Objective Function Coefficients

Variable Label	Lower Limit	Original Coefficient	Upper Limit
X1	5.2857	7	8.3333
X2	4.2000	5	11.6667
X3	No Limit	2	2.7500

Right-Hand-Side Values

Constraint Label	Lower Limit	Original Value	Upper Limit
C1	60	150	166.6667
C2	90	100	250.0000
C3	59.3750	160	No limit

15. The Washington Chemical Company produces chemicals and solvents for the glue industry. The production process is divided into several "focused factories," each producing a specific set of products. The time has come to prepare the production plan for one of the focused factories. This particular factory produces five products, which must pass through both the reactor and the separator. Each product also requires a certain combination of raw materials. Production data are shown in Table I.1.

    The Washington Chemical Company has a long-term contract with a major glue manufacturer that requires annual production of 3000 pounds of both products 3 and 4. More of these products could be produced because there is a demand for them.
    a. Determine the annual production quantity of each product that maximizes contribution to profits. Assume the company can sell all it can produce.
    b. Specify the lot size for each product.
16. The Warwick Manufacturing Company produces shovels for industrial and home use. Sales of the shovels are seasonal, and Warwick's customers refuse to stockpile them during slack periods. In other words, the customers want to minimize inventory, insist on shipments according to their schedules, and won't accept backorders.

    Warwick employs manual, unskilled laborers, who require only very basic training. Producing 1000 shovels costs $3500 on regular time and $3700 on overtime. These amounts include materials, which account for over 85 percent of the cost. Overtime is limited to production of 15,000 shovels per quarter. In addition, subcontractors can be hired at $4200 per thousand shovels, but Warwick's labor contract restricts this type of production to 5000 shovels per quarter.

    The current level of inventory is 30,000 shovels, and management wants to end the year at that level.

Holding 1000 shovels in inventory costs $280 per quarter. The latest annual demand forecast is

Quarter	Demand
1	70,000
2	150,000
3	320,000
4	100,000
Totals	640,000

Build a linear programming model to determine the *best* regular-time capacity plan. Assume that

- the firm has 30 workers now, and management wants to have the same number in quarter 4,
- each worker can produce 4000 shovels per quarter, and
- hiring a worker costs $1000, and laying off a worker costs $600.

17. The management of Warwick Company (Problem 16) is willing to give price breaks to its customers as an incentive to purchase shovels in advance of the traditional seasons. Warwick's sales and marketing staff estimates that the demand for shovels resulting from the price breaks would be

Quarter	Demand	Original Demand
1	120,000	70,000
2	180,000	150,000
3	180,000	320,000
4	160,000	100,000
Totals	640,000	640,000

Calculate the optimal production plan (including the work-force staffing plan) under the new demand

TABLE I.1 *Production Data for Washington Chemical*

Resource	Product 1	2	3	4	5	Total Resources Available
Reactor (hr/lb)	0.05	0.10	0.80	0.57	0.15	7,500 hr*
Separator (hr/lb)	0.20	0.02	0.20	0.09	0.30	7,500 hr*
Raw material 1 (lb)	0.20	0.50	0.10	0.40	0.18	10,000 lb
Raw material 2 (lb)	—	0.70	—	0.50	—	6,000 lb
Raw material 3 (lb)	0.10	0.20	0.40	—	—	7,000 lb
Profit contribution ($/lb)	4.00	7.00	3.50	4.00	5.70	

*The total time available has been adjusted to account for setups. The five products have a prescribed sequence owing to the cost of changeovers between products. The company has a 35-day cycle (or 10 changeovers per year per product). Consequently, the time for these changeovers has been deducted from the total time available for these machines.

schedule. Compare it to the optimal production plan under the original demand schedule. Evaluate the potential effects of demand management.

18. Briley Cosmetics manufactures skin care products. The operations manager seeks the minimum-cost strategy to supply 10,000 cartons of face cream, 5000 cartons of body cream, and 15,000 cartons of shampoo to satisfy next month's domestic market.

    The manufacturing process consists of a two-stage process and involves two types of raw materials. Briley's monthly production capacity (first shift) is 15,000 labor hours for stage 1 and 10,000 labor hours for stage 2. The first shift hourly wage rates are $8.50 at stage 1 and $9.25 at stage 2. A second shift also is available, with a 10 percent reduction in capacity and a 10 percent shift (wage) premium. Essential raw materials A and B are mined locally. Mine capacity limits raw material availability to 200,000 pounds of A per month and 150,000 pounds of B per month. Briley's cost for raw material A is $1 per pound and for raw material B is $1.50 per pound.

    Briley's domestic facility has neither the labor nor the raw materials needed to meet the demand projected for next month. An overseas joint venture company has an additional source of the essential raw materials and is licensed to produce Briley Cosmetics for international markets. Briley may import face cream and/or body cream from this source for $40 per carton and $55 per carton, respectively.

	Product		
	Face Cream	Body Cream	Shampoo
Labor (hr/carton)			
Stage 1	1.5	1.8	1.0
Stage 2	0.8	1.0	0.5
Raw Materials (lb/carton)			
A	5	8	3
B	7	4	9

a. What optimal production schedule minimizes total production costs while meeting projected demand?

b. What is the minimum value of the objective function?

c. What is the value of an additional hour of stage 1 labor? Stage 2 labor?

d. What is the value of an additional pound of raw material A? Raw material B?

e. Over what range is the shadow price for raw material B valid?

f. What would be the impact on the optimal solution if the demand for all three products were decreased by 10 percent each?

g. At what price would importing body cream enter the solution?

19. The product planning manager at Westlake Electronics wants to determine the optimal television product mix for the next quarter. The production capacities for the firm's three manufacturing facilities are

Facility	Fabrication (hr)	Assembly (hr)
1	10,000	50,000
2	15,000	60,000
3	5,000	35,000
Totals	30,000	145,000

Westlake can produce three different types of TVs: portable (20 inches), regular (27 inches), and home theater (40 inches). The gross profit and production requirements by type of TV are

Television	Gross Profit	Fabrication (hr/unit)	Assembly (hr/unit)
Portable	$75	3	9
Regular	$125	4	12
Home theater	$200	7	16

a. What product mix optimizes gross profit?

b. What is the maximum value of the objective function?

c. What is the value of an additional hour of fabrication time at facility 1?

d. What would be the impact on the optimal solution if the company were required to produce at least 1500 portable and 500 home theater TVs?

e. What would be the impact on the optimal solution if (in addition to the constraints of part d) the production capacities for all three plants were increased by 10 percent?

f. How would the product mix change in the original formulation of part a if equal utilization of capacity were required for all three plants?

20. The Bull Grin Company produces a feed supplement for animal foods produced by a number of companies. Sales are seasonal, and Bull Grin's customers refuse to stockpile the supplement during slack sales periods. In other words, the customers want to minimize inventory, insist on shipments according to their schedules, and won't accept backorders.

    Bull Grin employs manual, unskilled laborers, who require little or no training. Producing 1000 pounds of supplement costs $810 on regular time and $900 on overtime. These amounts include materials, which account for over 80 percent of the cost. Overtime is limited to production of 30,000 pounds per quarter. In addition, subcontractors can be hired at $1100 per thousand pounds, but only 10,000 pounds per quarter can be produced this way.

The current level of inventory is 40,000 pounds, and management wants to end the year at that level. Holding 1000 pounds of feed supplement in inventory costs $110 per quarter. The latest annual forecast follows.

Quarter	Demand (lb)
1	100,000
2	410,000
3	770,000
4	440,000
Total	1,720,000

The firm currently has 180 workers, a number that management wants to keep in quarter 4. Each worker can produce 2000 pounds per quarter, so regular-time production costs $1620 per worker. Idle workers must be paid at that same rate. Hiring one worker costs $1000, and laying off a worker costs $600.

Write the objective function and constraints describing this production planning problem, after fully defining the decision variables.

21. Inside Traders, Inc. invests in various types of securities. The firm has $5 million for immediate investment and wants to maximize the interest earned over the next year. Four investment possibilities are presented in the following table. To further structure the portfolio, the board of directors has specified that at least 40 percent of the investment must be in corporate bonds and common stock. Furthermore, no more than 20 percent of the investment may be in real estate.

Investment	Expected Interest Earned (%)
Corporate bonds	8.5
Common stock	9.0
Gold certificates	10.0
Real estate	13.0

Write the objective function and constraints for this portfolio investment problem, after fully defining the decision variables.

22. NYNEX has a scheduling problem. Operators work eight-hour shifts and can begin work at midnight, 4 A.M., 8 A.M., noon, 4 P.M., or 8 P.M. Operators are needed to satisfy the following demand pattern. Formulate a linear programming model to cover the demand requirements with the minimum number of operators.

Time Period	Operators Needed
Midnight to 4 A.M.	4
4 A.M. to 8 A.M.	6
8 A.M. to noon	90
Noon to 4 P.M.	85
4 P.M. to 8 P.M.	55
8 P.M. to 12 midnight	20

Selected References

Anderson, David R., Dennis J. Sweeney, and Thomas A. Williams. *An Introduction to Management Science: Quantitative Approaches to Decision Making.* St. Paul, Minn.: West, 1988.

Asim, R., E. De Falomir, and L. Lasdon. "An Optimization-Based Decision Support System for a Product-Mix Problem." *Interfaces,* vol. 12, no. 2 (April 1982), pp. 26–33.

Bierman, Harold, Charles P. Bonini, and Warren H. Hausman. *Quantitative Analysis for Business Decisions.* Homewood, Ill.: Richard D. Irwin, 1986.

Cook, Thomas M., and Robert A. Russell. *Introduction to Management Sciences.* Englewood Cliffs, N.J.: Prentice-Hall, 1993.

Krajewski, L. J., and H. E. Thompson. *Management Science: Quantitative Methods in Context.* New York: John Wiley & Sons, 1981.

Markland, Robert E., and James R. Sweigart. *Quantitative Methods: Applications to Managerial Decision Making.* New York: John Wiley & Sons, 1987.

Perry, C., and K. C. Crellin. "The Precise Management Meaning of a Shadow Price." *Interfaces,* vol. 12, no. 2 (April 1982), pp. 61-63.

Taylor, Bernard W., III. *Introduction to Management Science.* Needham Heights, Mass.: Allyn & Bacon, 1990.

Wagner, Harvey M. *Principles of Operations Research,* 2nd ed. Englewood Cliffs, N.J.: Prentice-Hall, 1975.

Chapter Fourteen

MATERIAL REQUIREMENTS PLANNING

they Products Corporation is a leading manufacturer of street sweepers, refuse haulers, and bulk materials handling and processing equipment for the municipal and construction markets. Street sweepers are a complex product, involving the purchasing, stocking, distribution, and assembly of 20,000 components from 1400 vendors. Most of the equipment sold is configured to each customer's order. Prior to installing a computerized material requirements planning system, the company determined its component production requirements manually. In addition, management did not have accurate financial data for costing the manufacturing process or preparing timely accounts payable and accounts receivable reports. For example, under the old system, accounts receivable took as long as a week to process, so managing account delinquencies was difficult. After the computerized system was installed, inventories were reduced by 33 percent, accounts receivable were recorded daily, and accurate financial and manufacturing data were available for

This Athey street sweeper is composed of approximately 20,000 separate components.

accounting reports and forecasting. In addition, the new system could quickly change a price quote on an order to a firm customer order, thereby reducing the time needed to process a customer order and improving customer service. This capability contributed to a 100 percent increase in Athey's replacement parts business. (Jernigan, 1993)

As the experiences of Athey Products Corporation demonstrate, the company that successfully balances customer service with inventory management and investment gains a competitive edge. Thus the ability to maintain an efficient flow of materials from suppliers and to effectively manage internal activities relating to materials is essential to a profitable operation. Operations management tries to ensure that all resources needed to produce finished products will be available at the right time. For a manufacturer this may mean keeping track of thousands of subassemblies, components, and raw materials.

We begin this chapter with a discussion of dependent demand and how it differs from independent demand. Then we review the benefits of material requirements planning (MRP), a system designed for managing inventories subject to dependent demands. Next, we discuss the major inputs to MRP systems: bills of materials, master production schedules, and inventory records. Finally, we explore the issues in implementation of an MRP system and how MRP principles can be used for distribution inventories.

◆ DEPENDENT DEMAND

To illustrate the concept of dependent demand, let's consider a Huffy bicycle produced for retail outlets. The bicycle, one of many different types held in inventory at Huffy's plant, has a high-volume demand rate over time. Demand for a final product such as a bicycle is called **independent demand** because it is influenced only by market conditions and not by demand for any other type of bicycle held in inventory. Huffy must *forecast* that demand using techniques such as those discussed in Chapter 10. However, Huffy keeps many items other than completed bicycles in inventory, including handle bars, pedals, frames, and wheel rims. Each of these items has a **dependent demand** because the quantity required is a function of the demand for other items held in inventory. For example, the demand for frames, pedals, and rims is *dependent* on the production decisions for completed bicycles. Operations can *calculate* the demand for dependent demand items once the bicycle production levels are announced. For example, every bicycle needs two wheel rims, so 1000 completed bicycles need 1000(2) = 2000 rims. There is no need to use statistical forecasting techniques for these items.

The bicycle, or any other good manufactured from one or more components, is called a **parent**. The wheel rim is an example of a **component**—an item that may go through one or more operations to be transformed into or become part of one or more parents. The rim may have several different parents because it might be used for more than one style of bicycle. The parent–component relationship can cause erratic dependent demand patterns for components. Suppose that every time inventory falls to 500 units, an order for 1000 more bicycles is placed, as shown in Fig 14.1(a). The assembly supervisor then authorizes the withdrawal of 2000 rims from inventory, along with other components for the finished product; demand for the rim is shown in Fig. 14.1(b). Consequently, even though customer demand for the finished bicycle is continuous and uniform, the production demand for wheel rims is "lumpy"; that is, it occurs sporadically, usually in relatively large quantities. Thus the *production* decisions for the assembly of bicycles, which account for the costs of assembling the bicycles and the projected assembly capacities at the time the decisions are made, determine the demand for rims.

Managing dependent demand inventories is complicated because some components may be subject to both dependent and independent demand. For example, operations needs 2000 wheel rims for the new bicycles, but the company also

FIGURE 14.1

Lumpy Dependent Demand Resulting from Continuous Independent Demand

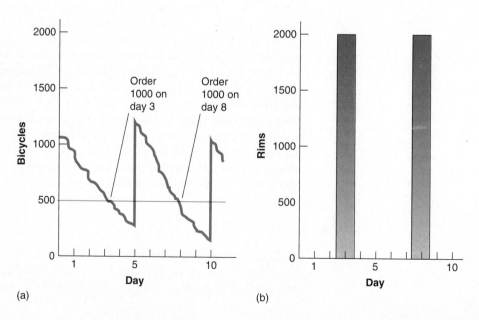

(a)   (b)

sells replacement rims for old bicycles directly to retail outlets. This practice places an independent demand on the inventory of rims. Material requirements planning addresses complex situations involving components that may have independent demand as well as dependent demand inventories.

◆ BENEFITS OF MATERIAL REQUIREMENTS PLANNING

Why should companies invest in an MRP system?

For years, many companies tried to manage production and delivery of dependent demand inventories with independent demand systems, but the outcome seldom was satisfactory. As a result, **material requirements planning (MRP)**—a computerized information system—was developed specifically to aid in managing dependent demand inventory and scheduling replenishment orders. The MRP system enables businesses to reduce inventory levels, utilize labor and facilities better, and improve customer service. For example, when American Sterilizer Company introduced MRP at its Hospital Products and Systems Group, it increased on-time customer deliveries from 70 to 95 percent. It also cut overtime by at least 50 percent, reduced component shortages by more than 80 percent, lowered indirect labor by 24 percent, and reduced direct labor by 7 percent.

Material requirements planning has three advantages.

1. Statistical forecasting for components with lumpy demand results in large forecasting errors. Compensating for such errors by increasing safety stock is costly, with no guarantee that stockouts can be avoided. MRP calculates the dependent demand of components from the production schedules of their parents, thereby providing a better forecast of component requirements.
2. MRP systems provide managers with information useful for planning capacities and estimating financial requirements. Production schedules and materials purchases can be translated into capacity requirements and dollar amounts and can be projected in the time periods when they will appear. Planners can use the information on parent item schedules to identify times when needed components may be unavailable because of capacity shortages, supplier delivery delays, and the like.
3. MRP systems automatically update the dependent demand and inventory replenishment schedules of components when the production schedules of parent items change. The MRP system alerts the planners whenever action is needed on any component.

A survey of industrial firms showed that, although such benefits are not always realized, neither are they unusual. The average MRP user increased inventory turns from 4.6 to 5.5 and cut delivery lead times from 17.5 to 13.5 weeks (see Cerveny and Scott, 1989). Research conducted by Greene (1988) indicated that about 34,000 manufacturing sites in the United States use MRP.

◆ INPUTS TO MATERIAL REQUIREMENTS PLANNING

The key inputs of an MRP system are bills of materials, master production schedules, and inventory records. Using this information, the MRP system identifies actions that operations must take to stay on schedule, such as releasing new production orders, adjusting order quantities, and expediting late orders.

FIGURE 14.2
Material Requirements
Plan Inputs

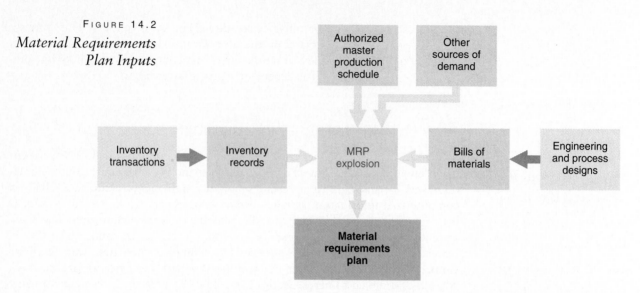

An MRP system translates the master production schedule and other sources of demand into the requirements for all subassemblies, components, and raw materials needed to produce the required parent items. This process is called an **MRP explosion** because it converts the schedules of various final products into a much larger number of schedules for components, as shown in Fig. 14.2.

Bill of Materials

Material requirements planning derives a component's requirements from the production schedules of its parents. Consequently the system needs accurate information on the parent–component relationships. A **bill of materials (BOM)** is a record of all the components of an item, the parent–component relationships, and usage quantities derived from engineering and process designs. In Fig. 14.3 the BOM of a simple ladder-back chair shows that the chair is made from a ladder-back subassembly, a seat subassembly, legs, and leg supports. In turn, the ladder-back subassembly is made from legs and back slats, and the seat subassembly is made from a seat frame and a cushion. Finally, the seat frame is made from seat-frame boards. For convenience we refer to these items by the letters shown in Fig. 14.3.

All items except A are components because they are needed to make a parent. Items A, B, C, and H are parents because they all have at least one component. The BOM also specifies the **usage quantity,** or the number of units of a component needed to make one unit of its immediate parent. Figure 14.3 shows usage quantities for each parent–component relationship in parentheses. Note that one chair (item A) is made from one ladder-back subassembly (item B), one seat subassembly (item C), two front legs (item D), and four leg supports (item E). In addition, item B is made from two back legs (item F) and four back slats (item G). Item C needs one seat frame (item H) and one seat cushion (item I). Finally, item H needs four seat-frame boards (item J).

Four terms frequently used to describe inventory items are end items, intermediate items, subassemblies, and purchased items. An **end item** typically is the final product sold to the customer; it is a parent but not a component. Item A in Fig. 14.3 is an end item. Accounting statements classify inventory of end items as

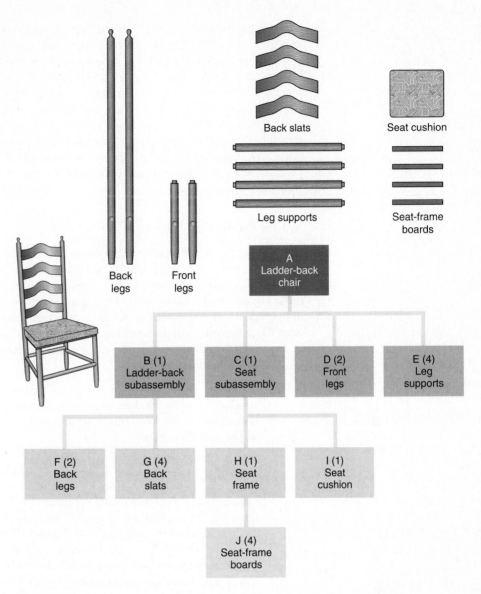

FIGURE 14.3

Bill of Materials for a Ladder-Back Chair

either work-in-process (WIP), if work remains to be done, or finished goods. An **intermediate item** is one such as B, C, or H that has at least one parent and at least one component. Some products have several levels of intermediate items; the parent of one intermediate item also is an intermediate item. Inventory of intermediate items—whether completed or still on the shop floor—is classified as WIP. A **subassembly** is an intermediate item that is *assembled* (as opposed to being transformed by other means) from *more* than one component. Items B and C are subassemblies. A **purchased item** has no components because it comes from a supplier, but it has one or more parents. Examples are items D, E, F, G, I, and J in Fig. 14.3. Inventory of purchased items is treated as raw materials in accounting statements.

A component may have more than one parent. **Part commonality,** sometimes called *standardization of parts* or *modularity,* is the degree to which a component has more than one immediate parent. As a result of commonality, the same item may appear in several places in the bill of materials for a product, or it may appear in the bills of materials for several different products. For example, the seat assembly from Fig. 14.3 is a component of the ladder-back chair and of a kitchen chair that is part of the same family of products. The usage quantity specified in the bill of materials relates to a specific parent–component relationship. The usage quantity for any component can change, depending on the parent item. Part commonality increases volume and repeatability for some items—which has several advantages for process design (see Chapter 3)—and helps minimize inventory costs. Today, almost 90 percent of manufacturing firms have products with at least some part commonality, with 44 percent reporting that it is extensive (Sharma, 1987).

Master Production Schedule

The second input is the **master production schedule (MPS)**, which details how many end items will be produced within specified periods of time. It disaggregates the aggregate production plan (see Chapter 13) into specific product schedules. Figure 14.4 shows how an aggregate plan for a family of chairs is disaggregated into the weekly master production schedule for each specific chair type. Time periods (called *time buckets*) are usually weeks, although hours, days, or even months may be used. The chair example demonstrates the following aspects of master scheduling.

1. The sums of the quantities in the MPS must equal those in the aggregate production plan. This constraint ensures consistency between the plans, a desirable result because of the economic analysis undertaken to arrive at the aggregate plan.
2. The aggregate production quantities must be allocated efficiently over time. The specific mix of chair types—the amount of each type as a percentage of the total aggregate quantity—is based on historic demand and marketing and promotional considerations. The planner must select lot sizes for each chair type, taking into consideration economic factors such as production setup costs and inventory carrying costs.
3. Capacity limitations, such as machine or labor capacity, storage space, or working capital, may determine the timing and size of MPS quantities. The planner must acknowledge these limitations by recognizing that some chair styles require more resources than others and setting the timing and size of the production quantities accordingly.

FIGURE 14.4

Master Production Schedule for a Family of Chairs

	April				May			
	1	2	3	4	5	6	7	8
Ladder-back chair		150				150		
Kitchen chair					120			120
Desk chair	200		200		200		200	
Aggregate production plan for chair family	550				790			

FIGURE 14.5

*Master Production
Scheduling Process*

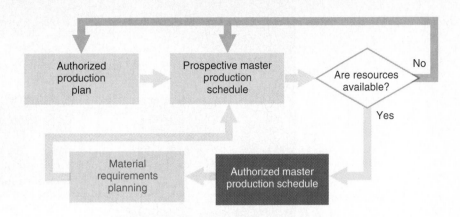

How do competitive priorities
affect the approach to master
production scheduling?

Master Production Scheduling Process and Strategies. Figure 14.5 shows the master production scheduling process. Operations must first create a prospective MPS to test whether it meets the schedule with the resources (e.g., machine capacities, labor, overtime, and subcontractors) provided for in the aggregate production plan. Operations revises the MPS until it obtains a schedule that satisfies all resource limitations or determines that no feasible schedule can be developed. In the latter event, the production plan must be revised to adjust production requirements or increase authorized resources. Once a feasible prospective MPS has been accepted by plant management, operations uses the authorized MPS as input to material requirements planning. Operations can then determine specific schedules for component production and assembly. Actual performance data are inputs to the next prospective MPS, and the master production scheduling process is repeated.

The master production schedule links the firm's broad strategies, as expressed in the aggregate production plan, to more specific tactical plans that will enable the firm to achieve its objectives. Three basic MPS strategies enable a firm to manage inventories in support of its competitive priorities. The strategy chosen will determine the manager's approach to master production scheduling.

1. *Make-to-stock strategy.* Product-focused firms tend to use a **make-to-stock strategy,** in which the firm holds end items in stock to minimize customer delivery times. This strategy is feasible because most product-focused firms produce relatively few standardized products, for which they can make reasonably accurate forecasts. Examples of products produced with a make-to-stock strategy include garden tools, electronic components, and chemicals. Thus these firms develop master production schedules for end items. Figure 14.6 demonstrates that make-to-stock operations typically produce a small number of finished products from a large number of different raw materials.

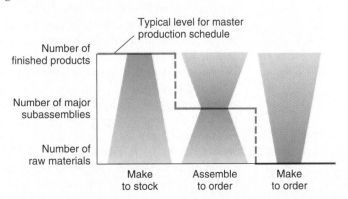

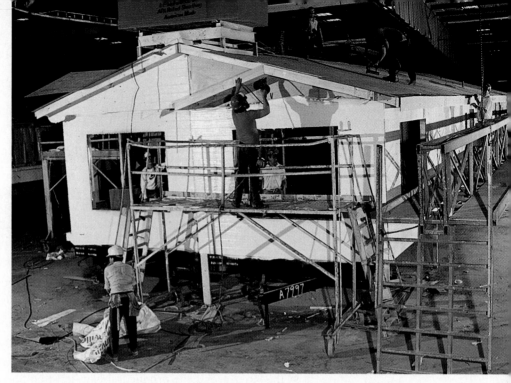

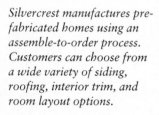

Silvercrest manufactures pre-fabricated homes using an assemble-to-order process. Customers can choose from a wide variety of siding, roofing, interior trim, and room layout options.

2. *Assemble-to-order strategy.* The **assemble-to-order strategy** is an approach to producing end items customized with many options from standard components and subassemblies upon receipt of customer orders. For example, an automobile manufacturer can literally produce millions of cars, no two alike, to meet the mix of options and accessories demanded by customers. Other such products include farm tractors, upholstered furniture, and automatic teller machines. The assemble-to-order strategy addresses two competitive priorities: customization and fast delivery time. Operations holds the major assemblies and components in stock until a specific order comes in, at which time it produces the end item. Stocking end items would be economically prohibitive because forecasts cannot accurately tell which of the options the customer will select.

As Fig. 14.6 shows, in an assemble-to-order strategy, operations produces a large number of different items from a relatively small number of components and major subassemblies. Suppose that an automobile manufacturer offers the following customer options: 3 engine sizes, 4 transmission types, 2 drive trains, 3 steering options, 3 tire sizes, 3 body styles, 2 body trim options, 4 interior options, and 2 brake systems. The body frame and certain other parts are common to every car. Based on these customer choices, you can produce $3 \times 4 \times 2 \times 3 \times 3 \times 3 \times 2 \times 4 \times 2 = 10,368$ different cars. However, there are only $3 + 4 + 2 + 3 + 3 + 3 + 2 + 4 + 2 = 26$ components and major subassemblies, plus a common assembly of parts needed for every car—a far smaller number than the total number of cars that can be produced. Demand for these components and major subassemblies is much easier to forecast than that for any completely assembled product. Consequently, operations bases master production scheduling on the components and major subassemblies, rather than on the end items.

3. *Make-to-order strategy.* Many process-focused firms use a **make-to-order strategy**, whereby operations produces end items to customer specifications. This strategy provides a high degree of customization. The many custom-made end items, subassemblies, and components are produced from a relatively smaller number of raw materials and purchased components, as illustrated in Fig. 14.6. Examples include specialized medical equipment, castings, and plastic bottles. For this strategy, the master production schedule generally

consists of orders for standard supplies and operating schedules (e.g., number of shifts and overtime) for crucial processes because the demand for supplies and capacity hours is easier to forecast from historical experiences than is demand for specific end items or major subassemblies. End-item scheduling becomes feasible only if customer orders allow sufficiently long delivery times.

Functional Interfaces. Operations needs information from other functional areas to develop an MPS that achieves production plan objectives and organizational goals. Although master production schedules are continually subject to revision, changes should be made with a full understanding of the consequences. Often, changes to the MPS require additional resources, as in the case of an increase in the order quantity of a product. Many companies face this situation frequently, and the problem is amplified when an important customer is involved. Unless more resources are authorized for the product, less resources will be available for other products, putting their schedules in jeopardy. Some companies require the vice-presidents of marketing and manufacturing jointly to authorize significant MPS changes to ensure mutual resolution of such issues. Managerial Practice 14.1 on the next page discusses how these functional interfaces were resolved in developing master production schedules at Hyundai.

Other functional areas can use the MPS for routine planning. Finance uses the MPS to estimate budgets and cash flows. Marketing uses it to project the impact of product mix changes on the firm's ability to satisfy customer demand and manage delivery schedules. Using rough-cut capacity planning, which we discuss later in the chapter, manufacturing can estimate the effects of MPS changes on loads at critical workstations. Personal computers, with their excellent graphic capabilities, give managers access to many MPS-related reports in readable and useful formats. PC programs allow managers to ask "what if" questions about the effects of changes to the master production schedule. However, these programs project only what may happen *if* the prospective MPS is implemented, not what *should* be done.

Developing a Master Production Schedule. The process of developing a master production schedule includes (1) calculating the projected on-hand inventory and (2) determining the timing and size of the production quantities of specific products. We use the manufacturer of the ladder-back chair to illustrate the process. For simplicity, we assume that the firm doesn't utilize safety stocks for end items, even though many firms do.

> **Step 1.** *Calculate projected on-hand inventories.* The first step is to calculate the **projected on-hand inventory,** an estimate of the amount of inventory available each week after demand has been satisfied:

$$\begin{pmatrix} \text{Projected on-hand} \\ \text{inventory at end of} \\ \text{this period} \end{pmatrix} = \begin{pmatrix} \text{On-hand} \\ \text{inventory} \\ \text{last period} \end{pmatrix} + \begin{pmatrix} \text{MPS quantity} \\ \text{due this} \\ \text{period} \end{pmatrix} - \begin{pmatrix} \text{Projected} \\ \text{requirements} \\ \text{this period} \end{pmatrix}$$

> In some periods there may be no MPS quantity for a product because sufficient inventory already exists. For the projected requirements for this period, the scheduler uses whichever is larger—the forecast or the customer orders booked—recognizing that the forecast is subject to error. If actual booked orders exceed the forecast, the projection will be more accurate if the scheduler uses the booked orders. Conversely, if the forecast exceeds booked

Managerial Practice 14.1

▶ *Master Production Scheduling at Hyundai Motor Company*

The Hyundai Motor Company produces 780,000 automobiles at a rate of 137 units per hour. The company offers approximately 4000 combinations of model, options, and interior color. Hyundai develops an annual business plan that is expressed in monthly sales volumes by model types and by engine and transmission types. This plan becomes the basis for the master production schedule, which is the responsibility of the production/sales control department. Each month, representatives from the sales, production planning, and materials departments meet to develop monthly production schedules. The production/sales control department, which reports to the vice-president of manufacturing, mediates conflicts between functional areas.

The MPS is developed on an eight-month rolling horizon basis; that is, each month the MPS is updated for the next eight months. During each meeting the schedule for the next month is confirmed and the following month's schedule is developed for the purpose of production planning and buying locally purchased parts. The rest of the monthly schedules are used as forecasts to give the purchasing department and suppliers enough lead time to acquire imported raw materials and parts.

Operations prepares separate MPSs for passenger and commercial vehicles. Hyundai develops a separate master schedule for each of its models, which is further broken down by destination and body trim. These schedules are used to plan the production at assembly lines dedicated to each model. Next, the MPS for each model is broken down by engine size and transmission type. This schedule is used as the primary input to the engine and transmission plant schedules. Finally, the MPS for each model is converted into a schedule that shows the monthly production volume requirements for the model (e.g., Excel 5 door) by body trim level (e.g., L, GL, or GLS) and by interior color (e.g., chestnut red or dark sapphire). This schedule is of primary importance to suppliers that deliver various parts and interior furnishings.

The production planning department uses the monthly schedules to develop weekly schedules specifying daily volumes by model and sequence. The materials department uses the schedules to calculate parts and materials requirements.

Source: Chan Hahn and Kee Young Kim, *Hyundai Motor Company: Manufacturing Strategies and Production Planning and Control Systems*, Bowling Green State University, 1989, pp. 53–68.

orders, we assume that it will provide a better estimate of requirements for the period. The manufacturer of the ladder-back chair produces the chair to stock and needs to develop an MPS for it. Marketing has forecast a demand of 30 chairs for the first week of April, but actual customer orders booked are for 38 chairs. The current on-hand inventory is 55 chairs. No MPS quantity is due in week 1.

Figure 14.7 shows a partial MPS record with these quantities listed. As actual orders for week 1 are greater than the forecast, the scheduler uses the figure for actual orders in calculating the projected inventory balance at the end of week 1:

$$\text{Inventory} = \begin{pmatrix} 55 \text{ chairs} \\ \text{currently} \\ \text{in stock} \end{pmatrix} + \begin{pmatrix} \text{MPS quantity} \\ (\text{zero for} \\ \text{week 1}) \end{pmatrix} - \begin{pmatrix} 38 \text{ chairs already} \\ \text{promised for} \\ \text{delivery in week 1} \end{pmatrix} = 17 \text{ chairs}$$

Because no MPS quantity is scheduled, it has no effect on the on-hand inventory for week 1.

Figure 14.8 shows marketing's forecast and actual orders for week 2. In week 2, the forecast quantity exceeds actual orders booked, so the projected

FIGURE 14.7

Master Production Schedule for Week 1

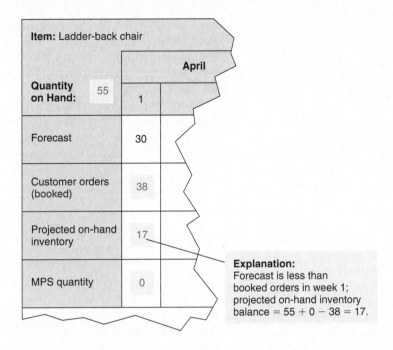

Item: Ladder-back chair

Quantity on Hand: 55	April 1	
Forecast	30	
Customer orders (booked)	38	
Projected on-hand inventory	17	
MPS quantity	0	

Explanation:
Forecast is less than booked orders in week 1; projected on-hand inventory balance = 55 + 0 − 38 = 17.

FIGURE 14.8

Master Production Schedule for Weeks 1 and 2

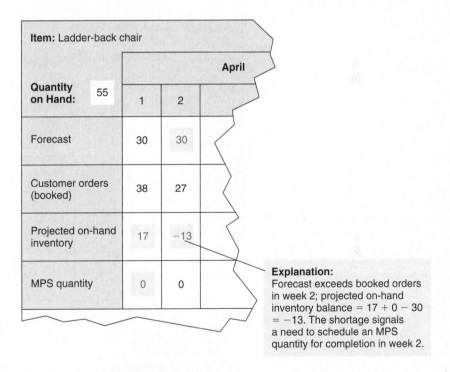

Item: Ladder-back chair

Quantity on Hand: 55	April 1	2	
Forecast	30	30	
Customer orders (booked)	38	27	
Projected on-hand inventory	17	−13	
MPS quantity	0	0	

Explanation:
Forecast exceeds booked orders in week 2; projected on-hand inventory balance = 17 + 0 − 30 = −13. The shortage signals a need to schedule an MPS quantity for completion in week 2.

on-hand inventory for the end of week 2 is 17 + 0 − 30 = −13. The shortage signals the need for more chairs in week 2.

Step 2. *Determine the timing and size of MPS quantities.* The goal of determining the timing and size of MPS quantities is maintaining a nonnegative projected on-hand inventory balance. As the scheduler projects shortages in inventory, she schedules MPS quantities to cover them. The first MPS quantity should be scheduled for the week when the projected on-hand inventory reflects a negative balance, such as week 2 in Fig. 14.8.* The scheduler adds the MPS quantity to the projected on-hand inventory and searches for the next period when a shortage occurs. This shortage signals a need for a second MPS quantity, and so on.

Figure 14.9 shows the master production schedule for the ladder-back chair. The order policy requires production lot sizes of 150 units. A shortage of 13 chairs in week 2 will occur unless the scheduler provides for an MPS quantity for that period. Once the MPS quantity is scheduled, the updated projected inventory balance for week 2 is:

$$\text{Inventory} = \left(\begin{array}{c} \text{17 units in} \\ \text{inventory at} \\ \text{end of week 1} \end{array} \right) + \left(\begin{array}{c} \text{MPS quantity} \\ \text{of 150 units} \end{array} \right) - \left(\begin{array}{c} \text{Forecast} \\ \text{of 30 units} \end{array} \right) = 137 \text{ units}$$

The scheduler proceeds column by column through the MPS record until reaching the end, filling in the MPS quantities as needed to avoid shortages. The 137 units will satisfy forecasted demands until week 7, when the pro-

FIGURE 14.9

Master Production Schedule for Weeks 1–8

Item: Ladder-back chair					Order Policy: 150 units Lead Time: 1 week			
		April			May			
Quantity on Hand: 55	1	2	3	4	5	6	7	8
Forecast	30	30	30	30	35	35	35	35
Customer orders (booked)	38	27	24	8	0	0	0	0
Projected on-hand inventory	17	137	107	77	42	7	122	87
MPS quantity	0	150	0	0	0	0	150	0
MPS start	150	0	0	0	0	150	0	0

Explanation:
The time needed to assemble 150 chairs is one week. The assembly department must start assembling chairs in week 1 to have them ready by week 2.

Explanation:
On-hand inventory balance = 17 + 150 − 30 = 137. The MPS quantity is needed to avoid a shortage of 30 − 17 = 13 chairs in week 2.

---

* In some cases, new orders will be planned before a negative balance is encountered. Two such instances are building safety stocks and building anticipation inventories.

jected inventory balance in the absence of an MPS quantity is $7 + 0 - 35 = -28$. This shortage signals the need for another MPS quantity of 150 units. The updated inventory balance is $7 + 150 - 35 = 122$ for week 7.

The last row in Fig. 14.9 indicates the periods in which production of the MPS quantities must *begin* so that they will be available when indicated in the MPS quantity row. In the upper right portion of the MPS record, a lead time of one week is indicated for the ladder-back chair; that is, one week is needed to assemble 150 ladder-back chairs, assuming that items B, C, D, and E are available. For each MPS quantity, the scheduler works backward through the lead time to determine when the assembly department must start producing chairs. Consequently, a lot of 150 units must be started in week 1 and another in week 6.

Available-to-Promise Quantities. In addition to providing manufacturing with the timing and size of production quantities, the master production schedule provides marketing with information that is useful in negotiating delivery dates with customers. The quantity of end items that marketing can promise to deliver on specified dates is called **available-to-promise (ATP) inventory**. It is the difference between the customer orders already booked and the quantity that operations is planning to produce. As new customer orders are accepted, the ATP inventory is reduced to reflect commitment of the firm to ship those quantities, but the actual inventory stays unchanged until the order is removed from inventory and shipped to the customer. An available-to-promise inventory is associated with each MPS quantity. The ATP in week 2 is the MPS quantity minus booked customer orders until the next MPS quantity, or $150 - (27 + 24 + 8 + 0 + 0) = 91$ units. The ATP tells marketing that, of the 150 units scheduled for completion in week 2, 91 units are uncommitted, and total orders up to that quantity can be promised for delivery as early as week 2. In week 7, the ATP is 150 units, because there are no booked orders in week 7 and beyond.

The procedure for calculating available-to-promise information is slightly different for the first (current) week of the schedule than for other weeks. The ATP inventory for the first week equals *current on-hand inventory* plus the MPS quantity for the first week, minus the cumulative total of booked orders up to (but not including) the week in which the next MPS quantity arrives. So, in Fig. 14.9, the ATP for the first week is $55 + 0 - 38 = 17$. This information tells marketing that it can promise as many as 17 units this week, 91 more units in week 2, and 150 more units in week 7. If customer order requests exceed ATP quantities in those time periods, the MPS must be changed before the customer orders can be booked.

Freezing the MPS. The master production schedule is the basis of all end item, subassembly, component, and materials schedules. For this reason, changes to the MPS can be costly, particularly if they are made to MPS quantities soon to be completed. Increases in an MPS quantity may cause delays in shipments to customers or excessive expediting costs because of shortages in materials. Decreases in MPS quantities can result in unused materials or components (at least until another need for them arises) and consumption of valuable capacities for something not needed. Similar costs occur when forecasted need dates for MPS quantities are changed. For these reasons many firms "freeze," or disallow changes to, a portion of the master production schedule.

How can accurate shipping dates be established for customers?

Freezing can be accomplished by specifying a **demand time fence,** which is the number of periods (beginning with the current period) during which few, if any, changes can be made to the MPS (i.e., the MPS is firm). The Ethan Allen Furniture Company uses a demand time fence of eight weeks. Thus, if the current period is period 1, the MPS is frozen for periods 1–8. Neither the master scheduler nor the computer can reschedule MPS quantities for this period without management's approval.

Other time fences can be specified that allow varying amounts of change. For example, another commonly used fence is the **planning time fence,** which covers a longer period than the demand time fence. The master scheduler—but not the computer—can make changes to the MPS quantities during this period of time. Beyond the planning time fence the computer may schedule the MPS quantities, based on the approved ordering policy. Figure 14.10 shows a demand time fence of two weeks and a planning time fence of six weeks for the ladder-back chair MPS. The MPS quantity in week 2 cannot be changed without management's approval. The MPS quantity in week 7 can be changed by the master scheduler without management's approval. The MPS quantities beyond week 8 can be changed by the computer, based on policies approved by management and programmed into the computer.

FIGURE 14.10

Master Production Schedule Time Fences

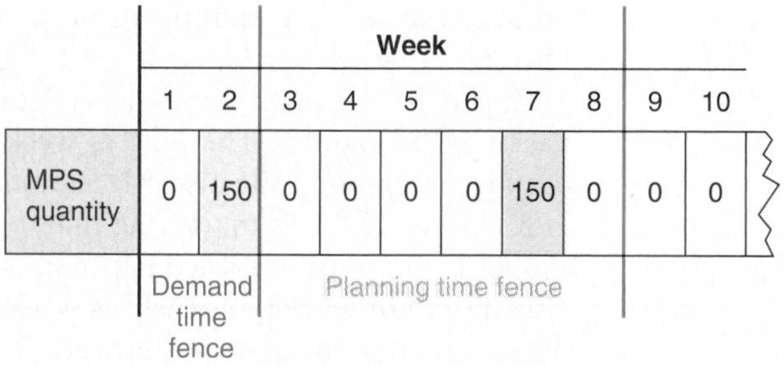

The number of time fences can vary. Black and Decker uses three time fences: 8, 13, and 26 weeks. The 8-week fence is essentially a demand time fence. From 8 to 13 weeks the MPS is quite rigid, but minor changes to model series may be made if components are available. From 13 to 26 weeks, substitutions of one end item for another are permitted as long as the production plan isn't violated and components are available. Beyond 26 weeks, marketing can make changes as long as they are compatible with the production plan (Vollmann, Berry, and Whybark, 1992).

The length of time fences should be reviewed periodically and adjusted as necessary. Although freezing the MPS reduces manufacturing costs and makes life easier for those responsible for scheduling components and materials, it tends to make the MPS less responsive to changes in customer demand. The costs of not being able to satisfy customers who place unexpected orders for delivery within the demand time fence must be weighed against the savings in production costs. Freezing should be considered only when the costs of meeting customer demand are prohibitive.

Rough-Cut Capacity Planning.   After developing a prospective master production schedule, operations must determine whether the MPS is feasible in terms of the firm's available resources (see Fig. 14.5). It does so by performing feasibility checks of the MPS with **rough-cut capacity planning,** so called because it gives only a rough approximation of actual resource requirements. Three approaches are common. **Capacity bills** are analogous to bills of materials for an end item except that they specify capacity requirements of critical resources (e.g., hours, square feet, or dollars) needed per unit of the end item, instead of usage quantities (measured in units) required by the immediate parent of a component. The routing and standard time for each component is needed to identify the machine and labor resources used. The MPS quantities for the end item are multiplied by these capacity requirements per unit to arrive at the total capacity requirements for each critical resource. **Resource profiles** use capacity bills to specify capacity requirements for critical resources for each period of the item's total manufacturing lead time. The resource profile approach, which additionally requires a manufacturing lead time for each component, provides a time-phased profile of capacity requirements in weekly time periods. Each resource's requirements are placed in the time period in which they would occur, relative to the time period in which the MPS quantity is required. The capacity bills approach is simpler and has less data requirements, but it groups all requirements for critical resources into the time period when the MPS quantity is required.

In this section we describe the **method of overall factors** because it provides a simple illustration of rough-cut capacity planning. We begin by multiplying each MPS quantity by its direct labor factor (such as direct labor hours per unit) for work performed at critical workstations. **Critical workstations** are operations that limit output because the need to use them frequently exceeds their capacity. The hours scheduled for work at these stations are called critical hours because they determine the feasibility of an MPS. Management tries to schedule time at critical workstations as efficiently as possible to maximize output. Thus if a critical workstation has 200 hours of capacity per week and for some reason has used only 150 hours this week, the lost 50 hours cannot be used next week, should 250 hours be required then. We use direct labor hours in our discussion, but in some situations machine hours may be more appropriate because they are the limiting resource at the critical workstations.

The total number of direct labor hours for all critical workstations in a period is multiplied by each critical workstation's load factor (the percentage of total direct labor hours at critical workstations typically spent at the workstation) to arrive at an estimate of total hours for that station. This estimate is called a *load profile*. The load profile is calculated for all future periods covered by the MPS. Management can compare the resulting load profile for each critical workstation to its capacity and then decide whether to keep the proposed schedule or modify it.

To illustrate, let's consider a company that produces three items, A, B, and C, to stock. Figure 14.11 on the next page shows an MPS for those items. To develop the load profile for this schedule, the scheduler needs to (1) identify the critical workstations, (2) estimate direct labor factors for each item, and (3) develop load factors for each critical workstation.

The method of overall factors involves the use of time standards (or gross estimates if standards aren't available) to estimate the number of direct hours required at each workstation to produce one unit of each item. Suppose that the scheduler has identified two critical workstations: 0810A and 0820B in our example. The scheduler then aggregates the hours for critical stations to obtain one direct labor factor and aggregates the hours for noncritical stations to obtain a second direct labor factor.

How can better estimates be obtained of cash flows and capacity requirements?

FIGURE 14.11

*Master Production
Schedule*

Item	Week								Total Units
	1	2	3	4	5	6	7	8	
A	25	25	25	25	35	35	35	35	240
B		50		50		50		50	200
C	72		75		56		68		271

Direct Labor Factors

Item	Critical Workstations (hr)	Noncritical Workstations (hr)	Total (hr)
A	1.60	0.00	1.60
B	6.07	8.00	14.07
C	5.04	4.00	9.04

To estimate the percentage of total labor hours that each critical workstation will require for an MPS, the scheduler must consult past records. First, the scheduler determines the total number of direct labor hours that each critical station required over a specific time period. The time period chosen should be long enough to give a representative total. Next, the scheduler calculates the percentage of total critical hours this quantity represents. The result is a load factor for each critical workstation, which can be used to estimate labor requirements.

Using the MPS, direct labor factors, and load factors, the scheduler can develop a **composite load profile**, which is an estimate of the direct labor hours for each critical workstation, the total for all critical workstations, and the total for the plant. The procedure involves the following steps.

Step 1.   For each time period, multiply each item's MPS quantity by its corresponding critical workstation's direct labor factor. Calculate a total critical direct labor requirement for each period. Do the same for the total (critical plus noncritical) workstation requirements.

Step 2.   For each time period, multiply each critical workstation's load factor by the total critical direct labor hours estimated in step 1.

EXAMPLE 14.1

*Developing a Load
Profile for an MPS*

Use the method of overall factors to develop a load profile for the MPS shown in Fig. 14.11.

Solution   First, we develop the load factors for the critical workstations 0810A and 0820B. The following table shows that the 4900 hours reported for workstation 0810A during the past year represent 34 percent of total direct labor hours for all critical workstations that year. Thus the load factor for 0810A is 34 percent. We assume that station 0810A will continue to get 34 percent of the load on all critical stations. Similar reasoning yields a load factor of 66 percent for station 0820B.

	Direct Labor Hours by Quarter					Load Factor
Workstation	1	2	3	4	Total	(%)
0810A	1,140	1,285	1,175	1,300	4,900	34
0820B	2,430	2,540	2,100	2,380	9,450	66
Total critical hours	3,570	3,825	3,275	3,680	14,350	100
Total noncritical hours	5,200	5,150	5,000	5,300	20,650	

Using the direct labor factors for items A, B, and C and the load factors just calculated, we develop a composite load profile for the MPS. In the first week, the MPS calls for production of 25 units of A and 72 units of C. We use the critical workstation labor factors for items A and C to obtain a combined critical direct labor requirement of $25(1.60) + 72(5.04) = 402.88$ hours. The total direct labor requirement is $25(1.60) + 72(5.04 + 4.00) = 690.88$ hours. We calculate labor requirements for the other weeks in a similar manner. The results (rounded to the nearest whole number) are shown in the bottom three rows of the following table. We then estimate that in the first week workstation 0810A will need $0.34(403) = 137.02$ hours and workstation 0820B will need $0.66(403) = 265.98$ hours (top two rows).

	Week								
Workstation	1	2	3	4	5	6	7	8	Total
0810A	137	117	142	117	115	122	136	122	1008
0820B	266	227	276	227	223	238	263	238	1958
Total critical hours	403	344	418	344	338	360	399	360	2966
Total noncritical hours	288	400	300	400	224	400	272	400	2684
Total labor hours	691	744	718	744	562	760	671	760	5650

By comparing load profiles to labor capacities approved in the production plan, a scheduler can determine whether the prospective MPS is feasible. If total direct labor requirements fall within authorized limits of regular time plus overtime—and if the schedule meets other criteria, such as shipping promises and financial requirements—management will likely authorize the MPS. If not, the scheduler will have to come up with a better schedule. Later we will discuss capacity reports that are generated from detailed information from the material requirements plan.

Inventory Record

Inventory records are the final input to MRP, and the basic building blocks of up-to-date records are inventory transactions (see Fig. 14.2). Transactions include releasing new orders, receiving scheduled receipts, adjusting due dates for scheduled receipts, withdrawing inventory, canceling orders, correcting inventory errors, rejecting shipments, and verifying scrap losses and stock returns. Recording such transactions is essential for maintaining the accurate records of on-hand inventory balances and scheduled receipts necessary for an effective MRP system.

The **inventory record,** like the master production schedule, divides the future into time periods called *time buckets*. It shows an item's lot size policy, lead time, and safety stock requirement, as well as various time-phased data. The purpose of the inventory record is to keep track of inventory levels and component replenishment needs. The time-phased information contained in the inventory record consists of

1. gross requirements,
2. scheduled receipts,
3. projected on-hand inventory,
4. planned receipts, and
5. planned order releases.

We illustrate the discussion of inventory records with the seat subassembly, item C, shown in Fig. 14.3. It is used in two products: a ladder-back chair and a kitchen chair.

Gross Requirements.   The **gross requirements** are the total demand derived from *all* parent production plans. They also include demand not otherwise accounted for, such as demand for replacement parts for units already sold. Figure 14.12 shows the MPS start dates for the ladder-back and kitchen chairs and a

FIGURE 14.12

Partially Completed Material Requirements Planning Record for the Seat Subassembly, Showing the Link Between Master Production Schedule Start Quantities and Gross Requirements

"MPS Start" Quantities

	Week							
	1	2	3	4	5	6	7	8
Ladder-back chair	150					150		
Kitchen chair				120			120	

Item: C
Description: Seat subassembly

Lot Size: 230 units
Lead Time: 2 weeks
Safety Stock: 50 units

		Week							
		1	2	3	4	5	6	7	8
Gross requirements		150	0	0	120	0	150	120	0
Scheduled receipts		230	0	0	0	0	0	0	0
Projected on-hand inventory	47	127	127	127	7				

Explanation:
Gross requirements are the total demand
for the two chairs. Projected on-hand inventory
in week 1 is 47 + 230 + 0 − 150 = 127 units.

partially completed inventory record for item C, the seat subassembly. Item C is produced in lots of 230 units, has a lead time of two weeks, and requires a safety stock of 50 units. The inventory record also shows item C's gross requirements for the next eight weeks. The seat subassembly's requirements exhibit lumpy demand: Operations will withdraw inventory in only four of the eight weeks.

The MRP system works with release dates to schedule production and delivery for components and subassemblies. Its program logic anticipates the removal of all materials required by a parent's production order from inventory at the *beginning* of the parent item's lead time—when the scheduler first releases the order to the shop. Note that in Fig. 14.12 item C's gross requirements are derived from the start row of the master production schedules for the ladder-back and kitchen chairs. Only one seat is required for a chair, so the gross requirements for the seat subassembly equal the MPS quantities of the chairs. If the usage quantity contained in the bills of materials of the chairs had been two seat subassemblies, for example, the gross requirements for item C would have been two times the MPS quantities.

Scheduled Receipts. Recall that **scheduled receipts** (sometimes called *open orders*) are orders that have been placed but not yet completed. For a purchased item, the scheduled receipt could be in one of several stages: being ordered by a buyer, being processed by a supplier, being transported to the purchaser, or being inspected by the purchaser's receiving department. If production is making the item in-house, the order could be on the shop floor being processed, waiting for components, waiting in queue, or waiting to be moved to its next operation. According to Fig. 14.12, one 230-unit order of item C is due in week 1. Given the two-week lead time, the inventory planner probably released the order two weeks ago. Such orders normally don't show up on a record further into the future than the item's lead time.

Projected On-Hand Inventory. The beginning inventory, shown as the first entry (47) in Fig. 14.12, indicates on-hand inventory available at the time the record was computed. As with scheduled receipts, transactions are made for each actual withdrawal and receipt to update the MRP database. Then, when the MRP system produces the revised record (typically once per week), the correct inventory will appear.

Other entries in the row show inventory expected in future weeks. Projected on-hand inventory is calculated as

$$\begin{pmatrix} \text{Projected on-hand} \\ \text{inventory balance} \\ \text{at end of week } t \end{pmatrix} = \begin{pmatrix} \text{Inventory on} \\ \text{hand at end of} \\ \text{week } t-1 \end{pmatrix} + \begin{pmatrix} \text{Scheduled} \\ \text{receipts due} \\ \text{in week } t \end{pmatrix} + \begin{pmatrix} \text{Planned} \\ \text{receipts in} \\ \text{week } t \end{pmatrix} - \begin{pmatrix} \text{Gross} \\ \text{requirements} \\ \text{in week } t \end{pmatrix}$$

Figure 14.12 shows on-hand inventory projected through week 4. The calculations for each week are

Week 1: $47 + 230 + 0 - 150 = 127$
Weeks 2 and 3: $127 + 0 + 0 - 0 = 127$
Week 4: $127 + 0 + 0 - 120 = 7$

In week 4 the balance drops to 7 units, or substantially below the desired safety stock of 50 units. This condition signals the need for a planned receipt.

Planned Receipts.   A **planned receipt** is a new order not yet released to the shop or the supplier. Planning for receipt of these new orders will keep the projected on-hand balance from dropping below the desired safety stock level. If no safety stock is called for (which often is the case for intermediate items), the purpose of these new orders is to avoid a negative projected on-hand balance in the inventory record. The record shows when order quantities should be received in both cases.

The planned receipt row is developed in much the same way as the MPS quantity row is developed.

1. Weekly on-hand inventory is projected until a shortage appears. Completion of the initial planned receipt is scheduled for the week when inventory would otherwise drop below the safety stock. The addition of the newly planned receipt should raise the projected on-hand balance so that it equals or exceeds the safety stock.
2. Projection of on-hand inventory continues until the next shortage occurs. This shortage signals the need for the second planned receipt.

This process is repeated until the end of the planning horizon by proceeding column by column through the MRP record—filling in planned receipts as needed and completing the projected on-hand inventory row. Figure 14.13 shows the

FIGURE 14.13

Completed Inventory Record for the Seat Subassembly

Item: C Description: Seat subassembly						Lot Size: 230 units Lead Time: 2 weeks Safety Stock: 50 units		
	Week							
	1	2	3	4	5	6	7	8
Gross requirements	150	0	0	120	0	150	120	0
Scheduled receipts	230	0	0	0	0	0	0	0
Projected on-hand inventory 47	127	127	127	237	237	87	197	197
Planned receipts				230			230	
Planned order releases		230			230			

Explanation:
Without a new order in week 4, inventory will drop below the 50-unit safety stock to 127 + 0 + 0 − 120 = 7 units. Adding the planned receipt brings the balance to 127 + 0 + 230 − 120 = 237 units. Offsetting for a two-week lead time puts the corresponding planned order release back to week 2.

Explanation:
The first planned order lasts until week 7, when projected inventory would drop to 87 + 0 + 0 − 120 = −33 units. Adding the second planned receipt brings the balance to 87 + 0 + 230 − 120 = 197 units. The corresponding planned order release is for week 5 (or week 7 minus 2 weeks).

planned receipts for the seat subassembly. In week 4 the projected on-hand inventory will drop below the safety stock of 50, so a planned receipt of 230 units is scheduled for week 4. The updated inventory on-hand balance is 127 (inventory at end of week 3) + 230 (planned receipt) − 120 (gross requirements) = 237 units. The projected on-hand inventory remains at 237 for week 5 because there are no scheduled receipts or gross requirements. In week 6 the projected on-hand inventory is 237 (inventory at end of week 5) − 150 (gross requirements) = 87 units. This quantity is greater than the safety stock requirement of 50 units, so no new planned receipt is needed. In week 7, however, a shortage will occur unless more seat subassemblies are received. With a planned receipt in week 7, the updated inventory balance is 87 (inventory at end of week 6) + 230 (planned receipt) − 120 (gross requirements) = 197 units.

Planned Order Releases. A **planned order release** indicates when an order for a specified quantity of an item is to be issued. The release date is found by subtracting the lead time from the receipt date; the procedure is similar to the one for calculating the MPS start row in the master production schedule. For uniformity, we always use the *midpoint convention*—the assumption that withdrawals and receipts occur at the middle of the week. The planned order release row simplifies deriving the gross requirements for an item's components that are farther down the bill of materials. These gross requirements come directly from the planned order release row: No additional time offsets are needed. Figure 14.13 shows the planned order releases for the seat subassembly.

◆ PLANNING FACTORS

The planning factors in an MRP record play an important role in the overall performance of the MRP system. By manipulating these factors, managers can fine-tune inventory operations. In this section we discuss the planning lead time, the lot-sizing rule, and safety stock.

Lead Time

The specification of an item's planning lead time determines the amount of time allowed to get the item into stock after the order has been issued. If the lead time is longer than necessary, the item may arrive in inventory sooner than needed, thereby increasing inventory holding costs. If the lead time is too short, stockouts, excessive expediting costs, or both may occur.

For purchased items, the planning lead time is the time allowed for receiving a shipment from the supplier after the order has been sent, including the normal time to place the order. Often the purchasing contract stipulates the delivery date. For items manufactured in-house, the planning lead time consists of estimates for

- setup time,
- process time,
- materials handling time between operations, and
- waiting time.

Each of these times must be estimated for every operation along the item's route. Estimating setup, processing, and materials handling time may be relatively easy, but estimating the waiting time for materials handling equipment or a machine to perform a particular operation may be more difficult. In a process-focused facility, such as a job shop, the load on the shop varies considerably over time, causing actual waiting times for a particular order to fluctuate widely. Because jobs spend much time in waiting lines in these environments, estimated waiting time typically is a large proportion of the planning lead time. However, in a product-focused facility, such as an assembly plant, product routings are more standard and waiting time is more predictable; hence waiting time generally is a less significant proportion of planning lead times.

Lot-Sizing Rules

How important is the choice of lot-sizing rules?

A lot-sizing rule determines the timing and size of order quantities. A lot-sizing rule must be assigned to each item before planned receipts and planned order releases can be computed. The choice of lot-sizing rules is important because they determine the number of setups required and the inventory holding costs for each item. We present three lot-sizing rules: fixed order quantity, periodic order quantity, and lot for lot.

Fixed Order Quantity.   The **fixed order quantity (FOQ)** rule maintains the same order quantity each time an order is issued. For example, the lot size might be the size dictated by equipment capacity limits, as when a full lot must be loaded into a furnace at one time. For purchased items the FOQ could be determined by the quantity discount level, truckload capacity, or minimum purchase quantity. Alternatively, the lot size could be determined by the economic order quantity (EOQ) formula (see Chapter 12). Figure 14.13 illustrates the FOQ rule. However, if an item's gross requirement within a week is particularly large, the FOQ might be insufficient to restore even the desired safety stock. In such unusual cases, the inventory planner must increase the lot size beyond the FOQ, typically to a size large enough to bring the projected on-hand inventory just up to the desired safety stock level. Another option is to make the order quantity an integer multiple of the FOQ. This option is appropriate when capacity constraints limit production to FOQ sizes (at most) and setup costs are high.

Periodic Order Quantity.   The **periodic order quantity (POQ)** rule allows a different order quantity for each order issued, but tends to issue the order at predetermined time intervals such as every 2 weeks. The order quantity equals the amount of the item needed during the predetermined time between orders and must be large enough to prevent stock from falling below the desired safety stock level. Specifically, the POQ is

$$\begin{pmatrix} \text{POQ lot size,} \\ \text{to arrive in} \\ \text{week } t \end{pmatrix} = \begin{pmatrix} \text{Total gross require-} \\ \text{ments for } P \text{ weeks,} \\ \text{including week } t \end{pmatrix} + \begin{pmatrix} \text{Desired} \\ \text{safety} \\ \text{stock} \end{pmatrix} - \begin{pmatrix} \text{Projected on-hand} \\ \text{inventory balance at} \\ \text{end of week } t - 1 \end{pmatrix}$$

This amount restores the safety stock and exactly covers P weeks' worth of gross requirements. That is, the projected on-hand inventory should equal the desired safety stock in the Pth week.

Figure 14.14 shows application of the POQ rule, with $P = 3$ weeks, to the seat subassembly inventory. The first order is required in week 4 because that is the first week when the projected inventory balance will fall below the desired

FIGURE 14.14

Inventory Record for the Seat Subassembly with POQ (P=3) Rule

Item: C					Lot Size: $P = 3$			
Description: Seat subassembly					Lead Time: 2 weeks			
					Safety Stock: 50 units			

	Week							
	1	2	3	4	5	6	7	8
Gross requirements	150			120		150	120	
Scheduled receipts	230							
Projected on-hand inventory 47	127	127	127	200	200	50	50	50
Planned receipts				193			120	
Planned order releases		193			120			

safety stock level of 50 units. The first order using $P = 3$ weeks is

$$\begin{pmatrix} \text{POQ} \\ \text{lot} \\ \text{size} \end{pmatrix} = \begin{pmatrix} \text{Gross require-} \\ \text{ments for weeks} \\ \text{4, 5, and 6} \end{pmatrix} + \begin{pmatrix} \text{Safety} \\ \text{stock} \end{pmatrix} - \begin{pmatrix} \text{Inventory at} \\ \text{end of week 3} \end{pmatrix}$$
$$= (120 + 0 + 150) + 50 - 127 = 193 \text{ units}$$

The second order must arrive in week 7, with a lot size of $(120 + 0) + 50 - 50 = 120$ units. This second order reflects only two weeks' worth of gross requirements—to the end of the planning horizon.

The POQ rule does *not* mean that operations must issue a new order every P weeks. Rather, when an order *is* planned, its lot size must be enough to cover P weeks. One way to select a P value is to divide the average lot size desired (such as the EOQ, as demonstrated in Chapter 12, or some other agreeable lot size) by the average weekly demand. That is, express the target lot size as a desired weeks of supply and round to the nearest integer.

Lot for Lot.   A special case of the POQ rule is the **lot-for-lot (L4L) rule**, under which the lot size ordered covers the gross requirements of a single week. Thus $P = 1$. This rule ensures that the planned order is just large enough to prevent a shortage in the single week it covers. The goal is to minimize inventory levels. The L4L lot size is

$$\begin{pmatrix} \text{L4L lot size,} \\ \text{to arrive in} \\ \text{week } t \end{pmatrix} = \begin{pmatrix} \text{Gross require-} \\ \text{ments for} \\ \text{week } t \end{pmatrix} + \begin{pmatrix} \text{Desired} \\ \text{safety stock} \end{pmatrix} - \begin{pmatrix} \text{Projected on-hand} \\ \text{inventory balance at} \\ \text{end of week } t - 1 \end{pmatrix}$$

The projected on-hand inventory combined with the new order will equal the desired safety stock (zero if none is required) in week t. Following the first planned order, an additional planned order will be used to match each subsequent gross requirement.

Figure 14.15 shows application of the L4L rule to the seat subassembly inventory. As before, the first order is needed in week 4:

$$\begin{pmatrix} L4L \\ lot \\ size \end{pmatrix} = \begin{pmatrix} Gross\ require\text{-} \\ ments\ in \\ week\ 4 \end{pmatrix} + \begin{pmatrix} Safety \\ stock \end{pmatrix} - \begin{pmatrix} Inventory \\ balance\ at\ end \\ of\ week\ 3 \end{pmatrix}$$
$$= 120 + 50 - 127 = 43$$

The stockroom must receive additional orders in weeks 6 and 7 to satisfy each of the subsequent gross requirements. The lot size for week 6 is $150 + 50 - 50 = 150$. Similarly, the lot size for week 7 is $120 + 50 - 50 = 120$.

FIGURE 14.15

Inventory Record for the Seat Subassembly with the Lot-for-Lot (L4L) Rule

Item: C Description: Seat subassembly						Lot Size: L4L Lead Time: 2 weeks Safety Stock: 50 units			
		Week							
		1	2	3	4	5	6	7	8
Gross requirements		150			120		150	120	
Scheduled receipts		230							
Projected on-hand inventory	47	127	127	127	50	50	50	50	50
Planned receipts					43		150	120	
Planned order releases			43		150	120			

Comparison of Lot-Sizing Rules. Choosing a lot-sizing rule can have important implications for inventory management. Lot-sizing rules affect inventory costs and setup or ordering costs. The three rules presented differ from one another in one or both respects. Let's compare the projected on-hand inventory averaged over the eight weeks of the planning horizon for the three rules: FOQ, POQ, and L4L. The data are shown in Fig. 14.13, 14.14, and 14.15, respectively.

$$\text{FOQ:} \quad \frac{127 + 127 + 127 + 237 + 237 + 87 + 197 + 197}{8} = 167 \text{ units}$$

$$\text{POQ:} \quad \frac{127 + 127 + 127 + 200 + 200 + 50 + 50 + 50}{8} = 116 \text{ units}$$

$$\text{L4L:} \quad \frac{127 + 127 + 127 + 50 + 50 + 50 + 50 + 50}{8} = 79 \text{ units}$$

The good performance of the L4L rule with respect to average inventory levels comes at the price of an additional planned order and its accompanying setup time and cost. We can draw three conclusions from this comparison.

1. The FOQ rule generates a high level of average inventory because it creates inventory *remnants*. A remnant is inventory that is carried into a week but is too small to prevent a shortage. Remnants occur because the FOQ doesn't match requirements exactly. For example, according to Fig. 14.13, the stockroom must receive a planned order in week 7, even though 87 units are on hand at the beginning of that week. The remnant is the 37 units in excess of the required safety stock of 50 units that the stockroom will carry for three weeks, beginning with receipt of the first planned order in week 4. Although they increase average inventory levels, inventory remnants introduce stability into the production process by buffering unexpected scrap losses, capacity bottlenecks, inaccurate inventory records, or unstable gross requirements.

2. The POQ rule reduces the amount of average on-hand inventory because it does a better job of matching order quantity to requirements. It adjusts lot sizes as requirements increase or decrease. Figure 14.13 shows that in week 7, when the POQ rule has fully taken effect, the projected on-hand inventory is the minimum allowed by the safety stock requirement. There are no remnants.

3. The L4L rule minimizes inventory investment, but it also maximizes the number of orders placed. This rule is most applicable to expensive items or items with small ordering or setup costs. It is the only rule that can be used for an item made to order rather than made to stock.

By avoiding remnants, both the POQ and the L4L rule may introduce instability by tying the lot-sizing decision so closely to requirements. If any requirement changes, so must the lot size, which can disrupt component schedules. Last-minute increases in parent orders may be hindered by missing components.

Safety Stock

An important managerial issue is the quantity of safety stock to require. It is more complex for dependent demand items than for independent demand items. Safety stock for dependent demand items with lumpy demand (gross requirements) is valuable only when future gross requirements, the timing or size of scheduled receipts, and the amount of scrap are uncertain. Safety stock should be reduced and ultimately removed as the causes of the uncertainty are eliminated. The usual policy is to use safety stock for end items and purchased items to protect against fluctuating customer orders and unreliable suppliers of components and to avoid it as much as possible for intermediate items.

◆ OUTPUTS FROM MATERIAL REQUIREMENTS PLANNING

Material requirements planning systems provide many reports, schedules, and notices to help managers control dependent demand inventories, as indicated in Fig. 14.16 on the next page. In this section we discuss the MRP explosion process, action notices that alert managers to items needing attention, and capacity reports that project the capacity requirements implied by the material requirements plan.

FIGURE 14.16
Material Requirements Planning Outputs

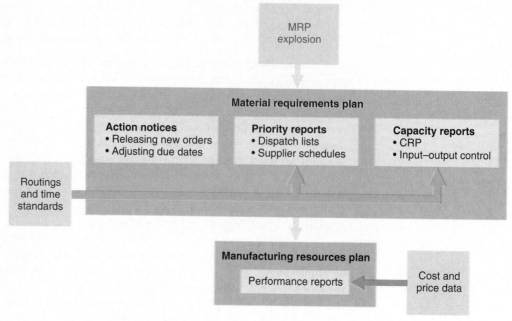

Material Requirements Planning Explosion

What information is available from MRP systems that will provide help in managing materials better?

MRP translates, or "explodes," the master production schedule and other sources of demand into the requirements for all subassemblies, components, and raw materials needed to produce parent items. This process generates the material requirements plan for each component item.

The Explosion Process. An item's gross requirements are derived from three sources:

1. the MPS for immediate parents that are end items,
2. the planned order releases for parents below the MPS level, and
3. any other requirements not originating in the MPS, such as the demand for replacement parts.

To accumulate the gross requirements for a particular component, the computer starts with the MPS and works downward through the bills of materials, calculating the planned order releases of all items as it goes. This procedure is called **level-by-level processing**.

The computer assigns a permanent *level code* to each item. Levels are denoted by a number; the lowest number, 0, represents the highest level to which an item can be assigned. By convention, all MPS items are assigned level 0. Those components having only an MPS item as an immediate parent are assigned level 1. Their components are assigned level 2, and so on. Sometimes an item appears at different levels in various bills of materials because it has more than one immediate parent or because its only immediate parent has more than one parent. In that case the item is assigned to the lowest level at which it appears in any bill of materials. Figure 14.17 shows the bills of materials for two end items, A and B. Both items are assigned to level 0. Intermediate item C has only one immediate parent, which happens to be an MPS item, and so is assigned to level 1. However,

Figure 14.17

Figure 14.17

Bills of Materials for End Items A and B, Showing Usage Quantities for C and D

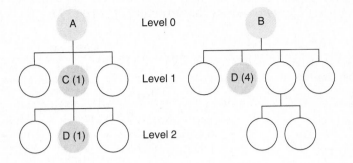

item D has two immediate parents: B and C. The *lowest* level at which D appears in any bill of materials is level 2; it is therefore assigned to level 2. When updating the inventory records in an MRP system, the computer proceeds with level-by-level processing, each time checking to ensure that all items with lower code numbers (higher assigned levels) have been processed before accumulating the gross requirements for an item. A component cannot be processed until all its parents have been processed.

Figure 14.18 on the next page shows an example of level-by-level processing. Given the MPS for items A and B at level 0 with the MPS start row for each item, the computer proceeds to scan all the immediate components of A and B to find those with a level 1 code. Item C satisfies the requirement (there may be others, but we haven't shown them). All the necessary information for accumulating the gross requirements for C is known, so we can proceed to update the MRP record for C. The bill of materials for A calls for a usage quantity of 1 for C, so the MPS quantity of 100 in the MPS start row in week 23 becomes a gross requirement of 100 for C in week 23. The on-hand inventory projection, planned receipts, and planned order releases for C can be calculated now that the gross requirements and scheduled receipts are known. The computer continues to process all items with a level 1 code, bypassing D because it has a lower level code.

When the processing gets to level 2, D's MRP record can be updated. At that time, the planned order releases from C can be combined with the MPS for B to arrive at the gross requirements for D. Note that 4 units of D are needed for each unit of B, so the MPS for B must be multiplied by 4 to arrive at the gross requirements for D. For example, the gross requirements for D are determined as follows.

$$\text{Week 24:} \quad \text{Gross requirement} = \begin{pmatrix} \text{Planned order release} \\ \text{from C in week 24} \times \\ \text{usage quantity} \end{pmatrix} + \begin{pmatrix} \text{MPS start for B} \\ \text{in week 24} \times \\ \text{usage quantity} \end{pmatrix}$$
$$= 150(1) + (5)4 = 170 \text{ units}$$

Week 26: Gross requirement = $0(1) + (10)4 = 40$ units
Week 28: Gross requirement = $0(1) + (15)4 = 60$ units
Week 29: Gross requirement = Service part order for 20 units

Remember that the gross requirements for a component come from the planned order releases (or MPS start quantities) of its parent items modified by the usage quantities, plus demand for previously sold product replacement parts.

FIGURE 14.18   *Deriving Gross Requirements for Item D*

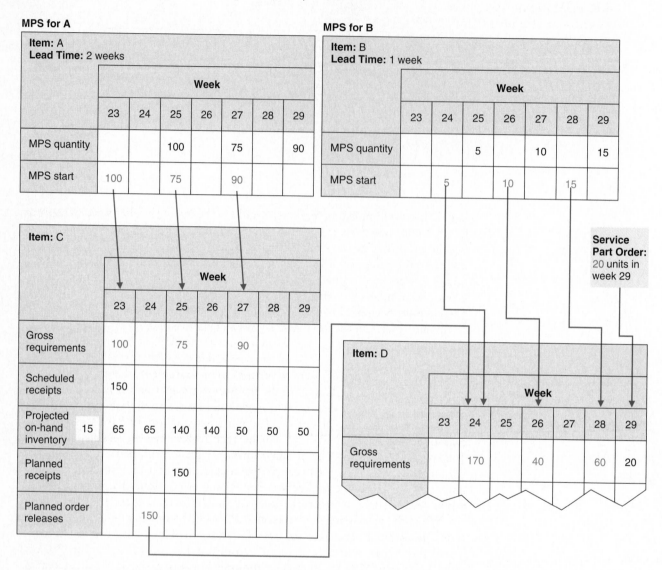

Types of MRP Systems.   There are two types of MRP systems. A **regenerative MRP system** periodically performs the explosion process, typically on a weekly basis, and completely recomputes all inventory records. After a week, the material requirements plan becomes outdated. The system then performs a new explosion based on the latest MPS, bills of materials, and information on scheduled receipts and on-hand balances. A **net change MRP system** recomputes records as needed. With each change in the MPS and with each transaction, the system executes a partial explosion to update the affected records. Net change systems tend to be preferred in more dynamic manufacturing situations. However, they may take more computer time and generate too many action notices (sometimes called "system nervousness"). Most new MRP users begin with a regenerative system.

Action Notices

Once computed, inventory records for each item appearing in the bills of materials can be printed in hard copy or displayed on a computer video screen. Inventory planners use a computer-generated memo called an **action notice** to make decisions about releasing new orders and adjusting the due dates of scheduled receipts. The action notice steers planners to items that need their attention. They can then view the full records for those items and take the necessary actions. An action notice can simply be a list of part numbers for items needing attention. Or it can be the full record for such items, with a note at the bottom identifying the action needed.

Releasing New Orders.   If there is a nonzero quantity in the first week's entry of the planned order release row, sometimes called the **action bucket,** the computer issues an action notice. An order in the action bucket is the call to release the planned order. When an order is released, paperwork is issued to the shop authorizing the withdrawal of all required materials from the inventory storeroom and the start of production. The date on which production actually begins depends on the amount of work already in the shop. Delaying the release one week will provide *less* than the planned lead time for producing the item. Releasing an order before it gets to the action bucket allows *more* than the planned lead time for production. Solved Problem 4 provides an example of action notices for releasing new orders.

Adjusting Due Dates of Scheduled Receipts.   If subtracting the scheduled receipt from the projected on-hand inventory for the week in which it is due does not cause inventory to drop below the desired safety stock, the scheduled receipt is arriving too early. In such a case, the inventory planner can delay the scheduled receipt. If the projected on-hand balance for the week prior to the arrival of the scheduled receipt is below the desired safety stock (negative if no safety stock is allowed), the scheduled receipt is arriving too late. In this case, the planner should expedite the arrival of the scheduled receipt. Mismatches in the planned due dates of scheduled receipts and their actual "need" dates occur because of changes in the item's gross requirements. Solved Problem 4 provides an opportunity to delay a scheduled receipt.

Making Decisions.   Although the computer generates action notices, *decisions* based on them are made by the inventory planner. The planner reviews the item's complete MRP inventory record, along with those of its components. If component inventory is available to support the order, the planner usually decides to release the order as planned. The planner would input an *inventory transaction* to change the computer record file by adding the quantity and due date of a new scheduled receipt. This new order would show up in the scheduled receipts row the next time the system generated the material requirements plan, and it would drop out of the planned order receipt row. When releasing a new order, the planner can also prepare documentation for tool requisitions, routings, or parts lists. For purchased items, a requisition is sent to the appropriate buyer, who in turn places the order with a supplier. These purchasing activities often are computer assisted. At times the planner may deviate from the lot size or timing specified in an item's planned order release.

Capacity Reports

By itself, the MRP system doesn't recognize capacity limitations when computing planned orders. That is, it may call for a planned order release that exceeds the amount that can be physically produced. An essential role of managers is to monitor the capacity requirements of material requirements plans, making adjustments to a plan when it cannot be met. In this section we discuss two sources of information for short-term decisions that materials managers continually make: capacity requirements planning reports and input–output reports.

Capacity Requirements Planning.   **Capacity requirements planning (CRP)** is a technique for projecting time-phased capacity requirements for workstations in order to match the material requirements plan with the plant's production capacity. The technique is used to calculate workload according to work required to complete the scheduled receipts already in the shop and to complete the planned order releases yet to be released. This task is accomplished with the use of the inventory records, which supply the planned order releases and the status of the scheduled receipts; the item's routing, which specifies the workstations that must process the item; lead times between each workstation; and the processing and setup times at each workstation. Using scheduled completion dates as a starting point, CRP traces back through an item's routing to estimate when the scheduled receipt or planned order will be at each workstation. The system uses the processing and setup times to estimate the load that the item will impose on each station. This process is followed for each planned order and scheduled receipt for all items. The workloads for each workstation are obtained by adding the time that each item needs at a particular workstation. Critical workstations are those at which the projected loads exceed station capacities.

Figure 14.19 shows a capacity requirements report for a lathe station that turns wooden table legs. There are four lathes, each scheduled for two shifts per day. The lathe station has a maximum capacity of 320 hours per week. The *planned* hours represent labor requirements for all planned orders for items that need to be routed through the lathe station. The *actual* hours represent the backlog of work visible on the shop floor—that is, scheduled receipts. Combining requirements from both sources gives *total* hours. Comparing total hours to actual

FIGURE 14.19

*Capacity Requirements
Report*

Date: Plant 01 Dept. 03: Lathe Station Capacity: 320 hours per week	Week: 32					
	Week					
	32	33	34	35	36	37
Planned hours	90	156	349	210	360	280
Actual hours	210	104	41	0	0	0
Total hours	300	260	390	210	360	280

Explanation:
Projected capacity requirements exceed weekly hours of capacity.

capacity constraints can give advance warning of potential problems. The planner must resolve any capacity problems uncovered.

The CRP report in Fig. 14.19 should arouse the planner's concern. Unless something is done, the current capacity of 320 hours per week will be exceeded in week 34 and again in week 36. Requirements for all other time periods are well below the capacity limit. Perhaps the best choice is to release some orders earlier than planned, so that they will arrive at the lathe station in weeks 32, 33, and 35 rather than weeks 34 and 36. This adjustment will help smooth capacity and alleviate projected bottlenecks. Other options might be to change the lot sizes of some items, use overtime, subcontract, off-load to another workstation, or simply let the bottlenecks occur.

Input–Output Control.   An **input–output control report** compares planned input (from prior CRP reports) with actual input and compares planned output with actual output. Inputs and outputs are expressed in common units, usually labor or machine hours. Information in the report indicates whether workstations have been performing as expected and helps management pinpoint the source of capacity problems. Actual outputs can fall behind planned outputs for two reasons:

1. *Insufficient inputs.*   Output may lag when inputs are insufficient to support the planned output rates. The problem can lie upstream at a prior operation, or it may be caused by missing purchased parts. In effect, not enough work arrives to keep the operation busy.
2. *Insufficient capacity.*   Output may lag at the station itself. Even though input rates keep pace, output may slip below expected levels because of absenteeism, equipment failures, inadequate staffing levels, or low productivity rates.

The input–output report in Fig. 14.20 has been prepared for a rough mill workstation at which desk chair components are machined. Management established a tolerance of ± 25 hours of cumulative deviations from plans. As long as cumulative deviations don't exceed this threshold, there is no cause for concern.

FIGURE 14.20

Input-Output Report

Explanation: Cumulative deviations between −25 hours and +25 hours are allowed.

Workstation: Rough Mill   **Week:** 32
Tolerance: ±25 hours

	Week Ending				
	28	29	30	31	32
Inputs					
Planned	160	155	170	160	
Actual	145	160	168	177	165
Cumulative deviation	−15	−10	−12	+5	
Outputs					
Planned	170	170	160	160	
Actual	165	165	150	148	160
Cumulative deviation	−5	−10	−20	−32	

Explanation: Cumulative deviation exceeds lower tolerance limit, indicating actual hours of output have fallen too far below planned hours of output and some action is required.

However, the report shows that in week 31 actual outputs fell behind planned outputs by a total of 32 hours. This cumulative deviation exceeds the 25-hour tolerance, so there is a problem. Actual inputs are keeping pace with planned inputs, so the lag results from insufficient capacity at the rough mill station itself. Temporary use of overtime may be necessary to increase the output rate.

MRP II: A COMPREHENSIVE INFORMATION SYSTEM

How can MRP be coupled to other functional areas?

To this point we have emphasized the attributes of MRP as an information system for aiding order-launching decisions in manufacturing. However, the databases created and maintained by MRP can be used to generate valuable reports for other functional areas.

Manufacturing resource planning (MRP II) ties the basic MRP system to the company's financial system. MRP II enables managers to test "what if" scenarios by using simulation. Management can project the dollar value of shipments, product costs, overhead allocations, inventories, backlogs, and profits. Information from the MPS, scheduled receipts, and planned orders can be converted into cash flow projections, broken down by product families. For example, the projected on-hand quantities in MRP inventory records allow the computation of future levels of inventory investment. These levels are obtained simply by multiplying the quantities by the per unit value of each item and adding these amounts for all items belonging to the same product family. Similar computations are possible for other performance measures of interest to management.

Information from MRP II is used by managers in manufacturing, purchasing, marketing, finance, and engineering. MRP II reports help these managers develop and monitor the overall business plan and recognize sales objectives, manufacturing capabilities, and cash flow constraints.

The Colorado Springs Division of Hewlett-Packard provides an example of the successful use of MRP II. This division, which makes a variety of complex electronic instruments, modified its MRP system to provide financial reports in step with its operational plans. Predictions are quite good, with production costs coming within 1 percent of predictions. Smaller companies also can use the system successfully. Managerial Practice 14.2 explains how MRP II is used by one of Hewlett-Packard's suppliers, a manufacturer of syringes and miniature valves.

IMPLEMENTATION ISSUES

Although thousands of firms have tried MRP, not all have been able to apply it successfully. A company can easily invest $500,000 in an MRP system, only to be plagued still by high inventories and late customer deliveries. What goes wrong? One possibility is poor implementation of the MRP system because of a lack of top management support. Success isn't automatic but is achieved only through the dedicated efforts of those involved in making the system function as intended. A second possibility, which we discuss later, is that the company's manufacturing environment doesn't give MRP a distinct advantage over other systems.

Managerial Practice 14.2

▶ *MRP II Implementation at Kloehn*

Kloehn is one of five manufacturers specializing in syringes, miniature valves, and computer-driven syringe assemblies found in scientific and medical instrumentation. Eighty percent of its output is specially produced for such customers as Abbott Labs and Hewlett-Packard. Kloehn employs about 100 people and has sales in the $10–$15 million range. Although sales volume today is rapidly expanding and the future looks bright, it has not always been so. To provide good customer service in the mid 1980s, Kloehn built up large inventories of raw materials and finished goods to meet anticipated customer demand. In 1987 customer demand fell off and Kloehn was left with a costly situation that could have put it out of business.

CEO Garth Kloehn decided that the company had to develop the capability to identify and track all costs and to design controls to keep costs in line with sales. Kevin Fox was hired as manager of production control and manufacturing information systems to implement an integrated manufacturing system. After extensive study, Fox selected IBM's Manufacturing Accounting Production and Inventory Control System (MAPICS). Within 60 days of completion of the first phase of implementation, manufacturing lead time had been cut by 20 percent, largely by integrating marketing and manufacturing using the order entry & invoicing and inventory management modules. In addition, inventory turns increased from 1.2 to 4, and profitability rose by 10 percent from 1989 to 1990.

With MRP II every department in the company is in some way integrated with the system. The following are some of the ways integration was achieved at Kloehn.

Engineering: The system automatically updates revisions as it generates new blueprints, ensuring that each job package contains the latest customer specs. The time needed to create a new product was reduced by 33 percent.

Research and Development: The system tracks existing product costs and holds information on the history of similar products.

Shop Floor: The system provides an accurate and efficient way to track labor hours and costs.

MRP II permits the instantaneous exchange of information among all departments, from the shop floor to R&D and marketing.

Marketing: The system checks the product status, stock availability, stock locations, and routings and can verify engineering drawings.

Accounting: The system provides financial analysis for budgeting and forecasting, departmentalization of costs, automatic journal entries, and financial ratio analysis.

Source: Jim Barnes, "For Kloehn, Good Customer Service Meant Controlling Its Own Growth," *APICS—The Performance Advantage* (August 1991), pp. 26–29.

Prerequisites

In addition to top management support, two prerequisites to successful implementation of an MRP system are computer support and accurate and realistic input.

Computer Support.   Successful implementation of MRP requires a careful assessment of computer requirements, such as the size of random access memory, the capacity of external data storage devices, the processing speeds of the central processing unit (CPU), and the number and types of individual computer workstations. Some MRP systems can be installed on personal computers. However, internal memory and processing speed limitations restrict the number of stock items that can be controlled. Processing speed can be a major consideration because completely exploding a master schedule with thousands of components and assemblies can take many hours of computer time. The system generates numerous reports, thus requiring adequate printing capabilities. Additional processing requirements might be imposed if the firm adopts a *net change system* to update frequently the data in the system.

Another consideration linked to computer support is the choice of software. Decisions must be made regarding the functions to be supported by the MRP system and the amount to be spent on the software package. Many packages are available, each containing various modules, ranging from accounting applications and production costing to capacity requirements planning. Software packages can cost anywhere from several thousand dollars for a PC-based system to $500,000 or more for a mainframe system.

Accurate and Realistic Input.   Any decision support system such as MRP rests on valid input data from the master production schedule, bills of materials, and inventory records. When MRP fails to live up to expectations, management should look first at these inputs. Are they accurate and realistic? Data accuracy makes a significant difference in whether MRP implementation is successful.

Cycle counting, or checking items periodically, is one of several ways to improve record accuracy (see Chapter 12). MRP inventory records are checked against the actual counts, and corrections are made to the inventory record file in the MRP system. But this activity can keep a group of cycle counters busy full time if the number of items in stock is large, and it can be tedious and time consuming. Consider the problem of counting thousands of transistors or resistors in a plant producing electronics products. In such cases, sensitive scales can be used to estimate the number of items in stock. Based on the weight of one or a small number of parts and the weight of their container, the scale can estimate the total number of parts in the container, with errors of less than 1 percent.

Favorable Environments for Material Requirements Planning

Some companies do not adopt an MRP system or are disappointed with its results because their manufacturing environment doesn't give MRP a distinct advantage over other systems. Cerveny and Scott (1989) reported that 40 percent of the firms they surveyed had not adopted an MRP system; of those that had, 67 percent said that the system was a success and 16 percent said that it was a failure. Four environmental characteristics are particularly important: number of BOM levels, magnitude of lot sizes, volatility, and manufacturing's positioning strategy.

Number of BOM Levels. MRP is most useful in managing large numbers of dependent demand items—that is, when there are many levels in the bills of materials. Thus the greatest numbers of MRP users are in the fabricated metals, machinery, and electric and electronic industries, which tend to have many BOM levels and consequently lumpy demand for components. The average user of MRP has more than six BOM levels.

Magnitude of Lot Sizes. Even with many levels, though, dependent demand patterns need not be lumpy. The other variable is the magnitude of lot sizes. The relative superiority of MRP is greatest with more BOM levels *and* larger lot sizes. When a firm works with extremely small lot sizes, changing over to MRP may not be beneficial.

Volatility. Firms operating in environments with little volatility are likely to achieve savings with MRP. A basic assumption underlying MRP systems is that projections of gross requirements, scheduled receipts, and planned order releases are realistic. This assumption isn't valid in a highly volatile manufacturing environment with high scrap rates, capacity bottlenecks, last-minute rush jobs, and unreliable suppliers.

Manufacturing's Positioning Strategy. MRP seems to be most attractive to firms that have positioned themselves with an intermediate strategy. They produce in batches, experience low to medium demand volumes, tend to offer numerous product options, and make products that have relatively short life cycles. Many firms with a strong process focus or a strong product focus have found that MRP isn't particularly valuable, although some use it effectively. In process-focused firms, annual demand for specific items is small, making products expensive, engineering needs great, and lead times long and uncertain. The number of customized products is large, making the job of maintaining files on bills of materials complicated. Product-focused firms using continuous processes (such as a paper mill) tend to have few BOM levels, high capital intensity, and tight constraints on equipment capacity. Here the focus of managerial concern is with the master production schedule. Only 3 percent of MRP system users operate continuous manufacturing processes (see Cerveny and Scott, 1989).

FIGURE 14.21

Distribution System, Showing Supply Links from Plants to Distribution Centers and Retail Stores

◆ DISTRIBUTION REQUIREMENTS PLANNING

The principles of MRP can also be applied to distribution inventories, or stocks of items held at retailers and distribution centers. Consider the distribution system in Fig. 14.21. The top level represents retail stores at various locations

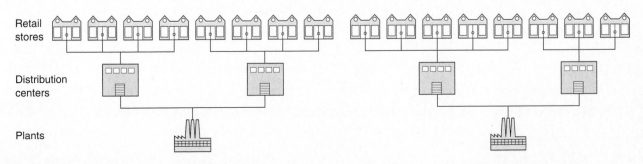

Retail stores

Distribution centers

Plants

throughout the country. At the middle level are regional distribution centers (DCs) that replenish retail store inventories on request. The bottom level consists of one or more plants that supply the DCs. In the past, plants tended to schedule production to meet the forecasted demand patterns of the DCs. The DCs, in turn, replenished their inventories based on past demand patterns of the retail stores, reordering stocks from the factory whenever the inventory position reached a predetermined reorder point. The retailers followed a similar procedure, ordering stock from the distributor.

To illustrate the shortcomings of this approach, let's suppose that customer demand for a product suddenly increases by 10 percent. What will happen? Because the retailers carry some inventory, there will be some delay before the DCs feel the impact of the full 10 percent increase. Still more time passes before the plants feel the effect of the full increase, reflected as higher demand from the DCs. Thus for months the plants could continue underproducing at their normal rate. When the deficiency finally becomes apparent, the plants must increase their output by much more than 10 percent to replenish inventory levels.

Can MRP be used for distribution inventories?

Distribution requirements planning (DRP) is an inventory control and scheduling technique that applies MRP principles to distribution inventories. It helps avoid self-induced swings in demand. An inventory record is maintained for each item at each location. The planned order releases projected at the retail level are used to derive the gross requirements for each item at the DC level from standard MRP logic and bills of materials. Next, planned order releases at the DC level are computed, from which the gross requirements for the plant level can be derived. This information provides the basis for updating the master production schedule at the plant.

Use of DRP requires an integrated information system. If the manufacturer operates its own DCs and retail stores, called forward integration, gathering demand information and relaying it back to the plants is easy. If the manufacturer doesn't own the DCs and retail stores, all three levels must agree to convey planned order releases from one level to the next. And open communication can be extended from manufacturers to their suppliers, giving suppliers a better idea of future demand. Reducing demand uncertainty can pay off in lower inventories, better service, or both.

CHAPTER REVIEW

Solved Problem 1

Refer to the bill of materials for item A shown in Fig. 14.22.

FIGURE 14.22

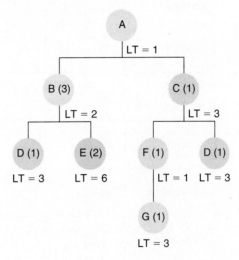

a. If there is no existing inventory, how many units of G, E, and D must be purchased to produce five units of end item A?
b. Use the lead time shown next to each component to determine the demand time fence at the lead time required for final assembly and the planning time fence at the cumulative lead time required to make the earliest purchase commitment.

Solution
a. Five units of G, 30 units of E, and 20 units of D must be purchased to make 5 units of A. The usage quantities shown in Fig. 14.22 indicate that 2 units of E are needed to make 1 unit of B and that 3 units of B are needed to make 1 unit of A; therefore 5 units of A require 30 units of E ($2 \times 3 \times 5 = 30$). One unit of D is consumed to make 1 unit of B, and 3 units of B per unit of A result in 15 units of D ($1 \times 3 \times 5 = 15$), plus 1 unit of D in each unit of C and 1 unit of C per unit of A result in another 5 units of D ($1 \times 1 \times 5 = 5$). The total requirements to make 5 units of A are 20 units of D ($15 + 5$). The calculation of requirements for G is simply $1 \times 1 \times 1 \times 5 = 5$ units.
b. The demand time fence is set at one week, which is the lead time required for final assembly of subassemblies B and C to produce end item A. The planning time fence is determined by the longest *time* path from the end item to the bottom of the bill of materials. The longest path, E–B–A, is nine weeks ($6 + 2 + 1$), or one week longer than G–F–C–A, which is eight weeks in duration.

Solved Problem 2

The order policy is to produce end item A in lots of 50 units. Using the data shown in Fig. 14.23 and the FOQ lot-sizing rule, complete the projected on-hand inventory and MPS quantity rows. Then complete the MPS start row by offsetting the MPS quantities for the final assembly lead time.

FIGURE 14.23

Item: A									Order Policy: 50 units Lead Time: 1 week	
	Week									
Quantity on Hand: 5	1	2	3	4	5	6	7	8	9	10
Forecast	20	10	40	10	0	0	40	20	30	10
Customer orders (booked)	30	20	5	8	0	2	0	0	0	0
Projected on-hand inventory	25									
MPS quantity	50									
MPS start										

FIGURE 14.24

Item: A									Order Policy: 50 units Lead Time: 1 week	
	Week									
Quantity on Hand: 5	1	2	3	4	5	6	7	8	9	10
Forecast	20	10	40	10	0	0	30	20	40	20
Customer orders (booked)	30	20	5	8	0	2	0	0	0	0
Projected on-hand inventory	25	5	15	5	5	3	23	3	13	43
MPS quantity	50		50				50		50	50
MPS start		50				50		50	50	

Solution The projected on-hand inventory for the second week is given by

$$\begin{pmatrix} \text{Projected on-hand} \\ \text{inventory at end of} \\ \text{second week} \end{pmatrix} = \begin{pmatrix} \text{On-hand} \\ \text{inventory last} \\ \text{week} \end{pmatrix} + \begin{pmatrix} \text{MPS} \\ \text{quantity due} \\ \text{second week} \end{pmatrix} - \begin{pmatrix} \text{Requirements} \\ \text{second week} \end{pmatrix}$$

$$= 25 + 0 - 20 = 5$$

where requirements are the larger of the forecast or actual customer orders booked for shipment this period. No MPS quantity is required.

Without an MPS quantity in the third period, the projected on-hand inventory is negative: $5 + 0 - 40 = -35$. Therefore an MPS quantity equal to the lot size of 50 must be completed in the third period. Then the projected on-hand inventory for the third week will be $5 + 50 - 40 = 15$.

Figure 14.24 shows the projected on-hand inventories and MPS quantities that would result from completing the MPS calculations. The MPS start row is completed by simply shifting a copy of the MPS quantity row to the left by one column to account for the one-week final assembly lead time.

Solved Problem 3

The Acme Rocket Company produces two products for crafty coyotes interested in a road-runner dinner. The harness rocket (HR) is designed for quick acceleration and low-level flying in pursuit of fleeing road runners. The shoe rocket (SR) is useful for high-speed chases over long, straight Arizona roads. The MPS shown in Fig. 14.25 has been proposed.

FIGURE 14.25

Item	Week 1	2	3	4	5	Total Units
HR	20	20	20	40	40	140
SR	30		30		30	90

The Acme Rocket Company has two critical workstations: powder packing (PP) and wick setting (WS). Historically, PP has had 70 percent and WS 30 percent of the critical workstation hours. The direct labor factors per unit follow.

Item	Critical Workstations	Noncritical Workstations	Total
HR	10.0	6.0	16.0
SR	7.2	3.5	10.7

a. Use the method of overall factors to create a load profile based on the proposed MPS.
b. Suppose that the production plan specified a total of 680 labor hours per week, including 420 hours at the critical workstations. What changes to the schedule would reduce potential problems with this MPS?

Solution a. Table 14.1 shows the load profile for weeks 1–5.

TABLE 14.1   *Load Profile*

| | **Week** | | | | | |
Workstation	1	2	3	4	5	Total
Powder packing (70%)	291	140	291	280	431	1433
Wick setting (30%)	125	60	125	120	185	615
Total critical hours*	416	200	416	400	616	2048
Total noncritical hours†	225	120	225	240	345	1155
Total labor hours	641	320	641	640	961	3203

*(MPS quantity for HR)(10.0 hr/unit) + (MPS for SR)(7.2 hr/unit).
†(MPS quantity for HR)(6.0 hr/unit) + (MPS for SR)(3.5 hr/unit).

b. Note that the proposed MPS schedule results in an uneven load on the factory. In particular, the week 2 load is about half that specified in the production plan, and the week 5 load is about one and a half times that specified in the production plan.

A change that would ease the MPS is to shift 30 units of SR production from week 5 to week 2, as shown in Table 14.2. This change increases the inventory holding cost of SR but satisfies the capacity constraints. (The profile for weeks 1, 3, and 4 doesn't change.) This change results in approximately 640 labor hours per week.

TABLE 14.2   *Load Profile After MPS Change*

| | **Week** | | | | | |
Workstation	1	2	3	4	5	Total
Powder packing (70%)	291	291	291	280	280	1433
Wick setting (30%)	125	125	125	120	120	615
Total critical hours	416	416	416	400	400	2048
Total noncritical hours	225	225	225	240	240	1155
Total labor hours	641	641	641	640	640	3203

Solved Problem 4

The MPS for product A calls for completion of a 50-unit order in week 4 and a 60-unit order in week 8. The MPS for product B calls for completion of a 200-unit order in week 5. The lead times are two weeks for A and one week for B. Develop a material requirements plan for the next six weeks for items C, D, E, and F, identifying any action notices that would be provided. The BOMs are shown in Fig. 14.26, and data from the inventory records are shown in Table 14.3.

Master Schedule

Item: End item A										Lead Time: 2 weeks
	Week									
	1	2	3	4	5	6	7	8	9	10
MPS quantity				50				60		
MPS start		50				60				

Master Schedule

Item: End item B										Lead Time: 1 week	
	Week										
	1	**2**	**3**	**4**	**5**	**6**	**7**	**8**	**9**	**10**	
MPS quantity					200						
MPS start				200							

FIGURE 14.26

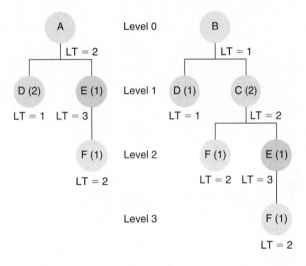

TABLE 14.3   *Inventory Record Data*

	Item			
Data Category	**C**	**D**	**E**	**F**
Lot-sizing rule	FOQ = 400	POQ ($P = 3$)	L4L	L4L
Lead time	2 weeks	1 week	3 weeks	2 weeks
Safety stock	0	50	0	20
Scheduled receipts	None	None	450 (week 1)	None
Beginning (on-hand) inventory	100	70	0	425

Solution   The lowest level code for each component is as follows: item C, level 1; item D, level 1; item E, level 2; and item F, level 3 (see Fig. 14.26). Therefore we begin with item C, then go to D, E, and F in that order (see Fig. 14.27 on the next page).

An action notice would call for delaying the scheduled receipt for item E from week 1 to week 2. Other action notices would notify planners that items D and F have a planned order release in the action bucket.

FIGURE 14.27

Item: C
Description:

Lot Size: FOQ = 400 units
Lead Time: 2 weeks
Safety Stock: 0 units

		Week									
		1	2	3	4	5	6	7	8	9	10
Gross requirements					400						
Scheduled receipts											
Projected on-hand inventory	100	100	100	100	100	100	100	100	100	100	100
Planned receipts					400						
Planned order releases			400								

Item: D
Description:

Lot Size: POQ ($P = 3$)
Lead Time: 1 week
Safety Stock: 50 units

		Week									
		1	2	3	4	5	6	7	8	9	10
Gross requirements			100		200		120				
Scheduled receipts											
Projected on-hand inventory	70	70	250	250	50	50	50	50	50	50	50
Planned receipts			280				120				
Planned order releases		280				120					

Item: E
Description:

Lot Size: L4L
Lead Time: 3 weeks
Safety Stock: 0 units

		Week									
		1	2	3	4	5	6	7	8	9	10
Gross requirements			450				60				
Scheduled receipts		450 →									
Projected on-hand inventory	0	450	0	0	0	0	0	0	0	0	0
Planned receipts							60				
Planned order releases				60							

Item: F
Description:

Lot Size: L4L
Lead Time: 2 weeks
Safety Stock: 20 units

		Week									
		1	2	3	4	5	6	7	8	9	10
Gross requirements			400	60							
Scheduled receipts											
Projected on-hand inventory	425	425	25	20	20	20	20	20	20	20	20
Planned receipts				55							
Planned order releases		55									

Chapter Highlights

- Dependent demand for component items can be calculated from production schedules of parent items.
- Material requirements planning (MRP) is a computerized scheduling and information system that offers benefits in managing dependent demand inventories because it (1) recognizes the relationship between production schedules and the demand for component items, (2) provides forward visibility for planning and problem solving, and (3) provides a way to change materials plans in concert with production schedule changes. MRP has three basic inputs: bills of materials, the master production schedule, and inventory records.
- A bill of materials is a diagram or structured list of all components of an item, the parent–component relationships, and usage quantities.
- A master production schedule (MPS) states the number of end items to be produced during specific time periods within an intermediate planning horizon. The MPS is developed within the overall guidelines of the production plan and the firm's competitive priorities. Typically, firms using a make-to-stock strategy schedule end items, firms following an assemble-to-order strategy schedule subassemblies, and firms using a make-to-order strategy schedule purchased components and critical resources. Changes to the MPS are managed by the use of time fences. The MPS inside the demand time fence may be considered to be frozen, whereas changes beyond the planning time fence are easily accommodated.
- Rough-cut capacity planning techniques, such as the method of overall factors, capacity bills, and resource profiles, are used to calculate load profiles for critical workstations. By comparing load profiles to labor capacities approved in the production plan, the scheduler can determine whether the prospective MPS is feasible.
- The material requirements plan is prepared from the most recent inventory records for all items. The basic elements in each record are gross requirements, scheduled receipts, projected on-hand inventory, planned receipts, and planned order releases. Several quantities must be determined for each inventory record, including lot size, lead time, and safety stock.
- The MRP explosion procedure involves level-by-level processing. Starting at the MPS level, the planned order releases of a parent, modified by usage quantities shown in the bill of materials, become the gross requirements of its components.
- MRP systems provide outputs such as the material requirements plan, action notices, capacity reports, and performance reports. Action notices bring to a planner's attention new orders that need to be released or items that have open orders with misaligned due dates.
- Capacity requirements planning (CRP) is a technique for estimating the work load required by a master schedule. CRP uses routing information to identify the workstations involved and MRP information about existing inventory, lead-time offset, and replacement part requirements to calculate accurate work load projections. The input–output control report monitors activity at the workstations and compares actual work loads to those planned by CRP. Discrepancies between the actual and the plan indicate the need for corrective action.
- Manufacturing resource planning (MRP II) ties the basic MRP system to the financial and accounting system. Advanced systems integrate management decision support for all business functions.
- Implementation of MRP systems is widespread. Significant inventory, customer service, and productivity benefits have been reported by many firms. Prerequisites to successful implementation are adequate managerial and computer support, accurate databases, and user knowledge and acceptance. The relative benefits of MRP depend on the number of BOM levels, the magnitude of lot sizes, environmental volatility, and positioning strategy.
- The principles of MRP can be extended to manage distribution inventory with a system called distribution requirements planning (DRP).

Key Terms

planned order release *683*   purchased item *667*   scheduled receipts *681*
planned receipt *682*   regenerative MRP system *691* subassembly *667*
planning time fence *676*   resource profiles *677*   usage quantity *666*
projected on-hand inventory *671*   rough-cut capacity planning *677*

Study Questions

1. How does independent demand differ from dependent demand?
2. What is the purpose of the master production schedule (MPS)?
3. How does an MPS differ from a production plan?
4. What are the advantages of linking the MPS and the production plan?
5. Briefly explain master production scheduling to your boss, who has not heard of it before. Why are the alternative schedules called prospective?
6. Why is rough-cut capacity planning important?
7. If you were a master production scheduler in a company using an assemble-to-order strategy, would you prepare a schedule for end items or for some group of intermediate-level items? Explain.
8. Why are competitive priorities important considerations in master production scheduling?
9. Comment on the statement "It is impossible to put together realistic marketing and financial plans without being able to set and achieve production plans."
10. How can the available-to-promise (ATP) inventory information be used?
11. How does the on-hand inventory balance differ from the ATP inventory?
12. MRP logic derives a component's gross requirements from the planned order releases of all its parents. Why does this necessitate a top-down processing of records?
13. How do scheduled receipts differ from planned receipts?
14. How is safety stock handled by MRP? How much should be carried? At what levels?
15. Efficient customer service, low inventory, and effective operations are conflicting objectives. How can MRP users report *simultaneous* improvements in inventory, customer service, and productivity?
16. Calculating planned order releases with a POQ rule is less complicated after the first one. For each subsequent planned receipt, the lot size is simply the gross requirements sum for the next *P* weeks. Safety stock and the previous week's projected on-hand balance can be ignored. Why?
17. Why do some companies fail to achieve any measurable improvements from MRP?
18. Suppose that a manufacturer decides to share planned order release information with its suppliers. What benefits can accrue to both parties? Might there be disadvantages? If so, what might they be?
19. Why can the reliability of time-phased gross requirements be reduced by last-minute changes in the MPS, unexpected scrap losses, late supplier shipments, unexpected capacity bottlenecks, or inaccurate inventory records?

Problems

1. Consider the bill of materials in Fig. 14.28.
   a. How many immediate parents (one level above) does item I have? How many immediate parents does item E have?
   b. How many unique components does item A have at all levels?
   c. Which of the components are purchased items?
   d. How many intermediate items does item A have at all levels?
   e. Given the lead times noted on Fig. 14.28, how far in advance of shipment is the earliest purchase commitment required?
2. Item A is made from components B, C, and D. Item B, in turn, is made from C. Item D also is an intermediate item, made from B. All usage quantities are 2, except that only 1 unit of item C is needed to make 1 unit of B. Draw the bill of materials for item A.

FIGURE 14.28

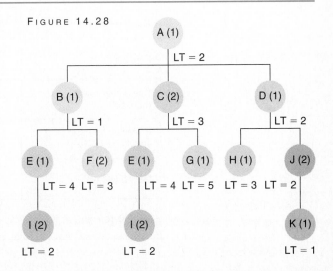

3. What is the lead time (in weeks) to respond to a customer order for item A, based on the BOM shown in Fig. 14.29 and assuming that there are no existing inventories?

FIGURE 14.29

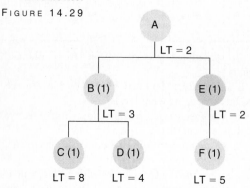

4. Item A is made from components B and C. Item B, in turn, is made from D and E. Item C also is an intermediate item, made from F and H. Finally, intermediate item E is made from H and G. Note that item H has two parents. The following are item lead times.

Item	A	B	C	D	E	F	G	H
Lead Time (weeks)	1	2	5	6	3	4	1	3

a. What lead time (in weeks) is needed to respond to a customer order for item A, assuming that there are no existing inventories?

b. What is the customer response time if items D, F, G, and H are in inventory?

5. Refer to Fig. 14.22 and Solved Problem 1. If there are 2 units of B, 1 unit of F, and 3 units of G in inventory, how many units of G, E, and D must be purchased to produce 5 units of end item A?

6. Complete the MPS record in Fig. 14.30 for a single item.

7. Complete the MPS record shown in Fig. 14.31 for a single item.

8. An end item's demand forecasts for the next 10 weeks are 30, 20, 35, 50, 25, 25, 0, 40, 0, and 50 units. The current on-hand inventory is 70 units. The order policy is to produce in lots of 75. The booked customer orders for the item, starting with week 1, are 22, 30, 15, 9, 0, 0, 5, 3, 7, and 0 units. At present, there are no MPS quantities for this item. The lead time is two weeks. Develop an MPS for this end item.

9. At present, there are 50 units of an end item in inventory. Order policy is fixed at 125 units.

a. Complete the MPS record in Fig. 14.32 for this end item.

b. The MPS in part a was not approved. During the approval process, the MPS quantity in week 9 was brought forward to week 2. Given this changed MPS, revise the projected on-hand inventory row in Fig. 14.32 and list the advantages and concerns associated with this change.

FIGURE 14.30

Item: A						**Order Policy:** 60 units **Lead Time:** 2 weeks		
		Week						
Quantity on Hand: 35	1	2	3	4	5	6	7	8
Forecast	17	15	25	25	20	27	30	35
Customer orders (booked)	15	16	5	11	9	0	5	0
Projected on-hand inventory								
MPS quantity								
MPS start								

FIGURE 14.31

Item: A						Order Policy: 100 units Lead Time: 1 week		
		January				February		
Quantity on Hand: 75	1	2	3	4	5	6	7	8
Forecast	75	65	50	45	65	65	75	75
Customer orders (booked)	40	10	55	0	35	70	0	0
Projected on-hand inventory								
MPS quantity	100							
MPS start								

FIGURE 14.32

Item: A							Order Policy: 125 units Lead Time: 1 week			
					Week					
Quantity on Hand: 50	1	2	3	4	5	6	7	8	9	10
Forecast	10	15	20	30	40	60	80	120	120	120
Customer orders (booked)	12	9	11	5	2	0	4	0	0	0
Projected on-hand inventory										
MPS quantity										
MPS start										

10. Figure 14.33 shows a partially completed MPS record for orange peelers.
    a. Develop the MPS for orange peelers.
    b. Four customer orders arrived in the following sequence.

Order	Quantity	Week Desired
1	500	4
2	100	5
3	300	1
4	350	7

Assume that you must commit to the orders in the sequence of arrival and cannot change the desired shipping dates or your MPS. Which orders should you accept?

11. Morrison Electronics has forecasted the following demand for one of its products for the next eight weeks: 70, 70, 65, 60, 55, 85, 75, and 85. The booked customer orders for this product, starting in week 1, are 50, 60, 55, 40, 35, 0, 0, and 0 units. The current on-hand inventory is 100 units, the order quantity is 150 units, and the lead time is 1 week.
    a. Develop an MPS for this product.
    b. The marketing department at Morrison has revised its forecasts. Starting with week 1, the new forecasts are 70, 70, 75, 70, 70, 100, 100, and 110 units. Assuming that the prospective MPS you developed in part a doesn't change, prepare a revised MPS record. Comment on the situation that Morrison now faces.

12. The Conestoga Wagon Company produces a single product: a motorized child-sized version of the original Conestoga wagon. The following MPS has been proposed.

Week	1	2	3	4	5	6
Units	50	50	40	30	30	50

There is one critical workstation in the shop: the frame-building station. Each wagon requires 3 direct labor hours at this critical workstation. The total direct labor requirement per unit is 18 hours.
    a. Use the method of overall factors to determine the direct labor requirements at the frame-building workstation.
    b. Assume that the MPS was designed to meet forecasted requirements exactly in each period and that there are no available on-hand inventories. Suppose that the available labor hours at the frame-building workstation are 150 hours per week for weeks 1 and 2 and 120 hours per week for weeks 3–6. Revise the MPS to ensure that no stockouts occur, capacity constraints are satisfied, and inventory is minimized.

FIGURE 14.33

Item: Orange peeler								Order Policy: 500 units Lead Time: 1 week			
		Week									
Quantity on Hand: 400		1	2	3	4	5	6	7	8	9	10
Forecast		550	300	400	450	300	350	200	300	450	400
Customer orders (booked)		300	350	250	250	200	150	100	100	100	100
Projected on-hand inventory											
MPS quantity		500									
MPS start											

13. Marshall Fans produces a lightweight desktop fan. An MPS for the fan has been proposed.

Month	Jan	Feb	Mar	Apr	May	Jun
Units	300	400	200	400	500	750

Two critical workstations are involved in the production of the fan: 401A and 401B. Historically, 401A has had 80 percent and 401B has had 20 percent of the total critical workstation hours. The direct labor hours per unit are as follows: critical workstations, 2.0; noncritical workstations, 3.0; and total, 5. Use the method of overall factors to determine the direct labor requirements for each critical workstation and for the entire plant.

14. The Karry Kart Company produces two products: a deluxe kart (DK) and a standard kart (SK). The following MPS has been proposed for the two products.

Item	Week 1	2	3	4	5	6	Total
DK	50	50	30	30	30	30	220
SK	60	—	60	—	60	—	180

The direct labor hours per unit are

Item	Critical Workstations	Noncritical Workstations	Total
DK	11.0	4.0	15.0
SK	6.0	4.0	10.0

There are three critical workstations: Z101, Z105, and Z107. Historically, Z101, Z105, and Z107 have accounted for 40 percent, 30 percent, and 30 percent of the direct labor hours, respectively.
a. Create a load profile based on the proposed MPS, using the method of overall factors.
b. Suppose that the production plan specifies a total of 1100 direct labor hours, of which 750 are at the critical workstations. What might be done to improve the MPS?

15. The partially completed inventory record in Fig. 14.34 shows gross requirements, scheduled receipts, and current on-hand inventory. Lead time and safety stock factors are also shown.
a. Complete the last three rows of the record by using an FOQ of 110 units.
b. Complete the last three rows of the record by using the L4L lot-sizing rule.
c. Complete the last three rows of the record by using the POQ lot-sizing rule, with $P = 2$.

FIGURE 14.34

Item: M405—X Description: Table top assembly											Lot Size: Lead Time: 2 weeks Safety Stock: 0 units
		Week									
		1	2	3	4	5	6	7	8	9	10
Gross requirements		90		85		80		45	90		
Scheduled receipts		110									
Projected on-hand inventory	40										
Planned receipts											
Planned order releases											

16. Figure 14.35 shows a partially completed inventory record. Gross requirements, scheduled receipts, and current on-hand inventory, as well as lead time and safety stock parameters, are shown.
   a. Complete the record by using an FOQ of 220 units.
   b. Complete the record by using the L4L rule.

   c. Complete the record by using the POQ rule, with $P = 3$.
17. The inventory record in Fig. 14.36 has been partially completed.
   a. Complete the last three rows by using an FOQ of 60 units. If there are action notices, what factors should you consider in responding to them?

FIGURE 14.35

Item: MQ—09
Description: Rear wheel assembly

Lot Size:
Lead Time: 1 week
Safety Stock: 50 units

		Week									
		1	2	3	4	5	6	7	8	9	10
Gross requirements		205		130	85		70	60	95		
Scheduled receipts		220									
Projected on-hand inventory	100										
Planned receipts											
Planned order releases											

FIGURE 14.36

Item: GF—4
Description: Motor assembly

Lot Size:
Lead Time: 3 weeks
Safety Stock: 30 units

		Week										
		1	2	3	4	5	6	7	8	9	10	11	12
Gross requirements			50		35		55		30		10		25
Scheduled receipts				60									
Projected on-hand inventory	40												
Planned receipts													
Planned order releases													

b. Revise the planned order release row by using the L4L rule.

c. Revise the planned order release row by using the POQ rule. Find the value of *P* that should (in the long run) yield an average lot size of 60 units. Assume that the average weekly demand for the foreseeable future is 15 units.

18. The BOM for product A is shown in Fig. 14.37, and data from the inventory records are shown in Table 14.4. In the master production schedule for product A, the MPS quantity row (showing *completion* dates) calls for 250 units in week 8. The lead time for production of A is two weeks. Develop the material requirements plan for the next six weeks for items B, C, and D.

FIGURE 14.37

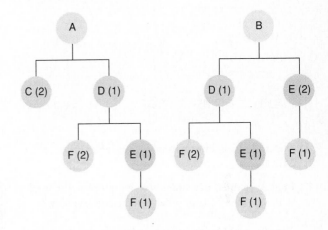

After completing the plan, identify any action notices that would be issued. (*Hint:* An item's gross requirements cannot be derived unless the planned order releases of all its parents are known.)

19. The BOMs for products A and B are shown in Fig. 14.38. Data from inventory records are shown in Table 14.5. The MPS calls for 85 units of product A to be completed in week 4 and 100 units in week 7 (the lead time is one week). The MPS for product B calls for 180 units to be completed in week 7 (the lead time is two weeks). Develop the material requirements plan for the next six weeks for items C, D, E, and F. Identify any action notices.

FIGURE 14.38

20. Figure 14.39 on the next page illustrates the BOM of product A. The master production schedule calls for 50 units of A in week 4, 65 units in week 7, and 80 units in week 10. The lead time for A is two weeks. Item C is produced to make A and to meet the forecasted demand for replacement parts. Past replacement part demand has been 20 units per week (add 20 units to C's gross requirements). The lead times for items F and C are one week, and for the other items the lead time is two weeks. A safety stock of 30 units

TABLE 14.4 *Inventory Record Data*

Data Category	B	C	D
Lot-sizing rule	L4L	FOQ = 1000	L4L
Lead time	2 weeks	1 week	3 weeks
Safety stock	0	100	0
Scheduled receipts	None	1000 (week 1)	None
Beginning (on-hand) inventory	0	200	0

TABLE 14.5 *Inventory Record Data*

Data Category	C	D	E	F
Lot-sizing rule	FOQ = 220	L4L	FOQ = 300	POQ = (*P* = 2)
Lead time	3 weeks	2 weeks	3 weeks	2 weeks
Safety stock	20	0	0	80
Scheduled receipts	280 (week 1)	None	300 (week 3)	None
On-hand inventory	25	0	150	600

is required for item C. No safety stock is required for items B, D, E, and F. The L4L lot-sizing rule is used for items B and F; the POQ lot-sizing rule ($P = 3$) is used for C. Item E has an FOQ of 600 units, and D has an FOQ of 250 units. On-hand inventories are 50 units of B, 50 units of C, 120 units of D, 70 units of E, and 250 units of F. Item B has a scheduled receipt of 50 units in week 2.

Develop a material requirements plan for the next eight weeks for items B, C, D, E, and F. What action notices will be generated?

FIGURE 14.39

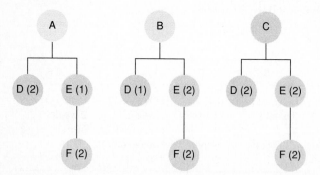

21. The following information is available about three MPS items.

   Item A: An 80-unit order is to be completed in week 4. A 55-unit order is to be completed in week 7.
   Item B: A 125-unit order is to be completed in week 7.
   Item C: A 60-unit order is to be completed in week 7.

   The lead times are one week for A, two weeks for B, and three weeks for C. Develop the material requirements plan for the next six weeks for items D, E, and F, identifying any action notices that would be provided. The BOMs are shown in Fig. 14.40, and data from the inventory records are shown in Table 14.6.

FIGURE 14.40

TABLE 14.6   *Inventory Record Data*

Data Category	Item		
	D	**E**	**F**
Lot-sizing rule	FOQ = 150	L4L	POQ = (P = 2)
Lead time	3 weeks	1 week	2 weeks
Safety stock	40	0	30
Scheduled receipts	250 (week 1)	120 (week 2)	None
Beginning (on-hand) inventory	150	0	100

22. At the beginning of week 45, production schedules at the chair assembly workstation called for the existing 60-hour backlog of work to be gradually reduced to 20 hours by the end of week 48. This reduction was to be accomplished by releasing an average of 310 hours of work per week to chair assembly while providing resources sufficient to complete 320 hours per week. At the beginning of week 49 the input–output report represented by Fig. 14.41 is brought to your attention.

FIGURE 14.41

Workstation: Chair assembly				**Week:** 49	
Tolerance: ±50 hours					
			Week		
	45	46	47	48	49
Inputs Planned Actual Cumulative deviation	310 305	310 285	310 295	310 270	320
Outputs Planned Actual Cumulative deviation	320 320	320 305	320 300	320 290	320
Planned ending backlog (hrs)	50	40	30	20	20
Actual backlog 60 hrs					

a. What triggered this report? (*Hint:* Complete the cumulative deviation rows.)
b. What problem is indicated by the data in the input–output control report? (*Hint:* Calculate the actual backlog row and compare it to the planned backlog row.)
c. What might be done to resolve this problem?

Advanced Problems

A computer package is useful for Problems 25 and 26.

23. Items A and B are dependent demand items. Item B's only parent is A. Three units of B are needed to make one unit of A. The current material requirements plans for A and B are shown in Fig. 14.42.

    a. Today the planner responsible for items A and B learned some good news and some bad news. Al-though the scheduled receipt of 90 units of A has been finished (the good news), only 45 units were put in the storeroom; the other 45 were scrapped (the bad news). Recalculate the two inventory records to reflect this event. (*Hint:* A scheduled receipt should no longer be shown for A, but its on-hand balance now is 65 units.)

    b. What action notices would be issued relative to the new material requirements plan?

FIGURE 14.42

Item: A
Description:

Lot Size: 90 units
Lead Time: 1 week
Safety Stock: 0 units

		Week						
		1	2	3	4	5	6	7
Gross requirements		85		50			110	60
Scheduled receipts		90						
Projected on-hand inventory	20	25	25	65	65	65	45	75
Planned receipts				90			90	90
Planned order releases			90			90	90	

Item: B
Description:

Lot Size: L4L
Lead Time: 3 weeks
Safety Stock: 0 units

		Week						
		1	2	3	4	5	6	7
Gross requirements			270			270	270	
Scheduled receipts			270					
Projected on-hand inventory	0	0	0	0	0	0	0	0
Planned receipts						270	270	
Planned order releases			270	270				

24. Figure 14.43 shows the BOMs for two end items, A and B. Table 14.7 shows the MPS quantity *start* date (already offset for lead time) for each one. Table 14.8 contains data from inventory records for items C, D, and E. Determine the material requirements plan for items C, D, and E for the next eight weeks. Identify any action notices that would be provided.

FIGURE 14.43

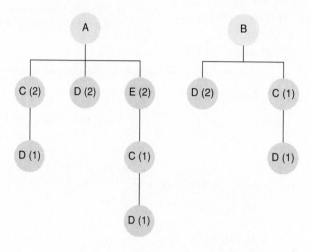

TABLE 14.7   *MPS Quantity Start Dates*

				Date				
Product	**1**	**2**	**3**	**4**	**5**	**6**	**7**	**8**
A		125		95		150		130
B			80			70		

TABLE 14.8   *Inventory Record Data*

	Item		
Data Category	**C**	**D**	**E**
Lot-sizing rule	POQ ($P = 3$)	FOQ = 800	L4L
Lead time	2 weeks	1 week	3 weeks
Safety stock	75	120	0
Scheduled receipts	None	800 (week 1)	200 (week 2)
On-hand inventory	625	350	85

FIGURE 14.44

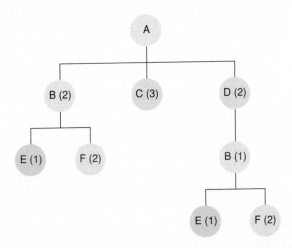

TABLE 14.9 *Inventory Record Data*

Data Category	Item				
	B	**C**	**D**	**E**	**F**
Lot-sizing rule	FOQ = 700	FOQ = 700	L4L	L4L	L4L
Lead time	4 weeks	3 weeks	3 weeks	2 weeks	1 week
Safety stock	50	100	0	100	0
Scheduled receipts	700 (week 1)	450 (week 2)	150 (week 2)	None	1400 (week 1)
Beginning (on-hand) inventory	215	105	125	750	0

25. The BOM for product A is shown above in Fig. 14.44. The MPS for product A calls for 120 units to be *started* (already offset for lead times) in weeks 2, 4, 5, and 8. Table 14.9 shows data from the inventory records. Develop the material requirements plan for the next eight weeks for each item. Would any action notices be issued? If so, identify them.

26. Develop the material requirements plan for all components and intermediate items associated with end item A for the next ten weeks. Refer to Solved Problem 1 (Fig. 14.22) for the bill of materials, Solved Problem 2 (Fig. 14.24) for the master schedule, and Table 14.10 for component inventory record information.

TABLE 14.10 *Inventory Record Data*

Data Category	Item					
	B	**C**	**D**	**E**	**F**	**G**
Lot-sizing rule	L4L	L4L	POQ (P = 2)	L4L	L4L	FOQ = 100
Lead time	2 weeks	3 weeks	3 weeks	6 weeks	1 week	3 weeks
Safety stock	30	10	0	0	0	0
Scheduled receipts	150 (week 2)	50 (week 2)	None	400 (week 6)	40 (week 3)	None
On-hand inventory	30	20	60	400	0	0

27. Items A and B are dependent demand items. Four units of B are needed to make one unit of A. Item B's only parent is A. The current material requirements plans for A and B are shown in Fig. 14.45. If 110 units of A are on hand, rather than 80 units, what is the new material requirements plan? Would there be any action notices? If so, identify them.

F I G U R E   1 4 . 4 5

Item: A
Description:

Lot Size: 90 units
Lead Time: 2 weeks
Safety Stock: 10 units

		Week									
		1	2	3	4	5	6	7	8	9	10
Gross requirements		120			70			85	90		70
Scheduled receipts		90									
Projected on-hand inventory	80	50	50	50	70	70	70	75	75	75	95
Planned receipts					90			90	90		90
Planned order releases			90			90	90		90		

Item: B
Description:

Lot Size: L4L
Lead Time: 4 weeks
Safety Stock: 0 units

		Week									
		1	2	3	4	5	6	7	8	9	10
Gross requirements			360			360	360				
Scheduled receipts			360								
Projected on-hand inventory	0	0	0	0	0	0	0	0	0	0	0
Planned receipts						360	360				
Planned order releases		360	360								

CASE

King Manufacturing

Last year a new MRP system was installed at King Manufacturing. Fred Neff, the vice-president of operations, worked closely with the task force created to bring MRP on line. He frequently attended the training sessions for selected employees, emphasizing how MRP should help King Manufacturing secure a competitive edge. When the system went up, there was an aura of tranquility and goodwill. As a symbolic gesture, King's complete supply of red expediting tags was discarded. The days of the informal system of fire fighting and expediting were over!

A year later, Neff's mood is quite different. Inventory and overtime levels have not dropped as much as expected. Customer service is as bad as ever, and complaints of late shipments are too numerous. Convinced that this shouldn't happen with MRP, Neff is having a new round of discussions with key members of the operations department. After all, "a problem well stated is one half solved."

Barbara Jones

Barbara Jones, the production and inventory control manager, assures Neff that inventory records and BOM files are now being faithfully maintained.

> With our regenerative system, there is a new explosion each week. This gives us an updated material requirements plan and action notices for launching new orders. Some of my group do think we should extend our outputs to get priority and capacity reports. As you know, we decided to get the order-launching capability well established before worrying about such refinements. Besides, most of our problems rest with the purchasing and marketing departments. We experience too many stockouts of purchased parts, even though we have worked closely with I. M. Beyer's group to get realistic lead-time estimates. As for marketing, they keep taking last-minute orders from favorite customers. This plays havoc with our production schedules.

Bill Hardy

Neff's conversation with Bill Hardy, the shop superintendent, suggests that the old informal system is still alive and well.

> I'm starting to wonder about this MRP system, even though it looks great on paper. Last week we had hardly any work, and I was forced to overproduce on several orders just to keep everyone busy. This week is just the opposite. So many new orders were released with short fuses that almost everyone will need to work overtime. It's either feast or famine. Why couldn't Jones's group have released some of these orders a couple of weeks ago?
>
> Another thing is the due dates assigned to each order. I know they never get updated because the dates the system shows for scheduled receipts don't change even though everyone knows the production schedules of their parents have changed. Things change pretty quickly around here, and morale is slipping. The only chuckle we get is when I. M. Beyer walks through the plant. Everyone knows that purchasing isn't doing the job. He should come down more frequently. Incidentally, we could use more expediters. We want to start using red tags again.

I. M. Beyer

Neff's conversation with the purchasing manager, I. M. Beyer, is equally disconcerting.

> Our buyers are really getting frustrated with this new system. There is no time for creative buying. Almost all of their time is spent following up on late orders. For example, yesterday we received an action notice to bring in 200 units of C130-A in just two weeks. We need three months of lead time for this item! We tried both possible suppliers, but they said that a delivery in two weeks was impossible. What are Jones's planners doing? The perplexing thing is that the planned lead time in the inventory record for C130-A is correctly stated as 12 weeks. Doesn't MRP offset for lead time?
>
> It is getting to the point that I avoid trips to the plant. Everyone out there seems to think that we are the cause of their problems.

Questions

1. Identify what is wrong at King Manufacturing. Is the problem with the system itself or how it is being used? Explain.
2. What steps should Neff and others take to improve operations?

Selected References

Berry, W. L., T. G. Schmitt, and T. E. Vollmann. "Capacity Planning Techniques for Manufacturing Control Systems: Information Requirements and Operational Features." *Journal of Operations Management,* vol. 3, no. 1 (November 1982), pp. 13–25.

Blackstone, J. H. *Capacity Management.* Cincinnati: South-Western, 1989.

Bruggeman, J. J., and S. Haythornthwaite. "The Master Schedule." *APICS—The Performance Advantage* (October 1991), pp. 44–46.

Cerveny, Robert P., and Lawrence W. Scott. "A Survey of MRP Implementation." *Production and Inventory Management Journal,* vol. 30, no. 3 (1989), pp. 31–34.

Chakravarty, A., and H. K. Jain. "Distributed Computer System Capacity Planning and Capacity Loading." *Decision Sciences,* vol. 21, no. 2 (Spring 1990), pp. 253–262.

Chung, C. H., and L. Krajewski. "Planning Horizons for Master Production Scheduling." *Journal of Operations Management,* vol. 4, no. 4 (August 1984).

Dougherty, J. R., and J. F. Proud. "From Master Schedules to Finishing Schedules in the 1990s." *American Production and Inventory Control Society 1990 Annual Conference Proceedings,* pp. 368–370.

Greene, Alice H. "MRP 96—Getting Another Perspective." *P&IM Review with APICS News* (November 1988), pp. 26–27.

Haddock, Jorge, and Donald E. Hubicki. "Which Lot-Sizing Techniques Are Used in Material Requirements Planning?" *Production and Inventory Management Journal,* vol. 30, no. 3 (1989), pp. 53–56.

Harl, Johannes E., and Larry P. Ritzman. "A Heuristic Algorithm for Capacity Sensitive Lot Sizing." *Journal of Operations Management,* vol. 5, no. 3 (May 1985), pp. 309–326.

Jernigan, Jeff. "Comprehensiveness, Cost-Effectiveness Sweep Aside Operations Challenges," *APICS—The Performance Advantage* (March 1993), pp. 44–45.

Orlicky, J. *Material Requirements Planning.* New York: McGraw-Hill, 1975.

Ormsby, Joseph G., Susan Y. Ormsby, and Carl R. Ruthstrom. "MRP II Implementation: A Case Study." *Production and Inventory Management,* vol. 31, no. 4 (4th Quarter 1990), pp. 77–82.

Ritzman, Larry P., Barry E. King, and Lee J. Krajewski. "Manufacturing Performance—Pulling the Right Levers." *Harvard Business Review* (March–April 1984), pp. 143–152.

Sharma, Deven. *Manufacturing Strategy: An Empirical Analysis.* Unpublished Ph.D. dissertation, Ohio State University, 1987.

Vollmann, T. E., W. L. Berry, and D. C. Whybark. *Manufacturing Planning and Control Systems.* Homewood, Ill.: Irwin, 1992.

Wight, Oliver W. *Manufacturing Resource Planning: MRP II.* Essex Junction, Vt.: Oliver Wight, Ltd., 1984.

Chapter Fifteen

JUST-IN-TIME SYSTEMS

arley-Davidson's motorcycle business was on the ropes in 1978, when it tried—and failed—to prove in court that its Japanese competitors were dumping their products on the market at prices below cost to gain market share. Harley management was amazed to learn that these Japanese companies actually were achieving operating costs 30 percent below theirs. The stark realization that their operations were highly inefficient led Harley management to implement the three Japanese practices that it believed were the key to success: quality circles, statistical process control (SPC), and just-in-time manufacturing. (We covered quality circles in Chapter 4 and SPC in Chapter 5.) Although the road to success at times was rocky, since implementing a just-in-time system in 1981 the company has reduced inventories by 40 percent, increased productivity (in terms of vehicles produced per employee) by 129 percent, reduced its supplier base by 30 percent, and reported improved net profits since

At Harley-Davidson's Milwaukee production facility, workers assemble wheel components.

1983. The turnaround has enabled management to close the gap between Harley and its competitors and improve its market share.

The Harley-Davidson story isn't unusual. **Just-in-time (JIT) systems,** which are designed to produce or deliver goods or services as needed and minimize inventories, require major changes in traditional operating practices. Often a crisis (such as being faced with going out of business or closing a plant) galvanizes management and labor to work together and effect the needed changes. Converting from traditional manufacturing to a just-in-time system brings up not only inventory control issues, but also process management and scheduling issues. In this chapter we identify the characteristics of just-in-time systems, discuss how JIT systems can be used for continuous improvement of operations, and indicate how manufacturing and service operations utilize JIT systems. We also address the strategic implications of such systems and some of the implementation issues that companies face. Finally, we discuss the choice of an appropriate production and inventory management system for a particular environment.

◆ CHARACTERISTICS OF JUST-IN-TIME SYSTEMS

Just-in-time systems focus on reducing inefficiency and unproductive time in the production process to improve continuously the process and the quality of the product or service. Employee involvement and inventory reduction are essential to JIT operations. Just-in-time systems are known by many different names, including *zero inventory, synchronous manufacturing, lean production, stockless production* (Hewlett-Packard), *material as needed* (Harley-Davidson), and *continuous flow manufacturing* (IBM). In this section we discuss the following characteristics of JIT systems: pull method of material flow, consistently high quality, small lot sizes, short setup times, uniform workstation loads, standardized components and work methods, close supplier ties, flexible work force, product focus, automated production, and preventive maintenance.

Pull Method of Material Flow

Just-in-time systems utilize the pull method of material flow. However, another popular method of material flow is the push method. To differentiate between these two systems, consider the production system for a Quarter Pounder at a McDonald's restaurant. There are two workstations. The burger maker is the person responsible for producing this burger: Burger patties must be fried; buns must be toasted and then dressed with ketchup, pickles, mayonnaise, lettuce, and cheese; and the patties must be inserted into buns and put on a tray. The final assembler takes the tray, wraps the burgers in paper, and restocks the inventory. Inventories must be kept low because any burgers left unsold after seven minutes must be destroyed.

The flow of materials is from the burger maker to the final assembler to the customer. One way to manage this flow is by using the **push method,** in which the production of the item begins in advance of customer needs. With this method, management schedules the receipt of all raw materials (e.g., meat, buns, and condiments) and authorizes the start of production, all in advance of Quarter Pounder needs. The burger maker starts production of 24 burgers (the capacity of the griddle) and, when they are completed, pushes them along to the final assembler's station, where they might have to wait until she is ready for them. The packaged burgers then wait on a warming tray until a customer purchases one.

The other way to manage the flow among the burger maker, the final assembler, and the customer is to use the **pull method,** in which customer demand activates production of the item. With the pull method, as customers purchase burgers, the final assembler checks the inventory level of burgers and, when they are almost depleted, orders six more. The burger maker produces the six burgers and gives the tray to the final assembler, who completes the assembly and places the burgers in the inventory for sale. The pull method is better for the production of burgers: The two workers can coordinate the two workstations to keep inventory low, important because of the seven-minute time limit. The production of burgers is a highly repetitive process, setup times and process times are low, and the flow of materials is well defined. There is no need to produce to anticipated needs more than a few minutes ahead.

Firms that tend to have highly repetitive manufacturing processes and well-defined material flows use just-in-time systems because the pull method allows closer control of inventory and production at the workstations. Other firms, such as job shops producing products in low volumes with low repeatability in the production process, tend to use a push method such as MRP. In this environment a customer order is promised for delivery on some future date. Production is started at the first workstation and pushed ahead to the next one. Inventory accumulates in anticipation of shipping the completed order on the promised date.

Under what circumstances can a just-in-time system be used effectively?

Consistently High Quality

JIT systems seek to eliminate scrap and rework in order to achieve a uniform flow of materials. Efficient JIT operations require conformance to product or service specifications and implementation of the behavioral and statistical methods of total quality management (TQM) outlined in Chapters 4 and 5. JIT systems control quality at the source, with workers acting as their own quality inspectors. For example, a soldering operation at the Texas Instruments antenna department had a defect rate that varied from zero to 50 percent on a daily basis, averaging about 20 percent. To compensate, production planners increased the lot sizes, which only increased inventory levels and did nothing to reduce the number of defective items. Engineers discovered through experimentation that gas temperature was a critical variable in producing defect-free items. They devised statistical control charts for the operators to use to monitor gas temperature and adjust it themselves. Process yields immediately improved and stabilized at 95 percent, eventually enabling management to implement a JIT system.

Management must realize the enormous responsibility this method places on the workers and must prepare them properly, as one GM division quickly learned. When Buick City began using JIT in 1985, management authorized its workers to stop the production line by pulling a cord if quality problems arose at their stations—a practice the Japanese call *andon*. GM also eliminated production-line inspectors and cut the number of supervisors by half. Stopping the line, however, is a costly action that brings a problem to everyone's attention. The workers weren't prepared for that responsibility; productivity and quality took a nose-dive. The paint on Le Sabres wasn't shiny enough. The seams weren't straight. The top of the dashboard had an unintended wave. Management, labor, and engineering formed a team to correct the problems. Work methods were changed, and the *andon* system was modified to include a yellow warning cord so that workers could call for help without stopping the line.

On Buick's LeSabre line, a worker moves the engine into place.

Small Lot Sizes

Rather than building up a cushion of inventory, users of JIT systems maintain inventory with lot sizes that are as small as possible. Small lot sizes have three benefits. First, small lot sizes reduce *cycle* inventory, the inventory in excess of the safety stock carried between orders (see Chapter 11). The average cycle inventory equals one-half the lot size: As the lot size gets smaller, so does cycle inventory. Reducing cycle inventory reduces the time and space involved in manufacturing and holding inventory. Figure 15.1 shows the effect on cycle inventory of reducing the lot size from 100 to 50 for a uniform demand of 10 units per hour: Cycle inventory is cut in half.

FIGURE 15.1

Implications for Small and Large Lot Sizes for Cycle Inventory

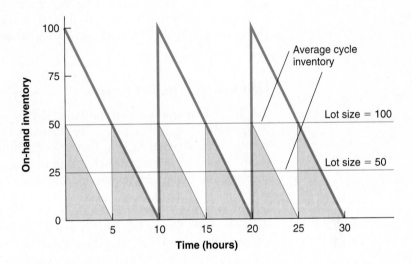

Second, small lot sizes help cut lead times. A decline in lead time in turn cuts pipeline (WIP) inventory because the total processing time at each workstation is greater for large lots than for small lots. Also, a large lot often has to wait longer to be processed at the next workstation while that workstation finishes working on another large lot. In addition, if any defective items are discovered, large lots cause longer delays because the entire lot must be inspected to find all the items that need rework.

Finally, small lots help achieve a uniform operating system workload. Large lots consume large chunks of processing time on workstations and therefore complicate scheduling. Small lots can be juggled more effectively, enabling schedulers to utilize capacities more efficiently. In addition, small lots allow workstations to accommodate mixed-model production (more than one item) by reducing waiting line times for production. We return to this point when we discuss uniform workstation loads.

Short Setup Times

Reduced lot sizes have the disadvantage of increased setup frequency. In operations where the setup times are normally low, as in the McDonald's example, small lots are feasible. However, in fabrication operations with sizable setup times, increasing the frequency of setups may result in wasting employee and equipment time. These operations must reduce setup times to realize the benefits of small-lot production.

Achieving low setup times often requires close cooperation among engineering, management, and labor. For example, changing dies on large presses to form automobile parts from sheet metal can take three to four hours. At Honda's Marysville, Ohio, plant—where four stamping lines stamp all the exterior and major interior body panels for Accord production—teams worked on ways to reduce the changeover time for the massive dies. As a result, a complete change of dies for a giant 2400-ton press now takes less than eight minutes. The Japanese goal of **single-digit setup** means having setup times of less than 10 minutes. Some techniques to reduce setup times include using conveyors for die storage, moving large dies with cranes, simplifying dies, enacting machine controls, using microcomputers to automatically feed and position work, and preparing for changeovers while the current job is being processed.

Uniform Workstation Loads

The JIT system works best if the daily load on individual workstations is relatively uniform. Uniform loads can be achieved by assembling the same type and number of units each day, thus creating a uniform daily demand at all workstations. Capacity planning, which recognizes capacity constraints at critical workstations, and line balancing are used to develop the monthly master production schedule. For example, at Toyota the aggregate production plan may call for 4500 Camrys per week for the next month. That requires two full shifts, five days per week, producing 900 Camrys each day, or 450 per shift. Three models of Camrys are produced: four-door sedans (S), two-door coupes (C), and wagons (W). Suppose that Toyota needs 200 sedans, 150 coupes, and 100 wagons per shift to satisfy market demand. To produce 450 units in one shift of 480 minutes, the line must roll out a Camry every 480/450 = 1.067 minutes.

Three ways of devising a master production schedule for the Camrys are of interest here. First, with big-lot production, all daily requirements of a model are produced in one batch before another model is started. The sequence of 200 S's, 150 C's, and 100 W's would be repeated once per shift. Not only would these big lots increase the average cycle inventory level; they also would cause lumpy requirements on all the workstations feeding the assembly line.

The second option uses **mixed-model assembly,** producing a mix of models in smaller lots. Note that the production requirements are in the ratio of 4 sedans to 3 coupes to 2 wagons, found by dividing the model's production requirements by the greatest common divisor, or 50. Thus the Toyota planner could develop a production cycle consisting of 9 units: 4 sedans, 3 coupes, and 2 wagons. The cycle would repeat in 9(1.067) = 9.60 minutes, for a total of 50 times per shift (480 min/9.60 min = 50).

A sequence of S–W–S–C–S–C–S–W–C, repeated 50 times per shift, would achieve the same total output as the other options. This option is feasible only if the setup times are very short. The sequence generates a steady rate of component requirements for the various models and allows the use of small lot sizes at the feeder workstations. Consequently, the capacity requirements at those stations are greatly smoothed. These requirements can be compared to actual capacities during the planning phase, and modifications to the production cycle, production requirements, or capacities can be made as necessary.

Standardized Components and Work Methods

The standardization of components, called *part commonality* or *modularity*, increases repeatability. For example, a firm producing 10 products from 1000 different components could redesign its products so that they consist of only 100 different components with larger daily requirements. Because the requirements per component increase, so does repeatability; that is, each worker performs a standardized task or work method more often each day. Productivity tends to increase because, with increased repetition, workers learn to do the task more efficiently. Standardization of components and work methods aids in achieving the high-productivity, low-inventory objectives of JIT systems.

Close Supplier Ties

Because JIT systems operate with very low levels of inventory, close relationships with suppliers are necessary. Stock shipments must be frequent, have short lead times, arrive on schedule, and be of high quality. A contract might require a supplier to deliver goods to a factory as often as several times per day. Purchasing managers focus on three areas: reducing the number of suppliers, using local suppliers, and improving supplier relations.

Typically, one of the first actions undertaken when a JIT system is implemented is to pare the number of suppliers. Xerox, for example, reduced the number of its suppliers from 5000 to just 300. This approach puts a lot of pressure on these suppliers to deliver high-quality components on time. To compensate, JIT users extend their contracts with these suppliers and give them firm advance-order information. In addition, they include their suppliers in the early phases of product design to avoid problems after production has begun. They also work with their suppliers' vendors, trying to achieve JIT inventory flows throughout the entire supplier chain.

Manufacturers using JIT systems generally utilize local suppliers. For instance, when GM located its Saturn complex in Tennessee, many suppliers clustered nearby. Harley-Davidson reduced the number of its suppliers and gave preference to those close to its plants—for example, three-fourths of the suppliers for the Milwaukee engine plant are located within a 175-mile radius. Geographic proximity means that the company can reduce the need for safety stocks. Companies that have no suppliers close by must have a finely tuned distribution system. For example, New United Motor Manufacturing, Incorporated (NUMMI), the joint venture between GM and Toyota in California, has suppliers in Indiana, Ohio, and Michigan. Through a carefully coordinated system involving trains and piggyback truck trailers, suppliers deliver enough parts for exactly one day's production each day.

JIT users also find that a cooperative orientation with suppliers is essential (Chapter 11). The JIT philosophy is to look for ways to improve efficiency and reduce inventories throughout the supplier chain. Close cooperation between companies and their suppliers can be a win–win situation for everyone. Better communication of component requirements, for example, enables more efficient inventory planning and distribution scheduling by the suppliers, thereby improving supplier profit margins. Customers can then negotiate lower component prices. Suppliers also should be included in the design of new products so that inefficient component designs can be avoided before production begins. Close supplier relations cannot be established and maintained if companies view their suppliers as adversaries whenever contracts are negotiated. Rather, they should consider suppliers to be partners in a venture where both parties have an interest in maintaining a long-term, profitable relationship.

Flexible Work Force

Workers in flexible work forces can perform more than one job. When the skill levels required to perform most tasks are low—at a McDonald's restaurant, for instance—a high degree of flexibility in the work force can be achieved with little training. In situations requiring higher skill levels, such as at the Texas Instruments antenna department, shifting workers to other jobs may require extensive, costly training. Flexibility can be very beneficial: Workers can be shifted among workstations to help relieve bottlenecks as they arise without resorting to inventory buffers—an aspect important to the uniform flow of JIT systems. Or they can step in and do the job for those on vacation or out sick. Although assigning workers to tasks they don't usually perform may reduce efficiency, some rotation relieves boredom and refreshes workers.

Product Focus

A product focus can reduce the frequency of setups. If volumes of specific products are large enough, groups of machines and workers can be organized into a product layout (see Chapter 9) to eliminate setups entirely. If volume is insufficient to keep a line of similar products busy, *group technology* can be used to design small production lines that manufacture, in volume, families of components with common attributes. Changeovers from a component in one product family to the next component in the same family are minimal.

Another tactic used to reduce or eliminate setups is the one-worker, multiple machines (OWMM) approach, which essentially is a one-person line. One worker operates several machines, with each machine advancing the process a step at a time. Because the same product is made repeatedly, setups are eliminated. For example, in a McDonald's restaurant the person preparing fish sandwiches uses the OWMM approach. When the signal is given to produce more fish sandwiches, the employee puts the fish patties into the fish fryer and sets the timer. Then while the fish are frying, he puts the buns into the steamer. When the buns are finished, he puts them on a tray and dresses them with condiments. When the fish patties are ready, he inserts them into the buns. The completed sandwiches are placed on the shelf for the final assembler to package for the customer. Then the cycle repeats itself.

Automated Production

Automation plays a big role in JIT systems and is a key to low-cost production. Sakichi Toyoda, the founder of Toyota, once said, "Whenever there is money, invest it into machinery." Money freed up because of JIT inventory reductions can be invested in automation to reduce costs. The benefits, of course, are greater profits, greater market share (because prices can be cut), or both. Automation should be planned carefully, however. Many managers believe that if some automation is good, more is better. That isn't always the case. When GM initiated Buick City, for example, it installed 250 robots, some with vision systems for mounting windshields. Unfortunately, the robots skipped black cars because they

Robots perform many operations on cars built at the NUMMI facility.

couldn't "see" them. New software eventually solved the problem; however, GM management found that humans could do some jobs better than robots and replaced 30 robots with humans.

Preventive Maintenance

Because JIT emphasizes finely tuned material flows and little buffer inventory between workstations, unplanned machine downtime can be disruptive. Preventive maintenance can reduce the frequency and duration of machine downtime. After the technician has performed routine maintenance activities, she can test other parts that might need to be replaced. Replacement during regularly scheduled maintenance periods is easier and quicker than dealing with machine failures during production. Maintenance is done on a schedule that balances the cost of the preventive maintenance program against the risks and costs of machine failure.

Another tactic is to make workers responsible for routinely maintaining their own equipment and develop employee pride in keeping their machines in top condition. This tactic, however, typically is limited to general housekeeping chores, minor lubrication, and adjustments. High-tech machines need trained specialists. Doing even simple maintenance tasks goes a long way toward improving machine performance, though.

◆ CONTINUOUS IMPROVEMENT WITH JUST-IN-TIME SYSTEMS

How can JIT systems facilitate continuous improvement?

By spotlighting areas that need improvement, JIT systems lead to continuous improvement in quality and productivity. Figure 15.2 characterizes the philosophy behind continuous improvement with JIT systems. In manufacturing, the water surface represents product and component inventory levels. In services, the water surface represents service system capacity, such as staff levels. The rocks represent problems encountered in manufacturing or service delivery. When the water surface is high enough, the boat passes over the rocks because the high level of inventory covers up problems. As inventory shrinks, rocks are exposed.

FIGURE 15.2

Continuous Improvement with JIT Systems

Ultimately, the boat will hit a rock if the water surface falls far enough. Through JIT systems, workers, supervisors, engineers, and analysts use the methods for continuous improvement discussed in Chapters 3, 4, and 5 to demolish the exposed rock. The coordination required for the pull system of material flows in JIT systems identifies problems in time for corrective action to be taken.

In manufacturing, eliminating the problem of too much scrap might require improving work methods, employee quality training, and supplier quality. The desire to eliminate capacity imbalances might focus attention on the master production schedule and work-force flexibility. Reducing unreliable deliveries calls for cooperating better with suppliers or replacing suppliers. Maintaining low inventories, periodically stressing the system to identify problems, and focusing on the elements of the JIT system lie at the heart of continuous improvement. For example, the Kawasaki plant in Nebraska periodically cuts safety stocks almost to zero. Problems are exposed, recorded, and later assigned as improvement projects. After the improvements have been made, inventories are permanently cut to the new level. The Japanese have used this trial-and-error process to develop more efficient manufacturing operations.

Service operations that are integral to both manufacturing and service organizations, including scheduling, billing, order taking, accounting, and financial tasks, also can be improved with JIT systems. As in manufacturing, continuous improvement means that employees and managers continue to seek ways to improve operations. However, the mechanics of highlighting the areas needing improvement are different. In service operations, a common approach used by managers to place stress on the system is to reduce the number of employees doing a particular operation or series of operations until the process begins to slow or come to a halt. The problems can be identified, and ways for overcoming them can be explored. We return to the use of JIT systems in services later. Managerial Practice 15.1 describes how one U.S. company used JIT to gain continuous improvements in operations.

Managerial Practice 15.1

▶ *Continuous Improvement at Northern Telecom*

Northern Telecom, which began operations only eight years after Alexander Graham Bell invented the telephone, produces central office switching equipment, transmission equipment, and private business exchanges (PBX) for the telephone industry. In the late 1970s Northern Telecom entered an extended, vigorous growth period when it introduced the first fully digital switch. By 1984 sales were $2.5 billion, an increase of 1200 percent from eight years before. The work force increased by 1500 employees, and for three consecutive years, output doubled. Then, in 1985, competitors introduced fully digital switches of their own, and pressure increased to produce high-quality, more sophisticated products at low cost. Although Northern Telecom was coping with the new competitive environment and had already implemented a JIT production philosophy in some plants, management decided that long-term success required a complete reexamination of the production process. Continuous improvements were needed in many areas. Three of the areas the company addressed first were manufacturing process improvement, new product introduction and change, and procurement.

Manufacturing Process Improvement

Northern Telecom introduced total quality control (TQC), which involved training in quality control for supervisors and line employees. The company empowered employees to shut down the line when quality problems surfaced (*andon* system). Manufacturing lot sizes were reduced, and the line was instructed to pull material as needed, with a target lot size of one unit, rather than push a week's worth of inventory to the line.

New Product Introduction and Change

By introducing cross-functional product teams, Northern Telecom reduced the time required to bring a new product to market in some divisions by as much as 50 percent. The teams consisted of representatives of various functions, including design, manufacturing, and marketing. While a product was still in the design phase, the team shared ideas about what was commercially important or difficult to manufacture. Consequently, the teams resolved problems earlier than before, reducing the necessity of making costly design changes later.

Procurement

Northern Telecom reduced its suppliers from 9400 in 1984 to 2500 in 1988. To do so, one division designed a certification program whereby suppliers had to meet stringent standards; the entire company now uses the program. Some suppliers had to change their operations significantly to win Northern Telecom's business. In addition, the company worked closely with its suppliers to ensure that quality standards were met and would then pull materials directly from successful suppliers to the assembly line. This effort reduced the receiving cycle time from three weeks to just four hours, the incoming inspection staff from 47 to 24, and problems on the shop floor caused by defective materials by 97 percent.

The table below shows how continuous improvement efforts at Northern Telecom resulted in significant operational benefits. The percentages are relative to the year the first measure was taken. For example, the manufacturing cycle time for central office equipment in 1989 was only 25 percent of that in 1986. All percentages are approximate.

			Percentage		
Performance Measure	**1985**	**1986**	**1987**	**1988**	**1989**
Manufacturing cycle time					
Central office switches		100%	48%	27%	25%
Transmission equipment		100%	50%	37%	30%
PBX		100%	49%	33%	30%
Aggregate inventory	100%	100%	73%	72%	70%
Operations overhead	100%	80%	75%	75%	65%

Source: Roy Merrills, "How Northern Telecom Competes on Time," *Harvard Business Review* (July–August 1989), pp. 108–114.

◆ THE KANBAN SYSTEM

How is the flow of materials in a factory controlled in a JIT system?

One of the most publicized JIT systems is the kanban system developed by Toyota. **Kanban,** meaning "card" or "visible record" in Japanese, refers to cards used to control the flow of production through a factory. In the most basic kanban system, a card is attached to each container of items that have been produced. This card represents a percentage of the daily requirements for an item. When the user of the parts empties a container, the card is removed from the container and put on a receiving post. The empty container is taken to the storage area. The card signals the need to produce another container of the part. When a container has been refilled, the card is put on the container, which is then returned to a storage area. The cycle begins again when the user of the parts retrieves the container with the card attached.

Toyota uses a two-card system, based on a withdrawal card and a production-order card, to control withdrawal quantities more closely. The withdrawal card specifies the item and the quantity the user of the item should withdraw from the producer of the item, as well as the stocking locations for both the user and the producer. The production-order card specifies the item and the production quantity to be produced, the materials required and where to find them, and where to store the finished item. Materials cannot be withdrawn without a withdrawal card, and production cannot begin without a production-order card. The cards are attached to containers when production commences. Figure 15.3 illustrates the two-card system. The container (red arrow) travels between the assembly line and the fabrication cell. The withdrawal card (green arrow) is used to get

FIGURE 15.3

Two-Card Kanban System

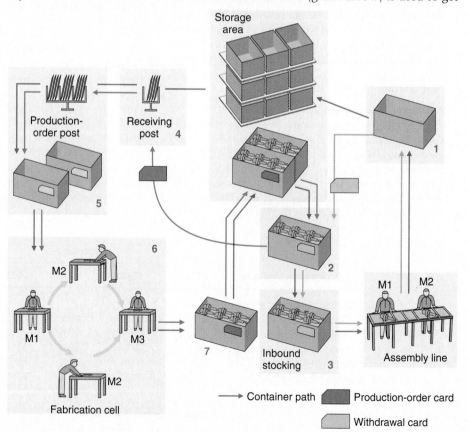

Container path →   ■ Production-order card

□ Withdrawal card

more materials for the assembly line. The production card (blue arrow) authorizes the fabrication cell to produce more parts and travels with the container.

For simplicity we describe a fabrication process that feeds an assembly line. Keep in mind, though, that the system works for any process that feeds another process. In all, seven steps are required, involving two loops—one for each type of card.

Step 1. Accumulated empty containers, with withdrawal cards attached, are taken from the assembly line to the storage area. Withdrawal cards are detached from the containers and retained for future reference (step 3).

Step 2. The empty containers are exchanged for full ones. The production-order card on each full container is detached and placed on the receiving post.

Step 3. The contents of the full containers are checked against the specifications on the withdrawal card, and if they are satisfactory, a withdrawal card is attached to each full container. The containers are moved to the inbound stocking location of the assembly line. This step completes the loop for the withdrawal card.

Step 4. The production sequence at the fabrication cell begins with removal of the production-order cards from the receiving post. They are reviewed and sorted before being placed on the production-order post.

Step 5. The parts are produced in the sequence of the production-order cards on the post. Production-order cards are attached to empty containers and taken to the fabrication cell.

Step 6. The production-order card and the container move as a pair through the fabrication process.

Step 7. In the last step the finished units are transported to the storage area to support the production requirements of the assembly line. This completes the loop for the production-order card.

All workstation and supplier tasks are coordinated similarly to provide just-in-time quantities of materials.

General Operating Rules

The operating rules for the two-card system are simple and are designed to facilitate the flow of materials, while maintaining control of inventory levels.

1. Each container must have a card.
2. The assembly line always withdraws materials from the fabrication cell. The fabrication cell never pushes parts to the assembly line because, sooner or later, parts will be supplied that are not yet needed for production.
3. Containers of parts must never be removed from a storage area without an authorizing withdrawal card.
4. The containers should always contain the same number of good parts. The use of nonstandard containers or irregularly filled containers disrupts the production flow of the assembly line.
5. Only nondefective parts should be passed along to the assembly line to make the best use of materials and workers' time.

6. Total production should not exceed the total amount authorized on the production-order cards in the system. Similarly, the quantity of parts withdrawn by the assembly line should not exceed the total amount authorized on the withdrawal cards in the system.

Determining the Number of Containers (Kanban Card Sets)

The number of authorized containers in a JIT system determines the amount of authorized inventory. Management must make two determinations: (1) the size of the containers and (2) the number of containers flowing back and forth between the supplier station and the user station. The first decision amounts to determining the lot size and may be compared to calculating the economic order quantity (EOQ).

The number of containers flowing back and forth between two stations directly affects the quantities of work-in-process inventory and safety stock. The containers spend some time in production, in a line waiting, in a storage location, or in transit. The key to determining the number of containers required is to estimate accurately the average lead time needed to produce a container of parts. The lead time is a function of the processing time per container at the supplier station, the waiting time during the production process, and the time required for materials handling. The number of containers needed to support the user station equals the average demand during the lead time plus some safety stock to account for unexpected circumstances, divided by the size of one container. Because a container cannot be withdrawn from storage without a withdrawal card and its replacement cannot be produced without a production-order card, determining the number of containers amounts to determining the number of kanban card sets (one of each type per container). Therefore the number of kanban card sets is

$$k = \frac{\text{Average demand during lead time } plus \text{ safety stock}}{\text{Size of container}}$$

$$= \frac{d(\overline{w} + \overline{p})(1 + \alpha)}{c}$$

where k = number of production-order/withdrawal card sets for a part

d = expected daily demand for the part, in units

$\overline{w}$ = average waiting time during the production process plus materials handling time per container, in fractions of a day

$\overline{p}$ = average processing time per container, in fractions of a day

c = quantity in a standard container of the part

α = a policy variable that reflects the efficiency of the workstations producing and using the part (Toyota uses a value of no more than 10 percent)

The kanban system allows management to fine-tune the flow of materials in the system in a straightforward way. For example, removing card sets from the system reduces the number of authorized containers of the part, thus reducing the inventory of the part.

The container quantity, c, and the efficiency factor, α, are variables that management can use to control inventory. Adjusting c changes the lot sizes, and adjusting α changes the amount of safety stock. The kanban system actually is a special form of the base-stock system described in Chapter 12. In this case, the stocking level is $d(\overline{w} + \overline{p})(1 + \alpha)$, and the order quantity is fixed at c units. Each time a container of parts is removed from the base stock, authorization is given to replace it.

EXAMPLE 15.1

Determining the Appropriate Number of Kanban Card Sets

The Westerville Auto Parts Company produces rocker-arm assemblies for use in the steering and suspension systems of four-wheel-drive trucks. A typical container of parts spends 0.02 day in processing and 0.08 day in materials handling and waiting during its manufacturing cycle. The daily demand for the part is 2000 units. Management believes that demand for the rocker-arm assembly is uncertain enough to warrant a safety stock equivalent of 10 percent of its authorized inventory.

    a. If there are 22 parts in each container, how many kanban card sets (production-order and withdrawal cards) should be authorized?

    b. Suppose that a proposal to revise the plant layout would cut materials handling and waiting time per container to 0.06 day. How many card sets would be needed?

Solution

    a. If $d = 2000$ units/day, $\overline{p} = 0.02$ day, $\alpha = 0.10$, $\overline{w} = 0.08$ day, and $c = 22$ units,

$$k = \frac{2000(0.08 + 0.02)(1.10)}{22} = \frac{220}{22} = 10 \text{ card sets}$$

    b. If $d = 2000$ units/day, $\overline{p} = 0.02$ day, $\alpha = 0.10$, $\overline{w} = 0.06$ day, and $c = 22$ units,

$$k = \frac{2000(0.06 + 0.02)(1.10)}{22} = \frac{176}{22} = 8 \text{ card sets}$$

    The average lead time per container is $\overline{w} + \overline{p}$. With a lead time of 0.10 day, 10 card sets are needed. However, if the improved facility layout reduces the materials handling time and waiting time, $\overline{w}$, to 0.06 day, only 8 card sets are needed. The maximum authorized inventory of the rocker-arm assembly is kc units. Thus in part a the maximum authorized inventory is 220 units, but in part b it is only 176 units. Reducing $\overline{w} + \overline{p}$ by 20 percent has reduced the inventory of the part by 20 percent.

Other Kanban Signals

Cards aren't the only way to signal the need for more production of a part. Other, less formal methods are possible, including container and containerless systems.

Container System.   Sometimes the container itself can be used as a signal device: An empty container signals the need to fill it. The amount of inventory of the part is adjusted by adding or removing containers. This system works well when the container is specially designed for a part and no other parts could accidentally be put in it. Such is the case when the container is actually a pallet or fixture used to position the part during precision processing.

Containerless System.   Systems requiring no containers have been devised. In assembly-line operations, operators having their own workbench areas put completed units on painted squares, one unit per square. Each painted square represents a container, and the number of painted squares on each operator's bench is calculated to balance the line flow. When the subsequent user removes a unit from one of the producer's squares, the empty square signals the need to produce another unit.

McDonald's uses a containerless system. A command from the manager or the final assembler starts production, or the number of hamburgers in the ramp itself signals the need. Either way, the customer dictates production.

◆ JIT II®

The JIT II concept was conceived and implemented by the Bose Corporation, producer of high-quality professional sound systems and speaker systems. In a JIT II system, the supplier is brought into the plant to be an active member of the purchasing office of the customer. The *in-plant representative* is on site full time at the supplier's expense and is empowered to use customer purchase orders. Typically, the representative's duties include

- issuing purchase orders to his or her own firms on behalf of Bose,
- working on design ideas to help save costs and improve manufacturing processes, and
- managing production schedules for suppliers, materials contractors, and other subcontractors.

The in-plant representative replaces the buyer, the salesperson, and sometimes the materials planner in a typical JIT arrangement. Thus JIT II fosters extremely close interaction with suppliers. Bose started the system in 1987, and by 1992 there were nine in-plant representatives billing about 25 percent of the total purchasing budget. Although more representatives will be added, the qualifications for a supplier to be included in the program are stringent.

In general, JIT II offers the following benefits to the customer.

- Liberated from administrative tasks, the purchasing staff is able to work on improving efficiencies in other areas of procurement.
- Communication and purchase order placement are improved dramatically.
- The cost of materials is reduced immediately, and the savings are ongoing.
- Preferred suppliers are brought into the product design process earlier.
- A natural foundation is provided for electronic data interchange (EDI), effective paperwork, and administrative savings.

In general, JIT II offers the following benefits to the supplier.

- It eliminates sales effort.
- Communication and purchase order placement are improved dramatically.

- The volume of business rises at the start of the program and continues to grow as new products are introduced.
- An evergreen contract is provided, with no end date and no rebidding.
- The supplier can communicate with and sell directly to engineering.
- Invoicing and payment administration are efficient.

Thus JIT II is an advance over other just-in-time systems because it provides the organizational structure needed to improve supplier coordination by integrating the logistics, production, and purchasing processes.

◆ JUST-IN-TIME SYSTEMS IN SERVICES

How can JIT systems be used in a service environment?

The just-in-time philosophy also can be applied to the production of services. We have already discussed some of the elements of the JIT system used in a McDonald's restaurant. In general, service environments may benefit from JIT systems if their operations are repetitive, have reasonably high volumes, and deal with tangible items such as sandwiches, mail, checks, or bills. In other words, the services must involve "manufacturinglike" operations. Other services involving a high degree of customization, such as haircutting, can also make use of JIT systems but to a lesser degree—basically utilizing elements of JIT systems in their operations.

The focus of JIT systems is on improving the process; therefore some of the JIT concepts useful for manufacturers are also useful for service providers. These concepts include the following.

- *Consistently high quality.* Benchmarking, service design, and quality function deployment can be used successfully in service operations. Service employees can be taught the value of providing defect-free services.
- *Uniform facility loads.* Reservation systems and differential pricing are two ways in which service providers can level the loads on their facilities.
- *Standardized work methods.* In highly repetitive service operations great efficiencies can be gained by analyzing work methods and standardizing improvements for all employees to use. For example, UPS consistently monitors work methods and revises them as necessary to improve service.
- *Close supplier ties.* Volume services such as fast-food restaurants and mass merchandisers such as Wal-Mart and Kmart require close supplier contacts to ensure frequent, short lead time and high-quality shipments of supplies.
- *Flexible work force.* The more customized the service, the greater is the need for a multiskilled work force. For example, stereo component repair shops require broadly trained personnel who can identify a wide variety of problems and then repair the defective unit. The employees at a sectional center post office have more narrowly defined jobs because of the repetitive nature of the tasks they must perform, and thus they do not have to acquire many alternative skills.
- *Automation.* Automation can play a big role in providing just-in-time services. For example, banks offer ATMs that provide various bank services on demand 24 hours a day.

Managerial Practice 15.2

▶ *Implementing a JIT System at Security Pacific*

The External Mail Services section of the Security Pacific Corporation processes approximately 5 million customer statements, notices, and other mailings monthly. Seven million checks must be sorted, enclosed in envelopes with statements, and mailed to 190,000 customers. Of this total, 30,000 customer statements have so many checks that they must be prepared manually.

In the spring of 1989, management decided to reduce the processing time and improve the accuracy of the 30,000 manually prepared month-end statements. Instead of taking the traditional approach of adding employees and quality inspectors, which would increase costs, management decided to redesign the system, incorporating JIT concepts.

Figure 15.4 shows the manual system design in 1989. Each check passed through four workstations:

1. *Marp (mismatch account report) table and check-filing area.* When the automatic sorter rejected checks because the magnetic ink encoding was unreadable, a report was generated that alerted a staff member to hand-sort the checks and file them in the correct customer account. They were then carted to the setup table.
2. *Setup table.* A clerk placed the corresponding printed statements for each batch of checks at the back of the tray. One tray, or lot size, could have thousands of items. The trays were moved to the statement stuffing cubicles.
3. *Statement cubicles.* Clerks matched checks with statements and inserted them into envelopes for mailing. The envelopes were moved to the metering area.

4. *Electronic scales and metering area.* The envelopes were weighed on electronic scales (e-scales) and posted.

The original system for the manually prepared statements created several problems. Statements had to travel 240 feet from first handling to final metering. Processing clerks had to walk from 10 to 30 feet to get more work or to deposit their output at the next station. In addition, several bottlenecks existed. Typically, 10,000 statements were in line at the marp/file area and 7500 customer accounts at the setup area. Metering commonly had 13,500 statements waiting for processing. Clearly, a better way had to be found.

Figure 15.5 shows the system after Security Pacific implemented a product focus. With the setup table placed near the marp and file area, carts now travel only 3 to 10 feet to the setup station, whereas in the past they had to travel 120 feet. Lot sizes were reduced to 250 statements per tray. This design facilitated a balanced staffing plan—two setup staff keep pace with five to six stuffing staff, who keep pace with two electronic scale operators. Work flows without a large buildup because it goes from station to station, usually by hand-off from one worker to the next.

Security Pacific realized the following benefits from implementing JIT concepts.

- Mail processing time was reduced by 33 percent.
- Mismatches were reduced by 94 percent.
- Salary costs were reduced by $32,400 annually.
- Floor space was reduced by 50 percent.
- In-process waiting lines were reduced by 75 to 90 percent.

Source: Paul Jackson, "White Collar JIT at Security Pacific," *Target*, vol. 7, no. 1 (Spring 1991), pp. 32–37. Figures reprinted with permission of the Association for Manufacturing Excellence, Wheeling, Ill.

- *Preventive maintenance.* Services that are highly dependent on machinery can make good use of routine preventive maintenance. For example, entertainment services such as Walt Disney World must have dependable people-moving apparatus to accommodate large volumes of customers.
- *Pull method of material flows.* Service operations where tangible items are processed, such as fast-food restaurants, can utilize the pull method.

FIGURE 15.4 *Manual Statement Stuffing—Security Pacific*

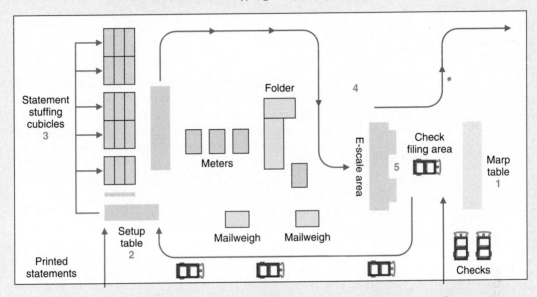

FIGURE 15.5 *Manual Statement Stuffing—Post JIT System Implementation*

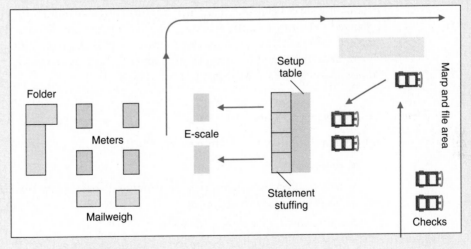

- *Product focus.* Managers of service operations can organize their employees and equipment to provide uniform flows through the system and eliminate wasted employee time. Managerial Practice 15.2 shows how the reorganization of the check-sorting operation played a major role in the implementation of a JIT system at a bank.

◆ STRATEGIC IMPLICATIONS OF JUST-IN-TIME SYSTEMS

When corporate strategy centers on dramatic improvements in inventory turnover and labor productivity, just-in-time systems can be the solution. Such systems form an integral part of corporate strategies emphasizing time-based competition because they focus on cutting cycle times, improving inventory turnover, and increasing labor productivity. In this section we consider competitive priorities and positioning strategy, as well as the overall benefits of JIT systems.

Competitive Priorities

Low cost and consistent quality are the priorities emphasized most often in JIT systems. Superior features and volume flexibility are emphasized less often. The ability to provide product variety depends on the degree of flexibility designed into the production system. For example, mixed-model automobile assembly lines allow variety in output from the standpoint of color, options, and even body style. Production to customized, individual orders, however, usually isn't attempted with a JIT system. Generally, end items are standards rather than specials, preproduced to inventory in support of a shipping schedule. The erratic demand and last-minute rush jobs of customized orders don't link well with a system designed to produce at a constant daily rate utilizing low inventory buffers.

Positioning Strategy

A just-in-time strategy involves a product focus to achieve high-volume, low-cost production. Workers and machines are organized around product flows and arranged to conform to the sequence of work operations. With line flows, a unit finished at one station goes almost immediately to the next station, thereby reducing manufacturing lead time and inventory. Process repetition makes opportunities for methods improvement more visible.

Operational Benefits

JIT systems have many operational benefits. They

- reduce space requirements;
- reduce inventory investment in purchased parts, raw materials, work in process, and finished goods;
- reduce manufacturing lead times;
- increase the productivity of direct labor employees, indirect support employees, and clerical staff;
- increase equipment utilization;
- reduce paperwork and require only simple planning systems;
- set valid priorities for production scheduling;
- encourage participation by the work force; and
- increase product quality.

One goal is to drive setup times so low that production of one end unit or part becomes economical. Although this goal is rarely achieved, the focus still is on small-lot production. In addition, constant attention is given to cutting safety stock and WIP inventory between manufacturing processes. The result is less need for storage space and inventory investment. Smaller lot sizes and smoothed flows of materials help reduce manufacturing lead times, increase work-force productivity, and improve equipment utilization.

A major operational benefit is the simplicity of the system: Product mix or volume changes planned by the MPS can be accomplished by adjusting the number of card sets in the system. The priority of each production order is reflected in the sequence of the production-order cards on the post. Production orders for parts that are running low are placed before those for parts that have more supply.

Just-in-time systems also involve a considerable amount of work-force participation on the shop floor. Small-group interaction sessions encourage worker participation and have resulted in improvements in many aspects of manufacturing, not the least of which is product quality. Overall, the advantages of JIT systems have caused many managers to reevaluate their own systems and consider adapting operations to the JIT philosophy.

◆ IMPLEMENTATION ISSUES

What can be done to make employees more receptive to the changes associated with just-in-time systems?

The benefits of JIT systems seem to be outstanding, yet problems can arise even after a JIT system has long been operational. Even the Japanese, who pioneered JIT practices in the automobile industry, aren't immune from problems: Tokyo is experiencing monumental traffic jams owing in large measure to truck deliveries to JIT manufacturers—small trucks make up 47 percent of Tokyo's traffic. In this section we address some of the issues managers should be aware of when implementing a JIT system.

Organizational Considerations

Implementing a JIT system requires management to consider issues of worker stress, cooperation and trust among workers and management, and reward systems and labor classifications.

Human Costs of JIT Systems.   Just-in-time systems can be coupled with statistical process control (SPC) to reduce variations in production. However, this combination requires a high degree of regimentation and sometimes causes stress in the work force. In a JIT system, workers must meet specified cycle times, and with SPC they must follow prescribed problem-solving methods. Such systems might make workers feel pushed and stressed, causing productivity losses or quality reductions. In addition, workers might feel that they have lost some autonomy because of the close linkages in material flows between stations with little or no safety stocks. Managers can mitigate some of these effects by allowing slack in the system through the judicious use of safety stock inventories and by emphasizing material flows instead of worker pace. Managers also can promote the use of work teams and allow them to determine their task assignments or rotations within the team's domain of responsibility.

Cooperation and Trust. In a JIT system workers and first-line supervisors must take on responsibilities formerly assigned to middle managers and support staff. Activities such as scheduling, expediting, and improving productivity become part of the duties of lower-level personnel. Consequently, organizational relationships must be reoriented to build close cooperation and mutual trust between the work force and management. Such cooperation and trust may be difficult to achieve, particularly in light of the typical adversarial positions taken by labor and management in the past. For example, the Mazda plant in Flat Rock, Michigan, was experiencing quality problems in August 1988. Greater absenteeism than the Japanese expected and inexperience of the work force were cited as major contributors. Some people felt that the real problem was a lack of understanding of the American culture by Japanese managers. As the president of UAW Local 3000 put it, "To the Japanese, work is the most important part of life, and they expect everybody to be as dedicated as they are. But to Americans, the job is there to support your life on the outside."

Reward Systems and Labor Classifications. In some instances the reward system must be revamped when a JIT system is implemented. At General Motors, for example, a plan to reduce stock at one plant ran into trouble because the production superintendent refused to cut back production of unneeded parts; his salary was based on his plant's production volume.

The realignment of reward systems isn't the only hurdle. Labor contracts traditionally have reduced management's flexibility in reassigning workers as the need arises. A typical automobile plant in the United States has several unions and dozens of labor classifications. To gain more flexibility, management in some cases has obtained union concessions by granting other types of benefits. In other cases management has relocated plants to take advantage of nonunion or foreign labor. In contrast, at Toyota management deals with only one company union, and there are only eight different labor classifications in a typical plant.

Process Considerations

Firms using JIT systems typically have a product focus or at least some dominant material flows. To take advantage of JIT practices, firms might have to change their existing layouts, as did Security Pacific. Certain workstations might have to be moved closer together, and cells of machines devoted to particular families of components. A survey of 68 firms using JIT systems indicated that the single most important factor in successful implementation is changing product flows and layout to a cellular design (Billesbach, 1991). However, rearranging a plant to conform to JIT practices can be costly. For example, whereas many plants now receive raw materials and purchased parts by rail, to facilitate smaller, more frequent JIT shipments, truck deliveries would be preferable. Loading docks might have to be reconstructed or expanded and certain operations relocated to accommodate the change in transportation mode and quantities of arriving materials.

Inventory and Scheduling

Firms need to have stable master production schedules, short setups, and frequent, reliable supplies of materials and components to achieve the full potential of the JIT concept.

MPS Stability. Daily production schedules must be stable for extended periods. At Toyota the master production schedule is stated in fractions of days over a three-month period and is revised only once a month. The first month of the schedule is frozen to avoid disruptive changes in the daily production schedule for each workstation; that is, the workstations execute the same work schedule each day of the month. At the beginning of each month, card sets are reissued for the new daily production rate. Stable schedules are needed so that production lines can be balanced and new assignments found for employees who otherwise would be underutilized. The JIT system cannot respond quickly to scheduling changes because little slack inventory or capacity is available to absorb these changes.

Setups. If the inventory advantages of a JIT system are to be realized, small container sizes must be used. However, because small containers require a large number of setups, companies must significantly reduce setup times. Some companies haven't been able to achieve short setup times and therefore have to use large-lot production, negating some of the advantages of JIT practices. Also, JIT systems are vulnerable to lengthy changeovers to new products because of the low levels of finished goods inventory. For example, Ford and GM are at a competitive disadvantage because of the time they need to change from one year's model to the next. GM required 87 days to change from the 1994 Chevrolet Lumina to the 1995 model, and Ford required 60 days to change from the 1994 Tempo to the Mystique, its 1995 replacement. In contrast, Toyota changed from the 1991 Camry to the 1992 version in 18 days, and Honda switched from the 1993 Accord to the 1994 model in only 3 days. Every month that a plant is shut down costs between $65 million and $85 million in pretax profits.

Purchasing and Logistics. If frequent, small shipments of purchased items cannot be arranged with suppliers, large inventory savings for these items can't be realized. In the United States such arrangements may prove difficult because of the geographic dispersion of suppliers.

The shipments of raw materials and components must be reliable because of the low inventory levels in JIT systems. A plant can be shut down because of a lack of materials. For example, in 1992, a strike at the GM plant in Lordstown, Ohio, caused the Saturn plant in Spring Hill, Tennessee, to shut down, losing the production of 1000 cars per day. Lordstown supplies parts to Saturn, which doesn't stockpile the parts because of JIT practices.

◆ CHOICE OF A PRODUCTION AND INVENTORY MANAGEMENT SYSTEM

What are the critical factors to consider in choosing a production and inventory control system?

In earlier chapters we presented the reorder point (ROP) system and the material requirements planning (MRP) system, and in this chapter we discussed just-in-time systems. Obviously, management has several systems from which to choose—and more will become available in the future. In this section we briefly compare these production and inventory systems and share some insights regarding how well these systems work in various environments.

Reorder Point Versus Material Requirements Planning Systems

The MRP system outperforms the ROP system in discrete-item manufacturing environments producing to stock, an advantage that increases as the number of levels in the bills of materials increases. Because the gross requirements of a component are the planned order releases of its parents, component gross requirements tend to become very lumpy, thereby deviating from the assumptions of the ROP system. The more levels in a system, the lumpier are the requirements at the bottom of the bills of materials because lot sizes tend to increase. Even when the two systems are compared for the same number of levels in the bills of materials, MRP's advantages over ROP increase as lot sizes increase. In general, MRP is the obvious choice unless lot sizes are small, there are few BOM levels, and demand requirements are stable.

Material Requirements Planning Versus Just-in-Time Systems

Is a choice between a push system and a pull system necessary? Actually, these methods aren't mutually exclusive, and the best solution often is a hybrid of the strengths of both approaches (Karmarkar, 1989). MRP II systems are good at overall materials planning and data management and can be used to support the informational needs of various functional areas in the firm. MRP systems can be used effectively to understand the implications of lot-sizing decisions and master scheduling changes on overall inventories and capacity. In contrast, JIT systems are a less expensive, more effective way to control material flows on the shop floor. A kanban system can be used to maintain low levels of inventory and to adjust production rates over time.

The nature of the production process determines the appropriate system. For line flows, order releases don't change from week to week, so a rate-based system such as JIT works well. Although MRP is an effective technique for scheduling production on a weekly basis, scheduling of daily requirements within each specific week is left to production supervisors. At this level, the shop floor level, a pull system is more useful than MRP. In a repetitive manufacturing environment with reasonably stable but varying schedules, a hybrid system may be appropriate. MRP could be used for order release, as schedules change, or for coordinating with suppliers on long-lead-time items. Pull methods could be used for actual material flows on the shop floor. Names such as synchro-MRP, rate-based MRP II, and JIT-MRP have been used to describe these hybrid systems.

In job shop environments, where material flows are complex and demands are highly variable, MRP is the system of choice. The material flows are too complex for a JIT system, and pull techniques can't cope with the demand and lead time variability. In addition, the shop floor requires sophisticated tracking and scheduling capability.

◆ THE MANUFACTURING ENVIRONMENT

In general, although the ROP, MRP, and JIT systems work well in certain environments, they may not work well in others. The choice of a system can affect inventory levels and customer service. High inventory levels strain a company's financial resources and can limit its capability to invest in needed capital improvements. Poor customer service affects market share and the company's ability to compete in the marketplace. Installing an inappropriate system can be an expensive mistake.

We have identified several specific factors of manufacturing that affect inventory investment, productivity, and customer service. Studies have concluded that reduced lot sizes and setup times have the greatest impact, followed by reduced yield losses and increased worker flexibility (Ritzman, King, and Krajewski, 1984). Firms can improve on these factors regardless of the system. Other aspects of manufacturing, such as capacity slack or safety stock, bills of materials, facility design, and supplier performance, have less impact on performance.

Nonetheless, firms should "get their houses in order" by working to improve these environmental factors for whatever production and inventory system they use. For example, reducing lot sizes and setup times will decrease investment and improve customer service, regardless of the system being used. The point is that any production and inventory system by itself will not set things right, but significant improvements in performance *can* be achieved by shaping manufacturing environments properly. A focus on continuous improvement is a key to shaping a manufacturing environment.

CHAPTER REVIEW

Solved Problem

A company using a kanban system has an inefficient machine group. For example, the daily demand for part L105A is 3000 units. The average waiting time for a container of parts is 0.8 day. The processing time for a container of L105A is 0.2 day, and a container holds 270 units. Currently, there are 20 kanban card sets for this item.

a. What is the value of the policy variable, α?
b. What is the total planned inventory (work in process and finished goods) for item L105A?
c. Suppose that the policy variable α were 0. How many card sets would be needed now? What is the effect of the policy variable in this example?

Solution a. We use the equation for the number of card sets and then solve for α:

$$k = \frac{d(\overline{w} + \overline{p})(1 + \alpha)}{c}$$

$$= \frac{3000(0.8 + 0.2)(1 + \alpha)}{270} = 20$$

and

$$(1 + \alpha) = \frac{20(270)}{3000(0.8 + 0.2)} = 1.8$$

$$\alpha = 1.8 - 1 = 0.8$$

b. With 20 card sets in the system and each container holding 270 units, the total planned inventory is $20(270) = 5400$ units.

c. If $\alpha = 0$,

$$k = \frac{3000(0.8 + 0.2)(1 + 0)}{270} = 11.11, \quad \text{or 12 card sets}$$

The policy variable adjusts the number of card sets. In this case the difference is quite dramatic because $\overline{w} + \overline{p}$ is fairly large and the container size is small relative to daily demand.

Formula Review

1. Number of kanban card sets:

$$k = \frac{\text{Average demand during lead time} + \text{Safety stock}}{\text{Size of container}}$$

$$= \frac{d(\overline{w} + \overline{p})(1 + \alpha)}{c}$$

Chapter Highlights

- Just-in-time systems are designed to produce or deliver just the right products or services in just the right quantities just in time to serve subsequent production processes or customers.

- Some of the key elements of JIT systems are a pull method to manage material flow, consistently high quality, small lot sizes, short setup times, uniform workstation loads, standardized components and work methods, close supplier ties, flexible work force, product focus, automated production, preventive maintenance, and continuous improvement.

- A two-card kanban system uses withdrawal and production-order card sets to control production flow. The authorized inventory of a part is a function of the number of authorized cards for that item. The number of cards depends on average demand during manufacturing lead time, the container size, and a policy variable to adjust for unexpected occurrences. Many other methods may be used to signal the need for material replenishment and production.

- The JIT II® system provides an organizational structure for improved supplier coordination by integrating the logistics, production, and purchasing processes.

- Just-in-time concepts have been applied to the production of services. Service organizations that have repetitive operations, maintain reasonably high volume, and deal with some tangible item are most likely to benefit from JIT practices.

- For operations having a product focus and competing on the basis of low cost and consistent quality, JIT system advantages include reductions in inventory, space requirements, and paperwork and increases in productivity, worker participation, and quality. However, implementation is such a massive task that organizations tend not to accept this challenge until bankruptcy becomes the only alternative. JIT systems require fundamental changes in the way *all* of the business functions are performed. Increasing cooperation and trust between management and labor, basing rewards on team rather than individual performance, and replacing adversarial supplier relationships with partnerships are some of the basic cultural changes involved in JIT system implementation.

- Reorder point, MRP, and JIT systems are the most common of the available choices for a production and inventory system, but they do not constitute an all-inclusive list. New approaches become available continually. Reducing lot sizes and setup times will decrease inventory investment, improve customer service, and increase productivity, regardless of the system in use.

Key Terms

just-in-time (JIT) systems 722
kanban 732

mixed-model assembly 726
pull method 723

push method 723
single-digit setup 726

Study Questions

1. Why is a JIT system considered a *pull system?* What competitive advantages do pull systems have over push systems?

2. Theory X states that employees resist work and that management must closely supervise them or they will accomplish nothing. Theory Y states that employees desire work and that management should empower employees to direct their own activities. Describe how push systems and pull systems relate to these theories.

3. Toyota's kanban system utilizes two main types of cards that authorize certain actions. Explain the purposes of these cards and describe how they are used.

4. Consider the formula for determining the number of kanban card sets for an item. If the process for that item is *inefficient,* which parameters in the equation might be larger than desirable? Why? If a supervisor wanted to increase the safety stock, which parameter would be adjusted?

5. In the ROP system the amount of safety stock depends on the standard deviation of demand during the lead time and the desired cycle-service level. How is safety stock determined in the kanban system?

6. What process is used in a JIT system to identify areas for improvement?

7. Why is a stable master production schedule essential to JIT systems? What options are available for changing production rates?

8. When JIT production goes well and the daily quota has been completed before the end of the shift, production is stopped for the rest of the day, but workers aren't sent home early. Why don't the lines continue production? Why aren't workers sent home?

9. Consider the statement "The just-in-time system is a total managerial concept, whereas the kanban system and systems like it are merely information systems designed to provide the basis for the timing and lot-sizing decisions of production quantities." Do you agree or disagree? Why?

10. What factors should management consider when deciding whether to use a JIT system in a particular manufacturing environment?

11. What are the similarities and dissimilarities of JIT applications in service firms and in manufacturing firms?

12. Some workers in JIT systems feel increased stress. What are the sources of this stress? Are push systems less stressful than pull systems? Why or why not?

13. Why does the choice of a production and inventory system have implications for the firm as a whole?

Discussion Questions

1. Compare and contrast the following two situations.
   a. A company's JIT system stresses teamwork. Employees feel more involved, and therefore productivity and quality have increased. Yet one of the problems in implementing the JIT system has been the loss of individual autonomy.
   b. A humanities professor believes that all students desire to learn. To encourage students to work together and learn from each other, thereby increasing involvement, productivity, and the quality of the learning experience, the professor announces that all students in the class will receive the same grade and it will be based on the performance of the group.

2. Which elements of JIT systems would be most troublesome for U.S. manufacturers to implement? Why?

Problems

1. The Hama motorcycle company produces three models: the Llama, a sure-footed dirt bike; the Yoka, a nimble cafe racer; and the Mama, a large interstate tourer. This month's master production schedule calls for the production of 54 Mamas, 42 Yokas, and 30 Llamas per seven-hour shift.
   a. What average cycle time for the assembly line to achieve the production quota in seven hours is required?
   b. If mixed-model scheduling is used, how many of each model will be produced before the production cycle is repeated?
   c. Determine a satisfactory production sequence for the ultimate in small-lot production: one unit.
   d. The design of a new model, the Hemn Hama, includes features from the Llama, Yoka, and Mama models. The resulting blended design has an indecisive character and is expected to attract some sales from the other models. Determine a mixed-model schedule resulting in 52 Mamas, 39 Yokas, 26 Llamas, and 13 Hemns per seven-hour shift. Although the total number of motorcycles produced per day will increase only slightly, what problem might be anticipated in implementing this change from the production schedule indicated in part b?

2. A fabrication cell at Spradley's Sprockets uses the pull method to supply gears to an assembly line. George Jitson is in charge of the assembly line, which requires 500 gears per day. Containers typically wait 0.20 day in the fabrication cell. Each container holds 20 gears,

and one container requires 1.8 days in machine time. Setup times are negligible. If the policy variable for unforeseen contingencies is set at 5 percent, how many card sets should Jitson authorize for the gear replenishment system?

3. You have been asked to analyze the kanban system of Le Jit, a French manufacturer of gaming devices. One of the workstations feeding the assembly line produces part K669B. The daily demand for K669B is 2000 units. The average processing time per unit is 0.001 day. Le Jit's records show that the average container spends 1.10 days waiting at the feeder workstation. The container for K669B can hold 270 units. Eleven card sets are authorized for the part. Recall that $\bar{p}$ is the average processing time per container, not per individual part.

   a. Find the value of the policy variable (α) that expresses the amount of implied safety stock in this system.

   b. Use the implied value of α from part a to determine the required reduction in waiting time if one card set were removed. Assume that all other parameters remain constant.

4. An assembly line requires two components: gadjits and widjits. Gadjits are produced by center 1 and widjits by center 2. Each unit of the end item, called a jit-together, requires 3 gadjits and 2 widjits, as shown in Fig. 15.6. The daily production quota on the assembly line is 800 jit-togethers.

FIGURE 15.6

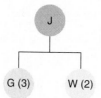

The container for gadjits holds 80 units. The policy variable for center 1 is set at 0.09. The average waiting time for a container of gadjits is 0.09 day, and 0.06 day is needed to produce a container. The container for widjits holds 50 units, and the policy variable for center 2 is 0.08. The average waiting time per container of widgits is 0.14 day, and the time required to process a container is 0.20 day.

   a. How many kanban card sets are needed for gadjits?

   b. How many kanban card sets are needed for widjits?

5. Gestalt, Inc. uses a kanban system in its automobile production facility in Germany. This facility operates eight hours per day to produce the Jitterbug, a replacement for the obsolete but immensely popular Jitney Beetle. Suppose that a certain part requires 150 seconds of processing at machine cell 33B and a container of parts averages 2.4 hours of waiting time there. Management has allowed a 10 percent buffer

for unexpected occurrences. Each container holds 20 parts, and 10 card sets are authorized. How much daily demand can be satisfied with this system? *Hint:* Recall that $\bar{p}$ is the average processing time per container, not per individual part.

6. A jittery U.S. Postal Service supervisor is looking for ways to reduce stress in the sorting department. With the existing arrangement, stamped letters are machine-canceled and loaded into tubs with 480 letters per tub. The tubs are then pushed to postal clerks, who read and key zip codes into an automated sorting machine at the rate of one tub per 480 seconds. To overcome the stress caused when the stamp canceling machine outpaces the sorting clerks, a pull system is proposed. When the clerks are ready to process another tub of mail, they will pull the tub from the canceling machine area. How many tubs should circulate between the sorting clerks and the canceling machine if 120,000 letters are to be sorted during an eight-hour shift, the safety stock policy variable, α, is 0.2, and the average waiting time plus materials handling time is 40 minutes per tub?

7. The master schedule at Isuzu calls for 1320 Isuzus to be produced during each of 22 production days in January and 960 Isuzus to be produced during each of 20 production days in February. Isuzu uses a two-card kanban system to communicate with Gesundheit, a nearby supplier of tires. Isuzu purchases four tires per vehicle from Gesundheit. The safety stock policy variable, α, is 0.15. The container (a delivery truck) size is 200 tires. The average waiting time plus materials handling time is 0.16 day per container. Assembly lines are rebalanced at the beginning of each month. The average processing time per container in January is 0.10 day. February processing time will average 0.125 day per container. How many kanban card sets should be authorized for January? How many for February?

8. Jitsmart uses a special case of the base stock system (see Chapter 12) to manage inventories of plastic action-figure toys. The action figures are purchased from Tacky Toys, Inc. and arrive in boxes of 48. Full boxes are stored on high shelves out of reach of customers. A small inventory is maintained on child-level shelves. Depletion of the lower-shelf inventory signals the need to take down a box of action figures to replenish the inventory. A reorder card is then removed from the box and sent to Tacky Toys to authorize replenishment of a container of action figures. The average demand rate for a popular action figure, Agent 99, is 36 units per day. The total lead time (waiting plus processing) is 11 days. Jitsmart's safety stock policy variable, α, is 0.25. What is the base stock level for Jitsmart?

CASE

Copper Kettle Catering

Copper Kettle Catering (CKC) is a full-service catering company that provides services ranging from box lunches for picnics or luncheon meetings to large wedding, dinner, or office parties. Established as a lunch delivery service for offices in 1972 by Wayne and Janet Williams, CKC has grown to be one of the largest catering businesses in Raleigh, North Carolina. The Williamses divide customer demand into two categories: *deliver only* and *deliver and serve*.

The deliver-only side of the business provides drop-off of boxed meals consisting of a sandwich, salad, dessert, and fruit. The menu for this service is limited to six sandwich selections, three salads or potato chips, and a brownie or fruit bar. Grapes and an orange slice are included with every meal, and iced tea can be ordered to accompany the meals. The overall level of demand for this service throughout the year is fairly constant, although the mix of menu items delivered varies. The planning horizon for this segment of the business is short: Customers usually call no more than a day ahead of time. CKC requires customers to call deliver-only orders in by 10:00 A.M. to guarantee delivery the same day.

The deliver-and-serve side of the business focuses on catering large parties, dinners, and weddings. The extensive range of menu items includes a full selection of hors d'oeuvres, entrées, beverages, and special-request items. The demand for these services is much more seasonal, with heavier demands occurring in the late spring–early summer for weddings and the late fall–early winter for holiday parties. However, this segment also has a longer planning horizon. Customers book dates and choose menu items weeks or months ahead of time.

Copper Kettle Company's food preparation facilities support both operations. The physical facilities layout resembles that of a job shop. There are five major work areas: a stove–oven area for hot food preparation, a cold area for salad preparation, an hors d'oeuvre preparation area, a sandwich preparation area, and an assembly area where deliver-only orders are boxed and deliver-and-serve orders are assembled and trayed. Three walk-in coolers store foods requiring refrigeration, and a large pantry houses nonperishable goods. Space limitations and the risk of spoilage limit the amount of raw materials and prepared food items that can be carried in inventory at any one time. CKC purchases desserts from outside vendors. Some deliver the desserts to CKC, others require CKC to send someone to pick up desserts at their facilities.

The scheduling of orders is a two-stage process. Each Monday, the Williamses develop the schedule of deliver-and-serve orders to be processed each day. CKC typically has multiple deliver-and-serve orders to fill each day of the week. This level of demand allows a certain efficiency in preparation of multiple orders. The deliver-only orders are scheduled day to day owing to the short order lead times. CKC sometimes runs out of ingredients for deliver-only menu items because of the limited inventory space.

Wayne and Janet Williams have 10 full-time employees: two cooks and eight food preparation workers, who also work as servers for the deliver-and-serve orders. In periods of high demand, the Williamses hire additional part-time servers. The position of cook is specialized and requires a high degree of training and skill. The rest of the employees are flexible and move between tasks as needed.

The business environment for catering is competitive. The competitive priorities are high-quality food, delivery reliability, flexibility, and cost—in that order. "The quality of the food and its preparation is paramount" states Wayne Williams. "Caterers with poor-quality food will not stay in business long." Quality is measured by both freshness and taste. Delivery reliability encompasses both on-time delivery and the time required to respond to customer orders (in effect, the order lead time). Flexibility focuses on both the range of catering requests that a company can satisfy and menu variety.

Recently, CKC has begun to feel the competitive pressures of increasingly demanding customers and several new specialty caterers. Customers are demanding more menu flexibility and faster response times. Small specialty caterers have entered the market and have targeted specific well-defined market segments. One example is a small caterer called Lunches-R-US, which located a facility in the middle of a large office complex to serve the lunch trade and competes with CKC on cost.

Wayne and Janet Williams have been impressed by the concepts of just-in-time operating systems, especially the ideas of increasing flexibility, reducing lead times, and lowering costs. They sound like what CKC needs to do to remain competitive. But the Williamses wonder whether JIT concepts and practices are transferable to a service business.

Questions

1. Are the operations of Copper Kettle Catering conducive to the application of JIT concepts and practices? Explain.
2. What, if any, are the major barriers to implementing a JIT system at Copper Kettle Catering?
3. What would you recommend that Wayne and Janet Williams do to take advantage of JIT concepts in operating CKC?

Source: This case was prepared by Dr. Brooke Saladin, Wake Forest University, as a basis for classroom discussion.

Selected References

Billesbach, Thomas J. "A Study of the Implementation of Just-in-Time in the United States." *Production and Inventory Management Journal* (Third Quarter 1991), pp. 1–4.

Billesbach, Thomas J., and M. J. Schniederjans. "Applicability of Just-in-Time Techniques in Administration." *Production and Inventory Management Journal* (Third Quarter 1989), pp. 40–44.

Ellis, Scott, and Bill Conlon. "JIT Points the Way to Gains in Quality, Cost and Lead Time." *APICS—The Performance Advantage* (August 1992), pp. 16–19.

Hahn, Chan K., Peter Pinto, and Daniel Bragg. "Just-in-Time Production and Purchasing." *Journal of Purchasing and Materials Management* (Fall 1983), pp. 2–10.

Hall, R. W. *Driving the Productivity Machine.* Falls Church, Va.: The American Production and Inventory Control Society, 1981.

Hutchins, D. "Having a Hard Time with Just-in-Time." *Fortune* (June 1986), pp. 64–66.

Karmarkar, U. "Getting Control of Just-in-Time." *Harvard Business Review* (September–October 1989), pp. 123–131.

Klein, J. A. "The Human Costs of Manufacturing Reform." *Harvard Business Review* (March–April 1989), pp. 60–66.

Krajewski, L. J., B. King, L. P. Ritzman, and D. S. Wong. "Kanban, MRP and Shaping the Manufacturing Environment." *Management Science*, vol. 33, no. 1 (January 1987), pp. 57–75.

McClenahen, John S. "So Long, Salespeople, and Good-bye, Buyers—JIT II Is Here." *Industry Week,* February 18, 1991, pp. 48–65.

Monden, Y. "What Makes the Toyota Production System Really Tick?" *Journal of Industrial Engineering* (January 1981), pp. 36–46.

Moody, Patricia E. "Bose Corporation: Hi-Fi Leader Stretches to Meet Growth Challenges." *Target* (Winter 1991), pp. 17–22.

Ritzman, L. P., B. E. King, and L. J. Krajewski. "Manufacturing Performance—Pulling the Right Levers." *Harvard Business Review* (March–April 1984), pp. 143–152.

Schonberger, R. J. *Japanese Manufacturing Techniques.* New York: Free Press, 1982.

Chapter Sixteen

SCHEDULING

The Homestead is a five-star hotel and restaurant in the secluded mountains of Hot Springs, Virginia. Scheduling plays a big role in maintaining the excellent customer service that the resort has long been known for. The restaurant offers a different menu each evening, providing guests several choices of gourmet entrées, appetizers, and desserts. Dinners are prepared to the individual customer's taste; consequently each customer order can be unique. A master chef schedules the "production" of the meal components so that they are completed together, assigns assistant chefs to workstations, and oversees the "assembly" of the meal for each guest. To achieve the process flexibility needed to cook the large variety of meals, the kitchen has a process focus, with workstations arranged by the functions performed at them. For example, at one station vegetables are prepared, at another the salads are made, and at still another an entrée is readied. A total of 60 assistant chefs work in the restaurant's kitchen, but all of them may not be working on a particular day. The assistant chefs are assigned to a particular station on a given evening and may be assigned to other cooking tasks by the master chef as needed. A chalkboard hangs over each workstation, describing the cooking task assigned to the station that evening. A computer screen, mounted in a position where all the assistant chefs can see it, posts the meal components that must be cooked as the customers order them. Some components that most people order with dinner, such as the "vegetables of the day," are processed in

Chefs at the Homestead pay meticulous attention to detail in food presentation so as to maintain the restaurant's reputation for providing a high-quality dining experience.

batches and kept warm until needed, whereas others, such as prime rib cooked medium rare, must be custom-prepared after the order is received. The master chef must coordinate the cooking of side dishes and entrée so that the components of the entire meal are ready at the same time and served while hot. Scheduling this operation is a challenging task because there may be hundreds of dinner orders in any evening, and the reputation of the Homestead depends on the performance of the kitchen.

As the Homestead example demonstrates, effective scheduling can be a competitive advantage for a firm. **Scheduling** allocates resources over time to accomplish specific tasks. Normally, scheduling is done after a number of other managerial decisions have been made. For example, planning emergency services such as fire protection first requires an analysis of the best location for fire stations, decisions about the type and quantity of fire-fighting equipment at each location, and a staffing plan for each station. Only then can specific work schedules for fire fighters be determined. Sound scheduling can help an organization achieve its strategic goals. For example, a fire department is better able to meet its objective of protecting the community if an adequate number of fire fighters are scheduled at all times.

In this chapter we discuss scheduling in both manufacturing and service organizations and some useful techniques for generating schedules. There are two basic types of scheduling: **work-force scheduling,** which determines when employees work, and **operations scheduling,** which assigns jobs to machines or workers to jobs. Both types of scheduling are used by manufacturing and service firms. For instance, at Ross Products, a manufacturer of infant foods, many different flavor options must be scheduled on the machines, and the associates who operate the machines must be scheduled on shifts. At Homestead, the master chef schedules the production of food items at the various workstations and prepares the work schedules for the assistant chefs. In manufacturing, operations scheduling is crucial because many performance measures, such as on-time delivery, inventory levels, the manufacturing cycle time, cost, and quality, relate directly to the scheduling of each production lot. Work-force scheduling is equally crucial because measures of performance such as customer waiting time, waiting-line length, utilization, cost, and quality are related to the availability of the servers. However, work-force scheduling usually is less complicated unless the firm employs a significant number of part-time workers or operates seven days a week.

◆ SCHEDULING IN MANUFACTURING

Operations schedules are short-term plans designed to implement the master production schedule. Operations scheduling focuses on how best to use existing capacity, taking into account technical production constraints. Often, several jobs (e.g., open orders for components) must be processed at one or more workstations. Typically, a variety of tasks can be performed at each workstation. If schedules aren't carefully planned to avoid bottlenecks, waiting lines may develop.

In this section we introduce the problem of scheduling by presenting a traditional manual tool for scheduling called the Gantt chart and then identifying the performance measures used for evaluating schedules. Next we focus on scheduling approaches used in two basic manufacturing environments: job shops and flow shops (see Chapter 2). A job shop specializes in low- to medium-volume batch production where the routings for jobs are jumbled. Tasks in this type of process-focused environment are difficult to schedule because of the variability in job routings and the continual introduction of new jobs to be processed. A flow shop designed for medium- to high-volume production is easier to schedule because in a product-focused facility the jobs have a common flow pattern through the system. Nonetheless, scheduling mistakes can be costly in either situation.

Gantt Charts

The **Gantt chart,** first devised by Henry L. Gantt in 1917, is a visual tool for sequencing work on machines and monitoring its progress. The chart takes two basic forms: the job or activity progress chart and the machine chart. Both types of Gantt charts present the ideal and the actual use of resources over time. The *progress chart* graphically displays the current status of each job relative to its scheduled completion date. For example, suppose that an automobile parts man-

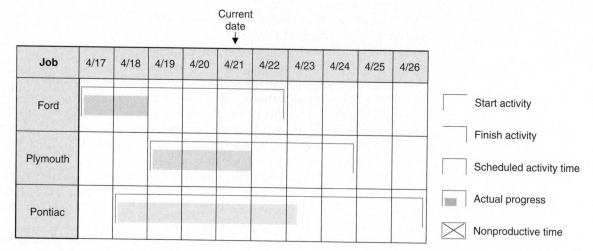

FIGURE 16.1

Gantt Chart of Job Progress for an Auto Parts Company

ufacturer has three jobs under way, one each for Ford, Plymouth, and Pontiac. The actual status of these orders is shown by the colored bars in Fig. 16.1; the red lines indicate the desired schedule for the start and finish of each job. For the current date, April 21, this Gantt chart shows that the Ford order is behind schedule because operations has completed only the work scheduled through 4/18. The Plymouth order is exactly on schedule, and the Pontiac order is ahead of schedule.

Figure 16.2 shows a *machine chart* for the automobile parts manufacturer. This chart depicts the sequence of future work at the two machines and also can be used to monitor progress. Using the same notation as in Fig. 16.1, the chart shows that for the current date of April 21, the Plymouth job is on schedule at machine 1 because the actual progress coincides with the current date. The Pontiac order has finished at machine 2, which is now idle. The plant manager can easily see from the Gantt machine chart the consequence of juggling the schedules. The usual approach is to juggle the schedules by trial and error until a schedule achieves satisfactory levels of selected performance measures.

FIGURE 16.2

Gantt Chart for Machines at an Auto Parts Company

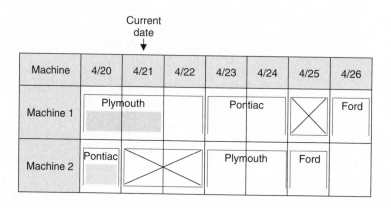

Performance Measures

The example of the auto parts manufacturer demonstrates a common problem in scheduling operations—in this case, how to schedule three jobs on two machines. In general, for n jobs, each requiring m machines, there are $(n!)^m$ possible schedules. In the case of the auto parts company, there are $(3!)^2 = 36$ possible schedules. Some might not be feasible because of individual job routings or because some jobs depend on the completion of others. Even so, in a typical job shop hundreds of scheduling decisions must be made every day.

From the manager's perspective, identifying the performance measures to be used in selecting a schedule is important. If the overall goals of the organization are to be achieved, the schedules should reflect managerially acceptable performance measures. The following list describes the most common performance measures used in operations scheduling, some of which will be familiar to you already. Each of these measures can be expressed as a statistical distribution having a mean and variance.

- *Job flow time.* The amount of shop time for the job is called **job flow time.** It is the sum of the moving time between operations, waiting time for machines or work orders, process time (including setups), and delays resulting from machine breakdowns, component unavailability, and the like.

$$\text{Job flow time} = \text{Time of completion} - \begin{array}{c}\text{Time job was available for first}\\\text{processing operation}\end{array}$$

Note that the starting time is the time the job was *available* for its first processing operation, not necessarily when the job began its first operation.

- *Makespan.* The total amount of time required to complete a *group* of jobs is called **makespan.**

$$\text{Makespan} = \text{Time of completion of last job} - \text{Starting time of first job}$$

- *Past due.* The measure **past due** can be expressed as the *amount of time* by which a job missed its due date or as the *percentage of total jobs* processed over some period of time that missed their due dates.

- *Work-in-process inventory.* Any job in a waiting line, moving from one operation to the next, being delayed for some reason, being processed, or residing in component or subassembly inventories is considered to be **work-in-process (WIP) inventory** or *pipeline inventory.* This measure can be expressed in units (individual items only), number of jobs, dollar value for the entire system, or weeks of supply.

- *Total inventory.* The sum of scheduled receipts and on-hand inventories is the **total inventory.**

$$\text{Total inventory} = \text{Scheduled receipts for all items} + \begin{array}{c}\text{On-hand inventories}\\\text{of all items}\end{array}$$

This measure could be expressed in weeks of supply, dollars, or units (individual items only).

- *Utilization.* The percentage of work time productively spent by a machine or worker is called utilization (Chapter 7).

$$\text{Utilization} = \frac{\text{Productive work time}}{\text{Total work time available}}$$

Utilization for more than one machine or worker can be calculated by adding the productive work times of all machines or workers and dividing by the total work time they are available.

These performance measures often are interrelated. For example, in a job shop, minimizing the mean job flow time tends to reduce work-in-process inventory and increase utilization. In a flow shop, minimizing the makespan for a group of jobs tends to increase facility utilization. An understanding of the interactions of job flow time, makespan, past due, WIP inventory, total inventory, and utilization can make scheduling easier.

Job Shop Dispatching

Just as there are many feasible schedules for a specific group of jobs on a particular set of machines, there also are many ways to generate schedules. They range from straightforward manual methods, such as manipulating Gantt charts, to sophisticated computer models for developing optimal schedules. One way of generating schedules in job shops—**dispatching procedures**—allows the schedule for a workstation to evolve over a period of time. The decision about which job to process next (or whether to let the station remain idle) is made with simple priority rules whenever the workstation becomes available for further processing. One advantage of this method is that last-minute information on operating conditions can be incorporated into the schedule as it evolves.

Dispatching procedures determine the job to process next with the help of **priority sequencing rules.** When several jobs are waiting in line at a workstation, priority rules specify the job processing sequence. These rules can be applied by a worker or incorporated into a computerized scheduling system that generates a dispatch list of jobs and priorities for each workstation. The following priority sequencing rules are commonly used in practice.

Which customers or jobs should have top priority?

- *Critical ratio.* The **critical ratio (CR)** is calculated by dividing the time remaining to a job's due date by the total shop time remaining for the job, including the setup, processing, move, and expected waiting times of all remaining operations, including the operation being scheduled. The formula is

$$CR = \frac{\text{Due date} - \text{Today's date}}{\text{Total shop time remaining}}$$

  A ratio less than 1.0 implies that the job is behind schedule, and a ratio greater than 1.0 implies that the job is ahead of schedule. The job with the lowest CR is scheduled next.

- *Earliest due date.* The job with the **earliest due date (EDD)** is scheduled next.

- *First come, first served.* The job that arrived at the workstation first has the highest priority under a **first come, first served (FCFS)** rule.

- *Shortest processing time.* The job requiring the **shortest processing time (SPT)** at the workstation is processed next.

- *Slack per remaining operations.* Slack is the difference between the time remaining to a job's due date and the total shop time remaining, including that of the operation being scheduled. A job's priority is determined by dividing the slack by the number of operations that remain, including the one being scheduled, to arrive at the **slack per remaining operations (S/RO).**

$$S/RO = \frac{(\text{Due date} - \text{Today's date}) - \text{Total shop time remaining}}{\text{Number of operations remaining}}$$

The job with the lowest S/RO is scheduled next.

There are many ways to break ties if two or more jobs have the same top priority. One way is to arbitrarily choose one of the tied jobs for processing next.

Although the priority sequencing rules seem simple, the actual task of scheduling hundreds of jobs through hundreds of workstations requires intensive data gathering and manipulation. The scheduler needs information on each job's processing requirements: the job's due date; its routing; the standard setup, processing, and expected waiting times at each operation; whether alternative machines could be used at each operation; and the components and raw materials needed at each operation. In addition, the scheduler needs to know the job's current status: its location (in line for a machine or being processed on a machine), how much of the operation has been completed, the actual arrival and departure times at each operation or waiting line, the actual processing and setup times, and many other pieces of information. The scheduler uses the priority sequencing rules to determine the processing sequence of jobs at a workstation and the remaining information for estimating job arrival times at the next workstation, determining whether an alternative machine should be used when the primary one is busy, and predicting the need for materials-handling equipment. Because this information may change throughout the day, computers are needed to track the data and to maintain valid priorities. Managerial Practice 16.1 on page 760 discusses the computerized system used by an aircraft manufacturer.

Sequencing Operations for One Machine

Any priority sequencing rule can be used to schedule any number of workstations with the dispatching procedure. For the purpose of illustrating the rules, however, we focus on scheduling several jobs on a single machine. We divide the rules into two categories: single-dimension rules and multiple-dimension rules.

Single-Dimension Rules. Some priority rules (e.g., FCFS, EDD, and SPT) base a job's priority assignment only on information on the jobs waiting for processing at the individual workstation. We call these rules **single-dimension rules** because they base the priority on a single aspect of the job, such as arrival time at the workstation, the due date, or the processing time. We begin with an example of single-dimension rules.

EXAMPLE 16.1

Comparing the EDD and SPT Rules

The Taylor Machine Shop rebores engine blocks. Currently, five engine blocks are waiting for processing. At any time, the company has only one engine expert on duty who can do this type of work. The engine problems have been diagnosed, and processing times for the jobs have been estimated. Times have been agreed upon with the customers as to when they can expect the work to be completed. The accompanying table shows the situation as of Monday morning. As Taylor is open from 8 A.M. until 5 P.M. each weekday, plus weekend hours as needed, the customer pickup times are measured in business hours from Monday morning. Determine the schedule for the engine expert by using (a) the EDD rule and (b) the SPT rule. For each, calculate the average hours early, hours past due, work-in-process inventory, and total inventory.

Engine Block	Processing Time, Including Setup (hr)	Scheduled Customer Pickup Time (business hr from now)
Ranger	8	10
Explorer	6	12
Bronco	15	20
Econoline 150	3	18
Thunderbird	12	22

Solution

a. The EDD rule states that the first engine block in the sequence is the one with the closest due date. Consequently, the Ranger engine block is processed first. The Thunderbird engine block, with its due date furthest in the future, is processed last. The sequence is shown in the following table, along with the job flow times, the hours early, and the hours past due.

Engine Block Sequence	Begin Work		Processing Time (hr)		Job Flow Time (hr)	Scheduled Customer Pickup Time	Actual Customer Pickup Time	Hours Early	Hours Past Due
Ranger	0	+	8	=	8	10	10	2	
Explorer	8	+	6	=	14	12	14		2
Econoline 150	14	+	3	=	17	18	18	1	
Bronco	17	+	15	=	32	20	32		12
Thunderbird	32	+	12	=	44	22	44		22

The flow time for each job equals the waiting time plus the processing time. For example, the Explorer engine block had to wait 8 hours before the engine expert started to work on it. The process time for the job is 6 hours, so its flow time is 14 hours. The average flow time and the other performance measures for the EDD schedule for the five engine blocks are shown below.

$$\text{Average job flow time} = \frac{8 + 14 + 17 + 32 + 44}{5} = 23 \text{ hours}$$

$$\text{Average hours early} = \frac{2 + 0 + 1 + 0 + 0}{5} = 0.6 \text{ hour}$$

$$\text{Average hours past due} = \frac{0 + 2 + 0 + 12 + 22}{5} = 7.2 \text{ hours}$$

$$\text{Average WIP inventory} = \frac{\text{Sum of flow times}}{\text{Makespan}} = \frac{8 + 14 + 17 + 32 + 44}{44}$$

$$= 2.61 \text{ engine blocks}$$

You might think of the sum of flow times as the total *job hours* spent by the engine blocks waiting for the engine expert and being processed. (In this example there are no component or subassembly inventories, so WIP inventory consists only of those engine blocks waiting or being processed.) Dividing this sum by the makespan, or the total elapsed time required to complete work on all the engine blocks, provides the average work-in-process inventory.

Finally,

$$\text{Average total inventory} = \frac{\text{Sum of time in system}}{\text{Makespan}} = \frac{10 + 14 + 18 + 32 + 44}{44}$$

$$= 2.68 \text{ engine blocks}$$

Total inventory is the sum of the work-in-process inventory and the completed jobs waiting to be picked up by customers. The average total inventory equals the sum of the times each job spent in the shop—in this example, the total job hours spent waiting for the engine expert, being processed, and waiting for pickup—divided by the makespan. For example, the first job to be picked up is the Ranger engine block, which spent 10 hours in the system. Then the Explorer engine block is picked up, after spending 14 job hours in the system. The time spent by any job in the system equals its actual customer pickup time because all jobs were available for processing at time zero.

b. Under the SPT rule, the sequence starts with the engine block having the shortest processing time, the Econoline 150, and ends with the one having the longest processing time, the Bronco. The sequence, along with the job flow times, early hours, and past due hours, is contained in the following table.

Engine Block Sequence	Begin Work	Processing Time (hr)		Job Flow Time (hr)	Scheduled Customer Pickup Time	Actual Customer Pickup Time	Hours Early	Hours Past Due
Econoline 150	0	+ 3	=	3	18	18	15	
Explorer	3	+ 6	=	9	12	12	3	
Ranger	9	+ 8	=	17	10	17		7
Thunderbird	17	+ 12	=	29	22	29		7
Bronco	29	+ 15	=	44	20	44		24

The performance measures are

$$\text{Average job flow time} = \frac{3 + 9 + 17 + 29 + 44}{5} = 20.4 \text{ hours}$$

$$\text{Average hours early} = \frac{15 + 3 + 0 + 0 + 0}{5} = 3.6 \text{ hours}$$

$$\text{Average past due hours} = \frac{0 + 0 + 7 + 7 + 24}{5} = 7.6 \text{ hours}$$

$$\text{Average WIP inventory} = \frac{3 + 9 + 17 + 29 + 44}{44} = 2.32 \text{ engine blocks}$$

$$\text{Average total inventory} = \frac{18 + 12 + 17 + 29 + 44}{44}$$

$$= 2.73 \text{ engine blocks}$$

Managerial Practice 16.1

▶ *Lockheed Aeronautical Systems' Computerized Scheduling System*

The defense industry faces reduced levels of government spending for major defense projects and greater competitive pressures to secure the few projects that will be authorized. The Lockheed Aeronautical Systems Company responded to these competitive pressures by designing production systems to cope with the problems of aircraft production in the twenty-first century. The company developed a paperless shop floor control system that provides factory workers with current, accurate electronic data and support documentation—in both text and graphics—needed to perform their jobs. The system tracks job progress and time at each operation and recommends the next job to process at a particular workstation.

The system works as follows. When a worker logs into the system and passes his or her identification badge through a magnetic reader, the system displays, in order of priority, the current orders that must be processed that day at that workstation. The system is updated continually as work is completed and new work arrives. The worker can select the first order on the list merely by touching it on the screen or can be authorized to override the system and select a different one. After the job has been selected, the system displays all pertinent work information for that job. The worker then gets the parts and verifies that the parts are the correct ones by wanding a bar code label on the attached tag. When the worker completes the job, the work is automatically dispatched to the next workstation.

Lockheed management believes that the successes to date demonstrate the potential benefits of the system, in-

With a computer to provide all relevant job information, workers at Lockheed no longer need to shuffle paper.

cluding increased shop floor control, improved scheduling, improved cost and quality performance, integration of other factory systems, increased learning rates for new shop floor workers, and rapid delivery of up-to-date data to the shop floor.

Source: Michael Sheehan, "Paperless Systems Boosting Performance, Reduce Costs," *Production and Inventory Management* (September 1991), pp. 37–40.

How important is the choice of priority dispatching rules to the effectiveness of the operating system?

As the solution of Example 16.1 shows, the SPT schedule provided a lower average job flow time and lower work-in-process inventory. The EDD schedule gave better customer service, as measured by the average hours past due, and a lower maximum hours past due (22 versus 24). It also provided a lower total inventory because fewer job hours were spent waiting for customers to pick up their engine blocks after they had been completed. The SPT priority rule will push jobs through the system to completion more quickly than will the other rules. Speed can be an advantage—but only if jobs can be delivered sooner than promised and revenue collected earlier. If they cannot, the completed job must stay in finished inventory, canceling the advantage of minimizing the average work-in-process inventory. Consequently, the priority rule chosen can help or hinder the organization in meeting its competitive priorities.

In Example 16.1, SPT and EDD provided schedules that resulted in different values for the performance criteria; however, both schedules have the same makespan of 44 hours. This result always will occur in single-operation scheduling for a *fixed number* of jobs available for processing—regardless of the priority rule used—because there are no idle workstation times between any two jobs.

Using simulation models of job shop systems, researchers have studied the implications of the single-dimension rules for various performance measures. In most of these studies, all jobs were considered to be independent, and the assumption was made that sufficient capacity generally was available. These studies found that the EDD rule performs well with respect to the percentage of jobs past due and the variance of hours past due. For a given set of jobs to be processed on a single machine, it minimizes the maximum of the past due hours of any job in the set. It is popular with firms that are sensitive to due date changes, although it doesn't perform very well with respect to flow time, work-in-process inventory, or utilization.

Often referred to as the *world champion,* the SPT rule tends to minimize mean flow time, work-in-process inventory, and percentage of jobs past due and to maximize shop utilization. For the single machine case, the SPT rule always will provide the lowest mean flow time. However, it could increase total inventory because it tends to push all work to the finished state. In addition, it tends to produce a large variance in past due hours because the larger jobs might have to wait a long time for processing. Also, it provides no opportunity to adjust schedules when due dates change. The advantage of this rule over others diminishes as the load on the shop increases.

Finally, though the first-come, first-served rule is considered fair to the jobs (or customers), it performs poorly with respect to all performance measures. Actually, it is a random rule with respect to operating performance measures.

Multiple-Dimension Rules. Priority rules such as CR and S/RO incorporate information about the remaining workstations at which the job must be processed, in addition to the processing time at the present workstation or the due date considered by single-dimension rules. We call these rules **multiple-dimension rules** because they apply to more than one aspect of the job. The following example demonstrates their use for sequencing jobs.

Example 16.2

Sequencing with the CR and S/RO Rules

The first five columns of the following table contain information about a set of four jobs presently waiting at an engine lathe. Several operations, including the one at the engine lathe, remain to be done on each job. Determine the schedule by using (a) the CR rule and (b) the S/RO rule.

Job	Operation Time at Engine Lathe (hr)	Time Remaining to Due Date (Days)	Number of Operations Remaining	Shop Time Remaining	CR	S/RO
1	2.3	15	10	6.1	2.46	0.89
2	10.5	10	2	7.8	1.28	1.10
3	6.2	20	12	14.5	1.38	0.46
4	15.6	8	5	10.2	0.78	−0.44

Solution

a. Using CR to schedule the machine, we divide the time remaining to the due date by the shop time remaining (measured in days here) to get the priority index for each job. For job 1,

$$\text{CR} = \frac{\text{Time remaining to due date}}{\text{Shop time remaining}} = \frac{15}{6.1} = 2.46$$

By arranging the jobs in sequence with the lowest critical ratio first, we determine that the sequence of jobs to be processed by the engine lathe is 4–2–3–1, assuming that no other jobs arrive in the meantime.

b. Using S/RO, we divide the difference between the time remaining to the due date and the shop time remaining by the number of remaining operations. For job 1,

$$\text{S/RO} = \frac{\text{Time remaining to due date} - \text{Shop time remaining}}{\text{Number of operations remaining}}$$

$$= \frac{15 - 6.1}{10} = 0.89$$

Arranging the jobs by starting with the lowest S/RO yields a 4–3–1–2 sequence of jobs.

Note that application of the two priority rules gives two different schedules. Moreover, the SPT sequence, based on operation times (measured in hours) at the engine lathe only, is 1–3–2–4. No preference is given to job 4 in the SPT schedule, even though it may not be finished by its due date. The FCFS sequence is 1–2–3–4, and the EDD sequence is 4–2–1–3. The CMOM computer printout below shows the comparative performance of the five dispatching rules.

Priority Rule Summary

	FCFS	Shortest Processing Time	Earliest Due Date	Critical Ratio	Slack per Remaining Operation
Avg Flow Time	17.175	16.100	26.175	27.150	24.025
Avg Early Time	3.425	6.050	0	0	0
Avg Past Due	7.350	8.900	12.925	13.900	10.775
Avg. W-I-P	1.986	1.861	3.026	3.139	2.777
Avg Total Inv	2.382	2.561	3.026	3.139	2.777

The S/RO rule is better than the EDD rule and the CR rule but much worse than the SPT rule and the FCFS rule for this example. However, the S/RO has the advantage of allowing schedule changes when due dates change. These results cannot be generalized to other situations because only four jobs are being processed.

Simulation studies have shown that S/RO is better than EDD with respect to the percentage of jobs past due but worse than SPT and EDD with respect to average job flow times. These studies also indicate that CR results in longer job flow times than SPT but less variance in the distribution of past due hours. Consequently, even though the multiple-dimension rules use more information, there is no clear-cut best choice. Each rule should be tested in the environment for which it is intended.

Multiple-Workstation Scheduling

Priority sequencing rules may be used to schedule more than one operation with the dispatching procedure. Each operation is treated independently. When a workstation becomes idle, the priority rule is applied to the jobs waiting for that operation, and the one with the highest priority is selected. When that operation is finished, the job is moved to the next operation in its routing, where it waits until it again has the highest priority. At any workstation, the jobs in the waiting line change over a period of time, so the choice of a priority rule can make quite a difference in processing sequence. Schedules can be evaluated using the performance measures already discussed.

Sequencing Operations for a Two-Station Flow Shop

Suppose that a flow shop has several jobs ready for processing at two workstations and that the routings of all jobs are identical. Whereas in single-machine scheduling the makespan is the same regardless of the priority rule chosen, in scheduling of two or more operations in a flow shop the makespan varies according to the sequence chosen. Determining a production sequence for a group of jobs so as to minimize the makespan has two advantages.

1. The group of jobs is completed in minimum time.
2. Utilization of the two-station flow shop is maximized. Utilizing the first workstation continuously until it processes the last job minimizes the idle time on the *second* workstation.

Johnson's rule is a procedure that minimizes makespan in scheduling a group of jobs on two workstations. Johnson showed that the sequence of jobs at the two stations should be identical and that therefore the priority assigned to a job should be the same at both. The procedure is based on the assumption of a known set of jobs, each with a known processing time and available to begin processing on the first workstation. The procedure is as follows.

Step 1. Scan the processing times at each workstation and find the shortest processing time among the jobs not yet scheduled. If there is a tie, choose one job arbitrarily.

Step 2. If the shortest processing time is on workstation 1, schedule the corresponding job as early as possible. If the shortest processing time is on workstation 2, schedule the corresponding job as late as possible.

Step 3. Eliminate the last job scheduled from further consideration. Repeat steps 1 and 2 until all jobs have been scheduled.

EXAMPLE 16.3

Scheduling a Group of Jobs on Two Workstations

The Morris Machine Company just received an order to refurbish five motors for materials-handling equipment that were damaged in a fire. The motors will be repaired at two workstations in the following manner.

Workstation 1: Dismantle the motor and clean parts.

Workstation 2: Replace parts as necessary, test the motor, and make adjustments.

The customer's shop will be inoperable until all the motors have been repaired, so the plant manager is interested in developing a schedule that minimizes the makespan and has authorized round-the-clock operations until the motors have been repaired. The estimated time for repairing each motor is shown in the following table.

	Time (hr)	
Motor	Workstation 1	Workstation 2
M1	12	22
M2	4	5
M3	5	3
M4	15	16
M5	10	8

Solution   The logic for the optimal sequence is shown in Table 16.1.

TABLE 16.1   *Establishing a Job Sequence*

Iteration	Job Sequence					Comments
1					M3	Shortest processing time is 3 hours for M3 at workstation 2. Therefore M3 is scheduled as late as possible.
2	M2				M3	Eliminate M3's time from the table of estimated times. The next shortest processing time is 4 hours, for M2 at workstation 1. M2 is therefore scheduled first.
3	M2			M5	M3	Eliminate M2 from the table. The next shortest processing time is 8 hours for M5 at workstation 2. Therefore M5 is scheduled as late as possible.
4	M2	M1		M5	M3	Eliminate M5 from the table. The next shortest processing time is 12 hours for M1 at workstation 1. M1 is scheduled as early as possible.
5	M2	M1	M4	M5	M3	The last motor to be scheduled is M4. It is placed in the last remaining position, in the middle of the schedule.

No other sequence of jobs will produce a lower makespan. To determine the makespan, we have to draw a Gantt chart, as shown in Fig. 16.3. In this case, refurbishing and reinstalling all five motors will take 65 hours. This schedule minimizes the idle time of workstation 2 and gives the fastest repair time for all five motors. Note that the schedule recognizes that a job can't begin at workstation 2 until it has been completed at workstation 1.

FIGURE 16.3   *Machine Chart for the Morris Machine Company Repair Schedule*

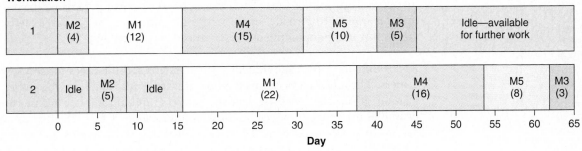

Workstation

Labor-Limited Environments

Thus far we have assumed that a job never has to wait for lack of a worker; that is, the limiting resource is the number of machines or workstations available. More typical, however, is a **labor-limited environment** in which the resource constraint is the amount of labor available, not the number of machines or workstations. In this case, workers are trained to work on a variety of machines or tasks to increase the flexibility of operations.

In a labor-limited environment, the scheduler not only must decide which job to process next at a particular workstation, but also must assign a worker to his or her next workstation. The scheduler can use priority rules to make these decisions, as we used them to schedule engine blocks in Example 16.1. In labor-limited environments, the labor-assignment policies, as well as the dispatching priority rules, affect performance. The following are some examples of labor-assignment rules.

- Assign personnel to the workstation having the job that has been in the system longest.
- Assign personnel to the workstation having the most jobs waiting for processing.
- Assign personnel to the workstation having the largest standard work content.
- Assign personnel to the workstation having the job that has the earliest due date.

◆ SCHEDULING IN SERVICES

What scheduling methods can be used to manage the capacity of a service system?

One important distinction between manufacturing and services that affects scheduling is that service operations cannot create inventories to buffer demand uncertainties. A second distinction is that in service operations demand often is less predictable. Customers may decide on the spur of the moment that they need a hamburger, a haircut, or a plumbing repair. Thus capacity, often in the form of employees, is crucial for service providers. In this section we discuss various ways in which scheduling systems can facilitate the capacity management of service providers.

Scheduling Customer Demand

One way to manage capacity is to schedule customers for arrival times and definite periods of service time. With this approach, capacity remains fixed and demand is leveled to provide timely service and utilize capacity. Three methods are commonly used: appointments, reservations, and backlogs.

Appointments.   An appointment system assigns specific times for service to customers. The advantages of this method are timely customer service and high utilization of servers. Doctors, dentists, lawyers, and automobile repair shops are examples of service providers that use appointment systems. Doctors can use the system to schedule parts of their day to visit hospital patients, and lawyers can set aside time to prepare cases. If timely service is to be provided, however, care must be taken to tailor the length of appointments to individual customer needs rather than merely scheduling customers at equal time intervals. This approach minimizes the schedule slippage. Appointment systems can backfire if there are a significant number of late arrivals or no-shows.

Reservations.   Reservation systems, although quite similar to appointment systems, are used when the customer actually occupies or uses facilities associated with the service. For example, customers reserve hotel rooms, automobiles, airline seats, and concert seats. The major advantage of reservation systems is the lead time they give service managers to plan the efficient use of facilities. Often reservations require some form of down payment to reduce the problem of no-shows. Many hotels require one night's payment when the reservation is made, and concerts usually require attendees to purchase tickets in advance.

Hertz offers a quick check-in service. The employee's hand-held computer is tied into the main reservation system. In addition to allowing quick customer service and a high degree of face-to-face contact, the system puts the car back into the pool of rentable cars immediately.

Backlogs. A less precise way to schedule customers is to allow backlogs to develop; that is, customers never know exactly when service will commence. They present their service request to an order taker, who adds it to the waiting line of orders already in the system. TV repair shops, restaurants, banks, grocery stores, and barber shops are examples of the many types of businesses that use this system. Various priority rules can be used to determine which order to process next. The usual rule is first come, first served, but if the order involves rework on a previous order, it may get a higher priority.

Scheduling the Work Force

Another way to manage capacity with a scheduling system is to specify the on-duty and off-duty periods for each employee over a certain time period, as in assigning postal clerks, nurses, or police officers to specific workdays and shifts. This approach is used when customers demand quick response and total demand can be forecasted with reasonable accuracy. In these instances, capacity is adjusted to meet the expected loads on the service system.

Recall that work-force schedules translate the staffing plan into specific schedules of work for each employee. Determining the workdays for each employee in itself doesn't make the staffing plan operational. Daily work-force requirements, stated in aggregate terms in the staffing plan, must be satisfied. The work-force capacity available each day must meet or exceed daily work-force requirements. If it doesn't, the scheduler must try to rearrange days off until the requirements are met. If no such schedule can be found, management might have to change the staffing plan and authorize more employees, overtime hours, or larger backlogs.

Constraints. The technical constraints imposed on the work-force schedule are the resources provided by the staffing plan and the requirements placed on the operating system. However, other constraints, including legal and behavioral considerations, also can be imposed. For example, an airline may be required to have at least a minimum number of flight attendants on duty at all times. Similarly, a minimum number of fire and safety personnel must be on duty at a fire station at all times. Such constraints limit management's flexibility in developing work-force schedules.

The constraints imposed by the psychological needs of workers complicate scheduling even more. Some of these constraints are written into labor agreements. For example, an employer may agree to give employees a certain number of consecutive days off per week or to limit employees' consecutive workdays to a certain maximum. Other provisions might govern the allocation of vacation, days off for holidays, or rotating shift assignments. In addition, preferences of the employees themselves need to be considered.

One way that managers deal with certain undesirable aspects of scheduling is to use a **rotating schedule,** which rotates employees through a series of workdays or hours. Thus over a period of time, each person has the same opportunity to have weekends and holidays off and to work days, as well as evenings and nights. A rotating schedule gives each employee the next employee's schedule the following week. In contrast, a **fixed schedule** calls for each employee to work the same days and hours each week.

How can an effective work-
force schedule be developed
for a service system?

Developing a Work-Force Schedule.   Suppose that we are interested in developing an employee schedule for a company that operates seven days a week and provides each employee two consecutive days off. In this section we demonstrate a method that recognizes this constraint. It is similar to one developed by Tibrewala, Philippe, and Brown (1972), but doesn't guarantee an optimal solution. The objective is to identify the two consecutive days off for each employee that will minimize the amount of total slack capacity. The work schedule for each employee, then, is the five days that remain after the two days off have been determined. The procedure involves the following steps.

Step 1.   From the schedule of net requirements for the week, find all the pairs of consecutive days that include the minimum daily requirements. Select the unique pair that has the lowest total requirements for the two days. Suppose that the numbers of employees required are as follows:

Monday:	8	Friday:	7
Tuesday:	9	Saturday:	4
Wednesday:	2	Sunday:	2
Thursday:	12		

The minimum capacity requirement is 2 employees, on Wednesday and Sunday. The pairs that contain the minimum requirement are Saturday–Sunday, Sunday–Monday, Tuesday–Wednesday, and Wednesday–Thursday. The pair having the lowest total requirements is Saturday–Sunday, with $4 + 2 = 6$.

Step 2.   If a tie occurs, choose one of the tied pairs, consistent with provisions written into the labor agreement, if any. Alternatively, the tie could be broken by asking the employee being scheduled to make the choice. As a last resort, the tie could be broken arbitrarily. For example, preference could be given to Saturday–Sunday pairs.

Step 3.   Assign the employee the selected pair of days off. Subtract the requirements satisfied by the employee from the net requirements for each day the employee is to work. In this case, the employee is assigned Saturday and Sunday off. After requirements are subtracted, Monday's requirement is 7, Tuesday's is 8, Wednesday's is 1, Thursday's is 11, and Friday's is 6. Saturday's and Sunday's requirements don't change because no employee is yet scheduled to work those days.

Step 4.   Repeat steps 1–3 until all requirements have been satisfied or a certain number of employees have been scheduled.

This method reduces the amount of slack capacity assigned to days having low requirements and forces the days having high requirements to be scheduled first. It also recognizes some of the behavioral and contractual aspects of work-force scheduling in the tie-breaking rules. However, the schedules produced might *not* minimize total slack capacity. Different rules for finding the days-off pair and breaking ties are needed to ensure minimal total slack capacity.

EXAMPLE 16.4

Developing a Work-Force Schedule

The Amalgamated Parcel Service is open seven days a week. The schedule of requirements is

Day	M	T	W	Th	F	S	Su
Number of employees	6	4	8	9	10	3	2

The manager needs a work-force schedule that provides two consecutive days off and minimizes the amount of total slack capacity. To break ties in the selection of off days, the scheduler gives preference to Saturday–Sunday if it is one of the tied pairs. If not, she selects one of the tied pairs arbitrarily.

Solution Although both S–Su and Su–M contain the minimum requirements, S–Su has the lowest total requirements. Therefore employee 1 is scheduled to work Monday–Friday. The revised set of requirements, after scheduling employee 1, is

Day		M	T	W	Th	F	S	Su
Number of employees		5	3	7	8	9	3	2

Note that the requirements for S–Su are carried forward because these are employee 1's days off. These updated requirements are the ones the scheduler uses for the next employee.

The unique minimum again is on S–Su, so the scheduler assigns employee 2 to a M–F schedule. She then reduces the requirements for M–F to reflect the assignment of employee 2.

The day-off assignments for the remaining employees are shown in Table 16.2.

TABLE 16.2   *Scheduling Days Off*

M	T	W	Th	F	S	Su	Employee	Comments
4	2	6	7	8	3	2	3	S–Su has the lowest total requirements. Reduce the requirements to reflect a M–F schedule for employee 3.
3	1	5	6	7	3	2	4	M–T has the lowest total requirements. Assign employee 4 to a W–Su schedule and update the requirements.
3	1	4	5	6	2	1	5	S–Su has the lowest total requirements. Assign employee 5 to a M–F schedule and update the requirements.
2	0	3	4	5	2	1	6	M–T has the lowest total requirements. Assign employee 6 to a W–Su schedule and update the requirements.
2	0	2	3	4	1	0	7	S–Su has the lowest total requirements. Assign employee 7 to a M–F schedule and update the requirements.
1	0	1	2	3	1	0	8	Three pairs have the minimum requirement and the lowest total: S–Su, M–T, and T–W. Choose S–Su according to the tie-breaking rule. Assign employee 8 a M–F schedule and update the requirements.
0	0	0	1	2	1	0	9	Arbitrarily choose Su–M to break ties because S–Su doesn't have the lowest total requirements. Assign employee 9 to a T–S schedule.
0	0	0	0	1	0	0	10	Choose S–Su according to the tie-breaking rule. Assign employee 10 a M–F schedule.

The schedule for the employees is shown in Table 16.3. With its substantial amount of slack capacity, the schedule isn't unique. Employee 9, for example, could have Su–M, M–T, or T–W off without causing a capacity shortage. Indeed, the company might be able to get by with one fewer employee because of the total of eight slack days of capacity. However, all 10 employees are needed on Fridays. If the manager were willing to get by with only 9 employees on Fridays or if someone could work one day of overtime on a rotating basis, he wouldn't need employee 10. As indicated in the table, the net requirement left for employee 10 to satisfy amounts to only one day, Friday. Thus employee 10 can be used to fill in for vacationing or sick employees.

TABLE 16.3   *Final Schedule*

Employee	M	T	W	Th	F	S	Su	Total
1	X	X	X	X	X	off	off	
2	X	X	X	X	X	off	off	
3	X	X	X	X	X	off	off	
4	off	off	X	X	X	X	X	
5	X	X	X	X	X	off	off	
6	off	off	X	X	X	X	X	
7	X	X	X	X	X	off	off	
8	X	X	X	X	X	off	off	
9	off	X	X	X	X	X	off	
10	X	X	X	X	X	off	off	
Capacity, C	7	7	10	10	10	3	2	50
Requirements, R	6	4	8	9	10	3	2	42
Slack, $C-R$	1	3	2	1	0	0	1	8

Computerized Work-Force Scheduling Systems.   Work-force scheduling often entails a myriad of constraints and concerns. In some types of firms, such as telephone companies, mail-order catalog houses, or emergency hotline agencies, employees must be on duty 24 hours a day, seven days a week. Sometimes a portion of the staff is part time, allowing management a great deal of flexibility in developing schedules but adding considerable complexity to the requirements. The flexibility comes from the opportunity to match anticipated loads closely by using overlapping shifts or odd shift lengths; the complexity comes from having to evaluate the numerous possible alternatives. Management also must consider the timing of lunch breaks and rest periods, the number and starting times of shift schedules, and the days off for each employee. An additional typical concern is that the number of employees on duty at any particular time be sufficient to answer calls within a reasonable amount of time.

Computerized scheduling systems are available to cope with the complexity of work-force scheduling. For example, L. L. Bean's telephone service center must be staffed with telephone operators seven days a week, 24 hours a day. The company uses 350 permanent and temporary employees. The permanent workers are guaranteed a minimum weekly workload apportioned over a seven-day week on a rotating schedule. The temporary staff works a variety of schedules,

Managerial Practice 16.2

▶ *Scheduling Police Officers in the San Francisco Police Department*

The San Francisco Police Department (SFPD) serves a population of 700,000 with about 850 officers on regular patrol duty. The city is divided into nine police precincts, each served by as many as 120 officers. In 1986 the SFPD was using a manual system to generate officer schedules and had no way of determining whether its trial-and-error schedules were the best that could be devised. More importantly, the manual system was too cumbersome to evaluate alternative policies for scheduling and deploying officers.

After extensive study, a task force decided that a new system was needed. The system had to be easy to use and capable of generating optimal and realistic schedules in less than 30 minutes on a microcomputer. It also had to use existing data sources and allow adjustments to suggested schedules in less than 60 seconds. An extensive review of the literature revealed that no such approach existed, so a new one had to be built. In addition to meeting the technical requirements mentioned, the system had to be capable of addressing various other issues:

- *A 10-hour day, 4-day week (4/10) versus an 8-hour day, 5-day week (5/8).* The Police Officers Association was very interested in the 4/10 option, but police management didn't know how that would affect coverage.
- *One officer per car versus two officers per car.* Many officers preferred the two-per-car option, but that too would affect coverage.
- *Fixed versus rotating schedules.* The rotating schedules, particularly when combined with the 4/10 option, were popular with the officers. However, rotating schedules tend to require more officers to achieve the same coverage because officers usually move in groups and groups must be ap-

proximately the same size. Assigning officers in groups poses problems in covering peak days because there could be either more or fewer officers than needed. This problem is avoided by the fixed schedule approach.

- *Number of start times.* Technically, a shift could start on any one of the 168 hours (24 × 7) of the week, but that would cause a nightmare for administrators. The more shift starting times that are available, however, the more closely officer capacity can match the anticipated load. Some balance was needed, and the new system had to enable evaluation of the alternatives.
- *Minimum number of officers on duty.* The system had to allow for constraints imposing a minimum number of officers on duty at certain selected times of the day and week.
- *Nonpatrol duties.* Training and station duties had to be accounted for in the workload.

The new system had three major components. First, it made use of an existing forecasting system. For each of the 168 hours of the week, the forecasting component translated the number of calls for service into the number of officers required, modified for the proportion of two-officer car teams. It also added in the nonpatrol duties. Second, a mathematical model determined the best schedule for the number of officers available. The final component allowed police personnel to modify the suggested schedules interactively.

The benefits accruing from the system are substantial. The SFPD now has 25 percent more patrol units available in time of need, the equivalent of adding 200 officers to the force at a cost of $11 million. In addition, response times have improved by 20 percent. Even traffic citations have increased, by $3 million annually.

Source: Phillip Taylor and Stephen Huxley, "A Break from Tradition for the San Francisco Police: Patrol Officer Scheduling Using an Optimization-Based Decision Support System," *Interfaces* (January–February 1989), pp. 4–24.

ranging from a full six-day week to a guaranteed weekly minimum of 20 hours. Bean uses a computer program to forecast the hourly load for the telephone service center, translate the workload into capacity requirements, and then generate week-long staffing schedules for the permanent and temporary telephone operators to meet these demand requirements. The program selects the schedule that minimizes the sum of expected costs of over- and understaffing.

Outdoor goods retailer L. L. Bean has developed loyal customers through its policy of maintaining high-quality customer service. The telephone service center is staffed with operators 7 days a week, 24 hours a day.

Another example of a difficult scheduling task is that faced by police departments. Requirements for police services vary considerably throughout the day. Needs can be as much as eight times greater from 10 to 11 P.M. than from 5 to 6 A.M. Managerial Practice 16.2 on page 771 describes the San Francisco Police Department's experience in developing a work-force scheduling system.

CHAPTER REVIEW

Solved Problem 1

The Neptune's Den Machine Shop specializes in overhauling outboard marine engines. Some engines require replacement of broken parts, whereas others need a complete overhaul. Currently, five engines with varying problems are awaiting service. The best estimates for the labor times involved and the promise dates (in number of days from today) are shown in the following table. Customers usually do not pick up their engines early.

Engine	Estimated Labor Time (days)	Promise Date (days from now)
50-hp Evinrude	5	8
7-hp Chrysler	4	15
100-hp Mercury	10	12
4-hp Sportsman	1	20
75-hp Nautique	3	10

a. Develop separate schedules by using the SPT and EDD rules. Compare the two schedules on the basis of average job flow time, percentage of past due jobs, and maximum past due days for any engine.
b. For each schedule, calculate average work-in-process inventory (in engines) and average total inventory (in engines).

Solution   a. Using the shortest processing time (SPT) rule, we obtain the following schedule.

Repair Sequence	Processing Time	Job Flow Time	Promise Date	Actual Pickup Date	Days Early	Days Past Due
4-hp Sportsman	1	1	20	20	19	
75-hp Nautique	3	4	10	10	6	
7-hp Chrysler	4	8	15	15	7	
50-hp Evinrude	5	13	8	13		5
100-hp Mercury	10	23	12	23		11
Total		49		81		

Using the earliest due date (EDD), we come up with this schedule.

Repair Sequence	Processing Time	Job Flow Time	Promise Date	Actual Pickup Date	Days Early	Days Past Due
50-hp Evinrude	5	5	8	8	3	
75-hp Nautique	3	8	10	10	2	
100-hp Mercury	10	18	12	18		6
7-hp Chrysler	4	22	15	22		7
4-hp Sportsman	1	23	20	23		3
Total		76		81		

Average job flow time is 9.8 (or 49/5) days for SPT and 15.2 (or 76/5) days for EDD. Percentage of past due jobs is 40 percent (2/5) for SPT and 60 percent (3/5) for EDD. The EDD schedule minimizes the maximum days past due but has a greater flow time and causes more jobs to be past due.

b. For SPT, inventory averages are as follows.

$$\text{Average WIP inventory} = \frac{\text{Sum of flow times}}{\text{Makespan}} = \frac{49}{23} = 2.13 \text{ engines}$$

$$\text{Average total inventory} = \frac{\text{Sum of time in system}}{\text{Makespan}} = \frac{81}{23} = 3.52 \text{ engines}$$

For EDD, they are

$$\text{Average WIP inventory} = \frac{76}{23} = 3.30 \text{ engines}$$

$$\text{Average total inventory} = \frac{81}{23} = 3.52 \text{ engines}$$

Solved Problem 2

The following data were reported by the shop floor control system for order processing at the edge grinder. The current date is day 150. The number of remaining operations and the total work remaining include the operation at the edge grinder. All orders are available for processing, and none have been started yet.

Current Order	Processing Time (hr)	Due Date (day)	Remaining Operations	Shop Time Remaining (days)
A101	10	162	10	9
B272	7	158	9	6
C105	15	152	1	1
D707	4	170	8	18
E555	8	154	5	8

a. Specify the priorities for each job if the shop floor control system uses slack per remaining operations (S/RO) or critical ratio (CR).
b. For each priority rule, calculate the average job flow time per job at the edge grinder.

Solution   a. We specify the priorities for each job using the two dispatching rules.

$$S/RO = \frac{(\text{Due date} - \text{Today's date}) - \text{Shop time remaining}}{\text{Number of operations remaining}}$$

$$E555: \quad S/RO = \frac{(154 - 150) - 8}{5} = -0.80 \quad [1]$$

$$B272: \quad S/RO = \frac{(158 - 150) - 6}{9} = 0.22 \quad [2]$$

$$D707: \quad S/RO = \frac{(170 - 150) - 18}{8} = 0.25 \quad [3]$$

$$A101: \quad S/RO = \frac{(162 - 150) - 9}{10} = 0.30 \quad [4]$$

$$C105: \quad S/RO = \frac{(152 - 150) - 1}{1} = 1.00 \quad [5]$$

The sequence of production for S/RO is shown above in brackets.

$$CR = \frac{\text{Due date} - \text{Today's date}}{\text{Shop time remaining}}$$

$$E555: \quad CR = \frac{154 - 150}{8} = 0.50 \quad [1]$$

$$D707: \quad CR = \frac{170 - 150}{18} = 1.11 \quad [2]$$

$$B272: \quad CR = \frac{158 - 150}{6} = 1.33 \quad [3]$$

$$A101: \quad CR = \frac{162 - 150}{9} = 1.33 \quad [4]$$

$$C105: \quad CR = \frac{152 - 150}{1} = 2.00 \quad [5]$$

The sequence of production for CR is shown above in brackets.
b. We are looking for the flow time of a set of jobs at a single machine, so each job's flow time equals the flow time of the job just prior to it in sequence plus its own processing time. Consequently, the average flow times are

$$\text{S/RO:} \qquad \frac{8 + 15 + 19 + 29 + 44}{5} = 23.0 \text{ hours}$$

$$\text{CR:} \qquad \frac{8 + 12 + 19 + 29 + 44}{5} = 22.4 \text{ hours}$$

In this example the average flow time per job is lower for the critical ratio rule, which isn't always the case. For example, the critical ratios for B272 and A101 are tied at 1.33. If we arbitrarily assigned A101 before B272, the average flow time would increase to $(8 + 12 + 22 + 29 + 44)/5 = 23.0$ hours.

Solved Problem 3

The Rocky Mountain Arsenal, formerly a chemical warfare manufacturing site, is said to be one of the most polluted locations in the United States. Cleanup of chemical waste storage basins will involve two operations.

Operation 1:	Drain and dredge basin.
Operation 2:	Incinerate materials.

Management has estimated that each operation will require the following amounts of time (in days).

	Storage Basin									
	A	B	C	D	E	F	G	H	I	J
Dredge	3	4	3	6	1	3	2	1	8	4
Incinerate	1	4	2	1	2	6	4	1	2	8

Because of the health danger, human access to the area has been severely restricted for decades. As an unintended result, the Rocky Mountain Arsenal has now become a prolific wildlife refuge, which now supports several endangered species. Management's objective is to clean up the area while minimizing disruption to wildlife. This objective can be translated as minimizing the makespan of the cleanup operations. First, find a schedule that minimizes the makespan. Then calculate the average job flow time of a storage basin through the two operations. What is the total elapsed time for cleaning all 10 basins? Display the schedule in a Gantt machine chart.

Solution   We can use Johnson's rule to find the schedule that minimizes the total makespan. Four jobs are tied for the shortest process time: A, D, E, and H. We arbitrarily choose to start with basin E, the first on the list for the drain and dredge operation. The ten steps used to arrive at a sequence are as follows.

Select basin E first (tied with basin H); put at the front.	E	—	—	—	—	—	—	—	—	—
Select basin H next; put toward the front.	E	H	—	—	—	—	—	—	—	—
Select basin A next (tied with basin D); put at the end.	E	H	—	—	—	—	—	—	—	A
Put basin D toward the end.	E	H	—	—	—	—	—	—	D	A
Put basin G toward the front.	E	H	G	—	—	—	—	—	D	A
Put basin C toward the end.	E	H	G	—	—	—	—	C	D	A
Put basin I toward the end.	E	H	G	—	—	—	I	C	D	A
Put basin F toward the front.	E	H	G	F	—	—	I	C	D	A
Put basin B toward the front.	E	H	G	F	B	—	I	C	D	A
Put basin J in the remaining space.	E	H	G	F	B	J	I	C	D	A

There are several optimal solutions to this problem because of the ties at the start of the scheduling procedure. However, all have the same makespan. The schedule would be as follows:

	Operation 1		Operation 2	
Basin	Start	Finish	Start	Finish
E	0	1	1	3
H	1	2	3	4
G	2	4	4	8
F	4	7	8	14
B	7	11	14	18
J	11	15	18	26
I	15	23	26	28
C	23	26	28	30
D	26	32	32	33
A	32	35	35	36
			Total	200

The makespan is 36 days. The average job flow time is the sum of incineration finish times divided by 10, or 200/10 = 20 days. The Gantt machine chart for this schedule is given in Fig. 16.4.

FIGURE 16.4

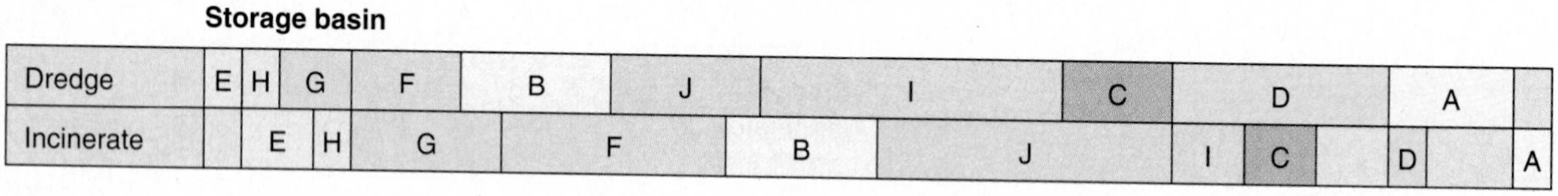

Storage basin

| Dredge | E | H | G | F | B | J | I | C | D | A | |
| Incinerate | | E | H | G | F | B | J | I | C | D | A |

Solved Problem 4

The Food Bin grocery store operates 24 hours per day, seven days per week. Fred Bulger, the store manager, has been analyzing the efficiency and productivity of store operations recently. Bulger decided to observe the need for checkout clerks on the first shift for a one-month period. At the end of the month, he calculated the average number of checkout registers that should be open during the first shift each day. His results showed peak needs on Saturdays and Sundays.

Day	M	T	W	Th	F	S	Su
Requirements	3	4	5	5	4	7	8

Bulger now has to come up with a work-force schedule that guarantees each checkout clerk two consecutive days off but still covers all requirements.

a. Develop a work-force schedule that covers all requirements while giving two consecutive days off to each clerk. How many clerks are needed? Assume that the clerks have no preference regarding which days they have off.

b. Plans can be made to use the clerks for other duties if slack or idle time resulting from this schedule can be determined. How much idle time will result from this schedule and on what days?

Solution   a. We use the method demonstrated in Example 16.4 to determine the number of clerks needed.

	Day						
	M	T	W	Th	F	S	Su
Requirements	3	4	5	5	4	7	8
Clerk 1	off	off	X	X	X	X	X
Requirements	3	4	4	4	3	6	7
Clerk 2	off	off	X	X	X	X	X
Requirements	3	4	3	3	2	5	6
Clerk 3	X	X	X	off	off	X	X
Requirements	2	3	2	3	2	4	5
Clerk 4	X	X	X	off	off	X	X
Requirements	1	2	1	3	2	3	4
Clerk 5	X	off	off	X	X	X	X
Requirements	0	2	1	2	1	2	3
Clerk 6	off	off	X	X	X	X	X
Requirements	0	2	0	1	0	1	2
Clerk 7	X	X	off	off	X	X	X
Requirements	0	1	0	1	0	0	1
Clerk 8	X	X	X	X	off	off	X
Requirements	0	0	0	0	0	0	0

The minimum number of clerks is eight.

b. Based on the results in part a, the number of clerks on duty minus the requirements is the number of idle clerks available for other duties:

	Day						
	M	T	W	Th	F	S	Su
Number on duty	5	4	6	5	5	7	8
Requirements	3	4	5	5	4	7	8
Idle clerks	2	0	1	0	1	0	0

The slack in this schedule would indicate to Bulger the number of employees he might ask to work part time (fewer than five days per week). For example, clerk 7 might work Tuesday, Saturday, and Sunday, and clerk 8 might work Tuesday, Thursday, and Sunday. That would eliminate slack from the schedule.

Formula Review

1. Performance measures:

$$\text{Job flow time} = \text{Time of completion} - \frac{\text{Time job was available for}}{\text{first processing operation}}$$

$$\text{Makespan} = \text{Time of completion of last job} - \text{Starting time of first job}$$

$$\text{Average WIP inventory} = \frac{\text{Sum of flow times}}{\text{Makespan}}$$

$$\text{Average inventory} = \frac{\text{Sum of time in system}}{\text{Makespan}}$$

$$\text{Total inventory} = \text{Scheduled receipts for all items} + \text{On-hand inventories of all items}$$

$$\text{Utilization} = \frac{\text{Productive work time}}{\text{Total work time available}}$$

2. Critical ratio:

$$CR = \frac{\text{Due date} - \text{Today's date}}{\text{Total shop time remaining}}$$

3. Slack per remaining operation:

$$S/RO = \frac{(\text{Due date} - \text{Today's date}) - \text{Shop time remaining}}{\text{Number of operations remaining}}$$

Chapter Highlights

- Scheduling is the allocation of resources over a period of time to accomplish a specific set of tasks. Two basic types of scheduling are work-force scheduling and operations scheduling.
- Gantt charts are useful for depicting the sequence of work at a particular workstation and for monitoring the progress of jobs in the system.
- No approach to scheduling is best for all situations. Performance measures that can be used to evaluate schedules include average job flow time, makespan, percentage of jobs past due, average amount of time past due per job, average work-in-process inventory, average investment in total inventory, and utilization of equipment and workers.
- Dispatching procedures allow a schedule to evolve from new information about operating conditions. Priority rules are used to make these decisions. The choice of priority rule can affect the schedule performance mea-

sures that are of concern to management.
- Labor-limited systems add another dimension to operations scheduling. In addition to determining which job to process next, the scheduler also must assign the work to an available operator having the required skills.
- Capacity considerations are important for scheduling services. If the capacity of the operating system is fixed, loads can be leveled by using approaches such as appointments, reservations, and backlogs. If service is determined by labor availability, work-force scheduling may be appropriate.
- A work-force schedule translates a staffing plan into a specific work schedule for each employee. Typical work-force scheduling considerations include capacity limits, service targets, consecutive days off, maximum number of workdays in a row, type of schedule (fixed or rotating), and vacation and holiday time.

Key Terms

critical ratio (CR) *756*
dispatching procedures *756*
earliest due date (EDD) *756*
first come, first served (FCFS) *756*
fixed schedule *767*
Gantt chart *753*
job flow time *755*
Johnson's rule *763*

labor-limited environment *765*
makespan *755*
multiple-dimension rules *761*
operations scheduling *753*
past due *755*
priority sequencing rules *756*
rotating schedule *767*
scheduling *752*

shortest processing time (SPT) *756*
single-dimension rules *757*
slack per remaining operations
    (S/RO) *756*
total inventory *755*
work-force scheduling *753*
work-in-process (WIP) inventory
    755

Study Questions

1. How does a schedule differ from a plan? Is scheduling a general or detailed activity? Is scheduling typically an activity of top management, middle management, or first-line managers?
2. Compare and contrast work-force scheduling with operations scheduling. Are they related in any way? If so, how?

3. What is the difference between the job flow time measure and the makespan measure? In what situation is makespan the same regardless of job sequence?
4. Which priority rule do you use in sequencing your homework? Why do first-come, first-served and shortest processing time rules perform poorly when demand approaches capacity? If you find that you have

more homework than there is time remaining to the end of the term, which priority rule will result in your completing all the homework?

5. Under which of the performance measures are multiple-dimension priority rules likely to outperform a single-dimension priority rule such as shortest processing time?

6. The shortest processing time (SPT) rule has been criticized because some jobs get through the production system quickly, whereas others (the ones that have long processing times) must spend considerable time waiting. Suggest a modification to the SPT rule to overcome this criticism.

7. You have just selected some ice cream from the freezer at the grocery store and joined the six-item-or-less, cash-only checkout line. Which priority rules are in effect here? Which of the performance measures does the cash-only line improve?

8. There is a problem with S/RO when more than one job in the waiting line has negative slack. For example, if job 1 has a slack of −1 with 1 operation remaining and job 2 has a slack of −2 with 10 operations remaining, S/RO would choose job 1 first because it has the smallest (most negative) ratio. Yet job 2 seems to be the one that should be processed next. Suggest a simple modification to the S/RO rule to overcome this difficulty.

9. Work-force schedules have various uses. Discuss these uses within the context of a service operation familiar to you.

Discussion Questions

1. Suppose that two alternative approaches for determining machine schedules are available. One is an optimizing approach that can be run once a week on the computer. The other is a dispatching approach that utilizes priority rules to determine the schedule as it evolves. Discuss the advantages and disadvantages of each approach and the conditions under which each approach is likely to be better.

2. Explain why management should be concerned about priority systems in manufacturing and service organizations.

Problems

1. The Studywell Company manufactures wooden desks. Management schedules overtime every weekend to reduce the backlog on the most popular models. The automatic routing machine is used to cut certain types of edges on the desktops. The following orders need to be scheduled for the routing machine.

Order	Estimated Machine Time (hr)	Due Date (hr from now)
AZ135	14	14
DM246	8	20
SX435	10	6
PC088	3	18

The due dates reflect the need for the order to be at its next operation.

a. Develop separate schedules by using the SPT and EDD rules. Compare the two schedules on the basis of average flow time, the percentage of past due jobs, and maximum past due hours for any order.

b. For each schedule, calculate average work-in-process inventory (in orders) and average total inventory (in orders).

c. Comment on the performance of the two rules relative to these measures.

2. The drill press is a bottleneck operation in a production system. Currently, five jobs are waiting to be processed. Following are the available operations data. Assume that the current date is week 5 and that the number of remaining operations and the shop time remaining include the operation at the drill press.

Job	Processing Time	Due Date	Operations Remaining	Shop Time Remaining (wk)
AA	4	10	3	4
BB	8	16	4	6
CC	13	21	10	9
DD	6	23	3	12
EE	2	12	5	3

a. Specify the priority for each job if the shop floor control system uses each of the following priority rules: SPT, S/RO, EDD, and CR.

b. For each priority rule, calculate the average flow time per job at the drill press.

c. Which of these priority rules would work best for priority planning with an MRP system? Why?

TABLE 16.4   *Manufacturing Data*

Job	Release Time	Lot Size	Processing Time (hr/unit)	Setup Time (hr)	Due Date
1	8:00 A.M. Tuesday	80	0.10	1	3:00 A.M. Wednesday
2	8:45 A.M. Tuesday	100	0.05	2	11:00 P.M. Tuesday
3	9:00 A.M. Tuesday	160	0.08	3	10:00 P.M. Tuesday
4	9:15 A.M. Tuesday	300	0.02	4	6:00 P.M. Tuesday

3. The machine shop at Blackwell Industries operates 24 hours a day and uses a numerically controlled (NC) welding machine. The load on the machine is monitored, and no more than 24 hours of work is released to the welding operators in one day. The data for a typical set of jobs are shown in Table 16.4. Management has been investigating scheduling procedures that would reduce inventory and increase customer service in the shop. Assume that at 8:00 A.M. on Tuesday the NC welding machine was idle.

   a. Develop schedules for SPT and EDD priority rules, and draw a Gantt machine chart for each schedule.

   b. For each schedule in part a, calculate the average past due hours per job and the average flow time per job. Keep in mind that the jobs are available for processing at different times.

   c. Comment on the customer service and inventory performance of the two rules. What trade-offs should management consider in selecting rules for scheduling the welding machine in the future?

4. Refer to the Gantt machine chart in Fig. 16.5.

   a. Suppose that a routing requirement is that each job must be processed on machine A first. Can the makespan be improved? If so, draw a Gantt chart with the improved schedule. If not, state why not.

   b. Suppose that there is no routing restriction on machine sequence, and that jobs can be processed in any sequence on the machines. Can the makespan in the chart be improved in this case? If so, draw a Gantt chart with your schedule. If not, state why not.

FIGURE 16.5

Machine

5. A manufacturer of sails for small boats has a group of custom sails awaiting the last two processing operations before the sails are sent to the customers. Operation 1 must be performed before operation 2, and the jobs have different time requirements for each operation. The hours required are as follows:

					Job					
	1	2	3	4	5	6	7	8	9	10
Operation 1	1	5	8	3	9	4	7	2	4	9
Operation 2	8	3	1	2	8	6	7	2	4	1

   a. Use Johnson's rule to determine the optimal sequence.

   b. Draw a Gantt chart for each operation.

6. Mighty Metal Company is under tremendous pressure to complete a government contract for six orders in 20 working days. The orders are for spare parts for highway maintenance equipment. According to the government contract, a late penalty of $500 is imposed each day the order is late. Owing to a nationwide increase in highway construction, Mighty Metal has received many orders for spare parts replacement and the shop has been extremely busy. To complete the government contract, the parts must be deburred and heat treated. The production control manager has suggested the following schedule.

	Deburr		Heat Treat	
Job	Start	Finish	Start	Finish
1	0	2	2	5
2	2	5	5	9
3	5	11	11	12
4	11	14	14	20
5	14	15	20	23
6	15	18	23	25

Is there a better schedule to avoid the late penalties? If so, show it.

7. Sharon Tepper is the operations manager of the machine shop of Universal Manufacturing. She has to schedule eight jobs that are to be sent to final assembly for an important customer order. Currently, all eight jobs are in department 12 and must be routed to department 22 next. Eric Koval, supervisor for department 12, is concerned about keeping his work-in-process inventory low and is adamant about processing the jobs through his department on the basis of shortest processing time. Pat Mooney, supervisor for department 22, pointed out that if Koval were more flexible the orders could be finished and shipped earlier. The processing times (in days) for each job in each department follow.

Job

	1	2	3	4	5	6	7	8
Department 12	2	4	7	5	4	10	8	2
Department 22	3	6	3	8	2	6	6	5

a. Determine a schedule for the operation in each department. Use SPT for department 12 and the same sequence for department 22. What is the average job flow time for department 12? What is the makespan through both departments? What is the sum of jobs times days spent in the system?

b. Find a schedule that will minimize the makespan through both departments, and then calculate the average job flow time for department 12. What is the sum of jobs times days spent in the system?

c. Discuss the trade-offs represented by these two schedules. What implications do they have for centralized scheduling?

8. John Mathews manages the Richland Distribution Center. After careful examination of his database information, he has determined the daily requirements for part-time loading dock personnel. The distribution center operates seven days a week, and the daily part-time staffing requirements are

Day	M	T	W	Th	F	S	Su
Requirements	6	3	5	3	7	2	3

Find the minimum number of workers Mathews must hire. Prepare a work-force schedule for these individuals so that each will have two consecutive days off per week and all staffing requirements will be satisfied. Give preference to the pair S–Su in case of a tie.

9. Arthur Tumble manages a ski school in a large resort and is trying to develop a schedule for instructors. The instructors receive little salary and work just enough to earn room and board. They do receive free skiing, spending most of their free time tackling the resort's notorious double black diamond slopes. Hence, the instructors work only four days a week. One of the lesson packages offered at the resort is a four-day beginner package. Tumble likes to keep the same instructor with a group over the four-day period, so he schedules the instructors for four consecutive days and then three days off. Tumble uses years of experience with demand forecasts provided by management to formulate his instructor requirements for the upcoming month.

Day	M	T	W	Th	F	S	Su
Requirements	5	4	4	5	5	7	6

a. Determine how many instructors Tumble needs to employ. Give preference to Saturday and Sunday off. *Hint:* Look for the group of three days with lowest requirements.

b. Specify the work schedule for each employee. How much slack does your schedule generate for each day?

10. The mayor of Massilon, Ohio, wanting to be environmentally progressive, has decided to implement a recycling plan. All residents of the city will receive a special three-part bin to separate their glass, plastic, and aluminum, and the city will be responsible for picking up the materials. A young city and regional planning graduate, Keith Raker, has been hired to manage the recycling program. After carefully studying the city's population density, Raker decides that the following numbers of recycling collectors will be needed.

Day	M	T	W	Th	F	S	Su
Requirements	12	7	9	9	5	3	6

The requirements are based on the populations of the various housing developments and subdivisions in the city and surrounding communities. To motivate residents of some areas to have their pickups scheduled on weekends, a special tax break will be given.

a. Find the minimum number of recycling collectors required if each employee works five days a week and has two consecutive days off. Give preference to S–Su when that pair is involved in a tie.

b. Specify the work schedule for each employee. How much slack does your schedule generate for each day?

c. Suppose that Raker can smooth the requirements further through greater tax incentives. The requirements then will be 8 on Monday and 7 on the other days of the week. How many employees will be needed now? Giving preference to S–Su when that pair is involved in a tie doesn't yield the optimal solution. Find a better solution in terms of minimal total slack capacity. Does smoothing of requirements have capital investment implications? If so, what are they?

Advanced Problems

We suggest the use of a computer for the following problem. Problem 22 in Supplement I is a scheduling problem that can be solved with linear programming.

11. The repair manager at Universal Electronics needs to develop a priority schedule for repairing eight IBM PCs. Each job requires analysis using the same diagnostic system. Furthermore, each job will require additional processing after the diagnostic evaluation. The manager doesn't expect any rescheduling delays, and the jobs are to move directly to the next process after the diagnostic work has been completed. The manager has collected the following processing time and scheduling data for each repair job.

Job	Work Time (days)	Due Date (days)	Shop Time Remaining (days)	Operations Remaining
1	0.25	5	1.5	5
2	1.75	4	2.5	7
3	1.50	6	3.0	9
4	2.00	5	3.5	12
5	1.50	4	2.0	8
6	0.75	7	1.5	6
7	1.25	6	2.0	9
8	1.00	4	1.5	3

a. Compare the relative performance of the FCFS, SPT, EDD, S/RO, and CR rules.
b. Discuss the selection of one of the rules for this company. What criteria do you consider most important in the selection of a rule in this situation?

12. Penultimate Support Systems makes fairly good speaker and equipment support stands for music groups. The assembly process involves two operations: (1) fabrication, or cutting aluminum tubing to the correct lengths, and (2) assembly, with purchased fasteners and injection-molded plastic parts. Setup time for assembly is negligible. Fabrication setup time and run time per unit, assembly run time per unit, and the production schedule for next week follow. Organize the work to minimize makespan, and create a Gantt chart. Can this work be accomplished within two 40-hour shifts?

Model	Quantity	Fabrication Setup (hr)	Fabrication Run Time (hr/unit)	Assembly Run Time (hr/unit)
A	200	2	0.050	0.04
B	300	3	0.070	0.10
C	100	1	0.050	0.12
D	250	2	0.064	0.60

13. Little 6, Inc., an accounting firm, forecasts the following weekly workload during the tax season.

	M	T	W	Th	F	S	Su
Personal tax returns	24	14	18	18	10	28	16
Corporate tax returns	18	10	12	15	24	12	4

Corporate tax returns each require 4 hours of an accountant's time, and personal returns each require 90 minutes. During tax season, each accountant can work up to 10 hours per day. However, error rates increase to unacceptable levels when accountants work more than five consecutive days per week.

a. Create an effective and efficient work schedule.
b. Assume that Little 6 has three part-time employees available to work three days per week. How could these employees be effectively utilized?

14. Eight jobs must be processed on three machines in the sequence M1–M2–M3. The processing times (in hours) are

	1	2	3	4	5	6	7	8
Machine 1	2	5	2	3	1	2	4	2
Machine 2	4	1	3	5	5	6	2	1
Machine 3	6	4	5	2	3	2	6	2

Machine M2 is a bottleneck, and management wants to maximize its use. Consequently, the schedule for the eight jobs, through the three machines, was based on the SPT rule on M2. The proposed schedule is 2–8–7–3–1–4–5–6.

a. It is now 4 P.M. on Monday. Suppose that processing on M2 is to begin at 7 A.M. on Tuesday. Use the proposed schedule to determine the schedules for M1 and M3 so that job 2 begins processing on M2 at 7 A.M. on Tuesday. Draw Gantt charts for M1, M2, and M3. What is the makespan for the eight jobs?

b. Find a schedule that utilizes M2 better and yields a shorter makespan.

15. The last few steps of a production process require two operations. Some jobs require processing on M1 before processing on M3. Other jobs require processing on M2 before M3. Currently, six jobs are waiting at M1 and four jobs are waiting at M2. The following data have been supplied by the shop floor control system.

Processing Time (hr)

Job	M1	M2	M3	Due Date (hr from now)
1	6	—	4	13
2	2	—	1	18
3	4	—	7	22
4	5	—	3	16
5	7	—	4	30
6	3	—	1	29
7	—	4	6	42
8	—	2	10	31
9	—	6	9	48
10	—	8	2	40

a. Schedule this shop by using the following rules: SPT, EDD, S/RO, and CR.

b. Discuss the operating implications of each of the schedules you developed in part a.

16. Return to Problem 8 and the work-force schedule for part-time loading dock workers. Suppose that each part-time worker can work only three days, but the days must be consecutive. Devise an approach to this work-force scheduling problem. Your objective is to minimize total slack capacity. What is the minimum number of clerks needed now and what are their schedules?

C A S E

Food King

Based in Charlotte, North Carolina, the Food King grocery supermarket chain stretches from the Virginias down the East Coast into Florida. As in the rest of the country, the grocery supermarket industry in the Southeast is very competitive, with average profit margins running at about 2 percent of revenues. Historically, the overriding competitive priority for all grocery chains was low prices. With profit margins so small, stores were continually looking for ways to reduce costs and utilize facilities efficiently. Several grocery chains still focus on low prices as their main competitive priority.

Food King, however, recently decided to focus its competitive positioning on enhancing the consumer's shopping experience. Food King's target market is the upscale food shopper, who has the following shopping priorities.

1. *Cleanliness.* The facility is clean and orderly, with items well marked and easy to find.
2. *Availability.* The selection of items is broad, and the customer has several choices for any one item.
3. *Timely service.* The store is open at convenient times, and customers don't have to wait in long checkout lines.
4. *Reasonable prices.* Although customers are willing to pay a small premium for cleanliness, availability, and good service, prices still must be competitive.

Marty Moyer had been the store manager of the Food King supermarket in Rock Hill, South Carolina, for the past three years. He had worked his way up from stockboy to manager of this medium-sized facility. Because of his success managing the Rock Hill facility, Moyer was promoted to the store manager's position at the large, flagship Food King store in Columbia. This facility had just instituted 24-hours-per-day, 7-days-a-week hours in response to competitive pressures.

After a month as manager at the Columbia store, Moyer has become familiar with the local market characteristics, store operations, and store personnel. His major challenge for the future is to align the store with the new competitive priorities established for the chain. An area he has identified as a particular concern is the scheduling of stockers and baggers. The cleanliness, availability, and service time priorities put added pressure on Moyer to have the appropriate number of stocking and bagging personnel available. Maintaining a high level of cleanliness requires more stocking personnel to keep the stock orderly on the shelves and the aisles clear and swept. The availability priority requires more frequent replenishment of shelves because the greater selection of items means less space is allocated to any one brand or item. Finally, the need for fast service requires baggers to be available to assist the cashier in serving customers quickly, especially during peak shopping periods when long waits could occur if cashiers had to bag and ring up the groceries.

Moyer knows that he can't solve the cleanliness, availability, and timely service issues just by adding stocking and bagging personnel to the payroll. To make a profit in a low-margin business environment, he has to control costs so that prices remain competitive. The trick is to develop a work schedule for the stocking and bagging personnel that satisfies competitive requirements, conforms to a reasonable set of work policies, and utilizes the personnel efficiently to minimize labor costs.

Moyers begins to address this problem by collecting information on existing scheduling policies and procedures along with a forecasted level of demand for personnel. The stocking and bagging positions can be filled with either full-time or part-time employees. Full-time employees work eight hours per day five days a week, with two consecutive days off each week. The eight-hour shifts usually are scheduled as consecutive eight-hour blocks of time; however, he can schedule an employee to two four-hour time blocks (with four hours off between them) within a particular day if there is a stocker and a bagger for the four-hour period between scheduled blocks of time.

All part-time employees are scheduled in four-hour blocks of time for up to 20 hours per week. Food King limits the number of part-time employees to 50 percent of the total number of full-time employees for each category of worker. Most of the part-time employees are utilized as baggers because they tend to be retired people who have difficulty with the heavy lifting required in stocking shelves. Food King likes to hire retired people because they are dependable, reliable, and more willing to work weekends than are teenagers. Full-time employees earn $5.25 per hour; part-time employees earn only $4.50 per hour.

For scheduling purposes, each day is divided into six four-hour time blocks beginning with 8:00 A.M. to 12:00 noon. Demand for stocking and bagging personnel varies quite a bit within a 24-hour period. Moyer developed a forecast of personnel needs by four-hour time blocks by analyzing customer activity data and supplier delivery schedules. The following table gives his estimate of the total number of stockers and baggers required for each four-hour block of time starting at the time indicated.

	Day						
Hour	M	T	W	Th	F	S	Su
8:00 A.M.	6	8	5	5	8	15	4
12:00 P.M.	6	8	5	5	10	15	6
4:00 P.M.	5	6	5	5	15	15	6
8:00 P.M.	4	4	4	4	8	6	4
12:00 A.M.	4	4	4	4	5	4	4
4:00 A.M.	8	4	4	8	5	4	4

The peak requirements occur during the heavy shopping periods on Friday and Saturday. More stocking personnel are required on Monday and Thursday evenings because of the large number of supplier deliveries on those days.

Moyer wants to determine the number of stocking and bagging personnel needed, the appropriate mix of full-time and part-time employees, and the work schedule for each employee. Going to a 24-hours-a-day operation has certainly complicated the scheduling task. He knows that younger, full-time employees probably will be best for the late night and early morning blocks of time. But the younger employees dislike working these hours. Somehow the schedule has to convey fairness for all.

Questions

1. Translate the four priorities of the shoppers into a set of competitive priorities for operations at the Rock Hill Food King store.
2. Develop a schedule of full-time and part-time stockers and baggers for Marty Moyer. Explain the strategy you used and the trade-offs you made to satisfy the Rock Hill store's competitive priorities.
3. What measures would you take to ensure that the schedule is fair to all employees?

Source: This case was prepared by Dr. Brooke Saladin, Wake Forest University, as a basis for classroom discussion.

Selected References

Andrews, B. H., and H. L. Parsons. "L. L. Bean Chooses a Telephone Agent Scheduling System." *Interfaces* (November–December 1989), pp. 1–9.

Ashton, James E., and Frank X. Cook, Jr. "Time to Reform Job Shop Manufacturing." *Harvard Business Review* (March–April 1989), pp. 106–111.

Baker, K. R. *Introduction to Sequencing and Scheduling.* New York: John Wiley & Sons, 1984.

Berry, W. L., and V. Rao. "Critical Ratio Scheduling: An Experimental Analysis." *Management Science,* vol. 22, no. 1 (October 1975), pp. 192–201.

Browne, J. J. "Simplified Scheduling of Routine Work Hours and Days Off." *Industrial Engineering* (December 1979), pp. 27–29.

Browne, J. J., and J. Prop. "Supplement to Scheduling Routine Work Hours." *Industrial Engineering* (July 1989), p. 12.

Cook, Thomas. "OR/MS: Alive and Flying at American Airlines." *OR/MS Today* (June 1989), pp. 16–18.

Hill, A. D., J. D. Naumann, and N. L. Chervany. "SCAT and SPAT: Large-Scale Computer-Based Optimization Systems for the Personnel Assignment Problem." *Decision Sciences,* vol. 14, no. 2 (April 1983), pp. 207–220.

Johnson, S. M. "Optimal Two Stage and Three Stage Production Schedules with Setup Times Included." *Naval Logistics Quarterly,* vol. 1, no. 1 (March 1954), pp. 61–68.

Kanet, J. K., and J. C. Hayya. "Priority Dispatching with Operation Due Dates in a Job Shop." *Journal of Operations Management,* vol. 2, no. 3 (May 1982), pp. 167–175.

Kiran, Ali S., and Thomas H. Willingham. "Simulation: Help for your Scheduling Problems." *APICS—The Performance Advantage* (August 1992), pp. 26–28.

Krajewski, L. J., and L. P. Ritzman. "Shift Scheduling in Banking Operations: A Case Application." *Interfaces,* vol. 10, no. 2 (April 1980), pp. 1–8.

Mabert, V. A. "Static vs. Dynamic Priority Rules for Check Processing in Multiple Dispatch–Multiple Branch Banking." *Journal of Operations Management,* vol. 2, no. 1 (May 1982), pp. 187–196.

Rhodes, Phillip. "Modern Job Shop Manufacturing Systems." *APICS—The Performance Advantage* (January 1992), pp. 27–28.

Tibrewala, R. K., D. Philippe, and J. J. Browne. "Optimal Scheduling of Two Consecutive Idle Periods." *Management Science,* vol. 19, no. 1 (September 1972), pp. 71–75.

Treleven, M. D. "The Timing of Labor Transfers in Dual Resource-Constrained Systems: Push versus Pull Rules." *Decision Sciences,* vol. 18, no. 1 (Winter 1987), pp. 73–88.

Vollmann, Thomas E., William Berry, and D. Clay Whybark. *Manufacturing Planning and Control Systems,* 3rd ed. Homewood, Ill.: Irwin, 1992.

Chapter Seventeen

MANAGING COMPLEX PROJECTS

The planning of the 1996 Summer Olympic Games in Atlanta, Georgia, exemplifies a large, complex project. The city of Atlanta, in conjunction with the Olympic Planning Committee, had to plan and execute a wide variety of tasks, including the construction of buildings to house some of the events, arrangement of housing and security for the athletes, organization of a transportation system for millions of spectators, and coordination of all the athletic events. More than 2000 athletic events had to be scheduled for the 15-day period of the games. Logical constraints, such as scheduling the semifinals before the finals and not scheduling two events for the same time and place, complicated the planning process. Traditions also had to be considered, such as running the marathon on the last day and ensuring that swimming and track and field did not go on at the same time. International TV networks also imposed conditions, such as having events popular with their home audiences take place in prime time. Of course, not all events could be run when the TV networks wanted because different countries in different time zones enjoy the

To plan the 1996 Atlanta Olympic Games, planners adapted software developed for the 1994 Games in Norway. The program, called LOLITA (Lillehammer On-Line Interactive Timing Acquisition), facilitated coordination of the many steps in developing the sites and schedules for the games.

same sports. Only careful project scheduling and control would enable the athletic events to take place on time and ensure the availability of the resources to run them properly.

Projects like the 1996 Summer Olympics are unique operations with a finite life span. Generally, many interrelated activities must be scheduled and monitored within strict time, cost, and performance guidelines. In this chapter we consider methods for managing complex projects. We begin with a general introduction to the basic project management tools and some of the managerial aspects of project scheduling and control. We then explore the use of network methods for managing projects and end with an assessment of their limitations.

◆ MANAGING PROJECTS

The Olympic Committee is responsible for scheduling and controlling a large project. We define a **project** as an interrelated set of activities that has a definite starting and ending point and that results in a unique product or service. Examples of large projects include constructing a building, ball park, road, dam, or oil pipeline; renovating a blighted urban area; developing a prototype for a new airplane; introducing a new product; organizing a state fair; and redesigning the layout of a plant or office.

Project management is goal oriented: When the team accomplishes its assigned objectives, it disbands. Team members might move on to other projects or return to their regular jobs. The project manager must motivate and coordinate the personnel assigned to the project to deliver the project on time. Complex projects such as organization of the Olympic games involve thousands of interrelated, often unique, activities. Thus the project manager may have difficulty falling back on prior experience or established procedures. The personnel come from diverse backgrounds and have many different skills. Furthermore, many team members will not be associated with the project for its full duration. They may view the project as disruptive to their regular work relationships and routines. Others will experience conflicts in loyalty or in demands on their time between their projects and department supervisors. But, despite these potential difficulties, working on projects offers substantial rewards: the excitement of dynamic work, the satisfaction of solving challenging problems, the status of membership on an elite team, and the opportunity to work with and learn from other skilled professionals.

Project managers must stay on top of their projects to meet schedules and keep costs within budget. Unexpected problems can cause delays, requiring rescheduling and reallocation of resources—and often resulting in severe financial repercussions. For example, Microsoft announced a delay in the release of Windows 95 because preliminary testing results unexpectedly uncovered "bugs" in the program. The problems had to be corrected before further tests could be conducted. The delay dealt a blow to third-party software developers, who also had to delay the release of their products. After the delay announcement, Microsoft's stock closed down 2¾ points on Nasdaq trading.

Frequently, managers must make quick decisions on the basis of incomplete information. **Network planning models** can help project managers maintain control, giving them the capability to evaluate the time and cost implications of resource trade-offs. As we discussed in Chapter 16, Gantt charts have long been used to schedule and control projects (see Figs. 16.1 and 16.2). For large projects, however, Gantt charts present difficulties: They don't directly recognize precedence relationships between activities, and they don't indicate which activities are crucial to completing the project on time.

What tools are available to schedule and control projects?

Two network planning methods were developed in the 1950s to deal with some of the shortcomings of Gantt charts. Both methods look at a project as a set of interrelated activities that can be visually displayed in a **network diagram,** which consists of nodes (circles) and arcs (arrows) that depict the relationships between activities. Working with a network diagram, an analyst can determine which activities, if delayed, will delay the entire project.

The **program evaluation and review technique (PERT)** was created for the U.S. Navy's Polaris missile project, which involved 3000 separate contractors and suppliers. Because many of the project's activities had never been performed before, PERT was developed to handle uncertain time estimates. In retrospect, PERT generally is credited with reducing the project's completion time by at least 18 months.

J. E. Kelly of Remington-Rand and M. R. Walker of Du Pont developed the **critical path method (CPM)** as a means of scheduling maintenance shutdowns at chemical processing plants. Because maintenance projects were routine in the chemical industry, reasonably accurate time estimates for activities were available. Thus CPM was based on the assumption that project activity times can be estimated accurately and do not vary.

Although early versions of PERT and CPM differed in their treatment of time estimates, today the differences between PERT and CPM are minor. Basically, either approach can cope with uncertainty. For purposes of our discussion, we simply refer to them collectively as PERT/CPM.

◆ NETWORK METHODS

Managing a complex project requires identifying every activity to be undertaken and planning when each activity must begin and end to complete the overall project on time. The degree of difficulty in scheduling a complex project depends on the number of activities, their required sequence, and their timing. Typically, managing projects with networks involves four steps:

1. describing the project,
2. diagramming the network,
3. estimating time of completion, and
4. monitoring project progress.

Describing the Project

The project manager must first describe the project in terms that everyone involved will understand. This description should include a clear statement of the project's end point. For example, the end point for a software development team would be publication of the completed software package. With the input of the team, the project manager must carefully define all project activities and precedence relationships. An **activity** is the smallest unit of work effort consuming both time and resources that the project manager can schedule and control. A **precedence relationship** determines a sequence for undertaking activities; it specifies that one activity cannot start until a preceding activity has been completed. For example, brochures announcing a conference for executives must first be designed by the program committee (activity A) before they can be printed (activity B). In other words, activity A must precede activity B.

Just what constitutes an activity will vary. For example, suppose a divisional vice-president is put in charge of a project to start manufacturing a product in a foreign country. Her list of activities may include "construct the plant." This item indicates that completion of construction will have a major bearing on when operations can begin. However, the construction supervisor's list of activities must include a greater level of detail such as "pour foundation" and "wire for electrical service." In general, a manager's project description should reflect only the level of detail that he or she needs in order to make scheduling and resource allocation decisions.

Diagramming the Network

Diagramming the project as a network requires establishing the precedence relationships between activities. For complex projects this task is essential because incorrect or omitted precedence relationships will result in costly delays. The precedence relationships are represented by a network diagram, consisting of nodes (circles) and arcs (arrows) that depict the relationships between activities. Two different approaches may be used to create a network diagram. The first approach, the **activity-on-arc (AOA) network**, uses arcs to represent activities and nodes to represent events. An **event** is the point at which one or more activities are to be completed and one or more other activities are to begin. An event consumes neither time nor resources. Because the AOA approach emphasizes activity connection points, we say that it is *event oriented*. Here, the precedence relationships require that an event not occur until all preceding activities have been completed. A convention used in AOA networks is to number events sequentially from left to right.

FIGURE 17.1   *AOA and AON Approaches to Activity Relationships*

AOA	AON	Activity Relationships
(a)		S precedes T, which precedes U.
(b)		S and T must be completed before U can be started.
(c)		T and U cannot begin until S has been completed.
(d)		U and V cannot begin until both S and T have been completed.
(e)		U cannot begin until both S and T have been completed; V cannot begin until T has been completed.
(f)		T and U cannot begin until S has been completed; V cannot begin until both T and U have been completed.

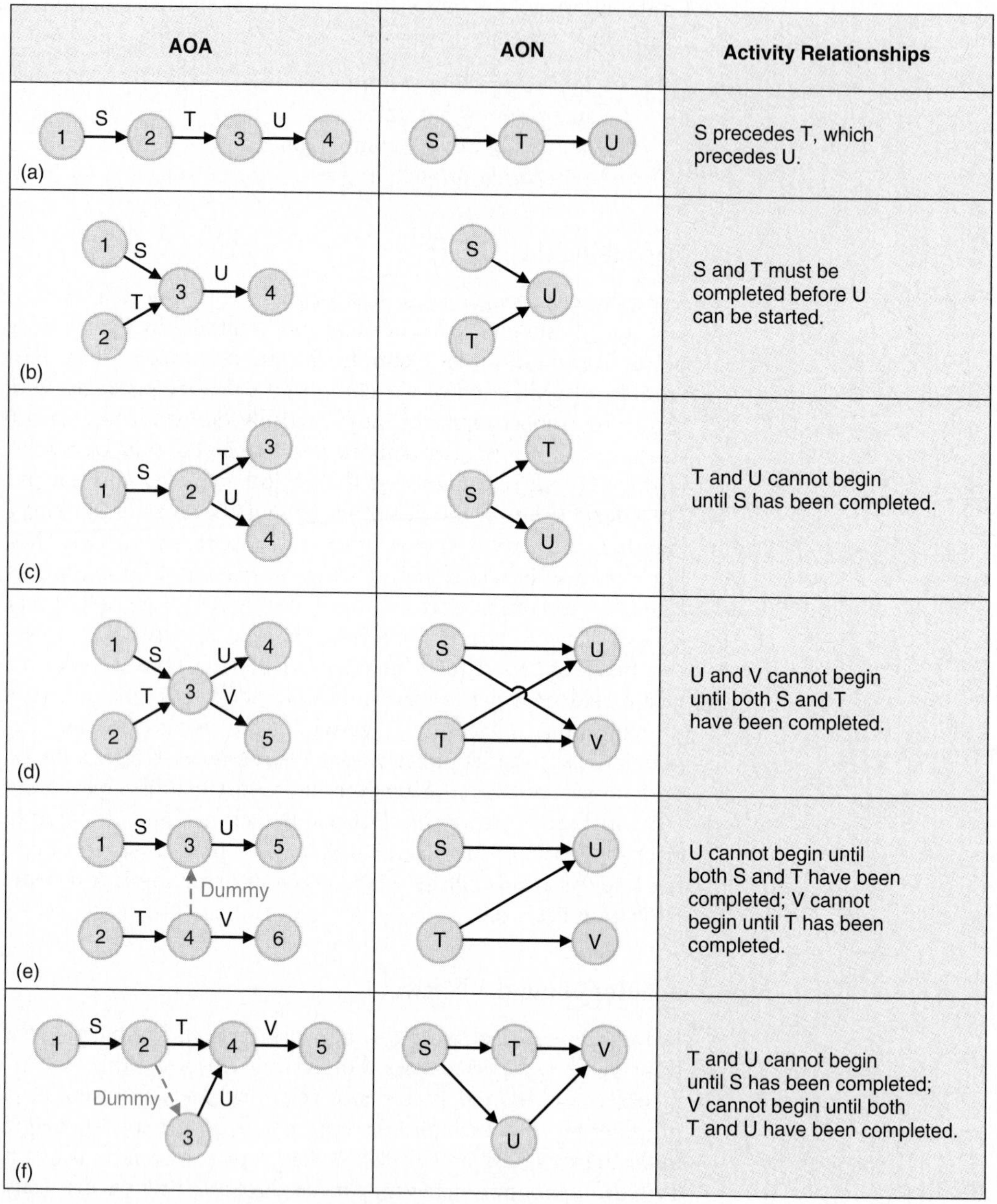

The second approach is the **activity-on-node (AON) network,** in which the nodes represent activities and the arcs indicate the precedence relationships between them. This approach is *activity oriented*. Here, the precedence relationships require that an activity not begin until all preceding activities have been completed. We used AON networks to describe assembly lines in Chapter 9.

Figure 17.1 shows the AOA and AON approaches for several activity relationships commonly encountered. In Fig. 17.1(a), activity S must be completed before activity T, which in turn must be completed before activity U can be started. For example, in the AOA diagram, event 1 might be "the start of the project," and event 2 might be "the completion of activity S." The arrows in the AOA diagram denote both precedence and the activity itself. The arrow for activity S starts from event 1 and ends at event 2, indicating that the sequence of events is from 1 to 2. In the AON diagram, the arrows represent precedence relationships only. The direction of the arrows indicates the sequence of activities, from S to T to U.

Figure 17.1(b) shows that activities S and T can be worked simultaneously, but both must be completed before activity U can begin. In Fig. 17.1(c), both activities T and U cannot begin until activity S has been completed. Multiple dependencies also can be identified. Figure 17.1(d) shows that U and V cannot begin until both S and T have been completed.

Sometimes the AOA approach requires the addition of a *dummy activity* to clarify the precedence relationships between two activities. Figure 17.1(e) shows an example of this situation. Activity U cannot begin until both S and T have been completed; however V depends only on the completion of T. A dummy activity, which has an activity time of zero and requires no resources, must be used to clarify the precedence between T and V and between S and T and U. A dummy activity also is used when two activities have the same starting and ending nodes. For example, in Fig. 17.1(f), both activities T and U cannot begin until S has been completed, and activity V cannot begin until both T and U have been completed. The dummy activity enables activities T and U to have unique beginning nodes. This distinction is important for computer programs because activities often are identified by their beginning and ending nodes. Without dummy activities, activities with identical beginning and ending nodes could not be differentiated from each other, which becomes important when the activities have different time requirements.

EXAMPLE 17.1

Diagramming a Hospital Project

In the interest of better serving the public in Benjamin County, St. Adolf's Hospital has decided to relocate from Christofer to Northville, a large suburb that at present has no primary medical facility. The move to Northville will involve constructing a new hospital and making it operational. Judy Kramer, executive director of the board of St. Adolf's, must prepare for a hearing, scheduled for next week, before the Central Ohio Hospital Board (COHB) on the proposed project. The hearing will address the specifics of the total project, including time and cost estimates for its completion.

With the help of her staff, Kramer has identified 11 major project activities. She also has specified the immediate predecessors (those activities that must be completed before a particular activity can begin) for each activity, as shown in the following table.

Activity	Description	Immediate Predecessor(s)
A	Select administrative and medical staff.	—
B	Select site and do site survey.	—
C	Select equipment.	A
D	Prepare final construction plans and layout.	B
E	Bring utilities to the site.	B
F	Interview applicants and fill positions in nursing, support staff, maintenance, and security.	A
G	Purchase and take delivery of equipment.	C
H	Construct the hospital.	D
I	Develop an information system.	A
J	Install the equipment.	E, G, H
K	Train nurses and support staff.	F, I, J

a. Draw the AON network diagram.   b. Draw the AOA network diagram.

Solution

a. The AON network for the hospital project, based on Kramer's 11 activities and their precedence relationships, is shown in Fig. 17.2. It depicts activities as circles, with arrows indicating the sequence in which they are to be performed. Activities A and B emanate from a *start* node because they have no immediate predecessors. The arrows connecting activity A to activities C, F, and I indicate that all three require completion of activity A before they can begin. Similarly, activity B must be completed before activities D and E can begin, and so on. Activity K connects to a *finish* node because no activities follow it. The start and finish nodes do not actually represent activities. They merely provide beginning and ending points for the network.

FIGURE 17.2   *AON Network for the St. Adolf's Hospital Project*

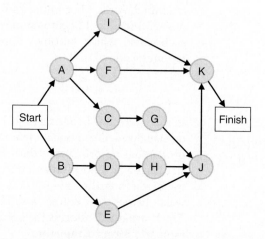

b. The AOA diagram is shown in Fig. 17.3. Event 1 is the start of the project. Activities A and B have no immediate predecessors; therefore the arrows representing those activities both have event 1 as their base. Event 2 signals the completion of activity A. As activities C, F, and I all require the completion of A, the arrows representing these activities leave the node

FIGURE 17.3 *AOA Network for the St. Adolf's Hospital Project*

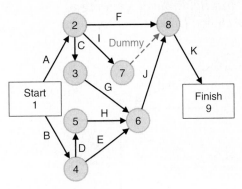

representing event 2. Similarly, the arrows for activities D and E leave the node for event 4, which signals the completion of activity B. The arrow for activity G leaves event 3, and event 6 is needed to tie activities G, H, and E together because they must be completed before activity J can begin.

Properly representing the relationship for activity K requires the use of a dummy activity. Activities I and F both emanate from event 2, and both must be completed before K can begin. Activities I and F will have the same beginning and ending nodes unless a dummy activity is used. Hence event 7 signals the end of activity I, and event 8 signals the end of activity F, with a dummy activity joining them. Now all activities are uniquely defined, and the network shows that activities F, I, and J must be completed before activity K can begin. Event 9 indicates the completion of the project.

Both the AON and the AOA approach can accurately represent all the activities and precedence relationships in a project. However, the AOA approach often requires fewer nodes than the AON approach. In Example 17.1, the AON diagram has 13 nodes whereas the AOA diagram has only 9. In contrast, the AON approach doesn't need dummy activities. Regardless of the approach used, modeling a large project as a network forces managers to identify the necessary activities and recognize the precedence relationships. If this preplanning is skipped, a project often experiences unexpected delays.

In the remainder of our discussion of PERT/CPM, we will use the AON convention, although AOA diagrams also can be applied to all the procedures.

Estimating Time of Completion

Project managers next must make time estimates for activities. When the same type of project has been done many times before, time estimates are apt to have a higher degree of certainty and are said to be **deterministic estimates.** If a project has never been done before, time estimates involve uncertainty and are called **probabilistic estimates.** For now, assume that the time estimates used in the St. Adolf's Hospital relocation problem are deterministic estimates. Figure 17.4 on the next page shows the estimated time for each activity of the St. Adolf's project.

Which activities determine the duration of an entire project?

FIGURE 17.4   *Network for St. Adolf's Hospital Project, Showing Activity Times*

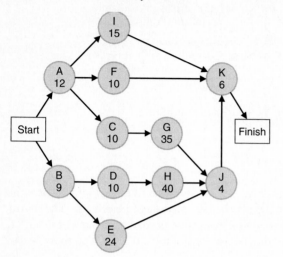

FIGURE 17.5   *Activity Paths for the Hospital Project, with the Critical Path Shown in Red*

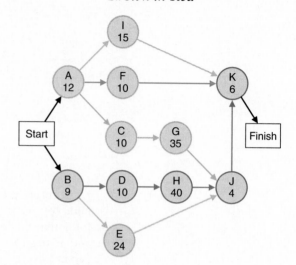

A crucial aspect of project management is estimating the time of completion. If each activity in relocating the hospital were done in sequence, with work proceeding on only one activity at a time, the time of completion would equal the sum of the times for all the activities, or 175 weeks. However, Fig. 17.4 indicates that some activities can be carried on simultaneously. We call each sequence of activities between the project's start and finish a **path.** Figure 17.5 shows that the network describing the hospital relocation project has five paths: A–I–K, A–F–K, A–C–G–J–K, B–D–H–J–K, and B–E–J–K. The **critical path** is the sequence of activities between a project's start and finish that takes the longest time to complete. Thus the activities along the critical path determine the completion time of the project; that is, if one of the activities on the critical path is delayed, the entire project will be delayed. The expected times for the paths in the hospital project network are

Path	Expected Time (wk)
A–F–K	28
A–I–K	33
A–C–G–J–K	67
B–D–H–J–K	69
B–E–J–K	43

The activity string B–D–H–J–K is expected to take 69 weeks to complete. As the longest, it constitutes the critical path for the hospital project and is shown in red on Fig. 17.5.

As the critical path defines the completion time of the project, Judy Kramer should focus on these activities in managing the project. However, projects can have more than one critical path. If activity A, C, or G were to fall behind by two weeks, the string A–C–G–J–K would be a second critical path. Consequently, managers should be aware that delays in activities not on the critical path could cause delays in the entire project.

Manually finding the critical path in this way is easy for small projects; however, computers must be used for large, complex projects. Computers calculate activity slack and prepare periodic reports for managers to monitor progress. **Activity slack** is the maximum length of time that an activity can be delayed without delaying the entire project. Activities on the critical path have zero slack. Constantly monitoring the progress of activities with little or no slack enables managers to identify activities that need to be expedited to keep the project on schedule. Activity slack is calculated from four times for each activity: earliest start time, earliest finish time, latest start time, and latest finish time.

Earliest Start and Earliest Finish Times.   The earliest start and earliest finish times are obtained as follows.

The **earliest finish time (EF)** of an activity equals its earliest start time plus its expected duration, t, or $EF = ES + t$.
The **earliest start time (ES)** for an activity is the earliest finish time of the immediately preceding activity. For activities with more than one preceding activity, ES is the latest of the earliest finish times of the preceding activities.

To calculate the duration of the entire project, we determine the EF for the last activity on the critical path.

E X A M P L E   17.2

Calculating Earliest Start and Earliest Finish Times

Calculate the earliest start and finish times for the activities in the hospital project. Figure 17.5 contains the activity times.

Solution   We begin at the start node at time zero. Activities A and B have no predecessors, so the earliest start times for these activities are also zero. The earliest finish times for these activities are

$$EF_A = 0 + 12 = 12 \quad \text{and} \quad EF_B = 0 + 9 = 9$$

Because the earliest start time for activities I, F, and C is the earliest finish time of activity A,

$$ES_I = 12, \quad ES_F = 12, \quad \text{and} \quad ES_C = 12$$

Similarly,

$$ES_D = 9 \quad \text{and} \quad ES_E = 9$$

After placing these ES values on the network diagram (see Fig. 17.6 on the next page), we determine the EF times for activities I, F, C, D, and E:

$$EF_I = 12 + 15 = 27, \quad EF_F = 12 + 10 = 22, \quad EF_C = 12 + 10 = 22$$

$$EF_D = 9 + 10 = 19, \quad \text{and} \quad EF_E = 9 + 24 = 33$$

The earliest start time for activity G is the latest EF time of all immediately preceding activities, so

$$ES_G = EF_C \qquad ES_H = EF_D$$
$$= 22 \qquad\qquad = 19$$

$$EF_G = ES_G + t \qquad EF_H = ES_H + t$$
$$= 22 + 35 \qquad\quad = 19 + 40$$
$$= 57 \qquad\qquad = 59$$

FIGURE 17.6   *Network for the Hospital Project, Showing Earliest Start and Earliest Finish Times*

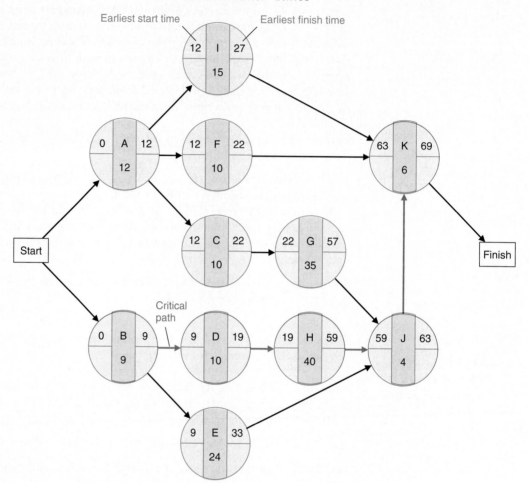

Activity J has several predecessors, so the earliest time activity J can begin is the latest of the EF times of any of its preceding activities: EF_G, EF_H, EF_E. Thus $EF_J = 59 + 4 = 63$. Similarly, $ES_K = 63$ and $EF_K = 63 + 6 = 69$. Because activity K is the last activity on the critical path, the earliest the project can be completed is week 69. The earliest start and finish times for all activities are shown in Fig. 17.6.

Latest Start and Latest Finish Times.   To obtain the latest start and latest finish times, we must work backward from the finish node. We start by setting the latest finish time of the project equal to the earliest finish time of the last activity on the critical path.

> The **latest finish time (LF)** for an activity is the latest start time of the activity immediately following it. For activities with more than one activity following, LF is the earliest of the latest start times of those activities.
> The **latest start time (LS)** for an activity equals its latest finish time minus its expected duration, *t*, or $LS = LF - t$.

For the hospital project, calculate the latest start and latest finish times for each activity from Fig. 17.6.

Solution We begin by setting the latest finish activity time of activity K at week 69, its earliest finish time as determined in Example 17.2. Thus the latest start time for activity K is

$$LS_K = LF_K - t = 69 - 6 = 63$$

If activity K is to start no later than week 63, all its predecessors must finish no later than that time. Consequently,

$$LF_I = 63, \qquad LF_F = 63, \qquad \text{and} \qquad LF_J = 63$$

The latest start times for these activities (See Fig. 17.7) are

$$LS_I = 63 - 15 = 48, \qquad LS_F = 63 - 10 = 53, \qquad \text{and} \qquad LS_J = 63 - 4 = 59$$

After obtaining LS_J, we can calculate the latest start times for the immediate predecessors of activity J:

$$LS_G = 59 - 35 = 24, \qquad LS_H = 59 - 40 = 19, \qquad \text{and} \qquad LS_E = 59 - 24 = 35$$

Figure 17.7 *Network for the Hospital Project, Showing Data Needed for Activity Slack Calculation*

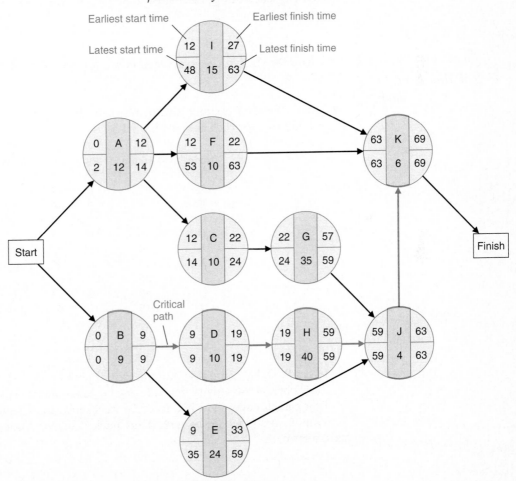

Similarly, we can now calculate latest start times for activities C and D:

$$LS_C = 24 - 10 = 14 \qquad \text{and} \qquad LS_D = 19 - 10 = 9$$

Activity A has more than one immediately following activity: I, F, and C. The earliest of the latest start times is 14 for activity C, so

$$LS_A = 14 - 12 = 2$$

Similarly, activity B has two immediate followers, D and E. The earliest of the latest start times of these activities is 9, so

$$LS_B = 9 - 9 = 0$$

This result implies that activity B must be started immediately if the project is to be completed by week 69. The latest start and latest finish times for all activities are shown in Fig. 17.7.

Activity Slack.   Information on slack is useful to project managers because it helps them make decisions regarding reallocation of resources. Activities with zero slack are on the critical path. Resources could be taken from activities with slack and given to other activities that are behind schedule until the slack is used up. Activity slack can be calculated in one of two ways for any activity:

$$S = LS - ES \qquad \text{or} \qquad S = LF - EF$$

EXAMPLE 17.4

Calculating Activity Slack

Calculate the slack for the activities in the hospital project. Use the data in Fig. 17.7.

Solution   We can use either starting times or finishing times. The following table shows the slack for each activity, $LS - ES$.

Node	Duration	ES	LS	Slack
A	12	0	2	2
B	9	0	0	0
C	10	12	14	2
D	10	9	9	0
E	24	9	35	26
F	10	12	53	41
G	35	22	24	2
H	40	19	19	0
I	15	12	48	36
J	4	59	59	0
K	6	63	63	0

Activities B, D, H, J, and K are on the critical path because they have zero slack.

The slack at an activity depends on the performance of activities leading to it. If the time for activity A had to be 14 weeks instead of 12 weeks, the slack for activities C and G would be zero. Thus slack is shared among all activities on a particular path.

Monitoring Project Progress

Even the best laid project plans can go awry. Monitoring slack time in the schedule can help managers control the activities along the critical path. Suppose that in the hospital project activity A is completed in 16 weeks rather than the anticipated 12 weeks and activity B takes 10 weeks instead of the expected 9 weeks. Table 17.1 shows how these delays affect slack times as of the sixteenth week of the project. Activities A and B aren't shown because they have already been completed.

TABLE 17.1 *Slack Calculations After Activities A and B Have Been Completed*

Activity	Duration	Earliest Start	Latest Start	Slack
C	10	16	14	−2
G	35	26	24	−2
J	4	61	59	−2
K	6	65	63	−2
D	10	10	9	−1
H	40	20	19	−1
E	24	10	35	25
I	15	16	48	32
F	10	16	53	37

Negative slack occurs when the assumptions used to compute the planned slack are invalid. Activities C, G, J, and K, which depend on the timely completion of activities A and B, show negative slack because they have been pushed beyond their planned latest start dates. The activities at the top of Table 17.1 are more critical than those at the bottom because they are the furthest behind schedule and they affect the completion time of the entire project. To meet the original completion target of week 69, the project manager must try to make up two weeks of time somewhere along path C–G–J–K. Moreover, one week will have to be made up along path D–H. If that time is made up, there will be two critical paths: C–G–J–K and D–H–J–K. Many project managers work with computer scheduling programs that generate slack reports such as that shown in Table 17.1.

◆ PROBABILISTIC TIME ESTIMATES

How can uncertainty in time estimates be incorporated into project planning?

To this point, we have assumed that the time estimates for the project were certain. Many times, however, managers must deal with uncertainty caused by labor shortages, weather, supply delays, or accidents. To incorporate uncertainty into the network model, probabilistic time estimates can be used.

With the probabilistic approach, activity times are stated in terms of three reasonable time estimates.

1. The **optimistic time** *(a)* is the shortest time in which the activity can be completed, if all goes exceptionally well.
2. The **most likely time** *(m)* is the probable time required to perform the activity.
3. The **pessimistic time** *(b)* is the longest estimated time required to perform an activity.

The following Big Picture describes some of the uncertainties in activity times that have to be dealt with in a major project.

THE BIG PICTURE: Coors Field Baseball Stadium Project

Play ball! is a familiar call in the spring, and the people of Denver, Colorado, wanted to hear those words directed at their own National League baseball team. The Denver Metropolitan Major League Baseball Stadium District, a political subdivision of the state, was created by the Colorado Legislature in June 1989. It was given the authority and responsibility to promote the acquisition of a major league franchise and develop a baseball stadium. A key requirement of the National League for granting a franchise is that the community have a state-of-the-art ballpark dedicated to baseball or commit to building one. One of the first challenges was to secure from the community a financial commitment to build a new stadium. The district prepared a financial plan and recommended using a sales tax levy contingent on the awarding of a baseball franchise. After the sales tax had been approved by the voters, the district entered into an agreement with the Colorado Baseball Partnership (team ownership group), which provided for building a state-of-the-art ballpark if the partnership succeeded in procuring a franchise. The partnership then proceeded with the application for the franchise. At the same time, the district proceeded with site selection. On July 5, 1991, the National League approved the partnership's application for the Colorado Rockies baseball franchise, allowing the district to initiate the tax levy, purchase the land, and proceed with the development of Coors Field. The Colorado Rockies began competition in April 1993, initially playing their games in Denver's Mile High Stadium. Following is a list of the major milestones in the project.

June 2, 1989	District legislation becomes effective
May 10, 1990	Architect selected
May 15, 1990	Request for proposals for site selection
July 11, 1990	Plan for finance prepared
August 14, 1990	Sales tax election—voters approve tax
September 1, 1990	National League deadline for franchise applications
September 18, 1990	Colorado delegation presentation to National League in New York
March 13, 1991	Lower downtown site selected
March 26, 1991	National League selection committee visit to Denver
July 5, 1991	National League awards franchise to Colorado Baseball Partnership, 1993, Ltd.
December 31, 1991	Largest portion of land purchased
February 13, 1992	Final lease negotiations start
April 1, 1992	Schematic design of ballpark starts
April 21, 1992	Contractor selected

October 8, 1992	Architect presents exterior elevations of ballpark to the public
October 16, 1992	Construction starts
November 11, 1992	Satellite site location of home plate
November 30, 1992	Mass excavation commences
February 2, 1993	Agreement on final terms of lease
February 15, 1993	Caissons and foundation start
June 8, 1993	Playing field turf planted at a farm in northeastern Colorado
July 14, 1993	Last parcel of land purchased
September 24, 1993	First steel raised
October 6, 1993	Final seating capacity set
March 11, 1994	First bricks placed
September 19, 1994	Scoreboard installed
October 25, 1994	Sod transplanted to playing field
February 27, 1995	Sports lighting turned on at night
March 31, 1995	Field ready for opening day

Construction of the stadium started on October 16, 1992. One of the techniques the contractor used to help manage the progress of the thousands of construction activities was the critical path method (CPM). However, planned start times and durations of many of the construction activities had to be altered because of non-construction-related occurrences. For example, land acquisition took longer than anticipated because one property owner refused to sell a parcel of land on the site that was slated to become the home-plate entrance to the stadium. Consequently, construction had to begin out of sequence in order to maintain construction progress and avoid changing the scheduled completion date. In addition, owing to the enthusiastic response of baseball fans to the Colorado Rockies, the district altered its estimates of needed seating capacity three times before finally settling on 50,000. Each change required a design modification, which then caused a change in construction activities. Eventually, the stadium took 29 months to construct and cost more than $215.5 million.

To ensure community input on key components of project design, District Executive Director John Lehigh and his staff held regular meetings with six different citizen advisory committees that represented traffic and transportation, stadium design, handicapped person accessibility, ballpark operations, environmental concerns, art and decorations, media access, and neighborhood interests and concerns. These meetings generated numerous recommendations, to which the project design team responded during the project. For example, neighborhood residents' concerns about the stadium location prompted extensive parking and traffic studies, resulting in a traffic management plan that helped mitigate the concerns.

On such a complex project, it is normal to develop a schedule of milestones at the beginning of the project to provide a framework for managing it. As the project proceeded and additional tasks become known, more detailed schedules were developed. Scheduling techniques such as CPM were important tools used by the project team to manage change. The results were good. On April 26, 1995, the citizens of Denver watched the Colorado Rockies beat the New York Mets in what has been billed as the finest ballpark in the major leagues; the Big Picture illustration on pages 802–803 shows its layout.

Construction of the ballpark required 57,000 cubic yards of concrete, 700,000 masonry blocks, 1,400,000 bricks, and 9000 tons of steel. Before construction could begin, quantities of these materials had to be estimated, suppliers selected, and delivery schedules determined. Quantities and schedules then had to be changed when the seating capacity was increased. Construction started in October 1992 and was completed in March 1995.

Seating (A). From the start in 1993, attendance figures at the Colorado Rockies games at Mile High Stadium consistently surpassed expectations, with average crowds of over 57,000 fans per game exceeding the seating capacity of 43,000 planned for Coors Field. The seating capacity was increased by 500, then by 1500, and finally by another 5000 one year after construction began on the stadium, resulting in a total of over 50,000 seats. The final design called for 18,300 seats in the main concourse, 3200 in left field, 2300 in center field, 2600 in right field, 18,500 in the upper deck, 4400 in the club mezzanine, and 700 in the suites. Included in these figures are 500 wheelchair seats with 500 companion seats and 500 seats without arms for disabled fans.

The Playing Field (B). Creating the playing field involved a number of sequential steps. Once the site had been excavated, 10,000 feet of drainage pipes were positioned throughout the site and 3000 tons of pea gravel spread on top to improve drainage. The pipes can drain 5 inches of rain an hour. The 3-acre playing field was made from 6000 tons of sand in an organic peat growing mixture. Forty-five miles of wire were installed beneath the surface to lengthen the growing season of the turf. The sod, a bluegrass/ryegrass blend, was planted at a turf farm in June 1993 and transplanted to Coors Field in October 1994.

Lighting (C). Coors Field is illuminated by 528 metal halide lamp fixtures, which can be individually controlled for optimal lighting. The 200-watt lights were attached to the structural steel support trusses prior to erection to reduce labor time.

Parking (D). A major component of the stadium project was planning efficient traffic flows and parking. A detailed analysis of vehicle access and parking was conducted before construction began. As the stadium seating capacity was increased after construction began, so was the parking capacity. The present parking capacity is 5500 on-site spots.

Entrance (E). The ballpark was designed to make access and egress convenient for the fans. The ballpark has two gentle sloping ramps, numerous stair towers, 11 passenger elevators, 7 escalators, and 2 freight elevators. To accommodate the fans during the game, the ballpark has 35 separate concession stands, numerous portable stands, 35 women's restrooms, 31 men's restrooms, and 8 family restrooms.

Calculating Time Statistics

With three time estimates—the optimistic time, the most likely time, and the pessimistic time—the manager has enough information to estimate the probability that the activity will be completed in the scheduled amount of time. To do so, the manager must first calculate the mean and variance of a probability distribution for each activity. In PERT/CPM, each activity time is treated as though it were a random variable derived from a beta probability distribution. This distribution can have various shapes, allowing the most likely time estimate (m) to fall anywhere between the pessimistic (b) and optimistic (a) time estimates. The most likely time estimate is the *mode* of the beta distribution, or the time with the highest probability of occurrence. This condition isn't possible with the normal distribution, which is symmetrical, as it requires the mode to be equidistant from the end points of the distribution. Figure 17.8 shows the difference between the two distributions.

FIGURE 17.8

Differences Between Beta and Normal Distributions for Project Analysis

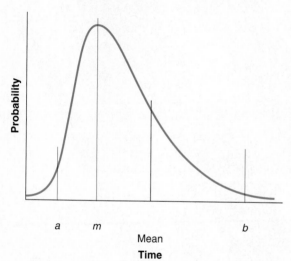

(a) **Beta distribution:** The most likely time (m) has the highest probability and can be placed anywhere between the optimistic (a) and pessimistic (b) times.

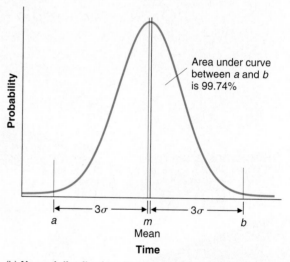

(b) **Normal distribution:** The mean and most likely times must be the same. If a and b are chosen to be 6σ apart, there is a 99.74 percent chance that the actual activity time will fall between them.

Two other key assumptions are required. First, we assume that a, m, and b can be estimated accurately. The estimates might best be considered values that define a reasonable time range for the activity duration, negotiated between the manager and the employees responsible for the activities. Second, we assume that the standard deviation, σ, of the activity time is one-sixth the range $b - a$. Hence the chance that actual activity times will fall below a or above b is slim. The assumption makes sense because, if the activity time followed the normal distribution, six standard deviations would span approximately 99.74 percent of the normal distribution.

Even with these assumptions, derivation of the mean and variance of each activity's probability distribution is complex. These derivations show that the mean of the beta distribution can be estimated by using the following weighted average of the three time estimates:

$$t_e = \frac{a + 4m + b}{6}$$

Note that the most likely time has four times the weight of the pessimistic and optimistic estimates.

The variance of the beta distribution for each activity is

$$\sigma^2 = \left(\frac{b - a}{6}\right)^2$$

The variance, which is the standard deviation squared, increases as the difference between b and a increases. This result implies that the less certain a person is in estimating the actual time for an activity, the greater will be the variance.

EXAMPLE 17.5

Calculating Means and Variances

Suppose that Judy Kramer has arrived at the following time estimates for activity B (site selection and survey) of the hospital project:

$$a = 7 \text{ weeks}, \quad m = 8 \text{ weeks}, \quad \text{and} \quad b = 15 \text{ weeks}$$

a. Calculate the expected time for activity B and the variance.
b. Calculate the expected time and variance for the other activities in the project.

Solution

a. The expected time for activity B is

$$t_e = \frac{7 + 4(8) + 15}{6} = \frac{54}{6} = 9 \text{ weeks}$$

Note that the expected time (9 weeks) doesn't equal the most likely time (8 weeks) for this activity. These times will be the same only when the most likely time is equidistant from the optimistic and pessimistic times. We calculate the variance for activity B as

$$\sigma^2 = \left(\frac{15 - 7}{6}\right)^2 = \left(\frac{8}{6}\right)^2 = 1.78$$

b. The following table shows expected activity times and variances for the activities listed in Kramer's project description. Note that the greatest uncertainty lies with the time estimate for activity I, followed by the estimates for activities E and G. The expected time for each activity will prove useful in determining the critical path.

	Time Estimates (wk)			Activity Statistics	
Activity	Optimistic (a)	Most Likely (m)	Pessimistic (b)	Expected Time (t_e)	Variance (σ^2)
A	11	12	13	12	0.11
B	7	8	15	9	1.78
C	5	10	15	10	2.78
D	8	9	16	10	1.78
E	14	25	30	24	7.11
F	6	9	18	10	4.00
G	25	36	41	35	7.11
H	35	40	45	40	2.78
I	10	13	28	15	9.00
J	1	2	15	4	5.44
K	5	6	7	6	0.11

Analyzing Probabilities

Because the time estimates for activities involve uncertainty, project managers are interested in determining the probability of meeting the project completion deadline. To develop the probability distribution for the project completion time, we assume that the duration time of one activity doesn't depend on that of any other activity. This assumption enables us to estimate the mean and variance of the probability distribution of the time duration of the entire project by summing the duration times and variances of the activities along the critical path. However, if one work crew is assigned two activities that can be done at the same time, the activity times will be interdependent. In addition, if other paths in the network have small amounts of slack, we should calculate the joint probability distribution for those paths as well. We discuss this point later.

Because of the assumption that the activity duration times are independent random variables, we can make use of the central limit theorem, which states that the sum of a group of independent, identically distributed random variables approaches a normal distribution as the number of random variables increases. The mean of the normal distribution is the sum of the expected activity times on the path. In the case of the critical path, it is the earliest expected finish time for the project:

$$T_E = \Sigma(\text{Activity times on the critical path}) = \text{Mean of normal distribution}$$

Similarly, because of the assumption of activity time independence, we use the sum of the variances of the activities along the path as the variance of the time distribution for that path. That is,

$$\sigma^2 = \Sigma(\text{Variances of activities on the critical path})$$

To analyze probabilities of completing a project by a certain date using the normal distribution, we use the z-transformation formula:

$$z = \frac{T - T_E}{\sqrt{\sigma^2}}$$

where
$$T = \text{due date for the project}$$
$$T_E = \text{earliest expected completion date for the project}$$

The procedure for assessing the probability of completing any activity in a project by a specific date is similar to the one just discussed. However, instead of the critical path, we would use the longest time path of activities from the start node to the activity node in question.

EXAMPLE 17.6

Calculating the Probability of Completing a Project by a Given Date

Calculate the probability that the hospital will become operational in 72 weeks, using (a) the critical path and (b) path A–C–G–J–K.

Solution

a. The critical path B–D–H–J–K has a length of 69 weeks. From the table in Example 17.5, we obtain the variance of path B–D–H–J–K: $\sigma^2 = 1.78 + 1.78 + 2.78 + 5.44 + 0.11 = 11.89$. Next, we calculate the z-value:

$$z = \frac{72 - 69}{\sqrt{11.89}} = \frac{3}{3.45} = 0.87$$

Using the normal distribution table in Appendix 2, we find that the probability is about 0.81 that the length of path B–D–H–J–K will be no greater than 72 weeks. Because this path is the critical path, there is a 19 percent probability that the project will take longer than 72 weeks. This probability is shown graphically in Fig. 17.9.

FIGURE 17.9 *Probability of Completing the Hospital Project on Schedule*

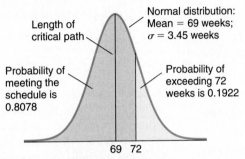

b. From the table in Example 17.5, we determine that the sum of the activity times on path A–C–G–J–K is 67 weeks and that $\sigma^2 = 0.11 + 2.78 + 7.11 + 5.44 + 0.11 = 15.55$. The z-value is

$$z = \frac{72 - 67}{\sqrt{15.55}} = \frac{5}{3.94} = 1.27$$

The probability is about 0.90 that the length of path A–C–G–J–K will be no greater than 72 weeks. However, this analysis implies that there is a 10 percent chance that this path will cause a delay in the project. It also demonstrates the importance of monitoring paths that have durations close to that of the critical path.

As Example 17.6 demonstrated, one or more network paths for a project may be shorter than the critical path but have enough variance in activity time estimates to become the critical path sometime during the project. In the hospital project, path A–C–G–J–K will become the critical path if its length equals or exceeds 69 weeks *or* if the length of path B–D–H–J–K equals 67 weeks or less. Figure 17.10 shows the considerable overlap between the probability distributions for these two paths. Computing the probability that path A–C–G–J–K will

FIGURE 17.10

Probability Distributions for the Critical Path and Next Longest Path for the Hospital Project

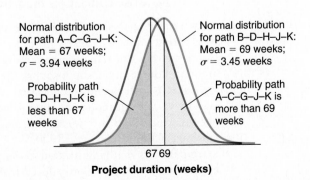

become the critical path requires the estimation of the joint probability that path A–C–G–J–K $\geq$ 69 weeks *and* that path B–D–H–J–K $\leq$ 67 weeks, as indicated by the shaded areas. The two paths are dependent on each other (share common activities), so the calculation of the joint probability requires computer simulation. Nonetheless, close attention to activities A, C, and G, in addition to activities B, D, H, J, and K, seems warranted. If a project has multiple critical paths, the critical path with the largest variance should be used in the denominator of the z-transformation formula. This approach allows the probability estimate to reflect the correct amount of uncertainty in the project duration.

COST CONSIDERATIONS

How do project planning methods increase the potential to control costs and provide better customer service?

Keeping costs at acceptable levels almost always is as important as meeting schedule dates. In this section we discuss the use of PERT/CPM methods to obtain minimum-cost schedules.

The reality of project management is that there are always time–cost trade-offs. For example, a project often can be completed earlier than scheduled by hiring more workers or running extra shifts. Such actions could be advantageous if savings or additional revenues accrue from completing the project early. Total project costs are the sum of direct costs, indirect costs, and penalty costs. These costs are dependent either on activity times or on the project completion time. Direct costs include labor, materials, and any other costs directly related to project activities. Managers can shorten individual activity times by using additional direct resources such as overtime, personnel, or equipment. Indirect costs include administration, depreciation, financial, and other variable overhead costs that can be avoided by reducing total project time. The shorter the duration of the project, the lower the indirect costs will be. Finally, a project incurs penalty costs if it extends beyond some specific date, whereas a bonus may be provided for early completion. Thus a project manager may consider *crashing*, or expediting, some activities to reduce overall project completion time and total project costs.

To assess whether crashing some activities would be beneficial — from either a cost or a schedule perspective—the manager needs to know the following times and costs.

1. The **normal time (NT)** is the time to complete the activity under normal conditions. Normal time equals the expected time t_e, calculated earlier.
2. The **normal cost (NC)** is the activity cost associated with the normal time.
3. The **crash time (CT)** is the shortest possible time to complete the activity.
4. The **crash cost (CC)** is the activity cost associated with the crash time.

Our cost analysis is based on the assumption that direct costs increase linearly as activity time is reduced from its normal time. This assumption implies that for every week the activity time is reduced, direct costs increase by a proportional amount. For example, suppose that the normal time for activity C in the hospital project is 10 weeks and is associated with a direct cost of $4000. If, by crashing activity C, we can reduce its time to only 5 weeks at a crash cost of $7000, the net time reduction is 5 weeks at a net cost increase of $3000. We assume that crashing activity C costs $3000/5 = $600 per week—an assumption of linear marginal costs that is illustrated in Fig. 17.11. Thus, if activity C were expedited by two weeks (i.e., its time reduced from 10 weeks to 8 weeks), the estimated di-

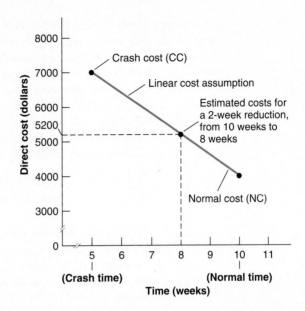

FIGURE 17.11

Cost–Time Relationships in Cost Analysis

rect costs would be $4000 + 2(\$600) = \$5200$. For any activity, the cost to crash an activity by one week is

$$\text{Cost to crash per week} = \frac{CC - NC}{NT - CT}$$

Table 17.2 contains direct cost and time data and the costs of crashing per week for the activities in the hospital project.

TABLE 17.2   *Direct Cost and Time Data for the Hospital Project*

Activity	Normal Time (NT)	Normal Cost (NC)	Crash Time (CT)	Crash Cost (CC)	Maximum Time Reduction (wk)	Cost of Crashing per Week
A	12	$ 12,000	11	$ 13,000	1	$ 1,000
B	9	50,000	7	64,000	2	7,000
C	10	4,000	5	7,000	5	600
D	10	16,000	8	20,000	2	2,000
E	24	120,000	14	200,000	10	8,000
F	10	10,000	6	16,000	4	1,500
G	35	500,000	25	530,000	10	3,000
H	40	1,200,000	35	1,260,000	5	12,000
I	15	40,000	10	52,500	5	2,500
J	4	10,000	1	13,000	3	1,000
K	6	30,000	5	34,000	1	4,000
	Totals	$1,992,000		$2,209,500		

The objective of cost analysis is to determine the project completion time that minimizes total project costs. Suppose that project indirect costs are $8000 per week. Suppose also that, after week 65, St. Adolf's incurs a penalty cost of $20,000 per week if the hospital isn't fully operational. With a critical path completion time of 69 weeks, the hospital faces potentially large penalty costs. For every week that the project is shortened—to week 65—the hospital saves one week of penalty *and* indirect costs, or $28,000. For reductions beyond week 65, the savings are only the weekly indirect costs of $8000.

In determining the **minimum-cost schedule,** we start with the normal time schedule and crash activities along the critical path, because the length of the critical path equals the length of the project. We want to determine how much we can add in crash costs without exceeding the savings in indirect and penalty costs. The procedure involves the following steps.

Step 1. Determine the project's critical path(s).

Step 2. Find the cheapest activity or activities on the critical path(s) to crash.

Step 3. Reduce the time for this activity until (a) it cannot be further reduced, (b) another path becomes critical, or (c) the increase in direct costs exceeds the savings that result from shortening the project. If more than one path is critical, the time for an activity on each path may have to be reduced simultaneously.

Step 4. Repeat this procedure until the increase in direct costs is less than the savings generated by shortening the project.

EXAMPLE 17.7

Finding a Minimum-Cost Schedule

Determine the minimum-cost schedule for the hospital project. Use the information in Table 17.2 and Fig. 17.7.

Solution   The projected completion time of the project is 69 weeks. The project costs for that schedule are $1,992,000 in direct costs, 69($8,000) = $552,000 in indirect costs, and (69 − 65)($20,000) = $80,000 in penalty costs, for total project costs of $2,624,000. The five paths in the network have the following normal times.

A–I–K:	33 weeks	B–D–H–J–K:	69 weeks
A–F–K:	28 weeks	B–E–J–K:	43 weeks
A–C–G–J–K:	67 weeks		

If all activities on A–C–G–J–K were crashed, the path duration would be 47 weeks. Crashing all activities on B–D–H–J–K results in a duration of 56 weeks. The *normal* times of A–I–K, A–F–K, and B–E–J–K are less than the minimum times of the other two paths, so we can disregard those three paths; they will never become critical regardless of the crashing we may do.

Stage 1

Step 1. The critical path is B–D–H–J–K.

Step 2. The cheapest activity to crash per week is J at $1000, which is much less than the savings in indirect and penalty costs of $28,000 per week.

Step 3. Crash activity J to its limit of 3 weeks because the critical path remains unchanged. The new expected path times are

A–C–G–J–K:	64 weeks	B–D–H–J–K:	66 weeks

The net savings are 3($28,000) − 3($1000) = $81,000. The total project costs are now $2,624,000 − $81,000 = $2,543,000.

Stage 2

Step 1. The critical path is still B–D–H–J–K.

Step 2. The cheapest activity to crash per week now is D at $2000.

Step 3. Crash D by two weeks. The first week of reduction in activity D saves $28,000 because it eliminates a week of penalty costs, as well as indirect costs. Crashing D by a second week saves only $8000 in indirect costs because, after week 65, there are no more penalty costs. These savings still exceed the cost of crashing D by two weeks. The updated path times are

A–C–G–J–K: 64 weeks   B–D–H–J–K: 64 weeks

The net savings are $28,000 + $8000 − 2($2000) = $32,000. The total project costs are now $2,543,000 − $32,000 = $2,511,000.

Stage 3

Step 1. After crashing D, we now have two critical paths. *Both* critical paths must now be shortened to realize any savings in indirect project costs. If one is shortened and the other isn't, the length of the project remains unchanged.

Step 2. Our alternatives are to crash one of the following combinations of activities—(A, B), (A, H), (C, B), (C, H), (G, B), (G, H)—or to crash activity K, which is on both critical paths (J has already been crashed). We consider only those alternatives for which the cost of crashing is less than the potential savings of $8000 per week. The only viable alternatives are (C, B) at a cost of $7600 per week and K at $4000 per week. We choose activity K to crash.

Step 3. We crash activity K to the greatest extent possible—a reduction of one week — because it is on both critical paths. The updated path times are

A–C–G–J–K: 63 weeks   B–D–H–J–K: 63 weeks

The net savings are $8000 − $4000 = $4000. The total project costs are $2,511,000 − $4000 = $2,507,000.

Stage 4

Step 1. The critical paths are B–D–H–J–K and A–C–G–J–K.

Step 2. The only viable alternative at this stage is to crash activities B and C simultaneously at a cost of $7600 per week. This amount is still less than the savings of $8000 per week.

Step 3. Crash activities B and C by two weeks, the limit for activity B. The updated path times are

A–C–G–J–K: 61 weeks   B–D–H–J–K: 61 weeks

The net savings are 2($8000) − 2($7600) = $800. The total project costs are $2,507,000 − $800 = $2,506,200.

Any other combination of activities will result in a net increase in total project costs because the crash costs exceed weekly indirect costs. The minimum-cost schedule is 61 weeks, with a total cost of $2,506,200. To obtain this schedule, we crashed activities B, D, J, and K to their limits and activity C to 8 weeks. The other activities remain at their normal times. This schedule costs $117,800 less than the normal-time schedule.

◆   RESOURCE LIMITATIONS

What is the effect of limited resources on project duration?

The project management approaches discussed so far consider only activity times in determining overall project duration and the critical path. An underlying assumption in the use of PERT/CPM is that sufficient resources will be available when needed to complete all project activities on schedule. However, developing schedules without considering the load placed on resources can result in inefficient resource use and even cause project delays if capacity limitations are exceeded.

For purposes of discussion, consider the project diagram in Fig. 17.12. Each of the five activities involves a certain amount of time and has a resource requirement. The critical path is A–B–E, and the total time to complete the project, ignoring resource limitations, is nine days.

FIGURE 17.12

Project Diagram, Showing Resource Requirements, Activity Times, and Critical Path

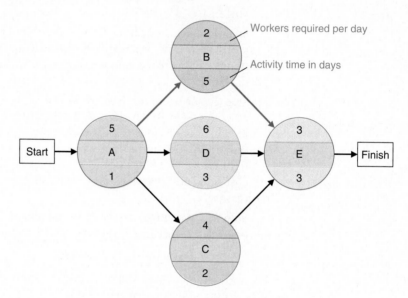

Although AON or AOA network diagrams are useful for displaying an entire project and showing the precedence relationships between activities, they aren't especially useful for showing the implications of resource requirements for a schedule of activities. Gantt charts are more helpful in this regard.

We want to generate a schedule that recognizes resource constraints, as well as the precedence relationships between activities. Let's suppose that we are limited to a small number of workers per day. Although we could use an optimizing approach, such as linear programming (see Supplement I), to derive a schedule under these conditions, a more useful approach is the following procedure, developed by Weist (1966).

1. Start with the first day of the project and schedule as many activities as possible, considering precedence relationships and resource limitations. Continue with the second day, and so on, until all activities have been scheduled.
2. When several activities compete for the same resources, give preference to the activities with the least slack, as determined with standard PERT/CPM methods.

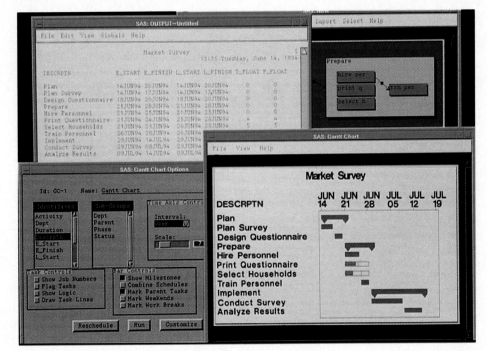

Gantt chart software may be used to schedule each step in a market survey project. This project has three phases: plan, prepare, and implement. Specific activities are shown under each phase. Some activities can be executed simultaneously, whereas others must be sequenced.

3. Reschedule noncritical activities, if possible, to free resources for critical or nonslack activities.

The intent of this procedure is to minimize total project time, subject to resource constraints.

EXAMPLE 17.8

Developing a Resource-Constrained Schedule

Generate a resource-constrained schedule for the project depicted in Fig. 17.12. Assume that only six workers per day are available.

Solution

Step 1. Schedule activity A first because all other activities depend on its completion.

Step 2. The choice is among activities B, C, and D because their predecessor has been scheduled. Activities C and D have slack, but activity B doesn't because it's on the critical path. Therefore schedule B next. So far, we have committed five workers on day 1 and two workers on days 2–6.

Step 3. We have a choice between activities C and D, but we must choose C next. It requires only four workers per day, and we can schedule it on days 2 and 3 without violating the resource constraint of six workers per day. Activity D requires six workers per day, but we have already scheduled activity B, which needs two workers.

Step 4. The remaining activities to schedule are D and E. We must schedule D first because of precedence constraints. The resulting schedule is shown in Fig. 17.13.

FIGURE 17.13   *Resource-Constrained Schedule*

Activity	Day											
	1	2	3	4	5	6	7	8	9	10	11	12
A	⑤											
B				②								
C			④									
D								⑥				
E											③	
Resource Requirements	5	6	6	2	2	2	6	6	6	3	3	3

This schedule results in the shortest project time possible under the resource constraints. Activity C can be delayed three days without delaying the completion of the project or exceeding the resource constraints. The critical path based on resource requirements *and* time estimates is A–B–D–E. However, the use of the procedure will not always be so successful. We can only say that it will generally produce solutions close to the optimum.

◆ BENEFITS AND LIMITATIONS OF PERT/CPM SYSTEMS

PERT/CPM systems offer a number of benefits to project managers. However, they also have limitations.

Benefits

We have already discussed the benefits of network planning models for large, complex projects. In summary, they include the following.

1. Considering projects as networks forces managers to organize the required data and identify the interrelationships between activities. This process also identifies the data to be gathered and provides a forum for managers of different functions to discuss the nature of the various activities and their requirements.
2. PERT/CPM computer packages provide graphic displays of the project diagram and progress reports.
3. Networks enable managers to estimate the completion time of the project, which can be useful in planning other events or in contractual negotiations with customers.
4. Reports highlight the activities that are crucial to completing the project on schedule. These reports can be updated periodically over the life of the project.
5. Reports also highlight the activities that have slack, thereby indicating resources that may be reallocated to more urgent activities.
6. Networks enable managers to analyze cost–time trade-offs.

Limitations

Let's now turn to the limitations of PERT/CPM.

Network Diagrams. The methods used in PERT/CPM are based on the assumption that project activities have clear beginning and ending points, that they are independent of each other, and that the activity sequence relationships can be specified in a network diagram. In reality, two activities may overlap, or the outcome of one activity may determine the time and resources required for another activity. Also, a network diagram developed at the start of a project may later limit the project manager's flexibility to handle changing situations. At times, actual precedence relationships cannot be specified beforehand because of some dependencies between activities.

Control. A second underlying assumption in PERT/CPM methods is that managers should focus only on the activities along the critical path. However, managers also must pay attention to *near-critical* paths, which could become critical if the schedules of one or more of the activities slip. Project managers who overlook near-critical paths may find their project's completion date slipping.

Time Estimates. A third assumption—that uncertain activity times follow the beta distribution—has brought a variety of criticism. First, the formulas used to calculate the mean and variance of the beta distribution are only approximations and are subject to errors of up to 10 percent for the mean and 5 percent for the variance. These errors could give incorrect critical paths. Second, arriving at accurate time estimates for activities that have never been performed before is extremely difficult. Many project managers prefer to use a single time estimate, arguing that pessimistic time estimates often are inflated and vary far more from the most likely time estimate than do the optimistic time estimates. Inflated pessimistic time estimates build a cushion of slack into the schedule. Finally, the choice of the beta distribution is somewhat arbitrary, and the use of another distribution would result in a different expected time and variance for each activity.

Resource Limitations. A fourth assumption of PERT/CPM is that sufficient resources will be available when needed to complete all project activities on schedule. However, managers should consider the load placed on resources to ensure efficient resource use and avoid project delays caused by exceeding capacity. Network diagrams don't show the implications of resource limitations for a schedule of activities.

Although PERT/CPM has shortcomings, its skillful application to project management can significantly aid project managers in their work.

◆ COMPUTERIZED PROJECT SCHEDULING AND CONTROL

Computerized network planning methods are used extensively for projects in government, construction, aerospace, entertainment, pharmaceuticals, utilities, manufacturing, and architectural engineering. Ford Motor Company used computerized network planning for retooling assembly lines, and Chrysler Corporation used it for building a new assembly plant. Other users include the San Francisco Opera Association, the Walt Disney Company, and Procter & Gamble. Managerial Practice 17.1 discusses the project scheduling software used by a large construction company.

Managerial Practice 17.1

▶ *Integrated Project Control at the M. W. Kellogg Company*

The M. W. Kellogg Company is one of the world's leading engineering contractors specializing in the engineering design and construction of petroleum and petrochemical facilities. Maintaining promised delivery dates of such large and complex facilities is a difficult task. The typical project involves 1500 engineering activities, 1100 materials requisitions and purchase orders, 4000 cost accounts, 150 project change notices, and 400,000 work hours. A project may cost anywhere from $10 million to $100 million, and delays can cost the customer millions in lost revenues. The Kellogg Company may have up to 20 of these projects ongoing at any point in time.

A sophisticated computer package with CPM at the core, called Artemis®, was purchased to assist managers with complex scheduling problems. When the company gets a new job, the following tasks are performed.

- A master schedule is developed with CPM and approved by management. This schedule contains the completion times of the various components of the project and becomes a commitment to the customer.
- Detailed engineering and procurement schedules are established, reviewed by management, and finalized. Approved budgets for each department are broken down into cost accounts and integrated with existing schedules and workloads.
- Performance is tracked every two weeks by measuring progress and actual hours used against the baselines provided by CPM. Schedule updates are distributed internally and to customers at least once a month.

The approach taken by the Kellogg Company provides an early warning system for detection of slippage in the schedule.

Source: Anita M. Hickman, "Refining the Process of Project Control," *Production and Inventory Management* (February 1992), pp. 26–29.

The M. W. Kellogg Company had to purchase a sophisticated software package because of the complexity of its scheduling problems. However, with the advent of personal computers, "off-the-shelf" project management software has become accessible to many companies. Large as well as small projects are routinely managed with the assistance of standard computerized scheduling packages. Software costs have come down, and the user interfaces are friendly. Standard software programs may differ in terms of their output reports and may include one or more of the following capabilities:

- *Gantt charts and PERT/CPM diagrams.* The graphics capabilities of software packages allow for visual displays of project progress on Gantt charts and PERT/CPM network diagrams. Most packages allow the user to display portions of the network on the video monitor to analyze specific problems.

- *Project status and summary reports.* These reports include budget variance reports that compare planned to actual expenses at any stage in the project, resource histograms that graphically display the usage of a particular resource over time, status reports for each worker by task performed, and summary reports that indicate project progress to top management.

- *Tracking reports.* These reports identify areas of concern such as the percentage of activity completion with respect to time, budget, or labor resources. Most software packages allow multiple projects to be tracked at the same time. This feature is important when resources must be shared jointly by several projects.

Almost any project requiring significant resources will be aided by the use of project management software. However, despite today's user-friendly packages, extensive employee training might be needed for an organization to benefit fully from these systems.

CHAPTER REVIEW

Solved Problem 1

An advertising project manager has developed the network diagrams shown in Fig. 17.14 for a new advertising campaign. In addition, the manager has gathered the time information for each activity, as shown in the accompanying table.

FIGURE 17.14   *Network Diagrams for an Advertising Program*

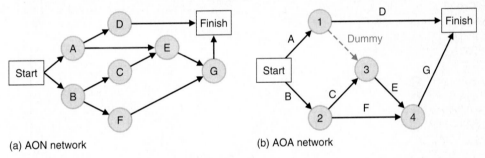

(a) AON network   (b) AOA network

a. Calculate the expected time and variance for each activity.
b. Calculate the activity slacks and determine the critical path using the expected activity times.
c. What is the probability of completing the project within 23 weeks?

| | Time Estimates (wk) | | | |
Activity	Optimistic	Most Likely	Pessimistic	Immediate Predecessor(s)
A	1	4	7	—
B	2	6	7	—
C	3	3	6	B
D	6	13	14	A
E	3	6	12	A, C
F	6	8	16	B
G	1	5	6	E, F

Solution   a. The expected time for each activity is calculated as follows:

$$t_e = \frac{a + 4m + b}{6}$$

Activity	Expected Time (wk)	Variance
A	4.0	1.00
B	5.5	0.69
C	3.5	0.25
D	12.0	1.78
E	6.5	2.25
F	9.0	2.78
G	4.5	0.69

b. We need to calculate the earliest start, latest start, earliest finish, and latest finish times for each activity. Starting with activities A and B, we proceed from the beginning of the network and move to the end, calculating the earliest start and finish times (shown graphically in Fig. 17.15 for the AON diagram):

FIGURE 17.15

AON Diagram with Earliest Start and Earliest Finish Times

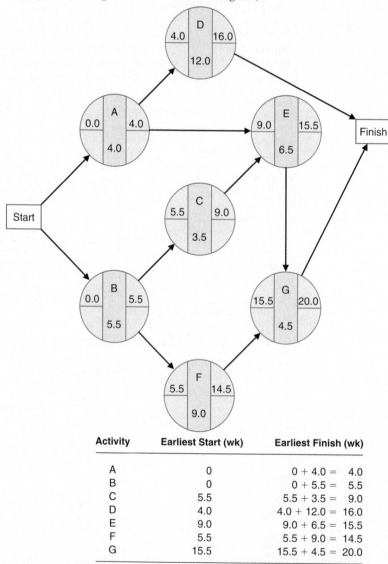

Activity	Earliest Start (wk)	Earliest Finish (wk)
A	0	0 + 4.0 = 4.0
B	0	0 + 5.5 = 5.5
C	5.5	5.5 + 3.5 = 9.0
D	4.0	4.0 + 12.0 = 16.0
E	9.0	9.0 + 6.5 = 15.5
F	5.5	5.5 + 9.0 = 14.5
G	15.5	15.5 + 4.5 = 20.0

Based on expected times, the earliest finish for the project is week 20, when activity G has been completed. Using that as a target date, we can work backward through the network, calculating the latest start and finish times (shown graphically in Fig. 17.16):

FIGURE 17.16

AON Diagram with All Time Estimates Needed to Calculate Slack

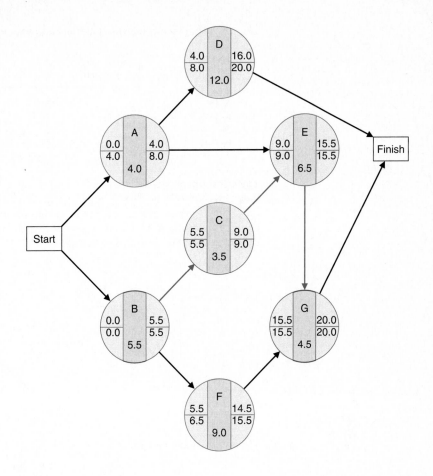

Activity	Latest Start (wk)	Latest Finish (wk)
G	15.5	20.0
F	6.5	15.5
E	9.0	15.5
D	8.0	20.0
C	5.5	9.0
B	0.0	5.5
A	8.0	12.0

We now calculate the activity slacks and determine which activities are on the critical path.

Activity	Start Earliest	Start Latest	Finish Earliest	Finish Latest	Activity Slack	Critical Path
A	0.0	4.0	4.0	8.0	4.0	No
B	0.0	0.0	5.5	5.5	0.0	Yes
C	5.5	5.5	9.0	9.0	0.0	Yes
D	4.0	8.0	16.0	20.0	4.0	No
E	9.0	9.0	15.5	15.5	0.0	Yes
F	5.5	6.5	14.5	15.5	1.0	No
G	15.5	15.5	20.0	20.0	0.0	Yes

The paths, and their total expected times and variances, are

Path	Total Expected Time (wk)	Total Variance
A–D	4 + 12 = 16	1.00 + 1.78 = 2.78
A–E–G	4 + 6.5 + 4.5 = 15	1.00 + 2.25 + 0.69 = 3.94
B–C–E–G	5.5 + 3.5 + 6.5 + 4.5 = 20	0.69 + 0.25 + 2.25 + 0.69 = 3.88
B–F–G	5.5 + 9 + 4.5 = 19	0.69 + 2.78 + 0.69 = 4.16

The critical path is B–C–E–G, with a total expected time of 20 weeks. However, path B–F–G is 19 weeks and has a large variance. In this solution we used the AON notation, showing the start and finish times within the node circles. The same results can be obtained with the AOA notation, except that the times typically are shown in a box drawn near the arc (arrow). For example:

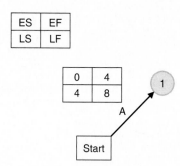

c. We first calculate the z-value:

$$z = \frac{T - T_E}{\sqrt{\sigma^2}} = \frac{23 - 20}{\sqrt{3.88}} = 1.52$$

Using Appendix 2, we find that the probability of completing the project in 23 weeks or less is 0.9357. Because the length of path B–F–G is very close to that of the critical path and has a large variance, it might well become the critical path during the project.

Solved Problem 2

Your company has just received an order from a good customer for a specially designed electric motor. The contract states that, starting on the thirteenth day from now, your firm will experience a penalty of $100 per day until the job is completed. Indirect project costs amount to $200 per day. The data on direct costs and activity precedence relationships are given in Table 17.3.

a. Draw the project network diagram.
b. What completion date would you recommend?

Solution   a. The AON network diagram, including normal activity times, for this procedure is shown in Fig. 17.17. Keep the following points in mind while constructing a network diagram.

- Always have start and finish nodes.
- Try to avoid crossing paths to keep the diagram simple.
- Use only one arrow to directly connect any two nodes.

TABLE 17.3   *Electric Motor Project Data*

Activity	Normal Time (days)	Normal Cost ($)	Crash Time (days)	Crash Cost ($)	Immediate Predecessor(s)
A	4	1000	3	1300	None
B	7	1400	4	2000	None
C	5	2000	4	2700	None
D	6	1200	5	1400	A
E	3	900	2	1100	B
F	11	2500	6	3750	C
G	4	800	3	1450	D, E
H	3	300	1	500	F, G

FIGURE 17.17

AON Diagram for the Electric Motor Project

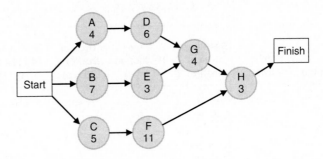

- Put the activities with no predecessors at the left and point the arrows from left to right.
- Use scratch paper and be prepared to revise the diagram several times before you come up with a correct and uncluttered diagram.

b. With these activity durations, the project will be completed in 19 days and incur a $700 penalty for lateness. Determining a good completion date requires the use of the minimum-cost schedule procedure. Using the data in Table 17.3, you can determine the maximum crash time reduction and crash cost per day for each activity. For example, for activity A:

Maximum crash time = Normal time − Crash time = 4 days − 3 days = 1 day

$$\text{Crash cost per day} = \frac{\text{Crash cost} - \text{Normal cost}}{\text{Normal time} - \text{Crash time}} = \frac{\text{CC} - \text{NC}}{\text{NT} - \text{CT}} = \frac{\$1300 - \$1000}{4 \text{ days} - 3 \text{ days}} = \$300$$

Activity	Crash Cost per Day ($)	Maximum Time Reduction (days)
A	300	1
B	200	3
C	700	1
D	200	1
E	200	1
F	250	5
G	650	1
H	100	2

Table 17.4 contains a summary of the analysis and the resultant project duration and total cost. The critical path is C–F–H at 19 days—the longest path in the network. The cheapest of these activities to crash is H, which costs only an extra $100 per day to crash. Doing so saves $200 + $100 = $300 per day in indirect and penalty costs. If you crash this activity two days (the maximum), the lengths of the paths are now

| A–D–G–H: | 15 days | B–E–G–H: | 15 days | C–F–H: | 17 days |

The critical path is still C–F–H. The next cheapest critical activity to crash is F at $250 per day. You can crash F only two days because at that point you will have three critical paths. Further reductions in project duration will require simultaneous crashing of more than one activity (D, E, and F). The cost to do so, $650, exceeds the savings, $300. Consequently, you should stop. Note that every activity is critical. The project costs are minimized when the completion date is day 15. However, there may be some goodwill costs associated with disappointing a customer that wants delivery in 12 days.

TABLE 17.4 *Project Cost Analysis*

Stage	Crash Activity	Resulting Critical Path(s)	Time Reduction (days)	Project Duration (days)	Project Direct Costs, Last Trial	Crash Cost Added	Total Indirect Costs	Total Penalty Costs	Total Project Costs
0	—	C–F–H	—	19	$10,100	—	$3,800	$700	$14,600
1	H	C–F–H	2	17	$10,100	$200	$3,400	$500	$14,200
2	F	A–D–G–H B–E–G–H C–F–H	2	15	$10,300	$500	$3,000	$300	$14,100

Solved Problem 3

A maintenance crew at the Woody Manufacturing Company must do scheduled machine maintenance in the fabricating department. A series of interrelated activities must be accomplished, requiring a different number of workers each day. Figure 17.18 shows the project network, the number of workers required, and the activity time. The company can devote a maximum of six maintenance workers per day to these activities.

FIGURE 17.18

Network for the Maintenance Project

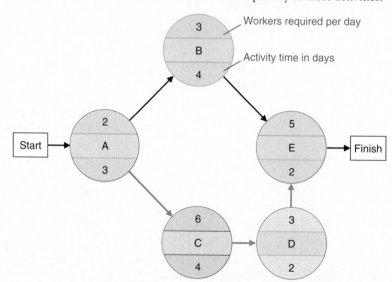

a. Use Weist's procedure to find a new schedule, and draw a Gantt chart for it.

b. How long will the project take and which activities are critical?

Solution   a. The critical path of this project (disregarding the resource constraint) is A–C–D–E at 11 weeks. Consequently, only activity B has slack. Figure 17.19 shows the schedule.

FIGURE 17.19   *Gantt Chart Schedule for the Maintenance Project*

Activity	Day												
	1	2	3	4	5	6	7	8	9	10	11	12	13
A		②											
B									③				
C					⑥								
D									③				
E												⑤	
Resource requirements	2	2	2	6	6	6	6	6	6	3	3	5	5

Step 1.   Schedule activity A first on day 1. We cannot schedule any other activities until day 4 because of the resource constraint.

Step 2.   Activities B and C are now tied. We schedule C next because it has no slack.

Step 3.   Activities B and D are tied. We choose D next because it has no slack. We must start it on day 8 because of the resource constraint.

Step 4.   We must schedule activity B next because of its precedence relationship to activity E.

Step 5.   Finally, we schedule E for days 12 and 13. It couldn't be started earlier because of the resource constraint.

b. The project will take 13 days, and every activity is critical. No activity can be shifted from its present schedule without violating the maintenance worker capacity limitation.

Formula Review

1. Start and finish times:

   ES = max [EF times of all activities immediately preceding activity]

   EF = ES + t

   LS = LF − t

   LF = min [LS times of all activities immediately following activity]

2. Activity slack:

   S = LS − ES   or S = LF − EF

3. Activity time statistics:

$$t_e = \frac{a + 4m + b}{6} \qquad \text{(expected activity time)}$$

$$\sigma^2 = \left(\frac{b - a}{6}\right)^2 \qquad \text{(variance)}$$

4. z-transformation formula:

$$z = \frac{T - T_E}{\sqrt{\sigma^2}} \quad \text{where} \quad \begin{aligned} T &= \text{due date for the project} \\ T_E &= \Sigma(\text{expected activity times on the critical path}) \\ &= \text{mean of normal distribution} \\ \sigma^2 &= \Sigma(\text{variances of activities on the critical path}) \end{aligned}$$

5. Project costs:

$$\text{Crash cost per unit of time} = \frac{\text{Crash cost} - \text{Normal cost}}{\text{Normal time} - \text{Crash time}} = \frac{CC - NC}{NT - CT}$$

Chapter Highlights

- Projects are unique operations having a finite life span. Network planning can help in managing a project. It involves (1) describing the project as a set of interrelated activities, (2) diagramming the network to show precedence relationships, (3) estimating time of completion by determining the critical path, and (4) monitoring project progress.
- PERT/CPM methods focus on the critical path: the sequence of activities requiring the greatest cumulative amount of time for completion. Delay in critical activities will delay the entire project. Uncertainty in activity times can be recognized by securing three time estimates for each activity, then calculating expected activity times and variances. Activity times are assumed to follow a beta distribution.
- PERT/CPM methods can be used to assess the probability of finishing the project by a certain date or to find the minimum-cost schedule with the assumption that marginal costs are linear.
- Computerized network planning methods are useful for managing large projects with many activities, when frequent updates or changes to the original project occur,

and when comparisons of actual versus planned time and resource usage are needed.
- The project duration may increase if sufficient resources aren't available when needed. Weist's procedure is a useful approach to deriving a project schedule subject to resource constraints.
- Criticisms of PERT/CPM methods focus on the validity of four assumptions in the network model. First, activities sometimes don't have clear beginning and ending points. Second, near-critical paths may become critical and affect project completion. Third, use of the beta distribution may not result in good estimates for the expected times and variances, and the underlying activity time estimates may be inaccurate. Fourth, ignoring resource capacity limitations may result in inefficient resource use and project delays.
- Skillful use of PERT/CPM can help managers (1) organize a project and identify activity interrelationships, (2) report progress, (3) estimate project completion time, (4) highlight critical activities, (5) identify slack activities and beneficial reallocation of resources, and (6) analyze cost–time trade-offs.

Key Terms

activity *789*
activity-on-arc (AOA) network *789*
activity-on-node (AON) network *791*
activity slack *795*
crash cost (CC) *808*
crash time (CT) *808*

critical path *794*
critical path method (CPM) *788*
deterministic estimates *793*
earliest finish time (EF) *795*
earliest start time (ES) *795*
event *790*
latest finish time (LF) *796*

latest start time (LS) *796*
minimum-cost schedule *810*
most likely time (*m*) *800*
network diagram *788*
network planning models *788*
normal cost (NC) *808*
normal time (NT) *808*

Study Questions

1. What constitutes effective project management?

2. What information is needed to construct the network diagram for a project? Can any project be diagrammed as a network?

3. When a large project is mismanaged, it makes news. Identify penalties associated with a mismanaged project in your experience or in recent headlines. If possible, identify the cause of the problem. For example, were the problems caused by inaccurate time estimates, changed scope, unplanned or improperly sequenced activities, inadequate resources, or poor management–labor relations?

4. A certain advertising agency is preparing a bid for a promotional campaign of a type never before attempted. The project comprises a large number of interrelated activities. Explain how you would arrive at three time estimates for each activity so that you could use a network planning model to assess the chances that the project can be completed when the sponsor wants it.

5. Why was the beta distribution chosen over the normal distribution for PERT/CPM analyses?

6. Why is the critical path of such importance in project management? Can it change during the course of the project? If so, why?

7. When determining the probability of completing a project within a certain amount of time, what assumptions are you making? What role do the lengths and variances of paths other than the critical path play in such an analysis?

8. Suppose that your company has accepted a project of a type that it has completed many times before. Any activity can be expedited with an increase in costs. There are weekly indirect costs, and there is a weekly penalty if project completion extends beyond a certain date. Identify the data that you would need and explain the analytic process that you would use to determine a minimum-cost schedule. What assumptions would you make in doing such an analysis?

9. Explain the usefulness of a slack-sorted list of activities.

10. Suppose that you are trying to convince management that methods such as PERT/CPM would be useful to them. Some of the managers have voiced the following concerns. Prepare a brief response to each of these concerns.

    a. There is a tendency for technicians to handle the operation of PERT/CPM; thus management will not use it often.

    b. It puts pressure on managers because everyone knows where the critical path is. Managers of activities along the critical path are in the spotlight, and if their activities are delayed, the costs of the delays are on their shoulders.

    c. The introduction of network planning techniques may require new communication channels and systems procedures.

Problems

In the following problems, network diagrams can be drawn in the AOA or AON format. Your instructor will indicate which is preferred.

1. Consider the following data for a project.

Activity	Activity Time (days)	Immediate Predecessor(s)
A	2	—
B	4	A
C	5	A
D	2	B
E	1	B
F	8	B, C
G	3	D, E
H	5	F
I	4	F
J	7	G, H, I

a. Draw the network diagram.
b. Calculate the critical path for this project.
c. How much slack is in activities G, H, and I?

2. The following information is known about a project.

a. Draw the network diagram for this project.
b. Determine the critical path and project duration.

Activity	Activity Time (days)	Immediate Predecessor(s)
A	4	—
B	3	A
C	1	A
D	3	C
E	4	B, D
F	3	E
G	2	E

3. A project has the following precedence relationships and activity times.

Activity	Activity Time (wks)	Immediate Predecessor(s)
A	8	—
B	10	—
C	10	A
D	15	B, C
E	12	B
F	4	D
G	8	E
H	7	F, G

  a. Draw the network diagram.

  b. Calculate the slack for each activity. Which activities are on the critical path?

4. The following information is available about a project.

Activity	Activity Time (days)	Immediate Predecessor(s)
A	3	—
B	4	—
C	5	—
D	4	—
E	7	A
F	2	B, C, D
G	4	E, F
H	6	F
I	4	G
J	3	G
K	3	H

  a. Draw the network diagram.

  b. Find the critical path.

5. The following information has been gathered for a project.

Activity	Activity Time (wk)	Immediate Predecessor(s)
A	6	—
B	9	A
C	3	A
D	7	C
E	11	B, C
F	3	E, D

  a. Draw the network diagram.

  b. Calculate the slack for each activity and determine the critical path. How long will the project take?

6. Consider the following project information.

Activity	Activity Time (wk)	Immediate Predecessor(s)
A	4	—
B	3	—
C	5	—
D	3	A, B
E	6	B
F	4	D, C
G	8	E, C
H	12	F, G

  a. Draw the network diagram for this project.

  b. Specify the critical path(s).

  c. Calculate the total slack for activities A and D.

  d. What happens to the slack for D if A takes five days?

7. Recently, you were assigned to manage a project for your company. You have constructed a network diagram depicting the various activities in the project (Fig. 17.20). In addition, you have asked various managers and subordinates to estimate the amount of time that they would expect each of the activities to take. Their responses are shown in the following table.

Activity	Time Estimates (days)		
	Optimistic	Most Likely	Pessimistic
A	5	8	11
B	4	8	11
C	5	6	7
D	2	4	6
E	4	7	10

FIGURE 17.20   *AON Project Diagram*

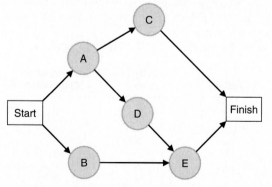

  a. What is the expected completion time of the project?

b. What is the probability of completing the project in 21 days?

c. What is the probability of completing the project in 17 days?

8. In Solved Problem 1, estimate the probability that the noncritical path B–F–G will take more than 20 weeks. *Hint:* Subtract from 1.00 the probability that B–F–G will take 20 weeks or less.

9. Consider the following data for a project never before attempted by your company.

Activity	Expected Time, t_e (wk)	Immediate Predecessor(s)
A	5	—
B	3	—
C	2	A
D	5	B
E	4	C, D
F	7	D

a. Draw the network diagram for this project.

b. Identify the critical path and estimate the project's duration.

c. Calculate the slack for each activity.

10. The director of continuing education at Bluebird University has just approved the planning for a sales-training seminar. Her administrative assistant has identified the various activities that must be done and their relationships to each other, as shown in Table 17.5.

TABLE 17.5 *Activities for the Sales-Training Seminar*

Activity	Description	Immediate Predecessor(s)
A	Design brochure and course announcement.	—
B	Identify prospective teachers.	—
C	Prepare detailed outline of course.	—
D	Send brochure and student applications.	A
E	Send teacher applications.	B
F	Select teacher for course.	C, E
G	Accept students.	D
H	Select text for course.	F
I	Order and receive texts.	G, H
J	Prepare room for class.	G

Because of the uncertainty in planning the new course, the assistant also has supplied the following time estimates for each activity.

	Time Estimates (days)		
Activity	Optimistic	Most Likely	Pessimistic
A	5	7	8
B	6	8	12
C	3	4	5
D	11	17	25
E	8	10	12
F	3	4	5
G	4	8	9
H	5	7	9
I	8	11	17
J	4	4	4

The director wants to conduct the seminar 47 working days from now. What is the probability that everything will be ready in time?

11. Table 17.6 contains information about a project. Shorten the project by finding the minimum-cost schedule. Assume that project indirect costs and penalty costs are negligible. Identify activities to crash while minimizing the additional crash costs.

TABLE 17.6 *Project Activity and Cost Data*

Activity	Normal Time (days)	Crash Time (days)	Cost to Crash ($ per day)	Immediate Predecessor(s)
A	7	6	200	None
B	12	9	250	None
C	7	6	250	A
D	6	5	300	A
E	1	1	—	B
F	1	1	—	C, D
G	3	1	200	D, E
H	3	2	350	F
I	2	2	—	G

12. Information concerning a project is given in Table 17.7. Indirect project costs amount to $250 per day. The company will incur a $100 per day penalty for each day the project lasts beyond day 14.

TABLE 17.7 *Project Activity and Cost Data*

Activity	Normal Time (days)	Normal Cost ($)	Crash Time (days)	Crash Cost ($)	Immediate Predecessor(s)
A	5	1000	4	1200	None
B	5	800	3	2000	None
C	2	600	1	900	A, B
D	3	1500	2	2000	B
E	5	900	3	1200	C, D
F	2	1300	1	1400	E
G	3	900	3	900	E
H	5	500	3	900	G

TABLE 17.8 *Data for the Fast-Food Outlet Project*

Activity	Description	Immediate Predecessor(s)	Time (wk) a	Time (wk) m	Time (wk) b
A	Interview at college for new manager.	—	2	4	6
B	Renovate building.	—	5	8	11
C	Place ad for employees and interview applicants.	—	7	9	17
D	Have new-manager prospects visit.	A	1	2	3
E	Purchase equipment for new outlet and install.	B	2	4	12
F	Check employee applicant references and make final selection.	C	4	4	4
G	Check references for new manager and make final selection.	D	1	1	1
H	Hold orientation meetings and do payroll paperwork.	E, F, G	2	2	2

a. What is the project's duration if only normal times are used?

b. What is the minimum-cost schedule?

c. What is the critical path for the minimum-cost schedule?

13. Hamilton Berger, district manager for Gumfull Foods, Inc., is in charge of opening a new fast-food outlet in the college town of Senility. His major concern is the hiring of a manager and a cadre of hamburger cooks, assemblers, and dispensers. He also has to coordinate the renovation of a building that previously was owned by a pet supplies retailer. He has gathered the data shown in Table 17.8.

Top management has told Berger that the new outlet is to be opened as soon as possible. Every week that the project can be shortened will save the firm $1200 in lease costs. Hamilton thought about how to save time during the project and came up with two possibilities. One was to employ Amazon, Inc., a local employment agency, to locate some good prospects for the manager's job. This approach would save three weeks in activity A and cost Gumfull Foods $2500. The other was to add a few workers to shorten the time for activity B by two weeks at an additional cost of $2700.

Help Ham Berger by answering the following questions.

a. How long is the project expected to take?

b. Suppose that Berger has a personal goal of completing the project in 14 weeks. What is the probability that this will happen?

c. What additional expenditures should be made to reduce the project's duration? Use the expected time for each activity as though it were certain.

14. The diagram in Fig. 17.21 was developed for a project that you are managing. Suppose that you are interested in finding ways to speed up the project at minimal additional cost. Determine the schedule for completing the project in 25 days at minimum cost. Penalty costs and project overhead costs are negligible. Alternative time and cost data for each activity are shown in Table 17.9.

FIGURE 17.21 *AON Network Diagram*

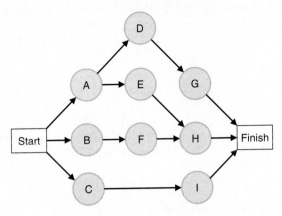

TABLE 17.9 *Project Activity and Cost Data*

Activity	Alternative 1		Alternative 2	
	Time (days)	Cost ($)	Time (days)	Cost ($)
A	12	1300	11	1700
B	13	1150	10	1500
C	20	3000	18	4500
D	9	2000	5	3000
E	12	550	9	900
F	10	700	8	1050
G	8	1550	6	1800
H	2	450	1	800
I	5	2500	2	4000

15. The construction crew of Johnson Homebuilders must frame a new house. The following data are available for the project.

Activity	Activity Time (days)	Workers Required (per day)	Immediate Predecessor(s)
A	4	2	—
B	1	6	—
C	3	3	A
D	2	3	B
E	3	5	C, D

a. Draw the network diagram for the project.
b. Determine the project's critical path and duration.
c. What is the slack for each activity?
d. Only six construction workers are available each day. Use Weist's procedure to find a new schedule and draw a Gantt chart for it. What is the critical path in this schedule? How long will the project take now?

16. The network shown in Fig. 17.22 includes the number of workers required per day for each activity, the name of each activity, and the time (in days) required. Use Weist's procedure to find a schedule that utilizes a maximum of 10 workers each day. Draw a Gantt chart for this schedule.
a. How long will this project take?
b. What is the critical path?

17. A line crew for the Alphabet Telephone Company must install some cable in a rural area. The following data are available for the project.

FIGURE 17.22 *Project Diagram*

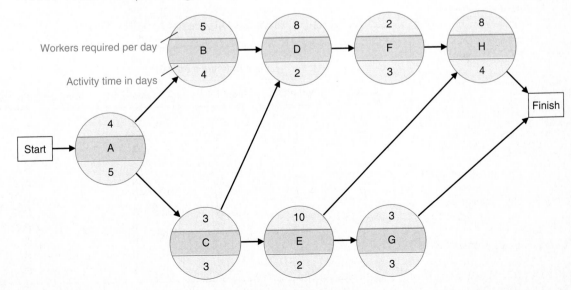

Activity	Activity Time (days)	Line Crew Required (per day)	Immediate Predecessor(s)
A	2	10	—
B	3	6	A
C	5	5	A
D	3	5	A
E	3	5	D
F	1	7	B, C, E

a. Disregarding capacity limitations, determine the critical path and calculate the slack for each activity. How long will the project take?

b. Suppose that there are only 10 crew members. Use Weist's procedure to find a schedule that doesn't exceed 10 workers per day on the project. Draw a Gantt chart for your schedule. What is the critical path now? What is the slack for each activity? How long will the project now take?

18. The following information concerns a new project your company is undertaking.

Activity	Activity Time (days)	Immediate Predecessor(s)
A	10	—
B	11	—
C	9	A, B
D	5	A, B
E	8	A, B
F	13	C, E
G	5	C, D
H	10	G
I	6	F, G
J	9	E, H
K	11	I, J

a. Draw the network diagram for this project.

b. Determine the critical path and project completion time.

Advanced Problems

A PERT/CPM computer program would be helpful in solving Problems 20–22.

19. The project manager of Good Public Relations has gathered the data shown in Table 17.10 for a new advertising campaign.

a. How long is the project likely to take?

b. What is the probability that the project will take more than 38 weeks?

c. Consider the path A–E–G–H–J. What is the probability that this path will exceed the expected project duration?

20. The new products manager at Webb Enterprise wants to evaluate the feasibility of a new computer-based learning system. Table 17.11 on the next page presents the tasks and corresponding time estimates (in weeks) for the proposed project.

a. What is the estimated completion time of the project?

b. Identify the critical path(s).

c. What is the probability of completing the project in 55 weeks? 60 weeks?

d. What is the impact on the critical time if task F is delayed by 1 week? 3 weeks?

TABLE 17.10   *Activity Data for Advertising Project*

Activity	Time Estimates (days)			Immediate Predecessor(s)
	Optimistic	Most Likely	Pessimistic	
A	8	10	12	—
B	5	8	17	—
C	7	8	9	—
D	1	2	3	B
E	8	10	12	A, C
F	5	6	7	D, E
G	1	3	5	D, E
H	2	5	8	F, G
I	2	4	6	G
J	4	5	8	H
K	2	2	2	H

TABLE 17.11 *Activity Data for the Project*

Activity	Description	Time Estimates Optimistic	Time Estimates Most Likely	Time Estimates Pessimistic	Immediate Predecessor(s)
A	Market research	5	7	10	—
B	R&D	12	18	25	—
C	Engineering	6	9	12	B
D	Prototype design	8	12	15	C
E	Costing	2	3	4	C
F	Testing	3	5	8	D
G	Market survey	2	4	7	A, D
H	Market analysis	2	3	4	G
I	Quality assurance	1	2	3	A, D
J	Financial analysis	3	3	4	E, F, H
K	Supplier analysis	2	2	2	E
L	Patent search	1	3	4	B
M	Internal assessment	2	2	2	A
N	Reporting	3	3	3	I, J, K, L
O	Decision making	1	2	3	M, N

21. The Los Angeles Transit Authority has recently awarded a contract to the Bridgeright Corporation. The contract calls for construction of an underground tunnel as part of L.A.'s ongoing rapid transit project. The contract specifies that the tunnel must be finished within 36 months. Additionally, there is a $1 million a month penalty for each month the project exceeds the time limit and a $250,000 per month bonus for each month the project is completed under the time limit.

Table 17.12 presents the activities, normal and crash times, normal and crash costs, and immediate predecessors(s).

a. Develop a plan that minimizes total cost. What completion time would you plan for? Why?

b. Discuss the role of the bonus in your suggested plan. What increase in the dollar amount of the bonus would make reducing the completion time of your planned project schedule advantageous?

TABLE 17.12 *Activity and Cost Data for the Rapid Transit Project*

Activity	Description	Normal Time (mo)	Crash Time (mo)	Normal Cost ($000)	Crash Cost ($000)	Immediate Predecessor(s)
A	Finalize plan.	4	3	200	250	—
B	Obtain permits.	6	4	500	800	A
C	Design tunnel.	8	6	800	1200	A
D	Specify equipment.	3	3	100	100	B
E	Order equipment.	4	3	200	350	D
F	Prepare route.	5	3	400	800	C
G	Evacuate tunnel.	15	10	1000	3500	E, F
H	Test system.	5	4	600	800	G
I	Certify system.	3	2	300	400	H

22. Bentonite Homes builds houses. Create a network showing the precedence relationships for the activities listed in Table 17.13.

23. Fronc is a wedding coordinator. Beatrice Wright and William Bach have asked Fronc to help them organize their wedding. Create a network showing the precedence relationships for the activities listed in Table 17.14.

24. The information in Table 17.15 is available about a large project.

TABLE 17.13   *Bentonite Home-Building Activities*

Activity	Description	Activity	Description
Start		M	Roughing-in plumbing
A	Appliance installation	N	Outside painting
B	Building permit	O	Interior painting
C	Carpets and flooring	P	Roof
D	Dry wall	Q	Siding
E	Electrical wiring	R	Final wood trim
F	Foundation	S	Pouring sidewalks, driveway, basement, and garage floors
G	Framing	T	Doors
H	Heating and air conditioning	U	Windows
I	Insulation	V	Bath fixtures
J	Kitchen and bath cabinets	W	Lawn sprinkler system
K	Lighting fixtures	X	Landscaping
L	Moving in		

TABLE 17.14   *Will & Bea Wright-Bach Wedding Activities*

Activity	Description	Activity	Description
Start	Accept proposal	O	Order cake, mints, cashews
A	Select and print announcements	P	Photographer
B	Blood tests	Q	Reserve reception hall
C	Color theme selection	R	Rings
D1	Wedding dress	S	Bachelor party
D2	Bridesmaids' dresses	T	Tuxedo rental
D3	Bride's mother's dress	U	Ushers
D4	Groom's mother's dress	V	Reserve church
E	Establish budget and net worth of parents	W	Wedding ceremony
F	Flowers	X	Select groomsmen, ring bearer
G	Gifts for wedding party	Y	Select bridesmaids, flower girls
H	Honeymoon planning	Z	Rehearsal and prenuptial dinner
I	Mailed invitations	AA	Prenuptial agreement
J	Guest list	BB	Groom's nervous breakdown
K	Caterer	CC	Register for china, flatware, gifts
L	Marriage license	DD	Dance band
M	Menu for reception	EE	Thank you notes
N	Newspaper picture, society page announcement	FF	Finish

a. Determine the critical path and the expected completion time of the project.

b. Plot the total project cost, starting from day 1 to the expected completion date of the project, assuming the earliest start times for each activity. Compare that result to a similar plot for the latest start times. What implication does the time differential have for cash flows and project scheduling?

TABLE 17.15 *Activity and Cost Data*

Activity	Activity Time (days)	Activity Cost	Immediate Predecessor(s)	Activity	Activity Time (days)	Activity Cost	Immediate Predecessor(s)
A	3	100	—	I	1	100	E
B	4	150	—	J	4	75	D, E
C	2	125	A	K	3	150	F, G
D	5	175	B	L	3	150	G, H, I
E	3	150	B	M	2	100	I, J
F	4	200	C, D	N	4	175	K, M
G	6	75	C	O	1	200	H, M
H	2	50	C, D, E	P	5	150	N, L, O

C A S E

The Pert Studebaker

The new director of service operations for Roberts's Auto Sales and Service (RASAS) started work at the beginning of the year. It is now mid-February. RASAS consists of three car dealerships that sell and service several makes of American and Japanese cars, two auto parts stores, a large body shop and car painting business, and an auto salvage yard. Vikky Roberts, owner of RASAS, went into the car business more than 20 years ago when she inherited a Studebaker dealership from her father. The Studebaker Corporation was on the wane when she obtained the business, but she was able to capitalize on her knowledge and experience to build her business into the diversified and successful "miniempire" it is today. Her motto, "Sell 'em today, repair 'em tomorrow!" reflects a strategy that she refers to in private as "Get 'em coming and going."

Roberts has always retained a soft spot in her heart for Studebaker automobiles. They were manufactured in South Bend, Indiana, from 1919 to 1966, and many are still operable today because of a vast number of collectors and loyal fans. Roberts has just acquired a 1963 Studebaker Avanti that needs a lot of restoration. She has also noted the public's growing interest in the restoration of vintage automobiles.

Roberts is thinking of expanding into the vintage car restoration business and needs help in assessing the feasibility of such a move. She also wants to restore her 1963 Avanti to mint condition, or as close to mint condition as possible. If she decides to go into the car restoring business, she can use the Avanti as an exhibit in sales and advertising and take it to auto shows to attract business for the new shop.

Roberts believes that many people want the thrill of restoring an old car themselves but don't have time to run down all the old parts. Still others just want to own a vintage auto because it is different, and many of them have plenty of money to pay someone to restore an auto for them.

Roberts wants the new business to appeal to both types of people. For the first group, she envisions serving as a parts broker for NOS ("new old stock"), new parts that were manufactured many years ago, packaged in their original cartons. It can be a time-consuming process to find the right part. RASAS could also machine new parts to replicate those that are hard to find or no longer exist.

In addition, RASAS could assemble a library of parts and body manuals for old cars, to serve as an information resource for do-it-yourself restorers. The do-it-yourselfers could come to RASAS for help in compiling their parts lists, and RASAS could acquire the parts for them. For others RASAS would take charge of the entire restoration.

Vikky Roberts asks the new director of service operations to take a good look at her Avanti and see what needs to be done to restore it to the condition it was in when it came from the factory more than 30 years ago. She wants to restore it in time to exhibit it at the National Studebaker Meet beginning July 15 in Springfield, Missouri. If the car wins first prize in its category, it will be a real public relations coup for RASAS—especially if Roberts decides to enter this new venture. Even if she doesn't, the car will be a showpiece for the rest of the business.

Roberts asks the director of service operations to prepare a report about what is involved in restoring the car and whether it can be done in time for the Springfield meet this summer. PERT/CPM is to be used to determine if the July 15 date is feasible. The parts manager, the body shop manager, and the chief mechanic have provided the following estimates of times and tasks that need to be done, as well as cost estimates:

Order all needed material and parts (upholstery, windshield, carburetor, and oil pump). Time: 2 days. Cost (phone calls and labor): $100.

Receive upholstery material for seat covers. Can't do until order is placed. Time: 30 days. Cost: $250.

Receive windshield. Can't do until order is placed. Time: 10 days. Cost: $130.

Receive carburetor and oil pump. Can't do until order is placed. Time: 7 days. Cost: $180.

Remove chrome from body. Can do immediately. Time: 1 day. Cost: $50.

Remove body (doors, hood, trunk, and fenders) from frame. Can't do until chrome is removed. Time: 1 day. Cost: $150.

Have fenders repaired by body shop. Can't do until body is removed from frame. Time: 4 days. Cost: $200.

Repair doors, trunk, and hood. Can't do until body is removed from frame. Time: 6 days. Cost: $300.

Pull engine from chassis. Do after body is removed from frame. Time: 1 day. Cost: $50.

Remove rust from frame. Do after the engine has been pulled from the chassis. Time: 3 days. Cost: $300.

Regrind engine valves. Have to pull engine from chassis first. Time: 5 days. Cost: $500.

Replace carburetor and oil pump. Do after engine has been pulled from chassis and after carburetor and oil pump have been received. Time: 1 day. Cost: $50.

Rechrome the chrome parts. Chrome must have been removed from the body first. Time: 3 days. Cost: $150.

Reinstall engine. Do after valves are reground and carburetor and oil pump have been installed. Time: 1 day. Cost: $150.

Put doors, hood, and trunk back on frame. The doors, hood, and trunk must have been repaired. The frame also has to have had its rust removed. Time: 1 day. Cost: $80.

Rebuild transmission and replace brakes. Do this after the engine has been reinstalled and the doors, hood, and trunk are back on the frame. Time: 4 days. Cost: $700.

Replace windshield. Windshield must have been received. Time: 1 day. Cost: $70.

Put fenders back on. The fenders must already have been repaired and the transmission rebuilt and the brakes replaced. Time: 1 day. Cost: $60.

Paint car. Can't do until the fenders are back on and windshield replaced. Time: 4 days. Cost: $1700.

Reupholster interior of car. Must have first received upholstery material. Car must also have been painted. Time: 7 days. Cost: $1200.

Put chrome parts back on. Car has to have been painted and chrome parts rechromed. Time: 1 day. Cost: $50.

Pull car to Studebaker show in Springfield, Missouri. Must have completed reupholstery of interior and have put the chrome parts back on. Time: 2 days. Cost: $500.

Roberts wants to limit the expenditures on this project to what could be recovered by selling the restored car. She has already spent $1500 to acquire the car.

In addition, she would like a brief report on some of the aspects of the proposed business, such as how it fits in with RASAS's other businesses and what RASAS's operations task should be with regard to cost, quality, customer service, and flexibility.

According to *Turning Wheels,* a publication for owners and drivers of Studebakers, and other books on car restoration, there are categories of restoration. A basic restoration gets the car looking great and running, but a mint condition restoration puts the car back in original condition—as it was "when it rolled off the line." When restored cars compete, a car in mint condition has an advantage over one that is just a basic restoration. As cars are restored, they can also be customized. This means that something is put on the car that couldn't have been on the original. Customized cars compete in a separate class. Roberts wants a mint condition restoration, without customization. (The proposed new business would accept any kind of restoration a customer wanted.)

A restored 1963 Avanti can probably be sold for $15,000. Thus, the total budget cannot exceed $13,500 ($15,000 minus the $1500 Roberts has already spent). Even though much of the work will be done by Roberts's own employees, labor and materials costs must be considered. All relevant costs have been included in the cost estimates.

Questions

1. Using the information provided, prepare the report Roberts requested, assuming that the project will begin in late February of the current year. This leaves 100 working days to complete the project, including

transporting the car to Springfield before the meet begins. Your report should briefly discuss the aspects of the proposed new business, such as the competitive priorities (see Chapter 2), that Roberts asked about.

2. Compose a table containing the project activities, with a letter assigned to each activity, the time estimates, and the precedence relationships from which you will assemble the network diagram.

3. Draw an AON network diagram of the project similar to Fig. 17.4. Determine the activities on the critical path and the estimated slack for each activity.

4. Prepare a project budget showing the cost of each activity and the total for the project.

Source: This case was prepared by and is used courtesy of Professor Sue Perrott Siferd, Arizona State University.

Selected References

Andreu, R., and A. Corominas. "SUCCESS 92: A DSS for Scheduling the Olympic Games." *Interfaces*, vol. 19, no. 5 (September–October 1989), pp. 1–12.

Denzler, David R. "A Review of CA-SuperProject." *APICS—The Performance Advantage* (September 1991), pp. 40–41.

Kerzner, Harold. *Project Management for Executives.* New York: Van Nostrand Reinhold, 1984.

Littlefield, T. K., and P. H. Randolph. "PERT Duration Times: Mathematical or MBO." *Interfaces*, vol. 21, no. 6 (November–December 1991), pp. 92–95.

"Project Management Software." *PC Magazine* (September 11, 1990), pp. 338–339.

Smith-Daniels, Dwight E., and Nicholas J. Aquilano. "Constrained Resource Project Scheduling." *Journal of Operations Management*, vol. 4, no. 4 (1984), pp. 369–387.

Sullivan, K. B. "Experts' Advice on Deciding When a PC May Help a Project." *PC Week* (January 21, 1986), p. 135.

Weist, J. D. "Heuristic Programs for Decision Making." *Harvard Business Review* (September–October 1966), pp. 129–143.

Financial Analysis

Many decisions in operations management involve large capital investments. Automation, vertical integration, capacity expansion, layout revisions, and installing a new computerized inventory system are but some examples. In fact, most of a firm's assets are tied up in the operations function. Therefore the operations manager should seek high-yield capital projects and then assess their costs, benefits, and risks.

Such projects require strong cross-functional coordination, particularly with finance and accounting. The projects must fit in with the organization's financial plans and capabilities. If a firm plans to open a new production facility in 2000, it must begin lining up financing in 1996. The projects must also be subjected to one or more types of financial analysis, to assess their attractiveness relative to other investment opportunities. This supplement presents a brief overview of basic financial analyses and the kinds of computer support available for making such decisions. See your finance textbook for a more comprehensive treatment of the subject.

◆ TIME VALUE OF MONEY

An important concept underlying many financial analysis techniques is that a dollar in hand today is worth more than a dollar to be received in the future. A dollar in hand can be invested to earn a return, so that more than one dollar will be available in the future. This concept is known as the **time value of money**.

Future Value of an Investment

If $5000 is invested at 10 percent interest for one year, at the end of the year the $5000 will have earned $500 in interest and the total amount available will be $5500. If the interest earned is allowed to accumulate, it also earns interest and the original investment will grow to $12,970 in 10 years. The process by which interest on an investment accumulates, and then earns interest itself for the remainder of the investment period, is known as **compounding interest**. The value of an investment at the end of the period over which interest is compounded is called the **future value of an investment**.

To calculate the future value of an investment, you first express the interest rate and the time period in the same units of time as the interval at which compounding occurs. Let's assume that interest is compounded annually, express all time periods in years, and use annual interest rates. To find the value of an investment one year in the future, multiply the amount invested by the sum of 1 plus the interest rate (expressed as a decimal). The value of a $5000 investment at 12 percent per year one year from now is

$$\$5000(1.12) = \$5600$$

If the entire amount remains invested, at the end of two years you would have

$$5600(1.12) = \$5000(1.12)^2 = \$6272$$

In general,

$$F = P(1 + r)^n$$

where F = future value of the investment at the end of n periods

P = amount invested at the beginning, called the principal

r = periodic interest rate

n = number of time periods for which the interest compounds

Present Value of a Future Amount

Let's look at the converse problem. Suppose you want to make an investment now that will be worth $10,000 in one year. If the interest rate is 12 percent and P represents the amount invested now, the relation becomes

$$F = \$10,000 = P(1 + 0.12)$$

Solving for P gives

$$P = \frac{F}{(1 + r)} = \frac{10,000}{(1 + 0.12)} = \$8929$$

The amount that must be invested now to accumulate to a certain amount in the future at a specific interest rate is called the **present value of an investment**. The process of finding the present value of an investment, when the future value and the interest rate are known, is called **discounting** the future value to its present value. If the number of time periods n for which discounting is desired is greater than 1, the present value is determined by dividing the future value by the nth power of the sum of 1 plus the interest rate. The general formula for determining the present value is

$$P = \frac{F}{(1 + r)^n}$$

The interest rate is also called the **discount rate**.

Present Value Factors

Although you can calculate P from its formula in a few steps with most pocket calculators, you also can use a table. To do so, write the present value formula another way:

$$P = \frac{F}{(1 + r)^n} = F\left[\frac{1}{(1 + r)^n}\right]$$

Let $[1/(1 + r)^n]$ be the *present value factor,* which is called pf and which you can find in Table A1.1. This table gives you the present value of a future amount of $1 for various time periods and interest rates. To use the table, locate the column for the appropriate interest rate and the row for the appropriate period. The number in the body of the table where this row and column intersect is the pf value. Multiply it by F to get P. For example, suppose that an investment will generate $15,000 in 10 years. If the interest rate is 12 percent, Table A1.1 shows that pf = 0.3220. Multiplying it by $15,000 gives the present value, or

$$P = F(\text{pf}) = \$15,000(0.3220)$$
$$= \$4830$$

APPENDIX ONE   *Financial Analysis*

TABLE A1.1   *Present Value Factors for a Single Payment*

Interest Rate (r)

Number of Periods (n)	0.01	0.02	0.03	0.04	0.05	0.06	0.08	0.10	0.12	0.14	0.16	0.18	0.20	0.22	0.24	0.26	0.28	0.30
1	.9901	.9804	.9709	.9615	.9524	.9434	.9259	.9091	.8929	.8772	.8621	.8475	.8333	.8197	.8065	.7937	.7812	.7692
2	.9803	.9612	.9426	.9246	.9070	.8900	.8573	.8264	.7972	.7695	.7432	.7182	.6944	.6719	.6504	.6299	.6104	.5917
3	.9706	.9423	.9151	.8890	.8638	.8396	.7938	.7513	.7118	.6750	.6407	.6086	.5787	.5507	.5245	.4999	.4768	.4552
4	.9610	.9238	.8885	.8548	.8227	.7921	.7350	.6830	.6355	.5921	.5523	.5158	.4823	.4514	.4230	.3968	.3725	.3501
5	.9515	.9057	.8626	.8219	.7835	.7473	.6806	.6209	.5674	.5194	.4761	.4371	.4019	.3700	.3411	.3149	.2910	.2693
6	.9420	.8880	.8375	.7903	.7462	.7050	.6302	.5645	.5066	.4556	.4104	.3704	.3349	.3033	.2751	.2499	.2274	.2072
7	.9327	.8706	.8131	.7599	.7107	.6651	.5835	.5132	.4523	.3996	.3538	.3139	.2791	.2486	.2218	.1983	.1776	.1594
8	.9235	.8535	.7894	.7307	.6768	.6274	.5403	.4665	.4039	.3506	.3050	.2660	.2326	.2038	.1789	.1574	.1388	.1226
9	.9143	.8368	.7664	.7026	.6446	.5919	.5002	.4241	.3606	.3075	.2630	.2255	.1938	.1670	.1443	.1249	.1084	.0943
10	.9053	.8203	.7441	.6756	.6139	.5584	.4632	.3855	.3220	.2697	.2267	.1911	.1615	.1369	.1164	.0922	.0847	.0725
11	.8963	.8043	.7224	.6496	.5847	.5268	.4289	.3505	.2875	.2366	.1954	.1619	.1346	.1122	.0938	.0787	.0662	.0558
12	.8874	.7885	.7014	.6246	.5568	.4970	.3971	.3186	.2567	.2076	.1685	.1372	.1122	.0920	.0757	.0625	.0517	.0429
13	.8787	.7730	.6810	.6006	.5303	.4688	.3677	.2897	.2292	.1821	.1452	.1163	.0935	.0754	.0610	.0496	.0404	.0330
14	.8700	.7579	.6611	.5775	.5051	.4423	.3405	.2633	.2046	.1597	.1252	.0985	.0779	.0618	.0492	.0393	.0316	.0254
15	.8613	.7430	.6419	.5553	.4810	.4173	.3152	.2394	.1827	.1401	.1079	.0835	.0649	.0507	.0397	.0312	.0247	.0195
16	.8528	.7284	.6232	.5339	.4581	.3936	.2919	.2176	.1631	.1229	.0930	.0708	.0541	.0415	.0320	.0248	.0193	.0150
17	.8444	.7142	.6050	.5134	.4363	.3714	.2703	.1978	.1456	.1078	.0802	.0600	.0451	.0340	.0258	.0197	.0150	.0116
18	.8360	.7002	.5874	.4936	.4155	.3503	.2502	.1799	.1300	.0946	.0691	.0508	.0376	.0279	.0208	.0156	.0118	.0089
19	.8277	.6864	.5703	.4746	.3957	.3305	.2317	.1635	.1161	.0829	.0596	.0431	.0313	.0229	.0168	.0124	.0092	.0068
20	.8195	.6730	.5537	.4564	.3769	.3118	.2145	.1486	.1037	.0728	.0514	.0365	.0261	.0187	.0135	.0098	.0072	.0053
21	.8114	.6598	.5375	.4388	.3589	.2942	.1987	.1351	.0926	.0638	.0443	.0309	.0217	.0154	.0109	.0078	.0056	.0040
22	.8034	.6468	.5219	.4220	.3418	.2775	.1839	.1228	.0826	.0560	.0382	.0262	.0181	.0126	.0088	.0062	.0044	.0031
23	.7954	.6342	.5067	.4057	.3256	.2618	.1703	.1117	.0738	.0491	.0329	.0222	.0151	.0103	.0071	.0049	.0034	.0024
24	.7876	.6217	.4919	.3901	.3101	.2470	.1577	.1015	.0659	.0431	.0284	.0188	.0126	.0085	.0057	.0039	.0027	.0018
25	.7798	.6095	.4776	.3751	.2953	.2330	.1460	.0923	.0588	.0378	.0245	.0160	.0105	.0069	.0046	.0031	.0021	.0014
26	.7720	.5976	.4637	.3607	.2812	.2198	.1352	.0839	.0525	.0331	.0211	.0135	.0087	.0057	.0037	.0025	.0016	.0011
27	.7644	.5859	.4502	.3468	.2678	.2074	.1252	.0763	.0469	.0291	.0182	.0115	.0073	.0047	.0030	.0019	.0013	.0008
28	.7568	.5744	.4371	.3335	.2551	.1956	.1159	.0693	.0419	.0255	.0157	.0097	.0061	.0038	.0024	.0015	.0010	.0006
29	.7493	.5631	.4243	.3207	.2429	.1846	.1073	.0630	.0374	.0224	.0135	.0082	.0051	.0031	.0020	.0012	.0008	.0005
30	.7419	.5521	.4120	.3083	.2314	.1741	.0994	.0573	.0334	.0196	.0116	.0070	.0042	.0026	.0016	.0010	.0006	.0004
35	.7059	.5000	.3554	.2534	.1813	.1301	.0676	.0356	.0189	.0102	.0055	.0030	.0017	.0009	.0005	.0003	.0002	.0001
40	.6717	.4529	.3066	.2083	.1420	.0972	.0460	.0221	.0107	.0053	.0026	.0013	.0007	.0004	.0002	.0001	.0001	.0000

$$P = \frac{F}{(1 + r)^n} = F(\text{pf})$$

where

P = present value of a single investment
F = future value of a single payment
n = number of periods for which P is to be invested
r = periodic interest rate
pf = present value factor for \$1 = $1/(1 + r)^n$

Annuities

An **annuity** is a series of payments of a fixed amount for a specified number of years. All such payments are treated as happening at the end of a year. Suppose that you want to invest an amount at an interest rate of 10 percent so that you may draw out $5000 per year for each of the next four years. You could determine the present value of this $5000 four-year annuity by treating the four payments as single future payments. The present value of an investment needed now, in order for you to receive these payments for the next four years, is the sum of the present values of each of the four payments. That is,

$$P = \frac{\$5000}{1 + 0.10} + \frac{\$5000}{(1 + 0.10)^2} + \frac{\$5000}{(1 + 0.10)^3} + \frac{\$5000}{(1 + 0.10)^4}$$

$$= \$4545 + \$4132 + \$3757 + \$3415$$

$$= \$15,849$$

A much easier way to calculate this amount is to use Table A1.2. Look for the factor in the table at the intersection of the 10 percent column and the fourth period row. It is 3.1699. For annuities, this present value factor is called af, to distinguish it from the present value factor for a single payment. To determine the present value of an annuity, multiply its amount by af, to get

$$P = A(\text{af}) = \$5000(3.1699)$$

$$= \$15,849$$

where
P = present value of an investment

A = amount of the annuity received each year

af = present value factor for an annuity

◆ TECHNIQUES OF ANALYSIS

You can now apply these concepts to the financial analysis of proposed investments. Three basic financial analysis techniques are

1. the net present value method,
2. the internal rate of return method, and
3. the payback method.

These methods work with cash flows. **Cash flow** is the cash that will flow into and out of the organization because of the project, including revenues, costs, and changes in assets and liabilities. Be sure to remember two points when determining cash flows for any project:

1. Consider only the amounts of cash flows that will change if the project is undertaken. These amounts are called incremental cash flows and are the difference between the cash flows with the project and without it.
2. Convert cash flows to *after-tax* amounts before applying the net present value, payback, or internal rate of return method to them. This step introduces taxes and depreciation into the calculations.

TABLE A1.2   *Present Value Factors of an Annuity*

Number of Periods (n)	Interest Rate (r)																	
	0.01	0.02	0.03	0.04	0.05	0.06	0.08	0.10	0.12	0.14	0.16	0.18	0.20	0.22	0.24	0.26	0.28	0.30
1	0.9901	0.9804	0.9709	0.9615	0.9524	0.9434	0.9259	0.9091	0.8929	0.8772	0.8621	0.8475	0.8333	0.8197	0.8065	0.7937	0.7812	0.7692
2	1.9704	1.9416	1.9135	1.8861	1.8594	1.8334	1.7833	1.7355	1.6901	1.6467	1.6052	1.5656	1.5278	1.4915	1.4568	1.4235	1.3916	1.3609
3	2.9410	2.8839	2.8286	2.7751	2.7232	2.6730	2.5771	2.4869	2.4018	2.3216	2.2459	2.1743	2.1065	2.0422	1.9813	1.9234	1.8684	1.8161
4	3.9020	3.8077	3.7171	3.6299	3.5460	3.4651	3.3121	3.1699	3.0373	2.9137	2.7982	2.6901	2.5887	2.4936	2.4043	2.3202	2.2410	2.1662
5	4.8534	4.7135	4.5797	4.4518	4.3295	4.2124	3.9927	3.7908	3.6048	3.4331	3.2743	3.1272	2.9906	2.8636	2.7454	2.6351	2.5320	2.4356
6	5.7955	5.6014	5.4172	5.2421	5.0757	4.9173	4.6229	4.3553	4.1114	3.8887	3.6847	3.4976	3.3255	3.1669	3.0205	2.8850	2.7594	2.6427
7	6.7282	6.4720	6.2303	6.0021	5.7864	5.5824	5.2064	4.8684	4.5638	4.2883	4.0386	3.8115	3.6046	3.4155	3.2423	3.0833	2.9370	2.8021
8	7.6517	7.3255	7.0197	6.7327	6.4632	6.2098	5.7466	5.3349	4.9676	4.6389	4.3436	4.0776	3.8372	3.6193	3.4212	3.2407	3.0758	2.9247
9	8.5660	8.1622	7.7861	7.4353	7.1078	6.8017	6.2469	5.7590	5.3282	4.9464	4.6065	4.3030	4.0310	3.7863	3.5655	3.3657	3.1842	3.0190
10	9.4713	8.9826	8.5302	8.1109	7.7217	7.3601	6.7101	6.1446	5.6502	5.2161	4.8332	4.4941	4.1925	3.9232	3.6819	3.4648	3.2689	3.0915
11	10.3676	9.7868	9.2526	8.7605	8.3064	7.8869	7.1390	6.4951	5.9377	5.4527	5.0286	4.6560	4.3271	4.0354	3.7757	3.5435	3.3351	3.1473
12	11.2551	10.5753	9.9540	9.3851	8.8633	8.3838	7.5361	6.8137	6.1944	5.6603	5.1971	4.7932	4.4392	4.1274	3.8514	3.6059	3.3868	3.1903
13	12.1337	11.3484	10.6350	9.9856	9.3936	8.8527	7.9038	7.1034	6.4235	5.8424	5.3423	4.9095	4.5327	4.2028	3.9124	3.6555	3.4272	3.2233
14	13.0037	12.1062	11.2961	10.5631	9.8986	9.2950	8.2442	7.3667	6.6282	6.0021	5.4675	5.0081	4.6106	4.2646	3.9616	3.6949	3.4587	3.2487
15	13.8651	12.8493	11.9379	11.1184	10.3797	9.7122	8.5595	7.6061	6.8109	6.1422	5.5755	5.0916	4.6755	4.3152	4.0013	3.7261	3.4834	3.2682
16	14.7179	13.5777	12.5611	11.6523	10.8378	10.1059	8.8514	7.8237	6.9740	6.2651	5.6685	5.1624	4.7296	4.3567	4.0333	3.7509	3.5026	3.2832
17	15.5623	14.2919	13.1661	12.1657	11.2741	10.4773	9.1216	8.0216	7.1196	6.3729	5.7487	5.2223	4.7746	4.3908	4.0591	3.7705	3.5177	3.2948
18	16.3983	14.9920	13.7535	12.6593	11.6896	10.8276	9.3719	8.2014	7.2497	6.4674	5.8178	5.2732	4.8122	4.4187	4.0799	3.7861	3.5294	3.3037
19	17.2260	15.6785	14.3238	13.1339	12.0853	11.1581	9.6036	8.3649	7.3658	6.5504	5.8775	5.3162	4.8435	4.4415	4.0967	3.7985	3.5386	3.3105
20	18.0456	16.3514	14.8775	13.5903	12.4622	11.4699	9.8181	8.5136	7.4694	6.6231	5.9288	5.3527	4.8696	4.4603	4.1103	3.8083	3.5458	3.3158
21	18.8570	17.0112	15.4150	14.0292	12.8212	11.7641	10.0168	8.6487	7.5620	6.6870	5.9731	5.3837	4.8913	4.4756	4.1212	3.8161	3.5514	3.3198
22	19.6604	17.6580	15.9369	14.4511	13.1630	12.0416	10.2007	8.7715	7.6446	6.7429	6.0113	5.4099	4.9094	4.4882	4.1300	3.8223	3.5558	3.3230
23	20.4558	18.2922	16.4436	14.8568	13.4886	12.3034	10.3711	8.8832	7.7184	6.7921	6.0442	5.4321	4.9245	4.4985	4.1371	3.8273	3.5592	3.3254
24	21.2434	18.9139	16.9355	15.2470	13.7986	12.5504	10.5288	8.9847	7.7843	6.8351	6.0726	5.4509	4.9371	4.5070	4.1428	3.8312	3.5619	3.3272
25	22.0232	19.5235	17.4131	15.6221	14.0939	12.7834	10.6748	9.0770	7.8431	6.8729	6.0971	5.4669	4.9476	4.5139	4.1474	3.8342	3.5640	3.3286
26	22.7952	20.1210	17.8768	15.9828	14.3752	13.0032	10.8100	9.1609	7.8957	6.9061	6.1182	5.4804	4.9563	4.5196	4.1511	3.8367	3.5656	3.3297
27	23.5596	20.7069	18.3270	16.3296	14.6430	13.2105	10.9352	9.2372	7.9426	6.9352	6.1364	5.4919	4.9636	4.5243	4.1542	3.8387	3.5669	3.3305
28	24.3164	21.2813	18.7641	16.6631	14.8981	13.4062	11.0511	9.3066	7.9844	6.9607	6.1520	5.5016	4.9697	4.5281	4.1566	3.8402	3.5679	3.3312
29	25.0658	21.8444	19.1885	16.9837	15.1411	13.5907	11.1584	9.3696	8.0218	6.9830	6.1656	5.5098	4.9747	4.5312	4.1585	3.8414	3.5687	3.3317
30	25.8077	22.3965	19.6004	17.2920	15.3725	13.7648	11.2578	9.4269	8.0552	7.0027	6.1772	5.5168	4.9789	4.5338	4.1601	3.8424	3.5693	3.3321
35	29.4086	24.9986	21.4872	18.6646	16.3742	14.4982	11.6546	9.6442	8.1755	7.0700	6.2153	5.5386	4.9915	4.5411	4.1644	3.8450	3.5708	3.3330
40	32.8347	27.3555	23.1148	19.7928	17.1591	15.0463	11.9246	9.7791	8.2438	7.1050	6.2335	5.5482	4.9966	4.5439	4.1659	3.8458	3.5712	3.3332

$$P = \frac{A}{(1+r)} + \frac{A}{(1+r)^2} + \cdots + \frac{A}{(1+r)^n} = A\sum_{j=1}^{n} 1/(1+r)^j = A(\text{af})$$

where

P = present value of a single investment

A = amount of annuity to be received at the end of each period

n = number of periods for which the annuity is received

r = periodic interest rate

af = annuity factor for an annuity of \$1 $= \sum_{j=1}^{n} 1/(1+r)^j$

Depreciation and Taxes

Depreciation is an allowance for the consumption of capital. In this type of analysis, depreciation is relevant for only one reason: It acts as a tax shield. Depreciation isn't a legitimate cash flow because it is not cash that is actually paid out each year. However, depreciation does affect how an accountant calculates net income, against which the income-tax rate is applied. Therefore depreciation enters into the calculation, as a tax shield, only when tax liability is figured. Taxes must be paid on pre-tax cash inflows *minus* the depreciation that is associated with the proposed investment. United States tax laws allow either straight-line or accelerated depreciation.

Straight-Line Depreciation. The **straight-line method** of calculating annual depreciation is the simplest and usually is adequate for internal planning purposes. First subtract the estimated salvage value from the amount of investment required at the beginning of the project, then divide by the number of years in the asset's expected economic life. **Salvage value** is the cash flow from the sale or disposal of plant and equipment at the end of a project's life.* The general expression for annual depreciation is

$$D = \frac{I - S}{n}$$

where
D = annual depreciation
I = amount of the investment
S = salvage value
n = number of years of project life

Accelerated Depreciation. If the tax shields come earlier, they are worth more. Tax laws allow just that, with what is called *accelerated depreciation*. Since 1986, the only acceptable accelerated depreciation method is known as the **Modified Accelerated Cost Recovery System** (MACRS). MACRS shortens the lives of investments, giving firms larger tax deductions. It creates six classes of investments, each of which has a recovery period or class life. Depreciation for each year is calculated by multiplying the asset's cost by the fixed percentage in Table A1.3.† The following are examples of the first four classes.

3-year class:	specially designed tools and equipment used in research
5-year class:	autos, copiers, and computers
7-year class:	most industrial equipment and office furniture
10-year class:	some longer-life equipment

Table A1.3 doesn't show the 27.5-year and 31.5-year classes, which are reserved for real estate. MACRS depreciation calculations ignore salvage value and the actual expected economic life. If there is salvage value after the asset has been fully depreciated, it is treated as taxable income.

---

*Disposal of property often results in an accounting gain or loss that can increase or decrease income tax and affect cash flows. These tax effects should be considered in determining the actual cash inflow or outflow from disposal of property.

†The table can be confusing because it allows a depreciation deduction for one more year than would seem appropriate for a given class. The reason is that MACRS assumes that assets are in service for only six months of the first year and six months of the last year. An asset in the second class still has a five-year life, but it spans six calendar years.

TABLE A1.3   *Modified ACRS Depreciation Allowances*

| Year | Class of Investment | | | |
	3-Year	5-Year	7-Year	10-Year
1	33.33	20.00	14.29	10.00
2	44.45	32.00	24.49	18.00
3	14.81	19.20	17.49	14.40
4	7.41	11.52	12.49	11.52
5		11.52	8.93	9.22
6		5.76	8.93	7.37
7			8.93	6.55
8			4.45	6.55
9				6.55
10				6.55
11				3.29
	100.0%	100.0%	100.0%	100.0%

Taxes.   The income-tax rate varies from one state or country to another. Calculation of the tax total should include all relevant federal, state, and local income taxes. When doing a financial analysis, you may want to use an average income-tax rate based on the firm's tax rate over the past several years, or you may want to base the tax rate on the highest tax bracket that applies to the taxpaying unit. The one thing you should never do is ignore taxes in making a financial analysis.

Analysis of Cash Flows

You now are ready to determine the after-tax cash flow for each year of the project's life. Use the following four steps to calculate the flow year by year.

1. Subtract the new expenses attributed to the project from new revenues. If revenues are unaffected, begin with the project's cost savings.
2. Next subtract the depreciation (D), to get pre-tax income.
3. Subtract taxes, which constitute the pre-tax income multiplied by the tax rate. The difference is called the net operating income (NOI).
4. Compute the total after-tax cash flow as NOI + D, adding back the depreciation that was deducted temporarily to compute the tax.

EXAMPLE A1.1
Calculating After-Tax Cash Flows

A local restaurant is considering adding a salad bar. The investment required to remodel the dining area and add the salad bar will be $16,000. Other information about the project is as follows.

1. The price and variable cost per salad are $3.50 and $2.00, respectively.
2. Annual demand should be about 11,000 salads.
3. Fixed costs, other than depreciation, will be $8000, which covers the energy to operate the refrigerated unit and wages for another part-time employee to stock the salad bar during peak business hours.
4. The assets go into the MACRS five-year class for depreciation purposes, with no salvage value.

5. The tax rate is 40 percent.
6. Management wants to earn a return of at least 14 percent on the project.

Determine the after-tax cash flows for the life of this project.

Solution The cash flow projections are shown in the following table. Depreciation is based on Table A1.3. For example, depreciation in 1996 is $3200 (or $16,000 × 0.20). The cash flow in 2001 comes from depreciation's tax shield in the first half of the year.

				Year			
Item	1995	1996	1997	1998	1999	2000	2001
Initial Information							
Annual demand (salads)		11,000	11,000	11,000	11,000	11,000	
Investment	$16,000						
Interest (discount) rate	0.14						
Cash Flows							
Revenue		$38,500	$38,500	$38,500	$38,500	$38,500	
Expenses: Variable costs		22,000	22,000	22,000	22,000	22,000	
Expenses: Fixed costs		8,000	8,000	8,000	8,000	8,000	
Depreciation (*D*)		3,200	5,120	3,072	1,843	1,843	922
Pre-tax income		$5,300	$3,380	$5,428	$6,657	$6,657	−$922
Taxes (40%)		2,120	1,352	2,171	2,663	2,663	−369
Net operating income (NOI)		$ 3,180	$ 2,028	$ 3,257	$ 3,994	$ 3,994	−$553
Total cash flow (NOI + *D*)		$6,380	$7,148	$6,329	$5,837	$5,837	$369

Net Present Value Method

The **net present value (NPV) method** is used to evaluate an investment by calculating the present values of all after-tax total cash flows and then subtracting the original investment amount (which is already a present value) from their total. The difference is the project's net present value. If it is positive for the discount rate used, the investment earns a rate of return higher than the discount rate. If the net present value is negative, the investment earns a rate of return lower than the discount rate. Most firms set the discount rate equal to the *overall weighted average cost of capital,* which becomes the lowest desired return on investment. If a negative net present value results, the project is not approved. The discount rate that represents the lowest desired return on investment is thought of as a hurdle over which the investment must pass and is often referred to as the **hurdle rate.**

Internal Rate of Return Method

A related technique involves calculating the **internal rate of return (IRR),** which is the discount rate that makes the NPV of a project zero. It is "internal" because it depends only on the cash flows of the investment, not on rates offered elsewhere. With this method, a project is acceptable only if the IRR exceeds the hurdle rate. The IRR is a single number that summarizes the merits of the investment. It can be used to rank multiple projects from best to worst, so it is particularly useful when the budget limits new investments in any year.

You can find the IRR by trial and error. Start with a low discount rate and calculate the NPV. If it exceeds 0, increase the discount rate and try again. The NPV will eventually go to 0 and later to a negative value. When the NPV is near 0, you have found the IRR.

Payback Method

The other commonly used method of evaluating projects is the **payback method,** which determines how much time will elapse before the total of *after-tax* cash flows will equal, or pay back, the initial investment.

Even though it is scorned by many academics, the payback method continues to be widely used, particularly at lower management levels. It can be quickly and easily applied and gives decision makers some idea of how long recovery of invested funds will take. Uncertainty surrounds every investment project. The costs and revenues on which analyses are based are best estimates, not actual values. An investment project with a quick payback isn't considered as risky as one with a long payback. The payback method also has drawbacks. A major criticism is that it encourages managers to focus on the short run. A project that takes a long time to develop but generates excellent cash flows later in its life usually is rejected under the payback method. The payback method also has been criticized for its failure to consider the time value of money. For these reasons, we recommend that payback analysis be combined with a more sophisticated method such as NPV or IRR in analyzing the financial implications of a project.

EXAMPLE A1.2

Calculating NPV, IRR, and Payback Period

What are the NPV, IRR, and payback period for the salad bar project in Example A1.1?

Solution   Management wants to earn a return of at least 14 percent on its investment, so we use that rate to find the pf values in Table A1.1. The present value of each year's total cash flow and the NPV of the project are as follows.

1996:	$6380(0.8772) = $5597
1997:	$7148(0.7695) = $5500
1998:	$6329(0.6750) = $4272
1999:	$5837(0.5921) = $3456
2000:	$5837(0.5194) = $3032
2001:	$ 369(0.4556) = $ 168

NPV of project

$$= (\$5597 + \$5500 + \$4272 + \$3456 + \$3032 + \$168) - \$16{,}000$$
$$= \$6025$$

Because the NPV is positive, the recommendation would be to approve the project.

To find the IRR, let's begin with the 14 percent discount rate, which produced a positive NPV above. Incrementing at 4 percent with each step, we reach a negative NPV with a 30 percent discount rate. If we back up to 28 percent to "fine tune" our estimate, the NPV is $322. Therefore the IRR is about 29 percent. The computer can provide a more precise answer with much less computation.

Discount Rate	NPV
14%	$6025
18%	$4092
22%	$2425
26%	$ 977
30%	−$ 199

To determine the payback period, we add the after-tax cash flows at the bottom of the table in Example A1.1 for each year until we get as close as possible to $16,000 without exceeding it. For 1996 and 1997, cash flows are $6380 + $7148 = $13,528. The payback method is based on the assumption that cash flows are evenly distributed throughout the year, so in 1998 only $2472 must be received before the payback point is reached. As $2472/$6329 is 0.39, the payback period is 2.39 years.

Managing by the Numbers

The precision and analytical detachment that come from using the NPV, IRR, or payback method can be deceiving. In fact, U.S. business has been accused of *managing by the numbers,* with a preference for short-term results from low-risk projects (see Hayes and Abernathy, 1980; Skinner, 1984). Part of the problem lies with managers who are on the fast track to the top of their organizations. They occupy a rung on the ladder for a short time and then move up, and so they perceive it to be in their career interests to favor investments that give quick results. They establish short paybacks and high hurdle rates. They ignore or forgo long-term benefits from technological advances, innovative product plans, and strategic capacity additions. Over the long run, this narrow vision jeopardizes the firm's competitive advantage—and even its survival.

Managing by the numbers has a second cause. Projects with the greatest strategic impact are likely to be riskier and have qualitative benefits that cannot be easily quantified. Consider an investment in some of the newer types of flexible automation. (See Supplement B after Chapter 3.) Benefits can include better quality, quicker delivery times, higher sales, and lower inventory. The equipment might be reprogrammed to handle new products not yet conceived of by the firm. Enough might be learned with the new technology that subsequent investments will pay off at an even higher rate of return. The mistake is to ignore these benefits simply because they cannot be easily quantified. Including risks and qualitative factors as part of the analysis is far better than ignoring them. The proliferation of microcomputers and the corresponding use of computer spreadsheets to perform financial analyses have made possible the rapid evaluation of many different scenarios relating to a project. They are referred to as "what if" analyses and allow an analyst to look at what would happen to cash flows if certain events or combinations of events were to occur. Using a preference matrix also may help an analyst recognize qualitative factors more explicitly.

The message is clear. Financial analysis is a valuable tool for evaluating investment projects. However, it can never replace the insight that comes from hands-on experience. Managers must use their judgment, taking into account not only NPV, IRR, or payback data but also how the project fits operations and corporate strategy.

Selected References

Brealey, Richard A., Stewart C. Meyers, and Alan J. Marcus. *Fundamentals of Corporate Finance*. New York: McGraw-Hill, 1995.

Brigham, Eugene F., and Louis C. Gapenski. *Financial Management: Theory and Practice,* 7th ed. Orlando: Dryden, 1994.

Hayes, Robert H., and William J. Abernathy. "Managing Our Way to Economic Decline." *Harvard Business Review* (July–August 1980), pp. 67–77.

Hodder, James E., and Henry E. Riggs. "Pitfalls in Evaluating Risky Projects." *Harvard Business Review* (January–February 1985), pp. 128–135.

Kieso, Donald E., and Jerry J. Weygandt. *Intermediate Accounting,* 4th ed. New York: John Wiley & Sons, 1983.

Ross, Stephen A., Randolph W. Westerfield, and Bradford D. Jordon. *Fundamentals of Corporate Finance*, 2nd ed. Homewood, Ill.: Irwin, 1993.

Skinner, Wickham. "Operations Technology: Blind Spot in Strategic Management." *Interfaces,* vol. 14, no. 1 (January–February 1984), pp. 116–125.

Woodward, Herbert N. "Management Strategies for Small Companies." *Harvard Business Review* (January–February 1976), pp. 113–121.

APPENDIX 2

Normal Distribution

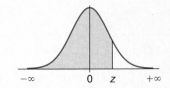

	.00	.01	.02	.03	.04	.05	.06	.07	.08	.09
.0	.5000	.5040	.5080	.5120	.5160	.5199	.5239	.5279	.5319	.5359
.1	.5398	.5438	.5478	.5517	.5557	.5596	.5636	.5675	.5714	.5753
.2	.5793	.5832	.5871	.5910	.5948	.5987	.6026	.6064	.6103	.6141
.3	.6179	.6217	.6255	.6293	.6331	.6368	.6406	.6443	.6480	.6517
.4	.6554	.6591	.6628	.6664	.6700	.6736	.6772	.6808	.6844	.6879
.5	.6915	.6950	.6985	.7019	.7054	.7088	.7123	.7157	.7190	.7224
.6	.7257	.7291	.7324	.7357	.7389	.7422	.7454	.7486	.7517	.7549
.7	.7580	.7611	.7642	.7673	.7704	.7734	.7764	.7794	.7823	.7852
.8	.7881	.7910	.7939	.7967	.7995	.8023	.8051	.8078	.8106	.8133
.9	.8159	.8186	.8212	.8238	.8264	.8289	.8315	.8340	.8365	.8389
1.0	.8413	.8438	.8461	.8485	.8508	.8531	.8554	.8577	.8599	.8621
1.1	.8643	.8665	.8686	.8708	.8729	.8749	.8770	.8790	.8810	.8830
1.2	.8849	.8869	.8888	.8907	.8925	.8944	.8962	.8980	.8997	.9015
1.3	.9032	.9049	.9066	.9082	.9099	.9115	.9131	.9147	.9162	.9177
1.4	.9192	.9207	.9222	.9236	.9251	.9265	.9279	.9292	.9306	.9319
1.5	.9332	.9345	.9357	.9370	.9382	.9394	.9406	.9418	.9429	.9441
1.6	.9452	.9463	.9474	.9484	.9495	.9505	.9515	.9525	.9535	.9545
1.7	.9554	.9564	.9573	.9582	.9591	.9599	.9608	.9616	.9625	.9633
1.8	.9641	.9649	.9656	.9664	.9671	.9678	.9686	.9693	.9699	.9706
1.9	.9713	.9719	.9726	.9732	.9738	.9744	.9750	.9756	.9761	.9767
2.0	.9772	.9778	.9783	.9788	.9793	.9798	.9803	.9808	.9812	.9817
2.1	.9821	.9826	.9830	.9834	.9838	.9842	.9846	.9850	.9854	.9857
2.2	.9861	.9864	.9868	.9871	.9875	.9878	.9881	.9884	.9887	.9890
2.3	.9893	.9896	.9898	.9901	.9904	.9906	.9909	.9911	.9913	.9916
2.4	.9918	.9920	.9922	.9925	.9927	.9929	.9931	.9932	.9934	.9936
2.5	.9938	.9940	.9941	.9943	.9945	.9946	.9948	.9949	.9951	.9952
2.6	.9953	.9955	.9956	.9957	.9959	.9960	.9961	.9962	.9963	.9964
2.7	.9965	.9966	.9967	.9968	.9969	.9970	.9971	.9972	.9973	.9974
2.8	.9974	.9975	.9976	.9977	.9977	.9978	.9979	.9979	.9980	.9981
2.9	.9981	.9982	.9982	.9983	.9984	.9984	.9985	.9985	.9986	.9986
3.0	.9987	.9987	.9987	.9988	.9988	.9989	.9989	.9989	.9990	.9990
3.1	.9990	.9991	.9991	.9991	.9992	.9992	.9992	.9992	.9993	.9993
3.2	.9993	.9993	.9994	.9994	.9994	.9994	.9994	.9995	.9995	.9995
3.3	.9995	.9995	.9995	.9996	.9996	.9996	.9996	.9996	.9996	.9997
3.4	.9997	.9997	.9997	.9997	.9997	.9997	.9997	.9997	.9997	.9998

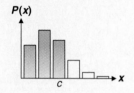

Cumulative Poisson Probabilities

$$P(x \le c) = \sum_{x=0}^{x=c} \frac{\lambda^x \cdot e^{-\lambda}}{x!}$$

np	0	1	2	3	4	5	6	7	8	9	10	11	12
.05	.951	.999	1.000										
.10	.905	.995	1.000										
.15	.861	.990	.999	1.000									
.20	.819	.982	.999	1.000									
.25	.779	.974	.998	1.000									
.30	.741	.963	.996	1.000									
.35	.705	.951	.994	1.000									
.40	.670	.938	.992	.999	1.000								
.45	.638	.925	.989	.999	1.000								
.50	.607	.910	.986	.998	1.000								
.55	.577	.894	.982	.998	1.000								
.60	.549	.878	.977	.997	1.000								
.65	.522	.861	.972	.996	.999	1.000							
.70	.497	.844	.966	.994	.999	1.000							
.75	.472	.827	.959	.993	.999	1.000							
.80	.449	.809	.953	.991	.999	1.000							
.85	.427	.791	.945	.989	.998	1.000							
.90	.407	.772	.937	.987	.998	1.000							
.95	.387	.754	.929	.984	.997	1.000							
1.0	.368	.736	.920	.981	.996	.999	1.000						
1.1	.333	.699	.900	.974	.995	.999	1.000						
1.2	.301	.663	.879	.966	.992	.998	1.000						
1.3	.273	.627	.857	.957	.989	.998	1.000						
1.4	.247	.592	.833	.946	.986	.997	.999	1.000					
1.5	.223	.558	.809	.934	.981	.996	.999	1.000					
1.6	.202	.525	.783	.921	.976	.994	.999	1.000					
1.7	.183	.493	.757	.907	.970	.992	.998	1.000					
1.8	.165	.463	.731	.891	.964	.990	.997	.999	1.000				
1.9	.150	.434	.704	.875	.956	.987	.997	.999	1.000				
2.0	.135	.406	.677	.857	.947	.983	.995	.999	1.000				
2.2	.111	.355	.623	.819	.928	.975	.993	.998	1.000				
2.4	.091	.308	.570	.779	.904	.964	.988	.997	.999	1.000			
2.6	.074	.267	.518	.736	.877	.951	.983	.995	.999	1.000			
2.8	.061	.231	.469	.692	.848	.935	.976	.992	.998	.999	1.000		
3.0	.050	.199	.423	.647	.815	.916	.966	.988	.996	.999	1.000		
3.2	.041	.171	.380	.603	.781	.895	.955	.983	.994	.998	1.000		
3.4	.033	.147	.340	.558	.744	.871	.942	.977	.992	.997	.999	1.000	
3.6	.027	.126	.303	.515	.706	.844	.927	.969	.988	.996	.999	1.000	
3.8	.022	.107	.269	.473	.668	.816	.909	.960	.984	.994	.998	.999	1.000
4.0	.018	.092	.238	.433	.629	.785	.889	.949	.979	.992	.997	.999	1.000